SPECIAL EDITION

USING
Macromedia®
Studio MX
2004

Michael Hurwicz

800 East 96th Street
Indianapolis, Indiana 46240

CONTENTS AT A GLANCE

Introduction

Part I: Getting Started with Macromedia Studio MX

1 Setup and Planning
2 Studio MX: A Bird's-Eye View
3 Introducing the MX Interface

Part II: Dreamweaver MX

4 What's New in Dreamweaver MX 2004
5 Working in the Dreamweaver Environment
6 Setting Up Sites, Pages, and Templates
7 Working Efficiently in Dreamweaver
8 Writing and Editing HTML, XHTML, and CSS
9 Professional Page Design
10 Adding Interactivity and Multimedia
11 Managing Your Site
12 Expanding Dreamweaver and Using Third-Party
   Software
13 Developing ColdFusion Applications in Dreamweaver

Part III: Flash MX

14 What's New in Flash MX 2004?
15 The Flash Environment and Tools
16 Working with Vector Graphics and Bitmaps
17 Working with Text
18 Animation, Interactivity, and Rich Media
19 Introduction to ActionScript
20 Basic ActionScript
21 Advanced ActionScript
22 External Communications
23 Using Flash for Dynamic Data

Part IV: Fireworks MX

24 What's New in Fireworks MX 2004?
25 Fireworks MX 2004 Environment and Tools
26 Creating Graphics, Rollovers, and Animations
27 Optimizing and Exporting Graphics and Web Pages
28 Automating and Extending Fireworks

Part V: FreeHand MX

29 FreeHand MX Environment and Tools
30 Using FreeHand in Web Site Planning and Creation
31 Integration with the Studio MX Suite

Part VI: ColdFusion MX

32 Understanding and Administering ColdFusion
33 ColdFusion Markup Language (CFML)

Part VIII: Appendixes

A ActionScript Reference
B Making Flash Accessible
Index

SPECIAL EDITION USING MACROMEDIA STUDIO MX 2004

International Standard Book Number: 0-7897-3042-1

Library of Congress Catalog Card Number: 2003106143

Printed in the United States of America

First Printing: April 2004

06   05   04   03   4   3   2   1

Trademarks

Warning and Disclaimer

Bulk Sales

Que Publishing offers excellent discounts on this book when ordered in quantity for bulk purchases or special sales. For more information, please contact

U.S. Corporate and Government Sales
1-800-382-3419
corpsales@pearsontechgroup.com

For sales outside of the U.S., please contact

International Sales
1-317-428-3341
international@pearsontechgroup.com

Acquisitions Editor
Shelley Johnston

Development Editor
Damon Jordan

Managing Editor
Charlotte Clapp

Project Editor
Andy Beaster

Copy Editor
Margo Catts

Indexer
Mandie Frank

Proofreader
Jennifer Timpe

Technical Editors
Lynn Baus
Steve Heckler

Publishing Coordinator
Vanessa Evans

Interior Designer
Anne Jones

Cover Designer
Anne Jones

Page Layout
Michelle Mitchell

TABLE OF CONTENTS

Introduction 1

What's New in Studio MX? 2

Who Should Read This Book? 3

How to Use This Book ꜱ 4

Conventions Used in This Book 6

I Getting Started with Macromedia Studio MX

1 Setup and Planning **11**

   Additional Software 12

      Web Service 12

      Database Management 12

   Planning and Design 13

      Using FreeHand for Mockups 13

      The Dreamweaver Bindings Panel 14

      Templates 14

      CSS 14

   Troubleshooting 15

2 Studio MX: A Bird's-Eye View **17**

   Studio MX: Choosing Your Tools 18

   The Basics: Words and Graphics 18

   Animation, Navigation and Interaction 19

   Dynamic Content 20

      Creating Server Behaviors 20

      Creating the Client Interface 21

3 Introducing the MX Interface **23**

   Studio MX: Family Resemblances 24

      Selecting Objects 29

   Main Menu Bar and Toolbar 30

   Panels 30

   Tools Panel Subsections 33

   Tools 33

      Strokes and Fills 33

      Setting Stroke and Fill Colors 34

      Working with Fills 35

      Working with Gradients 36

      Eyedropper 37

      Line 38

      Pencil 38

      Rectangle and Ellipse Tools 38

      The Pen Tool 39

      Optimizing Curves 42

Working with Text 42
  Adding Text 43
  Resizing Text Blocks 43
  Changing Text Globally 44

Character and Paragraph Attributes 45
  Font, Point Size, Color, and Styles 45
  Text Direction 46
  Kerning and Character Spacing 46
  Character Position 47
  Alignment and Justification 47

Keyboard Shortcuts 47

Troubleshooting 49

II Dreamweaver MX

4 What's New In Dreamweaver MX 2004 53

A New Dreamweaver User Interface 54
  New Quickstart Menu 54
  Streamlined Workspace 55
  Reorganized Panels 57

Siteless Page Editing 57

Enhanced CSS Support 57
  Integrated CSS 58
  Enhanced CSS Panel 58
  CSS Property Inspector 59
  CSS-Based Page Properties 60

Increased Integration with Other Suite Applications ...61
  Integrated Fireworks Image Editing 61
  Increased Integration With Flash 63

Enhanced Support for Dynamic Platforms 64

Copy and Paste from Microsoft Applications 65

Additional Coding Tools 66
  Dynamic Cross-Browser Compatibility Check 66
  Enhanced Find and Replace 67
  Right-Click Coding Tools 68

Enhanced Security Using FTP 69

Troubleshooting 70

Peer to Peer: Taking the Anxiety Out of CSS 70

5 Working in the Dreamweaver Environment 73

The Dreamweaver MX Interface, In Depth 74
  Workspace Layouts 74
  Exploring the Document Window 76
  Using the Property Inspector 81
  Working with Panels 81
  Code Inspector 93

Working with Text in the Document Window 93
   Paragraphs 94
   Line Breaks 94
   Styling Text 94
   Aligning Text 97
   Indenting Text 98

Creating Lists in Documents 98
   Unordered (Bulleted) Lists 98
   Ordered (Numbered) Lists 99

Troubleshooting 100

Peer to Peer: The Essence of Structure 101

6 Setting Up Sites, Pages, and Templates 103

Establishing a Web Site 104
   Defining the Site Locally 104
   Setting the Remote Information 106
   Importing an Existing Web Site 109

Managing Documents 111
   Creating a New Document 111
   Saving Files 113
   Deleting, Duplicating, and Renaming Documents 113
   Opening an Existing Document 114
   Using Design Notes to Track Changes to a Document 115

Pre-Design Page Setup 117
   Adding the Page Title 117
   Establishing Default Page Properties 118

Managing Pages with Templates 122
   Starting a New Template 123
   Saving a Document as a Template 124
   Creating Editable Regions 124
   Creating Optional Regions 125
   Creating Repeating Regions 127
   Making Attributes Editable 129

Using Templates 130
   Creating a New Page from a Template 130
   Making Changes to the Page 131
   Applying a Template to an Existing Page 131
   Editing a Template 132

Troubleshooting 133

7 Working Efficiently in Dreamweaver 135

Keeping Track of Site Components 136

Working with the Assets Panel 137

Creating a Favorites List and Favorites Folder 137
   Adding an Asset to the Favorites List 138
   Creating a New Favorites Folder 138

Asset Types 139
  Images 139
  Colors 139
  URLs 139
  Flash 140
  Shockwave 140
  Movies 140
  Scripts 140
  Templates 141
  Library 141

Adding an Asset to a Web Page 141

Maintaining the Assets Panel 141
  Refreshing and Rebuilding the Site Assets List 142
  Editing Assets in Other Programs 142
  Using the Assets Panel Between Sites 142

Creating Library Items 143
  Library Items and Server-Side Includes 144
  Library Items Versus Dreamweaver Templates 144

Using Library Items 146
  Editing Library Items 147
  Detaching from the Original 148
  Deleting Library Items 149
  Behaviors in the Librarys 149

Checking Your Page Code 150
  Cleaning Up Your HTML 150
  Estimating Download Speed 152
  Spell Checking 153
  Checking for Cross-Browser Compatibility 154
  A Final Manual Review 156

Testing Your Site Online 156
  Testing Download Speed 156
  Fixing Problems 157
  Editing on the Server 157

Troubleshooting 157

Peer to Peer: Standards and Search 158

8 Writing and Editing HTML, XHTML, and CSS 161

Browser Languages 162
  Macromedia and Markup 163
  Origin of the Species: SGML, HTML, XML, and XHTML .163

HTML 4 164

XHTML 167
  Document Conformance and Document Type Definitions 167
  Well-Formedness and Syntactical Rules in XHTML 1.0 168

HTML and XHTML Syntax 169
  Elements 169
  Attributes 170
  Values 170

CSS Styles: Background 171
   The Evolution of Style 172
   Cascading Style Sheets 173
   Inside CSS Markup 173
   Choosing a Style Sheet Editor 178
CSS in Dreamweaver MX 2004 179
   The CSS Styles Panel 180
   Managing Style Sheets 180
   Creating a New Style Definition 182
   Defining Styles 183
   Editing Style Sheets 185
Troubleshooting 187
Peer to Peer: Macromedia and the Web Standards Project 188
Peer to Peer: CSS Resources 189
   Articles 189
   Web Resources 189
   Books 189

9 Professional Page Design **191**
Table Elements 192
Using Layout Mode 193
   Drawing Layout Tables and Cells in Layout Mode 193
   Drawing a Layout Table 194
   Drawing a Layout Cell 194
   Nesting a Layout Table 195
   Formatting in Layout Mode 🆕 195
   Setting Layout Table and Cell Attributes 196
   Adding Content 197
   Moving and Resizing Layout Cells and Tables 198
About Frames 199
Building Framed Pages in Dreamweaver MX 2004 200
   Creating Framesets 200
   Using a Predefined Frameset 201
   Using Frame Selection Tools 203
Modifying Framesets and Frame Elements 205
   Modifying the Frameset Element 205
   Modifying Frame Elements in the Frameset 205
   Dreamweaver MX 2004 Frame Options in the Property Inspector 205
Targeting Windows 206
   Using the `target` and `name` Attributes to Link a Frame 206
   Using Reserved Target Names 207
Layout with Style 207
Layer Preferences 208
The Layer "Box" 209
   Creating a Layer 209
   Adding Content to the Layer 210
   Selecting, Moving, Aligning, and Resizing a Layer in Design View ..210

Selecting a layer 211
Resizing a Layer 212
Resizing Multiple Layers at the Same Time 213
Aligning Layers 213

Using the Layers Panel 213
Layer Visibility 213
Renaming Layers 214
Changing the Stacking Order 214
Nesting Layers 214
Layer Overlap 214

Setting Layer Attributes 215

Designing with Layers 216
Change Property 216
Set Text of Layer 217
Show-Hide Layers 217

Troubleshooting 218

10 Adding Interactivity and Multimedia **219**

Oh, Behave: JavaScript and Behaviors 220
Understanding JavaScript 220
Using JavaScript Snippets 221
Using Behaviors 221

Rollovers and Nav Bars 223
Creating a Rollover 223
Designing Remote Rollovers 225
Creating Navigation Bars 225

Interactivity and Layers 227
Showing and Hiding Draw Layers 227
Dragging a Layer 227
Timeline, R.I.P. 228

Plug-Ins, Applets, and Controls 229
Plug-ins 229
ActiveX Controls 232
Java Applets 234

Audio and Video for the Web 235
Using Dreamweaver to Add Sound Files to a Page 236
Inserting Video 238

Troubleshooting 239

Peer to Peer: Making Pages Containing Audio and Video Valid and Accessible 239

11 Managing Your Site **241**

Site Management Concepts 242

Compatibility and Accessibility Testing 242
What Are Web Standards, Really? 242
The Bottom Line: Time and Money 242
When to Switch? 243
Validating Documents 243

Cross-Browser Compatibility 244
Validating for Accessibility 245
Testing Accessibility with Macromedia Dreamweaver MX 246
Uploading Pages 🆕. 248
Going Online 249
Putting Files (Uploading) 250
Getting Files (Downloading) 251
Testing Your Site Online 251
Collaborating 252
Setting Up a Remote Site 252
Checking Files In and Out 252
Other Version Control Systems 254
Synchronizing Sites 255
Site Reports and Link Maintenance 256
Putting the Site Report to Work 256
Maintaining Link Integrity 258
Troubleshooting 261
Peer to Peer: Using Macromedia Extensions and Products for Accessibility Testing 262
Peer to Peer: Tracking Usage Statistics 262

12 Expanding Dreamweaver and Using Third-Party Software 263
Extending Macromedia Dreamweaver 264
About Macromedia Exchange 264
Managing Extensions 265
Adding an Extension 267
Downloading a Behavior 267
Installing Third-Party Plug-ins 268
Using Contribute 2 with Dreamweaver 268
About the Contribute Interface 269
Creating a New Page with Contribute 271
Importing Word and Excel Documents into a Page .272
Working with Text 273
Creating Lists 273
Working with Images 274
Creating a Table 274
Working with Links 274
Working with Frames 274
Publishing Your Drafts 274
Integrating Dreamweaver with Fireworks 274
Setting Fireworks as the Default Image Editor 275
Inserting or Creating a Fireworks Image 276
Launching Fireworks to Edit or Optimize an Image .276
Using the New Image Editing Toolbar 277
Integrating Dreamweaver with Flash 278
File Types and Object Properties 279
Inserting Flash Text 280

Adding Flash Buttons 281

Previewing, Editing, and Resizing Flash Buttons and Text .282

Microsoft Integration Features 🄽🄴🅆 283

Troubleshooting 284

Peer to Peer: Macromedia Extensions for Markup Compliance 285

Peer to Peer: Markup and Contribute 285

13 Developing ColdFusion Applications in Dreamweaver **287**

Dynamic Dreamweaver 🄽🄴🅆 288

Creating a Site for Dynamic Pages 289

Database Operations 290

Previewing Data 291

Retrieving Data 293

Using Dynamic Data 297

Live Data: Viewing Data While Editing 306

Using Server Behaviors to Modify Dynamic Data 306

Inserting, Updating, and Deleting Database Records 308

Drilling Down into Data with Master/Detail Pages 310

Making Client Access Easier: Web Services and Components 311

Creating a CFC 312

Invoking a Function in a CFC 312

Creating a Web Service CFC 314

Consuming Web Services 316

Troubleshooting 317

III Flash MX

14 What's New in Flash MX 2004? **321**

Faster Flash Files 322

3D, Text Effects, Graphs, Charts, and More... 322

Effects and Animation Made Easy 323

Speeding Up Common Tasks 323

A Tale of Two Versions 324

More and Better Components 325

Quick Take-off with Templates 326

Text: Spelling, Formatting, Translating 326

Better Importing 327

Searching Through Space and Time 327

The Find and Replace Feature 328

The History Panel 328

JavaScript for Flash (JSFL) 329

New Security Rules 330

A New Version of ActionScript 330

Troubleshooting 331

15 The Flash Environment and Tools 333

Panel Sets 334
   Panel Sets 334
Setting Document Attributes 334
The Timeline 334
   Frames 335
   Keyframes 335
   Layers and Layer Folders 336
   Onion Skinning and Multiple Frame Editing 338
The Toolbox 339
   Arrow Tool NEW 339
   Lasso Tool 339
   Brush Tool 340
   Free Transform Tool 341
   Fill Transform Tool 341
   Ink Bottle Tool 341
   Eraser Tool 342
Keyboard Shortcuts 342
The Library 343
   Creating Common Libraries 344
The Movie Explorer 344
Setting Flash Preferences 345
   General Preferences NEW 345
   Editing Preferences NEW 347
   Clipboard Preferences 348
   Warning Preferences NEW 348
   ActionScript Editor Preferences NEW 349
Troubleshooting 350

16 Working with Vector Graphics and Bitmaps 351

Understanding Vector Graphics 352
Editing and Adjusting Shapes 352
   Using the Selection and Subselection Tools 352
   Straightening and Smoothing 353
   Optimizing Curves 353
Using Layout Aids 353
   Snapping 353
   Grids, Guides, and Guide Layers 354
   Sizing Shapes Precisely 355
   The Align Panel 356
Creating a Mask 356
Working with Bitmaps 357
   Importing Bitmaps NEW 357
   Preparing Bitmaps for Import 357
   Tracing Bitmaps 358
   Optimizing Traced Bitmaps 361

Breaking Apart Bitmaps 362
Compressing Bitmaps 363
Animating Bitmaps 364

Troubleshooting 365

17 Working with Text 367

Working with Text 368

Displaying Clear, Sharp Text 368
Using Snap to Pixels to Automatically Align Text 369
Alignment and Justification 369
Turning Anti-Aliasing Off NEW 370

Dynamic and Input Text 370
Input Text 370
Dynamic Text 371
Using a Variable to Set and Get Text 372
Text Formatting Options NEW 372
Embedded and Device Fonts 373
Breaking Text Apart 374
Transforming Text 375

Best Practices for Using Text 376

Troubleshooting 377

18 Animation, Interactivity, and Rich Media 379

Symbols, Instances, and Library Assets 380
Understanding Symbols 380
Creating Symbols from Scratch 381
Editing Symbols 385
Instances 386
The Library 389

Animating in Flash NEW 390
Frames and Keyframes 391
Tweening 393
Timeline Effects NEW 400
Scrubbing Through the Timeline 403
Cartoon Animation in Flash: Panning 404
Nesting Symbols 404
Animation Guidelines 405

Using Sound 406
Understanding Sound NEW 406
Preparing Sounds for Flash 407
Stream Versus Event, External Versus Embedded 408
Importing Sounds 412
"Editing" Sounds 413
Controlling Sound 414
Optimizing Sounds 415
Turning Off Sound 417

Flash Interactivity 418
   Introduction to Flash Interactivity 418
   Easy ActionScripting with Behaviors NEW 418
   Embedded Video Behaviors 419
   Media Behaviors 419
   Projector Behavior 419
   Movieclip Behaviors 420
   Sound Behaviors 420
   Web Behavior 420
   Buttons 420
   Menus 424
Accelerating Application Development with Components 426
   Working with Components 428
   Skinning Components 430
Integrating Video NEW 431
   Video File Types 432
   Embedded Versus Linked Video 433
   The Video Import Wizard NEW 433
   Working with Imported Video 438
   Controlling Video Playback 439
Troubleshooting 439

19 Introduction to ActionScript **441**
Adding Interactivity with ActionScript NEW 442
   Accessing the Actions Panel 443
Using the Actions Panel 444
   Selecting Frame Actions or Object Actions 445
   Hiding and Un-hiding the Actions Toolbox 446
Understanding Object-Oriented Languages 446
The Three R's: Readability, Reusability, and Reachability 448
   Readability: Writing Readable Code 448
   Reusability: Modularizing Code 451
   Reachability: Organizing and Centralizing Code 453
Hint, Hint: Flash Helps You Code 456
Troubleshooting NEW 458

20 Basic ActionScript **459**
What Do You Mean, "Basic"? 460
Managing Variables, Data, and Datatypes 460
   Working with Variables 460
   Rules for Naming Variables (and Other Things) NEW 462
   Using Datatypes to Categorize Data NEW 464
   The Nine ActionScript Datatypes 464
   Explicit and Implicit Data Conversion 469
   Numbers and Strings versus Numeric and String Literals 470
   Object and Array Literals 470
   Using `null` and `undefined` 471

Working with Operands, Expressions, and Statements 471
    Using Operators 474
    Assignment and Compound Assignment 475
    Understanding Precedence, Associativity, and Operator Grouping 475
Control Blocks 476
    Understanding Program Flow Control 480
    Making Decisions with Conditionals and `switch` NEW......................480
    Using Loops to Repeat Actions 483
Combining Statements into Functions 486
    Function Basics: Creating Functions 486
    Calling Functions 488
    Using `var` to Create Local Function Variables 488
    Passing Information to Functions in Arguments 489
    Using Return Values to Retrieve Results 492
    Functions as Classes: Constructor Functions 493
    Using `Function.apply()` and `Function.call()` 493
    Explicit Scoping 494
    Automatic Scoping 497
Using Event Handlers to Trigger Action NEW..................................500
    Static and Dynamic Event Handlers 503
    System Events and User Input Events 504
    Registering Listeners 504
    Scoping and the `this` Keyword with Event Handlers 505
    Calling Event Handlers Explicitly 507
    Event Handlers and Focus 507
    Disabling and Deleting Event Handlers 507
    Button Events 508
    Key Events 511
    Mouse Events 512
    Movie Clip Events 513
    Selection Events 515
    Sound Events 515
    The Stage `onResize` Event 516
    `TextField` Events 516
Working with Movie Clips 517
    Flash MX 2004's New Movie Clip Features 518
    Creating and Removing Movie Clips 518
    Loading and Unloading External Content NEW..............................520
    Controlling the Visual Stacking Order of Movie Clips 524
    Using Levels for Visual Stacking NEW....................................525
    Using `Init` Objects to Give Properties to New Movie Clips 528
    Detecting Movie Clip Collisions 529
    Using `setInterval()` to Call a Function Repetitively 531
    Dragging and Dropping Movie Clips 533
    Working with Dynamic Masks NEW..534
Troubleshooting 535

21 Advanced ActionScript **539**

ActionScript 2.0: Real Class 540

Defining a Class 541

Creating Class Instances 541

Using Default (Prototype) and Instance Features 542

Static or Class Features 543

Using a Constructor Function to Initialize Attribute Values 544

Managing the "Visibility" of Class Features 546

Accessing and Modifying ("Getting" and "Setting") Attributes 546

Allowing or Disallowing the Creation of New Class Features 548

Creating Hierarchies of Classes 550

Facilitating the Creation of Standard Interfaces to Classes 552

Telling the Compiler Where to Look for Classes 554

Using the Core Classes 556

The `Array` Class 𝗡𝗘𝗪 557

`Boolean`, `Number`, and `String`: The Wrapper Classes 567

The `String` Class 569

The `Date` Class 569

The `Error` Class 𝗡𝗘𝗪 570

The `Function` Class 572

The `Object` Class 572

The `Math` Object 578

The `System` Object 𝗡𝗘𝗪 589

Movie-Related Classes and Global Objects 𝗡𝗘𝗪 592

The `Accessibility` Object 𝗡𝗘𝗪 593

The `Button` Class 593

The `Color` Class 594

The `ContextMenu` Class 𝗡𝗘𝗪 596

The `Key` Object 596

The `LocalConnection` Class 596

The `Mouse` Object 𝗡𝗘𝗪 600

The `PrintJob` Class 𝗡𝗘𝗪 600

The `Selection` Object 602

The `Shared Object` Class 602

The `Stage` Object 603

The `TextField` and `TextFormat` Classes 𝗡𝗘𝗪 605

The `TextSnapshot` Class 𝗡𝗘𝗪 611

Building Your Own Components 𝗡𝗘𝗪 612

Troubleshooting 615

22 External Communications **617**

Introduction to External Communications 618

Communicating Locally 618

Controlling the Browser 618

Calling JavaScript Functions 621

Controlling the Projector 622

Introduction to Network-Aware Communications 𝗡𝗘𝗪 623

Loading Text Data with LoadVars 625
    Completing LoadVars 625
    Embedding Data on the HTML Page 632

XML Data 634
    Introduction to XML 634
    Parsing XML Data 638
    Building XML Data 641
    Importing XML Documents 643
    Sending XML Documents to the Server 645
    XML Sockets 645

Customizing HTTP Headers with addRequestHeader() NEW....................646

NetConnection, NetStream, and the Rich Media Classes NEW...............647
    Using NetConnection and NetStream for Progressive Loading 648
    Working with .flv Files and the NetStream Object NEW...............649
    The Sound Class NEW..651
    The Video Class 656

Troubleshooting 657

23 Using Flash for Dynamic Data 661

Introduction to Dynamic Data in Flash MX 2004 NEW.......................662

Databinding and Components 664

Flash Remoting 666

Using and Modifying the DataGrid Component 668
    Removing a Column 668
    Changing Column Headers 669
    Changing a Row's Background Color 669
    Formatting Columns 670
    Responding to Clicks on Headers 670
    Responding to Rollovers 671

Web Services 672
    Creating Component Instances 674
    Setting Up Databindings 675
    Triggering the Data Source 678

Troubleshooting 679

IV Fireworks MX

24 What's New in Fireworks MX 2004? 683

Upgrading to Fireworks MX 2004 684

Performance Improvements 684
    Transform Tool Enhanced 684

Interface Enhancements 684
    Start Page 685
    Graphical Previews 685

New Tools 686
    Auto Shapes 686
    Red Eye Removal Tool 687
    Replace Color Tool 687
    Motion Blur Live Effects 688
Enhanced Roundtrip Editing 689
New Anti-Aliasing Options 689
New Effects 690
    Contour Gradients 690
    Dashed Strokes 690
    Add Noise Live Effect 691
JavaScript API Extensions 691
Full Unicode Support 691
Site Management 692
    Version Control 692
    Built-In FTP 692

25 Fireworks MX 2004 Environment and Tools **693**
Fireworks MX 2004 Environment 694
    A Quick Look at the Fireworks Environment 694
    The Major Interface Elements 695
Document Window 696
Tools Unique to Fireworks 698
    Select Tools Group 698
    Bitmap Tools 700
    Vector Tools 712
    Web Tools 719
Property Inspector 721
Main Menu 721
    File Menu 721
    Edit Menu 722
    View Menu 722
    Select Menu 722
    Modify Menu 723
    Text Menu 723
    Commands Menu 724
    Filters Menu 724
    Window Menu 725
    Help Menu 725
Customization with Preferences 725
    General Tab 726
    Editing Tab 726
    Launch and Edit 726
    Folders 727
    Import 727
Troubleshooting 728

26 Creating Graphics, Rollovers, and Animations 731

Graphics as Objects 732
   Bitmap Graphics .732
   Vector Graphics 733
   Paths Versus Strokes 734

Layers 734
   Layers Panel Basics 735

Frames 736
   Frames Panel Basics 736

Layers and Frames 737
   Shared Versus Unshared Layers .738
   Web Layer 738

Simple Rollover 738

Swap Image Behavior 739

Navigation Bars with Four-State Buttons 741

Fireworks and Animation 743
   Animation Planning 743

Building an Animation 744
   Frame-by-Frame Animation 744
   Tweened Animation 747
   Animation Symbols 748
   Optimizing Your Animation for Export as an Animated GIF 750
   Optimizing Your Animation for Export to Flash 751

Troubleshooting 752

27 Optimizing and Exporting Graphics and Web Pages 755

Optimization Fundamentals 756
   Compression 756

File Types 758

Using the Optimize Panel 758
   Optimize to Size Command 760
   Using Saved Settings 760
   Using Manual Settings 762

Exporting Fireworks Images 766
   Web Graphics 766
   Web Pages 769
   Integrating with Dreamweaver 771
   Integrating with Flash 772
   Integrating with Director 772

Troubleshooting 774

28 Automating and Extending Fireworks 775

Automating Tasks 776
   Find and Replace .776
   Batch Processing .778

Extending Fireworks 780
   Creating Commands with the History Panel 780
   Using the Extension Manager 781
Troubleshooting 782

V: FreeHand MX

29 FreeHand MX Environment and Tools **785**
FreeHand MX Environment 786
Document Window 786
Panels 787
   Property Inspector Group 788
   Mixers and Tint Panel Group 790
   Layers Panel Group 792
   Assets Panel Group 793
Tools Unique to FreeHand MX 795
   Page Tool 795
   Output Area Tool 796
   Variable Stroke Pen Tool 797
   Calligraphic Pen Tool 798
   Spiral 800
   Arc 801
   Scale 801
   Rotate 803
   Reflect 804
   Skew 805
   Freeform 806
   Roughen 808
   Bend 809
   Eraser 809
   Knife Tool 810
   Perspective Tool 810
   3D Rotation Tool 812
   Fisheye Lens Tool 814
   Extrude Tool 815
   Smudge Tool 818
   Shadow Tool 818
   Trace Tool 820
   Blend Tool 821
   Mirror Tool 822
   Graphic Hose Tool 823
   Chart Tool 826
   Action Tool 828
   Connector Tool 829

Toolbars Unique to FreeHand MX 830
    Xtra Operations Toolbar 831
    Xtra Tools 832
    Envelope Toolbar 833
Troubleshooting 834

30 Using FreeHand in Web Site Planning and Creation 837
Site Architecture 838
    Create a Site Map with the Connector Tool 838
Site Design 845
    Create a Multipage Document 845
    Design the Home Page 848
    Text Effects 849
    Actions 852
Troubleshooting 854

31 Integration with the Studio MX Suite 857
Moving Designs to the Web 858
    Web-Safe Colors 858
    Web Graphics 859
    HTML Pages 863
Working with Fireworks MX 865
    Importing Fireworks MX files into FreeHand MX 865
    Editing Fireworks MX Images in FreeHand MX 866
Working with Flash MX 867
    Using FreeHand MX Objects in Flash MX 868
    Using Flash MX Movies in FreeHand MX 868
    Exporting Flash MX Movies from FreeHand MX 869
    Editing Flash MX Movies in FreeHand MX 870
Troubleshooting 870

VI ColdFusion MX

32 Understanding and Administering ColdFusion 875
Introducing ColdFusion 876
ColdFusion Architecture 877
Using Flash to Access the ColdFusion Server 878
    Web Services 879
    Flash Remoting 879
Using the Built-in Web server 880
Configuring Data Sources 880
Troubleshooting 883

33 ColdFusion Markup Language (CFML) **885**

Introducing CFML 886

Variables and Scopes 888

Troubleshooting with Data Type Checking 888

Using `cftry/cfcatch` to Trap Errors 889

Managing Variables in Scopes 889

Using ColdFusion for Database Operations 891

Retrieving Data 891

Updating Records 892

Inserting Records 894

Deleting Records 895

Custom Tags 895

Custom Tag Basics 897

Passing Data to a Custom Tag 897

Returning Data from a Custom Tag 898

The `cf_scrape` Custom Tag 899

Creating and Using ColdFusion Components (CFCs) 903

Creating and Using Web Service CFCs 904

Troubleshooting 905

VIII Appendixes

A ActionScript Reference **909**

The `ContextMenu` Class 910

Datatype Conversion Rules 911

Converting to a Number 914

Using Implicit Datatype Conversion 916

The `MovieClip` Class 917

Notes on Movie Clip Methods and Attributes 922

`enabled` 923

`focusEnabled` 923

`hitArea` 924

`tabChildren` 924

`tabEnabled` 925

`tabIndex` 925

`trackAsMenu` 925

`useHandCursor` 926

Arithmetic Operators 926

The Special Value NaN ("Not a Number") 926

Incrementing and Decrementing 926

Addition and Subtraction 927

Working with the Polymorphic + Operator 928

Working with the Overloaded - Operator 928

Multiplication and Division 929

Modulo (%) Division 929

Understanding Bitwise Operators 930
  Bitwise Logical Operators 931
  Bit-Shift Operators 935
Assignment and Compound Assignment 938
Comparison Operators 939
  Understanding Equality Operators 939
  Automatic Datatype Conversions for Comparisons 940
  Deprecated Flash 4 Comparison Operators 942
Using Logical (Boolean) Operators 943
The Conditional Operator 946
The Comma Operator 947
Named Operators 948
  The new Operator 948
  The typeof Operator 948
  The instanceof Operator 948
  The delete Operator 949
  The void Operator 949
  Object Property Access: The Dot Operator 950
  The Array-Element/Object Property Operator 950
  The Parentheses/Function Call Operator 950
The Date Class 951
The Key Object 955
The Math Object 957
The TextField and TextFormat Classes 958
Wrapper Classes: Boolean, Number, String 968
The Camera Class 972
The Microphone Class 974

B Making Flash Accessible 977
Accessibility Guidelines 🆕 978
Introduction to Accessibility in Flash MX 2004 978
How to Make Content Accessible 979
Index 981

ABOUT THE AUTHOR

Michael Hurwicz is a freelance writer, developer, designer, animator, and musician living in Eastsound, WA. He is the Flash and 3D Guy at Late Night Design. He has been writing about technical topics for the computer trade press since 1985. Michael is president of Irthlingz, a nonprofit organization dedicated to environmental education and entertainment. You can e-mail Michael at `michael@hurwicz.com` as well as visit his Web sites at `http://www.latenightdesign.com`, `http://www.hurwicz.com`, `http://www.flashoop.com`, and `http://www.irthlingz.org`.

CONTRIBUTING AUTHORS

John Kuhlman is a full-time writer who plays graphic designer and Web developer while most normal people are sleeping. His more notable projects include *FreeHand MX* (Virtual Training Company, 2003) and a co-author role in *HTML/XHTML/XML Magic* (New Riders Publishing, 2001). In addition, he has written numerous articles on online marketing and public relations. John is also the founder of Kreativwerks (`www.kreativwerks.com`), a communications design studio specializing in online brand development.

Sean R. Nicholson is the network administrator and Web developer for the Career Services Center at the University of Missouri Kansas City. He and his development teams architect, develop, and manage foundation and backend execution for programs such as the CareerExec Employment Database (`www.careerexec.com`), UMKC Career Services Website (`www.career.umkc.edu`), UMKC's Virtual Career Fair (`www.umkc.edu/virtualfair`), and Kansas City United (`www.kansascityunited.com`). Sean also does private contract work and consulting on database and Web development with organizations and individuals. Sean's technical publications include *Dreamweaver MX 2004 and Databases*, *Dreamweaver MX Magic*, *Inside UltraDev 4*, *Discover Excel 97*, and *Teach Yourself Outlook 98 in 24 Hours*, and he has written several legal articles ranging in topics from Canadian water rights to the protection of historic artifacts lost at sea.

Emily Sherrill Weadock is an award-winning graphic artist, author, animator, and illustrator whose talent ranges from technical illustration to 3D animation and Web site design. She has illustrated eighteen books and written two, *Flash 5 Quick Reference For Dummies* and *Creating Cool PowerPoint 97 Presentations*. Before trading brushes for mice, Emily enjoyed success as a mixed-media construction artist. She studied art at SMU and Baylor University.

Glenn Weadock is president of Independent Software, Inc. (ISI), a Colorado-based computer consulting firm he co-founded in 1982. ISI provides Web design, technical training, and consulting services to clients such as Global Knowledge, Ernst & Young, and Avaya Communications. Glenn has taught advanced technical seminars all over the world, and has written twenty books published in five languages, including *Look & Learn Dreamweaver 4.*

Dedication

To A.A. Hurwicz, with love and respect

—Michael Hurwicz

Acknowledgments

Thank you, thank you, thank you, thank you to:

Shelley Johnston for firmly yet gracefully shepherding this project from start to finish; co-authors John Kuhlman, Glenn and Emily Weadock, and Sean Nicholson for coming through in every way possible; Margo Catts for tirelessly finding and correcting my mistakes, blunders, and omissions; and technical editors extraordinaire Steve Heckler and Lynn Baus, for catching mistakes, testing fixes, and writing extensive and thoughtful suggestions for additional material that greatly enriched this book.

My most excellent agent, David Fugate at Waterside Productions, for making and fostering the connection with Que.

Ralf Bokelberg (`http://www.QLOD.com`) for oxo.fla, also used as a basis for tictactoe_lc.fla and player_lc.fla on the CD (Chapter 21).

Adam Holden-Bache and Mark Lewis, CEO and CTO, respectively, of Mass Transmit (`http://www.masstransmit.com`), for dropdownmenu.fla on the CD (Chapter 20).

Gary Grossman, principal engineer, Macromedia Flash team, for the `makeHandler()` function in Chapter 20.

Helen Triolo (`http://i-Technica.com`) for trigdemo.fla on the CD (Chapter 21).

Peter Hall (`http://www.peterjoel.com`) for scratch.fla on the CD (Chapter 20).

Andy Hall (`ahall@panache.co.uk`) for spacelisten.fla on the CD (Chapter 20).

Ric Ewing (`rewing@riverdeep.net`) for drawmethods.fla and 4SegCircle.fla on the CD (Chapter 20) and for general support and assistance on the drawing API.

Keith Peters (`kp@bit-101.com`, `www.bit-101.com`) for 3Dcube.fla and test5.fla on the CD (Chapter 20).

Millie Maruani (`millie@noos.fr`, `http://millie.free.fr`) for api_flower.fla and api_cube.fla on the CD (Chapter 20).

—Michael Hurwicz

WE WANT TO HEAR FROM YOU!

As the reader of this book, *you* are our most important critic and commentator. We value your opinion and want to know what we're doing right, what we could do better, what areas you'd like to see us publish in, and any other words of wisdom you're willing to pass our way.

You can email or write me directly to let me know what you did or didn't like about this book—as well as what we can do to make our books better.

Please note that I cannot help you with technical problems related to the topic of this book.

When you write, please be sure to include this book's title and author as well as your name and email address. I will carefully review your comments and share them with the author and editors who worked on the book.

Email: feedback@quepublishing.com

Mail: Mark Taber
          Associate Publisher
          Que Publishing
          800 East 96th Street
          Indianapolis, IN 46240 USA

For more information about this book or another Que title, visit our Web site at www.quepublishing.com. Type the ISBN (excluding hyphens) or the title of a book in the Search field to find the page you're looking for.

INTRODUCTION

In this chapter

What's New in Studio MX?   2

Who Should Read This Book?   3

How to Use This Book   4

Conventions Used in This Book   6

Macromedia Studio MX 2004 is the latest version of a product suite that includes Dreamweaver MX 2004, Flash MX 2004, Fireworks MX 2004, FreeHand MX, and ColdFusion MX 6.1 Developer Edition.

Dreamweaver MX is the leading professional Web development tool, used for creating all kinds of Web sites.

Flash started years ago as a tool for creating simple Web animations, and has evolved into a development environment for Internet applications, whether they involve interactivity, rich media such as video, or database access. In addition to its intrinsic capabilities, Flash gains strength from the fact that it is the dominant authoring tool for the Flash Player, which is not only the most popular rich media plug-in, but the most widely installed browser plug-in of any sort.

Fireworks MX is a graphics editor optimized for the Web, focusing on bitmaps but also supporting vector graphics.

FreeHand MX is a vector graphics drawing program.

ColdFusion MX turns your current Web server into a database server.

Together, these five programs form a powerful, flexible, integrated suite for developing Internet applications.

WHAT'S NEW IN STUDIO MX?

Dreamweaver's new features include

- Full CSS integration, including a "Relevant CSS" tab that displays rules applied to the selected element, and more accurate CSS layout rendering in Design view
- Dynamic cross-browser validation, automatically performed each time you save a document
- Enhanced integration with Flash and Fireworks
- An image-editing toolbar for frequent graphics operations
- Intelligent cut-and-paste from Microsoft Office documents
- "Siteless" page editing, permitting you to work on a server without creating a full Dreamweaver site
- Secure FTP for safer server connections
- Enhanced code-editing tools, including an improved Tag inspector and a new Code View context menu
- Advanced find and replace

Flash's new features include

- Faster Flash files (SWFs)
- Third-party plug-ins supporting 3D, text effects, graphs, charts, and more

- Timeline Effects, which make it easy to add common effects such as fade-ins, fade-outs, wipes, drop shadows, blurs, position-rotation-scale animations, and fragmenting and "exploding" objects
- Behaviors for easy application of predefined ActionScript snippets
- More and better components, for faster construction of sophisticated user interfaces
- Templates that provide basic design and architecture for a project, saving you set-up time
- A spell-checker
- Enhanced find and replace
- A Video Import Wizard, including video clip editing
- A History panel that records previous actions, enabling flexible undo, redo, and command creation
- Tighter security rules in Flash Player 7
- ActionScript 2, implementing object-oriented programming (OOP) in a more standard way

Fireworks' new features include

- Improved performance
- Graphical previews that make it easier to select the right fill, brush, or texture
- An Auto Shapes tool that provides new shapes
- A Red Eye Removal tool that removes "red-eye" from photographs
- A Replace Color tool that makes it easier to change selected colors in bitmaps
- Motion blur effects
- Roundtrip editing for server-side file formats, such as ASP, CFM, and PHP, seamlessly reflecting Fireworks edits in other MX 2004 programs
- New anti-aliasing options
- A contour gradient feature that applies a gradient effect that matches an object's shape
- Six varieties of dashed and dotted lines
- An Add Noise Live Effect that applies "noise" to an image for a more natural look
- JavaScript API (Application Programming Interface) extensions

FreeHand MX and **ColdFusion MX** were not updated for Studio MX 2004.

WHO SHOULD READ THIS BOOK?

This book assumes that you have some background in graphics and/or Web design, and you've purchased (or are considering purchasing) Studio MX 2004 with the goal of producing professional-level work. You're looking for ways of using the software more efficiently and effectively. Perhaps you've played with the programs and looked at the tutorials and help files a bit, and you want something more.

While keeping proficiency and professionalism in mind as the goal, this book still tries to explain concepts and techniques completely. Nor does it assume that you know something about Studio MX 2004 before it is covered in these pages. The hope is that even a beginner—a motivated beginner, that is—could find this book valuable.

Starting with basics, not skipping anything, and still getting into advanced topics means packing as much useful information into each page as possible. Therefore, this book often does not walk you step by step through basic tasks. It assumes you are a motivated learner, willing to jump in and experiment.

HOW TO USE THIS BOOK

This book contains one major section for each of the five Studio MX 2004 programs. In addition, there is a preliminary section (Chapters 1–3) covering topics and features that apply to multiple programs in the Studio MX 2004 suite. All the later sections in this book assume familiarity with the first three chapters. Therefore, most readers will probably find it useful to look the first section over before proceeding to material specific to a particular program.

In particular, Chapter 3 serves as an introduction to the user interfaces of Dreamweaver, Flash, Fireworks, and FreeHand. This is possible because these programs have so much in common. Whichever program you are interested in, Chapter 3 is your jumping-off place.

Except for this dependency on the first section, each program-specific section can basically stand on its own. You can go right to the first chapter on Flash (Chapter 14) without having read any of the chapters on Dreamweaver (Chapters 4–13). Similarly, you won't have any problem reading the chapters on Fireworks (Chapters 24–28) if you haven't read any of the Dreamweaver or Flash material.

There are two other exceptions to this "each-section-is-an-island" principle. First, there are features that specifically target integration between two Studio MX 2004 programs. To grasp these features, you obviously have to have some understanding of both programs.

The second exception has to do with features that relate to database access. An online database application comes in three parts: a database server, application-specific services that run on the server, and clients that access those services. ColdFusion, Dreamweaver, and optionally Flash are natural allies in creating such a three-part online database application: ColdFusion for implementing the database server, Dreamweaver for creating application-specific services built on ColdFusion or other server technologies, and either Dreamweaver or Flash for creating client applications. Chapter 32 ("Understanding and Administering ColdFusion") in the ColdFusion section discusses this cooperative relationship in more detail. In the Dreamweaver section, Chapter 13 ("Developing ColdFusion Applications in Dreamweaver") shows how to create ColdFusion services and browser pages that access those services. Finally, in the Flash section, Chapter 23 ("Using Flash for Dynamic Data") uses one of the ColdFusion services created in Chapter 13 for examples involving Flash database clients. So there is a tight relationship between Chapter 13, Chapter 23, and the ColdFusion chapters. This is natural because an online database application simply cannot be constructed with Dreamweaver alone, Flash alone, or ColdFusion alone.

If your primary goal, for example, is to create a Flash client that accesses ColdFusion services or any online database service, it might makes sense to read the ColdFusion chapters first (even though they're at the end of the book), then Chapter 13 to create the service that the Flash client will access, and finally Chapter 23 to create the Flash client.

For most purposes, however, you can read this book from cover to cover or use it as a random-access reference. The same applies to each individual section: You can read sequentially or look for the particular feature that interests you. Within a section, however, later chapters may assume familiarity with earlier chapters.

First-time users will probably do well to dive into the programs and play a little bit before starting the book. Realistically, you will probably use this book largely as a reference, to help you solve problems as they arise. On the other hand, Dreamweaver MX 2004, Flash MX 2004, and Fireworks MX 2004 have enough new features that even experienced users may benefit from at least skimming these sections from beginning to end, looking for the "New in Studio MX 2004" icon:

 Where there are sample or reference files on the CD to accompany the text, be sure to look at them. In the case of sample files, try playing with them and modifying them. The hands-on experience will prove invaluable, and you may even be able to use a file as a partial basis for your own project.

Also, be sure to check out the many excellent Web resources for Studio MX 2004 developers. If you need a jumping-off place, go to http://www.hurwicz.com and click on Using Studio MX.

This book is divided into six parts:

I. Getting Started with Macromedia Studio MX 2004
II. Dreamweaver MX 2004
III. Flash MX 2004
IV. Fireworks MX 2004
V. FreeHand MX
VI. ColdFusion MX

Part I (Chapters 1–3) gives you an overview of the Studio MX 2004 suite. Chapter 3 goes into detail about common interface features.

Part II (Chapters 4–13) covers Dreamweaver MX 2004. Chapter 13 covers database access. Examples use ColdFusion services.

Part III (Chapters 14–23) is dedicated to Flash MX 2004. Chapter 23 shows you how to create Flash database clients; it and uses a ColdFusion service for examples.

Part IV (Chapters 24–28) covers Fireworks MX 2004, and Part V (Chapters 29–31) covers FreeHand MX.

Finally, Part VI (Chapters 32 and 33) focuses on ColdFusion MX, but includes material that may be helpful in understanding the database-related features of Dreamweaver and Flash.

CONVENTIONS USED IN THIS BOOK

In ordinary text (not code), italics indicate the initial definition of a new term or phrase. Initial caps indicate words that appear in the user interface, such as menu items, dialog box names, dialog box elements, and commands.

A monospace font is used to differentiate code—HTML, ColdFusion Markup Language (CFML) and ActionScript—from any other text with special emphasis. For example, you will see `<p align="right">` (HTML), `<cfoutput>` (ColdFusion) and `gotoAndPlay()` (ActionScript).

Within code, italicized words are placeholders for actual code that you will substitute. For example, in the ActionScript `Key.isDown(charCode)`, `charCode` is a placeholder for a character code that you will substitute. `Key.isDown(Key.UP)` is actual ActionScript, in which `Key.UP` represents the actual character code.

A common ActionScript convention, often used in this book, is to start object names with `my` when they represent new instances created by the programmer. For instance, `TextField` represents the built-in class of text fields, not created by the programmer. On the other hand, `myTextField` is a new text field instance created by the programmer.

Because using the mouse is different on Macs and Windows-based PCs, we have indicated the appropriate action for Mac users in parentheses, while PC useres should refer to the actions in brackets. For example, "To see the pop-up menu, (control+click) [Right-click] anywhere on the screen."

All the Studio MX programs except ColdFusion have a panel, at the bottom of the screen by default, labeled Properties. Macromedia now refers to this panel as the *Property inspector*. However, you may also see *Properties inspector* or *Property inspector*. *Panel*, *inspector*, and sometimes *tab* and even the old *palette* are often used interchangeably. These various bits of jargon all mean essentially the same thing—little boxes with particular specialties. In addition to the main text and screenshots, this book contains tips, cautions, notes, and cross-references. These are all designated with special icons, as follows:

TIP

Tips contain insights and techniques that will help you use Studio MX more effectively.

NOTE

> Notes contain extra information or alternative techniques for performing tasks that will enhance your understanding of the current topic.

CAUTION

> Cautions warn you about potential problems.

→ Cross-references direct you to complementary or supplementary information in other sections of the book, or on the CD that accompanies this book.

PART I

GETTING STARTED WITH MACROMEDIA STUDIO MX

1 Setup and Planning   11

2 Studio MX: A Bird's-Eye View   17

3 Introducing the MX Interface   23

CHAPTER **1**

SETUP AND PLANNING

In this chapter

Additional Software   12

Planning and Design   13

There are a couple of things I thought I should mention before diving into the details of Studio MX—namely, additional software you might need or want, and tools to help with the "noodling" stage of Web site design.

ADDITIONAL SOFTWARE

Studio MX is a fairly self-contained toolkit, providing everything you need to create Web pages. However, you might need or want some additional software to get the maximum benefit from Studio MX. Two main types of programs come to mind here: a Web server and a database management system (DBMS).

WEB SERVICE

You'll probably want a local Web server to test Web pages. To see whether you already have one running, type http://localhost in your browser address bar. If you have a local Web server running, you'll probably get a default page with various kinds of information about your Web server. Or you may just get an index of folders and files.

 Don't know if you have a local Web server? **See** *"How can I tell if I have a local Web server or not?" in the "Troubleshooting" section at the end of this chapter.*

Another option is to use the Web server that comes with ColdFusion Developer Edition. That's a good choice if you're planning to use ColdFusion and not ASP.NET, and if you need a Web server only for testing, not for actually hosting applications. The advantage of the Web server that comes with ColdFusion is that it is automatically configured during installation. If you use a non-ColdFusion Web server, you'll have to go through an extra step to configure it for use with ColdFusion. Note that the ColdFusion Web server operates by default on port 8500, so you have to put http://localhost:8500 in the address bar of the browser.

ASP.NET pages work only with Microsoft IIS 5 or higher, which runs only under certain versions of Windows (*not* Windows 98 or lower, for example). You can *create* ASP.NET pages on any computer running Studio MX. But you'll need IIS 5 to *test* them.

And as an alternative to running a local Web server, you can upload files via File Transfer Protocol (FTP) to a Web site hosted by an Internet Service Provider (ISP) and test them there. However, it's more efficient to be able to test on a Web server installed on your own local machine, or on a shared drive on a server on your local area network (LAN); it saves you the sometimes time-consuming step of uploading files.

→ For sources of information on this topic **see** "Installing a Web Server" on the CD accompanying this book.

DATABASE MANAGEMENT

Studio MX allows you to build Web applications that access databases via a ColdFusion server or other technologies such as PHP and ASP.NET. All you need is Dreamweaver to create the database-enabled Web pages, and one or more database files. Optionally, you can use Flash to build the user interface.

Someone has to create the database files using a database management system (DBMS). Microsoft Access and SQL Server are common DBMS choices for both Windows and Macintosh users. Shareware MySQL is included with Macintosh OS X 10.2.6, and can be downloaded free for Windows.

If someone else is handling the database design and implementation, you can get by without a database management system yourself. The database designer can give you the database file or files, ideally populated with some sample data. You can work with the files on your development machine without having the program that created them. If the structure of the data needs to change—for instance, the database has fields for a user's name, login ID, and password, and you want to add a field that defines a role for each user—the database designer makes the necessary changes and gives you a new database file. You yourself can use Dreamweaver, and optionally Flash, to create utilities to add, delete, or change data.

On the other hand, if you need to create database files yourself, or change their structure, you'll need a database management system. Microsoft Access and SQL Server are widely supported by ColdFusion hosting services, and are also the most common choices for use with ASP.NET. MySQL is often associated with PHP. Of course, there are many other DBMS options.

After you have the database file, you can select it as a content source in the Bindings panel in Dreamweaver.

→ For more on dynamic data in Dreamweaver, **see** Chapter 13, "Developing ColdFusion Applications in Dreamweaver," **page 287**.

→ For more on dynamic data in Flash, **see** Chapter 23, "Using Flash for Dynamic Data," **page 661**.

PLANNING AND DESIGN

Studio MX is primarily a tool set for actually creating Web sites, but you're also likely to use it for "noodling" ideas and experimenting—the equivalent of sketching on a napkin—when you (or your client) are not yet sure exactly what you want the site to look like or do. FreeHand can be particularly valuable at this stage. Other tools you might want to leverage include the Dreamweaver Bindings panel, templates, and Cascading Style Sheets (CSS).

USING FREEHAND FOR MOCKUPS

At the planning stage, when you're just experimenting with ideas, FreeHand has a number of features that recommend it for the job.

For instance, it is the only program in the suite that can handle multiple pages in one document and output them all as HTML in one operation (using Publish as HTML). You may or may not end up using this HTML in your final project, but it does allow you to generate and view multiple Web pages quickly and easily. So FreeHand is an efficient tool if you're making mockups or sketches of multiple Web pages.

FreeHand is also the only product that has built-in flowcharting, which uses its dynamically linked objects feature. Finally, Master Pages allows you to easily represent common elements, such as a logo or navigation bar, on multiple Web pages.

→ For more on using FreeHand for mockups, **see** Chapter 30, "Using FreeHand in Web Site Planning and Creation, " **page 837**.

THE DREAMWEAVER BINDINGS PANEL

If you're working with dynamic data, part of the planning/design process will be getting a feeling for how much room it will take up on the screen, how to present it legibly and usably, how it will harmonize with other design elements, and so on. Assuming you've already got your database installed, and you are successfully accessing it through the Bindings panel in Dreamweaver, populating HTML tables with data is a straightforward process in Dreamweaver. It's easy enough to create several different data layouts to see which one works best.

TEMPLATES

You may also want to spend some time browsing the templates in Flash and Dreamweaver. If you can decide early in the design process that you can adapt one of these to your needs, it can save you hours and hours of work. The template options show up when you start a new document file (File, New).

CSS

Cascading Style Sheets (CSS) can make it easy to experiment with different formats and see the changes in all your files, including text in Flash content.

CSS originated in the HTML world as a way of controlling formatting in any number of documents by editing one simple text file, the style sheet. One of Macromedia's major focuses for Dreamweaver MX 2004 was deeper support for CSS-based designs. Dreamweaver MX 2004 is an excellent tool for creating and maintaining style sheets. And now the style sheets you manage in Dreamweaver can easily be applied to text in Flash, too. Dreamweaver also provides templates for style sheets and for HTML documents based on style sheets.

Studio MX's CSS support isn't perfect. I'd like to see Flash use CSS for non-text design elements, such as background color. And I wish I could apply styles with one click in Dreamweaver MX 2004, the way I could in Dreamweaver MX. Nevertheless, I'm excited about Macromedia's clear commitment to making CSS central to the design process, and to expanding the power and convenience of CSS beyond HTML and Dreamweaver. Even Fireworks, with its Export to CSS Layers feature, enables you to export the layers of a Fireworks document to CSS layers, so that you can continue in Dreamweaver to move and re-size each layer individually, and even change which layer is on top of which.

CSS offers a low-maintenance way of keeping formatting in sync in any number of HTML files. That is particularly valuable during the early design stages, when you may have to make global changes repeatedly. Consider making CSS an integral part of your strategy early in the design cycle.

TROUBLESHOOTING

How can I tell whether I have a local Web server or not?

If you're on Windows, you may already be running Microsoft Internet Information Server (IIS) or Personal Web Server (PWS), a scaled-down version of IIS. One clue that you are running one of these is if your system drive contains an *Inetpub* folder; that's the PWS and IIS default folder.

Similarly, Macintosh OS X 10.2.6 and newer includes the popular shareware Apache HTTP Server. Try typing **http://localhost**. If you get a browser error—such as Page cannot be displayed—go into System Preferences, click Sharing, and enable Web sharing to activate Apache.

CHAPTER **2**

Studio MX: A Bird's-Eye View

In this chapter

Studio MX: A Choosing Your Tools   18

The Basics: Words and Graphics   18

Animation, Navigation, and Interaction   19

Dynamic Content   20

2

STUDIO MX: CHOOSING YOUR TOOLS

Studio MX 2004 represents an incredibly rich array of capabilities, reflecting the variety of Web sites and applications developers are called upon to create. Any particular Web site or Internet application is likely to use only a small subset of these capabilities. Some Studio MX features address common requirements, such as displaying pages containing words and/or images and navigating those pages. Others address specialized or advanced needs, such as displaying dynamic data, playing video and audio, or applying cinematic effects such as fade-ins and fade-outs.

In some cases, the choice of tool is clear. For video and audio, for example, use Flash. This chapter covers situations where you have more choices.

This chapter presents a high-level view of Studio MX, as well as some associated products, and what each of the Studio MX programs can do. This chapter also does double duty as a quick tour of Studio MX and environs, and as a guide for determining which tools and features you might use for a particular project. (I'll be talking as if you will be using all these tools yourself. Obviously, tasks may be divided up among the team members. However, the association of task to tool remains the same.)

There's a certain amount of overlap in what the Studio MX programs do. For those common functions, which program you choose for a given task may be mostly a matter of taste or experience. That's sometimes the case when choosing drawing tools, for instance.

At the same time, each of the programs clearly has unique strengths and limitations. Using the best tool for the job will help you work faster and provide more value to your client and the people accessing your site.

THE BASICS: WORDS AND GRAPHICS

Fundamental requirements for most Web sites include text and graphics.

For editing existing bitmaps, such as JPEGs or GIFs, use Fireworks. If you want to create bitmaps from scratch with drawing tools, you could use Fireworks, Flash, or FreeHand. All of them can export GIFs and JPEGs. FreeHand has the most powerful drawing capabilities. However, each program has some unique capabilities not found in the others.

→ For a comparison of the tools in Fireworks, Flash, and FreeHand, **see** Chapter 3, "Introducing the MX Interface," **page 23**. It's largely a discussion of similarities in the tools, but it also gets into differences.

All four Studio MX programs deal with text. Fireworks and FreeHand excel at applying special effects such as drop shadows, embossing, and blurring. Usually, applying the effect converts the vector text to a bitmap, so it can no longer be edited as text. Then the text is typically exported as a bitmap file, such as a GIF, to be used in a Web site.

Dreamweaver, on the other hand, works like a word processor in that it directly manipulates the system fonts provided by the operating system. There's no need to convert to or export to a bitmap format. However, when it comes to changing the appearance of the text, you're limited to just a few standard possibilities, such as bolding, italicizing, and changing the font size.

If you just want to get text online, use Dreamweaver. For instance, if you want to put a short story online, just type it and apply text formatting in Dreamweaver, save, and publish. Dreamweaver also provides the most straightforward means of combining text and graphics.

The main reason to use FreeHand or Fireworks with text is for effects such as drop shadows, embossing, and blurring. Each has some unique effects, such as 3D (extruding) in FreeHand and motion trail (comet tail) in Fireworks. If you want to use text effects, a couple of hours playing with them in both programs will be time well spent. (Fun, too.) Text with effects applied has to be exported in a bitmap or Flash (SWF) format. If you want to combine the text with an image, you can do that, too.

ANIMATION, NAVIGATION AND INTERACTION

You can create animation as a Dynamic HTML (DHTML) file, an animated GIF, or an SWF.

DHTML is the most limited in what it can do: just vary the style, position, and display of HTML elements, such as text or graphics. On the positive side, it uses standard JavaScript, so most modern browsers support it with no problems. Use Dreamweaver behaviors to apply DHTML without having to write any JavaScript.

Animated GIFs present even fewer potential compatibility problems—even older browsers support them. On the downside, GIF is a bitmap format; you can't use vector graphics to reduce file sizes. (Vectors define shapes using compact mathematical formulas, whereas bitmaps define the properties of each and every pixel, one by one. Bitmaps are often ten times as big as equivalent vectors. On the other hand, the Flash SWF vector format requires the Flash plug-in in the browser.) Files get bigger as animations get more complex, so animated GIFs are generally used only for very simple animations.

→ For more on the differences between vector and bitmap graphics, **see** " Understanding Vector Graphics," **page 352**, in Chapter 16, "Working with Vector Graphics and Bitmaps."

You can create animated GIFs in either Flash or Fireworks. Flash's "timeline effects" feature makes it ridiculously easy to apply effects such as bouncing, fading in or out, and exploding. Tweening offers a nearly infinite variety of animation possibilities, but does involve a learning curve, even with Macromedia's intuitive visual tools. (If you use ActionScript to apply animation, it is lost in animated GIFs.)

Fireworks animation is limited to varying the position, rotation, scale, and opacity of an object over a particular number of frames—much more limited than Flash, but very easy to use.

The SWF file format, which uses vector graphics, can reduce file sizes, so it is the usual choice for more complex or longer animations. On the other hand, people viewing your site must have the right version of the Flash Player installed in their browser.

Flash was created for making SWFs, and it offers stunning breadth and power for creating animations, using not just visual tools and tweening (as with animated GIFs), but also ActionScript. Almost anything that can be done on the Web today can be done with Flash and SWFs. The learning curve can be lifelong. On the other hand, you can also do the same

2

easy yet impressive things with SWFs that you can with animated GIFs, and the file sizes will likely be much smaller.

For FreeHand and Fireworks, SWF output is just a feature, not the central purpose of their existence. Fireworks offers the same position-rotation-scale-opacity functionality for SWFs as for animated GIFs. FreeHand enables you to use the Animate Xtra feature to animate the position of objects, and you can also apply some simple ActionScript to do things such as go to a particular frame and either stop or continue play, load movies or sounds, drag and drop movie clips, or go to a particular URL. These actions are more navigation/interaction than animation.

As with animation, there's not much you can't do with Flash when it comes to navigation and interaction. Flash supports drag-and-drop "behaviors" that enable you to easily create buttons to do things such as jump to a URL, play a sound, go to a particular frame of a movie, and pause a video stream—all without writing a line of ActionScript.

By dragging and dropping Flash components onto the Stage and setting a few parameters, you can create professional-quality user interface elements such as scrolling list boxes, drop-down menus, and combo boxes. Components can save you a lot of work. Most of them are useful only in the context of an ActionScript program.

DYNAMIC CONTENT

Dynamic content is generated or retrieved on the fly (dynamically) by a server-based application and integrated into a Web page before it is sent to the browser. For example, the server-based application may pull data from a database and display it in the Web page.

The developer (or development team) has to do two things: Create one or more server behaviors, such as retrieving a recordset from a database, and create client applications such as Web pages, possibly including Flash applications, that invoke those server behaviors and display the results.

CREATING SERVER BEHAVIORS

In Studio MX, you use Dreamweaver to create the server-side functionality. Dreamweaver can create Web pages supporting any of five major dynamic content technologies: Macromedia ColdFusion, Microsoft Active Server Pages (ASP), ASP.NET, JavaServer Pages (JSP), and PHP. Of these, this book focuses on ColdFusion.

You can use three basic approaches to create server behaviors. They're not mutually exclusive, and the first can serve as a gentle introduction to the second.

- First, Dreamweaver provides tools that make it easy to create simple, useful server behaviors, with little or no coding. These tools can ease the learning curve and speed up your workflow. The Dreamweaver tools are particularly powerful for creating ColdFusion-based server behaviors.

→ For more on Dreamweaver's tools for auto-generating ColdFusion server behaviors, **see** Chapter 13, "Developing ColdFusion Applications in Dreamweaver," **page 287**.

- Second, you can code in the server's native language. In the case of ColdFusion Markup Language (CFML), it's not too difficult to learn, especially if you already know some HTML, and the power you get in return is impressive.

→ For more on CFML, **see** Chapter 33, "ColdFusion Markup Language (CFML)," **page 885**.

- Third, you can use ColdFusion's Server-Side ActionScript (SSAS). This consists of just two functions: CF.query for database operations such as retrieving, inserting, updating, and deleting records; and CF.http for sending information to a remote server or passing variables to a ColdFusion page or CGI program and getting return data. It's just a tiny fraction of what CFML can do, but very often it's all an ActionScript programmer needs. Everything else can be done in Flash.

CREATING THE CLIENT INTERFACE

To develop the client functionality—making requests and receiving return values—you'll probaby use just Dreamweaver or just Flash, though there's no reason why you can't use both in a single application. Both Dreamweaver and Flash have easy-to-use, powerful tools for integrating dynamic data.

Dreamweaver is a little easier than Flash. Dreamweaver can almost instantly create a bare-bones user interface that incorporates dynamic data. For instance, in Chapter 13, you'll find an example of creating a client request in Dreamweaver just by dragging and dropping a server behavior.

→ For more on drag-and-drop client creation, **see** "Consuming Web Services," **page 316**, in Chapter 13, "Developing ColdFusion Applications in Dreamweaver."

Still, it's amazing how easy it can be to get the basics of dynamic data working in Flash MX Professional 2004. (And you should definitely use the Professional version for dynamic data, because of the special data components it includes.)

Both Dreamweaver and Flash can produce a wide variety of great-looking, powerful, highly usable client pages and applications that incorporate dynamic data. Realistically, they're both so good, I think most people will make the decision about which program to use based on factors other than their dynamic data functionality.

→ For more on dynamic data in Flash, **see** Chapter 23, "Using Flash for Dynamic Data," **page 661**.

→ For more on dynamic data in Dreamweaver, **see** Chapter 13, **page 287**.

→ There's also information on dynamic data in Chapter 32, "Understanding and Administering ColdFusion," **page 875**.

CHAPTER 3

INTRODUCING THE MX INTERFACE

In this chapter

Studio MX: Family Resemblances   24

Main Menu Bar and Tool Bar   30

Panels   30

Tools Panel Subsections   33

Tools   33

Working with Text   42

Character and Paragraph Attributes   45

Keyboard Shortcuts   47

STUDIO MX: FAMILY RESEMBLANCES

A number of features and user-interface elements are shared among all or a subset of the Studio MX family. (The features discussed here aren't relevant to ColdFusion, which is not a desktop application, and has only a browser-based administrative utility.) These common elements include

- A start page, offering likely initial actions, such as creating a new document, creating a document based on a template, or opening a recent document.
- A central workspace, called the Stage in Flash and the "document window" in the other programs.
- A main menu bar at the top of the screen, with File, Edit, View, Insert, Modify, Commands, Window, and Help menus.
- Many of the options on these menus.
- A main toolbar below the main menu bar. If the main menu bar is hidden, use Window, Toolbars, Main to display it.
- Many of the commands on the main toolbar.
- Panels and the way they work—how you open, close, minimize, maximize, dock, and undock them, for example.
- A Property inspector.
- Many of the object attributes on the Property inspector (for example, font styles such as bold and italic).
- A Tools panel on the left side of the screen.
- Tools panel subsections such as View and Colors.
- Many of the tools on the Tools panels (for example, selection, text, and drawing tools).
- Some keyboard shortcuts.

Figures 3.1–3.4 show the main interface features for Flash, Fireworks, FreeHand, and Dreamweaver respectively.

Figure 3.1
The Flash MX 2004 interface. The Rounded rectangle radius button in the lower-left corner rounds the corners of rectangles.

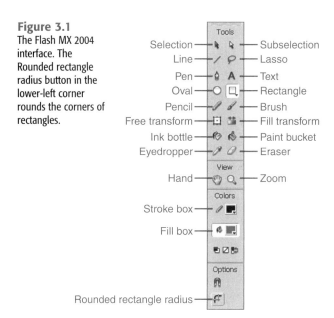

Selection — Subselection
Line — Lasso
Pen — Text
Oval — Rectangle
Pencil — Brush
Free transform — Fill transform
Ink bottle — Paint bucket
Eyedropper — Eraser
Hand — Zoom
Stroke box
Fill box
Rounded rectangle radius

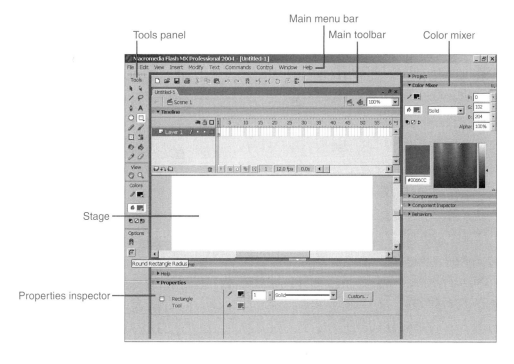

Tools panel
Main menu bar
Main toolbar
Color mixer
Stage
Properties inspector

Figure 3.2
The Fireworks MX
2004 interface.

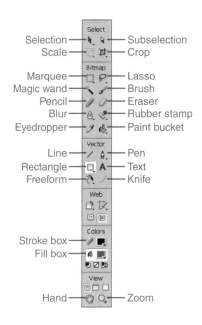

Selection — Subselection
Scale — Crop

Bitmap

Marquee — Lasso
Magic wand — Brush
Pencil — Eraser
Blur — Rubber stamp
Eyedropper — Paint bucket

Vector

Line — Pen
Rectangle — Text
Freeform — Knife

Web

Colors

Stroke box
Fill box

View

Hand — Zoom

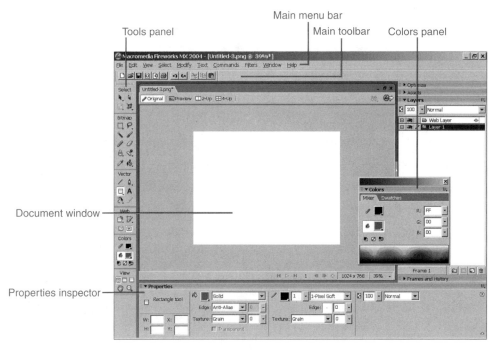

Main menu bar

Tools panel · Main toolbar · Colors panel

Document window

Properties inspector

Figure 3.3
The FreeHand MX interface. The rectangle in the document window has a linear gradient fill.

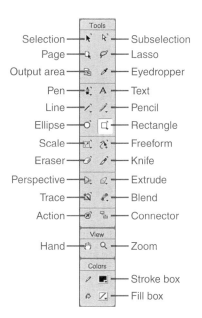

Selection — Subselection
Page — Lasso
Output area — Eyedropper
Pen — Text
Line — Pencil
Ellipse — Rectangle
Scale — Freeform
Eraser — Knife
Perspective — Extrude
Trace — Blend
Action — Connector
Hand — Zoom
Stroke box
Fill box

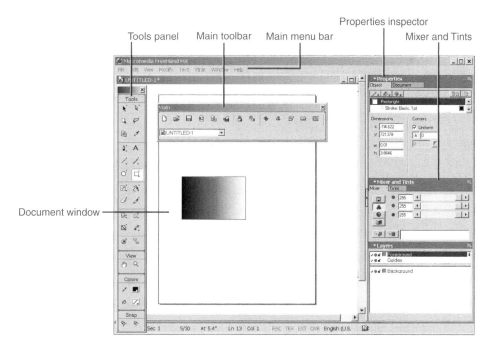

Tools panel
Main toolbar
Main menu bar
Properties inspector
Mixer and Tints
Document window

3

Figure 3.4
The Dreamweaver MX 2004 interface. Dreamweaver has a color picker, which comes up when you click the color box. Dreamweaver doesn't have a colors mixer for creating custom colors.

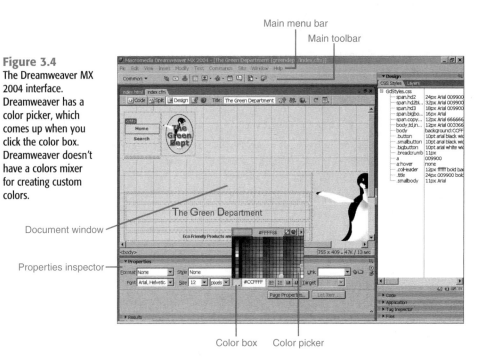

Table 3.1 shows which programs support each of the main interface features.

Main feature	Sub-feature/ option	Menu Options	Dreamweaver	Flash	Fireworks	FreeHand
Start Page	Open a recent item, Create new		x	x	x	
	Create from template		x	x		
Main menu bar			x	x	x	x
	File	Open, Close, Save, Import/ Export, Exit	x	x	x	x
	Edit	Undo/Redo, Cut/Copy/ Paste, Preferences (*), Keyboard Shortcuts	x	x	x	x

TABLE 3.1   LIST OF FEATURES SUPPORTED BY FLASH, FIREWORKS, DREAMWEAVER, AND FREEHAND

Main feature	Sub-feature/ option	Menu Options	Dreamweaver	Flash	Fireworks	FreeHand
	Modify	Arrange, Align	x	x	x	x
	Commands		x	x	x	
	Window					
	Help					
Main Toolbar	New, Open, Save, Print			x	x	x
Panels	Open, Close, Minimize, Maximize, Dock, Undock		x			
	Properties	Text	x	x	x	x
		Bitmaps	x	x	x	x
		Tools		x	x	x
		Document		x	x	x
	Tools	Tools (Selection, Subselection, Lasso, Line, Pen, Text, Rectangle, Ellipse, Eyedropper, Eraser, Brush)		x	x	x
		View (Hand, Zoom)		x	x	x
		Colors		x	x	x
Keyboard Shortcuts			x	x	x	x

(*) Preferences is on the Flash menu on the Mac.

SELECTING OBJECTS

To select objects in Flash, Fireworks, and FreeHand, you can use the Selection (Pointer), Subselection, and Lasso tools, or use keyboard shortcuts or menu commands. With the Selection and Subselection tools, you click and drag to create a rectangular selection box. With the lasso tool, you can create irregularly shaped selection boxes.

To use the Lasso, create a shape by clicking and dragging. When you release the mouse, the shape is automatically closed with a straight line, and everything within the resulting shape is selected. FreeHand shows you the straight line; Flash and Fireworks don't. In Flash, the

Lasso has a polygon mode, selectable in the Options section of the Tools panel, which constrains you to drawing straight lines, and requires you to click for each line segment, and double-click to end.

You can group objects (Modify, Group) so that you can select them as a single object.

Hold down the Cmd (Mac) or Ctrl (Windows) key to temporarily select the Pointer while using another tool.

While using the Selection, Subselection, or Lasso tools, hold down the Shift key to select multiple objects.

MAIN MENU BAR AND TOOLBAR

A main menu bar and toolbar at the top of the screen—as well as options for opening files, cutting and pasting, or printing—are common to a wide variety of desktop applications. (The main toolbar is not displayed in Flash by default, but is accessible via Window, Toolbars, Main.)

It can be hard to predict, for instance, where different applications will put dialogs for preferences or customizing keyboard shortcuts. It's handy to know that they will always be at the bottom of the Edit menu in Studio MX in Windows and on the menu with the application name (e.g. the Flash menu in Flash) on the Mac.

PANELS

Panels group related information into a few well-defined categories, such as Tools and Properties, making it easier to find what you're looking for. With a single click on the triangle to the left of the panel name, you can minimize or maximize panels, making it easier to keep your workspace uncluttered. A panel that is currently closed can be opened via the Window menu.

All panels can be docked and undocked, so you can arrange them the way you want. Position the cursor over the upper left corner of the panel. When the cursor turns into a "move" icon, click and drag to move the panel. (See Figure 3.5.) After a panel is undocked, you can move it around by clicking and dragging on the blue bar at the top of the panel, but you have to grab it by the upper left corner again to re-dock it. On the Mac, in Flash, you cannot dock panels to the Timeline or Stage, and the Property inspector floats on its own. By default, the Actions panel in Flash also opens free-floating on the Mac, but it can be docked.

Move icon

Figure 3.5
To dock or undock a panel, grab it by the upper left corner.

You can resize some panels by positioning the cursor at an edge or corner. If the cursor turns into a two-headed arrow, as shown in the lower-right corner in Figure 3.6, the panel is resizable. Click and drag to resize.

Figure 3.6
To resize a panel, grab it by an edge or corner. If the cursor turns into a two-headed arrow, you can resize.

— Two-headed arrow cursor

All the Studio MX programs have a Property inspector that provides contextual editing options based on the type of object selected, often giving you one-stop shopping for object editing. It's at the bottom of the screen, except in FreeHand, where by default all panels except Tools are on the right. (Refer to Figures 3.1–3.4.)

Sometimes the programs share just a few basic object attributes on the Property inspector. For instance, Dreamweaver, Fireworks, Flash, and FreeHand all work with bitmaps, but only two attributes—the width and height of the image—are common to all four programs. All but Dreamweaver also give the bitmap's position on an x-y coordinate grid. (See Figure 3.7.)

Figure 3.7
Clockwise from left: Bitmap properties in FreeHand, Flash and Fireworks.

3

Similarly, Fireworks, Flash, and FreeHand all have a "document" object, but the x and y dimensions of the document are the only common attributes. (See Figure 3.8.)

Figure 3.8
From top to bottom: Document properties in FreeHand, Flash and Fireworks.

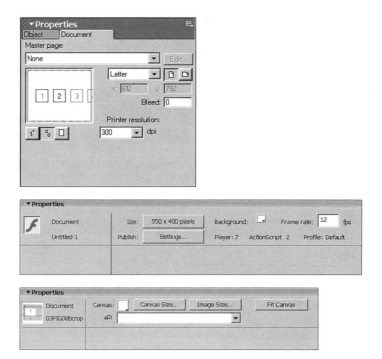

One area of significant overlap is manipulating text. There are half a dozen or so common attributes for text objects—including styles such as bold and italic, left-right-center alignment, font, size, and color—most of them expressed in standard symbols familiar from applications such as Microsoft Word. (See Figure 3.9.)

Figure 3.9
Common text attributes, shown here in the Dreamweaver Property inspector.

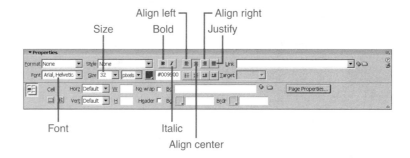

Even where individual attributes are not the same from program to program, though, it's still a great efficiency-booster just to have almost everything related to a particular type of object gathered in one place, as opposed to being scattered in half a dozen different palettes, as was often the case a couple of versions back.

TOOLS PANEL SUBSECTIONS

The Tools panel is divided into subsections, including a View section, a Colors section, and one or more sections for editing tools. Flash also has an Options section where you select options associated with the currently selected editing tool, such as the Round Rectangle Radius option shown in Figure 3.1. Fireworks also has a Web section, with tools for preparing graphics for use on the Web.

The View section contains tools to manipulate the view of the workspace, as opposed to objects in the workspace. The Hand tool and the Zoom tool are common to Flash, Fireworks, and FreeHand. (Refer to Figures 3.1, 3.2, and 3.4.)

Click and drag with the Hand tool to move the view—an alternative to the scroll bars on the bottom and side of the workspace.

Click with the Zoom tool anywhere in the workspace to zoom in. The spot where you click becomes the center of the view. Option-click (Mac) or Alt+click (Windows) to zoom out. You can also drag out a selection box around any area to zoom in on that area. In Flash, the options section enables you to select Zoom In or Zoom Out modes.

In Fireworks, the View section also contains options for viewing the workspace full-screen, with or without menus.

3

TOOLS

The broadest and deepest areas of overlap relate to the editing tools in the Tools panel. Selection, Subselection, Line, Lasso, Pen, Pencil, Text, Rectangle, Ellipse, Eyedropper, and Eraser tools are all found in Flash, Fireworks, and FreeHand. (Refer to Figures 3.1, 3.2 and 3.4.)

Many of the basic concepts and techniques for using these tools are the same in all three programs. Common elements include the basics of strokes, fills, and gradients, as well as the workings of tools such as Selection, Subselection, Line, Lasso, Pen, Text, Rectangle, Ellipse, and Eyedropper. The Eraser, though it has the same basic function in all Studio MX programs—deleting objects or portions of objects—differs enough among programs to deserve separate treatment for each. The same is true of the Brush tool, common to Flash and Fireworks.

STROKES AND FILLS

Vector drawing tools create shapes consisting of strokes, fills, or both. Strokes are lines, and fills are areas. In shapes containing both, strokes and fills are independent of one another: You can set their attributes separately and move them independently.

Flash is unique in that overlapping shapes drawn on the same layer interact. For instance:

- A shape drawn on top of another replaces any portions of the original shape that it obscures.

- Shapes of the same color merge where they touch, whereas shapes of different colors remain distinct (although overlapped portions are replaced, as described in the preceding bullet).

- New vertices are created where strokes intersect.

In Fireworks and FreeHand, no new vertices are created at stroke intersections, and overlapping shapes remain distinct and don't change one another.

SETTING STROKE AND FILL COLORS

In Flash, Fireworks, and FreeHand, to set the stroke or fill color, first click in a Stroke or Fill box in one of two places:

- The Colors section of the Tools panel.

- A color box in the Property inspector, after you have selected a tool. (In FreeHand, you also have to click on the paint bucket icon in the Object tab in the Property inspector to add a fill property to the object, as shown in Figure 3.10.)

Figure 3.10
Click on the paint bucket to add a fill in FreeHand.

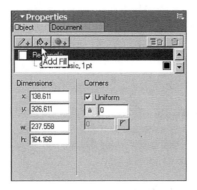

This brings up a color-selection panel. The simplest of these panels is the Web-safe color picker, which contains swatches for the 216 generic colors common to the two major browsers, Netscape and Internet Explorer, and the two major operating systems, Macintosh and Windows. A colors mixer (Color Mixer in Flash, Colors in Fireworks, Color Mixer and Tints in FreeHand) enables you to go beyond the Web-safe colors by mixing your own custom colors. Toggle the colors mixer on or off with Shift+F9 in all three programs. (Color mixers are shown in Figures 3.1, 3.2 and 3.4.)

There are a number of systems or modes for mixing colors. All three programs support RGB (red-green-blue) and HSB (hue-saturation-brightness). (HSB is called HLS, for hue-luminance-saturation, in FreeHand.) FreeHand and Fireworks also support several other modes.

RGB is the standard additive color model created for graphics viewed on computer monitors. Unless you are accustomed to using HSB color, stick with the RGB default.

In Flash and Fireworks, if you click on the upper-right corner of the colors mixer, as shown in Figure 3.11, you get a pop-up menu offering various color-related functions, including selecting a color mode (RGB or HSB) and saving a custom color as a swatch, which you can later retrieve from the swatches panel. FreeHand includes buttons on the Mixer and Tints panel for these functions. (See Figure 3.12.)

Figure 3.11
Click on the upper-right corner of the colors mixer in Flash and Fireworks for a pop-up menu of color-related options.

Figure 3.12
FreeHand color options, with RGB mode selected.

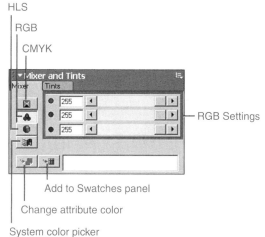

Dreamweaver, not being a graphics editor, does not work with strokes and fills. It has a Color Picker, which pops up whenever you click a color box, generally to specify an HTML color attribute. (Refer to Figure 3.3.)

WORKING WITH FILLS

Any closed shape can have a fill. The two basic types of fills are solid colors and gradients. A gradient contains two or more colors, blending smoothly from one to the next. Linear gradients display colors in a striped pattern. Radial gradients display colors in a circular pattern from the center outward; they can add depth to circular objects, for instance, making them appear three-dimensional. Solid colors and gradients are available in Flash, Fireworks, and FreeHand. Flash and Fireworks also support a third type of fill: bitmaps.

The programs do have a number of minor differences when it comes to working with fills. For instance:

- In all the programs, you select a gradient or solid fill by using a drop-down menu. In Flash, the drop-down menu and gradient definition bar are in the colors mixer. In Fireworks and FreeHand, they're in the Property inspector. In FreeHand, you have to click on the Fill property to get to the drop-down. (See Figure 3.13.)

- In Flash and Fireworks, shapes such as rectangles and circles are filled by default. In FreeHand, the default is no fill, represented by a white box with a diagonal red line through it, as shown in Figure 3.4. The "no fill" option is available in Flash and Fireworks, too.

- In Flash and Fireworks, you can edit a fill without first selecting the object, by clicking any enclosed area with the Paint Bucket tool. FreeHand doesn't have a Paint Bucket tool; you have to select the object before editing the fill.

Gradient definition bar

Fill mode selection drop-down

Figure 3.13
Selecting gradient fill mode in Flash.

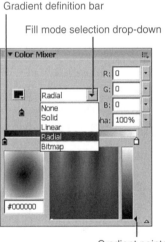

Gradient pointers

Working with Gradients

All the Studio MX programs except Dreamweaver can create gradient fills, with Fireworks offering a dozen varieties, FreeHand half a dozen, and Flash just the basic linear and radial gradients. You can also create custom gradients, specifying how many and which colors are used, by using a gradient definition bar and gradient pointers. (Refer to Figure 3.13.) Each pointer marks the spot where a particular color occurs in its non-blended form. To change the colors in the gradient, click on gradient pointers and assign new colors to them. To move a pointer, click and drag it.

Again, the programs show some minor differences in the interface. For instance, to create new gradient pointers in Flash and Fireworks, you click just below the definition bar, between the two original pointers. In FreeHand, you drag one of the end pointers into the middle; the original end pointer remains where it was, and a new pointer is created in the middle.

To change a gradient color, click on a pointer. In Fireworks and FreeHand, the Web-safe color picker pops up automatically. In Flash, access the color picker by clicking the color box at the top left of the Colors Mixer.

→ For more on gradients in Fireworks, **see** "Gradients," **page 710**, in Chapter 25.

→ For more on colors in FreeHand, **see** "Mixer Panel," **page 790**, in Chapter 29.

EYEDROPPER

The basic purpose of the Eyedropper tool is the same throughout Studio MX: It speeds up color selection by enabling you to copy stroke or fill attributes from one object in the work-space to another. (Dreamweaver can pick up colors from anywhere on the screen, even outside its own windows.) If you click on a bitmap with the Eyedropper tool, it picks up the color of the individual pixel you click on.

The Eyedropper is temporarily activated whenever you click on a color box. (This is the only way to activate the Eyedropper in Dreamweaver.) So throughout Studio MX, you can use the following procedure: Select the object or objects whose stroke or fill color you want to change. Click a Stroke or Fill color box. Click on a swatch or on an object to select the color you want.

It's possible to select the color before selecting the object or objects you want to edit. In FreeHand, you can do this simply by selecting the Eyedropper tool and dragging and dropping a color from one object to another. You can drag a stroke color to a fill, and vice versa. It's marvelously flexible and easy to use.

The Flash procedure is less flexible, in that it's only convenient for fill-to-fill or stroke-to-stroke copies. In Flash, instead of dragging and dropping, use the Eyedropper to click on the first object and then on the second. When you click on the stroke or fill that you want to copy, the Eyedropper changes to the Ink Bottle (for a stroke) or Paint Bucket (for a fill). When you click on the second object, its fill or stroke changes to that of the first object.

To do a stroke-to-fill copy in Flash, for instance, you can follow this procedure: Click on the fill color box in the Colors section of the Tools panel. Select the Eyedropper. Click on a stroke in the workspace. This changes the color in the fill color box to the color of the object's stroke. Finally, select the Paint Bucket and click the object or objects you want to change.

Fireworks doesn't have an Ink Bottle tool, and the most convenient way to change a stroke is just to click on the stroke first and then change the stroke color in the Colors section of the Tools panel.

LINE

The Line tool is the most basic of the drawing tools. It draws straight lines (strokes). Simply select the Line tool; then click and drag to create lines. Shift+dragging draws lines that are vertical, horizontal, or on a 45° slant.

You can, of course, use the Line tool to draw closed shapes such as squares or rectangles that can have fills applied to them. However, you must manually add a fill, using the Paint Bucket tool, after you have closed a shape. In FreeHand, join the lines (Modify, Join) and the fill will automatically be applied.

PENCIL

The Pencil tool enables you to draw freeform lines and shapes. Select the Pencil tool and then click and drag to sketch lines with the mouse. As with the Line tool, Shift+dragging constrains the angle to multiples of 45°. In Flash and Fireworks, after creating a closed shape, you can manually fill it by using the Paint Bucket tool. FreeHand automatically fills even open shapes created with the Pencil tool.

Flash has a unique feature in the three pencil modes in the Options section of the Toolbox: straighten, smooth, and Ink (maintain rough shapes).

RECTANGLE AND ELLIPSE TOOLS

The Rectangle and Ellipse ("Oval" in Flash) tools enable you to draw these simple shapes just by clicking and dragging. Use Shift+drag to draw perfect circles or squares.

In Fireworks, click and hold on the Rectangle to bring up a fly-out with the Ellipse tool, as well as a Polygon tool and a number of *Auto Shapes* such as a spiral, an arrow, a star and a doughnut.

→ For more on Auto shapes, **see** Chapter 24, "What's New in Fireworks MX 2004," **page 686**.

You can draw rectangles with rounded corners. The interfaces are slightly different for each program, but the result is the same. In Flash, after selecting the Rectangle tool, select the Round Rectangle Radius modifier at the bottom of the Tools panel. Enter a number in the corner radius field; the higher the number, the rounder the corners. In Fireworks, click and hold on the Rectangle tool and select the Rounded Rectangle smart shape from the fly-out that appears. (See Figure 3.14.) In FreeHand, enter a number in the Corners section of the Object tab in the Property inspector. The higher the number, the more rounding. In Figure 3.4, the number in the Corners section is zero, so there is no rounding.

→ For more on drawing rectangles with rounded corners, **see** "Sizing Shapes Precisely," **page 355** (Flash), in Chapter 16, "Working with Vector Grpahics and Bitmaps"; and "Rounded Rectangle," **page 717** (Fireworks) in Chapter 25.

Figure 3.14
The Fireworks
Rounded Rectangle
feature.

THE PEN TOOL

The Pen tool is an extremely powerful drawing tool. If you haven't used an illustration program before, the Pen tool will take some getting used to, particularly the way it draws curves. You'll be rewarded with precisely drawn curves and irregular shapes that cannot be achieved with any other tool.

The Pen tool draws by connecting anchor points. A straight line or curve connecting two anchor points is a *segment*. A *path* consists of one or more connected segments.

Select the Pen tool and move your mouse pointer onto the Stage. A small x appears to the right of the pen, as shown in Figure 3.15, indicating that you are placing the first anchor.

Figure 3.15
The Pen tool displays
a small x as you place
the first anchor point
of a shape.

DRAWING STRAIGHT LINE SEGMENTS

To draw a straight line segment, just click and release, move the mouse, and click again. Shift+clicking draws vertical, horizontal, or diagonal (45°) lines. To end an open path, double-click the final anchor point, or select a different tool. You can also Cmd-click (Mac) or Ctrl+click (Windows) off the path. To end a closed path, hold the Pen over the first anchor point. A small dot appears to the right of the Pen, indicating that you can close the path, as shown in Figure 3.16. Then click just once.

Figure 3.16
The Pen tool displays a small circle if you are correctly positioned to close a path.

DRAWING CURVED SEGMENTS

The Pen tool creates *Bezier curves*, controlled by *control handles*, as shown in Figure 3.17. The length and angle of the control handles determine the shape of the curve.

One simple way to create a curve segment is to click and release at the point where you want the segment to start, move to the point where you want it to end, and click and drag. Whichever way you drag, the curve is created in the opposite direction. To create another curve on the same path, move again, and click and drag again. Or you could make the next segment a straight line by just clicking, rather than clicking and dragging. Points created by clicking are *corner points* and do not have control handles. Points created by clicking and dragging are *curve points* and do have control handles. To end the path, move off the path and Cmd-click (Mac) or Ctrl+click (Windows). To convert a corner point to a curve point, and create curvature in the straight line segments, select the point with the Subselection tool, and Option-click (Mac) or Alt+click (Windows) and drag. To convert a curve point to a corner point, click on the point with the Pen tool. Clicking on a corner point with the Pen tool deletes the point.

Figure 3.17
The anatomy of a curve: two anchor points, each with two control handles.

To close a curved path, just click on the initial anchor point, or else click on the initial anchor point and drag away from the curve, as shown in Figure 3.18.

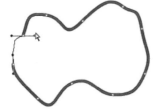

Figure 3.18
Click on the initial anchor point and drag away from the curve to close a curved path.

ADJUSTING ANCHOR POINTS AND HANDLES

The easiest way to work with the Pen tool is to complete a path and then move, add, and delete anchor points and adjust handles.

To adjust anchor points, you must first select them. Use the Subselection tool and click on a path to reveal the anchor points, as shown in Figure 3.19.

Figure 3.19
Click on a path with the Subselection tool to reveal anchor points.

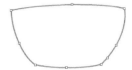

If you click directly on an anchor, you both select that point and reveal all others in the path. If you click on a path but not directly on an anchor point, you simply reveal the anchor points in the path and must then click directly on one to select it. Shift+click additional anchor points to add them to the selection. You can then click directly on an anchor to reveal any control handles. Click and drag anchor points to move them, as shown in Figure 3.20. You can also select an anchor point and use the arrow keys to nudge it.

3

Figure 3.20
Click and drag a control handle to alter the shape of a curve.

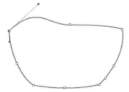

You can also add anchor points. Position the Pen tool on the path. A small plus sign appears next to the Pen tool. Click to create the anchor point.

You can delete anchor points by selecting them with the Subselection tool and hitting the Delete key.

ADJUSTING CURVED SEGMENTS

To adjust the size and angle of a curve without moving anchor points, use the Subselection tool to select the path, select the anchor point, and click and drag its control handles. Where two curved segments intersect, two control handles extend away from a common anchor point. Each handle controls a curve on either side of a common anchor point. Dragging one end of a double control handle changes the curves on both sides of the anchor point, which stays in place, as shown in Figure 3.21.

To adjust just the curved segment on just one side, rather than both, Option-drag (Mac) or Alt+drag (Windows) just one end of a double-control handle.

If a curve segment intersects a straight segment, you'll see a control handle just on the curve side of the anchor. Click and drag this handle with the Subselection tool to change the arc, or click and drag the anchor point to move the curve.

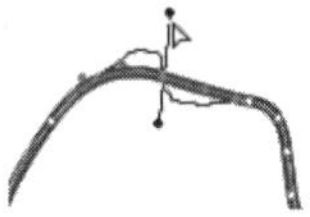

Figure 3.21
Dragging one end of a double control handle changes curves on both sides of the shared anchor point.

In Flash, you can also click and drag with the Selection tool to move segments. In Fireworks and FreeHand, clicking on a segment with the Selection tool selects the whole path, and dragging moves it.

OPTIMIZING CURVES

After you have created a curve, you can reduce the number of points that define it, keeping the same basic shape but smoothing it out. This is called *optimizing* or *simplifying* the curve. To do this in Fireworks and FreeHand, use Modify, Alter Path, Simplify. In Flash, use Modify, Shape, Optimize. You can set a slider to maximize or minimize optimization. In Fireworks and FreeHand, you can also set the optimization amount numerically. Flash gives you the option of running several smoothing passes in one operation.

WORKING WITH TEXT

The Studio MX programs have a lot in common in the way they deal with text, including many basic functions such as adding, editing, and deleting text, as well as assigning character attributes such as bold and italic, and paragraph attributes such as indentation and justification. Many of these functions are also similar to those of widely-used programs such as Microsoft Word.

Some functions, such as dynamic text (text loaded at runtime as opposed to authoring time) and user input fields (where the user can enter text), are restricted to Flash and Dreamweaver because only those programs have the means to control the runtime environment (that is, the Flash player or the browser).

Fireworks and FreeHand each offer special text effects, such as drop shadows that make the text appear to stand out from the page.

In the Property inspector, Dreamweaver offers only text attributes that are supported in HTML, such as bold, italic, color, font, indentation, and justification. Other attributes, such as spacing between characters, are not supported in HTML or Dreamweaver.

Flash MX 2004's support for a subset of Cascading Style Sheets (CSS) tags, used to format text, provides standard-based integration with Dreamweaver MX 2004, which is even more CSS-centric than then previous versions. This is an extremely useful feature. However, the procedures for using CSS in the two programs have little in common, so CSS features are covered separately, in the sections devoted to Flash and Dreamweaver respectively.

Adding Text

In Dreamweaver, to add text, you just click in the workspace and start typing. In the other three Studio MX programs, you need to select the Text tool first, and then either simply click in the workspace to create an auto-expanding text block, or click and drag in the workspace to create a fixed-width text block. The auto-expanding text block continues to grow wider until you hit the Enter key, setting the width and starting a new line of text. The width of the fixed-width text block is the width of the box you drag out. (The height is determined by the point size of the text, which is set in the Property inspector.)

As you type in a fixed-width text block, your text wraps and the text block grows in height to accommodate new lines.

Resizing Text Blocks

In Flash and Fireworks, you can resize text blocks using a handle, which is a circle for auto-expanding blocks and a square for fixed-width blocks, as shown in Figure 3.22. The block changes size when you drag the handle, and the text reflows to fit the box, changing the line breaks as necessary, but keeping the spacing between lines and between characters the same. If you use the Width and Height fields in the Property inspector to resize text blocks, the text stretches or squashes to fit the box, keeping the line breaks the same. Handles appear only when the Text tool is selected and the cursor is in the text block.

Use the handle to resize the text box.

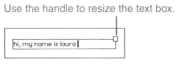

Figure 3.22
Drag a text box's handle to resize a text box.

CAUTION

In Flash and Fireworks, if you use the Width and Height fields in the Property inspector to resize text blocks, you'll stretch or squash the text.

FreeHand works almost exactly opposite to Flash and Fireworks when it comes to resizing text blocks. In FreeHand, the handles are small dark boxes at each corner and on each side of the text block, as shown in Figure 3.23. (The box in the corner is an overflow indicator, turning dark when there is more text than fits in the text block.) As you drag a handle, the block changes size, and the spacing between characters and lines also changes, while the line breaks stay the same. In FreeHand, to get the same effect as dragging handles in Flash and Fireworks, change the width and height properties in the Property inspector. Handles in FreeHand are visible whenever the text block is selected, but can be dragged only with the Selection or Subselection tool. If the Text tool is selected and you click on a text block handle, the Selection tool is automatically activated.

Figure 3.23
In FreeHand, the handles for resizing a text block are small dark boxes at each corner and on each side of the text block. The overflow indicator turns dark when there is more text than fits in the text block. There is no overflow in this case.

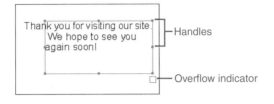

CHANGING TEXT GLOBALLY

You can set text attributes before you place text on the Stage by choosing the Text tool and making changes in the Property inspector.

After text has been created, to make global changes that affect all the text in the text block, use the Selection tool or Subselection tool to select the text block and then change the properties in the Property inspector, as shown in Figure 3.24.

Figure 3.24
Making global changes to a text block in the Property inspector in Flash. Text orientation options in Flash are Horizontal, Vertical Left-to-Right, and Vertical Right-to-left. Format includes indentation, line spacing, left margin, and right margin.

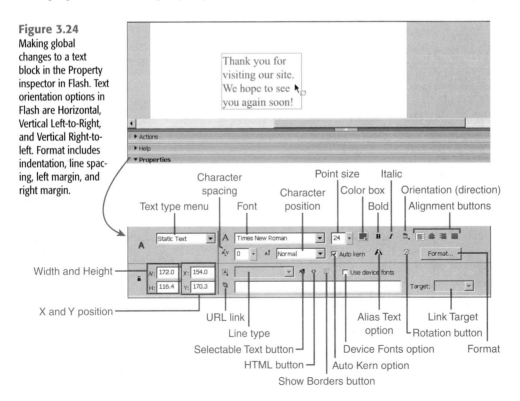

Some properties, such as text orientation (vertical, horizontal, left-to-right, right-to-left) in Flash and Fireworks, can only be changed globally. Such properties change for the whole text block, whether the Selection or Subselection tool has been used to select the text block as a whole, or whether the Text tool has been used to select particular characters or paragraphs.

To move a text block, click and drag with the Selection tool or Subselection tool.

TIP

> To quickly switch from the Selection tool to the Text tool when editing text, double-click a text block with the Selection tool. The arrow pointer changes to an insertion point, and the Text tool is active.

CHARACTER AND PARAGRAPH ATTRIBUTES

Text attributes can be divided into those that affect paragraphs and those that affect individual letters or characters. The most commonly used paragraph attribute is justification: aligned left, aligned right, centered, and justified (aligned left and right). Others include line spacing, first-line indent, and margins. Character attributes include font, point size, character position, character spacing, and kerning (pairwise character spacing).

To make paragraph-level changes, select the Text tool. Then, to make changes to just one paragraph, click anywhere in that paragraph. Alternatively, you can select any part of one or more paragraphs. Any subsequent paragraph-level changes made in the Property inspector affect all the chosen paragraphs.

To make character-level changes, click and drag with the Text tool to select the text you want to change, as shown in Figure 3.25. Any subsequent character-level changes made in the Property inspector affect just the selected characters.

Figure 3.25
Click and drag with the Text tool to edit individual letters within text blocks.

FONT, POINT SIZE, COLOR, AND STYLES

You can select a font from a drop-down menu (indicated as "Font" in Figure 13.9). In Flash and Dreamweaver, you can also type in the font name. If you type in the font name, you need to click at the insertion point in the workspace to be able to type your text. Otherwise, you enter your text into the Font selection field.

You can type in a font size in all four programs. All four also offer an alternative means to select the font size: a pop-up slider in Flash and Fireworks, a drop-down listing just the most commonly used font sizes in Dreamweaver and FreeHand. Typing in a size is generally the easiest way to set the font size. However, the sliders enable you to select text and quickly preview it at many different sizes.

Flash and Fireworks assign the fill color to your text. Dreamweaver doesn't distinguish between stroke and fill, so there's just one color selection box. FreeHand automatically assigns just a fill color to text, but allows you to add a stroke, so the text can be outlined in a different color.

You can also force font styles by using the Bold and Italic buttons. In Dreamweaver and Flash, consider creating and applying a CSS tag instead. That way, later on, you can make global changes to all bolded text just by changing the tag.

→ For more on applying CSS tags in Flash, **see** "Formatting Using CSS," **page 608**, in Chapter 21, "Advanced ActionScript." For CSS in Dreamweaver, **see** "CSS Styles: Background," **page 171**, and "CSS in Dreamweaver MX 2004," **page 179**, in Chapter 8, "Writing and Editing HTML, XHTML, and CSS."

In Flash, where you can include the font in the movie, it may be preferable to use a bold or italic version of a font rather than the Bold and Italic buttons, because you can lose much of the subtlety of a typeface by forcing a bold or italic style that it wasn't designed for. When working with text in Dreamweaver, you're using system fonts (fonts provided by the user's computer) and can't be sure that the bold or italic versions will be available on all machines. Therefore, it's common to just stick with standard fonts and use the bold and italic buttons in Dreamweaver.

TEXT DIRECTION

Flash and Fireworks allow you to control text direction: horizontal left-to-right, horizontal right-to-left (not available in Flash), vertical left-to-right, and vertical right-to-left. In Freehand, you control text direction by attaching the text to a path.

→ For more on reversing text direction in FreeHand, **see** "Text Effects," **page 849**, Chapter 30, "Using FreeHand in Web Site Planning and Creation."

Vertical directions are particularly useful for Asian languages. Figure 3.24 shows the text direction button in Flash.

KERNING AND CHARACTER SPACING

Kerning refers to the amount of space between two letters or characters, whereas *character spacing* applies to larger groups of characters or entire blocks of text. Both kerning and character spacing can be defined by positive or negative settings. Positive settings increase the amount of space between letters, and negative settings decrease space until letters eventually overlap, as shown in Figure 3.26. Zero is neutral. For general legibility in blocks of copy, it's best to work within a range of 0 to +5 or even less, depending on text size. The smaller the point size, the greater the effect of character spacing. Many fonts have desirable kerning built in. In Flash and Fireworks, you can use this kerning by selecting the Auto Kern option. FreeHand does this automatically. As already mentioned, Dreamweaver does not support these options.

Figure 3.26
Character spacing: +20 on the top, 0 in the middle, –5 at the bottom.

In Flash, Fireworks, and FreeHand, select letters, words, or entire text blocks, then enter a positive or negative number in the character spacing field. In Flash and Fireworks, you can also drag a slider to select the amount of spacing. When used with vertical text, character spacing determines the vertical amount of space between characters. In Flash, you can also set a preference to turn off kerning of vertical text; then character spacing affects only horizontal text.

CHARACTER POSITION

Character position refers to raising or lowering text in relation to a baseline, as with superscripts and subscripts. Most of the time you will use the default of Normal, which places text squarely on the baseline. (See Figure 3.27.) The superscript and subscript options are typically used with special characters or footnotes within text blocks.

Figure 3.27
The baseline is an implied line on which the characters sit. Superscript and subscript appear above or below the baseline.

ALIGNMENT AND JUSTIFICATION

In all four programs, use Alignment buttons to specify left-aligned, centered, right-aligned, or full justification of paragraphs. Full justification creates newspaper-style paragraphs that are aligned on both the left and right sides. When using full justification, be sure to check the amount of space that is created by the justification so that large, distracting gaps do not appear between words. Do not use full justification with bitmap fonts, or they will stretch and become blurry. These settings also apply to vertical text, in the programs that support that.

KEYBOARD SHORTCUTS

Studio MX provides keyboard shortcuts for selecting tools, opening panels, and selecting menu options. They can be real time-savers, so it's worthwhile to memorize the ones you use the most.

Table 3.2 lists keyboard shortcuts for accessing tools. These shortcuts, which consist of a single key, are common to Flash and Fireworks. (Dreamweaver doesn't have a Tools panel, and FreeHand has a different set of default keyboard shortcuts.)

TABLE 3.2 TOOLBOX SHORTCUTS

Tool	Keyboard Shortcut
Selection tool	V
Subselection tool	A
Line tool	N
Lasso tool	L
Pen tool	P
Text tool	T
Eyedropper tool	I
Eraser tool	E
Hand tool	H
Zoom tool	Z

Shortcuts for accessing panels are shown in Table 3.3. These shortcuts act as toggles, so you use the shortcuts once to launch a panel and a second time to hide the panel.

TABLE 3.3 PANEL SHORTCUTS

Panel	Mac	Windows	Notes
Help	F1	F1	Reference in Dreamweaver
Hide/Unhide All	F4	F4	
Tools	Cmd-F2	Ctrl+F2	Main Toolbar in Dreamweaver
Properties	Cmd-F3	Ctrl+F3	
Color Mixer	Shift-F9	Shift+F9	Snippets in Dreamweaver
Color Swatches	Cmd-F9	Ctrl+F9	Server Behaviors in Dreamweaver

TROUBLESHOOTING

If these programs are so similar, how do you know which one to choose for any given task?

This chapter focused on similarities, but the programs are fundamentally different.

Fireworks and FreeHand are all about creating and editing *content*. Neither is designed for authoring an entire *project*. Fireworks' strong point is creating and editing bitmap content, though it does have vector capabilities, too. FreeHand is primarily for vector drawing, and is also great for layout and storyboarding.

Flash, on the other hand, is fundamentally an authoring tool, designed for creating whole projects. It can also be used to create content for Web sites. Frequently, however, the Flash content dominates to the extent that the site is essentially created in Flash, with Dreamweaver just providing an HTML container.

Dreamweaver is an authoring tool almost exclusively. It is not designed to create content for use in the other authoring environments. (There are minor exceptions, such as creating HTML text or a CSS style sheet in Dreamweaver for use in Flash.) Dreamweaver itself can create only text, such as HTML, DHTML, XHTML, CSS and XML. You can use other content in Dreamweaver, but you create it outside of Dreamweaver.

PART II

DREAMWEAVER MX

4 What's New in Dreamweaver MX 2004   53

5 Working in the Dreamweaver Environment   73

6 Setting Up Sites, Pages, and Templates   103

7 Working Efficiently in Dreamweaver   135

8 Writing and Editing HTML, XHTML, and CSS   161

9 Professional Page Design   191

10 Adding Interactivity and Multimedia   219

11 Managing Your Site   241

12 Expanding Dreamweaver and Using Third-Party Software   263

13 Developing ColdFusion Applications in Dreamweaver   287

CHAPTER 4

WHAT'S NEW IN DREAMWEAVER MX 2004

In this chapter

A New Dreamweaver User Interface   54

Siteless Page Editing   57

Enhanced CSS Support   57

Increased Integration with Other Suite Applications   61

Enhanced Support for Dynamic Platforms   64

Copy and Paste from Microsoft Applications   65

Additional Coding Tools   66

Enhanced Security Using FTP   69

Peer to Peer: Taking the Anxiety Out of CSS   70

A NEW DREAMWEAVER USER INTERFACE

With the release of Dreamweaver MX, Macromedia introduced Web developers to a new way of laying out their design projects. In addition to various ways of viewing projects (for example, code view, design view, and split view), Macromedia added the capability to easily dock or undock panels, hide tools to maximize workspace, and provided access to tools such as code snippets and Cascading Style Sheets.

The development of the Dreamweaver design environment certainly did not stop with MX, however. With the introduction of Dreamweaver MX 2004, Macromedia has gone above and beyond in their efforts to create an environment that allows maximum access to development tools while enabling developers to easily create a customized environment with plenty of room to see the content of their pages.

In this chapter, we'll take a look at some of the new features that have been added to Dreamweaver MX 2004 and explain why they enhance the development process.

NEW QUICKSTART MENU

When you start Dreamweaver for the first time, you'll probably notice the new quickstart menu (see Figure 4.1), which provides easy access to a variety of project and document types, as well as access to any sites that might have been imported from previous versions of Dreamweaver that were installed on your workstation.

Figure 4.1
The new quickstart menu allows you to open recently viewed pages, create new pages, or build a new project from available samples.

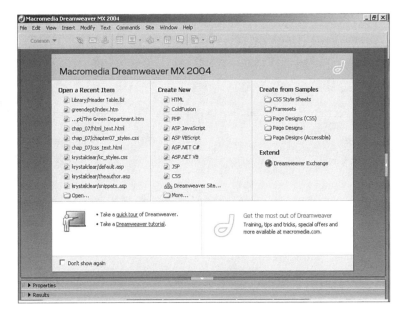

In addition, from the quickstart menu you can take a tour of the new features available or access the Dreamweaver Exchange, where you can download a wide variety of extensions to

Dreamweaver's capabilities. If you would rather Dreamweaver start with a blank page, rather than the quickstart menu, you can check the box in the lower-left corner that says Don't Show Again.

NOTE

If you turn off the quickstart menu, but later want to reactivate it, you can do so from the Preferences dialog box by choosing Edit, Preferences from the file menu. In the Preferences dialog box, check the box next to Show Start Page.

STREAMLINED WORKSPACE

The enhancements to the Dreamweaver environment don't stop with a simple quickstart menu. Those users familiar with previous versions of Dreamweaver will notice a distinct difference upon first glance in the fact that Dreamweaver MX 2004 uses a new color scheme, complete with gradient toolbar and panel headers and buttons (see Figure 4.2) that are much easier to read and identify than previous versions.

For instance, the buttons that allow you to switch between Code, Split, and Design view are now clearly marked, as opposed to the previous versions, which required that you hover over the button and read the tool tip to identify the function of the button.

Figure 4.2
Dreamweaver's new look and feel are more than just aesthetic changes. The changes help developers work smarter and faster.

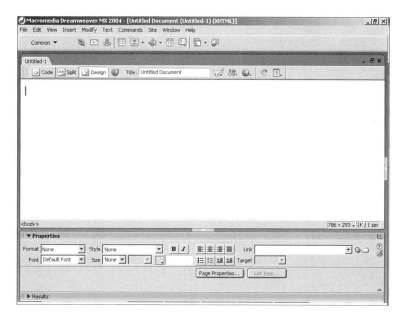

In developing the new user interface, it is readily apparent that Macromedia had one goal in mind: provide complete access to every tool included within Dreamweaver, but allow users to customize the desktop to maximize their workspace. Toward that goal, the panels in

Dreamweaver have been reorganized into logical groups that complement each other better than previous versions and also complement nearly every aspect of the development environment. These panels can be displayed (see Figure 4.3), hidden (see Figure 4.4), resized, and reorganized at the developer's whim to maximize workspace or increase accessibility of commonly-used tools.

Figure 4.3
Developers can choose to view all or some of the panels, toolbars, and inspectors available in the user interface, or…

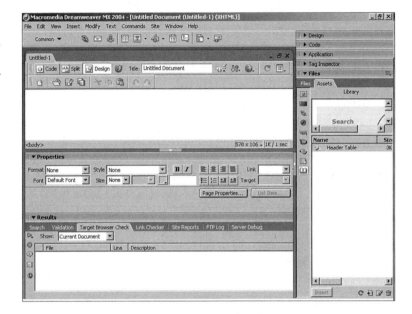

Figure 4.4
…the workspace can be maximized for development.

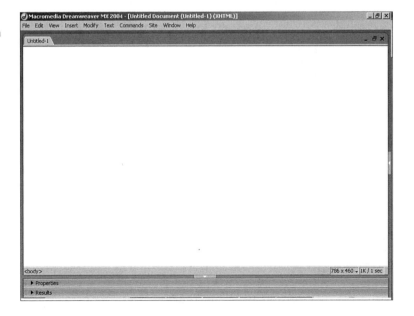

No matter how you choose to organize your workspace, the possibilities for designing an environment that maximizes your efficiency are nearly limitless, and your environment can be changed from project to project.

Reorganized Panels

As was briefly mentioned earlier, Macromedia has reorganized several of the panels in a manner that is more logical. For instance, the Site panel has been replaced by the Files panel, which serves basically the same purpose, but is a more suitable name because developers use this panel most frequently to manage their files, rather than their sites.

The functions of each panel and the individual changes are covered later in Chapter 5, "Dreamweaver Environment and Tools."

TIP

> Remember that just because Macromedia groups panels in a certain way doesn't mean that it will necessarily fit your needs. To recognize this, Dreamweaver includes the capability to rename categories and regroup the various panels in ways that better suit you.

Siteless Page Editing

One of the apparent reasons for renaming the Site panel to the Files panel is to accommodate one of Dreamweaver MX 2004's new features: siteless page editing. In prior versions of Dreamweaver, a site needed to be defined for relative linking to function properly. In 2004, however, Macromedia has enabled developers to create pages without having to build an entire site first. Although it might seem logical to build a Dreamweaver site for most projects, there are times when you might need to build a single page or edit another developer's work and not need to walk through the process of creating a site for such a small project. With the inclusion of this new feature, you can choose whether a Dreamweaver site is necessary for the project.

Enhanced CSS Support

The enhancement that will affect the majority of Dreamweaver users is the fact that Dreamweaver now uses Cascading Style Sheets (CSS) to control a much broader range of page and style elements, rather than elements such as <font> tags that were used in previous versions. As Web standards have shifted toward the adoption of CSS as the standard for formatting text, Macromedia has embraced those standards and made using style sheets as easy as possible.

TIP

> Dreamweaver MX 2004 is fully CSS 2 compliant. For details on the CSS 2 standards, check out the World Wide Web Consortium (W3C) at http://www.w3.org/TR/REC-CSS2/.

INTEGRATED CSS

For many Web developers, the mere mention of Cascading Style Sheets often sends a chill up the spine and induces a nervous twitch. The thought of hand-coding long, detailed style sheets just to format text may seem like fun to some, but usually causes many to avoid learning about CSS altogether. Macromedia, however, has taken the mystery out of style sheets and has integrated their functionality to the point that you can build pages in Dreamweaver, using custom styles, and never have to look at a style sheet.

By default, Dreamweaver now uses styles rather than HTML tags to format text and page properties such as link colors and page color. All you have to do is set the preferences in the Page Properties dialog box and Dreamweaver does the rest. For instance, imagine that you wanted to customize your page's background color. To accomplish this, you would

1. Open the Page Properties dialog box, shown in Figure 4.5, by choosing Modify, Page Properties from the menu bar.

Figure 4.5
Changing the background color of a page can easily be done with the Page Properties dialog box.

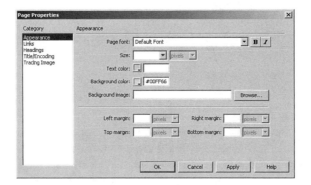

2. In the Page Properties dialog box, use the color picker to select a custom background color.
3. Click OK to apply the change.

When you click OK, Dreamweaver writes the code that changes the background color of the page. In previous versions, the code that would have been added would have been inside the <body> tag. However, as shown in Figure 4.6, Dreamweaver instead writes a style that controls the page color. In essence, you just used custom styles without ever having to develop or code a style sheet.

ENHANCED CSS PANEL

In addition to being able to add CSS to your pages automatically, Dreamweaver MX 2004 also enables you to customize your style sheets and classes via the Relevant CSS panel (see Figure 4.7). Now you can simply select any element on the page (including the page itself, by not selecting anything) and easily determine what styles are being applied in the page.

Figure 4.6
A style, rather than HTML tags, was used to modify the background of the page.

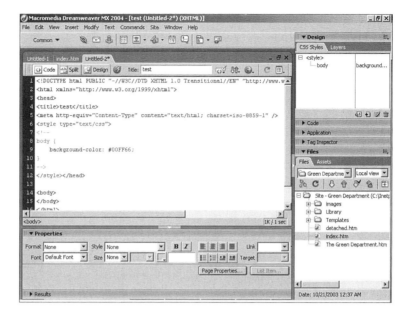

Figure 4.7
Using the enhanced Relevant CSS Panel, it is easy to see what styles are being applied to any particular page element.

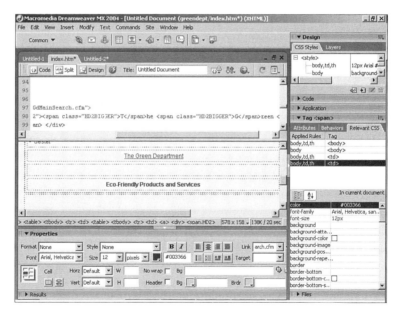

CSS PROPERTY INSPECTOR

With the integration of styles also comes updates to Dreamweaver's Property inspector (see Figure 4.8). When selected, the Format, Font, Size, and Color elements each automatically add the appropriate style code to your pages. If you select a unique combination of text, size, and color that has not been used in the page previously, Dreamweaver simply creates a new style for you, which you can reuse over and over.

Figure 4.8
The Property inspector may look similar, but it has become much more powerful through the integration of CSS.

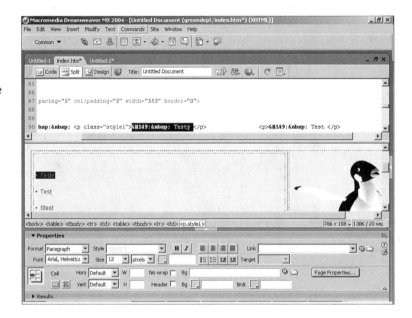

CSS-BASED PAGE PROPERTIES

As you saw earlier, changing page elements such as background color can be accomplished as easily as ever through the use of styles. Nearly every page attribute, however, can now be controlled just as easily. Elements such as page margins, link colors, and underline styles (see Figure 4.9), and even background images can all be controlled with styles and don't ever require a single line of hand-written code.

Figure 4.9
Using the Page Properties dialog box, you can use styles to customize your pages without ever having to create your own style sheets.

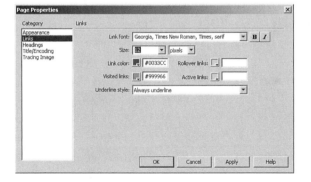

TIP

> As you will see in Chapter 5, you can still use the Font element if you have previously existing sites that use `<font>` tags to format text. Dreamweaver MX 2004 merely uses CSS as the default method of styling text, but it is still completely capable of developing sites that are not CSS-based.

INCREASED INTEGRATION WITH OTHER SUITE APPLICATIONS

Most Web projects rely upon professionally designed graphics or multimedia elements, and Macromedia's Fireworks and Flash have long been recognized as two of the most powerful applications for creating these elements. With Dreamweaver MX 2004, you now have more control over graphic and multimedia elements created with these two programs from within the Dreamweaver environment.

INTEGRATED FIREWORKS IMAGE EDITING

Dreamweaver's Property inspector now includes access to some of the fundamental (and often most used) graphic editing tools through the integration of Fireworks' technology. After selecting a graphic inserted into a page, you can now optimize, crop, rotate, adjust the brightness and contrast, and sharpen images without ever having to leave Dreamweaver.

For instance, suppose you have created a page and are ready to optimize it for dial-up users. You have discovered that your images are taking too long to load because of their file size and you want to optimize them. In the past, you would switch to Fireworks, open the file, optimize it, and re-export it to the appropriate directory. With the integrated Fireworks tools, however, that process is history. To optimize a file from within Fireworks, simply follow these steps:

1. Insert an image into any page and select it.
2. On the Property inspector, click the Optimize in Fireworks button (shown in Figure 4.10).
3. In the Find Source dialog box, shown in Figure 4.11, indicate whether you want to optimize only the graphic included in the page or a source graphic such as a Fireworks PNG file. In this case, click No to simply optimize the image located in the page.

NOTE

> If you don't want to be asked about source files each time you optimize a graphic, you can use the drop-down to indicate what pattern should be followed when the Optimize in Fireworks button is clicked.

Figure 4.10
The Optimize feature enables you to streamline your graphics without ever leaving Dreamweaver.

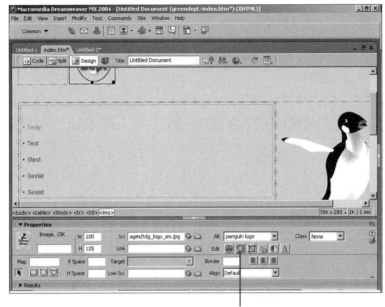

Optimize in Fireworks button

Figure 4.11
You can choose to optimize either just the individual image or the source file as well.

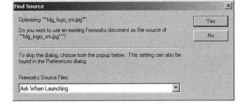

4. In the Optimize images dialog box, shown in Figure 4.12, modify the output settings that you prefer and click the Update button.

TIP

Using the Optimize images dialog box, you can also quickly modify the image's physical size using the File tab. After the update is done, however, you need to click the Refresh Size button, located on the Property inspector (next to the height and width fields) to apply the changes.

To learn why you should update your source files rather than updating images embedded in your pages, **see** *"Why Update My Source Files?" in the "Troubleshooting" section at the end of this chapter,* **page 70**.

If the basic editing tools integrated into Dreamweaver aren't enough for your project, you can take advantage of the Edit in Fireworks button located on the Property inspector (see Figure 4.12), which allows you to easily edit a graphic, export it, and update the image in your pages.

Figure 4.12
The Edit in Fireworks button gives you easy access to all the tools Fireworks has to offer.

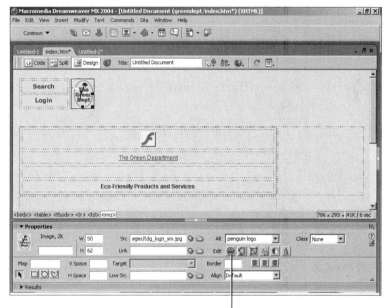

Edit in Fireworks button

INCREASED INTEGRATION WITH FLASH

Editing Flash movies with Dreamweaver's Property inspector is now just as easy as editing images. You can now select a movie located in a page, click the Edit button on the Property inspector (shown in Figure 4.13), and the source file is automatically opened in Flash (see Figure 4.14). After your edits have been made, simply publish the file and the updates will be applied to the Flash movie in your page.

Figure 4.13
Editing Flash movies is as simple as clicking a button on the Property inspector.

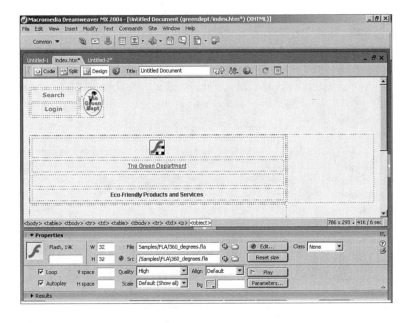

Figure 4.14
After you edit your movie in Flash, you can save your changes and they are applied to the movie placed in your Dreamweaver page.

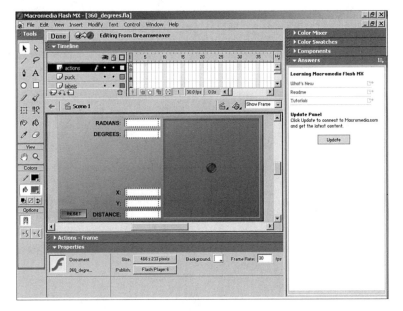

ENHANCED SUPPORT FOR DYNAMIC PLATFORMS

If you are planning to work with any of the various dynamic Web servers such as ColdFusion, Active Server Pages (ASP), ASP.NET, JavaServer Pages, or PHP, Dreamweaver continues to make things easy.

ColdFusion developers should be happy with the inclusion of several new features in Dreamweaver MX 2004. Dreamweaver now includes the latest release of HomeSite+, which provides complete support for ColdFusion 6.1 tags and includes a new Macro recorder for automating repetitive tasks. In addition, time-saving features such as the enhanced Snippet panel and siteless file editing have been integrated as well.

 To learn what happened to support for UltraDev 4 ColdFusion server objects, **see** *"Where Are The UltraDev 4 CF Server Objects?" in the "Troubleshooting" section at the end of this chapter,* **page 70**.

If ASP.NET is your platform of choice, you'll be happy to know that Dreamweaver MX 2004 fully supports ASP.NET 1.1. Using the Dreamweaver Server Behaviors, you can quickly connect your pages to a database, develop ASP.NET Webforms, and even create your own custom tags.

JavaServer Pages are also fully supported in the latest release of Dreamweaver. In addition, you can create a connection between Dreamweaver and JavaBeans to access the various JavaBean properties within Dreamweaver.

As the popularity of PHP continues to grow among Web developers, Macromedia has enhanced Dreamweaver's support for this platform. PHP developers can take advantage of many of the server behaviors that were previously available for other platforms, such as authenticating users, dynamic page navigation, and the quick creation of Master-Detail page sets.

NOTE

> Although ASP.NET is slowly replacing Active Server Pages as Microsoft's dynamic platform, additional features to support ASP 3.0 have not been included in the latest version of Dreamweaver. It is possible, however, to create or download custom extensions to Dreamweaver that support ASP 3.0

COPY AND PASTE FROM MICROSOFT APPLICATIONS

Any Web developer who has tried to copy and paste content from a Microsoft Word table or Excel spreadsheet should truly appreciate what Macromedia has accomplished in Dreamweaver MX 2004. No more rebuilding tables from content that was originally created in Word or Excel (WooHoo!). Instead, tables can be copied and pasted directly from Excel and Word (see Figure 4.15), and Dreamweaver constructs a table with the appropriate dimensions.

Figure 4.15
Tables can now be copied and pasted directly from Word or Excel.

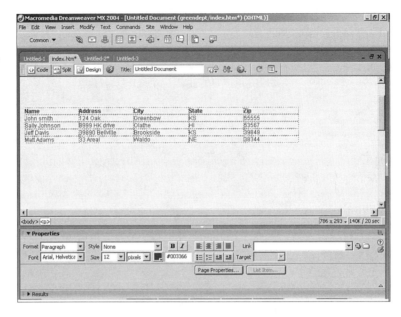

NOTE

Although it's great that Dreamweaver is now able to understand and accommodate the table structures used by Word and Excel, it's still a little early to expect too much out of the copy/paste relationship between Dreamweaver and Microsoft products. For instance, if you copy and paste a bulleted list from Word, Dreamweaver displays the list (bullets and all), but does not recode the content into an unordered list as it should be. Instead, you get content divided by paragraph breaks, using the Unicode character to symbolize the bullet. Although getting closer, the two applications still have a way to go before they are totally copy/paste compatible.

To learn why dynamic pages are much better than copying/pasting, **see** "Frequently Changing Content" in the "Troubleshooting" section at the end of this chapter, **p. 70**.

ADDITIONAL CODING TOOLS

Although Macromedia has done a great job creating an application that allows you to build pages without having to write code, the reality is the more access you have to your code and the more tools that are available for tweaking it, the easier the process becomes when you do need to manually write code. To make manual coding easier, Dreamweaver MX 2004 includes several features that help developers write the cleanest code possible.

DYNAMIC CROSS-BROWSER COMPATIBILITY CHECK

Coding pages for multiple browsers can be a time-consuming task, but one that ensures that your pages are presented properly to visitors. In the past, checking for compatibility meant building the page, previewing it the browser, and then adjusting the necessary code. Dreamweaver MX 2004, however, has added a new feature that alerts developers to potential issues at any time during the development process. By clicking on the Dynamic Cross-Browser Compatibility Check button, shown in Figure 4.16, you can see what code might cause problems in a wide variety of browsers.

Figure 4.16
The Dynamic Cross-Browser Compatibility Check helps you build pages that function in the most popular browsers.

Dynamic Cross-Browser Compatibility Check

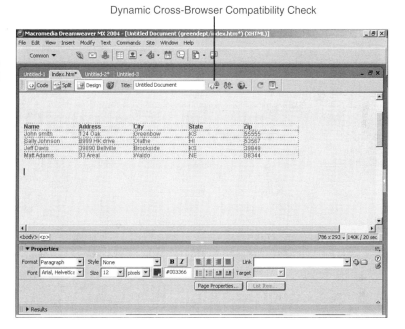

ENHANCED FIND AND REPLACE

Dreamweaver's Find and Replace can be a powerful tool when you're editing code, making page changes, or updating information across an entire site. Significant enhancements have been made to the Find and Replace interface (shown in Figure 4.17) in Dreamweaver MX 2004, making it even more powerful.

Using the Find and Replace panel, you can now conduct advanced text searches, indicating in what tags the code might be located (see Figure 4.18). In addition, you can save searches that you conduct frequently for later use by using the Save Query button. To retrieve a saved search, use the Load Query button to navigate and load the previously saved search parameters.

Save Query ─┐ ┌─ Load Query

Figure 4.17
The Find and Replace interface is even more powerful in Dreamweaver MX 2004.

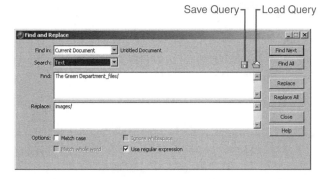

Figure 4.18
Advanced searches can be conducted, specifying the location of text within specific tags.

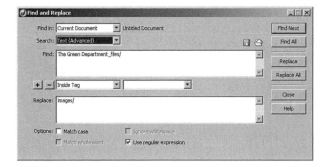

RIGHT-CLICK CODING TOOLS

Dreamweaver's new coding tools provide easy access to some of the most commonly used coding commands. In the Code view, you can now select a block of text and right-click to open a context menu. The menu, showing in Figure 4.19, enables you to perform actions such as indenting/outdenting code, converting the case of your code, and creating snippets with the click of your mouse.

Figure 4.19
The new coding tools provide access to commonly used coding commands.

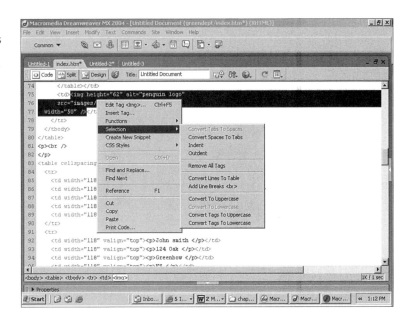

ENHANCED SECURITY USING FTP

In previous versions of Dreamweaver, secure FTP was accomplished with the installation of a Microsoft add-on called PuTTY. Dreamweaver MX 2004, however, now includes secure FTP connectivity using the OpenSSH protocol. Because SFTP is now an integral part of Dreamweaver, you can create secure connections when setting up a site by simply checking the SFTP box in the Site Definition dialog box (shown in Figure 4.20).

Figure 4.20
In Dreamweaver MX 2004, you can easily encrypt your FTP information with SFTP.

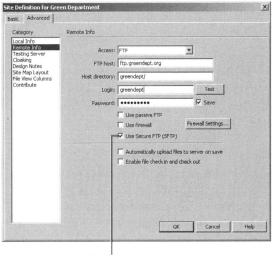

SFTP check box

TROUBLESHOOTING

WHY UPDATE MY SOURCE FILES?

I chose not to update my source file and decreased the size of my image. Now I want to increase the size of the image, but it's all blurry. What did I do wrong?

If you use the Optimize in Fireworks tool and choose not to update any source file, be careful if you choose to resize JPEG or GIF images. If you make an image smaller, but later want to return it to its original size, without the source file you'll end up with blurry graphics. JPEGs and GIFs are both raster images, which can't be easily increased in size without distortion. For this reason, it's always a good idea to keep your source files and save them in PNG format. PNG images are vector images and are less susceptible to distortion during the resizing process.

WHERE ARE THE ULTRADEV CF SERVER OBJECTS?

I manage a site that uses UltraDev 4 ColdFusion server objects and I don't see support for them in Dreamweaver MX 2004. Are they gone?

Macromedia has removed support for the UltraDev 4 ColdFusion server objects in Dreamweaver MX 2004, so if you are working with sites that contain these server objects, you need to update them to the Dreamweaver MX 2004 server objects for ColdFusion before you can edit those elements.

FREQUENTLY CHANGING CONTENT

Should I be using dynamic pages or copy/paste to update my pages that rely on data stored in Word documents or Excel spreadsheets?

If your page needs to display Word or Excel tables that won't change, copying and pasting can be effective. If, however, the information will be updated frequently and those changes need to be reflected in your pages, you should consider importing your information into an Access database and using Dreamweaver's database-connectivity tools rather than continually copying/pasting the data into your pages. If you use these tools, the dynamic pages are automatically updated whenever you make changes to the Access database, saving you the hassle of manually updating each page.

PEER TO PEER: TAKING THE ANXIETY OUT OF CSS

I'll admit it. I used to avoid Cascading Style Sheets at all costs. Frankly, all that extra time developing classes and coding the style sheets just never seemed worth it. Plus, there was just something scary about them. But with Dreamweaver MX 2004, there's really no excuse for not moving toward the future of Web standards and embracing style sheets. Dreamweaver makes them easy. So easy, in fact, that you can build your pages without really even knowing that Dreamweaver is using style sheets or worrying about whether or not they're correct. That's the great thing about Dreamweaver—clean, worry-free code.

The difficulty, however, comes in updating existing sites that rely on the Font element and <Body> tag to control page properties. Changing these sites to CSS can be a bit of a daunting task, but after you begin classifying your text and thinking in the terms of what style would be appropriate in which situation, you'll probably find that creating classes and style sheets isn't really the ominous task that you thought it would be.

In the long run, you'll find that Dreamweaver's new CSS integration can make your life a lot easier by allowing you to create portable style sheets that can be transferred from one site to another. After you become comfortable with the process of creating styles and applying them becomes second-nature, you'll most likely look back and wonder why you didn't begin the conversion to CSS sooner.

4

CHAPTER 5

Working in the Dreamweaver Environment

In this chapter

The Dreamweaver MX Interface, In Depth   74

Working with Text in the Document Window   93

Creating Lists in Documents   XX98

Peer to Peer: The Essence of Structure   101

THE DREAMWEAVER MX INTERFACE, IN DEPTH

Dreamweaver has so many tools and features it's unlikely that you'll use all of them for every site. Some you might not ever need at all, particularly if you're an advanced Web developer. However, knowing what's available in Dreamweaver will help you customize your workspace to put frequently used tools within easy reach as you remove extraneous toolbars and panels from view. After you know what features are available and how they work, you can then begin adding content to pages and putting those tools to work for you.

WORKSPACE LAYOUTS

If you're using Windows, your first decision is choosing a workspace layout. When you installed Dreamweaver, you were prompted to select an initial Workspace Setup (see Figure 5.1). Regardless of whether you chose the Designer or Coder workspace, Dreamweaver allows you to change your workspace at any time to meet the development style of the project you are working on.

Figure 5.1
The Workspace Setup dialog box appears when you first install Dreamweaver on a Windows system. You can also access Workspace Setup from the Preferences dialog box.

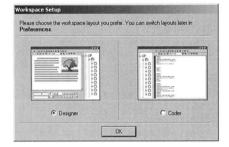

To change the workspace, do the following:

1. Select Edit, Preferences.
2. In the General category, click the Change Workspace button.
3. Select a workspace from the Workspace Setup dialog box.
4. Click OK to return to the Preferences dialog box.
5. Click OK to close out of the Preferences dialog box.

The changes you made to the workspace won't take effect until you exit and restart Dreamweaver.

The workspace layouts are

- **Designer Workspace**—All windows, panels, and inspectors are contained within one application window, in the same manner as in Fireworks and other Macromedia applications (see Figure 5.2). All panels are docked on the right side of the application window. Documents are opened in Design view by default, and multiple documents are tabbed at the top of the Document window.

Figure 5.2
The Designer workspace contains all documents, panels, and inspectors in one application window.

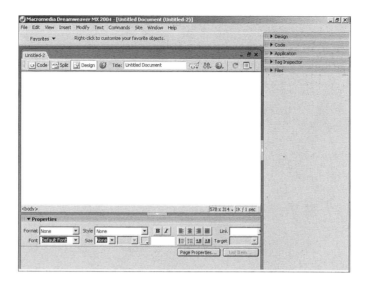

■ **Coder Workspace**—All panels are docked on the left in the same manner as in HomeSite and ColdFusion Studio (see Figure 5.3). This workspace opens all documents in Code view by default.

Figure 5.3
The Coder workspace is similar to that of the Designer workspace, but the panel groups are positioned on the left side of the window.

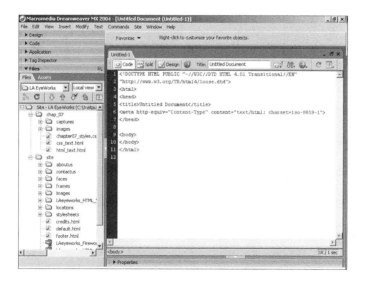

NOTE

Mac users have only the floating layout available.

No matter which workspace you choose, you can customize it to meet your needs by moving and changing Dreamweaver's various panels. Panels that are regrouped or undocked from the panel group remain in that new state even in future Dreamweaver sessions. The Property inspector is initially collapsed, showing only the most common options. If you expand the Property inspector, it remains expanded in future sessions unless you manually collapse it.

EXPLORING THE DOCUMENT WINDOW

The Document window is where most of the action takes place. The Document window contains a title bar, menus, toolbars, and a status bar. All the other panels, inspectors, and toolbars exist to add to or modify the contents of the Document window. The Document window is capable of displaying a visual representation of the site in Design view (see Figure 5.4), the HTML code for the site in Code view (see Figure 5.5), or a split window containing both the design and the code (see Figure 5.6).

Figure 5.4
Design view enables you to work in a what-you-see-is-what-you-get (WYSIWYG) atmosphere.

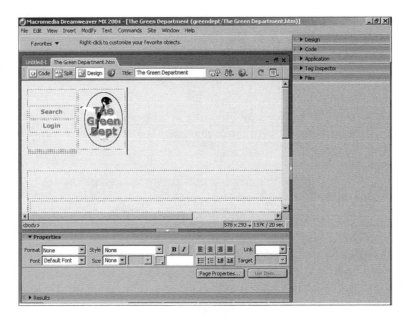

Regardless of your preference, it's likely that you will use all three views at some point or other. Even with the advancements of WYSIWYG development environments, it's still good to understand and be able to modify and write code by hand.

> **TIP**
>
> In Code and Design view, changes you make to the code aren't reflected in the Design pane unless you refresh the view. You can do this by clicking the Refresh button on either the Property inspector or the Document toolbar, or simply by pressing F5.

TITLE BAR

The Title bar displays the title and filename of the open document. Aside from being a reminder of the name of the page on which you're currently working, it can also serve as a reminder that you haven't yet given the page a title. As you work, an asterisk is appended to the filename, signifying that you've made unsaved changes to the document. Use the Save keyboard shortcut (Command-S) [Ctrl+S] or select File, Save to save your file.

Figure 5.5
Code view enables you to develop or edit the markup directly.

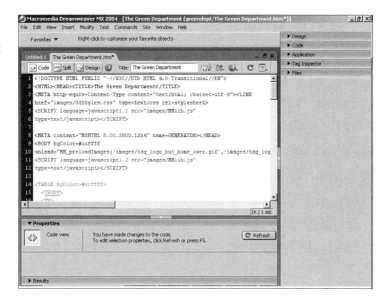

Figure 5.6
Code and Design view enables you to make changes to either pane and see how changes in one affect the other.

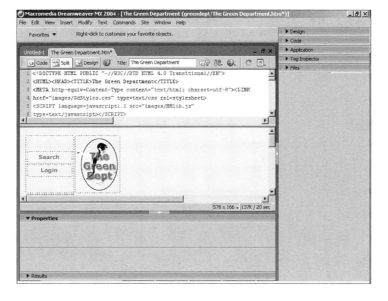

5

MENU BAR

The Menu bar contains nearly all the commands and features of Dreamweaver. Most of these commands are also accessible from panels or the Property inspector, as well as context menus that pop up when you (Control-click) [right-click] your mouse.

TOOLBARS

Three toolbars are available in the Document window. To toggle these toolbars from view, select View, Toolbars, and select from the three options. All the toolbars can be visible at the same time, but they will cut down on your workspace.

The Standard toolbar contains the usual File, Save, Copy/Cut, and Paste commands (see Figure 5.7). If you already know the keyboard shortcuts for these common commands— they're the same as those for most Windows or Mac applications—this toolbar simply takes up valuable real estate.

Figure 5.7
The Standard toolbar is useful for novices, but it takes up valuable screen real estate.

The Document toolbar, shown in Figure 5.8, also contains options available elsewhere in Dreamweaver, such as switching views or titling the document. Although you can access these features from the menu bar as well, it's usually convenient to have them at your fingertips through keyboard shortcuts.

Figure 5.8
The Document toolbar makes it easy to switch views, title the page, and preview the document in a browser.

The Insert toolbar, shown in Figure 5.9, enables you to easily insert elements into your pages. The available elements are divided into logical categories, which can be selected from the dropdown menu at the far left of the Insert bar. When selected, each category displays a unique set of buttons that allow you to add any specific element to your page with the click of your mouse.

Figure 5.9
The Insert toolbar allows you to easily add elements to your pages.

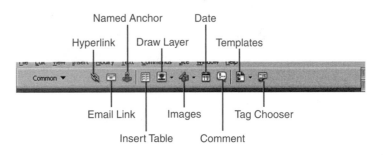

The Insert bar contains 8 categories, each containing icons for the most frequently used options in that category (see Table 5.1).

TABLE 5.1   INSERT BAR CATEGORIES

Category	Function
Common	Contains image, table, link, layer, third-party code (Fireworks), comment, and other commonly used objects.
Layout	Enables toggling of standard and layout views for creating tables and provides the tools to use Layout view to draw tables and cells.
Forms	Inserts form containers and elements.
Text	Adds text formatting, such as bold and italic, and paragraph formatting, such as headings and lists. It can also be used to access the Font Tag Editor to set multiple attributes at once.
HTML	Adds HTML elements, such as horizontal rules or frames, to your page.
Application	Enables you to build recordsets containing data from your database connections and display content from those recordsets on your pages.
Flash Elements	Enables you to control Flash elements stored within your pages.
Favorites	Enables you to create your own toolbar with buttons for your favorite elements.

To insert an element from one of the Insert bar categories, position the cursor in the page and then click the object button in the Insert bar (or drag the object button to the insertion point). In the case of inserting images or creating links, among others, a dialog box appears to help you complete the insertion, in which you can perform such actions as selecting an image file or defining the link parameters. To insert placeholders for these elements, when available (such as for images), press the (Option) [Ctrl] key while clicking the Object button. You can then select a final image or fill in other required attributes later in the development process.

5

STATUS BAR

The Status bar is located at the bottom of the Document window (see Figure 5.10). It provides information about the file size and download time for the document. Dreamweaver calculates an approximate download time based on the Connection Speed setting in the Status Bar category of the Preferences dialog box (Edit, Preferences). By default, Dreamweaver calculates page load times at 56 kilobits per second, but you can change these settings to calculate download time for faster or slower means of connection.

Figure 5.10
The Status bar displays the Tag selector, Window Size selector, and Download size/ speed indicator.

WINDOW SIZE SELECTOR   You can change the dimensions of your default screen size to match those of your typical site visitor. This enables you to design for a wide range of browser dimensions or to test the general appearance of the document in a specific configuration.

Choosing the Right Viewing Size

More and more Web visitors are using upgraded monitors, enabling them to view pages in a broader array of colors and at a higher resolution. As a result, many designers are now developing based on an 800×600 screen size or higher. For the most part, this is acceptable, but keep in mind that there are always those who are still satisfied with 640×480 displays. WebTV owners have a display size of only 560×384 (and an equally limited range of colors and other limitations).

TAG SELECTOR   The Tag Selector combines the best of working in Design view with the need to occasionally—and sometimes frequently—make changes to the underlying code by hand. The Tag Selector shows the HTML tags (see Figure 5.11) relative to the position of the cursor in Design view.

Figure 5.11
The Tag Selector gives you quick access to tags used in your document.

This feature is often overlooked because there are so many methods for accessing and editing code. But when you're working on nested tables or have multiple layers on the page, the Tag Selector can help you find your place in the code. Just click a tag in the Tag Selector to highlight the contents of the tag in Design view. You can then make modifications to that element in the Property inspector or by using the menus and panels. You can also select a tag from the Tag Selector, switch to Code view, and the element and its contents will be highlighted.

The Tag Selector also makes deleting blocks of content easy. You can delete tables or blocks of text easily by choosing their container tag in the Tag Selector and then pressing the (Backspace) [Delete] key to erase it.

 All your document content disappears upon deleting a tag? Find out why, and how to avoid this problem, in "Deleting Content" in the "Troubleshooting" section later in this chapter.

Finally, the Tag Selector can be used to edit tags. Select a tag, and then bring up the context menu (Ctrl-click) [right-click]. The context menu provides one of many methods for setting the class of a tag, used extensively with Cascading Style Sheets. You can also use the context menu to access the Quick Tag Editor by choosing Edit Tag.

NOTE

The Tag Selector isn't visible in Code view because other code tools are more useful in this environment. Thus, if you're using the Coder workspace, the Tag Selector doesn't appear at the bottom of the Document window.

USING THE PROPERTY INSPECTOR

The Property inspector is arguably the most important tool in Dreamweaver (see Figure 5.12). Whereas other panels place objects on the page, the Property inspector modifies the attributes of those objects. The context of the Property inspector changes depending on the selected element or view. As with all panels, the Property inspector can be moved. It can be docked either above or below the Document window or undocked to become a floating panel.

Figure 5.12
The Property inspector changes with the context of the selection.

The Property inspector is initially in a minimal state, containing only the most popular attributes for an element. In many cases, however, additional attributes are available in the expanded Property inspector. To expand the panel, click the arrow in the bottom-right corner.

In addition to the standard text fields and buttons, the Property inspector contains several other features. The color picker is used to select a color for text, table borders, and other objects. The Point-to-File and Folder icons are used to locate files to insert images or links; the Quick Tag Editor, signified by a pencil-and-paper icon on the right side of the Property inspector, enables you to add element attributes not found on the Inspector. Selecting the question mark icon launches the Using Dreamweaver help system.

WORKING WITH PANELS

Unless you've changed the default workspace to remove all the panels and inspectors from view, you'll see that the Document window is surrounded by groupings of additional options and site information. Some of these panels are critical to Dreamweaver's ease of use, whereas others can be removed without worry.

Panels are grouped by default in logical panel groups. Of course, this logic might or might not apply to your workflow, so the arrangement of panels into groups can be modified to meet your needs.

To open a panel group, click the arrow to the left of the panel group name or click the panel group name itself. (See Figure 5.13.)

ARRANGING PANEL GROUPS

Each panel group has several controls (see Figure 5.14). The icon to the right of the panel group name activates a drop-down options menu containing several commands within the context of the panels contained in the group. At the bottom of each menu is also a series of panel group commands.

5

Figure 5.13
Click the arrow next to panel groups to open and close panels. Here, you see the Design, Code, Application, Tag Inspector, and Files panels, with the Code and Application panel groups open.

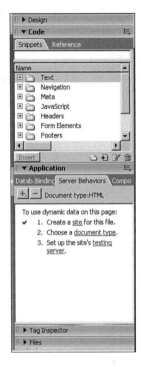

Gripper

Figure 5.14
The panel group controls include a gripper and a drop-down menu with group commands.

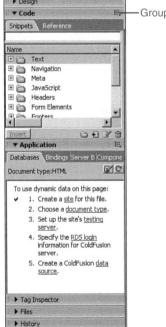

Group command dropdown

5

To the left of the group name is a tool called the *gripper*. Clicking and dragging the gripper for a group enables you to undock that panel group. These floating panels can then be moved around the workspace. To dock a floating panel group, drag it by its gripper until the insert indicator is positioned where you want in the panel dock. Thus, you can use the gripper to rearrange the order of the panel groups in the panel dock.

Panels can be moved into other existing or new panel groups. To do this, follow these steps:

1. Select the tab for the panel you want to relocate.

2. Open the options menu for the panel group in which the panel is currently located.

3. Select the Group [*panel name*] With command.

4. Select an existing panel group, or select New Panel Group to create a new panel group.

The moved panel immediately appears in its new group. Or, if you created a new panel group, open the Options menu in the new group and select Rename Panel Group to give it an appropriate name. You can then add other panels to the new group.

Panel groups can be sized to take up more or less space in the panel dock. When you position the mouse between panel groups, the cursor changes into a double-headed arrow, which can be clicked and dragged up or down to modify the size of expanded panel groups. To maximize a panel group to take up as much space in the panel dock as possible, select Maximize Panel Group from the Panel menu. This minimizes other open panel groups to give the select group full use of the vertical space.

Some panels—particularly the Reference panel, located in the Code panel group—benefit from additional horizontal space as well as vertical. Position the mouse cursor between the panel dock and the Document window until it becomes a double-headed arrow; then click and drag horizontally to give additional space to the panel dock. Keep in mind, however, that this decreases the size of the Document window.

5

> **TIP**
>
> If you're making extensive use of the Reference panel, move it into its own panel group and then undock that group. You can then expand the size of the panel without resizing the Document window. As an added benefit, the floating panel remains on top of the Document window even as you work on a page, eliminating the need to switch between viewing the panel and your document.

If you're not using a panel group at all, you can close it by selecting Close Panel Group from the Options menu for that group. To reopen a closed panel group, select it from the Window menu in the Document window.

DESIGN PANELS

The Design panel group contains panels that control the styles and behaviors of the elements on the page. The two panels in this group are CSS Styles (see Figure 5.15), and Layers (see Figure 5.16).

Figure 5.15
The CSS Styles panel is used to define and modify Cascading Style Sheets, which is the preferred method for establishing the presentation of elements.

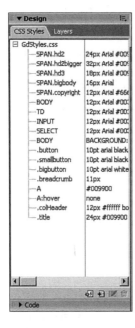

Figure 5.16
The Layers panel is used to control any layers that exist within the document.

CODE PANELS

The Code panels can be used in either Design or Code view and enable you to control code snippets and seek reference information about your code.

The Snippets panel contains predefined code snippets, grouped in related folders (see Figure 5.17). You can also add your own snippets and folders in this panel.

Figure 5.17
The Snippets panel contains small, reusable portions of code, which can be inserted into a page.

The Reference panel provides reference material for HTML, CSS, JavaScript, dynamic server technologies, and accessibility issues (see Figure 5.18).

Figure 5.18
The Reference panel is a tremendous resource for Web development information.

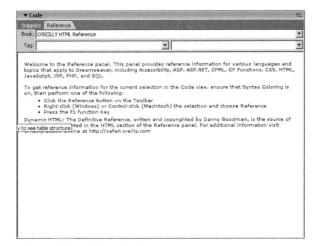

5

APPLICATION PANELS

When you're using databases and advanced server technologies to create dynamic pages, you'll want to open the Application panel. Initially, each of the panels in this group prompts you to configure the test server and other requirements (if you haven't already done so in the Site Definition).

Using the Databases panel (see Figure 5.19), you can easily create a connection to a database containing content for your site.

Figure 5.19
The Databases panel controls database connections.

The Bindings panel, shown in Figure 5.20, is used to create recordsets or datasets (depending on your platform) and allows you to drag and drop dynamic content into your pages.

Figure 5.20
The Bindings panel allows you to easily add dynamic text and elements to your pages.

The Server Behaviors panel (see Figure 5.21) gives you access to a broad range of dynamic server behaviors ranging from restricting access to your pages to repeating regions.

Figure 5.21
The Server Behaviors panel provides access to database-driven server behaviors.

Finally, the Components panel (see Figure 5.22) enables you to easily add Web Services or ColdFusion components to your page.

Figure 5.22
The Components panel provides access to ColdFusion components and Web Services.

5

NOTE

If you don't design dynamic pages, you can close this panel group entirely to save space.

TAG INSPECTOR PANELS

The Tag Inspector panel enables you to visualize how tags are nested within other tags within the document and what attributes are associated with each tag. By selecting an element within the page or choosing a tag from the Tag Selector and then choosing the Attributes panel (see Figure 5.23), you can view information about the tag, such as general attributes, any styles that are associated with it, the language in which the code is styled, and any uncategorized attributes associated with the tag.

Figure 5.23
The Attributes panel allows you to visualize attributes of specific code tags.

The Behaviors panel, shown in Figure 5.24, provides you with access to commonly used JavaScript behaviors that can be associated with tags within your document. For instance, after you create a hyperlink from text and select the <a> tag, the Behaviors panel provides access to numerous behaviors that are unavailable to non-linked text.

Similarly, the Relevant CSS panel displays information regarding Cascading Style Sheets that are linked to a particular tag.

FILES PANELS

The Files panel, shown in Figure 5.25, enables you to view and manipulate the files and folders located within your local site. The Files panel also allows you to create, edit, and delete Dreamweaver sites (which are covered in Chapter 6).

Figure 5.24
The Behaviors panel gives you access to JavaScript behaviors that can be applied to specific elements.

Figure 5.25
The Files panel enables you to manage the files and folders contained within your site.

The Assets panel allows you to easily organize elements located within your site, such as images, movies, rich content, and hyperlinks. Using the Assets panel can save you time because you simply drag and drop elements right into your page (see Figure 5.26).

Figure 5.26
The Assets panel organizes many of the elements contained within your site.

HISTORY PANEL

The History panel maintains a list of all your actions in the current document (see Figure 5.27). You can use this list to create new commands for repetitive, time-consuming actions. You can also use the History panel to undo multiple steps at once or to replay steps.

Figure 5.27
The History panel tracks every action you've performed on the current document since you opened it last.

5

The last item on the list is the most recent, and the panel scrolls upward. To undo the last several actions, drag the slider that's to the left of the steps upward to select the steps you want to undo. After you've made your selection, continue editing. The selected steps are not undone until you take another action that overwrites those steps in the history.

To repeat steps, use the slider to select them and then click the Copy Steps button.

NOTE

After you've undone multiple items and overwritten them with other steps, you cannot redo the original steps.

To create a command, select a series of steps with the slider and then click the Save Selected Steps as a Command button. You'll be prompted to give the command a name, and the new command will appear on the Commands menu.

NOTE

The History panel tracks only a limited number of steps per session. You can increase or decrease this number in the Maximum Number of History Steps field of the General Preferences settings.

RESULTS PANEL

The Results panel automatically appears to display the results of searches, validation checks, and various reports.

SEARCH PANEL   The Search panel is displayed at the bottom of the workspace whenever you issue a Find command (see Figure 5.28) that reaches beyond the active document (such as if you're conducting a site-wide search). This panel displays the results of a search and allows you to click the results to edit them in the Document window. Buttons on the left side of the panel enable you to initiate or cancel Find commands.

Figure 5.28
The Search panel lists the results of searches in a document or site.

VALIDATION PANEL   The Validation panel, shown in Figure 5.29, lists any coding errors in the site or document when you validate the site (by selecting File, Check Page, Validate Markup/Validate As XML). This validation can also be initiated directly from the panel, and corrections can be located from it.

Figure 5.29
The Validation panel lists coding errors.

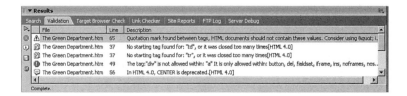

TARGET BROWSER CHECK PANEL   The Target Browser Check panel, shown in Figure 5.30, lists browser compatibility issues that have emerged in a running of the Check Target Browsers report (File, Check Page, Check Target Browsers or directly from the Target Browser Check panel). The panel provides options to save the report for future reference. By highlighting an item in the report and clicking the More Info button, you can view a dialog box explaining exactly why an item is marked. If you double-click an entry, it opens in the Document window in Code and Design view with the offending code highlighted.

Figure 5.30
The Target Browser Check panel lists elements that can't be viewed properly in the target browser.

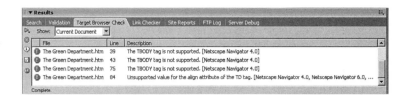

LINK CHECKER PANEL   The Link Checker panel, shown in Figure 5.31, lists the results of the Check Links report (File, Check Page, Check Links, or run from within the Link Checker panel). This report lists broken links, orphaned files within the site, and all external links.

Figure 5.31
The Link Checker panel enables you to fix broken links, eliminate orphaned files, and manually validate external links.

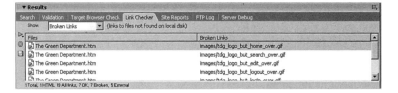

SITE REPORTS PANEL   The Site Reports panel, shown in Figure 5.32, displays the results of the Site Report (Site, Reports from either the Document window or Site panel menus). The Site Report can be quite extensive, depending on the options you choose when initiating the report. As with the other Results panels, you can use this report to get more information on the items listed and use the items to locate the specific code in question to make modifications.

FTP LOG PANEL   The FTP Log panel tracks communication with the remote server. You can also enter commands directly to the server from this panel, which is useful to experienced developers.

Figure 5.32
The Site Reports panel lists problems found with accessibility, incomplete tags, or missing *alt* attributes.

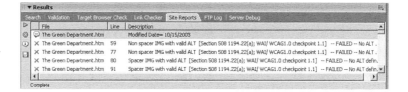

SERVER DEBUG PANEL   The Server Debug panel is used with dynamic pages to locate errors in the code. To use this feature, select View, Server Debug from the menu. The Server Debug panel displays the results of this command, including the server variables and values, execution time, and SQL queries on the page. If you didn't configure your testing server correctly, this panel prompts you through the required steps.

CODE INSPECTOR

The Code Inspector contains all the same features as the Code view, but is located on a floating panel (see Figure 5.33). The Code view was new in Dreamweaver 4, and the Code Inspector remains primarily for long-term Dreamweaver developers who were used to accessing their code in this manner. The Code Inspector can either be activated by choosing Window, Code Inspector or by pressing the F10 key.

Figure 5.33
The Code Inspector duplicates the functionality of the Code view in the Document window. The only advantage of the Code Inspector is its capability to be positioned elsewhere on the screen because it's a floating panel.

5

WORKING WITH TEXT IN THE DOCUMENT WINDOW

Now that you know what tools are available for your use, it's time to start putting them to use. Probably the most common element of all Web pages is text that conveys information. Because text itself does not convey emphasis or emotion, a variety of styles, fonts, sizes, and colors can be used to tailor the message to the audience.

You enter text into Dreamweaver by either typing directly in the Document window or cutting/copying and pasting text from another source. Text can be selected for editing or cutting and pasting within the document, using many of the same menu commands and keyboard shortcuts available in most word processors.

After the text is entered into the Document window, you have many options for formatting it.

PARAGRAPHS

A lot of the text in your documents is likely to be standard paragraphs. To create a paragraph break, simply press (Return) [Enter] and a blank line of whitespace is inserted below the paragraph.

> **NOTE**
>
> From a markup standpoint, Dreamweaver assumes your text is in paragraph format by default until you apply formatting to the contrary. All text within the <p>...</p> tag pair is formatted as one paragraph.

LINE BREAKS

Whitespace is important for control of design and readability. In most HTML editors, including Dreamweaver, when you press the (Return) [Enter] key, a new <p> tag is inserted. Dreamweaver also automatically inserts a new HTML paragraph with a nonbreaking space   entity between the opening and end tags. If you then type on this new line, the nonbreaking space is replaced with your content. If you leave the paragraph blank, however, the paragraph remains with a nonbreaking space. Because the tag is not empty, browsers correctly interpret this paragraph as a blank line.

Conversely, you might want to start a new line of text without that blank line inserted by the paragraph tags. To do this, use a line break. A *line break* inserts a carriage return in the text without closing the paragraph tag and, thus, without inserting extra space between the two lines.

To add a line break, follow these steps:

1. Position your cursor where you want to force a line break.
2. Select Insert, Special Characters, Line Break from the menu, or press (Shift-Return) [Shift+Enter].

The text is forced to a new line without additional whitespace between lines. Line breaks can also be used to force more whitespace within a paragraph if you add multiple breaks consecutively.

 Find out why you'll get a validation error if text isn't properly formatted in strict HTML or XHTML documents in "Validation Errors Related to Text," in the "Troubleshooting" section at the end of this chapter.

STYLING TEXT

Styling the text used to present your content is usually one of the easiest ways to spice up the presentation of your information. Until the last few years, the use of the font element as the preferred method of styling left Web developers with a very limited selection of "safe" fonts and attributes from which to choose. However, with the announcement of new

HTML 4.0 standards, the font element has been deprecated (meaning it's not recommended anymore) by the World Wide Web Consortium (W3C) and Macromedia has shifted the way that Dreamweaver MX 2004 applies font styling to pages from the use of <font> tags to Cascading Style Sheets (CSS).

NOTE

> Dreamweaver MX 2004 has not abandoned the use of the font element completely. If you have existing projects that already use the font element, you can continue applying font styling in that manner by choosing Edit, Preferences, and removing the check in the box next to Use CSS Instead of HTML Tags.

The nice thing about using CSS in Dreamweaver is you can have as much or as little control over them as you wish. If you're used to using the standard fonts that have traditionally been "safe" for Web use, then the Font dropdown in the Property inspector allows you to apply a font and never have to touch a style sheet. Now that's a full-service code generator!

If, however, you would like to work with new fonts and styles that are available with the adoption of CSS, then you can create custom style sheets that can easily be applied on a page-by-page basis or throughout your entire site. We'll cover CSS in-depth in Chapter 8.

 Want to use the font element and still follow best practices? Check out which HTML and XHTML document types allow you to use the font element in "Font Use" in the "Troubleshooting" section at the end of this chapter.

When applying a style to your text, there are several attributes that can be accessed easily via the Property inspector (see Figure 5.34).

Figure 5.34
The Property inspector puts the most common text style attributes within easy reach.

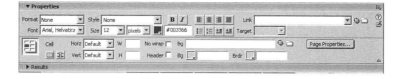

SETTING THE FONT FACE

In Dreamweaver, fonts are chosen from one of the defined font groups. Select a range of text, and then select a font group from the Font Type drop-down menu in the Property inspector.

To change the font of a block of text, follow these steps:

1. Highlight the text to which you would like to apply the font.
2. Click the Font drop-down list in the Property inspector.
3. Choose a font from the list.

SETTING THE FONT SIZE

Prior to the adoption of CSS as the preferred styling method, the font element used a set of arbitrary font sizes ranging from 1 to 7. The worst part about these sizes is that different browsers interpreted their sizes differently. This meant that text would appear differently in different browsers. Through the use of CSS, however, we can now control the exact pixel size of our fonts, ensuring that they are displayed consistently across every browser.

To set the font size for a block of text, do the following:

1. Select the text to be sized. If no text is selected, the size change is applied to subsequent text.
2. In the Property inspector, click the Size drop-down list.
3. Select a size from the list.

SETTING THE FONT COLOR

The default text color is set in the Page Properties dialog box. Unless you modified the page properties, the default color for text is black (#000000). To change the color of text from the default, select the text and then use the Color Picker in the Property inspector to select a new color (see Figure 5.35). The Text Color field uses the same Dreamweaver color picker as the Page Properties and other color tools. Alternatively, you can type the hexadecimal code in the text box to the right of the Color Picker.

Figure 5.35
Using the color picker to set the font color is a quick, visual way to colorize your fonts.

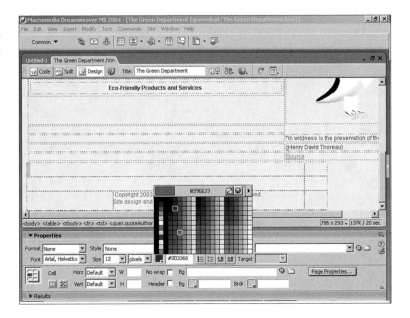

5

NOTE

To return text to the default text color, click the Color Picker and then click the white square with the red strikethrough button.

Setting Font Styles

A font style is formatting such as bold or italics applied to a font. The most typical font styles were shown in Figure 5.34 and can be applied from the Property inspector.

You can choose additional font styles by selecting Text, Style from the menu (see Table 5.2). You can also choose more than one style for the same text selection, such as when creating bold, italicized text.

TABLE 5.2   FONT FACES AND THEIR USES

Font Style	HTML Element	Used For
Bold	b	Adding bold emphasis
Italic	i	Adding emphasis with italicization
<u>Underline</u>	u	Adding emphasis with underline
~~Strikethrough~~	s or strikethrough	Editorial purposes
Teletype	tt	Monospaced font
Emphasis	em	Usually displayed as italics
Strong	strong	Stronger emphasis than just using the emphasis style, usually displays as bold
Code	code	Text that represents a computer program listing
Variable	var	Text that represents a program variable
Sample	samp	Text that represents sample output from a program
Keyboard	kbd	Text that represents user input
Citation	cite	Source of a quote
Definition	dfn	Text that is a definition
Definition	del	Text that has been deleted from the page
Definition	ins	Text that has been inserted into the page

If you select a style before typing, the style is applied to all subsequent text.

CAUTION

Remember, if you underline text on your pages, it can be confused with a link.

Aligning Text

Paragraph alignment is used to position text relative to its confining margins, whether those margins are the page margins, a table cell, or a layer. To change the alignment of text, follow these steps:

1. Select the text you want to align, or insert the cursor at the beginning of the text.
2. Click Align Left, Align Center, Align Right, or Justify on the Property inspector.

You can also align text by selecting Align from the Text menu.

NOTE

Alignment is considered presentational and therefore can be used only in HTML and XHTML transitional documents.

INDENTING TEXT

Text can be indented or outdented in several ways. Select the desired text and use one of the following methods to indent or outdent the text:

- Use the Property inspector and click the Indent or Outdent button.
- From the menu bar, select Text, Indent or Text, Outdent.
- If the text you highlight is a list, you can right-click it and select List, Indent or List, Outdent from the context menu.

Indents and outdents can be applied multiple times until the text is positioned where you desire. Although this is easy to do, it's not the preferred method for positioning text. A better solution is to use a table or CSS.

CREATING LISTS IN DOCUMENTS

5

Lists bring order and structure to text on the Web. Large blocks of text are difficult to read onscreen, so lists break things into manageable highlights.

Lists items are formatted in `<li>...</li>` tag pairs for each item. The list in its entirety also needs to be defined. The manner in which this is done depends on the type of list.

UNORDERED (BULLETED) LISTS

An unordered list is used when the sequence of the items isn't important. Bulleted lists can be created from text you've already entered, or the list can be created as you type the text. Here's how to make an unordered list:

1. To configure the list and then type the list items, position the cursor where you want to start the list. If you're converting existing text into a list, select the text.
2. In the Property inspector, click the Unordered List button. You can also select Text, List, Unordered List.
3. Type in the text of your list.
4. To end the list after you enter all the items, press (Return) [Enter] twice or click the Unordered List button in the Property inspector.

List items are spaced more closely together than paragraphs (see Figure 5.36). If you look at the Code view, the unordered list is contained within a <ul>...</ul> tag pair.

Figure 5.36
An unordered list is used for items that don't need to appear in a specific order.

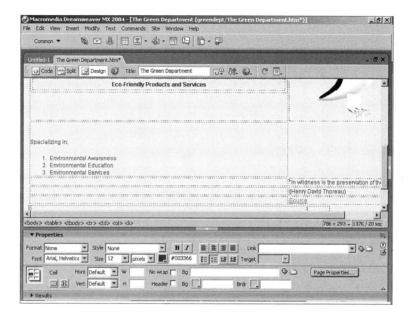

Font faces, colors, sizes, and styles can be applied to lists. Paragraph formatting, however, is likely to destroy the list layout, so it should be avoided. To remove list formatting, select the entire list and then click the Unordered List button in the Property inspector. The text itself remains, but the formatting of the list is deleted as is the markup that created the list.

ORDERED (NUMBERED) LISTS

Ordered lists are used when items should be followed sequentially. Create these lists in the same manner as unordered lists, but simply click the Ordered List button instead. Examining the code, you'll see that ordered lists are defined by the <ol>...</ol> tag pair.

One of the best features of an ordered list is its capability to renumber itself as items are added, deleted, or moved. To add an item to the list, position the insertion point at the end of the list item above where you want the addition to appear. Press (Return) [Enter] to add a new line; then type in the new item. To move an item in the list, either use the cut-and-paste method or highlight the list item and then drag it to its new location while holding down the left mouse button.

TROUBLESHOOTING

DELETING CONTENT

I selected a tag and deleted it, only to find all my content had disappeared. What happened?

You likely selected the body tag and pressed Delete while attempting to delete another tag or some portion of your content. When you use the Tag Selector for deletion, select the body tag, and then press Delete, the head content remains but the body tag returns to a completely empty state. Of course, this also means you should use this feature with care when selecting the body or other large containers on a page.

VALIDATION ERRORS RELATED TO TEXT

I'm getting validation errors related to text materials. Why?

This might be due to an issue with browser display.

Browsers rely on certain display models to interpret HTML and XHTML. Two such display models are referred to as *inline* and *block*. An element that is inline appears within the text itself, and therefore no carriage return is applied by the browser. Examples of inline elements include a, span, and any text formatting such as b, i, and u. Block elements are complete sections after which browsers apply a carriage return automatically. Examples of block elements include all headers, p, div, and table.

Strict forms of markup expect that the author will place all inline elements within a properly described block. This means that text should appear within a header, paragraph, list, or any other block element but should not appear alone. So, in a strict document, the following is incorrect and causes a validation error:

```
Send <a href="mailto:molly@molly.com" title="email molly">me</a> an e-mail.
```

To avoid errors, make sure your text is properly placed within a block element, such as a paragraph:

```
<p>Send <a href="mailto:molly@molly.com"
➥title="email molly">me</a> an e-mail.</p>
```

Interestingly, this problem doesn't occur with transitional DTDs, which do not require adherence to block and inline rules.

FONT USE

I want to use the font element and still have valid documents. Is that possible?

You can do so by following these DTDs:

- HTML 4.0 transitional
- HTML 4.01 transitional
- XHTML 1.0

You can't use the `font` element in any strict HTML or XHTML document or with the XHTML 1.1 public DTD. As you are already aware, the use of the `font` element is highly discouraged in favor of CSS.

PEER TO PEER: THE ESSENCE OF STRUCTURE

Text structuring provides an excellent example of why the goal to separate document structure from presentation rules is so important.

If you add elements to text in a haphazard way—such as using paragraph tags to create whitespace, using headers out of numeric order, and using `font` elements—the document has no structure. An `h1` header was labeled a "level one" with the precise goal in mind of labeling the content within the element as being a header of first-level priority, an `h2` a second-level priority, and so on. This hierarchy is part of what creates structure. Add to that properly formatted paragraphs, line breaks, the reduction or elimination of font tags, and the use of lists to organize a document, and you get to the heart of what a structured document is all about.

When you use the hierarchical and logical methods described previously to structure documents, those documents become much more accessible not only to those with disabilities, but also for alternative devices such as PDAs, pagers, mobile phones, and so on. Follow these general guidelines, and your pages will be extremely flexible in how they can be used. What's more, you'll have returned to the original vision of the Web: a platform-independent means of sharing documents.

CHAPTER **6**

SETTING UP SITES, PAGES, AND TEMPLATES

In this chapter

Establishing a Web Site   104

Managing Documents   111

Pre-Design Page Setup   117

Managing Pages with Templates   122

Using Templates   130

ESTABLISHING A WEB SITE

Before you start using Dreamweaver to design your Web site, you should first *define* your Dreamweaver site. Defining a site refers to setting up a directory structure locally and, when appropriate, on the remote server where the site will appear. After your site is defined, you can begin working on your new pages and sites in an organized fashion.

Most readers will already have an idea of how best to create directory structures, and many of you might be running Web servers of your own. This experience will be helpful to you as you proceed to set up both your computer and any remote server for Macromedia Dreamweaver. In fact, if you already have a Web server set up, you can jump right into the following tasks.

If you don't have a local or remote hosting service for your site, now would be a good time to begin looking into Web hosting options and finding the best situation for your needs.

> **NOTE**
>
> To learn more about the types of hosting available and to find a hosting provider, please see the following article in *The Web Host Industry Review*, http://thewhir.com/find/web-hosts/articles/.

DEFINING THE SITE LOCALLY

The first thing you'll need to do before being able to do any editing or design work with Dreamweaver is to create a local folder.

Follow these steps:

1. Make a new folder on your computer to store pages and Web site components. I called mine greendept. In that folder, create an images subfolder, where you can store any images you'll use with the site.

2. Open Dreamweaver, and from the main menu, select Site, Manage Sites.

3. In the Manage Sites dialog box, click the New button and choose Site. The Site Definition dialog box appears (see Figure 6.1) and you should see two tab options, Basic and Advanced.

4. Click the Advanced tab. To the left, you'll see a list of category definitions for the site you're creating. For now, you're concerned only with Local Info. You'll have the opportunity to add other definitions later in this chapter.

5. Be sure that Local Info is highlighted. In the Site Name text box, add a name to identify this specific site from others you may have already created, or will create in the future.

6. In the Local Root Folder text box, type in the path to the site folder that you created. If you can't remember the complete path to the folder or are unsure of it, click the folder icon to browse your computer for the folder. After you've found the new folder, highlight it and click (Choose) [Select]. You'll now see that the path has been added to the Local Root Folder.

Figure 6.1
For any site you work with, you'll use the Site definition dialog box to name the site and set options for how you want to use it. The Basic tab is a wizard to help easily guide you through; more advanced users can click the Advanced tab and enter their own parameters.

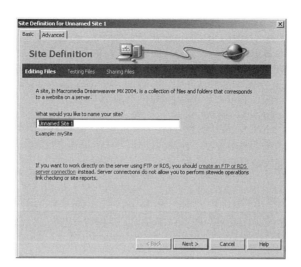

7. If the Refresh Local File List Automatically check box is unchecked, check it.

 Files not updating properly? See "Refreshing Files" in the "Troubleshooting" section at the end of the chapter.

8. Now add the path to the images folder by typing in the path to that folder in the Default Images Folder text box. You can also browse to the folder and add it. If you don't already have a folder defined, select Browse and then select a new folder through the dialog box. After you've created the new folder, you can select it and continue.

9. Leave the remainder of the dialog box as is, and click OK to apply your changes. You'll add the remote server information in the next section.

10. Click Done to close the Manage Sites dialog box.

To see the new site added, select Window, Files from the main menu.

Creating the Best File Structure

With simple sites comprising just a few pages and images, file structure isn't an area of extreme concern. However, when sites grow to contain hundreds, thousands, or even greater numbers of files, it becomes imperative to architect a good file structure system to accommodate them.

The use of a local root folder is a good beginning. In this area should be any top-level files, such as the index page, and the main pages for the site. But if your site contains a great number of articles and resources, you might have to break this down into much greater detail. Let's say you are an e-zine and regularly publish articles, columns, comics, and classifieds. It is in your best interest to create subfolders for each of these, keeping things organized by topic.

Similarly, if you are using media other than images on your site, you might want to create subfolders for various media, such as images, audio, video, and so on.

6

The one potential problem that can arise out of creating too many subdirectories is that the resulting URLs can be very long, which makes them difficult to remember and bookmark and, depending on the way they are fashioned, even likely to cause problems with page validation (see the Peer to Peer section at the end of this chapter for more information).

A good exercise is to sketch out the file structure ahead of time. This will provide you a blueprint from which to work as you proceed in the building of your site. Although it's not always easy to anticipate the future, keep in mind that the site, if successful, will grow in size and that growth will need to be accommodated.

Setting the Remote Information

Now that you have your local site established, the next step is to set up a connection to your remote server that allows you to transfer files between your local workstation and the server where your site is hosted. Gather all the information you have about your remote server. In most cases you'll be using FTP, but there are other connection options, as described in Table 6.1.

TABLE 6.1   REMOTE INFORMATION OPTIONS

Option	What It Does
None	Select this if you simply want to build your site on your local computer. You can always consider transfer options later.
FTP	This is the File Transfer Protocol. This method is in widespread use for transferring files from a local machine to a remote machine.
Local/Network	If you are working on a network or running Web server software locally, select this option.
RDS	This is Remote Development Services. It is used by people working with dynamic content in ColdFusion.
SourceSafe Database	A special Microsoft database that enables powerful management features for teams working on sites, SourceSafe must be installed and in use if you want to use this option.
WebDAV	Certain servers use the Web-based Distributed Authoring and Versioning tools. If you are using a WebDAV system, select this option.

In most instances, you'll be using FTP, which is the process discussed here. If you are certain that you'll be using a different method, simply select the necessary option from the drop-down menu. Select FTP if you plan on moving your files to a live Web server, or select None if you plan on creating your site locally and figuring out what to do with it later.

To set up FTP, you need to obtain the following information:

- FTP host name
- Login name (this is your user ID information)
- Password (this is a password selected by or provided to you by your service provider)
- Any additional information provided by your service provider regarding required settings

Typically, your service provider will have configured your login to default to the remote root folder. This folder corresponds to the local root folder because it will be the folder where the top-level documents and the subdirectories can be found.

With your FTP information in hand, you're ready to add the remote server information to the site you just defined. Follow these steps:

1. From the main menu, select Site, Manage Sites. The Manage Sites dialog box appears (see Figure 6.2).

Figure 6.2
Highlight the appropriate site in the Manage Sites menu to select it.

2. Highlight the site you want to modify by clicking it.

3. Click Edit. The Site Definition dialog box appears.

4. Select the Advanced tab, and under Category, highlight the Remote Info entry. A drop-down menu appears with a number of options. Select FTP. The dialog box updates with the necessary fields.

5. Enter your FTP host, host directory, login, and password. I recommend checking the Save check box. Unless your provider requires you to use passive FTP, leave the Use Passive FTP check box blank. Passive FTP is used for additional security but is not required in most cases (see Figure 6.3).

Figure 6.3
When you've finished filling out the Site Definition dialog box, your site will have most of the features necessary to manage the various files.

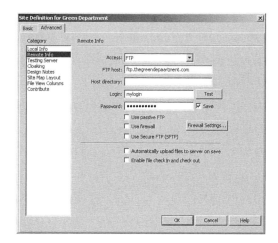

6

6. Click OK to apply the changes and click Done to close the Manage Sites dialog box.

In most cases, this will be enough information to get you started. Click the Test button to see whether, in fact, you get a connection. If you do, terrific! If not, carefully look over the information you entered and see whether everything is up to par. If it is and you are working from within a network and still having trouble, you might be behind a security firewall. If you are, you need to get those settings from your system administrator and enter them into the appropriate areas.

The two other options on the dialog box are as follows:

■ **Automatically upload files to server on save**—If you check this option, Dreamweaver automatically transfers the site to the remote server when you save the site. Because this can actually upload files that are in the process of being edited, I don't recommend choosing this option unless you are using an external versioning system such as SourceSafe.

■ **Enable file check in and check out**—If you want to enable this feature, click once in the check box. The advantage of enabling this feature is that if multiple people are working on the site, Dreamweaver helps you manage team files, preventing overwriting and the need for additional edits.

To connect to and view your remote site, do the following:

1. Make sure the Files panel is open (select Window, Files).

2. Select your site from the Site panel list by clicking it once to highlight it.

3. From the Files panel button bar, click the Connect button shown in Figure 6.4.

Connect/Disconnect icon

Figure 6.4
Clicking this icon connects you to a remote site. After you are connected, clicking it disconnects you.

4. Dreamweaver connects with the site. Select Remote View from the drop-down box found to the far right.

You'll now see the current structure of the remote site. This changes as you publish files to the server (see Figure 6.5).

Figure 6.5
Using the Files panel to set features on your remote site allows quick access and updates to the files within your project.

IMPORTING AN EXISTING WEB SITE

If you have existing Web sites on your local computer or a Web server you want to maintain with Dreamweaver, you'll need to first import them.

IMPORTING A LOCAL SITE

If you want to bring a site that resides on your local computer into Dreamweaver, follow these steps:

1. Select Site, Manage Sites. The Manage Sites dialog box appears.
2. Click the New button. The Site Definition dialog box appears.
3. Define the Site Name just as you did in the previous section.
4. Type in the path to the Local Root Folder for the site, or find the Root Folder for the site by using the browse feature. Highlight the site and click the Select button. Dreamweaver begins importing all the site files and directories. This might take a minute or two, depending on the size of the site you're importing.
5. After the import is complete, click OK. The Site Definition dialog box closes, leaving the Manage Sites dialog box open. You'll now see the name of the site you just defined in step 3.
6. Click Done.

6

Your site is now available from the Files panel, where you can see it in its entirety (see Figure 6.6).

Figure 6.6
The Files panel on the right shows the imported site.

IMPORTING A REMOTE SITE

If you have a site on a server and would like to add it to Dreamweaver for management and editing, here's how:

1. Begin by creating a local folder just as you did for a new site.

2. Create a new Dreamweaver site and add the remote site options into the remote info text boxes. This time, use the information matching the Web server and location within that server where your remote Web site resides. Click OK.

3. In the Files panel, find the newly added remote site, highlight it, and then connect to it by using the Connect button.

4. To import the entire site, click the root folder on the remote site.

5. Click the Site drop-down menu, and then select Get File(s) (the arrow pointing down). Dreamweaver asks whether you're sure you want to get the entire site. Because you do, click Yes; the site will now be transferred to the local folder you created in step 1. This might take a few minutes, depending on how large the remote site is.

After the site is resident on your local machine, you can edit it as you see fit and then later transfer the edited files back to the remote server (see Figure 6.7).

NOTE

> If you are working on only one section of the site, you might want to transfer only the directories and files you'll be working on. Generally speaking, having all a site's assets on hand helps you get the most out of Dreamweaver MX tools, such as site mapping.

6

Figure 6.7
The remote site is now available on your local drive.

MANAGING DOCUMENTS

After you have defined your site, you'll want to start working with the documents—opening them, adding new documents, and even deleting or renaming them.

CREATING A NEW DOCUMENT

With the site defined, opened, or imported into Macromedia Dreamweaver MX, you're ready to add pages to your site. The software is very powerful and offers a wide range of page types that have been preauthored and categorized for your needs. These page types include HTML, XHTML, CSS, XML, and even a WML (Wireless Markup Language) option. Dreamweaver also offers several page designs that can be extremely useful. What's more, all these documents are customizable and can be used to generate new templates that conform to your own designs.

> **NOTE**
>
> Select File, New, and check out the New Document dialog box, where you can explore all the file types and preconfigured documents available.

Follow these steps to create and save a new page:

1. Select File, New from the main menu. The New Document dialog box opens (see Figure 6.8).

Figure 6.8
A variety of file type options are available in the New Document dialog box, including HTML and CSS.

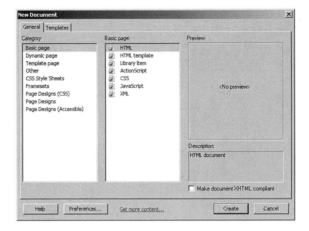

2. In the General tab, you'll see the list of page types. For a standard HTML page, highlight the Basic Page category and then select HTML. If you want to author your document in XHTML, check the Make Document XHTML Compliant check box. For another kind of page, move to that category and then highlight the file type you want.

3. Click Create to create the page and a new page is created (see Figure 6.9).

Figure 6.9 shows a newly created document in Design view.

Figure 6.9
Here's a newly created XHTML document in Design view.

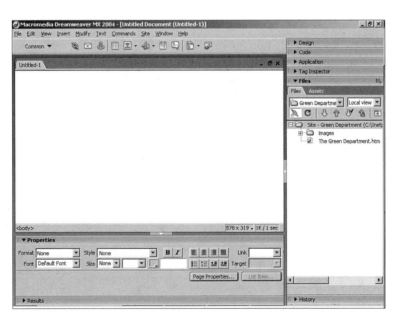

You can now add text, images—whatever you want—to the page.

SAVING FILES

After you've modified the page, you'll want to save the file. Here's how to do so:

1. Select File, Save As. The Save As dialog box appears.
2. Find the location where you want to save your file.
3. Name the file.
4. Click the Save button to save your changes.

Tips for saving data

File management is easy, but it can also be risky. You can overwrite files, lose data, and save files to the wrong area of your computer. You also can run the risk of saving files improperly. Dreamweaver's management tools help you a great deal with this, but there are still some good guidelines to follow.

Here are some tips for general saving and file management:

- **Save your work regularly**—Whenever you begin a new file, immediately name it properly and save it to the correct location in your directory structure.
- **Back up your work**—Whether you make a copy of the file to floppy disk, Zip disk, or CD is no matter—just make sure you keep a copy! There's no feeling more awful than when you lose your hard work.
- **Create your directory structure first, and save files to that area**—Use Dreamweaver's Site Definitions dialog box to ensure you set up your directory structure before trying to manage a project. This way you'll know where your files are, setting up a logical structure upon which to form the linking of pages and page assets within a given document.

Another problem with file management has to do with saving files to the wrong format. Let's say you're in Fireworks MX and want to save a file as a JPEG, but you mistakenly select another format. If you give the file the wrong suffix name, the program saves the file improperly.

This problem holds true when saving HTML, XHTML, and Cascading Style Sheets (CSS) files and related documents. It's important to remember that HTML, XHTML, and CSS are saved in ASCII, or *text* format. If you save a file as a binary file or transfer it as a binary file, the file will be corrupt. The same is true with binary formats—you can't try to save or transfer a GIF or JPEG file in ASCII, for example, because you will destroy the file's integrity.

DELETING, DUPLICATING, AND RENAMING DOCUMENTS

As you are developing your site or reworking an existing site, there will be times that you'll find it necessary to duplicate a document to create a new document with similar items, rename an existing document, or delete documents that you no longer need. To do this, you simply (Control-click) [right-click] the document in the Files window, choose the Edit submenu, and select the option to fit your needs (see Figure 6.10).

To delete a file, select the Delete option from the context menu. A pop-up window asks whether you really want to delete the selected file. Click OK. The file is now deleted.

Duplicating files is particularly handy when you want to use most of the information in a given page but modify some content. You can duplicate the page you want, make the modifications to the copy, and then rename the copy.

6

Figure 6.10
With the Site window open and a file selected, you can access a context menu with a variety of options, including Delete, Duplicate, and Rename.

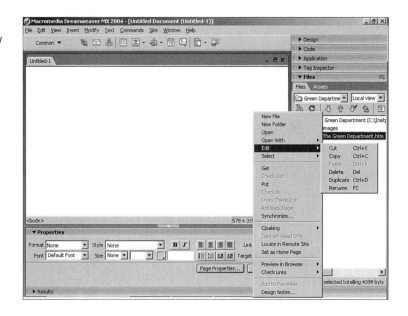

To duplicate a file, highlight the file to be duplicated in the Site panel. Then bring up the context menu and select Edit, Duplicate. A copy of the file immediately appears with the words copy of in front of the original filename.

To rename a file, bring up the context menu, select Edit, Rename, and type in the new name for the file.

CAUTION

When renaming files, be sure to provide the proper file extension. If you rename a file with a different extension (or without one altogether), the file will open improperly or not at all.

OPENING AN EXISTING DOCUMENT

To open an existing document located on your hard drive, begin by selecting File, Open. The Open dialog box appears; browse for your file. Highlight the file you want to open, and then click the Open button.

The file now opens and is available for your modifications.

You can also open documents from the Site panel by simply double-clicking the document you want to open.

NOTE

Files open in the view in which you're working. So, if you're in Design view, the file opens in Design view.

USING DESIGN NOTES TO TRACK CHANGES TO A DOCUMENT

As you work, you'll find there is information about the pages with which you're working that you'll want to jot down to remember later or to tell a co-worker about. Macromedia Dreamweaver MX 2004 provides a very handy tool called Design Notes that enables you to make notes for a page and save them to a separate file. You can also attach Design Notes to objects such as Flash files or applets, and you can use Design Notes in other programs such as Macromedia Fireworks MX. Here, the focus is on attaching a Design Note to a new or an existing document.

When adding Design Notes to a page, you can mark a file's status as follows:

- Draft
- Revision 1
- Revision 2
- Revision 3
- Alpha
- Beta
- Final
- Needs Attention

You can also create a basic Design Note with your page. To do so, follow these steps:

1. Be sure the page is saved because you will not be allowed to write a Design Note if it isn't. Select File, Design Notes. The Design Notes dialog box opens with the Basic tab activated.

2. Select a status option from the Status drop-down menu. I selected Needs Attention.

3. Type your notes into the Notes text box (see Figure 6.11).

Figure 6.11
Add status and comments to a Design Note. You can modify Design notes to show author, date, and customized comments.

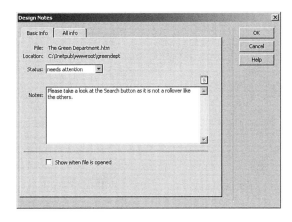

6

4. If you want the date to appear with your Design Note, click the Date icon above the Notes text box.

5. If you want the note to automatically show when the file opens, select the Show When File Is Opened check box.

6. Click OK.

Your Design Note is now saved with the page, and if you checked the Show When File Is Opened check box, the note opens every time the page is opened with Dreamweaver MX 2004. If you leave that option unchecked, you can always see a Design Note by selecting File, Design Notes, and if a Design Note is attached to the file, it appears. You can also see design notes by expanding the Site panel, which has a column indicating whether a given file has a note attached to it.

You can also use the All Info tab within the Design Notes dialog box to add name and value pairs to the notes. So, if you want to show that the author of the document is Harry, you can do so by adding the name of author and the value of Harry. Here's how:

1. With your page saved, select File, Design Notes.

2. When the Design Notes dialog box appears, fill in any basic information in the Basic tab; then click the All Info tab.

3. Click the plus (+) symbol (see Figure 6.12). Your cursor moves to the Name text box. Enter in a name that defines what you're trying to express—for example, **author**, **company**, or **project**.

Figure 6.12
Using the All Info feature with Design Notes enables you to quickly and easily provide helpful information regarding a page or object.

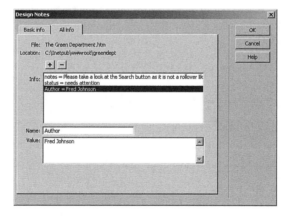

4. Move to the Value text box and type in the value, which would in this example be an author, a company, or a project name or description.

5. Click OK to save the Design Note.

You can edit your Design Note at any time by selecting File, Design Notes. When the Design Note appears, make modifications by using the Basic and All Info tabs. For example, if you want to remove a name-value pair entry, simply highlight it in the All Info tab and click the minus symbol.

PRE-DESIGN PAGE SETUP

Before you begin with the layout and content of your page, it's a good idea to set up the foundation of your page, including elements such as the page title, font preferences, and backgrounds.

ADDING THE PAGE TITLE

Titling your page is essential for numerous reasons. The page title is displayed in the browser window's title bar and is used to

- Denote bookmarks when a visitor bookmarks that page.
- Provide a marker for a browser's history feature.
- Promote better accessibility by assisting site visitors with orientation—your page title helps visitors know where on the Web they are, and specifically, where on your site they might be.
- Label the page, should it be printed out.

The title is ASCII text that resides in the title container in the head section of a Web page and can contain letters, numbers, and character entities as well as spaces.

NOTE

> Although you can use character entities (such as   and so on) in the title, you *cannot* use any HTML or XHTML itself. So, if you want to add quotation marks or a copyright symbol to your title, you can do so by using an entity. However, you can't use any formatting, such as bold or italic.

Whenever you create a new Web page in Macromedia Dreamweaver, it will have the default title Untitled Document.

To set your title, follow these steps:

1. In the Document window, highlight the default Untitled Document text located in the Title: field.
2. Type in the new title.
3. Click OK. Your title will be updated.

What happens when you don't add a title to your page? Find out in "Trouble with No Title Information" in the "Troubleshooting" section, later this chapter.

ESTABLISHING DEFAULT PAGE PROPERTIES

Dreamweaver enables you to easily customize each page's default properties. Through the Page Properties dialog box, you can establish elements such as text properties, link colors, page encoding, and much more.

SELECTING A BACKGROUND COLOR

Selecting the right background is important to the design process. You want to select a color that contrasts with the text (foreground) color so that reading is easier. If you decide to use a background image, use one that promotes readability, unless you are going for a completely visual effect. Selecting a background that is too distracting can cause eye strain, especially if the site has a lot of text to read.

New documents are set to white by default. You can see this by opening the Page Properties window. Right below the Background Image textbox you can see the Background option.

If you know the hexadecimal color value for the background of your page, type it into the Background text box and click Apply. To set a color value for your background with the color chip, follow these steps:

1. Open the Page Properties dialog box by choosing Modify, Page Properties from the Menu bar.

2. In the Page Properties dialog box, choose Appearance from the Category panel.

3. Click the Background color chip to open a color palette from which to choose your color (see Figure 6.13).

Figure 6.13
Type the color value in directly or select a color from the drop-down menu.

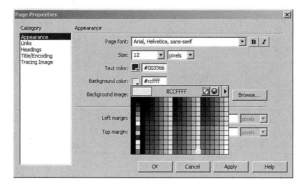

4. Move your pointer over the colors until you find one you like for your page. You'll see the hexadecimal value of the color appear in the top bar of the palette.

5. Click the desired color. The palette loads the hexadecimal value into the Background color text box, and the color chip is updated to reflect your color.

6. Click Apply in the Page Properties window to see the background color in action.

SETTING BACKGROUND IMAGES

Using a background image can enhance the page both aesthetically and functionally, such as when using a background with a colored section for navigation.

Image Formats for Page Backgrounds

Background images can be any type of image that browsers can display.

Generally, the image format you choose should be the one that compresses your image the most with the least loss of visual quality (for graphics with large areas of solid color, the GIF format, and for more complex images and photographs, the JPEG format).

You can use a PNG graphic in the background. However, a lot of browsers simply do not support PNG or poorly support PNG graphics. This makes the format a generally bad choice unless you know without a doubt that your audience is using browsers that have correct PNG support for your needs.

You can also use GIF animations as background graphics, but use background animations with extreme care and in special cases in which the visual or motion design of the page is more important than its readability.

All background graphics tile by default (see Figure 6.14). This means that your background graphic, no matter how large or small in dimension, will repeat horizontally and vertically across the page. So, when you create it, consider how it will look when placed end-on-end in two dimensions.

Figure 6.14
The Background image is automatically tiled behind all other content on the Web page.

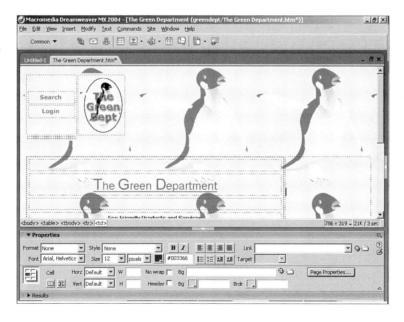

After you have created or chosen the background graphic you'd like to use, place it in your images folder. To add the background to your page by using the Page Properties dialog box, follow these steps:

1. In the Page Properties dialog box, click Choose (Mac) or Browse (Windows). This will open a browsing window.

2. Locate the file you just saved to your images directory and select it.

3. Click Apply to apply your background image to the current page.

CAUTION

> If the image file you selected is not within the current Web site's local root folder, you will be prompted by Macromedia Dreamweaver as to whether you want to move a copy of the image file into the Web site. This is usually a good idea because it avoids the risk of losing the image when you upload the site.

If the image dictated in the URL does not exist, no image is displayed—not even a broken image icon—and the background color is used instead.

WORKING WITH PAGE MARGINS

Page margins are considered to be between the edge of the viewable area of the browser window and the HTML content within it. Using Dreamweaver, you can control the top, bottom, and both side margins.

Macromedia Dreamweaver allows you to control the margins for a page using the Page Properties window. To do so:

1. Open the Page Properties window and choose the Appearance category.

2. Type the margin number (in pixels) you'd like to use for each of the margins for the page (see Figure 6.15).

3. Click OK and continue working.

Figure 6.15
Use the Page Properties dialog box to set margins.

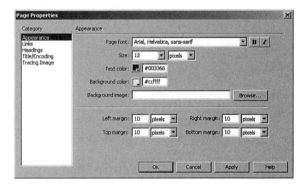

CHANGING THE DEFAULT TEXT COLOR

Text color is traditionally black for any text running longer than a few sentences. Black text on a white background provides the highest contrast possible and, arguably, is the easiest to read on screen and paper alike.

Of course, to create compelling designs, you might want to use other colors from your palette for the general text color. But remember that the higher the contrast, the better readability will result. What's more, many people are color blind and cannot see certain colors or combinations of colors. Your knowledge of audience and the intent of the site will help dictate your color choices.

To change the text color with the Page Properties window, follow these steps:

1. Click the Text color chip to bring up the color palette.

2. Find the color you'd like and click on it. The hex code for the color is entered into the Text color textbox, and the chip changes color from default black to the text color of your choice.

3. Click Apply to apply your text color changes to the document.

MANAGING LINK COLORS

By the Page Properties dialog box, you can also set colors for four different link states:

- **Link**—This is the color of the link in its normal state and is expressed with the attribute name `link`.

- **Visited link**—When a link had been visited by a site visitor, setting the `vlink` attribute changes that link color to denote that the link has already been followed.

- **Rollover link**—When a hover style is selected, the link changes to this color by default.

- **Active link**—This is the link color that displays as the visitor clicks on the link. Its attribute name is `alink`.

When a new document is opened in Macromedia Dreamweaver, no default link colors are set. If left unset, the browser sets the link colors to its own defaults or to user specifications. Generally, the browser's default link colors are blue for unvisited links, red for active links, and purple for visited links.

 Some concern exists over the coloring of links outside of the familiar browser defaults. Find out how this affects you in "Coloring Links" in the "Troubleshooting" section later this chapter.

As with other page properties, link colors can easily be set in the Page Properties window. To do so, follow these steps:

1. Open the Page Properties window and choose the Links category. Click the color chip next to Links, and select your link color. If you already know your color, simply type the hex value into the Links color text box (see Figure 6.16).

2. Move to the Visited Links option and either use the color chip or enter the known hex color into the text box.

3. Continue on to the Rollover Links option, making your changes by following the same steps as with other link options.

4. Finally, select a default color for the Active links option.

6

Figure 6.16
Select a color for the hypertext links on the page.

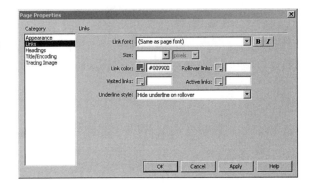

5. After you have all the link colors added, click Apply to apply them to your page, or click OK to continue working.

TIP

> Hypertext links need to stand apart from other text on the screen so that users can recognize them. To that end, the colors you choose should contrast sharply with the text color. Generally, it is best to select a more vibrant color for unvisited than for visited links.

MANAGING PAGES WITH TEMPLATES

Web sites tend to reuse many of the same elements and layout from page to page. This provides a consistent look and feel across the entire site. It also speeds up development time when you can reuse your images and code. You can, of course, cut and paste your images and layout elements from page to page. This approach, however, is not without its own problems. For example, changing the layout on one page means that you have to make the same changes by hand on all your pages, which can be tedious and prone to mistakes.

Dreamweaver's solution to this error-prone process of reusing page layouts is templates. Dreamweaver *templates* are special documents you can build that contain the layout for your site's pages. The template contains the structure and elements used for page layout, along with regions you designate as editable that will be used later for adding content.

When you use a template to create a page , it remains attached to that template even after the unique content of the page is added (unless you detach it yourself). This lets you make changes to the template document and have those changes applied to all pages that are attached to it, a very powerful ability that saves you time and helps prevent errors.

There are essentially two ways to create templates in Dreamweaver. You can create a template document from scratch or use an existing document as a template.

NOTE

> No matter which method you use to create a template—making it from scratch or saving an existing document as a template—Dreamweaver places the template in a folder named `Templates` in your site's root folder. If this folder does not exist, it is automatically created when you save your first template.

STARTING A NEW TEMPLATE

There are two ways to create a new template document in Dreamweaver. The first and most obvious method is to use the File menu, like so:

1. Select File, New.

2. In the New Document dialog box, select Template Page under the General tab.

3. Select the type of template page to create from the Template Page list. Unless you're using a server-side technology such as ASP or ColdFusion, select HTML Template.

The second way to create new templates is in the Assets panel. This is convenient because the Assets panel is also the place where you keep track of and use your templates. To use the Assets panel, do the following:

1. Select Window, Assets to open the Assets panel.

2. Select the Templates category (see Figure 6.17).

Figure 6.17
The Templates category of the Assets panel is the place to create and use templates for your site.

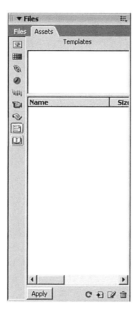

6

3. Click the New Template button at the bottom of the Assets panel, or select New Template from the context menu. An untitled template document is added to the list.

4. Enter a name for the template.

5. Click Edit to open the document.

SAVING A DOCUMENT AS A TEMPLATE

You can also choose to save an existing document as a template by following these steps:

1. Open the document in the Document window.

2. Select File, Save As Template.

3. In the Save As Template dialog box, enter a name for the template.

NOTE

If you add a template region to a document that is not already a template (using the Insert, Template Objects command, for example), Dreamweaver automatically converts the document into a template. Unless you disable it, a warning dialog box pops up informing you of this when you add a template region.

Either method you use to create templates places them in the Templates folder in the site's root folder.

CREATING EDITABLE REGIONS

After you have created a template and designed your layout, you need to indicate which sections can be edited in documents that use the template. When you choose which parts of the document are editable, the rest of the document is locked from accidental changes. All templates need to have at least one editable region to be useful. If you try to save a template with no editable region, Dreamweaver will give you a warning message.

An editable region must contain an entire block in your document. If you are using a table for layout, you can make the entire table editable or just an individual cell. You can make multiple cells of the table part of the same editable region if you don't make the entire table editable.

To create an editable region on a template, do the following:

1. Select the region you want to make editable.

2. Select Insert, Template Objects, Editable Region. You can also (Ctrl-click) [right-click] and select Templates, New Editable Region from the context menu or select the Editable Region button on the Templates category of the Insert bar.

3. In the New Editable Region dialog box, enter a unique descriptive name for the region (see Figure 6.18). You can use spaces, but not any characters that are used to define HTML or JavaScript elements such as question marks, quotation marks, curly brackets, or angle brackets.

Figure 6.18
A descriptive name for your editable region helps you easily identify the purpose for the section.

4. Click OK to finish adding the region. The editable region is displayed in the designer as a box with a tab showing the region's name (see Figure 6.19).

Figure 6.19
Editable regions are shown in the template as a box with a tab indicating the region's name.

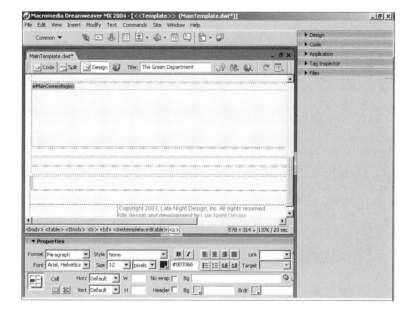

TIP

> You might decide later that a region you previously marked as editable should be locked. You can remove editable regions by selecting the region you want to detach and selecting Modify, Templates, Remove Template Markup.

CREATING OPTIONAL REGIONS

Dreamweaver allows you to mark regions as optional. Optional regions can be used to specify content that may or may not be shown in the final document. Thus, if certain pages need to show repetitive content—such as a disclaimer or copyright notice—and others don't, you can turn the optional regions on and off as each page requires. In Design view, the tab of the optional region is preceded by the word *if*. Based on the condition set in the template, a template user can define whether the region is viewable in pages she creates.

Here's how to insert an optional region:

1. Select the element or section you want to make optional.

2. Select Insert, Template Objects, Optional Region from the menu. You can also select Templates, New Optional Region from the context menu or click the Optional Region button on the Templates category of the Insert bar.

3. Specify the options for the region in the Optional Region dialog box. These options are described in the next section.

4. Click OK to create the optional region.

SETTING OPTIONAL REGION OPTIONS

Optional region options are set in the New Optional Region dialog box (see Figure 6.20). This dialog box is used to set template parameters and define the conditional statements that determine whether the optional region should be shown.

Figure 6.20
The New Optional Region dialog box is used to specify parameters and conditional statements used to control an optional region's display.

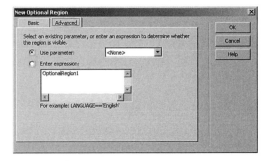

On the Basic tab of the New Optional Region dialog box, you can define a new template parameter for the region. Template parameter values can be set for each page that uses the template and are used to determine whether the region is displayed. If you have multiple optional regions, simply use the same parameter name for each one. To define a template parameter, do this:

1. Open the New Optional Region dialog box for an optional region.

2. In the Basics tab, enter the name of the parameter.

3. Make sure Show By Default is checked if you want pages created with this template to have this parameter set to TRUE by default. Uncheck it if you want the region to be hidden by default.

4. Click OK.

You can also choose existing template parameters from a pop-up menu by clicking the Advanced tab and selecting the parameter you want to use. Note that only existing parameters are displayed in this menu.

EDITABLE OPTIONAL REGIONS

Editable optional regions can be added as well. To add an editable optional region, follow these steps:

1. Position the pointer where you want the region positioned in the document. A selection can't be changed into an editable optional region, so do not select any elements or text.

2. Select Insert, Template Objects, Editable Optional Region, or click the Editable Optional Region button on the Templates category of the Insert bar.

3. Specify the options for the region in the Optional Region dialog box as described previously.

4. Click OK to create the editable optional region. It is shown in the editor with tabs for both the editable and optional content.

CREATING REPEATING REGIONS

Templates can also contain regions that repeat. Repeating regions are used to allow the template's user to expand sections of the document in a controlled manner. For example, a template might have a table to which the template author can add new rows. Making a row of the table repeatable enables the table to expand without requiring that you give up control of the layout.

REPEATING TABLES

A repeating table can be used to provide a structured way to expand a document. The table row can contain one or more editable cells that the template user can fill with content.

To insert a repeating table to a document, do the following:

1. Put the insertion point in the document where you want the table.

2. Select Insert, Template Objects, Repeating Table from the menu. The Insert Repeating Table dialog box appears (see Figure 6.21).

Figure 6.21
You can also click the Repeating Table button on the Templates category of the Insert bar to open the Insert Repeating Table dialog box.

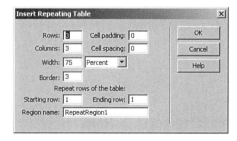

3. Enter the values for the table in the dialog box. Rows, Columns, Cell Padding, Cell Spacing, Width, and Border are standard table attributes that you can set accordingly. The following parameters are unique to repeating tables:

- **Starting Row**—Specifies the first row to use in the repeating region. By default this is row 1, but it can be changed if the first row contains information, such as column headings, that shouldn't be repeated.
- **Ending Row**—Specifies the ending row of the table to use as the repeating region. This can be the same as the starting row for simple tables, or it can be one or more rows later to repeat more complex table layouts.
- **Region Name**—Lets you specify a unique name for the region.

4. Click OK to insert the table.

REPEATING REGIONS

A more freeform repeating option is the repeating region. Repeating regions typically contain tables, but they can also contain other elements and attributes.

Repeating regions are not editable by themselves, but they can contain one or more editable regions inside themselves to allow the region to be customized. To create a repeatable region, do the following:

1. Either select the existing content you want to make into a repeating region or place the insertion point where you want it to go.
2. Select Insert, Template Objects, Repeating Region from the document menu, or (Control-click) [right-click] the document and select Templates, New Repeating Region from the context menu. The New Repeating Region dialog box appears (see Figure 6.22).

Figure 6.22
The New Repeating Region dialog box is used to give a unique name to a repeating section of a template. You can also open the dialog box by clicking the Repeating Region button on the Templates category of the Insert bar.

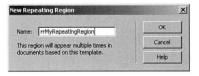

3. Enter a unique name for the region in the New Repeating Region dialog box.
4. Click OK.
5. Insert one or more editable regions in the repeating region to enable the template user to customize it.

MAKING ATTRIBUTES EDITABLE

To allow the template user to set certain attributes of an element, but not control anything else about it, you need to make certain attributes editable. For instance, you might want to allow a different iconic image in the heading of the page and allow the template user to specify a new value for the src attribute. You could make only this attribute editable while leaving other attributes locked, such as the height and width.

To create an editable attribute for an element, follow these steps:

1. Select the element in the Document window.

2. Select Modify, Templates, Make Attribute Editable from the main menu. The Editable Tag Attributes dialog box appears (see Figure 6.23).

Figure 6.23
Templates can have elements that are locked but contain editable attributes.

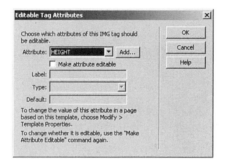

3. Select the attribute you want to make editable from the list. Only attributes that are currently defined for the element are shown—if the one you want isn't shown, click Add and enter the attribute name.

4. Check the Make Attribute Editable box.

5. Enter a descriptive label for the attribute in the Label field. This is necessary to make it easier to identify what the attribute is for when a template-based page is created.

6. Select the type of attribute. This tells Dreamweaver what type of data the attribute contains and how to prompt the template user for a value. Select one of the following:

   - **Text**—Specifies a text element. For example, use this for alignment attributes so the user can enter left, center, or right.

   - **URL**—Specifies a link or an image source attribute. Using this type enables Dreamweaver to automatically keep track of and update the link path.

   - **Color**—Specifies a color value. A color picker is used to prompt the template user to enter a color.

   - **True/False**—Specifies a Boolean value. Use this to set attributes that have only true or false values.

   - **Number**—Specifies a numeric value. For example, this could be used to specify an image height and width.

6

7. Enter a default value for the attribute. This should be a value consistent with the type you chose.

8. If you want to make other attributes of the element editable, you can repeat steps 3–7 without leaving the dialog box.

9. Click OK to apply the changes.

USING TEMPLATES

After your template layout is defined, you're ready to use it to create your site. You can use a template in one of two ways:

- Create a new document from a template.
- Apply template changes to an existing document.

CREATING A NEW PAGE FROM A TEMPLATE

The most common way to use a template is to create a new document in a site. A new document is created just like any other, but the document's content contains the template code along with any regions that are editable. If an editable region had text or other content in it in the template, that content is also included in the document.

To create a new page from the template, do one of the following:

- Select File, New from the document menu, and click the Templates tab in the dialog box. Select the site and a template (see Figure 6.24).
- Select a template from the Templates category of the Assets panel. (Control-click) [Right-click] the selected template to bring up the context menu. Select the New from Template option.

Figure 6.24
The New from Template dialog box lets you browse your sites for templates. It shows a thumbnail preview of the template to make finding the one you are looking for easier.

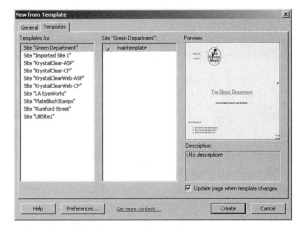

Controlling highlighting for templates is something you might want to do. See "Highlighting Template Code" in the "Troubleshooting" section at the end of this chapter.

Making Changes to the Page

After you have a document created with the template, editing it is a lot like editing any other document. The only difference is that you can modify only the content of the editable portions of the page.

To change content in an editable region, simply click the region and enter the new content. You can use any of the Dreamweaver editing features in this content region.

Repeatable regions have additional options. On the right side of the Region tab, you have the option to add, remove, or select a new repeating section.

Applying a Template to an Existing Page

Although creating new pages that automatically use a template layout is what templates are primarily about, it is also nice to be able to take an existing document and apply a template layout to it. Dreamweaver enables you to do this, and it does so by attempting to match the page content with the regions of the template.

Pages originally created with a previous version of the template are likely to have some regions that match the new template. Dreamweaver matches these regions automatically.

If you apply the template to a document that doesn't have matching editable regions, Dreamweaver allows you to select a template region to apply mismatched content to or to delete content that doesn't match. To apply a template to an existing document, do this:

1. Open the document to which you want to apply the template by using the Files panel or by selecting File, Open from the Document menu.
2. Select Modify, Templates, Apply Template to Page from the Document menu. You can also select a template in the Templates category of the Assets panel and click Apply, or you can drag a template from the Assets panel to the document.
3. If there is content that can't be matched to a template region, the Inconsistent Region Names dialog box is displayed (see Figure 6.25).
4. Select an editable region from the list. Then, using the Move Content to New Region drop-down menu, select a template region into which Dreamweaver should move the content.
5. Repeat step 4 for other editable regions of the document.
6. Click OK.

 Detaching a template is possible, too. See "Detaching a Template" in the "Troubleshooting" section at the end of this chapter.

6

Figure 6.25
When you apply a template to an existing page, the Inconsistent Region Names dialog box lets you choose which region of the template to use for existing content.

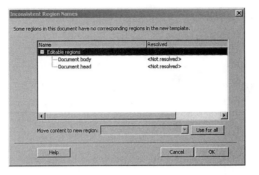

EDITING A TEMPLATE

Editing a template is similar to editing any other document. Double-click the template in the Assets panel to open it in the editor, or select it in the list and click the Edit button.

After you've made changes to a template, you need to apply the changes to any document that uses the template. If you specified the option to automatically update a page, the Update Template Files dialog box appears when you save the template and gives you the option of updating or not updating pages in your site. If you don't have a page marked to automatically update, apply the template to it by using the Apply button in the Assets panel. Any editable regions that can't be matched to regions in the new template cause the Inconsistent Region Names dialog box to be displayed.

You can use the Update Pages dialog box to quickly apply a template to all pages that use it in your site. To use this dialog box, do the following:

1. Select Modify, Templates, Update Pages. The Update Pages dialog box appears (see Figure 6.26).

Figure 6.26
The Update Pages dialog box enables you to quickly apply a template to any template pages on your site.

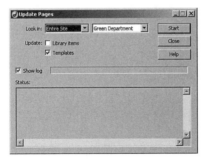

2. Select one of the following options:

- **Entire Site**—Select this option in the Look In list to update an entire site; then select the site in the drop-down list.

- **Files That Use**—Select this option in the Look In list to update only those pages that use a particular template file, then select the appropriate template from the drop-down list.

3. Leave the Show Log check box checked to see the changes that are made to your pages.

4. Click Start to update the pages.

The log window shows the pages that were updated. If any errors occurred in the update, they are shown in the log's status window as well.

TROUBLESHOOTING

REFRESHING FILES

How can I make sure my site files are always up to date?

To ensure that all files are automatically refreshed, be certain to select the auto refresh feature. This is a helpful feature because it updates new files as you add them to the site.

TROUBLES WITH NO TITLE INFORMATION

I'm not really sure what the title of my page should be. Is it really necessary?

If you leave title information out of your page, the title publishes to Dreamweaver's default `Untitled Document`. This gives your page visitors absolutely no help when trying to orient themselves to the page, figure out its purpose, and bookmark the page for further reference. Plus, the `title` element is required in HTML 4.0 and 4.01, and also in XHTML 1.0 and 1.1. Using a clear title is an important part of setting Page properties, so be careful not to overlook it!

COLORING LINKS

Are there any hard and fast rules for what color links should be? I'd like to make them match my site, but someone said that they have to be a certain color.

Many usability pundits—including Jakob Nielssen—have expressed that colored links other than browser defaults cause usability problems with navigation. Although this might be true for people very new to using the Web (and nowadays, newcomers see so many different link colors, the point is almost moot), it's highly unlikely that any experienced user will fail to recognize a link. Unless you are expressly asked by a client or superior to follow defaults, you should feel free to color links as you see fit.

HIGHLIGHTING TEMPLATE CODE

I want to see my editable regions. How can I ensure that I do?

Template editable regions are shown in your document as a colored border with a tab in the upper-left corner with the region name. For repeating regions, controls are also shown that enable you to add and remove repeating sections. These tabs are shown only while in the Designer—they don't appear on the live version of the page. You can control whether this highlighting is seen by selecting or deselecting View, Visual Aids, Invisible Elements.

CHAPTER **7**

WORKING EFFICIENTLY IN DREAMWEAVER

In this chapter

Keeping Track of Site Components   136

Working with the Assets Panel   137

Creating a Favorites List and Favorites Folder   137

Asset Types   139

Adding an Asset to a Web Page   141

Maintaining the Assets Panel   141

Creating Library Items   143

Using Library Items   146

Checking Your Page Code   150

Testing Your Site Online   156

Peer to Peer: Standards and Search   158

KEEPING TRACK OF SITE COMPONENTS

Designing and developing a working, growing Web site often means keeping track of an ever-increasing assortment of HTML pages, images, links, color schemes, templates, Flash, and multimedia. As your site grows, it's harder and harder to keep everything in one place. Even if you organize your site well with folders for images, multimedia, and style sheets, you'll soon find the need to add a separate folder for navigational images or perhaps another for movies or articles relating to a particular section of your site. Navigating to these separate folders time after time during the development process can become tedious and fraught with opportunities for mistakes.

Links and color schemes present different challenges, of course. These items aren't stored in files, so you can't just navigate the folders of your site to find the link you used on one page or that very color of blue you used on another. If the same color scheme isn't used from page to page, site consistency is lost. Templates can solve the color consistency issue to some extent, as can Cascading Style Sheets (CSS), but they certainly don't completely solve the problem.

Enter Dreamweaver's Assets panel (see Figure 7.1). Dreamweaver stores every major element of a site in a cache. The Assets panel is a complement to the Files panel, and indeed, they're both docked in the same Files panel group. The Files panel lists the tangible files for the site. The Assets panel lists the intangibles— the colors, URLs, templates, images, and multimedia used on the site's pages.

Figure 7.1
The Assets panel breaks the site cache into nine categories, each of which can be viewed as a site-wide list or a user-generated favorites list of oft-used assets.

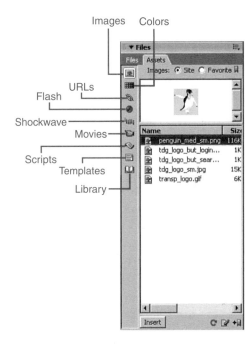

7

WORKING WITH THE ASSETS PANEL

The Assets panel doesn't recognize every asset type, but it does recognize many of the most common ones. The left side of the Assets panel has a column of buttons that let you choose the category of assets to display—Images, Colors, URLs, Flash, Shockwave, Movies, Scripts, Templates, and Library. The right side of the panel lists the assets within the selected category. A preview version of a selected asset is displayed above the list.

Unfortunately, Dreamweaver doesn't track assets such as audio files, Adobe Acrobat PDFs, or Java applets. Also, don't be misled by the generic Movies category because it doesn't list unsupported media formats such as Windows Media or RealVideo.

NOTE

You can expand the preview area by dragging the splitter bar between the preview and list areas.

CREATING A FAVORITES LIST AND FAVORITES FOLDER

The Assets panel has two different views. The Site list provides a complete list of all the assets in every folder and page of the site. The Favorites list displays only the assets you choose to put there (see Figure 7.2). If you create a well-planned Favorites list for your site, you'll have all the colors, URLs, and other elements within easy reach while still having convenient access to the less-used assets from the Site list. To change between the two views, click the Site or Favorites radio button at the top of the panel.

Figure 7.2
The Favorites list contains only assets you select, creating a specialized list for your most frequently used assets.

7

ADDING AN ASSET TO THE FAVORITES LIST

To add an asset to the Favorites list, follow these steps:

1. Select an item in the Site list.

2. Click the Add to Favorites button on the bottom right of the panel, or (Command-click) [right-click] and select Add to Favorites from the context menu.

You can also add images and media files to the Favorites list directly from the Site panel. Select an appropriate file and select Add to Favorites from the context menu. The exact name of this menu option changes depending on the type of asset—in the case of an image, the option is labeled Add to Image Favorites.

Assets added to the Favorites list remain on the list unless you manually remove them. Even if you refresh or re-create the site cache to update the Assets panel, the Favorites list remains the same. To remove an asset from this list, select it and then click the Remove from Favorites button.

NOTE

> Removing an asset from the Favorites list doesn't delete the asset from the site. It's still accessible from the Site list.

Have you ever designed a site and lost track of exactly which site belongs to which obscure URL or which shade of blue you're using for a particular item? This can happen even when using the Assets panel because URLs are often not descriptive even in a list, and all the hex values and slight color variations begin to blur in your mind. Find out how to avoid losing track of your site's stuff in the "Nicknaming Assets" topic of the "Troubleshooting" section, found at the end of this chapter.

CREATING A NEW FAVORITES FOLDER

Even when you're using the Favorites list, it's easy to become overwhelmed with assets, particularly on a large site. An advantage the Favorites list has over the Site list is that it enables you to organize assets into groups called Favorites folders.

Favorites folders can be useful for organizing and quickly locating images you want to use together on your pages. For example, on a cooking site, you might have movies with demonstrations of cooking techniques, gadgets, and recipes. By grouping these into Favorites folders, you'll know exactly where to look to find the movie you seek. For organizational overkill, you can even nest Favorites folders.

To create a Favorites folder, do the following:

1. Switch to the Favorites view of the Assets panel.

2. Click the New Favorites Folder at the bottom of the Assets panel.

3. Type in a name for the folder.

4. Drag assets from the Favorites list into the new folder.

Of course, this feature is purely for convenience. The actual location of the files within your local site remains the same.

ASSET TYPES

Along with their general usage as assets, each type of asset also has some specific purpose or limitations.

IMAGES

The Images category lists any image files that you've placed within your local site, even if you've not yet used them on a page. Dreamweaver recognizes GIFs, JPEGs, and PNG formats.

 Forget to give sliced-image portions a unique name? You can use the Assets panel to solve the problem. Please see "Sliced Images and the Assets Panel" in the "Troubleshooting" section at the end of this chapter.

COLORS

The Colors category lists any colors that have been used for text, backgrounds, or links on any page within the site. Dreamweaver does not include colors from images or media files.

You can add a new color to the Favorites list directly in the Assets panel by doing the following:

1. In the Favorites view, select the Colors category.
2. Click the New Color button.
3. Use the color picker to choose a new color.

URLs

A URL asset is a reference to an external URL to which a page in your site has a link. When the Assets list is created, every page in the site is scanned for HTTP, FTP, Gopher, HTTPS, JavaScript, email (`mailto`), and local file (`file://`).

As with colors, you can create new URLs directly in the Favorites list. Follow these steps:

1. In the Favorites list, select the URLs category.
2. Click the New URL button. (This is the same button used to add new colors; it's just renamed within the context of the category.)
3. Enter a URL and a nickname in the Add URL dialog box (see Figure 7.3).

7

Figure 7.3
Enter a URL and nick-
name for the new
asset. The nickname
can be used as the
source text for the link
when inserted into a
document.

4. Click OK.

If a URL has a nickname, the name is used as the source text if the asset is inserted into a
document, unless a selection of the link source has already been made.

FLASH

If your site contains Macromedia Flash (SWF) files, they'll be listed in the Flash category.
This list also includes Flash buttons or text objects that you create in Dreamweaver. The
Assets panel lets you preview your Flash content. When one of these assets is selected, a
small Play button appears in the upper-right corner of the preview area. Most likely, you'll
need to resize the Assets panel to view the Flash movie. Another way to preview the movie
is to double-click the file in the Assets list.

> **NOTE**
>
> The Assets panel doesn't list Flash source (FLA) files.

SHOCKWAVE

This category shows any movies in Macromedia Shockwave format. As with Flash movies,
Shockwave files can be previewed in the preview area or the standalone QuickTime player.

MOVIES

If your site has any movies in the MPEG or QuickTime format, they'll be displayed in the
Movies category. As with Flash and Shockwave movies, you can preview them in the Assets
panel or the standalone QuickTime player.

SCRIPTS

JavaScript and VBScript files are listed in the Scripts category. The list contains only scripts
in files with JS or VBS extensions—scripts contained in your HTML files aren't listed. The
text of the script file is displayed in the preview pane when you select the asset.

7

Inserting a script asset into a document creates a `<script src="file://...>` tag, with the `src` attribute containing a link to the script file.

TEMPLATES

This category lists Dreamweaver template (DWT) files. A *template* is a document you can use to provide a standardized layout for your pages. Templates are among the few assets you can create from the Site list.

LIBRARY

Library assets are elements you want to use in multiple pages. They are easily updated on all pages containing them when you edit the library item.

ADDING AN ASSET TO A WEB PAGE

Of course, the real power of the Assets panel is in its capability to streamline your development time. You can insert most types of assets directly into a document by dragging them to the Design view of the Document window or by using the Insert button at the bottom of the panel. On the Colors and Templates categories, the Insert button changes to the Apply button.

The asset is added to the page at the insertion point. In the case of colors, text typed after the insertion point appears in the selected color. If you've inserted a URL asset, the destination path of the URL appears as the source for the link; the source text can, of course, be modified.

For assets such as URLs and colors, you can also apply them to selected text in Design view. To do this, follow these steps:

1. Select the text to which the color or link should be applied.
2. Select the asset from the Assets panel.
3. Click Apply, or select Apply from the context menu.

To apply scripts to the head of the page, select View, Head Content; then drag the script from the Assets panel into the Head Content area of the Document window.

MAINTAINING THE ASSETS PANEL

The Assets panel requires regular maintenance to retain its value. As the site evolves, so do the assets, but the Assets panel lacks the capability to automatically keep up with its listings. Assets themselves might need to be updated. And, finally, sites might need to share assets already listed on another site.

7

REFRESHING AND REBUILDING THE SITE ASSETS LIST

The first time you open the Assets panel for a site, it scans for assets to build a site assets list. After the initial list is created, however, assets are not added to the list unless you refresh the Site list. To do this, follow these steps:

1. Make sure the site list is showing by clicking the Site button at the top of the Assets panel.

2. Click the Refresh Site List button at the bottom of the panel. You can also (Command-click) [right-click] the Assets panel and select Refresh Site List from the context menu.

Refreshing the site list updates the Assets panel with any assets that have been added or deleted within Dreamweaver. If you've made changes to the site outside Dreamweaver, however, these assets are not updated even when you use the Refresh Site List feature. Instead, the list must be re-created. To do this, hold down the Ctrl key when clicking the Refresh Site List button or select Recreate Site List from the context menu.

NOTE

> Proper updating within Dreamweaver suggests that, ideally, you will perform all maintenance on your site within the Dreamweaver application.

EDITING ASSETS IN OTHER PROGRAMS

To edit an asset, either double-click it in the Assets panel or select it and click the Edit button. Some assets, such as images, must be edited by an external application. The application to use is determined by the settings in the Dreamweaver Preferences tool. If you want to use a different application than the default, select Edit, Preferences and select the File Types/Editors category. Then, add the application you want to use to edit that file type.

Assets that don't reside in physical files but are, instead, scanned from your documents— such as URLs and colors—can be edited only in the Favorites list.

HTML-based assets, templates, and library items are edited in Dreamweaver. Double-clicking assets of this type opens a new Document window containing the asset.

USING THE ASSETS PANEL BETWEEN SITES

Assets are often useful on multiple sites. For an asset to be available to a site, the asset must first be copied to the Favorites list of the new site. To do so, follow these steps:

1. Select the asset or Favorites folder from the Assets panel.

2. (Command-click) [Right-click] and select Copy to Site from the context menu.

3. Select a site from the list of defined sites.

The assets are copied to the other site into folders corresponding to those on the source site.

CREATING LIBRARY ITEMS

As any experienced Web designer knows, site development often consists of placing the same elements on multiple pages to create a cohesive whole. Assets and templates help in these situations—as do snippets if you're code-inclined—but they aren't always the right tools for the job. Assets are very specific and apply to only one type of element or file. Templates are used to create entire pages. But what about reusing specific portions of a page?

Library items complete the triumvirate of design tools for accessing reusable elements. Despite being one of the Assets panel categories, Library items are used to re-create elements (or a group of elements) defined by the designer.

These can include anything from portions of text to an entire table structure. Library items can be used to add a copyright notice to the bottom of each page; this notice can then be updated each year by changing only the Library item instead of every page on the site. Library items can also be used to create a sidebar table structure that can then be inserted as needed on pages throughout the site.

When you create your first Library item, Dreamweaver generates a Library folder in your local site. This folder contains all the Library items for the site, each of which is identifiable to a Windows user by its .lbi extension.

Although you can edit library files directly in this folder, the best place to work with Library items is in the Library category of the Assets panel (see Figure 7.4). In this panel, you can create and edit Library items, insert them into pages, and even copy them to another site's library.

Figure 7.4
The Library category of the Assets panel displays a preview of the Library item and tools to create and edit items.

LIBRARY ITEMS AND SERVER-SIDE INCLUDES

If Dreamweaver Library items sound a lot like Server-Side Includes (SSIs), you're right—they essentially work the same way.

SSIs are small files that the server inserts when it delivers a page to a requesting browser. These small files contain the same information that a Dreamweaver Library item can—although SSIs are more flexible in that they allow you to include *any* portion of a document, including `head` elements (which Library items do not allow).

Any document that will receive the SSI must contain the `include` statement. This statement will look something like this (servers vary, as do the syntax for SSIs):

```
<!--#include virtual="/includes/footer.ssi" -->
```

Dreamweaver does allow you to create SSIs via the specific application you might be using: PHP, ASP, and so forth. To use SSIs, you need to check with your server administrator to ascertain proper syntax and usage.

NOTE

A comprehensive Webmonkey article on extending Dreamweaver also contains good information on using SSIs, including converting Library items to SSIs, `http://hotwired.lycos.com/webmonkey/99/11/index2a.html`.

LIBRARY ITEMS VERSUS DREAMWEAVER TEMPLATES

The biggest advantage Library items have is how easy they are to edit. Just as with templates, when the Library item is edited, every instance of the item on your site's pages is updated automatically. Also just like templates, Library items are coded into the document with comment tags. These tags surround the code for the Library item and contain a link back to the library source code.

The comment text for a Library item is distinguishable from that of template comments. The comments will appear as

```
<!--#BeginLibraryItem "/Library/Sidebar.lbi"-->
```

and

```
<!--#EndLibraryItem -->
```

The path included in the `#BeginLibraryItem` comment will reflect the name of the Library item.

Library items can comprise any element or combination of elements on a page, with the exception of `head` content (such as `script`, `style`, and `meta` tags).

To create a Library item, do the following:

1. Select the elements you want to create as a Library item. In my sample site, I've selected the Login/Search header table.

2. Drag the selection to the Library category of the Assets panel. Alternatively, click the New Library Item button at the bottom of the panel, or select Modify, Library, Add Object to Library from the menu (see Figure 7.5).

Figure 7.5
The New Library Item button can be used to create a Library item. You can also insert a Library item, refresh the site list, edit a Library item, or delete one by using the Assets panel Library options.

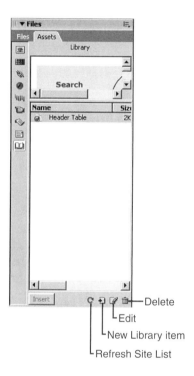

Delete
Edit
New Library item
Refresh Site List

3. Enter the Library item's name. The more descriptive, the better because this becomes the filename for the Library item.

When you create the Library item, the original selection becomes the first instance of your new object, linked to the new item you created from it. The Property inspector changes context to provide tools for editing the Library item, detaching the selected instance of the item from its source, or re-creating the item from the selected instance (see Figure 7.6).

7

Figure 7.6
The Library Item Property inspector enables you to modify the Library item and the selected instance of it on the page.

USING LIBRARY ITEMS

When you create your first Library item, you can immediately see how it appears in Design view when inserted into a page because the selected elements become a library instance (see Figure 7.7).

Figure 7.7
When you insert a Library item, the markup for the elements is inserted, surrounded by comment tags. The item appears highlighted in Design view to distinguish it from regular, editable content.

Inserted Library Item

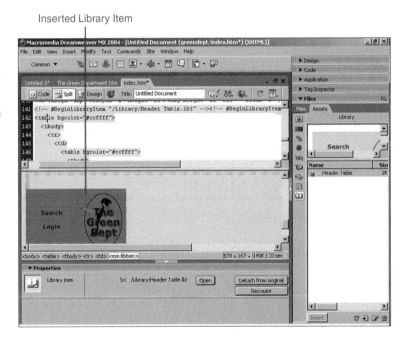

To insert the Library item elsewhere in the site, follow these steps:

1. Position the insertion point in the Document window where you want the Library item to be placed.
2. Open the Library category of the Assets panel.
3. Select the Library item you want to insert.
4. Click the Insert button at the bottom of the Assets panel, or drag the Library item to the Document window.

You can insert the Library item content and immediately detach it from the library by pressing the Ctrl key as you drag or click the Insert button. If you do this, the content will be copied into the document at the insertion point, but the inserted content assumes the same status as any other element on the page and must be manually changed in Design or Code view.

The status of the Library item itself remains unchanged. You can still insert the Library item elsewhere in the site, either retaining its attachment to the item or detaching it, as necessary.

EDITING LIBRARY ITEMS

As mentioned earlier, the advantage of the library is that modifications made to an item are updated site-wide.

Here's how to edit a Library item:

1. Select the item.
2. Click the Edit button in the Assets panel. You can also open the Library item for editing from the Property inspector when an instance of the item is selected in the Document window.
3. Edit the syntax and content as you require.

When you edit a Library item, the content of the item appears in a new document window. After making your changes, save the document. An alert box prompts you to update any pages containing the Library item (see Figure 7.8).

Figure 7.8
When you save changes to a Library item, you're prompted to update all instances of the item throughout the site.

If you don't update pages at this point, you can use Modify, Library, Update Current Page or Update Pages later. If you choose to update, the Update Pages dialog box appears and lists the number of updates made (see Figure 7.9). You can also use this opportunity to update the remainder of the site's library and template instances.

7

Figure 7.9
The Update Pages dialog box is used to update both Library items and templates used in the site.

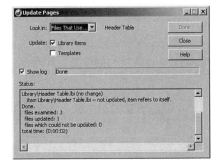

CAUTION

When editing Library items, you can't use Cascading Style Sheets (CSS) because they insert code into the `head` section of the page. Library items can insert a consecutive block of code only into the *body* of the document.

NOTE

Although you can't include style rules in a Library item, you can include class attributes. When the Library item is inserted, it assumes the styles set for that class in the attached internal or external style sheet, thus assuming the appearance of the rest of the site.

If the Library item is updated, all markup between the comment tags is modified to reflect the changes. In templates, certain regions can be locked so you don't inadvertently modify pieces of the template.

Library items, however, have no such constraints. Changing the content of the inserted Library item doesn't break the link to the library. However, if you manually modify the content of the Library item within the document—adding content to a table inserted using a Library item, for example—those changes will be lost when and if the Library item is updated. If you don't want your changes to be overridden, you need to detach the inserted Library item from the source.

DETACHING FROM THE ORIGINAL

To detach an instance of a Library item from the library and thereby prevent it from being edited and updated when the Library item itself is modified, you need to break the link between the document and the item.

To detach a Library item from the original, do the following:

1. Select the instance you want to detach in the Document window. The Property inspector modifies to manage your item.

2. Click Detach from Original (see Figure 7.10). The highlighting around the item disappears, signifying that the content is now simply a part of the document.

3. Save any changes.

7

Figure 7.10 shows the Detach button in the Property inspector.

Figure 7.10
Detaching a Library item from the original merges the content and code from that item with the document at hand.

DELETING LIBRARY ITEMS

To delete a Library item, follow these steps:

1. Make sure the Assets panel is open and the Library is selected. Then, select the item to be deleted.

2. Click the Delete button at the bottom of the Assets panel.

The item is deleted from the Assets panel, but any instances of it remain in their respective documents.

CAUTION

The delete process is irreversible. After a Library item is deleted, it is removed from the hard drive.

Did you accidentally delete a Library item? See "Re-creating Library Items" in the "Troubleshooting" section of this chapter.

BEHAVIORS IN THE LIBRARYS

When you create a Library item out of content containing Dreamweaver behaviors, the elements and event handlers are copied, but the associated JavaScript is not. Remember: The Library item can't update head content.

Fortunately, though, when you insert the Library item into a document, Dreamweaver is smart enough to know to add the appropriate JavaScript functions. If those functions are already in the head, Dreamweaver knows not to duplicate it.

You can't use the Open option in the Property inspector to edit behaviors. This option only opens the Library item itself, which won't contain the necessary JavaScript and access to the Behaviors panel.

Editing behaviors in a Library item, therefore, requires a workaround. Follow these steps:

1. Open a document that contains an instance of the Library item.

2. Select the Library item in the document.

3. Click Detach from Original in the Property inspector to make the item editable.

7

4. Use the Behaviors panel to change events and actions as necessary.

5. In the Library category of the Assets panel, delete the original Library item by clicking Delete at the bottom of the Assets panel.

6. In the Document window, select all the elements contained in the Library item.

7. In the Assets panel, click the New Library button, giving the Library item the same name as the original.

CAUTION

> Be sure to note the exact name of the original Library item before you delete it. If you give the new Library item a different name, the links to all other instances of the Library item will be broken.

After the Library item has been re-created in this manner, you need to update the site to bring all the other instances of the Library item up to date. To do this, select Modify, Library, Update Pages from the menu.

TIP

> Library items can be copied to another site in the same manner as any other asset on the Assets panel. Select the Library item, (Command-click) [right-click], and select Copy to Site from the context menu. A pop-out menu lists all the defined sites to which you can copy the Library item. If this is the first Library item being added to the other site, Dreamweaver creates a Library folder in the local site.

CHECKING YOUR PAGE CODE

Some developers view Web design as a race to get a site from the drawing board through the development process to the finish line—the live server. In actuality, there are many steps between developing the site's pages and putting out the virtual "Open" sign. The difference between a mediocre site and a great site is often the attention paid to these interim details.

By the time you've designed a table layout, added navigation, inserted images and text, and linked everything to the Web at large, you might be rather sick of looking at your site. It's worth resigning yourself, however, to a last look or two to ensure that everything's in place.

CLEANING UP YOUR HTML

As you well know, even the best Web developers sometimes have errors in their markup. Dreamweaver writes fairly tight markup, but when creating complex pages, it can sometimes leave behind extraneous or redundant nested tags. One method of fixing these mistakes is using the Find and Replace commands in a well-planned pattern to hunt down common problems. Dreamweaver offers a better solution, however. The Clean Up HTML/XHTML command has the following options:

- **Empty Container Tags**—Removes tags that don't have content between the opening and end tags (for example, `<i></i>`).

- **Redundant Nested Tags**—Removes tags that are nested redundantly within the exact same tag (for example, `<b>Most chefs <b>use </b>three basic knives.</b>`).

- **Non-Dreamweaver HTML Comments**—Removes comments inserted by developers. This command does not remove comment tags inserted by Dreamweaver to mark templates or library items, (for example, `<!--insert image of wildlife here when graphics are complete-->`).

 Do you prefer comments to Design notes? See "HTML Comments and Design Notes" in the "Troubleshooting" section at the end of this chapter to determine which is best for you.

- **Dreamweaver Special Markup**—Removes comments inserted by Dreamweaver to identify templates and library items. For example, `<!--TemplateBeginRepeat name="..." -->` is markup inserted by Dreamweaver to define a repeatable region in a template.

- **Specific Tag(s)**—Allows you to specify a tag or tags to remove. Any content that appears within that tag is preserved. Multiple tags can be separated with commas in the tag field. So, if you type **b, i** into the tag field, all instances of the `<b>` and `<i>` tags will be removed from the document.

- **Combine Nested `<font>` Tags when Possible**—Combines multiple `<font>` tags if they surround the same block of text. For example, `<font color="FFFFFF"><font size="3">assisting wildlife</font></font>` would be combined into `<font color="FFFFFF" size="3">assisting wildlife</font>`.

> **NOTE**
>
> This command does not combine redundant attributes from `<font>` tags that control only a subset of the text block, so the `<font color="FFFFFF" size="3">The <font color="00FF00" size="3">Green</font> Department thrives on assisting wildlife</font>` would not be combined.

- **Show Log on Completion**—Displays a report showing how many changes were made.

To use the Clean Up HTML command, do the following:

1. Open the document you want to clean up.
2. Select Commands, Clean Up HTML. If you're developing in XHTML, the Commands menu automatically changes this option to Clean Up XHTML.
3. Select the options for Dreamweaver to find and repair (see Figure 7.11).
4. Click OK.

7

Figure 7.11
The Clean Up HTML/XHTML dialog box lists the many options of this command.

If you select the Show Log on Completion option, Dreamweaver displays a report listing how many items were fixed or removed after the command is executed (see Figure 7.12). If you ran the Clean Up XHTML command, this report also states the number of img tags that don't have alt text attributes.

TIP

If the Clean Up XHTML command reports missing alt tags, it's a simple matter to use the Find command to search for img tags to find those without alt attributes.

Figure 7.12
This alert box details the number of changes made to the document after the Clean Up XHTML command is executed.

ESTIMATING DOWNLOAD SPEED

Even with the advent of broadband, download speed is still an issue for many Web surfers. If anything, faster Internet access has made visitors even more impatient for sites to load. You can estimate the speed at which a page will download by looking at the Download indicator at the bottom of the Document window (see Figure 7.13).

The Download indicator settings are controlled by the Status Bar category of the Preferences dialog box (accessed by selecting Edit, Preferences, and then clicking the Status Bar category). As you work, set this option to match that of the expected average visitor of your site. When your page is complete, you should set this preference at various connection speeds to get an estimate of the download times on both extremely fast and very slow connections.

If the download time appears significant, use the Clean Up HTML/XHTML command to remove any extraneous tags and comments. Be sure you've optimized all your images to their fullest without sacrificing too much quality.

Figure 7.13
The Download indicator displays the file size of the page and all its components and approximates the download time at a preselected connection speed.

NOTE

Remember, the Download indicator provides only an approximation of download speed. Dreamweaver can't assess factors such as traffic and server speed.

SPELL CHECKING

There are very few truly great spellers on the planet, and even the best spellers make mistakes. Dreamweaver's spell-check feature helps both the best and the worst spellers hide their flaws from public view. To run the spell-checker, do the following:

1. Select Text, Check Spelling from the Document window menu.

2. The spell-checker stops at the first word in the document that isn't in its dictionary. The word is highlighted in the document and is also displayed in the Check Spelling dialog box (see Figure 7.14).

3. If you know the word is spelled correctly, click the Add to Personal button to add the word to your dictionary.

Work for a specific industry or profession that uses many words not in a standard dictionary? No problem! See "Adding Dictionary Terms" in the "Troubleshooting" section at the end of this chapter.

4. If the word is spelled correctly, but you don't want to add it to your personal dictionary—such as when you're using an intentional misspelling to make a point within the context of your site—click the Ignore button. To ignore all instances of this spelling, click the Ignore All button.

5. If the word is indeed misspelled, either manually type the correct spelling in the Change To field or select one of the words in the Suggestions list. Click Change to replace the misspelled word with the new spelling. Or, click Change All to replace all instances of the same misspelled word.

6. When the Spelling Check Completed alert appears, click OK to end the spell-check.

NOTE

As with all spell-checkers, Dreamweaver won't catch misuse of homonyms (by, bye) or commonly misused words (affect, effect) .

7

Figure 7.14
The spell-check highlights the misspelled word so you can see it in context. The dialog box makes suggestions as to the proper spelling or allows you to manually type the correct word.

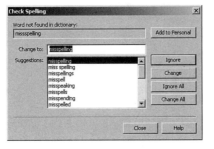

CHECKING FOR CROSS-BROWSER COMPATIBILITY

One of the biggest pitfalls Web developers become subject to is forgetting to check their sites for cross-browser compatibility. There's nothing worse than rolling out a great Web application and then having someone ask you why the pages don't load properly, the tables are out of alignment, or elements of the application don't function properly. By checking to be sure that your application works in both Internet Explorer and Netscape throughout the process, you'll save yourself the hassle of having to fix problems after the site is released to the public.

NOTE

> Checking for cross-browser compatibility means more than just opening the pages in IE and Netscape. If you really want to ensure that most visitors will be able to use your site, check the site in IE 4.0 and 6.0 (or later) and also check your site in Netscape Navigator 4.0 and 7.0 (or later). The combination of these four browsers will cover the vast majority of users out there.

To help you in creating pages that are cross-browser compatible, Dreamweaver has a couple of tools that make the process easier.

DYNAMIC CROSS-BROWSER COMPATIBILITY

During the page development process, you can check any page for browser errors by clicking the Dynamic Cross-Browser Compatibility button (see Figure 7.15) on the Document toolbar.

To check any page for errors, do the following:

1. Click the Cross-Browser Compatibility button on the Document toolbar.
2. From the dropdown menu, choose Check Browser Support. After the check is completed, Dreamweaver displays a tool tip with an error count (see Figure 7.16).

7

Figure 7.15
The Cross-Browser Compatibility button enables you to see any errors that your pages might encounter in specific browsers.

Dynamic Cross-Browser Compatibility Check Button

Figure 7.16
After the compatibility check is completed, a tool tip displays the error count.

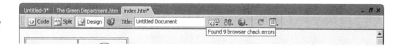

3. To view the code that is generating the error, click the Cross-Browser Compatibility button again and choose Next Error. Dreamweaver opens the Split view (see Figure 7.17) and highlights the first error. You can continue through the list by using the Next error menu option.

Figure 7.17
Using the Cross-Browser Compatibility tool, you can view the code that could potentially generate the error.

4. To see a complete list of the errors generated and the browsers that would potentially encounter the error, click Show All Errors from the menu.

CHECK TARGET BROWSERS

Another handy tool that helps you ensure your pages will function optimally in the various browsers is the Check Target Browser command. By choosing File, Check Page, Check Target Browser from the menu bar, you can run a report that displays each of the browser errors that the page would generate (see Figure 7.18).

TIP

You can edit the browsers that are included in the target browser check by clicking the Target Browser Check menu dropdown in the Results panel. From the menu, choose Settings and select the minimum browser levels you want included in the report.

7

Figure 7.18
The Target Browser Check displays each error that might be encountered and the browser that would cause the error.

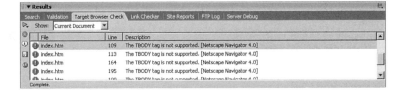

A FINAL MANUAL REVIEW

The Dreamweaver tools mentioned previously in this chapter all help you prepare your site for its final journey to the remote server. Nothing, however, beats a good eye. After you've cleaned up your HTML, spell-checked the site, and ensured that everything is optimized, it's worth taking one last look at each and every page of the site. Be especially on the alert for

- Table layouts that have gone awry as you inserted images and text
- Missing page titles, descriptions, and keywords
- Commonly misused words that wouldn't be picked up by the spell-checker
- Images that don't suit the final content
- Placeholder images that weren't replaced with final graphics
- Cross-browser compatibility and design integrity

TESTING YOUR SITE ONLINE

After the site has been transferred to the remote server, the testing process starts all over again. Although you've checked the site for approximate download speeds, accessibility, cross-browser compatibility, and code validation with Dreamweaver's tools, nothing can replace real-life experience.

TESTING DOWNLOAD SPEED

As mentioned earlier, the download speed provided by Dreamweaver in the status bar is only an approximation based purely on the size of the document and its components and the speed of the user's connection. After the site is on the server, you can test the accuracy of Dreamweaver's prediction. If you're using a broadband connection, it's very important to visit the site through a standard modem, especially if your intended audience will include a significant number of dial-up users.

Note, however, that even if you're testing the site at various speeds, the true test comes when the site is live. If you're lucky enough to have a high volume of visitors, you might be unfortunate enough to have slow-downs in access speed as the server struggles to keep up.

FIXING PROBLEMS

Putting the site onto the remote server also enables you to check for real-life cross-browser compatibility. Again, Dreamweaver can alert you if your code is not compatible with certain browsers or platforms, but even valid code can appear very different on various configurations. Even if you don't have the necessary platforms and browsers to personally test your pages, having the site on the remote server enables you to get the opinion of others with different configurations.

Taking a fresh look at the site can also draw your attention to other minor problems, such as typos or slow-loading images that you didn't catch in earlier testing.

EDITING ON THE SERVER

When you find mistakes, you can edit pages directly on the server. To do this, use the Connects to Remote Host button on the Site toolbar to connect to the server. If you're using the expanded Files panel, select a file from the Remote Site pane and open the file. If you're using the unexpanded Files panel, the view automatically changes to the Remote view upon connecting to the server. Select a file from this view, and open it. You can then edit the file as normal. When you save the file, it is automatically saved to both the remote server and the local folder, ensuring that your local folder remains an accurate replica of the live site.

TROUBLESHOOTING

NICKNAMING ASSETS

I'm getting so much stuff in my Assets panel that I can no longer remember what's what. Is there an easy way to keep things straight?

One of the more useful features of the Favorites list is the ability it gives you to nickname your assets. Instead of assets appearing in the list as "http://www.pendragn.com," you can nickname the asset as "Jenn's Site," which will hopefully jog your memory more easily.

To change an asset's nickname, be certain you're in the Favorites view, select the asset, and then select Edit Nickname from the context menu. You can also edit the Nickname by single-clicking the current nickname twice. After entering the nickname, press (Return) [Enter] or click elsewhere in the Assets panel. The actual filename, color, or URL will still appear in the Value column of the Favorites list, and the preview display will remain unchanged.

SLICED IMAGES AND THE ASSETS PANEL

How can I have more control over individual images I'm working with while constructing a table?

The display on the Assets panel is helpful when you're piecing a sliced image back into a table, particularly if you forgot to give each slice a unique name in your graphics application. Unlike selecting image files from the Insert Image dialog box or dragging from the Site panel at random, the Assets panel displays each image, so you can drag and drop the pieces into the table like a puzzle.

RE-CREATING LIBRARY ITEMS

I deleted a Library item and then realized I need it again. What can I do?

If you accidentally delete a Library item, your only recourse is to re-create it from one of its instances in a document. To do this, select an instance of the Library item and click the Recreate button in the Property inspector.

If there aren't any instances of the Library item in your site—which could occur if you made the original instance editable and either didn't create any other instances or made all of those editable, as well—you'll need to create a new Library item from scratch.

HTML COMMENTS AND DESIGN NOTES

Which is better, HTML comments or Design Notes?

Which do you prefer? Either HTML comments or Design Notes can provide useful information about a site and its various assets. Either way is a perfectly legitimate course. However, if you determine that you need to communicate information mostly with co-workers—*all* of whom are using Dreamweaver—then the Design Note method might be the better option because it reduces your overhead.

However, if you do use comments, you can use the Non-Dreamweaver HTML Comments command when cleaning up your HTML or XHTML. If you've used comments instead of Design Notes to communicate with other members of the development team or as reminders to yourself, this command removes all these comments. However, Design Notes are left intact. Comments might no longer be useful after the page is complete and might unnecessarily pad a page, thus increasing its download time. Design Notes do not affect a page's download time.

ADDING DICTIONARY TERMS

This spell-checker is driving me nuts! None of the words that come up as wrong are really misspelled. How can I get around this?

If you develop sites that are specific to a particular field, such as psychology or engineering, you can seed the dictionary by creating a document with a list of correctly spelled terms. Run the spell-checker and as it highlights each term, use the Add to Personal button to add them to the dictionary.

One very cool fact: The dictionary isn't site specific, so words you enter into the dictionary in one site are available in other sites.

PEER TO PEER: STANDARDS AND SEARCH

Sometimes, aspects of following best practices and standards can have unexpected but positive effects in other areas of the work.

A properly structured document complete with accessibility features, such as `alt` text and `noframes` content for framed pages, can enhance your search engine ranking. The reason is because a well-structured document contains a natural hierarchy of topical logic that you can tap into, placing keywords in helpful places.

Images should always contain `alt` text for accessibility reasons, but this can also be used to increase search engine rankings if you make judicious use of keywords in the text. Similarly, if headings using structured, hierarchical h1, h2,…tags contain keywords, this can increase the site's ranking with some engines. Other methods for increasing search engine rankings include ensuring that image maps have alternative text menus, putting essential text as close to the top of the page as possible by designing your table and frame layouts well, and putting `noframes` content on frameset pages.

Of course, nothing can beat a site where the content itself is well written, fits the description of the site, and makes good use of the site keywords in its text. Aside from increasing search engine rankings, good content increases word-of-mouth promotion by your site's visitors.

CHAPTER 8

WRITING AND EDITING HTML, XHTML, AND CSS

In this chapter

Browser Languages   162

HTML 4   164

XHTML   167

HTML and XHTML Syntax   169

CSS Styles: Background   171

CSS in Dreamweaver MX 2004   179

Peer to Peer: Macromedia and the Web Standards Project   188

Peer to Peer: CSS Resources   189

BROWSER LANGUAGES

You can certainly use Dreamweaver MX 2004 to create great-looking, functional Web sites without ever editing a single line of code. A big part of Dreamweaver's appeal is that you can lay out your work in an interactive, WYSIWYG fashion (What You See Is What You Get), and let Dreamweaver work behind the scenes to build the underlying *HyperText Markup Language* (*HTML*) that tells the browser how to draw the page.

When you get deeper into the program, however, you come to realize that certain operations are easier when you know a bit about HTML and its more recent successor, *Extensible HTML* (*XHTML*). For example, if you've already developed some facility with HTML, you may prefer to write or fine-tune parts of your Web pages directly in Dreamweaver's Code View. You may also have HTML code that you've already written and that you'd like to bring into Dreamweaver for editing and reuse. You may want to understand some of the differences between "bad" HTML and "good" (*well-formed*) HTML so that your pages work more predictably. Or you may just want to bring your Web code up to a more structured standard (XHTML) for better future upgradability and compatibility. In all these situations, and more besides, some familiarity with HTML and XHTML will stand you in good stead, even if you never become fluent, per se, in these languages.

Beyond HTML, and its evolutionary offspring XHTML, modern browsers (version 4 and higher) speak yet another language: *CSS*, short for *Cascading Style Sheets*. CSS started life as a way to bring some typographical flexibility to the admittedly boring HTML world. With CSS, you can specify fonts, point sizes, text colors, borders, backgrounds, indents, wrapping behaviors, and so on. Even better, you can create style definitions—combinations of attributes that you'd like to reuse without redefining each time.

Another very important aspect of CSS is its capability to create *layers*, regions on a Web page with precise dimensions and location. Layers (also called *CSS layers*) are actually nothing more than <div> tags with CSS positioning attributes, and that precise positioning feature is one of the key advantages that layers have over HTML tables. Layers give the Web designer a great option for page design when HTML tables just don't cut the mustard— even the enhanced table-mode layouts that programs such as Dreamweaver make so convenient.

CSS layers do have their problems. If you want maximum backward compatibility, HTML tables are still the way to go. Also, not every designer likes working with CSS layers, for they can be complex and a bit idiosyncratic in terms of how they behave in different browsers. However, Macromedia is so taken with them that the company has laced Dreamweaver MX 2004 with new CSS-related page layout features, not least of which is the opportunity to choose from a variety of attractive predefined CSS page designs. Dreamweaver MX 2004 also makes it easier than ever to apply and edit CSS styles, even if creating those styles still involves a certain amount of tedium. In addition, this latest Dreamweaver displays CSS layers and layouts with greater accuracy than prior versions did.

Clearly, Dreamweaver MX 2004 reflects a strong commitment on Macromedia's part to giving CSS styles and layers a higher profile, and the new user interface tools go a long way toward minimizing the headaches of using CSS.

MACROMEDIA AND MARKUP

Macromedia Dreamweaver was one of the first Web design tools to ensure that users can customize the way the program manages markup. The term *Roundtrip HTML* emerged to describe the ability to move HTML documents between editors, within Dreamweaver, and within Dreamweaver views with limited or no changes being made to your markup.

However, sometimes "improving" HTML is even more important than maintaining its original structure and format. Dreamweaver has some built-in facilities for correcting HTML so that it more closely follows W3C-recommended markup approaches. Doing so creates consistency between documents, saving time and frustration when trying to find errors within a document. What's more, when multiple people are working on a site, adhering to standard practices creates a much more efficient work environment. Documents become more interoperable, reducing testing time and increasing portability. Documents conforming to W3C recommendations pay attention to the needs of the disabled, ensuring that the information within them can be easily accessed and clearly understood. Formal markup also provides a means by which documents can be prepared to display in a variety of languages using different character sets.

As the world moves from Web to wireless and alternative means of accessing Web-based data, clean markup becomes an imperative. Markup adhering to current recommendations and approaches can easily be interpreted by a much wider range of user agents beyond the browser—making your information very widely accessible.

ORIGIN OF THE SPECIES: SGML, HTML, XML, AND XHTML

To understand HTML, step back to its parent markup language, the Standard Generalized Markup Language (SGML). SGML has been around for years and became a standard for document markup specialists in government, medicine, law, and finance. SGML is a *metalanguage*, that is, a collection of language rules that authors use to create their own document languages.

HTML is one of those resulting languages. From SGML, HTML took its structure, syntax, and basic rules. However, HTML—even in its current seemingly complex state—is much less complex and detailed than SGML. Especially in its early life, HTML was very simple. It existed to allow for some very basic markup of pages for the Web: paragraphs, line breaks, and headers. Remember, the Web was first a text-only environment. HTML was not developed with detailed presentation concerns in mind; rather, its goal was the simple structuring of data.

8

Enter the visual browser, which changed the Web environment from one constructed of text documents to one promising growing opportunities for visual design. HTML—and Web browsers themselves—were stretched out of proportion to accommodate the rapid-fire pace of the Web's visual and interactive growth. Designers were naturally more concerned with creating designs that were visually rich and aesthetically pleasing.

Trying to manipulate HTML to get it to do what you want is pretty frustrating. There are no consistent methods for creating layout. You have little control over whitespace—relying on workarounds such as single-pixel spacer GIFs—and there's essentially no stable way to manage type within HTML itself. HTML illustrates that the Web was never intended to be a visual environment. But it became one, and how to manage that reality has been a challenge ever since.

Another child of SGML is XML, the Extensible Markup Language. XML is also a meta-language and exists as a means of creating other languages. Although SGML is complex and detailed, XML is a streamlined meta-language suitable for creating Web markup languages that are customizable and flexible for the needs of specific applications. Examples of XML markup applications include Scalable Vector Graphics (SVG), Synchronized Multimedia Integration Language (SMIL), and Wireless Markup Language (WML).

People working on the evolution of markup languages via the W3C began to look at HTML and the problems it was facing because of this stretching and manipulating to accommodate design. HTML had become in many ways a linguistic mess. So, work was done to take the best of HTML and apply the strength and logic of XML. From this work came a new, refined markup language, the Extensible Hypertext Markup Language (XHTML).

XHTML is the reformulation of HTML as an XML application. The rules and methodologies of XML are applied to HTML, bringing syntactical strength back into HTML, which lost that strength during its rapid evolution from text document markup language to the de facto language of visual design. XHTML brings markup a lot closer to the interoperable, accessible, international, and growth-oriented goals mentioned at the beginning of this chapter.

HTML 4

To balance shifting trends in convention and approach the demand for better standardization across browsers, HTML 4 emerged with some potent rules. These rules, in their strictest incarnation, don't always work in cross-browser/cross-platform design, and they often are not backward compatible. To address these issues, HTML 4 has built-in accommodations for them.

These accommodations are found in the document type definitions (DTDs) found within the HTML 4 specification. DTDs are essentially laundry lists of all the elements, attributes,

8

and syntax conformance rules needed for a document to conform to the real language in question. In formal markup, the DTDs are declared within the document, which you'll see later.

The following DTDs exist in HTML 4:

- **Strict HTML 4**—This is the purest of HTML 4 interpretations. Anything deprecated (made obsolete) in this version of the language is not used, ever. Most presentational elements and attributes are left out of the interpretation—you can't use a font tag, for example, when writing a document that conforms to a strict interpretation.

- **Transitional, or "loose" HTML 4**—By combining aspects of the prior version of HTML (HTML 3.2) with elements from the strict HTML 4 standard, a more realistic, usable version of the language emerges. This is where you will find the most backward compatibility for many public and contemporary Web site designs. In transitional HTML, you can use font tags, attributes for presentation, and tables for layout, and the concern with document structure is slightly less demanding than in strict interpretations. Most readers will likely use transitional HTML (or XHTML 1.0) to accommodate their goals.

- **Frameset HTML 4**—This includes all the information within the transitional version, combined with the newly adopted frame-based elements such as frame, frameset, noframes, and iframe. The frameset interpretation exists as an interpretation to confirm the standardization of frames within HTML and offer a regulated method of using them.

The standard expects that you will insert the appropriate document version and the document type definition identifying the specification to which the document conforms. So, if you're creating a strict HTML document, the shell of the document should appear with the document version, as shown in Listing 8.1.

LISTING 8.1 SAMPLE HTML STRICT DOCUMENT

```
<!DOCTYPE HTML PUBLIC "-//W3C//DTD HTML 4.0//EN"
"http://www.w3.org/TR/REC-html40/strict.dtd">
<html>
<head>
<title>Strict HTML Sample Shell</title>
</head>
<body>

</body>
</html>
```

Transitional documents appear with the document type and structure, as demonstrated in Listing 8.2.

LISTING 8.2   SAMPLE HTML TRANSITIONAL DOCUMENT

```
<!DOCTYPE HTML PUBLIC "-//W3C//DTD HTML 4.0 Transitional//EN"
"http://www.w3.org/TR/REC-html40/loose.dtd">
<html>
<head>
<title>Transitional HTML Sample Shell</title>
</head>
<body>

</body>
</html>
```

Finally, any page you build with frames in HTML 4 should be denoted as being within the frameset interpretation. Frameset documents contain the frameset version information, as follows:

```
<!DOCTYPE HTML PUBLIC "-//W3C//DTD HTML 4.0 Frameset//EN"
"http://www.w3.org/TR/REC-html40/frameset.dtd">
```

Along with these interpretations are three primary concepts HTML 4 encourages authors to adopt to ameliorate problems and concerns with the language's past (and often current) use:

- **Separate document structure from presentation and style**—Much of HTML 4 focuses on taking any element from prior language versions used for presentation or style of information and setting it aside. Instead, style sheets for presentation and design are typically recommended.

- **Think carefully about accessibility and internationalization**—Because HTML was originally built for all people to access documents, including those on a variety of platforms, using different languages, using different user agents, and with a special concern for people having physical impairments, the standard asks that we keep these issues in mind when authoring code. A good example of this is adding `alt` attribute descriptions to `img` tags, which helps visually impaired users to better understand Web documents.

- **Make documents load more quickly via careful table design**—HTML 4 has several element additions that help tables render incrementally. In fact, HTML 4 highly encourages developers to move away from using tables for an underlying grid system, implementing the use of style sheet positioning in its place.

XHTML builds heavily on these foundations. Whether you choose to employ XHTML or HTML, you should use recommended markup rather than arbitrary markup. This is especially important when you move from HTML into the realm of XML and beyond, because without the foundational concepts and techniques, you run the risk of making mistakes such as introducing proprietary or even nonexistent markup into a document. If that happens, and you try to share that document with another colleague, company, or application, significant problems can ensue.

XHTML

As you delve more deeply into XHTML, you can begin to see how it uses aspects of both familiar HTML concepts and strict ideas influenced by XML. In XHTML, document conformance and DTDs are essentials. This is true, too, of HTML 4.

8

DOCUMENT CONFORMANCE AND DOCUMENT TYPE DEFINITIONS

For a document to conform to XHTML 1.0, it must adhere to the following:

- The document must validate against one of the three DTDs: strict, transitional, or frameset.
- The root element of an XHTML 1.0 document must be `<html>`.
- The root element must designate an XHTML namespace, using the `xmlns` attribute.
- A `DOCTYPE` (document type) definition must appear in the document prior to the root element.

In XHTML 1.0, as with HTML 4.0, there are only three preset DTDs. How you write your XHTML documents—and how they're validated by various tools—relies on the DTD you choose.

In XML, and for future versions of XHTML, DTDs can be customized. This adds a great deal of power to your toolkit because you can define the rules and the actual tags a document must use to conform to that common language. So, if a company makes a special product, it can create its own vocabulary to manage that product. Or entire industries, such as medical or financial, can share DTDs specific to their unique needs.

The three DTDs currently available for your use in XHTML 1.0 are

- Strict
- Transitional
- Frameset

These DTDs are the same as those in HTML 4.01. The actual vocabularies are somewhat different, however, reflecting the rigor and syntactical shifts that have occurred in XHTML.

XHTML 1.0 that follows the strict document type definition is the most rigorous—and the purest—of XHTML syntax. Transitional XHTML 1.0 is the more forgiving vocabulary within the standard. You must still follow syntax rules and the rules for well-formed documents, but you have leeway with certain elements, attributes, and code approaches; for example, you can use deprecated tags, such as `font` or `center`. Finally, the Frameset DTD denotes a document as a frameset. Any frameset you create in XHTML 1.0 must be declared as such; otherwise, it will not validate.

To convert an HTML document to XHTML in Dreamweaver MX 2004, select File, Convert, XHTML. (Incidentally, you must repeat this step for each file in a frameset.) To create a new document that uses XHTML, choose File, New, and select the Make Document XHTML Compliant check box.

WELL-FORMEDNESS AND SYNTACTICAL RULES IN XHTML 1.0

Any document you write must follow the correct order of elements and the correct method of writing those elements. As you probably realize, browsers forgive. So, if I were to write the following in HTML:

```
<b><i>Welcome to my Web site!</b></i>
```

A browser is likely to display my text as both bold and italic. However, look at the markup. It opens with the opening bold tag and then the italics tag. But instead of nesting the tags properly, the bold tag is closed first. This is improper nesting, and as a result, the code is considered poorly formed. To be well-formed, the code must be properly ordered:

```
<b><i>Welcome to my Web site!</i></b>
```

This is a well-formed bit of markup. "Well-formedness" (English majors, pardon the awkward construction!) is a critical concept in XHTML 1.0.

Some other issues related to markup in XHTML 1.0 include

- **All elements and attribute names must appear in lowercase**—HTML is not case sensitive. But in XHTML, every element and attribute name *must* be in lowercase: `<p align="right">`. Attribute values (such as `"right"` in this case, but also in case-sensitive filenames in URLs) can be in mixed case.

- **All attribute values must be quoted**—In HTML, you can get away without quoting values, as in:

  ```
  <img src="my.gif" height=55 width=65 alt="picture of me">
  ```

  Some attributes are quoted, some aren't. But when writing XHTML, you *must quote all attribute values*:

  ```
  <img src="my.gif" height="55" width="65" alt="picture of me">
  ```

- **All non-empty elements require end tags, and empty elements must be properly terminated**—A non-empty element is an element that might contain content or other elements. A paragraph is non-empty because within the tags exists text, images, or other media. In HTML, you could open a paragraph but not close it. In XHTML 1.0, you must close any non-empty element. Use this:

  ```
  <p>This text is content within my non-empty paragraph element.</p>
  ```

  not this:

  ```
  <p>This text is content within my non-empty paragraph element.
  ```

Empty elements, such as breaks, horizontal rules, and images, do not contain content. In XML, and thus in XHTML, a termination is required in the form of a slash after the element name, so `<br>` becomes `<br/>`. Because some browser bugs cause pages to render improperly, in XHTML 1.0 you must add a space before the final slash to ensure the page is readable:

```
<br />.
```

Remember that image element just a few paragraphs ago? Even with all the attributes quoted, it's not proper XHTML 1.0. Because it's an empty element, it must be terminated accordingly:

```
<img src="my.gif" height="55" width="65" alt="picture of me" />
```

HTML AND XHTML SYNTAX

Many Dreamweaver MX 2004 users might not have a clear understanding of the building blocks of HTML and XHTML: elements, attributes, and values. The following sections help clarify those building blocks.

ELEMENTS

All standard element identifiers are contained within angle brackets, as follows:

```
<link>
```

Note that there are no spaces between the symbols and the tag and no spaces between the letters that denote the tag.

Elements that appear in the body of a document are defined by the concepts of *block* or *inline*.

BLOCK

Block-level elements are structural. They can contain other block-level elements (as in a division containing paragraphs) and inline elements. Usually, block-level elements are rendered by browsers as beginning on a new line.

INLINE

Inline elements, also referred to as *text-level* elements, contain content. They can also contain other inline elements, but they should not contain block-level elements. Inline elements typically work within the content of a document without causing any line breaks.

In transitional HTML and XHTML, inline elements can appear alone. However, in strict HTML and XHTML, all inline elements must be contained within a reasonable block-level element. So, say you are using the `img` element and you do not place it within a division, paragraph, or other block-level element. In a transitional document, you have no problems with validation, but in a strict document, you get an error.

8

ATTRIBUTES

Many elements can act perfectly fine alone, but some tags must have *attributes* to function properly. An attribute consists of two properties: name and value.

Many attributes in HTML have historically had to do with modifying the way something on a page looks. (In the strict DTDs of HTML 4 and XHTML, any attribute that defines a style is not allowed; instead, you must use style sheets. However, you can use these attributes and their companion values in transitional HTML 4.01 and XHTML 1.0.) Other attributes are fundamental to the proper interpretation of an element and have nothing to do with presentation at all. Examples would be `src`, `alt`, and `href`.

Attribute names can be whole words, partial words, abbreviations, or even acronyms. Some whole word attributes include `align`, `color`, `link`, and `face`. Partial word examples include `src` for "source" and `vlink` for "visited link."

Attributes follow the tag and are separated by at least one space:

```
<body bgcolor...
```

These are then set by the attribute value before the tag is closed.

A tag can have more than one attribute, and some tags take on many attributes at the same time. In this case, the syntax follows the same concept: first the tag, then a space, then an attribute. The attribute receives a value, and then a space is again introduced *before* the next attribute:

```
<body bgcolor="#ffffff" text="#000000">
```

and so forth, until all the attributes and their values are included.

VALUES

Values, like attributes, can be made up of a whole word. All values are preceded by an = symbol (the equal sign), and the value is within quotation marks.

If you're using the `div`, or division, element and want to align all the information in that division in a transitional HTML or XHTML document, you can select from several values that modify the `align` attribute. Such values include `left`, `right`, `center`, and `justify`. A resulting statement would be

```
<div align="right">
</div>
```

Some attribute values are numeric, referring to pixels, percentages, browser-defined sizes, or hexadecimal numbers to define color. A pixel value example is well described by the `width` attribute:

```
<table width="768">
```

Using a percentage value in the same instance looks like this:

```
<table width="100%">
```

Browser-defined sizes are those sizes that the browser selects. In other words, you can't predetermine the exact size, such as with pixels, but you can approximate the size. The best example of this is with the deprecated font tag attribute size. The size attribute can opt to take a value ranging from 1 to 7, with 1 being the smallest and 7 the largest:

```
<font size="5">
```

Any text between this and the closing font tag takes on the browser's interpretation of a size 5.

An example of a numeric type of value is hexadecimal color codes:

```
<body bgcolor="#FFFFFF">
```

There are other kinds of values you should be aware of. One such value is a relative or absolute link to another document, meaning that a directory, series of directories, and specific filename can be included in certain attributes to fulfill a value:

```
<a href="http://www.molly.com/">Go to My Home Page</a>
```

This markup creates a link that, when activated, goes to Molly's home page. The a, or anchor element, creates a link; the attribute is href, or hypertext reference; and the value is the URL, http://www.molly.com/.

Similarly, I can point to a directory and an image:

```
<img src="images/molly.gif" />
```

In this case, the tag is img, or image (which, again, is an empty element and must be terminated in XHTML); the attribute is src ("source"); and the value is a combination of the path to the images directory and the specific file, molly.gif.

Another interesting example is alt. This appears in image or object tags and offers a description of the image or object for those who can't or don't want to see the image or object:

```
<img src="molly.gif" alt="picture of Molly" />
```

In this situation, the value assigned to the alt attribute is actually a series of words used to describe the picture. You can also see in this example how a tag can have multiple attributes with corresponding values.

CSS STYLES: BACKGROUND

In this section, we take a look at CSS's "reason for being," talk a bit about the versatility and structure of CSS markup, and explain some of the lingo you will need when working with CSS in Dreamweaver MX 2004. Afterwards, the final section in this chapter discusses the specifics of using CSS within Dreamweaver—specifics that have changed in some evolutionary and very useful ways since the previous version.

THE EVOLUTION OF STYLE

In the early days of HTML, tags were merely intended to provide structure for content, specifying that selected content should be contained in a table, for example. The actual display of this structure was left to the browser. Each browser had its own variations on the font size of a heading or whether it should appear in bold or italics.

When designers wanted to present their material in a visually appealing manner, new tags and attributes were developed and Web design became much more complex. The form and function of HTML pages became confusingly intertwined, and adherence to HTML standards went by the wayside.

Now the standards pendulum is swinging the other way, and the current movement in Web design is to separate document structure from presentation to achieve greater document formality. Web designers aren't about to give up their hard-won control over the visual presentation of their material, however, so leaving display totally up to the browser is unacceptable. Enter the Cascading Style Sheet (CSS).

DESIGNING BEYOND HTML

CSS meets the requirement of separating form and function while also expanding the design possibilities beyond HTML. Font control, color management, margin control, and page layout are only a few of the design elements that CSS improves.

Perhaps the greatest advantage of style sheets is their updatability. When presentation is intermingled with the content and structure of the page, each change to font color or size must be made individually. Using CSS, a change to the style sheet updates any and all iterations of that style. If you're using an external style sheet, changes can ripple through to every site page that's linked to that style sheet. In some cases, you can give a site an entirely new look without touching a single page of HTML.

CSS is one of the critical components of Dynamic HTML (DHTML), along with HTML and JavaScript. DHTML can make pages come alive with layers. It's also a means of providing interactivity for site visitors.

CSS VERSUS HTML STYLES

Dreamweaver has always offered both CSS and HTML Styles, but the MX 2004 version has deemphasized HTML Styles almost out of existence. Although they both control the style and appearance of a document, their functionality is quite different. You can apply CSS to a wide range of HTML tags, either by redefining the tag itself or by adding a class attribute. CSS can be defined within the HTML document or in an external file, which in turn can be linked to multiple HTML documents. You can also modify CSS by changing the CSS declaration itself, with those modifications automatically applied to each occurrence when rendered in the browser.

HTML Styles provide a way to describe presentational attributes from within HTML—not CSS—to stylize a page. These are much more limited. Rather than serving to separate structure from presentation, these styles let you more easily apply inline formatting. They can be applied only to paragraphs or blocks of selected text, so they can't be used to format the appearance of a table or layer. The styles are applied with font tags, which cannot be used in Strict HTML and XHTML.

HTML Styles are useful only if you're designing for really old browsers that most likely can't interpret CSS. Under more usual circumstances, however, CSS is far preferable as a means to apply style. Macromedia has even dropped the HTML Styles panel from Dreamweaver MX 2004, signifying that HTML styles are "out" and CSS styles are "in." Given that fact, in combination with the other limitations just mentioned, we won't go into HTML styles in more detail here.

CASCADING STYLE SHEETS

Although Cascading Style Sheets are far more powerful than HTML Styles and are the preferred method for applying styles to a site, no browser completely supports all of CSS, although the most recent versions of each major browser come close.

Unlike HTML Styles, CSS truly separates presentation from structure. Deprecated tags are avoided, making CSS the perfect choice to use with Strict DTDs. Styles can be applied to any tag or even to a specific class of that tag.

INSIDE CSS MARKUP

CSS properties can be applied to a wide range of elements. To use these properties, you first create a *rule* for the display of a particular tag. A rule is the fundamental unit of CSS, and is made up of the following components:

- **Selector**—The element to which you're applying the style. If you want to format the paragraph tag to display text in burgundy, for example, the selector is the <p> tag.
- **Declaration**—The properties and values that describe how to display the selector, including
  - **Property**—The property of the selector being modified, such as the color, size, font, margin, or position. For example, to display the burgundy paragraph text, you must modify the color property.
  - **Value**—The setting for the property. For burgundy paragraph text, for example, the value of the color property is #660033.

When you put these parts together, the result is a rule that looks like this:

```
p {color: #660033;}
```

Notice the declaration is enclosed in curly brackets. A rule can contain multiple declarations within the brackets, each separated with a semicolon, like this:

8

```
p {
color: #660033;
font-family: Trebuchet, san-serif;
font-size: 14pt;
text-align: center;
}
```

This results in centered, burgundy text in either the Trebuchet MS font or a similar sans-serif font in a 14-point size.

GROUPING

Declarations can also be used for multiple selectors at the same time, which is called *grouping*:

```
p, h1, h2 {color: #660033; font-family: Trebuchet MS;}
```

This rule defines a style for the paragraph, heading 1, and heading 2 tags.

NOTE

> The semicolon is important for separating declarations, but it's optional after the last declaration in a rule. If you forget to include a semicolon between declarations, the entire rule might be ignored by a browser. It's best to just get into the habit of always adding a semicolon to the end of declarations, including those at the end of a rule.

You can use grouping in style declarations, too, such as with font properties. A typical body style might look like this:

```
body {
font-family: Trebuchet MS, san-serif;
font-size: 13pt;
line-height: 14pt;
font-weight: bold;
font-style: normal;
}
```

Grouping the arguments can shorten the style to the following:

```
body {
font: bold normal 13pt/14pt Trebuchet, san-serif;
}
```

When grouping arguments, the order of the properties is very important. Although font-style is the last declaration in the expanded rule, it is the second value listed in the shorthand declaration. Also notice that no commas appear between the values, other than the one separating the font family values.

NOTE

> The ungrouped example also shows how an extensive style rule can be declared over multiple lines. The selector and opening curly bracket are placed on the first line, and each property/value group is displayed on another line, ending with the closing curly bracket on the last line.

NESTING STYLE

Let's say you want to define all paragraph text to be burgundy except when it's contained in a table—you want that text to be dark blue (#333366). The style sheet for these rules would appear like this:

```
p {color: #660033;}
td p {color: #333366;}
```

Unlike the structure of a rule being applied to multiple tags, the second rule in this style sheet doesn't separate the selectors with a comma. This lack of a comma is what tells the browser to render the style only when the tag is nested as such.

SELECTORS: HTML, CLASSES, AND IDs

Several types of selectors exist:

- **Element selectors**—Refer directly to an HTML element, such as p, h1, a, and so on.
- **Class selectors**—Class selectors can be considered "custom" selectors that you intend to use more than once within a document. They are defined with a name preceded by a period, such as .bodytext, followed by the style declaration. They are applied within the HTML document if you use the class attribute:

```
<p class="bodytext">This paragraph will take on the style you've defined
for the class selector "bodytext".</p>
```

- **ID selectors**—ID selectors begin with a hash mark (#) instead of a period. They are called on in the document with the id attribute. Unlike class selectors, a specific ID is used only once within a document.

Posting a recipe is an example of the use of class selectors. You might want the ingredients list to appear in a large font size in burgundy. The directions can appear in a smaller size in dark blue, and the nutritional information could appear in an even smaller size in black. You can declare each of these styles as a different class.

Class tags can be defined in two ways. If the style is to be applied only to paragraphs of a particular class, you can define the class within the paragraph selector. On the other hand, if you want the style to be available to a wide range of elements, such as to headings and list items as well as paragraphs, you can define the class as a selector itself. Thus, the style rules for the previous example could appear as follows:

```
.ingred {color: #660033; font-size: 13pt;}
p.direct {color: #333366; font-size: 11pt;}
p.nutri {color: #000000; font-size: 9pt;}
```

Notice in the example that the directions and nutrition information classes are defined as being a subset of the paragraph element, whereas the ingredients are defined as a standalone class. This is because ingredients can appear either in paragraph format or in lists. Defining the classes this way gives you the flexibility to apply the styles where they're best served.

In the HTML document, the classname appears wherever the style should apply:

```
<p class="direct">Directions</p>
```

To apply a class style to a selection instead of an entire paragraph, use the `<div>` and `<span>` tags with the class attribute. When giving recipe directions, the name of each ingredient can appear in the `.ingred` class style—yet another reason to define that class independently of a tag element. The directions would appear as such:

```
<p class="direct"> Heat oven to 300 degrees F. Place aluminum foil
on cookie sheet; generously brush with 1 tablespoon of the
<span class="ingred">oil</span>.
Arrange <span class="ingred">tomato halves</span>, cut sides up,
in single layer on foil; brush with 2 teaspoons of the oil. Sprinkle
with <span class="ingred">sugar</span>, <span class="ingred">salt</span>
and <span class="ingred">pepper</span>. </p>
```

Figure 8.1 shows how a recipe appears in the browser when this style sheet is used.

Figure 8.1
This recipe applies the three classes declared in the style sheet.

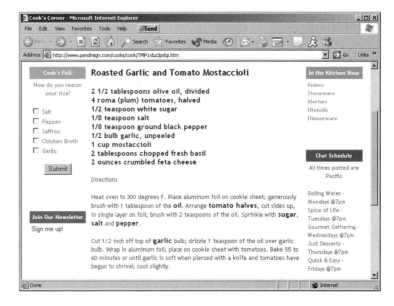

Link Classes

One of the most common uses of style is to format links to suit the design of a site. The a tag can be styled to remove the underlining on links. Links have four states—active, hover, link, and visited—and each of these states can be defined separately in a style sheet. The active state of the link is when it's clicked by a user. The hover state displays when the mouse is over the link, whereas the link state applies to links that have not been visited. The visited state is how links are displayed after they've been recently visited. You can customize these pseudo-classes in the Page Properties dialog box, now accessible via a button on the Property inspector.

STYLE INTEGRATION

HTML documents can use style sheets in three primary ways. The relating of a style sheet to a document is referred to as *integration*. The location of your style rules is just as important as the declarations within them.

EXTERNAL CSS   An external style sheet is also called a *linked* style sheet because it's a separate document that is linked to one or more HTML documents. This type of style sheet offers the greatest amount of flexibility because changes to the style sheet update the display of every page from which it's linked. You can create a new external style sheet from one of several Macromedia-supplied examples by choosing File, New, and selecting CSS Style Sheets in the Category column.

External style sheets simply contain the rules you define for your page or site, and they're saved with a .css extension. To apply the style sheet to an HTML document, you add a <link> tag to the head of the HTML document, such as

```
<link rel="stylesheet" href="cooksite.css" type="text/css">
```

This link must be added to the head of every HTML document that uses the style sheet. To modify the appearance of a site, simply edit the style sheet. Whenever a page is viewed in a browser, the current CSS rules are adopted.

NOTE

> Dreamweaver can display many styles in the Document window, whether they're applied internally or from an external style sheet. In fact, the latest version of Dreamweaver displays CSS styles with significantly greater accuracy than ever before. Some styles, however, can be displayed only in a browser. When testing your style sheets, use the Preview in Browser feature of Dreamweaver.

INTERNAL CSS   Internal style sheets, also known as *embedded* or *unlinked* style sheets, are used to control a single HTML document. The style rules are placed in the <head> of the document in a <style> tag pair, such as the following:

```
<head>
<title>Cook's Corner</title>
<style>
<!--
p {color: #660033;}
p.ingred {font: 12pt Trebuchet MS;}
-->
</style>
</head>
```

Notice the actual style rules are contained in a comment tag. This is to prevent them from being displayed as regular text in a browser that doesn't support the `<style>` element.

APPLYING STYLES IN A TAG   The third type of style, the inline style, is an attribute applied directly to a tag within the body of the HTML document, such as

```
<p style="color: #660033;">There are three new recipes.</p>
```

Inline styles can also be used in `<div>` and `<span>` tags to apply a style to a selection. This method gives you complete control over that particular instance of that specific element, but it doesn't apply the style anywhere else within either the document or the site. Thus, the inline style is most useful for exceptions to either the default display or an internal or external style sheet. It's far less easy to update inline styles, so they generally shouldn't be used as a matter of course.

UNDERSTANDING THE CASCADE ORDER

The three main types of style sheets aren't mutually exclusive. In fact, you can use various style sheets together to gain a great deal of control over the presentation of your site.

Using the cooking site as an example, the overall design of the site would use an external style sheet containing rules for sidebar text, body content, and other site-wide elements. The recipes appear on only one page, however, so the recipe styles can be embedded internally onto that page. If a particular recipe has special instructions you want to emphasize, you could apply an inline style to that selection of text.

The cascading nature of CSS means that we need a precedence convention when rules conflict. The closer a style declaration is to the content it's defining, the more precedence it has over that content. In other words, if an inline style contradicts an external style sheet, the inline style takes precedence because it's closest to the actual content.

Inheriting Properties

Certain HTML tags exist only within other tags. The `<body>` element contains all the page's content and its markup. The `<body>` tag is the parent, and all the tags within it are considered children of this element. For another example, table rows and cells appear only within `<table>` tags.

Children may inherit the style applied to their parent tag unless the child tag itself is defined. However, many style properties are not inherited; you'll see this effect in the new Relevant CSS tab of the revamped Tag Inspector, where non-inherited properties appear in a red strikethrough typeface.

Browsers are becoming better about their capability to keep the containment hierarchy intact when it comes to inheritance of style sheet rules. There are still inconsistencies, however, especially when applying styles to tables.

CHOOSING A STYLE SHEET EDITOR

Now that you have a better understanding of CSS, you need to choose an environment for developing and maintaining your style sheets.

Dreamweaver's Internal Editor

Dreamweaver enables you to create and edit style sheets in several ways. The Dreamweaver Document window can also serve as a text editor (see Figure 8.2). Thus, you can create an external style sheet by opening a new document, manually adding style rules, and saving the document with a `.css` extension.

Figure 8.2
This external style sheet can be modified in the Document window, as shown here, or in the CSS Styles panel.

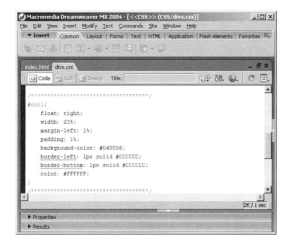

The most common method for managing both internal and external style sheets in Dreamweaver has been to use the CSS Styles panel in the Design panel group. The CSS Styles panel automates the style sheet process and offers an extensive array of style declaration options. In MX 2004, the panel has been enhanced in that you can now jump directly to style definitions in the code. However, you can no longer apply styles from the CSS Styles panel; you now use the Property inspector for that purpose.

Setting an External Style Sheet Editor

Although Dreamweaver offers powerful CSS tools, some experienced developers prefer to use a third-party style sheet application. The most popular of these applications is TopStyle by Bradbury Software (`http://www.bradsoft.com`). You can set Dreamweaver to use a third-party program for CSS editing (select Edit, Preferences, File Types/Editors), but before you do, make sure you familiarize yourself with MX 2004's new features. You may find, as we did, that the new Dreamweaver gives you most of what external CSS editors do, and more conveniently.

CSS in Dreamweaver MX 2004

Now that you have the basics of CSS under your virtual belt, this section examines how Dreamweaver lets you interact with CSS styles, with particular emphasis on evolutionary

8

enhancements to the Property inspector, the CSS Styles panel, and a welcome newcomer: the Relevant CSS tab of the Tag inspector, which may just be the coolest single new feature in this release.

THE CSS STYLES PANEL

The CSS Styles panel (see Figure 8.3) facilitates both the creation and editing (but no longer the application) of style rules for both external and embedded style sheets.

Figure 8.3
The CSS Styles panel lists all the internal and external styles available for the current document.

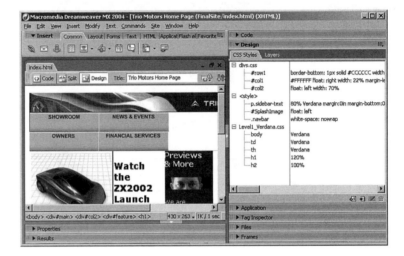

Unlike in Dreamweaver MX, the CSS Styles panel no longer offers the Apply Styles view. To apply a style, select a tag or block of text, (Option-click) [right-click] the style in the CSS Styles panel, and choose Apply. Alternatively, you can select the tag or block of text, then choose the style in the Property inspector's Style drop-down list.

MANAGING STYLE SHEETS

Styles can be created internally or externally. If you haven't attached an external style sheet to the page, new styles will be added internally to the HTML document by default. Before you can add styles to an external style sheet, you need to create a link to one.

CREATING AN EXTERNAL STYLE SHEET

The most convenient way to create a new external style sheet is to choose File, New, choose CSS Style Sheets under the Category column, then click an entry under the CSS Style Sheets column in the middle of the dialog box (see Figure 8.4). Dreamweaver offers a preview of the selected style sheet to the right. You can use these predefined style sheets as jumping-off points to create your own customized versions with new rules that you create.

Figure 8.4
Using the New Document dialog box is the easiest way to create a new external style sheet in the latest version of Dreamweaver.

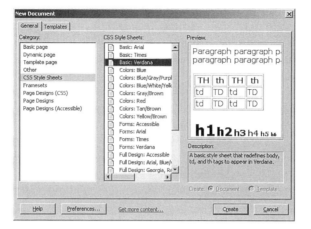

8

Another method for creating a new external style sheet is to click the New CSS Style button on the CSS Styles panel and select New Style Sheet File from the Define In field. This opens the File Selector dialog box, in which you can navigate to the folder where the new .css file should be stored and give the file a name.

Linking to an External Style Sheet

The process of linking an HTML document to an external style sheet is nearly identical to previous versions of Dreamweaver:

1. In the CSS Styles panel, select Attach Style Sheet.
2. In the Attach External Style Sheet dialog box, provide the name of the style sheet (see Figure 8.5).

Figure 8.5
The Attach External Style Sheet dialog box can be used to attach existing style sheets or kickstart the creation of new style sheets.

You can name the style sheet by using the following options:

- Type the name directly if you already know the complete path.
- Use the File Selector to navigate to the .css file.
- If you're creating a new style sheet, click the sample style sheets link to choose a .css file to start with, then save it to your site folder with the suggested name or with a new name of your choosing. Filenames must be in lowercase, contain no punctuation, and end in a .css extension.

3. Select either Link or Import as the method to attach to the external style sheet.

NOTE

> Link is the most common method for attaching external style sheets. Import is not supported by some browsers, so it should be used only in limited situations.

4. Click OK to create a link to the external style sheet.

After an external style sheet has been attached, you'll be able to choose to add new styles either internally in the HTML document or to the external sheet.

EXPORTING STYLES

You can also create an external style sheet by exporting the styles from an internal style sheet. Do the following:

1. Open the HTML document that contains the internal styles.
2. Select File, Export, Export CSS Styles.
3. In the Export Styles As CSS File dialog box, navigate to the folder in which the style sheet should be saved.
4. Give the new style sheet a name. The name should end with a `.css` extension.
5. Click Save.

CREATING A NEW STYLE DEFINITION

Whether you're using internal or external style sheets, the next step is to define the styles you need for your page or site. To create a new style, follow these steps:

1. From the CSS Styles panel, click the New CSS Style button.
2. The New CSS Style dialog box appears (see Figure 8.6). In the Define In field, choose to add the new style to an external style sheet or in This Document Only (an internal style sheet).

Figure 8.6
The New CSS Style dialog box determines the location of the new style as well as the type.

3. Select a style type:

- **Class (can apply to any tag)**—Creates a class style. If you select this option, you need to name the class in the Name field above the style type selector. If you don't precede the classname with a period (.), as is required by the style sheet, Dreamweaver adds it for you.

- **Tag (redefines the look of a specific tag)**—Applies a style to an HTML tag. When you select this option, you also must select a tag from the Tag field above the style type selector. These styles are automatically applied to the appropriate tags after they're defined. You won't see a difference in the code itself. Rather, the style to be applied to the tag is interpreted from the style sheet—whether external or embedded—and applied to all instances of the tag.

- **Advanced (Ids, contextual selectors, etc)**—Applies a style to one of the link types listed in the Selector field above the style type selector. These styles enable you to remove the underlining from links and otherwise change the appearance of the various link states. They're automatically applied after they're defined.

4. Click OK.

5. The CSS Style Definition dialog box opens. Set the style rules by choosing from the various style categories and options (explained later in this chapter).

6. Click OK to complete the style definition and return to the Document window.

NOTE

> To create a nested style or tag-specific class, use the Advanced option and then type in the selector(s). Type the tag names without angle brackets.

After you create a style, it's easy to apply. Styles defined for an HTML tag are automatically applied when viewed in a browser. Apply class styles by doing the following:

1. In the Document window, select the content to which you want to apply the class style.

2. In the CSS Styles panel, (Option-click) [right-click] a style from the list and choose Apply, or, in the Property inspector, choose the style from the Style drop-down list.

If the selection is only a small portion of content within a tag, the <span> tag is used with the class attribute. If the selection extends across multiple paragraphs or tag pairs, use the <div> tag to apply the style.

DEFINING STYLES

The Style Definition dialog box contains almost every available option for CSS. Some of these options can't be rendered in any browsers, as yet, but Dreamweaver makes them available to plan for future support. Most style options can be displayed in the Document window, but you should preview your documents in a browser to be certain they're rendering correctly.

8

To access the Style Definition dialog box, click the New CSS Style button in the CSS Styles panel. The New CSS Style dialog box appears. Name your style and complete the dialog box as per your needs, then click OK. The CSS Style Definition dialog box now appears (see Figure 8.7).

Figure 8.7
Using the Style Definition dialog box to manage a style sheet.

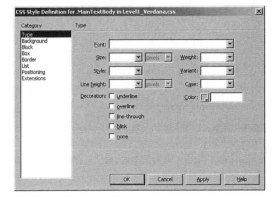

The Style Definition dialog box is divided into logical categories to group the style properties. You can choose freely among the categories and properties even within one style rule. Each category's options are detailed in the tables for Chapter 8 on the enclosed CD-ROM.

Setting the Type

The Type category contains properties pertaining to the appearance of text. If you're removing the underlining from links—one of the most common applications of CSS—select None in the Decoration properties.

Setting the Background

The Background category offers control over background images and colors. Not only do these styles ensure consistency throughout the site, but they also offer greater control over the repeating and scrolling of background images. Most background styles aren't supported in Netscape 4 but are fully supported in Netscape 6.

Setting the Block Properties

Block styles are used to control the alignment and spacing of text blocks. Support for these styles is, at best, spotty and buggy in Netscape 4 but is fully implemented in Netscape 6. Support in Internet Explorer is still rather limited.

Setting the Box Properties

Box styles are used to control the positioning and spacing of elements, much in the same way as tables. With appropriate browser support, which is still somewhat spotty even in the current browsers, you could design your entire site using box and positioning styles rather than tables.

Setting the Border

Border styles are used to set borders to surround an element. Each side of the rectangular border can have a unique line thickness and color. Borders can also be applied to only select sides of the element, creating text surrounded on the top and bottom while the sides remain open or similar combinations. Eight border styles exist, giving the border an inset, grooved, or dotted-line appearance. Unlike the line thickness and color, these styles are applied to all sides of the border. Many of the border properties are buggy in earlier browsers, so they should be applied cautiously and thoroughly tested.

Setting the List Properties

List styles offer control over the appearance of lists.

Setting the Position

Positioning styles control the exact placement of elements on the page. These properties form the basis of working with layers.

Setting Extensions

CSS extensions are specialty properties used to manage page breaks, cursor design, and add filters (which really are DHTML, rather than CSS).

Editing Style Sheets

The biggest benefit of using style sheets is being able to update the format of a site or page quickly. To edit your style sheets, follow these steps, which represent a welcome streamlining over earlier versions of Dreamweaver:

1. Click on the rule of interest in the CSS Styles panel to highlight it.
2. Click the Edit Style button in the CSS Styles panel.
3. The CSS Style Definition dialog box appears, from which you can change the style.

Want an even easier method? (Control-click) [right-click] the rule and choose Edit. If you'd rather use the new CSS Property inspector to edit your style sheets, click the rule and make your edits in the CSS Property inspector—discussed further at the end of this chapter.

Using Design Time Style Sheets

Design Time style sheets enable you to temporarily display or hide the effects of various style sheets within the site. This feature works only in the Document window; what the user actually sees in the browser is determined by the style sheets attached to the final HTML document. For development purposes, however, this tool can be quite convenient.

To use Design Time style sheets, do the following:

1. (Control-click) [right-click] in the CSS Styles panel to open the context menu.
2. Select Design Time.

3. In the Design Time Style Sheets dialog box, use the plus and minus buttons to open the File Selector and select which style sheets should be visible or invisible while you develop the site.

4. Click OK.

To see at a glance which style sheets are visible or hidden, look at the CSS Styles panel. You'll notice the word "design" or "hidden" next to the style sheet's name if you used the Design Time feature to set that style sheet.

USING THE NEW RELEVANT CSS TAB

One of the niftiest improvements in Dreamweaver MX 2004 is the Relevant CSS tab, also known in some Macromedia documents as the "rule inspector," which appears in the restructured Tag Inspector (see Figure 8.8). Click in your document, whether in Code view or Design view, and the Relevant CSS tab shows you which CSS rules apply to the current selection.

Figure 8.8
The Relevant CSS tab in the new Tag Inspector shows which CSS rules apply to the current selection.

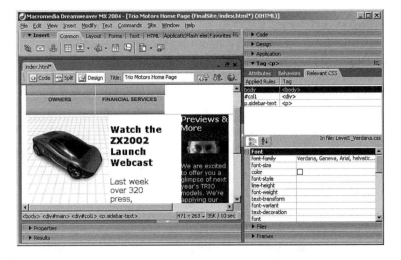

This tab has two halves: upper and lower. The upper half lists the rules affecting the current selection and the tags they affect. The bottom half lists the CSS properties of the current selection, with a handy color-coded system. Set properties show up in blue, and irrelevant properties appear in red (and a strikethrough font). Irrelevant properties are either those that don't inherit, or those that have been overridden according to the cascade precedence rules. You can find out which is the case by hovering the cursor over the irrelevant property.

If you double-click a rule in the Relevant CSS tab, Dreamweaver opens up the CSS code in the Document window so you can hand-edit it if you like. (If you were in Design view, Dreamweaver throws you into Split view.) The program also opens the CSS Properties tab (see Figure 8.9), a new and different way of defining and editing CSS styles. After you get used to the CSS Properties tab, you may find it quicker than navigating the various CSS Style Definition screens. If not, the old method is still available.

Figure 8.9
The CSS Properties tab shows the properties for a selected CSS rule, either in alphabetical view or in category view, and lets you edit them.

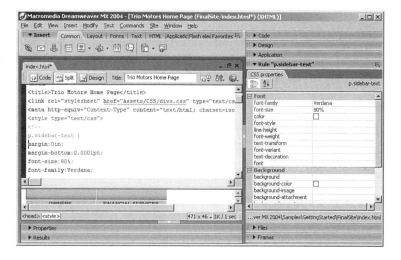

To get back to the Tag inspector from the CSS Properties tab, simply switch back to Design view and click anywhere on the page.

TROUBLESHOOTING

DREAMWEAVER HELP FOR XHTML

I just don't understand all this XHTML stuff. I need help!

There are several interesting ways that Dreamweaver MX shows its support for XHTML in terms of documentation. Open the Help section of Dreamweaver by selecting Help, Using Dreamweaver. After you're in the Help interface, click the Search tab and type **XHTML** into the search keyword field. Of special interest is the "About the XHTML Code Generated by Dreamweaver."

USING EXTERNAL EDITORS

I know Dreamweaver MX has a lot of options for working with markup, but I'm used to using a specific editor. Can I use an external editor with Dreamweaver?

Integrating external HTML editors for use with Dreamweaver is a very easy process. In fact, Homesite is distributed along with Dreamweaver for precisely this purpose.

BROWSERS AND THE id ATTRIBUTE

I inadvertently used id instead of class. It kept working, so I didn't realize I was doing something wrong. How'd this happen?

Despite the fact that IDs are supposed to be used only once in a document, browsers tend to forgive this. Therefore, you might see multiple IDs relating to the same rule in documents that render just as if the ID selector were a class selector. This is, however, not valid, and you will get errors when you go to validate such a document—to say nothing of causing problems with scripts that expect valid markup.

FONT CONCERNS

I set up a style sheet to control my fonts, yet the faces I chose are not appearing. Why is this?

Although fonts can be easily controlled by style sheets, CSS falls under the same limitation as HTML in font delivery: Namely, the specific typeface must be available on the computer viewing your page. As with the font element, style sheets allow you to stack font groups to maximize the possibility that a visitor's browser will be capable of seeing your text as you designed.

PEER TO PEER: MACROMEDIA AND THE WEB STANDARDS PROJECT

The Web Standards Project (WaSP) Dreamweaver Task Force was created in 2001 to accomplish two tasks of vital importance:

- To work with Macromedia's engineers to improve the standards compliance and accessibility of Web pages produced with Macromedia Dreamweaver.

- To communicate effectively within the online Dreamweaver community, raising awareness of Web standards and helping others discover how their tools can be used to create standards-compliant, accessible sites.

A special report by the WaSP Dreamweaver Task Force about Macromedia Dreamweaver MX can be found at `http://www.webstandards.org/act/campaign/dwtf/mxassessed.html`. The mission, history, and participants of the Task Force are described at `http://www.webstandards.org/act/campaign/dwtf/`.

PEER TO PEER: CSS RESOURCES

Here are a few references on CSS.

ARTICLES

The following articles will provide insight into CSS:

- "CSS: The True Language of Web Design. Part I: The separation of presentation from structure." `http://www.molly.com/articles/markupandcss/2002-02-truelanguage1.php`.
- "CSS: The True Language of Web Design. Part 2: Primary concepts and methods found in CSS." `http://www.molly.com/articles/markupandcss/2002-03-truelanguage2.php`.

WEB RESOURCES

The following is a valuable Web resource:

- The W3C style pages and CSS specifications can be found at `http://www.w3.org/Style/`.

BOOKS

Recommended readings on CSS include the following:

- Four books from Eric A. Meyer: *Cascading Style Sheets: The Definitive Guide* (O'Reilly & Associates, May 2000); *Cascading Style Sheets 2.0 Programmer's Reference* (Osborne/McGraw-Hill, March 2001); *CSS Pocket Reference* (O'Reilly & Associates, May 2001); and *Eric Meyer On CSS* (New Riders, June 2002).
- *Designing CSS Web Pages* by Christopher Schmitt (New Riders, 2002) is a good choice for designers seeking a better understanding of what CSS can do for them.
- *Sams Teach Yourself CSS in 24 Hours* by Kynn Bartlett is an easy-to-read, tutorial-style book.

PROFESSIONAL PAGE DESIGN

In this chapter

Table Elements   192

Using Layout Mode   193

About Frames   199

Building Framed Pages in Dreamweaver MX 2004   200

Modifying Framesets and Frame Elements   205

Targeting Windows   206

Layout with Style   207

Layer Preferences   208

The Layer "Box"   209

Using the Layers Panel   213

Setting Layer Attributes   215

Designing with Layers   216

When designing pages in Dreamweaver, you have many arrows in your quiver. Foremost among them, in chronological order of their appearance on the Web design scene, are tables, frames, and layers. This chapter discusses these three methods—their pros and cons, quirks and caveats—as well as how to implement them with specific Dreamweaver MX 2004 commands and tools.

This book naturally focuses on technology and tools, but to keep things in perspective, we should mention that a good eye is an important requirement for attractive Web page design. So, if you plan on doing some serious page layout work, you may want to look into some books and classes on the basics of visual aesthetics. Even this advanced version of Dreamweaver doesn't have a pop-up dialog box that warns you when a page looks ugly.

TABLE ELEMENTS

The first step in becoming aware of how best to use tables as a fundamental tool in Web design is to understand the HTML and XHTML elements used to create them (see Table 9.1).

TABLE 9.1   TABLE ELEMENTS IN HTML AND XHTML

Element	Purpose
table	The main table tag, it denotes the beginning and subsequent end of a table.
tr	The table row tag and its companion closing tag, <tr> ... </tr>.
td	The table data or table cell. This tag is used to define individual table cells.
th	Defines a cell with header information. Typically, this renders in bold.
caption	A caption describes the nature of a table. You are allowed only one caption per table. Captions are especially helpful for accessibility and are rarely used in table layout, but rather are reserved for table data.
thead	Table head, for table header information.
tfoot	Table foot, for footer information.
tbody	Table body.
colgroup	Defines a group of columns. There are two ways to specify the group. One is to use the span attribute to specify the number of columns to be grouped. The other way is to use the col element.
col	Used to define columns within a group.

The trick now is knowing when and how to use and modify these elements. Fortunately, Dreamweaver provides a lot of help. It is possible to create effective layout tables without ever interacting with the underlying HTML, although recognizing the tags makes certain operations—such as selecting tables—more convenient.

USING LAYOUT MODE

Dreamweaver's Layout mode is a special document view designed to make it easier to create cells and tables for page layout purposes, as opposed to creating tables for tabular, chart-type data. You can move portions of your design around the page with a freedom you would not have working in traditional Design view. The underlying markup is still tables, but you get more visual interface options along the way.

After you have created a table, you can see how it looks in Layout mode by following these steps:

1. If you're in Code view, switch to Design view. (You must first be in Design view to get to Layout mode.)

2. Click the Layout tab along the Insert bar and then click the Layout button. Alternatively, you can select View, Table Mode, Layout Mode from the main menu or press (Command-F6) [Ctrl-F6].

3. You'll notice that in Layout mode, your table now appears with a different "look"—that of a layout table rather than an HTML table.

You are now ready to modify your table using Layout mode's tools and options.

> **NOTE**
>
> To return to working on your tables outside of Layout Mode, select View, Table Mode, Standard Mode. Dreamweaver switches back to the Standard mode of Design view, where you can continue working or switch to Code view, as you prefer. You can also press Ctrl-F6 again.

DRAWING LAYOUT TABLES AND CELLS IN LAYOUT MODE

A layout cell is very similar to a table cell in that it contains your content. However, the purpose of layout tables and cells is to help you organize and move tables around in a way that would be prohibitively difficult if you were just inserting table cells and rows normally. Layout mode is especially helpful if you're using tables to create a visual structure, as opposed to a data chart.

As with table cells, layout cells cannot exist outside a layout table. If you create a layout cell, Dreamweaver automatically places it within a layout table, and will create a layout table if none exists. Create an additional layout table anywhere on the page where you want more control over that portion of the page.

> **NOTE**
>
> You can nest layout tables, enabling you to create more complex layouts.

DRAWING A LAYOUT TABLE

You can create one layout table at a time in Dreamweaver, or multiple tables one after another, as the following sections explain.

CREATING A SINGLE LAYOUT TABLE

Make sure you are in Layout mode. From the Layout tab of the Insert bar, click the Layout Table button. Position your cursor in the document; notice that it changes to a crosshair (+) when you move below any existing content. Now click and drag to create your layout table.

> **TIP**
>
> If the no-draw cursor appears while you are trying to draw a layout table below existing content, resize the Document window. Doing so creates more empty space between the bottom of the existing content and the bottom of the window.

CREATE MULTIPLE LAYOUT TABLES CONTINUOUSLY

Follow the steps in "Creating a Single Layout Table," but use (Control-drag) or [Command-drag]. As long as you continue to hold down (Control) or [Command], you can draw layout tables one after the other (see Figure 9.1). This prevents you from having to re-select the Layout Table button.

Figure 9.1
Each layout table appears in green, with a tab denoting Layout Table at the upper left.

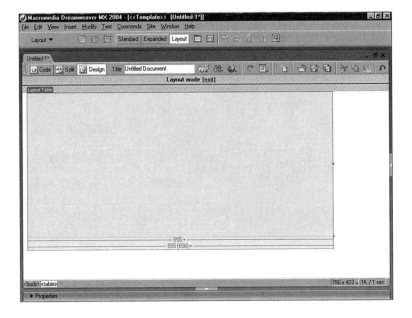

DRAWING A LAYOUT CELL

As with tables, you can draw layout cells one at a time, or in batches, as described in the following sections.

CREATING A SINGLE LAYOUT CELL

Make sure you are in Layout mode. From the Layout tab of the Insert bar, click the Draw Layout Cell button. Position your cursor in the document. Notice that it changes to a crosshair (+) when you move below any existing content. Position your cursor on the page where you want to start the cell, then drag to create. The cell appears on the page with a blue outline. (If no layout table already exists to host the cell, Dreamweaver creates one for you.)

CREATE MULTIPLE LAYOUT CELLS CONTINUOUSLY

Follow the procedure in "Creating a Single Layout Cell," but use (Control-drag) or [Command-drag]. As long as you continue to hold down (Control) or [Command], you can draw layout cells one after the other. This prevents you from having to re-select the Draw Layout Cell button. The cell appears on the page with a blue outline.

CAUTION

> Cell edges automatically snap to the edge of the surrounding layout table if you draw the cell too close to the edge of the layout table. To avoid this, temporarily disable snapping by holding down (Alt) or [Option] when drawing the cell.

NESTING A LAYOUT TABLE

Make sure you are in Layout mode. From the Layout tab of the Insert bar, click the Layout Table button. Position your cursor in the gray empty area of the existing layout table. Notice that it changes to a crosshair (+). Now click and drag to create your nested layout table.

CAUTION

> You can create a nested layout table only in the empty area of an existing layout table, or around existing cells. You can't create a layout table inside a layout cell.

FORMATTING IN LAYOUT MODE

A range of utilities is available to assist you in creating a great table design within Layout mode. You can use the Property inspector to modify your layout table and cell attributes; you can add content to a layout cell and modify that cell to more effectively manage that content; and you can let Dreamweaver help you make decisions about using spacer graphics for table layout integrity.

 Dreamweaver MX 2004 adds a new tables mode called "Expanded." (The button's between Standard and Layout on the Insert bar.) When you're in Expanded Tables mode, added cell padding and spacing is placed in all tables in a document temporarily. This increases the tables' borders for ease of editing, allowing you to select items within tables more easily, or

9

more precisely position the insertion point. For example, you might expand a table to make it easier to place the insertion point to the left or right of an image, without accidentally selecting the image or the table cell. Just be careful: After placing the insertion point, return to Standard or Layout mode to make your edits. Some visual functions, such as resizing, don't work correctly in Expanded Tables mode.

SETTING LAYOUT TABLE AND CELL ATTRIBUTES

Many options exist for modifying layout tables and cells. When you're working in Layout mode, these settings (such as width, height, background, no wrap, cell padding, and cell spacing) apply to the layout tables and cells, as well as to the way the markup will be generated to create the underlying table-based design. In addition, several options for layout tables and cells you might not have seen before include the following:

- **Fixed**—Allows you to specify a pixel value width for your table or table cell. In fixed design, you must never exceed a cell's parameters. If you have a cell that is 125 pixels wide, but you put a 200-pixel-wide graphic in it, the table renders it improperly.

- **Autostretch**—Results in the table or table cell having a percentage value. The resulting table or cell is therefore dynamic and will automatically flow to fill the available space.

- **Clear Row Heights**—Removes specific height settings for all the cells in the layout table.

- **Make Widths Consistent**—In fixed designs, matches the width of the cell to its contents. So, if you create a layout cell that is 300 pixels wide and the content is 250 pixels wide, this feature resets the cell width to 250.

- **Remove All Spacers**—Removes any spacers used in your layout. Spacers are transparent images, such as a single-pixel GIF file, that Dreamweaver uses to force cells to a particular width.

- **Remove Nesting**—Removes any nested layout tables without removing the content.

NOTE

> Because Dreamweaver adds heights as you work on your design in Layout mode, you will likely want to remove that markup. To do so, select the Clear Row Heights option from the Property inspector, or the Clear All Heights option from the drop-down menu at the top (or sometimes bottom) of the table in Layout view. Do this only after you've added the content to the cells within that row, to avoid deleting empty rows entirely.

SELECTING OPTIONS FOR A LAYOUT TABLE

Select the layout table by clicking the layout table's tab, or click the <table> tag in the tag selector at the bottom of the Document window. In the Property inspector, make modifications to the properties available. Press (Return) [Enter] at any time to apply a property. Save your file to update the changes.

SELECTING OPTIONS FOR A LAYOUT CELL

Select the layout cell by clicking the edge of the cell (which takes a certain amount of coordination!), or (Command-click) [Ctrl-click] anywhere in the cell. In the Property inspector, make modifications to the properties available. Press (Return) [Enter] at any time to apply a property. Save your file to update the changes.

ADDING CONTENT

You can add any kind of content you would like to a layout cell, just as you would with a traditional HTML table cell.

ADDING TEXT TO A LAYOUT CELL

Place your cursor in the layout cell where you want to add text. Start typing. The cell automatically expands as you type, if needed. You can also paste text copied from another document into a cell.

ADDING AN IMAGE TO A CELL

Place your cursor in the layout cell where you want to add the image. Now either choose Insert, Image, or, in the Common tab of the Insert bar, click the Images button, and select Image. The Select Image Source dialog box appears, where you can select an image file. Click OK. The image now appears in the layout cell.

You also can add other elements, such as objects and applets. Simply add them to the layout cell as you would to a normal document (see Figure 9.2).

Figure 9.2
This layout table has cells containing text, images, and Flash objects.

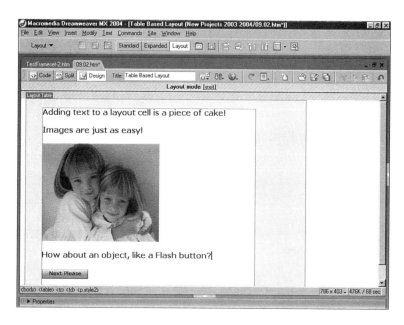

Trying to add content to a layout table but having difficulties? **See** *"Adding Content" in the "Troubleshooting" section of this chapter.*

MOVING AND RESIZING LAYOUT CELLS AND TABLES

Rare is the table or cell that satisfies the designer completely at first placement. Dreamweaver makes changing layout cells and tables easy.

RESIZING A LAYOUT TABLE

Clicking the tab at the top left of the table selects the table and displays selection handles around it. To resize the table, drag the selection handles.

MOVING A NESTED LAYOUT TABLE

You can't move a main layout table, but you can move a nested layout table. Clicking the tab at the top left of the table selects the table and displays selection handles around it. Now you can either drag the table to another location on the page, or press the arrow keys to move the table one pixel at a time. Holding down Shift while using an arrow key moves a table ten pixels at a time.

RESIZING A LAYOUT CELL

Select a cell by clicking the edge of the cell or by (Control-clicking) or [Command-clicking] anywhere in the cell. The selection handles now appear around the cell. Drag a selection handle to resize the cell. The cell edges automatically snap to align with other cells' edges, if any are present.

MOVING A LAYOUT CELL

Select a cell by clicking an edge of the cell or by (Control-clicking) or [Command-clicking] anywhere in the cell. Selection handles appear around the cell. Now either drag the cell to another location within its layout table, or use the arrow keys to move the cell one pixel at a time. Holding down Shift while using an arrow key moves a cell ten pixels at a time.

MOVING A NESTED LAYOUT CELL

Select a cell by clicking the edge of the cell or by (Control-clicking) or [Command-clicking] anywhere in the cell. Selection handles now appear around the cell; use them to resize.

NOTE

Layout cells, like table cells, cannot overlap, and a layout cell cannot be made smaller than its contents. Overlapping and clipping can be done with Draw Layers, if you need those features.

ABOUT FRAMES

Frames can be very empowering from a design perspective. Designers can keep sections of a page static while other parts of the page can be used to display other pages. Navigation is the most common reason to use frames, because you can specify a navigation area that is to remain in the same place at all times (see Figure 9.3). A designated area in a browser window that can display an HTML document independent of what's being displayed in the rest of the browser window is called a *frame*. An HTML file that defines the layout and properties of a set of frames is called a *frameset*.

Figure 9.3
This frame-based site keeps the left navigation area static, enabling new content to be loaded into the main window at right.

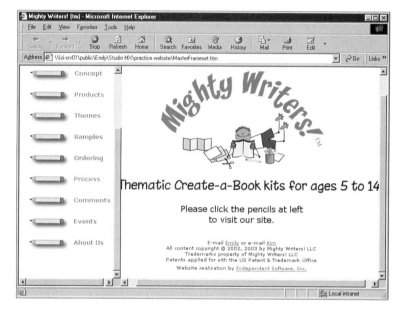

There are a couple of advantages to using frames:

- After your visitor has accessed your site, her browser doesn't need to reload the navigation-related graphics as she moves from page to page. This gives the site a feeling of continuity. It also saves the visitor from having to hunt for information that is sometimes buried several pages back (such as what site she is viewing, or company contact information.)

- If a frame's content is too large to fit into a window, the frame has its own scroll bar. Your visitor can use the scroll bar to scroll this frame independently and separately from the window. For example, if you have a long page of content in a frame, your visitor can scroll down to the end of the content. After he's at the bottom, he doesn't need to return to the top of the content to access the navigation bar if the navigation bar is in a different and static frame.

Having said that, frames are not without their downside. Bookmarking a framed page can prove problematic, as can printing it. Some testing may be in order for pages that you expect users to print or to add to Favorites lists.

 Concerned with issues related to linking to other Web sites from within your frames page? **See** *"Using Frames to Contain Other Sites" in the "Troubleshooting" section at the end of this chapter.*

BUILDING FRAMED PAGES IN DREAMWEAVER MX 2004

CAUTION

> The frameset is a conceptual replacement for the body in the frameset HTML or XHTML document. Therefore, *no* body tags should appear. The one exception to this is the noframes element, which allows you to place a body element within it.

In this section, you'll step through a series of exercises to get you working immediately with frame documents. The first exercise will be to create a frameset, and then you'll move on to build framed pages.

CREATING FRAMESETS

There are two ways to create a frameset in Dreamweaver MX 2004. You can create your own, or you can use a predefined frameset.

BUILDING YOUR OWN FRAMESET

Before you begin creating a frameset or working with frames, make the frame borders visible in the Document window's Design view by selecting View, Visual Aids, Frame Borders.

You can design your own frameset in Dreamweaver by adding "splitters" to the window.

CREATING A FRAMESET

Select Modify, Frameset, then select a splitting style from the submenu: Split Frame Left, Split Frame Right, Split Frame Up, or Split Frame Down. The window is automatically split into frames accordingly. If you currently have a document open, it will fill one of the frames. Figure 9.4 shows a frame being split.

If you want to use one of Dreamweaver's existing frame layouts, you can create a frameset more quickly by using the Insert bar. For details, see "Creating a Predefined Frameset to Display an Existing Document in a Frame", later in this chapter.

SPLITTING A FRAME INTO SMALLER FRAMES

To split the frame where the insertion point is, select the frame. Now choose a splitting style from the Modify, Frameset submenu (see Figure 9.4).

To split a frame or set of frames vertically or horizontally, move your mouse over the outer frame border until you see the two-arrow cursor. Now drag the frame border from the edge of the Design view into the middle of the Design view.

To split a frame by using a frame border that isn't at the edge of the Design view, position your cursor until you see a two-arrow cursor. Now Alt-drag a frame border.

To divide a frame into four frames, position your cursor in a corner until you see the four-arrow cursor. Now from the frame border, drag the cursor from the Design view into the middle of a frame.

DELETING A FRAME

Position your cursor on the frame border to be deleted, and drag the frame border off the page or to a border of the parent frame. (This remains one of the least intuitive operations in the Dreamweaver program—why not just right-click a frame in the Frames panel and choose Delete? No one knows.) Dreamweaver prompts you to save the document if there's unsaved content in a frame that's being deleted.

DELETING A FRAMESET

You cannot completely delete a frameset simply by dragging the borders off. Closing the Document window where it is displayed completely eliminates it. If the frameset file has been saved, the file needs to be deleted.

RESIZING A FRAME

There are two ways to resize a frame: approximately and exactly. To resize a frame approximately, position your cursor on the frame border and drag it in the Document window's Design view. To resize a frame exactly, set the options for the frameset dimensions in the Property inspector. (You may need to click the expander arrow in the inspector's lower-right corner to see the dimensions settings.)

If you are happy with the frameset you've created, save the file and continue working. If you'd like to create more splits, follow these steps:

1. Place your cursor into the frame you'd like to split.
2. Select Modify, Frameset, and again select a splitting option.
3. Continue to split frames by dragging the splitting items to the required location.

USING A PREDEFINED FRAMESET

There are two ways to create a predefined frameset. To create a new empty frameset, use the New Document dialog box. To create a frameset and display your current document in one of the new frames, use the Layout tab of the Insert bar.

Figure 9.4
Using splitting styles, you can break the frame up as you need to without ever worrying about how to generate the complex frameset markup.

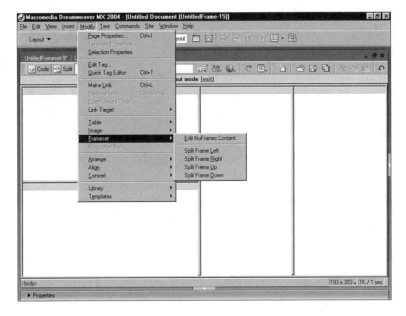

CREATING A NEW EMPTY PREDEFINED FRAMESET

Start by selecting File, New. Dreamweaver MX 2004 provides you with 15 different styles of predefined framesets at the opening window. Simply select the category titled Framesets from the Create From Samples category at the opening window.

Now select a Framesets style from the list in the New Document dialog box, and click Create. Dreamweaver MX 2004 generates the frameset and opens it into the Document window.

If you have activated the Frame Tag Accessibility Attributes dialog box in Preferences, it will appear. If so, complete the dialog box for each frame, clicking OK upon completion.

CREATING A PREDEFINED FRAMESET TO DISPLAY AN EXISTING DOCUMENT IN A FRAME

Place your cursor in the document and then select Insert, HTML, Frames and pick one of the styles from the cascading submenu; or from the Insert bar's Layout tab, select the Frames button and choose a predefined frameset (see Figure 9.5).

If you have activated the Frame Tag Accessibility Attributes dialog box in Preferences, it will appear. If so, complete the dialog box for each frame, clicking OK upon completion.

The frameset illustration provides a diagram of each frameset as it is applied to the current document. The area highlighted in blue represents the frame in which the current document content will appear.

Figure 9.5
This frameset design would normally be complicated to mark up, but using predefined frameset styles allows you great design options.

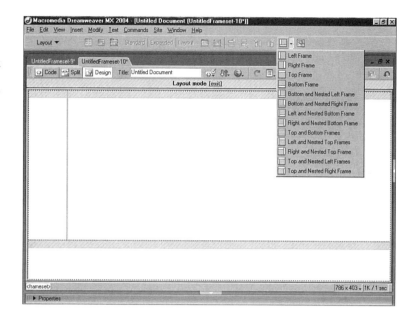

Dreamweaver MX 2004 automatically applies the frameset. This means that it has also generated the individual documents that are delivered to each individual frame. If you're starting from scratch, these should be saved because you will eventually be adding content to them.

You can now make modifications to the frameset, using the Property inspector.

USING FRAME SELECTION TOOLS

Dreamweaver MX 2004 provides you with two primary visual means to help you make selections when working with your framesets and frame elements. You can work in the Frames panel or the Document window. As a general rule, it's much more user-friendly to work with frames and framesets in the Frames panel.

To work in the Frames panel, select Window, Frames. A small diagram of the Design view appears on the Frames panel, providing an illustration of the frames within a frameset. After a frame is selected in the Frames panel, a black border surrounds it. After a frameset is selected in the Frames panel, a thick black line appears around the frameset. If the Property inspector is open, you can confirm your choice by viewing the frame or frameset name there.

SELECTING A FRAME IN THE FRAMES PANEL

Click inside the frame in the Frames panel. A selection outline appears around the selected frame in both the Frames panel and the Document window's Design view.

SELECTING A FRAMESET IN THE FRAMES PANEL

Click on the border that surrounds the frameset in the Frames panel. A selection outline appears around the frameset in both the Frames panel and the Document window's Design view.

After a frame is selected in the Document window's Design view, a heavy dotted line surrounds each frame. After a frameset is selected in the Document window's Design view, all the frames contained in that frameset are surrounded with a faint dotted line.

SELECTING A FRAME IN THE DOCUMENT WINDOW'S DESIGN VIEW

With your frameset document open, switch to Design view by selecting View, Design. To select a frame, (Option-Shift-click) [Alt-click] inside a specific frame.

SELECTING A FRAMESET IN THE DOCUMENT WINDOW'S DESIGN VIEW

To select a frameset, be sure the frame's visual borders are on so you can see what you're doing. Select View, Visual Aids, Frame Borders. Now click any of the frameset's borders (see Figure 9.6).

Figure 9.6
Select Dreamweaver MX 2004's visual frame border aids to make frame and frameset selections.

CAUTION

Simply clicking in a frame in the Document view does not select it. Instead, a single click in a frame enables you to edit the contents of that frame.

MODIFYING FRAMESETS AND FRAME ELEMENTS

There are many means by which you can modify framesets and frame elements in the frameset.

MODIFYING THE FRAMESET ELEMENT

To make any modifications to your frameset, open the frameset file and select the frameset in the Document window (click a frame border), or use the Frames panel (easier) by clicking on the frame and then clicking the `<frameset>` tag selector button for the appropriate parent frameset. Use the Property inspector to make any desired changes (see Figure 9.7).

Figure 9.7
When a frameset document is open and the frameset is selected, the Property inspector makes frameset-related options available.

MODIFYING FRAME ELEMENTS IN THE FRAMESET

How you set up your frames is important because the information in the frame element relates to the way in which these elements will behave.

DREAMWEAVER MX 2004 FRAME OPTIONS IN THE PROPERTY INSPECTOR

The following list discusses several frame properties of interest.

- **FrameName**—The name a link's target attribute or a script uses to refer to the frame. A frame name has to be a single word. When naming a frame, do not use periods (.), hyphens (-), or spaces. A frame name must start with a letter and not a numeral. Be aware that frame names are case sensitive. Don't use terms that are set aside for use in JavaScript (such as `top` or `navigator`).

- **Src**—Denotes the source document to display in the frame. Clicking the folder icon opens the Select HTML File dialog box, allowing you to browse and select a file.

- **Scroll**—Indicates whether scroll bars appear in the frame. Attribute values available are Yes (scroll is always available when needed), No (scroll is never available), Auto (scroll available only when needed), and Default. When the Default setting is selected, it doesn't set a value for the corresponding attribute, which allows each browser to use its default value. Because most browsers default to Auto, the scroll bars appear only when there is not enough room in a browser window to display all the contents of the current frame.

- **Borders**—Displays or hides the borders of the current frame when viewed in a browser. Attribute values available are Yes (provides a frame border), No (disallows a frame border), and Default. Most browsers default to showing borders, unless the parent frameset has Borders set to No. A border is hidden only when all frames that share the border have a Borders setting of No, or when the parent frameset's Borders property is set to No and the frames sharing the border have a Borders setting of Default. Selecting a Borders option for a frame from the Properties dialog box takes priority over the frameset's border settings.

- **NoResize**—Stops visitors from resizing the frames in the browser. Turn on or off by checking.

- **Border Color**—Adds a colored border to the frames. Clicking on the Color Box takes you to the Color Cubes color palette and the Continuous Tone palette, where you can use the eyedropper to choose a Web-safe color. All colors on the Color Cubes and Continuous Tone palettes are Web-safe. Clicking on the System Color Picker button takes you to the System Color Picker. This enables you to choose a custom color. Note that colors chosen from this palette are not Web-safe. The selected color applies to all borders that touch the frame, and overrides the frameset's specified border color.

- **Margin Width**—Defines the width in pixels for the left and right margins and directly affects the space between the frame borders and the content.

- **Margin Height**—Defines the width in pixels for the top and bottom margins and directly affects the space between the frame borders and the content.

TARGETING WINDOWS

To effectively use frames, a designer must decide where linked pages will load. For example, you might have set up your frameset to contain a menu on the left and a larger frame field on the right. The goal is to ensure that the links in the menu always load in the content area, unless you want a different behavior.

The following are two basic ways to link, or *target*, documents to specific windows:

- Combine `target` and `name` attributes to specifically target windows.
- Use a reserved target name, such as `self`.

The `target` and `name` attributes enable you to add pages to your framed site and target a specific window by naming that window and targeting the link.

 Trying to print out a frame in your framed page but having no success? **See** *"Printing Frames" in the "Troubleshooting" section of this chapter.*

USING THE `target` AND `name` ATTRIBUTES TO LINK A FRAME

To target a frame to open properly by using the `target` and `name` attributes, you first need to ensure that all your individual frames have been properly named in the frameset. Avoid naming standard targets with anything other than an accepted alphanumeric character; an underscore, or any other symbol, is ignored. Then, follow these steps:

1. Select a link or linked object in the frame where you'd like the link to reside. In our example, that would be the left menu, which is named `leftFrame`.

2. Provide the source file of the page you're going to have load in the main area by clicking the folder icon and navigating to the appropriate file.

3. In the Property inspector, you'll find the Target drop-down menu. If you named all your frame files and are working in the frameset, the name of your frame should appear in the list. Because you want the linked page to load in the `mainFrame` frame (the one to the right), select `mainFrame` as your target.

The target element has now properly been added to the link. When you click the link, the page you want to load in the main frame will do so.

Using Reserved Target Names

As you look at the Target drop-down menu, you'll find several predefined target names that cause certain actions to occur when a target link is created:

- `target="_blank"`—The targeted document opens in a completely new browser window. Use this only when a new window is absolutely necessary; otherwise, you run the risk of irritating visitors, who, depending on their settings, might end up with numerous, resource-draining browser windows on the desktop. Also, some browser add-ins automatically stifle pop-up windows to block advertising.

- `target="_self"`—The targeted document loads in the same frame where the originating link exists.

- `target="_parent"`—This loads the targeted document into the link's parent frameset.

- `target="_top"`—Use this attribute to load the link into the full window, overriding any existing frames. This is usually the correct choice when a link takes the visitor out of your framed site into a new site.

Layout with Style

Layers are rectangular containers on a Web page. Using Dreamweaver layers—a feature made possible through the use of Cascading Style Sheets (CSS)—designers can gain almost as much control over their pages as traditional print layout offers. Dreamweaver layers can be visible or hidden. When used with behaviors, they form the basis for pop-out menus on cutting edge sites. Layers can even be animated with timelines.

Although Dreamweaver treats layers as objects unto themselves, they are actually CSS constructs. A <div> or <span> tag is given an ID (to identify the layer from among multiple layers) and styled with positioning declarations. Code for a typical layer might look like this:

```
<div id="Layer1" style="position: absolute; left: 400px; top: 100px;
width: 100px; height: 75px; z-index: 3"></div>
```

The contents of the layer would appear within the <div> tag pair.

→ For more information on positioning styles in CSS, **see** Chapter 8, "Writing and Editing HTML, XHTML, and CSS," **page 161**.

LAYER PREFERENCES

Before you create layers for layout purposes, you should indicate your preferences for the default settings new layers should use. This is done in the Layers category of the Preferences dialog box (see Figure 9.8). Go to Edit, Preferences, Layers.

The preferences are as follows:

- **Visibility**—This sets a layer's visibility. Your options here are Default, Inherit, Visible, and Hidden. Default specifies that the browser default should be used, which gives control to the user but takes away some control from the developer. When no visibility is selected, most browsers default to Inherit. Inherit uses the visibility property of the layer's parent and should be used with nested layers. Visible displays the layer contents, regardless of the parent's value. Hidden hides the layer contents, regardless of the parent's value.

- **Width and Height**—This sets the default width and height (in pixels) for inserted layers (those created by dragging from the Draw Layer button in the Insert Bar or by selecting Insert, Layout Objects, Layer).

- **Background Color**—This sets the color used in the background of layers. Clicking on the Color Box takes you to the Color Cubes palette and Continuous Tone palette, where you can use the eyedropper to choose a Web-safe color. All colors on the Color Cubes and Continuous Tone palettes are Web-safe. Clicking on the color wheel button takes you to the System Color Picker, which allows you to choose a custom color—including ones that are not Web-safe.

- **Background Image**—This sets a default background image. Enter the image file to use in the text box, or click the Browse button to locate the file on your computer.

- **Nesting**—When you draw a layer within the boundaries of another layer, it becomes nested in that layer when this option is checked. Whatever you choose for this setting can be temporarily overridden if you hold (Option) [Alt] when drawing a layer.

- **Netscape 4 Compatibility**—Netscape 4 browsers have a known bug that causes layers to be positioned incorrectly when a user resizes his browser. This option inserts a JavaScript function into the document head that forces the page to reload whenever the browser window is resized. This option can also be toggled on and off by using the command Add/Remove Netscape Resize Fix on the Commands menu.

Figure 9.8
The Layers preferences control the default settings for layers.

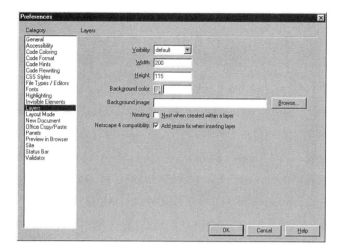

THE LAYER "BOX"

Dreamweaver provides several ways of creating layers.

> **TIP**
>
> Dreamweaver MX 2004 offers a number of predefined, layer-based page layouts that you can use as a jumping-off point for your own designs. To access these, choose File, New, choose Page Designs (CSS) in the Category column, then click through the individual designs in the center column, looking at the preview window until you find one that approximates your desired design.

CREATING A LAYER

To create a layer, do one of the following:

- To create a layer, select Insert, Layout Objects, Layer from the menu. A layer is created at the insertion point with the default size settings.

- You can also create a layer by dragging the Draw Layer option from the Layout tab of the Insert bar into the Document window. The layer is created in the closest position possible to where you release the button.

- To draw a layer, click the Draw Layer button in the Layout tab of the Insert Bar. Then click in your document where you want the layer to be positioned and drag from the upper-left corner to the lower-right corner of your intended layer (see Figure 9.9).

- To draw multiple layers, click the Draw Layer button in the Insert Bar. Then hold down the (Command) [Ctrl] key while you draw. This enables you to continue drawing layers without having to repeatedly click the Draw Layer button.

Figure 9.9
Draw a layer by clicking the Draw Layer icon in the Insert Bar; then click and drag in the Document window to define the layer's size and position.

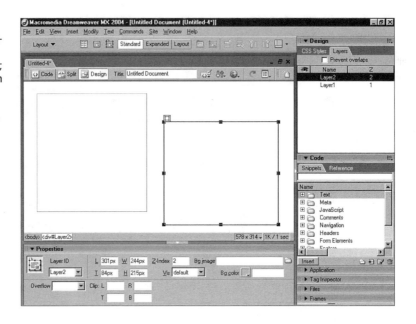

If you have Invisible Elements turned on (View, Visual Aids, Invisible Elements), and you've checked Anchor Points for Layers in the Edit, Preferences, Invisible Elements list, a layer marker appears in the Document window for each layer. Even if you move the layer box, the layer marker remains where it was originally positioned.

NOTE

When Invisible Elements are active and layer anchor points selected, the elements on your page can appear in a shifted position in Design view. Turn off this option to get a better idea of how your page will look in a browser.

ADDING CONTENT TO THE LAYER

You can insert elements into a layer just as you can with your base document. Before placing elements into a layer, you must first activate the layer by clicking anywhere inside its border. (Don't click the layer border itself, because that selects the layer for resizing or moving.)

When you activate a layer, the insertion point appears inside the borders of the layer box. Now any inserted object or typed text will go inside the layer (see Figure 9.10).

SELECTING, MOVING, ALIGNING, AND RESIZING A LAYER IN DESIGN VIEW

When you insert layers, they are rarely exactly where you want them to be. Fortunately, manipulating layers is easy. You can move, resize, or align layers in Design view, either "by sight" (see Figure 9.11) or via the Property inspector. You can select a layer or multiple layers in the Layers Panel or the Document window.

Figure 9.10
Activating a layer places the insertion point inside it. Any text or objects inserted here are placed within the layer.

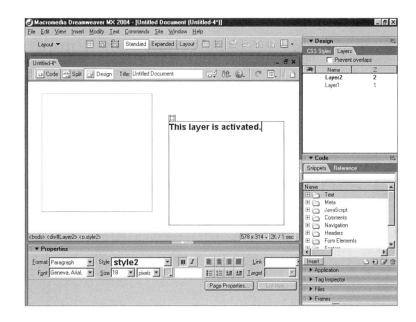

SELECTING A LAYER

You can select one or more layers in various ways.

USING THE LAYERS PANEL TO SELECT A LAYER

To use the Layers panel to select a layer, select Window, Layers and select the name of the layer.

SELECTING A LAYER IN THE DOCUMENT WINDOW

Click on the layer's border (the cursor turns into a four-headed arrow) and the resize handles appear, indicating that the layer is selected. Watch out: Clicking inside a layer causes the layer's selection handle to appear at the upper left, but does not actually select the layer. Always check the Property inspector to confirm that what you've selected is what you think you've selected.

USING KEYBOARD SHORTCUTS TO SELECT A LAYER

To use keyboard shortcuts to select a layer, select (Control-Shift-click) or [Command-Shift-click] from inside the layer.

USING THE TAG SELECTOR TO SELECT A LAYER

Click in a layer, then click the `<div>` tag in the Tag Selector to select a layer.

SELECTING MULTIPLE LAYERS

To select multiple layers with the Layers panel, Shift-click on as many layers as needed. The layers selected will stay highlighted.

SELECTING MULTIPLE LAYERS IN THE DOCUMENT WINDOW

To select multiple layers in the Document window, select Shift-click on the borders of two or more layers.

Figure 9.11
You can resize a layer by clicking its border and dragging one of the resize points around the edge. Move the layer by dragging on the drag box in the upper-left corner.

The Drag Box   A Resize Handle

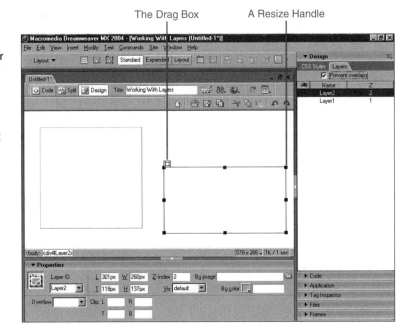

RESIZING A LAYER

RESIZING A LAYER WITH RESIZE HANDLES

In Design view, position the cursor over one of the eight resize handles on the sides and corners of the selected layer. A double-arrow cursor indicates the direction in which you can resize. Click and drag a handle to resize the layer.

RESIZING A LAYER ONE PIXEL AT A TIME

In Design view, hold down (Control) or [Option] while pressing an arrow key. This method allows only the right and bottom border to move; the left and top borders are fixed.

USING GRID SNAPPING INCREMENTS TO RESIZE A LAYER

In Design view, hold down (Shift-Control) or [Shift-Option] while pressing an arrow key.

RESIZING A LAYER BY SETTING THE VALUES

In Design view, type in the values in width (W) and height (H) in the Property inspector (Window, Properties).

RESIZING MULTIPLE LAYERS AT THE SAME TIME

Various techniques exist to resize multiple layers simultaneously.

RESIZING MULTIPLE LAYERS SO THEY CONFORM TO EACH OTHER

In Design View, select Modify, Align, Make Same Width or Modify, Align, Make Same Height. The first selected layers conform to the width or height of the last selected layer. The last layer selected is represented by solid resize handles on the border; the other layers are represented by hollow resize handles.

RESIZING MULTIPLE LAYERS SO THAT THE SAME SETTINGS APPLY

Select two or more layers. In the Property inspector, under Multiple Layers, enter the width and height values. The values are applied to all selected layers.

ALIGNING LAYERS

In Design view, select two or more layers. Select Modify, Align, and choose Left, Right, Top, or Bottom. All layers align with the last selected layer (highlighted in black). When aligning layers, child layers that aren't selected may move with a selected parent layer. The last layer selected is represented by solid resize handles on the border; the other layers are represented by hollow resize handles.

USING THE LAYERS PANEL

The Layers panel, located by default in the Design group, provides a convenient way to view and modify the layout properties for the layers in a page. Use Window, Layers to display it if it is not visible.

Layers appear in the list in the reverse order from which they were inserted, from the most recently inserted layers at the top to previously inserted layers at the bottom. Nested layers (layers contained within other layers) appear as a tree view descending from the parent layer. From the Layers panel, you can select layers, set their visibility, rename them, change their stacking order, nest them, and set the layer overlap setting.

LAYER VISIBILITY

The visibility of a layer can be changed by using the Layers panel. This is handy from a design standpoint because you can work on page layout with less clutter by hiding layers you don't need to see. The eye icon on the top left column of the panel indicates the current visible state for each layer. If the eye is open, the layer is visible; if closed, the layer is invisible; and if the eye icon does not appear, no visibility has been specified and the default value is applied as indicated in the Property inspector. You can toggle the initial visibility for the layer by clicking on the eye icon. Clicking the eye icon in the column header sets the visibility for all layers at once. You can also change layer visibility via behaviors, as discussed later in this chapter.

RENAMING LAYERS

Although Dreamweaver inserts unique IDs for layers it creates, you'll frequently want to rename the layers to make them easier to remember and indicate their purpose. This way, you can easily tell which layer is being targeted by a JavaScript operation or behavior.

To rename a layer from the Layers panel, double-click its name. The name then becomes editable, and you can simply type in a new name. You can also rename a layer from its Property inspector.

CHANGING THE STACKING ORDER

The stacking order for layers, otherwise known as the *z-order*, specifies which layer is seen on top when two layers overlap. Let's say you want to create content boxes that have a slight overlap. Layers with a higher z-index appear on top of layers with a lower number.

You can change the stacking order for layers in two ways:

- In the Layers panel, select the layer you want to change and drag it up or down the layer list to the desired position. A line is shown indicating the new layer position. Release the mouse button when the layer is in the correct position. Dreamweaver renumbers the values in the z-index column to reflect the new order.

- In the z column, click on the number for the layer you're changing. An edit box appears, and you can type a new number. Enter a higher number to move the layer up in the stacking order, or a lower number to move it down. Press (Return) [Enter], and the layer is then moved to the new position in the list.

NESTING LAYERS

Nested layers are layers contained within other layers. You can nest layers when creating them or by using the Layers panel. To nest a layer with the Layers panel, hold down the (Command) [Ctrl] key and drag a layer to the target layer. Careful here: Some browsers, especially certain versions of Netscape, do not properly display nested layers, so testing is in order!

LAYER OVERLAP

When individuals size their browsers, content layers often overlap. To prevent this from happening, you should indicate whether you want to allow layers to overlap. This is handled in two different ways:

- In the Layers panel, check the Prevent Overlaps box.
- Check the Modify, Arrange, Prevent Layer Overlaps menu item.

When the Prevent Layer Overlaps option is on, you cannot create a layer in front of another layer. If you move or resize a layer, it won't overlap other layers. Note, however, that when you activate this option, existing overlapping is not affected.

The Prevent Layer Overlaps option overrides the Snap to Grid option. If both are enabled and you move a layer, it doesn't snap to the grid if doing so would cause it to overlap another layer.

SETTING LAYER ATTRIBUTES

The Property inspector can be used to set attributes for layers after they're created. To view the Property inspector for a particular layer, select the layer in the Layers panel or click the layer border in the Document window (see Figure 9.12). Click the Property inspector expander button if you don't see all the options. The attributes available within the Layer Property inspector are listed in Table 9.2.

Figure 9.12
The Layer Property inspector lets you set layer options.

TABLE 9.2 LAYER PROPERTY INSPECTOR OPTIONS

Options	Purpose
Layer ID	Specifies the name of the layer to use for scripting and as identification in CSS. Every layer must have a unique name, and the name cannot contain any special characters (spaces, hyphens, or periods).
L and T	Specify the top-left coordinates relative to the top-left corner of the page or to the parent layer if nested. New values may be entered to change as well.
W and H	Specify the width and height of the layer box. These are the minimum sizes to use for the layer. If the layer's content exceeds the dimensions of the layer, the layer automatically expands to fit, depending on the Overflow setting.
Z-Index	Specifies a value to use for stacking layers. Layers with higher values for this option are shown in front of layers with lower values.
Vis	Specifies the initial visibility of the layer. This can be changed with behaviors, such as when creating a pop-out menu.
Bg Image	Specifies an image to use for the layer background. You can enter a filename directly into the text box or use the Browse button to locate it.

Table 9.2 Continued

Options	Purpose
Bg Color	Uses the color picker to select a background color for the layer.
Overflow	Specifies what happens if the content of a layer exceeds its dimensions. If Visible, the layer is resized to show all the content. If Hidden, any content exceeding the layer size is clipped. If Scroll, scrollbars are visible at all times in the layer, enabling the user to scroll through the layer's content. If Auto, scrollbars appear only when the content exceeds the layer dimensions.
Clip	Defines a layer's visible area. This can be used to cut content from the edge of a layer to focus on a specific area. The values represent the distance in pixels from the layer's boundaries, relative to the layer.

NOTE

Remember the rules of inheritance, discussed in Chapter 8, "Writing and Editing HTML, XHTML, and CSS." If the layer has a background color, that color is also applied to any content within the layer unless contradicted by another CSS rule.

To change the attributes of multiple layers simultaneously, press (Shift) [Ctrl] as you select the layers in the Layers panel or the Document window. The Property inspector changes to the Multiple Layers inspector. This inspector offers only a subset of the layer attributes— L and T, W and H, Vis, Tag, Bg Image, and Bg Color. These changes affect all the selected layers.

Designing with Layers

Among the many advantages of layers is that you can use them to create dynamic content. When JavaScript and behaviors are added to layers, they become incredibly powerful and enable interaction with your users.

→ For an introduction to JavaScript and working with behaviors in Dreamweaver, **see** Chapter 10, "Adding Interactivity and Multimedia," **page 219**.

Behaviors that can target layers include Change Property, Set Text of Layer, Show-Hide Layers, and Timelines. Layers can also be used in conjunction with other elements and behaviors to create advanced navigation systems.

Change Property

The Change Property action can be used to change the value of a layer's attributes (see Figure 9.13). You can use it to set the size, position, z-index, and other properties in recent browser versions.

Figure 9.13
The Change Property behavior is used to change the value of a layer's attributes.

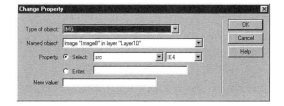

Other properties can be set as well:

- **Type of Object**—Select the kind of object you want to target. For layers, select one of the layer tags. This limits the name choices in the Named Object drop-down list.

- **Named Object**—This is a list of the objects in your document that match the type of object you choose.

- **Property**—You can select a target browser from the drop-down list on the right side, which provides a list of supported properties on the left. As an alternative, you can check Enter and enter the name of any property directly. This enables you to set properties you know about but that aren't listed as choices.

- **New Value**—Enter the value you want the property to have after the event is fired—for instance, a new color if you're changing a color property.

SET TEXT OF LAYER

The Set Text of Layer action enables you to completely replace a layer's content with new text that you supply. This text can be any valid HTML markup, and you can even embed JavaScript statements or function calls by enclosing them in braces, like this:

```
Today's date is {new Date()}.
```

SHOW-HIDE LAYERS

One of the most useful features of layers is their capability to be shown or hidden on demand. A page might have layers to make up pop-up menus, which become visible when the mouse is moved over the navbar buttons. The Show-Hide Layers behavior makes tying this process to a variety of events easy.

The Show-Hide Layers behavior lets you show, hide, or return to the default state any and all layers you choose with a single action.

TROUBLESHOOTING

USING THE GRID

I'm having trouble getting my layout to line up right. What tools in Dreamweaver will help?

Turning on the grid can provide a visual guide while you're working with layout tables. The grid also enables you to control snapping, which, when turned on, allows the elements on your page to snap to the grid's parameters rather than float randomly. To control the grid settings, select View, Grid, Grid Settings. When the Grid Settings dialog box appears, you can modify the display of the grid and the snap settings. If you want to turn on snapping, check the Snap to Grid check box. If you want to turn it off, make sure the check box is clear.

ADDING CONTENT

I'm having difficulties adding content to a layout table. What's the solution?

You can place content only in a layout cell, not a table. So, if you have no cells in the layout table, you need to create some for your content. Or you might be clicking outside the layout cell. Be sure that, if you have an existing layout cell, you are working within that cell. Cells will be white rather than gray.

USING FRAMES TO CONTAIN OTHER SITES

What if I want to keep part of my site available at all times while displaying content from an external site? Can I just link the external site into one of my own frames?

Can you? Technically speaking, yes. Legally speaking? Questionable. People have argued over this very issue, and the general sense is that if doing this isn't exactly illegal, it demonstrates a complete lack of etiquette, and may also confuse newcomers to the Web. There have been court cases in which framed content has been considered copyright infringement when incorporated into someone else's site, so it is recommended that you do not use this practice without explicit permission.

PRINTING FRAMES

How can I make my framed pages easily printable?

Provide a link to a printable format, a downloadable text file, an HTML or XHTML document, or even a Portable Document Format (PDF) file.

CONVERSION CONCERNS

I'm attempting to use the conversion feature to convert layers to tables, but my design isn't being preserved. Any suggestions?

If your layers overlap, are on a timeline, or are hidden, as in pop-out menus, the conversion process can't preserve your design. You'll still need to make considerable modifications to the converted file to make it acceptable for viewing.

ADDING INTERACTIVITY AND MULTIMEDIA

In this chapter

Oh, Behave: JavaScript and Behaviors   220

Rollovers and Nav Bars   223

Interactivity and Layers   227

Plug-Ins, Applets, and Controls   229

Audio and Video for the Web   235

Peer to Peer: Making Pages Containing Audio and Video Valid and Accessible   239

Ask any ten Web designers to name two things that can make the difference between a boring site and an interesting one, and you'll probably get ten different answers. But certainly interactivity and multimedia are likely to come up often.

Interactivity refers to the user's capability to perform some sort of operation with the mouse or keyboard that produces some sort of result from the browser. The most basic interaction is clicking a link to display new content, but Dreamweaver MX 2004 can go far beyond that—for example, with rollovers, navigation bars, movable layers, and many other effects, all made possible by pre-built JavaScript "behaviors."

Multimedia has come to mean virtually anything involving audio, video, animation, or some combination thereof. Although the results of successful multimedia integration can be brilliant, developing multimedia Web sites in a multi-browser, multi-platform world, with its variety of playback software technologies and "plug-ins" and "applets," can be a major challenge. Bringing audio and video clips into Dreamweaver via Flash is therefore a popular approach.

We won't devote time to writing your own JavaScript code here, nor will we guide you in the nuances of digital video production. We will, however, introduce you to the nuts and bolts of how Dreamweaver implements interactivity and multimedia within its user interface.

OH, BEHAVE: JAVASCRIPT AND BEHAVIORS

Scripts give you the power to specify actions that should occur when certain events happen on the screen. For example, a simple script might change a graphic when the viewer passes her mouse pointer over it. Such scripts are most often JavaScript (or some version thereof) but can be Visual Basic Script (VBScript) or other languages. Scripting, along with HTML and CSS, comprises the combination of technologies we refer to as "Dynamic HTML" or DHTML.

UNDERSTANDING JAVASCRIPT

Dreamweaver can react to many types of browser events. Table 10.1 provides a sampling.

TABLE 10.1—A FEW COMMON EVENT HANDLERS

Event Handler	Event
onBlur	Element is deselected.
onClick	Element is clicked.
onKeyPress	Any keyboard key is clicked.
onLoad	An element loads (including the Web page).
onMouseOut	Mouse pointer passes out of an element.
onMouseOver	Mouse pointer passes over an element.

If you want to create your own JavaScript code, you can use the Script icon in the Insert panel's HTML tab. If you aren't a JavaScript programmer yourself, never fear: Dreamweaver can take much of the drudgery out of adding JavaScript functions to a Web page. The program offers two features for this purpose: *snippets*, which allow you to add and customize preprogrammed chunks of JavaScript, and *behaviors*, which allow you to quickly add common actions for a variety of common events.

Using JavaScript Snippets

Snippets are self-contained JavaScript code fragments and functions that perform common tasks, including everything from displaying interactive "tool tips" to opening a new pop-up window (see Figure 10.1). Macromedia has tested the snippets to ensure cross-browser compatibility, but you should do your own testing to be sure.

Figure 10.1
The code snippet panel. Each snippet has a brief description to the right of its name.

Using Behaviors

Dreamweaver also offers prebuilt JavaScript programs in the form of *behaviors*. You attach behaviors to HTML tags on the page that define particular elements. A user triggers a behavior by doing something that the browser registers as an *event*, such as mousing over an image. Whenever the specified event happens to that element—whether it is the entire Web page, a graphic, or a text link—the associated action is performed. In Dreamweaver-speak, then, a behavior is the combination of an *event* and its subsequent *action*.

Dreamweaver comes with several built-in actions to choose from, all of which have been tested to be as cross-browser and cross-platform compatible as possible. (Different browsers generate different events, and not all actions work in all browsers.) These include actions such as Call JavaScript, Control Shockwave or Flash, Drag Layer, Open Browser Window, Play Sound, and Show-Hide Layers. (See Table 10.A on this book's CD-ROM for a more thorough list.). In addition, you can build your own behaviors or download additional behaviors from the Internet.

THE BEHAVIORS PANEL

Behaviors are added to elements/objects on the page (or to the page itself) through the Behaviors panel (see Figure 10.2), which you can open by selecting Window, Behaviors. This panel lets you associate new behaviors with existing tags, edit existing behaviors, and (for tags that have multiple behaviors) change the sequence in which the behaviors execute.

Figure 10.2
In this figure, the Behaviors panel appears in the upper right of the workspace. The Add Action button is the "+" in the upper-left corner of the Behaviors panel.

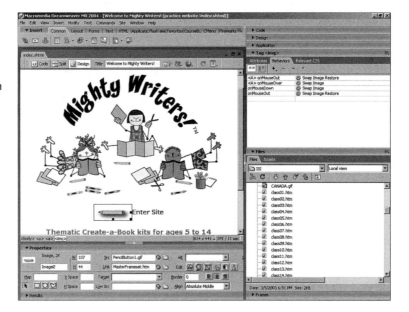

ATTACHING BEHAVIORS

You can attach behaviors to links, images, form elements, or any of several other HTML elements. You can also use the <body> tag in Code or Design view to attach them to the entire document.

When behaviors or events are grayed out, they are unavailable. Because some events are relevant to only some page elements, not all behaviors and events are available all the time.

The target browser selected determines which events are supported for a given element. For Example, Internet Explorer 4.0 has a greater selection of events for each element than Netscape Navigator 4.0 or any 3.0 browser. Generally, later browsers support all the events of earlier browsers.

To attach a behavior, select Window, Behaviors to open the Behaviors panel. Select an object on the page. Click the Plus (+) button on the tab and choose an action from the Actions pop-up menu. A dialog box appears, specific to the selected action. This box includes fields, allowing you to customize the parameters of the action, and instructions. Make changes and click OK. The action now appears in the right column of the Behaviors panel.

> **TIP**
>
> To attach a behavior to the entire page, while in Code view, click the `<body>` tag in the tag selector located at the bottom left of the Document window.

The default event to trigger the action appears in the Events column on the left of the Behaviors panel. If this is not the trigger event you want—and often it isn't—select another event from the Events drop-down menu. Click in the Events column on the event to be changed, then click the down arrow that appears, and select the desired event from the drop-down menu.

> **TIP**
>
> You can set Dreamweaver MX 2004 to show only events that work in particular browsers by selecting the Show Events For option at the bottom of the Actions pop-up menu and selecting a browser and version.

10

ROLLOVERS AND NAV BARS

One of the most common and powerful ways to achieve interesting navigation schemes is to use JavaScript *rollovers*. JavaScript rollovers allow you to swap a linked image on the fly. With image swapping, you can add visual cues to indicate which link the user is about to click and even add information about the link.

A more advanced form of the rollover is termed the *navigation bar*. Dreamweaver allows you to quickly assemble a collection of menu options with rollovers, which you can conveniently edit at any time.

Dreamweaver's built-in rollover capabilities can save you hours of coding time. However, Fireworks MX 2004 has even more sophisticated rollover capabilities. If you spend much time creating rollovers, learning Fireworks may be worth your while. Meanwhile, this section gives you a look at Dreamweaver's rollover and navigation bar features.

CREATING A ROLLOVER

The concept behind creating a rollover is simple: When the visitor places her mouse over a linked image, the browser replaces that image with another image. Then, when the visitor moves her mouse away from the image, the browser replaces the new image with the first image.

You can use behaviors to hand-script rollovers, but that can be time-consuming, tedious, and error-prone. One misplaced semicolon can take hours to track down in a really complex script. Macromedia Dreamweaver's controls make setting up and editing rollovers easy.

CREATING THE IMAGES

You need two graphics to create a rollover with Macromedia Dreamweaver: An *off* state image and an *on* state image. The off state is how the image appears when the page first loads and how it should appear after a rollover. The on state is how the image looks during the rollover. The on and off rollover images should be the same size to avoid distortion. You can use any program to create the images as long as they can be saved in a Web-ready format (GIF or JPEG are recommended).

One way to create consistent rollover graphics is to use the Layers features available in your favorite graphics editor. For example, in Adobe Photoshop, you can set up a layer for each rollover state but keep the same background image. This is crucial because it allows you to keep a consistent background for all the states, and ensures that all the images will be the same size when saved. No matter how you create these images, save them as separate graphic files with filenames that help you remember what they are and which state is which.

ADDING A ROLLOVER TO YOUR PAGE

After you have created your rollover graphics, add them to your Web page. To begin, open the Web page to which you want to add the rollover, and select Design view.

To insert the rollover, do one of the following:

- Place an insertion point in your document. In the Insert bar's Common tab, select the Image drop-down menu and click the Rollover Image option.
- Drag the aforementioned Rollover Image icon to the desired location in the Document window.
- Select Insert, Image Objects, Rollover Image.

In the Insert Rollover Image dialog box, type a new name for the rollover, even if you've already given names to the two individual images you plan to use. The rollover object will have its own name independent of those two.

Specify the location of the "original image" (used during off state) and the "rollover image" (which appears during on state). You'll also usually want to select the Preload Rollover Image box because it prevents the pausing that can occur while the rollover image is being loaded after the onMouseOver event.

Add the URL for the link in the When Clicked, Go to URL field. If this rollover is not a link, leave this field blank; Macromedia Dreamweaver automatically fills in the link with a pound sign (#) to indicate a null link.

If you need to make changes to the rollover—for example, if you want to change the link URL—select the image and make your changes in the Property inspector.

Designing Remote Rollovers

Although rollovers are most often used to change the image being rolled over, you can use a rollover of one link (image or text) to change any remote graphic on the screen as long as the image being changed has a unique ID. For example, you could roll over a text link to change the contents of a floating glossary layer. This is referred to as a *remote rollover* or a *disjoint rollover*. To create this sort of rollover, you need to use the Behaviors panel, as described earlier in this chapter, with the Swap Image and Swap Image Restore behaviors.

Creating Navigation Bars

Most Web sites include a menu to help visitors navigate the site, and such menus often use rollovers to help communicate what is going on. Simple rollovers are helpful but limited for this task, so Macromedia Dreamweaver includes a navigation bar to collect menu options into one element and provide four rollover states: *up, over, down,* and *over while down*.

Creating the Navigation Bar Graphics

First, create the menu images in a graphics program such as Photoshop or Fireworks. The obvious difference between the rollovers already discussed and the navigation bar rollovers is that you need to create four different states for each menu item in a navigation bar, versus just two states for a simple rollover.

- **Up**—The "off" state for the link. This should let the visitor know that it can be clicked but should not overwhelm other elements on the screen. For example, use light text here.

- **Over**—The "on" state for the link. This should convey that the link is ready to be clicked. You can communicate this through color changes, shifting size, shifting position, and so on. The idea is for an obvious change to occur between the up and over states. For example, text could become black with a drop shadow.

- **Down**—The currently selected menu option. This should be clearly contrasted from the up state; for example, black text.

- **Over While Down**—The "on" state for an element currently in the down state. Because the element is already down, indicating that it is selected, you need to either communicate to the visitor that this link is already active or simply leave it looking the same as the down mode. Red text could be used here.

Adding the Navigation Bar

Unlike a simple rollover, every menu option requires between two and four images. After you've made them, adding the bar to Dreamweaver is straightforward:

1. Open the Web page on which you want your navigation bar, place your cursor where you want the bar, and from the Insert bar's Common tab, click the Navigation Bar option from the Image drop-down menu to open the Insert Navigation Bar dialog box (see Figure 10.3).

Figure 10.3
The Navigation Bar button opens the Insert Navigation Bar dialog box.

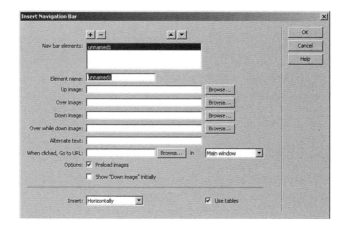

10

NOTE

You can also use Insert, Image Objects, Navigation Bar to insert a navigation bar.

2. When the Insert Navigation Bar dialog box opens, it automatically creates a blank default button, called unnamed1. Type a new and unique name for the first navigation element (button), replacing the default value.

3. Specify the images to be used for the four states by typing the path to the image or by using the Browse button.

4. Enter the URL to which the button should link and specify where the link should target. If you are working with a frames document, the frames appear in the targeting list.

5. Select whether you want the graphics for this element to be preloaded. This is generally recommended for responsiveness.

6. Select whether this element should initially be in the down state.

7. Add as many navigation bar elements as desired by clicking the plus sign and following steps 2–6 for each.

8. Select whether you want the navigation bar to run horizontally or vertically and whether you want to use tables to create the layout.

After you have added all the navigation bar elements, click OK; the new navigation bar appears on your Web page.

EDITING THE NAVIGATION BAR

You can use only one navigation bar per Web page with Dreamweaver, but you *can* change and add to the navigation bar as much as you want. You can edit the navigation bar in four ways: via the Navigation Bar button, via the Property inspector, in Code view (editing the JavaScript directly), and with the Behaviors panel.

In the Behaviors panel, each element in the navigation bar has four events associated with it: `onMouseOver`, `onMouseOut`, `onClick`, and `onLoad`. Each of these events has a `Set Nav Bar` action associated with it. You can edit the Set Nav Bar action for each of these separately by double-clicking the behavior to open the Set Nav Bar Image dialog box.

INTERACTIVITY AND LAYERS

It's one thing to create a layer and add content to it, but a layer really comes to life when you add behaviors to it. A few special behaviors are used exclusively with layers: Showing, Hiding, and Dragging.

SHOWING AND HIDING DRAW LAYERS

Unlike images, layers cannot simply have their sources changed to change their appearance. Instead, they must have their visibility changed to make them either hidden or visible. You can turn on one layer while turning off another layer.

10

To add the Show-Hide behavior to control a layer's visibility, do the following:

1. Select an image or a link on the Web page (either in or out of a layer), and in the Behaviors panel, select the Show-Hide Layers behavior from the Add Behavior drop-down.

2. In the Show-Hide Layers dialog box that appears, select the layer you want to influence, then choose whether you want to make that layer show, hide, or use the default display.

3. Click OK. The behavior is now associated with the image or link you selected in step 1.

Text links default to using the `onClick` event, whereas images default to using the `onLoad` event (depending on the browser version for which you've chosen to display behaviors). You may well wish to choose a different event. When the event is triggered, the browser either hides or shows the layer.

DRAGGING A LAYER

You can set layers so that your site visitors can reposition them, giving those visitors a great deal of customization power. (You've no doubt seen such applications on portal pages, where you can move information boxes around the page to suit your tastes.) A visitor simply clicks the layer and drags to freely reposition it on the Web page.

The Drag Layer behavior is either on or not, so it is best associated with the `onLoad` event handler for the Web page or an element in the layer being moved. To add repositioning capability for a layer, follow these steps:

1. Select an image or a link on the Web page, either in or out of a layer. In the Behaviors panel, select the Drag Layer behavior from the Add Behavior drop-down, which opens the Drag Layer dialog box.

2. In the dialog box are two tabs, Basic and Advanced. In the Basic tab, select the layer you want to make draggable (see Figure 10.4).

Figure 10.4
These are Basic options for a dragged layer. The motion has been constrained so that the object moves only left and right.

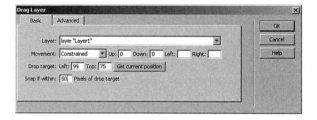

3. Choose whether the motion should be unconstrained or constrained (if constrained, set the maximum amount the layer can move up, down, left, or right from its current position).

4. Enter the target zone for dropping the layer and whether the layer should snap into that zone if it's within a certain number of pixels.

5. In the Advanced tab, select which part of the element can be clicked to be dragged (either the object generating the event or the entire layer).

6. Select whether the layer should be brought to the front as the user drags it and dropped to the back after she releases it.

7. Specify any JavaScript that you want to loop during the drag operation, such as a position monitoring routine.

8. Specify any JavaScript that you want to run when the layer is dropped.

9. Click OK.

The behavior is now associated with the image or link you selected in step 1. Text links default to using the onClick event, whereas images default to using the onLoad event. The layer can now be moved about the screen.

TIMELINE, R.I.P.

DHTML provides for the animation of layers. DHTML animation moves a layer slightly (maybe only by a few pixels) and then moves it again and again. If done quickly enough, say every few tenths of a second or so, this creates the illusion that the Draw Layer is moving.

DHTML animation is processor intensive, meaning that the visitor's computer controls how smooth the animation is. However, DHTML animations are faster to download than GIF animations because only one graphic or HTML text is used. In addition, DHTML animations are easier to change.

Dreamweaver used to feature a special Timeline available for designers wishing to use DHTML layer animation. It was complex, nonintuitive, and produced inefficient code; but some designers built entire Web sites around it, and it could do things that are difficult to accomplish any other way—for example, animating nonlinear motions, and using keyframing to trigger behaviors.

In Dreamweaver MX 2004, Macromedia has dropped the Timelines panel, probably at least in part because many designers nowadays use Flash when they want to move objects around on the page. However, if you still want or need to do DHTML-style layer animation, check out the free "Layer Animagic" extension by Project Seven. It's available on the Macromedia Exchange Web site, and at www.projectseven.com.

PLUG-INS, APPLETS, AND CONTROLS

Although client-side scripting is a versatile way of extending Web pages beyond the capabilities of standard HTML/XHTML, browser plug-ins, Java applets, and ActiveX controls take client-side functionality a step further, enabling you to add multimedia and dynamic interaction features to your site.

PLUG-INS

Plug-ins are small programs that extend the capabilities of the browser. Plug-ins work only on the platform for which they are designed. This means users must download a plug-in specific to their platforms (Windows, Mac, Unix, and others) to view the specialty content that the plug-in facilitates.

When you use a plug-in on a Web page, you are not actually embedding the plug-in itself into the document. Instead, you're inserting a reference to a content file with a specific Multipurpose Internet Mail Extension (MIME) type. The browser then uses the MIME type to determine which plug-in to use.

Unfortunately, this means that only one plug-in can be installed to play back a particular MIME type. For example, the multimedia player wars between Apple, Microsoft, and Real Networks, among others, have all produced plug-ins that can play back many of the same file formats, so you can never know for sure which player a particular user has installed.

Also, browser technology changes from version to version. For example, with Netscape 6, the plug-in API (Application Program Interface) changed to such an extent that many Netscape 4.x plug-ins no longer work.

CHECKING FOR PLUG-INS

An easy, albeit imperfect, way to detect plug-ins is with the use of a Dreamweaver behavior. The Check Browser behavior can be attached to a link or a body tag to provide an alternative page to use if the plug-in can't be supported. Table 10.2 presents some common plug-ins.

10

TABLE 10.2—COMMON PLUG-INS

Name	Use	URL
Apple QuickTime	The Apple QuickTime plug-in plays a variety of multimedia content formats, including QuickTime audio, video, and VR panoramas.	`http://www.apple.com/quicktime/download/`
Adobe Acrobat Reader	Adobe Acrobat is a popular format for ransmitting documents over the Web.	`http://www.adobe.com/products/acrobat/readstep2.html`
Macromedia Flash and Shockwave	The most popular format for creating vector and image-based animations on the Web.	`http://www.macromedia.com/software/flashplayer/`
Macromedia Shockwave	An advanced multimedia format used for graphics, audio and video, and even games.	`http://www.macromedia.com/software/shockwaveplayer/`
RealOne Player	The latest version of Real Network's player plug-in for many multimedia formats, including Real Audio, Real Video, and MP3.	`http://www.real.com`
Windows Media Player	Plays popular audio and video formats, including MP3, AVI, Windows Media Audio (WMA), and Active Streaming Format (ASF) .	`http://www.microsoft.com/Windows/windowsmedia/download/plugin.asp`

EMBEDDING A PLUG-IN

To embed plug-in content into a page, do one of the following:

- Place the cursor where you want the plug-in content to be inserted in the document. From the Common tab of the Insert bar, click the Media button and choose Plugin from the drop-down menu.

- Drag the Plugin icon from the menu to the location on the page where you want to embed the content.

- Place the cursor where you want to insert the control, and select Insert, Media, Plugin from the menu.

SETTING PLUG-IN PROPERTIES

Click the plug-in's placeholder in Design view to open the Plugin Property inspector (see Figure 10.5).

Figure 10.5
The Plugin Property inspector sets properties for the *<embed>* tag and allows you to preview the plug-in in Design view.

A few plug-in options are worthy of note:

- **Plugin Name**—Identifies the tag for scripting.
- **Src**—Specifies the data file to play with the plug-in.
- **Plg Url**—Specifies the URL of the site where the user can download the plug-in. If an appropriate plug-in to play the data file is not installed, the browser attempts to download it from this location.
- **Align**—Sets how the plug-in or applet should be aligned on the page. The various alignment options are the same as those for images and other elements and are covered in those chapters specific to those elements.

SETTING PLUG-IN PARAMETERS

The Parameters button on the Plugin Property inspector activates the Parameters dialog box, where you can enter any custom parameters that the control might need. These parameters are specified by the documentation or sample HTML code that comes with the plug-in developer's documentation.

FOCUS ON FLASH

Given its importance in the context of Studio MX 2004, we should address a few comments to the Flash plug-in. After you have a Flash movie source file, `.swf`, you can add it to a Web page using Dreamweaver in one of three ways:

- Open the Media drop-down menu on the Insert bar's Common tab, and click the Flash option.
- Drag the Flash icon from the menu to the point in the document where you want the Flash movie to appear.
- Select Insert, Media, Flash.

Whichever method you select causes the Select File dialog box to appear. Search your hard drive for the correct file, and click OK. The Flash placeholder appears. Dreamweaver inserts both the `object` and `embed` tags for Flash to work properly in multiple browser types.

After the movie has been added, you can make adjustments to its attributes by selecting the Flash placeholder and changing any of the properties in the Property inspector.

You can preview your work in the Document window by selecting the Flash placeholder, and using the Play and Stop buttons in the Property inspector. Of course, you can and should also preview the page in the target browser(s).

TIP

> Now that Flash can handle a variety of media types, including sound and video, many Web designers are opting to place their media files into Flash movies, and then embed those Flash movies into Dreamweaver pages. This can make life a lot simpler in that you don't have to worry about guessing which playback software any given user might have, pointing users to the proper download sites for plug-ins, and testing under a wide variety of possible scenarios. Check out the Flash MX 2004 chapters in this book for details on importing sound and video into Flash.

You can use behaviors to have the visitor's browser control a Flash movie when the user clicks a graphic, null text link, or other HTML object. Use the Control Shockwave or Flash behavior for this purpose.

FOCUS ON SHOCKWAVE

The Director interface is more complex than Flash. Nevertheless, some features make Director Shockwave appealing in certain cases for Web designers, including

- **Total control of presentation**—Flash has to limit the types of media and images it can use to properly compress for Web delivery. Shockwave enables you to create, import, and export a wide range of formats.

- **3D design**—Shockwave enables you not only to create 3D designs, but also to do so in a real-time rendering environment.

- **Greater interactivity**—With the Shockwave Multiuser server, you can create sophisticated, real-time, Web-based games and chat rooms.

NOTE

> Want to explore Shockwave applications? Check out Shockwave.com, http://www.shockwave.com, for a firsthand look at Shockwave features for the Web.

As with Flash, if you have a Shockwave movie and want to add it to your page, place your cursor where you want the content to appear, and choose Insert, Media, Shockwave. (You can also do this via the Media icon on the Common tab of the Insert bar.) Find the file (it will have a .dcr extension) and click OK.

ACTIVEX CONTROLS

ActiveX controls were developed by Microsoft and perform many of the same functions as plug-ins, but they are limited to Internet Explorer 3.0 or higher on the Windows platform. Netscape cannot run ActiveX controls without the aid of a third-party add-on.

Often, an ActiveX control provides more flexibility than its plug-in counterpart. Also, you can write your page in such a way that the ActiveX control is used on the Windows platform and the Netscape plug-in is used on others transparently, thereby providing the best possible experience to your site visitors no matter which browser they are using.

> **NOTE**
>
> To find recent ActiveX controls, check out C:Net's Download.Com section for components, at `http://download.com.com/2001-2206-0.html`.

Adding an ActiveX Control

To add an ActiveX control to a page, do one of the following:

- Place the cursor where you want the control to be inserted in the document. Open the Common tab of the Insert bar, click the Media button, and click ActiveX in the drop-down menu.
- Drag the ActiveX icon from the Insert bar's Media menu to the location on the page where you want to embed the control.
- Place the cursor where you want to insert the control, and select Insert, Media, ActiveX from the menu.

> **NOTE**
>
> The `object` element is used to add ActiveX controls to a page. The `object` element is current and active in all versions of HTML and XHTML.

Setting ActiveX Control Properties

Click the ActiveX control's placeholder in Design view to open the ActiveX Property inspector.

Table 10.3 describes a few Dreamweaver options of note regarding ActiveX controls.

TABLE 10.3   ACTIVEX CONTROLS

Option	Description of Action
ActiveX Name	The name attribute sets the name of the control, mainly for use in scripting.
ClassID	The `ClassID` property is unique to ActiveX controls. It specifies a 32-character unique identifier that is specific to the control. The Class ID to use is provided with the documentation accompanying the control, or is shown in sample HTML code that uses the control.

10

TABLE 10.3   CONTINUED

Option	Description of Action
Embed	The embed element is used to specify an alternative Netscape-style plug-in to use for browsers that don't support ActiveX.
Base	The Base property sets the codebase attribute for the object. This gives the browser a URL from which an ActiveX control can be downloaded if it isn't already installed on the user's system.
ID	The ID attribute sets a unique identifier for the object.
Data	Data is used to specify the data file the control should open. This is typically used for ActiveX controls that play a media file.

SETTING ACTIVEX CONTROL PARAMETERS

The Parameters button on the ActiveX Property inspector activates the Parameters dialog box, which lets you enter any custom parameters the control might need. If a control that you download requires any special parameters, it should come with documentation that explains them.

Unlike plug-in parameters, which use attributes, param tags are used to add ActiveX control parameters. To enter a parameter, click the Plus (+) button. Enter the name of the parameter in the Parameter column and a value in the Value column. You also can remove parameters by using the minus (–) button or rearrange them by clicking one and using the arrow buttons to move it up or down in the order.

USING ACTIVEX CONTROLS AND PLUG-INS AT THE SAME TIME

The Embed option of the ActiveX Property inspector is used to insert a plug-in into the control's object tag code. This enables Netscape and other browsers that ignore the object tag to see just the plug-in; Internet Explorer knows to ignore any plug-ins inside the object tag. This gives you a simple way to support both plug-ins and ActiveX controls without having to use a client (or server-side) script or a custom page for each browser.

JAVA APPLETS

Java applets, like plug-ins, enable you to extend the capabilities of a page beyond what can be accomplished with DHTML and client-side scripting. Java's "write once–run anywhere" philosophy and relatively small code size made it a natural fit for browser-embedded applications that could conceivably run on any hardware and operating system platform. Java applications designed to be run on the client use a subset of the Java language and are known as *applets*.

Java applets consist of class files that can be downloaded individually or in an archive (known as a Java Archive, or JAR, file). These class files consist of compiled Java code that is interpreted and run by a virtual machine. The virtual machine is the only component that must be written specifically for a particular host platform. After the user has it installed, along with the base Java classes, any Java applet should run.

EMBEDDING JAVA APPLETS

Dreamweaver's extensive support for plug-ins extends to Java applets as well. You insert Java applets just like plug-ins and ActiveX controls, but using the Applet selection instead of the Plug-in or ActiveX selection. It's the button that looks like a cup of coffee—naturally! An `applet` tag (which again looks like a cup of coffee in Design view) is inserted in your document.

SETTING APPLET PROPERTIES

The following options in the applet Property inspector are worth noting:

- **Applet Name**—This unique name can be used for controlling some applets via scripting.
- **W**—Width, in pixels or percent, specifies how much space you want the applet to occupy.
- **H**—Height specifies the applet height in pixels or percent.
- **Code**—The Code attribute specifies the filename of the file containing the applet's Java code.
- **Base**—The Base property specifies the path to the folder containing the applet. This path is relative to the site root, so it can remain blank if the Java applet file is located in the same folder as the document.
- **Alt**—The Alt property can be used to specify alternative content to display in the event that the client browser doesn't support Java applets or has disabled them.

SETTING APPLET PARAMETERS

The Parameters button on the Applet Property inspector activates the Parameters dialog box, which lets you enter any custom parameters that the applet you are embedding might have. If a Java applet that you download requires any special parameters, it should come with documentation that explains them. The Java parameters dialog box adds param tags to the applet in the same way that it does for ActiveX controls.

AUDIO AND VIDEO FOR THE WEB

With the growing access worldwide to broadband, the use of audio and video on Web sites has become more realistic. Technological advances in compression and streaming (the capability to send the audio or video data in a constant stream from the server to the client) have also increased the desirability of audio and video, where appropriate, on Web sites. You should still be careful, however, in using audio and video where bandwidth and user control is limited.

As much fun as it is, we can't get into the details of audio and video production in this book. If you're recording your own sound samples, you need a good microphone (or two), amplification (such as the Midiman Audio Buddy), capture hardware, and sound editing software (Audition from Adobe Systems is a great do-it-all package, and so is Sound Forge from Sony Pictures Digital, if you add the Noise Reduction plug-in.) For video, you need a high-quality capture device, a zippy computer, gobs of disk space, and encoding and editing software (such as Adobe Premiere). Today's hardware and software tools make A/V production more affordable than ever, but the software typically has long and steep learning curves. Hollywood makes it all look easy, but it isn't, so budget some time to educate yourself.

To play audio and video files, you and your site visitors must have plug-in software. Some of the primary plug-ins you may want to have (and encourage your site visitors to get) include Apple QuickTime, Microsoft Media Player, Real's RealOne Player, and the Beatnik Player. However, if you import your audio and video clips into Flash, it could be that the Flash player is the only one you and your visitors will need.

The importance of choosing appropriate file formats is hard to overemphasize. For audio, MP3 (Motion Picture Experts Group Audio Layer-3) files have very good quality, small size, can stream, and are extremely popular. AIFF (Audio Interchange File Format) features good quality and compatibility, but with larger file sizes. MIDI (Musical Instrument Digital Interface) files can have very good quality and offer very low file sizes, but they're for instrumental music only. RealAudio files offer small size and streaming. Rich Music Format (RMF) provides good quality and compression, and requires the Beatnik plug-in. WAV (Waveform Extension) files offer good quality and compatibility but large file sizes.

For video, MPEG and QuickTime tend to be popular choices. Many platforms support MPEG, and it provides a strong combination of high quality and high compression ratios. QuickTime tools and plug-ins are popular, especially on the Macintosh, but PCs can also play QuickTime movies, which offer a variety of quality and compression settings and have the file suffix .mov. AVI tends to be Microsoft-centric, and although it runs inline in the IE browser, support varies with other browsers. WMF (Windows Media Format) is another popular PC video format but it isn't cross-platform.

USING DREAMWEAVER TO ADD SOUND FILES TO A PAGE

Now, back to Dreamweaver. After you have your sound files, you can choose either to *link* to them so a user can download the file, or *embed* them so they will play in the browser or launch the required plug-in and play upon receipt of the file. Linking and embedding are described in the following sections, but you should also be aware of two other options.

First, you can attach sounds to HTML objects with the Play Sound JavaScript behavior. We covered behaviors earlier in this chapter, so take a look at that section if you skipped it. Second, you can choose to load the sound into a Flash movie, then embed the Flash object into your page. The latter is especially convenient, given that you don't have to worry about special sound plug-ins or variations in playback software at the client. As long as the visitor has the Flash player, she'll hear the sound as you intend it to be heard. We take a look at embedding Flash objects earlier in this chapter.

LINKING TO A SOUND FILE

Linking gives your site visitor the option to save the sound file to the local hard drive for playback at a later time, or play it right away. Linking is a good option when you are unsure of your audience's preferences and capabilities. However, you don't have as much control over the sound's behavior as you do with embedding.

To link to a sound file, follow these steps:

1. Place the text (or image or other media) you want to link to the sound file.
2. In Design view, select the text or media by highlighting it.
3. In the Property inspector, click the folder icon (to the right of the Link field) and find the audio file. Click to select it.
4. Click OK. Your file is now linked.

Typically, when a site visitor activates a link of this type, the file begins to download and play in the associated player. Alternatively, visitors can save the file to their hard drives to play at a later time.

EMBEDDING SOUND

If you want your sound files to play inline and you want to have the most control over how and when the sounds play, you should embed them. A variety of attributes is available in Dreamweaver when you embed a sound file, including

- **Plugin**—Enter a value here for name and id, which is necessary if you want to add behaviors or scripting to the sound file and player.
- **W**—Width is best controlled by pixels, but you can use a percentage to describe how much space within the browser frame you want the plug-in player to occupy.
- **H**—The Height attribute determines the height of the embedded sound file's plug-in player.
- **Src**—Location of the file.
- **Plg URL**—You can set a URL that takes users who don't have the correct plug-in to a plug-ins page to download it.

To embed a sound file on a page, follow these steps:

1. Open the document to which you want to add the sound file in Design view.
2. Place your cursor in the location where you want to add the file. On the Common tab of the Insert bar, click the Media button. Then click the plug-in icon. Alternatively, you can select Insert, Media, Plugin from the main menu. (If you know your audience will be using only Internet Explorer on the Windows platform, you could choose Insert, Media, ActiveX and specify the Windows Media Player class ID in the ActiveX Property inspector.) The Select dialog box appears.

10

3. Find the file you want to embed, and select it. In Design view, you'll now see an icon that represents your file.

4. The media file is now embedded. To manage its attributes, either select the plug-in icon in Design view or click within the embedded sound file in Code view. The Property inspector activates.

Make any modifications you want using the Property inspector. For example, you'll typically want to tweak the width and height settings if you want the user to be able to see the sound's helper application. You may also want to set some parameters, such as *hidden* or *autoplay*. When you're finished, save your file and test it by clicking Play from within the Property inspector. Then preview it in your target browsers.

INSERTING VIDEO

Adding video to your page works just the same way that adding audio does—at least from the authoring perspective. You can link to a video file, or you can embed the file. As with sound, linking to video gives the user more options, whereas embedding video can make the experience of the page more cohesive and give the creator more control over how and when it plays.

Linking and embedding video follows precisely the same steps as embedding sound, discussed earlier, with the difference that you'll select a video file rather than a sound file.

Additional Attributes for Embedding Audio and Video
Additional attributes are available for embedding audio and video. They include

- `autoplay="true/false"`—Answer with `true`, and your movie starts when the page is first accessed. Answer with `false`, and the user must click the Play button on the console for the movie to play.

- `controller="true/false"`—This adds user controls to the movie. If you set this to `true`, you must find out how many pixels your controller needs for the display and then add that amount to the height of your movie.

- `loop="true/false/palindrome"`—If you want the movie to play repeatedly, set this to `true`. If you want to play it once and stop, set it to `false`. `palindrome` plays from beginning to end and backwards in a continuous loop.

To add these attributes, bring up the Tag Inspector (select Window, Tag Inspector). Find the `embed` tag (for example, on the Status bar) and highlight it. All the attributes that you are currently using and that you might like to use are found there. Click in the value section found next to the attribute name and fill in the value of these attributes manually. Dreamweaver automatically updates them to the code.

Be aware that different playback applications support different parameters. For example, Windows Media Player supports parameters such as `showcontrols`, `showpositioncontrols`, `clicktoplay`, `showtracker`, and many others. Other multimedia players have their own sets of parameters; you'll have to research them, for example, by consulting the vendor's Web site.

TROUBLESHOOTING

PRELOADING IMAGES

I've heard that preloading images is a recommended practice. Why is this so?

Speed. Preloading means that the browser caches these images, so when you move from page to page, they aren't downloaded again. This speeds up the entire navigation process, yet provides your site visitors with a pleasant visual experience.

LEARNING MORE ABOUT WEB AUDIO AND VIDEO

I'm having a difficult time getting more details about using Web audio and video. Where can I go for more information?

A lot of online resources are available. Be sure to stop by the comprehensive About.Com section on home recording at `http://homerecording.about.com`. It's filled with excellent tutorials and references.

CONTROLLING MUSIC ON YOUR PAGE

I would like my music to load immediately with the page or be attached to another event after the page has loaded. Can I do this, and if so, how?

You can do so by tapping into the power of Dreamweaver behaviors. But, you can do so only in IE browsers. Netscape and Mozilla do not support this particular behavior.

To add a sound for immediate loading, do the following:

1. Open the Tag inspector and click the Behaviors tab.
2. Click the Plus sign and select Play Sound from the drop-down menu.
3. The Play Sound dialog box appears. Use the folder icon to browse your computer for the sound file. Highlight it and then click OK.
4. The sound file will be embedded into the document, along with some JavaScript.

The default event is `onLoad`, but you can change this by selecting the `sound` object and then highlighting `onLoad` in the Behaviors panel. A drop-down menu appears, and you can then select from one of the many event options.

PEER TO PEER: MAKING PAGES CONTAINING AUDIO AND VIDEO VALID AND ACCESSIBLE

Using the `embed` tag is actually forbidden in HTML and XHTML. Instead, the `object` tag is supposed to be used, but support for this element is limited to newer browsers, especially Internet Explorer.

So, how do you make a document that uses the embed element valid? Unless you're willing to write your own Document Type Definition in Modular XHTML (which is beyond the scope of this book), you can't. So, either insert all audio using the object tag or make the choice to have an invalid document.

The other concern with audio and video is accessibility. People who are blind, visually impaired, deaf, or hearing impaired will miss out on aspects of audio and video content. (See http://www.section508.gov for some details on making sites accessible.) The "best practice" here is to ensure that you *do not rely* on audio and video to express your main point. Also, add descriptive text near the audio or video that provides context and adds detailed information about what you are displaying or playing for your visitors, no matter their physical abilities.

10

CHAPTER **11**

MANAGING YOUR SITE

In this chapter

Site Management Concepts   242

Compatibility and Accessibility Testing   242

Uploading Pages   248

Collaborating   252

Site Reports and Link Maintenance   256

Peer to Peer: Using Macromedia Extensions and Products for Accessibility Testing   262

Peer to Peer: Tracking Usage Statistics   262

SITE MANAGEMENT CONCEPTS

Chapter 6, "Setting Up Sites, Pages, and Templates," discussed the key issues surrounding the design of a Dreamweaver MX 2004 site. Here, we talk about how you can use Dreamweaver to help manage your site after you've designed it.

The old adage that "nothing manages itself" is particularly true of Web sites, which require ongoing care and feeding as you update and enhance them. Another, more academic epithet we remember from engineering school is that "everything tends towards chaos," and that has a certain relevance to Web sites, too! Thankfully, Dreamweaver offers some helpful tools to help you keep your sites from devolving into the horror of randomness and confusion.

The key topics include compatibility testing, uploading files to a remote server, collaborating with other developers, running site reports, and maintaining the integrity of your site's links.

COMPATIBILITY AND ACCESSIBILITY TESTING

This section looks at the why, when, and how of validating your site documents for adherence to published standards, for compatibility with various target browsers, and for accessibility by visitors with one or more disabilities.

WHAT ARE WEB STANDARDS, REALLY?

We use the term *Web standard* to refer to what is actually a series of specifications and recommendations created by the World Wide Web Consortium (W3C). The W3C is not an authoritative standards body per se; its primary functions are to research, develop, and publish information on technologies and activities related to the Web.

THE BOTTOM LINE: TIME AND MONEY

Standards definitely can save time. Compliance probably saves money for everyone in the Web site development chain--from site owner to developer to ISP. Longer term, working with standards provides other benefits:

- **Technical advantages**--Technically, Web sites will be more easily maintained and also readily available for many platforms beyond the Web.
- **Creative advantages**--Creatively, you can apply style sheets that easily make a site look good on a computer screen, on a PDA screen, and even in print.
- **Social advantages**--Socially, we remove barriers to access by cleaning up our hacked markup and paying attention to accessibility concerns.

WHEN TO SWITCH?

Good times to look at introducing XHTML, layout with CSS, and validation of documents include

- **During a Web site redesign**--Much of the work being done by Web design firms and Web designers individually is redesigning of sites. This is an excellent time to introduce best practices and standards.

- **Upon creation of a new Web site**--Following the guidelines in this book will help ease you into Web standards.

NOTE

> The World Organization of Webmasters (WOW) provides certification, community, and educational resources for all Web professionals. This nonprofit organization works to provide you with the resources you'll need throughout your career. For more information, see www.joinwow.org.

VALIDATING DOCUMENTS

One of the first ways you can begin learning about Web standards is to validate your HTML or XHTML documents.

USING DREAMWEAVER MX VALIDATION TOOLS

Dreamweaver MX 2004 comes complete with several built-in validators. The validators provide helpful warnings (suggestions to consider) and errors (things you really should fix) to assist you in ensuring your documents pass muster.

 Trying to validate but having problems? Find out why in "Validator Trouble" in the "Troubleshooting" section at the end of this chapter.

Before you begin validating documents, you may want to go to Edit, Preferences, Validator. This lets you tell Dreamweaver what form(s) of validation you want to perform in the event that the document does not include a valid DOCTYPE declaration. Also, click the Options button to tell Dreamweaver what you'd like to see in the reports: errors, warnings, custom messages, and so on.

After that chore is done, open the document in Dreamweaver. Follow these steps to continue the validation process:

1. Select File, Check Page, Validate Markup. (If you are validating an XHTML document, select Validate as XML instead.) Dreamweaver runs its validator.

2. The Results panel, if not already open, opens and displays any warnings or errors (see Figure 11.1). Using the buttons on the left, click More Info to see the full description, Browse Report to see the report in HTML format, or Save Report to save it.

Figure 11.1
The Results panel's Validation tab alerts you to errors and warnings after a compatibility check.

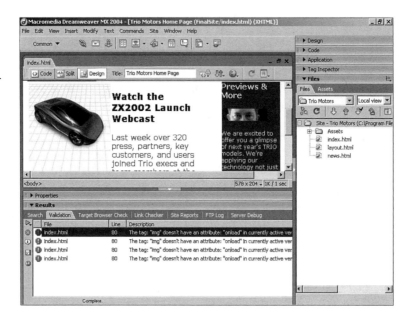

3. Examine the errors and make changes as you see fit.

4. Run the report against your entire site by clicking the green Validate button and choosing Validate Entire Site. Alternatively, select some files in the Files panel, click the green Validate button, and choose Validate Selected Files in Site.

Validation provides you with the following information:

- **File**--The name of the file being validated.

- **Line**--Helps you find the exact line where the associated problem to which the error or warning is referring resides. Double-click on any error or warning to go directly to the line in Code view where the problem is.

- **Description**--Provides a description of the problem and ideas on how to fix it.

If your document passes with no errors, you can assume you have a valid document.

CROSS-BROWSER COMPATIBILITY

You can use Dreamweaver to test for browser compatibility--whether the specific browser is installed on your system or not. Happily, Dreamweaver now also tests for CSS compatibility at the same time. The quick method is to click the new Browser Check icon on the Document toolbar, then examine the Results panel's Target Browser Check tab.

➔To learn more about dynamic cross-browser validation, and how to set this feature for specific browsers, **see** Chapter 7, "Working Efficiently in Dreamweaver," **page 135**.

It's also recommended that you have at least two testing computer platforms: Windows and Macintosh. Macintosh versions of Web browsers differ in their capabilities from Windows versions.

VALIDATING FOR ACCESSIBILITY

As it does with markup, Dreamweaver MX provides a means to test and report accessibility problems. Several other public validators are available, as well.

Before you attempt to validate for accessibility, you should examine your documents to see whether they adhere to the Web Accessibility Initiative (WAI) priority guidelines. The WAI of the W3C has an official document involving 14 guidelines for Web developers. The guidelines are as follows:

- **Provide equivalent alternatives to auditory and visual content**--If you're using sound or graphics, include text descriptions and employ HTML-based aids, such as the `alt` attribute in images, wherever possible.

- **Don't rely on color alone**--Because many people cannot see color, have problems with color blindness, or are accessing the Web via noncolor devices, relying solely on color to convey information is problematic. Make sure that foreground and background colors have high contrast.

- **Use markup and style sheets, and do so properly**--This guideline is an important one! It encourages the creation of well-formed documents in accordance with recommendations. The more separation you can get between presentation and document structure, the more accessible your pages will automatically become.

→For more information on markup, **see** Chapter 8, "Writing and Editing HTML, XHTML, and CSS," **page 161**.

- **Clarify natural language usage**--Any foreign pronunciations, acronyms, or abbreviations should be spelled out or accommodated through the use of the `title` attribute in related elements.

- **Create tables that transform gracefully**--Ideally, you're using tables now only for tabular data. Tables present specific problems, such as screen reader software reading across table cells, which can be very confusing.

→To work effectively with tables, **see** Chapter 9, "Professional Page Design," **page 191**.

- **Ensure that pages featuring new technologies transform gracefully**--All pages should be accessible no matter which technologies are being employed.

- **Ensure user control of time-sensitive content changes**--Many users with disabilities are adversely affected by things that move and blink. Other people have mobility impairments and cannot keep up with any kind of moving object. Anything that moves, blinks, or auto-updates should have controls that allow the user to stop, start, and pause the object to make the page more effective and usable.

- **Ensure direct accessibility of embedded user interfaces**--If you're placing an embedded object within your page, such as an applet or Flash design, be sure that users have access to the interface of that embedded object.

11

- **Design for device independence**--Individuals accessing the Web might be doing so through a number of devices, including keyboards, mice, voice commands, a head or mouth stick, and so on. General guidelines to manage this issue include using client-side imagemaps rather than server-side maps and providing tab order mechanisms in forms for easier navigation.

- **Use interim solutions**--Older browsers and assistive devices often do not operate properly, yet many are in abundance in various government organizations, including those that provide services to disabled communities. So, if I wrote a document with a consecutive list of links (very common in navigation schemes), my screen reader might read the link as one uninterrupted link and attempt to resolve it, to no avail. Another problem is the pop-up window, which these days is often used in advertising.

- **Use W3C technologies and guidelines**--The W3C provides recommendations for all browser and tools manufacturers as well as Web authors.

- **Provide context and orientation information**--The more complex a page or site, the more helpful it is to ensure that visitors know what they are doing at a given location and why.

- **Provide clear navigation mechanisms**--Clear and consistent navigation not only is an imperative in accessibility, but is also an imperative in user interface design. Links should be clearly identified and organized, and graphical options should have appropriate alternatives available.

- **Ensure that documents are clear and simple**--The easier your content is to understand, the more you'll get your point across, no matter who the audience is.

TESTING ACCESSIBILITY WITH MACROMEDIA DREAMWEAVER MX

Macromedia Dreamweaver MX provides several means of helping you to ensure that your documents are accessible. After you believe your document (or a section of a document) is ready to be tested, you can run an accessibility report.

RUNNING A DOCUMENT REPORT

To run an accessibility report on a document, follow these steps:

1. Open the document in Dreamweaver.
2. Select File, Check Page, Check Accessibility. The checker runs and provides a report in the Results panel, this time in the Site Reports tab.
3. Use the report to find and correct problems in the document.

NOTE

Context-sensitive explanations are at your fingertips. Right-click (control-click on the Mac) a report entry and choose More Info to open the Reference panel and see details about that specific accessibility problem.

As with the markup validation report, you will see the filename, line number where the error resides, and a description of the problem with a suggestion for fixing it (see Figure 11.2) .

Figure 11.2
Dreamweaver MX 2004 provides a detailed accessibility report in the Results panel.

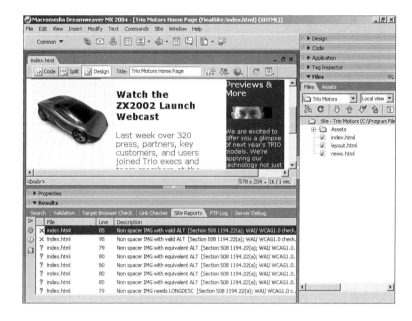

RUNNING A SITE REPORT

You can run accessibility reports for an entire site, too, although the procedure is different. Select Site, Reports to display the Reports dialog box, choose Entire Current Local Site in the drop-down list, then click Accessibility (see Figure 11.3).

Figure 11.3
Performing a site-wide accessibility report.

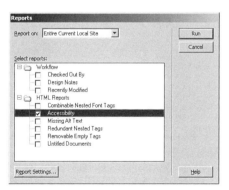

If you want to specify feature-specific settings, click the Report Settings button and enable or disable the features in which you're interested (see Figure 11.4). Finally, click the Run button to generate the report. It will appear in the Site Reports tab of the Results panel.

Figure 11.4
Setting detailed features for an accessibility report.

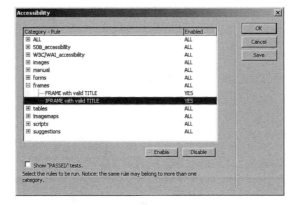

UPLOADING PAGES

After testing comes uploading. If you defined your remote server information when you defined the initial site, you're ready to go online. If you left the remote information blank, you'll need to edit your site definition to add this information. Follow these steps:

1. Select Site, Manage Sites from either the Document window or the Files panel.
2. Select the name of the site from the Manage Sites dialog box.
3. Click the Edit button to open the Site Definition dialog box.
4. Edit the Remote Info category, as described in Chapter 6, "Setting Up Sites, Pages, and Templates."

NOTE

If you've used external FTP utilities in the past, take another look at what Macromedia provides. For example, you can now specify *Secure FTP* (*SFTP*) in your site definition's Remote Info page. Secure FTP helps protect both authentication credentials and file content via encryption; you formerly had to use third-party software if your remote site required SFTP.

5. Click OK to close the Site Definition dialog box.
6. Click Done to close the Edit Sites dialog box.

NOTE

In the past, you had to set up a site to connect to a remote server. You can now perform "siteless" file editing by creating an entry in the Files panel for "FTP & RDS Server." Display the Desktop in the panel, then right-click (control-click on the Mac) FTP & RDS Servers, and choose New FTP Server. Fill out the Configure Server dialog box. Henceforth, the command File, Save to Remote Server lets you save files to that FTP server. Just remember that working siteless means you can't run site reports, link checking, and link replacement commands; you still need a full-fledged Dreamweaver site for that.

GOING ONLINE

At this point, most of your work will involve the Files panel. If you're still editing and tweaking pages, keep the panel docked to quickly move between views. Otherwise, use the Expand/Collapse button on the Files panel to open the site window (see Figure 11.5). The larger site view enables you to quickly move between the local and remote file lists and use drag-and-drop to upload and download files.

Figure 11.5
Unless you're still editing pages as you go, the expanded site window makes transferring files between the local and remote servers easier.

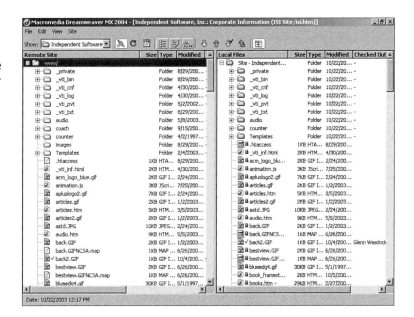

The site window is divided into two panes: the local file list and the remote server. The Remote Site pane remains empty until you connect to the remote server to update the file view. To connect to the remote server, click the Connects to Remote Host button on the site window toolbar (see Figure 11.6). When you connect to the remote server, the Remote Site pane is automatically updated with a current file list. Use the same button to disconnect from the server.

Figure 11.6
The site view toolbar contains the most important options of the upload/download process.

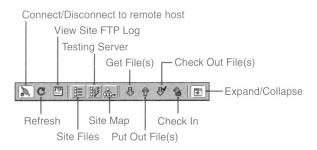

Toggling the Local/Remote Views

One key advantage of the site window is its display of both the local and remote file lists in the same window. After your site is live and you're doing more maintenance and updating than initial development, however, the Files panel might be more convenient. The upside of the Files panel is that it shares the screen real estate with the Document window, making it easy to edit files on the fly and then immediately upload them without changing views. The downside is that the Files panel can display only one file list at a time. To switch views, use the Files panel view drop-down menu.

PUTTING FILES (UPLOADING)

Until you upload files to the remote server, the Remote Site pane will be remarkably empty. Unless you're working in a development group, the commands you use to transfer files are Get (download from the remote server) and Put (upload to the remote server).

Initially, you'll most likely want to upload the entire site to the remote server. To do this, simply click the Put button on the site window/panel toolbar. Because this can be a lengthy process, Dreamweaver asks whether you want to proceed.

CAUTION

> You *must* select the site's root folder in the local pane to upload all the files and directories within the site. If you choose only one file or directory, just that element transfers.

To put individual files onto the remote server, follow these steps:

1. Highlight the file or files you want to transfer in the Local Files pane.

2. Click the Put File(s) button on the toolbar. (If the file hasn't been saved, Dreamweaver prompts you to save it.) The program asks whether you want to include any dependent files.

3. Click Yes or No. You can also choose to suppress this option from appearing in the future by selecting the Don't Show Me This Message Again check box. The transfer then begins.

TIP

> Use the (Shift) [Ctrl] key to select multiple files in the list.

NOTE

> If you're using the site window as suggested, you can also select the files in the Local Files pane and drag them to the Remote Site pane, which automatically initiates the Put command.

More About Dependent Files

Because Web pages are rarely self-contained in one file, it's important to upload the images, multimedia, and CSS style sheet files to the remote server as well. Dreamweaver helps in this area by asking whether you want to upload dependent files when putting a document on the remote server. This feature is extremely useful when you upload pages initially. Later, however, you should use this option only if you've changed several of these dependent files. If only the document itself has changed--or if you've changed only one or two dependent files--it's much less time-consuming to upload only those files that have changed.

Set your preference in the Site category of the Preferences dialog box. A common setting is to get/download/check out dependent files only when prompted, but to automatically put/upload/check in dependent files. The rationale for this setting is that the most current version of an image or other dependent file usually resides in the local folder, thus you don't want it automatically overwritten by an older version on the remote server when you get a file. However, you do want to upload the most current version of a dependent file when you put the page on the server.

Getting Files (Downloading)

The opposite process to uploading is getting pages from the remote server to work with them locally. To download, select a file or files in the Remote Site pane and click the Get File(s) button on the site view toolbar, or drag and drop the files into the local folder.

Testing Your Site Online

After the site has been transferred to the remote server, the testing process starts all over again. Although you've checked the site for approximate download speeds, the download speed provided by Dreamweaver in the status bar is only an approximation based on the size of the document and the speed of the connection. After the site is on the server, you can test the accuracy of this estimate.

If you're using a broadband connection, visit the site using a standard modem, especially if your intended audience will include a significant number of dial-up users. Even if you're testing the site at various speeds, the true test comes when the site is live. If you're lucky enough to have a high volume of visitors, you might have slow-downs in access speed as the server struggles to keep up.

Putting the site onto the remote server also enables you to check for real-life cross-browser compatibility. Having the site on the remote server enables you to get the opinion of others with different configurations.

When you find mistakes, you can edit pages directly on the server. To do this, connect to the server by using the Connects to Remote Host button on the Files toolbar. If you're using the site view window, select a file from the Remote Site pane and open the file. If you're using the Files panel, the view automatically changes to the Remote view upon connecting to the server. Select a file from this view, and open it. You can then edit the file as

11

normal. When you save the file, it is automatically saved to both the remote server and the local folder.

COLLABORATING

You may manage some sites entirely by yourself, but others you may need to manage with colleagues, friends, customers, vendors, volunteers, or some combination thereof. In this section, we take a look at two kinds of version control: the basic but effective kind that Dreamweaver provides via the check-in/check-out facility, and two more sophisticated kinds to which Dreamweaver can connect. We also discuss how to synchronize a site between local and remote locations, an especially important activity when multiple people work on the same site.

SETTING UP A REMOTE SITE

Working as part of a design team presents additional challenges. You must learn to work with others to perform some tasks you've already learned to do on your own. The most common concern is maintaining control over files when multiple developers are working on the same pages. Communication is another critical factor so the project proceeds smoothly.

When one member of the team opens a file, it must be locked to prevent others from editing the same file. Dreamweaver uses a minimal form of version control when Check In/Check Out are enabled. The remote server shows that a file is currently checked out and lists the name of the team member who currently has access to the file. Other developers can still access the file, but only in a read-only state.

Let's take a look at that feature, then examine two other technologies for handling the multiple-developer scenario. (Incidentally, the Check In/Check Out feature is available for developers working with Flash MX 2004 and Fireworks MX 2004.)

NOTE

Speaking of collaborating: If you've set up a Web site that requires periodic content updating, you may want to look into a new product from Macromedia called *Contribute*. This package lets users who aren't Web designers update a site created in Dreamweaver. You can use Dreamweaver to create templates that limit what users can edit. The great benefit is that designers don't have to spend their time performing simple content edits. To learn more, search on "contribute" in the Dreamweaver MX 2004 help system.

CHECKING FILES IN AND OUT

Even if your development team isn't using version control software, Dreamweaver has tools to keep your project running smoothly. When you set up the Remote Info in the Site Definition dialog box, there are options at the bottom of this box to enable Check In/Out. Check In is similar to the Put or upload command, whereas Check Out is similar to the Get or download command.

The advantage of using these tools instead of the default Get and Put commands is that Check In/Out tracks which files are currently in use by other members of the team. If a file is in use, the Remote Site list of the Site window/panel shows that the file is checked out, designated by a check mark in the file list. Dreamweaver achieves this magic by creating *.LCK files, containing user contact information, on the server and the local computer when you check a file out. Dreamweaver deletes these files when you check the file back in.

N O T E

> The Check In/Out options are useful for individual developers who work on multiple machines and platforms. If you forget to upload changes to the remote server, the file will appear as checked out when you try to retrieve it on another machine, thus enabling you to avoid having multiple copies of the same file, each with different revisions.

If you're using FTP in a team environment, it's important that every member of the team uses Dreamweaver's built-in FTP tools. If not, the Check In/Out features will be rendered ineffective. Dreamweaver will have no way of knowing when files are downloaded by an external FTP application.

To enable Check In/Out, select the Enable File Check In and Check Out box in the Remote Info category of the Site Definition dialog box. When you select this option, additional selections appear in the dialog box (see Figure 11.7).

Figure 11.7
When the Enable File Check In and Check Out option is selected, other options become available, as well.

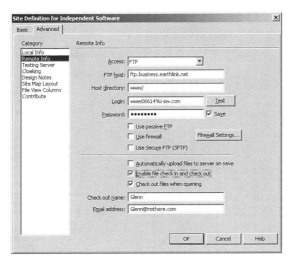

Select the Check Out Files when Opening option to automatically check out files when you double-click.

To make the Check In/Out feature most effective, Dreamweaver needs to be capable of tracking who has checked out the files. This allows other members of the team to communicate directly with the person who's currently working on a file that might be needed by someone else. To enable this feature, fill in the Check Out Name field with a unique user-name. If you also enter an email address where indicated, team members can click the address in the Remote Site list to open an email addressed to the appropriate developer.

After the Check In/Out options have been selected, their use is identical to the Get and Put commands. The same Get/Check Out and Put/Check In buttons are used to upload and download files.

 If you're having trouble with certain transfers, read "Checking the Transfer Log" in the "Troubleshooting" section later this chapter.

OTHER VERSION CONTROL SYSTEMS

Larger development houses often use more sophisticated version control systems such as Visual SourceSafe and WebDAV. Not only do version control systems such as Visual SourceSafe and WebDAV protect against overwritten files, but they also keep a historical record for each file in the project. This enables you to revert to previous versions of a document.

MICROSOFT VISUAL SOURCESAFE

Microsoft Visual SourceSafe is a Windows-based version control system. To use SourceSafe as your method of interacting with the remote server, follow these steps:

1. Open the Site Definition dialog box for your site by using the Site, Manage Sites command to open the Edit Sites dialog box. Click the site name, then click Edit.
2. Select the Remote Info category.
3. In the Access drop-down menu, select SourceSafe Database.
4. Click the Settings button to open the Open SourceSafe Database dialog box (see Figure 11.8).
5. In the Database Path field, enter the location of the SourceSafe database.
6. In the Project field, enter the name of the project, as it's referenced by the SourceSafe database.
7. Enter your username and password to access the project.
8. Click OK.

WEBDAV

Web-Based Distributed Authoring and Versioning (WebDAV) is another version control system. Because it is an open standard, it has a growing audience. To set WebDAV as your method of access to the remote server, use the Site Definition dialog box (steps 1 and 2 in the previous procedure) to set the Access field to WebDAV. Click Settings to open the WebDAV Connection dialog box. Enter the URL of the WebDAV server and your user-name and password to access it.

Figure 11.8
The SourceSafe
Database settings give
Dreamweaver access
to the project data-
base.

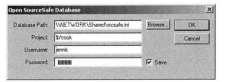

VERSION CONTROL LIMITATIONS IN DREAMWEAVER

Version control software is useful, but it has its limitations. If you're using VSS or WebDAV with Dreamweaver, the Synchronize and Select Newer Files options are unavailable because Dreamweaver can't obtain an accurate timestamp from the remote server. Also, depending on how your collaborative environment is configured, it's still possible to overwrite an updated file with one that's outdated if your local folder isn't current.

CLOAKING FILES AND FOLDERS

Often when you're making changes to the content of pages, the images and other elements of the site remain the same. When you've completed revisions and are ready to synchronize the local folder with the remote server, it's a waste of time to re-upload the image folder or other folders if no changes have taken place to the contents of those folders. Cloaking allows you to specify that certain folders are exempt from site-wide operations. (You can't cloak individual files, by the way.)

The Cloaking category of the Site Definition dialog box enables or disables cloaking for the site. After it is enabled, you can also set an entire file type to be cloaked, regardless of the directory in which it's located on the site. To cloak a folder, activate cloaking using Site, Cloaking in the Site window or Files panel.

SYNCHRONIZING SITES

As files are checked in and out by various developers, your local folders can quickly become outdated. To bring the local and remote sites back into sync, use the Synchronize tool:

1. From the Files panel or the site view window (but not the Document menu), select Site, Synchronize.

2. In the Synchronize dialog box, choose to synchronize only selected local files or the entire site (see Figure 11.9).

3. Choose whether to replace only the files on the remote server with their updated local counterparts, to replace only the files in the local folders with their more recent remote counterparts, or to synchronize in both directions as needed.

4. Decide whether to delete files that don't have a counterpart on the other server.

5. Click Preview to begin the synchronization process.

6. In the preview dialog box, verify which files should be uploaded, downloaded, or deleted. All files are selected by default for action. If you want to leave a particular file as is, deselect it.

7. Click OK to complete the synchronization.

Figure 11.9
The Synchronize dialog box determines the direction and scope of the synchronization process.

SITE REPORTS AND LINK MAINTENANCE

This section looks at tasks you should perform not only before your initial upload, but all throughout your site's lifetime, to ensure that as your site evolves, it does not deteriorate in terms of reliability, efficiency, or ease of use.

> **NOTE**
>
> One Dreamweaver feature you may want to explore as a site maintenance aid is the *map view* window. You can open this window by clicking Map View from the Files panel's drop-down view list, or by clicking the Site Map button from the site window's toolbar and choosing Map Only or Map and Files. Dreamweaver shows your site's structure two levels deep, and highlights broken links with red text and a broken-link icon. Files that you've checked out show up with a green check mark; files that others have checked out show up with a red check mark. A lock icon denotes a read-only file, and blue text with a globe icon indicates a file that lives on a different site. You can use map view to fix some site maintenance problems on a smaller site, but the site reports are generally quicker for this purpose on medium to large sites.

PUTTING THE SITE REPORT TO WORK

Site analysis begins with the markup itself. More than just a matter of wanting to write the best markup possible, HTML complications can have a tremendous impact on the usability of your site.

Consider the implications. If a site is laden with empty or redundant tags, the pages will take longer to load and might produce unexpected results in some browsers. If the pages don't have informative titles, visitors could become disoriented. Page titles also affect search engine rankings, which potentially makes this a return on investment issue, as well. If the images on the site don't have descriptive alt text, and if the site as a whole doesn't pass accessibility tests, potential visitors are lost.

The Site Report feature brings all these code issues together. To run a Site report, follow these steps:

1. Select Site, Reports from the Document window, the Files panel menu, or the site window menu.

2. The Reports dialog box contains a list of categories. Select the scope of the Report—the current document, the entire current local site, or selected files/folders.

3. Select the reports you require.

4. If the selected report(s) require additional settings, use the Report Settings button. Click this button in conjunction with each selected report that requires additional information.

5. Click Run to start the report process.

The site report options are in Table 11.1.

TABLE 11.1   SITE REPORT OPTIONS

Report Name	Purpose	Report Settings
Checked Out By	Lists all documents checked out by a specified user.	Specify the user name. If no username is entered into the Report Settings, the report lists all files checked out by each user.
Design Notes	Lists all Design Notes attached to the site (or selected documents).	Enter search constraints to find Design Notes related to a particular user, revision, or file type.
Recently Modified	Lists files that have changed within a particular time span.	
Combinable Nested Font Tags	Generates a list of font tags that define the same block of text that can be combined.	
Accessibility	Checks the site's compliance with Section 508 of the 1998 Rehabilitation Act for Accessibility.	Each of the accessibility rules can be enabled or disabled for the report.
Missing Alt Text	Lists images that have not been assigned an `alt` text attribute to make the content accessible.	
Redundant Nested Tags	Reports on instances where a tag (and attributes) are nested within the exact same tag.	
Removable Empty Tags	Lists extraneous tags that contain no content.	
Untitled Documents	Generates a list of all pages in the site that are untitled, either because they retain the default page title or because the <title> tag is missing.	

11

NOTE

> When you run the tag-related reports, Dreamweaver validates the site and reports other problems in a pop-up warning box.

The Clean Up XHTML command is useful for correcting some of the common coding problems, but it doesn't replace the need for the Reports tool because it addresses only a limited range of issues and can be used only one page at a time. It can and should be used in conjunction with the Site Report tool, however, to clean up the mistakes identified in the Report.

You can have Dreamweaver sort site reports by filename, line number, or problem description. The fastest method for fixing problems is usually to sort by filename. As you scroll through the report results, right-click (control-click on the Mac) an entry you want to address and select Open File. The file will be opened in the Document window in the split Design/Code view.

After you've made revisions to your site based on the report results, you should run the Site Report tool again. Your changes might have raised other issues.

MAINTAINING LINK INTEGRITY

Another essential site analysis chore is keeping diligent watch over the links within the site. As you already know, the Web changes so quickly that external links you create today can be outdated by tomorrow. Most Web design experts state that you should check external links at least once a month.

Internal linking, although not as common a problem because of Dreamweaver's capability to update links as pages are moved within the site's folder structure, is still fraught with some dangers. As you revise the site, it's not uncommon for pages to be *orphaned*—still available on the server but not linked from any other page of the site. Internal links can also break down if you edit a page in an external HTML editor or rename a page without electing to update the links to or from that page. Links to images are the most common type of internal link breakage because images are often deleted or renamed outside Dreamweaver.

CHECKING LINKS IN A SITE

The Check Links feature makes short work of these assorted link problems. Similar to the Site Report feature, the Check Links tool compiles a report of all broken links and orphaned files.

There are three types of Link reports, and each is accessed from a different menu:

- From the Files panel or site view window, select Site, Check Links Sitewide to check links throughout the entire site.

- From the main menu, select File, Check Page, Check Links to validate links within the current document.
- Select specific files and folders in the Site panel; then select Check Links, Selected Files/Folders from the context menu to check links only in those files and folders.

You can also access all three link report types by navigating to the Results panel's Link Checker tab and clicking the green arrow at the upper left of that tab.

The report appears in the Link Checker panel of the Results panel group. The report can be filtered to list only broken links, external links, or orphaned files if you use the Show drop-down menu in the Link Checker panel. As with site reports, the link report results can be saved to an XML file or used directly to help you locate and repair the problems.

 Want to validate external links? Find out what to do in "Validating External Links" in the "Troubleshooting" section later this chapter.

Repairing Links

To repair links using the Link Checker report, follow these steps:

1. Run the Check Links tool for the current page, selected pages/folders, or site-wide.
2. In the Broken Links column of the Link Checker report, select a broken link (see Figure 11.10).
3. Enter the correct path and filename or use the Browse icon to navigate to the correct file.
4. Press Enter or click another link to save the change.
5. If prompted to apply the same change to other broken links to this file, click Yes to automatically make the updates or No to change only the specific reference in question (see Figure 11.11). If you click Cancel, your change will be undone.

As you repair each link, it disappears from the report. If you filter the report to show only each type of link at a time, you can work methodically through the list of broken links and orphaned pages without being distracted by external links. When the broken link and orphaned page reports are empty, all the internal links have been validated. Because there's no way to validate external links in Dreamweaver, those links will always appear in an external link report.

You can also repair links directly in the document. Simply double-click the File column of a broken link, and the document opens in the Document window with the specific link selected. The link can then be modified in the Property inspector. Although this process is more time-consuming, it's useful when you want to see the link in context or make additional changes to it (such as modifying the source text) .

11

Figure 11.10
A Browse icon appears next to a broken link when it's selected for repair. Use this button to navigate to the file's correct location.

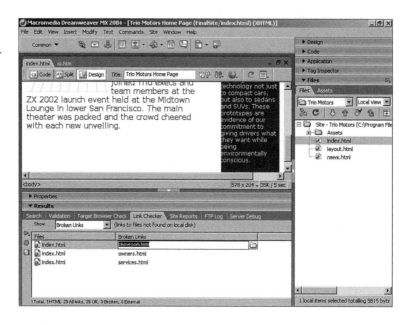

Figure 11.11
If other broken links to the same file exist, Dreamweaver asks whether those should also be updated.

CHANGING LINKS THROUGHOUT A SITE

Even if a link isn't broken, it might need to be updated to refer to a different destination file. If you change email addresses, for example, you'll want to change all the mailto links in the site to point to the new address.

To change a link site-wide, do the following:

1. Select Site, Change Link Sitewide from the Files panel menu, the site window menu, or the Document window.

2. In the Change Link Sitewide dialog box, enter the current link destination in the Change All Links To field (see Figure 11.12). Use the Browse icon if you're unsure of the path.

3. Enter the new link destination in the Into Links To field.

4. Click OK.

Figure 11.12
Changing links site-wide saves time and ensures that you don't miss any stragglers.

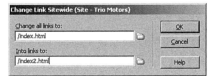

TROUBLESHOOTING

VALIDATOR TROUBLE

I tried to run my page through the validator, but it won't work. What's wrong?

For documents to be validated, they must contain the proper DOCTYPE declaration. Check your document.

CHECKING THE TRANSFER LOG

I'm having transfer problems. What's going on?

Whether you're getting/putting or checking in/out, Dreamweaver logs every FTP transaction between the local and remote sites. This log can help you track down transfer problems. To display the FTP log, select View, Site FTP Log from the Files panel or click the View Site FTP Log button from the site window. On the Mac, the Site FTP Log is under the Site menu. The log lists any error messages received in the Results panel.

SITE REPORT VISIBILITY

I'm trying to use the Site Report features, but the display is limited. How can I get to the complete report?

One of the limitations of the Site Report is the size of the panel on the screen. Unless you manually adjust the panels to take up more than the default screen real estate, some of the report explanations are truncated. Use the More Info option to read the complete text of the problem, or pull up relevant details in the Reference panel.

VALIDATING EXTERNAL LINKS

I need to validate links to other sites. Can Dreamweaver help me do that?

Dreamweaver does not validate external links. The Check Links report will, however, provide you with a list of external links. You can then go down the list and manually check each one.

PEER TO PEER: USING MACROMEDIA EXTENSIONS AND PRODUCTS FOR ACCESSIBILITY TESTING

Macromedia has recently joined forces with accessibility experts to create a product called LIFT. This product can be downloaded from www.usablenet.com/lift_dw/lift_dw.html, and it will run complete reports on your sites and assist you with making appropriate changes.

Some extensions are available for assisting you with ensuring that you are including important accessibility features in your documents. Be sure to check the Macromedia Exchange site's accessibility section for a range of utilities to assist you with the accessibility validation process.

PEER TO PEER: TRACKING USAGE STATISTICS

After the site is complete and live, your site analysis changes emphasis from the development of the site to its usage, and it is critical that you track this information if you want to truly serve your visitors and achieve best practices.

Dreamweaver, however, doesn't offer any tools for tracking usage statistics. The Macromedia Exchange contains some extensions to enable counters, but these are commercial products that charge a fee to be enabled on your site.

Many Web hosting services offer tools to allow their clients to track usage on their sites. Also, several free and commercial services are available to track these statistics. It generally requires some manual labor to insert the necessary code into your site, but they'll provide you with additional information about your site's usage and the demographics of your visitors.

To learn more about statistics, check first with your Web service provider or systems administrator to see whether preexisting tools are on your servers. If not, you might want to look into a free service, such as www.freestats.com.

CHAPTER **12**

EXPANDING DREAMWEAVER AND USING THIRD-PARTY SOFTWARE

In this chapter

Extending Macromedia Dreamweaver   264

Using Contribute 2 with Dreamweaver   268

Integrating Dreamweaver with Fireworks   274

Integrating Dreamweaver with Flash   278

Microsoft Integration Features   283

Peer to Peer: Macromedia Extensions for Markup Compliance   285

Peer to Peer: Markup and Contribute   285

Web design tools—even sophisticated, late-model ones such as Dreamweaver MX 2004—were never intended to be Swiss Army knives that provide every tool you need to build a Web site. Rather, their nature is to act as an integrator, bringing together content from multiple sources and applications, and doing so in such a way that the seams don't show! These integrated applications may include the following:

- Add-in code from other independent developers and experts, such as the extensions you can find via Macromedia Exchange.
- Collaborative tools such as Macromedia Contribute 2, which lets non-experts participate in Website design and upkeep.
- Bitmap-oriented graphics programs such as Macromedia Fireworks, which let you create, edit, and optimize images for Web deployment.
- Vector-oriented programs such as Macromedia Flash and Freehand, which let you create scalable images, animations, and multimedia presentations.
- Day-to-day office productivity programs, such as Microsoft Word and Excel, which form the source for much repurposed content.
- (Insert your favorite development tool here!) You can specify third-party image editors and code editors via Dreamweaver's Edit, Preferences command.

This chapter takes a look at all these tools. Two of the applications, namely Fireworks and Flash, receive detailed treatment in other sections of this book; here, we focus on how those tools integrate with Dreamweaver.

EXTENDING MACROMEDIA DREAMWEAVER

12

Programmers, especially those with JavaScript, XML, and C++ programming, can create *extensions* to Dreamweaver and share or sell them. Extensions can expand on existing features in Dreamweaver MX 2004, or they can provide entirely new capabilities. Extensions can help you with workflow, design, and development.

Many extensions are available for you to download and install. After they are installed, extensions become integrated into Dreamweaver as part of the program. (If you are thinking about writing your own extensions, check out Help, Extensions, Extending Dreamweaver. The help file that appears contains a wealth of detail for extension developers.)

ABOUT MACROMEDIA EXCHANGE

Macromedia Exchange is the Macromedia-run Web site where most extensions are submitted and are available for download (see Figure 12.1). Unlike in the past, the Exchange site contains both free software and software you must buy.

Figure 12.1
The Macromedia Exchange Web site is a rich environment for designers and developers to share and create extensions.

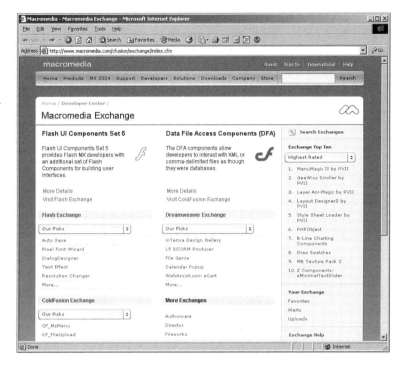

The Exchange Web site exists to provide a repository of extensions to Macromedia products, provide community and support via discussion groups, enable users of extensions to rate and review individual extensions, and provide information for designers and developers interested in writing their own extensions.

If you are interested in more extensions and components than you can find on Exchange, you may want to look into the DevNet Resource Kits (DRK's) from Macromedia. You can buy the quarterly CDs, subscribe to the service, or both.

NOTE

To access the Exchange site, point your browser to `http://exchange. macromedia.com/`. To go directly to the Dreamweaver Exchange, use this URL: `http://exchange.macromedia.com/dreamweaver/`.

MANAGING EXTENSIONS

If you'd like to add extensions to Dreamweaver, you first need to register at the site. After that, you should download and install the Extension Manager, a free program Macromedia provides to help you quickly add and install extensions. Then look through the variety of extension resources available to you, and download and install those of interest to you.

Registration is a simple process that provides you with several resources, including regular news updates via email regarding Macromedia resources and products, product tracking, and full access to Exchange services. To register for Macromedia Exchange, visit `http://www.macromedia.com/membership/`. Membership is free and instant.

Next, before you can download any extensions, you need to download and install the Extension Manager. To do so, point your browser to `http://exchange.macromedia.com/`. After you are a registered user, you will be welcomed by the Exchange and provided with a page that helps you access both the Exchange and the program version you require. Note that the minimum version of the Extension Manager that Macromedia recommends for use with Dreamweaver MX 2004 is 1.6.

To launch the Exchange from Dreamweaver MX 2004, select Commands, Manage Extensions. The Macromedia Extension Manager dialog box appears (see Figure 12.2). In the dialog box, you'll see a list of any extensions you might have downloaded in the past.

Figure 12.2
Here you see the Macromedia Extension Manager with a number of extensions installed.

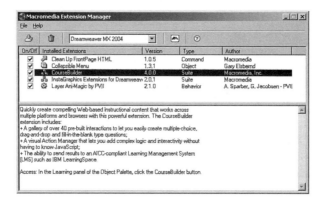

The Extension Manager dialog box provides the following options:

- **On/Off**—This option, found in the main window, allows you to check or uncheck a given extension to ensure that it is either activated or deactivated.

- **Installed Extension**—This feature lists by name all the extensions you've downloaded.

- **Version**—Here, you can find the numeric version release of the extension you're using. This is helpful when determining whether an upgrade to a given extension you might have had for some time is necessary.

- **Type**—This field describes the means by which the extension is accessed. For example, Command means the option is available to you from the Command menu.

- **Author**—Because the Exchange is an open-distribution system, authors are acknowledged in this field. Some authors include their email addresses so you can email them if you have any concerns or problems.

NOTE

> To see a description of the extension in question, highlight it in the Extension Manager dialog box; a description appears in the lower box, along with information on how to access the extension.

EXTENSIONS AT A GLANCE

Many extensions are available for Macromedia Dreamweaver. They are organized into categories so you can easily find those extensions most suited to your needs. The categories, at this writing, include accessibility, app servers, browsers, DHTML/layers, extension development, Fireworks, Flash media, learning, navigation, productivity, rich media, scripting, security, style/format, tables, text, commerce, content, and Web analysis.

GETTING HELP WITH EXTENSIONS

The Macromedia Web site provides terrific support to all designers and developers using Dreamweaver MX, as well as those using and creating extensions. Support is delivered via Macromedia newsgroups (Web-based and standard newsgroups) and the Web site in general.

To access general support, point your browser to `http://www.macromedia.com/devnet/community/` and click the Dreamweaver link. To access Dreamweaver online forums, where you'll find the Dreamweaver Exchange Extensions forum, point your browser to `http://webforums.macromedia.com/dreamweaver/` and click the Dreamweaver Exchange Extensions link. Support that comes through these channels is typically swift and most frequently provided by peers rather than Macromedia.

ADDING AN EXTENSION

After you have your membership, have downloaded and installed the Macromedia Extension Manager, and are oriented to the site, you can download and install your first extension. The procedure is simply a matter of browsing to the Exchange site, choosing an extension that looks interesting, reading about it, then clicking the Download button. After you've saved the downloaded extension, install it by opening Extension Manager, choosing Dreamweaver MX 2004 from the drop-down menu, and choosing File, Install Extension. You'll probably need to restart Dreamweaver to gain access to the new extension.

DOWNLOADING A BEHAVIOR

Downloading a behavior is similar to downloading any other extension. However, you begin the process by opening the Behaviors panel. From the Actions (+) menu, select Get More Behaviors. Your default Web browser will open, and the Macromedia Exchange Web site will be available. Browse to a behavior of interest and download it, then install the extension as described above. Again, you will generally need to restart Dreamweaver before using the new behavior. You'll see it in the Behaviors panel when you click the (+).

12

Many extensions are really mini-applications in and of themselves. If you invoke a given command or behavior, either that extension will automatically execute or its related dialog box will appear so you can customize and control the extension's features.

INSTALLING THIRD-PARTY PLUG-INS

Just as a site visitor must have a plug-in installed to display certain features such as Flash movies, so must you. Every time you start Dreamweaver, it performs a quick search to find out which plug-ins are available locally, looking in your browser folders for the information.

If you want to directly install a plug-in for use in Dreamweaver, download it from the plug-in's home Web site. (An example would be downloading the SVG plug-in from Adobe.) When prompted to save the plug-in to a particular location, select Browse and find the `Dreamweaver MX 2004/Configuration/Plugins` folder. When the download is complete, you might need to double-click the executable file for the plug-in to finish the installation process.

 Have you downloaded a plug-in and can play the associated media in Dreamweaver MX 2004 but not your browser? Find out why in "Plug-in Availability" in the "Troubleshooting" section.

USING CONTRIBUTE 2 WITH DREAMWEAVER

Macromedia Contribute 2 is a lightweight program that enables almost anyone to create and edit documents on existing Web sites. Contribute can be used along with features in Dreamweaver to help you—and co-workers who might not otherwise have extensive design or development experience—complete a range of tasks, including

- Maintenance and updates
- Adding new pages by using a blank page, a Contribute "starter" page, or a template created in Dreamweaver MX
- Publishing documents created in other applications, including Microsoft Word and Microsoft Excel
- Adding or removing text, graphics, and other media on your existing sites
- Sharing site connections in a team environement

Macromedia Contribute can be used by anyone creating sites in Dreamweaver MX, production team members, and anyone responsible for updating content to existing Web sites. Contribute provides the designer and developer quick and easy access to pages so as to allow for general updates to content, including text, images, and media. Team members not otherwise tasked with design or development can also use Contribute for these updates.

Business users and content editors will especially enjoy Contribute because it enables them to rapidly update pages without having to use Dreamweaver MX itself, much less know how to work with complex code and layout structures. For these users, Contribute is especially attractive because its easy-to-use interface is very similar to a word processing program.

Consider the marketing manager who wants to update text to reflect a recent promotion, an online magazine section editor who wants to add a new article, or even a company's CFO who'd like to publish an Excel spreadsheet to the corporate intranet. Most of these people aren't designers, developers, or Web authors. Their job is to get the content published to the Dreamweaver-designed site without having to deal with the more complex features of Dreamweaver, which are far outside the scope of what these individuals need to achieve.

As the site designer, developer, or project manager, you can empower both yourself and anyone working on the site that you design by using Contribute for those situations or individuals in which the objective is to get the content online within the context of the site's design.

Contribute operates while connected to the Internet. You can work offline on certain tasks, but most tasks are best carried out in the live connection environment.

Automatically installed with Contribute 2 is the FlashPaper Printer utility. FlashPaper easily converts documents, such as Microsoft Office, Microsoft Project, Visio, and PDFs to a Flash movie file, allowing them to be viewed in a browser. This is a great feature because Flash movie files are normally smaller than other document types and load more quickly when viewed in a browser. Content in your FlashPaper document is also better protected because it can't be selected and copied. Any printable document can be saved as a FlashPaper document and inserted into a Web page.

Windows XP and Windows 2000 operating systems support the FlashPaper Printer utility. FlashPaper documents that you generate are cross-platform compatible and can be viewed in any browser that supports Flash.

CAUTION

> FlashPaper documents can't be edited. To edit your document, you must make changes to the original document, then convert it again to a FlashPaper document.

12

ABOUT THE CONTRIBUTE INTERFACE

Interestingly, Contribute 2 works as a Web browser and page editor. The following two modes are available in Contribute:

- **Browse mode**—In this mode, Contribute acts as a Web browser, allowing you to open online Web pages, follow links, and even set bookmarks.

- **Edit mode**—You can browse to an existing page, switch into Edit mode, and begin making edits to the page.

Contribute is, as mentioned, very lightweight and extremely easy to use interface-wise. It contains a title bar, menu bar, toolbar, page navigation panel (which lists links and indicates published pages), Quick Help section, and document window. Figure 12.3 shows the Contribute workspace.

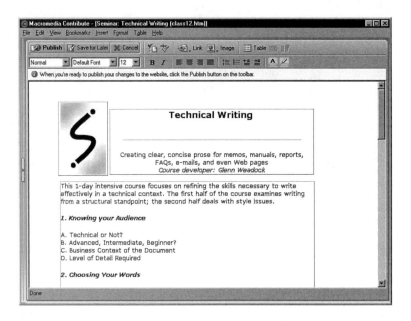

The editing toolbar options are available to help you achieve numerous editing options. You can

- Handle common file operations
- Set page properties
- Check spelling
- Insert content: links, images, and tables
- Add rows and columns
- Modify text style
- Set text alignment
- Create lists
- Modify indenting
- Make color changes

 Is the Edit Page button disabled? Find out why in "Disabled Edit Button" in the "Troubleshooting" section at the end of this chapter.

To edit a page in Contribute, follow these steps:

1. Enter the Web address in the browser toolbar. Alternatively, you can click the Home Page button and then select the site to navigate to the page you want to edit.

2. Click the Edit Page button to switch from Browse mode to Edit mode.

3. Make your editorial changes. When you're ready to publish the page, click Publish on the edit toolbar.

Contribute will publish your changes to the Web server.

CREATING A NEW PAGE WITH CONTRIBUTE

You can use two different methods to create new pages in Contribute. The first is to use the Insert Link method, and the second is to use the Add a Page button.

USING INSERT LINK

This method enables you to create a link from an existing page and create the new page for the link. To create a page using the Insert Link method, follow these steps:

1. Browse to the page you want to link to your new page.
2. Click Edit, and place the insertion point onto the page where you want the link to be.
3. Select Insert, Link. Choose the desired operation from the submenu, Drafts and Recent Pages, which creates a link on your page to a draft that you are currently editing or to a recently published page on your site; Create New Page, which creates a link to a new Web page on your site automatically created by Contribute at the same time that it creates the link; E-mail Address, which creates a link to an email address; or File on My Computer, which creates a link to a file on your computer or network.
4. The Insert Link dialog box appears.
5. Enter text in the Link Text box, if you did not select text or an image in your draft.

CAUTION

> Text box not available? If you selected text or an image in the draft, this box cannot be accessed.

6. In the File To Link To text box, click the Browse button to navigate to the file to which you want to link, then Select to close the dialog box.
7. To set advanced options, expand the dialog box by clicking the Advanced button, then set the options, which are Editing the URL for a Link; Setting a Target for Your Page; and Linking to a Specific Place in a Page.
8. Click OK. Contribute 2 performs the proper operation.

The link appears in the referring page, and the new page shows up in My Drafts. The page is automatically saved to the same location as the file that is linking to it. You can now add content to that page as is, use a template created in Dreamweaver MX for the design, and publish when ready.

CREATING A NEW PAGE WITH THE ADD A PAGE BUTTON

If you want to create a page within Contribute that is independent from a referring page, here's how:

12

1. Go to the folder where you want to create the new page.

2. Click the New Page button; the New Page dialog box appears.

3. In the Create New Page From section, select the type of page you want to create: Blank Web Page creates a blank page, and Copy of Current Page creates a copy of the page you are currently viewing.

CAUTION

> When the page contains frames or the page is a draft in the Contribute editor, you cannot create a copy of the current page. Likewise you cannot copy a page from one Web site to another Web site.

4. Select a page from either the Sample Web Pages folder, which creates a copy of a fixed sample page; or from the Templates folder, which creates a new page based on a Dreamweaver template; or on a Web site page that your administrator has designated as a template. A preview and description now appear.

5. Click the Refresh Templates button to update your list of templates, if necessary.

6. In the Page title text box enter a page title.

7. Click OK.

The new page opens in Edit mode so you can begin working on it with Contribute right away.

CAUTION

> Unless you designated another Web site in step 2, Contribute 2 puts the new page in the same folder as the page you were viewing when you created the page. If you need to, you can change the folder location when you publish the new page.

IMPORTING WORD AND EXCEL DOCUMENTS INTO A PAGE

One of the most useful features of Contribute 2 is that it enables you to quickly import Word and Excel content to your site. This is powerful because you don't have to re-create a table or content—Contribute does the work for you via a very simple, fast process. The online help system provides details.

Follow these steps:

1. To select the page where you want the content to appear, browse to an existing Web page, click the Edit Page button, and place the insertion point in the draft where you want to add the content or create a new page.

2. Now select the file by selecting Insert, Microsoft Office Document; by browsing to the file from the Open dialog box and clicking Open; or by dragging the file from its current location to the Contribute draft where you want the content to appear. If the

Insert Document dialog box appears, click Insert The Contents Of The Document Into This Page, and then click OK.

The content of the Word or Excel document now appears within your draft.

CREATING A DRAFT

As soon as you open a page in Edit mode, it is saved as a draft. You can see any drafts listed in the Drafts section of the sidebar's Places section. The advantage of a draft is that you can leave it in your Drafts section, close out of Contribute, and return to editing it later. All drafts stay in this section until you either publish or cancel your page.

You can save your draft by selecting File, Save. If you decide to close a draft and return to it later, you can do so by clicking the Web tab and browsing or editing as necessary. When you're ready to return to the draft, you can click the draft, which is found in the Places sidebar.

WORKING WITH TEXT

Contribute enables anyone to easily add and format text. Even though you might be using Dreamweaver to create your complex page designs, co-workers without the professional experience can easily make changes to those pages they are responsible for updating without having to deal with the complexity of Dreamweaver.

> **NOTE**
>
> Contribute recognizes and honors Dreamweaver templates and editable regions. Therefore, a Dreamweaver designer can specify in a template which parts of the page others may modify using Contribute. This is a key feature in that it prevents inexperienced contributors from wreaking havoc with your carefully crafted designs. Similarly, you can restrict the user to a list of defined styles.

There are several ways to add text to a page. You can do any of the following:

- Type the text directly into the document you're editing.
- Copy and paste text from another application.
- Drag text from another application.

You can change a variety of text features while using Contribute in Edit mode, including text style, font, font size, font style, text alignment, indent/outdent, list formats, text color, and highlight. To apply any of these options, simply select the text you want to modify and use the button or drop-down list for the option in question. You can also make these and other changes through the Format menu on the main toolbar.

CREATING LISTS

Lists are, of course, a very important means of organizing and presenting text on the Web. Contribute lets you create numbered lists, bulleted lists, definition lists, and sublists.

WORKING WITH IMAGES

Contribute allows you quick access to edit, add, and delete images from the pages in your site.

CREATING A TABLE

Tables are easily created in Contribute. You can insert a custom table and modify it, or you can create a table and apply a preset style from Contribute.

WORKING WITH LINKS

As with Dreamweaver, Macromedia Contribute enables you to create a variety of links, including text links, mail links, and linked images. You can also test your links from within Contribute.

NOTE

> For site-wide link checking, the tools in Macromedia Dreamweaver MX 2004 are much more sophisticated. However, this method is a quick and easy way of testing links on one or several pages at a time.

WORKING WITH FRAMES

Although you cannot create framed sites with Macromedia Contribute, you can edit frame content. So long as your site administrator has properly set permissions, you can access any frame page directly via the Contribute workspace—you don't have to browse to the individual frame page to edit it.

PUBLISHING YOUR DRAFTS

After you're finished editing your draft pages, you might want to perform a number of checks and then publish it to the live Web site. Some of the options you'll consider before publishing include

- Preview in Browser
- Spell and Link Check
- Making the draft available for review, approval, and feedback

NOTE

> For more information about Contribute, visit www.macromedia.com/products/contribute.

INTEGRATING DREAMWEAVER WITH FIREWORKS

Given that Macromedia developed both Dreamweaver and Fireworks, you might expect some nifty integration features between the two applications, and you'd be correct.

You can set Dreamweaver to use Fireworks as the default external image editor, insert an exported Fireworks image in such a way that Dreamweaver "knows" about the original Fireworks file or files, and launch the full Fireworks program for serious image editing. Perhaps most usefully, you can now perform a number of common image editing functions without having to load Fireworks in its entirety. Let's look at each of these capabilities.

SETTING FIREWORKS AS THE DEFAULT IMAGE EDITOR

Dreamweaver MX 2004 lets you specify that you want Fireworks to be the default (in Macromedia parlance, "primary") image editor for edit-and-launch capability. You can also tell Dreamweaver that you want Fireworks available, but not as the default, for example, if you're more used to working with another tool such as Photoshop or ImageReady.

Change or confirm these settings by choosing Edit, Preferences. Click File Types/Editors in the left column, and add Fireworks (and any other editors you'd like to have available from the context menu) in the right part of the dialog box by using the + button, for PNG, GIF, and JPG file types (see Figure 12.4). Your primary image editor will launch whenever you double-click an image in the Document window; you can launch a secondary image editor from the image's context menu (via a right-click on the PC or a control-click on the Mac).

Figure 12.4
For maximum integration within Studio MX 2004, choose Fireworks as your primary image editor in the Preferences dialog box.

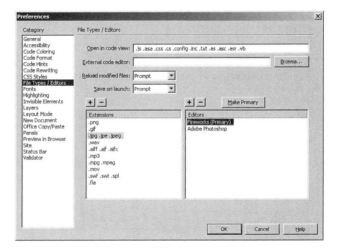

12

TIP

> You should also enable Design Notes for your Dreamweaver sites, and in Fireworks, export images to the site folder. Studio MX 2004 uses Design Notes for program-to-program communication; for example, Dreamweaver can find the original PNG file for a given exported image because Fireworks creates a Design Note containing that information during export. Exporting into a Dreamweaver site folder ensures that you and other collaborators have access to the image files for editing from the Dreamweaver user interface.

INSERTING OR CREATING A FIREWORKS IMAGE

You can insert a Fireworks image into a Dreamweaver document in two basic ways: via the normal Insert, Image command (or its Insert bar equivalent), and by updating a Dreamweaver *placeholder*. Dreamweaver lets you use placeholders when you're laying out a page and you know the size of the image you want, but you don't yet have the image file ready to insert.

In the first case, you would normally first use Fireworks to create the image and export it in a Web-friendly format such as GIF or JPG, then point Dreamweaver to the exported image. In the second case, you can simply right-click (control-click on the Mac) the placeholder and choose Create Image In Fireworks. Fireworks then launches in "Editing from Dreamweaver" mode.

When creating an image that began life as a placeholder, Fireworks honors the preset image size, image ID, attached behaviors (some, anyway), and attached links. After working your artistry in Fireworks, click the Done button and Fireworks prompts you to save the original image in PNG format and then export the image to GIF or JPG.

LAUNCHING FIREWORKS TO EDIT OR OPTIMIZE AN IMAGE

When working in Dreamweaver MX 2004 with an image that you'd like to edit in Fireworks, do one of the following:

- Right-click (PC) or Control-click (Mac) the image and choose Edit with Fireworks.
- Click the image and choose the Edit button on the Property inspector's new image toolbar.
- Control-double-click (PC) or Command-double-click (Mac) the image.

Whichever method you prefer, Fireworks opens in "Editing from Dreamweaver" mode (see Figure 12.5). If you've chosen an image slice that is part of a Fireworks table, assuming you've enabled Design Notes, Dreamweaver will find the original PNG file and open that in Fireworks for editing.

Figure 12.5
When you've launched Fireworks from within Dreamweaver, you can see the "Editing from Dreamweaver" notation in the Fireworks window.

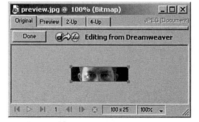

If you'd like to edit the image specifically to optimize its size-versus-quality tradeoff, you can save some time by selecting the image and choosing Commands, Optimize Image in

Fireworks. (There's also a new button for this on the Property inspector's new image toolbar, and a right-click command is available as well.) Fireworks opens in the Options panel, where you can fine-tune the compression settings and preview the results.

When you're finished editing or optimizing the image in Fireworks, simply click Done or Update (if you are editing or optimizing, respectively). Fireworks makes the appropriate changes to the original image file or files; exports the image, along with any accompanying HTML, for Dreamweaver's use; and returns the focus to Dreamweaver.

Macromedia calls the facility for maintaining the edits to the original file, as well as updating the Dreamweaver content, *roundtrip editing*. It's a major timesaving workflow feature.

USING THE NEW IMAGE EDITING TOOLBAR

Many Web designers need a few quick-and-dirty image editing capabilities but rarely need the power of a full-fledged graphics editor such as Fireworks. One of our favorite improvements in Dreamweaver MX 2004 is the addition of the image editing toolbar in the Property inspector (Figure 12.6), which lets you perform common operations on JPG and GIF files.

We put discussion of this toolbar here, in the integration section, because it does provide a convenient way for you to launch Fireworks for editing or optimization; however, you don't have to install Fireworks to use the toolbar's other features (crop, resample, brightness/contrast, and sharpen).

Here's a concise explanation of what these toolbar buttons do for you:

- **Edit**—Opens the image in Fireworks for editing. You must have Fireworks installed to use this button.

- **Optimize in Fireworks**—Identical to using Commands, Optimize Image in Fireworks: Opens Fireworks to the Options panel, where you can tweak compression settings. You must have Fireworks installed.

- **Crop**—Draws a bounding box around the image with resize handles that you can click and drag to crop the image to exclude areas you don't want.

- **Resample**—Performs a high-quality readjustment of pixels after you have resized an image (the button is grayed out until you perform the resize); dramatically improves quality and reduces file size. You don't need Fireworks installed to use this button.

- **Brightness and Contrast**—Opens a dialog box with two slider controls so you can make an image look more clearly as you want it. Fireworks need not be installed.

- **Sharpen**—Presents a slider control with which you can increase edge contrast to make bitmap images appear more detailed and focused; used mostly with JPG images. Fireworks need not be installed.

12

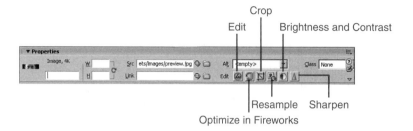

Figure 12.6
The new image editing toolbar appears on the Property inspector when you select an image.

If you find that you made a change that you don't like, the Edit, Undo command can reverse the change.

INTEGRATING DREAMWEAVER WITH FLASH

Macromedia Flash is a vector-based animation tool that has taken the Web by storm in the last several years. Dreamweaver lets you use Flash text and buttons in your pages without ever having to open Flash itself, or even know much about it.

You can also place Flash *movies* and *elements* (a new Flash file type) into a Dreamweaver document, them modify them from within Dreamweaver.

- To edit a Flash movie, launch Flash directly from the Design view via the Edit button on the Property inspector.

- To change a Flash element's parameters, use the Parameters button on the Property inspector. (The parameters that will be available for you to modify are set in advance, and [we hope!] documented for you, by the component's creator.)

In another example of Dreamweaver-to-Flash integration, you can update links in Flash files from the Dreamweaver site window. Open the Site Map view; choose View, Show Dependent Files; then change the links that appear beneath the SWF file icons. Dreamweaver automatically updates the SWF when you make such a change, and will offer to update the source Flash document (FLA) the next time you open it.

CAUTION

> Some users have reported problems updating links in SWFs created outside Dreamweaver, as opposed to Flash buttons created in Dreamweaver. Test your changed links to ensure that they work.

As with Fireworks integration, Flash integration works best if you enable Design Notes in your Dreamweaver site, and save any Flash movies to the site folder when you're working in Flash MX 2004.

FILE TYPES AND OBJECT PROPERTIES

Two primary types of Flash objects are available for your use in Dreamweaver MX 2004, whether or not you have Flash MX 2004 installed: text and buttons. This section takes a closer look at these popular Web page additions.

UNDERSTANDING FLASH FILE TYPES

Four Flash file types are important to know about. Table 12.1 shows these file types and explains their purposes.

TABLE 12.1   FLASH FILE TYPES

File Type	File Extension	Purpose
Flash Document	.fla	The source file for any Flash project. This file type requires Flash MX to open so you can export the file as an .swf or .swt file for delivery to Web browsers.
Flash Movie	.swf	This is a Web-ready compressed version of the .fla file. You can view this in a browser with the proper support, but you can't edit the file in Flash. The .swf file type is used when you create Flash buttons and text in Dreamweaver MX.
Flash Template	.swt	These templates provide a means for you to make modifications to an .swf file. In Dreamweaver MX, this file type is used to create and modify buttons, which are then saved as .swf files for use on a Web page.
Flash Component	.swc	Flash components, also called elements, are movies designed with customizable parameters that you can edit from within Dreamweaver without launching Flash. Download some from Macromedia Exchange, then insert them via the Flash Elements tab on the new Insert bar.

12

FLASH OBJECT PROPERTIES

Certain properties are available for you when working with Flash text and Flash buttons, as well. When you insert a Flash object into your document, you can select the object and set specific properties for that object.

The following properties are common to both text and buttons:

- **Name**—Identifies the button or text object so it can be used with scripts and behaviors.
- **Width**—Specifies the width of the object in pixels, picas, points, inches, millimeters, centimeters, or percentages.
- **Height**—Specifies the object's height. You have the same measurement options available as for width.

- **File**—The location and filename of the Flash object. You can browse for the file or, if you know the path, simply type it into the available field.

- **Edit**—Click this button, and the Flash object dialog box opens so you can modify your Flash button or text.

- **Reset Size**—Use this feature to reset the object to its actual size. (Resized Flash objects may look bad!)

- **Vertical Spacing**—Specifies, in pixels, the amount of whitespace above and below the object.

- **Horizontal Spacing**—Specifies, in pixels, the amount of whitespace to the left and right of the object.

- **Quality**—The higher the quality of an object, the better it will look. However, high-quality Flash objects—especially complex ones—take longer to load and require more processing power to work well. Available settings are Low, which is good for speed with a lower-quality appearance, and High, which opts for appearance over speed. Auto Low emphasizes speed but delivers higher quality wherever possible. Conversely, Auto High emphasizes quality *and* speed but opts for speed over quality if achieving both is not possible.

- **Scale**—Specifies how the movie will display. One option is *Default*, which makes the full object appear within the area defined by the width and height attributes. In this instance, the aspect ratio remains intact, preventing distortion. If you choose *No Border*, borders will be cropped. *Exact Fit* means that the object will fit into the exact width and height you determine, even if that's not its original size.

- **Align**—Specifies the object's alignment.

- **Background Color**—Specifies a background color for the object.

- **Play/Stop**—Allows you to preview your work. If you're in the preview, you can click the button, which will now be labeled Stop, to stop the preview.

- **Parameters**—To add or modify object parameters, click this option to open the Parameters dialog box.

INSERTING FLASH TEXT

Flash text is a Flash movie with only text in it that can be inserted into your Web pages in Dreamweaver. The advantage of Flash text is that you have more control over the typographic choice and quality because of the inherent nature of vector graphics. Vector type tends to be smoother and crisper, which improves readability.

Note that you do not need to have Flash MX 2004 installed to create Flash text in Dreamweaver MX 2004.

To insert a Flash text object, follow these steps:

1. Open a previously saved document, or save any new document or a document in progress.

2. Place your cursor where you'd like the text object to appear.

3. Select the Media drop-down menu on the Insert bar's Common tab. You can click the Flash Text icon, shown in Figure 12.7, or drag and drop it onto the page where you'd like the text object to appear. Alternatively, you can select Insert, Media, Flash Text. The Insert FlashText dialog box appears (see Figure 12.8) .

Figure 12.7
The Media menu on the Insert bar's Common tab contains three important icons relative to Flash objects: Flash, Flash Button, and Flash Text.

Figure 12.8
The Insert Flash Text dialog box contains numerous styling options.

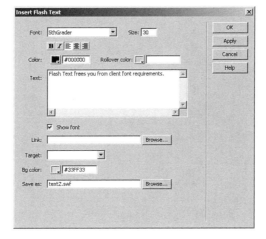

4. Add text into the text box labeled Text.
5. Modify the text as per your needs.
6. Customize a name for the Flash object file in the Save As field.
7. Click Apply or OK.

The Flash text is now inserted into your document.

ADDING FLASH BUTTONS

If you'd like to get a little more adventuresome and add Flash buttons to your page, Dreamweaver MX 2004 makes it remarkably easy to do so—as easy as adding and modifying Flash text. Some of the advantages of Flash buttons include smoother text, built-in mouseovers, and other effects.

Do the following to insert a Flash button object:

1. As with Flash text, make sure the file with which you are working is updated and saved.

2. Place your cursor where you'd like the button object to appear in the document.

3. Select the Media drop-down menu on the Insert bar's Common tab. You can click the Flash button icon or drag and drop it onto the page where you want the button object to appear. Alternatively, you can select Insert, Media, Flash Button. The Insert Flash Button dialog box appears (see Figure 12.9).

Figure 12.9
The Insert Flash Button dialog box provides everything you need to create a Flash button in Dreamweaver MX.

4. In the dialog box, browse to find the button style you'd like. Several styles are available, and you can get more from the Macromedia Exchange site by clicking the Get More Styles button found on the right side of the dialog box.

5. In the Button Text area, type in the text you want to appear on the button.

6. Customize the text style by using the Font and Size options. As with Flash Text objects, you can make a Flash button object a link.

7. You can select a background color for your button. As soon as you are happy with your choices, name your file and click Apply or OK to insert the button.

Dreamweaver MX now creates the button and inserts the Flash button object into the document.

PREVIEWING, EDITING, AND RESIZING FLASH BUTTONS AND TEXT

As you are working with Flash buttons and text objects, being able to preview their features is helpful. You can do this easily in Dreamweaver. You can also easily make additional edits and sizing changes to your objects, perfecting them as you work on your page.

PREVIEWING FLASH BUTTONS AND TEXT

To preview your Flash button or text object, make sure you're in Design view, select the Flash object, then click the Play button in the Property inspector. The Flash button or text object is now active, and you can test it out (for example, to see a rollover effect). Click Stop at any time to end the preview.

NOTE

Dreamweaver MX does not let you edit a Flash object while in preview mode.

EDITING FLASH OBJECTS

Here are several ways to open a Flash button or text object for editing:

- Double-click the object.
- Click the Edit button in the Property inspector.
- (Control-click) [Right-click] and select Edit from the context menu.

In the case of a Flash text object, the Insert Flash Text dialog box appears. If you are working with a button, the Insert Flash Button dialog box appears. In the case of a Flash movie, Flash MX 2004 itself launches for editing. You can now make any required modifications to the object.

RESIZING FLASH OBJECTS

Resizing Flash objects is easy and can be accomplished in Design view. First, select the object; then use the visual resize handles. In many cases, preserving the object's aspect ratio (its width and height relationship) is required. To do this, be sure to hold down the Shift key while resizing.

CAUTION

Not preserving an object's aspect ratio can result in a distorted or blurry display of that object.

12

If, at any point, you want to return the object to its original size, simply click the Reset Size button in the Property inspector.

MICROSOFT INTEGRATION FEATURES

Microsoft software is ubiquitous, and Macromedia has made some attempts over the years to accommodate that fact. For example, Dreamweaver has had for a long time a command to clean up the overweight HTML that Microsoft Word generates. It has also been possible to download extensions to clean up FrontPage HTML. For the past few versions,

Dreamweaver has been able to import tables built from exported Excel spreadsheets (or any other brand of spreadsheet offering basic text file export capability). However, integration with Microsoft's office productivity products has never been a huge selling point for Dreamweaver.

 That situation may be slowly changing. Dreamweaver MX 2004 brings an enhanced capability to import HTML from both Word and Excel. The big news here is that when you import such files (assuming you do it just right!), Dreamweaver preserves CSS styles. That is, for example, if you've created some Word styles in your Word document, Dreamweaver rebuilds these styles as internal (embedded) styles when you bring the content into a Dreamweaver document. This capability can dramatically reduce your reformatting time after an import operation. (It does require that you're using Office 2000 or newer, however.)

The trick in maintaining CSS styles is to copy a selection from the Microsoft Office application and paste it into your Dreamweaver document by using the command Edit, Paste Formatted. We found that using the commands File, Import, Word Document (or File, Import, Excel Document) do *not* trigger the CSS import, as you might reasonably expect them to do. These File commands do, however, perform an adequate job of converting a native .doc or .xls file to HTML, which is undeniably convenient compared to the old method of saving HTML files or comma-delimited files from the Microsoft applications before bringing them into Dreamweaver. (You can still use the File, Import, Word Document command to bring in a file that was exported as HTML from Word, by the way.)

CAUTION

Also be aware that merely formatting text in color in Word or Excel is not enough to maintain that color information when copying and pasting to Dreamweaver. The color must be part of a defined style for this feature to work.

TROUBLESHOOTING

PLUG-IN AVAILABILITY

My plug-in is not working outside of Dreamweaver. Why?

If you install a plug-in directly into Dreamweaver rather than to your browser, it might not be available in your Web browsers. You need to reinstall the plug-in to its recommended browser location for it to be available in your Web browser.

DISABLED EDIT BUTTON

The Edit Page button in Contribute is disabled, but I believe I have permission to edit the page. What's going on?

Another person is using Contribute or Dreamweaver to edit the page.

PEER TO PEER: MACROMEDIA EXTENSIONS FOR MARKUP COMPLIANCE

Macromedia Exchange extension authors have written several important extensions related to proper markup. They include

- **DMX Tidy**—This is an extension version of Dave Raggett's famous HTML Tidy program, used to tidy up problems in HTML and XHTML, and even convert HTML to XHTML.

- **Entity Converter**—This extension converts characters into entities, and vice versa.

- **DOCTYPE Inserter**—Inserts the appropriate DOCTYPE declarations into your documents.

PEER TO PEER: MARKUP AND CONTRIBUTE

Because Contribute is meant for a variety of people who do not necessarily have Web design and development experience, the program has very little sophistication when it comes to markup. Text formatting uses font tags and the like. You can't edit style sheets, and although layer content is editable, the layers themselves are not.

As a result, it becomes imperative to have a style guide or other method with which to achieve conformance. The site designers and developers, if adhering to standards, can provide editors with guidelines as to which Contribute features to use and which to not use.

What's more, if compliance is a concern, either content editors should be given some guidelines on how to validate a page and make edits external to Contribute, or the designers and developers working on the site should perform validation tasks.

DEVELOPING COLDFUSION APPLICATIONS IN DREAMWEAVER

In this chapter

Dynamic Dreamweaver   288

Creating a Site for Dynamic Pages   289

Database Operations   290

Making Client Access Easier: Web Services and Components   311

DYNAMIC DREAMWEAVER

Dreamweaver MX 2004 has a number of features designed to help you create Web pages that pull data from databases via ColdFusion. (It also supports other dynamic data technologies, such as PHP, ASP, ASP.NET, and JSP. This chapter focuses exclusively on ColdFusion, however.) Many of these features are based on auto-generation of HTML and ColdFusion Markup Language (CFML).

> **NOTE**
>
> ColdFusion Markup Language (CFML) is the HTML-like language for giving instructions to the ColdFusion server. CFML tags are highly intuitive for someone who already knows some HTML.

Some features generate individual words, such as the name of a database table or column, which you can drag and drop into the document window. Some generate blocks of code, complete pages, or even multiple pages for database interactions such as previewing, inserting, updating, and displaying data. Dreamweaver auto-generates code for dynamic tables, input forms, links to other files, conditional "if-else-then" logic, error trapping, and many other HTML and CFML features. For instance, to create a dynamic table (a table populated with data from a database), you press a button and fill in a few parameters on a dialog screen. Dreamweaver auto-generates an ordinary HTML table, with a little CFML thrown in to do the database work.

Among the most advanced and useful Dreamweaver features are those that auto-generate ColdFusion components (CFCs) that make ColdFusion functions more easily accessible to clients, including Flash clients that use Macromedia's Flash Remoting technology and Web services clients that use Simple Object Access Protocol (SOAP). Creating useful CFCs and Web services requires programming in CFML or Server-Side ActionScript. However, Dreamweaver and ColdFusion make the mechanics of creating and deploying CFCs and Web services very, very easy.

→ For more on Flash Remoting and Web services, **see** "Flash Remoting," **page 666**, and "Web Services," **page 672**, both in Chapter 23, "Using Flash for Dynamic Data."

 When they're created, dynamic objects (such as the dynamic table) are not formatted in any way, so they look very plain. For clarity's sake, I've left objects in their simplest forms in this chapter. However, because they are ordinary HTML objects, you can use standard HTML formatting techniques, including CSS, to make them look nice.

Dreamweaver MX 2004 doesn't bring any new features for developing ColdFusion applications. However, the interface you use to get to those features has changed somewhat, mainly in the redesign of the Dreamweaver Insert bar, which now gives you a choice between a tabbed and a menu interface. (Before it was always tabbed.) There's also a new Favorites category on the Insert bar, which you can populate with your most frequently used objects.

The other main interface to dynamic data-related features, the Application panel, has not changed.

→ For more on the redesigned Insert bar, **see** "Exploring the Document Window," **page 76**, in Chapter 5, "Working in the Dreamweaver Environment."

CREATING A SITE FOR DYNAMIC PAGES

When you're creating a new site in Dreamweaver (Site, Manage Sites, New), there's just one step that's specific to creating a site that includes ColdFusion pages: In the Testing Server category of the Site Definition dialog, choose ColdFusion as the server model, as shown in Figure 13.1.

Figure 13.1
When creating a new site that will contain ColdFusion pages, choose ColdFusion in the "Server model" drop-down menu in the Testing Server category of the Site Definition dialog.

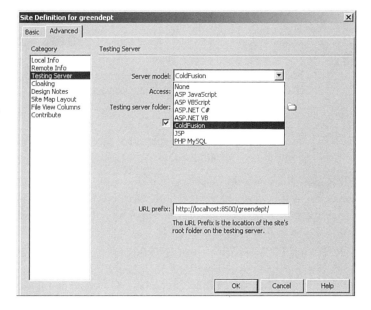

NOTE

Before doing any of the things discussed in the rest of this chapter, you have to do two things:

- Create or obtain a database. Databases are created with database management systems such as Microsoft Access, Microsoft SQL Server, or MySQL. The CD accompanying this book includes a Microsoft Access database, greendept.mdb, which was used to create the examples in this chapter.

- Put the database somewhere where ColdFusion can find it—usually on the ColdFusion server itself. ColdFusion runs only under Windows. For development purposes, if you're on a Windows machine, it's convenient to install the ColdFusion

continues

continued

> server and the database on your local machine. If you're running Dreamweaver on a Mac, then the ColdFusion server and the database will be on a Windows machine that you access over the network. (Caution: Some early testers found this to be an unstable configuration.) Either way, a System DSN (Data Source Name) must be created on the Windows machine, so that Windows applications can access the database. You'll probably find it easiest to use the ColdFusion Administrator to create the System DSN.

DATABASE OPERATIONS

If you want to use ColdFusion to integrate data into your Web pages, but you're not an expert in databases, CFML, or Structured Query Language (SQL), Dreamweaver can make your life a lot easier.

NOTE

> Structured Query Language (SQL, usually pronounced SEE'-KWUL) is the standard programming language for interacting with databases.

Specifically, here are three important tasks that Dreamweaver automates, often so successfully that they become almost instantaneous:

- Databases organize data into tables, and within tables into fields or columns. This organization is the *schema* of the database. Dreamweaver displays the schema in a hierarchical tree format that makes it easier to see how the data is organized. Dreamweaver also allows you to preview the data itself.

- CFML extends HTML with a set of tags, the most important of which are database-related. For four basic operations—retrieving, updating, inserting, and deleting data—Dreamweaver automatically produces the CFML code. The CFML code, which you can see in Code View mode in the document window, is a database command enclosed in CFML tags—specifically, `<cfquery> </cfquery>` tags.

- The database command inside the `<cfquery>` tags is expressed as a SQL statement, which the ColdFusion server passes on to the database, which performs the desired operation. The `<cfquery>` tag is similar for all these operations, but the SQL commands and syntax change depending on the operation. Dreamweaver produces the SQL statement automatically, so you don't have to know any SQL.

You can modify, delete, or move the CFML and SQL code produced by Dreamweaver. Do this in Code View mode in the document window.

→ For more on CFML and ColdFusion architecture, **see** Chapter 32, **page 875**, and Chapter 33, "ColdFusion Markup Language (CFML)," **page 885**.

PREVIEWING DATA

Before you can do any of the things described in the rest of this chapter, ColdFusion must be up and running. See Chapter 32 for a discussion of what this may entail, beyond just installing ColdFusion.

Dreamweaver offers a quick, convenient way to look at your data. You might want to do this, for example, to get an idea what the data will look like when you display it. Data is displayed 25 rows (records) at a time. Here's the procedure for previewing data:

1. Go to the Databases panel in the Application panel group. Here you'll find a listing of all the databases for which a system DSN has been defined on your machine.

   The databases are grayed out and inaccessible until you open a document. For previewing data, any kind of Dreamweaver document will do. The document is not used for previewing the data. A ColdFusion document is used in the next section on retrieving data. To open a ColdFusion document, click on ColdFusion in the Create New column of the startup page, or select File, New, Dynamic page, ColdFusion.

2. Click the plus sign to the left of the database name to expand the first level of the tree displaying the database's schema (structure). (Also loads the schema if it's not already loaded.)

3. Click the plus sign to the left of Tables to see a list of tables. (Figure 13.2 shows the greendept database expanded to show the fields in the Products table.)

4. Select the table you want to preview, bring up the context menu (right-click on the PC or Control-click on the Mac) and choose View Data, as shown in Figure 13.3. Figure 13.4 shows the preview of the Categories table in the greendept database.

NOTE

> Where the PC uses plus signs and minus signs to expand and collapse hierarchical trees, the Mac uses right-facing triangles and downward facing triangles, similar to those for maximizing and minimizing panels.

13

Click the plus or minus signs to expand or collapse the tree. Clicking the plus sign to the left of a database (such as greendept) both loads the database schema and expands the tree. The Refresh button reloads the database schema, so any changes you've made will show up. The Modify data sources button takes you to the ColdFusion Administrator, where you can manage system DSNs.

Figure 13.2
The Databases panel in the Application panel group.

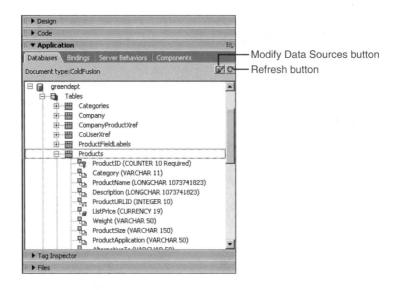

Figure 13.3
The context menu (right-click on the PC, Control-click on the Mac) options for a database table.

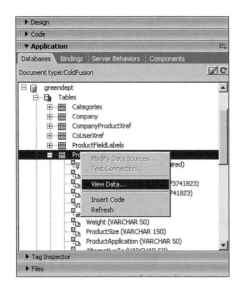

Choose View Data to browse the data in the table. Other options are

- Modify Data Sources (grayed out because it is active only for databases, not database tables) takes you to the ColdFusion Administrator, where you can add, delete, or modify system DSNs.

- Test Connection is grayed out for ColdFusion. For other server models, it tests the connection to the database. Not necessary for ColdFusion.

- Insert Code, active only in Code View, inserts the name of the selected database, table, or field into the code.

- Refresh reloads the database schema, so that the Databases panel reflects any changes made since the last load.

Figure 13.4
The View data screen as the Categories table was being built in the greendept database. To get this kind of display, select the table, right-click (PC) or Control-click (Mac) and choose View Data, as shown in Figure 13.3.

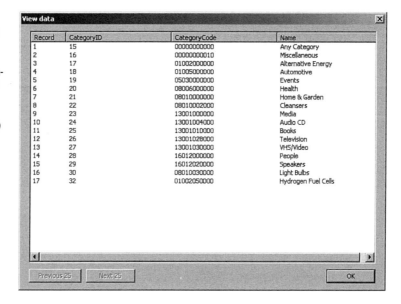

 Getting a timeout error when trying to view data? There are several possible solutions in the "Troubleshooting" section at the end of this chapter.

If, after loading the database schema (step 2 in the procedure just described), you change something in the schema—add or delete a table, for instance, or change the fields in a table—you will need to refresh the Databases panel to have those changes show up there. You can do this in one of two ways: by using the Refresh button in the upper right of the Databases panel (see Figure 13.2), or by selecting Refresh in the context menu for the database, a table, or a field.

RETRIEVING DATA

Unlike previewing data, in which you do not use a Dreamweaver document in any way, you retrieve data by coding and running a ColdFusion document. So if you do not have a ColdFusion document open yet, click ColdFusion in the Create New column of the startup page, or select File, New, Dynamic page, ColdFusion. If you were coding by hand, you would retrieve data by enclosing an SQL SELECT statement within a ColdFusion <cfquery> tag. Instead, you can use the Dreamweaver Bindings panel in the Application panel group to create the SQL and CFML code automatically.

13

NOTE

> You can create CFML by dragging and dropping from the Bindings panel into the document window. For instance, in Figure 13.8, dragging ProductID into the document creates this CFML code: `<cfoutput>#qProducts.ProductID#</cfoutput>`. This displays the ProductID of the first record in the Recordset.

NOTE

> You can drag and drop from the Databases panel into the document window, too. In Code View, the *name* of the table or column is created in the document, which helps you avoid typos. In Design View, dragging a table brings up the Recordset dialog configured for that table.

Here's the procedure for retrieving data:

1. Go to the Bindings panel in the Application panel group. If you have already created one or more Recordsets, they're listed here. If you haven't created any Recordsets yet, you see the list of instructions shown in Figure 13.5, the final instruction being to press the + button and choose Recordset.

2. Press the + button and choose Recordset, as shown in Figure 13.6. This brings up the Recordset dialog, shown in Figure 13.7.

3. Fill in the Recordset dialog, as shown in Figure 13.7. Provide an arbitrary name for the query that you are creating (qProducts in the figure). Choose the appropriate system DSN from the Data source drop-down menu (greendept in the figure). If the database is password-protected, provide the username and password (not required in this example). Select the columns that you want to retrieve. Optionally, select a field and a value on which to filter. In the figure, the only records selected will be those for which the Category field is equal to 13001010000 (the category code for books). Without this filter, all products would be retrieved; with it, only books are retrieved.

4. Click the OK button in the upper-right corner of the Recordset dialog. The Recordset is created in the document, as shown in the document window (on the left) in Figure 13.8. The Recordset is also represented visually in the Bindings panel, as shown on the right in Figure 13.8.

Figure 13.5
This is what you'll see in the Bindings panel in the Application panel group prior to creating any Recordsets.

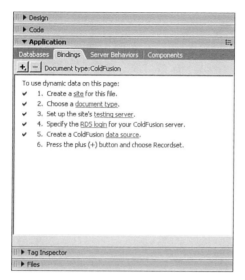

Figure 13.6
Press the + button and choose Recordset to bring up the Recordset dialog, which automates the process of creating CFML and SQL code for retrieving data.

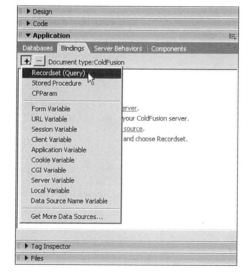

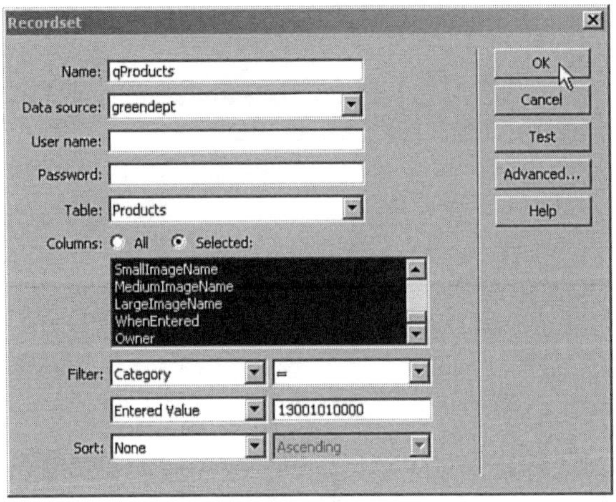

Figure 13.7
The Recordset dialog, which automates the process of creating CFML and SQL code for retrieving data.

Figure 13.8
The completed Recordset, in the document window on the left (within the `<cfquery>` tags), and represented visually in the Bindings panel on the right. Click the Refresh button in the upper right corner to update the Bindings panel if you add, edit, or delete a Recordset in the document window.

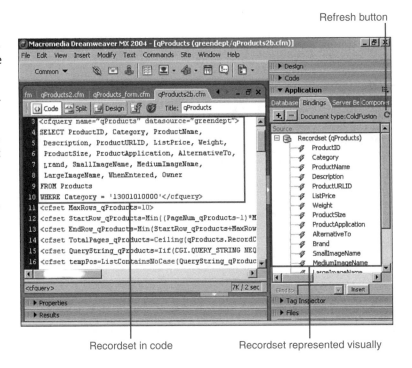

Refresh button

Recordset in code   Recordset represented visually

If you want to edit a Recordset, you have two options: If you are comfortable with the CFML and SQL involved, you can edit the code manually in Code View in the document window. Alternatively, you can double click any of the text associated with the Recordset in the Bindings panel. You have to click on text, not an icon. For example, in Figure 13.8, you would click on Recordset (qProducts) or any of the field names below that (ProductID and so on). This brings up the Recordset dialog (Figure 13.7), allowing you to edit the Recordset.

Note that all the columns in the Products table have been selected in this example. Clicking the All radio button in the Recordset dialog could have accomplished this. (Refer to Figure 13.7.) Instead, the Select radio button was clicked and then all the columns were selected. If the All radio button had been clicked, the SQL statement in Figure 13.8 would have begun SELECT * FROM Products. The asterisk is a wild-card meaning "all columns." This works fine in Microsoft Access. However, some other databases may automatically create other columns that you do not want to retrieve. If you were to use your code with those databases, you would retrieve the unwanted columns. Therefore, to make your code more flexible and portable across database systems, it is better to list each column individually.

Notice that the Bindings panel has a Refresh button in the upper-right corner. Click this button to update the view in the Bindings panel after you modify a Recordset.

If you load the page just created (qProducts.cfm in Figure 13.8, also available on the CD accompanying this book) into a browser, nothing is displayed. By itself, a Recordset displays nothing. It simply retrieves and holds data for possible use elsewhere in the document. The next section shows various ways to use the Recordset data in the document.

By default, the Recordset data is available only in the document that contains the Recordset. To access the Recordset from other documents, you can store the Recordset in a ColdFusion variable that persists across documents, such as a client, session, or application variable. Another possibility is to pass individual pieces of data from page to page as URL variables.

NOTE

> Dreamweaver enables you to create development-time variables for pages that need a form variable, URL variable, or other variable. While in the dynamic page, click + on the Bindings panel and choose the variable type. Variables created here exist only in Dreamweaver.

USING DYNAMIC DATA

After you have created a Recordset, you can either display the data in the browser or use it "behind the scenes" to determine whether a check box is checked, for instance, or whether an item on a selection list is selected.

Dreamweaver makes it easy for you to insert data anywhere in your Web page as text, in a table, or as an item on a menu or selection list. You can also use retrieved data to determine whether a check box is checked, or whether a radio button or list item is selected.

13

In addition, there is a Live Data feature that enables you to see the data in Dreamweaver while editing the page in Design View.

With the exception of the Live Data feature, the features illustrated in this section are all data insertion features. You get to them via the Insert menu on the main menu bar, or via the Insert toolbar. The Insert toolbar is generally quicker. Here, we'll look at six features reached via the Dynamic Data button on the Insert bar, shown in Figure 13.9. This is a multi-purpose button: Click the downward-facing triangle on the right side of the button to display these six options, then select the option you want. The button remains associated with that option until you change it, even if you the exit and restart Dreamweaver.

Figure 13.9
The Dynamic Data button on the Insert bar.

CREATING AND EDITING A DYNAMIC TABLE

The first option, Dynamic Table, uses an HTML table, combined with a little CFML, to display either all the data in the Recordset, or a configurable number of records starting from the beginning of the Recordset. It also allows you to set three standard HTML table attributes (border, cell padding, and cell spacing), as shown in Figure 13.10. After you've created the table, you can edit it in Code View or Design View.

Figure 13.10
The Dynamic Table dialog. As configured here, the dynamic table will show the first 10 records retrieved. For navigation to subsequent records, add a Recordset Navigation Bar, as shown in Figure 13.11.

Figure 13.11 shows a portion of the dynamic table displaying the qProducts Recordset.

VCR-style Recordset Navigation Bar

Figure 13.11
A portion of the dynamic table configured in Figure 13.10, displayed in a browser. Above the table, the Recordset Paging button on the Insert bar (shown in Figure 13.12) was used to add a Recordset Navigation Bar.

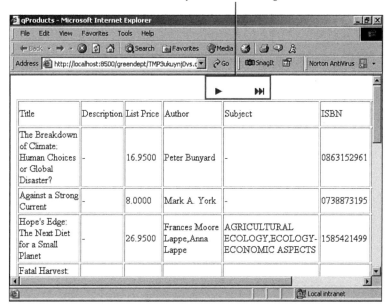

A dynamic table by itself does not include any navigation. However, you can easily add navigation by using the Recordset Paging button on the Insert bar, shown in figure 13.12. This is the procedure:

1. Click at the point in the document where you want to insert the Recordset navigation control.

2. Click on the Recordset Paging button on the Insert bar, bringing up the Recordset Navigation Bar dialog. Both the button and the dialog are shown in Figure 13.12.

3. On the Recordset Navigation Bar dialog, choose a Recordset and select either text or images, to show the navigation controls as text or VCR-style visual controls. The latter are illustrated at the top of Figure 13.11.

4. Click the OK button.

After you've created the dynamic table, you can edit it in Code View. For instance, if there are columns that you don't need, it's easy to eliminate them. In Figure 13.10, for example, ProductID, Category, and ProductURLID would not be meaningful to a user. (In the database, they are used as links to other tables that do provide meaningful information.) It's easy to eliminate them.

A Dreamweaver dynamic table is an HTML table with two rows. The first row is pure HTML. It contains the column headings, taken from the field names in the database. The second row contains ColdFusion variables, enclosed in pound signs, like this:

13

#qProducts.ProductID#. (In ColdFusion, pound signs indicate a variable as opposed to ordinary, literal text.) The second row also has CFML cfoutput tags around it, to display the data.

Figure 13.12
The Recordset Paging button, and the Recordset Navigation Bar dialog it brings up, enable you to add navigation for a dynamic table.

In the following HTML/CFML listing of the qProducts table, you'd delete the six bolded lines to eliminate the three columns that are not useful to the end user.

```
<table border="1">
  <tr>
    <td>ProductID</td>
    <td>Category</td>
    <td>ProductName</td>
    <td>Description</td>
    <td>ProductURLID</td>
    <td>ListPrice</td>
    <td>Weight</td>
    <td>ProductSize</td>
    <td>ProductApplication</td>
    <td>AlternativeTo</td>
    <td>Brand</td>
    <td>SmallImageName</td>
    <td>MediumImageName</td>
    <td>LargeImageName</td>
    <td>WhenEntered</td>
    <td>Owner</td>
  </tr>
  <cfoutput query="qProducts"
    startRow="#StartRow_qProducts#" maxRows="#MaxRows_qProducts#">
    <tr>
      <td>#qProducts.ProductID#</td>
      <td>#qProducts.Category#</td>
      <td>#qProducts.ProductName#</td>
      <td>#qProducts.Description#</td>
```

```
      <td>#qProducts.ProductURLID#</td>
      <td>#qProducts.ListPrice#</td>
      <td>#qProducts.Weight#</td>
      <td>#qProducts.ProductSize#</td>
      <td>#qProducts.ProductApplication#</td>
      <td>#qProducts.AlternativeTo#</td>
      <td>#qProducts.Brand#</td>
      <td>#qProducts.SmallImageName#</td>
      <td>#qProducts.MediumImageName#</td>
      <td>#qProducts.LargeImageName#</td>
      <td>#qProducts.WhenEntered#</td>
      <td>#qProducts.Owner#</td>
    </tr>
  </cfoutput>
</table>
```

At the same time, you could "clean up" some of the other headings. For instance, ListPrice would be better as List Price.

If you try this exercise with greendept.mdb from the CD, you'll see that other headings look just plain wrong: For instance, the Weight heading has peoples' names under it, and the text in the ProductSize column clearly has nothing to do with size. This database is designed to hold any type of product, service or event. Rather than try to design a single set of fields to fit all the possible categories, it was decided to re-purpose fields as needed for each category. For books, for instance, we don't need to know the weight, but we do need to know the author. Therefore, the Weight field was re-purposed to hold the author's name.

Although there are ways to use CFML to put in correct headings, you can just manually edit the headings here. Because this Recordset contains only books, change Weight to Author, and ProductSize to Subject in the first row. Make changes only in the first row. ColdFusion will still think of the author's name as #qProducts.Weight#, for example, so nothing in the second row should change.

On the CD accompanying this book, qProducts2.cfm has the unaltered version of the qProducts dynamic table, whereas qProducts2b.cfm has an edited version. (If you're curious, the ProductFieldLabels table has headings for all categories and would form the basis for automating the process of applying the right headings.)

INSERTING DYNAMIC TEXT

Dynamic text is most commonly used when a Recordset is known to contain only one row. If the Recordset contains more than one row of data, as in the case of the qProducts Recordset, the dynamic text by itself displays data from the first row only. One way to display data from multiple rows is to use a dynamic table.

Figure 13.13 shows the Dynamic Text configuration dialog, the resulting CFML, and a typical result in the browser. On the configuration dialog, select a field name and optionally apply a format. Dreamweaver automatically creates the code in the Code box. You can also edit the code in the Code box, before clicking OK. After you've created the dynamic text, you can edit it in Code View or Design View.

Figure 13.13
Inserting dynamic text: the configuration dialog, the resulting CFML, and a typical result in the browser.

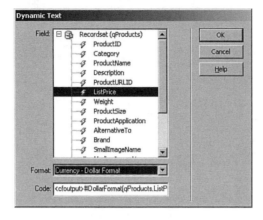

```
<cfoutput>#DollarFormat(qProducts.ListPrice)#</cfoutput>
```

$16.95

USING DYNAMIC DATA IN FORMS AND MENUS

Using dynamic data in forms and menus can simplify site maintenance. For instance, if a group of menu options appears on many pages, you can change the options on all those pages by editing the data in one place: in the database. The same principle holds for radio buttons, check boxes, text fields, and images.

Two common to ways of using Recordset data in a form are displaying the data and using it to determine the state of a visual control. Dreamweaver auto-generates code for both of these uses. The data can be displayed in a text box or selection list. In addition, it can be used to decide whether a check box should be checked by default, or whether a radio button, menu item, or list item should be selected by default.

Before adding dynamic data functionality, you must create a form. Select the Forms category by using the menu at the left of the Insert bar. Create the form with the Form button and add other form elements as desired by using the buttons on the Insert bar, shown in Figure 13.14. The left-most eight form elements on the Insert bar can use dynamic data, either displaying the data (Text Field and Text Area) or containing the data without showing it (Hidden Field), or they can use the data to determine the state of the form control (Check Box, Radio, and Radio Group). List/Menu and Jump Menu can both display data and use data to determine which item or items in the list or menu are selected initially.

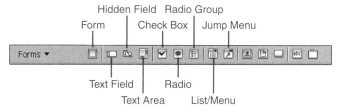

Hidden Field   Radio Group

Form   Check Box   Jump Menu

Text Field   Radio

Text Area   List/Menu

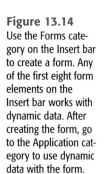

Figure 13.14
Use the Forms category on the Insert bar to create a form. Any of the first eight form elements on the Insert bar works with dynamic data. After creating the form, go to the Application category to use dynamic data with the form.

The basic procedure for using dynamic data in forms is the same for all types of form elements: After creating the form, go to the Application category and select one of the bottom four Dynamic Data button options, shown earlier in Figure 13.9. Each of the four works only with particular form elements. For example, Dynamic Text works with Text Field, Hidden Field, and Text Area. Dynamic Checkbox works with the Checkbox form element. Dynamic Radio Group works with Radio and Radio Group. List/Menu works with the List/Menu and Jump Menu form elements.

Dreamweaver looks at all the forms in your document, determines which of the form elements in your document can be used with the dynamic data feature you have chosen, and presents you with a configuration dialog listing those elements so that you can choose one. The configuration dialog also lets you specify from which Recordset field to get the data.

The dynamic Text Field just displays the data in the database Field that you select. (See Figure 13.15.) The auto-generated code looks like this:

```
<input value="<cfoutput>#qProducts.ProductName#</cfoutput>"
    name="productName" type="text">
```

This code uses the ColdFusion `cfoutput` tag to display the dynamic data. (All the sample code in this section is in `qProducts_form.cfm`, on the CD accompanying this book.)

The dynamic check box is checked if the dynamic data that you select is equal to a value that you enter in the dialog. (See Figure 13.16.)

Here's the code Dreamweaver auto-generated based on the dialog shown in Figure 13.16.

```
<input <cfif (#qProducts.Category# EQ 13001010000)>checked</cfif>
    name="isBook" type="checkbox" value="">
```

This code uses the ColdFusion `cfif` tag to include the `checked` attribute only if the stated condition is met, namely that the dynamic data, `qProducts.Category`, is equal to 13001010000.

13

The text field you select here...

Figure 13.15
The Dynamic Text dialog, which enables you display dynamic data in a text field. (An example of auto-generated code is shown in Figure 13.17.)

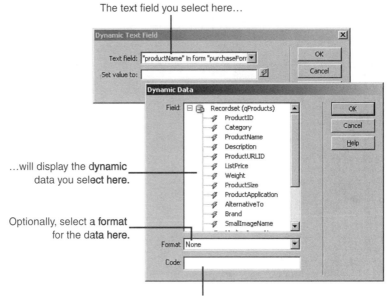

...will display the **dynamic data** you select **here**.

Optionally, select a **format** for the **data here**.

Dreamweaver shows you editable code here.

The checkbox you select here will be checked...

Figure 13.16
The Dynamic Checkbox dialog, which enables you to use dynamic data to determine whether a check box is checked.

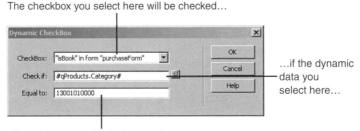

...if the dynamic data you select here...

...is equal to the value that you enter here.

13

Radio buttons are checked if the dynamic data that you select is equal to the value assigned to the radio button in the original form. (See Figure 13.17.)

Here's code for one radio button, auto-generated by Dreamweaver based on the dialog shown in Figure 13.17:

```
<input <cfoutput>#Iif(qProducts.Category EQ "14005000000",DE("CHECKED"),DE(""))#
    </cfoutput> type="radio" name="Shipping" value="14005000000">
```

This code uses the ColdFusion `iif` tag to include the `CHECKED` attribute only if the stated condition is met, namely that the dynamic data, `qProducts.Category`, is equal to 14005000000, the value assigned to the radio button in the original HTML-only form:

```
<input type="radio" name="Shipping" value="14005000000">
```

Radio buttons in the radio group
you select here will be checked…

Figure 13.17
The Dynamic Radio
Group dialog, which
allows you to use
dynamic data to
determine the
checked/unchecked
state of a radio button
or buttons.

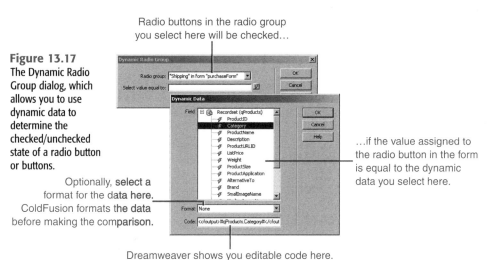

…if the value assigned to
the radio button in the form
is equal to the dynamic
data you select here.

Optionally, **select a**
format for the data here.
ColdFusion formats the data
before making the comparison.

Dreamweaver shows you editable code here.

When you create a dynamic list or menu, you specify (from top to bottom on the dialog shown in Figure 13.18):

1. The list or menu.
2. Optional static values that will be submitted to the server when the form is submitted, and display labels to accompany those static values.
3. The Recordset to use for dynamic data.
4. A dynamic data item that determines the value returned to the server when the form is submitted.
5. A dynamic data item for generating display labels.
6. A comparison value, which can be either entered manually or generated dynamically. If the value in step 4 equals the comparison value, the list or menu item will be pre-selected when the page is initially loaded.

Here's code for a selection list, auto-generated by Dreamweaver based on the dialog shown in Figure 13.18.

```
<select name="productList" size="10" multiple>
  <cfoutput query="qProducts">
    <option value="#qProducts.ProductID#"
     <cfif (qProducts.ProductID EQ 1)>selected</cfif>>
     #qProducts.ProductName#</option>
  </cfoutput>
</select>
```

This code uses the ColdFusion `cfif` tag to include the `selected` attribute only if the stated condition is met, namely that the dynamic data, `qProducts.ProductID`, is equal to 1. It also uses the ColdFusion `cfoutput` tag to display the items in the Recordset as the items on the selection list.

13

This list or menu will:

• Submit to the server the static values you enter here

• Display static labels you enter here

• Use the qProducts Recordset as the source for dynamic data

• Submit the ProductID to the server when the form is submitted

• Display the ProductName to the user

• Pre-select items for which the ProductID is equal to 1. You can either enter a value here (like 1) or use dynamic data.

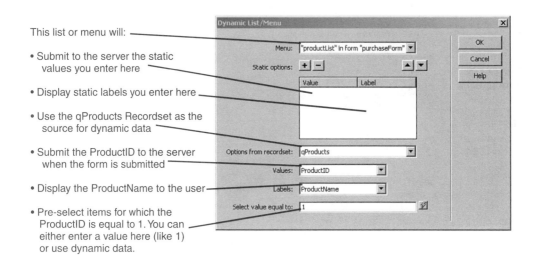

Figure 13.18
The List/Menu dialog enables you display dynamic data in a list or menu and determine which items are pre-selected.

LIVE DATA: VIEWING DATA WHILE EDITING

By default, Design View shows static content, but not dynamic data. However, because users will be seeing the dynamic data, you may want to see it while you're working, too. You can do that by clicking the Live Data button. Figure 13.19 shows qProducts_form.cfm (on the CD accompanying this book) with and without live data.

NOTE

Links don't work in Live Data mode. You have to view the page in a browser to test links.

Most normal Dreamweaver editing tasks can be performed in Live Data mode. For instance, you can edit or delete static text, or change the properties of a table or a list/menu in the Property inspector. In addition, you can modify dynamic content by editing server behaviors, as described in the next section.

USING SERVER BEHAVIORS TO MODIFY DYNAMIC DATA

After you have created any of the dynamic content objects (dynamic table, text, text field, check box, radio group, list/menu), you can edit them in the Server Behaviors panel in the Application panel group. In the Server Behaviors panel, you can see a list of all the dynamic objects on the current page. Double-click on any one of them to bring up the same dialog that you used to create the object originally. Make any changes you want, click OK, and the object will be modified.

Figure 13.19
A dynamic text field, check box, radio group, and list/menu before and after selecting the Live Data option. After modifying dynamic content on the Server Behaviors panel, click the Refresh button to redisplay dynamic content. Alternatively, enable Auto Refresh by clicking the check box, and dynamic content will redisplay automatically.

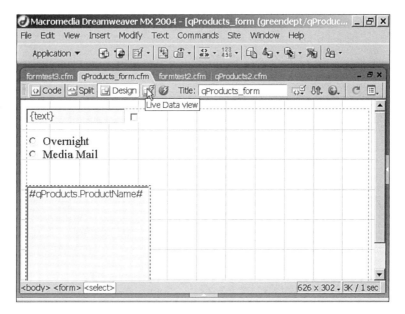

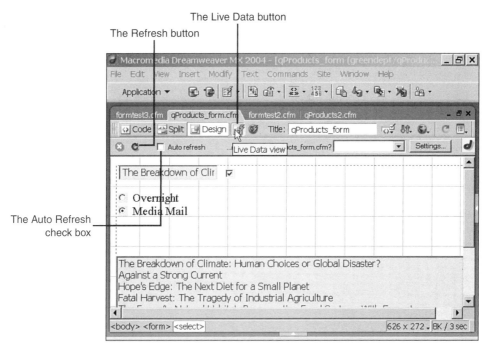

You can also delete objects in the Server Behaviors panel. Just select the object and press the Delete key. If other objects in the document depend on the object you are about to delete (for instance, you're about to delete a Recordset that is used to populate a dynamic table), Dreamweaver warns you, and you have to confirm the deletion.

When you make changes to the dynamic data, Dreamweaver normally stops displaying live data. To display live data again, click the Refresh button in the upper-left corner of the screen. (Refer to Figure 13.19.) To save yourself the trouble of clicking the Refresh button, enable auto-refresh by checking the Auto-refresh check box to the right of the Refresh button. (Again, refer to Figure 13.19.) A potential downside of auto-refresh is a delay while dynamic data is refreshed.

INSERTING, UPDATING, AND DELETING DATABASE RECORDS

Dreamweaver makes it relatively easy to create pages to insert, update, and delete database records. For all three operations, you start by creating a new page (File, New). Choose the Dynamic Page category in the first column, choose ColdFusion in the second column, and click the Create button.

With just a few mouse clicks, you can create a record insertion page that contains a form allowing the user to fill in information to populate a record. It also contains ColdFusion code for inserting the new record into the database.

In the Application category of the Insert bar, select Record Insertion Form Wizard by using the Insert Record button. (It's the fourth button from the right—see Figure 13.20.)

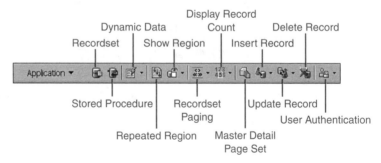

Figure 13.20
The Application category on the Insert bar provides access to many commonly used dynamic data features. Buttons with downward-facing triangles are multipurpose buttons. Click the triangle to expand the list of options associated with the button. Selections persist until you change them.

The Record Insertion Form dialog appears, as shown in Figure 13.21. The only fields that are always required are the data source and a table. If the database is password protected, you'll also need a username and password. All the fields in the table are included in the insertion form by default. Select a field and click the minus sign to remove that field from the record insertion form. When the new record is inserted, that field either is blank or has the default content defined by the database. Click the plus sign, pick one or more field names on the Add Columns dialog, and click OK to re-include those fields in the insertion form. You can also define a page where the user is redirected after inserting the record.

When you click OK on the Record Insertion Form dialog, Dreamweaver creates the form.

Figure 13.21
Using the information you provide on the Record Insertion Form, Dreamweaver auto-generates code for inserting a record in the database.

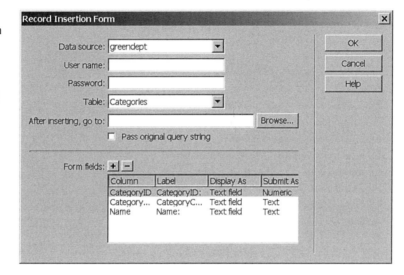

A record update page presents the user with a form showing the data currently contained in a record. The user can use the same form to change the data in one or more fields. When the user is satisfied with all changes, he or she clicks an Update record button to update the record.

Before you can create a page to update a record, you first have to create a Recordset containing the record you want to update. Then choose Record Update Form Wizard by using the Update Record button on the Insert bar. (The third button from the right in Figure 13.20.)

The Record Update Form dialog appears. The information required is similar to the Record Insertion Form, except that you also have to specify a Unique key column, a column (field) containing data that uniquely identifies each record in the table. This would typically be a primary key with no duplicates, such as ProductID in the Products table in the greendept database. The dialog provides a drop-down list of columns that could be used. Often there is only one such column, in which case it is automatically selected. This unique column is used in the record update form to unambiguously identify the record to update.

13

To create a page to delete a record, click on the Delete Record button and provide the name of the database (for example, greendept) and the name of the table (for example, Products). Optionally, you can also specify a page to go to after the record is deleted. (See Figure 13.22.)

Figure 13.22
The Delete Record dialog creates a page for deleting a record from a database.

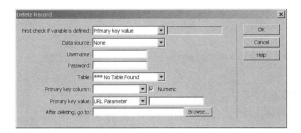

The Delete Record button doesn't create a form. Instead, it creates a block of ColdFusion code to delete a record. The record to be deleted must be identified by a primary key column, which is passed as a URL parameter to the page that performs the deletion. For example, the code for deleting a record from the Products table in the greendept database looks like this:

```
<cfif IsDefined("URL.ProductID") AND #URL.ProductID# NEQ "">
  <cfquery datasource="greendept">
  DELETE FROM Products WHERE ProductID=#URL.ProductID#
  </cfquery>
</cfif>
```

This code says, "If there is a URL parameter named ProductID, and it's not blank, then delete the record in the Products table in which the ProductID field is equal to the value passed in the URL parameter."

DRILLING DOWN INTO DATA WITH MASTER/DETAIL PAGES

A common way to give users convenient access to data is to first show a master page providing brief identifying information for a number of records, along with links that allow the user to drill down to a detail page for any selected record. For example, the master page might have just the title and the author for a number of books. For any selected book, the user could drill down to get more detailed information, such as the publisher, the publication date, and so on. Dreamweaver can do much of the heavy lifting for creating such pages, auto-generating a master page (with multi-screen navigation, if necessary) and a detail page—all based on one relatively simple dialog screen, shown in Figure 13.23.

Both the master and detail pages are dynamic tables and can be edited in Code View or Design View.

→ Editing dynamic tables is discussed earlier in this chapter under "Creating and Editing a Dynamic Table," **page 298**.

Before you can create master/detail pages, you first have to create a Recordset. Then choose Master Detail Page Set on the Insert bar. (The fifth button from the right in Figure 13.20.) Figure 13.23 explains how to fill in the Master Detail Page Set dialog.

You can browse to an existing page, and use that as the detail page. If you type in the name of a page that does not exist (for example, see detail in Figure 13.23), Dreamweaver creates it and opens it.

ColdFusion needs a unique key to pass from the master page to the detail page, to uniquely identify the desired record. For instance, ProductID is the unique key in Figure 13.23. ColdFusion passes the data in the unique key to the detail page as a URL parameter, such as recordID=240 here:

```
http://localhost:8500/greendept/Detail.cfm?recordID=240
```

Figure 13.23
The Master Detail Page Set dialog. Dreamweaver uses this information to auto-generate both a master and a detail page. If there are more records than can fit on one master page screen, Dreamweaver auto-generates navigation controls among master page screens.

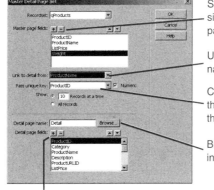

Select a column and click the minus sign to remove it from the master page. Click plus to add it back again.

Users click the product name to navigate to the detail page.

ColdFusion passes the ProductID to the detail page to uniquely identify the desired record.

Browse to a filename, or type in a new filename.

Select a column and click the minus sign to remove it from the detail page. Click plus to add it back again.

MAKING CLIENT ACCESS EASIER: WEB SERVICES AND COMPONENTS

Web services, using Simple Object Access Protocol (SOAP), are the emerging standard for making application services available over the Internet.

The Dreamweaver/ColdFusion combination may be the easiest way currently available to create and deploy a Web service. Dreamweaver can also help you build HTML/CFML pages that consume (use) Web services.

In ColdFusion, a Web service is embodied in a ColdFusion component (CFC), a data structure containing functions that clients can call. Every CFC is not a Web service, but every Web service in ColdFusion is a CFC. First, we'll see how Dreamweaver can help you create and invoke a CFC. Then we'll look at Dreamweaver's features for creating a Web service.

→ For more on CFCs, **see** "Creating and Using ColdFusion Components (CFCs)," **page 903**, in Chapter 33.

CREATING A CFC

You can create a working CFC in Dreamweaver by choosing File, New, selecting Dynamic Page and ColdFusion Component, and clicking Create. The CFC contains one function, myFunction, which takes one argument, myArgument, and returns the string "foo" to the client.

> **NOTE**
>
> A function is a block of code embodying a procedure.

> **NOTE**
>
> An argument is a data object passed to a function.

It looks like this:

```
<cfcomponent>
    <cffunction name="myFunction" access="public" returntype="string">
        <cfargument name="myArgument" type="string" required="true">
        <cfset myResult="foo">
        <cfreturn myResult>
    </cffunction>
</cfcomponent>
```

This code is meant to be used as a template for creating more useful CFCs. For example, as it stands, the function doesn't even do anything with the argument that is passed to it. However, creating a useful function would involve programming in CFML, which is not our focus here. Therefore, I'll use this component as an example. All you have to do to create the component is save the file you have just created. Dreamweaver automatically uses the extension .cfc. (In the examples that follow, the file is named myCFC.cfc.)

INVOKING A FUNCTION IN A CFC

After the CFC has been created, the next step is to create a page that invokes (calls) a function in the CFC. This is a simple two-step process:

1. Create a ColdFusion page: Select File, New to bring up the New Document dialog. In the Category column on the left, select Dynamic Page. In the Dynamic Page column on the right, select ColdFusion. Finally, click the Create button in the lower-right corner of the the New Document dialog.

2. Find the function on the Components panel in the Application panel group, and drag and drop the function into the document window. In the case of myCFC, there is just one function: myFunction.

The second step involves selecting CF Components in the drop-down menu at the top left of the Components panel, if it is not already selected. All the sites containing components will be listed. Expand the site that contains the component, and expand the component itself, so that you can see its functions. In Figure 13.24, for instance, the greendept site and the myCFC component are expanded, revealing the myFunction function.

Figure 13.24
The Components panel. Drag and drop a function from a CFC into the document window, and Dreamweaver auto-generates the code to invoke that function.

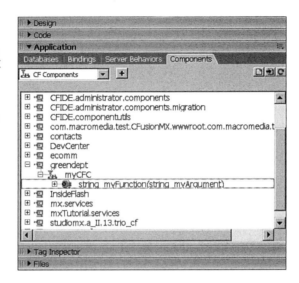

When that function is dragged into the document window, this code is automatically created:

```
<cfinvoke
 component="greendept.myCFC"
 method="myFunction"
 returnvariable="myFunctionRet">
     <cfinvokeargument name="myArgument" value="enter_value_here"/>
</cfinvoke>
```

Substitute a value where Dreamweaver auto-generates enter_value_here. The value you enter gets passed to the function as an argument. In a real-world application, you would also make some use of the return value, myFunctionRet, in your Web page. One possible use is simply to display the return value ("foo") by using cfoutput. You can do this at any point in the body of your document following the function invocation. For instructions, see the sidebar, "Using the Insert Bar to Create Instant CFML Tags."

13

Using the Insert Bar to Create Instant CFML Tags

The CFML category on the Insert bar allows you to create CFML tags by filling in values on dialogs. After you are familiar with the tags, the use of the dialogs is intuitive. For instance, to display the return value, myFunctionRet, you can use the following procedure:

1. On the Insert bar, select the CFML category.

2. Type **myFunctionRet** in the document window and select it.

3. Click the Surround with # button (the fourth button from the right). Dreamweaver auto-generates pound signs around myFunctionRet, making it a variable.

4. Leaving the selection highlighted, click the Out button (the third button from the left). Leave all the fields on the Tag Editor dialog blank and click OK. Dreamweaver auto-generates `<cfoutput></cfoutput>` tags around the selection.

This results in:

```
<cfoutput>#myFunctionRet#</cfoutput>
```

This will display the return value in the browser when the page is loaded.

CREATING A WEB SERVICE CFC

Dreamweaver can auto-generate a CFC designed specifically for use as a Web service. A Web service CFC can be somewhat complex, and one has to understand those complexities to fully understand the Dreamweaver interface for creating a Web service CFC.

→ For more on Web Service CFCs, **see** "Creating and Using Web Service CFCs," **page 904**, in Chapter 33.

In this section, however, I'll just illustrate the Dreamweaver workflow for creating a simple Web service CFC. Here's the procedure:

1. On the Components panel, with CF Components selected in the drop-down menu, click the plus sign to the right of the drop-down menu. The Create Component dialog appears (Figure 13.25). This dialog has four sections: Components, Properties, Functions, and Arguments. We'll just use Components and Functions here.

2. In the Components section, the only required fields are the component name (the name of the CFC file) and the component directory. In Figure 13.25, there is also a Display Name, a name formatted for display to the end user.

3. In the Functions section (Figure 13.26), click the plus sign at the top. The word "Function" will appear in the Functions box and in the Name box.

4. In the Name box, select the word "Function" and change it to the name of your function. Click the plus sign again, and the name will change in the Function box, as well. In Figure 13.26, the name was changed to `getSiteName`.

5. In the Access drop-down menu, select Remote. This enables remote clients to access your CFC via an HTTP URL.

6. Select an appropriate return type, depending on what type of value the function returns, such as a number, a date, or a string. You must select a return type!

7. Click OK. A Web service–ready CFC will be generated and opened for editing (`getSiteName.cfc` in this case).

NOTE

Be sure to declare a return type. The CFC requires it to work as a Web service.

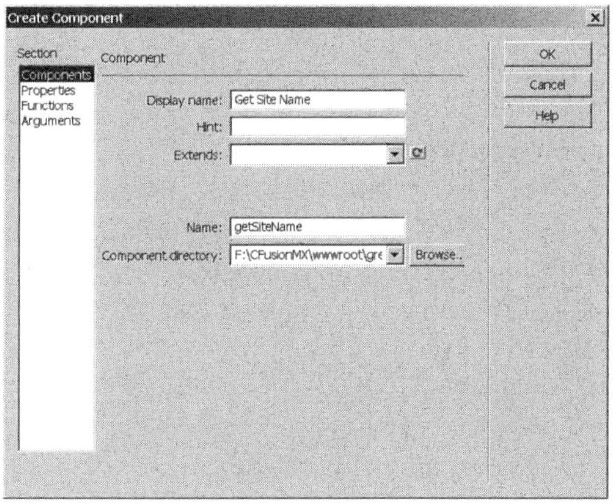

Figure 13.25
The Components section of the Create Component dialog. The lower two parameters, Name and Component directory, are required. Others are optional.

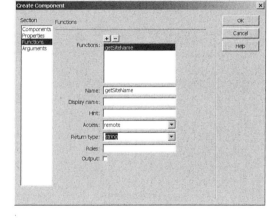

Figure 13.26
The Functions section of the Create Component dialog. You can add as many functions as you want. Access must be set to remote, so that remote clients can access the Web service. A Return type is also a requirement for the CFC to work as a Web service.

You can add as many functions as you want by repeating steps 3 and 4.

In general, CFCs generated using the Create Component dialog are used as templates, and fleshed out with more CFML coding to create a useful component. The getSiteName CFC needs a little bit of editing to be even minimally useful. Here's the completed code. Only the words "The Green Department" were added by hand. Everything else was generated by Dreamweaver.

```
<!--- Generated by Dreamweaver MX 2004 7.0.2052   (Win32) -
➥Mon Sep 15 19:26:23 GMT-0500 (Central Daylight Time) 2003 --->

<cfcomponent displayName="Get Site Name">
    <cffunction name="getSiteName" access="remote" returnType="string"
➥output="false">
        <!--- getSiteName body --->
        <cfreturn "The Green Department">
    </cffunction>
</cfcomponent>
```

13

You can drag and drop the `getSiteName` function into the document window from the Components panel to create a page that invokes the function, as illustrated in the previous section with myCFC.

In addition, the `getSiteName` function is formatted to work as a Web service, with four parameters: name, access, returnType, and output. Nothing more needs to be done to the CFC to make it accessible as a Web service. However, on the client side you need to create a proxy and a page with code that invokes the `getSiteName` function. Dreamweaver makes both tasks straightforward, as demonstrated in the next section.

Consuming Web Services

As discussed in Chapter 32, the Web services architecture requires the client to consume the Web service via a proxy.

→ For an overview of the ColdFusion Web services architecture, **see** "Using Flash to Access the ColdFusion Server," **page 878**, in Chapter 32.

Dreamweaver makes it easy to create the required proxy. Here's the procedure:

1. On the Components panel, select Web Services in the drop-down menu, if it is not already selected.

2. Click on the plus sign. The Add Using WSDL dialog appears.

3. Enter a URL. For most Web services, this will be the URL of a Web Service Description Language (WSDL) file. For instance, for the BabelFish translation service, the URL is `http://www.xmethods.net/sd/2001/BabelFishService.wsdl`. For a CFC, however, give the URL of the CFC, followed by ?wsdl. For instance, to add the getSiteName CFC as a locally accessible Web service, you use the following URL, as shown in Figure 13.27: `http://localhost:8500/greendept/getSiteName.cfc?wsdl`

   If the CFC were deployed on the Internet, it might be specified like this:

   `http://www.myDomain.com/greendept/getSiteName?wsdl`

4. Click OK. The Web service proxy is created in the ColdFusion server, and the Web service (getSiteNameService in this case) appears in the Components panel.

After you have created the proxy, creating a page to access a Web service function is easy: Just drag and drop the function into the document window. Here's the auto-generated code for the getSiteName function:

```
<cfinvoke
 webservice="http://localhost:8500/greendept/getSiteName.cfc?wsdl"
 method="getSiteName"
 returnvariable="aString">
</cfinvoke>
```

As before, you now have a return variable that you can use on your Web page. For instance, `<cfoutput>#aString#</cfoutput>` following the invocation displays the words "The Green Department".

Figure 13.27
The Add Using WSDL dialog creates a proxy on the ColdFusion server, enabling clients to access the CFC as a Web service. The name of the service appears in the Components panel.

TROUBLESHOOTING

When trying to preview data, I'm getting a Dreamweaver error saying "A server timeout has occurred." As the message suggests, I've checked to make sure that my Web server is up and running, and that there is an ODBC DSN on the testing server. What next?

You may get a timeout when there is a lot of data in the table you're trying to preview.

First, try viewing another table that you know has less data in it. If you can view that table, then your database and DSN are working properly. The problem could well be a table with too much data in it.

The best solution, which will allow you to work more efficiently and reliably here and elsewhere, is to use representative sample data for development, with no large tables.

Other possibilities are

- Build your own query in Dreamweaver and view the data in the browser.
- Use the appropriate database management system, such as Microsoft Access, to view the data.
- Increase the Page Timeout and/or Max Buffer Size for the DSN, using ColdFusion Administrator, Data Sources, Edit (button on the far left), Show Advanced Settings.

PART III

FLASH MX

14 What's New in Flash MX 2004? 321

15 The Flash Environment and Tools 333

16 Working with Vector Graphics and Bitmaps 351

17 Working with Text 367

18 Animation, Interactivity, and Rich Media 379

19 Introduction to ActionScript 441

20 Basic ActionScript 459

21 Advanced ActionScript 539

22 External Communications 617

23 Using Flash for Dynamic Data 661

CHAPTER 14

What's New in Flash MX 2004?

In this chapter

Faster Flash Files   322

3D, Text Effects, Graphs, Charts, and More…   322

Effects and Animation Made Easy   323

Speeding Up Common Tasks   323

A Tale of Two Versions   324

More and Better Components   325

Quick Take-off with Templates   326

Text: Spelling, Formatting, Translating   326

Better Importing   327

Searching Through Space and Time   327

JavaScript for Flash (JSFL)   329

New Security Rules   330

A New Version of ActionScript   330

This chapter provides an overview of the new features in Flash MX 2004. If you are still using the previous version of Flash MX, this chapter may help you decide whether the upgrade is worth it, and if so, which version of Flash MX 2004 you want. If you have already purchased Flash MX 2004, this chapter will orient you to new features.

FASTER FLASH FILES

Probably the most fundamental improvement in Flash MX 2004 is that your Flash files (SWFs) will run about a third faster. For some functions, such as XML parsing, it can be five times faster!

Much of this improvement is due to the Flash Player. Macromedia says, "Player runtime performance has been improved by a factor of two to five times for video, scripting, and general display rendering."

Performance improvement is more marked when you publish your files specifically for the latest version of the Flash Player, version 7. But it's also true to some extent if you publish for the previous version, Flash Player 6, but run the SWF in Flash Player 7.

Flash developers go to great lengths in pursuit of faster executables. With Flash MX 2004, the extra speed is automatic and effortless.

3D, TEXT EFFECTS, GRAPHS, CHARTS, AND MORE...

Flash now supports third-party extensions or add-ins. At press-time, nearly a dozen of these were available, supported by the original developers but sold exclusively through Macromedia's online store. A few examples:

- *Swift 3D Xpress* from Electric Rain. Helps you create 3D animation, complete with lighting, materials, specular highlights, shadows, and reflections. If you are familiar with the stand-alone Swift 3D product, you'll feel comfortable using this add-on. And, as with stand-alone Swift 3D, you'll be able to achieve some pleasing effects with a minimum amount of effort.

- *Distort FX, Text FX* and *Pixel FX* from Red Giant Software, and *SWiSH Power FX* from SWiSHzone.com. Includes text and button effects such as distortion, drop shadows, blurring, and extruding.

- *Swiff Chart* from GlobFX. Provides charting and graphing capabilities, including many variations of traditional line and bar graphs, pie charts, as well as more exotic formats such as donuts or combined styles.

These add-ons expedite bread-and-butter tasks like creating a rotating logo, attracting attention to a text block by stylizing and animating it, or creating a bar chart. Many effects that were either time consuming or took specialized knowledge are now quick and within anyone's reach.

The only drawback to add-ins is the cost. Individually, they cost $50 to $150, but each one addresses a limited range of functionality. It would be great to have them all. Unfortunately, just looking at the initial batch available at press time, you would end up paying more for add-ins than for Flash itself. Prices may reflect the vendors' need to avoid cannibalizing the market for their stand-alone products.

EFFECTS AND ANIMATION MADE EASY

Learning Flash can be challenging for first-time and occasional users. Absorbing the concepts and workflow of timeline-based animation can be difficult initially. Scripting with ActionScript can be even more intimidating.

With Behaviors and Timeline Effects, even first-time users can create interesting and useful effects easily, without scripting or working on the timeline.

Timeline Effects automatically create timeline-based animations. Just apply an effect to a movie clip, set a few parameters on a configuration screen, and you're finished. You can create fade-ins, fade-outs, wipes, and simple position-rotation-scale animations. You can explode, expand, and squeeze objects, as well as apply drop shadows and blurs.

There are limitations to how far you can go with this approach. For instance, if you combine effects, only the most recent effect is editable via its configuration screen. You have to adjust other effects on the timeline.

→ For more on combining Timeline Effects, **see** "Timeline Effects," **page 400** in Chapter 18, "Animation, Interactivity, and Rich Media."

Still, Timeline Effects simplify the workflow for simple effects tremendously. They ease the learning curve for beginners. And they can be time-savers even for experienced users.

Similarly, Behaviors make it easy to create simple interactivity. For instance, clicking a button can take the user to a designated point in the movie, load a graphic, cause a sound to play or stop playing, or open the browser and take the user to a Web site. In the background, each of these behaviors is implemented as ActionScript code. You can examine the code to learn from it. You can edit it. Or you can leave it alone. Thus, Behaviors can be a gentle introduction to ActionScript or a way of avoiding it.

SPEEDING UP COMMON TASKS

There are a number of seemingly minor enhancements that, because they speed up tasks that you perform over and over again, may save you a significant amount of time. For instance, you can now configure Flash's behavior at start-up, so that it automatically opens a new blank document, opens all recently-opened documents, or displays a start page that presents you with various options such as opening a new document or opening recently opened documents. Previously, none of these options was available: Flash simply started with no document open and no start page. (This behavior is still available, too.)

If you have several documents open at the same time, a tabbed interface allows you to select any one of them with a single click. (For some reason, the Macintosh version lacks this feature.) Previously, you had to use either the Window menu (click once on the menu, click

14

again on the filename) or a keyboard shortcut. The tabbed interface may not sound like a big deal, but it is actually a significant improvement.

Another feature that falls into the "little things mean a lot" classification is the Save and Compact option on the File menu. Flash developers have always had to deal with the fact that source (FLA) files only get bigger with each save (File, Save). If you delete a movie clip, for example, and save the FLA, Flash does not reclaim the space formerly occupied by the movie clip. In previous versions of Flash, you had to save under a new name (File, Save As) to get Flash to reorganize the file more efficiently, thus reducing its size. In Flash MX 2004 you have the option of doing a normal save (File, Save), which is usually instantaneous, or a Save and Compact, which may take a little longer for large files but reduces the file size.

A TALE OF TWO VERSIONS

Flash now comes in two versions: Flash MX 2004 and Flash MX 2004 Professional. The main reason to get Professional is for its dynamic data capabilities. Other features limited to the Pro version include a video export plugin (the FLV Exporter), many user interface components, "slide-based" programming (ideal for PowerPoint-style presentations), forms-based programming, and project management (version control and document check-out/check-in).

There's no universal rule for deciding who should get which version. "Professional for developers, standard version for designers" has some superficial plausibility, because of Professional's database support and forms-based programming. On the other hand, slide shows (also found only in Pro) might typically be associated more with designers.

The FLV Exporter, which works only with Professional, may actually be more useful for non-professionals. The FLV Exporter enables you to export FLV (Flash Video) files directly from programs such as Adobe After Effects and Discreet cleaner. FLV files are necessary if you want to use Flash's new progressive external video loading feature, which gives you much better control of the download/display process, as reflected in the new Media components: Display, Controller, and Playback (available in Flash Professional only). The Media components work only with .flv and .mp3 files, not other video formats such as .avi or .mov. The Media components allow you, for example, to set cue points to coordinate video with other events in your movie.

Previously, to get cue point functionality, you needed a communication server such as Flash Communication Server, which meant added cost and complexity.

However, using a standalone compression utility like Sorenson Squeeze for Macromedia Flash MX to produce the FLV will give better results than the FLV Exporter. Squeeze is likely to give you better quality at the same file size, or a smaller FLV file with the same quality, than the FLV Exporter. Professionals won't sacrifice size or quality to save the time it takes to run a file through Squeeze. So most people will continue with the current standard workflow: exporting a QuickTime or AVI file from After Effects or cleaner, and then using Squeeze to produce an FLV.

14

MORE AND BETTER COMPONENTS

Components are self-contained, portable building blocks for applications. Components make it easy for programmers to deliver internally complex functionality in an easy-to-use modular form. They implement functions that you use over and over again in many applications. Rather than build the functionality from scratch each time, you can just drag and drop a component onto the Stage, perhaps customize the component's appearance, and set a few parameters. Using components also helps you maintain consistency within an application.

Flash MX shipped with 7 components. Flash MX 2004 ships with 13. Flash MX 2004 Professional comes with 30 components!

In addition, Flash MX 2004 introduces a new generation (V2) of faster-loading, better-behaved components:

- *Faster-loading.* The V2 components initialize and resize more quickly than the V1 components that came with Flash MX, so the user sees the first screen of the application more quickly, and the components feel more responsive. They're also faster to work with in the authoring environment.

- *Better-behaved.* The V1 components sometimes had problems managing behaviors such as depth (whether an object is "in front of" or "behind" other objects) and focus (whether an object is selected or not). For instance, after you tabbed into a component, it was sometimes impossible to tab out of it. Now there are non-visual, automatically loaded components called *managers* to help address such problems. The managers are FocusManager, DepthManager, PopUpManager, and StyleManager.

In the V2 component architecture, components are compiled, so you can't get at their source code through the component itself, whether to modify the component or learn from it. Macromedia, however, has included the source code separately for the standard components (though not the Flash Pro data components) as part of the Flash MX 2004 install.

→ For a link to information on the location of the source code for components, **see** componentSource.htm on the CD accompanying this book.

Unfortunately, it's not advisable to use V2 and V1 components in the same application. V1 components are supported in Macromedia Flash MX 2004, but you have to publish to a version 6 SWF file when you use Actionscript 1.0. So, porting existing component-based applications into Flash MX 2004 can be a bit of a pain. More so because Macromedia neglected to make a V2 version of the V1 Scrollbar component. A scrollbar is part of the ScrollPane component, as well as the new TextArea component, so you still have scrollbars where you most need them when building applications from scratch. (The recommended solution for creating scrolling text in Flash MX 2004 is to use the TextArea component.)

The standard version of Flash MX 2004 has 13 user interface (UI) components—visible controls such as RadioButton, CheckBox, and TextInput that enable a user to interact with an application. In addition to 21 UI components, Professional has 3 media components (UI

14

controls for displaying and controlling playback of FLV and MP3 files) and six non-displaying data components (for accessing Web Services and XML data sources).

The first V2 component you drop on the Stage includes about 25KB of standard infrastructure, which can be shared by all subsequent components. That 25KB is a heavy price to pay if you use just one or two components. Spread over a dozen components, it becomes negligible. Still, user interface controls custom-designed for a particular application will always be lighter weight than general-purpose components.

→ For more on using components, **see** "Accelerating Application Development with Components," **page 426** in Chapter 18.

QUICK TAKE-OFF WITH TEMPLATES

When you create a new document (File, New), you can click on the new Templates tab to choose a template for the file. Templates provide basic design and architecture for a project, saving you set up time.

Some templates are very simple. For example, you can use a Banner Ad template to automatically configure the size of the Stage to 468×60 pixels. Setting the size of the Stage in this way is much faster than using Modify, Document, and typing in the numbers manually. There are ten templates for configuring standard sizes defined by the Interactive Advertising Bureau (www.iab.net).

Other templates are more complex, saving you even more time. For example, the Photo Slideshow template sets up a whole slide show, complete with images, captions, title, and frame, and as well as a controller component for slide-to-slide navigation. You can substitute your images for the ones that are there, type in new captions, and configure a delay time for the auto-play feature that displays all the images round-robin fashion.

There are templates for quizzes, and for mobile devices, such as Compaq's iPaq Pocket PC computer, various smart phones, and the Nokia CLIE PDA. When you install Flash Remoting, it also installs a template, which includes the ActionScript necessary to get a basic Remoting connection up and running.

Several types of templates are usable only in Flash MX 2004 Professional. These include templates for query-response applications (Form Applications), a special version of slide presentations (Slide Presentations), and a screen for choosing high, medium, or low bandwidth for a video stream (Video). The Pro-only templates appear on the Templates list in the standard version of Flash, too, but descriptive text says that you can use them only with Professional, and you get an error message if you try to use them with the standard version.

TEXT: SPELLING, FORMATTING, TRANSLATING

There are a number of features dealing specifically with text. For instance, Flash now includes a spell checker.

Another new feature allows you to use Cascading Style Sheets (CSS) to format text: the `TextField.StyleSheet` object in ActionScript. It's just a small subset of the full CSS that you can use with HTML tools such as Dreamweaver, but you can set all the common text attributes such as color, size, font, style (normal, italic, oblique), and weight (normal, bold, lighter). Flash CSS also supports a few other standard HTML tricks like making the font of a hypertext link change when the mouse pointer is over it. The CSS feature enables you to maintain a level of consistency between Flash and HTML files. It allows you to create one stylesheet and apply it in both environments.

In Flash Player 7 and later, you can also include images (JPEGs, SWFs, or movie clips, but not GIFs) as part of a text block.

→ For more on including images in text, **see** "Text Formatting Options," **page 372**, in Chapter 17, "Working with Text."

The new Alias Text button allows you to force aliasing (or disable anti-aliasing, depending on how you want to look at it). Anti-aliasing smoothes the edges of letters, so that they don't appear jagged. However, anti-aliasing can blur smaller fonts. The Alias Text feature can prevent this blurring.

→ For more on the Alias Text button, **see** "Turning Anti-Aliasing Off," **page 370**, in Chapter 17.

The new Strings panel facilitates publishing Flash content in multiple languages. You can set things up so that whenever you save, test, or publish your application, Flash creates folders with external XML files for each specified language. Translators can either work in the Strings panel in the Flash authoring environment, or use an XML editor directly on the XML files.

Better Importing

Being able to import external files (File, Import) with high fidelity can save you work, because it eliminates editing or re-creating the content in Flash. You can now import Adobe PDF files, Adobe Illustrator files, and EPS files, preserving an accurate vector representation of the source files.

→ For more on the importing files, **see** "Importing Bitmaps," **page 357,** in Chapter 16, "Working with Vector Graphics and Bitmaps."

The Video Import wizard (File, Import) not only makes it easier to get video into your project, it helps you perform editing tasks such as trimming the clip, creating multiple clips, and reordering clips.

Searching Through Space and Time

The new Find and Replace feature enables you to search your document. The History panel allows you to search backwards in time for previous actions.

14

The Find and Replace Feature

You can use the new Find and Replace feature (Edit, Find and Replace) to find and replace a text string, a font, a color, a symbol, a sound file, a video file, or an imported bitmap file in your Flash document. It's powerful, and it's easy to use because it's like find and replace features in common applications such as Microsoft Word.

The History Panel

The History panel shows a list of the things you've done since creating or opening the current document. Whether you draw an object, place a component on the Stage, set a component property, or select a frame, every move you make that affects the document is recorded in the History panel. You can use a simple slider to go backward any the number of steps, up to a specified maximum (100 by default), and then come forward again. It's like having a rewind and fast forward button for your document. Used in this fashion, the History panel provides a much more convenient way to undo (Edit, Undo) and redo (Edit, Redo) large numbers of steps.

> **NOTE**
>
> In previous versions of Flash, there was a separate set of undo steps for different interface areas, such as the Stage, movie clips, and Library. In Flash MX 2004, there is just one undo stack for the whole document. Some designers see this as a significant loss, and say that the History panel is not really a substitute.

There are also more complex ways to use it, such as saving a series of steps as a command, so that you can repeat them any time you want. You can also copy steps from one segment of the slider "timeline" and replay them at another point. Such uses are complicated by three factors.

First, some actions (marked with a red x on the History panel) can't be copied, replayed, or saved. For instance, the History panel shows you that you selected a frame, or that you set a property of a component, but it can't copy, replay, or save those actions. So those actions get skipped on copies, replays, and saves (though not on undos and redos that use the slider). These missing parts can cause the whole sequence of actions to have a different result.

Second, you can't reorder items on the History panel.

These two limitations make it much more difficult to create useful commands.

Finally, any time you go back and change something in the "past," everything after that point is wiped out. So you can't go back and correct one mistake but preserve everything that came after it, for example.

These limitations can be overcome to some extent, but only if you're willing to tackle JavaScript programming for the Flash environment, as discussed in the next section.

JAVASCRIPT FOR FLASH (JSFL)

You can customize the Flash environment in a number of ways by using Flash JavaScript (JSFL). The basic procedure is to create a .jsfl file and save it in an appropriate directory.

If you have installed Flash MX 2004, search for files with the extension .jsfl on your hard disk, and you will see that they are used in a number of subdirectories of the "First Run" directory. For example, in a typical Windows installation, if you put a .jsfl file in the `C:\Program Files\Macromedia\Flash MX 2004\<language>\First Run\Commands` folder (where <language> is the abbreviation for your language, such as en for English), the file-name (minus the .jsfl extension) will appear as a command on the Command menu.

On Windows systems, commands that you create with the Save As Command function in the History panel are saved in `C:\Documents And Settings\<user name>\Local Settings\Application Data\Macromedia\Flash MX 2004\<language>\Configuration\Commands`, where <user name> is your username and <language> is the abbreviation for your language. By default, the Local Settings folder is hidden.

You can also use .jsfl files to create behaviors, effects, tools, and screen types such as forms and slides.

Macromedia had not yet released JSFL documentation as this book went to press.

→ `JSFLlink.htm` on the CD accompanying this book contains a link to JSFL information, including a link to the Macromedia page with the official JSFL documentation.

You can see JSFL code by clicking the options menu in the upper-right corner of the History panel and selecting View, JavaScript in Panel. To edit the JSFL code, select the items you want from the History panel, click the Copy Selected Steps to the Clipboard button at the bottom of the panel (see Figure 14.1), and paste the JSFL code into the Flash Professional script editor (File, New, Flash JavaScript File) or any text editor.

Figure 14.1
Use the Copy Selected Steps to the Clipboard button to cut and paste JSFL code into a text editor or the Flash Professional script editor.

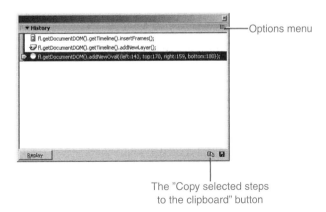

Options menu

The "Copy selected steps to the clipboard" button

14

In the Flash Professional script editor, you can press the + in the upper left to see a menu of JSFL language elements. (See Figure 14.2.)

Figure 14.2
Press the + in the upper left of the Flash Professional script editor to see a menu of JSFL language elements.

NEW SECURITY RULES

There are also changes in the security rules that determine whether one SWF file can access another SWF file and how external data can be loaded.

When Flash Player 7 is running inside a browser over HTTP, domains must be identical for data transfer to succeed. Even a sub-domain can no longer read data from a parent domain and vice versa. So, for example, `http://myServer.myDomain.com` cannot exchange data with `http://www.myDomain.com`.

One way to overcome this restriction is to create a small XML file called a *cross-domain policy file* (and named `crossdomain.xml`) on the machine providing the data.

→ `crossDomainPolicyFiles.htm` on the CD accompanying this book contains a link to information on cross-domain policy files, including a link to the Macromedia tech note discussing this issue.

There is also a new restriction that prevents an SWF file that is loaded using nonsecure (non-HTTPS) protocols from accessing content that is loaded using a secure (HTTPS) protocol, even when both are in exactly the same domain.

→ For more on these security issues, **see** Chapter 22, "External Communications," **page 617**, Chapter 23, "Using Flash for Dynamic Data," **page 661**, and `security2004.htm` on the CD accompanying this book.

A NEW VERSION OF ACTIONSCRIPT

ActionScript has been massively overhauled, giving birth to a brand-new version, ActionScript 2 (AS2), which implements object-oriented programming (OOP) in a more standard way than before.

→ For more on object-oriented programming (OOP), **see** "Understanding Object-Oriented Languages," **page 446**, in Chapter 19, "Introduction to ActionScript."

This section provides a high-level overview of these changes. See the chapters on ActionScript for details.

AS2 makes it easier to develop and debug object-oriented programs, especially for programmers familiar with other object-oriented languages, such as Java. Conversely, if you're new to programming, learning AS2 will give you more of a head start on learning other object-oriented languages.

14

One major new feature is strict data typing. When you create a variable, strict typing lets you declare that the variable can represent only a particular type of object, such as a number, a date, or a text string. Then, when you test your program, if you use a variable improperly—for instance, you use a number in a context that requires a text string—you get an error message. (AS2 does not *insist* that you declare all variable types, however.)

You can also use strict data typing and still publish for the Flash Player 6. Data types are checked only when you compile, not at runtime, so this feature is fundamentally independent of the Flash Player.

Flash MX 2004 doesn't force you to use any new ActionScript features. You can continue to code just as you did before, as long as you publish for the Flash Player 6. Macromedia is to be congratulated for finding a way to implement such sweeping changes in ActionScript and yet maintain perfect backward compatibility for existing scripts.

If you want to publish for Flash Player 7, you may need to modify your existing scripts. The modifications are conceptually minor, mainly involving case sensitivity and new reserved words.

One issue is that if you publish for Flash Player 7, ActionScript is case sensitive. Previously, ActionScript saw `myVar` and `MyVar` as the same thing, but no more.

There are also some new reserved words, such as `ContextMenu`, `Error`, `PrintJob`, and `throw`. In ActionScript 1, you are free to use these words as you wish. In AS2 they are part of the language, so you shouldn't use them for your own purposes. New reserved words include `class`, `extends`, `implements`, `interface`, `intrinsic`, `dynamic`, `static`, `public`, `private`, `get`, `set`, and `import`.

TROUBLESHOOTING

I'm modifying an existing .fla file to use AS2 syntax, and although I'm not getting any compiler errors, my program is not working as expected either! I think I'm doing everything right, but it's not working right!

If you modify an existing .fla file to use AS2 syntax, make sure AS2 is specified in the Publish Settings (File, Publish Settings). If it's not, the file may compile incorrectly, although Flash may not generate compiler errors. (Or it may generate compiler errors even though everything seems to be correct in your program.)

The problem here is that when you open a file created in a previous version of Flash, the Publish Settings are automatically set to match the file that you open, meaning it will always be ActionScript 1 and a version of the Player previous to 7. If you use features that require ActionScript 2 or Flash Player 7, problems result.

Hey, where's the Scale and Rotate Dialog?

For reasons best known to Macromedia, the Scale and Rotate Dialog was removed from from Flash MX 2004. In its place, Macromedia substituted...nothing. The Scale and Rotate dialog enables you to use keyboard input to do precise relative scaling and rotation. For instance, you could click on a movie clip and then rotate it exactly 60° and scale to exactly 150% of its previous size.

Luckily, Zé Fernando, an intrepid Brazilian programmer (http://www.fatorcaos.com.br), created a substitute dialog in JSFL:

http://newsfeed.fatorcaos.com.br/000024.html

CHAPTER 15

The Flash Environment and Tools

In this chapter

Panel Sets   334

Setting Document Attributes   334

The Timeline   334

The Toolbox   339

Keyboard Shortcuts   342

The Library   343

The Movie Explorer   344

Setting Flash Preferences   345

15

PANEL SETS

The interface consists of the same basic elements as the other Studio MX programs: a main menu bar and tool bar, the Stage, the Toolbox, the Property inspector, and numerous other panels. The basic operation of these elements is described in Chapter 3, "Introducing the MX Interface," and the interface you see when you start Flash is pictured in Figure 3.1.

→ For more on the common Studio MX 2004 interface, **see** Chapter 3, "Introducing the MX Interface," **page 23**.

PANEL SETS

Panel sets are a unique feature of Flash MX 2004 that allows you to instantly bring up any desired panel configuration. Just create the panel layout you want; choose Window, Save Panel Layout; give the new layout a name; and save it. Any time you want to bring it back, go to Window, Panel Sets, and select it. There is also a Default set, which returns you to the layout you see when you first install the program, often a good neutral starting point.

SETTING DOCUMENT ATTRIBUTES

You can access document attributes from the Property inspector or by choosing Modify, Document. The Property inspector shows the Document attributes by default when you open a new document, or you can access them by clicking on an empty portion of the Stage with the Selection or Subselection tool. The Size button launches a mostly redundant Document Properties pop-up dialog box, where you can specify the Stage dimensions (by typing in numbers, by choosing the default dimensions, or by matching the dimensions to the printer or the Stage contents), background color, frame rate, and ruler units. The Publish button launches the Publish Settings dialog box, where you determine what kinds of files to publish (for example, SWF, HTML) and various attributes of those files (such as the version of the Flash Player for the SWF, or the alignment of the Flash content within the HTML file). The Background Color box provides drop-down color swatches to specify the background color of the Stage. The frames per second (fps) option specifies the speed at which the movie plays; you can enter the speed directly into the Frame Rate field.

NOTE

Document and *movie* are interchangeable terms in Flash. *Document* may be used more often when referring to both visual and non-visual aspects of the movie. *Movie* feels right when referring to specifically cinematic features such as scenes and frames.

THE TIMELINE

There are two basic ways to use Flash: through visual tools (the "designer" approach) and through ActionScript (the "developer" approach). The Timeline is Flash's main visual organizing tool, allowing you to arrange your content in both time (frames) and space (layers). It contains the playhead, which indicates the current frame (see Figure 15.1).

Both approaches can be used together, but frequently one is emphasized over the other. In particular, application-oriented developers frequently use Timeline layers for organizing content, but timing of events is more often determined by scripting than by frames.

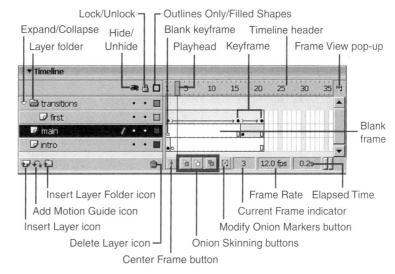

Figure 15.1
The Timeline controls and organizes frame-based animation.

FRAMES

A frame is the smallest discrete visual time element of the movie. (ActionScript can use sub-frame time intervals.) The simplest form of animation (conceptually, at least), frame-to-frame animation, works like flip-book animation. Each page is a static drawing, but flipping through them quickly in a series creates the illusion of movement. Frames allow you to control the sequencing and pace of your movie, and define the overall length. As with film, animations that take place over fewer frames (at a given frame rate) will appear faster in the final movie than those that occur over many frames. To insert frames, choose Insert, Frame, or press the keyboard shortcut F5.

KEYFRAMES

Keyframes indicate changes in an animation. Frames display the content of the keyframe that precedes them. It is only when a new keyframe is encountered that the contents of the Stage within a particular layer will change.

To insert a keyframe, choose Insert, Timeline, Keyframe, or press keyboard shortcut F6. When you insert a keyframe after an existing keyframe, the new keyframe initially displays the content of the preceding keyframe; you can then make changes to that original content in the new keyframe. To add a keyframe that provides you with a blank slate, you must choose Insert, Timeline, Blank Keyframe, or press F7. Create new content in the blank keyframe, and the movie will suddenly "cut" to that content when it reaches that frame. Keyframes are indicated by filled dots on the Timeline, whereas blank keyframes appear as empty dots.

→ The Timeline, frames, and keyframes are covered in greater depth in Chapter 18, "Animation, Interactivity, and Rich Media, " **page 379**.

LAYERS AND LAYER FOLDERS

Layers enable you to stack content. Think of each layer as a piece of clear acetate. Anywhere there is no content within a layer, you can see through that layer to the ones below it. Where there is content, it obscures the layers below it.

Layers allow you to organize and separate content. Layers also provide the organizing framework for a number of important features, such as applying animation visually (tweening), aligning objects or animating motion along a path (guide layers), and using one object to create a "window" to another object (mask layers). A quirk of Flash is that it merges simple, nongrouped shapes (but not symbols) that coexist on a single layer if they intersect. For example, if two red balls on the same layer touch, they become a single object, as shown in Figure 15.2.

→ For more on symbols, **see** "Symbols, Instances, and Library Assets," **page 380**, in Chapter 18.

→ For more on merging objects, **see** "Strokes and Fills," in Chapter 3, **page 33**.

→ For more on tweening, **see** "Animating in Flash," **page 390**, in Chapter 18.

→ For more on guide layers, **see** "Using Layout Aids," **page 353**, in Chapter 16, "Working with Vector Graphics and Bitmaps," and "Motion Guides," **page 395**, in Chapter 18.

→ For more on mask layers, **see** "Creating a Mask," **page 356**, in Chapter 16.

Adding layers does not increase the file size for your published movie, so you can use them as needed to organize your content.

Figure 15.2
Simple, nongrouped shapes on the same layer merge, forming a single shape, if they intersect. This is not true of symbols.

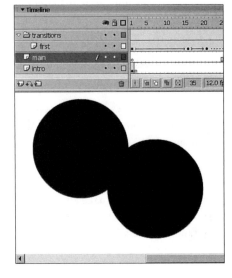

Flash automatically names layers as they are created and numbers them according to the order in which they are created. Double-click on a layer name, such as Layer 1, on the left side of the Timeline to rename it. Take the time to name your layers well, keeping the names short and descriptive. Well-named layers are signposts directing you to your objects. Large projects can quickly turn into bad road trips as layers multiply, but if you name your layers well, you need never get lost.

The icons to the right of each layer allow you to hide, lock, and show layers as outlines, as shown in Figure 15.3. It's a good idea to lock any layer you aren't currently working with so that you don't inadvertently move content. Option-click (Mac) or Alt+click (Windows) the dot on your layer that's under the lock icon to lock all other layers, or individually click the dots in the lock column to lock and unlock layers. Locked layers display the lock icon. You can also hide layers, using the dots under the eye icon, to see content that is obscured by upper layers. Again, Option-click or Alt+click the visibility dot on any layer to hide all other layers. Hidden layers are represented by red Xs in the left column under the eye icon. You can also display layer content as outlines, which can be helpful when you have many over-lapping elements on different layers. The solid square in the right column changes to a square with no fill when a layer is displayed as outlines.

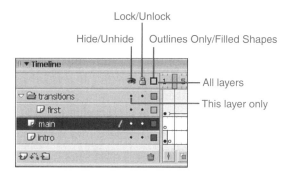

Figure 15.3
Layer icons enable you to hide, lock, or show layers as out-lines.

A pencil icon between the layer name and Hide/Unhide column indicates which layer is currently selected and being edited. Keep in mind that you cannot edit a layer that has been hidden. If you select a hidden layer, the pencil icon appears crossed out, as shown in Figure 15.4.

To rearrange layers, click and drag on a layer name and release it into a new position. You can also Shift+click layers to select more than one layer at a time.

The icons at the bottom of the Layers area of the Timeline window enable you to add a new layer, add a guide layer, or insert a layer folder. Guide layers help you to align objects. They can be used for static alignment of elements, such as for aligning objects on other lay-ers to objects or custom grids created on guide layers, or can be used as motion guides to keep animated objects on a path as they move. You can turn any layer into a guide layer by clicking the Motion Guide Layer icon. Guide layers do not appear in published Flash movies.

15

Pencil icon crossed out

Figure 15.4
You cannot edit a hidden layer, as shown by the crossed-out current layer icon.

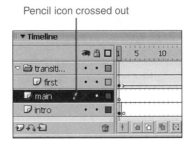

Layer folders group and organize layers into folders. Not only can you more easily find elements in your movies, but you also can save a lot of screen real estate by expanding just the folders containing layers you're currently working with. To place layers in folders, simply drag layers onto folder layers. Click the arrow to the left of the folder names to expand and contract layer folders.

ONION SKINNING AND MULTIPLE FRAME EDITING

Flash shows only one frame at a time on the Stage. To facilitate alignment in frame-by-frame animation, you can use onion skinning to display a series of frames simultaneously. The onion-skinning buttons, which allow you to configure onion-skinning, are located at the bottom of the Stage and appear as three sets of overlapping squares. The Onion Skin button, as shown in Figure 15.5, displays frames concurrently. The current frame (beneath the playhead) appears in full color, while the surrounding frames are dimmed and cannot be edited. You can change the number of frames that are visible by dragging the Start Onion Skin and End Onion Skin markers, which are in the Timeline header (with the playhead). Moving the playhead changes the current frame and the place where the range of onion-skinned frames begins and ends.

Onion Skin Outlines button

Onion Skin button   Edit Multiple Frames button

Figure 15.5
Drag the onion skin markers to display several frames simultaneously.

Modify Onion
Markers drop-down

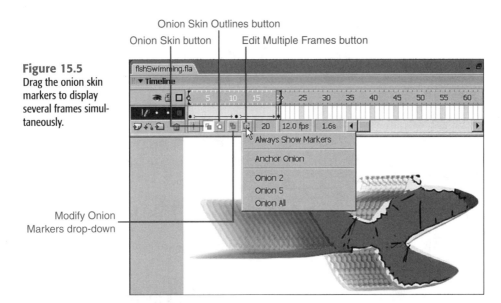

The Onion Skin Outlines button displays the onion-skinned objects as outlines. To edit all the frames that are onion skinned, select the Edit Multiple Frames button. Finally, there is a Modify Onion Markers button. It is a drop-down with options to anchor markers so that they don't move as the current frame changes. You can also specify a range of frames to onion skin: Onion 2 (two frames), Onion 5 (five frames), or Onion All (all frames) .

THE TOOLBOX

The Toolbox is covered in Chapter 3 because so many of its features are common to Fireworks and/or FreeHand. Figure 3.1 shows the Toolbox. Still, there are a couple of features that are unique to the Flash Toolbox, and those are covered here.

→ The Subselection, Line, Text, Pen, Oval, Rectangle, Paint Bucket, and Eyedropper tools, as well as the View Section and the Colors Section of the Toolbox, are all covered in Chapter 3, **page 23**.

ARROW TOOL

When the Arrow tool is selected, you'll notice that three modifiers are displayed in the Options section at the bottom of the Toolbox. The first, which looks like a magnet, is the Snap to Objects modifier. (There are two other ways to get to the same function: on the main menu, via View, Snapping, Snap to Objects; and on the main toolbar at the top of the screen, with the magnet icon.) Snapping makes it easy to position objects at a particular distance from one another (the "snap tolerance"), or exactly touching at edges, centers, or bounding boxes.

NOTE

> The bounding box is the smallest rectangular area that completely encloses the shape.

 There are separate horizontal and vertical snap tolerances (see Figure 15.6), as well as a snap tolerance from the edge of the Stage. These distances are configured on the Snap Align dialog (View, Snapping, Edit Snap Align), shown in Figure 15.7. Dotted lines appear when you are at the snap tolerance (whether or not snapping is on), as shown in Figure 15.6, making it easy to align objects.

When all or part of an object is selected on the Stage, the other modifiers, Smooth and Straighten, can be activated. Select a line or part of a shape outline and then click these modifiers to either add points to smooth a shape or remove points to straighten.

LASSO TOOL

→ For Lasso Tool basics, **see** "Selecting Objects," **page 29**, in Chapter 3.

The Lasso tool has three modifiers. The top two are the Magic Wand and Magic Wand Properties. They allow you to select portions of bitmaps that have been broken apart. Clicking on a bitmap selects pixels according to color range. Continue clicking to add to

15

the selection. The settings include threshold, which determines how sensitive the wand is to color differences in adjacent pixels. Lower numbers result in more precise selections, whereas higher numbers include a broader range of colors. Smoothing determines how much the borders of selections will be smoothed. The last modifier is Polygon mode, which draws lasso selections with straight edges.

Figure 15.6
The small box in the upper right (dark lines) is being dragged toward the larger box in the lower left. The lighter box in the upper right is the current position of the dragged box. The dotted lines indicate that the snap tolerance has been reached. These snap tolerances are configured in Figure 15.7.

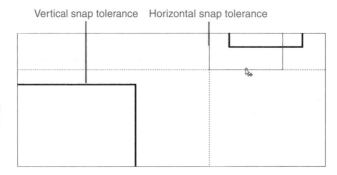
Vertical snap tolerance   Horizontal snap tolerance

Figure 15.7
The Snap Align dialog. The horizontal snap tolerance is set to 50, the vertical snap tolerance to 10. See Figure 15.6 to see these snap tolerances in action.

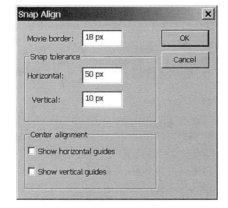

BRUSH TOOL

The Brush tool modifiers enable you to select a brush mode, size, and shape, and to lock a fill color. The Brush Mode modifier allows you to paint normally over strokes and fills. It can also be used like a stencil, to protect parts of objects. The Paint Fills modifier paints fills and empty sections of the Stage, leaving strokes unchanged. Paint Behind protects objects and paints only empty parts of the Stage. Paint Selection allows you to restrict the Paint tool to just the fill of an object that has been selected on the Stage—an automatic "keep within the lines" command. Unlike simply selecting a filled area and applying a new fill, which changes the whole fill, Paint Selection enables you to paint just part of the fill with a new color. The final Brush Mode modifier is Paint Inside, which allows you to paint roughly over an object and apply the color just to the object's fill, not to the stroke or the Stage.

If you have a pressure-sensitive tablet, the Pressure modifier varies the brush stroke according to how hard you press as you draw. The harder you press, the wider the stroke.

FREE TRANSFORM TOOL

Flash is the only Studio MX 2004 program with a Free Transform tool, which allows you to apply transformations individually or in combination to objects, groups, instances, and text blocks. Just select an object on the Stage and click the Free Transform tool. A bounding box appears around your selected object and, as you move your mouse around, the various transform methods are indicated by changes in the pointer.

The modifiers include Rotate and Skew, Scale, Distort, and Envelope. Distort simulates perspective by allowing you to click and drag the corner or edge handles on the bounding box, realigning the adjoining edges, as shown in Figure 15.8.

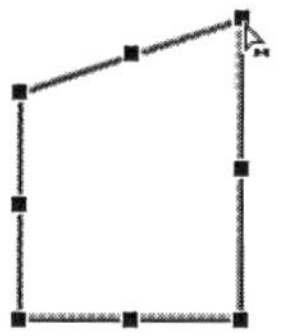

Figure 15.8
The Distort modifier reshapes and realigns shapes, simulating perspective.

As you can see in Figure 15.9, Envelope lets you warp and distort selected objects. Selections are contained within an *envelope*, and you can pull or push Bezier handles to warp the envelope contents. You can even convert the warping into individual keyframes so that it occurs incrementally over time.

FILL TRANSFORM TOOL

The Fill Transform tool, also unique to Flash, enables you to adjust gradient and bitmap fills. When you click on a gradient or bitmap fill, the bounding box and center of the fill are indicated by circles and boxes that can be dragged. If you hold the pointer over one of these handles, the pointer changes to indicate your editing options. You can reshape, rotate, scale, and skew bitmaps and gradients. You can even tile a bitmap fill.

INK BOTTLE TOOL

Flash is unique in using the Ink Bottle tool to modify an existing stroke. When you use this tool in conjunction with the Property inspector, you can edit stroke color, thickness, and style. You also can change any of these settings and click an existing stroke to implement changes.

15

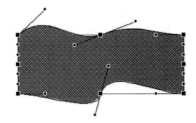

Figure 15.9
The Envelope modifier warps and distorts objects.

ERASER TOOL

Using the Eraser tool, you can erase objects in whole or part. Simply dragging the Eraser tool erases everything along its path. The Eraser Mode modifiers allow you to specify parameters, such as strokes and fills on the same layer (Erase Normal), fills only (Erase Fills), strokes only (Erase Lines), or only fills that have been selected (Erase Selected Fills). Using Erase Inside, you can start erasing a fill, and as long as you hold the mouse button down, only that one fill will be erased; other objects may seem to be erased, but they will reappear when you release the mouse button. The Faucet modifier removes strokes or fills in their entirety with a single click. The Eraser Shape modifier specifies a shape and size for the Eraser.

CAUTION

> The Faucet pointer has an irregular shape. The drop of water, *not* the faucet itself, makes selections. When you're working with small objects, position the drop of water over what you want to select.

KEYBOARD SHORTCUTS

Most keyboard shortcuts are covered in Chapter 3 because they are common to the MX 2004 family.

Table 15.1 lists a few keyboard shortcuts that are unique to Flash, in most cases because the tool itself is unique to Flash.

TABLE 15.1   TOOLBOX SHORTCUTS

Tool	Keyboard Shortcut
Free Transform tool	Q
Fill Transform tool	F
Ink Bottle tool	S
Paint Bucket tool	K

15

Because the MX 2004 family has only a few panels in common, there are many unique shortcuts to toggle panel visibility. These are shown in Table 15.2. Panel access shortcuts shared with other MX 2004 programs are covered in Chapter 3.

TABLE 15.2   PANEL SHORTCUTS

Panel	Mac	Windows
Timeline	Option-Cmd-T	Alt+Ctrl+F2
Property inspector	Cmd-F3	Ctrl+F3
Answers	Option-F1	Alt+F1
Align	Cmd-K	Ctrl+K
Info	Cmd-I	Ctrl+I
Scene	Shift-F2	Shift+F2
Transform	Cmd-T	Ctrl+T
Actions	F9	F9
Debugger	Shift-F4	Shift+F4
Movie Explorer	Option-F3	Alt+F3
Reference	Shift-F1	Shift+F1
Output	F2	F2
Accessibility	Option-F2	Alt+F2
Components	Cmd-F7	Ctrl+F7
Component Parameters	Option-F7	Alt+F7
Library	F11, Cmd-L	F11, Ctrl+L

THE LIBRARY

The Library provides a home for your document's symbols and imported assets, including bitmap graphics, sound files, and video clips.

NOTE

> A *symbol* is a reference to an object—a graphic, button, or movie clip—that you create in Flash. Using a reference rather than the actual object allows you to display the symbol many times with negligible effect on the size of your SWF file.

NOTE

> When you drag a symbol onto the Stage from the Library, you create an *instance* of the symbol on the Stage.

The Library panel lets you organize library items in folders, see how many times an item is used in a document, and sort items by type.

The Library displays a list of its contents, with each item preceded by an icon that indicates the type of content. Items can be grouped into folders, which can be selectively expanded to limit the amount of scrolling required to view the Library contents. Like layers, Library items rapidly multiply over the life of a project and can become the bane of a project if not carefully organized.

> **TIP**
>
> Try to anticipate the kinds of assets and symbols that a project will require. Create folders and decide on naming conventions before you begin to import assets.

CREATING COMMON LIBRARIES

Flash offers the capability to store permanent Library collections, known as Common Libraries. You can create your own project-specific Common Libraries to ensure that team members are using the same assets.

Flash MX 2004 also comes with some Common Libraries containing sample buttons, classes, and learning interactions, which you can access by choosing Window, Other Panels, Common Libraries.

THE MOVIE EXPLORER

The Movie Explorer offers a hierarchical view of every element in your Flash document. It enables you to display the entire contents of your document by frame, layer, or scene, as shown in Figure 15.10. That's every symbol, instance name, and line of code and text used, and you can search and replace it all. If you've lost something, you can find it here. You can even print it and have a complete map of your document's structure and elements.

To access the Movie Explorer, choose Window, Other Panels, Movie Explorer. You can filter what's displayed by using the buttons at the top of the window. The first shows text, the next shows symbols, then scripts, video/sounds/bitmaps, frames, and the last button enables you to customize what is shown. Just below the icons is the search field.

Navigate through document elements by using the filter buttons; then double-click to select individual elements in the list. If you double-click text, you can edit it within the Movie Explorer. The options menu (the drop-down list on the upper right) enables you to rename instances and symbols; to edit symbols in place on the Stage or in a new window; or to go to the frame, layer, or scene where a selected element is located. Double-clicking a line of code takes you to that code in the ActionScript Editor.

Options drop-down menu

Figure 15.10
The Movie Explorer displays the complete contents of your document.

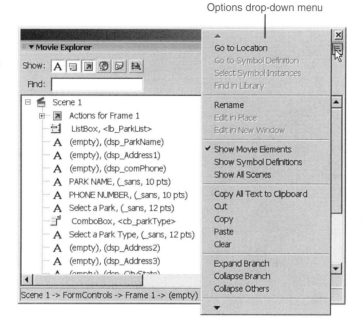

SETTING FLASH PREFERENCES

Preferences enable you to customize global aspects of the working environment. You access them by choosing Edit, Preferences (PC) or Flash, Preferences (Mac). Most preferences are simply that—a matter of personal preference. You will find the styles you like and are accustomed to, perhaps that mirror other applications with which you are more familiar, and can set your preferences accordingly. Adjusting the preferences is all about creating your preferred working environment.

GENERAL PREFERENCES

On the first tab, General Preferences, the first preference is Undo Levels, which determines the number of undo and redo levels that are kept in memory for each work session. The range is 0 to 200, with a default of 100. The higher the number, the more memory will be required to store the information necessary to achieve the undos and redos. It's best to strike a balance between the number of undos and the memory you have available on your system.

For Windows users, the next preference is Printing Options, with the option Disable PostScript, which is turned off by default. If you have problems printing to a PostScript printer, select this option but be aware that your printing will be slower. The Printing Options are not available on Macintosh.

Next are the Selection Options: Shift Select and Show Tooltips. Both of these options are turned on by default. Enabling Shift Select allows for a single selection only when clicking on the Stage. To select additional objects, you must Shift-select them. If Shift Select is disabled, any objects clicked on the Stage are automatically added to the selection.

Show Tooltips provides contextual information about tools, including keyboard shortcuts, if there are any, when you mouse over tools. This feature is especially helpful when you're first using Flash MX 2004.

You can choose from three Timeline Options. Disable Timeline Docking prevents the Timeline from docking with the Stage so that it floats freely. This feature can be useful for maximizing the Stage if screen real estate is limited. Disable Timeline Docking is turned off by default.

When Span Based Selection is enabled, clicking a frame in the Timeline selects the entire span of frames, either between keyframes (as shown in Figure 15.11) or from beginning to end if there are no keyframes. In the case of consecutive keyframes, clicking selects an individual keyframe. To select a single non-keyframe, you must Cmd-click (Mac) or Ctrl+click (Windows) or right-click the frame. With Span Based Selection disabled, which is the default, clicking a frame selects just that frame.

Figure 15.11
Span Based Selection selects spans of frames with a single click.

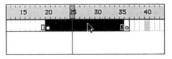

Selecting Named Anchor on Scenes allows you to add named anchors so that the Forward and Back browser buttons jump between scenes in a movie. You also can place anchors to jump from frame to frame, but you must set them manually. When Named Anchor on Scenes is enabled, Flash MX 2004 automatically places a named anchor on the first frame of each scene in a movie.

CAUTION

For named anchors to work, you must select the Flash with Named Anchors option from the Template drop-down menu within the HTML portion of the Publish Settings dialog box.

The Highlight Color options determine the color of the bounding box that appears around items as they are selected. Use This Color enables you to select any Web-safe color from a swatches palette. Use Layer Color assigns the color that is assigned to the layer on which the object is located. Each layer, as it is created, is assigned a color code, which is represented by a colored square to the right of the layer name. Choosing Use Layer Color enables you to quickly determine on which layer an object is.

Flash prompts you to replace missing fonts when you open a document that contains fonts not installed on your system. The Font Mapping Default preference enables you to select a default font to use when substituting missing fonts.

 The start page is a new feature in Studio MX 2004. In the On Launch section, you can choose to display the start page, a new document, a list of recently opened documents, or just the workspace with no document in it.

EDITING PREFERENCES

The Editing Preferences encompass pen and drawing settings as well as vertical text options. All the Editing Preferences are disabled by default.

The Pen Tool options include Show Pen Preview, which previews line segments as you draw before an endpoint is created. The segments appear to stick to the Pen tool until you click to add an endpoint. Otherwise, segments are not shown until an endpoint is created.

Show Solid Points makes unselected anchor points appear solid and selected anchor points appear hollow. When this option is not selected, which is the default, selected anchor points appear solid and unselected points are hollow.

Show Precise Cursors displays the Pen tool as a cross-hair pointer on the Stage, which makes it easier to place anchor points precisely. The default displays the Pen tool icon. You can also use the Caps Lock key to toggle between these settings while drawing.

You can create text that is oriented horizontally or vertically by using the Text Direction button in the Property inspector. The Vertical Text options allow you to make vertical text the default by using the Default Text Orientation option. Additionally, you can choose a Right to Left Text Flow option and a No Kerning option. If the No Kerning preference is enabled, you can still kern horizontal text by using the Property inspector.

The Drawing Settings allow you to customize tolerances and specify snapping, smoothing, and straightening of objects. All the defaults are set to Normal.

Connect Lines determines how close an endpoint being drawn can be to another line without snapping to it. Additionally, it determines the sensitivity of horizontal and vertical line recognition, or how near to horizontal or vertical a line must be drawn to snap to precise horizontal or vertical alignment. The options are Must Be Close, Normal, and Can Be Distant.

When you're drawing in Straighten or Smooth mode, Smooth Curves specifies how much smoothing or straightening is applied to curves or lines. Smoothing removes points from curves, creating gentler arcs, whereas Straighten flattens curved lines. The options are Off, Rough, Normal, and Smooth.

Recognize Lines determines Flash's threshold for recognizing rough Pencil-drawn line segments as lines, which it then makes perfectly straight. The options are Off, Strict, Normal, and Tolerant.

15

Recognize Shapes determines how precisely shapes must be drawn to be recognized as geometric shapes. They include circles, ovals, squares, rectangles, and arcs. The options are Off, Strict, Normal, and Tolerant.

Click Accuracy sets a threshold for how close the mouse must be to an object to select it. The options are Strict, Normal, and Tolerant.

NEW Flash MX 2004 Professional has a Project panel where you create and manage projects. Project settings enable you to choose to close open files associated with a project when you close the project in the Project panel (on by default) and to automatically save project files when you test or publish the project (off by default).

NEW Flash MX 2004 enables you to input Asian characters (Japanese, Chinese and—new in Flash MX 2004—Korean) on the Stage with a standard Western keyboard by using Input Method Editors (IMEs). Input Language Settings allows you to choose Japanese, Chinese, or Korean.

CLIPBOARD PREFERENCES

The Clipboard Preferences affect how objects are copied to the Clipboard and are platform-specific, with the exception of the FreeHand Text option.

For Windows, the settings are for Bitmaps and Gradients. With Bitmaps, you can specify Color Depth and Resolution parameters, apply anti-aliasing by selecting Smooth, and set a Size Limit for the amount of RAM used when bitmaps are copied to the Clipboard. A Size Limit of None can be used if memory is limited.

The Gradients setting enables you to specify the quality of gradients copied to the Clipboard and pasted into other applications. This setting does not affect the quality of gradients pasted within Flash, which is always full quality.

The Macintosh has PICT Settings for Type, Resolution, and Gradients. Type specifies the format that is preserved for copied artwork: Objects for vector art or Bitmaps with a range of bit-depth settings. Resolution specifies the dots per inch (dpi) of copied images, and there is a check box option to include PostScript data. Gradients specifies gradient quality in PICTs copied and pasted outside Flash. The default is Normal, and the options are None, Fast, Normal, and Best. The higher the quality setting, the longer it takes to copy artwork. As with the Gradients setting on the Windows platform, this setting does not affect the quality of gradients pasted with Flash, where the full gradient quality will be maintained.

There is a single FreeHand Text option: Maintain Text as Blocks. Selecting this check box enables you to paste text from FreeHand and preserve it as editable text.

WARNING PREFERENCES

The Warning Preferences enable you to customize when you will receive warnings. All the warnings are enabled by default.

- **Warn on Save for Macromedia Flash MX Compatibility**—Alerts you if you try to save files with MX 2004 content in MX format.

- **Warn on Missing Fonts**—Gives an alert if you try to open a file containing fonts that are not installed on your system.

NEW ■ **Warn on URL Changes in Launch and Edit**—Alerts you if the URL for a document has changed since the last time you opened and edited it. This occurs, for instance, if you select Last Documents Open on the General Preferences tab, and launch Flash after one of those documents has been moved.

- **Warn on Reading Generator Content**—Displays a red X over any Generator content. Note that Generator objects are no longer supported.

- **Warn on Inserting Frames When Importing Content**—Notifies you when the Timeline must be extended to accommodate content you are attempting to import.

NEW ■ **Warn on Encoding Conflicts when Exporting .as Files**—Alerts you when selecting Default Encoding for the Save/Export option on the ActionScript preferences tab could lead to data loss or character corruption. (For example, if you try to save a document with Chinese, Japanese, or Korean characters in Default Encoding on an English system, the Asian characters will be corrupted.)

NEW ■ **Warn on Conversion of Effect Graphic Objects**—Gives an alert when you attempt to edit a symbol that has Timeline effects applied to it. If you edit a symbol with Timeline effects, you lose the ability to edit the symbol's settings.

- **Warn on Exporting to Flash Player 6 r65**—Warns you when you export (File, Export) to this version of the Flash Player. If you select Flash Player 6 on the Flash tab (File, Publish Settings), you get an option to optimize for Flash Player 6 r65. SWFs published with this option must be played in Flash Player 6 r65 or later. If you enable Warn on Exporting to Flash Player 6 r65, you will get a warning when you publish with the optimization enabled. The warning is given just once per work session for each source file (FLA), the first time you publish that file. If you close the FLA, open it again, and publish, you will get the warning again.

- **Warn on Sites with Overlapped Root Folder**—Warns you when you create a site (File, Edit Sites, New) in which the local root folder overlaps with another site (Flash MX 2004 Professional only).

- **Warn on Behavior Symbol Conversion**—Warns you when conversion from one type of symbol to another (for example, movie script to button) will cause a behavior to be deleted from an object.

- **Warn on Symbol Conversion**—Warns you when conversion from one type of symbol to another could cause problems.

ActionScript Editor Preferences

You also can access the ActionScript Editor Preferences from the Actions panel by choosing Preferences from the pop-up menu.

Editing Options enable you to customize formatting within the Actions panel. Automatic Indentation indents code, and you can enter a number (up to 4, which is the default) in the Tab Size field to determine the tab amounts. Code Hints displays coding hints as you type. The Delay slider allows you to specify a time delay before hints appear; the default is 0.

NEW Open/Import determines the encoding of files you open or import. Save/Export determines the encoding of files you save or export.

Text enables you to specify a font and size to display in the Actions panel.

Syntax Coloring enables you to customize text color for syntax elements such as foreground, background, keywords, comments, identifiers, and strings.

NEW Language enables you to define one or more Classpaths, where Flash will look for Class files used in ActionScript.

All the ActionScript Editor Preferences have default settings, and you can return to the defaults by selecting the Reset to Defaults button at the bottom of the Preferences window.

TROUBLESHOOTING

As I was experimenting with panel sets and layouts, I inadvertently hid a panel. Help!

Don't panic. You can easily restore panels. Here are several options:

- Manually go to the Window menu and select a panel you want to display.
- Use the appropriate keyboard shortcut to display a given panel.
- If all panels suddenly disappear, you've probably accidentally pressed F4. Press it again, and your panels should reappear.
- You can always restore the default panel set by choosing Window, Panel Sets, Default Layout.

CHAPTER 16

WORKING WITH VECTOR GRAPHICS AND BITMAPS

In this chapter

Understanding Vector Graphics   352

Editing and Adjusting Shapes   352

Using Layout Aids   353

Creating a Mask   356

Working with Bitmaps   357

UNDERSTANDING VECTOR GRAPHICS

Flash was originally designed as an animation application to translate old-style, incremental animation to the Web. Given its roots in cel animation, drawing has always been at the core of Flash. Although perhaps not as sexy as the scripting and complex interaction now possible, drawing is still essential to getting the most out of Flash.

Though computer *screens* always display pixels, computer *software* can define shapes in two ways: vector and bitmap. A bitmap is defined by a grid of *pixels*, like tiles forming a mosaic. Bitmaps contain color information for each pixel, plus the dimensions for the image, and define images pixel by pixel. Bitmaps are great for displaying subtle variations in color, such as photographic images. But what if you want to change the size of a bitmap image? Well, you either have to re-create the image at the desired dimensions or stretch the image, usually with undesirable results.

By comparison, vector graphics store a series of commands necessary to create an image through the use of elements such as lines, curves and fills. The commands, called *vectors*, dictate element attributes such as thickness, direction, color, and position, which your computer then calculates. Vector graphics allow for much finer detail and can be resized without losing definition, just by revising the formulas in the vectors. When you edit a vector graphic, you can simply change the attributes of the elements that make up the graphic. Vector graphics are best for displaying simple shapes with flat areas of color, such as icons, logos, and cartoon-style drawings.

A Flash movie can display both vector and bitmap graphics, but vectors have smaller file sizes, and the Flash Player can draw them more quickly and efficiently. Bitmap file size and download time are directly tied to an image's dimensions. With vector graphics, file size and rendering speed are determined by the complexity of the instructions, not the size of the graphic.

EDITING AND ADJUSTING SHAPES

Drawing shapes, especially with a mouse, can be far from exact. The best strategy, especially if you are new to the Flash drawing environment, is to draw quick approximations of shapes and then perfect them through editing. Editing an existing shape is far easier than drawing it perfectly from scratch.

→ Drawing tools are introduced in Chapter 3, "Introducing the MX Interface," in the section on "Tools," **page 33**, and discussed further in Chapter 15, "The Flash Environment and Tools," in the section on "The Toolbox," **page 339**.

USING THE SELECTION AND SUBSELECTION TOOLS

The Selection (Arrow) and Subselection tools can be used to adjust shapes. Simply click and drag segments or points. Dragging an anchor point changes the anchor position and the size and shape of the adjoining segments. Dragging a segment changes the segment's shape, while the anchor points on either side of it remain in place.

Straightening and Smoothing

You can also smooth and straighten irregular shapes and paths. For example, you may have drawn freeform curves with the Pencil tool, and your curves may have too many bumps and irregularities. To correct this, select a path or shape with the Selection tool; then click the Smooth modifier in the Options section at the bottom of the Toolbox. (This works best if you draw the curve with the Smooth modifier on in the first place.)

You can repeatedly click either modifier to produce greater changes. Not surprisingly, straight lines or shapes with straight sides are unaffected by the Straighten modifier. Ovals and perfect circles are likewise unaffected by the Smooth modifier.

Optimizing Curves

The more anchor points used in drawing curves, the more calculations it requires to draw them. In extreme cases this can result in larger file sizes as well as slower rendering. Curves can be optimized to reduce the number of anchor points. This results in smoother curves. The goal is to use only as many anchor points as needed to create your desired shape, and no more.

To optimize your curves, select a shape and choose Modify, Shape, Optimize. The Optimize Curves dialog box, shown in Figure 16.1, contains a smoothing slider and options to use multiple passes and to show a totals message. Make your selections and click OK. Smoothing reduces the number of points used in the shape. To dramatically reduce the number of points, choose Multiple Passes. Points are removed and the shape further refined in each pass until no further optimization is possible. The totals message compares the original number of curves with the optimized number of curves.

Figure 16.1
Using the Optimize Curves dialog box, you can smooth curves.

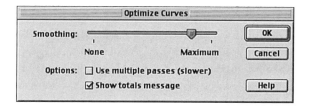

USING LAYOUT AIDS

To help you draw with precision and create unified layouts, Flash provides several aids, including snapping, the drawing grid, guides, guide layers, and the Align panel.

Snapping

One way to align elements is to use snapping. Pixel snapping is particularly useful. Because Flash is vector based, you can easily and inadvertently place objects in between whole pixels. These seemingly insignificant pixel fractions can throw off alignment and create problems, particularly with text.

→ For more on pixel alignment for text, **see** "Displaying Clear, Sharp Text," **page 368,** in Chapter 17, "Working with Text."

When you drag an object by its registration point (which appears as a crosshair when the object is selected), pixel snapping forces the object into alignment with a grid that has one-pixel spacing between guidelines.

→ For more on the registration point, **see** "Registration," **page 382,** in Chapter 18, "Animation, Interactivity, and Rich Media."

In addition, with pixel snapping enabled (View, Snapping, Snap to Pixels), any object you create or place on the Stage will snap to a whole pixel coordinate, avoiding many alignment problems. Unfortunately, pixel snapping is off when you open a new Flash document; you have to remember to turn it on.

NOTE

> At 400% magnification (View, Magnification, 400%), Flash displays the pixel snapping grid. To temporarily hide the grid, press and hold X. The grid reappears when you let go.

To temporarily disable pixel snapping, press and hold C. It reactivates as soon as you release C.

GRIDS, GUIDES, AND GUIDE LAYERS

This section provides an overview of the drawing grid, guides, and guide layers, which help you to align elements within your layouts, helping to create an overall sense of order, intention, and unity.

→ For more instructions on accessing and implementing grids and guides, **see** the next section, "Sizing Shapes Precisely," **page 355**.

Grids and guides provide vertical and horizontal guidelines to which objects can be aligned or snapped. The grid option displays uniformly placed horizontal and vertical lines that cover the Stage, appearing behind any artwork. Guides are individual, manually placed horizontal and vertical lines. Guide layers allow you to create your own visual alignment aids. Neither grids, guides, nor guide layers are exported, so they are not visible in your final movie, nor do they increase in size.

Guides are most useful for marking the alignment of recurring elements that give structure to your layout, such as menu bars or columns of text. To use the guides, you must show the rulers, which appear along the top and left side of the Stage. To add a horizontal guide, click on the horizontal ruler at the top of the Stage and drag down from it. Click and drag across from the vertical ruler on the left to create a vertical guide. To move a guide, click and drag it with the Selection tool. To remove a guide from the Stage, drag it with the Selection tool back to its originating ruler.

Guide layers allow you to create irregular guides. Grids and guides produce guidelines that are horizontal and vertical and that extend from one end of the Stage to the other. What's special about guide layers is that they allow you to use any of the drawing tools to create your guides. With guide layers, you are not limited to perpendicular guidelines, or even to lines at all. In a guide layer, you could draw a diagonal line, or hexagonal shapes, to use for alignment. Click the Guide icon below the Timeline layers to create a guide layer. Draw your guide shapes and then use the Align panel to position elements on other layers to elements on your guide layers.

SIZING SHAPES PRECISELY

With all of Flash's sophisticated drawing capabilities, you'd think you could specify that you want to draw a square that is 15 pixels by 15 pixels, but you can't. There are, however, a number of ways to achieve precise dimensions for your shapes—using rulers, the drawing grid, guides, and the arrow keys. Here are your options:

- **Use rulers**—Turn on rulers (View, Rulers) and use them as a reference as you draw. Zoom in as much as is convenient. You may not get 100% accuracy using rulers alone, but you can come close.

- **Use guides**—Drag horizontal and vertical guides from the rulers onto the Stage. Turn them on (View, Guides, Show Guides). Turn snapping on for guides (View, Snapping, Snap to Guides) and other kinds of snapping off. Use arrow keys to move the guides. Lock the guides when you've got them where you want them (View, Guides, Lock Guides).

- **Use the drawing grid**—Configure the grid to the desired size (View, Grid, Edit Grid), turn on the grid (View, Grid, Show Grid), and draw with grid snapping on (View, Snapping, Snap to Grid) and other kinds of snapping off.

- **Set width and height numerically**—Draw a shape, approximating the desired size, then select and resize it by entering the correct width and height in the Property inspector or the Info panel. This approach is workable with squares, rectangles, and circles. However, if you try it with rectangles with rounded edges, for example, your curves can become distorted.

- **Use the arrow keys**—For rectangles with rounded corners, use the Subselection tool to select the anchor points around two adjacent corners, as shown in Figure 16.2, and nudge them with the arrow keys until the rectangle is the correct size. This approach preserves the corner radius of your rounded corners as you resize.

Figure 16.2
You can use the Subselection tool to resize rectangles with rounded corners without distorting the corner radius.

16

THE ALIGN PANEL

Using the Align panel (Window, Design Panels, Align), you can align objects to each other or to the Stage. First select two or more objects to align. To align objects to the Stage—for example, to center them or to align them to the left side of the Stage—select the To Stage button on the right side of the panel, as shown in Figure 16.3. To align objects to each other, deselect the To Stage button. Use the Align buttons to align the objects' right or left edges, centers, or tops or bottoms, or to center them vertically. The Distribute buttons distribute a series of objects evenly, measuring from their top or bottom edges, centers, left or right edges, or vertical centers.

NOTE

When Flash aligns objects to each other, it notes which edge you want to align and uses the edge farthest in that direction to align all selected objects.

Figure 16.3
The Align panel aligns objects to each other or to the Stage.

CREATING A MASK

Masks are like windows or cut-outs: They reveal parts of images in layers below. For example, you can use text as a mask to reveal parts of an image within the shapes of the letters, as shown in Figure 16.4. Creating a mask is easy. Draw simple shapes on a layer above the layer you want to mask. When your mask shape is in place, (Ctrl+click) [right-click] the layer and then select Mask from the context menu. This applies the mask to the layer below and locks both the mask layer and the masked layer below it. To mask another layer with the same mask, drag and drop it under the mask layer. You can also (Ctrl+click) [right-click] the layer you want to mask, and select Properties, Masked.

→ For more details on using masks, **see** "Working with Dynamic Masks," **page 534**, in Chapter 20, "Basic ActionScript."

Figure 16.4
Text can be used as a mask.

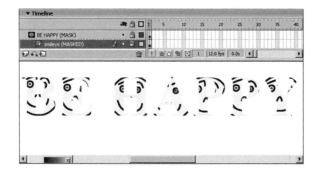

WORKING WITH BITMAPS

Flash enables you to import and transform bitmaps and use them as fills. You can also *trace* bitmaps, converting them to vectors. Finally, you can break bitmaps apart, which permits you to edit portions of the bitmap, rather than just transform the whole bitmap.

IMPORTING BITMAPS

Flash can import files in a variety of formats. Many depend on having QuickTime 4 or higher installed; you can download it free at `www.apple.com`.

 With QuickTime 4, both Windows and Macintosh can import the following vector or bitmap formats: BMP, EPS, GIF and Animated GIF, JPEG, PDF, PNG, Adobe Illustrator (AI, versions 6.0 to 10.0), AutoCAD DXF (DXF), FreeHand (FH7, FH8, FH9, FH10, FH11), FutureSplash Player (SPL), MacPaint (PNTG), PhotoShop, PICT, QuickTime Image, Silicon Graphics Image, SWF files (for Flash Player 6 or 7), TGA, TIFF, and Windows Metafile (WMF). Windows can also import Enhanced Windows Metafile (EMF). (PDF and EPS import are new in Flash MX 2004.)

> **NOTE**
>
> Although you can import Photoshop files via QuickTime, the layers are flattened upon import.

Flash stores imported assets in the Library. You can import multiple assets into the Library (File, Import, Import to Library) and then place them individually on the Stage. Alternatively, you can import directly to the Stage (File, Import, Import to Stage). This approach places an instance on the Stage and the imported file in the Library.

With either approach, the Import dialog box is just like an ordinary File Open dialog, allowing you to navigate to the file that you want to import.

PREPARING BITMAPS FOR IMPORT

Flash is not designed for editing bitmaps. Therefore, bitmaps should be prepared prior to import. Most importantly, bitmaps should be cropped and resized to the desired dimensions.

Avoid resizing bitmaps in Flash. If you scale a bitmap down in Flash, even if it looks fine, you won't have eliminated any bytes in your SWF. Scale the bitmap down in Fireworks or another graphics editor, and the graphics file becomes smaller, making your SWF smaller, too.

In addition, image quality decreases if you resize bitmaps, especially if you attempt to enlarge them. Bitmaps contain a finite number of pixels. When you enlarge them, they lack the color information necessary to fill the added pixels, so new pixels are created in tones that are halfway between existing pixels. This produces the strange artifacts that appear in many poorly created bitmaps on the Web. Plan for the inclusion of bitmaps in your movies, and import them at the correct size, so that you don't have to resize them in Flash.

16

Flash provides an Edit button in the Property inspector that can launch an external image-editing program to edit your imported bitmap. With an imported bitmap selected, click the Edit button to open the bitmap in the application that edited it. You can then edit the bitmap and save it, and your image in Flash is updated.

The more thoroughly you know an image-editing program, the better your results will be using bitmaps in Flash. For instance, you can decrease the size of imported bitmaps by taking advantage of alpha channels in programs such as Fireworks and PhotoShop. Alpha channels are layers that are added to bitmaps to create transparency. By exporting with an alpha channel, you may be able create smaller PNG (or GIF) files to import into Flash, resulting in a smaller SWF.

Any bitmap can be assigned as a fill. Because they tile (repeat multiple times to cover the entire fill area of an object), bitmaps produce unusual fills and are used infrequently. To create a bitmap fill, click the Fill Color box (the one with the Paint Bucket icon) at the top of the Color Mixer. Then select Bitmap from the Fill Style drop-down menu (just to the right of the Fill Color box). The Import to Library dialog box appears, as shown in Figure 16.5, prompting you to select a bitmap.

Figure 16.5
The Import to Library dialog box appears when you select Bitmap as the Fill Style.

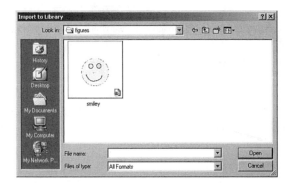

The bitmap is displayed as your current color in the Fill Color box at the top left of the Color Mixer and is applied as a fill to selected shapes (see Figure 16.6).

TRACING BITMAPS

Bitmaps can be *traced* (converted to vector graphics), which reduces file size for suitable bitmaps. Not all bitmaps are good candidates for tracing, though. Precise tracing of any highly detailed photographic image results in a vector graphic with a larger file size than the original bitmap. In addition, the user's computer has to perform all those complex vector calculations. The original bitmap would not only have a smaller file size but would put much less stress on the user's processor.

Figure 16.7 offers an example of a good candidate for tracing. The best candidates are simple shapes with large blocks of color.

Figure 16.6
Apply bitmap fills
using the Color Mixer.

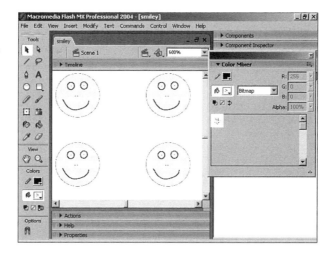

Figure 16.7
The simple shape of
this flower and its
few color gradations
make it a good
candidate to trace.

Images with complicated patterns, such as the one in Figure 16.8, or many color gradations are best left as bitmaps.

Figure 16.8
This image, with its
complex patterns and
shadows, is best left
as a bitmap.

TIP

Although simple shapes are most easily converted to vectors, you can simplify complex bitmaps and create abstract, stylized vector graphics by using less precise tracing settings.

To trace a bitmap, select the bitmap instance on the Stage and then choose Modify, Bitmap, Trace Bitmap. The Trace Bitmap dialog box opens, as shown in Figure 16.9.

Figure 16.9
The Trace Bitmap dialog box offers control over how a bitmap is traced.

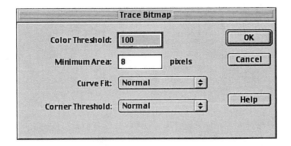

There are four settings for tracing. The Color Threshold, a number ranging from 1 to 500, determines how much color detail will be preserved in the traced bitmap. The Minimum Area option specifies the number of surrounding pixels, from 1 to 1000, that will be considered when assigning color to an individual pixel. The lower these numbers, the larger the file, and the longer tracing takes. On the other hand, very high numbers result in blurred, muddy images. The goal is to find the highest numbers that still yield acceptable color gradation and image detail. These are often fairly low numbers, not too far from the defaults of 10 (Threshold) and 8 (Area).

The Curve Fit option determines how closely arcs in curves are adhered to during tracing. The options range from Pixels, the tightest and most intricate tracing, down through Very Tight, Tight, Normal (the default), Smooth, and finally Very Smooth, the least detailed.

The Corner Threshold option similarly determines how precisely corners are traced—Many Corners, Normal (the default), or Few Corners. Start with the default settings and click OK to get a baseline trace for your bitmap. If you want to adjust the results, choose Edit, Undo, or press Cmd-Z (Mac) or Ctrl+Z (Windows). Trace the bitmap again and experiment with the different settings.

Less precise settings produce smaller file sizes and more impressionistic images, as shown in Figure 16.10.

More precise settings create larger files, but the image can appear very similar to the original bitmap, as shown in Figure 16.11.

Figure 16.10
Traced bitmaps can produce impressionistic effects.

16

Figure 16.11
Lower tolerance settings produce more detailed tracings that more closely resemble the original bitmaps.

OPTIMIZING TRACED BITMAPS

If you have to wait more than a couple of seconds while Flash traces a bitmap—and you're not on a slow computer—check your file size. Most likely your settings are too precise.

To see how complicated a tracing is, select a traced bitmap and choose View, Preview Mode, Outlines to display the tracing outlines. (See Figure 16.12.) To return to Normal view, choose View, Preview Mode, Fast.

The extreme detail of the tracing on the right is probably too much to deliver over the Internet. One way to reduce the detail in a tracing is to optimize curves. To do so, choose Modify, Shape, Optimize to access the Optimize Curves dialog box, as shown in Figure 16.13.

Figure 16.12
You can view tracing outlines to evaluate the complexity of a traced bitmap.

Figure 16.13
By adjusting the settings in the Optimize Curves dialog box, you can simplify a traced bitmap.

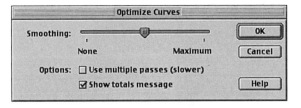

Drag the Smoothing slider and experiment with different settings. Select Show Totals Message to monitor the number of curves that are removed and click OK. The Totals message appears, as shown in Figure 16.14.

Figure 16.14
The Totals message details the overall reduction in curves.

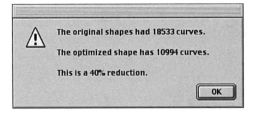

The Optimize Curves feature is powerful, but if optimization exceeds 40% to 50%, image quality will probably be excessively degraded. In that case, undo and trace again.

BREAKING APART BITMAPS

Breaking apart a bitmap (Modify, Break Apart) separates a bitmap into its component pixels, which can then be selected and modified individually. Unless a bitmap is broken apart, it can only be selected and manipulated globally, as a whole. After a bitmap is broken apart, you can use the drawing and painting tools to edit individual pixels.

You can use the Lasso tool with the Magic Wand modifier to select portions of a broken-apart bitmap according to color range. Click on a pixel and all surrounding pixels of the same or similar color are selected. The Threshold option in the Magic Wand Settings dialog box, as shown in Figure 16.15, determines how closely a color must match the pixel that is clicked to be included in the selection. The range is from 0 to 200. The higher the number, the greater the range of included colors. Entering 0 selects only pixels of exactly the same color. The Smoothing option determines how accurate the edges of selections are. From most to least accurate, the choices are Pixels, Rough, Normal, and Smooth. Clicking on different parts of the image with the Magic Wand adds to the selection; you don't have to hold the Shift key down, as you do when selecting multiple objects with the Selection tool, for example. When a selection has been made, you can use the Fill controls and Paint Bucket tool to change colors.

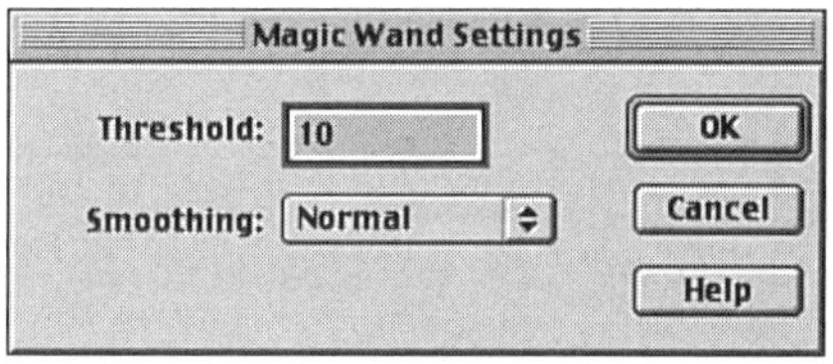

Figure 16.15
The Magic Wand Settings dialog box allows you to refine the way selections are made.

COMPRESSING BITMAPS

Because bitmaps can significantly increase file size, it's vital to compress them as much as possible. By default, the original compression settings of a bitmap are used when a movie is published. However, you may be able to improve upon the original compression by tweaking a bitmap's properties, especially if a bitmap has been traced. To access the Bitmap Properties dialog box, select a bitmap in the Library and either click the Properties button, as shown in Figure 16.16, or Ctrl-click (Mac) or right-click (Windows) and choose Properties.

Figure 16.16
With a bitmap selected in the Library panel, click the Properties button at the bottom of the Library panel and choose Properties to access the Bitmap Properties dialog box.

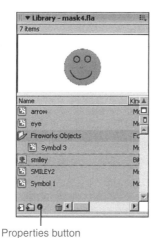

Properties button

The Bitmap Properties dialog box appears, as shown in Figure 16.17. Choose Photo (JPEG) in the Compression drop-down menu to compress the bitmap in the JPEG format, which will discard pixel information during compression. To maintain the original compression settings of the imported bitmap, check Use Imported JPEG Data. Each time a JPEG is compressed, data is discarded, so image quality becomes progressively worse. Typically, it is best to use the imported JPEG data to prevent image deterioration. You can specify a new JPEG quality setting, but you cannot increase the quality of an imported JPEG and will instead reduce the quality further. To specify a new JPEG quality setting, uncheck Use Imported JPEG Data and enter a number between 1 and 100 in the Quality field. If you specify a new JPEG setting, be sure to check the image quality to ensure that it does not noticeably degrade. Use JPEG with bitmaps that have photographic detail and wide tonal variations.

Figure 16.17
In the Bitmap Properties dialog box, you can specify compression settings for imported bitmaps.

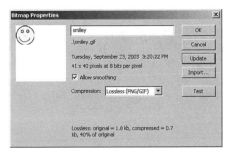

To compress without discarding pixel information, choose Lossless (PNG/GIF) in the Compression drop-down menu. Use Lossless with traced bitmaps that have simple shapes and fewer colors.

Click Test to compare the compressed file size to that of the original, as shown in Figure 16.18. Then click the Update button to preview the effects of your settings on the image preview in the upper left of the dialog box. Take the time to experiment with different settings to find the best compromise between image quality and file size. When you're satisfied with your compression settings, click OK.

Bitmaps can greatly enhance Flash movies. When used in combination with native vector art, bitmaps help to create textured, engaging designs and are indispensable for conveying photographic detail. Use bitmaps carefully to manage file size.

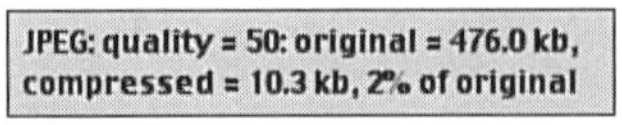

Figure 16.18
Clicking Test compares the resulting file size after compression with the original.

> JPEG: quality = 50: original = 476.0 kb,
> compressed = 10.3 kb, 2% of original

ANIMATING BITMAPS

Flash does not interpolate bitmap information as easily or as well as it does vector information. Remember, bitmaps map each pixel in an image, so there is much more information to interpolate. Bitmap tweens can dramatically increase file size and can produce unwanted effects such as slight stuttering during playback.

Use bitmap animation sparingly and keep the animation simple for best results. Faster, shorter bitmap tweens such as quick zooms are best, and can disguise stuttering. Smaller bitmaps affect file size less, as will confining animation to as small an area of the Stage as possible. Also, try to confine file-size–intensive effects such as bitmap animation to frames where there are few other effects, or users will have to wait even longer for content to download as movie elements compete for scarce bandwidth. If bitmap animation is crucial, you can experiment with setting a higher frame rate for better quality, but this also increases file size. As always, test several frame rates to make the best compromise between image quality and file size.

TROUBLESHOOTING

When I click and drag a shape, why does the stroke get left behind?

Clicking to select a shape that has both a stroke and a fill selects only the stroke or the fill, depending on which has been clicked. You must double-click a shape to select both. Alternatively, you can click and drag with the Selection tool to drag a selection marquee around both.

Why do bitmaps appear blurry in my published movie?

Check the Properties of bitmaps that appear blurry (Ctrl+click or right-click in the Library and choose Properties). Make sure that the Allow Smoothing option is unchecked. Smoothing anti-aliases a bitmap by smoothing the edges, which can make images appear blurry or out of focus. Also, in the Publish Settings dialog box, select the HTML tab and set the quality to Best.

Is there any way to trace a bitmap so that it is more detailed in some areas of an image and less so in others?

The trace settings only work globally, producing a standard level of detail throughout an image. However, it is possible to trace the same image twice, with differing amounts of detail, and combine the two by aligning the images on top of each other and erasing the unwanted portions. In this way, you can create a simple tracing for the majority of an image and include more detail in selected areas. This method does increase file size, so use it sparingly.

CHAPTER 17

WORKING WITH TEXT

In this chapter

Working with Text   368

Displaying Clear, Sharp Text   368

Dynamic and Input Text   370

Best Practices for Using Text   376

WORKING WITH TEXT

Macromedia Flash MX 2004 offers a tremendous range of options for manipulating text—from simple static text to highly stylized and animated text. *Static* text is entered by the developer at authoring time. *Input* text is input by the user (in a form, for example), whereas *dynamic* text is pulled in dynamically from an external source at runtime.

Many of the basics of creating and formatting text, which are similar in all the MX programs, are covered in Chapter 3, "Introducing the MX Interface."

→ For text basics, **see** Chapter 3, "Working with Text," **page 42**.

DISPLAYING CLEAR, SHARP TEXT

Despite the variety and sophistication of Flash's text features, the seemingly simple and basic goal of having text appear clear and sharp can be difficult to achieve. The basis of this problem is the fact that computers display text in square pixels. This shape is especially unfortunate for displaying letters. Most letters are not blocky but are instead composed of graceful curves. But the only way computers can transmit the letterforms is to convert curves into pixels, and much is lost in that translation.

Anti-aliasing is an attempt to regain some of the subtlety of curves in a pixel environment. With anti-aliasing, transitional pixels that are intermediate in color and tone are added between the type and the background, which results in smoother, although potentially fuzzy, letterforms. Say you have black text on a white background. Anti-aliasing adds some gray pixels around curved areas in the black letters, as shown in Figure 17.1.

Figure 17.1
The letter on the right is anti-aliased, with gray pixels added on the curves to display smoother letters.

Unfortunately, anti-aliasing can make text look fuzzy, particularly at small sizes, as you can see in Figure 17.2.

Enter bitmap fonts, also called pixel fonts. These fonts are designed without curves, specifically for computer display. Because they lack curves, there is no need to anti-alias. However, because these fonts are designed to the pixel, they must be used at the specific sizes for which they were designed and must be positioned precisely on whole pixels.

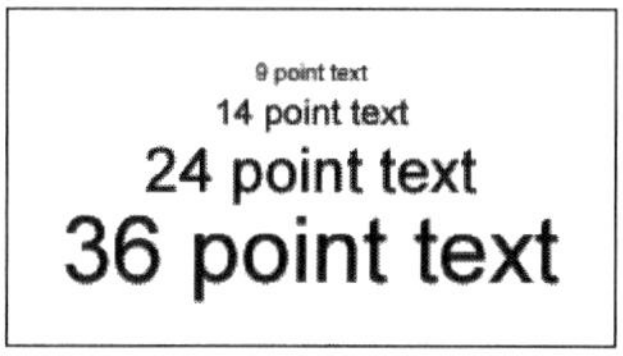

Figure 17.2
Anti-aliasing works best with relatively large type sizes; otherwise, it makes text appear fuzzy. Notice how the top line here looks slightly grayed out or blurred.

9 point text
14 point text
24 point text
36 point text

Quality bitmap fonts are becoming more widely available, thanks in large part to the growing popularity of Flash. One of the best sources is www.miniml.com, which features a wide variety of bitmap typefaces, including fonts designed specifically for body text (copy) and headers, plus a serif font.

Bitmap Font Resources
Bitmap fonts are increasingly popular, and new ones are being introduced all the time. Here are some good sources:

http://cgm.cs.mcgill.ca/~luc/pixel.html provides an exhaustive list of links to fonts—a fantastic resource.

http://www.miniml.com offers a large range of quality styles in multiple sizes. A few free fonts are available, or a 2004 Access Pass provides unlimited access to and use of fonts created in the calendar year for $100.

http://www.fontsforflash.com/ offers a variety of fonts for sale. A few free fonts are offered; you can purchase the rest individually. Their user guide offers some useful information on using pixel fonts in Flash: http://www.fontsforflash.com/userguide/

This site offers free pixel fonts: http://www.dsg4.com/04/extra/bitmap/index.html

USING SNAP TO PIXELS TO AUTOMATICALLY ALIGN TEXT

Before you begin to type, make sure that Snap to Pixels is turned on (View, Snapping, Snap to Pixels) and all other types of snapping are off. This ensures that bitmap fonts align exactly to whole pixels and, when text is placed directly on the Main Timeline, prevents fuzziness. However, when text is embedded within symbols and then placed on the Main Timeline, pixel snapping does not guarantee sharp text.

 *To learn more about preventing blurry fonts within instances of symbols, **see** the "Troubleshooting" section at the end of this chapter, **page 377**.*

ALIGNMENT AND JUSTIFICATION

If you are using bitmap fonts, the default left alignment is the safest option. Right-alignment may also work. Centering and full justification are likely to force bitmap fonts into sub-pixel alignment (that is, alignment on fractional coordinates, as opposed to integer coordinates) so that they appear blurry. The greatest culprit is full justification, which stretches fonts onto sub-pixel coordinates even when Snap to Pixels is enabled.

TURNING ANTI-ALIASING OFF

The Alias Text button on the Property inspector, a new option in Flash MX 2004, allows you to turn anti-aliasing off. (See Figure 17.3.) This sometimes makes text look crisper and more readable. For some serif fonts, such as Times Roman, it works best from font sizes 12 to 24. (At smaller sizes, fonts begin to blur. At larger sizes, they appear jaggy.) For some sans-serif fonts, Alias Text works well for smaller sizes. For example, Verdana size 10 is noticeably clearer with Alias Text selected. Alias Text may not work well below size 10, ensuring a continued role for bitmap fonts.

> **NOTE**
>
> Serifs are little extra strokes at the end of the main vertical and horizontal strokes of some letters. Sans serif means "without serif." (See Figure 17.5.)

DYNAMIC AND INPUT TEXT

Static text does not allow for any user input. To change the text, changes must be made in the Flash source file (FLA). Input and dynamic text fields are populated at runtime. To do anything useful with them, you have to access or manipulate the text fields with ActionScript.

With input and dynamic text, you create placeholder text fields in the FLA to designate where text will be placed and how it will appear during playback. Input and dynamic text attributes, like static text attributes, are assigned in the Property inspector.

INPUT TEXT

To create an input text field, click the Text tool, select Input Text from the pop-up Text type menu in the Property inspector, and drag out a text field on the Stage where the user can enter text. Or you can convert an existing text block by selecting it and changing the text type to Input Text. The borders of input text fields appear as dotted lines when not selected. Assign text attributes such as font, point size, and font color in the Property inspector as you would with static text. To preview text appearance, type something in the input text field. If you leave text in the field, it will remain there until the user replaces it. For example, you might want the field to initially contain a hint about what the user should enter ("Type your name here").

There are two ways to indicate to users where they should click to enter input text. You can turn on borders around your input text field by clicking the Show border around text button, shown in Figure 17.3.

Alias Text button

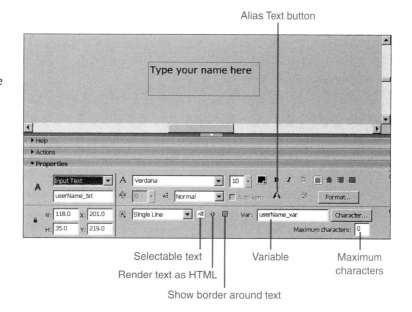

Figure 17.3
Text field attributes. All the attributes shown here, with the exceptions of Selectable and Alias Text, are applicable only to input and dynamic text fields.

Selectable text

Render text as HTML

Show border around text

Variable

Maximum characters

17

Your input text field appears with a black border and a white background. If this is undesirable, you can position an input field without borders over a shape that can indicate your input boundaries, as shown in Figure 17.4. Alternatively, you can use ActionScript to set the background and border colors.

Figure 17.4
Position your input text field over graphic elements to indicate the borders without having a white background appear.

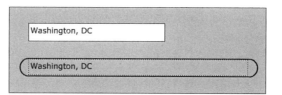

DYNAMIC TEXT

Dynamic text is loaded into your movie at runtime from an external source, such as a text file, a database, or a live feed from a server, rather than assembled in advance in the FLA. This is a good option for content that changes frequently, such as news stories, because content can be updated without edits to the FLA.

You create a dynamic text field just like an input text field, except that you select Dynamic Text from the Text type menu.

You can type in a dynamic text field to preview text appearance. If you leave text in the field, the user will see that text until other text dynamically replaces it.

Because dynamic text boxes use system fonts, you need to chose a system/device font or standard serif or san serif font like Verdana or Times. The alternative is to embed the outlines of a different font.

USING A VARIABLE TO SET AND GET TEXT

One way to control the text in an input or dynamic text field is by associating a variable name with the field. Any value assigned to the variable with ActionScript will appear in the field. Any reference to the variable in your scripts is interpreted by ActionScript as a reference to the text in the field.

Use the Var field in the Property inspector to assign the variable. For example, in Figure 17.3, the variable name userName_var was been assigned to the input text field, userName_txt.

TEXT FORMATTING OPTIONS

Several text formatting options are specific to input and dynamic text. You must give these text fields instance names to be able to use ActionScript to access their properties. To do so, enter a unique instance name in the Instance Name field, which is beneath the Text type drop-down in the Property inspector. For instance, in Figure 17.3, the instance name was userName_txt.

Using the Line type drop-down option, you can specify whether a dynamic or input text field can contain more than a single line of text. The options are Single Line; Multiline, which displays multiple lines of text; and Multiline No Wrap, which displays multiple lines only if the user enters hard breaks with Return (Mac) or Enter (Windows).

The Maximum Characters field, as shown in Figure 17.3, allows you to limit the number of characters that can be entered into an input text field.

The Render Text as HTML button allows you to use some HTML formatting in the text field. When this option is selected, Flash applies the appropriate formatting to the text at runtime. (This does not work for text you enter in the FLA.) The supported tags include links, bold, break (new line), italic, underline, paragraph, font color, font face, and font size.

In Flash Player 7 and later, you can also include images in the form of JPEGs, SWFs, or movie clips (not GIFs). The ActionScript is simple:

```
userName_var = "Enter user name: <img src = \"test.jpg\">";
```

Supported HTML attributes include leftmargin, rightmargin, align indent, and leading. You can also set Render as HTML in ActionScript by using the html property of the TextField object.

Finally, this panel contains an option to allow users to select the text. It is turned on by default, as shown in Figure 17.3. If you don't want users to be able to select your text—to copy and paste it, for example—deselect the Selectable text button.

EMBEDDED AND DEVICE FONTS

When you create text in Flash, all the fonts installed on your system are at your disposal. However, other users may not have your installed fonts, and different fonts are available on different platforms. Does this mean that your careful formatting of text will go to waste? No, but you need to take steps to ensure that users see the typefaces you want them to see.

You have two options. One is to embed font outlines. Embedding allows you to save the outlines of your fonts so that text is displayed in the specified font even if it is not installed on a user's system. Flash anti-aliases embedded fonts unless you select Alias Text. Embedding fonts does add to the overall file size of movies.

With static text, you don't need to embed the fonts because the outlines are automatically saved. Fonts used in dynamic and input text fields are by default not embedded and therefore not anti-aliased. To embed fonts, click the Edit character options button just to the right of the Var field. The Character Options dialog box launches. You can choose to embed all the characters in the font. Or you can embed just selected subsets of the font, such as uppercase, lowercase, or numerals. To reduce your file size, embed only the characters you need. For instance, you don't need to embed characters other than numerals for a text field that will contain the year in four-digit format.

Not all fonts can be embedded and exported with your movie. Sometimes Flash doesn't recognize font outline information. To test whether a font can be embedded, select the text and click the Alias Text button on and off. If you see no change, Flash does not recognize the font's outlines and cannot embed it.

The alternative to embedding fonts is using device fonts. Computer operating systems include a limited number of fonts that are automatically installed. These fonts are different on Macintosh and Windows platforms, but each platform includes a sans serif, a serif, and a typewriter typeface. (See Figure 17.5.) Typewriter typefaces are monospaced, meaning that each letter occupies an identical amount of space. Note that both the capital *A* and the lowercase *i* in the typewriter typeface in Figure 17.5 occupy equal amounts of space. Compare this to the serif and sans serif examples.

Figure 17.5
Device fonts utilize system fonts that include serif, sans serif, and typewriter typefaces.

Serif   Sans Serif   Typewriter

When device fonts are specified, outlines are not embedded, and the Flash Player displays the most similar font that is installed on the user's system. Three device fonts are available: _sans, which typically uses Helvetica (Mac) or Arial (PC); _serif, which typically uses Times or Times New Roman; and _typewriter, which uses fonts similar to Courier. To specify device fonts, select them from the Font pop-up list, as shown in Figure 17.6.

Figure 17.6
You can select device fonts from the Font pop-up list in the Property inspector.

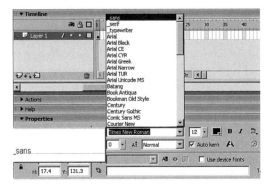

Device fonts produce smaller file sizes than embedded fonts, but there is an element of uncertainty; if a user doesn't have installed fonts that correspond to specified device fonts, strange and unexpected substitutions may occur. Device fonts are not anti-aliased, so they work best at small sizes where anti-aliasing can make characters appear fuzzy. They may appear noticeably jagged at large sizes because they are not anti-aliased.

BREAKING TEXT APART

You can break apart text by using Modify, Break Apart, placing each character into a separate text block. Individual characters in words can then be animated separately. If you break apart the same text a second time, you convert it into graphic shapes. (See Figure 17.7.)

Figure 17.7
Break apart text once to place each character into its own text box or a second time to convert text blocks to shapes.

After text is converted to shapes, it is no longer recognized as text and cannot be edited as text.

With text broken apart, Flash allows you to quickly distribute the character blocks to separate layers. Select the text blocks with the Arrow tool and then choose Modify, Timeline, Distribute to Layers. Flash places each letter on a separate layer, named for each character.

Naming Distributed Layers
Flash assigns each distributed layer the name of the letter it contains. If a word uses a letter more than once, you end up with several layers with the same name. This quickly becomes confusing, so be sure to add numbers or otherwise create distinctions between layers containing the same letters.

TRANSFORMING TEXT

After your text is broken apart into shapes, it can be dramatically transformed. You can use the Subselection tool to select points and move them, changing the shapes of letters, as shown in Figure 17.8. Such transformations can be used to create unique letter shapes and can be animated over time through the use of shape tweens.

→ For more information about creating animation and shape tweens, **see** Chapter 18, "Animation, Interactivity, and Rich Media," **page 379**.

Figure 17.8
After your text is broken apart into shapes, you can use the Subselection tool to drag anchor points and reshape letters.

You can also use the new Distort and Envelope transform modifiers to really push the boundaries of text distortion. You cannot use these modifiers on groups or symbols: These tools are grayed out until you convert the text to shapes. Then you use either the Arrow tool or the Free Transform tool and drag over shapes that create a word to transform the word as a whole. If you use the Arrow tool, select the Transform tool; then select the Distort or Envelope modifiers of the Free Transform tool at the bottom of the Toolbox, and select and drag the transform handles that appear around your word, as shown in Figure 17.9.

Figure 17.9
Use the Distort modifier of the Free Transform tool to create perspective text effects.

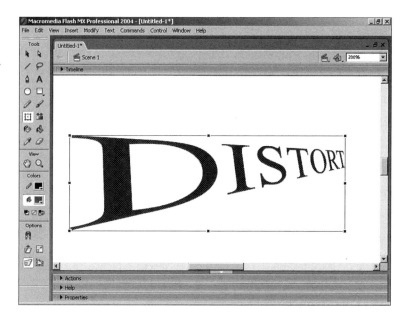

The Envelope modifier creates the most dramatic transformation and can completely change the shapes of letters, as shown in Figure 17.10. Use this powerful capability carefully because letters can become so misshapen that they are no longer recognizable or legible.

Figure 17.10
Use the Envelope modifier of the Free Transform tool for more psychedelic text effects.

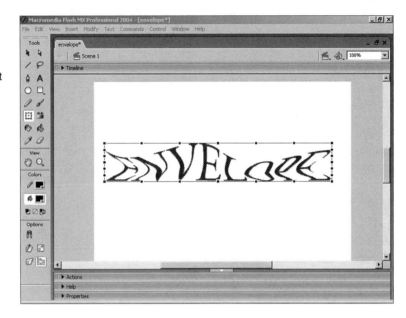

BEST PRACTICES FOR USING TEXT

It is crucial to ensure that your text can be read. Attributes that affect legibility include

- Contrast between text color and background color
- Serif typefaces
- Point size
- Letter spacing and line spacing

These attributes are especially important when bitmap fonts are used. The point size is predetermined for bitmap fonts and is often small. It is therefore even more important to ensure that there is sufficient contrast between font color and background color. Dark text on light backgrounds is most easily read, although light text can be used on dark backgrounds if the colors are carefully chosen to ensure sufficient contrast. Avoid combining text and background colors that are similar in brightness, especially with text at small sizes, such as body copy set in bitmap fonts.

Another rule of thumb is to avoid the use of serif typefaces at small sizes. Serifs are delicate lines, much finer than the main strokes of letters, and at small sizes it is difficult to distinguish such fine detail. Anti-aliasing exacerbates the problem. Miniml offers a bitmap serif font, Cerif, which is more legible at small sizes.

- For more information about Miniml fonts and other bitmap fonts, **see** the "Bitmap Font Resources" sidebar, earlier in this chapter, **page 369**.

If you are not using bitmap fonts, you can control the point size of your text. Preview your text at different sizes and formatting to find the optimum size, letter spacing, and line spacing. Also, have someone else read your text to ensure that a viewer who is unfamiliar with the content can comfortably read it.

Give Text Fields Unique Instance Names

If you need to create several input or dynamic text fields that are the same size and have the same attributes, it's fastest to copy and paste a single text field. However, copied text fields have identical attributes, *including* instance and variable names. This will really mess up your scripting, so you must–I repeat *must*–then assign unique instance and variable names for each text field. Be compulsive about naming.

Similarly, if you're having a problem with a script dealing with multiple text fields, check your instance and variable names for repetition. Because you can display the attributes of only one text field at a time in the Property inspector, use the Movie Explorer or the List Variables option in the Debugger (Debug, List Variables) to view the entire list of variables at once.

TROUBLESHOOTING

BLURRY MAIN TIMELINE FONTS

Why do bitmap fonts placed on whole pixel coordinates in a movie clip appear blurry when placed on the Main Timeline?

Check to be sure that your movie clip is placed on whole pixel coordinates in the Main Timeline. Placement on the Main Timeline determines the coordinates of the text embedded within a movie clip. Even though your text may reside on whole coordinates (x.0) in a nested clip, if the clip is placed on sub-pixel coordinates on the Main Timeline (for example, x.5), the text is in fact displayed at the sub-pixel (fractional) coordinate: x.0 + x.5 = x.5.

Also, when you publish a movie containing bitmap fonts, be sure to select No Scale from the Scale options within the HTML Publish Settings. If the movie is allowed to scale, its dimensions are determined by the size of the browser window, causing the SWF to stretch or shrink. Any text also stretches or shrinks and displays at sizes different from those specified in your FLA. Bitmap fonts are mapped to specific pixels and must be displayed at precise sizes to render correctly.

Bitmap fonts are especially problematic when used in components. The reason is that the movie clips within components that contain text are not positioned on whole pixels. Branden Hall has scripted a workaround that rounds the pixel placement. You can find it at:
`http://www.waxpraxis.org/archives/000017.html`

BOLD OR ITALIC TEXT IN DYNAMIC TEXT FIELDS

Why am I unable to use bold or italic text in a dynamic text field?

You can run into problems if you use HTML formatting with an embedded font. Embedding fonts includes embedding the font outlines in the published movie. However, bold and italic fonts are distinct, separate outlines that must also be embedded to display. Embedding bold and italic font outlines increase the size of your movie significantly—you are tripling the font information that is contained in a movie. Also, you may have to trick Flash into including these outlines. To embed the outlines, you must create a text field to specify each outline. You can do so by creating text fields outside the viewable Stage area that specify alternative outlines—one for bold, one for italic, and so on. You can limit the embedded characters if you know the types of characters that will be used in your dynamic text fields. (In the Property inspector, click the Character button to specify which subsets of the entire typeface you want to include.) Still, embedding additional outlines increases the file size of your movie noticeably.

CHAPTER 18

ANIMATION, INTERACTIVITY, AND RICH MEDIA

In this chapter

Symbols, Instances, and Library Assets   380

Animating in Flash   390

Using Sound   406

Flash Interactivity   418

Accelerating Application Development with Components   426

Integrating Video   431

SYMBOLS, INSTANCES, AND LIBRARY ASSETS

Symbols are the basic building blocks of a well-designed Flash movie, allowing you to reduce the size of your SWF file and organize movie assets conveniently in the Library.

UNDERSTANDING SYMBOLS

Any time you draw a shape, place an imported bitmap, or animate an object, your published movie must store the information required to render these elements. Symbols allow you to store each asset just once in the Library. You can then display each asset on the Stage as many times as you want without significantly increasing the movie's size. Smaller movies mean faster downloads and better performance. In addition, when you need to make changes, you can make them in a single place and affect many parts of your movie. If a client doesn't like the color scheme you've used for a project, you may be able to change it very quickly just by editing a few symbols.

When you drag a symbol from the Library to the Stage, each "appearance" of the symbol on the Stage is called an *instance*. Each instance is independent and can be manipulated freely without affecting the Library symbol or other instances.

Think of instances as Flash Lego blocks. The trick is to learn to separate the elements of your movies into component parts—Lego blocks—that can be snapped together to form complex animations and interface systems.

You can create symbols directly in the Library. In addition, any object on the Stage can be converted to a symbol. (Select the object and choose Modify, Convert to Symbol. Or use F8.)

There are three types of symbols: graphic, button, and movie clip. Each has its own time-line, Stage, and layers.

GRAPHIC SYMBOLS

Graphic symbols are the most basic and least powerful symbols, best used with static images, such as backgrounds. Graphics can be animated but cannot contain sounds or interactive elements. Further, because it is controlled by the Timeline of the movie or movie clip in which it resides, a graphic symbol plays only for the duration of the Timeline. Use movie clips for animation; reserve graphic symbols for static elements that are reused.

BUTTON SYMBOLS

Buttons are interactive symbols that respond to user interaction, such as mouse clicks and rollovers. Buttons have unique timelines containing Up, Over, Down, and Hit frames, as shown in Figure 18.1. These frames represent button states. Button timelines don't unfold over time like other timelines, but instead respond and move among the four frames according to user interaction.

Figure 18.1
Buttons have unique timelines containing Up, Over, Down, and Hit frames.

The four button states are as follows:

- **Up**—Defines how the button appears with no user interaction.
- **Over**—Provides a rollover state when the mouse pointer hovers over the button.
- **Down**—Defines the appearance of the button when it is clicked.
- **Hit**—Defines the area that responds to the mouse. Content in the Hit frame is not displayed.

You don't need to create all four states for every button. Button states can contain graphics, sounds, and even movie clips.

→ To learn more about buttons, **see** "Buttons," in this chapter, **page 420**.

Movie Clips

Movie clips are self-contained movies, with their own independent timelines that are not tied to the Main Timeline. Think of the Main Timeline as a master "container" movie clip. Like the Main Timeline, movie clips can contain graphics, buttons, and scripted interactive controls, sounds, videos, and even other movie clips. Nesting movie clips inside other movie clips permits complex interactivity and nonlinear narrative flow.

→ To learn about the Movie Clip object in ActionScript, **see** "Working with Movie Clips," **page 517**, in Chapter 20, "Basic ActionScript."

Creating Symbols from Scratch

There are two ways to start creating a symbol from scratch:

- Make sure that nothing is selected on the Stage. On the Main Menu, choose Insert, Symbol, or press Cmd-F8 (Mac) or Ctrl+F8 (Windows).
- Click in the upper right corner of the Library panel, and choose New Symbol.

NOTE

> Be on the lookout for opportunities to convert artwork into component parts that can be reused. Symbols increase your efficiency and reduce SWF size, so take the fullest possible advantage of them.

Either of these actions will bring up the Create New Symbol dialog box, as shown in Figure 18.2.

18

Figure 18.2
In the Create New Symbol dialog box, you can name your symbol and choose its type.

18

Type in a name for your symbol, and choose the type of symbol: movie clip (the initial default), button, or graphic. Then click OK. Your symbol is added to the Library and is opened in the work area in symbol-editing mode. The name of your symbol appears in the Information bar above the upper-left corner of the Stage, and a crosshair icon appears in the middle of the Stage, indicating the symbol's registration point, as shown in Figure 18.3. You can now add content to your symbol.

Figure 18.3
When you create a new symbol, it is placed in the Library and opened in symbol-editing mode.

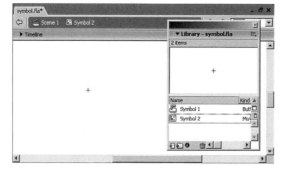

REGISTRATION

The registration point, which appears as a crosshair when you select an object, is the point of reference used when you position a symbol using the Align panel, or when you choose to snap to grids, guides, pixels or objects. In fact, snapping works only if you drag an object by its registration point. When you use ActionScript to position an object numerically , it's the registration point that gets placed at the specified (x,y) coordinates. (When you use the Property inspector or the Info panel to position an object numerically, the upper-left corner is the reference point.)

There are nine standard points of registration: each of the four corners, the center point, and the midpoint on each edge of an object. The registration point determines the 0,0 point—0-x and 0-y—for that symbol.

NOTE

The nine standard points of registration are the available options when you convert artwork to a symbol. In addition, you can edit a symbol to change its registration point to any point within the symbol.

Coordinate systems map a two-dimensional plane, allowing you to plot objects to specific coordinates. The x-axis is the horizontal axis, and the y-axis is the vertical axis. In the main "container" movie, 0,0 (x,y) is the upper-left corner of the Stage. Upper left is the default registration for artwork converted into a symbol, as well. However, when you create a new movie clip from scratch, 0,0 (x,y) is the center point by default.

As an object moves to the right, its x-value increases. As it moves down, its y-value increases (inverted from the normal Cartesian coordinate system). Negative x-values occur when the object crosses to the left of the y-axis (which is off the Stage in the main movie). Negative y-values occur when the object crosses above the x-axis (also off the Stage in the main movie) .

CONVERT TO SYMBOL

To convert an existing object on the Stage to a symbol, select it and choose Modify, Convert to Symbol, or press F8.

Choosing this option launches the Convert to Symbol dialog box, which is nearly identical to the Create New Symbol dialog box with an important exception—it contains a Registration setting, as shown in Figure 18.4.

Figure 18.4
The Convert to Symbol dialog box enables you to convert an object on the Stage to a symbol and set its registration point.

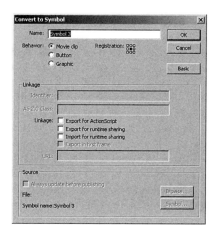

Click one of the squares in the Registration grid to set the registration point. In general, positioning objects according to their upper-left corner is easiest. If you change the registration in the Convert to Symbol dialog box, that setting becomes the default, even if you exit and restart Flash.

Give your symbol a name, select the type of symbol, and click OK. The symbol is added to the Library, and the selection on the Stage becomes an instance of the symbol, as indicated by the square bounding box that appears. The crosshair indicates the symbol's registration point.

→ For more on the Library, **see** "The Library," later in this chapter, **page 389**.

You can also duplicate an existing symbol to use it as a template for a new symbol. Select an instance on the Stage and choose Modify, Symbol, Duplicate Symbol. You can name the new symbol in the Symbol Name dialog box that appears. This creates a copy of the symbol in the Library, where you can select and edit it.

EDITING TRANSFORMATION POINTS

The small empty circle within a selected symbol is the transformation point, the point around which rotate, scale, and skew transforms are performed.

You may need to change a symbol's transformation point. A common example is a scripted status bar, used in a preloader to indicate the progress of a download to users. In this example, the status bar is a rectangle that is scripted to extend, or grow wider, to represent the progress of a download. If the transformation point is the center of the status bar symbol, changes in the width of the progress bar occur from the center in either direction, as shown in Figure 18.5, which is probably not the effect you intend.

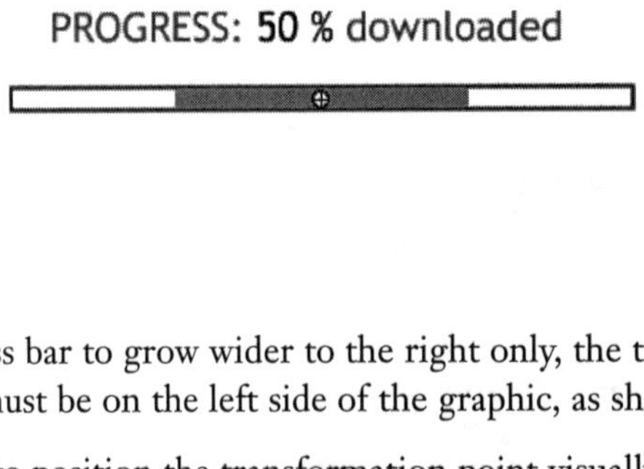

Figure 18.5
If a symbol's transformation point is its center, any transformations occur from that point.

PROGRESS: 50 % downloaded

For a progress bar to grow wider to the right only, the transformation point of the status bar symbol must be on the left side of the graphic, as shown in Figure 18.6.

A quick way to position the transformation point visually is to select a symbol instance on the Stage and then select the Rotate and Skew tool or the Scale tool in the Main Toolbar. The transformation point circle appears white within the selected instance. You can click and drag the circle to relocate the transformation point anywhere within the workspace (even off the Stage).

Figure 18.6
The status bar symbol's transformation point is on the left side, so changes in its width occur from the left.

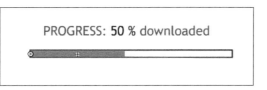

EDITING SYMBOLS

You can edit symbols in three ways: in place, in a new window, or in symbol-editing mode.

EDIT IN PLACE

The Edit in Place command enables you to edit a symbol in the context of other objects on the Stage. The other objects are slightly dimmed, and are not selectable. You can tweak size, color, or shape, for example, and see how the changes look in the context of the other objects on the Stage, without worrying about accidentally selecting and modifying another object.

To edit in place, double-click a symbol on the Stage, or select a symbol and choose Edit, Edit in Place, or Ctrl-click (Mac), or right-click (Windows) and select Edit in Place from the pop-up menu.

For instance, say you are creating a circle to use as the "O" in a tic-tac-toe game, as shown in Figure 18.7. As you can see, the circle symbol is too big for the tic-tac-toe grid. The Edit in Place command enables you to scale the circle within the context of the grid, without worrying about accidentally selecting the grid.

18

Figure 18.7
Edit in Place allows you to edit symbols within the context of other objects on the Stage.

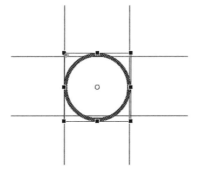

After you finish editing, click the Back button or the current scene name in the Information bar above the upper-left corner of the Stage, click the current scene in the scene pop-up menu, or choose Edit, Edit Document. Ctrl+E (Windows) or Cmd-E (Mac) also works.

EDIT IN NEW WINDOW

You can also edit symbols in a new window. Editing in a new window launches the symbol's timeline in a new window while the main movie remains open in the original window. You can go back and forth between the main movie and the symbol timeline, editing the symbol without the distraction of surrounding objects, but still checking to see what it looks like in context.

To edit a symbol in a new window, select the symbol on the Stage and Ctrl-click (Mac) or right-click (Windows) and select Edit in New Window from the pop-up menu. The symbol opens in a separate window. Edit as needed and then click the Close button in the upper-left corner (Mac) or the upper-right corner (Windows) to close the separate window and return to the Main Timeline.

SYMBOL-EDITING MODE

Editing in symbol-editing mode takes you from the main work area—whichever timeline you may be working in—into the symbol's timeline. If you need to make extensive changes to a symbol, it may be easiest to edit it in isolation. You can access symbol-editing mode in any of the following ways:

- Select the symbol on the Stage. Then Ctrl-click (Mac) or right-click (Windows) and select Edit from the pop-up menu.
- Select the symbol on the Stage and choose Edit, Edit Symbols.
- Double-click the symbol's icon (located to the left of the symbol's name) in the Library.
- Select the symbol in the Library and choose Edit from the Library options pop-up menu. Alternatively, Ctrl-click (Mac) or right-click (Windows) and select Edit from the context menu.

Edit as needed and then, to return to the Main Timeline, do one of the following:

- Click the Back button in the Information bar.
- Choose Edit, Edit Document.
- Use a shortcut key: Ctrl+E (Windows) or Cmd-E (Mac) .

INSTANCES

Symbols reside in the Library. When you place a symbol on the Stage, you create an *instance* of the symbol: a reference to the symbol that takes up almost no memory or storage. Changing the original symbol in the Library changes every instance of that symbol. However, instances are independent of their original symbols. For example, you can transform (rotate, skew, or scale) an instance without changing the symbol itself or affecting any other instances of the same symbol.

For example, if you select an instance and use the Scale tool to scale it, you change the dimensions of that instance only. To change the dimensions of the symbol itself, you would need to edit the symbol, using one of the methods outlined in the previous section.

You can also change an instance's type. Say you have an instance of a graphic symbol that you want to animate independently of the Main Timeline. You can easily change that instance from a graphic to a movie clip. Select the instance and, in the Property inspector, use the drop-down menu to change the instance type, as shown in Figure 18.8.

Figure 18.8
Use the Instance Type drop-down menu in the Property inspector to change instance behavior.

CHANGING INSTANCE PROPERTIES

An instance's brightness, tint, and alpha (transparency) are independent of its original symbol, as are its advanced color settings. You access these properties by using the Color drop-down menu on the Property inspector, as shown in Figure 18.9.

Color Drop-down

18

Figure 18.9
The Color drop-down enables you to manipulate an instance's color properties.

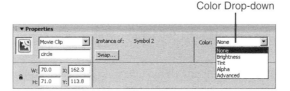

Use the Brightness option to make an instance lighter or darker. Enter a value directly in the Brightness field or drag the slider (see Figure 18.10) to change the relative brightness of an instance from 100% (white) to –100% (black) .

The Tint option enables you to change the hue of an instance by manipulating its red, green, blue, and alpha values. First, click the color box to select the tint color, and either enter its values in the red, green, and blue fields or use the Color box to select a Web-safe color. Then adjust the alpha setting to change the saturation of the tint, as shown in Figure 18.11.

Brightness slider

Figure 18.10
Change the brightness setting using the numerical type-in or the slider.

Brightness numerical type-in

Color box ┐ ┌ Alpha slider

Figure 18.11
Change the red, green, blue, and alpha settings within the Tint option to change an instance's hue.

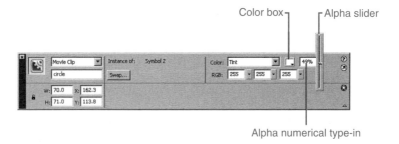

Alpha numerical type-in

The Alpha option changes an instance's transparency, from 100% (opaque) to 0% (completely transparent). Enter a numerical value in the Alpha field or use the slider to select a setting.

The Advanced option allows you to manipulate the red, green, blue, and transparency values separately, producing more subtle effects than tint. To launch the Advanced Settings dialog box, select Advanced from the Color pop-up menu and click the Settings button on the right to launch the Advanced Effect dialog box.

You can adjust values either by percentages (using fields in the left column) or by absolute values (using fields in the right column), as shown in Figure 18.12.

Figure 18.12
In the Advanced Effect dialog box, you can manipulate settings by percentages or by numeric values.

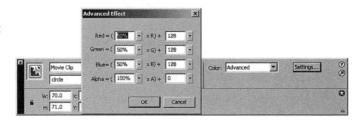

Advanced effects work by taking the current red, green, and blue values and multiplying them by the percentages entered in the left column. These amounts are then added to the values in the right column, producing new color values. Don't be intimidated by the Advanced Color settings; just take the time to experiment with them. You'll find these subtle effects work best with the range of color values found in bitmaps.

Swapping Symbols

As you develop a movie, you may want to swap an instance of one symbol for an instance of a different symbol—for example, to swap graphics. To swap a symbol instance, select the instance and click Swap in the Property inspector to launch the Swap Symbol dialog box. The Swap Symbol dialog box displays all the symbols in the Library. Select a substitute image and click OK.

Instance Names

You can give movie clip and button instances unique instance names, which allow you to access symbol instances using ActionScript. Symbol instances can then be manipulated pro-grammatically. Scripting provides much greater control over symbol instances and enables you to create content that can change in response to user actions.

➔ For more information about using ActionScript to access instances, **see** "Working with Movie Clips," **page 517**, in Chapter 20.

To assign an instance name, select a button or movie clip instance on the Stage and type a unique name in the Instance Name field in the Property inspector, as shown in Figure 18.13.

18

Instance Name

Figure 18.13
Instance names enable you to access individual movie clip and button instances with ActionScript.

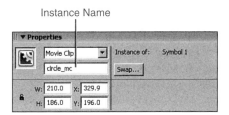

The Library

Symbols are housed and organized in the Library. To open the Library, choose Window, Library. You'll need to have the Library open to drag symbol instances to the Stage, so you may want to dock the Library with the other panels you keep open as you work. The Library panel consists of a preview window at the top, below which is a scrolling list of symbols and imported assets. You can expand the Library by clicking the Wide Library View button, as shown in Figure 18.14, to see more information about symbols, such as their Linkage identifiers, use counts (how many times the symbol is used in the movie), and last modification date.

Normal Library
View button

Wide Library
View button

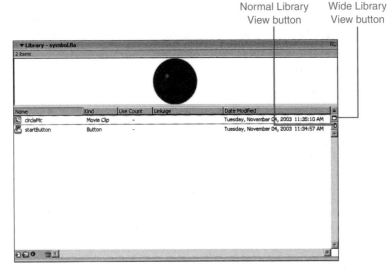

Figure 18.14
Click the Wide Library
View button to
expand the Library
panel.

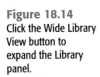

To change the sort order in the Library, click on the column headers to sort by name, kind (type), use count, linkage, or date modified. Sorting by use count is helpful in identifying symbols that are no longer used in your movies. By default, you have to explicitly request updating of the Use Count by selecting Update Use Counts Now from the Library options pop-up menu. You can keep use counts constantly updated by choosing Keep Use Counts Updated from the Library options pop-up.

The contents of the Library can be organized into folders. Simply click the New Folder icon at the bottom left of the Library panel to create a new folder. As with layer folders, using Library folders helps to conserve scarce screen real estate. You can also use folders to organize the contents of the Library. You might have a folder for imported assets, one for navigation symbols, and so on. The number of items in the Library can quickly mushroom when you're working on big projects, and you can waste a lot of time scrolling through the contents of the Library to locate a particular symbol if you do not use folders to organize your symbols and assets.

ANIMATING IN FLASH

Animation is the illusion of movement created by a progressive sequence of still images. The emphasis is on the *sequence*. In producing the illusion of movement, the quality of the sequence is the crucial ingredient, and is more important than the quality of the images. This is true because animation is not the art of moving objects and drawings, but instead is the art of drawing and capturing motion. The art is in the action.

Macromedia Flash is uniquely equipped to produce animation. The vector format is perfectly suited for cartoon-like animation. Vector graphics produce shapes that can be easily and precisely transformed while maintaining small file sizes. Vector graphics offer the capability to zoom in and out on shapes, which helps to create convincing animation. Bitmaps can also be animated in Flash. Flash's symbol system is also ideal for animation. Symbols allow you to break animations into component parts and create complex animations using nested symbols.

Flash MX 2004 brings one major new feature in the area of animation: Timeline Effects. This feature allows you to create effects, most of them animated, just by setting parameters on configuration screens. Effects include fade-ins, fade-outs, wipes, drop shadows and blurs; simple position-rotation-scale animations; and just for good measure, fragmenting and "exploding" objects!

FRAMES AND KEYFRAMES

The Timeline is divided horizontally into *frames*—discrete units of time. The Timeline is also divided into layers, which simulate depth—whether objects are "in front of" or "behind" other objects.

The playhead displays a single frame at a time, and a nearly unlimited number of layers within each frame. Within a single timeline, you have to put content on different layers to animate objects individually using the techniques described in this chapter. (With ActionScript, separation on different layers is not a requirement for animating objects individually.) For instance, you might have a stationary background and several layers with content that animate at different points in your movie.

The Magic Number: 16,000
Have you ever wondered how big a Flash movie can be? Well, 16,000 is something of a magic number in Flash. It's the maximum number of frames (any more and playback will stop), symbol instances, layers, and loaded movies.

→ For more on Flash size limits, **see** "How big can a Flash movie be?," `http://www.macromedia.com/support/flash/ts/documents/bigflash.htm`.

A frame is a static slice of time—the contents of the Stage at a particular moment. *Keyframes* are critical junctures where you define how you want the contents of the Stage to change. Flash creates animation by tracking change: where the contents of the Stage change—keyframes—and between frames in which the contents either remain the same (in frame-to-frame animation) or gradually approach the states defined in the next keyframe (in animations that use *tweening*) .

ADDING, EDITING, DELETING, AND COPYING FRAMES

When you create a new document, Flash provides a single layer with one frame. You add frames to define when the contents of a layer are visible. The overall length of a movie is determined by the highest frame number that occurs in any layer. Adding frames to a layer keeps content on the Stage longer. Deleting frames reduces the time that content is visible.

To add frames to a layer, click to select a frame in the Timeline and then press F5 to insert frames.

When content is added to the Stage, Flash converts the current frame to a keyframe, because the new content represents a change. Ordinary frames display the content of the keyframe that precedes them. Content remains static between keyframes unless a *tween* has been added.

Tweening

"Tween" comes from the term "inbetweening." In classic animation, senior artists would sketch frames where crucial action occurs, and junior artists would fill in the intermediate frames, or "inbetweens." Similarly, when you create a tween in Flash, Flash acts as your junior artist, interpolating the changes between keyframes.

To add a keyframe, click to select a frame in the Timeline; then press F6 to insert a keyframe, which is displayed as a hollow circle, as shown in Figure 18.15.

Blank keyframe

Keyframe with content

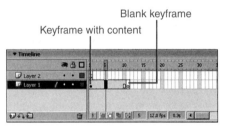

Figure 18.15
Blank keyframes are displayed as hollow circles, and keyframes with content are shown as filled circles.

To delete frames or keyframes, select the frame or frames you want to delete, Ctrl-click (Mac) or right-click (Windows), and select Remove Frames from the context menu. To change a keyframe to an ordinary frame, removing the changes that occur in that keyframe without deleting the frame, select a keyframe, Ctrl-click (Mac) or right-click (Windows), and choose Clear Keyframe from the context menu.

To select multiple frames, click and drag across frames. You also can copy and paste frames. Select frames and/or keyframes, Ctrl-click (Mac) or right-click (Windows), and select Copy Frames from the context menu. Select another frame in the Timeline, and Ctrl-click (Mac) or right-click (Windows) and select Paste Frames from the context menu. You can copy and paste frames across layers. If you copy frames from multiple layers, they will paste into multiple layers.

MANIPULATING KEYFRAMES

Keyframes can be added anywhere within a layer. Flash inserts frames, if necessary, to fill the distance between an existing keyframe and a new keyframe. A keyframe newly created with F6 displays the content of the preceding keyframe and allows that content to be changed. To clear the contents of the Stage on a particular layer, add a blank keyframe by selecting a frame and pressing F7.

Adding a keyframe extends the Timeline by one or more frames. You can also convert existing frames to keyframes or blank keyframes. Select one or more frames, Ctrl-click (Mac) or right-click (Windows), and select Convert to Keyframes or Convert to Blank Keyframes.

To move keyframes in the Timeline, select one or more keyframes, release, and click and drag the keyframe(s) to a new position, even to a new layer.

FRAME RATE

The speed of motion is determined by your movie's frame rate and the number of frames over which the motion takes place. Flash allows you to set the frame rate, in number of frames per second, for your movie. It's best to set the frame rate for a document as soon as you open it, or you may have to tweak the length of your animations later if you change the rate. The easiest way to set the frame rate is as follows:

1. Click an unoccupied portion of the Stage. The document properties appear in the Property inspector, as shown in Figure 18.16.

Frame Rate

Figure 18.16
The frame rate of a movie is accessed in the document settings displayed in the Property inspector.

2. Click in the Frame Rate field and enter a number. The default fps (frames per second) is 12. Anything between 8 and 18 is acceptable for the Web. If you set higher rates, insufficient bandwidth and/or a processing-intensive movie may make the configured rate only intermittently achievable, resulting in random variations in the actual rate.

The higher the frame rate, the smoother the animation, and the larger the SWF. If you know your audience has higher bandwidth and faster computers, you have the luxury of using higher frame rates. In most cases, however, it's best to err on the side of caution and use lower frame rates. If a download takes too long, your audience may leave in frustration and never see your animation.

With the frame rate set, you can focus on the timing of your animations. Animations that unfold over a greater number of frames appear slower, whereas those that take place over few frames appear rapid.

TWEENING

There are two types of animation in Flash: *frame-by-frame* and *tweened*. Frame-by-frame animation changes the contents of the stage in keyframes only. Frame-by-frame animation is both labor and file-size intensive but gives you complete control at every moment. Tweened animation consists of keyframes for critical changes, with Flash creating the intermediate steps between keyframes.

There are two types of tweens: *motion* and *shape*. Motion tweens interpolate changes in position, scale, rotation, color, and transparency of a single shape. Shape tweens interpolate differences between two shapes on a single layer, allowing you to morph or change one into the other.

Tweened objects must be symbols or groups on a single layer. If you attempt to tween simple shapes without converting them to symbols, a dotted line appears between keyframes and a caution symbol appears in the Property inspector, as shown in Figure 18.17.

Figure 18.17
A dashed line in the Timeline and a caution symbol in the Property inspector indicate incomplete tweens.

These symbols indicate that the tween is incomplete, and if you preview your animation, you'll see that your intended tween does not occur.

MOTION TWEENING

To create a simple motion tweened animation of a ball falling, follow these steps:

1. Open a new document by choosing File, New or by pressing Cmd-N (Mac) or Ctrl+N (Windows).

2. Select the Oval tool, and choose a fill color with no stroke.

Different Strokes

When animating solid shapes, use strokes only when necessary, that is, when the stroke is a different color than the fill. A stroke that is the same color as the fill is indistinguishable from the fill and requires Flash to perform unnecessary calculations that increase rendering time and file size.

---

3. Shift+drag with the Oval tool near the top of the Stage to draw a circle.

4. Select the circle and convert it to a symbol by pressing F8. Name the symbol `ball`, choose Graphic for the behavior, and click the center square in the registration grid. Click OK to close the Convert to Symbol dialog box.

5. Go to frame 12 and press F6 to insert a keyframe. Notice that nothing on the Stage has changed yet.

6. Using the Selection tool, click and drag the ball to move it to the bottom of the Stage, as shown in Figure 18.18.

Figure 18.18
Insert a keyframe in frame 12 and use the Selection tool to move the ball to the bottom of the Stage.

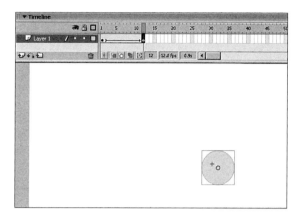

7. Play your movie within the work area by pressing Return (Mac) or Enter (Windows). Notice that the ball is positioned at the top of the Stage for 11 frames and jumps to the bottom of the Stage only in frame 12. Without tweening, frames 2–11 just display the content of the keyframe in frame 1.

8. To make your ball appear to gradually fall to the bottom of the Stage, select any frame between frames 1 and 12. Ctrl-click (Mac) or right-click (Windows) to access the context menu. Select Create Motion Tween. (Alternatively, you can select Motion from the Tween drop-down menu in the Property inspector.)

9. Play your movie again by pressing Return (Mac) or Enter (Windows). The ball now gradually falls over the course of all 12 frames.

10. Save your animation as ball.fla. You will be using it again later in this section.

You could have created the ball animation using frame-by-frame animation, but given the simple path of the animation, tweening works fine, reducing both effort and file size.

MOTION GUIDES   When you create a motion tween, Flash follows the shortest path between positions in keyframes. This saves file size but isn't always desirable. For instance, suppose you want the ball in the previous example to bounce rather than merely fall. You can accomplish this with the help of a motion guide, by following these steps:

1. Open ball.fla.

2. Select frame 12.

3. Use the Selection tool to drag the ball instance to the right on the Stage.

4. Play your animation by pressing Return (Mac) or Enter (Windows). The ball travels at an unnatural angle from the top of the Stage to the lower right, as shown in Figure 18.19. You need to create a motion guide to overcome this problem.

Figure 18.19
With motion tweens, Flash follows the shortest path between positions in keyframes, as revealed in Onion Skin mode.

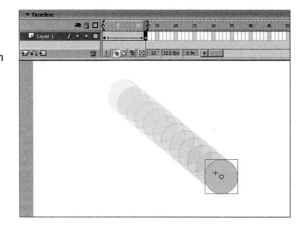

5. Select the ball layer and choose Insert, Timeline, Motion Guide. A motion guide layer is added above the selected layer, as shown in Figure 18.20.

Figure 18.20
To create a motion guide, select a layer and choose Insert, Motion Guide.

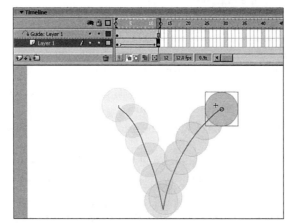

6. In the guide layer, use the Pencil or Pen tool to draw the path along which you want the ball to bounce. (Refer to the V-shaped line in Figure 18.20.)

7. Select frame 1 in the ball layer and check the Property inspector to ensure that Snap is checked, as shown in Figure 18.21. When Snap is selected, the registration point of a tweened object is snapped to the path of the motion guide. Your ball should appear snapped to the end of the motion guide.

Figure 18.21
Select Snap in the Property inspector to snap the registration point of a tweened object to a motion guide.

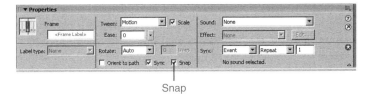

Snap

8. Select frame 12 in the ball layer and, using the Selection tool, click and drag the ball to the end of the motion guide path until it snaps to the end.

9. Save your file as ball2.fla. Play your animation by pressing Return (Mac) or Enter (Windows). Your ball should follow the arc of your motion guide.

A motion guide works only if objects are snapped to the beginning and end of the motion guide path. The path is not visible in your published movie, so feel free to draw it in a color that contrasts with your tweened object to facilitate the snapping process.

 For more information about motion guides, **see** the "Troubleshooting" section at the end of this chapter, **page 439**.

EASING   When Flash creates a motion tween, it spaces the movements evenly over the frames between keyframes. To create gradual acceleration and deceleration, which often appears more natural, you can adjust *easing* in your tweens. Positive easing values (between 1 and 100) cause motion tweens to start quickly and decelerate near the end. This is known as *easing out*. Negative easing values (between -1 and -100) create tweens that speed up as they progress, known as *easing in*.

To change the Ease settings in the bouncing ball animation, follow these steps:

1. Open ball2.fla.

2. Click in the ball layer to select a frame in the motion tween.

3. Click the Onion Skin button in the Timeline so you can preview your animation, and click the Onion Marker button and select Onion All from the pop-up menu, as shown in Figure 18.22.

Figure 18.22
Onion skinning options enable you to preview your animations by showing the contents of multiple frames simultaneously.

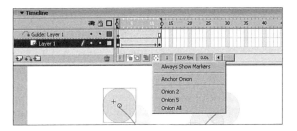

4. In the Property inspector, click on the Ease slider and drag it upward until the animation on the Stage appears slower near the end, as shown in Figure 18.23. With onion skinning turned on, you'll notice changes in speed represented by varying distances between objects in different frames.

Figure 18.23
Onion skinning reveals changes in easing as varying distances between objects in different frames.

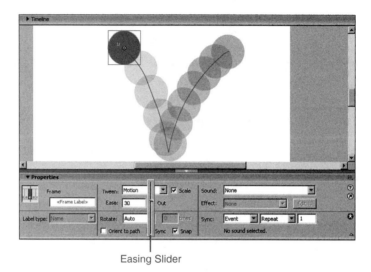

Easing Slider

5. Save your file as ball3.fla and play or test your movie by hitting Enter or choosing Control, Test Movie.

Onion Skinning

Normally only one frame at a time is visible on the Stage. Onion skinning, however, allows you to see many frames simultaneously, as you saw in the preceding exercise. This ability to see frames in context is invaluable when you're creating animations. Turn on onion skins frequently as you create tweens to check alignment and easing.

Onion skins are also helpful in perfecting the timing of animations. When onion skins show no overlap in objects across frames, the animation is so rapid that it appears to jump, and detecting the continuity of movement is difficult.

SHAPE TWEENS   Flash can interpolate dramatic changes in the shapes of objects. Shape tweens create the illusion of one shape morphing into another. Unlike motion tweens, shape tweens work only with simple shapes. You have to break apart a symbol instance, group, or bitmap to apply a shape tween to it.

To create a simple shape tween, follow these steps:

1. Open a new document by pressing Cmd-N (Mac) or Ctrl+N (Windows).

2. Click on the Stage and change the movie dimensions to 400×200 in the Property inspector.

3. Select the Rectangle tool, and choose a fill color and no stroke. Click and drag on the Stage to draw a large rectangle.

4. Press Cmd-K (Mac) or Ctrl+K (Windows) to open the Align panel. Select the rectangle on the Stage, and in the Align panel, select To Stage and center the rectangle horizontally and vertically, as shown in Figure 18.24, by clicking the second and fifth buttons in the Align row.

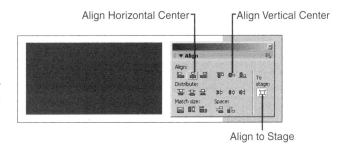

Align Horizontal Center ⌐ ⌐ Align Vertical Center

Figure 18.24
Select To Stage in the Align panel and center the rectangle vertically and horizontally.

Align to Stage

5. Select frame 15 in the Timeline and press F7 to insert a blank keyframe.

6. Select the Text tool, and choose a bold typeface and a large point size, such as 72, in the Property inspector. Click with the Text tool on the Stage and type your name.

7. Click the text with the Selection tool to select it. Use the Align panel to center it horizontally and vertically as you did in step 4.

8. With the text selected, choose Modify, Break Apart to break the text block into letters.

9. Choose Modify, Break Apart a second time to break letters apart into shapes.

10. Select a frame between keyframes, and in the Property inspector, choose Shape from the Tween pop-up menu, as shown in Figure 18.25.

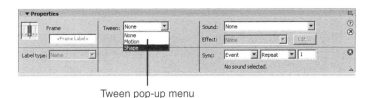

Figure 18.25
Select a frame between keyframes and choose Shape from the Tween pop-up menu in the Property inspector.

Tween pop-up menu

11. Save your movie and test it by choosing Control, Test Movie. The rectangle morphs into your name.

Easing can be applied to shape tweens. There is an additional option for *blending*, as shown in Figure 18.26. Blending is either distributive, which smoothes shapes during interpolation, or angular, which preserves the hard edges of shapes. Angular is appropriate for shapes with pronounced edges and angles.

Figure 18.26
Shape tweens have a blending option, which either smoothes shapes or preserves angles during tweening.

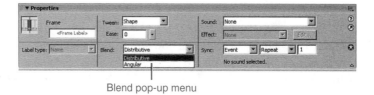

Blend pop-up menu

Shape tweens can inflate file sizes, so don't use them indiscriminately.

SHAPE HINTS

In shape tweens as in motion tweens, Flash creates the simplest interpolation between shapes. This can produce strange and sometimes undesirable effects. For instance, parts of shapes can turn inside out during interpolation. You may be able to correct problems by identifying *shape hints*—points that should correspond in the beginning and ending shapes.

To use shape hints, follow these steps:

1. Select the first shape in a shape tween sequence.
2. Choose Modify, Shape, Add Shape Hint. The beginning shape hint appears as a red circle containing the letter *a*.
3. Click on the shape hint with the Selection tool and drag it to the point you want to mark.
4. Click in the final frame of the shape tween. The corresponding shape hint appears in a similar position on the final shape.
5. Test your movie again to see how the shape hint affects the tween.

You can add as many as 26 shape hints.

TIMELINE EFFECTS

Timeline effects, new in Flash MX 2004, allow you to manipulate graphics or symbols by setting parameters—no ActionScript, Toolbox tools or tweening required. The preview window shows what the effect will look like with your new settings, before you commit to the effect.

To add a Timeline effect, follow this procedure:

1. With the Selection tool, click the object on the Stage.
2. Either select Insert, Timeline Effects, and then choose an effect; or else right-click (Windows) or Control-click (Macintosh) and select Timeline Effects, and then choose an effect from the context menu.
3. Select parameters.
4. If you change parameters, click Update Preview to view the effect with the new settings.

5. When you are satisfied with your effect, click OK.

6. Choose Control, Test Movie to test.

There are limitations to how far you can go with this approach. For instance, if you combine effects, only the most recent effect is editable via its configuration screen. You have to adjust other effects on the Timeline.

Table 18.1 shows all the Timeline Effects and their parameters.

TABLE 18.1   TIMELINE EFFECT SETTINGS

Effect	Description	Settings
Copy to grid	Duplicates selected object in a grid.	Number of rows
		Number of columns
		Distance between rows, in pixels
		Distance between columns, in pixels
Distributed duplication	Duplicates a selected object with gradual transforms, and with the final copy reflects the parameters entered in the settings.	Number of copies
		Offset distance, x position, in pixels
		Offset distance, y position, in pixels
		Offset rotation, in degrees
		Offset start frame, in frames across Timeline
		Exponential scaling by x, y scale, in delta percentage
		Linear scaling by x, y scale, in delta percentage
		Final alpha, a percentage
		Change color, select/deselect
		Final color, in RGB hex value (final copy has this color value; intermediate copies gradually transition to it)
		Duplication delay, in frames (results in pause between copies)

continues

TABLE 18.1 CONTINUED

Effect	Description	Settings
Blur	Creates a motion blur effect by changing the alpha value, position, or scale of an object over time.	Effect duration, in frames
		Allow horizontal blur
		Allow vertical blur
		Direction of blur
		Number of steps
		Starting scale
Drop shadow	Creates a shadow below the selected element.	Color, in hex RGB value
		Alpha transparency, a percentage
		Shadow offset, in x, y offset in pixels
Expand	Expands, contracts, or expands and contracts objects over time. Groups objects or text in a movie clip or graphic symbol.	Expand duration, in frames
		Expand, squeeze, both
		Expand direction, to left, from center, to right
		Fragment offset, in pixels
		Shift group center by, x, y offset, in pixels
		Change fragment size by, height, width, in pixels
Explode	Fragments and "explodes" object.	Effect duration, in frames
		Direction of explosion, upward to left, center, or right, downward to left, center, or right
		Arc size, x, y offset in pixels
		Rotate fragments by, in degrees
		Change fragments size by, in degrees
		Final alpha, a percentage

Effect	Description	Settings
Transform	Changes position, scale, rotation, alpha, and tint of the selected objects. Used for Fade In/Out, Fly In/Out, Grow/Shrink, and Spin Left/Right effects.	Effect duration, in frames
		Move to position, x, y offset, in pixels
		Change position by, x, y offset, in pixels
		Scale, lock to equally apply change, a percentage, unlock to apply x and/or y axis change separately, a percentage
		Rotate, in degrees
		Spin, number of times
		Times, counterclockwise, clockwise
		Change color, select/deselect
		Final color, in RGB hex value
		Final alpha, a percentage
		Motion ease
Transition	Wipes In, Wipes Out, Fades In, Fades Out selected objects.	Effect duration, in frames
		Direction, toggle between in (e.g. Fade In) and out (e.g. Fade Out), select up, down, left, or right
		Fade, select/deselect
		Wipe, select/deselect
		Motion ease

18

SCRUBBING THROUGH THE TIMELINE

Previewing your animations in motion as you work is essential. *Scrubbing* refers to manually moving the playhead back and forth within the Timeline, allowing you to preview the progression of a movie. Simply click and drag the playhead (the red rectangle just above the top layer in the Timeline) and move it across frames to preview them. You can move as quickly or as slowly as you want. A red line extends from the playhead down through frames in the Timeline to indicate the current frame.

You can use the Control menu options or keyboard shortcuts to preview your movie. For instance, you can choose Play or press Return (Mac) or Enter (Windows), to play the movie Timeline once. You can choose Test Movie or Cmd-Return (Mac) or Ctrl+Enter (Windows) to play the movie continuously. You can step through a movie a frame at a time, using the period key to go forward and comma key to go backward.

CARTOON ANIMATION IN FLASH: PANNING

Flash's vector format is ideally suited to cartoon animation. Vector graphics resemble cartoon-style drawings and can be easily and accurately transformed in Flash. Many traditional cartooning techniques can be translated into Flash.

A classic animation strategy that can be translated to the Web is panning. Panning creates the illusion of depth of field and a continuous background. In film this would be achieved by panning the camera, or moving the camera across a scene at a fixed height to capture the full sweep of a distant background. In animation, this effect is simulated by moving the background across the fixed Stage.

The secret to creating a convincing pan is to create background elements that are animated at different rates. The most distant element should move at the slowest rate. Objects in the foreground appear to move relative to the scene behind them, creating the illusion of depth.

To produce a pan effect, follow these steps:

1. Create a background element that is wider than the Stage. Ideally, the left and right edges of the background should match up so that the background appears seamless when it loops while in motion.

2. Tween the background element across the Stage so that in the first keyframe the right edge of the background is flush with the right edge of the Stage. In the final keyframe, the left edge of the background should be flush with the left edge of the Stage. This effect creates the illusion of continuous motion and a sprawling, vast backdrop.

NESTING SYMBOLS

The easiest way to create complex character animation is to use nested symbols. Isolate each moving part into a separate symbol that can be assembled in the master symbol.

The human walk cycle is one of the most difficult animations to achieve realistically. With care, you can construct it in nested symbols for maximum efficiency and realism. Start by dissecting the movements of a person walking in profile. The highest level is a movie clip symbol for the walking cycle. It contains layers for the head, torso, and legs. The head could be a single graphic. The torso movie clip contains two animated instances of an arm symbol, and the legs movie clip consists of two animated instances of a leg symbol. Collectively, the symbols that comprise the walking cycle make up a complete stride that repeats continuously and automatically.

ANIMATION GUIDELINES

Any style of animation—from classic cartoon-style characters to scripted physics-based movement—can benefit from some classic animation principles:

- **Timing and Motion** —Timing gives meaning to movement. The speed at which a movement happens can imbue the same motion with different meaning. Think of a punch. If it is delivered rapidly, with the person on the receiving end snapping back, it is a painful event. The same motion, delivered more slowly with a minimal reaction from the receiver, could be seen as playful.

  You can manipulate timing to give objects life and convey their attributes: For instance, heavy objects are difficult to move and take longer to accelerate and decelerate.

  Pacing is also crucial. There is a delicate balance between anticipation, action, and reaction. If the pace is too slow, the viewer will lose interest, but if it is too fast, the action may be confusing and open to misinterpretation. Also, experiment with the length of each stage—they should not be of equal lengths or carry the same emphasis. Action typically is the focus, but you can confound that expectation to great effect. Lengthy anticipation followed by quick action and reaction can produce comic or dramatic effect.

- **Anticipation** —Movement is most dynamic and realistic if it is anticipated. Runners rock backward slightly before hurtling themselves forward. Try adding slight movement in the opposite direction at the beginning of a motion.

- **Follow-through** —Movement does not stop instantaneously. Runners do not stop as soon as they cross the finish line, but continue on as they decelerate. Think of the follow-through of a pitcher's arm after a ball is released. Whenever you initiate a movement, try to follow it through slightly beyond the "goal" of the movement.

- **Squash and Stretch** —Few objects are completely rigid while in motion. Most objects are slightly deformed by motion and collision. To make our ball bounce even more realistic, we could scale the ball (as part of the motion tween) so that it stretches as it falls and squashes on impact.

- **Overlapping Action** —Avoid beginning or ending different actions simultaneously. Stagger movement: Have a second object begin to move before the first object has stopped, when possible.

- **Secondary Motion** —Animation is most effective if it produces a ripple effect; movement should rarely happen in isolation. Secondary motion results directly from primary action, echoing and reinforcing the main action. For example, if an ant character turns its head suddenly, its antennae may oscillate slightly.

- **"Un-perfecting" animation**—The mathematical precision of Flash's vector graphics can become impersonal and therefore less interesting. In the natural world, shapes have imperfections and movement is often irregular. To create the most compelling animations with Flash, tweak shapes to make them slightly irregular; use easing to create variety in pacing; and introduce intermediate keyframes in tweens and combine frame-by-frame and tweened animations for more realistic effects. Above all, take inspiration from the imperfect world around you.

18

USING SOUND

Sound adds depth and resonance to your Flash movies. Even before it was possible to incorporate sound tracks with movies, live music was used as accompaniment to accent action and stir emotion during silent movies. To appreciate all that sound adds to visual experiences, try to imagine *Jaws* without the menacing sound track.

UNDERSTANDING SOUND

There are two important audio-related enhancements in Flash MX 2004: the ability to retrieve ID3 metadata from MP3 files and the ability to load .flv files, which may contain only audio. Both are covered in other chapters.

→ For more on .flv loading, **see** "NetConnection, NetStream, and the Rich Media Classes," **page 647**, and "Working with .flv Files and the NetStream Object," **page 649**, in Chapter 22, "External Communications." For ID3 metadata, **see** "Sound Events," **page 515** under "Sound.ID3 Attributes."

There are some critical differences in the way you perceive visual information and the way you perceive sound. Because you blink somewhere in the neighborhood of 20 times per minute, with each blink lasting approximately a quarter of a second, your brain is accustomed to interruptions in the flow of visual data and is extremely adept at filling in gaps in visual information. This ability to connect the visual dots is what allows you to perceive film as continuous motion, when it is actually a series of static images shown in quick succession.

Your brain is not nearly so forgiving of or able to compensate for gaps in audio information. On the contrary, you are especially sensitive to variations in sound. Whereas film visuals are delivered in static frames, film sound is delivered in a continuous stream or sound track. Content delivery over the Web, however, makes it difficult to emulate a continuous sound track.

Sound is produced when objects vibrate. These vibrations displace the molecules of a gas, liquid, or solid, and travel through these substances as sound waves. When these waves hit your eardrums, the brain perceives the vibrations as sound. As shown in Figure 18.27, you differentiate between sounds according to variations in two characteristics of the sound wave:

- **Frequency**—How quickly the pressure fluctuates; a higher rate of fluctuation is perceived as a higher pitch.
- **Amplitude**—The level of pressure; higher levels are perceived as louder.

Flash must reproduce these characteristics of sound waves to be able to deliver sound.

Figure 18.27

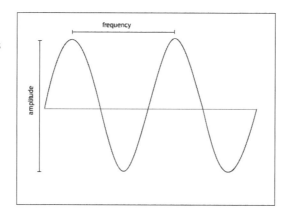

The anatomy of a sound wave: Frequency determines pitch and amplitude determines loudness.

PREPARING SOUNDS FOR FLASH

To reproduce sound digitally, sound waves are *sampled*. Sampling is the process of measuring and recording the characteristics of a sound at fixed time intervals. Each measurement produces one sample. For digital reproduction, the characteristics of the sample are used as the characteristics of the entire time interval. This is always a simplification of reality, because the digital reproduction goes by discrete steps, rather than changing smoothly, as shown in Figure 18.28. The more samples you take, the more closely the digital reproduction approximates the real sound wave. The number of samples captured per second, known as the *sampling rate* and measured in hertz (Hz), is one of the primary factors in determining digital audio quality.

18

Figure 18.28
Sound sampling: The gray bars represent samples of a sound wave.

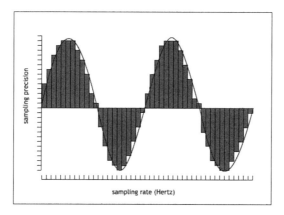

The sampling process should sound familiar because it echoes the process of creating animation using frames. The sampling rate is similar to the frame rate of a movie, in frames per second. It is also similar to pixel resolution. Table 18.2 shows standard sampling rates and the associated fidelity, or sound quality.

TABLE 18.2   SOUND SAMPLING RATES

Sampling Rate	Sound Quality
44.1kHz	CD quality
22.05kHz	FM radio quality; popular Web playback choice
11.025kHz	Lowest recommended quality for short music clips; high quality for speech
5kHz	Minimum quality for speech

Sampling precision, or *bit depth*, determines how many discrete amplitude levels are possible when sampling a sound. This is analogous to the bit depth of bitmap images. The higher the bit depth, the more accurate the representation of the amplitude. Table 18.3 shows standard sound bit depths and the comparable sound quality.

TABLE 18.3   SOUND BIT DEPTH AND ASSOCIATED QUALITY

Bit Depth	Sound Quality
16	CD
12	Near CD
8	FM radio
4	Lowest acceptable for music

As you might expect, higher sampling rates and bit depths result in larger sound file sizes. However, these two components of reproduced sound can be independently manipulated to create smaller files. Compared to music, speech has fewer variations in pitch, but may have greater fluctuation in amplitude or volume because of pauses between words and sentences. Unwanted hissing or noise can occur during these pauses. Therefore, speech requires a lower sampling rate with a higher bit depth to reduce the occurrence of noise or hissing during pauses.

Conversely, music has a greater range in pitch, or frequency, requiring a higher sampling rate to reproduce the pitch variation. Music typically has a narrower range of volume than speech does, so the bit depth can be lower.

Similarly, the choice between stereo and mono sound has a large impact on file size. Naturally, two audio channels make for twice the file size.

STREAM VERSUS EVENT, EXTERNAL VERSUS EMBEDDED

There are two different ways of classifying sounds in Flash. One has to do with how sounds are synchronized within the Flash movie. The other has to do with how they are loaded into the Flash movie in the first place. However, these two classifications are not entirely independent of one another, which creates room for confusion.

Let's start with how sound files are loaded. There are two possibilities here: *embedded* and *external*. Embedded sound files are *imported* into the FLA and reside in the Library and perhaps also on the Timeline at authoring time; they are contained in the SWF at runtime. External files are not imported and continue to reside outside both the FLA and the SWF. Embedded files can come in a wide variety of formats. External sound files must be either MP3 or FLV. This chapter focuses on embedded sound files.

→ To learn more about externally loaded sounds, which are loaded and controlled with ActionScript, **see** "Sound Events," **page 515**, in Chapter 20, and "The Sound Class," **page 651**, in Chapter 22.

Moving on to synchronization within the Flash movie, embedded sounds are divided into two types: *event* sounds and *stream* sounds. Event sounds are triggered by events such as the mouse rolling over a button, or the playhead entering a particular frame. After that, they are *not* synchronized with the Timeline. They simply continue playing, independently of whatever else happens in the movie. In fact, they keep playing even if the movie stops. (Like all other sounds, you can stop event sounds with an ActionScript `stopAllSounds()` command.) A minute-long event sound can play within a one-frame movie. An event sound is stored in its entirety in the first frame in which it appears. Only changes, such as fade-ins and fade-outs, are stored in subsequent keyframes.

With a stream sound, in contrast, a small, precisely-measured piece of the sound is stored in each frame where it is supposed to play. Thus, stream sounds are tightly synchronized with the Timeline. If the movie stops, the stream sounds stops, too. If the movie jumps to a different frame, the stream sound at that frame plays. The movie has to have enough frames to accommodate all the stream sound that you want to play.

External sound files always behave like event sounds in terms of synchronization within Flash. They have no relationship with the Timeline, do not care which frame is currently playing, and continue to play even if the movie stops. What can be confusing is that when you load an external MP3 (using the `loadSound()` method of the Sound class), you can choose to load it as an event sound or as a streaming sound. This does not affect synchronization in any way!

What does it affect, then? With external MP3s, the event versus streaming distinction determines whether the whole sound file has to download before it can start to play. If you download as an event file, the whole file must download before it can start to play. Playback has to be explicitly initiated; it's not automatic. If you download as a streaming file, there is just a short wait while the streaming buffer fills, and then the file starts to play. Playback begins automatically. (Audio-only FLV files are always loaded as streaming files in this sense.)

Event- and stream-embedded sounds follow the same rule about starting to play, with one slight complication. The basic idea is that embedded event sounds download completely before you can start to play them, and require a trigger to start. The user experiences a wait in the frame where the sound first appears. Embedded-stream sounds start immediately and automatically, after a short pause to fill the streaming buffer; they don't have to download completely to start playing, and they don't require any event to start playing.

18

The complication is that you can configure embedded sounds to export in the first frame of the movie. If you do that, both embedded-event sounds and embedded-stream sounds must load completely before they can start playing. The user experiences a wait before the movie starts. Event sounds still have to be triggered by an event, and stream sounds still don't require an event.

How event sounds are triggered differs for embedded and external files. An embedded-event sound typically starts when the playhead enters the frame that the sound is in. For external MP3s loaded as event sounds, you initiate playback by scripting, using the start() method of the Sound class.

With both embedded and external sound files, if you set things up so that the entire file loads before starting to play, there is a reward: The quality of the sound is likely to be optimal. If, on the other hand, the file is continuing to download while it plays, a slow Internet connection can degrade the quality of the sound. (The likelihood of this occurring can be greatly reduced for FLVs if you configure a large streaming buffer.)

Another area of similarity between embedded and externally loaded sounds is how they behave if playback is re-initiated while the sound is already playing: With embedded or external streaming, the first instance stops when the second instance starts playing. With event sounds, whether embedded or external MP3, that's not necessarily true: The first instance of the sound may continue while the second instance plays simultaneously.

I say "not necessarily" because, once again, there is a wrinkle for embedded files: As discussed in the following section, you can use the Sync field in the Property inspector to configure an embedded event sound so that the first instance stops playing when the second instance starts.

Table 18.4 summarizes some of the important differences between embedded event sounds and embedded stream sounds.

One other characteristic shown in this table is whether the global sound settings configured via File, Publish Settings override similar settings that can be applied to individual sounds in the Sound Properties dialog. For event sounds, the override behavior is configured using the Override Sound Settings check box on the Flash tab in Publish Settings. With stream sounds, the situation is more complex. If the stream sound is *not* exported in the first frame, Publish Settings always overrides settings in the Sound Properties dialog. If the stream sound *is* exported in the first frame, behavior is inconsistent, and you should make sure that both the global and the individual settings are the same, so that you know what you're going to get.

→ Sound settings and the Sound Properties dialog are discussed later in this chapter, under "Optimizing Sounds," **page 415**.

TABLE 18.4   EMBEDDED SOUNDS: EVENT VERSUS STREAM

		Exported in First Frame	Not Exported in First Frame
Event	Publish Settings Override Sound Properties	Configured in Publish Settings	Configured in Publish Settings
	Download fully before starting to play	Yes	Yes
	Synced to timeline	No	No
	Automatic start	No	No
	Assured quality	Yes	Yes
Stream	Publish Settings Override Sound Properties	Inconsistent	Publish Settings always override
	Download fully before starting to play	Yes	No
	Synced to timeline	Yes	Yes
	Automatic start	Yes	Yes
	Assured quality	Yes	No

From here on, this chapter discusses only embedded sounds.

SYNCHRONIZATION OPTIONS

When you place a sound on the Stage, you can select a synchronization option in the Property inspector. The synchronization options are Event, Start, Stop, and Stream. Event makes the sound an event sound. Start prevents an event sound from overlapping if the triggering event is repeated. Start sounds play only one at a time. Stop silences the sound to which it's applied and any event sounds. Stream synchronizes the sound to the animation.

When you place a sound on an empty Timeline, it occupies just a single frame. That's all an event sound requires to play in its entirety. Stream sounds, however, play only during frames that contain the sound. If you are using stream sound, you need to add frames to your sound layer to display and play the sound fully. Select the last frame in the sound layer that you want to contain the sound, and press F5 to insert frames.

The waveform of your sound will appear across the frames it occupies, as shown in Figure 18.29. For long and/or low-amplitude sounds, you may need to increase the height of the layer to see the waveform. Right-click (Windows) or Ctrl-click (Mac) on the layer name or icon, select Properties from the context menu, and select 200% to 300% from the Layer Height drop-down menu.

18

Figure 18.29
A sound waveform in the Timeline.

IMPORTING SOUNDS

Flash allows you to import assets that cannot be created within Flash, such as sounds or bitmaps, and use them in your movies. Sounds that are imported into Flash are placed in the Library. The following sound file formats can be imported into Flash MX 2004:

- **WAV (Windows only)**—The Waveform Audio File Format was developed for the Windows platform and is the standard sound file format for Windows.

- **AIFF (Macintosh only)**—The Audio Interchange File Format developed by Apple is the standard sound file format used on the Macintosh.

- **MP3 (Macintosh and Windows)**—(MPEG-1 Audio Layer-3) offers tremendous compression of sound data without sacrificing sound quality. Original CD data can be compressed by a factor of 12 using MP3 compression.

If you have QuickTime 4 or higher installed, you can also import the following formats:

- Sound Designer II (Macintosh only)
- Sound Only QuickTime Movies (Windows or Macintosh)
- Sun AU (Windows or Macintosh)
- System 7 Sounds (Macintosh only)

MP3 is the only sound format you can import that is precompressed. Therefore, MP3 file sizes are smaller than WAV or AIFF files. To import a sound, choose File, Import, Import to Library. (If you choose Import to Stage, Flash still imports only to the Library!)

Select a sound and click Open. The sound is added to the Library. To preview a sound, select it in the Library and click the black arrow that appears over the sound waveform in the window.

The best approach is to place a sound on its own layer. With an empty layer selected, drag a sound from the Library onto the Stage. The sound is placed on the selected layer.

Sound properties are shown in the Property inspector, as shown in Figure 18.30. Notice that the sound sampling rate, number of sound channels, bit depth, length in seconds, and file size are displayed in the bottom right of the Property inspector (22kHz Stereo 16 Bit 232.2 seconds 1858KB, in this case) .

Figure 18.30
Sound attributes can be accessed and edited in the Property inspector.

"EDITING" SOUNDS

Flash does not allow true sound editing—changing the sound wave itself. However, you can change the way Flash plays a sound. The Effect pop-up menu in the Property inspector (refer to Figure 18.30) allows you to manipulate volume effects such as fading in and out, and offers some control over stereo channels.

None, the default option, applies no effects or removes previously set effects. Left Channel/Right Channel allows you to play only one of the sound channels. Fade Left to Right/Fade Right to Left shifts the sound from one channel to the other, creating a pan effect. Fade In gradually increases the volume (amplitude) of a sound over its duration. Fade Out gradually decreases the volume of a sound.

Selecting Custom or clicking the Edit button brings up the Edit Envelope dialog box, shown in Figure 18.31, for more flexible volume control.

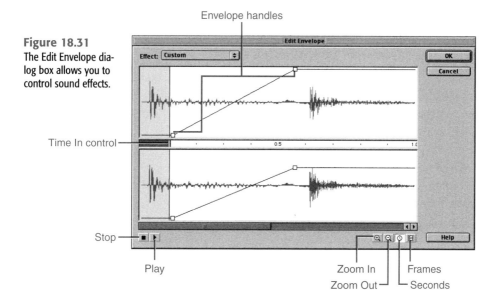

Figure 18.31
The Edit Envelope dialog box allows you to control sound effects.

To "cut" a section at the beginning of the sound, drag the Time In control toward the middle of the Edit Envelope dialog box. You'll find a corresponding Time End control at the end of the sound. The sound starts immediately at the new start point, and ends at the new end point. If there is silence, for instance, at the beginning or end of an audio clip, use this feature to eliminate the silence and reduce the size of the SWF.

Envelope handles, draggable square icons that appear on a sound channel, allow you to control the volume in a given channel. Each channel has a single envelope handle when the Edit Envelope dialog box is launched. Click and drag the Envelope handle up or down to change the overall volume of the sound. To create a fade in or fade out, click on the envelope lines to create additional envelope handles, up to a maximum of eight total handles. These additional handles allow you to independently drag and control the volume for portions of your sound.

Use the Zoom buttons to zoom in on portions of your sound or zoom out to view a sound in its entirety. Click the Seconds or Frames buttons to view your sound in seconds or according to the number of frames. Use the Play and Stop buttons to preview your edits. When you're satisfied with your edits, click OK.

Sounds can also loop (repeat indefinitely) or else repeat a designated number of times. With a sound selected, select Repeat or Loop from the Loop Sound drop-down menu in the Property inspector. If you select Repeat, you can also designate a number of times to repeat. Loop repeats indefinitely.

CAUTION

> If you loop a streamed sound, frames are added to the end of your movie to accommodate the looping, increasing the size of the SWF.

CONTROLLING SOUND

You can control when a sound plays and ends by using keyframes in the timeline or by using ActionScript to access the Sound object. Although sound is time-based, you can force it to begin and end in relation to content in other frames by utilizing keyframes. In this way, you can synchronize sound to animation. The Sound object allows you to extend some control of sound playback to the user.

KEYFRAMES

You use keyframes to start and stop sounds in sync with animation. To add a sound to an animation, follow these steps:

1. Create a new layer for the sound and then insert a keyframe in the sound layer to correspond with the place where you want your sound to begin.

2. With the keyframe on the sound layer selected, drag your sound from the Library to the Stage to add the sound to the Timeline.

3. Insert a keyframe at a later frame in your sound layer where you want the sound to end.

4. Click on a frame within the sound, and select a synchronization setting in the Property inspector.

It is especially important to preview your sound if you're truncating it—stopping it before the sound is over—to be sure it does not seem to end prematurely or abruptly (unless, of course, that is the desired effect) .

LINKAGE AND THE SOUND OBJECT

It is possible to control embedded sounds by using the Sound object in ActionScript. Using the Sound object, you can allow your users to control the delivery of sound in your movies. The Sound object allows you to turn sounds on and off, change the volume or the panning of sounds, or start a sound after another sound ends.

To use the Sound object to access an embedded sound, you must assign a Linkage identifier to your sound in the Library. Open the Library panel and select your sound. To access the Linkage Properties dialog box, Ctrl-click (Mac) or right-click (Windows) the symbol name and choose Linkage from the pop-up menu, or choose Linkage from the Library options pop-up menu at the upper-right corner of the Library panel.

Click in the Export for ActionScript check box. Selecting this option places the symbol name for your sound in the Identifier field and also automatically selects the Export in first frame check box, as shown in Figure 18.32.

Figure 18.32
Select Export for ActionScript to enter a Linkage identifier in the Linkage Properties dialog box.

You may prefer to edit the Identifier string that is automatically filled in with your symbol name. Keep your Identifier name simple and descriptive. Don't use spaces.

When you're finished, click OK to close the Linkage Properties dialog box.

You use the Linkage identifier with the `Sound.attachSound()` method to instantiate the sound on the Stage. Sounds loaded in this fashion are always event sounds.

OPTIMIZING SOUNDS

Because sounds can add significantly to the SWF file size, it is important to optimize them. Ideally, optimization begins before you import your sounds. Flash provides only modest sound-editing capabilities, so take advantage of sound-editing programs if you have access to them.

Embedded sounds, whether event or stream, can be compressed individually. To create individual compression settings, double-click a sound symbol's icon in the Library, or Ctrl-click (Mac) or right-click (Windows) and select Properties from the context menu to launch the Sound Properties dialog box, as shown in Figure 18.33.

18

Figure 18.33
By selecting settings in the Sound Properties dialog box, you can compress sounds individually.

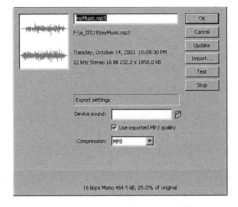

You can choose from several compression options. The first, Default, uses the global compression settings selected in File, Publish Settings (MP3 16-bit mono by default) .

ADPCM

ADPCM, or Adaptive Differential Pulse Code Modulation, compresses 8-bit or 16-bit sound data. It gives you some control over sample rate and a bit depth, and it sounds good with most sounds. However, it can sound very gritty and harsh. For this reason, it is often reserved for short, non-musical, non-speech event sounds, such as button clicks.

Selecting Convert Stereo to Mono compresses two mixed sound channels into one. Mono sounds are unaffected by this setting.

A sample rate of 22kHz is standard for the Web and is half the standard CD rate of 44kHz. You cannot increase a sound's original kHz rate.

You can decrease the bit depth, reducing the range of amplitude variation within sound samples. Lower bit depths and sample rates reduce file size and also decrease sound quality. Be sure to click the Test button to preview your sound at different settings.

MP3 COMPRESSION

MP3 usually offers the best compromise between audio quality and file size, so it is the setting you will choose most often. It is the best option for longer sounds.

Choose MP3 from the Compression menu. You can either use the original MP3 compression settings of your imported sound (check Use Imported MP3 Quality) or refine those settings.

To edit the settings, be sure that Use Imported MP3 Quality is not checked; then select a bit rate to determine the bits per second for your exported sound. Choose 16Kbps or higher to maintain sound quality.

You can also use MP3 to compress stereo tracks into mono. MP3 compression does not allow stereo output at 16Kbps or lower. To get stereo MP3 output, choose a bit rate of 20Kbps or higher and uncheck the Convert Stereo to Mono check box.

Finally, you can choose from three quality settings: Fast, Medium, and Best. Test your sound at various quality settings to find the best compression.

NOTE

> Even though you can set individual compression for stream sounds, all stream sounds within a movie are exported together in a single stream, which uses one setting.

OTHER COMPRESSION OPTIONS

The Raw option exports with no compression. This is the best quality, but the file size is usually unacceptable for the Web.

Speech compression uses a specially licensed algorithm for speech from Nellymoser Inc. (www.nellymoser.com).

TURNING OFF SOUND

You may want to allow the user to turn off sounds. The last thing you want is to drive visitors away from your Flash sites because they dislike your music. To provide this option, follow these steps:

1. Drag a button component to the Stage (from the UI Components category of the Components panel).

2. With the button selected, open the Property inspector and click on the word "Button" in the label field and type in a new label, like "Stop Sounds".

3. With the button selected, open the Behaviors panel, click the blue plus sign, go to the Sound category, and click on Stop All Sounds. You'll get a prompt describing the purpose of this behavior (as if it's not obvious from the name).

4. Click OK. With the button selected, check in the Actions panel, and you should see the following code:
```
on (click) {
    //stopAllSounds Behavior
    stopAllSounds();
}
```

5. Test your movie by pressing Cmd-Return (Mac) or Ctrl+Enter (Windows). Press your button, and all sounds should stop.

18

FLASH INTERACTIVITY

Flash offers a unique fusion of graphics, animation, and interactivity. Not only can you use Flash to create intricate graphics and animated content, but you can also use ActionScript, Flash's scripting language, to enable the users to control the delivery of that content.

INTRODUCTION TO FLASH INTERACTIVITY

You can script Flash movies to respond to a variety of user behaviors, from mouse clicks to typed input in text fields. Interactivity can be as simple as a button click shifting the play-back to a different frame or as complex as dynamically loaded menus.

EASY ACTIONSCRIPTING WITH BEHAVIORS

Behaviors make creating interactivity easier than ever in Flash MX 2004 by completely automating the process of adding ActionScript to objects such as buttons, movie clips, text fields, and video and sound files.

Only a limited set of behaviors ships with Flash MX 2004. These are handy for the scripter and a godsend for the non-scripter. In addition, programmers can create behaviors, using XML with embedded ActionScript, via Macromedia's new XML-to-UI application programming interface (API). Thus, new behaviors will be available, like other Flash extensions, through Macromedia Exchange.

The basic procedure for applying a behavior is as follows:

1. Select the object to which you want to apply the behavior.

2. On the Behaviors panel, click the blue plus sign and roll down through the various categories.

   As you roll over each category, the behaviors in that category display in a pop-up menu. The behaviors that appear may change depending on various factors. For instance, if you have a movie clip selected on the Stage, the Movie clip category will have a dozen options. If you don't have a movie clip selected, eight of these dozen options (Bring Forward, Bring to Front, Duplicate Movie clip, Send Backward, Send to Back, Start Dragging Movie clip, Stop Dragging Movie clip, and Unload Movie clip) are not present, because they don't make any sense.

3. Highlight and click on the behavior you want to apply.

   You may get a warning if the behavior is about to do something you may not expect. For example, if you select the "Go to Web Page" behavior in the Web category with no button or movie clip selected, the behavior creates a new empty movie clip and attaches the ActionScript to it. However, before doing that, it warns you, giving you a chance to cancel.

   You also get a dialog that typically allows some configuration. For instance, for the Go to Web Page behavior, you enter the URL of the Web page and select an Open In option to open the Web page in the same browser page that is already open, the parent of that page, a new page, or the top-level parent of the current page.

DATA BEHAVIORS

There is just one Data behavior, Trigger Data Source, available in Flash MX 2004 Professional. It causes a data component, such as the WebServiceConnector or the XMLConnector, to retrieve data.

→ For an example of using the Trigger Data Source behavior with the WebServiceConnector, **see** "Web Services," **page 672**, in Chapter 23, "Using Flash for Dynamic Data."

EMBEDDED VIDEO BEHAVIORS

Embedded Video Behaviors include three standard VCR-type controls: Pause, Play, and Stop. In addition, there are two commands to hide the video and make it visible again: Hide and Show.

MEDIA BEHAVIORS

Four behaviors work with the Flash Professional Media Components. The four functions are as follows:

- Associate a MediaController component with a MediaDisplay component.
- Associate a MediaDisplay component with a MediaController component.
- Implement cue-point navigation based on frame labels.
- Implement cue-point navigation for slides.

Cue points are a great new feature: They enable video playback to trigger events. For example, you could have sounds, images, and text change based on what is happening in the video. To create a cue point, select the component and click the + (plus) sign in the cue point panel at the bottom of the Component Inspector. Enter the name of a slide or frame label (Name) and a time (Position). Then, using the Behavior panel, create a Media behavior implementing cue point navigation for either frame labels or slides. The named label or slide is displayed when the video reaches the specified time.

You can also use ActionScript to listen for cue-point events. Each cue point is a property of a MediaDisplay component or a MediaController component. A cue point is an object with two properties: a time and a name. When the playhead reaches a cue point time, the cue point object broadcasts a cuePoint event. Listeners for this type of event receive the name, which can be used to go to a frame or a slide of the same name, or to perform any other desired action.

PROJECTOR BEHAVIOR

There is just one Projector behavior, Toggle Full Screen Mode, available only when a movieclip or button is selected. When you publish as a projector, as opposed to an SWF, it is often desirable to operate in full-screen mode, so that there is no other distracting content on the screen. This behavior does that for you.

18

MOVIECLIP BEHAVIORS

When a clip is selected, available Movieclip behaviors are Bring Forward, Bring to Front, Duplicate Movieclip, Goto and Play at Frame or Label, Goto and Stop at Frame or Label, Load External Movieclip, Load Graphic, Send Backward, Send to Back, Start Dragging Movieclip, Stop Dragging Movieclip, and Unload Movieclip.

Typically, a movie clip behavior occurs only when the user clicks the movie clip to which the behavior is applied. For example, if a "Bring" or "Send" behavior is applied, then when the movie clip is clicked, it changes its *depth* in the indicated way. For example, "Bring to Front" makes it appear in front of all other clips.

→ For more information on depth management, **see** "Visual Stacking for Siblings: Depth Numbers," **page 526**, in Chapter 20.

Behaviors that can be applied to the Main Timeline, such as the "Goto and Play at Frame or Label" behavior, do not require a click when applied to the Main Timeline.

SOUND BEHAVIORS

There are five Sound behaviors. Table 18.5 shows the behaviors and their ActionScript equivalent.

TABLE 18.5   SOUND BEHAVIORS

Behavior	ActionScript
Load Sound from Library	`Sound.attachSound()`
Load Streaming MP3 File	`Sound.loadSound()`
Play Sound	`Sound.start()`
Stop All Sounds	`StopAllSounds()`
Stop Sound	`Sound.stop()`

→ For step-by-step instructions for using the `StopAllSounds()` global function, **see** "Turning Off Sound," **page 417**, earlier in this chapter .

WEB BEHAVIOR

There is just one Web behavior: "Go to Web Page."

→ **See** details on the "Go to Web Page" behavior at the beginning of this "Behaviors" section, **page 418**.

BUTTONS

Buttons are interactive, four-frame movie clips. They provide feedback to users by changing in reaction to the users' actions, alerting the users that they can perform some new action. They are used much less now than in previous years, having been to a great extent replaced by button movie clips and the Button component. However, the traditional button is still a useful and usable tool.

→ The process for creating a button movie clip is described in "Movie Clip Events," **page 513**, Chapter 20.

When you create a button symbol, Flash automatically opens a four-frame button timeline. The four frames represent the button's Up, Over, Down, and Hit states. These frames can contain simple graphics, animated movie clips, or sounds. Although you can use different graphics for the different button states, it is important to maintain some sort of consistent button appearance. If a button changes dramatically in response to users' mouse movements, users may not experience the button as a single, unified object.

SIMPLE BUTTONS

Simple buttons employ graphic variation, such as changes in color, to create the visual button states—Up, Over, and Down—and provide visual cues to the users that they can perform an action and exercise some control over the movie's playback. To create a simple button containing static graphics, follow these steps:

1. Choose Insert, New Symbol or press Cmd-F8 (Mac) or Ctrl+F8 (Windows). The Create New Symbol dialog box launches.

2. Type a name for your button in the Name field and select Button for the behavior.

3. Click OK. A four-layer button timeline is created with a keyframe in the first frame, the Up state.

4. Use the drawing tools to create a visual form for your button in the Up frame. Button symbols can have multiple layers, so you can separate button graphics onto separate layers, as shown in Figure 18.34.

Figure 18.34
Use any of the drawing tools to create a graphic form for your button in the Up frame.

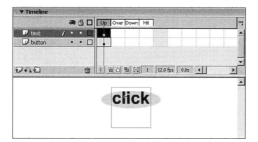

5. The Over state enables you to create rollovers. Click to select the frame beneath the Over label. If you want to change graphics in multiple layers to create your rollover effect, Shift+click to select frames in more than one layer. Choose Insert, Keyframe or press F6 (to add keyframes to those layers. Your button graphics from the first frame appear on the Stage.

6. Select the button graphics on the Stage and make changes to create a rollover state.

7. To create a click state for your button, select the frame(s) beneath the Down label; then repeat steps 5 and 6. Try offsetting your graphics by moving them down and to the right by a few pixels in the Down frame. This movement creates the illusion that a button is being depressed.

8. The Hit state defines the clickable area of your button. Add a keyframe beneath the Hit label in the layer that contains your button shape. Be sure that your shape covers the entire area that should register a button click. You might need to draw a separate shape in the Hit frame to cover the entire button area.

Hit Me

Hit states must be well defined for your button to be usable. Often a button graphic defines the area you want to be clickable, such as a rectangular box behind your button text. Then it's easy to use the same graphic in the Hit frame.

However, if a button consists solely of text, it's vital to draw a generous shape in the Hit frame that encompasses the text. Otherwise, users must click exactly within the letterforms for a click to register.

---

9. Click the Back arrow beneath the folder icons or choose Edit, Edit Document to exit symbol-editing mode and return to the Main Timeline.

10. Choose Window, Library or press Cmd-L (Mac) or Ctrl+L (Windows) to open the Library panel.

11. Locate your button in the Library and drag an instance onto the Stage.

12. Choose Control, Enable Simple Buttons to preview your button on the Stage. Move your mouse cursor over the button and click to see the Over and Down states. The Hit state is not visible during playback, but it defines the area of your button graphic that responds to the mouse and triggers the Over and Down states.

Your simple button graphics are complete, but your button doesn't actually do anything at this point. You need to add ActionScript so that your button does more than change appearance in response to the user's mouse.

The easiest way to assign a simple action to a button is to use Behaviors. Any behavior can be applied to a button.

→ For more on Behaviors, **see** "Easy ActionScripting with Behaviors," **page 418**, earlier in this section.

ADVANCED BUTTONS

Buttons can react to user interaction in myriad ways. Advanced buttons go beyond simple graphics and use sound or animated movie clips to denote button states. You can add sound to any of the button frames in place of or in addition to simple graphics. Sound is typically added to the Over or Down frames. Follow these steps to add sound to a button:

1. Insert a new layer in your button symbol. Name it sound. It's best to place a sound on its own layer.

2. Within the sound layer, insert a keyframe under the button state to which you want to add your sound.

3. With the keyframe selected, drag an instance of a sound from the Library to the Stage. The sound is added to the button frame.

4. In the Property inspector, set the sound synchronization to Event.

You can also create animated buttons by placing movie clips in button frames. It's best to use short animations and to limit your animations to a single button state; otherwise, the animations can become distracting and make it difficult to differentiate the different button states. To add an animation to a button state, follow these steps:

1. Create a movie clip for a button state.

2. Create a button and add a keyframe to the frame where you want to create an animated state.

3. Drag an instance of your movie clip from the Library to the Stage. Be sure to align your movie clip with graphics in other button frames so that the button appears in a consistent form. Use guides to mark the placement of your button across frames, to avoid unintended movement of your button when it is clicked or rolled over.

NOTE

> Alignment of elements, particularly text, across button frames is crucial. If elements are not aligned, they appear to jump between button states.

→ For more information about using guides and alignment, **see** "Grids, Guides, and Guide Layers", **page 354**, in Chapter 16, "Working with Vector Graphics and Bitmaps."

4. After you finish making other button frames, return to the Main Timeline and drag an instance of your button onto the Stage.

5. Test your movie by choosing Control, Test Movie.

CAUTION

> You cannot preview embedded movie clips in the Flash editor, which displays a single timeline at a time. Only the first frame of an embedded movie clip is visible within the Main Timeline.

You can also create invisible buttons—buttons that consist of a Hit state only. Why would you use an invisible button? Invisible buttons have been used to create hotspots, or clickable areas of graphics or movie clips. As you can do with imagemaps in HTML, you can place a series of invisible buttons over a graphic that you want to use for navigation. By using invisible buttons, you avoid having to create individual buttons containing slices of the graphic. However, the improved MX object model allows you to assign button interactivity directly to movie clips. Then you can use ActionScript to check for the mouse location. Also, using invisible buttons to create imagemaps is a disaster in terms of accessibility, because invisible buttons do not contain any text for screen readers and other assistive technologies to read.

→ For more information about Flash accessibility, **see** Appendix B, "Making Flash Accessible," **page 977**.

MENUS

Menus enable users to navigate through your movies and to choose when and in what order content is delivered. Menu-based navigation is vital to much Web-delivered content. There is no single standard for navigating Web content, such as turning pages in a book, or for neatly chunking Web content into easily indexed sections, such as individual pages within a book.

Flash's capacity for nested timelines means that there can be multiple paths through movies, and Web conventions such as breadcrumbs, which detail a user's path to a particular Web page, are not standard in Flash. Flash content can also be separated into individual SWFs, which can be loaded on demand to conserve bandwidth. For example, an online clothing retailer would be wise to separate different clothing lines into separate movies so that users looking for women's clothing need only wait for the desired Women's line to download, not the entire line from Men's to Children's. It's important to plan your movies well, with navigation that allows users to maneuver both within and between SWFs.

USING THE TIMELINE TO STRUCTURE DOCUMENTS

A simple way to structure interactions within your movie, requiring minimal scripting, is to place movie clips containing sections of your Flash content at keyframes on the timeline. These keyframes can be given corresponding frame labels, which can then be accessed using ActionScript.

Content sections of your movie can be placed into separate movie clips. For example, you could have Home, Services, Portfolio, About, and Profiles movie clips to correspond with menu items for a Flash site. You can then assemble the sections of your site on separate layers on the Main Timeline, as shown in Figure 18.35.

Figure 18.35
Sections of your movie can be assembled on separate layers on the Main Timeline.

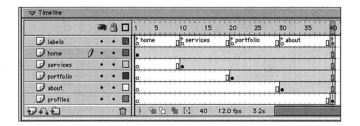

Each section needs its own layer, keyframe, and frame label. So, create a layer for each section. It's important to isolate each section on a different frame number so that you can write a script instructing the playhead to stop on a particular frame to access that section's content. Doing so requires staggering keyframes for the sections so that each occurs on a different frame number. Create a new layer for your labels, and add keyframes with labels corresponding to each of your section keyframes. You could simply assign your scripts according to frame number, but should you need to add new sections to your site, you'll have to change your scripts. Using labels allows you to easily add new content without having to update your existing scripts.

You can stagger the content keyframes so that the sections are placed on consecutive keyframes, but if you do, you won't be able to read the corresponding frame labels on the timeline. However, you can space out the keyframes so that your labels are legible within the timeline for quick reference.

Then, when you create your navigation system, you can assign button actions to access the different sections of your site by moving the playhead to the different section frame labels.

TRACK AS BUTTON AND TRACK AS MENU ITEM

Two important criteria for creating a Flash menu are available space and type of menu data. How much physical space does your layout allow for menu items? Will menu items change? If so, how often? Will menu data need to be dynamically loaded from external sources?

A simple series of menu buttons—the classic Web menu, shown in Figure 18.36—can be used if your site is small, with few menu items that should not require frequent updates.

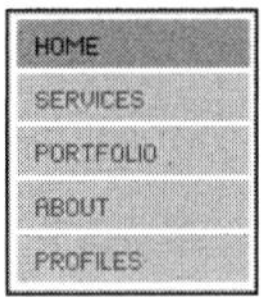

Figure 18.36
Simple, static menus can consist of a series of buttons.

When you create a button instance, you can set its properties in the Property inspector to Track as Button or Track as Menu Item. Track as Button, the default, defines a button's events independently of any other buttons. If a user clicks and drags from one button to another, the rollover is triggered only on the original button; the second button is independent of the first and does not track mouse events that occur on other buttons. Track as Menu Item, however, allows button events to be triggered by mouse events that may have started on other buttons. If a user clicks and drags from one button to another, releasing the mouse over the second button, the second button's rollover and click states are triggered. Buttons that are menu items should be set to Track as Menu Item.

Menus can also be extremely complex, triggering advanced scripts, even involving the loading of external data and XML. Dynamic menus can be completely generated on demand.

→ To learn more details about integrating XML data into Flash movies, **see** "XML Data," **page 634**, in Chapter 22.

18

ACCELERATING APPLICATION DEVELOPMENT WITH COMPONENTS

You can easily use symbols to create interactive buttons and movie clips. In addition, Flash MX 2004 introduces a new generation of prebuilt components: movie clips with predefined parameters for standard elements such as buttons, form elements, and display elements.

→ Components are introduced in "More and Better Components," **page 325** in Chapter 14, "What's New in Flash MX 2004?"

You can use components to quickly create buttons, forms that gather user input, progress bars, or display windows.

→ For an example that uses a button component, **see** "Turning Off Sound," **page 417**, earlier in this chapter.

If you have Flash Professional, you also have a rich set of Data components to assist you in retrieving and displaying data.

→ Two Data components, WebServiceConnector and DataGrid, are used extensively in Chapter 23. **See** "Databinding and Components," **page 664**, "Using and Modifying the DataGrid Component," **page 668**, and "Web Services," **page 672**.

Flash Professional also includes Media Components, used to display streaming `.flv` and `.mp3` files.

→ Media components are introduced in "A Tale of Two Versions", **page 324**, in Chapter 14.

Accelerating Help Development with RoboHelp

While we're on the subject of accelerating development, if you want to create a help feature patterned after popular desktop applications such as Microsoft Word, check out eHelp's RoboHelp. RoboHelp has a FlashHelp feature that enables you to create help systems entirely in Flash. (You can also use RoboHelp to create help systems using just HTML and JavaScript.) Macromedia liked it so much, they bought the company!

RoboHelp isn't cheap (just under US$1000 suggested retail, not including a support contract), but it does enable you to create a richer, more robust help feature in a fraction of the time you'd otherwise require.

See `http://www.ehelp.com`, and `http://www.ehelp.com/products/robohelp/flashhelpsamples.asp`.

Table 18.6 lists the 13 components that come with both versions of Flash MX 2004. Many more components are available for download from Macromedia. You can also create custom components.

→ For an introduction to creating custom components, **see** "Building Your Own Components," **page 612** in Chapter 21, "Advanced ActionScript."

TABLE 18.6   USER INTERFACE (UI) COMPONENTS IN BOTH VERSIONS OF FLASH MX 2004

Component	Description
Button	Triggers a one-time action. Can also be configured to act as an on/off toggle.
CheckBox	Registers a yes/no choice.
ComboBox	Registers a one-among-many choice. Choices appear in a scrolling list. Can have a blank text field at the top, into which the user can type a new choice.
Label	Displays a single line of non-editable text.
List	Registers a choice of one or more options from a scrolling list.
Loader	Contains a loaded SWF or JPEG file.
NumericStepper	Uses two clickable arrows to increment and decrement a number.
ProgressBar	Displays the progress of a process, such as loading a file.
RadioButton	Registers a choice among two or more mutually exclusive options. Each radio button represents one choice. Used in groups of two or more radio buttons.
ScrollPane	Displays movies, bitmaps, and SWF files in a box that can have scroll bars.
TextArea	Displays one or more lines of optionally editable text. Multi-line text input.
TextInput	Displays one line of optionally editable text. Single-line text input.
Window	Displays content, such as an SWF or JPEG. Has a title bar and optional Close button. Draggable.

Components are housed in the Components panel, which is part of the default Flash MX 2004 layout. To open the Components panel, choose Window, Development Panels, Components, or press Cmd-F7 (Mac) or Ctrl+F7 (Windows).

Simply drag and drop the component into your movie. Typically, the most important parameters determining component behavior and appearance appear in the Property inspector. The Component Inspector has a complete list of parameters. Often, you select component parameters from drop-down menus, so that you don't have to know what the options are in advance, and you can't choose an invalid option.

There are some components that do not require any ActionScript to be useful. For example, you can display an SWF or JPEG in a Window or ScrollPane, or text in a Label or TextArea, without needing any ActionScript.

On the other hand, several components require either databinding or some ActionScript to be useful. Databinding is the process of using a component to either receive data from or supply data to another component.

→ For more on databinding, **see** "Databinding and Components," **page 664**, in Chapter 23.

The basic ActionScript required is a *listener*, a function that fires automatically when the user changes the component. The listener receives an event object that gives you the key information that the user provided through the component. For example, if the user makes a selection from a ComboBox, the event object tells you what that selection was. If the user checks or unchecks a CheckBox, the event object will tell you whether the CheckBox is checked or unchecked. If the user selects a RadioButton, you can find out which one it was.

→ For more on listeners, **see** "Using Event Handlers to Trigger Action," **page 500**, in Chapter 20.

After you have the information, you still have to do something with it. That also requires ActionScript. You put the actions that you want to perform within the body of the listener function.

For example, suppose you create a calendar application, and you want to use a ComboBox to enable the user to select the month to display. You put each month's calendar on a different frame of the Timeline, with appropriate frame labels, such as jan, feb and so on. The listener receives an event object containing the month. You put a gotoAndStop() action in the listener body to go to the appropriate frame.

The next section gives step-by-step instructions for setting up such an application, and you can see a finished example in calendar.fla on the CD.

WORKING WITH COMPONENTS

To add a component, you simply drag and drop it onto the Stage. Or you can double-click a component in the Components panel, and an instance of the component is placed on the Stage, where you can reposition it as needed.

Follow these steps to add a ComboBox component:

1. Click to select the ComboBox component in the Components panel. Drag an instance to the Stage. The Property inspector displays the ComboBox component parameters, as shown in Figure 18.37.

Figure 18.37
Component attributes are displayed in the Property inspector.

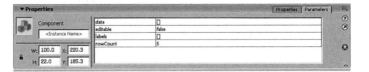

2. Assign an instance name of myComboBox to the ComboBox.

3. The Editable parameter is set to false by default, meaning that the contents of the ComboBox list are static. When this parameter is set to true, the user can enter an item that does not appear in the predefined list. Leave Editable set to false.

4. Double-click in the column next to Labels to launch the Values dialog box. Click the plus sign 12 times to create 12 values for the 12 months, as shown in Figure 18.38. Click each defaultValue and enter a month, until you've entered the months January through December. These labels define what will be displayed in the ComboBox.

Figure 18.38
Enter list items for the
ComboBox compo-
nent in the Values
dialog box.

5. Double-click in the column next to Data to launch the Values dialog box. Click the plus sign 12 times to create 12 values for the 12 months. Click each defaultValue and type in a list item for each month, jan through dec.

These data items are received by the event object, but (unlike the labels entered in step 4) are not displayed to the user. Therefore, you can use any convenient abbreviations for the months in this step. It is often handy to have one item (the label) that you display to the user, but a different item that you use with ActionScript. Data items allow you to do that.

6. Insert a layer (Insert, Timeline, Layer). Name it labels. In each of 12 consecutive frames on the labels layer, insert a keyframe (F6) and create a frame label corresponding to a data item, jan through dec.

The event object receives both the labels and the data. In this case, either one could do. Adding these data items allows us to use shorter labels on the Timeline.

7. Insert another layer. Name it calendar. In 12 consecutive frames on the calendar layer, place the calendar for that month. In calendar.fla, this is represented by an empty Window component titled with the appropriate month.

8. Insert a layer and name it actions. Type in the following ActionScript:

```
form = new Object();
form.change = function (eventObject){
    var frameLabel:String = eventObject.target.selectedItem.data;
    _root.gotoAndStop(frameLabel);
}
myComboBox.addEventListener("change", form);
stop();
```

9. Save your movie, and test it by choosing Control, Test Movie. The values you added to the ComboBox component are displayed in a drop-down list, as shown in Figure 18.39. When you select a value from the ComboBox, the movie goes to the appropriate frame.

18

Figure 18.39
The ComboBox component produces a scrollable drop-down list in your exported movie.

To find out which events (such as change in this example) the component will broadcast, go to the Actions toolbox on the left side of the Actions panel. All the components are listed in the Components category. Expand the component you're interested in, and click on Events.

As one of the properties of the event object, every component listener will receive target, which represents the component instance. To find out what attributes target will have (such as selectedItem in this example), look in the Actions panel under Properties for that component.

You do not have to create a new form object for each component. The form object represents the entire form, and you should use it for all components in the form. For example, if you were to add a CheckBox component to this form, you would add only the code for implementing the listener, like this:

```
myCheckBox.addEventListener("click", form);
form.click = function (eventObject){
        trace(eventObject.target);
        trace(eventObject.target.selected);
}
```

There is a check box in calendar.fla, so you can see how this works.

SKINNING COMPONENTS

Skins are graphic symbols or movieclips that determine how components look. Most skins contain visual elements, though a few contain only ActionScript code to draw the component.

With the previous generation of components, you changed their appearance by working in the Library. The new V2 components are compiled clips, so you cannot work with them in the Library. Instead, you have to work with FLA files containing the components' skins. These FLA files are called *themes*. They differ in appearance and behavior, but use the same symbol names and linkage identifiers for the skins. So, when you bring a theme into a document, the new symbols with their new linkage identifiers replace the previous symbols of the same name. Presto! All the components in your document that use that skin now look different.

Here's a simple example illustrating one way to apply a theme:

1. Create or open an FLA with a ComboBox component in it. I use the calendar that was created in the previous section. Save the file under a new name. I'll use calendar2.fla here.

2. Go to the First Run\ComponentFLA directory. For example, in a typical English-language Windows installation, this is C:\Program Files\Macromedia\Flash MX 2004\en\First Run\ComponentFLA

3. Open SampleTheme.fla and save it under a new name. I'll use theme1.fla.

4. Drag a ComboBox component onto the Stage in theme1.fla.

5. In the theme1.fla Library, open the following hierarchy of folders: Flash UI Components 2, Themes, MMDefault, ComboBox Assets, States. Here you can find the movieclips for the arrow that you click to expand the ComboBox.

6. Double-click on ComboDownArrowDown to edit it. This movieclip is the skin.

7. On the Stage, double-click on the arrow to open the SymDownArrow movieclip for editing.

8. Use the Paint Bucket tool to change the color of the down arrow and save theme1.fla.

9. Drag the Flash UI Components 2 folder from the theme1.fla Library to the calendar2.fla Library.

10. Test calendar2.fla. Any ComboBox in calendar2.fla displays the new color that you assigned in theme1.fla.

Dragging the Flash UI Components 2 folder into your Library makes the calendar2.fla much bigger. However, Flash uses only what it needs for the SWF, so there is not a comparable increase in the size of the SWF.

Note that some components share skins, so changing one skin can affect multiple component types.

INTEGRATING VIDEO

Flash MX 2004 support for video enables you to incorporate live action content such as corporate announcements, movie trailers, instructional videos, and news and sports coverage into your Flash movies. Users can control the delivery of video content—and not simply by using playback controls. As an example, with careful editing and compression to keep file size down, multiple video clips can offer user-controlled non-linear narratives. Further, it is possible to employ Flash text to offer optional video subtitles in multiple languages. Combining video and Flash can provide a highly individualized video experience.

With Flash MX 2004, you can embed video at authoring time or load external Flash Video (FLV) files at runtime.

→ There's actually a third option, *linking* video, discussed in this chapter. **See** "Embedded Versus Linked Video," **page 433**.

The ability to load external FLV files at runtime is new in Flash MX 2004. Progressive loading of FLVs at runtime offers a number of advantages, including reduced memory requirements, which improves overall performance; the flexibility to use different frame rates for different clips within the "container" movie; more control, such as the ability to set the size of the video buffer; and less likelihood that the loaded video will interrupt the movie into which it is loaded.

→ For more on loading external video at runtime, **see** "NetConnection, NetStream, and the Rich Media Classes," **page 647**, in Chapter 22.

This chapter discusses embedding video. There are still at least four good reasons why you might want to embed video, as opposed to loading FLVs: First, embedded video enables you to distribute your application as one SWF, rather than as an SWF plus one or more .flv files. Second, embedding can be easier: Implementing embedded video can be as easy as importing a video file and placing it on the Stage. Embedding video also enables you to work with video on the Timeline and transform it using Flash's tools, such as the Scale and Rotate tool. Finally, embedding standard video formats such as .avi or .mov enables you to use the Video Import Wizard, new in Flash MX 2004. (The Import Wizard does not work with FLVs.)

VIDEO FILE TYPES

Flash can import video in a variety of formats if either QuickTime 4 (QT) or higher or DirectX 7 or higher (Windows) is installed, as shown in Table 18.7. Macromedia Flash Video format, .flv, the format created by Sorenson Spark, can be imported without QT or DirectX installed.

TABLE 18.7   VIDEO IMPORT FILE FORMATS

File Type	Minimum Required Drivers	Platform
Audio Video Interleaved (.avi)	QuickTime 4, DirectX 7	Macintosh, Windows
Digital Video (.dv)	QuickTime 4	Macintosh, Windows
Motion Picture Experts Group (.mpg, .mpeg)	QuickTime 4, DirectX 7	Macintosh, Windows
QuickTime Movie (.mov)	QuickTime 4	Macintosh, Windows
Windows Media File (.wmv, .asf)	DirectX 7	Windows

Flash uses the Sorenson Spark codec to import and export video. *Codec* is an abbreviation for *coder-decoder*, and refers to a software module that compresses and decompresses video. To compress video, the codec reduces the number of bits needed to represent video data. The codec then decompresses, or recovers the original data, during playback. Video files are notoriously data intensive, so compression is vital.

Sorenson Spark

Sorenson Spark is a powerful compression application. Video files are huge—far too large for Internet delivery without intensive compression being applied. Codecs compress data for faster downloads and then decompress video data during playback. The Spark codec is integrated into the Flash Player, so no external players or plug-ins are required to display video content.

The standard edition of Sorenson Spark is integrated into Flash MX and is used to import and compress video files. A professional edition is also available; it provides more robust compression options, including two-pass Variable Bit Rate compression. You can purchase Sorenson Spark Pro at `http://www.sorenson.com`.

Video data can be compressed in two ways: spatially and temporally. Spatial (or intraframe) compression compresses data in each frame independently of other frames. Temporal (or interframe) compression compares data in successive frames and stores only the differences between frames. Sorenson Spark takes advantage of both types of compression. Whenever possible, Sorenson Spark utilizes temporal compression to create the smallest file sizes. However, when significant changes occur in a video frame, spatial compression is used in creating a video keyframe. Video keyframes mark points of change and are similar to Flash keyframes. A video keyframe becomes the reference point for subsequent temporal compression. Video keyframes are created during import into Flash.

EMBEDDED VERSUS LINKED VIDEO

You can either embed video directly into a Flash movie or else link video to a Flash movie. Embedded videos become part of the Flash document. Linked videos remain external to the Flash document. If you link to a QuickTime video, you must publish your Flash movie as a QuickTime movie. Video content is then displayed in QuickTime, outside the Flash Player. Embedding video integrates it seamlessly into your Flash movies, and no external players are required to view video content.

THE VIDEO IMPORT WIZARD

 The Video Import Wizard walks you through the process of importing a video. It allows you to apply basic compression settings, such as a bandwidth or quality setting, as well as advanced settings affecting the color, dimensions, and other options. You can save your settings in a preset for future use. The new clip editing feature enables you to trim material from the beginning and end of your clip, reducing the size of the SWF. You can also create multiple clips, reorder clips, and export the audio from the video clip.

The Video Import Wizard has two main functions: editing and encoding. There are both basic and advanced encoding options.

Here are the basic steps for importing and embedding a video clip:

1. Choose File, Import, and then Import to Stage or Import to Library. The Import or Import to Library dialog box launches.

2. Navigate to the location of the file you want to import, select the file, and click Open. If the imported file is a QuickTime movie (.mov), a QuickTime dialog box opens, prompting you to embed or link the video. Select Embed Video in Macromedia Flash Document.

3. A prompt asks whether you want to import the entire video, or edit the video first. If you choose to import the entire video, skip step 4 and go directly to step 5.

4. If you choose to edit the video first, the Editing dialog appears, as shown in Figure 18.40. When you are finished editing, click Next. The basic encoding screen, shown in Figure 18.41, appears.

Figure 18.40
The Editing dialog for the Video Import Wizard.

Figure 18.41
The basic Encoding dialog for the Video Import Wizard.

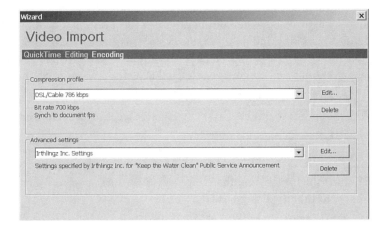

5. On the basic encoding screen, you can select an existing profile of one of two kinds: either a basic compression profile (top half of the screen) or a custom preset that you created with advanced configuration options (bottom half of the screen). You can also create new basic compression profiles in the top half of the screen. You create a new profile by clicking the Edit button, in either the top or bottom half of the screen.

6. Click Finish. You'll get an Importing dialog box with a progress bar, showing total import time on the right, and an updated count-down to zero on the left.

7. If you chose Import to Stage and the Timeline does not contain a sufficient number of frames to display the imported video, you are prompted to extend the Timeline. Click Yes to extend the Timeline or No to maintain the current number of frames. Any frames in the imported video that exceed the number of frames in the Timeline are not displayed during playback.

The video is imported to the Library, and an instance is also placed on the Stage if you chose Import to Stage.

To check the size of your imported video, save your movie and test it by choosing Control, Test Movie. Choose View, Bandwidth Profiler to preview your movie. Also, choose View, Simulate Download to preview how long users will have to wait for content to download.

EDITING

The Editing dialog, shown in Figure 18.40, enables you to cut your clip up into sub-clips, toss what you don't want, and reorder what's left. The four basic functions are creating a sub-clip, managing sub-clips in the scroll pane, updating an existing sub-clip, and previewing a sub-clip.

- **Creating a sub-clip.**

  To define the points where a sub-clip begins and ends, you can use either the In and Out points (the triangles below the scrubber bar) or the In and Out buttons (on the left below the scrubber bar).

  To use the In and Out points, just moved them to the desired start and end points and click Create Clip.

  To use the In and Out buttons, move the playhead to the desired start point and click the In button, then move the playhead to the desired end point and click the Out button. (You can reverse the order, too, setting the end point first.) Click Create Clip.

  The clip appears in the scroll pane on the left of the Editing dialog, represented by the name of the original clip. Rename it by double-clicking and typing a new name.

- **Managing sub-clips in the scroll pane.**

  There are three controls above the scroll pane: The trash can allows you to delete the selected clip. The up and down arrows enable you to move a clip up or down in the list. The order of the clips is particularly significant if you choose to combine the clips into a single library item after import, by clicking the check box in the lower right corner. In

18

that case, the clips are "spliced" into a single clip, in the order that they appear in the scroll pane.

- **Updating an existing sub-clip.**

  The most recently created clip appears in the central Editing pane. If you have created several clips, and you want to go back and change the In and/or Out point of a previous clip, select the clip in the scroll pane and click Update Clip. That Clip will appear in the central Editing pane, and you can change its In and/or Out points.

- **Previewing a sub-clip.**

  The familiar VCR-style controls allow you to step one frame backward, play from the current position, stop the video, or advance by one frame. To return to the start of the clip and play, click Preview Clip.

BASIC ENCODING

If you click the Edit button at the top of the Encoding dialog (refer to Figure 18.41), you can set basic encoding options, as shown in Figure 18.42.

Figure 18.42
Basic encoding options for the Video Import Wizard.

18

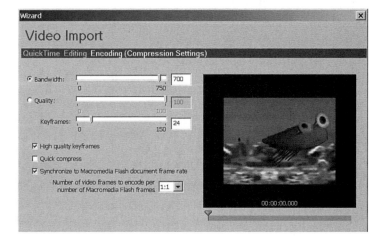

The basic encoding options are as follows:

- The Bandwidth slider specifies the bandwidth that the video will consume when downloading. Video quality may vary to keep bandwidth constant.

- The Quality slider specifies the quality at which the video will be exported, and is similar to the JPEG export settings. The quality range is from 0 to 100, although 60 is usually a minimum setting for acceptable output. To keep video quality the same, bandwidth requirements may vary.

- The Keyframes slider determines how often Sorenson Spark creates keyframes. Remember, complete frame data is stored only where keyframes occur. More keyframes result in larger file sizes. The number that you are setting here is the interval between keyframes, so lower values insert more keyframes. However, a setting of 0 inserts no keyframes. Experiment with this setting to find the best balance between image quality and file size.

- The High quality keyframes option, when selected, ensures consistent image quality in keyframes. If you've chosen the Bandwidth option at the top of the dialog, the quality of keyframes may be degraded if you do not choose this option.

- The Quick compress option enables you to speed up compression with the possible consequence of degraded image quality.

- Select Synchronize to Macromedia Flash document frame rate to match the playback speed of the imported video to the playback speed of the Main Timeline. You can also adjust the ratio of the video frame rate to the main Timeline frame rate, to drop frames from the imported video during playback. The default of 1:1 preserves the original frame rate of the imported video. Try not to go below a frame rate of 12fps, or the video may appear choppy.

If possible, import video with a compatible frame rate and synchronize the embedded video with the Main Timeline. Incompatible rates can cause frames to be dropped or duplicated, resulting in noticeable discontinuities on playback. The most likely form of non-compatible video is NTSC video with a frame rate of 29.97 frames per second. Deselecting the Synchronize option prevents frames from being dropped in the embedded video and eliminates discontinuities.

ADVANCED ENCODING

The Advanced Encoding dialog has three sections: Color, Dimensions, and Track options, as shown in Figure 18.43.

Figure 18.43
The Advanced Encoding dialog for the Video Import Wizard.

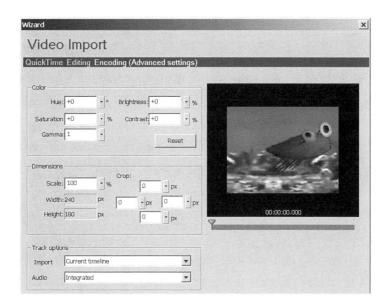

COLOR OPTIONS   Color options allow you to set Hue, Saturation, Gamma, Brightness, and Contrast. Each of these can be set numerically or controlled by a slider, located at the right of the numerical input box.

Hue lets you change the video's basic color, through all the colors of the rainbow (or "color wheel," if you want to sound professional). Values go from –180° to +180°.

Saturation can make your colors look more intense or deeper, or it can "wash out" the colors until they are colorless and gray. Saturation is measured as a percentage of gray from –100% to +100%. Lower values make the colors more gray.

Brightness lightens and darkens the video, all the way from pure white to pure black. It's measured from –100 to +100. Lower values make the image more black.

Contrast measures the contrast between dark and light in the image, and can affect how distinct or sharp objects appear. It's measured as a percentage from –100% to +100%. Lower values mean less contrast.

Gamma is a type of brightness adjustment that affects shadows, midtones, and highlights differently. For instance, it may be possible to lighten or darken the midtones without significantly changing the shadows and highlights, or to lighten the highlights without affecting the shadows. Values go from 0.1 to 1.8. A smaller value makes the image darker.

Reset resets all Color options to their default values.

DIMENSIONS   The Scale slider enables you to reduce the pixel dimensions of the imported video. The Output properties displayed below the slider update to reflect changes in the Scale setting. Values go from 0% to 100%. The default is 100%. Enlarging the video, which would degrade quality, is not possible.

The Crop section enables you to reduce the image by any desired number of pixels on any side or combination of sides.

TRACK OPTIONS   The Import option enables you to import the video to the current Timeline, as a movie clip, or as a graphic. You can browse the video on a timeline and manipulate the movie clip or graphic in all the usual ways, as discussed in the next section.

The Audio option enables you to import audio as a separate sound object, integrated with the video, or not at all.

WORKING WITH IMPORTED VIDEO

Embedded video instances can be transformed much like other objects. You can rotate, skew, apply color effects, mask, and even tween a video instance. Simply select the video instance and use the Free Transform tool to apply transformations. To mask a video, move the layer containing the video beneath a mask layer. To animate or apply color effects to a video instance, embed the video in a movie clip symbol and apply color effects or a tween to the symbol. Combine animation and video sparingly, though, as both can increase file size dramatically.

After a video is imported, you can replace or update it like other symbols. To replace an embedded video clip, follow these steps:

1. Within the Library, click to select the embedded video clip.
2. Click the upper-right corner of the Library panel to launch the Library Options pop-up menu, and choose Properties. The Embedded Video Properties dialog box appears.
3. Click Import to import a new clip to replace the embedded clip.

To update a clip that has been edited externally since import into Flash, select the clip in the Library and access the Embedded Video Properties as outlined in the preceding steps. Instead of clicking Import, click Update.

You can place video clips on the Stage and move them about like other objects. The Property inspector enables you to assign an instance name for a clip and to access its coordinates and dimensions.

CONTROLLING VIDEO PLAYBACK

After video is embedded, it can be controlled much like any other content that is on the Stage. Video frames are converted to Flash frames, and you can drag the playhead to scrub through the Timeline and preview video content. If your video content is lengthy, such as a presentation, it's a good idea to add buttons to allow users to control the playback of the video. You control video playback by using ActionScript to control the playback of the Timeline in which the video is placed. However, in Flash MX 2004, there's no longer any need to hand-code the ActionScript to control video. You can use the Embedded Video behaviors on the Behaviors panel to quickly apply the desired actions to buttons that look like VCR controls. You can find a selection of such buttons under Window, Other Panels, Common Libraries, Buttons.

Flash movies start to play automatically, and the video should also begin to play as soon as it loads, assuming it's in the first frame. You can prevent the movie (and therefore the video) from automatically playing by inserting a `stop()`; action in frame 1. Similarly, looping can be stopped if you add a `stop()`; action in the last frame.

TROUBLESHOOTING

How can I copy a symbol from one movie into another movie?

If you have more than one FLA open, the Libraries for all open documents appear in the Library panel. The title bars in the Library panel display the name of each FLA.

To copy a symbol from one Library to another, you can just copy (Cmd-C on the Mac or Ctrl+C on the PC) and Paste (Cmd-V on the Mac or Ctrl+V on the PC) from one library to another. Alternatively, you can undock one of the libraries, and simply drag and drop the symbol from one library to another. You can also drag a symbol onto the Stage in another FLA, which automatically adds the symbol to the other FLA's Library as well.

If you want to use multiple symbols from another movie, you can also open an FLA as a library, which opens just the Library of a selected FLA and not the Timeline or Stage. Choose File, Import, Open External Library and select an FLA.

Why do I receive the prompt Resolve Library Conflict?

Flash is protecting you from unwittingly overwriting an existing symbol in the Library. If you attempt to drag or copy a symbol to a Library, and the new symbol has the same name as an existing symbol, you are prompted to either replace or not replace the existing symbol. If you choose not to replace, the drag or copy operation is canceled. You can then go into the other Library, rename the symbol, and try again.

I've created a motion guide layer and motion path to animate along. Why isn't it working?

Animation moves along motion guides only if shapes are snapped to the beginning and end of the guide path. Check your beginning and ending keyframes and ensure that your shapes are squarely snapped to the path.

I'm unable to add a shape tween. Why isn't it working?

Check whether the objects you're attempting to tween are symbols. Although objects need to be symbols or grouped for *motion* tweens, you cannot perform a *shape* tween on groups or symbols. You can work around this problem by breaking apart a symbol instance. Simply select the instance on the Stage and press Cmd-B (Mac) or Ctrl+B (Windows) to convert a symbol to an object. If a symbol contains nested symbols, you may need to break it apart more than once. This affects just the symbol instance; the symbol itself remains intact in the Library.

CHAPTER **19**

INTRODUCTION TO ACTIONSCRIPT

In this chapter

Adding Interactivity with ActionScript   442

Using the Actions Panel   444

Understanding Object-Oriented Languages   446

The Three R's: Readability, Reusability, and Reachability   448

Hint, Hint: Flash Helps You Code   456

ADDING INTERACTIVITY WITH ACTIONSCRIPT

ActionScript is a programming language, a way of sending both commands and questions to the Flash Player about timelines, movie clips, and objects such as buttons.

NEW Flash MX 2004 introduces a new version of ActionScript, ActionScript 2 (AS2), which enhances productivity and supports better coding practices. To take advantage of AS2 features, you must publish for Flash Player 7 (FP7).

→ For a summary of key new features in AS2, **see** "A New Version of ActionScript," **page 330**, in Chapter 14, "What's New in Flash MX 2004?"

Existing AS1 scripts may have problems when published for FP7. It should be safe, however, to publish existing scripts for Flash Player version 6 (FP6) and play them in FP7.

What kinds of problems? For instance, there are some new objects and procedures whose names are now "reserved" by the ActionScript compiler: In movies published for FP6, they cause no problems. In movies published for FP7, you use them at your peril. Examples include ContextMenu, Error, and PrintJob.

In addition, AS1 seldom cared about capitalization. AS2, in contrast, is case sensitive. So, for instance, myTxt and MyTxt were considered the same variable in AS1, but not in AS2.

There are several other ways in which FP7 is stricter or more "correct" than FP6. ActionScript that depended on FP6's laxness may "break" in FP7.

→ The CD accompanying this book has a table of some key new ActionScript requirements for FP7: ASPlayerDifferences.htm.

 Having problems converting an old Flash file to use AS2? **See** *the "Troubleshooting" section later in this chapter, **page 458**.*

Often, you can accomplish tasks easily with ActionScript that would be difficult or impossible without it. Without ActionScript, you can access only a small portion of Flash's capabilities. For example, you need some ActionScript to get any kind of interactivity, such as responding when the user clicks on a button or presses a key on the keyboard. ActionScript is also the only way to get Flash to go to a particular frame of a timeline and either start or stop playing.

Flash's visual (non-scripting) tools enable you to create animations. ActionScript adds interactivity and enables you to animate with more control, often while consuming fewer processor cycles. With ActionScript, you can create navigation systems, listen for and gather user input, collect data, make calculations, examine the computer environment, and transform graphics, sound, and video.

NEW Behaviors, new in Flash MX 2004, make it easy to put simple interactivity in your movie without actually having to type one line of ActionScript code. But all behaviors do is automatically apply ActionScript.

NOTE

> Do not confuse behaviors with components. A component is a ready-made object such as a button, check box or drop-down menu (combo box). Components can (and usually do) have both ways of behaving (implemented in ActionScript) and a visual appearance (implemented in movieclips). A behavior is basically just a snippet of ActionScript that you can apply to appropriate objects with a couple of mouse clicks. A behavior in itself doesn't have any visual appearance.

Useful as they are, behaviors don't begin to illustrate the richness, flexibility, and endless possibilities that ActionScript opens up to the Flash developer. ActionScript is Flash's native language; behaviors are like a phrase book—extremely useful, but still limited. The phrase book may not have exactly what you want to say, and it limits itself to quite simple "ideas."

There are other advantages to ActionScript. For instance, when used for animation, ActionScript usually gives you smaller SWF files and better performance than tweening. Another advantage is that you can perform tasks with more precision, such as moving a movie clip to a precise position on the Stage.

NOTE

> ActionScript is based on the ECMA-262 standard, which JavaScript also implements. ActionScript and JavaScript are siblings, one of which chose a life in Flash, the other in the browser. Naturally, each is optimized for its environment, but they still bear a close family resemblance. AS2 is based on ECMA-262 version 4.

ActionScript offers endless possibilities, and you can easily get started using it. The place to start is the Actions panel.

ACCESSING THE ACTIONS PANEL

To display or maximize the Actions panel, do one of the following:

- From the Window menu, choose Actions.
- Press F9.

The Actions panel maximizes or becomes visible. Or, if it was behind another window, it comes to the front. In the default layout, the Actions panel is docked with the Property inspector, as shown in Figure 19.1. (If you want to restore the default layout, choose Window, Panel Sets, Default Layout.)

19

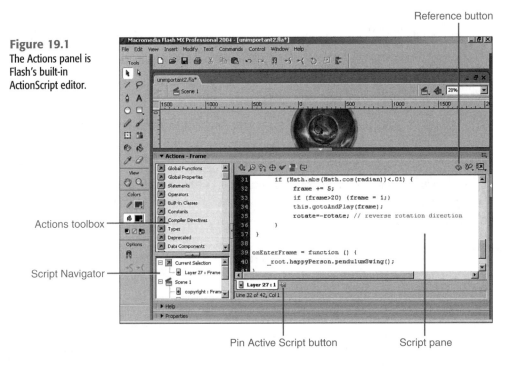

Figure 19.1
The Actions panel is
Flash's built-in
ActionScript editor.

The Actions panel is Flash's built-in ActionScript editor. It displays menu-style code hints if you use appropriate suffixes for object instances, such as _mc for movie clips. You can "pin" the current script (keep it in the Actions panel) by using the Pin Active Script button.

USING THE ACTIONS PANEL

You enter all your ActionScript in the Actions panel. ActionScript can be attached to a frame in a timeline, or to a button, movie clip, or component on the Stage. To attach the script to the correct item, click on the frame, button, movie clip, or component before starting to type in the Script pane on the right side of the Actions panel.

Adding a behavior just automates this process, as you can confirm by adding a behavior and then—without deselecting the frame or object with the behavior—opening the Actions panel, if it's not already open. You'll see the ActionScript for the behavior.

On the left side of the Actions panel is the Actions toolbox. (There's also a Script Navigator below the Actions toolbox, which represents the structure of your FLA file in a hierarchical format.) The Actions toolbox is like an ActionScript dictionary, except that it is organized functionally (by the way you use each item), rather than alphabetically. You can save keystrokes by dragging and dropping items from the Actions toolbox into the Script pane. Alternatively, right-click on any entry in the Actions toolbox, and select either Add to Script to copy that item into the Script pane, or View Help to bring up the help file (if one exists) for that item. Clicking the Reference button (refer to Figure 19.1) is another way to bring up the help file.

SELECTING FRAME ACTIONS OR OBJECT ACTIONS

A given block of actions can be attached either to an object (button, movie clip, or component) or to a frame. When you click on an object or a frame, the title bar at the top of the Actions panel changes to say "Actions—Frame," "Actions—Movie Clip," "Actions—Button" or just "Actions" (for a component).

In general, frame actions execute when the playhead reaches the frame to which the actions are attached. Object actions, on the other hand, are executed when a designated event occurs involving that object. For instance:

- **Frame action**. Suppose you put a `trace` action in a frame, such as

  ```
  trace("hello");
  ```

  The word `hello` will be displayed in the Output window each time the playhead reaches that frame.

- **Object action**. Movie clips have an "enter frame" event that occurs when the movie clip is on the Stage and the playhead enters a frame. So, for example, if your movie is running at 12 frames per second (fps), the "enter frame" event for that movie clip occurs 12 times per second when the movie clip is on the Stage. You can "hook into" this event by creating an event handler for it. Any ActionScript code that you put in your event handler will execute every time the event occurs. An "enter frame" event handler attached to an object looks like this:

  ```
  onClipEvent(enterFrame) {
      // your code goes here!
  }
  ```

In general, the ActionScript in a frame executes when the playhead reaches that frame. There are two notable exceptions, however:

- A *function* is a named block of code that implements a particular procedure. For instance, `gotoAndPlay()` is a built-in movie clip function that causes a movie to go to a particular frame in its Timeline and start playing.

  You can define your own custom functions anywhere that you can write code—within a frame or within an event handler. When the playhead reaches a frame or executes an event handler containing a custom function definition, the function becomes defined and available, but it does not actually execute. You have to *call* the function to cause it to execute.

→ For more information on functions, **see** "Combining Statements into Functions," **page 486**, in Chapter 20, "Basic ActionScript."

- In addition, there is another format for event handlers that allows you to enter object event handlers "in-line" with other code in a frame, rather than attached to an object. For instance, the following "enter frame" event handler is attached to a frame, but it works as if it were attached to the movie clip named `myClip`:

  ```
  myClip.onEnterFrame = function () {
      // your code goes here!
  };
  ```

19

When the playhead reaches a frame where an in-line event handler is defined, Flash starts "listening" for the event. However, like an attached event handler, the in-line event handler fires (executes the code it contains) only when the event occurs. With the "enter frame" event, this is likely to be immediate. However, there are other events, such as onRollOver() (the mouse rolling over the object) which might never occur at all.

Note that you cannot successfully assign an in-line event handler to an object unless the object exists in the workspace in the frame where you define the event handler. (The object could be in the offstage area, and thus not visible.) You can put the code in the frame, but it has no effect.

→ In the preceding example, myClip is the instance name of a movie clip. Movie clip instances are covered in Chapter 18, "Animation, Interactivity, and Rich Media," in the "Symbols, Instances, and Library Assets" section, **page 380**.

→ Event handlers that continue to fire when they're not performing any useful function can slow down your program. If you want to disable an event handler, **see** "Disabling and Deleting Event Handlers," **page 507**, in Chapter 20, and disableHandler.htm on the CD accompanying this book.

HIDING AND UN-HIDING THE ACTIONS TOOLBOX

You can hide the Actions toolbox, thus gaining more space for the Script pane, by clicking the triangle between the Actions toolbox and the Script pane. (Refer to Figure 19.1.) To un-hide the Actions toolbox, click the triangle again. (You can collapse the panels on the right side of the screen similarly by using the triangle on that side.)

UNDERSTANDING OBJECT-ORIENTED LANGUAGES

ActionScript is an object-oriented programming (OOP) language. AS2 is even more strongly object-oriented than AS1. For approximately the last 40 years, OOP has been gaining ground as the programming paradigm of choice. In this chapter, I explain why and give some simple examples. Subsequent chapters go into more detail.

"Object-oriented" means "based on objects." An *object* is a data structure that enables you to do in programs what you do in everyday life: group complex phenomena under simple headings.

For instance, suppose I want my friend Joe to come to my party and bring his guitar. Both Joe and his guitar have many capabilities and characteristics, but I just call Joe and say, "Hey, are you free Saturday night? Great! Come to my party and bring your guitar!" I don't have to tell him how to come to my party or what his guitar is; Joe already knows those things.

Joe, in this case, is analogous to a programming object. I'm dealing with two of his properties: One property is a function, namely, coming to a party. The other property is an object: Joe's guitar. (Joe, in this analogy, is also an object. So you have an object as a property of an object.)

You can use objects in ActionScript to organize the complex behaviors and characteristics of your programs and give yourself simple interfaces to them. Like Joe, an object is something that you can refer to by a single name, even though it may have many properties and behaviors. By summarizing related functions and data properties under object names, you make your programs easier to work with and understand.

Every movie clip in Flash is an object. Thus, if you have even a little experience with Flash, the terminology of objects may be new, but objects themselves are not.

Let's look at the three basic building blocks of objects: primitive data, functions, and data structures. This discussion will constitute a whirlwind tour of the elements that make up an ActionScript program. Most of the remainder of this section is devoted to filling in the details.

The simplest form of data—data primitives—includes numbers and character strings. For instance, the number 6 is a primitive datum (piece of data), as is the string `"Hello world!"`. A third primitive data type is Boolean. A Boolean datum can have only one of two values, namely, `true` or `false`.

→ If you want more information about primitives, **see** the section in Chapter 20 on "The Nine ActionScript Datatypes," **page 464**.

A *function*, as defined earlier in this chapter, is a named block of code embodying a procedure.

Primitive data and functions can be grouped into data structures. One type of data structure is an *array*, which is basically a numbered list, starting at zero. Thus, `myArray[0]` is the first element in the array named `myArray`. In an array containing the names of months, you would have `myArray[0] = "January"`.

→ If you want more information about arrays, **see** "Using the Core Classes," in Chapter 21, "Advanced ActionScript," **page 556**.

Objects are another way of grouping data and functions into structures. Instead of accessing things via numbers, as you do in an array, you use names to access the items (called *properties*) in an object.

The following are examples of some movie clip properties. They are all "read-write" properties: You can read them to determine the current state of the movie clip, or you can change them and thus control the movie clip.

- `_currentFrame`—A number; the movie clip's current frame on the Timeline.
- `_rotation`—A number; the number of degrees the movie clip has been rotated from its original position.
- `_visible`—A Boolean; controls the visibility of the movie clip.
- `_name`—A string; the name of the movie clip instance.

You access the elements of an array via the square bracket notation: `myArray[0]`. You typically access the properties of an object via "dot syntax," in which the name of the object and the name of the property are separated by a dot, as in these examples:

```
myClip._currentFrame
myClip._visible
myClip._name
myClip._rotation
myClip.gotoAndPlay()
```

In summary, objects are collections of properties. Each object has a name, and each property within an object has its own separate name. The property name refers either to a function or to data. The data may be a data primitive or a data structure such as an array or another object.

Data can also be stored in a *variable*, which is a container that is outside any data structure. For instance, the following statement stores the number 10 in a variable named x:

```
x = 10;
```

Functions in Objects Are Methods

Both arrays and objects can contain functions. However, object properties that refer to or contain functions are called *methods*. A function that is an element of an array is still just called a *function*.

Methods come under the grab-bag term *actions*, which also include global functions such as `eval` that are not associated with any object, statements such as `break` that control program flow, and directives such as `include` that give instructions to the ActionScript compiler. *Methods* is a more precise term.

THE THREE R's: READABILITY, REUSABILITY, AND REACHABILITY

Each Flash programmer tends to develop his or her own style of writing, organizing, and commenting programs. Companies that employ Flash programmers also have different standards. However, whatever your individual style, you probably want to write code that is readable, reachable, and perhaps reusable. The longer and more complex your programs are, the more important it is to think about these goals before and as you write.

READABILITY: WRITING READABLE CODE

When you go back to change, enhance, or debug a program, it's nice to have code that you can decipher without too much strain on your eyes or brain. Readability is partly just a matter of spacing, indentation, and capitalization. Comments can also add a lot to readability, as can the use of meaningful names for functions, variables, arrays, and objects. Finally, the best (and hardest) way of making code more readable is by solving coding problems in more elegant, simpler ways.

SPACING, INDENTATION, AND CAPITALIZATION

With few exceptions, ActionScript is very flexible about spacing and indentation. FP6 (and FP7 when playing movies published for FP6) is also forgiving when it comes to capitalization.

For example, when playing movies published for FP6, these two functions look the same to the ActionScript interpreter (the software that interprets SWF files):

```
function addonetobasescore(basescore){return basescore+1;}

function addOneToBaseScore (baseScore) {
    return baseScore + 1;
}
```

Whitespace, capitalization, and indentation make the second significantly more readable, and thus make it easier for you to understand and edit your program.

Remember, however, when publishing for FP7, capitalization affects the way your program works, not just the way it looks.

ADDING COMMENTS TO YOUR SCRIPT

Just formatting the code is seldom enough to make it clear what's going on in a complex program. Comments are usually necessary, too. Single-line comments are marked by double slashes:

```
// input: base score, returns: one more than the base score
```

A comment can also follow code:

```
baseScore += 1; // baseScore declared frame 1, main timeline
```

Enclose multiline comments like this:

```
/*
ADD ONE TO BASE SCORE
Michael Hurwicz  - January, 2004 - www.greendept.com
baseScore is an integer
*/
```

Some people prefer double slashes on every line because they make it clear that each line is still part of the comment:

```
/////////////////////////////////////////////////////////////////
// ADD ONE TO BASE SCORE
// Michael Hurwicz  - January, 2004 - www.greendept.com
// baseScore is an integer
/////////////////////////////////////////////////////////////////
```

In the Script pane, comments are color-coded, so you know where they start and stop. You can customize the color coding by selecting Edit, Preferences, ActionScript, and clicking in a color swatch in the Syntax coloring section. A selection of color swatches pops up, and you can select one. In this way, you can use colors for displaying foreground, background, keywords, comments, identifiers, and strings.

CREATING READABLE NAMES

You've seen that ActionScript programs have several types of elements that require names, such as functions, arrays, objects, and variables. What makes such names readable?

19

You've already encountered one aspect of readability for names: capitalization. Reading `addOneToBaseScore` is easier than reading `addonetobasescore`. Traditionally, by the way, most names in Flash begin with lowercase letters. An initial capital indicates a class.

Another good technique is to give things names that you (and others, if necessary) will understand intuitively. For instance, you probably won't have to examine the details of the `addOneToBaseScore` function to remember what it does.

SIMPLIFYING, STANDARDIZING, AND OPTIMIZING CODE

The best way to make your code more readable is to come up with straightforward ways of accomplishing your programming goals. Simple code will make your life as a programmer much easier. Of course, creating masterfully elegant code is easier said than done, but it's a worthy objective.

Better Coding with Pseudo-Code

One tool that may help you write simpler, more elegant code is pseudo-code. Pseudo-code represents your program, or some part of it, in your own words, but with as much specificity and detail as possible, and by trying to follow the flow and layout of the program as you envision it. Pseudo-code enables you to focus on the logic of your program, without getting bogged down in the mechanics of ActionScript. It allows you to mentally experiment with different approaches to a problem, without wasting time implementing approaches that you ultimately reject. When you do start coding, the pseudo-code serves as a detailed outline for the finished product, helping you stay on track.

Here's a very simple example, taken from leglift.fla, which is discussed in the next section. The central function in leglift.fla is `lift()`, which is called repetitively to gradually lift a leg off the ground or lower it back down. It can also stop the leg from moving. Movements are accomplished by rotating the leg at the hip. Here is the pseudo-code:

function `graduallyApproachGoal()` *receives a parameter (*goal*).*

If the current rotation of the leg is less than goal*, increase the rotation of the leg one degree.*

If the current rotation of the leg is greater than goal*, decrease the rotation of the leg one degree.*

If the current rotation is the same as goal*, do nothing. (The leg will not move.)*

You can see this function implemented as `lift()` on page 451 in the next section.

Trying to standardize your code is also helpful so that you can use the same techniques or syntax over and over. You'll understand blocks of code at a glance because you'll be so familiar with the techniques and syntax involved.

Simpler code also usually performs better than more complicated code. Because you will, of course, standardize on your best code examples, standardization is likely to make your program run better all around. Concise coding will also permit faster debugging and easier editing.

In some cases, however, a conflict occurs between fast code and easy-to-read code. In those cases, one approach is to actually use the fast code in the program but retain the easy-to-read code as a comment.

Reusability: Modularizing Code

Most programmers reuse code to some extent. After all, programming is essentially problem-solving. If you've solved a problem before, why reinvent the wheel? The techniques used to achieve reusability also make code more readable and easier to debug. Any time you find yourself typing similar code over and over, or cutting and pasting code, look for a better approach.

The two main vehicles of reusability are functions and objects. Both allow you to package functionality in modules that you can reuse both within a program and among multiple programs. Arrays can also play the same role, if you want access via numeric indices.

In addition, packaging functionality in functions and objects makes your code more readable. For instance, suppose you find this code inside an "enter frame" event handler attached to the left leg of a figure:

```
degrees++;
if (degrees < 30) {
    _rotation++;
}
```

You know that every time the movie clip enters a frame, the ActionScript interpreter is going to do whatever this code says. But what is that, exactly?

Compare that example to the following line, which invokes a `lift()` function, passing it an argument of 30.

NOTE

> An *argument* is data that you pass to a function, enclosed in parentheses after the function name.

```
lift (30);
```

You don't need to be a genius to guess that the figure is probably lifting its left leg, and that the argument, 30, has something to do with how much it's lifting the leg. You get that increase in readability just by putting the less intuitive code in a function with an intuitive name.

Now, let's make that leg part of an object named guy, with a `leftLeg` property. The `leftLeg` property is also an object, with a `lift()` method:

```
guy.leftLeg.lift(30);
```

It's practically a full sentence, with subject, object, verb, and adjective: A guy is lifting his left leg.

How do you make the leg part of an object named guy? You take advantage of the fact that movie clips are objects. Here, guy is a movie clip, and leftLeg is a clip within it. The `lift()` function becomes a method of leftLeg when it is defined as a property of the leftLeg object.

Both `lift()` and `guy.leftLeg.lift()` assume that somewhere else in your program you have defined a function called "lift" that does something similar to the less intuitive code shown on page 451. If you look at that function definition, you can get a more precise idea about what lifting means in this context—namely, that it has to do with rotating the clip:

```
function lift (degrees) {
    if (_rotation > degrees) {
        _rotation--;
    }
}
```

Add a comment to the function definition—"used to lift leftLeg"—and you have some very readable code.

The sample program leglift.fla shows a slight elaboration of this approach. It adds a second part to the `lift()` function so that the function lowers the leg if _rotation is less than degrees and raises the leg if _rotation is greater than degrees. If degrees equals _rotation, the function does nothing; that's the basis for stopping the leg.

```
// used to raise, lower and stop left leg
    function lift(degrees) {
        if (_rotation < degrees) {
            _rotation++; // lower the leg
        }

        if (_rotation > degrees) {
            _rotation--; // raise the leg
        }
    }
```

The sample also defines three functions that change the degrees variable, thus raising, lowering, or stopping the leg:

```
function raise() { degrees = 20; }
function lower() { degrees = 68; }
function halt() { degrees = _rotation; } // lift() will do nothing
```

These three functions are invoked from three buttons on the Stage. The "enter frame" event handler of the leg clip is constantly executing the `lift()` function, so the appropriate action is triggered as soon as degrees changes.

Using functions and objects also tends to make you a better programmer. This goes back to the fact that programming is problem-solving, and the first steps in problem-solving are defining the problem domain and defining the problem itself.

In the process of defining objects, you also define problem domains precisely. In the leg lift example, for instance, the domain of your problem is `guy.leftLeg`. Similarly, in the process of defining a function, you also define the problem. For instance, the previous function defines the problem as lifting the leg a certain number of degrees.

Functions and objects also help you break down large problems into smaller problems. Suppose you want a cartoon figure to walk across a room. A `walkAcrossTheRoom()` function might be relatively complicated. Perhaps you could write a `takeOneStep()` function and repeat it until the figure gets across the room. So, what is involved in taking one step? The figure has to swing an arm, move a leg, and move a certain distance forward.

If you keep going like this, eventually you'll come to problems that are small and precise enough to get your mind around and solve. You may start by implementing your solutions as functions. You could then combine these functions into more complex functions, objects, or sections of code. Objects and functions are great problem-solving tools because they help you solve dauntingly complex problems one simple step at a time.

 Ready to start programming, but don't know where to start? **See** *the "Troubleshooting" section later in this chapter,* ***page 458***.

Avoiding the supposed complexities of functions and objects is like avoiding the complexities of folders when you're managing email or files on a hard disk. As the number of messages or files grows, the lack of organization begins to hamper your ability to work efficiently. Similarly, objects and functions are basic to organizing ActionScript. They should make your life easier, not harder.

REACHABILITY: ORGANIZING AND CENTRALIZING CODE

There are two aspects to reachability: the interpreter's ability to find functions and variables at runtime (when your program is running) and your ability to find physical lines of code when you need to edit them.

By bundling functions and variables into objects and classifying objects in different classes, OOP provides the infrastructure that allows the ActionScript interpreter to find what it needs while your program is running. For instance, there is a concat() method (function) for arrays and a concat() method for text strings. In each case, the definition of the method is stored in the class definition, so the interpreter knows just where to look for it and doesn't get the two confused.

There are also *scoping* rules that determine whether a variable, function, or object in one part of the program is directly "visible" from another part of the program. By centralizing code—putting as much of it in one place as possible—you avoid possible scoping problems.

For instance, if all your code is within a single frame, you don't have to worry about scoping. Putting all your code in one frame was sometimes difficult or undesirable in Flash 5. In Flash MX, because of in-line event handlers, it is much easier and generally has few drawbacks. (In-line or *dynamic* event handlers are defined in frames rather than having to be attached to movie clips.)

For instance, the sample program leglift.fla on the CD is a bit hard to dissect because the small amount of code it contains is attached to several different objects and can be difficult to find. Sample program leglift2.fla centralizes all the code in one frame, making it easier to find and understand. The main change required was using in-line event handlers instead of event handlers attached to movie clips.

→ In-line event handlers are introduced in "Selecting Frame Actions or Object Actions," earlier in this chapter, **page 445**. They are discussed at more length in Chapter 20, in the "Using Event Handlers to Trigger Action" section, **page 500**.

19

→ For an example of making your code more readable, reusable, and reachable, **see** unimportant.htm on the CD.

Another important issue is your ability to find and conveniently edit code. In any somewhat complex program, Flash provides many nooks and crannies where you can "hide" code. If code is scattered around in too many places, maintaining your program can become hard.

Suppose you need to add a second argument to a function. The function itself is defined in just one place, so you can change it easily enough. However, you must also find every reference to that function in your program and add a second argument there, as well. If all your code is centralized in one place, you can search on the function name and probably find all the references in minutes. If your code is scattered around in 20 different places, you have a longer, more tedious job in front of you.

Centralizing code is perhaps the most important factor in easy program maintenance. Through in-line event handlers, Flash MX makes it easier to avoid the "scatter-gun" effect that makes programs difficult to maintain.

 *Have you centralized all your ActionScript and now want to keep it in the Actions panel while working on graphics in other frames? To find out how, **see** the "Troubleshooting" section later in this chapter, **page 458**.*

USING MOVIE CLIPS TO ORGANIZE DATA AND FUNCTIONS

Prior to Flash MX, nearly every scripted Flash program used movie clips for organizing code. The clips containing code were often "dummy" clips with no graphical content. Although you may still find it convenient to attach code to movie clips from time to time, this strategy is much less necessary in Flash MX than it was in Flash 5. Anything that you would formerly have put in an onClipEvent(enterFrame) event handler (attached to a movie clip) can now go in an in-line onEnterFrame event handler (in a frame). Similarly, there are in-line formats for other event handlers.

When considering whether to attach code to movie clips, think about this: If you have 20 movie clips on the Stage in frame 1 of your movie, you can put an action in the "enter frame" event handler of every movie clip, and the Flash interpreter will execute every one of those actions, round-robin style, before going on to frame 2. Or, you can put one in-line onEnterFrame event on the first frame of the Main Timeline and put all the actions in that one clip. Flash will execute all the actions in the in-line event handler before going on to frame 2. In other words, exactly the same thing gets accomplished, but your program may be 20 times easier to maintain.

USING TIMELINES TO ORGANIZE CODE

You can also use a timeline to organize code. Each frame can serve the purpose of a function, holding a block of code that accomplishes a particular task. You "invoke the function" with a play(), gotoAndPlay(), or gotoAndStop() action that sends the playhead to the appropriate frame.

At the same time, you can animate, add, or remove movie clips in that frame.

Better yet, put each block of code into a function and just call the function on the frame. This makes each frame more readable. It also allows you to centralize the bulk of the code. For instance, you can put all the functions in the first frame of a single layer.

However, because you must edit code separately in each frame, organizing code on a timeline doesn't really centralize the code. It's almost as tedious to "peek" into multiple frames on a timeline as it is to look in multiple movie clips.

Though still used, this technique is largely a holdover from earlier versions of Flash, which did not support functions. It is a viable technique, especially for simple movies, but it can become a hindrance in more complex ones.

USING THE MOVIE EXPLORER TO FIND ACTIONSCRIPT

The Movie Explorer can help you find the ActionScript in Flash source (.FLA) files. Start by deselecting all the buttons except the ActionScript button in the Show section near the upper left of the Movie Explorer panel (see Figure 19.2). The Movie Explorer then displays only movie clips and buttons that contain ActionScript.

Buttons, Movie Clips, Graphics

Text | ActionScript

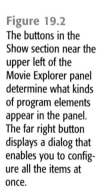

Figure 19.2
The buttons in the Show section near the upper left of the Movie Explorer panel determine what kinds of program elements appear in the panel. The far right button displays a dialog that enables you to configure all the items at once.

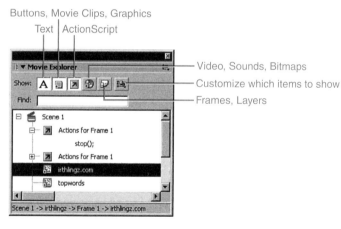

Video, Sounds, Bitmaps
Customize which items to show
Frames, Layers

19

→ For more details about the Movie Explorer, **see** Chapter 15, "Flash Environment and Tools," **page 344**.

The buttons in the Show section in the upper left of the Movie Explorer panel determine which types of movie elements the Movie Explorer displays. From left to right, they control text; buttons, movie clips, and graphics; ActionScript; video, sounds, and bitmaps; and frames and layers. The magnifying glass on the right provides a single panel for customizing all aspects of the Movie Explorer display.

To display the ActionScript in a particular button or movie clip, click on the button or movie clip name in the Movie Explorer display list. The name is highlighted. Then click on the options menu (in the upper-right corner of the Movie Explorer panel), and select

Expand Branch. Alternatively, you can click on the plus sign to the left of the movie clip or button icon in the display list. However, you might have to click on several plus signs before you get down to the ActionScript.

HINT, HINT: FLASH HELPS YOU CODE

Code hints act as a friendly expert watching over your shoulder as you create ActionScript, and giving you hints as you go along. Code hints come in two forms: *tooltips* and menu-driven *code completion*.

Tooltips show you formats after you have typed a portion of the action, or inserted an action via another means. For instance, in Figure 19.3, a `gotoAndPlay()` action has just been dragged from the Actions toolbox into the Script pane, and a tooltips hint has automatically appeared showing that this action requires a `frame` parameter indicating which frame to go to.

Figure 19.3
The action *instanceName. gotoAndPlay()* has just been dragged into the Script panel (on the right) from the Actions toolbox (on the left). The tooltip, "MovieClip. gotoAndPlay(`frame`)" shows the required format for the action.

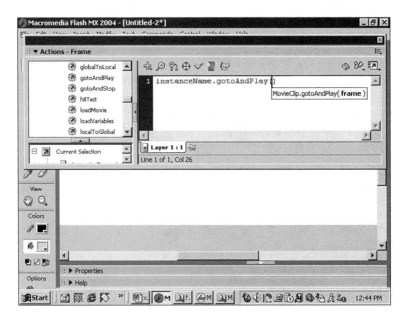

Code completion saves you typing by displaying a menu of possible choices, as shown in Figure 19.4.

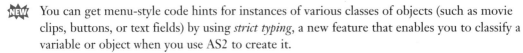 You can get menu-style code hints for instances of various classes of objects (such as movie clips, buttons, or text fields) by using *strict typing*, a new feature that enables you to classify a variable or object when you use AS2 to create it.

→ For more on strict typing, **see** "Managing Variables, Data, and Datatypes," in Chapter 20, **page 460**.

Figure 19.4
Code completion displays a menu of choices (_alpha, _focusrect, and so on, in this case) appropriate to the code you have begun to type.

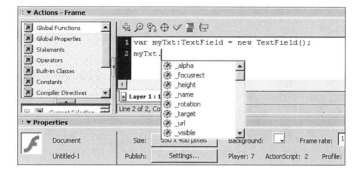

Figure 19.4 shows the Actions panel with two lines of code. The first line, `var myTxt:TextField = new TextField();`, creates a strictly typed text field object. The second line, `myTxt.`, is an incomplete statement that starts with the name of the new text object, followed by a period. There are only a limited number of ways to complete this statement, according to the rules of ActionScript syntax. As soon as you type the period, Flash lists appropriate possibilities.

An alternative way to get menu-style code hints, which works with AS1 as well as AS2, is to add a class-specific suffix to the name of the object or variable. When you create an object or variable with ActionScript, add the suffix to the object or variable name. If you create an object, such as a movie clip, text with a field, or button, by placing a symbol on the Stage, add the suffix to the instance name. For example, in Figure 19.5, the suffix _mc has been added to the instance name manystars, forming the name manystars_mc.

Figure 19.5
Flash provides menu-style code hints because a class-specific suffix, _mc (for "movie clip") has been added to the name of the object, manystars.

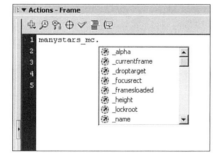

➔ The CD accompanying this book has a table of all the code hint suffixes. **See** `Code Hint Suffixes.htm`.

Both tooltips and menu-style code hints are enabled by default, but can be disabled if you select Edit, Preferences, ActionScript, and click in the "Code hints" check box. If code hints are enabled, you can enable and disable just tooltips by selecting Edit, Preferences, General, and clicking in the "Show tooltips" check box.

TROUBLESHOOTING

I know what I want my program to do, but where do I start?

If you find yourself completely stymied about how to approach a problem in ActionScript (or any programming language), you may not have broken down the problem into small enough component problems yet. Define sub-problems and sub-sub-problems. When you hit tasks that you can accomplish with a few lines of code, you're on your way.

A related approach is to attempt to solve a greatly simplified version of the problem you're really interested in. Then approach your goal by successive approximations.

Okay, I've centralized all my ActionScript. Now, how do I keep it in the Actions panel while I'm working on graphics in other frames?

Normally, when you click on a frame, the Actions panel displays whatever ActionScript is in that frame—even if that's no ActionScript at all. Then you have to go back and click in the frame that does have ActionScript in it. Annoying.

There is a solution: the Pin Active Script button. It's the button with the push pin symbol on it in the lower-left corner of the Actions panel. (Refer to Figure 19.1.) While your script is in the Actions panel, click on the Pin Active Script button. Your ActionScript is "pinned" in the Actions panel and will stay there, no matter what frame you are in, until you click the button again to "unpin" the ActionScript.

 In previous versions of Flash, you could pin only one script at a time. In Flash MX 2004, you can pin multiple scripts simultaneously. Tabs appear along the bottom of the Script pane. Click a tab to see the associated pinned script.

When you pin a script, the pin icon changes so the head is facing toward you. Click the changed icon to unpin the script.

I'm converting an old Flash project to use the AS2. But it's just not working! What's wrong?

Most probably, Flash MX 2004 recognized an older FLA and automatically configured the Publish Settings to AS1, and perhaps also for an older version of the Flash Player. The solution: Choose File, Publish Settings. On the Flash tab, select Flash Player 7 in the Version combo box, and ActionScript 2.0 in the ActionScript version combo box.

CHAPTER **20**

BASIC ACTIONSCRIPT

In this chapter

What Do You Mean, "Basic"?   460

Managing Variables, Data, and Datatypes   460

Working with Operands, Expressions, and Statements   471

Control Blocks   476

Combining Statements into Functions   486

Using Event Handlers to Trigger Action   500

Working with Movie Clips   517

WHAT DO YOU MEAN, "BASIC"?

By "basic" ActionScript, I mean ActionScript that deals with the fundamental building blocks of Flash movies and interactivity: movieclips, the mouse, the keyboard, buttons, sounds, text fields, and the Stage.

→ For discussion of these fundamental objects, other core ActionScript objects such as Date, Number, and String, and custom objects (belonging to classes that are not built in but created by a programmer), **see** Chapter 21, "Advanced ActionScript," **page 539**.

To work up to these basic building blocks, this chapter also covers variables, data, datatypes, operators, statements, and functions.

MANAGING VARIABLES, DATA, AND DATATYPES

A variable is a name that you assign to a datum (data item). It's called a *variable* because what it names can vary. For instance, a variable named myScore may equal 10 now. A moment later, after you've scored a point in a game, myScore may equal 11. However, in ActionScript, the variability of variables can go far beyond that: Unless you use *strict data typing*, you can assign different types of values to the same variable. For example, myScore could represent the number 11, then the string "foo", and finally an array of strings and numbers.

Unintentionally changing a variable's data type can lead to errors. Strict data typing helps you avoid this potential problem, which is why strict data typing is one of the most important new features in ActionScript 2 (AS2).

WORKING WITH VARIABLES

You can *declare* variables using the var keyword, as follows:

```
var x; // declares the variable x with no initial value
```

Implement strict typing by following the variable name with a colon and a data type, such as Number:

```
var x:Number; // declares the variable x as a Number with no initial value
```

You declare a variable, at most, once. Then you can use it as many times as you want throughout your program. For example:

```
var x:Number = 10; // declares the variable x and sets it equal to 10
trace  (x); // displays "10" in the Output window
var y:Number = x + 10; // declares the variable y and sets it equal to x + 10
trace (y); // displays "20" in the Output window
```

In many programming languages, you must declare a variable before you can use it. In ActionScript, if you use a variable that has not been declared, the ActionScript interpreter creates the variable on the fly (*implicitly*) .

It's good to get into the habit of declaring variables explicitly, however, and including a comment about how and where you use each variable. This coding practice makes your code more readable, and more importantly, it allows you to explicitly control the scope of variables—that is, where within a program a variable is defined or accessible.

→ This section touches on the issue of scope. "Combining Statements into Functions," later in this chapter, deals with scope in more depth. **See** "Explicit Scoping," **page 494**, and "Automatic Scoping," **page 497**.

In addition, explicit declarations can be more centralized and thus easier to find. Declaring variables implicitly is like leaving tools scattered around a workshop. You can never find the one you need when you're looking for it, and you are liable to trip over one you don't want when you least expect it.

→ For more details on declaring variables, **see** "Where to Declare Variables" below.

ASSIGNING VALUES TO VARIABLES

You can assign values to variables by using the assignment operator (=) or the set statement. For example, both of the following statements set the variable firstName equal to "John":

```
firstName = "John";
set (firstName , "John");
```

The value on the right can also be a complex expression:

```
x = y + 10;
set (x, y + 10);
```

In the preceding examples, set adds nothing but unnecessary complexity. However, if you want to use an expression to form the variable name, set enables you to do that, whereas the assignment operator alone does not. For example, this set statement works fine:

```
var i:Number = 4;set("day"+i+"night", "a French movie");
trace (day4night); // "a French movie"
```

But this statement generates an error:

```
"day"+i+"night" = "a French movie"; // ERROR!!!
```

→ For more on the assignment operator, **see** "Using Operators," later in this chapter, **page 474**.

WHERE TO DECLARE VARIABLES

Two issues generally predominate when you're deciding where to declare variables:

- Your ability to find your variables. This is an issue of *lexical* program design—how (or in this case *where*) you write things down.

- The capability of the ActionScript interpreter to find your variables when you want it to—and *not* find them when you don't want it to. "Findability" or scope management is an issue of *logical* program design—how the program works when it's running.

The Macromedia-recommended "best practice" from the lexical perspective is to put all or most of your code in one frame, such as the first frame of the top layer of the Main Timeline.

You can access Main Timeline variables from subclips by using _root as the path. For instance, suppose this line is on the Main Timeline:

```
myVar =  20;
```

Then you can access myVar from a subclip like this:

```
trace(_root.myVar); // displays "20"
```

→ You can run into problems using _root in a movie that is going to be loaded into another movie. Flash Player 7 (FP7) offers a solution in the _lockroot property of the MovieClip class. For more information, **see** "Loading and Unloading External Content," later in this chapter, **page 520**.

In a few situations, total centralization doesn't work. When it does work, you still have to organize your code within that single container to maximize readability and minimize errors.

WHEN *NOT* TO CENTRALIZE CODE

Program design works against code centralization in at least three situations:

- **When you use a preloader**, you want to get the preloader up quickly and then, in the background, do other things to initialize your program. The preloader and its variables typically take up one or more frames at the beginning of the movie. The main movie and its variables come on frame 2 or later.

- **When you use components**, which combine graphics and code, you cannot centralize the component code.

- **When you use AS2 classes**, each class definition is in its own file, in its own location.

The typical programmer never needs to delve into component or class code.

HOW TO ORGANIZE VARIABLES ON THE MAIN TIMELINE

Keeping a huge list of individual variables in a timeline can be like keeping kitchen utensils, piano-tuning accessories, and car repair tools all in the same drawer. Lexically, this can be hard to read. Reduce the confusion by dividing variables into categories using comments. Code for each category can also be stored and edited in an external file. You can load external files using the #include directive.

Writing all variables in one place raises logical design issues, too. For instance, each movie clip, including both its timeline and its event handlers, defines a single *scope*. The same applies to the Main Timeline. Within a single scope, no two program elements can have the same name. If they do, the more recently defined element will usually overwrite the one that existed previously. (In some cases, the existing name incapacitates the newer name.)

RULES FOR NAMING VARIABLES (AND OTHER THINGS)

A variable name is an ActionScript *identifier*, and as such must follow three naming rules, or you risk encountering serious problems:

- Use only letters, numbers, underscores, and dollar signs. Do not use spaces; punctuation marks such as periods, commas, hyphens, parentheses, brackets, exclamation points, or question marks; or symbols such as the following:

    ~ @ # % ^ & * = + / \ < >

- Use a letter, underscore, or dollar sign for the initial character. Do not use a number.
- Do not use reserved words.

ActionScript's reserved words are as follows:

add(*)	function	private
and(*)	ge(*)	public
break	gt(*)	return
case	if	static
catch	implements	super
class	import	switch
continue	in	tellTarget(*)
default	instanceof	this
delete	interface	throw
do	le(*)	try
else	lt(*)	typeof
eq(*)	ne(*)	var
export	new	void
finally	not(*)	while
for	or(*)	with

(*) Flash 4 reserved words deprecated since Flash 5

The following list shows words that may become reserved words in the future; you can use a word from this list now, but your program may "break" if a future version of ActionScript claims the word as its own.

abstract	enum	package
boolean	final	protected
byte	float	short
char	goto	synchronized
const	int	throws
debugger	long	transient
double	native	volatile

20

Other things being equal, you should follow these rules for movie clip instance names, too. Even though they are *not* officially identifiers, movie clip instance names often play the role of identifiers when you use them in ActionScript, and you may get errors if you don't follow the rules.

Having trouble with code that involves a movie clip name? **See** *the "Troubleshooting" section at the end of this chapter,* **page 535***.*

Many programmers also follow identifier-naming rules for other names, such as frame labels and layer names.

In movies published for FP6, only reserved words are case sensitive. Other identifiers are not. In movies published for FP7, all identifiers are case sensitive. Thus, myVar, myvar, and Myvar do *not* define different variables in FP6 movies, but *do* in FP7 movies. Case sensitivity is required by the ECMA-262 standard and could become a requirement in future versions of ActionScript.

In either AS1 or AS2, there is at least one case-related guideline that most programmers follow: Identifiers traditionally begin with lowercase letters. The one exception is class names. Constants (variables that always retain the same value) are often written in all uppercase letters.

→ **See** Chapter 21, **page 539**, for more information on classes.

Following some consistent capitalization rules is also a good idea to make your programs more readable.

USING DATATYPES TO CATEGORIZE DATA

The most basic piece of information to know about a variable is its datatype.

In AS1, mysterious errors often result from using the wrong datatype (using a text string where ActionScript requires a number, for instance), and keeping track of datatypes can be tricky because the ActionScript interpreter sometimes does automatic datatype conversions to try to make things work. You need to understand the logic of those conversions to predict which datatypes you will end up with.

In AS2, such problems can be eliminated by always using strict data typing. Then if you use the wrong data type, you will get an error message when you test or publish your movie.

THE NINE ACTIONSCRIPT DATATYPES

ActionScript has nine basic types of data. The five *primitive* datatypes, of which the most common are number and string, contain just a single primitive datum, such as a number or a single text string. The four *composite* datatypes (object, array, movieclip, and function) contain multiple pieces of data. For instance, a movie clip contains a _currentFrame property, a _name property, a _visible property, and many others.

You can determine the datatype of the value currently assigned to any variable by using the typeof operator, as follows:

```
var x:Number;
trace (typeof x); // no value assigned; displays "undefined" in Output window
x = 2;
trace (typeof x); // displays "number" in the Output window
```

Table 20.1 shows the ActionScript datatypes, with their `typeof` return values, examples of variable assignments, and legal values for the datatypes.

TABLE 20.1   ACTIONSCRIPT DATATYPES

Datatype	typeof **Value**	**Assignment Example**	**Legal Values**
number	"number"	var x:Number = 6;	Any number
string	"string"	var x:String = "foo";	Any character string
Boolean	"boolean"	var x:Boolean = true;	true, false
object	"object"	var x:Object = myObj;	Any object
array	"object"	var x:Array = myArray;	Any array
null	"null"	var x = null;	null
movieclip	"movieclip"	var x:MovieClip = myClip;	Any movie clip instance
function	"function"	var x:Function = myFunc;	Any function
undefined	"undefined"	var x;	undefined

Note that the variable assignment examples in Table 20.1 assume that the object, array, movie clip, and function already exist.

Also note that strict typing does not support the `null` or `undefined` values.

NUMBER

The two most important kinds of numbers are *integers*, which have no fractional component (such as in –10, 0, 2, 856), and *floating-point numbers* (*floats*) which do have a fractional component (such as in –10.2, .01, 635.8916).

Special values for the `number` datatype include

- NaN ("not a number"), which identifies non-numeric data in a datum of the `Number` datatype.
- `Number.MAX_VALUE`, which is the largest number that ActionScript can represent (1.79769313486231e+308).

Scientific Notation

To represent very large or very small floats (whether positive or negative), ActionScript uses scientific notation, consisting of a base and an exponent, separated by the letter e (*exponent*). For instance, 123,000,000,000,000 is 1.23e+15. You can use scientific notation in your programs, too, using any float as a base. For instance, you can write 126e+3 instead of 126,000.

NOTE

Flash uses *double-precision* floats, meaning they can have up to 15 *significant digits*. Thus, in scientific notation, Flash will never use more than 15 digits in the base.

20

- `Number.MIN_VALUE`, which is the smallest positive number that ActionScript can represent (5e-324).

- `Infinity` (positive infinity), which is an indeterminate number larger than `Number.MAX_VALUE`.

- `-Infinity` (negative infinity), which is an indeterminate number more negative than `Number.MIN_VALUE`.

- Constants, such as `pi` and the square root of 2, which are properties of the `Math` object.

→ For more information on the `Math` object as well as more details on manipulating numbers with built-in functions, **see** "The `Math` Object," **page 578**, in Chapter 21.

STRINGS

A string is any sequence of alphanumeric characters enclosed in quotation marks.

N O T E

> Alphanumeric: "consisting of alphabetic and numerical symbols and of punctuation marks, mathematical symbols, and other conventional symbols used in computer work." *American Heritage Dictionary of the English Language, New College Edition.* Published by Houghton Mifflin Company.

Flash MX supports the double-byte character set (DBCS), or Unicode character set, for text and user interface strings.

→ For more on Unicode, **see** unicode.htm on the CD accompanying this book.

BOOLEANS

The `Boolean` datatype permits only two values: `true` and `false`. The `true` and `false` values assigned to the variable can represent other concepts, such as yes and no, black and white, or up and down. The `Boolean` datatype is commonly used with `if` statements for decision-making. For instance, if the logic of your program is, "If the answer is yes, then..." you would probably declare the answer variable as a Boolean:

```
var answer:Boolean = true; // means the answer is "yes"
```

MODELING PROBLEM DOMAINS USING OBJECTS

`Object` is the most flexible ActionScript datatype, and the most fundamental composite datatype. The simplicity and flexibility of the `Object` datatypeObject datatype make it suitable for modeling almost any problem domain.

The `Object` datatype represents an unordered collection of properties, each of which is a `name:value` pair. An object property can contain any type of data that ActionScript supports.

Many of the operators commonly used with primitive datatypes don't apply to objects or other composite datatypes. For instance, you can't add, subtract, or multiply objects.

On the other hand, one operator applies only to objects (including movie clips): You use the dot (.) operator—officially known as the "object property access" operator—to...how did you guess?...access object properties. You can also use square brackets—officially the "array-element/object-property" operator—to access object properties. The general format is as follows:

```
object[property name string]
```

Note that the property name must be a string, meaning it must be enclosed in quotation marks. So, _root.myObj["name"] is the same as _root.myObj.name. Objects are properties of the timelines they are on, so a third way of writing the same thing is _root["myObj"]["name"]. The property name can also be represented by a variable, in which case the quotes are not present: _root.myObj[nameVar].

You create a datum of the object type by using the new operator, like this:

```
var myObj:Object = new Object();
```

Many classes of objects, such as the following three, simply display object as a typeof value.

```
var badAcctError:Error = new Error(); // new object in the Error class
var newsFeedXML:XML = new XML(); // new object in the XML class
var myArray:Array = new Array(); // new object in the Array class
```

ARRAY

An *array* is an ordered list. For instance, you could use an array to store the names of days of the week or months of the year. Items in the list (*elements*) are accessed via numerical indices. In ActionScript, the initial index is always 0. Here, you assign a value, "Monday", to the first element of an array, myArray, and display that value in the Output window:

```
myArray[0] = "Monday";
trace (myArray[0]); // "Monday"
```

The array is actually a special case of the Object datatypeObject datatype. As with objects, you use the new operator to create arrays. You can use all the same operators with arrays as with objects, with the exception of the dot (.) operator, which is reserved for objects (including movie clips).

Like objects, arrays can hold any kind of ActionScript data.

→ The numerical indices used to access arrays offer some possibilities that do not exist with objects. These possibilities are discussed in "The Array Class," **page 557**, in Chapter 21, "Advanced ActionScript").

null

The null datatype permits just one value: the primitive value null. You assign this value to a data container (such as a variable, object property, or array element) to indicate that the container is empty. You can also assign the null value to an identifier used as a function name, thus disabling the function.

20

The null datatype is closely related to the undefined datatype, as shown by the fact that the ActionScript interpreter sees them as equal:

```
trace (null == undefined); // "true"
```

There is nothing else (except null itself) that the interpreter considers equal to null. For example:

```
trace (null == ); // "false" - the empty string is not equal to null
```

→ For more information on the distinction between null and undefined, **see** "Using null and undefined," later in this chapter, **page 471**.

movieclip

The MovieClip datatype is familiar to every Flash programmer. Its main distinguishing features are a timeline and graphical content, which can be controlled via the movie clip's properties. Thus, for instance, a movie clip is the only built-in object in Flash that has color, position, rotation, scale, size, or transparency. Adding this datatype is one of the ways in which Macromedia went beyond the ECMA-262 standard in creating a scripting language for Flash.

FUNCTION

A *function* is a named block of ActionScript code that performs a particular task. A number of *global* functions, such as trace(), are not properties of any object. Functions that are properties of objects are called *methods*. For instance, gotoAndStop() is a MovieClip method that causes a movie clip to go to a particular frame in its timeline and stop.

Often, a function takes one or more *arguments* as input and returns a datum. For example, isNaN() is a global function that takes any expression as an argument and returns a Boolean true if the expression, when treated as a number, resolves to the special value NaN (not a number), or false if the expression does not resolve to NaN.

Although it's not usually as evident as it is with arrays, the Function datatype is actually a special case of the Object datatype, too. For example, although programmers don't often take advantage of this capability, functions can have properties, accessible via the same dot and square bracket operators used for the Object datatype.

Despite these object-like characteristics, you can't create or remove functions programmatically: The new and delete operators do not work with functions.

undefined

Like the null datatype, the undefined datatype indicates an absence of data. However, whereas you assign the null value yourself, the intention is that only the ActionScript interpreter will assign the undefined value as a default when you don't assign a value to a variable or other data container. For example:

```
var middleName:String;
trace (middleName);  // "undefined"
```

The ActionScript interpreter also returns `undefined` if you reference a variable or other data container that does not exist. (JavaScript generates an error under these conditions.)

→ **See** "Using `null` and `undefined`," **page xxx**, later in this chapter, for more details on the distinction between `null` and `undefined`.

EXPLICIT AND IMPLICIT DATA CONVERSION

After a variable has been declared, whether with or without strict data typing, you can explicitly change its datatype, a process called *casting* (or *typecasting*). You typecast using functions such as `Boolean()`, `Number()`, `String()`, and `toString()`. For instance, if you declare var `mc:MovieClip;` with no value, then, in Flash Player 7

- `Boolean(mc)` is equal to `false`, because `undefined` becomes `false` as a Boolean.

- `String(mc)` is equal to the string `"undefined"`. (In FP6, it's equal to the empty string.)

- `Number(mc)` is equal to `NaN`, because `undefined` becomes `NaN` as a Number. (In FP6, it becomes zero.)

> **NOTE**
>
> Because of differences in the ways different versions of the Flash Player evaluate `undefined`, **you should use the** `typeof` operator to determine whether a datum is of the `undefined` datatype:
> ```
> if (typeof middleName == "undefined");
> ```

Casting doesn't always work as you might expect or hope. For instance, the string `"six"` cannot be successfully converted to a number (it becomes `NaN`), but the numeral 6 can. On the other hand, any number can be converted to a string; for instance, the number 6 becomes the string `"6"`.

However, casting never yields an error, even if you're using strict data typing. Instead, the ActionScript interpreter assigns a new value to the variable based on its own rules, some of which are illustrated in the previous examples.

→ Datatype conversion rules are discussed in Appendix A, "ActionScript Reference," under "Datatype Conversion Rules," **page 911**.

The same rules apply if you're not using strict data typing or casting, and you simply use a variable in a new context. This is called *implicit* datatype conversion.

Implicit datatype conversion can happen without your being aware of it and therefore may produce results you aren't expecting. That's why it's helpful to use strict data typing.

Explicit datatype conversion (that is, casting) is less likely to cause trouble because you are always aware that you have done it.

20

NUMBERS AND STRINGS VERSUS NUMERIC AND STRING LITERALS

A *variable* is an abstract representation of a datum. It in no way resembles the datum itself. In contrast, a *literal* represents a datum literally, not abstractly, and the ActionScript interpreter actually creates the datum using only the literal as a blueprint.

In the following example, x is a variable. "Howdy Pete" is a string literal:

```
x = "Howdy Pete!"
```

A variable is a number if its assigned value is a numeric literal. It is also a number if its assigned value is a complex expression that can be reduced to a numeric literal. For instance:

```
x = 3 + 3; // can be reduced to a numeric literal: 6
```

Literals cannot span multiple lines of code. For instance, the following will not work:

```
test = "Howdy
Pete!";
```

You can use the plus (+) operator to get around this limitation:

```
test = "Howdy " +
    "Pete!";
```

A string or numeric literal may be used for a temporary purpose, without being stored. If you want to reuse the datum represented by a string or numeric literal, you must store it in a variable, array element, or object property. Unless it is stored, a literal does not persist and is of no further use.

OBJECT AND ARRAY LITERALS

An *array* is a named, ordered list whose elements are accessed via numeric indices. An *array literal* is a comma-separated list of the elements, enclosed in square brackets, without the array name or the indices. For instance, here are the first three values of an array of strings representing the months:

```
months[0] = "January";
months[1] = "February";
months[2] = "March";
```

The corresponding array literal looks like this:

```
["January" , "February" , "March"]
```

You can create an array by assigning the anonymous, nameless array literal to a variable, which thereby becomes an array name:

```
months = ["January" , "February" , "March"];
```

Similarly, an *object* is a named, unordered list whose properties are accessed by name. For instance, here are the properties of a computer object:

```
computer.monitor = "SVGA";
computer.processor = "Pentium 4";
computer.price = 1700;
```

The corresponding object literal is a comma-separated list of properties enclosed in curly braces, without the object name. Each property consists of a name and a value, separated by a colon. For instance:

```
{ monitor : "SVGA" , processor : "Pentium 4" , price : 1700 }
```

You can assign the object literal to a variable, which thereby becomes an object name:

```
computer = { monitor : "SVGA" , processor : "Pentium 4" , price : 1700 };
```

As with string and numeric literals, array and object literals are lost if they are not assigned to a variable or stored in an array element or an object property.

NOTE

> The object literal format provides a good visual representation of an object, and the *property*:*value* syntax is a concise way of referring to objects and properties.

USING null AND undefined

Both null and undefined are extremely useful to the programmer, but their uses are different, even though both indicate an absence of data. The null value is used in messages from the programmer to the interpreter. The undefined value should be reserved for messages from the interpreter to the programmer.

The ActionScript interpreter assigns the undefined datatype as a default when you don't assign any content to a declared variable. A declaration of this sort is shown in line 1 in the following example. The interpreter also returns undefined if you ask for the type of a variable that does not exist. This is illustrated in line 7.

Assigning the value undefined to a variable is legal but not recommended. (This poor practice is shown in line 5.) If you refrain from assigning the undefined datatype, you will always know when you see it that the interpreter has assigned it automatically. When you want to assign a value to a variable to indicate that it contains no data, use null. Then undefined will always indicate exactly what the word implies: something that has never been defined.

```
1: var x:Number;               // OK
2: trace (typeof x);       // "undefined"
3: x = null;               // OK
4: trace (typeof x);       // "null"
5: x = undefined;          // legal but poor practice !!!
6: trace (typeof x);       // "undefined" : no value assigned
7: trace (typeof y);       // "undefined" : doesn't exist
```

WORKING WITH OPERANDS, EXPRESSIONS, AND STATEMENTS

Operators are symbols and keywords that change, access, create, remove, analyze, and organize data. Most operators come from the fields of mathematics and logic. A number of them are old friends from grade-school arithmetic. For instance, the multiplication operator (*) multiplies two values; the addition operator (+) adds two values; the division operator (/) divides one value by another.

In some instances, an operator's form in ActionScript is different from that of grade-school arithmetic. For instance, the ActionScript multiplication operator is an asterisk (*), not ×. Similarly, the division operator is a forward slash (/), not the ÷ symbol.

Although operators are very basic, they're also powerful and can be tricky. There are a lot of them—52 in all, 51 of which are listed in Table 20.2.

Forty operators fall into five major categories:

- *Arithmetic* operators operate on numeric operands to produce a numeric result.
- *Assignment* operators assign a result to a variable, object property, or array element; *reassignment* operators also include an arithmetic or bitwise operation with the assignment.
- *Bitwise* operators operate on individual bits within a byte.
- *Comparison* operators compare two values.
- *Logical* (Boolean) operators reduce expressions to Boolean values (`true` or `false`) and return results based on those values.

In addition, 12 "one-of-a-kind" operators don't fall into any category: array-element/object-property, comma, conditional, `delete`, dot, function call, grouping, `new`, `typeof`, `instanceof`, `void`, and `super`.

TABLE 20.2   ACTIONSCRIPT OPERATORS

Operator	Category	Usage	Precedence	Associativity
x++	arithmetic	postfix increment	16	L-R
x--	arithmetic	postfix decrement	16	L-R
.	N/A	object property access	15	L-R
[]	N/A	array-element/ object-property	15	L-R
()	N/A	parentheses, grouping	15	L-R
function()	N/A	parentheses, function call	15	L-R
++x	arithmetic	prefix increment	14	R-L
--x	arithmetic	prefix decrement	14	R-L
-	arithmetic	unary negation	14	R-L

Operator	Category	Usage	Precedence	Associativity
~	bitwise	bitwise NOT	14	R-L
!	logical	logical NOT	14	R-L
new	N/A	create object/ array	14	R-L
delete	N/A	remove object/ property/array element	14	R-L
typeof	N/A	determine datatype	14	R-L
void	N/A	return undefined value	14	R-L
*	arithmetic	multiply	13	L-R
/	arithmetic	divide	13	L-R
%	arithmetic	modulo divide	13	L-R
+	arithmetic string	add (number) concatenate (string)	12	L-R
-	arithmetic	subtract	12	L-R
<<	bitwise	bitwise left shift	11	L-R
>>	bitwise	bitwise signed right shift	11	L-R
>>>	bitwise	bitwise unsigned right shift	11	L-R
<	comparison	less than	10	L-R
<=	comparison	less than or equal to	10	L-R
>	comparison	greater than	10	L-R
>=	comparison	greater than or equal to	10	L-R
instanceof	N/A	determine class	10	L-R
==	comparison	equality	9	L-R
!=	comparison	inequality	9	L-R
===	comparison	strict equality	9	L-R
!==	comparison	strict inequality	9	L-R

20

continues

TABLE 20.2   CONTINUED

Operator	Category	Usage	Precedence	Associativity
&	bitwise	bitwise AND	8	L-R
^	bitwise	bitwise XOR	7	L-R
¦	bitwise	bitwise OR	6	L-R
&&	logical	logical AND	5	L-R
¦¦	logical	logical OR	4	L-R
?:	N/A	conditional	3	R-L
=	assignment	assignment	2	R-L
+=	assignment	add and reassign	2	R-L
-=	assignment	subtract and reassign	2	R-L
*=	assignment	multiply and reassign	2	R-L
/=	assignment	divide and reassign	2	R-L
%=	assignment	modulo divide and reassign	2	R-L
<<=	bitwise	bit-shift left and reassign	2	R-L
>>=	bitwise	bit-shift right and reassign	2	R-L
>>>=	bitwise	bit-shift right (unsigned) and reassign	2	R-L
&=	bitwise	bitwise AND and reassign	2	R-L
^=	bitwise	bitwise XOR and reassign	2	R-L
¦=	bitwise	bitwise OR and reassign	2	R-L
,	N/A	comma	1	L-R

USING OPERATORS

Table 20.3 illustrates some typical uses of operators.

TABLE 20.3 USING OPERATORS

Statement	Operator(s)	Operator Name(s)	Operand(s)	Result
x = 3 + 7;	= +	Assignment, Addition	3, 7	x is set to 10
x = "Bed #"+6;	= +	Assignment, Concatenation	"Bed", "6"	x is set to "Bed #6";
x = a - b;	= -	Assignment, Subtraction	a, b	x is set to a less b
x = 3 * 7;	= *	Assignment, Multiplication	3, 7	x is set to 21
x++;	++	Unary Increment	x	x is incremented by 1
x--;	--	Unary Decrement	x	x is decremented by 1

A few definitions:

- *Operands* are what operators operate on.

- Operators combined with operands form *expressions*. An expression is a section of code that resolves to a single value.

- The *statement* is the smallest unit of ActionScript code that can actually cause something to happen. Often, all that's required to turn an expression into a statement is a semicolon. For instance, x++ is an expression, but x++; is a statement. (If you leave the semicolon off, the ActionScript interpreter tries to guess where it should go. But this is not a good practice. Officially, it's not a statement without the semicolon.)

ASSIGNMENT AND COMPOUND ASSIGNMENT

The assignment operator (=) stores the result of an expression in a variable, array element, or object property, as in these examples:

```
x = 2; // stores the number 2 in the variable x
month[11] = "December";// 12th element of the month array is "December"
car.color = 0xFF0000; // color property of car object is 0xFF0000 (red)
```

The ten *compound assignment operators* provide a concise notation for combining the assignment operator with various arithmetic or bitwise operators. For instance, the "add and reassign" operator (+=) combines assignment and addition. Each compound assignment operator performs an operation that involves two operands. The result is stored in the left operand. For instance, x += 2 adds 2 to x and stores the result in x. This is equivalent to x = x + 2.

UNDERSTANDING PRECEDENCE, ASSOCIATIVITY, AND OPERATOR GROUPING

When one statement includes multiple operators, the ActionScript interpreter has two simple rules by which it determines which operators to evaluate first:

20

- Each operator has a precedence value, as shown in Table 20.2. The interpreter evaluates operators in order of precedence, with higher precedence operators first.

- Operators with the same precedence are evaluated according to their *associativity*, either left to right (L–R) or right to left (R–L). Table 20.2 also shows the associativity of each operator.

Examples of precedence include the following:

```
1 + 2 * 10 // 21 - multiplication happens before addition
--6 * 100 // 500 - decrement happens before multiplication
```

The following *grouping operators*, which are parentheses, allow you to override the default order of evaluation:

```
(1 + 2) * 10 // 30 - addition happens before multiplication
--(6 * 100) // 599 - multiplication happens before decrement
```

You can also use parentheses to make the order of evaluation more obvious, even if they don't actually change anything. For instance:

```
1 + (2 * 10) // 21 - doesn't really change anything
```

Here's an example of associativity: The "add and reassign" (+=) and "subtract and reassign" (-=) operators have the same precedence and right-to-left associativity. Therefore, in the expression a += b -= c, the interpreter starts by evaluating the operator on the right, so a += b -= c is the same as a += (b -= c). For instance, in the following example, the interpreter evaluates b -= c first, making b equal to –1. Then it evaluates a += b, making a equal to 0, as shown here:

```
a = 1;
b = 2;
c = 3;
a += b -= c; // result: a == 0, b == -1, c == 3
```

→ For details of operators, **see** Appendix A, "ActionScript Reference," **page 909**.

CONTROL BLOCKS

A *statement* is the "sentence" of coding; that is, it is the smallest unit of code that communicates a complete command to the ActionScript interpreter. There are two basic kinds of statements: standalone statements and control blocks. So far, you've seen standalone statements, such as x = 3 * 7;. A control block is a statement that can contain other statements.

There are two kinds of control blocks: looping (or *iterative*) and non-looping. The looping control blocks (while, do-while, for, and for-in) repeat the statements they contain until a condition is met. The non-looping control blocks (if-else, ifFrameLoaded, and with) execute the statements they contain just once.

→ Sample movie dropdownmenu.fla on the CD accompanying this book generates a drop-down menu using a for-in loop. Notes are in dropdownmenu.htm.

A typical control block consists of a *keyword* (reserved word, such as `if` in the following examples), a *parenthesized control construct*, and a *body* consisting of zero or more statements. The keyword defines the type of statement (such as an `if` statement); the control construct determines under what conditions the body is executed; the body determines what actions the control block performs.

If two or more statements appear in the body, they must be enclosed in curly braces. You can write a statement on multiple lines for readability, without affecting what it does. For instance, these two statements are equivalent:

```
if (allDone) quit;
```

```
if (allDone)
    quit;
```

So are these two:

```
if (allDone) {cleanup(); quit;}
```

```
if (allDone) {
    cleanup();
    quit;
}
```

The `do-while`, `for-in`, and `if-else` statements contain two keywords. In a `do-while` or `if-else` statement, the second keyword follows the body. (Note that the "else" in the `if-else` construction is optional.) In the case of `for-in`, the second keyword is in the control construct.

Table 20.4, which lists keywords used in statements, shows each of these formats.

The keyword and the control construct together make up the *header* of the control block.

The following example displays numbers from 0 to 49:

```
for (var i:Number = 0; i < 50; i++) {
    trace(i);
}
```

Here, `for` is the keyword, `(i = 0; i < 50; i++)` is the control construct, and `trace(i);` is the single statement in the body. Therefore, `for (i = 0; i < 50; i++)` is the header.

20

TABLE 20.4   THE ACTIONSCRIPT STATEMENT KEYWORDS

Keyword(s)	Format	Description	Flow Control
break	break;	Cancel the current loop	loop
call	call(*frame*);	Execute the script on another frame	call

continues

TABLE 20.4   CONTINUED

Keyword(s)	Format	Description	Flow Control

class (*)	class *className*
	{
	// class definition here
	}
		Declare a static AS2 class	call

continue	continue;	Restart the current loop	loop
do-while	do { *statements* } while (*expression*);	Repeat statements while *expression* is true	loop
none (empty statement)	;	Hold a place for a statement	default

for	for (*init*; *test*; *next*) {
	    statements
	}
		Repeat statements while *test* is false	loop

for-in	for (*property* in *object*) {
	    statements
	}
		Enumerate properties of *object*	loop

function	function *name* (*parameters*) {
	    statements
	}
		Declare a function	call

	function *name*
	    (*parameters*):*Datatype* {
	    statements
	}
		Declare a function with a return type	call

if/else – if/else	if (*condition1*) {
	    statements
	} else if (*condition2*) {
	    statements
	} else {
	    statements
	}
		Execute statements based on one or more conditions	conditional

ifFrameLoaded	ifFrameLoaded (*frame*) {
	    statements
	}
		Execute statements if *frame* has been loaded (deprecated)	conditional

import (*)	import *className*; import *packageName*;	Make an AS2 class *or* group of classes (package) referencable by class name alone (no path required)	call

20

Keyword(s) Control	Format	Description	Flow
return	return; return *expression*;	Exit a function Return a value from a function	call
set	set (*variable*, *value*);	Assign a *value* to a dynamically named *variable*	default

switch/case/default	switch(*expression*) {
	case *value* : *block*
	default : *block*
	}
		Execute
		statement(s)
		starting with
		block where *value*
		matches *expression*
		(if no match,
		execute *default*)
			conditional

try/catch/finally	try {
	  statement(s)
	  if (*errorCondition*) {
	    throw new Error (*error*)
	  }
	} catch(*error*) {
	  error handling: block
	} finally {
	  statement(s)
	}
		In FP7, execute
		statement(s).
		If *errorCondition*
		occurs, execute
		catch block with
		error object/text
		parameter.
		With or without
		error, execute
		finally block.
			conditional

var	var *variableName*; var *variableName:Datatype*; var *variableName:Datatype* = *expression*;	Declare a variable, optional datatype, and optional value	default

while	while (*expression*) {
	  statements
	}
		Repeat statements
		while *expression*
		is true
			loop

with	with (*objectName*) {
	  statements
	}
		Execute statements
		in the context
		of a given object
			loop

(*) Covered in Chapter 21. Require Flash Player 6 or greater. The class *statement has other optional formats.*

UNDERSTANDING PROGRAM FLOW CONTROL

By default, the ActionScript interpreter executes statements sequentially, from top to bottom. However, most statements can change the default program flow. The exceptions are the empty statement, set, and var, which don't affect program flow.

The three basic types of flow control in ActionScript are *call*, *conditional*, and *loop*.

> **NOTE**
>
> The *call* paradigm of flow control is represented by function calls, including function calls within classes, and by the deprecated call statement. In this paradigm, the call interrupts the interpreter's sequential processing. The interpreter executes a block of code elsewhere in the program and then returns and continues processing at the point where it left off.

> **NOTE**
>
> System events also execute in a definite order in relation to the Main Timeline and the timelines of any child movie clips. For more on this topic, see timelineExecution.htm on the CD accompanying this book.

Conditional and *loop* flow control are the focus of the next section.

MAKING DECISIONS WITH CONDITIONALS AND switch

When the ActionScript interpreter encounters a conditional statement, it evaluates a condition in the control structure and, if the condition is true, executes the statements in the body.

There are two types of conditional statements: if-else and the deprecated ifFrameLoaded. if-else can be broken down into simple if statements and if-else statements.

THE if STATEMENT

The simplest conditional is an if statement. The syntax is straightforward:

```
if (expression) {
    statement1;
    statement2;
}
```

If *expression* resolves to a Boolean true, the statements in the body are executed. Otherwise, they are not executed.

Note that any array, object, or movie clip evaluates to true. Therefore, you can use an if statement to test for the existence (or nonexistence) of an array, object, or movie clip. For instance:

```
// if array exists, set variable len to length of array
if (myArray) {
```

20

```
    len = myArray.length;
}
```

THE if-else STATEMENT

An if-else statement is actually two separate but related statements: An if statement tells the interpreter what to do if the expression is true, and an else statement tells the interpreter what to do if the expression is false. For instance, in the following example, if the array myArray already exists, the program sets the variable newArray to false. If the array does not exist, the program creates the array first and then sets newArray to true.

```
if (myArray) {
    newArray = false;
} else {
    myArray = new Array();
    newArray = true;
}
```

"MULTIPLE-CHOICE" CONDITIONALS

You can test for a number of different conditions sequentially, by using multiple "else-if" clauses. For instance:

```
if (day == "Monday") {
    trace("is fair of face");
} else if (day == "Tuesday") {
    trace("is full of grace");
} else if (day == "Wednesday") {
    trace("is full of woe");
}
```

To make the last trace action a default, substitute the following for the last three lines:

```
} else trace("is full of woe");
```

THE switch/case STATEMENT

In the previous example, each conditional statement uses the variable day in an equality test. This type of conditional logic can also be expressed using a switch statement, like this:

```
switch (day) {
    case "Monday":
        trace("is fair of face");
        break;
    case "Tuesday":
        trace("is full of grace");
        break;
    case "Wednesday":
        trace("is full of woe");
}
```

20

The interpreter tests the same expression (in this case, the variable day) against each of a series of expressions (in this case, the string literals "Monday", "Tuesday", and "Wednesday"). When it finds a match, it starts executing statements, beginning with the statement following the matched value.

If the interpreter does not find a match, it looks for a `default` statement. For instance, to make the last `trace` action the default, substitute the following for the last three lines:

```
default:
    trace("is full of woe");
}
```

The `default` statement does not have to be the last statement in the `switch` body, though it almost always is.

Unlike the "multiple-choice" conditionals in the previous section, the `switch` statement uses strict equality (`===`) in comparing values. This means `switch` does not convert datatypes when making a comparison. To be considered equal, the operands must be of the same datatype to begin with.

Both the test value (`day`) and the `case` values (`"Monday"`, `"Tuesday"`, and `"Wednesday"`) can be any valid expressions, as long as each one resolves to a single value. However, the values are usually just string or numeric literals.

Note the `break` statement in each case. Each `case` statement specifies a beginning point for code execution. It does *not* specify any ending point. The `break` statements cause the interpreter to exit the `switch` statement after executing the statements associated with a single case. If multiple cases are executing one after another, you may have omitted `break` statements.

→ If a `case` statement isn't executing as expected, **see** the "Troubleshooting" section at the end of this chapter, **page 535**.

THE `try/catch/finally` STATEMENT

The `try/catch/finally` statement, which requires Flash Player 7, provides a standard framework for testing for and responding to errors. It consists of three blocks of code:

- In the `try` block, you attempt to do something and then test for an error condition. If an error occurs, you use the `throw` keyword to generate an error call. The `throw` call passes an argument, which is often just a text string, but can be any ActionScript object.

- The `catch` block automatically receives the call made in the `throw` block, including the passed parameter. Within the `catch` block, you respond to the error.

- The `finally` block executes whether or not an error occurs.

In the following fully functional example (tryCatch.fla on the CD), the `getCustomerInfo()` function (line 1) simulates an error condition by returning 1. Within the `try` block, line 4 tests for an error return (any return to other than 0). The `throw` statement on line 5 passes a text string, which is "caught" on line 7, in this case just displaying the text string in the Output window.

```
1:  function getCustomerInfo() { return (1); }
2:  try {
3:    var returnVal = getCustomerInfo();
4:    if(returnVal != 0) {
```

```
5:      throw new Error("Error getting Customer information.");
6:    }
7:  } catch (e) {
8:    trace(e); // error processing goes here
9:  }
10: finally {trace("finally")}; // "clean-up" or other final actions
```

If a function returns specific error codes (say 1, 2, and 3), you can have a `switch` statement or multiple `if` statements in the `try` block, testing for specific error returns and passing a different parameter, depending on which error has occurred.

THE ifFrameLoaded STATEMENT

The `ifFrameLoaded` statement is deprecated (supported for now but not forever), but it is still popular. The `ifFrameLoaded` statement offers compatibility with Flash 3. The recommended substitute, `_framesLoaded`, requires at least Flash 4.

The `ifFrameLoaded` statement is a special case of the `if` statement, which checks whether a specific frame (optionally in a specific scene) has loaded yet. It is used to make preloaders for movie clips.

For instance, if you put the following code on the first two frames of a movie clip, the clip loops through the first two frames until frame 60 has loaded. Then it will start playing from frame 5.

```
//frame1:
ifFrameLoaded (60) {
    gotoAndPlay (5);
}
//frame2:
gotoAndPlay (1);
```

The recommended substitute for `ifFrameLoaded (60)` is the `framesLoaded` property of the movie clip:

```
if (_framesLoaded == 60)
```

With `ifFrameLoaded`, you can also include a scene name:

```
ifFrameLoaded ("intro", 60) {
```

One limitation of `ifFrameLoaded` is that it does not support an `else` statement (whereas `_framesLoaded` does). The two-frame structure uses a two-frame loop to mimic an `else` clause.

USING LOOPS TO REPEAT ACTIONS

The loop statements, `while`, `do-while`, `for`, and `for-in`, are used to perform repetitive actions. Each repeatedly evaluates a condition and uses the result of the evaluation to decide whether to continue looping through the body. For example, a loop could be used to repetitively check whether a certain amount of time has elapsed, or to repetitively duplicate a movie clip until a certain number of clips has been created.

20

The four loop statements are closely related. The while and for statements are basically two ways of doing the same thing: Which you use is often a matter of taste. The Flash compiler translates both into while loops in the SWF. And do-while is just a minor variation of while.

THE while STATEMENT

The while statement is the basic statement for performing repetitive actions. The format for the while statement is

```
while ( expression ) {
    statement1;
    statement2;
    statement3;
}
```

The interpreter loops through the statements as long as the expression is true, unless it encounters a break statement, in which case it exits the loop. For instance, the following while loop puts a half-second (500 millisecond) delay into the program. It is based on the fact that elapsed time is the current time (obtained using getTimer()) minus the initial time:

```
initialTime = getTimer();
while (elapsedTime < 500) {
    elapsedTime = getTimer() - initialTime;
}
```

It is common to implement a while statement with a counter (i in the following example), which is initialized before the while loop and incremented within the while loop, until it reaches the count (500 in this case) defined in the control block:

```
var i:Number = 0;
while (i < 500) {
    i++;
    // do something 500 times
}
```

THE do-while STATEMENT

The body of a while loop does not execute even once if the condition is false from the beginning. To make the while loop execute at least once, use the do-while statement. For example:

```
do {
    statement1;
    statement2;
    statement3;
} while (expression);
```

→ Looping statements present the danger of infinite loops, if *expression* remains true forever. For an example of an infinite loop, **see** infiniteLoop.htm and recursion.htm on the CD accompanying this book.

THE for STATEMENT

A while loop can have a counter that is initialized and updated. The for statement makes initialization and updating part of the parenthesized control structure. The format of the for statement is as follows:

```
for (initialization; condition; update) {
    statement1;
    statement2;
    statement3;
}
```

For instance, the following is the most recent while shown previously, put into the form of a for loop:

```
for (var i:Number = 0; i < 500; i++) {
    // do something 500 times
}
```

Whether you use the while loop or the for loop is a matter of taste. The for loop is more concise. Its structure also reminds you to include the increment. Leaving the increment out of a while loop is a common error that leads to an infinite loop. On the other hand, the while loop allows you to comment the initialization, condition, and increment expressions separately.

THE for-in STATEMENT

The for-in statement enumerates or lists the properties of an object. It can be extremely useful for investigating existing objects that you did not define, such as built-in objects or objects associated with components. Its format is as follows:

```
for (variable in objectName) {
    statement1;
    statement2;
}
```

The variable name in the control structure is an arbitrary name that you pick, such as prop in this example. As the for-in statement loops, it contains the name of each property in succession (title, author, and language in the example).

```
myBook = {
 title : "Huckleberry Finn",
 author : "Mark Twain",
 language : "English"}; //create object, myBook
for (prop in myBook) {
     trace(prop+" : "+myBook[prop]);
}
```

This will display, on three lines, title : Huckleberry Finn, author : Mark Twain, language : English.

Note that the variable in the control structure contains the *name* of the property, not the *value* of the property. You can easily access the value when you have the name. For instance:

```
trace(myBook.title); // "Huckleberry Finn"
```

myBook["title"] is another way of expressing myBook.title. In a the example, myBook[prop] is equivalent first to myBook["title"], then to myBook["author"], and finally to myBook["language"].

→ **See** "The Object Class," **page 572,** "The PrintJob Class," **page 600,** and "Other Handy Flash CSS Features," **page 611**, in Chapter 21, for more examples that use the for-in statement.

COMBINING STATEMENTS INTO FUNCTIONS

A *function* is an entire block of code that you can call, or invoke, from anywhere in a program. Calling the function causes the code in the function to execute. You can call a function using its name, if it has one. You can also call functions via variables, array elements, or object properties. All these ways of referring to a function are much more concise than the body of the function itself. These ways of referring to functions give you short, convenient "handles" for potentially complex behaviors.

Functions make it much easier to maintain programs. For instance, suppose you create a displayError() function to display error messages. If you ever want to change your error display function, you can make the change in only one place, in the displayError() function declaration. If instead you repeat a block of code multiple times, you have to edit each duplicate block individually.

Functions greatly improve both readability and reusability. They also make SWF files smaller by substituting a short function call for a longer repeated block of code. In addition, object-oriented programming (OOP) is founded on functions.

→ For an introduction to functions, readability, reusability, and OOP, **see** Chapter 19, "Introduction to ActionScript," **page 441**.

FUNCTION BASICS: CREATING FUNCTIONS

There are two basics in using a function: creating it and calling it.

You can create a function in one of two ways, depending on whether or not you want it to have a permanent name of its own:

■ To create a function with its own permanent name, you *declare* the function.

■ To create a function with no permanent name of its own, you create a *function literal*. A function literal must be stored in a variable, an array element, or an object property to be referenceable.

DECLARING FUNCTIONS

When you declare a function, you permanently associate a function name with a block of code. The basic format for declaring a function is

```
function identifier(list):datatype {
    statement1;
    statement2;
}
```

where function is a keyword, *identifier* is the name of the function, *list* is an optional comma-separated list of *arguments* passed to the function, *datatype* is the data type of the value returned by the function, and *statement1* and *statement2* represent a series of ActionScript statements. The series can contain any number of statements.

The datatype is optional. If included, it applies strict data typing to the value returned by the function. You will get an error when you publish or test your program if the function returns a value of a different type than the declared datatype.

→ The name of the function must be a valid identifier, formed according to the rules set forth in "Rules for Naming Variables (and Other Things)" earlier in this chapter, **page 462**.

Use Void to type a function that doesn't return anything. For instance, here is a declaration of a function with no arguments and no return value:

```
function displayError():Void {
    errorText = "Error!";
    // error handling code
}
```

The idea is that this function updates a timeline variable that is displayed in a text field, notifying the user of an error.

USING FUNCTIONS WITHOUT NAMES: FUNCTION LITERALS

A literal is an expression that represents a datum *literally*, as opposed to *abstractly*. It embodies the datum rather than naming it. A function literal is a function that you write out without giving it a name. Here's an example of a function literal:

```
function () {
    errorText = "Error!";
    // error handling code
}
```

It looks just a like a function declaration with no name.

As with other literals, you need to store the function literal somewhere as soon as it's created, or it will be lost. You can store function literals in variables, for instance:

```
displayError = function () {
    trace("Error!");
};
```

In addition, you can store function literals as properties of objects:

```
myObj = {prop1 : function(){trace("prop1");} ,
         prop2 : function(){trace("prop2");} };
```

The following is another way of accomplishing the same thing. The first line creates an empty object. The second and third lines add properties to it. Each property refers to a function.

```
myObj = {}; // create empty object
myObj.prop1 = function(){trace("prop1");};
myObj.prop2 = function(){trace("prop2");};
```

The following example assigns the same functions as properties of an array:

```
myArray = []; // create empty array
myArray[0] = function(){trace("prop1");};
myArray[1] = function(){trace("prop2");};
```

20

CALLING FUNCTIONS

Declaring a function doesn't actually make anything happen in the program. To do that, you need to *call* or run the function. You call a function by using the function call operator, which is a pair of parentheses: (). The syntax for calling a function is straightforward:

```
identifier(list);
```

Here, `identifier` is the name of the function, and `list` is an optional comma-separated list of arguments.

Many ActionScript "actions" are built-in functions that you can call without declaring them. For example, `nextFrame()` is a built-in function that sends the playhead to the next frame and stops it. If a function has no arguments, the parentheses are left empty. Adding a semicolon completes the statement, as shown here:

```
nextFrame();
```

You call custom functions (ones that you have created) in exactly the same way:

```
displayError(); // invokes displayError() function
```

USING var TO CREATE LOCAL FUNCTION VARIABLES

Most functions contain one or more variables used only within the function. For instance, suppose you're writing a function, `greet()`, that returns one of three greetings ("good morning," "good afternoon," or "good evening") depending on the time of day. To determine the time in ActionScript, you create both a `Date` object (such as `myDate`) and a variable to hold the time (such as `hours`). You want to use `myDate` and `hours` only within the `greet()` function, but you may want to use those *names* again elsewhere in the program to refer to different objects or variables. Looking to the future, you also want to be able to drop this function into other programs and know that it will not cause a "name conflict" by using a name that is already in use in that program and therefore affect the items (such as variables or objects) in the other program with which it now inadvertently shares the name.

In a situation like this, you can use the var keyword to declare a *local* variable within a function. A local variable is available only within the function. A local variable does not change or refer to a variable of the same name outside the function. For instance:

```
function greet():String {
    var hours:Number;
    var myDate:Date;
    // code to get the time and return greeting
    // all uses of hours and myDate remain local to the function
}
```

In the following example, the trace (`myVar`) statement displays the local variable, not the timeline variable of the same name:

```
var myVar:String = "timeline";
function myFunc():Void {
    var myVar:String = "local";
    trace (myVar); // "local"
}
```

If you change var `myVar:String = "local"` to `myVar = "local"` the statement in the function *refers to and changes* the timeline variable of the same name! If you have a variable that you want to use just within a function, always declare it with var. Declaring it this way prevents you from inadvertently changing a timeline variable of the same name.

→ Arguments are also treated as local variables. Arguments are discussed later in this chapter, in the "Passing Information to Functions in Arguments" section below.

THE var KEYWORD DOESN'T WORK OUTSIDE FUNCTIONS

Anywhere on a timeline other than inside a function, the var keyword has no effect. This includes event handlers! You can use var in an event handler, but it doesn't change anything. For instance, if you create a variable in a load event handler, as shown in the following example, it *can* change and be changed by statements on the movie clip timeline, in other event handlers, or on associated buttons:

```
onClipEvent(load) {
    var c = 10; // the "var" doesn't change anything
}
```

ACCESSING TIMELINE VARIABLES WITHIN A FUNCTION

If you have a function on a timeline, and you use var to create a local variable within the function, you can refer to a timeline variable of the same name by using the this keyword. Here, this refers to the current timeline. Variables created within the timeline are properties of that timeline, and therefore can be referenced using the dot operator. For example:

```
myVar = "timeline";
function myFunc() {
    var myVar = "local";
    trace  (myVar); // "local"
    trace (this.myVar); // "timeline"
}
```

PASSING INFORMATION TO FUNCTIONS IN ARGUMENTS

The displayError() function in the "Calling Functions" section earlier in this chapter can display only one message: "Error!". Suppose you want to give the user more specific information about the error. You can do that, without creating a separate function for each error, by passing an *argument* to the displayError() function. In the following example, the argument is named arg. The arg parameter exists in memory only for the duration of the function. When the function terminates, arg disappears. It has completed its task in changing the errorText variable.

```
function displayError(arg) {
    var errorText:String = arg;
    // error handling code
}
```

Then you can call the function for different errors, like this:

```
displayError("Error: required field, cannot be left blank");
displayError("Error: password must be 8 or more characters");
displayError("Error: invalid zip code");
```

20

Adding arguments like this makes `displayError()` much more flexible and useful. In addition, it makes the function more reusable. For instance, you could easily plug in different error messages for a different program.

Note that declaring arguments does not limit the number of arguments that you can pass to a function. However, only arguments that are declared can be referred to within the function by name. You can access other arguments via the `arguments` object, as described in the section after next.

PASSING ARGUMENTS BY VALUE AND BY REFERENCE

When a primitive datum is passed to a function as an argument, it is passed *by value*. That is, the interpreter allocates a new space in memory and copies the value of the datum into it. The function never sees the original datum, only the copy. If you change the copy within the function, the original is not affected.

On the other hand, composite data types (objects, arrays, functions) are passed *by reference*. That is, the interpreter creates a pointer to the original item and passes it to the function. Any changes made within the function *do* affect the original.

THE `arguments` OBJECT

When a function is invoked, it automatically gets a property named `arguments`, which is an array (or, in Macromedia Flash 5, an array-like object), with elements that can be accessed via numeric indices (starting with 0), and a `length` property specifying the number of array elements.

Each time a function is called, `arguments` is created and populated with all the arguments passed to the function. In addition, `arguments.length` is set to the number of arguments.

In Flash Player 5 and earlier, array methods such as `push()` and `pop()` do not work with the `arguments` property. In the Flash 6 Player and later, `arguments` is a real array with all the associated methods. In addition, the `arguments.callee` property shows up in a `for-in` loop in the Flash 5 Player, but not in the Flash Player 6 and later.

The `arguments` property is available only inside the function, while the function is executing. It can be referred to simply as `arguments`. Alternatively, it can be preceded by the function name—for instance, `myFunc.arguments`.

In the following function, `myFunc()`, the `trace(arg1)` statement and the `trace(arguments[0])` statement do exactly the same thing, namely, display the value of the first (and only) argument:

```
function myFunc(arg1) {
    trace(arg1); // displays "this is the argument"
    trace(arguments[0]); // displays "this is the argument"
}
myFunc("this is the argument");
```

The arguments object has three properties:

- length—The length of the arguments array
- callee—The function that is currently executing
- caller—The function that called the currently executing function

NOTE

arguments.caller is available only in the Flash 6 Player and later, not the Flash 5 Player.

The preceding are *properties* of the object, not *elements* of the array. These three properties are present even if the arguments array has no elements—that is, even if no arguments are passed.

USING THE arguments.length PROPERTY

One use of the arguments.length property is to accommodate a variable number of arguments. For instance, the following avg() function returns the average of any number of arguments. The arguments array and the arguments.length property allow the avg() function to cope with a variable number of arguments:

```
function avg():Number {
    var sum:Number = 0;
    // add up all the arguments
    for(var i:Number = 0; i < arguments.length; i++) {
        sum = sum + arguments[i];
    }
    // divide the sum by the number of arguments -- that's the average
    var average:Number = sum/arguments.length;
    return average;
}
trace("Average = " + avg(2,4,6)); // display "Average = 4"
trace("Average = " + avg(10,20,30,40,50)); // display "Average = 30"
```

USING THE callee PROPERTY

The arguments.callee property gives you a way of calling a function from within the function, without using the function name. One use of arguments.callee is to make code more generic so that you can cut and paste more easily within and between programs.

With ordinary, named functions, using arguments.callee to create generic code is just a convenience. Each function has a fixed name, and you can always use it. In contrast, an anonymous function created by a function literal has no fixed name. At any given moment, it may be assigned to a particular variable, array element, or object property. But that assignment could change. In this case, using arguments.callee to create generic code is a safety measure—it insures that your reference to the function will continue to work, no matter what the function's current name is.

→ For an example of the type of problem that arguments.callee can prevent, **see** callee.htm on the CD accompanying this book.

20

Using the `caller` Property

The `caller` property gives you a way to call the function that called the currently executing function. For instance:

```
function calleeFunc() {
    arguments.caller(); // call the caller back
}
```

In using `arguments.caller`, be sure that the caller will not call the callee right back, creating an infinite loop.

Using Return Values to Retrieve Results

Sometimes, you want a function not only to perform a task but also to return a value to you. For instance, if you write a function to double numbers, you don't just want it to double the numbers; you want it to pass the doubled numbers back to you so that you can do something with them. Functions supply return values in a `return` statement. A `return` statement with a return *value* returns that value to the caller, as in the following example, in which a function returns twice the value passed to it:

```
function doubleIt(numberToBeDoubled:Number):Number {
    return numberToBeDoubled * 2;
}
```

Notice that strict data typing is used twice in the preceding function declaration: The first `Number` says that the argument has to be a number. The second `Number` says that the function must return a number.

A function does not need to have a `return` statement. If it doesn't have one, the function will just execute its statements sequentially, top to bottom, and terminate when it comes to the final curly brace. A `return` statement terminates the function immediately on the line that contains the return statement. A `return` statement with no return value returns `undefined`.

 Does part of your function seem "disabled"? Perhaps you're suffering from a premature `return` *statement.* ***See*** *the "Troubleshooting" section at the end of this chapter,* ***page 535***.

There are two ways to use a return value:

- Assign the return value to a variable and use the variable in some way.
- Use the function call itself as an expression.

For example, using the `doubleIt()` function, this is an example of the first approach:

```
twicefour = doubleIt(4);
trace(twicefour); // displays 8
```

And this is an example of the second approach:

```
trace(doubleIt(4)); // displays 8
```

Both examples accomplish the same task. The second approach is half the size of the first, both in the source code and in the SWF. However, the second approach does not create a variable that you can continue to use. The first approach does.

Not getting the return you expect? **See** *the "Troubleshooting" section at the end of this chapter,* **page 535**.

FUNCTIONS AS CLASSES: CONSTRUCTOR FUNCTIONS

ActionScript 1 uses *constructor functions* as its only embodiment of classes. ActionScript 1 uses the constructor function, in combination with the new operator, to create new objects belonging to a class. This is no longer recommended. If you are going to be creating classes with Flash MX 2004, use the ActionScript 2 approach.

→ If you need to use the ActionScript 1 approach to creating classes (for compatibility with Flash Player 5, for instance), **see** functionsAsClasses.htm on the CD accompanying this book. You may also want to consult *Special Edition Using Flash MX*, published by Que in 2003.

→ For more on ActionScript 2 methods of creating classes, **see** "ActionScript 2.0: Real Class," **page 540,** in Chapter 21.

USING Function.apply() AND Function.call()

The apply() and call() methods, which are defined for all functions, enable you to call a function or method as if it were a method of any designated object. You specify the object as the first argument of the apply() or call() method. Inside the called function, the this keyword refers to the designated object.

Without the apply() and call() methods, when you call a function or method, you're stuck with a default value for this. For example, if you call a method, this refers to the object to which the method belongs. If you call a function on a timeline, this refers to the timeline.

→ For more details on this, **see** "Explicit Scoping with the this Keyword," later in this chapter, **page 495**.

With apply() and call(), you can make this refer to any object you want.

You can also pass any number of parameters to the called function. The only difference between apply() and call() is that apply() passes parameters in an array, whereas call() passes a comma-delimited list.

The format looks like this:

```
myFunction.apply(myObject, myArray);
myFunction.call(myObject, myArg1, myArg2, myArg3);
```

The apply() or call() method receives whatever return value the function normally returns.

If the first argument is null, the default value of this is used. In this case, apply() and call() behave like normal function calls, except that apply() passes its parameters in an array.

You can also set the second argument to null, to show that you're deliberately not passing any parameters. This technique has the same effect as omitting the second argument completely.

20

The apply() method does not support *associative arrays* (arrays indexed by names rather than numbers) as its second argument. The named properties of the associative array are lost, and the called function receives only numerically indexed elements.

→ For more information on associative arrays, **see** "Named Array Elements: Associative Arrays," **page 561**, in Chapter 21, "Advanced ActionScript."

You can use the arguments property of a function as the second argument of apply(). For instance, the following example first calls the myHandler() function with two arguments: 1 and 2. The myHandler() function, in turn, calls the myDelegate() function. The myHandler() function "forwards" its arguments by using its arguments property as the second argument of the apply() method.

Notice how the return value returns from myDelegate() to myHandler() and then back to the original call.

The this keyword in myDelegate() refers to the timeline because the first argument of the apply() method was null. Thus, in the final trace action, p0 and p1 show up as ordinary timeline variables.

```
function myDelegate ():Boolean {
    this.p0 = arguments[0];
    this.p1 = arguments[1];
    return true;
}

function myHandler():Boolean {
    ret = myDelegate.apply (null, arguments); // "forwarding" arguments
    return ret;
}

result = myHandler(1,2);
trace (result); // true
trace (p0 + " " + p1); // 1 2
```

EXPLICIT SCOPING

Scoping is telling the ActionScript interpreter where to look for a variable, movie clip, object, or array. The interpreter can look in a *class*, in a *function*, in an *object*, in a *timeline*, in the Object object, or in _global. You can tell it specifically where to look, and then it looks in just that one place. That is *explicit* scoping, the subject of this section. Or you may deliberately *not* tell the interpreter where to look, and then it follows its own automatic scoping rules. That type of scoping is covered next, in the "Automatic Scoping" section.

Scope is like a sophisticated filing system. You can use it both to find things and to keep things private. Unfortunately, misfiling is also possible: Subtle bugs can result when the ActionScript interpreter is unable to find something or finds the wrong thing.

NOTE

In this section, *timeline* or *movie clip* means a movie clip timeline and any attached event handlers and buttons.

20

One way to avoid this type of problem is to use explicit scoping to tell the ActionScript interpreter exactly where to look. With explicit scoping, you use dot syntax (or deprecated *slash* syntax) to tell the ActionScript interpreter where to look for the data item that you're referencing. For instance:

```
_root.myClip.myFunc(); // tells interpreter to look in a movie clip "myClip"
_global.myVar = 10; // look in _global
```

THE LIMITATIONS OF HARD-CODING

Using the name of a class, movie clip, function, object, or the _global identifier to specify the *path* (location) of a datum, as in the previous examples, is an example of *hard-coding*. Though clear and often easy to use, hard-coded paths make code less reusable. In the root.myClip.myFunc(); example, for instance, if you want to use the myFunc() function in another project but need to use it somewhere other than a movie clip named myClip in _root, you need to do some recoding. The same holds true in the second example, if you want to reuse myVar but don't want it to be a global variable.

You may be able to avoid hard-coding by using *relative references* or by using the this keyword. Another possibility is to use automatic rather than explicit scoping.

EXPLICIT SCOPING WITH RELATIVE REFERENCES

When you're scoping to a movie clip, a common way of making code more reusable is to use *relative references*. That is, use the _parent property of the current movie clip to indicate the movie clip to look in. For instance:

```
_parent.myFunc(); // look in the parent of the clip this appears in
_parent._parent.myFunc(); // look in the "grandparent" of this clip
```

Suppose, for example, myFunc() is in a movie clip named mc1 on the main timeline, making the *absolute* path of the clip _root.mc1. (Any path that begins with _root is called an "absolute path," because it gives you the location of the movie clip starting from the Main Timeline, not relative to any other movie clip.) Now, if you want to reference myFunc() from a child clip—say, _root.mc1.mc2—you can use _parent.myFunc(). In a grandchild clip—say, _root.mc1.mc2.mc3—you can use _parent._parent.myFunc(). Later, if you use this code with movie clips myClip1, myClip2, and myClip3, nothing about the code needs to change to accommodate the different instance names of the movie clips.

20

EXPLICIT SCOPING WITH THE this KEYWORD

The third type of explicit scoping uses the this keyword. With one major exception, this refers to the movie clip where the statement is located. The next section gives some examples of the general rule. The section after that covers the exception.

In a timeline (including attached event handlers and buttons), this usually refers to the timeline. You can use the this keyword in movie clips to get the ActionScript interpreter to recognize that you're invoking a MovieClip method, as opposed to the global function of the same name. For instance, if you put this code on a timeline, the ActionScript interpreter thinks you're invoking the global `duplicateMovieClip()` function, which requires three parameters. Because there are only two parameters here, you get an error:

```
duplicateMovieClip("myClip",1); // ERROR!!!
```

By inserting the `this` keyword, you invoke the `MovieClip` method, which requires only two parameters, and all is well:

```
this.duplicateMovieClip("myClip",1); // no problem
```

The following example shows three uses of `this` on a timeline, each of which causes a variable to scope to the timeline:

- The variable is in a property of an object on the timeline.
- The variable is referenced inside a function.
- The variable is referenced in the movie clip directly.

The three `trace` statements at the end prove that the interpreter sees `this` as the timeline in each case. If `c` equals `300`, you can conclude that the statement is "seeing" a and b on the timeline. If it were seeing the a and b properties in the `myObj` object, for example, `c` would equal 3, not `300`.

```
a = 100; // variable declared on movie clip timeline
b = 200; // variable declared on movie clip timeline
c = a + b; // variable declared on movie clip timeline
myObj = {a : 1, b : 2, c : this.a + this.b} // #1 "this" in a property
function myFunc() {
     trace(this.c); // #2 this in a function
}
trace(this.c); // # 3 this on the timeline - displays 300
trace(myObj.c); // displays 300 - in an object
myFunc(); // displays 300 - in a function
```

The variable scopes to the timeline that it is on, even if it is used inside an object or function. Perhaps surprisingly, the interpreter does *not* check within the object first for properties that match the referenced name.

EXCEPTION: SCOPING TO THE OBJECT

In the previous section, you saw that, in most situations, if you see `this` as the path of a variable on a timeline, `this` means the timeline. There is one notable exception—namely that *within a method of an object*, `this` scopes to the object.

Other than that, the scoping rules for functions are the same as for variables. That is, on a timeline (or associated event handlers and buttons), or within a function on the timeline, `this.myFunc()` scopes to the timeline.

The following example does basically the same thing as the previous example, using functions instead of variables. The four function calls at the end (lines 10–13) tell the story. The first one shows that when you reference `this.a()` on the timeline, the interpreter looks for a() on the timeline. Similarly, when you reference a() within b(), as in the function invoked on line 11, the interpreter looks for a() on the timeline. The third function call (line 12) shows that invoking this.a() from within a function, myFunc(), on the timeline, doesn't change anything: The interpreter still looks for a() on the timeline. The final function call, however, shows that when you say this.a() within a method, the interpreter looks for a() in the object the method belongs to.

```
1: function a () {trace ("function a");}
2: function b () {this.a();} // "this" scopes to timeline here
3: myObj = {
4:      a : function () {trace ("object function a");},
5:      b : function () {this.a();} // this scopes to the object!
6: };
7: function myFunc() {
8:      this.a(); // "this" scopes to timeline here
9: }

10: this.a(); // displays "function a" - "this" scopes to timeline here
11: b();// displays "function a"
12: myFunc(); // displays "function a"
13: myObj.b(); // displays "object function a"
```

FUNCTION ALIASES RETAIN THEIR OWN SCOPE

If you set a variable equal to a function or method, the variable maintains its own scope as a variable. It does *not* adopt the scope of the function or method. Therefore, a variable that is supposedly "equal to" a function may behave very differently from the function, because of its different scope. For instance, in the following example, the variable myAliasFunc is set equal to the function myObj.myFunc. Executing myObj.myFunc() displays prop1 correctly because it uses the method, which scopes to the object. However, executing myAliasFunc() displays undefined (or, in Flash 5, a blank line) because myAliasFunc scopes to the timeline, where there is no such variable as prop1.

```
myObj = new Object();
myObj.myFunc = function () {
  trace(this.prop1);
}
myObj.prop1 = 1;
myAliasFunc = myObj.myFunc;
myObj.myFunc(); // displays "1"
myAliasFunc (); // undefined, this.prop1 is undefined in the timeline
```

AUTOMATIC SCOPING

With automatic scoping, you simply make a direct reference to the variable, function, object, or array, with no dot syntax. You let the ActionScript interpreter scope your datum automatically.

For example, this is a direct reference:

```
myFunc(); // does not tell the interpreter where to look for myFunc()
```

In this case, the interpreter starts its search wherever you make the data reference. From there, it may search in movie clip timelines (including associated event handlers and buttons), functions, or objects, including inheritance chains. As a last resort, it looks in _global.

By default, ActionScript *scope chains* are very simple. The scope chain is the list of objects to be searched. Unless you create a more complicated structure by using the object-oriented programming (OOP) techniques, the scope chain is usually global-Object-timeline or _global-Object-timeline-function. The interpreter searches these chains from right to left—for instance, the function first, then the timeline, then Object, and finally the _global object.

Longer chains do occur, such as _global-Object-timeline-outer function-inner function, in which the inner function is declared within the outer function.

You temporarily lengthen the scope chain when you use the with statement, which tacks on another object at the lowest level of the scope chain. That tacked-on object (the object in the with statement) is always checked first within the with statement. It is removed from the scope chain when the with statement terminates.

The following three examples show a starting point (where the variable or function is declared) and the typical resulting scope chain:

- Start on a *timeline* (or attached event handler or button).

  Example:

  ```
  myFunc; // on a timeline
  ```

  Scope chain: _global-Object-timeline.

  Note: The scope chain does not include other timelines.

- Start in an *object property* or *array element* on a timeline.

  In this example, the myVar variable is declared on the timeline and referenced as the myObj.myProp1 property. That property is then displayed in two ways: using a method of the object, myMethod(), defined on line 4 and called on line 5; and using a trace statement on the timeline, on line 6.

  ```
  1: myVar = "main";
  2: myObj = { myVar : "myVarObj",
  3:           myProp1 : myVar,
  4:           myMethod : function () {trace(this.myProp1);}};
  5: myObj.myMethod(); // displays "main"
  6: trace(myObj.myProp1); // displays "main"
  ```

  Scope chain: _global-Object-timeline.

  Note 1: If the value of myProp1 on line 3 is this.myVar (note the added this), the scope chain is still _global-Object-timeline.

  Note 2: The scope chain does not include "sibling" properties or elements. For instance, line 2 contains a myObj.myVar property, but it is ignored.

- Start in a *function* or *method* declaration.

  In the following example, the myVar variable, after being declared on the timeline (line 1), is referenced first in a function declaration that is on the timeline (line 3) and then in a method myObj.myFunc() (line 5). (Note: myVar : 99 does not reference the timeline variable. Instead, it defines an object property of the same name.)

```
1: myVar = 10;
2: function myFunc() {
3:      trace(myVar);
4: }
5: myObj = {myVar : 99 , myFunc : function() { trace(myVar);} }
6: myFunc(); // 10
7: myObj.myFunc(); // 10
```

Scope chain: _global-Object-timeline-function.

Note: The scope chain does not include "sibling" properties. For instance, the interpreter ignores the myVar : 99 property (line 5) .

The last statement (line 7), myObj.myFunc(), works identically in Flash Player 5 and later players, assuming it is on the same timeline as the declaration of myObj above it (line 5). However, if you tried to execute the myObj.myFunc() method from another timeline, it would fail in Flash Player 5 (or display a myVar variable on the other timeline, if one existed). In Flash Player 6 and later, you can execute the myObj.myFunc() method from another timeline, and it displays the myVar variable on the timeline where myObj is defined.

For instance, suppose the preceding code is on the Main Timeline, and you have a "circle" clip on the Main Timeline with the following statements on its timeline:

```
myVar = "circle";
_parent.myObj.myFunc(); // displays "circle" in Flash 5, 10 in Flash MX
```

The second statement displays "circle" in Flash Player 5. It displays "10" in Flash Player 6 and later. In Flash Player 6 and later, a method consistently takes the scope of the timeline where it is defined, never the timeline from which it is called. (Flash Player 6 and later conform to ECMA-262 in this respect, whereas Flash Player 5 deviated from it.)

Also in Flash Player 6 and later, a function literal defined within a function takes the scope of the outer function. In Flash Player 5, it took the scope of the timeline.

In the following example, innerFunction() refers to a function literal within outerFunction(). In Flash Player 6 and later, the function literal is scoped to outerFunction() and thus has access to the parameter arg. Therefore, when the function literal is returned in line 4, it includes the argument, which is displayed when the function executes in line 5. In Flash Player 5, innerFunction() is scoped to the timeline, on which arg is undefined, so line 5 displays "Argument was: ".

```
1: function outerFunction (arg) {
2:      return innerFunction = function () {trace ("Argument was: "+arg);}
3: }
4: myFunc = outerFunction("myArg");
5: myFunc(); // in Flash MX, displays "Argument was: myArg"
```

This is an example of a five-link scope chain: _global-Object-timeline-outer function-inner function.

The following makeHandler() function shows how you can use this FP6 and later functionality to attach event handler functions to a movie clip programmatically. The makeHandler()

function returns the `name` argument in FP6 and later. In FP5, it would return `undefined` (assuming there is no `name` variable on the timeline) because the inner function would not scope to the outer function.

```
// thanks to Gary Grossman, principal engineer, Macromedia Flash team!
function makeHandler(name) {
    return function () {
      trace("Handler  "+ name +"  invoked.");
    };
  }
  function makeHandlers(mc, names) { // mc is a movie clip instance
    for (var i=0; i<names.length; i++) {
      mc[names[i]] = makeHandler(names[i]);
      mc[names[i]](); // displays "Handler  onPress  invoked." etc.
    }
  }
  makeHandlers(mc, ["onPress", "onRelease", "onReleaseOutside",
            "onRollOver", "onRollOut", "onDragOver", "onDragOut"]);
```

 See the "Troubleshooting" section, **page 535**, later in this chapter for a discussion of the possibility of timing (position on the timeline) making a variable or function inaccessible even within a single timeline.

USING EVENT HANDLERS TO TRIGGER ACTION

The Flash Player generates an event to signal that something potentially significant has happened in your program. An event is like an announcement. Some object has to be listening for the event and respond to it for it to have any effect. Many built-in objects automatically listen for certain types of events. However, they never respond automatically. You enable a response by giving the responding object an *event handler* or *callback function* for a particular event.

If an object doesn't listen for a particular type of event by default, it may be possible to *register* the object to be a *listener* for that type of event. You register the object with the designated *broadcaster* for that type of event. For the example, you can register to receive all Mouse events or all Key (keyboard) events.

Many events don't accept registrations. Either an object is a potential responder or it's not. Even if an object is a potential responder, it still needs an appropriate callback function to actually respond.

General-Purpose Event Engines
The event model discussed in this chapter allows you to listen for a limited set of events, such as key presses, mouse clicks, text field changes, and Stage resizing. However, situations may arise in which you want to listen for other events, typically associated with objects or components that you have created. A general-purpose event engine allows you to do this. For instance, the new V2 components include such an event engine, UIEventDispatcher. Another is AsBroadcaster, added in the previous version of Flash MX; it's discussed in AsBroadcaster.htm on the CD.

Let's take two examples: the user releasing the mouse button and a movie clip named myClip entering a new frame.

Objects in your movie do not automatically respond when these events occur. However, if you add an onClipEvent(enterFrame) or an onEnterFrame() event handler to myClip, the statements in the event handler are executed each time myClip enters a new frame. myClip receives or *traps* the event, using an event handler or *callback* function specific to the enterFrame event.

For instance, you can define an onEnterFrame event handler for myClip by putting this line of code in a frame on the timeline containing myClip:

```
myClip.onEnterFrame = function () {trace("just testing");};
```

The Flash Player calls your callback function every time the movie enters a new frame. In this case, it displays "just testing" in the Output window once per frame.

There is no way for any object other than a movie clip to receive this event. There is no way to register to listen for the enterFrame event.

Similarly, you can add an onMouseUp event handler to a movie clip. In that case, the event handler is called when the mouse button is released:

```
myClip.onMouseUp = function () {trace("mouse button released");};
```

In addition, any other object can create an onMouseUp callback function and then register as a listener with the Mouse object (the broadcaster) to receive this event. Registration is accomplished using the addListener() method of the Mouse object. The following three lines form a working program that creates an object named myObj, creates an onMouseUp callback function for myObj, and registers myObj to receive the onMouseUp event:

```
myObj = new Object();
myObj.onMouseUp = function() {trace("myObj received the event");};
Mouse.addListener(myObj);
```

From that point on, myObj.onMouseUp fires whenever the mouse button is released.

The names of callback functions are predetermined: They always begin with on, as in onEnterFrame. The circumstances under which they are called are also predetermined. However, it is totally up to you to decide what statements to put in the callback function. For instance, your callback function might display a new graphic when a button is pressed, rearrange items on the Stage when the Stage is resized, check the value of a variable after a movie clip containing the variable has loaded, or check the contents of a changed text field and take action based on the text.

All callback functions belong to responding objects: they are *methods* of those objects. If the object is a movie clip, button, or text field, the callback function executes only if the object is currently on the Stage.

In some cases, it's easy to describe the relationship between an event and an object or class. For example, the Stage object broadcasts the onResize event. No one listens for this event

20

by default, but other objects can register, using the `addListener()` method of the Stage object, to receive the `onResize` event.

Other classes that have no default "audience" but offer registration for their events include ContextMenu and MovieClipLoader, both new in Flash MX 2004.

NEW The `onSelect` event of the ContextMenu class is called when a user brings up a custom context menu (Windows: right-click, Mac: Ctrl-click) that you have created, before the menu actually displays. There is one `onSelect` event for your entire custom menu, and one `onSelect` event for each custom item on the menu.

→ For more on the `ContextMenu` class, **see** Appendix A "ActionScript Reference," **page 910**, and contextMenu.fla on the CD accompanying this book.

NEW The `MovieClipLoader` class has five events (`onLoadComplete`, `onLoadError`, `onLoadInit`, `onLoadProgress`, `onLoadStart`) used to give you more control when loading SWFs and JPGs.

→ For more on MovieClipLoader, **see** "Loading and Unloading External Content," in this chapter, **page 520**.

As Table 20.5 shows, relationships between classes and events may be a little more complicated. Each row represents an event handler. Each column represents an object class. In the table, an E (for "Event") indicates that the event is received by objects in that class by default; all you have to do is create the event handler (no registration required). An L (for "Listener") indicates that the object accepts registrations for that event.

A blank entry indicates that the object does not receive that event by default. In that case, you can scan the row to see whether any object accepts registrations for the event.

Note that the table does not include the static on and `onClipEvent` event handlers.

TABLE 20.5   RELATIONSHIPS BETWEEN DYNAMIC EVENT HANDLERS AND OBJECTS

	Button	Key	LoadVars	MovieClip	Mouse	Selection	TextField	Sound	XML	XML Socket
onChanged							E,L			
onScroller	E			E			E,L			
onSetFocus	E			E		L	E			
onKillFocus	E			E			E			
onRollOver	E			E						
onRollOut	E			E						
onPress	E			E						
onRelease	E			E						
onReleaseOutside	E			E						
onDragOut	E			E						
onDragOver	E			E						

	Button	Key	LoadVars	MovieClip	Mouse	Selection	TextField	Sound	XML	XML Socket
onMouseUp				E	L					
onMouseDown				E	L					
onMouseMove				E	L					
onMouseWheel				E	L(**)					
onKeyUp		L		E						
onKeyDown		L		E						
onUnload				E						
onEnterFrame				E						
onLoad			E	E				E	E	
onData				E					E	E
onConnect									E	E
onClose									E	E
onSoundComplete								E		
onID3								E		

Legend:

(**)Windows only. (New in Flash MX 2004.)

E = object receives this event by default

L = object accepts registrations for this event

STATIC AND DYNAMIC EVENT HANDLERS

Event handlers can be object actions or frame actions.

➔ "Selecting Frame Actions or Object Actions," **page 445**, in Chapter 19, explains the difference between object actions and frame actions. Chapter 19 also shows how to create movie clip event handlers, using object actions.

There are just two basic event handlers that are object actions: on (for buttons) and onClipEvent (for movie clips). For each of these, the parameter after the event handler name determines which event they trap. For instance, on(press) traps a button press, and onClipEvent(enterFrame) traps the enterFrame event. To attach an event handler to an object, click on the button or movie clip on the Stage; then use the Actions pane to create the event handler. You cannot attach these two event handlers programmatically while the movie is running, nor can you change or delete them at runtime. They are *static* or *immutable*.

In contrast, event handlers in frames are attached programmatically while the movie is running. For instance, to use the XML onLoad event handler, you first create an XML object programmatically and then attach the event handler, also programmatically, like this:

20

```
myXML = new XML(); // create XML object
myXML.onLoad = function(success) {trace("loaded !")}; // attach handler
```

→ For more information on XML, **see** "XML Data," **page 634**, in Chapter 22, "External Communications."

Event handlers that are created programmatically can also be changed or deleted program-matically at runtime. They are *dynamic*.

Whereas static events are associated only with buttons and movie clips, you can create an event handler dynamically for a wide variety of object classes, including all those shown in Table 20.5. Every static on and onClipEvent event has a dynamic equivalent. For instance, onEnterFrame is the dynamic equivalent of onClipEvent(enterFrame) .

SYSTEM EVENTS AND USER INPUT EVENTS

The two basic kinds of events in Flash are *system* events and *user input* events. System events are generated by the movie. They include a movie clip entering a frame, for example, or an external data load operation completing.

User input events, on the other hand, begin with a mouse click or a keypress. Or, more pre-cisely, they arrive through the mouse or keyboard interfaces, which can also accommodate other input methods such as voice. User input events include all events associated with the Button, Key, Mouse, Stage, and TextField classes. Many movie clip events are also user input events because they duplicate the functionality of Button, Key, Mouse, and TextField events.

REGISTERING LISTENERS

Every dynamic event handler function is a property of an object. The object may belong to a built-in class, such as those shown in Table 20.5. In that case, the object probably receives one or more events by default. You just create the callback function for the particular object instance, and you're finished.

If you want an object that belongs to a built-in class to receive events it doesn't receive by default, or if you want a custom object that you have created to receive events, another step is involved: You must register the object as a listener.

You register an object as a listener by using the addListener method of the class with which you're registering. For example, a movie clip normally receives onKeyUp and onKeyDown events only when it has keyboard focus. To make it receive these events under all circum-stances, you create callback functions and register the movie clip as a listener with the Key class, like this:

```
myClip.onKeyUp = function () {trace("onKeyUp fired");};
myClip.onKeyDown = function () {trace("onKeyDown fired");};
Key.addListener(myClip);
```

Dynamic event handlers have a number of advantages over static ones:

- The dynamic approach is more flexible because you can decide programmatically at runtime which listeners to register and which events to create event handlers for. With the static approach, you need to decide which objects get which event handlers when you're authoring the movie.

- The dynamic approach allows you to put your code wherever you want. It doesn't force you to attach it to the movie clip. You might be able to centralize all your code on the main timeline, for instance, making it easier to find and edit.

- Dynamic event handlers are real functions, whereas static event handlers are not. That means that you can call dynamic event handlers explicitly, pass them parameters, and define local variables within them. None of those things are possible with static event handlers.

- There are just 9 static movie clip events, implemented as parameters to onClipEvent. There are 18 dynamic movie clip events.

- For both movie clips and buttons, there are no static equivalents for onSetFocus and onKillFocus. Thus, you can't programmatically control the way the static event handlers relate to keyboard focus.

- The dynamic onPress and onRelease event handlers can make a movie clip act like a button, firing its events only when it has focus, and displaying a hand icon. Achieving the same effect with the static mouseUp and mouseDown events takes more work.

NOTE

> You can turn an ordinary movie clip into a "button movie clip," because movie clips can take all the same events and have all the same behaviors as buttons, with the fortunate exception of scope. A *button movie clip* is a movie clip that acts like a button but offers more flexibility and retains its own scope rather than scoping to the timeline it's on.

→ The process for creating a button movie clip is described in "Movie Clip Events," later in this chapter, **page 513**.

Finally, using a movie clip just to trap events is like using a Swiss Army knife just for the corkscrew. A custom object uses less memory than an empty movie clip because it doesn't contain movie clip properties that are irrelevant to trapping events.

The only compelling reason to use static clip events is to use onClipEvent(load) for movie clips that are manually placed on the Stage at authoring time. The dynamic onLoad event does not work in this case.

' For more details on onLoad and onClipEvent(load), **see** "Movie Clip Events," later in this chapter, **page 513**.

20

SCOPING AND THE this KEYWORD WITH EVENT HANDLERS

Inside the static event handlers, on and onClipEvent, both the this keyword and direct references (with no path specified) refer to the Timeline of the clip to which the event handler is attached. For instance, the following are equivalent:

```
onClipEvent(enterFrame) {
    _x++;
}
onClipEvent(enterFrame) {
    this._x++;
}
```

With dynamic event handlers, however, the situation is more complex. Every dynamic event handler is a method of an object, and inside the event handler, this refers to the object. Direct references, on the other hand, scope to the Timeline on which the event handler function is defined. Thus, if the following code is placed on the Main Timeline, this.myVar refers to myClip.myVar, whereas myVar refers to _root.myVar, as you can verify by clicking the mouse:

```
_root.createEmptyMovieClip("myClip",1);
myVar = "main timeline";
myClip.myVar = "myClip";
myClip.onMouseUp = function() {
     trace(this.myVar); // "myClip"
     trace(myVar); // "main timeline"
}
```

As with other methods, you can define local variables in dynamic event handlers. For example, you could add the following as the first line of the myClip.onMouseUp function in the preceding example:

```
var myVar:String = "local";
```

The trace(myVar) statement in the last line then displays "local" rather than "main timeline".

You can point another object's event handler at myClip.onMouseUp, and the value of the this variable inside myClip.onMouseUp changes to the other object. The direct reference to myVar, on the other hand, still scopes to the Timeline on which the function literal is defined.

NOTE

> When the scope of a variable or other data item is the scope in which it is defined, the item is said to be *lexically* scoped—scoped where it's written.

For instance, suppose you create another clip named myClip2, give it its own myVar property, and give it an onMouseDown property referencing the myClip.onMouseUp event handler defined in the previous example. Here's the code:

```
myClip2.myVar = "myClip2";
myClip2.onMouseDown = _root.myClip.onMouseUp;
```

Although myClip.onMouseUp and myClip2.onMouseDown refer to the same function literal, myClip2.onMouseDown fires when the user *depresses* the mouse button, and this means myClip2 inside the function. It displays "myClip2" and "main timeline". On the other hand, myClip.onMouseUp fires when the user *releases* the mouse button, and this means myClip, so it displays "myClip" and "main timeline". In both cases, direct references still refer to the Main Timeline. To summarize: The value of the this variable is the object associated with the calling method, whereas the direct reference to myVar scopes lexically.

Calling Event Handlers Explicitly

Even though event handlers have the special property of being called automatically by the Flash Player under predetermined circumstances, invoking event handlers explicitly is also legal. You might want to invoke them, for instance, if you have created an event handler in one object and want to execute it on another object. Using the `Function.apply()` or `Function.call()` method allows you to specify the meaning of `this` within the call.

→ For examples of explicit invocations of event handlers, **see** invokeHandlersExplicit.htm on the CD accompanying this book.

Event Handlers and Focus

Text fields, buttons, and button movie clips all support the `onSetFocus` and `onKillFocus` events, which fire when the object gets or loses keyboard focus.

By default, `onKeyUp` and `onKeyDown` event handlers associated with these objects do not fire unless the object has keyboard focus—that is, unless the keyboard cursor is on the object. (The static equivalents, `onClipEvent(keyUp)` and `onClipEvent(keyDown)`, fire regardless of keyboard focus.)

Alternatively, you can use an `addListener` statement to register an object to receive a particular class of events. In that case, the object's dynamic event handlers for that class will always fire, whether or not the object has focus.

Thus, say you have a movie clip, `myClip`, and you want it to trap `onKeyUp` and `onKeyDown` events. First, create the callback functions:

```
myClip.onKeyUp = function () {trace("onKeyUp");};
myClip.onKeyDown = function () {trace("onKeyDown");};
```

Then you have two options. One possibility is to make `myClip` into a button movie clip. The callback functions are enabled when `myClip` has keyboard focus.

The other possibility is to make `myClip` a listener of the `Key` class, like this:

```
Key.addListener(myClip);
```

The callback functions are continuously enabled.

Disabling and Deleting Event Handlers

Deleting an event handler is easy because it's just an ordinary variable. Here's an example:

```
delete myClip.onKeyDown;
```

If you've registered a listener for a class from which you're no longer going to trap any events, you should remove the listener, as well, like this:

```
Key.removeListener(myClip);
```

→ If you want to temporarily disable an event handler so that it doesn't use up processor cycles when it isn't performing any useful function, **see** disableHandler.htm on the CD accompanying this book.

20

BUTTON EVENTS

Flash has eight static button events: press, release, releaseOutside, rollOver, rollOut, dragOut, dragOver, and keyPress.

It has nine dynamic button events: onPress, onRelease, onReleaseOutside, onRollOver, onRollOut, onDragOut, onDragOver, onKillFocus, and onSetFocus.

Notice that buttons do not receive dynamic Key events by default. However, you can make a button a listener of the Key class so that it can receive onKeyUp and onKeyDown events, the dynamic equivalents of keyPress.

All button events fire only in response to the primary mouse button. There is no reaction to a secondary mouse button.

All mouse-related button events (which include all button events except keyPress) fire just once, at a transition point. For instance, even though the user holds down the mouse button, the press event occurs just once, when the button is first pressed.

Except for the first paragraph on focus events, each of the following paragraphs covers just a single event, which may be trapped by either a static or a dynamic event handler. Thus, referring to "the press and onPress events," for example, is a bit like saying "the radio and TV news." There is just one event, but you're finding out about it through two different channels. You can also say "the press events," meaning "the press event, whether captured statically or dynamically."

onKillFocus, onSetFocus

The onSetFocus event occurs when a button gets keyboard focus. Keyboard focus changes when the user presses the Tab or Shift+Tab keys to navigate among text fields and buttons on a page. The onKillFocus event occurs when the button loses keyboard focus. Focus events were implemented primarily for input text fields. They provide a convenient hook for any necessary pre- and post-processing as the user fills in the fields. These events can also be useful for buttons and button movie clips. For instance, if you're using a Submit button, when the button gains focus, you could check to make sure the user has filled in all the fields properly. When the button loses focus, you could generate a Thank You message.

press / onPress

The press and onPress events occur when the user presses the primary mouse button while the mouse pointer is within the hit area of the button. This event provides the fastest possible reaction because it fires when the mouse button is pushed down, as opposed to when it is released. On the other hand, this does not allow the user to change his or her mind after pushing the mouse button. This event is most appropriate for games (where reaction time is critical), and it also works for checkboxes, where the user can undo the choice just by clicking the checkbox again.

release / onRelease

The `release` and `onRelease` events occur when the primary mouse button is both pressed and released while the mouse pointer is within the hit area of the button. These events allow the user to change his or her mind by moving the pointer outside the hit area before releasing the mouse button.

releaseOutside / onReleaseOutside

The `releaseOutside` and `onReleaseOutside` events occur when the user presses the mouse button while the pointer is within the hit area, and then moves the pointer outside the hit area and releases the button. If the user needs to drag something from one place to another, for instance, you could put actions within these event handlers to determine whether the mouse pointer is in the correct place when the user releases it.

rollOver / onRollOver

The `rollOver` and `onRollOver` events fire when the mouse pointer moves into the hit area while the mouse button is up (not depressed). Although the Over state of the button and the corresponding _over frame of a button movie clip handle the visual aspects of rollover, the event handler allows you to do something programmatically at this point, as well. For instance, if you want to do something just before the user presses a button, you can use these events.

rollOut / onRollOut

The `rollOut` and `onRollOut` events fire when the mouse pointer moves out of the hit area while the mouse button is up (*not* depressed). *Up* and _up handle the visual aspects of rollout, but the event handler allows you to do something programmatically. This event can be used, for instance, to do something after the user finishes interacting with a particular button.

dragOut / onDragOut

The `dragOut` and `onDragOut` events fire when the mouse pointer moves out of the hit area while the mouse button *is* pressed.

dragOver / onDragOver

The `dragOver` and `onDragOver` events fire when the user performs a `dragOut`-type action, does *not* release outside, and then moves the pointer back inside the hit area and releases.

keyPress

The `keyPress` event occurs when the user presses a key on the keyboard. The format is as follows:

```
on (keyPress key) {
    statement1;
```

```
    statement2;
}
```

key is a string in quotation marks representing the key pressed. For alphanumeric keys, *key* represents the key literally, like this:

```
on (keyPress "a") {
    trace("a pressed");
}
```

Alternatively, *key* can be one of 14 special keywords representing nonalphanumeric keys, such as arrow keys, the spacebar, and the Enter key:

<Backspace>	<Delete>	<Down>	<End>	<Enter>
<Home>	<Insert>	<Left>	<PgDn>	<PgUp>
<Right>	<Space>	<Tab>	<Up>	

You use the keywords like this:

```
on (keyPress "<Space>") {
    trace("space bar pressed");
}
```

Unlike mouse-related button events, keyPress typically occurs repeatedly if the user holds down the key, though this could vary with the keyboard and the operating system configuration.

The keyPress event handler must be attached to a button instance. In addition, the Flash Player must have mouse focus for key-related event handlers to fire. Movies get mouse focus automatically in the Flash Player or in a projector, but not in the browser. Therefore, for browser compatibility, you might want to make users click a button before beginning keyboard input.

> **TIP**
>
> In the Flash authoring environment, you may need to click in an input text field to give the movie keyboard focus.

> **TIP**
>
> Because keyboard focus behaves differently in the authoring environment, Flash Player, and browser, you should test any movie that involves keyboard focus in all the environments where it may be used.

In almost every way, the keyPress event is more limited and less flexible than the onKeyUp and onKeyDown events associated with the Key object. For instance, keyPress doesn't support function keys, Caps Lock, or the Cmd (Mac) or Ctrl (Windows) keys. Nor does it support listeners. Probably most importantly, keyPress requires that you check for a specific key; it does not allow you to get an event when any key is pressed and then determine which one it was. The Key object overcomes all these limitations.

The `keyPress` event does have one unique capability that the `Key` object events don't: It can disable the Tab key for focus shifting. To prevent users from using the Tab key to shift focus in the standalone player, projector, and browser, you attach the following to a button:

```
on(keyPress "<Tab>") {
     // must have some statement here
     dummy = null;
}
```

Then, if you want, you can use `Key` object events to detect the Tab key and `Selection.setFocus` to explicitly change focus.

The `Key` object events, on the other hand, allow you to capture the Tab key without disabling it for focus shifting.

KEY EVENTS

`onClipEvent(keyDown)` fires when the user presses any key on the keyboard, and `onClipEvent(keyUp)` fires when the user releases any key.

Four methods associated with the `Key` object allow you to determine which key was pressed:

- `Key.getCode()` returns the keycode of the last key pressed.
- `Key.getAscii()` returns the ASCII code of the last key pressed.
- `Key.isDown(keycode)` returns `true` if the specified key is being pressed now.
- `Key.isToggled(keycode)` returns `true` if the specified key (Caps Lock or Num Lock) is toggled on now.

You can use the `Key.isDown()` method by itself in an `enterFrame` event handler, to check for a key on every frame. For instance, this code checks for the Tab key on every frame:

```
myClip.onEnterFrame = function () {
     if (Key.isDown(Key.TAB)
          trace("Tab key pressed");
}
```

This code could be appropriate in a game, for example, where catching keypresses as fast as possible is a primary design goal.

Notice the use of the `TAB` constant in caps.

Unless you're checking on every frame, using `Key.isDown()` alone is an unreliable method of detecting keypresses because the user could press the key in a frame where you're not checking for it. To get around this problem, use a `Key` event handler to detect the keypress and one of the `Key` methods to find out which key it was. The following example uses the `onKeyDown` event handler with the `Key.getAscii()` method—and the `String.fromCharCode()` method—to translate the ASCII code into an alphanumeric character:

```
myClip.onKeyDown = function () {
     trace( String.fromCharCode(Key.getAscii()) );
};
```

20

When the Flash Player has focus, on(keyPress) will always fire when the appropriate key is pressed. Events associated with the Key object, however, may or may not fire, depending on two factors: keyboard focus and listener registration.

You can get Key-related event handlers to fire in two ways:

- Any object's Key-related event handlers will fire, regardless of keyboard focus, if the object is registered as a listener with the Key object

- If a button or button movie clip has keyboard focus, its Key-related event handlers will fire. It does *not* have to be registered as a listener with the Key object.

Table 20.6 summarizes these two rules.

TABLE 20.6   WHEN Key-RELATED EVENT HANDLERS FIRE

	Object Registered as Key **Listener**	**Object Not Registered as** Key **Listener**
Object has keyboard focus	Any object's Key events will fire.	Button and button movie clip's Key events will fire.
Object doesn't have keyboard focus	Any object's Key .events will fire.	Key events will not fire.

MOUSE EVENTS

There are static and dynamic versions of mouseDown, mouseUp, and mouseMove. For example, for mouseDown, the dynamic version is onMouseDown, and the static version is onClipEvent(mouseDown). They fire when the user presses the primary mouse button, when the user releases the button, and whenever the mouse moves, respectively. mouseMove may also fire when a movie loads.

Although Mouse events can now be associated with buttons, they fire no matter where the mouse pointer is on the Stage, ignoring both keyboard focus and button hit areas. In addition, unlike Button events, Mouse events do not change the mouse pointer to a hand cursor.

One use of mouseMove or onMouseMove is to "wake up" a program after an idle period. If you're using mouseMove or onMouseMove in a limited context like this, consider setting them equal to null while they're not being used. Otherwise, they can generate large numbers of events in a short time, taking up a lot of processor cycles.

One common use of Mouse events—in conjunction with the two Mouse methods, show() and hide(), which make the mouse pointer visible or invisible—is to create a custom mouse pointer. You hide the standard pointer, use _root._xmouse and _root._ymouse to check for mouse position whenever a Mouse event occurs, and then consistently display the custom mouse pointer at that position.

MOVIE CLIP EVENTS

Movie clips receive all the Button, Key, and Mouse events. In addition, movie clips receive enter frame, load, unload, and data events. The dynamic forms of these events—onEnterFrame, onLoad, onUnload, and onData—can be associated with the Main Timeline. The static forms can be attached to movie clips, but not to the Main Timeline. Movie clip events sometimes make things more straightforward. For instance, they eliminate the need to put code on a movie clip just because you want to execute some action on every frame.

enterFrame

The enterFrame event has already appeared many times in this book. It occurs each time the playhead enters a frame, and it is the most commonly used event in Flash.

data AND onData

The data and onData events fire when external data loads into a movie as a result of a loadVariables() or loadMovie() function.

→ The XML class also has an onData event, which is covered in "XML Data," **page 634**, in Chapter 22.

The loadVariables() function fires a single data event when an entire batch of variables finishes loading. In contrast, loadMovie() fires a series of data events up to a maximum of one per frame, as the movie loads. Thus, with loadVariables(), the data event tells you that you have all the data and can start to work with it. With loadMovie(), a data event tells you that some portion of the loaded movie has arrived, but you may need to check whether enough of it has arrived for your purposes. To check, you can use the getBytesLoaded() and getBytesTotal() functions, the _framesloaded and _totalframes movie clip properties, or—for Flash 4 compatibility—the deprecated ifFrameLoaded() function.

Sample movie ondata.fla on the CD provides a simple example of using the onData event with loadVariables().

→ The data event is covered in "The LoadVariables() Global Function," **page 626**, in Chapter 22.

load AND onLoad

The load or onLoad event fires when a movie clip is initially loaded into your movie.

→ The LoadVars object also has an onLoad event. **See** Chapter 22, **page 625**.
→ The Sound object has an onLoad event, too, covered in "Sound Events," later in this chapter, **page 515**.

The clip may have been manually created with the authoring tool, created when another clip was duplicated with duplicateMovieClip(), loaded from the Library with attachMovie(), or loaded as an external SWF with loadMovie().

In most cases, dynamic and static event handlers provide almost identical functionality. Dynamic event handlers provide advantages such as greater flexibility, easier code centralization, and local scoping. Still, anything that can be done with dynamic event handlers can usually also be done with static event handlers, and vice versa. Not so with the load and onLoad events. In fact, when you first start trying to apply the onLoad event, it appears nearly useless. Why?

20

The problem is that the onLoad event handler must be created before the clip loads. However, if the clip hasn't loaded, there is nothing to assign the onLoad event handler to. Thus, if a clip named myClip is manually created on the Stage, and you place the following code on the first frame of the Main Timeline, the clip will already have loaded by the time the interpreter gets to your code:

```
myClip.onLoad = function () {trace("myClip loads");}; // will never fire
```

On the other hand, if you're going to load the clip programmatically, using attachMovieClip(), should you declare the onLoad event handler before or after the attach? If before, the clip does not exist yet, so you can't define an event handler for it. If after, the clip has already loaded, and it's too late.

One way to get a dynamic onLoad event to fire successfully is to inherit it from the class. When a new object is created, there is a time when the object is still unnamed and "unborn" but already endowed with all the shared methods and properties from the class. When the object is "born," if one of those shared methods is an onLoad event handler, it will fire.

→ The ActionScript 1 approach to inheriting the onLoad method from the class is shown in AS1onLoad.fla and AS1onLoad2.fla on the CD accompanying this book.

→ For the ActionScript 2 approach to inheriting the methods from the class, **see** "ActionScript 2.0: Real Class," **page 540**, in Chapter 21.

unload AND onUnload

The unload and onUnload events occur when you use unloadMovie() or unloadMovieNum() to unload a clip that has been loaded.

The unload event is a good place to free up resources, such as listeners, that have been associated with a movie clip. For instance:

```
onClipEvent(load) {
    Mouse.addListener(this);
}
onClipEvent(unload) {
    Mouse.removeListener(this);
}
```

 Can't get a dynamic movie clip event to work? **See** *the "Troubleshooting" section at the end of this chapter,* **page 535***.*

CREATING A BUTTON MOVIE CLIP

Movie clips receive button events by default. This provides the foundation for creating a button movie clip. There are three other pieces of functionality that you want in a button:

- A *hand cursor*, so that the user gets a visual indication when the button is clickable. By default, if you assign a button event handler to a movie clip, the clip immediately starts displaying the hand cursor when the mouse pointer is over it.

- A *hit area*, defining the area of the Stage in which the button is clickable. Movie clips have a hitArea property that allows you to designate any movie clip as the hit area of the button movie clip.

- *Up, over, and down states*, so that the button changes appearance when the cursor enters the hit area and when the user presses the button. You can give _up, _over, and _down labels to frames in the button movie clip's timeline, and they will automatically provide the desired behaviors. Alternatively, you can use onRollOver, onRollOut, and onRelease or onPress event handlers to implement these behaviors.

→ On the CD accompanying this book, sample movie dynamicButtonMovie.fla (by Helen Triolo) and sample buttonMovie.fla demonstrate two approaches to accomplishing these tasks.

SELECTION EVENTS

The primary purpose of the Selection object is to help you manage keyboard focus.

Any object can receive notification of all focus changes if you register the object with the Selection object, using addListener, and define an onSetFocus event handler.

The Selection.onSetFocus event handler has the following format:

```
onSetFocus (oldFocus, newFocus) {
    statements
}
```

The following sample code creates an object and makes it listen for all onSetFocus events:

```
myObj = new Object();
myObj.onSetFocus = function() {trace("focus set event occurred");};
Selection.addListener(myObj);
```

This is different from the onSetFocus event handlers available by default (no addListener required) for instances of the Button, MovieClip, and TextField classes. A default onSetFocus event handler fires only when *the instance it belongs to* gets focus. Therefore, a default onSetFocus event handler needs only one argument, which is the old focus. The new focus is always the instance to which the handler belongs. So the format for a default onSetFocus event handler is as follows:

```
onSetFocus (oldFocus) {
    statements
}
```

If an instance of Button, MovieClip, or TextField uses addListener to register with the Selection object, the instance's onSetFocus event handler receives both kinds of notifications. This "double-barreled" onSetFocus event handler fires *twice* when the instance gets focus, but only once when any other object gets focus.

Sample movie selection.fla on the CD illustrates these points.

SOUND EVENTS

The Sound object has three events: onLoad, onSoundComplete and onID3. The onLoad event fires when the sound loads, and onSoundComplete fires when the sound completes playing.

20

The onID3 handler fires each time new ID3 data is available for an MP3 audio file loaded using Sound.attachSound() or Sound.loadSound(). If both ID3 1.0 and ID3 2.0 tags are present in a file, the onID3 handler fires twice.

As shown in sample movie sound.fla on the CD, you simply create the Sound object, define the event handlers, and load the sound.

> **TIP**
>
> Defining the event handlers *before* loading the sound is essential.

THE STAGE onResize EVENT

The Stage object has just one event: onResize, occurring when the user resizes the Stage. The Stage.resize event is typically used to adjust the dimensions, layout, or contents of the movie to fit the new size of the Stage.

The user can resize the Stage by clicking on boxes in the upper left (Mac) or upper right (Windows) of the Flash Player or the browser. The user can maximize the Stage or restore down or up. All these actions trigger an onResize event. Another way to resize is to drag the edges of the Player or browser window. This triggers multiple onResize events as the window continuously changes size. In the Flash Player or authoring environment, selecting View, Magnification, 100% also triggers an onResize event, but minimizing or zooming in or out does not. In addition, one or more Stage.resize events may fire when a movie is initially loaded, whether in a browser or in the Flash Player or authoring environment.

The scaleMode property of the Stage object determines how graphics are scaled and cropped as the Stage resizes. In the browser, parameters in the HTML file also affect scaling and cropping.

Although there are many combinations of scaleMode and HTML settings, here's a setup that will generally trigger the onResize event reliably:

1. Choose File, Publish Settings. On the HTML tab, select Percent in the Dimensions combo box, leaving Width and Height at the default values of 100%. Also on the HTML tab, select Default (Show All) in the Scale combo box.
2. Set Stage.scaleMode to "noScale" and Stage.align to "TL". You set these programmatically, as shown in stageResize.fla on the CD accompanying this book.

TextField EVENTS

The four TextField events in Flash are as follows:

- onSetFocus occurs when the keyboard focus is not on the text field and the user gives focus to it by clicking on it or entering it using the Tab or Shift+Tab keys. It has one argument: the previous focus.

■ onKillFocus occurs when the keyboard focus is on the text field and the user takes focus away from it by clicking outside it or leaving it using the Tab or Shift+Tab keys. It has one argument: the new focus.

→ For more information on onKillFocus and onSetFocus, **see** "Selection Events," earlier in this chapter, **page 515**.

 *Pressing Tab to change focus, but nothing is happening? **See** the "Troubleshooting" section at the end of this chapter, **page 535**.*

■ onChanged fires each time text in the field changes. Thus, it occurs every time the user types a letter in the text field and every time the user deletes a letter. Cutting a block of text or pasting in a block of text triggers just one onChanged event. This event has one argument: the text field instance name.

■ onScroller fires when the text scrolls, whether the user clicks the mouse on a scrollbar, uses the up and down arrow keys, or enters text into the text field. This event has one argument: the text field instance name.

Sample movie textfieldEvents.fla demonstrates each of these events. It contains an input text field, myText, with onChanged and onScroller events that increment variables (myChanged and myScroller) that are displayed in dynamic text fields.

WORKING WITH MOVIE CLIPS

The movie clip is by far the most important and commonly used object. It is also unique. Although the MovieClip class was created to bring movie clips under the umbrella of the object-oriented programming (OOP) framework introduced in Flash 5, movie clips are not like other objects and require special treatment in many ways.

For example, you can't create new MovieClip instances by using the new operator, as you can for most other classes. This statement, for instance, does *not* create a new movie clip:

```
myClip = new MovieClip(); // does NOT create a new movie clip!!
```

Unlike other constructor functions, the MovieClip class alone doesn't come close to being a complete factory for making movie clips. Instead, to create a new empty movie clip programmatically, you use the createEmptyMovieClip() method of the MovieClip class. The createEmptyMovieClip() method is necessary because the movie clip class has its roots in the pre-OOP era, and many of the most basic properties of a movie clip (such as _x, _y, _xscale, _yscale) have no connection to the MovieClip class but are built into the interpreter.

Movie clips are also unique in having a *timeline* with one or more *keyframes*—that is, frames in which you either add ActionScript or add or change a graphic, a button, a text field, or another movie clip. Many movie clip methods (such as gotoAndPlay(), stop() and prevFrame()), three movie clip properties (_currentframe, _framesloaded, and _totalframes), and the ubiquitous onEnterFrame event relate to the Timeline.

20

NOTE

> Buttons also have a specialized type of Timeline, although this Timeline does not support ActionScript. Nor are any methods, properties, or events associated with it.

Other than the Stage, the only objects that can contain graphical content in Flash are buttons and movie clips. Graphic symbols contain graphics, but graphic symbols are not objects.

→ **See** Appendix A, "ActionScript Reference," **page 909**, for a full listing of the methods and properties belonging to the MovieClip class (except the drawing methods, which are covered in drawing.htm on the CD accompanying this book) .

FLASH MX 2004'S NEW MOVIE CLIP FEATURES

Flash MX 2004 adds two new movie clip properties and four new methods, falling into four categories:

- Replacing or extending the standard context menu—The new menu property enables you to use the ContextMenu class to create a new context menu for a movie clip.

→ For more on the ContextMenu class, **see** "Using Event Handlers to Trigger Action," earlier in this chapter; Appendix A, "ActionScript Reference," **page 909**; and contextMenu.fla on the CD accompanying this book.

- Managing child clip depth—getNextHighestDepth and getInstanceAtDepth give you information you need to intelligently assign depth numbers to new movie clips, as you create them on a Stage, so that clips are visually "stacked" correctly, and so that you do not accidentally destroy existing content when you load new content, whether external content or content from the Library.

→ For more information on depth management, **see** "Visual Stacking for Siblings: Depth Numbers," later in this chapter, **page 526**.

- Loading external content—The new _lockroot property and the getSWFVersion method help you manage the process of loading external content, such as SWFs and JPEGs. Even more important in this regard is the MovieClipLoader class, which replaces the loadMovie method for content targeting FP7.

→ The content-loading features are covered later in this chapter, under "Loading and Unloading External Content," **page 520**.

- Managing static text—The new getTextSnapshot method returns a TextSnapshot object containing the static text in a movie clip, or an empty string if the clip contains no static text. This works in FP7 only, though the clip with the static text can be targeted for FP6 or FP7.

→ The TextSnapshot object is covered in "The TextSnapshot Class," **page 611**, in Chapter 21.

CREATING AND REMOVING MOVIE CLIPS

You can create movie clips in four ways. Each has implications for how the new clip fits into the hierarchy of clips and where it is positioned on the Stage.

You can also remove a movie clip, displace it with another clip, or remove just the graphical contents of a clip, while the movie clip object remains.

NOTE

Clip positioning is managed via the *registration point*, indicated by a cross-hatch that appears when a clip is edited in the Library. By default it's in the center of a clip, but in the upper left of the Main Timeline.

The Parent-Child Hierarchy

The hierarchy of clips in Flash, which determines their *visual stacking order*, is based on *parent-child* relationships.

A parent-child relationship between two movie clips is a "container-contained" relationship: The parent contains the child. A parent can have any number of children, but a child can have only one parent. Two children of the same parent are *siblings*.

→ For more details on the visual stacking order, **see** "Controlling the Visual Stacking Order of Movie Clips," later in this chapter, **page 524**.

CREATING MOVIE CLIPS

As mentioned earlier, you create a clip in one of four ways. Each of the following examples creates clip2 as a child of clip1. The last three examples also give clip2 a *depth number* of 1.

The four ways of creating a clip are as follows:

- **Manually**—For instance, while you're authoring, if clip1 and clip2 already exist in the Library, you open clip1 in the Library panel by double-clicking on the symbol icon, and then you drag and drop clip2 into clip1. You can also create and select a graphic inside clip1; select Modify, Convert to Symbol; type **clip2** in the Name field; click the Movie Clip radio button; and click OK to convert the graphic into a movie clip named clip2.

- **Using the `attachMovie()` method of the `MovieClip` class**—At runtime, if clip1 is on the Stage and a clip in the Library has the linkage ID clip, for example, the following statement creates a clip named clip2, position clip2, on the Stage with its registration point aligned with the registration point of clip1, and makes clip2 a child of clip1:
  ```
  clip1.attachMovie("clip", "clip2", 1);
  ```

- **Using the `duplicateMovieClip()` method of the `MovieClip` class or the `duplicateMovieClip()` global function**—At runtime, if myClip is on the Stage and is a child of clip1, either of the following statements creates a clip named clip2, position clip2, on the Stage with its registration point aligned with the registration point of myClip, and makes clip2 a child of clip1:
  ```
  myClip.duplicateMovieClip("clip2", 1);
  duplicateMovieClip("myClip", "clip2", 1);
  ```

20

- **Using the `createEmptyMovieClip()` method of the `MovieClip` class**—At runtime, if `clip1` is on the Stage, the following statement creates a clip named `clip2`, position `clip2`, on the Stage with its registration point aligned with the registration point of `clip1`, and makes `clip2` a child of `clip1`:

  ```
  clip1.createEmptyMovieClip("clip2",1);
  ```

  If you use `createEmptyMovieClip()` to create a movie clip in the root, the new clip's registration point is aligned with the upper-left corner of the Stage.

`attachMovie()`, `duplicateMovieClip()`, and `createNewMovieClip()` return references to the clips they create. Creating references to frequently used movie clips can be helpful, because evaluating a reference is less processor-intensive than evaluating a string. Here's an example with a return reference, `ref`:

```
ref = clip1.attachMovie("clip", "clip"+i, i);
```

NOTE

> `attachMovie()` can be used to attach buttons. Buttons can't be duplicated programmatically. In addition, they cannot be removed. Neither `removeMovieClip()` nor `unloadMovie()` works with buttons.

REMOVING MOVIE CLIPS

You can use the `removeMovieClip()` method of the `MovieClip` class to remove a clip created with `attachMovie()`, `duplicateMovieClip()`, or `createEmptyMovieClip()`. If you no longer need the graphics or code contained in a movie clip, removing it gives Flash a chance to reclaim the memory that the clip is using, and (especially if there are a lot of such clips to be removed) make your program run more efficiently. Here's an example:

```
myClip.removeMovieClip(); // myClip is gone
```

In addition, you can displace any existing clip by creating a new sibling with the same depth number as the existing clip.

You can remove the graphical content from a movie clip, leaving an "empty" movie clip object behind, using `unloadMovie()`. The empty clip could be used as a "container" to attach clips from the Library, for instance, or to load external content.

In contrast, `removeMovieClip()` completely removes the clip, leaving nothing behind. If you remove a clip using `removeMovieClip()`, you can't attach anything to it or load anything into it; it is simply not there.

LOADING AND UNLOADING EXTERNAL CONTENT

With the advent of `attachMovie()` in Flash 5, loading external SWFs became much less of a necessity. However, in some situations, you still might want to load external SWFs.

Suppose a Flash application provides access to several SWFs and/or JPEGs, and each user is likely to access only a small portion of the content. It doesn't make sense to force every user to download all the content, as happens when you store the content in the Library and use `attachMovie()`.

Or you might want to provide alternative "skins" for an application, each of which will be used by only a minority of users.

Or you might be asked to "frame" an existing SWF, perhaps adding an introduction, new music, or credits at the end. The easiest way to accomplish this task may be to write an application that contains the additional material and loads the existing SWF.

Another reason to load external SWFs might be to give the user a choice between different versions of your content—for instance, a large, high-resolution image and a small, low-resolution one.

You can load an external SWF or JPEG in four ways: using MovieClipLoader (highly recommended, but the loading movie can run only in FP7), the `loadMovieNum()` and `loadMovie()` global functions, or the `loadMovie()` method of the `MovieClip` class.

Whichever approach you use, it's primarily the process of loading that differentiates `MovieClipLoader` from the other approaches. The results are the same. That means that there are some facts of life about working with loaded content that remain the same, too. For instance, you can't duplicate clips containing external content, and loaded movies can attach *only* from their own libraries.

After you load content into a movie with `loadMovie()`, you cannot duplicate that movie. There is one minor exception to this rule: If you execute `duplicateMovieClip()` in the same code block as `loadMovie()`, you can use `duplicateMovieClip()` to duplicate the clip *with its original content* (not the newly loaded content). For instance, the following example does work but does *not* duplicate the loaded content as you might expect:

```
loadMovie("test.swf", _root.clip1);
_root.clip1.duplicateMovieClip("dupetest", 1);
```

Neither the rule nor the exception applies to `loadMovieNum()`, which does not load into a movie clip.

If you use `loadMovie()` to load content into `myClip`, you can no longer attach clips from `myClip`'s Library to `myClip`. You *can* attach content from the Library associated with the loaded content.

 *If you're having trouble attaching a movie from the Library of a loaded SWF or accessing a variable, movie clip, or function in a loaded SWF, **see** the "Troubleshooting" section at the end of this chapter, **page 535**.*

LOADING/UNLOADING SWFS AND JPEGS: FP6 OR EARLIER

Here's an example of each of the three ways to load content into FP6 and earlier:

```
loadMovieNum("test.swf", 1); // global function
loadMovie("test.swf","myClip"); // global function
myClip.loadMovie("test.swf"); // MovieClip method
```

20

With `loadMovieNum()`, either you assign the SWF or JPEG to an existing level, or you can create a new level for it. With the `loadMovie()` method of the `MovieClip` class, the external file loads into an existing clip, so its level is that of the existing clip.

→ For more details on levels, **see** "Controlling the Visual Stacking Order of Movie Clips," later in this chapter, **page 524**.

You can use the `loadMovie()` global function to load content into a *movie clip*, as shown in the preceding example. You can also use the `loadMovie()` global function to load into a *level*, using a string or a numeral to indicate the level:

```
loadMovie("test.swf","_level1"); // string "_level1"
loadMovie("test.swf", 1); // numeral 1
```

You can't use a variable to indicate the level. For instance, the following code doesn't work:

```
x = 15;
loadMovie("test.swf", x); // DOESN'T LOAD !!
```

Some reasonable-looking nonstring values cause the `loadMovie()` global function to load the content into level 0, replacing everything in your movie. For instance, the following is an innocent-looking implement of mass destruction:

```
loadMovie("test.swf",_level1); // LOADS INTO LEVEL 0 !!
```

External SWFs or JPEGs loaded with `loadMovie()` can be unloaded with `unloadMovie()`. You can use the global function for both loading and unloading, the `MovieClip` method for both, or the global function for one and the `MovieClip` method for the other. Here are some examples:

```
loadMovie("test.swf", _root.clip1); // load "test.swf" into _root.clip1
_root.clip2.loadMovie("test.swf"); // load "test.swf" into _root.clip2
unloadMovie("_root.clip2"); // unload whatever is in _root.clip2
clip1.unloadMovie(); // unload whatever is in clip1
```

Similarly, you can load with `loadMovieNum()` and unload with `unloadMovieNum()`:

```
loadMovieNum("test.swf", 1);
unloadMovieNum(1);
```

`unloadMovie()` leaves an empty movie clip. For instance, even after you have executed the `clip1.unloadMovie()` statement, `clip1` remains and you can attach content to it again:

```
clip1.loadMovie("new.swf");
```

You can also just load the new content without ever having executed `clip1.unloadMovie()`. Loading new content into a clip automatically unloads the old content.

You can use `unloadMovie()` to unload the graphical content from a manually created clip, leaving an empty movie clip.

The `unloadMovie()` **Global Function**
It is generally best to use a string to specify a movie to `unloadMovie()`.

The `unloadMovie()` global function can also take as a parameter a reference to a movie clip, rather than a string. For instance, this statement is legal:

```
unloadMovie(_root.clip2); // unload whatever is in _root.clip2
```

However, if you provide a reference to a clip that does not exist, the `unloadMovie()` global function unloads the content from whatever Timeline the statement is on. It's safer to use only strings as parameters for the `unloadMovie()` global function.

LOADING/UNLOADING SWFS AND JPEGS IN FP7: MOVIECLIPLOADER

 You can create a single `MovieClipLoader` object to handle all the loading and unloading in your movie, or you can create multiple `MovieClipLoader` objects.

`MovieClipLoader` has five events. In the order in which they are typically invoked, they are

- `MovieClipLoader.onLoadStart()`—Invoked when loading starts.
- `MovieClipLoader.onLoadError()`—Invoked if the clip cannot be loaded.
- `MovieClipLoader.onLoadProgress()`—Invoked as loading progresses.
- `MovieClipLoader.onLoadComplete()`—Invoked when the file has completely downloaded.
- `MovieClipLoader.onLoadInit()`—Invoked after the actions in the first frame of the clip execute.

In addition, `MovieClipLoader` has five methods:

- `MovieClipLoader.loadClip()`—Initiates the loading process.
- `MovieClipLoader.unloadClip()`—Removes movies/images loaded with `MovieClipLoader.loadClip()` or cancels a load operation in progress.
- `MovieClipLoader.addListener()`—Enables other objects to "tune in" on the process.
- `MovieClipLoader.removeListener()`—Removes a listener created with `addListener()`.
- `MovieClipLoader.getProgress()`—Allows you to explicitly request a progress report on downloaded file(s), instead of or in addition to onLoadProgress().

There are five basic steps or phases to using `MovieClipLoader`:

1. Create one or more instances of the `MovieClipLoader` class, using the new keyword.
2. Create the event handlers: `onLoadStart`, `onLoadError`, `onLoadComplete`, `onLoadInit`, and optionally `onLoadProgress`.
3. Load clips using `loadClip()`, and monitor progress from `onLoadStart` to `onLoadInit`.
4. Use the clips in your program.
5. Unload clips using `unLoadClip()`.

These are demonstrated in sample movie MCL.fla on the CD.

20

> **N O T E**
>
> MovieClipLoader does not report bytes loaded if you load a local file—only if you load a file from a Web site.

One nice feature of MovieClipLoader is that it is flexible and robust when it comes to how you specify the movie clip or level into which the content should be loaded. All these formats work:

```
myMCL_obj.loadClip("http://www.myDomain.com/test1.swf","_root.myMC1");
myMCL_obj.loadClip("http://www.myDomain.com/test1.swf","_level0.myMC1");
myMCL_obj.loadClip("http://www.myDomain.com/test1.swf", 1);//loads into level 1
myMCL_obj.loadClip("http://www.myDomain.com/test1.swf", _level0.myMC1);
myMCL_obj.loadClip("file:///C:/bigproject/images/testing.jpg", "_level0.myMC4");
```

Other advantages include

- You find out immediately whether loadClip() executed successfully or not.
- You can receive specific errors such as "URL not found."
- Checking progress is easy, and you can use either a listener or an explicit request for a progress report.

You don't get any of these features with MovieClip.onLoad() and loadMovie(). For gory details, go to http://www.moock.org/blog/archives/000010.html.

CONTROLLING THE VISUAL STACKING ORDER OF MOVIE CLIPS

Movie clips in a Flash document appear as if on clear pieces of acetate, so that where there is no graphical content at a higher stratum, elements on lower strata are visible. To control which movies appear in front of or behind other movies on the Stage, referred to as the *visual stacking order*, you need to understand how clips in a Flash document are arranged hierarchically.

The movie clip hierarchy combines two paradigms: the "sandwich" and the "tree." Specifically, a Flash document is organized into one or more sandwich-like *levels*. Within each level, clips are organized into a tree-like hierarchy, with clips vertically organized in a *parent-child hierarchy*, and the visual stacking order of siblings (child clips of the same parent) managed with depth numbers. Thus, the overall Flash document is a "sandwich of trees." If a movie has only one level, you deal with just one tree-like structure.

The _root identifier refers to the base of each tree. Each level has its own _root, or Main Timeline. Thus, two references to _root.myClip1 refer to two entirely different clips if the references occur on two different levels. For instance, one of the clips might be _level0.myClip1, and the other might be _level1.myClip1. References that begin with a level are unambiguous.

20

The initial hierarchical arrangement of movie clips is determined by five factors:

- The chronological order in which you manually place multiple clips into any single timeline layer
- The relative positions of timeline layers containing clips
- Parent-child relationships among clips
- Whether the clip was created with `duplicateMovieClip()`, `attachMovie()`, or `createEmptyMovieClip()`
- On which levels clips reside

Using Levels for Visual Stacking

The overall Flash document hierarchy consists of one or more numbered *levels*, starting with `_level0`. The level hierarchy is a simple "sandwich" structure, with a higher level number indicating a higher position in the hierarchy. For instance, `_level2` is in the foreground compared to `_level1`, and `_level1` is in the foreground compared to `_level0`.

Every document must have a `_level0`, and beyond that it can have any number of levels up to a total of more than 16,000. There is no harm in having gaps in level numbers. For instance, you can have content on levels 0, 100, and 1,000, with nothing on other levels.

You assign —and perhaps create —levels beyond `_level0` when you load an external SWF or JPEG using the `loadMovieNum()` or `loadMovie()` global function, or using `MovieClipLoader`'s `loadClip` method with a level number. Unless you deliberately create a new level using one of these three, your document will have only one level, `_level0`.

Visual Stacking for Nonsiblings: The Parent-Child Hierarchy

Within each level, the visual stacking order is determined by two factors: the parent-child hierarchy and depth numbers.

In the parent-child hierarchy, every sibling is the founder of a "family line." When you look vertically within a family line, the visual stacking order of parents and children is simple: A child always appears in the foreground in comparison with its parent.

Each family line forms a unit for purposes of visual stacking order, just as it does for setting rotation, scale, or position. When you're working with two sibling movie clips, you don't have to think about the fact that each one may be composed of child clips and grandchild clips and so on. The way that visual stacking order works is consistent with other operations in Flash: If you rotate a clip, any family line within it is rotated, too. If you move a clip, the whole family line is moved. Similarly, if one clip is placed "behind" another clip in the visual stacking order, that placement applies to any family line within each of those clips, too. In short, when you're working with a clip, you can treat it as a unit.

20

VISUAL STACKING FOR SIBLINGS: DEPTH NUMBERS

The other factor determining the visual stacking order within each level is *depth numbering*. Flash uses depth numbers to track several factors that together determine the visual stacking order of siblings. A siblings with a higher depth number appears in the foreground, in comparison with a sibling with a lower depth number.

The maximum number of depths that can be assigned in a single timeline is 16,384. Legal depth numbers range from –16,384 to 1,048,575.

NOTE

> Flash 5 apparently put no lower limit on depth numbers, but a Flash 6 SWF can't go below –16,384. The Flash 6 Player will make exceptions for older SWFs.

In the past, developers often used very high depth numbers, in an attempt to make sure that they didn't accidentally use an existing depth number for a new clip, which would cause the new clip to displace an existing clip.

Now, thanks to the new `getInstanceAtDepth` and `getNextHighestDepth` methods of the `MovieClip` class, the guessing games are over. You can use `getInstanceAtDepth` to test before you assign a depth number to a new movie clip. If you get back anything but `undefined`, you know there is already a clip there. `getInstanceAtDepth` also tells you the instance name of the clip, in case you need to make a decision based on that. Another approach is to use `getNextHighestDepth` to get the next unused depth number in sequence, and then use that.

These two methods are welcome complements to the existing `getDepth`, which allows you to determine the depth of any movie clip.

→ **See** Appendix A, "ActionScript Reference," **page 909**, for a listing of `MovieClip` methods and properties, including `getInstanceAtDepth` and `getNextHighestDepth`).

Together, these methods enable you to implement safe practices when assigning depth numbers, to make sure that you don't displace any existing content.

AUTOMATIC AND EXPLICIT DEPTH NUMBERING   Depth numbers may be assigned automatically or explicitly:

- Flash automatically assigns depth numbers to movie clips that you manually place on the Stage at authoring time. The numbering depends on three factors: the chronological order in which you place multiple clips into any single Timeline layer, the relative positions of Timeline layers containing clips, and parent-child relationships among clips. Automatically assigned depth numbers are always negative, starting at –16,384 for _root and going up, possibly with gaps (for example, –16,383, –16,382, –16,380).

- You must explicitly assign a depth number to each movie clip that you create using `duplicateMovieClip()`, `attachMovie()`, or `createEmptyMovieClip()`. Flash reserves numbers in the range from 1 to 16,384 for this purpose and does not automatically assign numbers in this range.

- You can explicitly "swap" the depth numbers of two existing clips, or assign a currently unused depth number to a clip, using the `swapDepths()` method of the `MovieClip` class.

  For instance, the following line assigns `myClip` a depth number of 1. If a sibling already has a depth number of 1, the sibling is assigned `myClip`'s current depth number.

  ```
  myClip.swapDepths(1);
  ```

  The following line gives `otherClip`'s depth number to `myClip` and vice versa:

  ```
  myClip.swapDepths(otherClip);
  ```

If you explicitly assign only depth numbers greater than 0, automatically assigned numbers and explicitly assigned numbers will never conflict because automatically assigned numbers are never greater than 0.

ASSIGNING _ROOT'S DEPTH TO CREATE NEW BACKGROUNDS DYNAMICALLY   You can dynamically place a background behind all content, including author-time content, by giving a new clip the depth of the _root (–16,384), like this:

```
_root.attachMovie ("newBackground", "myBG", -16384);
```

AUTOMATIC DEPTH NUMBERING   Flash follows just two key rules when automatically assigning depth numbers:

- A sibling in a higher timeline layer gets a higher depth number than a sibling in a lower timeline layer.

  > **NOTE**
  >
  > For automatically assigned depth numbers, "higher" means "less negative." For instance, –16,380 is higher than –16,382.

- A new sibling gets a higher depth number than any existing sibling. This means, for instance, if you manually place multiple clips into a single timeline layer, Flash automatically puts the more recently placed clips higher in the visual stacking order.

The relative depth numbers of parents and children don't matter. Depth numbers determine only how clips "stack up" in relation to their siblings. Nonsiblings can even have the same depth number because the parent-child hierarchy determines their visual stacking order.

20

APPLYING LEVELS AND DEPTHS

With Timeline layers, depth numbering, the parent-child hierarchy, and the object-oriented framework to help you organize content, using levels as an organizing tool may seem unnecessary. Here are some reasons why you might prefer to use movie clips rather than levels as load targets:

- A movie clip can have a meaningful name, making your program more readable. Levels always have the generic names `_level0`, `_level1`, and so on.

- Movie clips offer more fine-grained control of the visual stacking order via layers, the parent-child hierarchy, and depth numbers. If you load into a movie clip, the _root of the loaded SWF becomes the clip into which it is loaded, displacing anything that was there previously but retaining the movie clip's depth number, layer position, and position in the parent-child hierarchy. (Similarly, a JPEG loaded into a movie clip effectively becomes the movie clip.)

- You can't specify a depth, and you can't use depth to control what you displace, when you load into a level. The _root of an SWF loaded into a level using the loadMovieNum() or loadMovie() global function becomes the _root of the level into which it is loaded, visually displacing anything that was there previously.

On the other hand, levels can have some advantages:

- Sometimes loading into a level provides the kind of "clean sweep" change that you want. For instance, if you load a movie into _level0, all levels are unloaded, and the new movie becomes _level0. If you then load movies into other levels, the movie in _level0 sets document properties such as frame rate, background color, and frame size for all levels. Loading into _level0 can thus provide some basic consistency for a team of developers, for instance.

- Movie clip properties such as _visible and alpha can be applied to a level without affecting other levels. This capability provides an easy way to change properties for multiple clips, while still excluding other clips.

- You can get a streaming sound to play across multiple scenes if you load the SWF containing the sound into a level.

- For FP6 and earlier, if you're loading an SWF that uses the _root identifier in ActionScript statements, the loaded SWF has the best chance of working unchanged if loaded into a level because the _root of the loaded SWF becomes the _root of the level. Loading into a movie clip can cause many problems in this case. For instance, the SWF's _root variables could overwrite existing _root variables of the same name. In FP7, this problem is solved by the _lockroot property of the MovieClip class.

USING Init OBJECTS TO GIVE PROPERTIES TO NEW MOVIE CLIPS

Both the attachMovie() and duplicateMovieClip() methods of the MovieClip class allow you to specify an init object when creating a movie clip. Flash automatically gives the new clip all the local properties of the init object. This feature is an advantage of the duplicateMovieClip() method over the duplicateMovieClip() global function.

In the following example, myClip is the clip you're attaching to, linkageID is the linkage ID of a clip in the Library, newInstance is the name of the new clip, 1 is the depth of the new clip, and initObj is the name of an object:

```
myClip.attachMovie("linkageID", "newInstance", 1, initObj);
```

The result is that the newly created movie clip, newInstance, will have all the local properties of initObj. newInstance will *not* have properties that initObj inherits from its class prototype object.

You can use a function literal for an init object, like this:

```
myClip.attachMovie("linkageID", "newInstance", 1, {_x:300, _y:200 } ) ;
```

DETECTING MOVIE CLIP COLLISIONS

You can use the hitTest() method of the MovieClip class to determine whether any part of a movie clip overlaps either another movie clip or a particular point. The hitTest() method returns true if they coincide, otherwise false. Either or both of the clips, or any child clip, can have its _visible property set to false without affecting the hit test.

In the case of two movie clips, hitTest() checks whether their *bounding boxes* overlap. The bounding box is the smallest rectangle that contains all the graphics in the clip.

Determining a Movie Clip's Bounding Box

To find a movie clip's bounding box, use the getBounds() method of the MovieClip class. Here's an example:

```
boundsObject = myClip.getBounds(coordinateSpace);
```

boundsObject is an object with four properties—xMin, xMax, yMin, and yMax—that contain the left, right, top, and bottom coordinates, respectively, of myClip relative to the registration point of the Timeline named by coordinateSpace. Thus, in the example, boundsObject.yMin is the top of myClip.

If you don't supply a value for the coordinate space, the clip itself (myClip in the example) is used. If you don't supply a value for the clip itself, the current Timeline is used. Thus, these two statements are equivalent:

```
getBounds();
this.getBounds(this);
```

If you need to find only one of the four properties, you can get it like this:

```
topOfMyClip = myClip.getBounds().yMin;
```

You can use MovieClip.getBounds() for collision detection. In comparison with hitTest(), getBounds() is more flexible, both because it allows you to test separately for each of the four bounds of the clip, and because you are free to adjust the test point. Rather than use yMin for testing, for example, you could use yMin-10 or yMin+10.

Sample movie getbounds.fla on the CD illustrates the use of getBounds().

20

The format for checking for a collision between two movie clips is as follows:

```
myClip1.hitTest(myClip2)
```

When checking for a collision between a movie clip and a point, you can use either the bounding box of the movie clip or just the areas that actually contain graphics. Set the Boolean "shape flag" parameter to false to use the bounding box or to true to use just the graphics. The format is

```
target.hitTest(x, y, shapeFlag)
```

For instance, you can use the "point-check" approach to check whether the mouse pointer is over a movie clip:

```
myClip1.hitTest(_xmouse, _ymouse, true)
```

The "point-check" approach can also be used to check whether a movie clip overlaps the registration point of another movie clip.

→ *If you're having trouble using the "point-check"* hitTest *approach to check whether a movie clip overlaps the registration point of a movie created with* createEmptyMovieClip(), **see** *the "Troubleshooting" section at the end of this chapter,* **page 535**.

The hitTest() method is typically used with an if statement. In addition, you usually need to test for the collision repetitively. That means putting the test in an event handler. The following block of code checks in every frame whether any part of the graphics in myClip overlaps the point (100, 200) on the Timeline where the block of code resides.

```
_root.onEnterFrame = function () {
    if (myClip.hitTest(100, 200, true)) {
        // do something
    }
};
```

The x and y values used in a "point-check" hit test are interpreted as x and y points on the main Stage. If you want to check whether one movie clip has collided with a point in another movie clip, you need to use the localToGlobal() method of the MovieClip class to translate the coordinates of the point into main Stage coordinates.

THE localToGlobal() AND globalToLocal() MOVIE CLIP METHODS

Local movie clip coordinates are measured from the movie clip's registration point. Global coordinates are measured from the upper-left corner of the main Stage. To convert from local to global coordinates, or vice versa, you first create an object with two properties, x and y:

```
myObj = new Object();
myObj.x = 100;
myObj.y = 200;
```

Then you use this object as a parameter to the localToGlobal() or globalToLocal() method of the MovieClip class. The localToGlobal() method treats the x and y values as local coordinates and changes them to global ones. The globalToLocal() method treats the x and y values as global coordinates and changes them to local ones.

The methods do not return anything. Instead, they convert the actual x and y values in the object. For example, the following statement converts myObj.x and myObj.y from local coordinates within myClip to global coordinates:

```
myClip.localToGlobal(myObj);
```

REDUCING HIT TEST "MISSES" WITH "INVISIBLE CHILDREN"

If you check for a collision only once per frame, movie clips that are small in comparison with their relative speed can easily appear to "go through" each other without triggering a hit. For instance, suppose you have two movie clips, each 10 pixels square, moving toward one another at a rate of 20 pixels per frame. If the movie clips are 10 pixels apart in frame three, they will have "gone through" one another by frame four. No hit will be detected.

One way to reduce the number of "misses" is to create an invisible child clip (a clip with its _visible property set to `false`) inside one or both of the clips involved in the hit test. If the children are bigger than the parents, the bounding boxes of the parents are those of their invisible children. If the parents are moving at a constant rate relative to one another, you should be able to find some size for the children that consistently triggers hits. If the relative speed of the parents is variable, you can scale the children up as the relative speed increases.

CREATING THE ILLUSION OF A PERFECT HIT

When an "invisible child" or a "hit distance" is larger than a visible graphic, your program may detect a collision before the visible graphics collide. If the movie clips are moving fast enough, the fact that the graphics do not actually "touch" may not be obvious to the eye. On the other hand, there is usually a limit to how large "invisible children" or "hit distances" can be before the illusion of the graphics "bumping into one another" is no longer convincing. You can address this problem by moving the movie clips into the desired positions immediately after detecting the collision.

EXECUTING MULTIPLE HIT TESTS PER FRAME

An option that may work in some applications is to put the hit test in a mouse event handler, such as `onMouseMove`. Mouse event handlers can fire multiple times per frame.

Another possibility is to use the `setInterval()` global function to both move the movie clips and execute a hit test multiple times per frame. Performing a new hit test is useless, of course, if you haven't moved the clip since the last test. You should also use the `updateAfterEvent()` function to refresh the screen.

→ The `setInterval()` global function is covered in the next section, "Using `setInterval()` to Call a Function Repetitively," **page 531**.

CAUTION

> Executing hit tests multiple times per frame is processor-intensive and runs the risk of slowing down your application to an unacceptable degree.

20

USING `setInterval()` TO CALL A FUNCTION REPETITIVELY

The `setInterval()` global function calls a function or method repetitively at regular intervals while a movie plays. You provide a parameter that specifies an interval in milliseconds. The two formats are as follows:

```
setInterval(function,interval[,arg1, arg2, ...,argn] )
setInterval(object, methodName,interval[,arg1,arg2, ..., argn] )
```

For instance:

```
setInterval(myFunc,100);
setInterval(myObj, myMethod, 100);
```

This function looks straightforward enough. In reality, however, as the following two examples illustrate, the relationship between the interval you specify and the actual interval of execution is anything but obvious.

■ If the specified interval is less than the frame length (the time required to play one frame), the function or method is called at some point after the interval expires. However, the actual interval is often *10 times* the specified interval.

For instance, a frame rate of 1 frame per second (fps) is equivalent to a frame length of 1000 milliseconds (1 second). If you specify an interval of 10 milliseconds at 1 fps, the actual interval may be 100 milliseconds—10 times the interval you specified.

In addition, the interval can vary depending on how processor-intensive the function or method is, what other processing is competing with it, and how powerful the computer is.

■ If you specify an interval that is greater than the frame length, the function executes on the next frame transition. For example, at 1 fps, if you specify 1500 ms (a frame and a half), the function executes every other frame.

DETERMINING THE ACTUAL INTERVAL

You can use the following function to determine the actual interval resulting from any given specified interval. Just change the `interval` value in the first line.

```
interval = 100;
clearVal = setInterval(measureInterval, interval);
function measureInterval () {
    if (restart == undefined) restart = 0;
    else restart = start;
    start = getTimer();
    var elapsed = start - restart;
    trace("interval:  "+ elapsed);
    updateAfterEvent();
}
```

Note the `updateAfterEvent()` function in the last line, which refreshes the screen.

STOPPING OR "CLEARING" THE REPEATING FUNCTION CALL

`setInterval()` returns an *interval identifier* that you can pass to the `clearInterval()` method to stop the function from executing. For instance, in the code in the previous section, the interval identifier is `clearVal` in the second line. Thus, the following line cancels the execution of `measureInterval()`:

```
clearInterval(clearVal);
```

CAUTION

setInterval() can degrade the performance of your movie. The more intervals that you run simultaneously, the more the performance of your movie is likely to suffer.

DRAGGING AND DROPPING MOVIE CLIPS

The capability to "pick up" a graphic on the screen, move it to another location, and "drop" it is useful in graphical user interfaces and also in games.

startDrag() AND stopDrag()

You can implement drag-and-drop behavior by attaching two event handlers to a movie clip: an onPress event handler containing a startDrag() statement and an onRelease event handler containing a stopDrag() statement.

When you press the mouse button, the movie clip named in the startDrag() statement is "locked" to the mouse pointer and moves as the mouse pointer moves. When you release the mouse button, the stopDrag() statement in the onRelease event handler executes, and any currently draggable movie clip is no longer draggable.

Notice that the stopDrag() method does *not* apply just to the movie clip named in the stopDrag() statement. It disables dragging for any currently draggable clip. Thus, it is exactly equivalent to the stopDrag() global function. The movie clip name is like a comment, reminding you which clip you believe should currently be draggable.

The stopDrag() method takes no parameters. For instance, here's the stopDrag() portion of a typical drag-and drop implementation:

```
myClip.onRelease = function () {
    myClip.stopDrag();
};
```

Here's the startDrag() portion of a typical drag-and drop implementation:

```
myClip.onPress = function () {
    myClip.startDrag();
};
```

The optional parameters for startDrag() are discussed in the next section.

startDrag() OPTIONS

startDrag() has optional parameters to accomplish these two goals:

- Locking the movie clip's registration point to the mouse pointer. This locking occurs if the optional lock parameter is true. If lock is false, the movie clip and the mouse pointer retain the spatial relationship they had when the user first pressed the mouse button. If you don't supply a lock argument, it is treated as false.

- Constraining the area within which the movie clip can be dragged. The area is specified by four parameters: *left, top, right, bottom*. For instance, this statement constrains

20

`myClip` to a rectangle starting at the upper-left corner of the stage and going 100 pixels to the right and 200 pixels down:

```
myClip.startDrag(true, 0, 0, 100, 200);
```

→ Flash developer Andy Hall's spacelisten.fla on the CD provides an interesting example of drag-and-drop functionality in Flash MX.

USING THE _droptarget MOVIE CLIP PROPERTY

When a user drags and drops something, *where* the user drops it is often critical. Dropping a file into the trash triggers something quite different in a program than dropping it into a folder. The read-only _droptarget movie clip property gives you an easy way to test where a user has dropped, or may be about to drop, a movie clip.

If the registration point of a dragged clip is over any part of another clip (whether or not the mouse button has been released), the _droptarget property contains the path of that clip. If the dragged clip is not over any other clip, the _droptarget property is undefined.

The _droptarget property goes back to Flash 4, and it provides the path as a string in Flash 4 "slash notation," as shown in these examples:

```
/myClip
/myClip/child
```

WORKING WITH DYNAMIC MASKS

You can manually create a mask layer that reveals those portions of lower layers that are under graphics in the mask layer. Where the mask layer has no graphics, content in underlying layers is hidden.

→ For more information on setting up masking manually, see "Creating a Mask," **page 356**, in Chapter 16, "Working with Vector Graphics and Bitmaps."

You can use ActionScript to animate masks. For instance, you can move, rotate, and scale masks.

The setMask() method of the MovieClip class allows you to designate one clip as a mask for another clip programmatically. For instance, in the following statement, myMaskedClip is the instance name of a movie clip to be masked, and myMask is the instance name of the masked movie clip:

```
myMaskedClip.setMask (myMask);
```

Mask and maskee form an exclusive "monogamous" pair: You can have only one mask per maskee and only one maskee per mask. As soon as you set a new mask on a clip, any previous mask stops functioning as a mask. Usually, this limitation is not severe because both the mask and the masked movie clips can have multiple frames, multiple layers, and multiple scripted child clips internally.

If you want to turn off masking for a particular masked clip without designating a new mask, use null for the mask clip parameter, as shown here:

```
myMaskedClip.setMask (null); // myMaskedClip is no longer masked
```

Here are some points to remember about dynamic masking:

■ Masks are always invisible, *while they are masks*. As soon as a mask clip is no longer being used as a mask, it becomes visible—not usually the behavior you want. Therefore, before taking a mask out of service, you should probably make it invisible, like this:

```
myMaskedClip.setMask (myMask);
myMask._visible = false;
myMaskedClip.setMask (null);
```

■ You can use the drawing API to create masks. However, just as strokes (lines) have no effect in masks that you create manually, lines created with the drawing API are useless in masks. Only the filled portions of the clip have the capability to mask.

→ For more on the drawing API, **see** drawing.htm on the CD accompanying this book.

 ■ In Flash MX, device fonts in a masked movie clip were displayed but not masked. They showed up, even though they were not under the mask. You had to embed fonts to cure this problem. In FP7, device fonts are masked properly. See the sample files (Help, Samples, Using Device Font Masking) for more information.

■ Setting a movie clip to mask itself accomplishes nothing, as in this example:

```
mc.setMask(mc); // does nothing
```

→ Peter Hall's scratch.fla on the CD uses the drawing API and dynamic masking to create a scratch-and-win game.

TROUBLESHOOTING

Why can't I reference a variable on the Main Timeline from a subclip?

If you store variables in the Main Timeline and access them from subclips, don't forget to use _root when referencing the variables. Here's a common error: You look at the variable where it is declared in the Main Timeline and don't see _root there, so you forget to include _root when you reference the variable.

The operands are not equal, so why do they test equal?

One of the most common mistakes in ActionScript is using the assignment operator (=) when you should use the equality operator (==). The assignment operator sets a variable, array element, or object property equal to a value. The equality operator tests whether two expressions are equal. Your familiarity with standard arithmetic notation works against you here. Too often, you write if (x = 10), a statement that the ActionScript interpreter sees as always true, when you mean if (x == 10), a statement that is true only when x equals 10.

Why is my switch statement failing to execute any case statement?

Remember, switch comparisons use strict equality. Are you sure your test value and case value are of the same datatype? If you're using a variable as a test value, an error may have caused your test value to be undefined. As a debugging measure, use the typeof operator to confirm the datatype of your test value just prior to the switch statement.

Why can't I access a variable or function on the same timeline?

If the playhead has never once entered the frame containing a particular variable or function, the ActionScript interpreter doesn't know about that variable or function.

Say you put this event handler on frame 1:

```
_root.onEnterFrame = function() {
    trace(x);
};
```

You also put the statement x = 10; on frame 2 of the same timeline. In that case, the trace(x) statement in the event handler will display undefined the first time it executes (in the first frame) because x hasn't been defined yet. After the interpreter "sees" x (that is, after the playhead enters the second frame), it will always "remember" it, and the trace(x) statement in the event handler will display "10" upon entering all frames, even frame 1, from then on.

Note that all functions in a frame become known to the ActionScript interpreter as soon as it enters the frame. Thus, you can execute a function before you declare it, within a single frame:

```
test(); // displays "hi"
function test() {
    trace("hi");
}
```

Why am I getting an undefined return?

Functions return undefined when there is no return statement, when there is a return statement without a return value, or when you return a variable that hasn't been initialized. Check for one of these situations. In both of the following cases, for instance, what you want is return result;.

No return statement:

```
function doubleIt(numberToBeDoubled) {
    result = numberToBeDoubled * 2;
}
```

No return value:

```
function doubleIt(numberToBeDoubled) {
    result = numberToBeDoubled * 2;
    return;
}
```

Part of my function never runs! Why?

If part of your function never seems to run, perhaps a return statement is getting in the way. Here's a simple example of the problem:

```
1: function showRoomNumber(floor, num) {
2:     if (num < 0)
3:         err = "negative numbers not supported";
4:         return(err);
5:     return ("Your room number is "+floor+num); // this line never executes
6: }
```

The problem is that there are no curly braces around the two statements that are intended to be the error return (lines 3 and 4). Thus, line 4 always executes, causing the function to return. Line 3 is skipped if num is greater than or equal to 0. If line 3 doesn't execute, err isn't defined, and line 4 returns undefined. Meanwhile, line 5, which would return the room number, never executes at all.

The function should look like this:

```
function showRoomNumber(floor, num) {
    if (num < 0) {
        err = "negative numbers not supported";
        return(err)
    }
    return ("Your room number is "+floor+num);
}
```

I'm pressing Tab to change focus, but nothing is happening.

This is standard behavior in the authoring environment. Try testing your SWF in the browser and in the Flash Player.

Why can't I access information in my loaded SWFs?

You should be able to attach a movie from the Library of a loaded SWF, and access variables, movie clips, and functions defined in the loaded SWF.

If you cannot, you might not be referring to the items correctly. To view the paths and identifiers associated with the items, do the following:

- Select Debug, List Variables to list variables.
- Select Debug, List Objects to list objects.

If you're referring to the items correctly, you might be trying to access them before the SWF has loaded completely. Ideally, use MovieClipLoader to avoid this. If you need FP6 compatibility, try to make sure the file has loaded completely by doing one of the following:

- Put in an adequate delay. For instance, you could put the code that accesses the items a number of frames after the code that loads the SWF. This assumes some level of predictability in load time, however.
- Use the data event of the loadMovie() function in combination with the getBytesLoaded() and getBytesTotal() methods of the MovieClip class, the _framesloaded and _totalframes movie clip properties, or the deprecated ifFrameLoaded() function.

I'm using the "point-check" hitTest() approach to check whether a movie clip overlaps the registration point of a movie I created using createEmptyMovieClip(). Why isn't it working?

When you create movie clips manually, it is natural to create the graphics around the registration point and then position the movie clip on the Stage. Thus, you may become accustomed to the idea that the registration point is at the center of the graphics.

When using `createEmptyMovieClip()`, you use the drawing API to create the graphics, and you can create and position the graphics in one step without changing the registration point. For instance, using the `makeTriangle()` function in Helen Triolo's dynamicButtonMovie.fla sample movie, you can create and position the triangle in one line without changing the registration point. If you change the registration point, three lines are required to achieve the same visual effect. For instance, in the following listing, the result looks the same whether you use lines 12 through 14 or just line 15:

```
 1: function makeTriangle(x1, y1, x2, y2, x3, y3, zdepth) {
 2:     this.createEmptyMovieClip ("triangle", zdepth);
 3:     with (triangle){
 4:             beginFill (0x0000FF, 50);
 5:             moveTo (x1, y1);
 6:             lineTo (x2, y2);
 7:             lineTo (x3, y3);
 8:             lineTo (x1, y1);
 9:             endFill();
10:     }
11: }
12: /* makeTriangle(0, 0, 60, 130, -50, 1);
13: triangle._x = 200;
14: triangle._y = 200; */
15: makeTriangle(200, 200, 260, 330, 250, 1);
```

You can easily forget, when using the more efficient syntax, that the registration point is nowhere near the graphic. Then, if you do something where the registration point is important, you may get surprising results. For instance, the following hit test tells you when `myClip` overlaps `triangle`'s registration point; however, `myClip` will be nowhere near the triangle graphic at that time:

```
makeTriangle(200, 200, 260, 330, 250, 1);
myClip.hitTest(triangle._x, triangle._y);
```

CHAPTER 21

ADVANCED ACTIONSCRIPT

In this chapter

ActionScript 2.0: Real Class   540

Using the Core Classes   556

Movie-Related Classes and Global Objects   592

Building Your Own Components   612

ACTIONSCRIPT 2.0: REAL CLASS

Because it bundles functions and variables into objects and classifies objects in different classes, object-oriented programming (OOP) is designed to make complex programs easier to build and maintain. Classes are the most basic infrastructure for OOP.

With ActionScript 2.0, Macromedia has accomplished something wonderful: They have radically simplified the task of creating and using classes, and allowed us to use the new approach for real-world applications immediately, because it works in movies targeting Flash Player 6 (which most people have by now), rather than requiring Flash Player 7 (which some laggards may not have installed yet).

Macromedia was able to do this because in the SWF, the classes are still exactly the same as before. Another way of saying this is that AS2 classes "compile into" AS1 classes. Or, if you want to sound intelligent, say that the new system is just a "syntactic formalization" of the previous system: Macromedia changed the way that we give instructions to the Flash compiler; they didn't change the compiled code. The new instructions are simpler, more efficient and more foolproof.

→ This chapter talks only about the ActionScript 2 approach to creating classes. If you need to use the ActionScript 1 approach to creating classes (for compatibility with Flash Player 5, for instance), **see** functionsAsClasses.htm on the CD accompanying this book. There are also some files on the CD, such as drawing.htm and associated .fla files, which illustrate the ActionScript 1 approach to OOP. You may also want to consult *Special Edition Using Flash MX*, published by Que in 2003.

This section discusses basic techniques and best practices in

- Defining classes
- Creating class instances
- Using a constructor function to initialize attribute values when creating instances
- Managing the "visibility" of class features (methods and attributes defined in the class)
- Accessing and modifying ("getting" and "setting") attributes in classes
- Allowing or disallowing the creation of new class features at runtime
- Creating hierarchies of classes and subclasses
- Facilitating the creation of standard interfaces to classes
- Telling the compiler where to look for classes

Terminology

The term *member* is commonly used in the Flash environment to denote a method or attribute belonging to a class. I like "feature" more, because it has always seemed intuitively to me that a "member" of the MovieClip class (for instance) should mean a movie clip—an object belonging to the class, like a member of a club. But that's not the way it is. A movie clip is an *instance*, not a member, of the MovieClip class. Members are methods and attributes (that is, functions and data).

Property is officially another synonym for "feature" or "member," but even the Flash MX 2004 documentation often uses "property" to mean "attribute" instead. It doesn't cause any confusion if it's used in a context such as "properties and methods." Nevertheless, I try to use "property" to mean any kind of member, and use "attribute" when I want to make it clear that I mean a non-method property.

Class *features* = methods and attributes

Class *members* = same as class features

Class *properties* = same as class features

Class *instances* = objects belonging to the class, for example, `myDog` in the `Dog` class

Methods = functions

Attributes = data (variables)

DEFINING A CLASS

You create a new class by creating a file with the extension .as. (Not all files with the `.as` extension are classes. But all classes are embodied in files with the `.as` extension.) The file must have the same name as the class. Within the file is the class definition and nothing else—one class per file.

Always put your `.as` files either in the project folder (the one with the `.fla` file in it) or into a common class library folder that you create. Never put them in any existing Flash MX folder that contains classes from Macromedia as this can cause problems. A common practice is to create a new subdirectory under the Classes directory under Documents and Settings, below which reside all the Macromedia Flash classes. A common convention for creating classpaths is to base the folder structure on the reverse of the domain name. For instance, for greendept.org, you might store classes in org\greendept\Classes.

Here's a minimal class definition, for a `Dog` class:

```
class Dog {
// class definition goes here
}
```

That's it: The keyword `class`, the name of the class (capitalized by tradition), and the class definition in curly braces. The class definition consists entirely of `function` and `var` statements, declaring methods (functions) and attributes (variables) respectively. For example:

```
class Dog {
    var sound = "bow wow";
    function getSound() {
        return sound;
    }
}
```

By convention, all the attributes are declared first, then all the methods.

This class doesn't follow best practices by a long shot. (Much of the rest of this section is devoted to explaining its deficiencies.) But it does work.

CREATING CLASS INSTANCES

You create class instances by using the `new` statement. Here's the simplest form of it:

21

```
var myDog = new Dog();
```

However, you should never use this simplest form, because you should always specify the data type of the object you're creating, like this:

```
var myDog:Dog = new Dog();
```

Note that the data type is simply the class. By declaring the data type in this way, you tell the ActionScript compiler what kind of object myDog is, making it possible for the compiler to warn you if you use myDog improperly. This is an example of strict typing, which was introduced in Chapter 20.

→ For more on strict data typing, **see** "Managing Variables, Data, and Datatypes," **page 460** and "Declaring Functions," **page 486**, in Chapter 20, "Basic ActionScript."

The previous statement creates an instance of the Dog class, in much the same way that dragging and dropping a movie clip from the Library onto the Stage creates an instance of the movie clip.

Here is an abstract representation of the previous new statement:

```
var newInstanceName:Type = new ClassName();
```

After you've created an instance of a class, you use that instance to access the features of the class. (At least those that are publicly available. In the preceding Dog class, all the features are publicly available. That's one of the problems with it. We'll get back to that in a minute.) You use the dot (.) operator—known in this context as the *property access operator*—to access class features.

For instance, the preceding Dog class has two features: a sound attribute and a getSound method. We can test them like this:

```
trace ( myDog.getSound() ); // displays "bow wow"
trace ( myDog.sound ); // displays "bow wow"
```

USING DEFAULT (PROTOTYPE) AND INSTANCE FEATURES

ActionScript implements an efficient, transparent system for conserving memory when storing the methods and attributes that instances access through expressions like myDog.getSound() and myDog.sound. The essence of the system is this: A default value for each feature is stored in a central place that all instances can access. If the default value works for everyone, that's the only place the feature needs to be stored. On the other hand, an instance can create its own *instance copy* of any feature, and use that instead of the default. This takes up memory in that one instance, but not in other instances. At any time, the instance can delete its instance feature and go back to using the default, freeing up the memory that was used by the instance copy.

The "central place" where the defaults are stored is the *prototype* attribute of the class (which is an object, so that it can store any number of attributes itself). When an instance references a feature (as in myDog.getSound() or myDog.sound), if the compiler can't find the feature in the instance itself, it looks in the prototype of the class.

Consider the following code, which uses the previously defined Dog class:

```
1: var myDog:Dog = new Dog();
2: var myDog2:Dog = new Dog();
3: trace(myDog.sound); // "bow wow"
4: trace(myDog2.sound); // "bow wow"
5: myDog2.sound = "grrr";
6: trace(myDog2.sound); // "grrr"
7: trace(myDog.sound); // still "bow wow"
```

In lines 3 and 4, both instances are still using the default prototype feature. That's because, so far, they haven't done anything but "read" the feature. As long as that remains the case, the feature will be stored only in the prototype, and neither instance will have an instance copy of it. In line 5, however, myDog2 "writes" (or sets) the feature—gives it a new value. As soon as that happens, myDog2 gets its own instance copy of the feature. In line 6, myDog2 displays its instance copy. In line 7, myDog still displays the prototype feature, because myDog has never set this feature.

Now, let's delete myDog2's instance copy:

```
delete (myDog2.sound);
trace (myDog2.sound); // "bow wow"
```

Voila! The compiler, not finding an instance of sound associated with myDog2, looks in the prototype, finds the sound feature there, and displays its value.

The prototype object is also the basis for creating hierarchies of classes, a topic that we will go into later in this section.

STATIC OR CLASS FEATURES

Features stored in the prototype object are (or at least can be) shared by the whole class. However, they are generally accessed only through individual instances, such as myDog and myDog2. There is another kind of shared feature that cannot be accessed through individual instances, but must be accessed through the class itself. These features are called *static* or *class* features. For these features, there is never more than one copy for the whole class. If the feature is changed, it changes for all instances of the class.

The static keyword is a standard, used in other languages such as Java as well. However, it is perhaps not an ideal term, because these features are not unchanging. They can be changed, though you have to refer to them directly through the class (for example, Dog.sound), not through the instance (for example, myDog.sound). One approach is illustrated in the following example, which shows one .as file and two .fla files:

```
// StaticDog.as
class StaticDog {
    static var sound = "bow wow";
    function getSound() {
        return Dog.sound;
    }
    function setSound(newSound) {
        Dog.sound = newSound;
    }
```

21

```
}
// StaticDog.fla
trace (StaticDog.sound); // bow wow
StaticDog.sound = "yip yip";
trace (StaticDog.sound); // yip yip
// myDogs.fla
var myDog: StaticDog = new StaticDog();
var myDog2: StaticDog = new StaticDog();
trace(myDog.getSound()); // bow wow
trace(myDog2.getSound()); // bow wow
myDog.setSound("yip yip");
trace(myDog.getSound()); // yip yip
trace(myDog2.getSound()); // yip yip
```

StaticDog.fla doesn't even create an instance of the Dog class: It just sets the Dog.sound attribute directly. In contrast, myDogs.fla creates instances of the Dog class and uses getSound and setSound methods, which in turn manipulate Dog.sound. Notice that in myDogs.fla, even though only one instance changed the sound (third line from the end), the sound changed for both instances (as demonstrated in the last two lines) .

USING A CONSTRUCTOR FUNCTION TO INITIALIZE ATTRIBUTE VALUES

The Dog class, as you've seen, can give an initial value ("bow wow") to the instance attribute sound, by declaring it like this:

```
var sound:String = "bow wow";
```

Instances can create their own unique values for this feature. But what if you want each dog, from the moment it's created, to have its own unique sound? You can accomplish this using a *constructor function*, which effectively "builds" each dog when the dog is created. In the new statement, you pass parameters to the constructor function to provide values for attributes or to provide other data or references that the constructor function may need. You use parameters to tell the instance "factory" (the constructor function) what special features you want on the instance that you're "ordering."

The constructor function resides inside the class. It must have the same name as the class. It has no return statement and cannot have a return type, but it nevertheless returns an instance of the class, which you typically assign to a variable such as myDog or myDog2. In fact, a constructor function has been used throughout this chapter, but it wasn't obvious, because the compiler created the constructor function automatically when I didn't define one in the class. The auto-generated constructor function is "empty" and doesn't do anything except return an instance of the class. Here's an example of a Dog class (not found on the CD) with a constructor function that does do something: namely, create a sound feature based on a parameter:

```
// Dog.as
class Dog {
    private var sound = "bow wow";
    function Dog ( sound:String ) {
        this.sound = sound;
    }
    function getSound() :String {
```

```
        return sound;
    }
    function setSound(newSound:String) {
        sound = newSound;
    }
}
```

Notice within the constructor function the use of the keyword `this`, which refers to the instance being created. Thus, `this.sound = sound;` creates a new instance feature (`this.sound`) and assigns to it the value of the sound parameter (`sound`).

The first statement in the class (`var sound = "bow wow";`) creates a sound attribute in `Dog.prototype`. You need this attribute in this case. Otherwise, the constructor function tries to add a new sound attribute to a non-dynamic class, which doesn't work. The `this.sound = sound;` statement in the constructor function fails with the error, `There is no property with the name 'sound'`. If you make the class dynamic, you don't need the `var sound = "bow wow";`.

→ For more on dynamic classes, **see** "Allowing or Disallowing the Creation of New Class Features" in this chapter, **page 548**.

You may also want to make use of the sound attribute in the prototype. As it stands now, however, the prototype attribute will never be accessed: Every instance will have its own instance sound attribute. Even if the `new` statement creating the instance doesn't pass a parameter, the sound attribute will be created with the `undefined` value. However, you can modify the constructor function slightly, so that it doesn't do anything if no value or a null value is passed to it. Here's what that looks like:

```
function Dog ( sound ) {
    if (sound)
    this.sound = sound;
}
```

Now a statement like `var myDog:Dog = new Dog();` or `var myDog:Dog = new Dog(null);` does not cause any instance attribute to be created. Therefore, a statement like `trace(myDog.getSound());` accesses the prototype property. The following code illustrates this:

```
var myDog:Dog = new Dog("ruff");
var myDog2:Dog = new Dog();
trace(myDog.getSound()); // ruff
trace(myDog2.getSound()); // bow wow (from the prototype)
myDog.setSound("yip yip");
trace(myDog.getSound()); // yip yip
trace(myDog2.getSound()); // bow wow (from the prototype)
```

Without the `if (sound)` statement in the constructor function, the lines above that display `bow wow` from the prototype would display `undefined`.

A class can contain only one constructor function. Some languages allow more than one, and let the compiler figure out which constructor function to use based on how many and what types of parameters get passed in—a process called *overloading* constructor functions. ActionScript 2.0 doesn't support overloading in this context. (One of the few places that

21

ActionScript does support overloading is with the + operator, which determines whether it should be adding numbers or concatenating strings, based on the types of data it is used with.)

The only keywords that work in front of constructor functions are `public` and `private`. These two keywords are discussed in the next section.

MANAGING THE "VISIBILITY" OF CLASS FEATURES

I mentioned earlier that it is not a good thing that all the `Dog` class's features are publicly accessible. In a well-designed OOP application, each class publicizes *what it can do*, but it hides the details of *how* each task is accomplished (it *encapsulates* the functionality), and what *data* is maintained in connection with each task (known as *information hiding*). This principle usually translates into publicizing only methods, not attributes. (Some methods may also be hidden.)

The *visibility* of a feature describes the ability or inability of client code to access that feature directly, using the dot (.) property access operator. There are two kinds of visibility in ActionScript: public and private.

With public visibility, clients can access the feature using the property access operator. With private they can't. By convention, the visibility keyword is the first word in the declaration, like this:

```
private static var sound = "bow wow";
private var sound = "bow wow";
public static function getSound() { return sound; }
public function getSound() { return sound; }
```

Public visibility is the default. So if you don't declare any visibility, the feature will be public. Thus, the following two statements are functionally equivalent:

```
public var sound = "bow wow";
var sound = "bow wow";
```

The `public` keyword tells anyone reading the program that you deliberately made the feature public. You didn't just neglect to declare a visibility.

You will get the following compiler error if you try to access a private feature from client code (that is, in your .fla file): `The member is private and cannot be accessed.`

Private features are accessible from within the body of a method within the class. In Flash, this also applies to methods in subclasses. (Which makes *private* in Flash equivalent to *protected* in Java.)

21 ACCESSING AND MODIFYING ("GETTING" AND "SETTING") ATTRIBUTES

If you follow the recommended practice of hiding attributes by declaring them private, you need to create methods within the body of the class to access those attributes. This is done through "get" and "set" methods. Every attribute that is used by clients has at least a get method, or some method that "reads" the attribute. Private attributes with only a get method are in effect read-only.

Creating get and set methods does entail some extra work. The benefit is more flexibility as your program evolves. If you need to change the underlying data structure, for example, you may only have to modify your get and set methods to accommodate the change. If clients were to access attributes directly, you would have to modify every piece of code where such an access occurred. The get and set methods also provide a natural place to manipulate data before passing it on to clients. For these reasons, get and set methods are considered an essential part of good OOP design.

Some attributes may be used only for internal "housekeeping" within the class. They don't need get/set methods, though you may decide to use get/set methods anyway, for your own convenience in maintaining the class.

One potential disadvantage of get and set methods is losing the elegant, concise syntax of the dot operator. This:

```
trace(myDog.sound);
```

is shorter and easier to read than this:

```
trace(myDog.getSound());
```

Similarly, this:

```
myDog.sound = "grrr";
```

is shorter and easier to read than this:

```
myDog.setSound("grrr");
```

In ActionScript, you can have your cake and eat it, too. The get and set keywords allow you to create get and set methods that support access via the dot operator. Here's a bare-bones class declaration that does not use the get and set keywords, and therefore does not support access via the dot operator.

```
class Dog {
    private var sound:String = "bow wow";
    function getSound ():String {
        return sound;
    }
    function setSound ( newSound:String ) :Void {
        sound = newSound;
    }
}
```

For the preceding class, you need to use statements like trace(myDog.getSound()); and myDog.setSound("grrr");.

Here's the same class, using the get and set keywords:

```
// Dog.as
class Dog {
    private var __sound:String = "bow wow";
    function get sound ():String {
```

```
        return __sound;
    }
    function set sound ( newSound:String ):Void {
        __sound = newSound;
    }
}
```

Now, if `myDog` is an instance of the `Dog` class, the `trace(myDog.sound);` statement actually calls the first function, which gets the __sound attribute. Similarly, a statement like `myDog.sound = "grr";` calls the second function, which sets the __sound attribute.

A get method cannot take any parameters. A set method takes exactly one required parameter.

Notice that inside the class we have changed the name of the attribute by adding double underscores before it. The ActionScript compiler does not allow you to use the same name for two different members of a class; you'll get an error if you try. Using the same name but with double underscores added makes it visually clear to you which attribute is associated with the get and set methods. It is recommended that you use some naming convention that achieves the same goal. However, there are no hard and fast rules about how to do that.

Similarly, when naming the parameter passed to the set method, it's common to use the attribute name with "new" (for example, "newSound") tacked on at the beginning. But it's by no means obligatory. Many programmers take the "less is more" approach and just use the first letter of the attribute for the parameter name (like "s" for sound). Again, some consistent naming conventions will speed up your programming and make your code more readable.

There are few if any disadvantages to using get/set methods. Use them whenever you can because they eliminate most of the pain associated with information hiding.

Get/set methods are accessible within other methods in the class. If you refer to `sound`, for instance, elsewhere in the `Dog` class, the compiler may very well take it as a reference to the `get` or `set` function. Therefore, avoid using the names of the get/set methods elsewhere in the class unless you want to invoke the get/set methods.

One final note: When a set method runs, the corresponding get method runs automatically immediately afterwards. It doesn't do any harm, but it can drive you batty when you're debugging your program, if you don't know that it's expected behavior.

ALLOWING OR DISALLOWING THE CREATION OF NEW CLASS FEATURES

In the `Dog` class that we've been looking at, instances have the features defined in the class, and only those features. If you try to do something like this:

```
myDog.col = "brown" // col is the dog's color
```

you'll get a compiler error: `There is no property with the name 'col'`, indicating that there is no col attribute defined in the `Dog` class. You get this error because, by default, ActionScript classes are not *dynamic*: That is, they do not allow you to add new features to instances at runtime. Instances have the features defined in the class, and that's it.

Sometimes, however, you may want to leave open the possibility of adding new features to instances at runtime. For example, if other programmers are going to use your class, you may want them to have the flexibility of adding new members easily. Macromedia made the `MovieClip` class dynamic, for example, because some ActionScript programs rely heavily on adding features to movie clips.

You make a class dynamic by putting the word `dynamic` in front of the word `class` in the class declaration, like this:

```
dynamic class DynamicDog {
// details omitted - file on the CD
}
```

Now `myDog.col = "brown"` causes no problems. It adds a `col` attribute to the `myDog` instance. Other instances of the `Dog` class are not affected; they do not have a `col` attribute.

There are two reasons to avoid using dynamic classes:

- You can unknowingly create a new feature with a slip of your fingers on the keyboard. For instance, with the following line, you might inadvertently create a new feature named soumd:

  ```
  myDog.soumd = "grr";
  ```

  In a non-dynamic class, the compiler would have caught this typo, warning you that there was no such member.

- New features cannot be strongly typed. You cannot use the var keyword when creating dynamic attributes, so there is simply no opportunity for strong typing. For example, the following client code generates a compiler syntax error:

  ```
  var myDog.col = "brown"; // Syntax error!
  ```

  Therefore, you cannot do something like this:

  ```
  var myDog.col:String = "brown";
  ```

  If you create a function to set the new feature, strong typing will not work for that either. For instance, in the following example, the `setColor` function declares a string parameter, but the compiler does not generate an error if you execute `setColor` with a number as the parameter. For example, if `Dog` is a dynamic class:

  ```
  // myDynamicDog.fla
  var myDog: DynamicDog = new DynamicDog();
  myDog.col = "brown";
  myDog.setColor = function (newColor:String) { // try strongly typing
      myDog.col = newColor;
  };
  myDog.setColor( 16777215 ); // the compiler accepts this! :(
  trace ( myDog.col ); // 16777215
  ```

When you create hierarchies of classes, as described in the next section, all subclasses of a dynamic class are also dynamic.

Dynamic classes are often a convenient, "quick and dirty" way of getting the job done. However, especially for your own internal use, there are usually other ways of accomplishing

21

the same thing that don't sacrifice strong typing and typo-catching. Chief among those ways is creating hierarchies of classes.

CREATING HIERARCHIES OF CLASSES

If you want some, but not all, instances of the Dog class to have a col attribute, you can accomplish this by creating a *subclass* of the Dog class. You create a subclass by using the extends keyword in the class definition, like this:

```
// DogOfColor.as
class DogOfColor extends Dog {
    private var __col:String;
    public function get col ():String {
        return __col;
    }
    public function set col ( newColor:String ):Void {
        __col = newColor;
    }
}
```

Then simply create an instance in the usual way:

```
var myDog:DogOfColor = new DogOfColor();
```

myDog will have all the features from the prototype of the Dog class (the superclass) and all the features of the DogOfColor class (the subclass). If the two classes have any features with the same names, instances of the subclass will be created with the features defined in the subclass, whereas instances of the superclass will be created with the features defined in the superclass.

The extends keyword gives only prototype features from the Dog class to DogOfColor instances. What if the Dog class also has a constructor function that creates instance features that you want your DogOfColor instance to have, too? This can be accomplished by using the super operator at the beginning of the DogOfColor constructor function, like this:

```
function DogOfColor() {
    super();
    // other details omitted
}
```

The super statement actually runs the Dog constructor function. If the Dog constructor function requires parameters, you can pass those with super. Usually, you will take parameters passed to the DogOfColor constructor and pass them on to the Dog constructor.

For example, let's say the DogOfColor subclass needs a parameter for the dog's color, and the Dog superclass needs a parameter for the sound. Then the statement that creates the DogOfColor would typically take both parameters (sound and color), like this:

```
var myDog:DogOfColor = new DogOfColor("ruff", "tan");
```

In the DogOfColor constructor function, you would pass the sound parameter to the superclass constructor and set the color with the color parameter, like this:

```
function DogOfColor ( newSound:String , newCol:String ) {
```

```
    super ( newSound )
    if ( newCol )
        this.col = newCol;
}
```

If you want to pass all the parameters on, you can do that using the arguments object, like this:

```
function DogOfColor ( ) {
    super ( arguments );
}
```

Then, in the superclass constructor function, you can reference the parameters like this:

```
function Dog ( ) {
    if (arguments[0])
        this.sound = arguments[0];
    if (arguments[1])
        this.col = arguments[1];
}
```

This last example shows a situation in which you don't want to create any instance features in the subclass constructor. You want to create all of them in the superclass constructor. In that case, all that the subclass constructor has to contain is super(arguments);. Notice that when you use the arguments object, you don't have to put anything in the function parentheses, because the arguments object is automatically created and named by the compiler.

To make sure you get the proper instance features in subclass instances, running super must be the very first thing that happens in the constructor function. That way, superclass instance features are created first. When the subclass instance features are created later, if there are any with the same names as superclass instance features, the subclass features overwrite the superclass instance features, which is what you want. If you could run super after subclass instance features are created, superclass instance features could overwrite subclass instance features, which would tend to defeat the purpose of creating a subclass. If you put the super statement anywhere but at the beginning, the compiler will complain: The superconstructor must be called first in the constructor body.

Notice that I used the term "overwriting," not "overriding," in the previous paragraph. *Overriding* is something that occurs between features that reside at different levels in the class hierarchy, such as an instance feature and a prototype feature. It refers to a situation where the compiler finds a feature with a particular name lower down in the hierarchy (in the instance, for example), and therefore does not keep searching to find a feature of the same name at a higher level in the hierarchy (in the class prototype, for example). Both values continue to exist, but in different locations. *Overwriting*, on the other hand, takes place at a single level—at the instance level in the preceding paragraph, for example. There's only one feature and therefore just one value for the feature. When the feature gets set a second time, the value that was set the first time is permanently wiped out.

Here is a Dog superclass and a DogOfColor subclass illustrating much of what you've looked at so far in this chapter. (This is available on the CD as Dog.as and DogOfColor.as. The myDogOfColor.fla file "exercises" these classes.)

21

```
// Dog.as superclass
class Dog {
    private var __sound = "bow wow";
    function Dog ( newSound:String ) {
        if ( newSound ) {
        this.sound = newSound;
        }
    }
    public function get sound ( ):String {
        return __sound;
    }
    public function set sound ( newSound:String ):Void {
        __sound = newSound;
    }
}
// DogOfColor.as subclass
class DogOfColor extends Dog {
    private var __col = "brown";
    public function DogOfColor ( newSound:String , newCol:String ) {
        super ( newSound );
        if ( newCol ) {
            this.col = newCol;
        }
    }
    public function get col():String {
        return __col;
    }
    public function set col(newColor:String):Void {
        __col = newColor;
    }
}
```

Given these classes, a statement like this:

```
var myDog:DogOfColor = new DogOfColor("ruff", "tan");
```

results in a new `DogOfColor` object with access to all the prototype features from `Dog` (the private __sound attribute and the corresponding get and set methods) and all the prototype features from `DogOfColor` (the private __col attribute and the corresponding get and set methods). The prototype attributes __col and __sound (with the values "brown" and "bow wow," respectively) are overriden by instance attributes of the same names (with the values "tan" and "ruff," respectively).

FACILITATING THE CREATION OF STANDARD INTERFACES TO CLASSES

It sometimes happens that you want to use the same function call to get the same basic service from two different classes. For example, perhaps you have an `Employee` superclass, with subclasses that include `Executive`, `Hourly` (employees paid by the hour) and `Contractor`. It makes sense to have the superclass, because there are a lot of identical tasks you need to perform for all employees, such as keeping track of their names and phone numbers. There may also be tasks that are unique to certain subclasses, such as managing per-project contracts with contractors. In addition, there may be tasks which are conceptually the same, but differ in their internal details. For example, computing the employee's monthly check may be conceptually simple: Perhaps you just want a method that takes the month and the employee's Social Security number (or Employer Identification Number, in the case of a business) and returns a dollar amount. It might look something like this:

```
function computeMonthlyPay(month:String, SSN:Number):Number {//details omitted}
```

However, the internal details of the calculation will be very different for the three subclasses. Each class needs its own version of the method, but you'd like to ensure that they all use the same method name, parameter types, and return type. That way, you can use the same function call to get the same piece of information.

You can enforce such consistency among multiple classes by using an *interface*. (And, by the way, the classes do not have to be subclasses of a single superclass as in the previous example. They can be completely unrelated as far as the class hierarchy goes. In fact, interfaces are often used precisely because you want to enforce some consistency among multiple classes without forcing them into the same class hierarchy.)

An interface is embodied in an `.as` file containing an `interface` statement of the following form:

```
interface interfaceName {
 // interface method declarations
}
```

An interface method declaration looks like a normal function declaration, except that it lacks the function body (the curly braces and everything in them) and is terminated by a semicolon. By convention, the interface name usually begins with a capital I. For example, here is an interface containing a single method declaration:

```
// IEmployee.as
interface IEmployee {
    function computeMonthlyPayment(month:String, SSN:Number):Number;
}
```

The interface can contain as many of these "abstract" (bodiless) functions as you want, but that is all it can contain: no variable declarations, and no functions with bodies.

You use the `implements` keyword to assign an interface to a class. Then, of course, you also have to include the method itself in the class to conform to the interface. If you don't, the compiler gives you an error, such as `The class must implement method 'computeMonthlyPayment' from interface 'IEmployee'`. If you implement the function with the wrong data types, you will get an error like `The implementation of the interface method doesn't match its definition`.

Here's an example of an `Hourly` class subclassing `Employee` and implementing the `IEmployee` interface:

```
// Hourly.as
class Hourly extends Employee implements IEmployee {
    // other details omitted
    function computeMonthlyPayment (month:String, SSN:Number):Number {
    // other details omitted
    }
}
```

21

(The preceding example assumes that there is an `Employee.as` file embodying the `Employee` class. We have not shown that here.)

TELLING THE COMPILER WHERE TO LOOK FOR CLASSES

When it comes time to compile the SWF, the ActionScript compiler has to be able to find all the classes referenced in the `.fla` file. It can find them automatically if you put the class file in the same directory as the `.fla` file. In that case, you don't have to use any path when you create a new instance:

```
var myDog1:Dog = new Dog ( new Array() , 3 ) ;
var myDog2:Dog = new Dog ( new Array() , 4 ) ;
```

This is fine for small projects, or when you're just experimenting.

For more complex projects, and for classes that you want to use in multiple projects, you'll want to organize classes in their own dedicated directories. In that case, you have to do two things: enter a classpath to tell the compiler where to look for the `.as` files, and put an `import` statement in your `.fla` file.

There are two places to enter classpaths. You can use either or both. One sets *global* classpaths, which will be applied to every project. The other sets *project* classpaths just for the one `.fla` that you are publishing. Set global classpaths under Edit, Preferences. Go to the ActionScript tab and click the ActionScript 2.0 Settings button. Set project classpaths under File, Publish Settings. Go to the Flash tab and click on the Settings button next to the ActionScript version drop-down menu.

The classpath can give just the drive, or the full path to the class files, or anything in between. Whatever part of the path you don't include in the classpath definition, you must state explicitly in the class declaration in the `.as` file. The `import` statement duplicates the classpath in the `.as` file, and may explicitly state the class to import, or may end in an asterisk, indicating that all classes in the directory should be imported. (A directory used to hold classes is known as a *package*. An asterisk indicates that you want to import the entire package.) If no classpath is required in the `.as` file, no `import` statement is required; the compiler automatically imports all the classes in the directory. This latter arrangement makes your classes more portable, because they don't include any classpath. It also relieves you of the necessity of including `import` statements.

Table 21.1 illustrates some of the possibilities. For instance, in the second row, if the classpath is F:\org\greendept\, then the the import statement would be either `import Classes.Dog` or `import Classes.*`.

TABLE 21.1   IMPORT STATEMENTS AND CORRESPONDING CLASSPATHS

import	.as	global or project settings
None required	Dog	F:\org\greendept\Classes\
Classes.Dog	Classes.Dog	F:\org\greendept\
Classes.*	Classes.Dog	F:\org\greendept\
greendept.Classes.Dog	greendept.Classes.Dog	F:\org\
greendept.Classes.*	greendept.Classes.Dog	F:\org\
org.greendept.Classes.Dog	org.greendept.Classes.Dog	F:\
org.greendept.Classes.*	org.greendept.Classes.Dog	F:\

For both global and project classpaths, you can define multiple directories to be searched, and within each category (global and project), you can tell the compiler the order in which classpaths should be searched.

The interface, shown in Figure 21.1, is the same in both places. There are five buttons that you use to add, remove, and reorder classpaths. From left to right, they are Add New Path (+), Remove Selected Path (-), Browse To Path, Move Path Up, and Move Path Down. To add a new path, click on Add To Path and either type in a path, or else click Browse To Path to use a Windows Explorer-style interface to select a path. To delete a path, select the path and click Remove Selected Path. To move a Path up or down in the list, select the Path and then click the Move Path Up or Move Path Down button. Double-click on an existing entry to edit it.

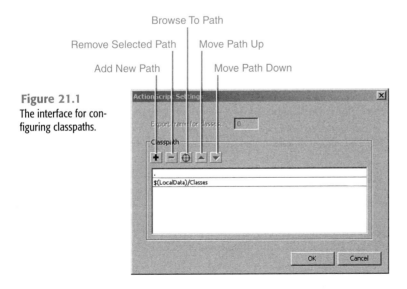

Figure 21.1
The interface for configuring classpaths.

The default classpaths are misconfigured as shipped, and you should change them. The search order you want is

- Paths you explicitly set in Publish Settings
- The implicit project path, that is, the path of the `.fla` file
- The implicit built-in global path

The actual order is

- Paths you explicitly set in Publish Settings
- The implicit built-in global path
- The implicit project path, that is, the path of the `.fla` file

The correct order maximizes your flexibility in overriding existing classes, that is, substituting your own class for an existing class. You do this by creating a new class of the same name as the existing class, and getting the Flash compiler to find your new class before it finds the existing class. The as-shipped search order makes it impossible for you to override a built-in class by placing a class of the same name in the project path. The desired search order enables that.

On the screen for setting default classpaths (Edit, Preferences, ActionScript tab, ActionScript 2.0 Settings), you should see two entries. The first should be something like `$(UserConfig)/Classes` or `$(LocalData)/Classes`. This is the global path. The second will be a period (.). This is the current working directory, that is, the project path.

The `$(UserConfig)` path is the per-user configuration directory. In Windows, this is usually `c:\Documents and Settings\username\Application Data\Macromedia\Flash MX 2004\en\Configuration`. On the Macintosh, it is `volume:Users:username:Library:Application Support:Macromedia:Flash MX 2004:en: configuration`.

`$(LocalData)` resolves to the `First Run` directory of your Flash installation.

Click on the first entry and click the Move Path Down button (the down arrow). The path moves down, so the dot is on top. Then click OK to exit.

(Thanks to Grant Skinner, `www.gskinner.com` and Phil Chung, `www.philterdesign.com`, for pointing this out.)

USING THE CORE CLASSES

Macromedia classifies 11 of Flash's built-in classes, shown in Table 21.2, as *core* classes. Of these, `arguments` is covered in Chapter 20. The others are covered in this section.

The core classes provide basic data-manipulation capabilities useful for a wide variety of programming tasks.

TABLE 21.2   CORE OBJECTS

Object	Represents
arguments	Function arguments (in an array)
Array	Ordered list
Boolean	True/false or other duality
Date	Calendar date/time
Error	An error condition
Function	A function
Math	Math functions and constants
Number	Numbers
Object	Unordered collection
String	Alphanumeric data
System	The computer system on which the SWF is running

THE Array CLASS

An *array* is an ordered, numbered collection of data items. You use an array like a filing cabinet for data. Each *element* (item in the array) is like a file drawer labeled with an *index* number. Indexes start at 0 and count up through the positive integers. The whole array also needs to be contained in a data item so that you can refer to it as a single object.

Table 21.3 summarizes the three types of data required to work with an array: elements, indexes, and a data container for the whole array.

TABLE 21.3   THREE TYPES OF DATA NEEDED FOR WORKING WITH ARRAYS

Type of Data	Filing Cabinet Analogy	Acceptable Values
The array *elements*	Each element is like the contents of one file drawer	Any valid expression
An *index* for each element	A numbered label on each file drawer	Any expression that resolves to an integer from 0 to Number.MAX_VALUE, inclusive
A *data container* for the whole array	A label for the entire filing cabinet	A variable, array element, or object property that refers to the array

An array element can contain any simple or composite data item: a number, string, Boolean, function, object, or array. Any valid expression can be used to define an element of an array.

21

> **NOTE**
>
> An *expression* is an ActionScript phrase that resolves to a single datum.

A single array can contain data items of various types.

An index can be any non-negative integer, or any expression that resolves to a non-negative integer. The highest valid index is `Number.MAX_VALUE`. If you go over `Number.MAX_VALUE`, Flash uses `Number.MAX_VALUE` as the index.

> **NOTE**
>
> `Number.MAX_VALUE` is the largest number that ActionScript can represent (1.79769313486231e+308).

The data container that allows you to reference the entire array as a single object can be a variable, array element, or object property.

CREATING ARRAYS

You can create arrays in two ways: using an array literal and using the `Array()` constructor function with the `new` keyword.

Here's the format using an array literal:

```
container = [expression1, expression2, expression3];
```

In the preceding format example, `container` is the variable, array element, or object property that references the entire array, and the expressions inside the square brackets are the expressions defining the elements of the array. Here are some examples:

```
var myArray:Array = ["John", "Mary", "Peter", "Pat"]; // container is a variable
var students:Object = new Object();
students.scores = [98, 95, 87, 65]; // container is an object property
var myMixedArray:Array = ["John", 98, "Mary", 95]; // array, mixed data types
```

You can create an array in three ways, using the `Array()` constructor function:

- You can call the constructor with no arguments:
  ```
  myArray:Array = new Array();
  ```
  This approach creates an *empty* array. Do this when you want to define the elements later.

- You can call the `Array()` constructor function with a single numeric argument:
  ```
  myArray:Array = new Array(8);
  ```
  All that actually happens here is that the array's `length` property is set to the number you specify. This approach has the effect of creating an array with the specified number of elements, each of which has the value `undefined`. However, an empty array also

21

returns `undefined` for any element you reference, so only the `length` property of the array distinguishes an empty array (no elements) from an array of empty elements (undefined elements).

■ You can call the `Array()` constructor function with arguments that provide values for array elements. The first argument becomes the value of the first element in the array. The second argument becomes the value of the second element in the array, and so on. For example:

```
myArray:Array = new Array(8, 10, 12);
myArray:Array = new Array("John", "Matt", "Mary", myVar, myArray, myObj) ;
```

If the `Array()` constructor function sees just one numeric argument, it assumes method 2 and sets the `length` property. If it sees one non-numeric argument or multiple arguments, it uses the arguments as values for array elements (method 3) .

REFERENCING ARRAY ELEMENTS

You use the index to reference array elements. The format is as follows:

`container[index]`

Thus, the first element in `myArray` is `myArray[0]`, the second element is `myArray[1]`, and so on.

You can both read and write array elements using this format. Here are some examples of reading:

```
myVar = myArray[2]; // read the element into a variable
myObj.myProp = myArray[6]; // read the element into an object property
```

Here are some examples of writing:

```
myArray[2] = myVar; // write the variable into the element
myArray[6] = myObj.myProp; // write the object property into the element
```

Here's an example of reading from one array and writing into another:

```
myArray[3] = myOtherArray[0];
```

The fact that you can reference array elements using numbers gives arrays much of their power. A common technique is to use an index variable and the array's `length` property to set up a `for` loop that searches through all the elements in the array, tests each one in some way, and takes an action based on the result of that test. The following example searches through an array of names, testing each name to see whether it equals a particular name, and then replaces that name after finding it:

```
var nameArray:Array = new Array("John Jones", "Mary Peterson", "Michael Smith");
for (var i:Number = 0; i < nameArray.length ; i++) { // the setup
    if (nameArray[i] == "Mary Peterson") {  // the test
        nameArray[i] = "Mary Laliberte"; // the action based on the test
    }
}
```

21

Notice that you need to say i < nameArray.length, not i <= nameArray.length ("less than" not "less than or equal to"), because the last index in an array is *one less* than the array's length property.

If you have a particular array operation that you perform more than once, you can reduce it to a function. For instance, you could turn the "search and replace" operation shown in the previous example into a function like this:

```
function searchAndReplace(inThisArray, findThis, replaceWithThis) {
    for (var i:Number = 0; i < inThisArray.length ; i++) { // the setup
        if (inThisArray [i] == findThis) {  // the test
        inThisArray[i] = replaceWithThis; // the action based on the test
    }
}
```

The var keyword in var i:Number = 0; makes i a local variable to the searchAndReplace() function, preventing it from interfering with other uses of i as a variable elsewhere in the program.

→ For more information on the var keyword, **see** "Using var to Create Local Function Variables," **page 488**, in Chapter 20.

ADDING ARRAY ELEMENTS

You can add a new element to an array just by assigning a value to it. The following example creates an empty array and then adds an element at index position 4:

```
myArray = new Array();
myArray[4] = "testing";
```

This also sets myArray.length to 5.

The preceding example illustrates a *sparse* array, an array in which elements with values are interspersed among elements to which no value has been assigned. Flash allocates memory only for elements with assigned values. Thus, Flash imposes no penalty for using sparse arrays.

As illustrated in the previous section, the same syntax used for adding an element to an array also replaces an existing element at the specified index position.

REMOVING ARRAY ELEMENTS

When removing an array element in the middle of an array, you want to accomplish these two goals:

- Change the value of the element to undefined.
- Deallocate the memory previously used to store the value in the element.

The delete operator takes care of both tasks. For instance:

```
delete myArray[6];
```

When removing the *last* element in an array, you want to perform both of these tasks and probably also reduce the `length` property of the array by one. You can accomplish all three objectives using the `pop()` method of the `Array` class:

```
myArray.pop(); // deletes last element, decrements length
```

The `pop()` method also returns the value of the element deleted.

→ For more details on the `pop()` method, **see** "`pop()` and `push()`," later in this section, under "Array Methods," **page 564**.

NAMED ARRAY ELEMENTS: ASSOCIATIVE ARRAYS

An array is actually an object in thin disguise. One result is that arrays can have named properties, just as objects can. An array with named properties is an *associative array* or *hash*.

You can assign or retrieve named properties in an array in two ways: using a string in the square brackets, or using the dot operator and an identifier. The following example shows two ways to define a property named `"Mary"` in the `myPhones` array:

```
myPhones ["Mary"] = "555-555-1212";
myPhones.Mary = "555-555-1212";
```

Similarly, you can retrieve the property using either syntax:

```
trace( myPhones ["Mary"] ); // 555-555-1212
trace( myPhones.Mary ); // 555-555-1212
```

You can mix and match these two approaches. For instance, a property defined with a string can be retrieved using the dot operator. The property name must be a legal identifier, or an expression that yields a legal identifier, for both approaches. With the first approach, you supply the identifier as a string; in the second approach, as an identifier.

You can remove named properties using the `delete` operator. For instance, either of the following statements removes the property named `"Mary"` and deallocates the memory associated with it:

```
delete myPhones["Mary"];
delete myPhones.Mary;
```

The `length` property of an array does not reflect any named properties. An array to which you have added 100 named properties but no numbered properties still has a `length` of 0. In addition, the array methods, such as `push()` and `pop()`, discussed in the next section, do not work with named array properties.

You can access the named properties of an array, like the properties of any object, using a `for-in` loop.

→ The `for-in` loop is covered in "The `for-in` Statement," **page 485**, in Chapter 20.

By the way, you can also give an object numbered properties, as in this example:

```
myObj = new Object();
myObj[0] = "hello world";
```

21

However, assigning numbered properties does not make myObj an array. For instance, myObj still doesn't have a length property or work with the Array methods.

ARRAY METHODS

In addition to its length attribute, the Array class has 12 methods of its own: concat(), join(), pop(), push(), reverse(), shift(), slice(), sort(), sortOn(), splice(), unshift(), and toString(). All Array properties are listed in Table 21.4. In addition, it inherits the methods of the Object class.

TABLE 21.4 ARRAY METHODS AND ATTRIBUTES

Name	Method/ Attribute	Syntax	Description
concat	M	myArray.concat (value0,value1,...valueN)	Concatenates the arguments and returns them as a new array.
join	M	myArray.join([separator])	Joins all elements of an array into a string.
pop	M	myArray.pop()	Removes the last element of an array and returns its value.
push	M	myArray.push (value0,value1,...valueN)	Adds one or more elements to the end of an array and returns the array's new length.
reverse	M	myArray.reverse()	Reverses the direction of an array.
shift	M	myArray.shift()	Removes the first element from an array and returns its value.
slice	M	myArray.slice (startIndex, endIndex)	Extracts a section of an array and returns it as a new array.
sort	M	my_array.sort()	Sorts an array in place.
	M	myArray.sort ([compareFunction])	
	M	my_array.sort(option I option I...)	
	M	my_array.sort(compareFunction, option I option I...)	
sortOn	M	myArray.sortOn(fieldName)	Sorts an array alphabetically based on a field in the array.

21

Name	Method/ Attribute	Syntax	Description
	M	*my_array*.sortOn("*fieldName*", *option* | *option* |...)	
	M	*my_array*.sortOn(["*fieldName*" , "*fieldName*" , ...])	
	M	*my_array*.sortOn(["*fieldName*" , "*fieldName*" , ...] , *option* | *option* |...)	
splice	M	myArray.splice(*start*, *deleteCount*, *value0*,*value1*... *valueN*)	Adds and/or removes elements from an array.
toString	M	myArray.toString()	Returns a string value repre senting the elements in the Array object.
unshift	M	myArray.unshift (*value1*,*value2*,...*valueN*)	Adds one or more elements to the beginning of an array and returns the array's new length.
length	A	myArray.length	The number of elements in the array, including empty or undefined elements.

→ For more information on the methods of the Object class, **see** "The Object Class," later in this chapter,
page 572.

join() AND toString()   The join()method converts all the elements of an array to strings
and concatenates them. That much is exactly the same behavior as the Array.toString()
method. However, with the join() method, you can specify a *delimiter* character or characters to separate the strings. The toString() method doesn't offer the delimiter option.

The format for join() is as follows:

```
myArray.join(delimiter);
```

If you don't specify a delimiter with join(), Flash uses a comma, exactly duplicating the
toString() method. For example:

```
myArray = new Array("John", "Matt", "Joe");
names = myArray.join();
```

The output is a string, John,Matt,Joe.

The delimiter option gives you some ability to format the output. For instance, if you want
a space after the comma, you can specify a two-character delimiter that consists of a comma
and a space:

```
myArray = new Array("John", "Matt", "Joe");
names = myArray.join(", "); // names = "John, Matt, Joe"
```

21

The toString() method is used to convert any nested arrays (arrays within the array) to strings. Therefore, these conversions use the simple comma delimiter, not any delimiter that you specify. For example:

```
myArray = new Array("John", "Matt", ["Peter","Mary","Sue"],"Joe");
names = myArray.join("--"); // names = "John--Matt--Peter,Mary,Sue--Joe"
```

The join() method does not change the array on which it operates.

pop() AND push()   The pop()and push() methods treat an array as a *stack*, and more particularly, a *last-in-first-out* (LIFO) stack. Imagine a cook stacking pancakes on your plate as they come off the grill. Each time the cook puts one or more pancakes on the stack, that's a push(). When you eat the top pancake on the stack, that's a pop(). In this analogy, the *top* of the stack of pancakes is the *end* of the array.

Both of these methods operate on the array *in place*. That is, they modify the existing array.

The push() method appends one or more new elements to the end of an array. It returns the new length of the array.

When invoked with no arguments, the push() method appends an empty element to the array (one whose value is undefined). This is equivalent to incrementing the length property of the array by 1.

You can use any expression to determine the value to push onto the array.

The pop() method deletes the last element in an array and returns the value of the element that is deleted. In addition, it decrements the length property of the array.

Here's an example in which we push a value onto an array and then pop it off:

```
myArray = new Array();
var x:Number = 3;
var y:Number = 4;
myArray.push ( x + y );
myVal = myArray.pop ( );
trace (myVal) ;
```

reverse()   The reverse() method reverses the order of the elements in an array. It does the reversal in place, modifying the existing array. In addition, it returns the reversed array, as shown in this example:

```
myArray = new Array (3, 2, 1);
returnArray = myArray.reverse(); // myArray is now [1,2,3}
trace (returnArray); // 1,2,3
```

sort() AND sortOn()   The sort() and sortOn()methods of the Array class gained five new options in Flash MX 2004, giving you more flexibility in how you sort arrays. The options can be referred to by numerals or by constant expressions (strings representing numbers, written in all caps by convention). Table 21.5 shows the five new options.

TABLE 21.5   NEW ARRAY SORT OPTIONS

Description	Numeral	Constant Expression
Not case sensitive (a precedes Z), rather than case sensitive (Z precedes a).	1	Array.CASEINSENSITIVE
Descending (b precedes a) rather than ascending (a precedes b).	2	Array.DESCENDING
Limited to arrays in which no two elements have the same sort order, as opposed to sorting any array, even if multiple elements have the same the sort order (and are therefore are placed consecutively in the sorted array in no particular order).	4	Array.UNIQUE
Returns a new array rather than returning nothing and modifying the array in place.	8	Array.RETURNINDEXEDARRAY
Numbers are treated as strings, so 1000 is "lower" than 9, because "1" is a lower string value than "9".	16	Array.NUMERIC

When called with no arguments, the sort() method sorts array elements in alphabetical order, *temporarily* converting them to strings first, if necessary. Any undefined elements are sorted to the end of the array. Use the Array.NUMERIC option to sort numerically.

To sort on some other basis, you need to provide a *comparison function* as an argument to the sort() method. The comparison function takes two required arguments. They represent any two elements of the array. It's as if you have been asked, "Given any two elements of this array, which one should come first?" You must answer this question with your comparison function.

The function must return a negative number if the first element should come first in the sorted array. If the second element should appear first, the comparison function must return a positive number. If the comparison function returns 0, it says that it doesn't matter which element comes first.

In the following example, the byVotes() comparison function sorts an array of objects representing candidates according to which candidate object has the larger number in its votes property. The comparison function returns a positive number if the second object received more votes than the first. Thus, this function effectively says, "Put the object with the most votes first." The same thing could have been accomplished if a negative number were returned if the first object received more votes than the second. The result of the following example is a candidates array with c3 and c2 in the 0 and 1 positions, and c1 and c4 following in no particular order (because they have the same number of votes).

21

```
var c1:Object = {fname: "Bob", lname: "Smith", votes: 2};
var c2:Object = {fname: "Charles", lname: "Boitier", votes: 30};
var c3:Object = {fname: "Dave", lname: "Meeks", votes: 100};
var c4:Object = {fname: "Abbey", lname: "Smith", votes: 2};
var candidates:Array = [c1, c2, c3, c4];
function byVotes (a, b) {
    return b.votes - a.votes;
}
candidates.sort(byVotes);
```

The sortOn() method provides a more concise notation for sorting objects in an array based on the value of a property of each object, eliminating the necessity for a comparison function. Prior to Flash MX 2004, sortOn() would not work in the previous example because sortOn() was limited to alphabetic sorting. Now, however, you can use the numeric option to make it sort numerically. So this single line accomplishes the same thing as the previous example:

```
candidates.sortOn("votes", Array.NUMERIC);
```

You can use an array of field names, for primary and secondary sorts. For instance, sorting on last name and first name:

```
candidates.sortOn(["lname", "fname"]);
```

concat()   The concat()method appends one or more values to an array. It returns a new array rather than modifying an existing array. For example:

```
myArray = new Array (3, 2, 1);
myArray.concat(4,5,6); //  returns [3,2,1,4,5,6]
```

If one of the arguments is an array, it will be "flattened" and appended. Therefore, the following has the same result as the previous example:

```
myArray = new Array (3, 2, 1);
myArray.concat( 4, [5,6] ); //  returns [3,2,1,4,5,6]
```

Nested arrays, however, are not flattened:

```
myArray.concat( [ 4, [5,6] ] ); //  returns [3,2,1,4,[5,6] ]
```

slice()   The slice() method returns a new array that is a "slice" or subarray of the original array. It does not change the original array. The slice() method takes two arguments: The first specifies the index of the first element to be returned, and the second is one greater than the index of the last element to be returned. If you provide only one argument, the slice contains all the elements of the array, starting at the index position indicated by the argument. A negative argument indicates an index position relative to the end of the array, starting with -1 for the last element in the array. Here are some examples:

```
myArray = [1,2,3,4,5,6];
myArray.slice(1,2); // 2
myArray.slice(1,-1); // 2,3,4,5
myArray.slice(0,3); // 1,2, 3
```

splice()   The splice() method can be used to add, remove, or both add and remove elements in a single operation. It modifies an existing array rather than returning a new array.

The format for the `splice()` method is as follows:

```
myArray.splice(startIndex, deleteCount, value0,value1...valueN)
```

All arguments except the first are optional. With only the `startIndex` argument, it deletes all elements beginning with `startIndex`. It returns the deleted elements. For instance:

```
myArray = [1,2,3,4,5,6];
trace(myArray.splice(1)); // returns : 2,3,4,5,6 -- these were deleted
trace(myArray); // 1 -- this is all that's left
```

The second parameter tells the `splice()` method how many elements to delete. Remaining elements are shifted downward (toward lower index numbers) to fill the gap. For instance:

```
myArray = [1,2,3,4,5,6];
trace(myArray.splice(1,2)); // 2,3 -- it just deleted two elements
trace(myArray); // 1,4,5,6 -- leaving four elements in the array
```

The rest of the arguments provide values for elements to insert into the array, beginning at the index position following `startIndex`. Existing elements are shifted upward in the array to accommodate the new elements. For example:

```
myArray = [1,2,3,4,5,6];
trace(myArray.splice(1,2,"flowers","teakettles")); // 2,3 - the deleted elements
trace(myArray); // 1,flowers,teakettles,4,5,6 - the new array
```

`unshift()` AND `shift()`   The `unshift()` and `shift()` methods are similar to `push()` and `pop()`, except that they insert and remove elements at the *beginning* of the array rather than at the *end*.

The `unshift()` method inserts one or more elements at the beginning of the array and returns the new length. Existing elements are shifted upward. For example:

```
myArray = [1,2,3,4,5,6];
trace(myArray.unshift("flowers","teakettles")); // 8 -- the new length
trace(myArray); // flowers,teakettles,1,2,3,4,5,6 -- the new array
```

The `shift()` method removes the first element in the array, returning the deleted element. Existing elements are shifted downward to fill the gap. For example:

```
myArray = [1,2,3,4,5,6];
trace(myArray.shift()); // 1 -- returns the deleted element
trace(myArray); // 2,3,4,5,6 -- here's what's left
```

Boolean, Number, AND String: THE WRAPPER CLASSES

The `Boolean`, `Number`, and `String` classes are "wrapper" classes for the corresponding primitive datatypes. An instance of a wrapper class contains a primitive datum in an inaccessible internal property. Unlike the primitive datum, an instance of a class can have properties and methods, both local and inherited. In the three core wrapper classes, all the built-in methods and properties but one are inherited from the class prototype object. The one exception is the `length` property of the `String` class: Obviously, each string needs to have its own `length` property.

21

→ For a complete table of methods and properties of the wrapper classes, **see** Appendix A, "ActionScript Reference," under "Wrapper Classes: `Boolean`, `Number`, `String`," **page 968**.

THE `Boolean` CLASS

The `Boolean` class is the simplest class in ActionScript. Instances have just two attributes: `__proto__`, which references the class prototype object, and `constructor`, which references the class constructor function. Every object has these properties. From now on, I usually won't bother to mention them.

The `Boolean` class has just two methods, which are also inherited from the Object class:

- `toString()` returns the Boolean value (`true` or `false`) as a string.

- `valueOf()` returns the primitive Boolean datum, allowing you to compare the values contained in the objects.

Comparing Objects

Two objects do *not* compare as equal just because they have the same properties with the same values. By default, two object references compare as equal only if they refer to *the same object*. Flash MX follows the ECMA-262 standard in comparing objects by *reference*, not by *value*. For instance, here we have two Number objects, both with the value 1, but they don't compare as equal:

```
trace( a == b ); // false
```

For `Boolean`, `Date`, `Number`, and `String` objects, you must use the `valueOf()` method to compare their contents:

```
trace( a.valueOf() == b.valueOf() ); // true
```

For other objects, a specific method may be required to get the values. To compare the colors stored in two instances of the `Color` class, for instance, you can use `getRGB()`.

→ For more details on the distinction between "by reference" and "by value," **see** "Passing Arguments by Value and by Reference," **page 490**, in Chapter 20.

The `toString()` method is seldom needed because ActionScript typically performs automatic conversion to the string datatype when appropriate. It can be used to force the use of a string or just to make absolutely sure that you are dealing with a string. However, the global `String()` conversion function performs the same task and allows you to use the same format with both objects and primitive data.

→ For more information on the `toString()` and `valueOf()` methods, **see** "The `Object` Class," later in this chapter, **page 572**.

→ For more details on the global conversion functions `String()`, `Number()`, and `Boolean()`, **see** "Explicit and Implicit Data Conversion," **page 469**, in Chapter 20.

THE `Number` CLASS

The `Number` class has `toString()` and `valueOf()` methods, which, respectively, return the string equivalent of the number and the primitive number datum.

In addition, the `Number` class has five constants: `NaN` ("not a number"), `Number.MAX_VALUE`, `Number.MIN_VALUE`, `Number.POSITIVE_INFINITY`, and `Number.NEGATIVE_INFINITY`.

→ The `Number` constants are discussed under "Number," **page 465** in Chapter 20.

THE `String` CLASS

The `String` class has a `valueOf()` method, which returns the primitive string datum. Each member of the `String` class has an instance attribute, `length`. In addition, the `String` class has a dozen string manipulation methods, which are among the most frequently used in ActionScript. They are also among the most processor-intensive, inspiring programmers to write alternative optimized methods.

String methods can be divided into four categories: searching for a character or character sequence, retrieving a portion or portions of a string, converting to lower- or uppercase, and generating characters from character codes or vice versa.

The `String.split()` method splits a string into substrings. The first argument, *delimiter*, is the character string that marks the places to make the splits. When the delimiter is the empty string, `String.split()` returns an array in which each element is one character in the string. For instance:

```
var myString:String = "Joe";
var i = myString.split("");
trace (i); // J,o,e
trace (i.length); // 3
```

An optional second argument, *limit*, specifies the maximum number of substrings.

The `String.substring()` method returns a substring starting at *startIndex* and ending one character before *endIndex*. The Flash 6 Player introduced a bug into this method. If *startIndex* is greater than *endIndex*, the Flash interpreter swaps them before running the function. However, *startIndex* must always be less than the length of the string. If it is equal to the length or greater, there's no swapping, and the empty string is returned.

THE `Date` CLASS

The `Date` class allows you to determine the current time and date and store times and dates in objects. All times and dates in ActionScript are stored in the form of a single number: the number of milliseconds before or after midnight of January 1, 1970 UTC (Coordinated Universal Time, which is the same as Greenwich Mean Time). This number is returned by the `Date.valueOf()` method.

You can use `Date` class methods to get and set the date/time as a single object, or to get and set the year, month, date, day, hour, minute, second, and millisecond independently, in local or UTC time. You can also retrieve the number of minutes between UTC and local time by using `getTimezoneOffset()`.

There is also a `toString()` method, which returns full date information in a human-readable form like the following: `Sun Jun 16 18:04:58 GMT-0600 2002`. The `Date()` global function does the same thing: `myDate.toString()` yields the same result as `Date(myDate)`. Neither is needed very often because of automatic datatype conversion.

→ For a listing of `Date` methods, **see** Appendix A, under "Methods of the `Date` Class," **page 951**.

You can use the `Date` constructor in three ways:

- `myDate = new Date();` sets `myDate` to the current date and time.

- `myDate = new Date(1000000);` sets `myDate` to the date and time one million milliseconds after midnight of January 1, 1970.

- `myDate = new Date(2004, 1, 2, 3, 4, 5, 6);` sets `myDate` to January 2, 2004, at 3:04 a.m., plus 5 seconds and 6 milliseconds. Thus, the format is `new Date (year, month, date, hour, minute, second, millisecond);`.

In the last format, all parameters except *year* and *month* are optional and are set to zero if not supplied. Hours are set on a 24-hour clock, where midnight is 0 and noon is 12. For the year, a value of 0 to 99 indicates 1900 though 1999. For years beyond 1999, you need to specify all four digits of the year.

THE Error CLASS

The `Error` class, new in Flash MX 2004, is used in conjunction with `try/catch/finally` and the `throw` keyword to implement a standard means of error trapping in Flash MX.

→ The `try/catch/finally` statement is introduced in Chapter 20, under "The `try/catch/finally` Statement," **page 482**.

It's a simple class, with two attributes and one method:

- `message`—The error message, a string

- `name`—A name you assign to the error class, a string

- `toString()`—A method that returns `message`

Both `message` and `name` default to "Error".

Here's a fully functional example (tryCatch.fla on the CD), in which an error condition is simulated in the `getCustomerInfo()` function by a return value of 1. (The idea is that the function would return to 0 if all went well, but we're only simulating the error condition here.)

```
1:  function getCustomerInfo() { return (1); }
2:  try {
3:    var returnVal = getCustomerInfo();
4:    if(returnVal != 0) {
5:      throw new Error("Error getting Customer information.");
6:    }
7:  } catch (e) {
8:    trace(e.name+" : "+e); // error processing goes here
9:  }
10: finally {trace("finally")}; // "clean-up" or other final actions
```

Line 1 simulates an error condition by returning 1. Within the `try` block, line 4 tests for an error return (any return other than 0). The `throw` statement on line 5 is where the `Error` class comes in. The new `Error` object will have the text string `"Error getting Customer information."` as its message attribute. The Error object is "caught" on line 7. On line 8, the `trace` statement displays the Error object's `name` attribute ("Error" in this case). Also on line 8, displaying the `Error` object itself (the e at the end of the `trace` statement) automatically invokes the `Error` object's `toString()` method, displaying the `message` value in the Output window.

You can create different error classes by subclassing the `Error` class, like this:

```
// CustErrorNoSuchCust.as
class CustErrorNoSuchCust extends Error {
    private var name:String = "NoSuchCustomer";
    private var message:String =
        "Error getting Customer information: No such customer.";
}

// CustErrorInactiveAcct.as
class CustErrorInactiveAcct extends Error {
    private var name:String = "InactiveAcct";
    private var message:String =
        "Error getting Customer information: Inactive Account.";
}
```

Notice that you can make name and message private, and you will still be able to access them, because you are inheriting get/set methods from the `Error` class.

In a real application, `getCustomerInfo()` would be a method of a class, such as a `Customer` class. Here's a minimal version, hard-coded for this example to return the "no such customer" error:

```
//Customer.as
class Customer {
    private var noSuchCustomerCondition:Boolean = true;
    private var inactiveAcctCondition:Boolean = false;
    function getCustomerInfo() {
      if (noSuchCustomerCondition) {
        throw new CustErrorNoSuchCust();
      }
      if (inactiveAcctCondition) {
        throw new CustErrorInactiveAcct();
      }
    }
}
```

Then the `.fla` looks like this:

```
// tryCatch2.fla
var myCustomer:Customer = new Customer ();
try {
    myCustomer.getCustomerInfo();
  }
catch (e:CustErrorNoSuchCust) {
    trace(e.name+" : "+e.toString());
    // more processing specific to the "no such customer" error
```

21

```
    }
catch (e:CustErrorInactiveAcct) {
    trace(e.name+" : "+e.toString());
    // more processing specific to the "inactive account" error
    }
finally {trace("finally")}; // "clean-up" or other final actions
```

All the files for the preceding example are available on the CD, with the names indicated in the comment at the top of each section of code.

THE Function CLASS

The Function class is a "nonconstructive" constructor: You can't create usable new instances with the new keyword. The Function class has just two built-in methods: apply() and call().

→ The apply() and call() methods, as well as the syntax for creating a function, are covered in "Combining Statements into Functions," in Chapter 20, **page 486**.

THE Object CLASS

The Object class is the foundation for all other classes in ActionScript. All other classes inherit from it and thus share its properties and methods. An instance property assigned by this class, and therefore present in every ActionScript object, is __proto__, which points to the prototype of the object's class.

The Object class has 11 properties, all hidden by default. You can use the undocumented ASSetPropFlags() function to "unhide" 10 properties of the Object class:

```
ASSetPropFlags(Object.prototype, null, 8, 1);
for (a in Object.prototype) trace (a);
```

The 10 properties are constructor, isPropertyEnumerable(), isPrototypeOf(), hasOwnProperty(), toLocaleString(), toString(), valueOf(), addProperty(), unwatch(), and watch(). Every object created with the new operator inherits these properties, the last 9 of which are methods.

The eleventh property is the registerClass() method, which is not covered here because it is used only in AS1, not in AS2.

Object properties are summarized in Table 21.6.

TABLE 21.6   METHODS AND ATTRIBUTES OF THE Object CLASS

Name	Method/ Attribute	Format	Description
addProperty	M	myObject.addProperty ("myProp", getMyProp, setMyProp)	Creates a getter/setter property named myProp.
constructor	A	myObject.constructor	Points to the constructor function of the class.

Name	Method/ Attribute	Format	Description
`hasOwnProperty`	M	`myObject.hasOwnProperty` `("myProp")`	Returns true if `myObject` has an instance property named `myProp`; otherwise, returns `false`.
`isPropertyEnumerable`	M	`isPropertyEnumerable` `(property)`	Returns true if `property` is an instance property that would be enumerated by a for-in loop.

`isPrototypeOf`	M	`protoObject.`
		`isPrototypeOf`
		`(instanceObject)`
			Returns true if `instanceObject` uses `protoObject` as the prototype object from which it gets shared properties. Otherwise, it returns `false`.

`registerClass`	M	`Object.registerClass` `("linkageID", MyClass);`	Preregisters a movie clip for membership in a class.
`toLocaleString`	M	`myObject.` `toLocaleString()`	Returns a string appropriate to a particular country or area; by default, returns the string `[object Object]`.
`toString`	M	`myObject.toString()`	Returns the string `[object Object]`.
`unwatch`	M	See Table 21.8	Removes the registration that a `watch()` method created.
`valueOf`	M	`myObject.valueOf()`	In the `Object` class, returns the object itself by default. Child classes, such as `Boolean`, `Date`, `Number`, and `String`, may define more useful `valueOf()` methods.
`watch`	M	See Table 21.8	Registers a callback function to be invoked when a specified property of an object changes.

21

Undocumented properties are `constructor`, `isPropertyEnumerable()`, `isPrototypeOf()`, `hasOwnProperty()` and `toLocaleString()`. The behavior of any undocumented feature is subject to change in future versions of Flash. However, of the eleven properties of the `Object` class, seven are defined in the ECMA-262 standard and are also found in JavaScript. (Though both have `propertyIsEnumerable()`, not `isPropertyEnumerable()`.) The four properties that are Flash-specific are `addProperty()`, `registerClass()`, `unwatch()`, and `watch()`.

constructor

The purpose of the `constructor` property is to point to the constructor function of the class. The `constructor` property can therefore be used to determine an object's class:

```
mySound = new Sound();
if ((typeof mySound == "object") && (mySound.constructor == Sound))
    // then do something with the Sound object
```

Each instance of the class has its own local `constructor` property, and the `prototype` object of the class (like any other object) also has a `constructor` property.

toString()

The purpose of the `toString()` method is to return a string that represents the object in some manner. ActionScript invokes this method when it needs to convert an object into a string. Some built-in objects come with class-specific `toString()` methods. They are listed in Table 21.7.

TABLE 21.7   RETURN VALUES OF `toString()` METHODS OF BUILT-IN OBJECTS

Class	Return Value of `toString()` Method
`Array`	A comma-separated list of the array's elements converted to strings
`Boolean`	`true` or `false` as a string
`Date`	The full date and time in the form `Sun Jun 16 18:04:58 GMT-0600 2002`(*)
`Button`, `MovieClip`, `TextField`	The absolute path to the instance
`Number`	The number as a string
`Object`	The string `[object Object]`
XML node object or XML document	XML source code

(*) GMT is the Greenwich Mean Time (same as UTC) offset.

Classes that do not have class-specific `toString()` methods use the one they inherit from the `Object` class, which returns the string `[object Object]`. You can assign a class-specific `toString()` method to get a more meaningful return, as in this example:

```
Sound.prototype.toString = function () {return "Sound";};
```

When you create a class, you may want to create a `toString()` method that will return information that you can use either for debugging or in your program.

toLocaleString()

The `toLocaleString()`method is an alternate, implementation-specific version of the `toString()` method. Its purpose is to provide a *localized* version of the string representing the object. Localization refers to adapting to various countries and languages. The `toLocaleString()` method in the `Object` class prototype returns the same thing as the `toString()` method. However, you can define `toLocaleString()` methods for built-in classes.

isPropertyEnumerable()

The `isPropertyEnumerable()`method takes one argument, which is a property of the object, and returns `true` for *instance properties* that would be enumerated by a `for-in` loop. If the property does not exist, if it is not an instance property, or if it would not be enumerated by a `for-in` loop, `isPropertyEnumerable()` returns `false`.

isPrototypeOf()

The `isPrototypeOf()`method takes one argument, which is an object. The format is as follows:

`protoObject.isPrototypeOf(instanceObject);`

If *instanceObject* uses *protoObject* as the `prototype` object from which it gets shared properties, `isPrototypeOf()` returns `true`. Otherwise, it returns `false`. The `isPrototypeOf()` method depends on the __proto__ property of the instance object to find the instance object's prototype.

valueOf()

Just as the `toString()` method represents the object as a string, the `valueOf()` method represents the object as another primitive datatype. The default `valueOf()` method in the `Object` class returns the object itself—which is something like buying a dollar bill for a dollar. However, a class can define a useful `valueOf()` method. For instance, the `Date` class has a `valueOf()` method that returns the number of milliseconds between the time of the `Date` object and midnight, January 1, 1970. For dates prior to that time, the number is negative. (This method is equivalent to the `Date.getTime()` method.)

```
myDate = new Date();
trace (myDate.valueOf()); // 1024275924859
trace (myDate); // Sun Jun 16 18:05:24 GMT-0700 2002
```

The `Boolean`, `Date`, `Number`, and `String` classes define `valueOf()` methods that return the primitive datum, allowing you to compare these primitive values.

21

hasOwnProperty()

The `hasOwnProperty()`method takes one string argument specifying a name of a possible local property. The method returns `true` if the object has an instance property with that name. Otherwise, it returns `false`. The format looks like this:

```
myTextField.hasOwnProperty("myProp")
```

findValueOf.fla on the CD accompanying this book creates a global `findValueOf()` function, using the `hasOwnProperty()` method to determine whether an object or any of the `prototype` objects it inherits from has a `valueOf()` method.

addProperty()

The `addProperty()` method makes it easier to use get/set functions with ActionScript 1. In external class files (with AS2), you can use `get` or `set` instead.

The `addProperty()` method allows you to add a property and associate get/set functions with it in one step. Thereafter, the dot syntax will actually call the get/set functions.

The format of the `addProperty()` method is as follows:

```
myObj.addProperty( "myProp", getMyProp, setMyProp )
```

Instead of the names of get and set functions, you can use function literals, as shown in sample movie addpropliteral.fla on the CD.

For more information, see addProperty.htm on the CD.

watch() AND unwatch()

The `watch()` and `unwatch()` methods register and unregister a callback function that is called whenever an attempt is made to change a particular property. This is a powerful capability, but one that comes at a cost: If you watch a property that is constantly changing, the callback function fires constantly, creating an excessive processing load.

The `watch()` method is useful for debugging. It can also be used as a kind of general-purpose event generator, like an `addListener()` for changes in properties. However, you can have only one watchpoint at a time on any given property. If you set a second watchpoint, it replaces the previous one. This contrasts with listeners: You can have as many listeners as you want for any given event. With `watch()`, you could implement your own event model so that any number of objects could "get the news" when the property changes.

The `watch()` method is not recommended for use with getter/setter properties. Although it may work to some extent, it could miss some changes, and there is a potential for creating excessive processing loads. Most built-in properties are getter/setter properties.

To start to watch a property, take these two steps: Define a callback function and execute the `watch()` statement. Table 21.8 shows formats for both steps, as well as the format for terminating the `watch()` with `unwatch()`.

TABLE 21.8   watch, callback, **AND** unwatch

Method/Function	Format	Parameters
watch	myObj.watch(property, callback, userData);	*property*—Specifies the property to watch (a string) *callback*—Specifies a callback function (a reference) *userData*(optional)—Specifies data to be sent to the callback function
callback function	function myFunc (property, oldval, newval, userData) { // statements }	*property*—Contains the property that changed *oldval*—Contains the previous value of *property* *newval*—Contains the new value of *property* *userData*—Contains data defined in the userData parameter of the watch() statement
unwatch	myObj.unwatch (property);	*property*—Specifies the property to stop watching

Both watch() and unwatch() return true if successful; otherwise, they return false.

The callback function is invoked as a method of the object containing the watched property (such as myObj in Table 21.8). Inside the callback function, this refers to myObj.

The object, such as myObj, that contains the property to be watched must exist when you set the watchpoint, and the watchpoint disappears if you delete the object. However, the watchpoint exists independently of the *property* it is watching. You can create a watchpoint on a property that does not yet exist, and the watchpoint will go into effect when you create the property. Similarly, you can delete a property for which a watchpoint has been set without destroying the watchpoint. If you later re-create the property, the watchpoint will still be in effect. To remove a watchpoint without deleting the object, use the unwatch() method.

The sample movie watch.fla contains a statusObj object with a property named isOkay:

```
statusObj = new Object();
statusObj.isOkay = "okay";
```

The following line sets a watchpoint on the isOkay property:

```
statusObj.watch("isOkay", setStatusText);
```

The callback function setStatusText() is as follows (I omitted the fourth parameter, *userData*, because it's not used):

```
function setStatusText (prop, oldval, newVal) {
    statusField.text = newVal;
    if (newVal == "okay") {
        statusField.setTextFormat(okayFormat);
```

21

```
    }
    else {
        statusField.setTextFormat(errorFormat);
    }
}
```

If the new value for the isOkay property is "okay", the status field text format is set to the okayFormat. If the new value for the isOkay property is anything other than "okay", the status field text format is set to the errorFormat.

The callback function is triggered by an *attempted* change in a property value. However, any actual change in that property is under the control of the callback function. If the callback function does *not* return a value, the property value is set to undefined. This is always the case with the setStatusText() function just shown, for instance. It never returns anything, so the watched property is always undefined.

If the callback function *does* return a value, the property is set to the return value. Because the callback function gets the previous value as its second parameter, it can nullify the change simply by returning the previous value. The watch() method's capability to control the value of the property or nullify the change distinguishes it from the addProperty() method.

THE Math OBJECT

Math is not actually a class but a singleton, that is, an instance of a class that can have only one instance.

Often, mathematical functions are the most straightforward way to achieve a desired motion or effect, whether smooth and natural or wildly and wonderfully unnatural. In addition, Math functions are often more flexible than any other approach, including tweening; that is, you can accomplish a broader range of tasks with them.

NOTE

> Combining the drawing methods and the math methods can yield marvelous results. On the CD, see drawing.htm and examples from Keith Peters (3Dcube.fla and test5.fla) and Millie Maruani (api_flower.fla and api_cube.fla).

The Math object has enough methods with varied uses to fill a book by itself. I'll give examples of some of the most common methods and some of the most powerful ones.

For a full listing of math functions, **see** "Math Methods and Attributes" in Appendix A, **page 957**.

COMMON Math FUNCTIONS

Among the most commonly used methods of the Math object are floor(), random(), and round().

floor() The floor() method truncates a decimal number and returns just the integer portion. For example:

```
x = Math.floor (8.21) // result: 8
x = Math.floor (8.5) // result: 8
x = Math.floor (-8.21) // result: -9
x = Math.floor (-8.5) // result: -9
```

random() The random() method returns a decimal number greater than or equal to 0 and less than 1, usually with 14 to 17 digits. For example:

```
x = Math.random();
/*
Sample results:
0.236938397510414
0.102950482211518
0.274189059284604
0.585484127786702
0.00277895387391511
0.80261959452304
*/
```

round() The round() method rounds a decimal number to the nearest integer. Here are some examples:

```
x = Math.round (8.21) // result: 8
x = Math.round (8.5) // result: 9
x = Math.round (8.6) // result: 9
x = Math.round (-8.21) // result: -8
x = Math.round (-8.5) // result: -8
x = Math.round (-8.6) // result: -9
```

In the following example, mcPercent is the integer percent of myClip that has been loaded:

```
mcPercent = Math.round(
    (myClip.getBytesLoaded() / myClip.getBytesTotal()) * 100
);
```

To round decimal fractions, first multiply by a power of 10, round, and then divide by the same power of 10. The power of 10 you use determines the number of decimal places you round to. For instance, the following example rounds y to one decimal place:

```
y = .12;
yr = Math.round(10*y)/10; // yr is .1
```

In the preceding example, if y is any positive decimal fraction, yr will be 0.0, 0.1, 0.2, 0.3, 0.4, 0.5, 0.6, 0.7, 0.8, 0.9, or 1.0.

GENERATING A RANDOM INTEGER FROM 0 TO 9, INCLUSIVE

You can combine random() and round() to produce random integers. This code executes the steps one by one:

```
for (i = 0; i < 10; i++) {
    x = Math.random(); // generate random number less than 1
    x *= 10; // multiply by 10
```

21

```
        x = Math.round(x); // round off
        trace(x);
}
```

Here's a shorter, faster form, replacing the whole body of the preceding `for` loop:

```
trace(Math.round(Math.random()*10));
```

USING `Math.sqrt()` TO GET AND SET RELATIVE POSITIONING

The `Math.sqrt()` (square root) method can be used both to determine and to control the position of one movie clip relative to another, or relative to any known point on the Stage. For instance, `Math.sqrt()` can be used to keep a draggable movie clip a fixed distance from a point, thus constraining the clip's movement to an arc.

This use of the `Math.sqrt()` method to control position is founded on the fact that the position of a movie clip on the Stage is completely determined by two numbers: its x position and its y position. Therefore, you can constrain a draggable clip to any path if you can come up with a formula that will give you one of these numbers if you have the other.

In Figure 21.2, if I give you an x position within the range of the arc, you can tell at a glance what y position you would have to assign to the mouse to keep it on the arc.

Figure 21.2
The `Math.sqrt()` function keeps the mouse a constant distance from the center point of the arc, thus keeping it on the arc.

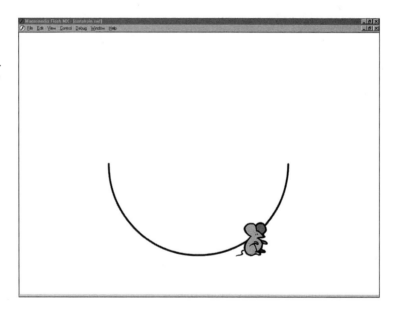

So perhaps it's not surprising that there is a mathematical equation that can do the same thing. By putting this equation into the mouse movie clip's *enter frame* event handler, you can force the mouse onto the arc in every frame where the x position permits it. This technique is demonstrated in sample movie constrain.fla.

The equation gets the mouse's _x property and then sets its _y property appropriately. The equation uses the fact that every point on the arc is the same distance from the center of the arc, namely, half the width of the arc movie clip. This distance is the radius of the arc, r in the formula. Here's the ActionScript:

```
onClipEvent(load){
    var r = root.arc._width/2; // the radius of the arc
    var ctr_x = 400; // the x position of the arc's center
    var ctr_y = 300; // the y position of the arc's center
}
onClipEvent(enterFrame) {
    y = Math.sqrt( (r * r) - ( (_x - ctr_x) * (_x - ctr_x) )) + ctr_y;
}
```

How was the formula derived?

Start from the fact that the distance between any two points on the Stage can be reduced to an x difference and a y difference. For example, in Figure 21.2, to get from the mouse to the center of the half circle, instead of going directly, you could go up (the y difference) and then left (the x difference).

Similarly, if you're given the x and y differences, the direct route is obvious. These three distances form a triangle, and given any two sides of a triangle, the third one is always obvious. Mathematically, if you know the direct distance from the mouse to the center of the arc and the x difference from the mouse to the center of the arc, you can calculate the y difference.

In this case, the distance from the mouse to the center of the arc is the radius of the arc, r; it is half the width of the arc movie clip (arc._width / 2). The x difference is _x minus ctr_x, _x being the x position of the mouse (you don't have to specify the movie clip instance name because the code is inside the mouse event handler), and ctr_x being the x position of the center point of the arc. Similarly, the y difference is _y minus ctr_y.

The equation that gives you the y difference is a form of the *Pythagorean theorem*, which says that $y^2 = r^2 - x^2$, where y is the y difference, r is the radius, and x is the x difference.

In ActionScript, the equation is as follows:

```
(y - ctr_y) * (y - ctr_y) = r * r - (x - ctr_x) * (x - ctr_x);
```

Taking the square root of both sides, you get the following:

```
y - ctr_y = Math.sqrt (r * r - (x - ctr_x) * (x - ctr_x));
```

Adding ctr_y to both sides gives the desired formula:

```
y = Math.sqrt( (r * r) - ( (_x - ctr_x) * (_x - ctr_x) )) + ctr_y;
```

BASIC TRIG METHODS: Math.sin() AND Math.cos()

The trigonometry methods, of which the most commonly used are sine (Math.sin) and cosine (Math.cos), are perhaps the most versatile methods of the Math object. These are

21

demonstrated in several `.fla` files on the CD. For instance, sample movie treeshadow.fla uses the `_rotation` property of a movie clip to make a "tree" topple, and animates its lengthening shadow as it falls, using the cosine (`Math.cos`) method, while calculating how far the top of the tree is from the ground, using the sine (`Math.sin`) method.

Sample movie enemy.fla uses trig to determine whether a gun is pointing at an enemy. You could use a similar approach to determine how many degrees (`_rotation`) to open a monster's jaws to accept an object of a given size.

The triangle in the circle on the left side of Figure 21.3 provides a visual representation of the sine and cosine functions. The sample movie, Helen Triolo's trigdemo.fla, brings it to life: On the left side of the figure, the sine and cosine functions are shown as legs of a triangle in a "unit circle," in which radius r is one unit in length. The radius is the hypotenuse (longest leg) of the triangle. The radius and the horizontal leg of the triangle form an angle, *[Θ] (theta)*. As the radius rotates around the circle, the horizontal leg of the triangle is the cosine, and the vertical leg is the sine, of the angle [theta] (theta). On the right side of the figure, you see how the sine function, in going up and down, traces a sine wave over time.

theta

Figure 21.3
A screenshot from trigdemo.fla. (Source: Helen Triolo)

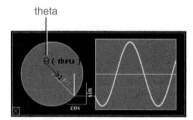

Officially, the sine is the ratio of the vertical leg to the hypotenuse (y/r), but if the hypotenuse measures one unit ($r = 1$), then y/r is just y. Similarly, the cosine is the horizontal leg over the hypotenuse (x/r), which equals x if r equals 1.

CAUTION

Flash measures `_rotation` *clockwise*, whereas the unit circle assumes *counterclockwise* rotation. You can reverse Flash's natural rotation direction to get it to match trigonometry functions better.

CAUTION

The unit circle assumes that zero degrees rotation is at 3 o'clock on the circle. Zero degrees rotation for a movie clip is whatever position it starts in. If a movie clip representing a tree starts with the tree upright, the tree will point to 90° (12 o'clock) on the unit circle when its `_rotation` is zero degrees.

21

By visualizing your movies within this unit circle, you can see how to produce the effects mentioned in the first paragraph of this section. See trigdemo.fla and trigdemo.htm on the CD for more details.

USING TRIG TO GET AND SET WIDTH AND HEIGHT

Sample movie treeshadow.fla uses the _rotation property of a movie clip to make a "tree" topple, as shown in Figure 21.4, and animates the tree's lengthening shadow as it falls, using the cosine (Math.cos) method, while calculating how far the top of the tree is from the ground, using the sine (Math.sin) method.

Figure 21.4
Using trig to lengthen a shadow and measure distance from the ground.

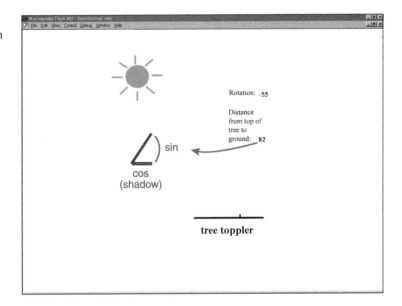

The toppling tree is the radius rotating (treeHeight in the program). This happens to be the *width* of the tree movie clip because the tree starts out lying down horizontally on the Stage. The shadow the tree casts is the cosine. The decreasing distance from the top of the tree to the ground as it falls is the sine.

Because this is not a unit circle (treeHeight is not equal to 1), you have to divide the horizontal leg of the triangle by the radius (treeHeight) to get the cosine. So, when the tree has fallen halfway to the ground (45°), you get

```
shadow / treeHeight = cos(45)
```

Multiplying both sides by the length of the tree, you get

```
shadow = cos(45) * treeHeight
```

The following line from sample movie treeshadow.fla uses shadow._xscale instead of an absolute value for setting the shadow width. However, because the _root.shadow clip is 100

21

pixels wide, setting its _xscale is the same as setting its _width. (See "Sizing Clips via Scale Instead of Height and Width," in trigdemo.htm on the CD.) The following code also converts the rotation measurement from degrees to radians for use by the cosine function:

```
_root.shadow._xscale = Math.cos(deg2rad(_root.tree._rotation))*treeHeight;
```

Radians and Degrees

In ActionScript, the trigonometry functions require angle measurements in *radians*. If you prefer to work in degrees, use a function that translates degrees into radians. The formula is

```
radians = degrees * pi / 180
```

Thus, in the sample movie, treeshadow.fla, to find the cosine of the rotation of a falling tree, you use

```
function deg2rad(degrees) {
    return degrees * Math.PI/180;
}
Math.cos(_root.deg2rad(_root.tree._rotation)
```

Table 21.9 gives some examples of rotation measurements in degrees and their radian equivalents.

> **NOTE**
>
> The number pi (Π), represented in ActionScript by `Math.PI`, is the ratio of the circumference to the diameter of a circle, approximately 3.14.

TABLE 21.9   DEGREES AND RADIANS

Degrees	Radians
Full circle (360)	2 * Math.PI
Half circle (180)	Math.PI
Quarter circle (90)	Math.PI/2
Eighth circle (45)	Math.PI / 4

Similarly, the sine is the vertical distance divided by the radius, so you can start with

```
distance from ground / treeHeight = sin(45)
```

Multiplying both sides by the length of the tree, you get

```
distance from ground = treeHeight * sin(45)
```

The sample movie rounds off the distance to display it more easily. It also uses `Math.abs` to take the absolute value, to compensate for Flash's reversed rotation direction. Finally, it subtracts 1, which causes it to round to 0 instead of rounding to 1 at each extreme of the tree's fall.

```
_root.distanceFromGround = Math.round(Math.abs
➥(Math.sin(deg2rad(_root.tree._rotation)) *_treeHeight)-1) ;
```

USING TRIG TO GET AND SET DIRECTION

To determine whether a gun is pointing at an enemy, use the gun's pivot point as the center of the unit circle, as shown in Figure 21.5.

Figure 21.5
Sample movie enemy.fla uses the `Math.sin()` method to determine when a gun is pointing at any enemy. (Source for robot graphic: Poser 4, Curious Labs. Gremlin source: DAZ Productions.)

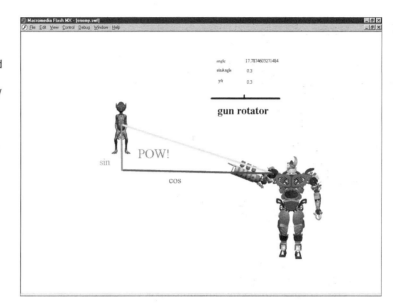

The unit is the direct distance from the gun to the enemy. Begin with the gun in a horizontal position and rotate the gun while checking in each frame whether the sine of the rotation equals the y difference between the enemy and the gun:

```
if (Math.sin(angle) == y)
```

In sample movie enemy.fla, it was necessary to add a couple of extra steps. For one, the movie starts with the gun at a nonzero rotation. The initial rotation is subtracted before the sine is taken. This effectively "zeroes out" the rotation.

```
angle = _root.gun._rotation - gunRotationStart;
```

Of course, there is the usual translation to radians:

```
sinAngle = Math.sin(deg2rad(angle));
```

The final test is completely straightforward:

```
if (sinAngle == yr)
```

The yr variable in this statement is the y difference between the gun and the enemy, expressed in terms of r:

```
var y = _root.gun._y - _root.enemy._y;
var yr = Math.round(((10*y) / r))/10;
```

Note the rounding of the y distance to one decimal place, using the `round()` method.

→ Rounding to one decimal place is discussed in "`round()`," earlier in this chapter, **page 579**.

The sine is similarly rounded:

```
sinAngle = Math.round(10*sinAngle)/10;
```

Both the sine and the y distance had to be rounded off, or they would never test equal because of minute differences.

CONTROLLING POSITION WITH `Math.sin()`

Using the `Math.sin()` method, you can vary any property of a movie clip by substituting the property for y in this equation, which represents the general format of the `Math.sin()` method:

```
y = Math.sin(x);
```

Figure 21.6 shows the result of moving the butterfly to the right (incrementing the _x property of the movie clip) the same amount in each frame, while moving the butterfly vertically (incrementing or decrementing the _y property of the movie clip) with the `Math.sin()` function.

Figure 21.6
The `Math.sin()` method can control position, speed, and rotation to produce natural, gentle transitions and effects. Here, the `Math.sin()` method controls the vertical position of the butterfly. (Human figure produced with Poser 4, Curious Labs.)

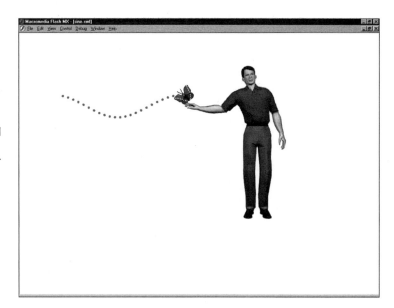

In the figure, the dots show the *sinuous* path followed by the butterfly. Here is the logic of the code controlling the butterfly's movement, expressed in pseudocode:

```
onClipEvent (enterFrame) {
    if (butterfly hasn't reached the target yet) {
        move butterfly one increment to the right;
```

```
            move b'fly vertically - amount depends on sine of x;
    }
}
```

The sine function goes through one full cycle (from peak to peak) as the x argument goes from 0 to 360 (traditionally visualized as the degrees of a circle). This example makes the butterfly go through one full sine wave by varying _x from 0 to 360.

Sample movie sine.fla expresses this logic in ActionScript. It has to make two adjustments: It adds a "y adjustment" variable (yadj), which increases the amplitude of the sine wave. Without this adjustment, the movement of the butterfly up and down would be very slight. It also uses the deg2rad() function to convert the degree measurement to radians. Here's the code:

```
// converts degrees to radians
function deg2rad (degrees) {
    return degrees * Math.PI/180;
}
bfly.startx = 0; // x starting point
bfly.endx = 360; // x ending point
bfly.starty = 112;
bfly._x = startx; // position the bfly at start
bfly._y = starty; // position the bfly at start
bfly.xinc = 16; // x increment for movement to the right in each frame
bfly.yadj = 8; // y adjustment - increases amplitude of sine wave
}
bfly.onEnterFrame = function() {
    if (bfly._x < bfly.endx) {
        bfly._x += bfly.xinc; // move bfly one increment to the right
        // move bfly vertically, amount depends on sine of x
        bfly._y += bfly.yadj * Math.sin(deg2rad(bfly._x));
    }
}
```

CONTROLLING SPEED WITH Math.sin()

You can apply the sine function to get the clip to speed up and slow down in a smooth, natural-looking way, too. Figure 21.7 shows what happens if, instead of moving the butterfly to the right the same amount in each frame, you vary the increment using the Math.sin() function. Instead of _x += xinc, you use _x += xinc + (xadj * Math.sin(deg2rad(_x))). This includes an x adjustment variable (xadj), set to 8 here, which exaggerates the amount of speed-up and slow-down. From 0–180°, the sine is positive, so the butterfly speeds up while moving down. From 180–360°, the sine is negative, so the butterfly slows down while moving up.

Remember that, in Flash, "moving down" means _y is getting larger. "Speeding up" means increasing the amount added to _x in each frame. Thus, a positive sine makes the butterfly move downward and speed up. Conversely, a negative sine makes the butterfly move upward and slow down. The changes in speed are indicated by the horizontal distances between the dots.

21

The slow-down means that the butterfly is in the 180–360° range for more frames than it is in the 0–180° range. (In Figure 21.7, each dot is one frame. Notice how many more dots there are in the second half of the butterfly's journey.) Thus, `_y += yadj *` `Math.sin(deg2rad(_x))` is executed more times with a negative sine than with a positive sine, making the butterfly move up farther than it moves down. Compensate for this by starting lower, substituting `var starty = 175` for `var starty = 112`. (See sample movie sine2.fla on the CD.)

Figure 21.7
Controlling speed using the
`Math.sin()`
method. The butterfly slows down as it moves up. (Human figure produced with Poser 4, Curious Labs.)

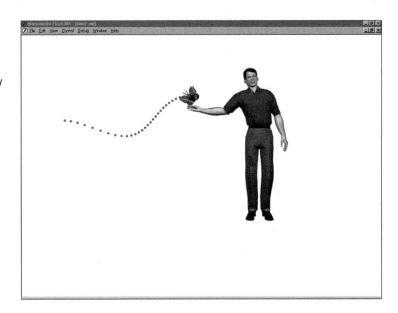

OTHER TRIG METHODS

Here are the other trig methods, specified in terms of the sine and cosine of a unit circle. Substitute `y/r` for `sin` and `x/r` for `cos` if r does not equal 1. The angle `theta` is specified in radians in all cases.

The arcsin (`asin`) method returns the angle given the sine:

```
theta = asin(sin)
theta = Math.asin(y/r);
```

The arccos (`acos`) method returns the angle given the cosine:

```
theta = acos(cos)
theta = Math.acos(x/r);
```

The tangent (`tan`) method returns the sine divided by the cosine:

```
sin/cos = tan(theta)
y / x = Math.tan(theta);
```

The arctangent (atan) method returns the angle given the tangent:

```
theta = atan(sin/cos)
theta = Math.atan(y/x) ;
```

THE System OBJECT

 The System object (which is a singleton, like the Math object) represents the computer (or other device, such as a PDA) on which the Flash Player is running. In Flash MX, the System object had only one property, capabilities, with 10 documented properties. In Flash MX 2004, the capabilities object has 26 properties, listed in Table 21.10.

TABLE 21.10 System.capabilities **PROPERTIES**

Properties	Meaning	Example	Comment
avHardwareDisable	Gets enabled/disabled status of camera and microphone	true	true means disabled (n)
hasAccessibility	Supports accessibility features	false	
hasAudio	Has audio capabilities	true	
hasAudioEncoder	Has an audio encoder	true	
hasEmbeddedVideo	System supports embedded video	true	(n)
hasMP3	Can play MP3 files	true	
hasPrinting	Has printing capability	true	(n)
hasScreenBroadcast	Supports development of screen broadcast applications (through Flash Communication Server)	false	(n)
hasScreenPlayback	Can play back screen broadcast applications (through Flash Communication Server)	false	
hasStreamingAudio	Can play streaming audio	true	(n)
hasStreamingVideo	Can play streaming video	true	(n)
hasVideoEncoder	Has a video encoder	true	
isDebugger	Debugger is active (special debugging version of Flash Player)	true	(*)
language	Gets the language, two-character code defined in ISO 639-1	en	(*)English
localFileReadDisable	Disabled/enabled status for local file reading	true	true means disabled (n)
manufacturer	Gets the manufacturer's string	Macromedia Windows	(*)

21

continues

Table 21.10 Continued

Properties	Meaning	Example	Comment
os	Gets the operating system	Windows 2000	(*)
pixelAspectRatio	Gets the pixel aspect ratio	1	
playerType	Gets type of Flash Player	"StandAlone", "External", "PlugIn", "ActiveX"	(n)
screenColor	Gets color, black & white (bw), or grayscale (gray) screen type	color	
screenDPI	Gets screen dots per inch in pixels	72	
screenResolutionX	Gets horizontal screen resolution (pixels)	1024	
screenResolutionY	Gets vertical screen resolution (pixels)	768	
serverString	Gets the string to send to server	A=t&MP3= t&AE=t& VE=t&ACC= f&DEB=t& V=WIN%206 %2C0%2C21 %2C0& M= Macromedia Windows& R=1024x768 &DP=72& COL=color &AR=1.0& I=point&OS= Windows 2000& L=en-US	(*)
version	Gets the version of Flash Player	WIN 7,0,0,231	(*)
windowlessDisable	Enabled/disabled status of browser's windowless modes	true	true means disabled (n)

(*) in Comment column indicates feature was present but undocumented in Flash MX.
(n) in Comment column indicates new feature, not present in Flash MX.

All the System.capabilities properties are effectively read-only. Although you may be able to set (change) them, it doesn't accomplish anything.

The serverString summarizes all the system capabilities in a single string that can be sent to a communications or application server. Note that serverString has been broken up into multiple lines so that it fits into Table 21.10. In practice, you receive it as a single, unbroken string, and that is how it is sent to the server, as well.

In addition, new features in Flash Player 7 include an onStatus event, two methods (setClipboard and showSettings), two Boolean attributes (useCodepage and exactSettings), and the security object, which has two methods (allowDomain and allowInsecureDomain).

The onStatus event is a "catch-all" event that can trap onStatus events for LocalConnection, NetStream, or SharedObject objects. Any time you don't create an onStatus event for any of these objects, the event will be trapped by the System.onStatus event handler, assuming you have created one.

➔ SharedObject and LocalConnection are covered later in this chapter under "The Shared Object Class," **page 602**, and "The LocalConnection Class," **page 596**. For more on the NetStream class, **see** "NetConnection, NetStream and the Rich Media Classes," **page 647**, in Chapter 22, "External Communications."

The setClipboard method allows you to write text to the system clipboard.

The showSettings method shows the settings in the Flash Player settings panel.

The useCodepage attribute tells the Flash Player whether external text files will be encoded using the default single-byte character codes associated with the Windows or Mac operating system (the default, true), or whether they will use double-byte Unicode (false).

➔ For more on Unicode, **see** unicode.htm on the CD accompanying this book.

The rest of the features all pertain to security.

The exactSettings attribute determines whether several URLs in the same main domain (for example, http://myHost.ourDomain.com and http://yourHost.ourDomain.com) access local settings (such as camera or microphone access permissions) or locally persistent data (shared objects) from a single source (http://ourDomain.com), or whether each URL does so from its own individual local source. The default is true for SWFs published for Flash Player 7 (requiring the local settings to be stored separately for each subdomain), and false for SWFs published for Flash Player 6 (allowing shared storage for the local settings).

The allowDomain method specifies which domains are allowed to access objects and variables in movies in the same domain as the movie executing the allowDomain method (which includes the movie executing the method itself). In Flash Player 6, you can just specify the main domain name, like this:

```
System.security.allowDomain("yourDomain.com");
```

In Flash Player 7, you need to specify full domain names:

```
System.security.allowDomain("www.yourDomain.com", "yourHost.yourDomain.com");
```

In movies published for Flash Player 6, allowDomain allows a container SWF loaded via HTTPS (HTTP Secure) to be accessed by SWFs loaded via non-secure HTTP. This is a lax behavior, which was eliminated for movies published for Flash Player 7, where objects

21

and variables in HTTPS-based SWFs can by default be accessed only by other HTTPS-based SWFs. If you want to relax this rule to allow insecure SWFs to access secure SWFs in movies published for Flash Player 7, you must use `allowInsecureDomain`.

MOVIE-RELATED CLASSES AND GLOBAL OBJECTS

ActionScript defines a number of classes and global objects (singletons) designed specifically for creating Web animation. Sixteen such classes are categorized as Movie-related and listed under Built-in Classes, Movie in the Macromedia Flash MX Toolbox list (on the left side of the Actions panel). These 15 Movie objects are as follows: `Accessibility`, `Button`, `Color`, `ContextMenu`, `Key`, `LocalConnection`, `Mouse`, `MovieClip`, `PrintJob`, `Selection`, `Sound`, `Stage`, `TextField`, `TextFormat` and `TextSnapShot`. Three of these, `ContextMenu`, `PrintJob` and `TextSnapShot`, are new in Flash MX 2004.

These Flash-specific objects are not defined in the ECMA-262 standard or implemented in JavaScript. Nevertheless, they include some of the most widely used classes in ActionScript, such as `MovieClip`, `TextField`, and `TextFormat`.

All the movie-related classes and objects are listed in Table 21.11.

TABLE 21.11   MOVIE-RELATED OBJECTS

Object	Represents	Singleton?	Comments
`Accessibility`	Screen reader program	Y	
`Button(n)`	Onscreen buttons	N	(*)
`Color`	Colors	N	
`ContextMenu`	Flash Player context menu	N	(n)
`Key`	Keystrokes	Y	
`LocalConnection`	Local inter-movie communication	N	
`Mouse`	Mouse cursor and clicks	Y	
`MovieClip`	Movie clip	N	(*)
`PrintJob`	Printing	N	(n)
`Selection`	Edit text selection and focus	Y	
`Sound`	Sound/music	N	
`Stage(n)`	The Stage	Y	
`TextField`	Text fields	N	
`TextFormat`	Formatting for text in text field	N	
`TextSnapShot`	Static text	N	(n)

(n) new in Flash MX 2004
(*) not a singleton, but can't create new instances with new keyword

21

THE Accessibility OBJECT

 The Accessibility object represents the ability of the Flash Player to make Flash movies accessible to the visually impaired. Flash accessibility relies on screen reader software that supports Microsoft Active Accessibility (MSAA). Screen reader software interprets text and certain other screen elements and reads them out loud. Window-Eyes from GW Micro is currently the most popular screen reader that supports Active Accessibility.

The Accessibility object has two documented properties:

The isActive() method checks whether an MSAA-compliant screen reader is active. Based on this information, you can load a more accessible interface into your movie or steer the user to a special accessible site. You should wait a second or two after your movie has loaded before executing isActive(). Otherwise, you may get a false return, even though a screen reader is active.

 You use the updateProperties() method after you have changed an accessibility property. The updateProperties() method causes Flash Player to update its description of all accessible objects and notify screen readers of any changes.

 There is also an _accProps variable, which can be used as a global variable applying to the whole movie, or as an attribute of a movie clip, button, dynamic text field, or input text field. It lets you set accessibility options, overriding those set in the Accessibility Panel at authoring time.

There are five accessibility properties. Three of them, name, description, and shortcut (keyboard shortcut) are self-explanatory. The other two are as follows:

- silent—Whether the movie or object "talks"—that is, whether it has been made accessible; true means it is *not* accessible.

- forceSimple—Whether child movies or objects are accessible; true means they are *not* accessible.

You can use the System.capabilities.hasAccessibility property to determine whether the system supports MSAA (even though the reader may not be currently active).

→ For more information on accessibility, **see** http://www.macromedia.com/macromedia/accessibility/features/flash/ and Appendix B, "Making Flash Accessible," **page 977**.

THE Button CLASS

The Button class has five properties (enabled, tabEnabled, tabIndex, trackAsMenu, and useHandCursor) and nine dynamic events (onPress, onRelease, onReleaseOutside, onRollOver, onRollOut, onDragOut, onDragOver, onKillFocus, and onSetFocus).

→ Button events are covered in "Button Events," **page 508**, in Chapter 20. The Button properties are the same as those for movie clips, described in the table of movie clip properties in Appendix A, "ActionScript Reference."

The Button class has only one method, getDepth(), which returns the depth of the button instance.

21

The `Button` constructor function cannot create new buttons. You have to create buttons manually or by using `attachMovie()`. (However, the `initObject` argument of `attachMovie()` does not work with buttons.)

THE Color CLASS

Each instance of the `Color` class programmatically controls the color and transparency (alpha) of a particular movie clip or of the main movie. You can use color changes to simulate various conditions. For instance, continuously darken the color of an entire movie to simulate nightfall, or add yellow and white when a spotlight hits something. Alpha can be used for fade-ins and fade-outs, and to simulate something semi-transparent like a veil.

In Flash, color has four components: red, green, blue, and alpha (or transparency).

You can work with color in ActionScript in two basic ways:

- Set or get a new color, replacing any existing color and not affecting alpha. To do so, use the `setRGB()` and `getRGB()` methods.

- Use `setTransform()` to modify an existing color, or use `getTransform()` to determine how the color is currently transformed. Using the transform approach, you can set and get alpha in addition to color.

Either way, you first need to create a color object for a particular movie clip, by using the target movie clip's instance name as the single string parameter to the `new` statement:

```
myColor = new Color("myClip");
```

setRGB() AND getRGB()

You can set the color of a movie clip using `setRGB()` and a six-digit hexadecimal number representing three pairs of digits. The pairs represent red, green, and blue values, respectively. Here are some examples:

```
myColor.setRGB(0xFF0000); // sets myColor to red
myColor.setRGB(0x00FF00); // sets myColor to green
myColor.setRGB(0x0000FF); // sets myColor to blue
```

→ For more details on hexadecimal notation, **see** hexadecimal.htm on the CD accompanying this book.

Web developers are familiar with hexadecimal numbers from HTML syntax like the following:

```
<BODY BGCOLOR="#00FF00">
```

In Flash, the fill-color box (indicated by a Paint Bucket icon in the Colors section of the Toolbox) gives you a handy way to determine the hexadecimal values of colors. Click on the fill-color box and then run the Eyedropper over the color swatches. As the Eyedropper passes over a swatch, the hexadecimal value of the color appears in the input box at the top of the fill-color box.

The `getRGB()` method returns the currently assigned color. For instance, to compare the colors stored in two instances of the `Color` class, you can use `getRGB()`.

The getRGB() method returns the color as a decimal number. To transform that into a hexadecimal number, use the toString() method of the Number class, like this:

```
hexColor = myColor.getRGB().toString(16);
```

setTransform() AND getTransform()

The setTransform() method allows you to transform all the colors and the alpha of a given movie clip. For instance, if you have a movie clip that contains 100 other clips of various colors, you can remove a little red and add a little blue on all of them in one operation by using setTransform(). In contrast, with setRGB(), you can only set them all to the same color. The setTransform() method is most useful for making changes to bitmaps, which contain many colors that you cannot address individually. The setTransform() method allows you to achieve subtle changes in tint exactly the same as those achievable via the Advanced Effect panel. (In the Properties Panel, select Advanced in the Color combo box, and then click the Settings button.)

Before you can use setTransform() and getTransform(), you need to create a *transform object*, which has eight properties corresponding to the eight input boxes on the Advanced Effect panel.

Both the Advanced Effect panel and the transform object contain four pairs of numbers, corresponding to red, green, blue, and alpha. The first number in each pair, the *transformation percentage*, is an integer from -100 to 100, which serves as a percentage multiplier for the existing color. The second number in each pair, the *offset*, is an integer from -255 to 255, which represents a color value. You take the result from the percentage multiplication and add the offset color value. Expressed in an equation, it looks like this:

```
newColor = ( oldColor × transformationPercentage ) + offset
```

This equation is, in fact, shown on each of the four lines in the Advanced Effect panel.

The transformation percentage multipliers are ra, ga, ba, and aa, for red, green, blue, and alpha, respectively.

The offset color values are rb, gb, bb, and ab, for red, green, blue, and alpha, respectively.

The following line of code creates a transform object, using an object literal:

```
myTransform = {ra:100,rb:255,ga:100,gb:255,ba:100,gb:255,aa:100,ab:255};
```

After you create a transform object, you can apply it to any instance of the Color class, as follows:

```
myColor.setTransform(myTransform);
```

The color of the movie clip associated with myColor changes.

Multiple setTransform() operations are *not* cumulative. Each transform operates on the original color values, assigned at authoring time or using the drawing API.

The getTransform() method returns a copy of the current transform object—the one set with the most recent setTransform().

21

THE CONTEXTMENU CLASS

 Creating the ContextMenu object itself using the customItems attribute (an array of ContextMenuItem objects) is covered in Appendix A, "ActionScript Reference." ContextMenu events are covered in " Using Event Handlers to Trigger Action" in Chapter 20. Also see contextMenu.fla on the CD accompanying this book.

THE Key OBJECT

The Key object represents user input via the keyboard.

The Key object has just four methods: getAscii(), getCode(), isDown(), and isToggled().

→ For an explanation of the four Key object methods, and for examples of using Key class methods with and without listeners, **see** "Key Events," in Chapter 20, **page 511**. Just preceding the "Key Events" section in Chapter 20, the last item in the "Button Events" section is an explanation of the on(keyPress) button event, **page 508**.

Eighteen constants, such as Key.BACKSPACE and Key.TAB, allow you to conveniently refer to commonly used keys without having to use their numeric codes. For instance:

```
if (Key.isDown(Key.UP)) {
    // then do things
}
```

→ For a listing of methods and constants associated with the Key object, see Appendix A, "ActionScript Reference," under "Key Object Methods and Constants."

If you need to determine the keycode of a particular key, you can create a keycode tester with the following code (also included on the CD as keytester.fla):

```
_root.createTextField("myTextField", 1, 50, 50, 100, 50);
myTextField.variable = "kc";
myTextField.setNewTextFormat(new TextFormat(null,20,0x000000,true));
_root.onEnterFrame = function () {
    kc = String.fromCharCode(Key.getCode())+" : "+Key.getCode();
};
```

When you press a key, its numeric code is displayed in the text field.

If you want to test keycodes within the authoring environment, select Control, Disable Keyboard Shortcuts while the movie is running. Disabling keyboard shortcuts allows the preceding code to pick up keys such as Backspace and Tab that are normally "trapped" by the keyboard shortcut feature.

THE LocalConnection CLASS

→ For more on LocalConnection, **see** tictactoe.htm, tictactoe_lc.fla, and player_lc.fla on the CD accompanying this book.

The LocalConnection class makes it possible for multiple SWFs running on the same computer to communicate. A movie can trigger an event handler in another movie, and movies can exchange arbitrary data. The local connection feature is browser independent and thus works regardless of JavaScript support in the browser. It also works in the Flash 6 Player and in Flash projectors.

To enable a movie to communicate over a local connection, you must first create an instance of the `LocalConnection` class. You can use that one instance to communicate over any number of *connections* or virtual channels. Each connection has its own name and is a one-to-one communication channel with another movie. To send over a connection, you use the `send()` method of the local connection instance. To receive, you use the `connect()` method.

The format for the constructor function is straightforward:

```
myLocalConnection = new LocalConnection();
```

The `LocalConnection` class has four methods: `send()`, `connect()`, `close()`, and `domain()`. You use both `send()` and `connect()` whenever you use a local connection, though some SWFs may only send, whereas others may only receive.

In addition, if the communicating movies are not in the same domain, you need to create an `allowDomain` or `allowInsecureDomain` handler in the receiving movie to validate domains from which you are willing to receive. You can also define an `onStatus` event handler in the sending movie, which receives a notification of success or failure when you invoke the `send()` method. The `onStatus` event handler is invoked when a `send()` command returns `true`. (The `send()` command returning `true` indicates that the format of the command was acceptable, but *not* that the data was actually dispatched.) The `onStatus` event handler receives as a parameter an object with a string property named `level`. If the value of the level property is `status`, the data was dispatched successfully. If the value of the level property is `error`, the data was *not* dispatched successfully. This occurs, for instance, if there is no one "listening" on that connection.

The following code, from tictactoe_lc.fla on the CD, displays the connection status in a text field, along with a name identifying the SWF:

```
myName = "tictactotallyautomatic";
xLC.onStatus = function(infoObject) {
    if (infoObject.level == "error") {
        _root.statusField.text = myName+" Connection xLC failed.";
    }
    else _root.statusField.text = myName+" Connection xLC succeeded.";
}
```

See Table 21.12 for a listing of `LocalConnection` methods and event handlers.

TABLE 21.12   `LocalConnection` **METHODS AND EVENT HANDLERS**

Name	Method/ Event Handler	Format	Description
send	M	`myLocalConnection.send` `(connectionName,` `method[, p1... pN])`	Sends data over *connectionName*. Returns `true` if the format of the command is acceptable.
connect	M	`myLocalConnection.` `connect(connectionName)`	Starts listening on *connectionName*.

21

continues

TABLE 21.12 CONTINUED

Name	Method/ Event Handler	Format	Description
close	M	`myLocalConnection.close` `(connectionName)`	Removes connection. Returns true if successful, `false` if no such connection exists.
domain	M	`myLocalConnection.` `domain()`	Returns a string containing the name of the domain of the SWF containing the `LocalConnection` instance. For example, `macromedia.com`.
allowDomain	E	`myLocalConnection.` `allowDomain = function` `(senderDomain) { }`	Created on the receiver, should return `true` if senderDomain is an acceptable sending domain.
onStatus	E	`myLocalConnection.` `onStatus = function` `(infoObject) { }`	Provides notification, via the `infoObject.level` property, of success or failure of a `send()` command.

The format for the `send()` method is as follows:

```
myLocalConnection.send(connectionName, method[, p1... pN])
```

Both connectionName and method are strings. The optional parameters supplied as p1 through pN may be of any datatype. The movie that is "listening" on the connection named in connectionName automatically executes the event handler named in method. Parameters p1 through pN are passed to the method.

Here's a `send()` example, also from tictactoe_lc.fla, using a local connection instance named xLC, a connection named xmove, an event handler named move(), and a variable named num.

```
xLC.send("xmove", "move", num);
```

On the receiving end, the `connect()` method is used to associate the event handler method with a particular connection. The format is simple:

```
myLocalConnection.connect(connectionName);
```

Here's an example that uses a local connection instance named oLC and a connection named xmove:

```
oLC.connect("xmove");
```

Receiving movies use the `allowDomain()` or `allowInsecureDomain()` method to accept or reject connections, based on the sender's domain. The ActionScript interpreter passes the domain name to the `allowDomain()` event handler as a parameter. If the `allowDomain()` method returns `true`, the connection is allowed. In the following example, only connections from allowedDomain.com are accepted:

```
xLC.allowDomain = function(senderDomain){
     return (senderDomain == "allowedDomain.com");
}
```

Senders and receivers can specify the sender's domain explicitly, as in the following examples:

```
xLC.send("flashoop.com:xmove", "move", num);
the oLC.connect("flashoop.com:xmove");
```

If the connection name contains a colon, it is assumed that you have provided the domain name explicitly.

If the connection name does not contain a colon, by default it is prefixed with the domain of the movie containing the LocalConnection instance. Thus, two SWFs running in the same domain can use a connection name with no domain name, as in the following examples:

```
xLC.send("xmove", "move", num);
oLC.connect("xmove");
```

For SWFs loaded from the local hard disk, the domain is localhost. For example, the following two statements are equivalent if the sending movie was loaded from the local hard disk:

```
oLC.connect("xmove");
oLC.connect("localhost:xmove")
```

When you're loading SWFs from different domains, if you want to accept the connection without checking the domain name, take these two steps:

- Start the connection name with an underscore character. Messages will be sent with no domain name. Here are examples:

  ```
  oLC.connect("_myConnection");
  xLC.send("_myConnection", "move", num);
  ```

- Create an allowDomain() handler for the receiver that always returns true, as in the following example:

  ```
  oLC.allowDomain = function(senderDomain){
       return true;
  };
  ```

Connections whose names begin with an underscore character are also accepted if the actual domain is localhost, even with no allowDomain() method.

There is no built-in multicasting for local connections. Thus, for instance, if three movies must all communicate with one another, each movie uses three connections: one to "listen" on and one to talk to each of the other movies. For instance, one movie might be listening on a connection named incominga, one on incomingb, and one on incomingc. In that case, the relevant code in the first movie would look like this:

```
1: myLocalConnection = new LocalConnection();
2: myLocalConnection.connect("incominga");
3: myLocalConnection.onReceive = function(message) {
```

21

```
4:        // your event handler code goes here
5: }
6: function sendAll() {
7:        myLocalConnection.send("incomingb", "onReceive", _root.input.text);
8:        myLocalConnection.send("incomingc", "onReceive", _root.input.text);
9: }
```

The code in the second movie would look the same, except that it would have `incomingb` on line 2 and `incominga` on line 7. The third movie would have `incomingc` on line 2 and `incominga` on line 8.

THE Mouse OBJECT

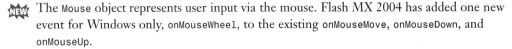 The `Mouse` object represents user input via the mouse. Flash MX 2004 has added one new event for Windows only, `onMouseWheel`, to the existing `onMouseMove`, `onMouseDown`, and `onMouseUp`.

→ For a discussion of `Mouse` events, see "Mouse Events," **page 512**, in Chapter 20. Also see the "Button Events" section, **page 508**. Most button events are mouse-related.

Beyond its event-related capabilities, covered in Chapter 20, the `Mouse` object has two methods: `show()` and `hide()`. The `hide()` method allows you to hide the standard mouse cursor. Then you can substitute a custom mouse cursor. The `show()` method makes the standard mouse cursor visible again.

For instance, say you want your cursor to look like a magic wand. Create a movie clip containing the magic wand graphic. Then, if the clip's instance name is `magicWand`, the code looks like this:

```
Mouse.hide();
_root.onEnterFrame = function () {
        magicWand._x = _root._xmouse
        magicWand._y = _root._ymouse
}
```

Then, to go back to the standard cursor, do this:

```
magicWand._visible = false;
Mouse.show();
```

THE PrintJob CLASS

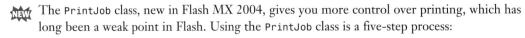 The `PrintJob` class, new in Flash MX 2004, gives you more control over printing, which has long been a weak point in Flash. Using the `PrintJob` class is a five-step process:

1. Create a new `PrintJob` instance, using the `new` keyword.

2. Use the `start` method to display the operating system Print dialog to the user. If the user cancels or an error occurs, the start method returns `false`. Otherwise, the user has chosen to print, and the start method returns `true`.

3. Use the `addPage` method one or more times to add pages to the print queue.

4. Use the `send` method to initiate printing. This brings up the standard operating system Print dialog, giving the user the opportunity to print or cancel.

5. Delete the `PrintJob` instance.

After the user has chosen to print, five attributes are set to show the page setup characteristics the user has chosen. These are shown in Table 21.13. These attributes can only be set automatically; they are "read-only" from your point of view as a programmer.

TABLE 21.13   PAGE SETUP ATTRIBUTES

Property	Type	Units	Comments
`myPrintJob.paperHeight`	Number	Points	Paper height
`myPrintJob.paperWidth`	Number	Points	Paper width
`myPrintJob.pageHeight`	Number	Points	Height of printable area (ignores any user-defined margins)
`myPrintJob.pageWidth`	Number	Points	Width of printable area on the page (ignores any user-defined margins)
`myPrintJob.orientation`	String	n/a	`portrait` or `landscape`

Only the `addPage` method has any complexity to it, in that it allows you to print just a portion of the screen, just a particular level or frame, to limit printing to a particular movie clip, as well as to use a `printAsBitmap` option that captures transparency and color effects of bitmaps. (By default Flash prints in a vector mode.)

Here is a minimal `addPage` method call, which prints level zero, in the default vector mode, including the whole Stage, and not limiting the printing to any particular movie clip:

```
myPrintJob.addPage(0);
```

Here's as example that limits printing to a particular area of the screen. The numbers are given in pixels, measured from the registration point, which is the upper left for the root and the midpoint for child movie clips. Thus, this will give you an area starting at the upper left and including 500 pixels over to the right and 400 pixels down.

```
(myPrintJob.addPage(0, {xMin:0,xMax:500,yMin:0,yMax:400}))
```

This adds printing in the bitmap mode, and printing only frame 3 of level 2:

```
myPrintJob.addPage(2, {xMin:0,xMax:500,yMin:0,yMax:400}, {printAsBitmap:true}, 3)
```

If you want to skip one option, but use a subsequent option, use `null` for the skipped option. For instance, to print frame 3 but use the default full-screen and vector printing:

```
myPrintJob.addPage(0, null, null, 3)
```

The `addPage` method returns `true` if the call was successful (that is, the page was added to the queue), and `false` if it was unsuccessful (nothing was added to the queue).

21

Here's a complete print job session:

```
var myPrintJob = new PrintJob();
ok = myPrintJob.start();  // user prints or cancels job
if (ok) {
    trace ("user chose to print the job");
    for (i in myPrintJob) trace (i+" : "+myPrintJob[i]); // show page setup
    success = myPrintJob.addPage(0);
    if (success) trace ("page added to queue");
    myPrintJob.send();
}
else trace ("job cancelled")
delete myPrintJob;
```

THE Selection OBJECT

The Selection object controls the edit text selection and focus.

→ Events for the Selection object are covered in "Selection Events," **page 515**, in Chapter 20. For more details on selection and focus, also look in "Event Handlers and Focus," **page 507**; "Button Events," **page 508**; and "Key Events," **page 511**.

In addition to its event-based capabilities, the Selection object has three methods dealing with the currently selected text, or *selection span*. Each of these methods returns an index into the selected text. The index is zero-based. That is, the first position is 0, the second position is 1, and so on.

getBeginIndex() returns the index of the beginning of the selection span.

getEndIndex() returns the index of the end of the selection span.

In both cases, if the method fails to find a valid index (for example, because there is no currently focused selection span), the method returns -1.

getCaretIndex() returns the index of the blinking cursor position. If no blinking cursor is displayed, the method returns -1.

For instance, to find out whether the cursor is at the end of a selected text field, you do the following:

```
if ( Selection.getCaretIndex() == Selection.getEndIndex() )
    // do something
```

THE Shared Object CLASS

The Shared Object class creates persistent storage of ActionScript objects on the user's local hard drive. The typical usage of this class is similar to that of "cookies" for browsers, namely, to store user-specific information on the user's computer, in such a way that the user can exit the application and even turn off the computer, without destroying the stored information. The next time the user starts the application, the application is able to access the shared information. For instance, a shared object could be used to store a username, password, or preferences. Information is both stored as and retrieved as an ActionScript object.

The ActionScript programmer has no access to the local file system, so shared objects create no security vulnerability from the user's point of view.

The Shared Object class was designed with the Flash Communication Server in mind. For instance, the onSync event is designed to synchronize all clients of the Flash Communication Server that have a shared object with a particular name. It fires whenever there is any change in the data in the shared object on any client. Each client receives a list of changes in the onSync event. Clients can then update their local shared objects accordingly. That's how the object is shared among all clients.

→ For more information on The Flash Communication Server, **see**
http://www.macromedia.com/devnet/mx/flashcom/.

Here's an example that creates a local shared object (line 1), stores an attribute in the shared object (line 2), writes the shared object to disk (line 3), accesses the shared object by name (line 4), and retrieves and displays the data that was previously stored (line 5):

```
1: mySO = SharedObject.getLocal("userInfo");
2: mySO.data.userName = "John Smith";
3: mySO.flush();
4: backAgain = SharedObject.getLocal("userInfo");
5: trace (uName = backAgain.data.userName); // "John Smith "
```

Notice that a shared object is created with a getLocal method, not a new statement, as shown in line 1. Data is stored as attributes of the data object, as shown in line 2. If you don't flush the information to disk, as in line 3, it will be written to disk before or when the application terminates normally.

The last two lines of the preceding example could occur at a different time, such as after exiting the application or turning the computer off. They can even be part of a different application, as long as an application knows the shared object name to request ("userInfo").

THE Stage OBJECT

One of its main purposes of the Stage object is to allow other objects to listen for the Stage.onResize event. The Stage.onResize event handler is typically used to adjust the dimensions or layout of the movie to fit the new size of the window.

→ For more details on the Stage.onResize event, **see** "The Stage onResize Event," **page 516**, in Chapter 20. "Basic ActionScript").

The Stage object has five properties, two of which are read-only:

- height—Specifies the height in pixels (read-only).
- width—Specifies the width in pixels (read-only).
- showMenu —Determines whether the File-View-Control-Help menu bar is displayed at the top of the standalone Flash Player.
- align—A string property that determines how graphical content on the Stage is aligned. The eight possible values are Top Left (TL), Top (T), Top Right (TR), Left (L), Right (R), Bottom Left (BL), Bottom (B), and Bottom Right (BR).

21

Here's the arrangement:

```
TL T TR
L    R
BL B BR
```

For example:

```
Stage.align = "B"; // align at the bottom center
```

The ActionScript interpreter is extremely forgiving of extraneous elements in the string you provide: It simply looks for the first occurrence of one of the acceptable strings, as in this example:

```
Stage.align = "^&*&%$#@WBF"; // sets Stage.align to "B"
```

If none of the acceptable strings is present in the string you supply, Stage alignment is set to fully centered (the missing space between L and R in the middle row of the preceding text "diagram"), and the `Stage.align` property is set to the empty string. For example:

```
Stage.align = ""; // align fully centered
```

■ scaleMode—Specifies the scaling mode of the Flash movie within the Stage. This string property has four legal values: `"exactFit"`, `"showAll"`, `"noBorder"`, and `"noScale"`. For instance:

```
Stage.scaleMode = "noScale";
```

In the standalone Flash Player (and in the authoring environment), the scaleMode property affects three characteristics of the graphics in a Flash movie: whether the graphics distort or remain proportional; whether the graphics scale when the user changes the size of the Player window; and if the graphics do scale, whether they scale to fit the larger or smaller dimension of the Player window, or both.

`"exactFit"` distorts to fill the Stage. That is, it scales to both the larger and the smaller dimension and does not crop the graphic.

`"showAll"` remains proportional and scales to prevent cropping. That is, it scales to fit the smaller dimension.

`"noBorder"` eliminates any "empty" border at the edges of the stage and scales to the larger dimension. Therefore, it may be cropped in the smaller dimension.

`"noScale"` does not scale and therefore may crop in both dimensions.

If you do not set a scaleMode value, it defaults to `"showAll"` in the standalone Flash Player and `"noScale"` in the authoring environment. In the browser, the default `Stage.scaleMode` is typically `"showAll"`.

The behavior that the default scaleMode causes in the browser depends on the setting of the Scale option on the HTML tab in the Publish Settings dialog box.

Four options on the HTML tab in the Publish Settings dialog box parallel the scaleMode options. (Select File, Publish Settings, and the Scale combo box.) The option you select on the HTML tab affects only parameters in tags in the HTML file. They determine what happens if you edit the HTML file and change the original WIDTH and

HEIGHT parameters in the OBJECT tag. The HTML Scale settings do *not* allow the Flash movie to adjust on the fly as the user changes the size of the browser window.

The HTML tab setting and Stage.scaleMode do interact. There may be browser and platform (such as Windows versus Mac) dependencies. In general, if Stage.scaleMode is set to "noScale" and the HTML Scale setting is either No scale or Default (Show All), you can change the values of the WIDTH and HEIGHT parameters in the OBJECT tag of the HTML file, and the SWF will not distort to fit the new size.

Table 21.14 shows some sample settings and what happens if you change the values of the WIDTH and HEIGHT parameters in the OBJECT tag of the HTML file. (Tested with IE 5.5. in Windows.) For instance, the first row of the table tells you that, if Stage.scaleMode is exactFit and the Scale setting on the HTML tab in Publish Settings is No scale, Exact fit, or Default (Show All), the graphic will be scaled to fit both the WIDTH and HEIGHT parameters in the OBJECT tag of the HTML file, distorting the graphic if necessary. On the other hand, if the Scale setting on the HTML tab is No Border, the graphic will scale proportionately (no distortion allowed), so that it fully occupies the larger of the WIDTH and HEIGHT parameters in the OBJECT tag. For instance, if WIDTH is 50 and HEIGHT is 100, the graphic will be 100 pixels high. If the proportionately scaled width is more than 50 pixels, the graphic will be cropped in the horizontal direction.

TABLE 21.14   Stage.scaleMode AND **HTML TAB SCALE SETTING INTERACTION**

Stage.scaleMode	HTML Tab "Scale" Setting	Result in IE 5.5
"exactFit"	No scale, Exact fit, or Default (Show All)	Nonproportional scaling (distort shape to fit height and width)
	No Border	Proportional scaling to larger dimension, cropping as necessary
"noScale"	Exact fit or No border	Proportional scaling to larger dimension, cropping as necessary
	No scale or Default (Show All)	No scaling
None (default)	No scale or Default (Show All)	No scaling
	Exact fit	Nonproportional scaling (distort shape to fit height and width)
	No border	Proportional scaling to larger dimension, cropping as necessary

THE TextField AND TextFormat CLASSES

 In addition to the menu attribute, used with the ContextMenu class, the TextField class has two new Boolean attributes (condenseWhite and mouseWheelEnabled). The big development, however, is the new StyleSheet class, which allows you to create a StyleSheet object to apply Cascading Style Sheets (CSS).

StyleSheet is the last topic in this section.

condenseWhite determines whether extra "white space" (which includes spaces, line breaks, and paragraph breaks) in an HTML text field should be removed when the field is displayed in a browser. The default value is false. If you set condenseWhite to true, you must use HTML tags such as <BR> and <P> to get line breaks and paragraph breaks in the text field. condenseWhite applies only to HTML text; therefore, if the html property of the text field is false, condenseWhite is ignored.

mouseWheelEnabled determines whether multiline text fields scroll when the mouse pointer is over a text field and the user turns the mouse wheel. By default, mouseWheelEnabled is true.

There are three basic steps to dynamically creating a text field. The steps are as follows:

1. Create the text field.
2. Set one or more properties of the field.
3. Format the field.

The first two come into play for every text field that you create dynamically. The last, formatting, is optional; you can just use default formatting.

DYNAMICALLY CREATING A TEXT FIELD

You create a text field dynamically, using the createTextField method of the MovieClip class. The format is as follows:

```
myClip.createTextField ("myTextField",depth,x,y,width,height)
```

myClip is the movie clip in which you are creating the new text field. myTextField is the instance name of the new text field. depth is the depth of the text field. x and y are the x and y coordinates of the text field, measured in pixels from the registration point of myClip. width and height are the width and height of the text field, measured in pixels.

For instance:

```
myClip.createTextField ("myTextField",2,100,100,25,12);
```

This example creates a new, empty text field named myTextField that is a child of myClip, at a depth of 2, 100 pixels to the right of and 100 pixels down from myClip's registration point. The text field is 25 pixels wide and 12 pixels high.

The newly created text field has a number of properties. For instance, Flash sets the _x and _y properties of the text field equal to the x and y parameters passed to createTextField(). Similarly, Flash sets the _width and _height properties of the text field equal to the width and height parameters passed to createTextField(). Flash also sets the type property to dynamic. All newly created text fields are dynamic unless and until you explicitly set the type property to input.

For a complete list of text field attributes, methods, and events, **see** Appendix A, "ActionScript Reference," under "TextField Attributes, Methods, and Events."

21

SETTING PROPERTIES OF THE TEXT FIELD

A new text field needs to have at least one attribute set, and possibly several, before it becomes useful. You need to do one or more of the following:

- Set the `variable` attribute for the text field.

    Because new text fields are automatically *dynamic* (as opposed to *input* or *static*) text fields, all you need to do is set the `variable` attribute, and the text field will immediately start displaying the value of the variable you specify.

- Set the `text` attribute for the text field.

    The `text` attribute determines what text will be displayed in the field. Both dynamic and input text fields display the text in their `text` properties.

- Make the field an input field by setting the `type` attribute equal to `"input"`.

> **NOTE**
>
> You cannot create "static" type text fields dynamically. You can, however, use "dynamic" type text fields exactly like static text fields.

You can have both a `variable` and a `text` attribute associated with a single dynamic or input text field, and display the `variable` and `text` properties alternately.

Other text field properties you might want to set include the following:

- `border = true` to give the text field a border
- `multiline = true` to allow the text field to display multiple lines of text, as opposed to just a single line
- `wordWrap = true` so that lines of text that are too long for the text field will "wrap" (display on the next line down) automatically

FORMATTING USING A `TextFormat` OBJECT

The text field properties mentioned in the preceding section do not format the text. For example, they do not underline, bold, or italicize text. Nor do they set the font, size, or color of the text. To do these types of things, you can create a `TextFormat` object and apply it to the text field. `TextFormat` is a class. Use it with the `new` keyword to create a `TextFormat` object, as follows:

```
myTextFormat = new TextFormat( font, size, color, bold, italic, underline, url,
➥ target, align, leftMargin, rightMargin, indent, leading);
```

All `TextFormat` parameters are optional and may be set to `null` to indicate that they are not defined. Trailing parameters (parameters that come after the last parameter you want to set) can be omitted entirely. Here's an example of creating a new `TextFormat` object, with red, bold text:

```
myTextFormat = new TextFormat(null,null,0xFF0000,true);
```

21

You can set `TextFormat` properties individually after creating the `TextFormat` object, as in this example:

```
myTextFormat.underline = true;
```

Though not as concise, setting properties individually is more readable.

→ For a complete list of `TextFormat` attributes and the only `TextFormat` method, `getTextExtent()`, see Appendix A, "ActionScript Reference," under "`TextFormat` Attributes and Methods."

You associate a new `TextFormat` object with a text field by using the `setTextFormat` method of the `TextField` class. For example:

```
myTextField.setTextFormat(myTextFormat);
```

To associate a new `TextFormat` object only with new text entered into a text field (for example, when a user is filling in an input field), use the `setNewTextFormat()` method of the `TextField` class, as shown in this example:

```
myTextField.setNewTextFormat(myTextFormat);
```

 *Losing formatting when you load new text into a text field? **See** the "Troubleshooting" section at the end of this chapter, **page 615**.*

Text Format Tags Embedded in HTML Text

You can embed text format tags in HTML text. Embedded tags can be used in addition to, or as an alternative to, `TextFormat` objects. Embedded tags make it easy to apply an attribute to just part of the text. For instance, in the sample movie htmltags.fla, which follows, the LEFTMARGIN and INDENT attributes apply to both paragraphs of HTML text, whereas the BLOCKINDENT attribute applies to only the second paragraph. Note that everything from line 4 onward is one long line of code.

```
1: _root.createTextField("mytext", 1, 50, 50, 300, 100);
2: myText.html = true;
3: myText.wordwrap = true;
4: myText.htmlText = "<TEXTFORMAT LEFTMARGIN=\"12\" INDENT=\"6\">
➥<P ALIGN=\"LEFT\"><FONT FACE=\"_sans\" SIZE=\"20\" COLOR=\"#FF0000\">
➥This is the first paragraph, with no block indent.
➥</FONT></P><TEXTFORMAT BLOCKINDENT=\"30\">
➥<P ALIGN=\"LEFT\"><FONT FACE=\"_sans\" SIZE=\"20\"
➥COLOR=\"#000000\"> This is the second paragraph, with a block indent.
➥</FONT></P></TEXTFORMAT></TEXTFORMAT>";
```

FORMATTING USING CSS

→ Formatting using CSS is briefly introduced under "Text: Spelling, Formatting, Translating," **page 326**, in Chapter 14, "What's New in Flash MX 2004?"

→ For a list of `StyleSheet` methods and the only `StyleSheet` event, see Appendix A, "ActionScript Reference," under "StyleSheet Methods and Event."

Formatting using CSS is basically a three-step process:

1. Create a new `StyleSheet` object.

2. Add one or more styles to the `StyleSheet` object.

3. Apply the `StyleSheet` object to a `TextField` object.

CREATE A NEW StyleSheet OBJECT   You create a new StyleSheet object with a typical new statement:

```
var myStyleSheet:TextField.StyleSheet = new TextField.StyleSheet();
```

Notice that the StyleSheet object is a property of the global TextField object—not of a particular text field.

ADD ONE OR MORE STYLES   You can add styles to a StyleSheet object either by loading an external stylesheet (.css file) using the load method, or by using the setStyle or parseCSS methods in ActionScript, with no external file.

Using an external file is usually preferable. For one thing, you don't have to cut and paste to reuse the same styles in another project. In addition, other programs such as Dreamweaver may be able to use the same external file.

However, the setStyle or parseCSS methods may be useful for adding styles to, or modifying styles loaded from, an existing stylesheet that you don't want to modify. In addition, they allow you to work with no external stylesheet, which may be quicker, and makes your project more self-contained.

The load method has an associated onLoad event that is called after the load completes, either successfully or unsuccessfully. It receives a Boolean parameter, set to true if the load was successful, and to false if the load was unsuccessful.

Here's an example of loading an external stylesheet, with an onLoad callback function that displays the style names if the load is successful:

```
myStyleSheet.onLoad = function(success) {
  if (success) {
    // display style names
    trace(this.getStyleNames());
  } else {
    trace("CSS load unsuccessful");
  }
}
myStyleSheet.load("SEUStudioMX.css")
```

Here are a couple of setStyle statements:

```
myStyleSheet.setStyle("h2", {
  fontSize: '24'
});
myStyleSheet.setStyle(".REF",
  { fontSize: '12',
    color: '#00FF00' }
  );
```

Note the use of single quote marks around the CSS values ('24'), which are not required in .css files. Also note that the CSS properties are separated by commas, not by semicolons, as they are in a .css file.

You can also create a "style object," giving it attributes that correspond to the ActionScript CSS properties, like this:

21

```
var myStyleObj:Object = new Object();
myStyleObj.color = '#FF0000';
myStyleObj.fontWeight = 'bold';
myStyleSheet.setStyle("em", myStyleObj);
delete myStyleObj;
```

You can delete the style object after using it in the setStyle method, and you should do so to reclaim the memory that it is using.

The parseCSS method allows you to use standard CSS syntax, using CSS property names rather than ActionScript property names, and using semicolons between properties. In the following example, we create a text string containing a standard CSS style tag named "ref" and then parse it with parseCSS:, adding the "ref" style to the myStyleSheet StyleSheet object. Note that the string starting with ".ref"—and shown here on the second and third lines—must actually be written all on one line.

```
var cssText:String =
    ".ref {color:#ff0000; font-size:20px;
    ➥[ccfont-style:italic;  text-decoration: underline; }";
myStyleSheet.parseCSS(cssText);
```

Flash MX supports only a limited subset of CSS properties, shown in Table 21.15.

TABLE 21.15   CSS PROPERTIES SUPPORTED IN FLASH PLAYER 7

CSS property	ActionScript property	Supported values
text-align	textAlign	left, center, right
font-size	fontSize	
text-decoration	textDecoration	none, underline
margin-left	marginLeft	(*)
margin-right	marginRight	
font-weight	fontWeight	normal, bold
font-style	fontStyle	normal, italic
text-indent	textIndent	(*)
font-family	fontFamily	
color	color	Hexadecimal color values
display	display	inline, block, none

(*)Flash looks at the number and applies that to the text, just as if you entered that number in the Properties Panel. It does not distinguish between points (pt) and pixels (px): You can use the number alone, as far as Flash is concerned.

When specifying the font family, mono is converted to _typewriter, sans-serif is converted to _sans, and serif is converted to _serif.

Only hexadecimal color values are supported. RGB colors (color: rgb(0,102,153)) and named colors (blue) are ignored, and the text remains the default black.

Flash is case sensitive when interpreting ActionScript CSS property names, such as fontSize. If you don't capitalize the *S* in the middle, for instance, you'll get the default font size.

For CSS properties read from an external .css file, Flash requires them to be all lowercase. This differs from the most browsers, which are not case sensitive when interpreting .css files. This is one reason you frequently have to edit .css files to use them successfully with Flash.

APPLY THE StyleSheet OBJECT TO A TextField OBJECT   Applying a StyleSheet object to a TextField object is simple: Just set the styleSheet attribute of the TextField object to the stylesheet, like this:

```
myTextField.styleSheet = myStyleSheet;
```

CSS styles work only on HTML text, so assign the text you want to format to the htmlText attribute of the TextField object, as in the following example:

```
_root.createTextField("myTextField",10,200,300,400,100);
myTextField.styleSheet = myStyleSheet;
myTextField.htmlText =
    "Here is <span class='REF'>REF style</span> and here is <h2>h2 style</h2>.";
```

OTHER HANDY FLASH CSS FEATURES   You can get the names of all the styles in a StyleSheet object by using the getStyleNames method. The names are returned in an array. Here's an example:

```
var myNameArray:Array = myStyleSheet.getStyleNames();
trace(myNameArray.join("\n"));
```

You can get the style object associated with any style, using the getStyle method. The style object is similar to the style object shown previously, used for setting a style. The following code gets a style object and displays all its properties by using a for-in loop:

```
emStyleObject = myStyleSheet.getStyle("em");
for (i in emStyleObject) trace (i+" : "+emStyleObject[i]);
```

You can use the clear() method to clear all the CSS properties from all the styles in a stylesheet, like this:

```
myStyleSheet.clear();
```

The names of the properties remain in the StyleSheet object. After you have cleared the CSS properties, getStyle returns null for all styles.

THE TextSnapshot CLASS

 The TextSnapshot class is designed to let you examine the static, non-selectable text in a movie clip. Instead of being created with a new statement, a TextSnapshot object is returned by the MovieClip.getTextSnapshot method, like this:

```
myTextSnapshot = myClip.getTextSnapshot();
```

The following code (textSnap.fla on the CD) should create a TextSnapshot object (line 2), search for the word "test" in it (line 3), set a "select color" of red to highlight selected text (line 4), select the word "test" (line 5), and display the selected text (line 6). It actually does all of that, except set the select color. Apparently, that feature doesn't work as advertised.

```
1: searchWord = "test";
2: var myTextSnapShot:TextSnapshot = myMC.getTextSnapshot();
3: foundIndex = myTextSnapShot.findText(0,searchWord,false);
4: myTextSnapShot.setSelectColor(0xFF0000);
5: myTextSnapShot.setSelected(foundIndex,foundIndex+searchWord.length,true);
6: trace(myTextSnapShot.getSelectedText());
```

BUILDING YOUR OWN COMPONENTS

→ For an introduction to V2 components, which are new in Flash MX 2004, **see** Chapter 18, "Animation, Interactivity, and Rich Media," **page 379**.

 A V2 component is essentially a custom class with a number of specific attributes and methods. Thus, the basics of creating components are the same as the basics of creating classes, described at the beginning of this chapter.

Building a component is typically a five-step process:

1. Create a movie clip in the Library and set its Linkage and AS 2.0 Class properties.

2. Create visual assets, and put them in the second frame of the new movie clip's Timeline, with a stop() action in the first frame.

3. Set Component Definition properties in the Library.

4. Create an .as class file, which embodies the component.

5. Export the component as an SWC (compiled SWF) file and put it in a specific directory where Flash will find it and include it on the Components Panel, where it's easily accessible for use in projects.

If that sounds pretty simple, it actually can be. From the coding perspective, the complexity of building a component is all in creating the .as file, which is where all the ActionScript goes. (No ActionScript for the component is contained in the .fla file.) If the ActionScript required is simple, creating the component is simple, too.

I am going to illustrate this by walking through the steps of creating what I believe may be the World's Simplest Component. The CD contains a finished example, in worldsSimplestComponent.fla and WorldsSimplestComponent.as.

Open a new .fla file and save it under whatever name you wish. I'll be using worldsSimplestComponent.fla here.

Create a new movie clip symbol in the Library, giving it any name you wish. In the Create New Symbol dialog, click the Export for ActionScript check box, and clear the Export in

First Frame check box by clicking it. In the Linkage section, enter an Identifier; I'm going to use worldsSimplestComponent. For the AS 2.0 Class, enter the name of the class (the name of the .as file, but without the .as extension), which will hold the ActionScript for your component. I'll use WorldsSimplestComponent. Remember that class names are capitalized by convention.

That completes step 1.

Because this component doesn't have any visual assets, we get to skip step 2.

Right-click on the movie clip in the Library, and go to the Component Definition option. Type the class name (for example, WorldsSimplestComponet) under AS 2.0 Class. Click the Display in Components Panel check box, and click OK. Notice that we didn't add any parameters at the top of the dialog. Flash will do that for us automatically when we create the class.

That completes step 3.

Now comes what would be the hard part, if this weren't possibly the World's Simplest Component: creating the .as file. In this case, however, it will be pretty straightforward. If you read the first section of this chapter, there will only be a couple of the new items here.

Here's what the .as file looks like:

```
// WorldsSimplestComponent.as
 1:   import mx.core.UIComponent;
 2:   class WorldsSimplestComponent extends mx.core.UIComponent{
 3:       var className:String = "WorldsSimplestComponent";
 4:       static var symbolOwner:Object = WorldsSimplestComponent;
 5:       static var symbolName:String = "WorldsSimplestComponent";
 6:
 7:       private var __message:String =
              "Am I the World's Simplest Component, or What?";
 8:       [Inspectable(defaultValue="World's Simplest Component", verbose=1,
category="Other")]
 9:     public function get message ():String {
10:           return __message;
11:       }
12:
13:       function WorldsSimplestComponent()
14:       {
15:           trace ("Creating World's Simplest Component");
16:       }
17:       function size(Void):Void
18:        {
19:           trace( "size" );
20:           super.size();
21:       }
22:
23:       function draw(Void):Void {
24:           var container:MovieClip =
                  this.createEmptyMovieClip( "container_mc", 0 );
25:           container.createTextField("message_txt",10,-100,-100,400,100);
26:           container.message_txt.htmlText = message;
27:       }
28:  }
```

21

Much of the preceding code is standard equipment for a component, including:

- Importing mx.core.UIComponent (or whatever class the component is inheriting from) in first line.
- The class declaration with the extends keyword.
- The attributes on lines 3–5, which must have the names shown (className, symbolOwner, and symbolName), and should be given values reflecting the name of the class itself, as shown.
- A constructor function, on lines 13–16. This is most often left empty for components. Here, it contains a trace statement for testing purposes.
- A size() method, as shown on lines 17–21. The purpose of this function is to react to changes in the component's size. In this case, all we are doing here (other than displaying a trace for testing purposes) is running the size() method of the super class.
- A draw() method, shown on lines 23–27. This is the method that "draws" the component on the stage. In this case, it contains the component's only functionality: creating an empty movie clip, creating a text field in the movie clip, and assigning a string variable to the htmlText property of the text field.

Providing the data infrastructure for the draw() method, we have a private variable (__message), which contains the text to display (line 7), and a get function for that variable (lines 9–11).

That leaves just one unexplained element, on line 8. This is a *metadata tag*, one of seven possible tags that provide component-specific information. This one, the *Inspectable* tag, causes the component feature that follows it (the get method in this case) to be exposed to users in the Component Inspector panel.

That concludes step 4.

If you drag the component from the Library onto the Stage now, you will see the trace message from the constructor function, saying Creating World's Simplest Component.

Right-click on the movie clip in the Library, and select Export SWC File. Give it a name (WorldsSimplestComponent.SWC in this case), and Flash will create an SWC file in the current directory.

All that remains now is to copy the SWC file to the Components directory (in Windows: Program Files\Macromedia\Flash MX 2004\en\First Run\Components\) and create a new directory with any name you wish. Copy the SWC file into the new directory.

Exit Flash and restart it. Open the Component Inspector, and you will see your directory as a category of components. Your new component will be in it. Drag it onto the Stage and watch it perform.

Running Superclass Initialization Code

Many component classes have initialization code, embodied in an `init()` function. In that case, when subclassing the component class, you would usually include an `init()` function in your subclass that runs the superclass `init()` function. Here's an example:

```
function init(Void):Void {
    super.init();
    // subclass-specific initialization code goes here
}
```

As indicated by the comment in the preceding example, you can also include subclass-specific initialization code after running the superclass `init()` function.

→ If you would like to advance to the next step by creating a slightly more complex component, and with visual assets, but still following very much the same steps outlined here, **see**
http://www.macromedia.com/devnet/mx/flash/articles/footer_component.html.

TROUBLESHOOTING

Why are my trig functions going crazy?

When trig functions give wildly unexpected results, one common reason is that you forgot to convert degree measurements into radians. Although Flash measures _rotation in degrees, all the Flash trigonometry functions require angles to be measured in radians.

→ Measuring angles in radians and degrees is discussed in the sidebar "Radians and Degrees," earlier in this chapter, **page 584**.

Why am I losing formatting when I load new text into a text field?

Say you've created a text field named `myText`, set the `text` attribute, and applied a format named `myTextFormat`. It works fine. When you change the text by assigning a new value to the `text` attribute, the text field reverts to its original configuration from the Properties Panel.

You need to use `setNewTextFormat()` in addition to `setTextFormat()`. This sets the format for new incoming text. You need to set it only once.

The following example shows the way to set the format. The problem, when the formatting reverts, is that you don't have a line like line 7.

```
1: _root.createTextField ("myText",2,100,100,200,20);
2: myTextFormat = new TextFormat()
3: myTextFormat.Color = 0xFF0000;
4: myTextFormat.font="verdana";
5: myText.text = "Original text";
6: myText.setTextFormat(myTextFormat);
7: myText.setNewTextFormat(myTextFormat);
8: myText.text="Here's some new text." ;
```

CHAPTER **22**

EXTERNAL COMMUNICATIONS

In this chapter

Introduction to External Communications   618

Communicating Locally   618

Introduction to Network-Aware Communications   623

Loading Text Data with `LoadVars`   625

XML Data   634

Customizing HTTP Headers with `addRequestHeader()`   646

`NetConnection`, `NetStream` and the Rich Media Classes   647

22

INTRODUCTION TO EXTERNAL COMMUNICATIONS

A Flash movie is capable of two basic types of external communications: local and network-aware. By "local" communication, I mean methods of communication that work only within the boundaries of a single computer. This primarily means communicating with the environment in which the movie is running. Movies typically run either in the Flash Player in a browser, or else as a stand-alone projector (a self-contained executable application). Which you generate depends on whether you choose to output as a Flash movie (SWF) or a projector in the Publish Settings dialog (File, Publish Settings).

By "network-aware" communication, I mean methods of communication that *can* reach outside a single computer through the use of network protocols, such as HTTP. That most importantly means communicating with servers, such as Web servers. However, the same techniques that are used, for instance, to download files from Web servers, can also be used to "download" files from the file system on the computer where the movie is running.

COMMUNICATING LOCALLY

Your Macromedia Flash movies can run in one of several environments. The most common environment is the Flash Player in a Web browser. You can also run a Flash movie as a standalone projector or inside a Macromedia Director movie. In all these cases, the movie can communicate with the environment in a number of ways. In this section, you'll look at how the movie can communicate with the local environment if it is running in the Flash Player in a browser or as a projector.

→ Two important means of communicating locally, Shared Object and LocalConnection, are covered in Chapter 21, "Advanced ActionScript," under "The Shared Object Class," **page 602**, and "The LocalConnection Class," **page 596**.

→ You can embed Flash MX movies into Macromedia Director MX as cast members. This is one of the most powerful aspects of both Flash and Director. To find out more about using Macromedia Director, **see** *Special Edition Using Macromedia Director MX* by Gary Rosenzweig (ISBN: 0789729032) .

CONTROLLING THE BROWSER

Flash movies can work just like the HTML <A HREF> tag when viewed in a Web browser, acting as a navigation control for the browser and changing the page being shown in the browser. They can also affect the page being shown in other browser windows and frames.

USING getURL()

The main tool for controlling the browser is the getURL() global function. This global function sends a message to the browser to tell it to load a new page from a specified URL. Calling the getURL() global function is just like a user clicking a link in an <A HREF> tag in the browser.

The following button script uses the getURL() global function to load a page named newpage.html:

```
on (release) {
    getURL("newpage.html");
}
```

N O T E

The Flash Player does not perform the actual page loading. It sends a message to the browser. It is then up to the browser to do the work.

A URL is a Uniform Resource Locator. It is the one required parameter of the getURL() global function.

There are two types of URLs: relative URLs and absolute URLs. A relative URL can be a local file, such as the newpage.html file in the previous example. It can also be a relative path to a file or directory.

An example of a relative URL that specifies a file in a directory below the current one is myfolder/newpage.html. This example specifies the file newpage.html, which is found in the folder named myfolder.

An absolute URL is a complete path to a file or directory on a server. An example of an absolute URL is http://www.mysite.com/newpage.html.

You can use getURL() with a relative URL to load a page on the same server as the current Web page. You can also use a relative URL to load a page on your local hard drive when the page is on the hard drive or when the movie is running as a projector.

You can use an absolute URL in getURL() only if you have an Internet connection because it usually calls out to a site on a Web server, not a page on your local machine.

Because the power of getURL() is not in Flash, but rather in the Web browser, you can use anything as a parameter that the browser understands as an address. For instance, if you want to make the browser list the files on an FTP server, you can use a URL such as ftp://ftp.myserver.com/. The browser lists the files there, as long as the browser supports FTP and the FTP site supports anonymous FTP, presuming no username or password is required.

TARGETING WINDOWS AND FRAMES

A second parameter that you can give getURL() is a target. This target can be a browser window, a browser frame, or a special command.

All Web browsers can have multiple windows open, each showing a different URL. These windows can be different sizes and have different toolbars, depending on how they were opened and how the user has adjusted them. You can also have multiple URLs visible in the same browser window by dividing it into frames. This is done at the HTML level with special HTML tags. Each frame in the window holds a separate URL and can be altered

22

without affecting the other frames. Most browsers can also accept special commands in their address fields as alternatives to URLs. These commands change the browser's behavior or get information about the browser.

To give getURL() a window or frame name, you first have to name your browser frames and windows. Naming them takes some planning when you create your HTML pages.

Suppose you have a two-frame page with a small navigation bar on the left and a large content frame on the right. The content frame can be named contentFrame. The navigation frame can have a Flash movie in it with navigation buttons. One of these buttons can direct the contentFrame to go to a new page like this:

```
on (release) {
  getURL("newpage.html","contentFrame");
}
```

Targeting a frame is as simple as that. The same command would even allow one browser window with a Flash movie to control the URL shown in another window. You could have a movie in the main browser window that controls a smaller pop-up window.

CREATING NEW BROWSER WINDOWS

If you use getURL() with a target that doesn't exist, the browser creates a new window to hold the content. For instance, if you target newWindow, and no window has that name, a new window named newWindow opens.

When this window exists, you can continue to address it by this name. So you can use newWindow as a target over and over again. The first time you use newWindow, the browser creates the window. Each time after that, you just change the content in the window. So a new window can be created, and you can also change its content later by using the same name. You can show HTML content to the user by creating and reusing the same window.

USING SPECIAL TARGETS

In addition to using your own names for targets, you can also use one of four special targets. Their names all begin with an underscore character. Here is a list of these special targets:

- _self—This target is the same as using no target parameter at all. It targets the current window or frame.
- _parent—This target refers to the frameset one level up from the current page.
- _top—This target refers to the window where the current frame or page is located. The page replaces all the frames in the current window.
- _blank—This target creates a new window. Using this target is the only way to guarantee that a new window will open, regardless of what any current windows are named.

To open a new window with a button, you could use a script such as this:

```
on (release) {
    getURL("newpage.html", "_blank");
}
```

CALLING JAVASCRIPT FUNCTIONS

Although getURL() allows you to load new pages with your Flash movie, you can take almost complete control of the browser by using the fscommand() global function. Using this global function, you can send messages to JavaScript in the browser. In addition, your Flash movie can receive messages from JavaScript on the Web page as well.

PROBLEMS WITH JAVASCRIPT

Before you consider using Flash-to-JavaScript communication, you should know about JavaScript's shortcomings. Mainly, it doesn't work in several browser variations.

To communicate between Flash and JavaScript, you need to have a piece of software that facilitates this communication. For Internet Explorer on Windows, this piece of software is called ActiveX. For older versions of Netscape Communicator, this piece of software is called LiveConnect. Both of these pieces of software are built-in parts of their respective browsers.

Although ActiveX is a part of Internet Explorer in Windows, it is not a part of Internet Explorer for the Mac. LiveConnect is a part of Netscape browser versions 4.7 and earlier, but it is not a part of Netscape 6 on either Mac or Windows. This leaves quite a few browser/platform variations where the fscommand() will not work: Windows users with Netscape and most Mac users. You can assume that any other browser, such as iCab or Opera, also does not support this communication. For this reason alone, most developers avoid Flash-to-JavaScript communication.

> **TIP**
>
> If you decide to use fscommand(), put a warning on your site for Mac and Netscape users so they understand the movie will not work completely with their browsers.

→ For more on calling JavaScript functions, **see** javascript_ch22.htm on the CD accompanying this book.

ALTERNATIVE TECHNIQUES

Another way to communicate from Flash to the browser relies on the fact that most browsers accept JavaScript commands in the Address field at the top of the window. You can use this technique to get around the Mac and Netscape limitations for standard JavaScript communication as mentioned earlier in the chapter.

For instance, you can open your browser and type **javascript: window.alert('Hello!');**. When you press Return (Mac) or Enter (Windows), the JavaScript after the colon should run, displaying an alert box.

22

When Flash executes a getURL() function, it is really just sending a string to the Address field in the browser. So, by using javascript: plus some JavaScript, you should be able to trigger the browser to do just about anything.

You can issue JavaScript commands or even call JavaScript functions that have been defined on the page. This technique works in most browsers, including more recent versions of Netscape on Windows and Internet Explorer on Mac. You can quickly test any browser by using a javascript: command in the Address field.

Although this technique is a good way to send messages from Flash to the browser, it doesn't help you send messages from the browser to Flash. It also has other drawbacks: For example, it frequently replaces the contents of the current browser window with the results of the JavaScript function you called.

CONTROLLING THE PROJECTOR

fscommand() has a completely different functionality if the Flash movie is running inside a projector. In that case, you're sending messages to the projector player, which accepts a limited, but useful, set of commands. For instance, you can force the projector to resize itself or quit when the user presses a button.

MODIFYING THE WINDOW

When using fscommand() in a projector, you still give it two parameters: command and arguments. The commands, however, are hard-coded into the projector, so you need to choose from a small set.

The fullscreen command enlarges the projector to the full size of the user's monitor. It stretches the contents of the Flash movie to fit this new window size. The result is that the movie takes over the whole screen. There aren't even any window borders or a title bar left.

To enlarge the projector to full screen, use this command:

```
fscommand("fullscreen", true);
```

To return the projector to its original size, use this one:

```
fscommand("fullscreen", false);
```

You can also adjust whether the movie inside the window scales. To turn off scaling, use the following:

```
fscommand("allowscale", false);
```

Then, when the projector is full screen, the movie remains its original size, centered in the window. This is also true when the user clicks and drags the window corner to enlarge or shrink the window. You can turn scaling back on by using the following command:

```
fscommand("allowscale", true);
```

HIDING THE CONTEXT MENU

In a projector, a user can Cmd-click (Mac) or right-click (Windows) to bring up a context menu. This menu allows the user to pause the movie or change the volume. You can disable this feature in a projector by using this command:

```
fscommand("showmenu", false);
```

You should disable this menu if you don't want the user controlling different aspects of your movie. You can turn it back on by using this command:

```
fscommand("showmenu", true);
```

Note that turning off this feature does not turn off the context menu completely. The user can still access Settings and About categories, but he cannot control the movie.

If you want to turn off these context menus when the movie is playing in the browser, you can turn off the Display Menu option in the HTML Publish Settings. This inserts a `menu` parameter with a value of `false` in the `OBJECT` and `EMBED` tags. Or you can insert these tags in the HTML yourself.

OTHER COMMANDS

The `quit` command simply exits a projector. Although it doesn't need a second parameter, `fscommand()` insists on a second parameter, so you can give it anything:

```
fscommand("quit", "");
```

You can also launch external applications with `fscommand()`. All you need to do is feed the command `"exec"`, plus the path to the application:

```
fscommand("exec", "test.bat");
```

Because of the `exec` command's potential for misuse, Macromedia has limited it to running from a subdirectory named `fscommand`. You must create a subdirectory named `fscommand` under the directory where your projector will run. Put the `.exe`, `.bat`, or other files that you wish to execute in the `fscommand` subdirectory. Do not put the projector itself in a subdirectory. As shown in the preceding example, you do not include the subdirectory name in the `exec` call.

INTRODUCTION TO NETWORK-AWARE COMMUNICATIONS

Flash offers six types of network-aware communication. In most cases, when you're communicating with a server, the same class permits two-way communication, both into and out of your movie. You can use

- MovieClip methods, such as `loadMovie` and `loadMovieNum` (for FP6), or the `MovieClipLoader` class (for FP7) to load SWF or JPEG files.

→ For more on loading SWF or JPEG files, **see** "Working with Movie Clips," **page 517**, in Chapter 20, "Basic ActionScript."

- The `LoadVars` class, or its predecessor `LoadVariables()`, to transfer simple text files or data from an HTML page.

- The `src` and `movie` parameters of both the `OBJECT` and `EMBED` tags (in the HTML file) to embed short pieces of text data on an HTML Page.

- The `XML` class to transfer structured information formatted in XML (Extensible Markup Language).

- The `NetConnection` and `NetStream` classes to load `.flv` video/audio files. (This is two-way only when using the Flash Communication Server.)

- Dynamic data, using Web Services or Flash Remoting, both covered in Chapter 23, "Using Flash for Dynamic Data," page 661.

In the all these cases except the last, the server, if there is one, is a Web server, and the basic communication protocol is typically HTTP. In the case of `NetConnection` and `NetStream`, the server, if there is one, is the Flash Communication Server (FCS), and the communication protocol is Macromedia's proprietary RTMP (Real-Time Messaging Protocol).

Flash MX 2004 brings three new developments in the area of network-aware external communications:

- Faster XML parsing (decoding or reading). Thank you, Macromedia!

- The ability to use `NetConnection` and `NetStream` to load external `.flv` files without FCS.

→ FLV files are introduced in "A Tale of Two Versions," **page 324**, in Chapter 14, "What's New in Flash MX 2004?".

- New `addRequestHeader()` methods for the `LoadVars` class and the `XML` class. These methods enable you to add or change HTTP *request headers*. These headers include widely-used standard headers that give the server a variety of information, such as what MIME content types (for example, text, video, audio) or character set the browser prefers or expects; special-purpose headers such as the SOAPAction header that indicates the intent of a SOAP HTTP request; and custom headers that you define yourself.

MIME Types

Browsers and Web servers classify transferred and stored content according to its MIME type. For instance, data-handling applications usually have to specify the MIME type `application/x-www-form-urlencoded` when sending data to Flash, or Flash can't use the data.

→ The use of `application/x-www-form-urlencoded` is demonstrated later in this chapter, under "Loading Dynamic Data with `LoadVars`," **page 627**.

→ The `addRequestHeader()` methods are covered at the end of this chapter, under "Customizing HTTP Headers with `addRequestHeader()`," **page 646**.

LOADING TEXT DATA WITH LoadVars

To get a piece of information from the server, you need to create the LoadVars object and then execute a load() method as follows:

```
var myLoadVars = new LoadVars();
myLoadVars.load("data.txt");
```

The preceding code uses data.txt as an example of the filename to be loaded. This text file should have a special format, consisting of any number of name/value pairs: *propertyName=propertyValue*&. The two special characters here are the equal sign and the ampersand. The equal sign divides the property name and its value. The ampersand serves as a delimiter between name/value pairs. You can place as many name/value pairs in the text file as you like. The following is an example:

```
a=7&b=42.8&c=Hello World!&
```

(The final ampersand in the preceding line is not necessary but also does no harm.)

Do not use quotation marks to indicate strings: The quotation marks will be loaded as part of the property value. In addition, you can have line breaks inside strings, and they will be included in the property value, as in the following example:

```
a=7&myString=This is a test
of a multi-line variable
passed to Flash&
```

When this data is loaded, an attribute is added to the LoadVars object for each name/value pair. For instance, in the previous examples, the attribute a is added with the value 7. You can display the a attribute in the Output window like this:

```
trace(myLoadVars.a);
```

COMPLETING LoadVars

When you use the load() method, you don't see the results instantly. First, Flash requests the file from the server; then it must wait until the file arrives. Only then can it read the information in the file. This process could take a fraction of a second or several seconds.

So how do you know when the load() is complete? There are two ways.

You can just check to see whether the loaded property of the LoadVars object is true, but doing so requires you to loop and check the loaded property over and over again. Instead, you can use the onLoad event of the LoadVars object to create a function that executes automatically when the loading is done. Here is an example:

```
myLoadVars = new LoadVars();
myLoadVars.onLoad = function() {
    results = myLoadVars.toString();
}
myLoadVars.load("loadVarsData.txt");
```

→ For more on events, **see** "Using Event Handlers to Trigger Action," **page 500**, in Chapter 20.

The preceding code segment, which you can find in the button in the sample movie named load.fla on the CD, sets the value of the variable results to the result of the toString() function. This function, when used with a LoadVars object, shows you the properties of the object in one long string. The result is as follows:

```
c=Hello%20World%21&b=42%2E8&a=7&onLoad=%5Btype%20Function%5D
```

The file loadVarsData.txt contains the following:

```
a=7&b=42.8&c=Hello World!&
```

The display order of the toString() method is the reverse of the order in which the variables are stored in the file. Also, the characters are converted to use escape characters similar to those used with Internet data. For instance, %20 stands for hexadecimal number 20, which is the decimal number 32, which is the character code for a space.

While you're waiting for a large data file to load, you can use ActionScript to track its progress. The LoadVars object includes getBytesTotal() and getBytesLoaded() methods. You can use them to create a progress display. However, in most cases, the data file is too small to need such a display.

Security Issues

By default, the Flash Player can read information only from the same domain where the Flash movie is located. (FP7 is stricter than FP6 in its interpretation of what "the same domain" means.) This is not true when you're testing a movie in Flash MX or using a standalone projector, but this restriction is enforced when you're viewing the movie over the Internet. So, by default, you cannot use Flash to load information from one Web site to another. A *policy file* on the server from which you're downloading can overcome this limitation.

→ For more on security, **see** "New Security Rules," **page 330**, in Chapter 14, "What's New in Flash MX 2004?." **Also see** crossDomainPolicyFiles.htm and security2004.htm on the CD accompanying this book.

THE LoadVariables() GLOBAL FUNCTION

It is worth mentioning the LoadVariables() global function, which is the "old-school" way of getting information from the server.

→ The use of LoadVariables is demonstrated in onData.fla on the CD accompanying this book.

LoadVariables() is similar to the LoadVars object, but instead of storing the data it receives inside an object, it creates and populates variables of the movie clip it is in, or the root level if it is at the root level. It looks like this:

```
this.LoadVariables("data.txt");
```

If the data.txt file is the same as in the previous example, variables a, b, and c will be created and populated.

You'll discover two major disadvantages to using LoadVariables(). The data is scattered into variables at the current level, rather than stored neatly inside the LoadVars object. The other disadvantage is that there is no event that can be used to deal with the variables when they have been loaded. That is, LoadVariables() has no event comparable to the onLoad event for LoadVars. Instead, to get a callback when variables have loaded, you must use onClipEvent(*data*), which is not always convenient.

An even more serious problem with LoadVariables() is that when you use it to send data (with an optional second parameter of POST or GET), it sends all the variables from the current timeline. This means you usually must create a special movie clip to hold only the data that LoadVariables() should send. LoadVars is much easier to deal with in such situations. You'll learn how to use LoadVars to send information back to the server later in this chapter.

LOADING DYNAMIC DATA WITH LoadVars

You can also use the LoadVars object to get data from a dynamically generated source. To accomplish this, you must write server-side programs, also called Common Gateway Interface scripts, or CGI scripts. CGI scripts are written with a variety of languages, such as Perl, C, and Java. Because teaching you any of these languages is beyond the scope of this book, I'll try to keep the examples as simple as possible. I'll use Perl because it is widely available and easy to understand.

Consider the example of getting the current server time. A Perl program to get the current server time and return it (time.pl on the CD) looks like this:

```perl
#!/usr/bin/perl  # tell Unix systems where Perl interpreter is
use CGI;  # use CGI.pm for easy parsing
$query = new CGI;  # create query object
print $query->header({"Content-Type: text/html"});  # declare content type

$time = localtime();
print "$time\n"; # \n is equivalent to a carriage return in the HTML
exit 0;
```

NOTE

In Perl, pound signs (#) precede comments. The "shebang" line (for example, #!/usr/bin/perl—the name is related to "bang," meaning "exclamation point") is a special case, used by Unix systems to locate the Perl interpreter. When I quote lines of Perl programs, I leave out the comments, except the shebang line.

The first line (#!/usr/bin/perl), the "shebang" line, is required on Unix systems, to tell the server where the Perl interpreter is. On Windows systems running ActivePerl, you may not need a shebang line at all, or you may need a different shebang line.

The next line (use CGI;), as the comment notes, tells the script to use the CGI.pm module, a Perl5 CGI library which provides robust parsing and interpreting of query strings passed to CGI scripts.

The third line ($query = new CGI;) creates a query object, through which you reference CGI.pm functions.

22

The fourth line (`print $query->header({"Content-Type: text/html"});`) "prints" (which really just means "outputs," in this case to the browser) a header line, telling the browser what kind of content to expect.

The heart of the program is the last three lines, which get the local server time and store it in a variable (`$time`), print the variable to the browser, and exit.

If you want to try this Perl program on your server, you need to take several steps. You can find this script, named time.pl, on the CD. Upload it to your Web server. If your server allows CGI scripts to work only in a special cgi-bin directory, you must place it there. You may have to set the permissions of the file to allow it to execute.

Creating a CGI program

If you are already lost, you have probably never created a CGI program. I strongly recommend that you get help from someone with CGI experience. Slight differences in server configurations could make running CGI scripts impossible if you don't have the help of someone with experience.

NOTE

A CGI script file from a Unix system may not run on a Windows system, because of the Unix line breaks in the file. The problem can be corrected by opening and re-saving the file with a Windows text editor.

→ If you want to teach yourself Perl, check out "*Sams Teach Yourself Perl in 21 Days*," by Laura Lemay, Richard Colburn, and Robert Kiesling, ISBN 0672320355.

Now point your browser to the Web location of the CGI program. You should see a page that looks something like this:

```
Sat Jan 24 12:13:02 2004
```

If you see an error message, perhaps your server is not configured to run CGI programs. Or you may have not set the permissions properly for the directory in which the CGI program resides. Permissions may have to be configured both for the operating system and for the Web server. There are also other minor reasons why the Perl program might not work: Perl is not installed on the server; it is at a different location than /usr/bin/perl; the time.pl file was not uploaded as text; and so on. Finding someone who has used such programs before is the best way to solve these problems.

Now that you have a Perl program that generates a simple Web page that a browser can use, you can alter it so that Flash can use it.

The first step is to use the proper MIME type for the returned information. This is the fourth line of the code. Right now it is `text/html`, but you want it to be `application/x-www-form-urlencoded`.

The next step is to format the output in the `propertyName=propertyValue` format. Assume that the movie is looking for the variable `currentTime`. Here is the resulting program (flash-time.pl on the CD):

```
#!/usr/bin/perl
use CGI;
$query = new CGI;
print $query->header({"Content-Type: application/x-www-form-urlencoded"});

$time = localtime();
print "currentTime=$time";
exit 0;
```

22

For your Flash movie to read this data, use a LoadVars object. As usual, you have to do three things to use LoadVars: create the LoadVars object, create an onLoad event for the LoadVars object, and execute a load() for the LoadVars object. Using a button with the instance name getTime_btn to execute the load(), the following code performs these three actions:

```
myLoadVars = new LoadVars();
myLoadVars.onLoad = function() {
        currentTime = this.currentTime; // "this" is myLoadVars
}
getTime_btn.onRelease = function () {
    myLoadVars.load("flashtime.pl");
}
```

The preceding code assumes that flashtime.pl is in the same directory as the SWF. If that is not the case, you need to provide a full URL to the Perl script.

You can see this code in the sample movie flashtime.fla. When the user presses the button, the movie calls out to flashtime.pl and gets the value it returns. The result should be something like currentTime=Sat Jan 24 12:13:02 2004.

Then the myLoadVars property currentTime (this.currentTime on line three in the preceding program) is copied to the root-level variable currentTime. This variable is linked to a dynamic text field, so you can see the result.

To get this movie working on your server, you need to upload flashtime.pl, flashtime.html, and flashtime.swf. They should all be placed in the same directory. You may need to set permissions for the directory, so that Perl scripts can run there.

The time displayed in the Flash movie is a reflection of the real time on the server. So the time is different each time you run the movie.

Setting the time is the simplest example of using dynamic information. From here, using such information all depends on your ability as a server-side programmer (or your connections with one). You can replace this simple Perl program with one that reads from a database and returns some complex data. For instance, it could return a random set of trivia questions or the latest stock quotes.

→ Sending email directly from Flash is another example of what can be done with Perl and CGI. **See** flashEmail.fla, flashEmail.pl, and flashEmail.html on the CD accompanying this book. (This script uses Unix sendmail and doesn't work on systems that don't support this capability.)

SENDING DATA WITH LoadVars

Sending information back to the server from Flash is similar to sending it back to the server from an HTML page. A CGI program must be at the other end to accept and record the information sent. Either of two commands may be used: GET or POST.

The GET method is the simplest. You can see it clearly in the Address field of your browser when it's in use. For example, this field might contain a URL that uses GET to send information to the server:

```
http://myserver.com/myscript.cgi?id=Mike&password=secret&
```

The preceding line of code sends two pieces of information to the script named myscript.cgi. It is up to that script to do something with the data.

The following example (collect.pl on the CD) is such a script. This Perl script grabs the GET input string and writes it to a file named Collect.txt. It also returns the text success! to the browser.

```
#!/usr/bin/perl
use CGI;
$q = new CGI;

$id = $q->param('id');
$password = $q->param('password');

open(OUTFILE,">>collect.txt");
print OUTFILE "$id\t$password\n";
close(OUTFILE);

print $q->header({"Content-Type: text/html\n\n"});
print "success!";
exit 0;
```

The original URL could come from something that the user hand-typed, from a standard HTML link, or from an HTML form using the GET method.

The data is taken from the portion of the URL after the question mark, also called the *query string*, represented in the preceding Perl script by the CGI object ($q). The open command opens the file named collect.txt with a >> option, which means that new data will be appended to the existing data in the file.

> **N O T E**
>
> The collect.txt file *must already exist* before you run collect.pl. The Perl script does *not* create collect.txt if it does not already exist.

The information is then written out, followed by a new line character. After the file is closed, the word success! is written out to the browser. This message replaces the current Web page in the browser. It gives you an indication that the CGI program did its job.

To get this script working on your server, you need to upload the collect.pl file and the empty text file collect.txt. As usual, the directory (and perhaps individual file) permissions need to be correctly configured. You can then test them in your browser by entering different text after the question mark in the URL. Whatever you put there should be recorded in the file.

If you cannot write to the file, the most likely problem is incorrect directory or file permissions. It could also be that the Perl script needs to specify the full local path to the collect.txt file (something along the lines of c:\inetpub\mydomain\cgi-bin\collect.txt, for example), rather than just the file name.

You can write to this file with Flash by using a LoadVars object. In addition to a load() method, LoadVars also has a send() method. The following ActionScript, attached to a button, collects three variable values in a LoadVars object and sends them to the CGI script:

```
on (release) {
    myLoadVars = new LoadVars();
    myLoadVars.name = username;
    myLoadVars.age = userage;
    myLoadVars.comment = usercomment;
    myLoadVars.send("collectNameAgeComment.pl","_self","GET");
}
```

This is the basic strategy employed in collectNameAgeComment.fla on the CD. (The main difference is that collectNameAgeComment.fla uses TextInput components rather than text fields. Therefore, username, userage and usercomment become username.text, userage.text and usercomment.text.)

The first parameter of the send() method is the location of the CGI program. The second parameter is the target window, which will hold the results printed by the CGI program. In this case, "_self" indicates that the results should replace the current page, including the Flash movie. The third parameter is either a "GET" or a "POST", depending on the method expected by the CGI program.

Suppose you don't want to replace the page and Flash movie with the results. Instead, suppose you want the Flash movie to continue. You would then use sendAndLoad() instead of send(). The sendAndLoad() method's second parameter is not a browser target, but another LoadVars object.

The initial LoadVars object holds the variables to be sent. The second LoadVars object contains the returned information. Here is an example:

```
on (release) {
    myLoadVars = new LoadVars();
    myLoadVarsReceive = new LoadVars();
    myLoadVars.id = userid;
    myLoadVars.password = userpassword;
    myLoadVars.onLoad = function() {
        // do something with information here
    }
    myLoadVars.sendAndLoad("flashCollect.pl", myLoadVarsReceive, "GET");
}
```

This approach is illustrated in flashCollect.fla and flashCollect.pl on the CD.

You can also use the POST method for sending variable values to the server. As a matter of fact, this approach is preferable because POST allows you to send long strings. The GET method limits string sizes depending on the browser and server.

With CGI.pm, the same Perl code retrieves both GET and POST information: You don't have to change a thing. However, in your Flash movie, you need to change load(), send(), or sendAndLoad() to use POST instead of GET.

EMBEDDING DATA ON THE HTML PAGE

Perhaps the most reliable and efficient way to send information from the server to your movie is to embed the information in the Web page in a place where your movie can get to it. You can do so by placing information in the src/movie parameters of both the OBJECT and EMBED tags on the Web page. For instance, a typical OBJECT movie parameter would look like this:

```
<param name="movie" value="frompage.swf">
```

You also can place a question mark and a list of variable definitions after the name of the movie like this:

```
<param name="movie" value="frompage.swf?var1=7&var2=42.8&var3=Hello!">
```

The result is that those three variables, starting with var1, are set to their respective values. This happens immediately after the movie is loaded, so you can expect these values to be present when your scripts begin. All the variables will be at the root level.

Including Variables with loadMovie
The technique of placing variables after the movie filename also works in loadMovie() commands. You can tell your Flash movie to load a new movie in its place and include a question mark and then variable declarations. The new movie loads with these variables set. Here is an example:

loadMovie("mynewmovie.swf?a=7&b=42.8", this);

You also need to include the same information after the src parameter of the EMBED tag. Otherwise, only Windows users who have Internet Explorer will get the variables. The following is a complete OBJECT/EMBED tag with the variables set for both parts of the tag:

```
<object classid="clsid:D27CDB6E-AE6D-11cf-96B8-444553540000"
codebase="http://download.macromedia.com/pub/
shockwave/cabs/flash/swflash.cab#version=7,0,0,0"
WIDTH="550" HEIGHT="400" id="frompage">

<param name="allowScriptAccess" value="sameDomain" />
<param name="movie"
value="frompage.swf?var1=7&var2=42.8&var3=Hello!" />

<param name="quality" value="high" />
<param name="bgcolor" value="#FFFFFF" />
```

```
<embed src="frompage.swf?var1=7&var2=42.8&var3=Hello!"

quality="high" bgcolor="#ffffff"
width="550" height="400" name="frompage" align=""
type="application/x-shockwave-flash"
pluginspace="http://www.macromedia.com/go/getflashplayer" />
</object>
```

You can see this HTML page in action by using the Frompage.html and frompage.fla sample files. Run Frompage.html, which loads frompage.swf, which in turn reads and displays the variables from Frompage.html.

This technique is powerful even without any server-side support. For instance, you could make a Flash title movie for your Web site. Inside the movie, you could have a place to display the title of the page where the movie appears. This dynamic text field can be linked to a variable that is set on the Web page. So on one page, titleText could be My Home Page, and on another page titleText could be My Links. Both pages use the same Flash movie, but with a different value for titleText set in the src/movie parameters. You could run the same title movie on all your Web pages.

You could also send dynamic data to your movie by using this technique. A simple example is to send the current time to a movie. The Date object relies on the user's computer's time, which is usually set correctly but can easily be changed to anything. If you have a popular Web site, chances are good that people with incorrect dates and times will access your site every day. Even those site visitors with correct times may live in different time zones. What if you need to display the accurate date and time as it stands on your server?

You can display the correct time with a server-side include. A server-side include is a little tag that is put inside a Web page to add a bit of information, or a complete file, before it is sent to the user. The user gets a complete page that doesn't appear to be any different from a normal Web page, but the HTML on your site is specially coded so that the server knows what to include and where.

Server-Side Includes
Server-side includes are not turned on in all Web servers. Check with your server administrator or ISP to find out whether they are turned on, or whether there are any special settings required. For instance, many servers are set to not use server-side includes for .html files, but only for .shtml files.

To use server-side includes to send the time to Flash, you need to alter the src/movie parameter to look like this:

```
timefrompage.swf?timeVar=<!--#echo var="DATE_LOCAL" -->&
```

The server-side include is the <!--#echo var="DATE_LOCAL" -->& part. If the server is correctly parsing the file for server-side includes, it will see this and replace it with the date and time. The result might look similar to Sunday, 24-Feb-2002 10:18:19 MST.

When Double Quotes = Double Trouble

If the server-side include code is part of a block of text enclosed in double quotes, the double quotes around DATE_LOCAL may cause problems if the SSI doesn't work. On some Web servers, such as Apache, you can avoid this problem by using single quotes, like this:

```
<PARAM NAME=movie
VALUE="timefrompage.swf?timeVar=<!--#echo var='DATE_LOCAL' -->">
```

Unfortunately, in my testing on Microsoft IIS, the SSI did not work if I used single quotes. So you are stuck using double quotes on IIS. However, be aware that if you do use double quotes around DATE_LOCAL and the SSI doesn't work, the browser may become confused and not display the Flash file at all.

The server makes the change before sending the page to the user. If you view the page's source in the browser, you will see the actual date and time, and no hint that a server-side include tag actually appears there on the real HTML page.

The sample files timefrompage.shtml and timefrompage.fla do not work if you run them from your hard drive or the accompanying CD-ROM because you are not passing them through a Web server. Upload the .shtml and .swf files to a test directory on your site to see them in action. If you don't see a date and time in the dynamic text field in the movie but instead see the echo tag, you know that server-side includes have not been turned on.

Using server-side includes is probably the least sophisticated way to add dynamic information to your Web pages. Other systems are very popular now—for example, Active Server Pages (ASP), JavaServer Pages (JSP), PHP, WebObjects, and ColdFusion. You could use any one of these examples to generate dynamic Web pages that include custom variables to be passed in to the Flash movie.

The main disadvantages of sending information to your movie with the src/movie tags are that the information typically needs to be short and that any user can see it if she simply views the source of the Web page she is visiting.

XML DATA

XML has been a hot topic among computer developers for the past few years. Macromedia Flash MX includes an extensive set of functions that allow you to import, export, and process XML data. It is one of the most powerful features of Flash.

INTRODUCTION TO XML

XML, which stands for Extensible Markup Language, is a simple way of storing a database of information. The data is stored in a simple text file. Tags are used to describe the data, much as they are used to describe the information in an HTML page.

XML looks like HTML. Looking at XML in this light is a good way to quickly understand what XML is about, but you also need to know that XML and HTML are different in many

22

ways. HTML is used to describe a Web page. XML can be used to describe anything at all. HTML has a predefined set of tags such as `<P>`, `<IMG>`, and `<A>`, whereas XML does not have any predefined tags.

Now consider this simple XML document. The following is the inventory of a produce store that has five apples, seven oranges, and two peaches:

```
<inventory>
    <fruit>
        <apples>5</apples>
        <oranges>7</oranges>
        <peaches>2</peaches>
    </fruit>
</inventory>
```

The tag surrounding the entire document has the name `inventory`. A well-formed XML document can have only one top-level tag.

The hierarchical structure of an XML document is referred to as a *tree*. Within the tree, each pair of similarly named tags demarcates a *node*. The node includes the tags themselves and everything between them. So, all the preceding XML code can be considered as one node, demarcated by the `<inventory>` tags. Within that node, there are other nodes, demarcated by other tags. Nodes one level down in the hierarchy are *child* nodes. The `inventory` node has one child node, `fruit`. `fruit` has three child nodes: `apples`, `oranges`, and `peaches`. Even the numbers 5, 7, and 2 are nodes. They are children of `apples`, `oranges`, and `peaches`, respectively.

The terms *node* and *element* are often used interchangeably. Strictly speaking, however, an element is a type of node. Table 22.1 shows some of the most common node types.

TABLE 22.1   COMMON XML NODE TYPES

Node Type	Example
Document type	`<!DOCTYPE produce SYSTEM "produce.dtd">`
Processing instruction	`<?xml version="1.0" encoding="iso-8859-1"?>`
Element	`<oranges type="navel">5</oranges>`
Attribute	`type="navel"`
Text	5

Each component of the tree structure is defined in a Document Type Definition (DTD) or *schema*. The DTD describes the structure of the data XML document, and the document is considered *valid* if it conforms to its DTD.

22

Flash: A Bit Too Forgiving?

The ActionScript XML parser is not a validating parser: It does not attempt to determine whether a document conforms to its DTD. In fact, Flash doesn't even read DTDs. The Flash parser just reads the DOCTYPE declaration and stores it in the docTypeDecl property; it does not validate the document. This is not a flaw in Flash. Many parsers are non-validating. This choice was made to keep the size of the Flash Player to a minimum. A document that is not valid can still be a legal or well-formed XML document.

In addition, however, the Flash parser accepts some mal-formed XML documents, such as documents with multiple top-level nodes. It would be better if Flash generated errors for such documents, at least warning you that other programs may not accept them.

Nodes like inventory, fruit, and apples are called *XML nodes*. Nodes like 5, 7, and 2 are called *text nodes*. An XML node has a node name but no value. Instead of a value, it usually has more child nodes. A text node, on the other hand, has no name, but it does have a value.

Figure 22.1 shows a graphical representation of the sample XML document. Each box represents a node. When a box is inside another box, the one inside is a child of the larger box.

Figure 22.1
A graphical representation of the produce store XML document.

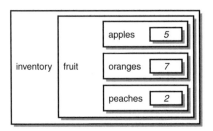

The first step toward using XML documents is understanding how to navigate inside one. For instance, inventory is the primary node. fruit is the only child of that node. fruit has three children, the first of which is apples. apples has one child, a text node with the value 5 in it.

So the 5 is the first child of apples, which is the first child of fruit, which is the first child of inventory, which is the first child of the document. Another way to say it is that 5 is the first child of the first child of the first child of the first child.

This description sounds wordy, so you may think that dealing with XML documents means that you'll have to deal with long associations like this. However, there is a way to shorten it. A fundamental rule of XML turns complex documents into simple ones: All XML nodes are, in fact, smaller XML documents.

So think of the apples node as its own document. The primary node is apples, and the child of that node is the text node with 5 in it. You'll use this technique to dissect XML data throughout the rest of the chapter.

FUNDAMENTALS OF XML

One of the most important aspects of XML is that it is readable by both computers and humans. This makes it different from other database-like files, which are either in binary code or arranged in an unreadable fashion.

So you can easily generate and edit simple XML documents all by yourself, using just a text editor such as Notepad or TextPad. But most of the time, XML documents are created by other programs. Many server-side database programs can send XML data. Some database applications that you run on your local machine have an Export to XML function.

To ensure that Flash will be able to read an XML document, make sure it is *well-formed*. This means it needs to follow a certain set of rules, some of which are obvious.

All tags in an XML document must have matching closing tags. So `<apples>` needs `</apples>`. Plus, these tags need to be in the proper order. So `<fruit><apples>2</apples></fruit>` is correct, but `<fruit><apples>2</fruit></apples>` will cause an error and the document will not be parsed correctly.

You can place your entire XML document in one line, with no tabs or line breaks. However, using just one line can make a document that is unreadable by humans. So Flash MX 2004 has the capability to ignore whitespace such as tabs and line breaks.

Tags in XML can have not only values or child nodes, but also attributes. For instance, if you want to specify more information than just `oranges` in the tag, you can use an attribute to get more specific:

```
<oranges type="navel">5</oranges>
```

You can use attributes exclusively, with no text node. Here's an example:

```
<employee name="John Doe" gender="male"></employee>
```

When there is no text node, you can also use an abbreviated syntax that combines the opening and closing tags in a single tag, like this:

```
<employee name="John Doe" gender="male" />
```

It's typically considered better XML style (and a file size reducer) to use the latter form.

USING XML IN FLASH

You use XML in Flash for two reasons. The first reason is that you can communicate with other systems easily. For instance, if your movie is to get data from a medical database, chances are that the person in charge of that database is not familiar with Flash but does know about XML. You can agree on an XML format for the data and then use XML to transfer information. In many cases, the database or communications network that you want Flash to access already uses XML.

22

The other reason to use XML in Flash is that the XML functionality is more suited for large and complex data handling than other parts of Flash.

For instance, if you want to read in an array of data, how would you do it without XML? You could use LoadVars to read in a large string and then split to break it into an array. But this approach is super-slow. Even writing your own alternative to split is slow. Or you could read in dozens or hundreds of variables, but this approach would be harder to create outside Flash and organize inside Flash.

With the XML object, you can read in large amounts of data quickly and access it quickly. This approach is ideal for getting database information and displaying it. For instance, you could use it to read in a set of trivia questions for a game or display user information in a user database. Doing these things with normal variables and arrays would be much more difficult and much slower.

PARSING XML DATA

So how do you get XML data into Flash? To do that, a text XML document must be brought into Flash and converted to an XML object that ActionScript can use. Converting text to another format like this is called *parsing*. The following sections describe the basic XML object functions and how to use them to get and read XML data.

CONVERTING TEXT INTO XML

The easiest way to make an XML object is to convert a small piece of properly formatted text into XML. You can do this just by creating a new XML object and feeding it the text:

```
myText = "<inventory><fruit><apples>5</apples><oranges>7</oranges>";
myText += "<peaches>2</peaches></fruit></inventory>";
myXML = new XML(myText);
```

You can also use the parseXML() command to do the same thing:

```
myText = "<inventory><fruit><apples>5</apples><oranges>7</oranges>";
myText += "<peaches>2</peaches></fruit></inventory>";
myXML = new XML();
myXML.parseXML(myText);
```

Although creating XML from text already inside the Flash movie has limited use, this approach is very good for learning about XML. Later in this chapter, you'll learn how to import larger XML documents from external files and programs.

EXAMINING XML DATA

If you test produce.fla on the CD, it displays inventory in the output window. This is the node name of the first child of the document loaded from the produce.xml file, which contains the produce store example shown earlier in this chapter and in Figure 22.1. The inventory node is the first child of the XML object.

The line of ActionScript code that displays inventory in the output window is

```
trace(myXML.firstChild.nodeName);
```

→ This line of code is in produce.fla on the CD. For a discussion of this line and the code surrounding it, **see** "Importing XML Documents," later in this chapter, **page 643**.

The `firstChild` property returns the first child node of the XML document. You can get any child node by using the array-like property `childNodes`. So `firstChild` and `childNodes[0]` are exactly the same thing.

Remember that a node of an XML object is another XML object. Nodes can be either XML nodes with a name and more children, or text nodes with no name or children, but a value.

You can use the `nodeName` property to get the name of an XML node and the `nodeValue` property to get the value of a text node.

NOTE

> When discussing XML, be aware that many terms mean the same thing. For example, an *XML document* and an *XML object* are the same thing in Flash. A *node* of an XML object is another *XML object*.

The following is a list of all the different XML properties that you can use to get children, names, and information from XML objects:

- `firstChild`—Returns the first child of a node. This is the same as using `childNodes[0]`.
- `hasChildNodes`—Returns `true` if the node has children.
- `lastChild`—Returns the last child of a node. You can get the number of children by using `childNodes.length`.
- `nextSibling`—Returns the next node, if any.
- `nodeName`—Returns the tag name of an XML node or `null` if it is a text node.
- `nodeType`—Returns `1` if the node is an XML node or `3` if it is a text node.
- `nodeValue`—Returns the value of a text node or `null` if it is an XML node.
- `parentNode`—Returns the parent node of a node.
- `previousSibling`—Returns the previous node, if any.
- `attributes`—Returns a variable object containing the attributes, if any, of a node.
- `childNodes`—Returns an array-like structure of child nodes. You can use `length` to get the total number of nodes and square brackets to specify a specific node.

Although simple examples, like the previous one, use `firstNode`, it is more common to use `childNodes` in all cases to navigate through an XML document. So the following few examples will help you understand how to use `childNodes` to get the information that you need. Follow along with Figure 22.1 or the text that precedes it.

This line returns `inventory`:

```
myXML.childNodes[0].nodeName
```

This line returns `null` because the first node is an XML node that has a name and contains children, but has no value itself:

```
myXML.childNodes[0].nodeValue
```

This line returns `fruit`:

```
myXML.childNodes[0].childNodes[0].nodeName
```

This line returns `apples`:

```
myXML.childNodes[0].childNodes[0].childNodes[0].nodeName
```

This line returns `null` because the `apples` node is still an XML node and has no value, only a name and children:

```
myXML.childNodes[0].childNodes[0].childNodes[0].nodeValue
```

To get the `5` contained in the `apples` node, you need to look at its child, which is a text node. This line returns `5`:

```
myXML.childNodes[0].childNodes[0].childNodes[0].childNodes[0].nodeValue
```

Because text nodes have no name, you get a `null` when trying to get the name of a text node:

```
myXML.childNodes[0].childNodes[0].childNodes[0].childNodes[0].nodeName
```

The `fruit` node contains three children. You can determine this by examining the `length` property of `childNodes`. This line returns `3` because there are three children of the `fruit` node:

```
myXML.childNodes[0].childNodes[0].childNodes.length
```

You can get the name of the second node of the fruit node, which is `oranges`, like this:

```
myXML.childNodes[0].childNodes[0].childNodes[1].nodeName
```

If you want to determine whether a node is an XML node or a text node, you can use `nodeType`. For instance, the `apples` node is an XML node. It returns `1`:

```
myXML.childNodes[0].childNodes[0].childNodes[0].nodeType
```

On the other hand, the node with the `5` in it is a text node and returns `3`:

```
myXML.childNodes[0].childNodes[0].childNodes[0].childNodes[0].nodeType
```

MAKING XML REFERENCES EASIER

Some of the lines in the previous examples get to be quite long. And this is a *simple* XML document. Imagine if the document contained a few more levels. You would have lines with half a dozen `childNodes` references. All these references could make for code that is quite long and confusing.

Fortunately, there is a simpler way to dig down to get the information you need. For example, suppose you want to get the number of apples in the store. Here's some code that could get that number:

22

```
inventory = myXML.childNodes[0];
fruit = inventory.childNodes[0];
apples = fruit.childNodes[0];
appleCount = apples.childNodes[0];
numApples = appleCount.nodeValue;
```

Although this code isn't really any shorter than a long string of `childNodes` references, it is much easier to understand. Plus, if you want to get the number of oranges next, you already have the `fruit` variable ready to go.

REFERENCING ATTRIBUTES

In addition to having children, XML nodes can also have attributes. For instance, the following XML document has an attribute named `type` that has a value 4:

```
<test type='4'>123</test>
```

To get an attribute's value, you need to know its name. The following is a piece of code that references the attribute in the previous example:

```
myXML.childNodes[0].attributes.type
```

The `attributes` property actually returns a variable object. This is a list of property names and values. If you want to see all the property names and values of an attribute listed, you could use code like this:

```
myAttributes = myXML.childNodes[0].attributes;
for(attribute in myAttributes) {
    trace(attribute+": "+myAttributes[attribute]);
}
```

BUILDING XML DATA

ActionScript also enables you to build an XML document from scratch or alter an existing document. After creating an empty object, you can use a variety of commands to add nodes.

But the process for making an XML object is a little confusing. Start with a simple example and create this small XML document that will look like this:

```
<test>123</test>
```

First, you must create the XML object, as follows:

```
myXML = new XML();
```

Next, you must add the node named `test`. You need to do this in two steps. The first step is to create the node:

```
testNode = myXML.createElement("test");
```

This step creates a node named `test`. Even though this node is part of `myXML`, it is sort of hanging out in the middle of nowhere. You have to attach it to a node. Because this is a new, empty XML object, you have only the object itself as a node:

```
myXML.appendChild(testNode);
```

To create the text node that will be a child of the `test` node, you need to use a slightly different command:

```
textNode = myXML.createTextNode("123");
```

Now, you have to add it as a child of the `test`. Fortunately, you still have the variable `testNode` to use to reference that node:

```
testNode.appendChild(textNode);
```

To test your series of commands, you can use the `toString()` function to send the XML document to the Output window:

```
trace(myXML.toString());
```

Check out the sample movie Build.fla, which uses only ActionScript to build the fruit stand example.

The following are other commands that you can use to modify an XML object:

- `appendChild(node)`—Adds a node that has been created with `createElement` or `createTextNode`.

- `cloneNode(deep)`—Creates a copy of a node. If *deep* is `true`, it also copies all its children and descendants.

- `createElement(nodeName)`—Makes a new XML node. This node is not part of the document until you use `appendChild` or `insertBefore`.

- `createTextNode(nodeValue)`—Makes a new text node. This node is not part of the document until you use `appendChild` or `insertBefore`.

- `insertBefore(nodetoInsert, nodeNum)`—Inserts a node (*nodetoInsert*) that has been created with `createElement` or `createTextNode`. The new node is a sibling of *nodeNum* and precedes it in the tree.

- `removeNode(nodeNum)`—Deletes a child node.

CREATING AND MODIFYING ATTRIBUTES

What seems to be left out of the XML modification commands is a way to add or modify attributes. Modifying attributes is beyond simple. All you need to do is assign a value to a node to create or modify one. For instance:

```
myXML.childNodes[0].attributes.myAttribute  = 42;
```

To create a simple XML object with attributes, like `<test type="4">7</test>`, you could use the following:

```
myXML = new XML();

testNode = myXML.createElement("test");

testNode.attributes.type = 4;
myXML.appendChild(testNode);
```

```
text = myXML.createTextNode("7");
testNode.appendChild(text) ;
```

IMPORTING XML DOCUMENTS

Most of the time you will be using XML documents you will actually be importing them from outside the Flash movie. XML documents can be text files sitting on your server, or they can be generated by server-side CGI programs.

CAUTION

> The same security restrictions that apply to downloading other types of data apply to downloading XML documents.

The XML object, in some ways, is like the LoadVars object. It can use load() to load in data from an external file or program.

However, rather than use the property=value& format, the file should be in XML format. If it is a proper XML document, it is parsed immediately into the XML object as data.

Now consider this example, which creates a new XML object and loads it in. Between these two commands, I set the ignoreWhite property to true. This means that the tabs and line breaks in the document are ignored. If you didn't set this property, you would have to write the XML document with no whitespace at all, or you would have all sorts of unwanted text nodes in the XML object.

```
myXML = new XML();
myXML.ignoreWhite = true;
myXML.load("produce.xml")
```

The load() method does not finish its task immediately. You have to wait for it to download the text file and parse it. Even if the files are all on your local hard drive, it does not happen fast enough for the next line to be able to access the data.

The XML object has an onLoad event just like the LoadVars object. You can define a function that will run as soon as loading is complete. Here's an example:

```
myXML = new XML();
myXML.ignoreWhite = true;
myXML.load("produce.xml")
myXML.onLoad = function() {
    trace(myXML.firstChild.nodeName);
}
```

Another way to tell whether the XML file has been loaded is to use the loaded property of the XML object. It returns true only after the import is complete. You have to keep testing the loaded property repetitively, which typically makes it less convenient than the onLoad event, which does not require repetitive testing but fires automatically when the load completes.

22

In addition, you can use several properties to monitor the progress of loading a large XML document. Here is a complete list:

- getBytesLoaded—Gives you the total number of bytes loaded so far.
- getBytesTotal—Gives you the total number of bytes in the XML file.
- loaded—Returns true only after the entire document has been loaded.
- status—Returns 0 if the load was successful. Other possible values are shown in Table 22.2.

TABLE 22.2   XML.status RETURN VALUES

Code	What It Means
0	Parse completed without errors.
-2	A CDATA tag not completed.
-3	XML declaration processor instruction (PI) tag not completed. Example of XML declaration PI: <?xml version="1.0"?>
-4	DOCTYPE tag not completed.
-5	A comment was not completed.
-6	Malformed XML element.
-7	Out of memory.
-8	Attribute value not terminated with a closing quote or double quotes.
-9	No end tag to match a start tag.
-10	End tag found without a start tag.

The onLoad event occurs after two things happen. The first is that the text file with the XML in it is fully downloaded. The second is that the XML document is parsed into the XML object.

However, you can intercept the XML text before it is parsed. To do this, use the onData event. This event allows you to capture the data before it gets *parsed*. You can then parse the data yourself, perhaps performing some custom functions on it beforehand. Here's an example:

```
myXML.onData = function(xmlText) {
    myXML.parseXML(xmlText);
}
```

This example doesn't do anything that a normal load() wouldn't do. However, you can see how you might be able to perform some unusual tasks. For instance, if your server-side program returns an XML document with an extra line at the beginning, you could trim that line from the xmlText parameter before passing it into parseXML().

After an XML document is parsed, either by load() or parseXML(), you can get some miscellaneous information from it by using one of these two properties:

- xmlDecl—If you're using XML standards, every XML document should have an XML tag at the beginning. This property gives you a string that contains that tag.

- docTypeDecl—Another standard tag for XML documents is the !DOCTYPE tag. This property returns a string with the value of that tag.

SENDING XML DOCUMENTS TO THE SERVER

After building an XML document with ActionScript, you may want to send it back to a server-side program for storage or processing. You can do this with the send() and sendAndLoad() commands.

These two commands work just as they do for the LoadVars object. The send() method sends a complete XML object back to a server address. If you use an alternate second parameter, as in the following example, the server's returned text is sent to another browser frame or window:

```
myXML.send("http://www.myserver.com/getxml.cgi","_self");
```

The preceding line uses "_self" as the return target, which means that the entire Web page is replaced by whatever the server program returns. If you simply leave out the second parameter, the operation is silent and the Flash movie continues.

NOTE

> If you need to use a specific MIME type to send your XML data to the server, you can set the contentType property of the XML object to that MIME type before using send() or sendAndLoad().

Using the sendAndLoad() method means that the second parameter should be another XML object. This new object receives the returned XML from the server just as if it had been used in a load() method.

```
returnXML = new XML();
myXML.sendAndLoad("http://www.myserver.com/getxml.cgi, returnXML);
```

If you want to monitor the progress of the load into returnXML, you must use onData or onLoad handlers of the returnXML object, not the myXML object.

→ For an example of a simple XML program, **see** books.fla and books.xml on the CD accompanying this book. For a description of books.fla, **see** books.html on the CD.

XML SOCKETS

XML sockets are a topic related to the XML object only in that they both use XML-formatted data. However, the XML Socket object does not use load() and send() commands to get and share its data. Instead, it uses connect() to connect to a server program.

22

A socket server program is unlike a CGI program in that it can maintain a continuous connection with the client through multiple requests. With CGI, the client issues a request and gets a response, but there is no continuous connection between requests. For a socket-based connection, the Flash movie uses `connect()` to make a connection. After a connection is established, XML data can be sent back and forth in real time. The server can actually send data to the movie even if the movie hasn't requested it. This is also known as *push* technology.

Most of what you need to know to use XML Sockets is not part of Flash or ActionScript. You'll have to write a server-side program, usually with Java or C++. You also need to be fairly knowledgeable about how servers and sockets work. For this reason, I will not go into any more detail about XML Sockets.

If you're using a third-party Flash-to-Sockets program, that third-party software provider should give you documentation on how to use XML Sockets to communicate with its product.

CUSTOMIZING HTTP HEADERS WITH addRequestHeader()

 New `addRequestHeader()` methods for the LoadVars class and the XML class allow you to add or change HTTP *request headers*. You can use these headers for a wide variety of standard purposes, such as telling the server what MIME content types (for example, text, video, audio) or character set the browser prefers or expects, or indicating what language you prefer (for servers supporting multiple languages). There are also special-purpose headers such as the SOAPAction header, which indicates the intent of a SOAP HTTP request. And you can define custom headers yourself.

Server scripting languages such as ColdFusion Markup Language (CFML), PHP, and ASP can be used to retrieve all headers. For example, in CFML you use the built-in `GetHttpRequestData()` function, like this:

```
<cfset x = GetHttpRequestData()>
```

You add the headers to the `LoadVars` or `XML` object in Flash. Methods such as `send()` or `sendAndLoad()` are used to automatically send headers to the server when the request is made.

There are two formats for the `addRequestHeader()` method. One provides a single header name, and a single value for that name. The other provides an array, which contains a name, a value, a name, a value, and so on for as many name/value pairs as you wish to send.

Here's an example of adding a single SOAPAction header with the value `"GetLastSellingPrice"`.

```
myLoadVars.addRequestHeader("SOAPAction", "GetLastSellingPrice");
```

Here's an example with two name/value pairs in an array. The first header, Content-Type, is a standard one. The second, X-ClientAppType, is a custom header, which you would have to write a program to capture, interpret, and use on the server. This example creates an array named myHeaders and then passes the array as an argument to addRequestHeader().

```
var myHeaders = ["Content-Type", "text/plain", "X-ClientAppType", "Flash"];
myXML.addRequestHeader(myHeaders);
```

If, before making the request to the server, you add the same header name more than once, only the last one counts.

Primarily for security reasons, you cannot use addRequestHeader() to add or change some standard HTTP headers . They include Accept-Ranges, Age, Allow, Allowed, Connection, Content-Length, Content-Location, Content-Range, ETag, Host, Last-Modified, Locations, Max-Forwards, Proxy-Authenticate, Proxy-Authorization, Public, Range, Retry-After, Server, TE, Trailer, Transfer-Encoding, Upgrade, URI, Vary, Via, Warning, and WWW-Authenticate.

NetConnection, NetStream, AND THE RICH MEDIA CLASSES

Six classes, listed in Table 22.3, fall into the Media category.

TABLE 22.3 MEDIA CLASSES

Object	Represents	Singleton
Camera	Video cameras (Webcams)	Y
Microphone	Microphones	Y
NetConnection	Network Connection	N
NetStream	Channel within a Connection	N
Sound	Sound/music	N
Video	Video source	N(*)

(*) not a singleton, but can't create new instances with new keyword

In Flash MX, these classes, with the exception of Sound, were used almost exclusively with the Flash Communication Server (FCS). This is still true for Microphone and Camera.

→ For a complete list of attributes, methods, and events associated with the Microphone and Camera objects, **see** Appendix A, "ActionScript Reference."

The other four Media classes are still used with FCS, too. For instance, the Video class can represent a real-time video/audio stream captured by a Webcam/microphone and broadcast via FCS, and the Sound class can represent just the audio portion of that stream. NetConnection is used to establish a connection to the server, and NetStream is used to manage individual video/audio streams.

22

→ For a complete list of attributes, methods, and events associated with the `NetConnection` and `NetStream`, **see** Appendix A.

In addition to the FCS-related application of these classes, in Flash MX 2004, the `Sound`, `Video`, `NetConnection` and `NetStream` classes, working together, can be used to manage *progressively loaded* FLV files.

USING `NetConnection` AND `NetStream` FOR PROGRESSIVE LOADING

Progressively loaded `.flv` files give you some of the advantages of streaming video without the video server required for true streaming video.

For instance, one of the big advantages of streaming video is that the video starts to play before it has completely loaded into the player, reducing the amount of time the user has to wait before the video starts playing. As the video plays, loading continues in parallel. A small amount of video/audio content is stored in a memory buffer, giving the player a "head start," with the goal of ensuring that there is always content to play, even if the download halts momentarily.

Progressively loaded `.flv` files provide all these same advantages. In fact, the resemblance is so close that the progressively loaded `.flv` is managed as a stream in Flash, using the same `NetStream` object used to manage streaming video from the Flash Communication Server (FCS).

→ For an introduction to the new progressive FLV feature, **see** "A Tale of Two Versions," **page 324**, in Chapter 14.

There are five basic steps required to start playing an `.flv` file:

1. Create a `NetConnection` object. For example, `var myNetConnection:NetConnection = new NetConnection();`

2. Tell the Flash Player you're not connecting to any FCS application by executing `myNetConnection.connect(null);`

3. Create a network stream over the connection. For example, `var myNetStream:NetStream = new NetStream(myNetConnection);`

4. Attach the stream to a `Video` object on the Stage. For example, `myVideo.attachVideo(myNetStream);`. Note that before you can do to do this, you have to create the `Video` object in the Library, and drag and drop it onto the Stage. To create a new `Video` object, click the top-right menu of the Library panel and choose New Video. Select the `Video` object on the Stage and give it an instance name, such as `myVideo`, in the Property inspector.

→ For an example of a Video in the Library loaded with `attachVideo()`, **see** keepwater_embed.fla on the CD.

5. Use `myNetStream.play(flvFileName)` to tell the stream which `.flv` file to play. This can be a local file, or a remote file specified using a URL (for example, `http://www.myDomain.com/myFile.flv`).

The NetStream object is your main tool for managing a video stream—one stream per NetStream object. When the stream is coming from Flash Communication Server MX, you have to manage the connection with the server, as well; you use a NetConnection object to do that. One connection can contain any number of streams. When you're just loading an .flv file, there's really no management required for the connection. However, you still have to create a NetConnection object to contain the NetStream object(s). The NetConnection object has only one method, connect(), when used with .flv files. You use connect() with a null parameter to tell the Flash Player that you're not connecting to any server application. Thus, the NetConnection-related code looks like this:

```
var connection_nc:NetConnection = new NetConnection();
connection_nc.connect(null);
```

You can publish the preceding code, and the rest of the code in this section, for Flash Player 6. If you take out the strong data typing, you could also publish for ActionScript 1. Basically, Macromedia just took the existing streaming media framework and applied it to .flv files. There's nothing new about the ActionScript syntax used for "streaming" .flv files.

The NetStream-related code is equally straightforward. The following code creates a new NetStream object in the connection_nc NetConnection object, attaches the stream to an existing video object on the Stage, and plays a file, myFile.flv, from a Web site:

```
var stream_ns:NetStream = new NetStream(connection_nc);
myVideo.attachVideo(stream_ns);
stream_ns.play("http://www.someDomain.com/myFile.flv");
```

If you want to control the sound separately from the video, create a Sound object associated with the clip, like this:

```
var mySound:Sound = new Sound(this);
```

Then you can use that Sound object to control volume or other characteristics of the sound.

→ For more on the Sound class, **see** "The Sound Class" later in this chapter, **page 651**.

For example, the following line sets the sound volume in the video to zero:

```
mySound.setVolume (0); // set volume to zero
```

In netstream.fla on the CD accompanying this book, you'll find working sample code incorporating NetConnection and NetStream, as well as code that controls audio, using a Sound object associated with a movie clip.

WORKING WITH .flv FILES AND THE NetStream OBJECT

In Flash MX, you had two choices for playing a video file in your movie: you could *embed* it (store it in the SWF) or you could *stream* it (get real-time video or video on demand from FCS). Embedding lets you see the individual video frames on the Timeline and work with the video using Flash's visual design tools.

Flash MX 2004 supports embedding with the new Video Import Wizard, which provides fine control over encoding options, scaling and cropping presets, as well as color and brightness settings.

However, with embedding, the browser has to download the entire SWF before the video starts to play. In addition, after about two minutes of continuous video playback, users may experience audio sync problems.

With FCS, video playback starts after a configurable initial pause to fill the video buffer (5 seconds by default). Audio sync is not a problem. However, you have the added expense and complexity of FCS.

Progressive loading offers a third choice: progressive loading of external .flv files either directly from a Web site using HTTP, or locally—but in either case, without embedding and without the aid of a special-purpose communication server.

One advantage of .flv files is that you can control them with NetStream objects. NetStream objects have a time property that tells you where the playhead is in the video file. Using this information, you can implement time-based control of the video clip or other elements of your movie. For example, you could pause the video clip at 5.5 seconds and display some text relating to the displayed image. Previously, the time-based kind of control was not easy to achieve without FCS.

Another advantage of .flv files is that they enable you to use the new Media Components (and the accompanying Media Behaviors) that come with Flash Professional. The Media Components implement control via time-based Cue Points, which is possible only with NetStream, and therefore only with the file formats supported by NetStream (.flv and .mp3).

Progressively loaded FLV files have other advantages, as well: For instance, they also require less memory than embedded video files; using less memory improves overall movie performance. In addition, rather than running at the same rate as the container movie, as embedded movies do, external FLVs retain their original frame rates, giving you the flexibility to use different frame rates for different clips within the container movie.

Another very useful feature of the NetStream object is the NetStream.setBufferTime() method. The NetStream buffer is a constantly-refilled "reservoir" that provides video to the Video object at a steady rate, compensating for the variable rates at which files typically load. The buffer should be large enough to continue streaming video even if download stops momentarily. The NetStream.setBufferTime() method enables you to set the size of the buffer in seconds. The longer the buffer time, the longer the initial delay while the buffer fills before the video starts playing. However, this initial delay is usually well worth it if it prevents the NetStream buffer from "running dry." If the buffer runs empty, the video pauses while the buffer refills.

You can create an onStatus event handler for the NetStream object that is playing the FLV. The onStatus event fires when a video/audio clip starts or stops playing, and when the clip automatically restarts (which happens if the NetStream buffer runs dry and a pause is required to refill it). For instance, the onStatus event handler receives the NetStream.Play.Start event when loading a particular video. You could use this opportunity to display some informational text about the video.

→ Both onStatus and setBufferTime are used in netstream.fla on the CD accompanying this book. They are also discussed later in this chapter under "The Video Class," **page 656**.

THE Sound CLASS

The Sound class represents sounds such as music, sound effects, or speech.

The most notable enhancement to the Sound class in Flash MX 2004 is the ability to retrieve ID3 metadata from MP3 files. ID3 metadata embedded in the .mp3 file provides information such as the artist, the genre, and the name of the song. The onID3 event of the Sound class fires when ID3 information is received within a downloaded MP3 file. You access specific metadata items by using the Sound.ID3 object, which has over 40 attributes, listed in Appendix A, under "Sound.ID3 Attributes."

→ Sound events are introduced in "Sound Events," **page 515**, in Chapter 20. Sample movie sound.fla on the CD shows how the sound events are used.

Sound capabilities can be divided into five major categories: creating the Sound object, loading sounds, getting information about sounds, controlling sounds, and using sound events.

CREATING THE Sound OBJECT

You can create a new Sound object in two ways. One creates a Sound object that controls all sounds in your movie. The other creates a Sound object that controls sounds in a particular movie clip (or on the root). The following examples illustrate these two methods:

```
allSounds = new Sound(); // controls all sounds in your movie
mcSounds = new Sound("mc1"); // controls sounds in the "mc1" movie clip
```

LOADING AND ATTACHING SOUNDS

ActionScript offers two basic options for accessing sounds: attaching them from the Library or loading them externally. When loading externally, you can either load .mp3 files by using the loadSound() method of the Sound class, or else load .flv files (which may contain only audio) by using NetConnection and NetStream.

→ Using NetConnection and NetStream to load .flv files is described earlier in this chapter, under "NetConnection, NetStream, and the Rich Media Classes," **page 647**, and "Working with .flv Files and the NetStream Object," **page 649**.

→ There is also a non-ActionScript approach to implementing audio in your movie, which involves importing sounds into the Library manually, and dragging and dropping them onto the Stage. **See** "Importing Sounds," **page 412**, in Chapter 18.

You can also load an SWF that contains manually imported audio, loads external audio, or attaches audio from the Library. That approach enables you, for example, to use the MovieClipLoader class to load sound.

You load an external MP3 using the `loadSound()` method, as follows:

```
mySound.loadSound("myTune.mp3", false);
```

The first parameter, which is the name of the sound file to load, is in URL format. Here's an example of a full path to a local file, `D:\sound\myTune.mp3`:

```
mySound.loadSound("file:///DI/sound/myTune.mp3", 1);
```

Using a domain name:

```
mySound.loadSound("http://www.somedomain.com/somesound.mp3", 1);
```

And an IP address and port number:

```
mySound.loadSound("http://205.188.234.33:8006", 1);
```

The second parameter passed to the `loadSound()` method determines whether the sound loads as a *streaming* sound (`true` or `1` in the second parameter) or an *event* sound (`false` or `0` in the second parameter).

A streaming sound starts playing as soon as the Flash Player has buffered enough of the sound file to play the number of seconds specified in the `_soundbuftime` global property—5 seconds, by default. You can change this time as follows:

```
_soundbuftime = 15; // buffer enough for 15 seconds of audio
```

An event sound doesn't start playing until it is completely loaded.

With a streaming sound, you don't have to tell it to start to play. It does so automatically. Thus, these two lines on a timeline start a sound playing:

```
mySound = new Sound();
mySound.loadSound ( "cantata.mp3", true ); // streaming
```

Event sounds, on the other hand, need an explicit call to the `start()` method to start playing. Because an event sound cannot start playing until it is fully loaded, the usual strategy is to put the start method inside an `onLoad` event handler. The event handler fires when the sound is fully loaded, triggering the `start()` method, as in this example:

```
mySound = new Sound(this);
mySound.onLoad = function () {
    this.start();
};
mySound.loadSound ( "cantata.mp3", 0 ); // event sound
```

You should define the `onLoad` handler *before* you load the sound.

The `onLoad` event also fires if the sound fails to load. To check for failure, use the parameter that is passed to the `onLoad` callback function. The parameter is a Boolean: `true` for success and `false` for failure. For example:

```
mySound.onLoad = function (success) {
    if (success) {
        this.start();
    }
    else {
```

```
    // handle the error here
  }
};
```

You use the `attachSound()` method to attach sounds from the Library, as follows:

```
mySound.attachSound("ByeBye.wav");
```

The single parameter for `attachSound()`is the linkage ID of the sound file in the Library. You must execute the `start()` method to start playing an attached sound.

There is another potential source for audio material that can be associated with a `Sound` object: a real-time audio stream originating either from a local audio source such as a microphone or from the Flash Communication Server.

Here is a complete, working program that creates a movie clip (line 1), assigns the audio stream from the default local microphone to a variable (line 2), attaches the audio stream to the movie clip (line 3), creates a `Sound` object that controls all sounds in the movie clip (line 4), and uses the `Sound` object to set the volume of the sound to `0`, thereby completely muting the sound (line 5).

```
1: createEmptyMovieClip ("aud", 1);
2: inputMic = Microphone.get(); // capture audio stream
3: aud.attachAudio(inputMic); // attach audio stream to movie clip
4: mySound = new Sound("aud"); // controls all sounds in "aud " movie clip
5: mySound.setVolume (0); // set volume to zero
```

 Having trouble playing a sound in a movie loaded with `MovieClip.loadMovie()`*?* **See** *the "Troubleshooting" section at the end of this chapter, **page 657**.*

CONTROLLING SOUNDS

You can start and stop a sound, as well as control volume, speaker balance, and stereo separation.

When you start a sound, you can optionally specify a starting point in the sound file, in seconds. There is a second optional parameter, as well, which specifies the number of times to loop the file. The format for the `start()` method is as follows:

```
mySound.start(secondOffset, loop)
```

In the following example, the sound starts one second into the sound file and loops 10 times. The offset parameter does *not* cause a delay. The Flash Player simply skips over the designated amount of audio.

```
mySound.start(1,10);
```

The `onSoundComplete` event does not fire until the sound has looped the specified number of times.

The `stop()` method has two formats. When executed without a parameter, the `stop()` method stops all sounds controlled by a particular `Sound` object. For example:

```
mySound.stop(); // stops all sounds controlled by mySound
```

22

Which sounds are controlled by a particular Sound object depends on how the Sound object was created, as in these examples:

```
mySound = new Sound(); // controls all sounds in the movie
mySound.stop(); // stops all sounds in the movie
mySound = new Sound("mc1"); // controls all sounds in "mc1" movie clip
mySound.stop(); // stops all sounds in  "mc1" movie clip
```

→ As described earlier in this chapter, in "Creating the Sound Object," **page 651**, a Sound object may control either all sounds in your movie, or just sounds in a particular movie clip.

You can also use a stopAllSounds() global function, which stops all sounds in a movie.

The stop() method has an optional parameter, used only with sounds attached using the attachSound() method. The parameter is the same linkage ID used to attach the sound originally:

```
mySound.attachSound("ByeBye");
mySound.stop("ByeBye");
```

When you use the stop() method with a linkage ID parameter, the Sound object on which you execute the stop() method does not have to be the same Sound object that the sound was attached to (mySound in the preceding example). However, it must be a Sound object that controls the same sounds as mySound. For instance, in the following example, both globalSound1 and globalSound2 control all sounds in the movie. In the following example, when globalSound2 ends, it also stops a sound that is attached to globalSound1.

```
globalSound1 = new Sound();
globalSound2 = new Sound();
globalSound1.attachSound("MyTune.mp3");
globalSound2.attachSound("ByeBye");
globalSound1.start(0,2);
globalSound2.start();
globalSound2.onSoundComplete = function() {
    globalSound2.stop("MyTune.mp3");
}
```

The same approach works if both Sound objects control sounds in the same movie clip.

You set the volume using the setVolume() method, which takes as a parameter a number from 0 to 100, inclusive. The default is 100. For instance, the following sets the volume to half of full volume:

```
mySound.setVolume(50);
```

You control speaker balance, the relative loudness of each speaker, using the setPan() method. The setPan() method takes one argument, a number from -100 to 100, inclusive. If the parameter is negative, the amount is subtracted from the right speaker, while the left speaker remains at 100% of the maximum volume. Thus, mySound.setPan(-50) results in the left speaker being on at 100% of maximum, while the right speaker is on at 50% of maximum. Similarly, if the parameter is positive, the number is subtracted from the left speaker, and the right speaker remains at 100% of maximum. Thus, mySound.setPan(25) results in the right speaker being on at 100% of maximum, while the left speaker is on at 75% of maximum.

The maximum volume is either the default of 100 or whatever you have set via `setVolume()`. Thus, if you set the volume to 0 with a statement like `mySound.setVolume(0)`, it doesn't matter what you do with `setPan()` or `setTransform()`: No sound will be heard.

Here's an example:

```
mySound.setPan(100); // left speaker off, right speaker at 100% of max
```

With the `setPan()` method, if you are working with stereo sound, all the sound in the left speaker represents the left stereo channel, and all the sound in the right speaker represents the right stereo channel.

You use the `setTransform()` method to control stereo separation. To use this method, you first create a generic object with four attributes: `ll`, `lr`, `rl`, and `rr`. Each property contains a number from 0 to 100, inclusive. The first letter in the property name indicates which speaker the property controls. The second letter indicates which stereo channel the property controls. Thus, `ll` is left speaker/left channel; `lr` is left speaker/right channel; and so on.

The following example uses an object literal to create a sound transform object. This sound transform object, when applied to a Sound object, completely suppresses the left speaker and puts 100% of both the left and right channels in the right speaker. This is impossible to accomplish with `setPan()`, which never puts the left channel in the right speaker.

```
soundTransform = { ll : 0 , lr : 0 , rl : 100 , rr : 100 };
```

You apply the `soundTransform` object to a Sound object as follows:

```
mySound.setTransform(soundTransform);
```

Getting Information About Sounds

You can monitor the progress of loading sounds, determine when a sound has completed playing, and check speaker balance and stereo separation. You can also find out the duration of a sound and how much of the sound has already played.

You monitor the progress of loading sounds by using the `getBytesLoaded()` method. You can combine it with the `getBytesTotal()` method to determine what percentage of the total sound has loaded:

```
percentLoaded = getBytesLoaded() / getBytesTotal() * 100;
```

You could, for instance, use the `percentLoaded` variable in the preceding example to determine the size of a progress bar in a sound preloader, providing a visual indication of progress in loading the sound.

The read-only `duration` and `position` attributes of the Sound object tell you how long the sound is and how long it has been playing, respectively. Both provide a measure in milliseconds. Both are getter/setter properties, so you shouldn't use the `Object.watch()` method with either of them. In the following example, the `percentPlayed` variable could be used to provide a progress bar for playing a sound, as opposed to loading one:

```
percentPlayed = mySound.position / mySound.duration * 100;
```

22

THE Video CLASS

The Video class has just two methods and four properties. You already saw, earlier in this chapter, how the attachVideo() method is used to associate a NetStream object with a Video object to stream an .flv file.

→ For an example of using the attachVideo() method, **see** "NetConnection, NetStream and the Rich Media Classes," earlier in this chapter, **page 647**.

Before using attachVideo(), you have to create a new Video object. In the top-right menu of the Library panel, click on New Video to create a Video object in the Library. Place an instance of the Video object on the Stage, and give the instance an instance name in the Property inspector.

The attachVideo() method can also be used with a Camera object, but that's typically not useful unless you have a way to broadcast the video stream. For instance, if the instance name is myVideo, this code, placed on the Timeline, gets the video stream from the local default camera:

```
myVideo.attachVideo(Camera.get());
```

If you have a Webcam but are not connected to a communication server, the preceding line of code enables you to watch yourself on the screen of your own computer. Have fun!

Tables 22.4 and 22.5 list the properties and methods, respectively, of the Video object.

TABLE 22.4 Video PROPERTIES

Property	Description
deblocking	A number that specifies the behavior for the deblocking filter applied by the video compressor when streaming video. 0 (the default) allows the video compressor to apply the deblocking filter as needed. 1 disables the deblocking filter. 2 forces the compressor to use the deblocking filter. Read-write.
smoothing	A Boolean; the default is false. Specifies whether video should be smoothed (interpolated) when it is scaled. The player must be in high-quality mode for smoothing to work. Read-write.
height	Height in pixels. Read-only.
width	Width in pixels. Read-only.

The deblocking and smoothing attributes of the video object configure video filters to mitigate the "blocky" appearance of highly compressed video. The deblocking filter degrades playback performance, especially on slower machines, and is usually not necessary for high-bandwidth video.

TABLE 22.5 *Video* METHODS

Name	Format	Description
attachVideo()	myVideoObject.attachVideo (*source* | null)	Specifies a video stream to be displayed in a myVideoObject. *source* is either a NetStream object or a Camera object that is capturing a video stream. The NetStream object could be playing an FLV file or a stream from FCS. If *source* is null, the connection to the video object is dropped. This method is unnecessary if the stream is audio-only. myNetStream.play() plays the audio portion of the video stream automatically.
clear	myVideoObject.clear()	Clears the image currently displayed in myVideoObject. Useful, for example, when the connection to the communication server breaks and you want to display standby information without having to hide the video object.

TROUBLESHOOTING

Why can't I get ActionScript-to-JavaScript communication to work?

You need to complete several steps before this communication will work: Set the ID parameters of both the OBJECT and EMBED tags, set the swLiveConnect parameter of the EMBED tag, and include a JavaScript function to get the message and a VBScript function to pass the message from VBScript to JavaScript. If any one of these elements is missing or contains a mistake, the communication does not work. Also, check to make sure your browser supports this communication.

I can get ActionScript-to-JavaScript communication to work on my machine, but it doesn't work for others.

Chances are the users are using browsers that do not support this type of communication. They also could have simply turned off JavaScript or ActiveX in their browsers. Some organizations have this feature turned off by default in all their browsers for security reasons.

I can't get Perl scripts to run on my server. What am I doing wrong?

It is important to realize that CGI programming is a different skill than Flash programming. If an electrician needs to have some water pipes moved to be able to run some wires, he would usually call a plumber to do the job rather than move them himself. Some Flash programmers can take on the extra skill of CGI programming, whereas others find it difficult to learn. If you're having trouble, you will definitely want to team up with someone else to get the job done.

I am including variables in the OBJECT movie parameter. They work fine in Internet Explorer for Windows, but other browsers don't get them.

You probably forgot to add the variables to the src parameter of the EMBED tag, or there is a typo in the EMBED tag but not the OBJECT tag. Internet Explorer for Windows uses the OBJECT tag and ignores the EMBED tag, whereas Netscape and other browsers use the EMBED tag but ignore the OBJECT tag.

I'm sure that my CGI program is done right and should work, but I still can't get Flash to load data from it.

You can and should always test your CGI programs from your browser with HTML. That is, you should browse an HTML page that submits to the CGI script or contains a Flash movie that submits to the CGI script. Place the HTML, SWF, and CGI files on the server and browse them through an http:// URL. For GET method programs, you can add the variables to the browser's address line. For POST method programs, you can create a simple HTML page with a form that calls the CGI program just as you would expect the Flash movie to do. The only change to the CGI program would be to have it set the MIME type to text/html. If you test the CGI program this way, you can determine whether the problem lies with the CGI program or your Flash movie.

XML

After importing an XML document, I can't find the nodes that I expect to be there. Is there a way to verify that the import worked?

There are many ways to verify a document after import. The easiest is to use the toString() function with trace to send the XML object to the Output window. You can also check the status property of the object. If either shows problems, your XML document must have errors in it. You can go through it line by line to find the missing or misspelled tag, or you can use a third-party XML creation tool to check for errors. You can also open the document in Microsoft Internet Explorer, which catches some basic problems, such as multiple top-level nodes.

After importing an XML document, I end up with a lot of blank text nodes. Why is that?

Any whitespace in your document, such as returns or tabs, is converted to little useless text nodes unless you set the ignoreWhite property of the XML object to true before parsing.

I can get the name of a node, but I can't seem to get the value of that same node. Why not?

Nodes don't have names *and* values; they have names *or* values. Chances are that the value you seek is actually the text node that is a child of the node with the name.

Why can't I access the sound in my loaded movie?

Here's a typical problem scenario: You have a movie—call it soundsInHere. The soundsInHere.fla movie has a sound file in its Library with the linkage name `"ByeBye"` and code on the Main Timeline that looks like this:

```
mySound = new Sound();
mySound.attachSound("ByeBye");
mySound.start();
```

When you test the soundsInHere movie on its own, the sound plays fine. But when you use `loadMovie()` to load the soundsInHere.swf file into another movie, the sound doesn't play.

The solution is to add the keyword `this` in the soundsInHere.fla file, as follows (with the keyword emphasized in bold):

```
mySound = new Sound(this);
mySound.attachSound("ByeBye");
mySound.start();
```

If you publish the soundsInHere.swf file again, it should work.

This was an issue in Flash 5, and it's still an issue in Flash MX 2004. You can find a tech note on it at www.macromedia.com/support/flash/ts/documents/attached_sound.htm

CHAPTER **23**

Using Flash for Dynamic Data

In this chapter

Introduction to Dynamic Data in Flash MX 2004   662

Databinding and Components   664

Flash Remoting   666

Using and Modifying the DataGrid Component   668

Web Services   672

INTRODUCTION TO DYNAMIC DATA IN FLASH MX 2004

This chapter focuses on using Flash MX 2004 for accessing databases. Although most of the material on Flash in this book is applicable to either the Standard or Professional version, this chapter uses three components available only in Flash MX 2004 Professional: the WebServiceConnector, DataSet, and DataGrid components. Data components such as these make the Professional version of Flash MX 2004 the clear choice for anyone planning to work with databases.

A Flash movie can access a database at runtime and either display the data or use it internally for decision-making. The Flash Player supports two fundamentally different database access technologies:

- Flash Remoting, which is unchanged from Flash MX and uses Macromedia's proprietary Action Message Format (AMF) communication protocol. AMF is highly efficient and optimized for the Flash client. The Flash client receives replies as ActionScript objects.

- Web services, based on the WebServiceConnector component, new in Flash MX 2004 Professsional. The WebServiceConnector uses Simple Object Access Protocol (SOAP). SOAP is an open standard, but somewhat verbose, meaning that its packets are large, and therefore data transfer is relatively inefficient. SOAP is not optimized for the Flash client. The Flash client receives replies as XML documents and must transform the XML into ActionScript objects to use the data in the ActionScript environment.

→ For a brief introduction to dynamic content in Studio MX 2004, **see** "Dynamic Content," **page 20**, in Chapter 2, "Studio MX: a Bird's-Eye View."

Even for the relatively small and simple recordset used as an example in this chapter, and using the local host (the Web server running on the same machine as the Flash client), I find Flash Remoting to be noticeably faster than Web services. When the service is accessed over the network (as in all real-world situations), the speed advantage of Flash Remoting usually becomes much more evident. Flash Remoting is also more mature and therefore tends to be more robust.

SWFs are also substantially smaller with Flash Remoting, perhaps because the Web services approach requires two data components (WebServiceConnector and DataSet) that are not required for Flash Remoting. For example, this chapter features two applications that do exactly the same thing, one with Flash Remoting, the other using Web services. The SWF for Flash Remoting is around 65KB. The SWF for Web services is around 125KB.

From the user's perspective, the only difference between Flash Remoting and Web services is that the latter is slower. On the other hand, as a developer, you have to consider the fact that Flash Remoting locks you and your client into a Macromedia solution on the server side: You can access data on a server only if the server has the Macromedia Flash Remoting Gateway (FRG) installed. The FRG can be installed in a variety of environments, falling into four major categories, summarized in Table 23.1.

TABLE 23.1 MAJOR ENVIRONMENTS SUPPORTING FLASH REMOTING GATEWAY

Environment	Service Implementation
J2EE	Enterprise JavaBeans (EJBs), JavaBeans, Plain Old Java Objects (POJOs), Java Management Extension (JMX) MBeans
.NET services	ASP.NET technologies, ADO.NET data-binding adapters, .NET assemblies (DLLs), .NET Web services
Server pages	Microsoft ASP pages, Java Server Pages (JSP) and Servlets, Macromedia ColdFusion components (CFCs)
XML objects	SOAP-based Web services exposed through WSDL files, org.w3c.dom.Document objects, and other serialized XML objects

NOTE

WSDL is Web Services Description Language, a standard XML-based language for describing Web services.

As you can see from Table 23.1, the FRG offers great flexibility in choosing a server technology. However, sites that you do not control are more likely to make services available as Web services than to implement the FRG. Thus, using the Web services approach on the Flash client gives you access to a wide variety of publicly available services, ranging from information about books and products from Amazon.com to the free translation service from BabelFish.

The ability to access Web services is extremely useful. From a technical perspective, the Web services approach is best suited to applications where the amount of data is small. From a practical perspective, you may have to use it whenever you do not control the server, and thus cannot install the FRG.

→ For a discussion of Flash Remoting and Web services in the ColdFusion context, **see** "Using Flash to Access the ColdFusion Server," **page 878**, in Chapter 32, "Understanding and Administering ColdFusion."

CAUTION

The same security restrictions that apply to downloading other types of data apply to Flash Remoting and Web services.

→ For more on security, see "New Security Rules," **page 330**, in Chapter 14, "What's New in Flash MX 2004?". Also **see** crossDomainPolicyFiles.htm and security2004.htm on the CD accompanying this book.

Before you can get hands-on with any of the features discussed in this chapter, you must have access to a server with a service that is implemented using one of the technologies shown in the right column of Table 23.1. In the examples in this chapter, the server is ColdFusion, so the implementation is a CFC. To make the examples in this chapter work on your system as they are shown in this chapter, you need to have ColdFusion up and running, and you need to copy qProducts.cfc from the CD into the //CfusionMX/wwwroot/ greendept folder (creating the greendept folder first, if necessary).

→ For a discussion of other things you may need to do to have a functional ColdFusion development environment, **see** "Introducing ColdFusion," **page 876**, in Chapter 32.

→ Chapter 13 of this book ("Developing ColdFusion Applications in Dreamweaver"), **page 312**, gives instructions for creating several ColdFusion Components (CFCs), one of which I adapt for the examples in this chapter. If you are not familiar with CFCs, I recommend that you read Chapters 13 and 32.

I will assume that you are running the services on your local host (e.g. http:// localhost:8500/greendept/myCFC.cfc). Except for security considerations (primarily cross-domain access), putting a service up on the Web after testing it locally is a simple matter of uploading the .cfc file to the ColdFusion server and changing the domain in the URL that is used to access the service (for example, `http://www.myDomain.com/greendept/myCFC.cfc`).

DATABINDING AND COMPONENTS

The DataGrid component, which we're going to use to display data in a sortable table, is based on the rather complex DataGrid class, which has 19 events, 31 methods, and 33 properties (attributes) documented. However, all you need to create the sortable table, fully populated with data, as in Figure 23.1, is one method, `setDataProvider()`, which sets one attribute: `dataProvider`. As the name implies, this attribute references an object that provides the data for the DataGrid.

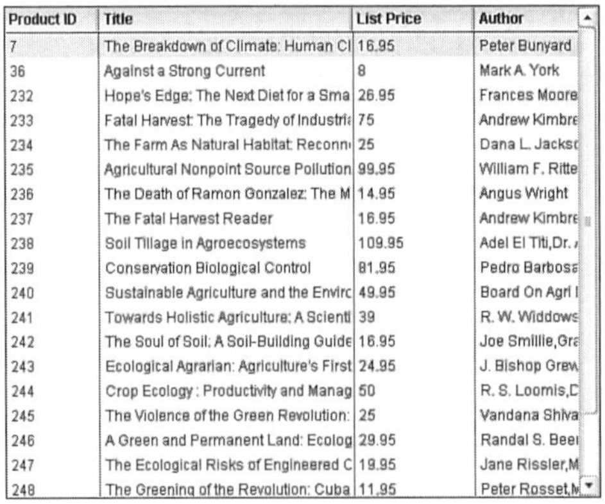

Figure 23.1
A DataGrid component displaying data from the qProducts.cfc Web service.

Product ID	Title	List Price	Author
7	The Breakdown of Climate: Human Cl	16.95	Peter Bunyard
36	Against a Strong Current	8	Mark A. York
232	Hope's Edge: The Next Diet for a Sma	26.95	Frances Moore
233	Fatal Harvest: The Tragedy of Industri	75	Andrew Kimbre
234	The Farm As Natural Habitat: Reconn	25	Dana L. Jacks
235	Agricultural Nonpoint Source Pollution	99.95	William F. Ritte
236	The Death of Ramon Gonzalez: The M	14.95	Angus Wright
237	The Fatal Harvest Reader	16.95	Andrew Kimbre
238	Soil Tillage in Agroecosystems	109.95	Adel El Titi,Dr.
239	Conservation Biological Control	81.95	Pedro Barbosa
240	Sustainable Agriculture and the Enviro	49.95	Board On Agri
241	Towards Holistic Agriculture: A Scienti	39	R. W. Widdows
242	The Soul of Soil: A Soil-Building Guide	16.95	Joe Smillie,Gra
243	Ecological Agrarian: Agriculture's First	24.95	J. Bishop Grew
244	Crop Ecology: Productivity and Manag	50	R. S. Loomis,C
245	The Violence of the Green Revolution:	25	Vandana Shiva
246	A Green and Permanent Land: Ecolog	29.95	Randal S. Beel
247	The Ecological Risks of Engineered C	19.95	Jane Rissler,M
248	The Greening of the Revolution: Cuba	11.95	Peter Rosset,M

The `dataProvider` attribute is actually a complex object in its own right, with a long list of methods and attributes. However, for our purposes right now, you can think of the `dataProvider` as an array of objects, with each object representing a row of data. For example, in Figure 23.1, the second row would be represented by the following object:

```
{ProductID: 36,
   ProductName: "Against a Strong Current",
   ListPrice: 8,
   Weight: "Mark A. York"}
```

NOTE

A row of data in a DataGrid object is officially referred to as an *item*.

(This data comes from the greendept.mdb database on the CD. To minimize the number of fields in the database, the Weight field was used to hold the author's name. It's not necessary to track weight for books, so instead of creating a separate Author field, the unused Weight field was pressed into service.)

→ **See** "Changing Column Headers," **page 669** in this chapter, to see how you can change the "WEIGHT" header to display "Author" so that users won't be confused.

Setting the dataProvider property is an example of *databinding*, because it binds the data source to the DataGrid. You can do databinding purely in ActionScript, or you can use the Component Inspector and not have to code at all.

The ActionScript for databinding is extremely simple. For example, the following line of code sets the dataProvider property for a DataGrid object whose instance name is books_dg. (You can create such a DataGrid object by dragging and dropping a DataGrid component from the UI Components section of the Components panel onto the Stage and typing in **books_dg** for the Instance Name in the Property inspector.) In the following example, the data will come from the array of objects referenced by the result variable:

```
books_dg.setDataProvider(result);
```

The result variable must reference an appropriate data source. If it doesn't, most likely you will see nothing in the DataGrid at all. Specifically, result should reference an array whose objects can be interpreted as representing rows of data. Most importantly, in the name/value pairs that make up the object, the *names* should be the same in each row. Only the *values* should change from row to row. Thus, in Figure 23.1, the attribute names in every row will be the same: ProductID, ProductName, ListPrice, and Weight. The values associated with the names will change from row to row.

Writing the ActionScript to bind a data source to the dataProvider attribute is easy: One little line of ActionScript, and you're done. Knowing *which data source is appropriate* for a particular component is not always easy, because you have to understand both the requirements of the component and the data structure of the source. That's where the Component Inspector comes in: It gives you a visual interface that shows you everything you need to know to make intelligent databinding decisions, even if you've never used the component before and/or are not familiar with the data source.

In qProducts.cfc, the getBooks() function returns the results of the qProducts query, which is a recordset. In ActionScript, the recordset becomes an array of objects, in which each object represents a record or row from the database. In other words, the result returned by the `getBooks()` function is a perfect source for binding to the `dataProvider` attribute. In the next section, on Flash Remoting, we will take advantage of this knowledge and just use ActionScript to do the binding. In the section on Web services, we'll use the Component Inspector to do the binding, so you'll have a chance to see how that works.

FLASH REMOTING

Before you can use Flash Remoting, you must download and install the Flash Remoting components from the Macromedia site (`http://www.macromedia.com`). These are non-visual components, with which you never interact directly in any way. After you install them, you can forget about them. However, they are required for creating Flash Remoting applications.

In the examples in this chapter, the ColdFusion server accesses the greendept.mdb database through the System DSN (Data Source Name) `greendept`. You can create the System DSN with the ColdFusion Administrator.

→ For step-by-step instructions for adding a System DSN, **see** "Configuring Data Sources," **page 880,** in Chapter 32.

It takes just a few lines of ActionScript to create a Flash Remoting connection with a particular service. After that connection is established, a single line of ActionScript can execute any operation (method or function) offered by the service.

Here's the ActionScript needed to set up the Flash Remoting connection with qProducts.cfc, residing on the ColdFusion server:

```
#include "NetServices.as"

NetServices.setDefaultGatewayUrl
                ("http://localhost:8500/flashservices/gateway");
gateway_conn = NetServices.createGatewayConnection();
myService = gateway_conn.getService("greendept.qProducts", this);
```

NetServices.as is a simple file (less than a dozen lines of code) defining the NetServices class used to create Flash Remoting connections. Note the empty line between the `include` statement and the rest of the program. It's always a good idea to have an empty line after any `include` statement; the ActionScript compiler can become confused if you don't.

The path `"http://localhost:8500/flashservices/gateway"` is the URL at which you will connect to the FRG. This may differ for different versions of the gateway. For instance, on a .NET installation, `"flashservices/gateway"` becomes `"flashservices/gateway.aspx"`.

The `flashservices/gateway` path is not an actual folder on the ColdFusion server. It is a logical mapping referencing the FRG. It is automatically created by the ColdFusion server. The FRG, in turn, automatically uses the wwwroot folder (for example, c:\CFusionMX\ wwwroot\) as its root. Note that your local server URL may be slightly different from the one shown in the preceding code. In particular, the port number may be something other than 8500. You may also have the option of using `127.0.0.1` instead of `localhost`.

The second-to-the-last line creates a new connection with the FRG. The NetServices class does not have a typical constructor function; you do not create new gateway connections using the new keyword. The createGatewayConnection() method is as close as you'll come to a constructor for Flash Remoting connections.

Finally, the last line creates a service (myService) that allows the Flash client to interact with the service on the server (qProducts.cfc, in the greendept folder, in this example). Notice that dots are used instead of slashes when specifying the path to the service on the server, and the ".cfc" is left off (greendept.qProducts).

The qProducts.cfc component is based on the qProducts query in qProducts.cfm in Chapter 13. However, the qProducts query in the CFC selects only ProductID, ProductName, ListPrice and Weight, instead of selecting all the fields in the Products table. The getBooks() function in the CFC simply returns the recordset created by the qProducts query.

23

Here's what qProducts.cfc looks like:

```
<cfcomponent>
 <cffunction name="getBooks" access="remote" returntype="query" output="false">
      <cfquery name="qProducts" datasource="greendept">
      SELECT ProductID, ProductName,
      ListPrice, Weight
      FROM Products
      WHERE Category = '13001010000'</cfquery>
      <cfreturn qProducts>
 </cffunction>
</cfcomponent>
```

Four ColdFusion tags are used to create this component: The <cfcomponent> tag identifies it as a component. The <cffunction> tag creates the getBooks() function. The <cfquery> tag retrieves records from the greendept database when the getBooks() function is executed. The <cfquery> tag stores the retrieved recordset in the qProducts query. Finally, the <cfreturn> tag returns the qProducts query when the function is executed.

To make use of this CFC, you need to do two things in the Flash client: create a callback function to get the result and call the getBooks() function. The result will be an ActionScript object representing the qProducts query. When you get the result, you'll bind it to the dataProvider attribute of a DataGrid object.

You use the Flash Remoting service that you created, myService, to execute the getBooks() function, like this:

```
myService.getBooks();
```

This works because functions in the CFC effectively become methods of myService.

To simplify this example, the getBooks() function was designed to take no arguments. However, you can design CFCs that do take arguments, in which case the function call would look something like this:

```
myService.myFunc(arg1,arg2);
```

→ For more on creating CFCs with arguments, **see** "Creating and Using ColdFusion Components (CFCs),"
page 903, in Chapter 33, "ColdFusion Markup Language (CFML)."

The Flash client's callback function for the `getBooks()` function must have a specific name: `getBooks_Result`. All we're going to do in the callback function in this example is databinding. Here's what it looks like:

```
function getBooks_Result ( result )
{
        books_dg.setDataProvider(result);
}
```

In this example, `books_dg` is the instance name of the DataGrid object. When `getBooks()` returns a result, `getBooks_Result()` fires, binding the result to the `books_dg.dataProvider` attribute, causing the data in the recordset to appear in the DataGrid.

In getBooks_rem.fla on the CD accompanying this book, the `getBooks()` function is called when you click the Get Books button. At that point, the Flash Remoting connection has done its job. After that, you will just work with the data in the DataGrid object.

TIP

> If you want to quickly create a "skeleton" program to create a Flash Remoting connection, choose File, New. Then go to the Templates Tab and select Remoting, Basic Remoting. You can edit the template to reflect the instance name of the components you are using, the name and path of the service you are accessing, and so on.

Using and Modifying the DataGrid Component

As soon as the DataGrid instance has data in it, it automatically has "stretchable," sortable columns. With "stretchable" columns, the user can position the mouse cursor in the header row on the vertical line between any two columns. The cursor turns into a two-headed arrow pointing right and left, as shown in Figure 23.2. The user can then click and drag to move the boundaries of the two columns left or right. (Microsoft Word tables and Excel spreadsheets have a similar feature.) The user can click once in the header, in any column, to sort the DataGrid based on the values in that column.

In addition to these default DataGrid features, you can use the methods of the `DataGrid` class, or the `DataGridColumn` class, to modify the DataGrid or individual columns in various ways. For instance, you can remove a column, change the header text in a column, or highlight a row.

Removing a Column

The `ProductID` field returned by `getBooks()` is not particularly useful to the user. You can remove it using the `removeColumnAt()` method of the DataGrid class. Because this is the left-most column, which is column 0, the statement looks like this:

```
books_dg.removeColumnAt(0);
```

Figure 23.2
The two-headed arrow cursor indicates that you can click and drag to stretch or shrink the adjacent columns, moving the boundaries between the two columns.

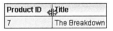

In getBooks_rem.fla on the CD accompanying this book, you trigger this action by clicking the Clear 1st Column button.

The `removeColumnAt()` method removes a column *after* the column has already been displayed. You can prevent a column from displaying in the first place by setting the `columnNames` attribute of the DataGrid to an array containing the names of the columns you want to display. Here's an example, found on line 8 of getBooks_rem.fla:

```
books_dg.columnNames = ["ProductName","ListPrice","Weight"];
```

The preceding line is commented out in the sample file. Just uncomment it if you want to see how it works. You may also want to uncomment lines 13 and 14 to space the three columns equally.

 If you are using the `columnNames` *attribute to predetermine the columns that appear in the DataGrid, and nothing is appearing in one or more columns,* **see** *the "Troubleshooting" section at the end of this chapter.*

CHANGING COLUMN HEADERS

DataGrid header text defaults to the names of the database fields. You can set the text in the headers to something more readable or understandable by setting the column's `headerText` attribute. To get a reference to the column, use the `getColumnAt()` method of the DataGrid class. For example, the following statement changes the header text on column 0 (the leftmost column) to "Product ID":

```
books_dg.getColumnAt(0).headerText = "Product ID";
```

In getBooks_rem.fla on the CD accompanying this book, the header text on all columns is changed when you click the Change Labels button.

CHANGING A ROW'S BACKGROUND COLOR

You can change the background color of a DataGrid row by using the `setPropertiesAt()` method of the DataGrid class. For example, the following statement changes the `backgroundColor` property of row 0 to green:

```
books_dg.setPropertiesAt(0, {backgroundColor:0x00FF00});
```

In the preceding line, the first parameter is the index of the DataGrid row. The index here is 0, which is the first row below the header.

FORMATTING COLUMNS

To format columns, use the `setStyle()` method of the `DataGridColumn` class. For instance, the following lines set the left-most column's background color to red, and the font in that column to bold, underlined, size 14:

```
books_dg.getColumnAt(0).setStyle("backgroundColor",0xff0000);
books_dg.getColumnAt(0).setStyle("fontWeight","bold");'
books_dg.getColumnAt(0).setStyle("textDecoration","underline");
books_dg.getColumnAt(0).setStyle("fontSize",14);
```

RESPONDING TO CLICKS ON HEADERS

The events associated with the DataGrid class allow you to create callback functions that fire when the user interacts with the DataGrid in various ways. For example, if you want to do something whenever the user clicks on a header, you can use the `headerRelease` event like this:

```
var myListener:Object = new Object();
myListener.headerRelease = function(eventObject){
    // your code goes here
}
books_dg.addEventListener("headerRelease", myListener);
```

In the `headerRelease()` callback function, the `eventObject` parameter has four attributes. The first two are standard for all DataGrid callback functions.

- `type`—The type of event, "headerRelease" in this example
- `target`—The object broadcasting the event, `books_dg` here
- `columnIndex`—The clicked column
- `view`—An object responsible for rendering the DataGrid

The view object is an extremely rich one. (In the Flash MX 2004 authoring environment, click on any header in the DataGrid displayed by getBooks_rem.fla, and all the properties of the `view` object will the displayed in the Output window. It takes up several pages of output.) By examining the properties of the `view` object, you can find out anything you need to know about the DataGrid object. Similarly, by using the methods of the `view` object, you can modify the DataGrid object. For example, this underlines all the text in the DataGrid:

```
eventObject.view.setStyle("textDecoration","underline");
```

To underline just the text in the column that was clicked, use the `columnIndex` attribute of `eventObject`:

```
i = eventObject.columnIndex;
eventObject.view.getColumnAt(i).setStyle("textDecoration","underline");
```

The preceding two code snippets are included (though commented out) in getBooks_rem.fla. What is actually implemented in the `headerRelease` event (and not commented out) is numeric sorting for columns with numeric data. Otherwise, by default, numeric columns sort alphabetically.

The alternate sort uses the `sortItems()` method of the `DataGrid` class. This method is inherited from the `List` class, and is identical to the `sort()` method of the `Array` class.

→ For information on the `sort()` method of the `Array` class, **see** "`sort()` and `sortOn()`," **page 564**, in Chapter 21, "Advanced ActionScript."

To implement the numeric sort, you need to do two things: create a numeric sort function, and tell the `DataGrid` object to use it.

If the numeric sort function is `numericSortFunc()`, then within the `releaseHeader` event, the following line tells the `DataGrid` object to use the numeric sort function:

```
eventObject.target.sortItems(numericSortFunc);
```

When the user clicks on a column header, the numeric sort function is called numerous times, to compare each row in the DataGrid to every other row. Two items (row objects) are passed to the numeric sort function each time it is called. The numeric sort function compares the values for the clicked column in the two items. Here is the essence of the numeric sort function, which closely parallels the `byVotes()` comparison function in Chapter 21:

```
function numericSortFunc (a , b) {
  var colName:String = eventObject.target.columnNames[eventObject.columnIndex];
  return b[colName] - a[colName];
}
```

The preceding function first gets the name of the column (`colName`) and then uses that name to retrieve the value for that column in each item. One value is then subtracted from the other, and the result is returned.

In getBooks_rem.fla, the numeric sort function is somewhat more complex, for two reasons:

First, we want to sort only *numeric* columns numerically. Columns containing *string* data should still be sorted alphabetically. In getBooks_rem.fla, the items in the column are examined after the header is clicked, and only numeric columns are sorted numerically.

Second, the default behavior for the *DataGrid* object is to re-sort the column each time it is clicked, alternating between sorting in ascending and descending order. This behavior is duplicated for the numeric sort, which makes it necessary to keep track of the current sort state for each column.

The ActionScript code associated with these enhancements is commented in getBooks_rem.fla.

RESPONDING TO ROLLOVERS

By default, the DataGrid highlights a row (that is, changes the background color) as you roll over it. You can capture the `itemRollOver` event and add to or change that default behavior. The index of the row is received as the `index` property of the event object. The following code captures the `itemRollOver` event. The callback function first resets the background color to white for all rows in lines 2 and 3, and then changes the background color for the rollover row to sky blue (0xCCFFFF) in line 4:

```
1: myListener.itemRollOver = function (eventObject) {
2:    for (i = 0 ; i < books_dg.rowCount ; i++)
3:        books_dg.setPropertiesAt(i, {backgroundColor:0xFFFFFF});
4:    books_dg.setPropertiesAt(eventObject.index, {backgroundColor:0xCCFFFF});
5: }
6: books_dg.addEventListener("itemRollOver", myListener);
```

WEB SERVICES

23

This section describes a procedure for accessing qProducts.cfc as a Web service using the WebServiceConnector component in Flash MX 2004 Professional. Unfortunately, if you use the DataSet component that comes with the Flash MX 2004 Professional 7.0.1 update, the final result does not display correctly: Of four columns of data that should be displayed in the DataGrid component, only two display. If you use the pre-update DataSet component, everything works correctly.

I considered just describing something much simpler, such as a situation in which the Web service returns a string, which is then displayed in a TextArea component. This scenario seems to work reliably most of the time, with both pre-update and post-update components. However, there are already excellent tutorials available on the Web that cover this simple scenario.

→ Here is a good tutorial on the WebserviceConnector: "Building a Tip of the Day Application," by Jen DeHaan, http://www.macromedia.com/devnet/mx/flash/articles/tipoday.html. Be sure to check out part two, which is where it gets into the WebServiceConnector.

By the time you read this, a de-bugged DataSet component may be available from the Macromedia or elsewhere. (Check http://www.flashoop.com for news.)

In the end, I decided that I would be contributing more to the sum total knowledge by leaving this section as is than by repeating what has already been excellently done elsewhere. The procedure described here is (theoretically) correct, and there is a working example on the CD (getBooks_wc.fla), which incorporates the pre-update DataSet component.

Before getting into details, let me note that the procedure I am about to describe assumes that you want to access a Web service that you have never previously defined in the Flash MX 2004 authoring environment. You can tell whether you have previously defined a Web service by going to the Web Services panel (Window, Development Panels, Web Services). If the service you want to access is already defined in the Web Services panel, you can save yourself a couple of steps. The catch is that the service may be defined in the Web Services panel, even if you've *never used the Web Services panel*. When you place a WebServiceConnector in the workspace and define a Web service in the Property inspector, that Web service automatically shows up in the Web Services panel, too.

→ If you want to access a Web service that is already defined in the Web Services panel, **see** "The Web Services Panel" sidebar, **page 673**, in this chapter.

The Web Services Panel

The Web Services panel (Window, Development Panels, Web Services) displays information about Web services in an easy-to-digest format. You can use it to define and explore a new service, or to explore a previously defined service. Very importantly, you can use it to quickly create and configure a WebServiceConnector to access an operation of a defined Web service.

To define a new Web service, you have to provide the WSDL URL for the Web service. You can enter the URL in the Property inspector with a WebServiceConnector selected, or you can use the Web Services panel itself. To enter the URL in the Web Services panel, click on the Define Web Services button in the upper left of the panel. (See Figure 23.3.)

In the Web Services panel, each Web service is represented by a globe icon, followed by an identifier formed from the name of the service with the word "Service" tacked on the end. Thus, the qProducts Web service becomes qProductsService, and the BabelFish Web service becomes BabelFishService.

If the service has any operations defined, there will be a small plus sign to the left of the globe icon. Click on the plus sign to expand the hierarchical display for the Web service.

The first level of the hierarchy shows the names of the operations the Web service offers. For instance, in Figure 23.3, the Web Services panel shows that the qProducts service offers just one operation, getBooks(). Similarly, the BabelFish service offers one operation, BabelFish().

The next level down shows params (parameters) and results. For instance, we can see that the getBooks() operation takes no parameters and returns a ColdFusion query, which is equivalent to an Array object in Flash.

For BabelFish, the Web Services panel shows that the operation does take parameters and returns a string.

The next level down provides additional information. For instance, under params, it provides the names and datatypes of any parameters. For example, for BabelFish, the parameters are sourcedata (the string to be translated) and translationmode (a short code, indicating the type of translation to be performed, such as English to French, French to German, and so on). It may also provide more information about results.

You can quickly create and configure a WebServiceConnector by right-clicking (Windows) or Ctrl-clicking (Mac) on any operation, such as getBooks() or BabelFish() in Figure 23.3, and selecting Add Method Call from the context menu. A WebServiceConnector component is created on the Stage, and the WSDLURL and operation fields are automatically filled in the Property inspector, all in a single operation.

Figure 23.3
The Web Services panel.

Define Web Services

Refresh Web Services

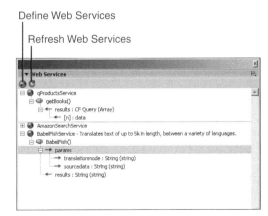

This procedure, which requires no hand-coded ActionScript, has three basic phases: creating component instances, setting up the databindings, and creating a triggering mechanism for the data source. In slightly more detail, the process can be broken down into seven basic steps:

1. Drag and drop a WebServiceConnector component into the workspace and give it an instance name.

2. In the Property inspector, set two WebServiceConnector component properties: the WSDL URL and the operation (function) that you want to call.

3. Drag and drop a DataSet component into the workspace and give it an instance name.

4. Drag and drop a DataGrid component onto the Stage and give it an instance name.

5. Set up databindings in the Component Inspector between the WebServiceConnector and the DataSet.

6. Set up databindings in the Component Inspector between the DataSet and the DataGrid.

7. Drag and drop a Button component onto the Stage and apply a Behavior that will "trigger" the data source (the WebServiceConnector) when the user clicks on the button.

Triggering the data source brings the data from the ColdFusion server into the WebServiceConnector, which provides the data to the DataSet, which in turn provides the data to the DataGrid. The DataGrid displays the data.

CREATING COMPONENT INSTANCES

Drag and drop a WebServiceConnector component from the Data Components section of the Components panel into the workspace. The WebServiceConnector component isn't a visual component, so it does not need to be on the Stage. You may prefer to position it off the Stage, so that what you see on the Stage as you're working more closely represents what users will see. With the component selected, give it an instance name in the Property inspector. For this example, we will use the instance name books_wc.

In the Property inspector, type **http://localhost:8500/greendept/qProducts.cfc?wsdl** into the WSDLURL field. (As with Flash Remoting, the localhost:8500 part of the URL may vary—especially the port number.) The question mark followed by wsdl causes the ColdFusion server to dynamically generate and return a WSDL *file* that contains a description of the Web service interface, allowing Flash MX 2004 to determine what operations are supported, what parameters the operations require, and what results the operations return. Flash MX 2004 uses this information to build the display in the Web Services panel and to populate the Component Inspector.

Click in the blank operations field and click on the down arrow to get a list of operations. There is just one operation in this case: getBooks. Select the operation from the drop-down menu. Or, you can just type **getBooks** in the operation field.

Drag and drop a DataSet component into the workspace and give it an instance name (we'll use books_ds). Again, this is a non-visual component, so it doesn't have to be on the Stage. Why do we need the DataSet component? Because If you bind a WebServiceConnector component directly to a DataGrid, the DataGrid's column sorting feature does not work. However, if you bind the WebServiceConnector to a DataSet component, and bind the DataSet component to the DataGrid, the sorting works. The DataSet component acts as a middleman between the WebServiceConnector and the DataGrid.

Drag and drop a DataGrid component onto the Stage and give it an instance name. For this example, we use books_dg. Change the DataGrid's width and height in the Property inspector, so that it fills most of the Stage. (But leave room for the button.) You may even want to make the Stage bigger (Modify, Document, Dimensions).

Drag and drop a Button component onto the Stage, anywhere where it doesn't overlap with the DataGrid component. It doesn't need an instance name.

SETTING UP DATABINDINGS

The first step is to bind the WebServiceConnector result to the DataSet dataProvider. When the WebServiceConnector returns data, it is stored initially in the DataSet.

To set up this binding, start by selecting the WebServiceConnector. In the Component Inspector, in the Bindings tab (which is present only in Flash Professional), click on the blue plus sign (the Add Binding button).

The Add Binding dialog pops up, enabling you to choose between params and results. params represents parameters passed to the WebServiceConnector.

However, in this case, the getBooks() function doesn't take any parameters, so do not select the params option.

Instead, select results and click OK. You have now indicated that you are going to bind the WebServiceConnector results (the recordset it gets from the ColdFusion server) to something. Next, you need to choose that something: the DataSet dataProvider.

In the name/value area at the bottom of the Component Inspector, click in the empty value box to the right of the bound to name. A magnifying glass icon appears on the right side of the value box, as shown in Figure 23.4. Click on the magnifying glass icon.

You get the Bound To dialog (Figure 23.5), listing all the components in the scene in the Component Paths section on the left side of the dialog. Click on the DataSet component. In the Schema Location section on the right side of the dialog are four attributes of the DataSet that are candidates for binding. The top one, dataProvider, is already selected. Leave it that way and click OK.

23

Figure 23.4
The Component
Inspector. Clicking on
the magnifying glass
brings up the Bound
To dialog.

Figure 23.5
The Bound To dialog.

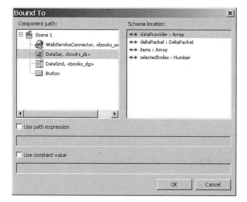

You've just completed one binding, feeding the results of the Web service call into the DataSet. The Component Inspector should look like Figure 23.6. The next step is binding the DataSet to the DataGrid.

Select the DataSet component in the workspace. The Bindings tab of the Component Inspector reflects the binding that you just created (Figure 23.7).

Figure 23.6
The Component
Inspector, showing
the WebService-
Connector bound
to the DataSet.
WebService-
Connector,
<books_wc> at the
top of the Component
Inspector indicates
that the
WebServiceConnector
is selected in the
workspace.

Figure 23.7
The Component
Inspector, showing
the DataSet bound to
the WebService-
Connector. *DataSet,*
<books_ds> at the
top of the Component
Inspector indicates
that the DataSet is
selected in the work-
space.

Click the blue plus sign in the Bindings tab of the Component Inspector. In the Add
Binding dialog, choose the dataProvider and click OK. You now have the dataProvider
twice on the Bindings tab. Click in the value box to the right of the bound to name. Click
on the magnifying glass. In the Bound To dialog, select the DataGrid in the Component
Paths section on the left. On the right, in the Schema Location section, dataProvider is
already selected. Click OK. The Component Inspector should look like Figure 23.8.

Figure 23.8
The Component
Inspector, showing
the DataSet bound to
the DataGrid.
DataSet,
<books_ds> at the
top of the Component
Inspector indicates
that the DataSet is
selected in the work-
space.

All the databinding is now complete.

TRIGGERING THE DATA SOURCE

All that remains now is to create a means of "triggering" the data source—a way to tell the WebServiceConnector to call the getBooks() function. We'll use the Button component to implement this feature. Start by selecting the Button component on the Stage.

To set up the triggering capability, use the Behaviors panel. If the Behaviors panel is not already visible, select Window, Development Panels, Behaviors. In the Behaviors panel, click on the blue plus sign (the Add Behavior button). Roll down to the Data category (the first category). Roll over to Trigger Data Source, the only option in the Data category, as shown in Figure 23.9. Click once.

Figure 23.9
Selecting the Trigger
Data Source behavior
on the Behaviors
panel.

The Trigger Data Source dialog is displayed, with only one possible data source to select, books_wc, the WebServiceConnector. Click on books_wc to select it, and click OK.

That's it. The behavior is now applied to the button.

You're now ready to test your movie. When you click the button, it should trigger the WebServiceConnector and data should display in the DataGrid.

getBooks_wc.fla on the CD illustrates the completed project, with several DataGrid manipulation options, such as removing the left-most column, changing the header text, and highlighting every other row for easier scanning.

→ After the DataGrid is displaying data, all the techniques for manipulating the DataGrid are exactly the same as those described previously in this chapter. **See** "Using and Modifying the DataGrid Component," **page 668**, earlier in this chapter.

TROUBLESHOOTING

I used the columnNames attribute of the DataGrid object to predetermine which columns are displayed. However, one or more columns is empty! What did I do wrong?

If you are publishing for Flash Player 7, column names are case sensitive. Thus, if you provide Listprice (with a small p) as the column name when it should be ListPrice (with a capital P), you create a column for a non-existent data field, and nothing displays.

PART IV

FIREWORKS MX

24 What's New in Fireworks MX 2004?   683

25 Fireworks MX 2004 Environment and Tools   693

26 Creating Graphics, Rollovers, and Animations   731

27 Optimizing and Exporting Graphics and Web Pages   755

28 Automating and Extending Fireworks   775

CHAPTER **24**

WHAT'S NEW IN FIREWORKS MX 2004?

In this chapter

Upgrading to Fireworks MX 2004   684

Performance Improvements   684

Interface Enhancements   684

New Tools   686

Enhanced Roundtrip Editing   689

New Anti-Aliasing Options   689

New Effects   690

JavaScript API Extensions   691

Full Unicode Support   691

Site Management   692

UPGRADING TO FIREWORKS MX 2004

There's a new Fireworks MX in town. If you're already a Fireworks MX user and want to know whether the newest version is worth upgrading to, read on. (Hint: It is.) If you've never used Fireworks or are considering upgrading from an earlier version, you will be impressed with what the folks at Macromedia have done to improve a program that already excels at designing, optimizing, and integrating Web graphics.

Unlike Photoshop which started its life for print image editing, Fireworks was designed from the beginning to create and manipulate Web graphics. Each successive version of this program has continued to improve the software's image optimization and creation/editing capabilities. In this chapter you will learn about what the folks at Macromedia have done to enhance an already robust Web graphics program.

PERFORMANCE IMPROVEMENTS

Perhaps the most significant changes to Fireworks MX 2004 are the ones under the hood. The new program is noticeably faster than its predecessors that had a tendency to operate like molasses on a cold winter day. Macromedia claims that large image manipulations and other processor-intensive tasks can now be handled up to 85% faster—and they appear to be right.

Batch processing is where the performance improvements are most noticeable. Resizing multiple images, for instance, as a batch process is definitely a much faster operation.

TRANSFORM TOOL ENHANCED

Macromedia has also enhanced the Transform tool (see Figure 24.1) to resize, stretch, and rotate objects with greater precision and speed. You can also scale text in point sizes.

In previous versions, you had to jump through a few hoops if you wanted to edit a JPEG and save the file in its original format. Before MX 2004, you had to save the image as a PNG, and then export it to JPEG. Fireworks MX 2004 now gives you the option to save a file in its native JPEG or GIF format.

INTERFACE ENHANCEMENTS

Although the interface improvements are most noticeable when moving from previous versions of Fireworks to Fireworks MX, there are still a few worthwhile enhancements in the latest version of the program.

→ For more on MX 2004 interface enhancements, **see** Chapter 3, "Introducing the MX Interface," **page 23**.

Figure 24.1
Improved performance means increased speed and precision with the Transform tool.

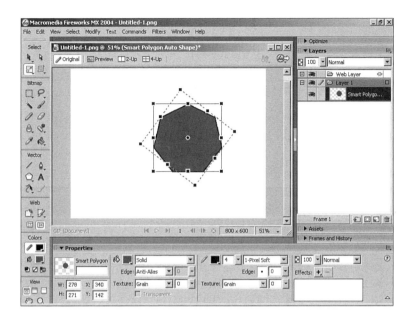

START PAGE

The Start page (see Figure 24.2) allows you to quickly access recently used files, create new files, or even access help and tutorials—all from one convenient location. This page appears when you launch Fireworks MX 2004 and when a document is not open.

Figure 24.2
The new Start page that greets you when you launch Fireworks MX 2004.

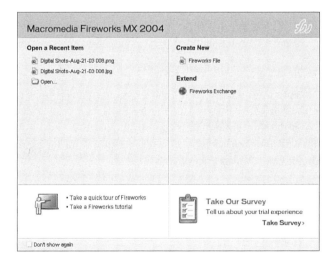

GRAPHICAL PREVIEWS

The Property inspector now includes graphical previews (see Figure 24.3) to make it easier to select the right fill, brush, or texture. This is a nice feature to have when you're not sure exactly which texture will look best, which brush stroke will match the design, or which gradient will achieve the desired effect.

Figure 24.3
Graphical previews have been added to the Property inspector.

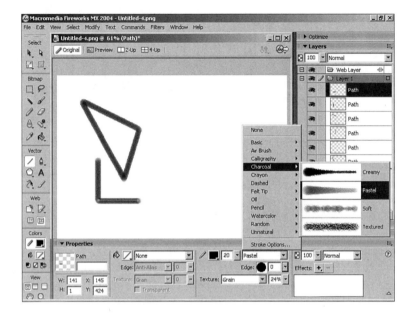

NEW TOOLS

Fireworks MX 2004 has added a few new tools to the image-editing tool box. Although these tools don't do anything that you could not have done in previous versions of Fireworks, they increase your efficiency. What took several steps now takes one or two.

AUTO SHAPES

The new Auto Shapes tools are one of the most appreciated additions to Fireworks MX 2004. A look at the Auto Shapes tools (see Figure 24.4) will reveal a slew of new shapes that you can use in your designs. Even better, you can modify these shapes by using the control handles, as well as change their stroke and fill properties. Auto Shapes can also be ungrouped and modified as individual objects.

The Auto Shapes panel (see Figure 24.5) also lets you create your own shapes, as well as use shapes from third-party developers.

Figure 24.4
Auto Shapes simplifies the process of creating complex shapes by giving you "canned" shapes that can be modified.

Figure 24.5
Shapes in the Auto Shapes panel that are shipped with Fireworks MX 2004.

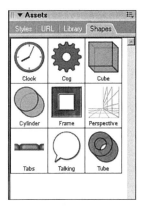

RED EYE REMOVAL TOOL

The Red Eye Removal tool enables you to remove that irritating red from the pupils of your Aunt May's birthday party photos (see Figure 24.6). Many designers have created their own workarounds to counter this photography phenomenon, but Macromedia has now given us the tools to simplify this process. The new tool works great on most red eye images, but gets a bit sketchy if the red eye leaks over to the iris.

REPLACE COLOR TOOL

The Replace Color tool lets you easily replace colors in bitmap images by painting with an adjustable brush-size cursor. Replacing image colors in previous versions of Fireworks required selecting pixels and then using the Paintbucket or Brush tool to modify the color. The new Replace Color tool allows you to select the color you want to change, set the color you want to change to, and then use the brush to make the switch (see Figure 24.7).

Figure 24.6
The Red Eye Removal tool provides a quick way to touch up photos affected by red eye.

Figure 24.7
The Replace Color tool gives you professional-level photo retouching capabilities so you can get funky with photos.

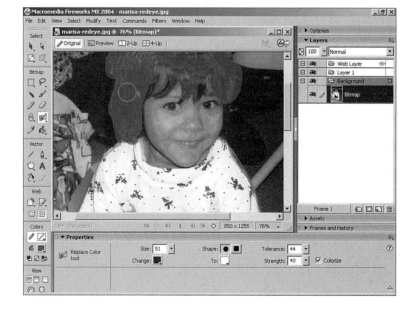

Motion Blur Live Effects

New in the Live Effects panel are some great new motion blur effects (see Figure 24.8). As with other effects, these "filters" can be applied, modified, and removed as you see fit.

Figure 24.8
The new Motion Blur Live Effects in action.

ENHANCED ROUNDTRIP EDITING

Fireworks MX 2004 now includes roundtrip support for server-side file formats, such as ASP, CFM, and PHP. Roundtrip refers to a powerful feature integrating Fireworks with other MX programs where you can make changes in one application and have those changes seamlessly reflected in the other.

NEW ANTI-ALIASING OPTIONS

Macromedia also enhanced Fireworks' anti-aliasing capabilities. The capability to create custom anti-alias settings and to use system anti-aliasing is a huge step forward in improving the way that Fireworks will render small text on the screen. Historically, Fireworks has not been a stellar performer when it comes to work with font sizes less than 12 points. The new custom anti-aliasing enables you to control the output of your text and makes it possible to make small adjustments that can lead to big improvements (see Figure 24.9).

Figure 24.9
Freehand MX 2004 offers complete customization of anti-alias settings.

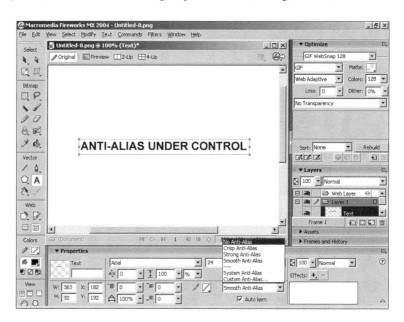

NEW EFFECTS

CONTOUR GRADIENTS

The contour gradient from FreeHand is now available in its suite-mate, Fireworks. A contour gradient follows the outline of a shape, applying the gradient effect to match the shape itself. Although the effect works best on complex shapes, the basic examples in Figure 24.10 should give you an inkling of what can be done with contour gradients.

Figure 24.10
Fireworks MX 2004 now enables you to apply contour gradients to objects.

DASHED STROKES

At long last, Fireworks now offers the capability to create dotted and dashed lines. No more typing in dashes or custom strokes to create these frequently used lines. Simply choose from six varieties of dashed and dotted lines, as shown in Figure 24.11.

Figure 24.11
Six new dashed and dotted lines you can use in your documents.

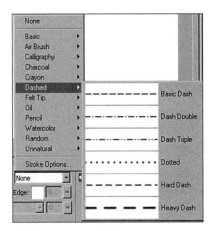

ADD NOISE LIVE EFFECT

The new Add Noise Live Effect brings your art closer to the world of hand rendering. Applying a bit of noise to an image that you created with vector tools can give the image a more natural look (see Figure 24.12).

Figure 24.12
Add Noise to your images to make them appear more organic.

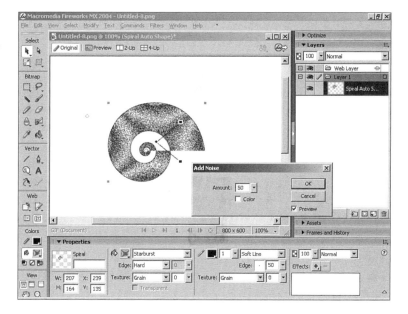

JavaScript API Extensions

Fireworks MX 2004 lets you extend functionality and automate tasks by creating commands that combine JavaScript extensibility API with interfaces from Macromedia Flash MX 2004. JavaScript API enables you to reduce repetitive tasks by writing your own JavaScript in a text editor to run within Fireworks. You can control nearly every command or setting in Fireworks through JavaScript.

→ For more on working with JavaScript extensions, **see** Chapter 12, "Expanding Dreamweaver and Using Third-Party Software," **page** 263.

Full Unicode Support

Unicode support has been improved to make it easier to use text in languages other than the one set up as your primary language on your computer. This feature is helpful to those who create Web sites in multiple languages and need to include characters other than those found in the standard character sets on their computers.

SITE MANAGEMENT

In regard to site management, the folks at Macromedia have empowered Fireworks users with the ability to manage Web sites directly through the program without having to launch Dreamweaver or a third-party FTP program. These new features not only give Fireworks some extra clout as a member of the MX family, they just make life downright easier.

VERSION CONTROL

You can now open files in a site that Dreamweaver has enabled as Check In/Check Out. Previous versions of Fireworks would not allow you to open a file that the Dreamweaver Site Manager had marked as locked down. Now you can Check In or Check Out files directly from Fireworks without having to launch Dreamweaver to get its permission to work on your files.

BUILT-IN FTP

Another new feature that will make your work more efficient is Fireworks' FTP capabilities. Rather than launching Dreamweaver to upload a modified graphic, you can now post the graphic directly to the Web server from Fireworks. You can also FTP a graphic from the server to your hard drive. The only catch is that you need to have the site defined in Dreamweaver MX 2004.

CHAPTER 25

FIREWORKS MX 2004 ENVIRONMENT AND TOOLS

In this chapter

Fireworks MX 2004 Environment   694

Document Window   696

Tools Unique to Fireworks   698

Property Inspector   721

Main Menu   721

Customization with Preferences   725

FIREWORKS MX 2004 ENVIRONMENT

In this chapter you will explore the Fireworks work environment which is comprised of the Document window, Property inspector, menus, tools and other panels. If you've used any of the other Macromedia MX programs, there's a good chance the Fireworks environment will look familiar with its Document window, Toolbar, Main Menu, and docked panel groups. In this chapter, we'll cover some of the features unique to the Fireworks MX 2004 environment.

→ For more information on the MX interface in general, **see** Chapter 3, "Introducing the MX Interface," **page 23**.

A QUICK LOOK AT THE FIREWORKS ENVIRONMENT

When you open Fireworks, you'll be greeted with something new, the Start Page (see Figure 25.1), which is common in all MX 2004 programs. The Start Page allows you to open a recent file, create a new file, access Fireworks tutorials, as well as hop on the Web with Fireworks Exchange to add new capabilities to the program. If you don't care for the Start Page, simply check the Don't Show Again box, located in the bottom left corner of the page.

Figure 25.1
New in Fireworks MX 2004 is the Start Page.

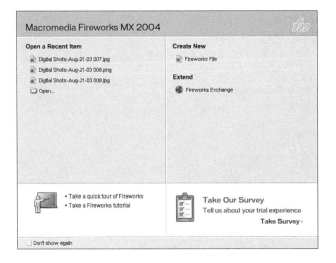

Use the Start Page to create a new file by selecting the Fireworks File under the Create New heading, or use the main menu (File, New). The New Document dialog box (see Figure 25.2) appears, where you can select the dimension for your new document.

After you've set the canvas size and canvas color for the document, you'll see an interface that looks similar to most of the other programs in the MX suite (see Figure 25.3) .

Figure 25.2
The New Document dialog box lets you control the canvas size and canvas color for each new document.

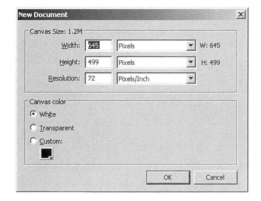

Figure 25.3
The MX interface puts nearly everything you'll need at your fingertips.

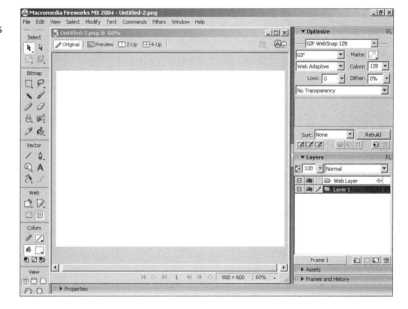

THE MAJOR INTERFACE ELEMENTS

The Fireworks MX interface comprises five elements, each with its own features.

- **Document window**—The Document window contains the canvas and the additional work area surrounding the canvas. The canvas is the "live" area where your images appear. Assets in the gray area are not exported unless you drag them back onto the canvas. At the top of the Document window are Original, Preview, 2-Up Preview, and 4-Up Preview buttons (see Figure 25.4). The preview buttons display the graphic as it would appear in a browser based on optimization settings.

Figure 25.4
The Preview buttons let you see how your graphics will look at various optimization settings.

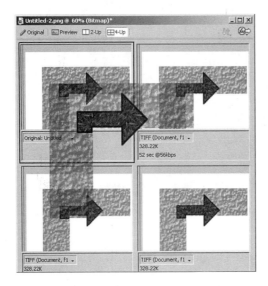

- **Tools**—Also referred to as the Toolbar, the Tools panel contains several tools that enable you to create and edit a variety of graphics, including text, vector objects, bitmaps, and Web objects.

- **Property inspector**—The Property inspector is a panel that changes the tools and modifiers displayed based on the object selected.

- **Menu**—Common to nearly all graphical interface is a top row of menus and submenus to group common commands.

- **Panels**—Like other MX programs, the panels in Fireworks are docked to the right of the screen. The default panels include Optimize, Layers, Assets, and Frames and History.

DOCUMENT WINDOW

The Document window contains the image or asset on which you are working, as well as a few other goodies. The most important part of the Document window is the canvas and the gray work area that surrounds it. As described earlier, the canvas represents the actual document as it would be exported. Graphics, or assets, in the gray area will not be visible in the exported document. The work area is handy to store graphics or to use for bleeds.

In the top-right corner of the Document window is the Send To menu (see Figure 25.5). This menu is used to quickly send your graphics to other Macromedia programs such as Dreamweaver, Flash, FreeHand, or Director, or even to enable you to preview it in a Web browser.

Send to menu

Figure 25.5
The Send To menu sends assets to other Macromedia programs.

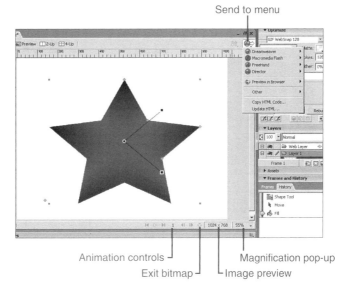

Animation controls ┘

Exit bitmap ┘

└ Image preview

Magnification pop-up

The bottom of the Document window contains animation controls that are activated if you are working with multiple frames.

The grayed out X circle to the right of the animation controls is used to exit bitmap mode and is also activated only if you are working in bitmap mode.

Moving farther right is the page preview, which shows a keyline image preview as well as the image's pixel width, height, and resolution, as shown in Figure 25.6.

Figure 25.6
The Page Preview window gives you a snapshot of your document's width, height, and resolution.

Width: 640
Height: 498
Resolution: 72.00 pixels/inch

At the far right-lower corner is the magnification pop-up menu, where you can see and change the magnification at which you view your document. Click the down arrow to change the magnification to one of 14 preset magnifications (see Figure 25.7).

25

Figure 25.7
The page magnifica-
tion pop-up menu lets
you control the mag-
nification of your can-
vas from 6–6400%.

TOOLS UNIQUE TO FIREWORKS

Many of the tools used in Fireworks are similar to tools found in other Studio MX programs, particularly FreeHand. For instance, there is little variation in how the selection and
drawing tools work between the programs. There are, however, a few "administrative" tools
specific to Fireworks, as well as some robust image modification tools we'll discuss in the
following sections.

SELECT TOOLS GROUP

As the name indicates, the Select tools are used to select objects, as well as reposition and
resize assets.

SELECT BEHIND

Unique to Fireworks is the Select Behind tool (see Figure 25.8), which enables you to select
objects beneath or stacked behind other objects.

Figure 25.8
The Select Behind
tool enables you to
select objects placed
behind other objects.

DISTORT

The Distort tool enables the user to distort objects by arbitrarily resizing points and sides,
as well as by rotating them. Select the object you want to modify, then use the Distort tool
(see Figure 25.9) to move one of the object handles.

Figure 25.9
The Distort tool
enables you to distort
and rotate objects.

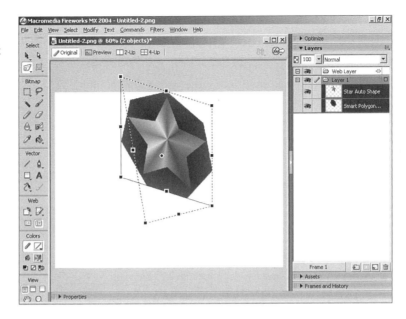

EXPORT AREA

The Export Area tool (see Figure 25.10) is used to define an area on the canvas for export. Select the tool and click and drag to define the export area. Release the mouse button and press the Enter key. The Export Preview dialog box appears, enabling you to control the export settings.

Figure 25.10
The Export Area tool
enables you to define
an area for export.

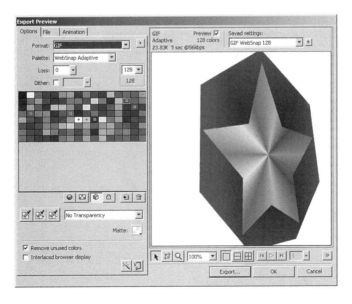

25

→ For more information on exporting images, **see** Chapter 27, "Optimizing and Exporting Graphics and Web Pages" **page 755**.

BITMAP TOOLS

The Bitmap group contains 19 tools that are used to modify bitmap images.

MARQUEE

The Marquee tool, or "marching ants," is used to define a rectangular area of pixels. Select the Marquee tool and click and drag to create a rectangular area that you can modify (see Figure 25.11). After you've released the mouse button, a new bitmap layer is created. To deselect the area, use Select, Deselect.

When you use any of the Marquee or Lasso tools, as well as the Magic Wand tool, the Property inspector displays three Edge options for the tool:

- **Hard**—Creates a selection with a defined edge.
- **Anti-alias**—Reduces jagged edges in the selection.
- **Feather**—Softens the edge of the selection.

When you choose the Marquee or Oval Marquee tool, the Property inspector also displays three style options:

- **Normal**—Creates a marquee in which the height and width are independent of each other.
- **Fixed Ratio**—Sets the height and width to a defined ratio.
- **Fixed Size**—Constrains the height and width to a defined dimension.

Figure 25.11
The Marquee tool defines a bitmap area where a new fill was applied.

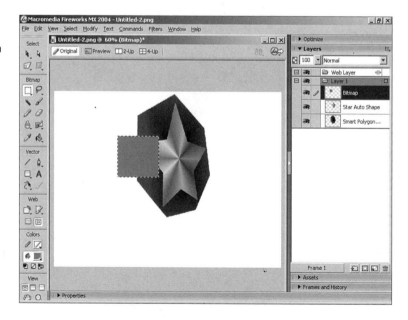

Oval Marquee

The Oval Marquee tool is identical to the Marquee tool except that it defines an elliptical area of pixels.

Lasso

The Lasso tool enables you to draw a freeform selection area. This is handy if you are selecting pixels in complex shapes (see Figure 25.12).

Figure 25.12
The Lasso tool is used to select pixels often found in complex shapes.

Polygon Lasso

The Polygon Lasso tool enables you to draw a polygonal selection area with numerous points (see Figure 25.13). This is better to use than the Lasso tool if you need to select areas with straight lines.

Magic Wand

The Magic Wand tool is probably one of the most used tools in image editing. Using this tool, you can select contiguous pixels of a similar color (see Figure 25.14). Using the Property inspector, you can control the Tolerance (0–255) and Edge (Hard, Anti-Alias, or Feather).

Figure 25.13
The Polygon Lasso tool is used to select a polygonal pixel area.

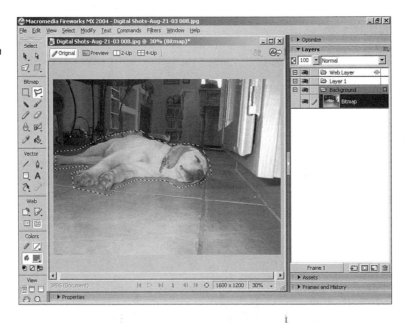

Figure 25.14
The Magic Wand tool is used to select pixels that are similar in color.

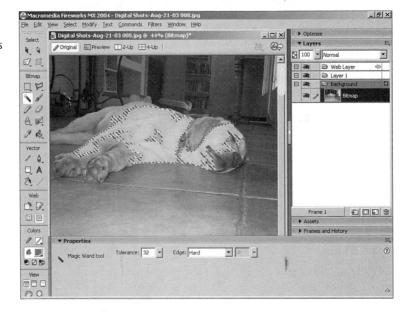

Adjusting the tolerance setting controls the tonal range of colors that are selected when you click a pixel with the Magic Wand. If you enter 0 and click a pixel, only adjacent pixels of exactly the same tone are selected. Conversely, if you enter 255, all colors in the object will be selected.

BRUSH

Like its real-world counterpart, the Brush tool (see Figure 25.15) is used to apply paint to a canvas. Rather than applying acrylic, oil, or watercolor paint, the Fireworks Brush tool applies pixels with a variety of settings.

Figure 25.15
The Brush tool is used like an artist's brush to apply colored pixels to your digital canvas.

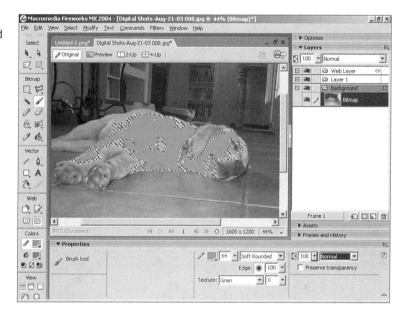

The power of the Brush tool can be utilized when you use the Property inspector (see Figure 25.16), the Stroke Options pop-up menu, and the Edit Stroke dialog box to add incredible control over every aspect of the brush. You adjust pixel color, brush size, edge effect, brush shape, texture, and transparency. In fact, there are more than 50 types of brush strokes you can use.

PENCIL

The Pencil tool is a less adept version of the Brush tool. The Pencil tool is constrained to be a 1-pixel brush (see Figure 25.17). Using the Property inspector, you can control the Pencil tool's color, anti-alias, and transparency.

ERASER

The Eraser tool (see Figure 25.18) is used to remove pixels from an image. Think of it as the anti-Brush tool. Using the Property inspector, you can control the Eraser tool's size, edge, shape, and transparency.

The Eraser tool, however, is not a universal eraser. Note that it is a bitmap tool and erases only pixels. It does not erase vector graphics such as shapes you create with the vector tools. This nuance has driven many to near insanity until they realized they were trying to use the wrong tool for the job.

Figure 25.16
The Property inspector gives you incredible control over the Brush tool's properties.

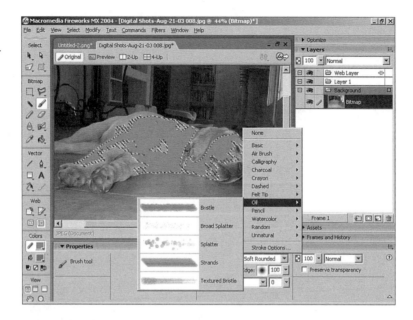

Figure 25.17
The Pencil tool is a 1-pixel brush.

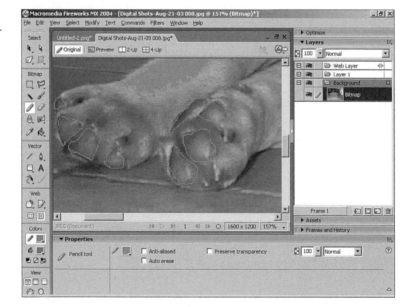

Figure 25.18
The Eraser tool removes pixels from an image.

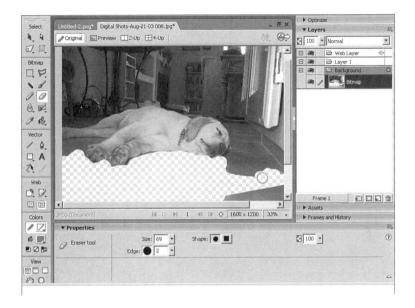

Blur

The Blur tool (see Figure 25.19) creates the effect of blurring pixels, much like a soft or out-of-focus effect. The Property inspector enables you to control the size, shape, edge, and intensity of the blur.

Figure 25.19
The Blur tool is being used to blur the fur on the puppy's ear.

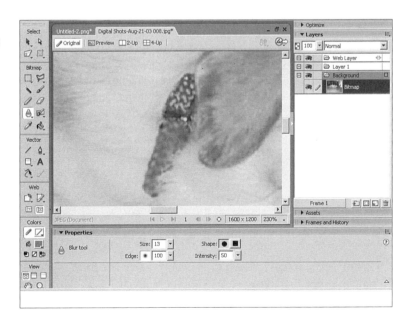

SHARPEN

The Sharpen tool (see Figure 25.20) increases the contrast between pixels and is useful for repairing out-of-focus images. The Property inspector enables you to control the size, shape, edge, and intensity of the effect.

Figure 25.20
The Sharpen tool increases contrast between pixels.

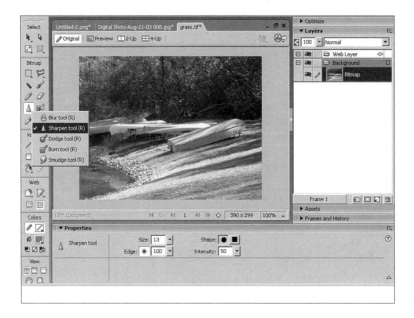

DODGE

A throwback to the darkroom days of photography, the Dodge tool is used to lighten pixels on the image (see Figure 25.21). Dodging areas of an image is useful to bring out more detail in darker pixels. The Property inspector enables you to control the size, edge, shape, range, and exposure of the dodge. You can apply the Dodge tool to three tonal ranges:

- **Shadows**—Change the dark portions of the image.
- **Highlights**—Change the light portions of the image.
- **Midtones**—Change the middle range of the image.

The exposure ranges from 0% to 100%. Specify a lower percentage value for a lessened effect, and a higher percentage for a stronger effect.

BURN

Another darkroom tool brought to the digital age is the Burn tool (see Figure 25.22). The Burn tool is used to darken pixels in the image. As with the Dodge tool, the Property inspector enables you to control the size, edge, shape, range, and exposure of the burn.

Hold down Alt (Windows) or Option (Macintosh) as you drag the tool to switch back and forth between the Burn tool and the Dodge tool.

Figure 25.21
The Dodge tool lightens pixels.

Figure 25.22
The Burn tool darkens pixels.

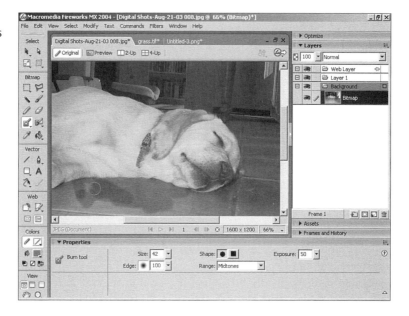

SMUDGE

The Smudge tool (see Figure 25.23) smears and displaces images. Visually, the effect is similar to that of the Blur tool. However, think of taking your finger and rubbing the wet ink on your freshly printed image. That's the Smudge tool. The Property inspector allows you to set the size, shape, edge, and pressure of the stroke. It also allows you to use a specified color at the beginning of each smudge stroke. If the smudge color is checked, the color under the tool pointer is used. If the Use Entire Document check box is selected, the tool uses color data from all objects on all layers to smudge the image.

Figure 25.23
The Smudge tool smears colors and allows this dog to go from no dreams to sweet dreams.

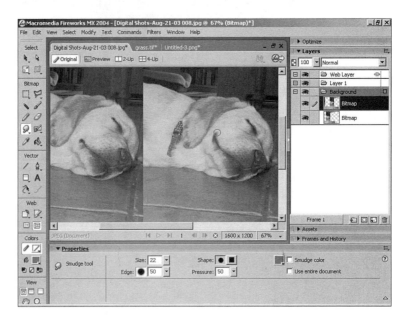

RUBBER STAMP

The Rubber Stamp tool takes pixels from one area of your image and paints them in another. Select the Rubber Stamp tool and click the area you want to clone. The sampling pointer turns into crosshairs. Move to a different part of the image and drag the pointer. You will now see two pointers. The first one is the source and the second is the Rubber Stamp. As you drag the second pointer, pixels beneath the first pointer are copied and applied to the area beneath the second (see Figure 25.24).

Use the Property inspector to control the Rubber Stamp tool's size, edge, and transparency. When Source Aligned is selected, the sampling pointer moves vertically and horizontally in alignment with the second. When Source Aligned is deselected, the sample area is fixed, regardless of where the second pointer is moved. If the Use Entire Document check box is selected, the tool samples from all objects on all layers. When this option is deselected, the Rubber Stamp tool samples from the active object only.

REPLACE COLOR

The Replace Color tool (see Figure 25.25) lets you select one color and paint over it with a different color. To use the Replace Color tool, click the Change color well in the Property inspector to select the color, and choose a color from the pop-up menu. You can also click in the image to choose the color you want to replace.

Figure 25.24
The Rubber Stamp tool clones pixels and can be used to clone objects like this row boat.

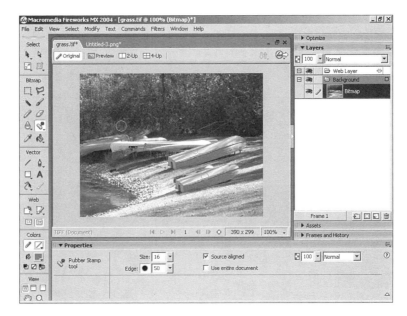

Click the To color well in the Property inspector to select the replacement color, then choose a color from the pop-up menu. You can also select a color from the image. Drag the tool over the color you want to replace.

25

Figure 25.25
The Replace Color tool replaces specific colors in an image.

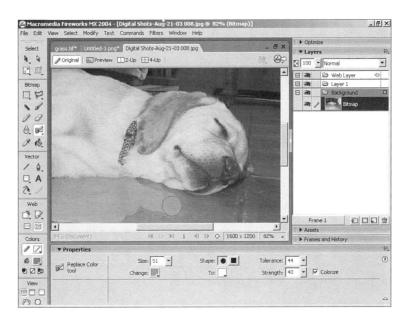

The Property inspector enables you to control brush size and shape, as well as color tolerance and strength. Select Colorize to replace the Change color with the To color. Deselect Colorize to tint the Change color with the To color, leaving some of the Change color intact.

RED-EYE REMOVAL

The Red-Eye Removal tool is used to correct the red-eye effect in photographs. This tool is essentially a stripped down version of the Replace Color tool in that it paints only red areas of an image and replaces the red pixels with grays and blacks (see Figure 25.26).

Figure 25.26
Get the red out with the Red-Eye Removal tool.

Select the Red-Eye Removal tool and drag or click the red pupils in the photograph to replace the red pixels. Use the Property inspector to set stroke attributes, brush tip size, brush tip shape, and tolerance (0 replaces only red; 255 replaces all hues that contain red). Strength sets the darkness of the grays used to replace reddish colors.

GRADIENT

The Gradient tool works like the Paint Bucket tool, but fills an object with a gradient rather than a solid color. To use the Gradient tool, select the Gradient tool from the Paint Bucket pop-up menu. Before you apply the gradient, you need to set the gradient attributes in the Property inspector (see Figure 25.27).

- **Fill Options**—Enables you to choose a gradient type.
- **Fill Color box (when clicked)**—Displays the Edit Gradient pop-up window, where you can set a variety of color and transparency options.

- **Edge**—Lets you select a hard, anti-aliased, or feathered fill edge. If you choose a feathered edge you can specify the amount of the feathering.

- **Texture**—Provides several textures to choose from, including Grain, Metal, Hatch, Mesh, or Sandpaper.

Click and drag the pointer to establish a starting point for the gradient, as well as the direction and length of the gradient.

Figure 25.27
Fireworks MX 2004 provides plenty of gradient options and controls.

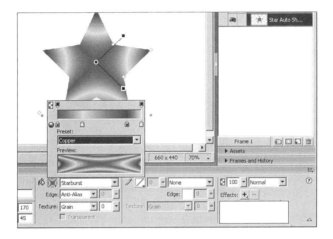

New in Fireworks MX 2004 is the contour gradient. A contour gradient follows a shape's outline, applying the gradient effect to match the shape itself. Although the effect works best on complex shapes, the examples in Figure 25.28 should give you an idea of what can be done with contour gradients.

Figure 25.28
New in Fireworks MX 2004 is the ability to create contour gradients.

But wait, there's more.

To edit a gradient, select the object with the gradient. Click the Fill Color box to view the Edit Gradient pop-up window. To add a color swatch, click the area below the gradient color ramp. To add an opacity swatch, click the area above the gradient color ramp.

To remove a color or opacity swatch from the gradient, simply drag the swatch away from the Edit Gradient pop-up window.

You can change the color of a color swatch by clicking the color swatch and choosing a color from the pop-up window.

You can adjust the transparency of an opacity swatch by clicking the opacity swatch and dragging the slider to the percentage of transparency, (0 is transparent and 100 is opaque) or by entering a numeric value from 0–100.

When you have finished editing the gradient, press Enter or click outside the Edit Gradient pop-up window. The gradient fill appears in any selected objects.

After the gradient is applied, you can still move, rotate, skew, and change the width of the gradient. When you use the Pointer or Gradient tools to select an object with a gradient fill, a set of handles appears on or near the object. You can drag these handles to adjust the object's fill.

To move the fill within an object, drag the round handle, or click in a new location in the fill with the Gradient tool. To rotate the fill, drag the lines connecting the handles. To adjust the fill width and skew, just drag a square handle.

VECTOR TOOLS

Although working with photographs and imported images revolves around bitmaps, Fireworks still has some powerful vector tools that allow you to unleash the illustrator within. This section looks at Fireworks' vector tools and what they can do.

LINE

The Line tool (see Figure 25.29) is used to draw straight lines. To draw a straight line, select the Line tool and then click on the canvas and drag to create the line. Hold down the Opt/Alt key while dragging to constrain the line to 45° increments. The Property inspector enables you to numerically adjust the width and height of the line, as well as its position on the canvas. You can also control the stroke settings and transparency attributes.

PEN TOOL

The Pen tool is used to draw complex shape and vector paths. You can draw straight lines by clicking plot points. It's as simple as playing connect-the-dots, as shown in Figure 25.30. Select the Pen tool and start clicking on the canvas. When you plot the next point, the previous line segment is deselected, as indicated by a hollow white center plot point. A straight line, representing the path, connects the two points.

Figure 25.29
A small sampling of some of the lines you can create with the Line tool.

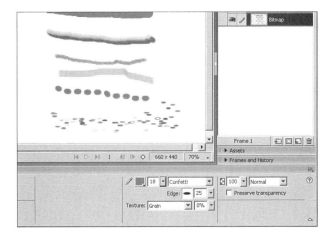

Figure 25.30
The Pen tool can draw lines by plotting a series of points.

To draw an open path, plot the points until the path is complete and then click the Pointer tool or any other tool. To draw a closed path, plot the points until the shape is complete and return to click on the first point again. When you hover over the first point, a hollow circle appears to the right of the Pen tool cursor. Clicking on the first point closes the path.

To draw a curve, press and hold the the mouse button down to position the control handles as you draw. Drawing curves is easy. Drawing curves that actually represent what you had in your mind's eye is not (see Figure 25.31). Practice drawing curves by tracing images or other rounded objects.

Figure 25.31
The brave can use the
Pen tool to draw
curved lines as well.

Use the Property inspector to control your line characteristics.

VECTOR PATH

The Vector Path tool is the vector version of the Pencil tool. Points are automatically inserted as you draw. To use the Vector Path tool, select the tool from the Pen pop-up menu and start drawing. Like the Pen tool, the Vector Path tool is easy to play with, but difficult to master.

The drawing in Figure 25.32 shows a quick application of the Vector Path tool and why I'll never be asked to write a book on illustration. Naturally, a graphics tablet would dramatically improve your drawing abilities.

Use the Property inspector to control your line characteristics.

REDRAW PATH

The Redraw Path tool is used to extend a segment of a previously drawn path. Using this tool to extend the segment retains the path's stroke, fill, and effect characteristics (see Figure 25.33).

Select the Redraw Path tool, located in the Pen tool pop-up menu, and move the pointer directly over the path. The pointer changes to the Redraw Path pointer. Drag to extend the path segment and the new portion of the path is highlighted in red. Release the mouse button and you're good to go.

Figure 25.32
The Vector Path tool is the freehand vector drawing tool.

Figure 25.33
The Redraw Path tool is used to extend a previously drawn line segment.

RECTANGLE

The Rectangle tool is used to draw rectangles and squares. To draw a rectangle, select the Rectangle tool and drag on the canvas to draw. Release the mouse button when you are finished and modify the rectangle's characteristics as needed in the Property inspector. To draw a perfect square, hold down the Shift key as you draw.

ELLIPSE

The Ellipse tool is used to draw ellipses and circles. To draw an ellipse, select the Ellipse tool from the Rectangle pop-up menu and drag on the canvas to draw. Release the mouse button when you are finished and modify the ellipse's characteristics as needed in the Property inspector. To draw a perfect circle, hold down the Shift key as you draw.

POLYGON

The Polygon tool is used to draw polygons and stars (see Figure 25.34). To draw a polygon, select the Polygon tool from the Rectangle pop-up menu and drag on the canvas to draw. Release the mouse button when you are finished and modify the polygon's characteristics as needed in the Property inspector.

Figure 25.34
Polygons and stars created with the Polygon tool.

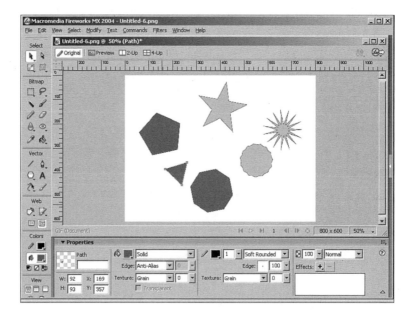

The nuisance about this tool is that you can't change the number or angle of sides after you've drawn the polygon or star. To make those changes, you need to do so before you draw the shape. Make sure no other items are selected on the canvas when you select the Polygon tool, or the Polygon tool options will not be displayed in the Property inspector. When you can get the tool options displayed (see Figure 25.35), you can select Polygon or Star for the Shape, the number of Sides, and the Angle for the sides.

AUTO SHAPES

The Auto Shapes tools are new to Fireworks MX 2004. A look at the Auto Shapes tools (see Figure 25.36) will reveal a slew of new shapes that you can use in your designs. Even better, you can modify these shapes by using the control handles, as well as change their stroke and fill properties. Auto Shapes can also be ungrouped and modified as individual objects.

Figure 25.35
Polygon tool options are accessed in the Property inspector as long as no item on the canvas is selected.

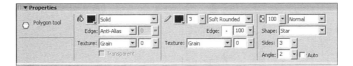

Select an Auto Shape from the Polygon pop-up menu and click and drag to draw your shape. Use the Property inspector and other vector drawing tools to modify the shape.

Fireworks comes with the following Auto Shapes:

- **Arrow**—Draws simple arrow shapes of any proportions.
- **Bent Arrow**—Draws right-angled arrow shapes of any proportions.
- **Beveled Rectangle**—Draws rectangles with beveled corners.
- **Chamfer Rectangle**—Draws rectangles with corners that are rounded to the inside of the rectangle.
- **Connector Line**—Draws three-segment connector lines like those used flowcharts.
- **Doughnut**—Draws filled ring shapes.
- **L-Shape**—Draws corner shapes with right angles.
- **Pie**—Draws pie charts.
- **Smart Polygon**—Draws equilateral polygons with 3 to 25 sides.
- **Rounded Rectangle**—Draws rectangles with rounded corners.
- **Spiral**—Draws open spirals.
- **Star**—Draws stars with any number of points from 3 to 25.

Figure 25.36
Auto Shapes simplifies the process of creating complex shapes by giving you "canned" shapes that can be modified.

The Auto Shapes panel (see Figure 25.37) also lets you create your own shapes, as well as use shapes from third-party developers.

Figure 25.37
Shapes in the Auto Shapes panel that are shipped with Fireworks MX 2004.

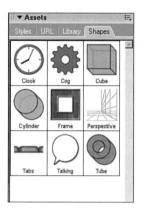

You can add new Auto Shapes by using the Fireworks Exchange Web site. To add new Auto Shapes, display the Shapes tab in the Assets panel. Click the Options menu and choose Get More Auto Shapes. Fireworks connects to the Fireworks Exchange Web site (see Figure 25.38). Follow the onscreen instructions to select new Auto Shapes and add them to Fireworks.

Figure 25.38
Add new Auto Shapes from the Fireworks Exchange Web site.

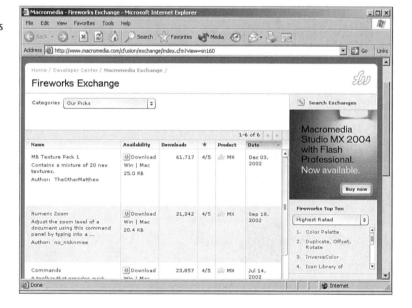

FREEFORM

→ For more information on using the Freeform tool, **see** Chapter 29, "FreeHand MX Environment and Tools," **page 806**.

→ For more information on using the Reshape Area tool, **see** Chapter 29, **page 808**.

PATH SCRUBBER-ADDITIVE & SUBTRACTIVE

Use the Path Scrubber tools to change the appearance of a path with varying pressure from a pressure-sensitive tablet or speed if you're using a mouse. Path scrubber properties, which include stroke size, angle, ink amount, scatter, hue, lightness, and saturation, can be specified by using the Property inspector (see Figure 25.39). You can also specify how much pressure and speed affects these properties.

Figure 25.39
Control the pressure and speed of the Path Scrubber tools in the Property inspector.

WEB TOOLS

Fireworks is the Web designer's best friend when it comes to creating graphics for the online medium. Because many Web graphics are used in interactions (links, rollovers, and so on), Fireworks has set aside several dedicated Web objects and tools in the Web category of the Tools panel.

HOTSPOT

The Rectangle, Circle, and Polygon Hotspot tools (see Figure 25.40) create hotspots, or image maps, specific to their shape. To create a hotspot, simply drag the Hotspot tool to draw a hotspot over an area of the graphic. Hold down Option/Alt key to draw from a center point. You can adjust a hotspot's position while you are drawing. While holding down the mouse button, press and hold down the Spacebar, then drag the hotspot to another location on the canvas. Release the Spacebar to continue drawing the hotspot.

The Polygon Hotspot tool draws a hotspot by connecting a series of points; it's similar to the Pen tool, but without the Bezier handles.

After you've created the hotspot, use the Property inspector to add the link URL, Alt tag, and Target (None, _blank, _self, _parent, _top) (see Figure 25.41).

SLICE AND POLYGON SLICE

Sliced Web objects are not really considered images, but HTML code—even though they represent an image. To create a slice, select the Slice tool and drag to draw the slice object (see Figure 25.42). The slice object appears on the Web Layer, and the slice guides appear in the document.

25

Figure 25.40
Use the Polygon Hotspot tool to create an odd-shaped image map.

Figure 25.41
Modify the hotspot or link settings in the Property inspector.

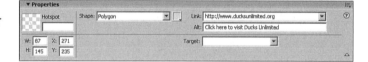

Figure 25.42
Create an image slice with the Slice tool or Polygon Slice tool.

Use the Polygon Slice tool to create a slice by connecting a series of points, similar to the Pen tool.

The Property inspector enables you to select an image type for the slice as well as set link properties.

HIDE AND SHOW SLICES

Use the Hide and Show Slices buttons (see Figure 25.43) to respectively hide or display your slices on the canvas.

Figure 25.43
Hide or show image slices by using the Hide or Show Slices buttons.

PROPERTY INSPECTOR

The Property inspector made its debut in Fireworks MX and it's been a hit with designers ever since. The Property inspector is a context-sensitive panel that changes options as you change your work. Choose a tool from the Tools panel, and the Property inspector displays tool options. Select a vector object, and it displays stroke and fill information. The inspector also displays effects, blending modes, and opacity, saving you tons of time and energy in opening other panels or dialog boxes.

This dynamic panel displays many of the common options for a selected object or tool. When no object or tool is selected, document options appear. The Property inspector in Fireworks MX is similar to the ones found in Dreamweaver MX and Flash MX.

MAIN MENU

The Main Menu (see Figure 25.44) is chock full of commands that enable you to do everything from opening a file to applying sophisticated effects to your images. Because an encyclopedia could be written on just this topic alone, the following sections simply summarize the important commands in each menu.

FILE MENU

Fireworks' File menu is similar to that of just about every other program. As the name suggests, commands in this menu affect whole files or documents. Some special File menu commands include

- Reconstitute Table, HTML Setup, and Update HTML are used to integrate Fireworks files with Web pages in Dreamweaver. These commands are explored more in Chapter 27, page 769.

- Batch Process allows you to automate a series of customizable commands, such as image resizing, on a large group of files, all with the click of a couple buttons.

Figure 25.44
Fireworks' Main menu is home to dozens of robust commands.

EDIT MENU

The Edit menu contains a few specialized commands for inserting Fireworks objects. Some unique Fireworks commands include

- Insert Fireworks objects, such as a New Button, Symbol, Hotspot, Slice, Layer, or Frame.

- Clipboard Variations, which enables you to Copy HTML Code, Paste Inside, Paste as Mask, and Paste Attributes.

- Preferences, which enables you to customize your workspace. Editing Preferences is discussed later in this chapter.

VIEW MENU

The View menu is home to commands that control how you look at your workspace. In addition to the typical magnification, ruler, and guides commands is the Windows/Macintosh Gamma command. Computers that run Windows and Macintosh operating systems use different gamma settings, which typically results in Windows screens being darker than their Mac counterparts. Big whoop, you say. Well, what can happen is that the graphic that looks fine on your Windows screen will appear slightly washed out on the Macintosh screen. Likewise, the graphic that works on a Macintosh screen will be darker on the Windows screen. Use the Windows/Macintosh Gamma command to toggle between the two gamma settings and see whether it does make a difference on your graphics.

SELECT MENU

The Select menu debuted in Fireworks MX and is split up into four categories:

- Vector path and selection tools, which are used to select and edit vector points and paths.

- Pixel selection tools, which are used to modify pixels of similar colors, feather selections, or invert selections.

- Pixel region selection tools, which are used to expand, contract, and smooth selected regions of pixels.

- Save bitmap selection tools, which are used to save and restore single bitmap selections.

MODIFY MENU

The Modify menu is the most frequently used menu in Fireworks. This menu contains commands that enable you to alter object attributes, stacking order, and grouping. Other commands of interest include

- Pop-Up Menu, which launches a wizard that enables you to create pop-up menus.

- Masks, which provide several masking effects in a submenu.

- Combine Paths, which gives you the Union, Intersect, Punch, and Crop commands to play with ways to combine separate shapes.

TEXT MENU

The Text menu provides common commands for modifying font, style, paragraph settings, alignment, and even spelling. Some unique commands include

- Attach to Path, which allows you to attach text to a vector path (see Figure 25.45).

Figure 25.45
Use the Attach to Path command (Text, Attach to Path) to make text follow the contour of a vector path.

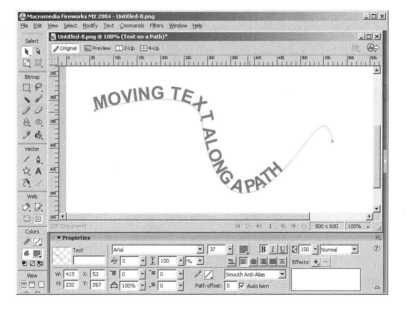

- Convert to Paths, with which you can change text to vector objects so you can modify text as a graphic object.

COMMANDS MENU

The Commands menu is where you can really see the flexibility of Fireworks. Within the Commands menu are several ready-made commands, or macros, that you can use to make your life simpler. You can also create your own commands, if you have the programming know-how.

Some interesting Commands included in Fireworks are

- Convert to Grayscale, which is found in the Creative submenu. This is similar to the popular command found in Photoshop.

- Resize Selected Objects, which provides a pop-up window that gives you a graphical interface with which to resize an object (see Figure 25.46). Nothing really special about this, except it looks cool.

Figure 25.46
The Resize Selected Objects command provides a visually slick way of resizing objects.

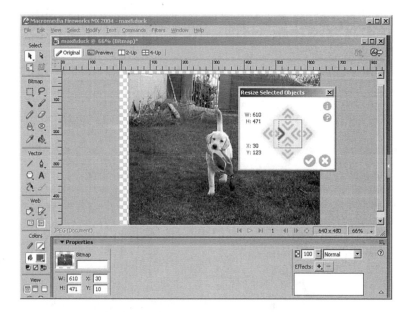

- Twist and Fade, which is also found in the Creative submenu. This third-party command enables you to create a vortex effect with any vector or bitmap graphic (see Figure 25.47). Be careful, though. It's addictive and resource intensive and could lock up the program if you call for too many steps.

FILTERS MENU

The Filters menu contains all the bitmap filters. Included are filters that handle color adjustment, blurring, levels, curves, unsharp mask, add noise, and so on. After it is applied to an image, a filter effect cannot be removed unless you use the Undo command (Edit, Undo Filter Image).

Figure 25.47
The Twist and Fade command adds some more special effects to your graphics arsenal.

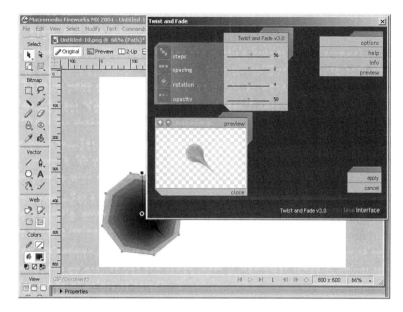

WINDOW MENU

The Window menu provides a list of all the panels and toolbars available in Fireworks. Think of it as your interface repository.

HELP MENU

Learn to appreciate the guidance and wisdom found within the Help menu. Here you can find the entire Fireworks MX 2004 manual in HTML format. You can search for answers to those aching questions about how to draw those pesky Bezier curves with the Pen tool.

You can also access online support from the Fireworks Help Center, as well as exchange ideas on the Macromedia Online Forums. Visiting the forums becomes a daily part of your life if you're interested in expanding your Fireworks capabilities.

CUSTOMIZATION WITH PREFERENCES

It's a fact of life that no two designers are alike. How you like to organize your workspace will be different from how I organize mine. The copy of Fireworks MX 2004 you installed on your desktop has pre-set preferences that the folks at Macromedia thought you'd enjoy. You may like what they've done, and you may be yearning to go in and tailor the program to fit your style.

Most people don't bother messing with customizing their preferences unless they use the program on a daily basis. If you do have a hankering to make some changes, read on.

For the most part, the preference settings are self-explanatory. I'll review a few key preferences that you may want to consider changing. Note that you will need to restart Fireworks for the new preferences to take effect.

GENERAL TAB

The General tab (see Figure 25.48) contains settings that influence the basic aspects of the Fireworks environment. One setting worth changing is the number of Undo Steps. The default setting is 20. The higher the setting, the more RAM is sucked up. The lower the setting, the less RAM is used, but the more hampered you are by your mistakes. It's a balancing act and you will have to determine what's best for you. I like to set my Undo Steps to 10.

Figure 25.48
The General Tab enables you to customize basic aspects of the Fireworks environment.

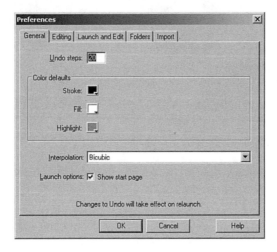

EDITING TAB

The Editing tab settings (see Figure 25.49) affect workflow. You can change cursor styles, hide edges, display striped borders, and so on. Most of these settings are customized based on personal preferences. Checking the Pen Preview, however, is handy if you're just learning how to use the Pen Tool because the next line segment is displayed while you're drawing.

LAUNCH AND EDIT

Launch and Edit settings are used to control how Fireworks integrates with other Macromedia programs such as Dreamweaver. Because most Fireworks graphics comprise an editable graphic (Fireworks PNG) and an exported graphic (JPEG or GIF), the launch and edit settings enable you to select one of the following three options:

■ Always Use Source PNG opens the source PNG file. When you're finished with the file, the original optimization settings are used when it's exported again.

- Never Use Source PNG to open the exported JPEG or GIF in Fireworks.

- Ask When Launching prompts you to decide what to do on a case-by-case basis.

Because I believe there are few absolutes in life, I keep the default Ask When Launching setting.

Figure 25.49
The Editing Tab enables you to customize workflow settings.

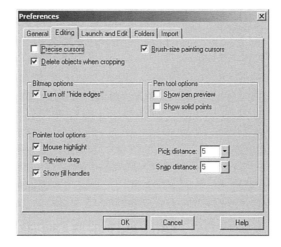

FOLDERS

The Folders tab enables you to designate where plug-ins, textures, and patterns are stored. After re-starting Fireworks, the program loads all plug-ins, textures, and patterns in those folders.

IMPORT

The Import tab provides controls on how Photoshop objects are imported into Fireworks:

- The Layers section dictates how Photoshop layers are brought into Fireworks. They can be imported as Fireworks Objects or as Fireworks Frames. The Share Layer Between Frames option imports the Photoshop layers as Fireworks sublayers and also designates those layers as shared.

- The Text section enables you to decide whether or not you want to retain editability or appearance. If you want to preserve the font style from the Photoshop object but don't have the font, select Maintain Appearance. If you want to edit the text, select Editable.

- The Use Flat Composite Image option flattens and merges all Photoshop layers.

TROUBLESHOOTING

HOW DO I BEND TEXT?

Unlike other graphics or image editing programs, there doesn't seem to be a way I can bend text around a shape. Can you do this in Fireworks?

Certainly. It just takes a couple of steps. First, trace a path with the pen tool. Then select your text and the path you have just drawn and use the Attach to Path command found in the Text menu. You can tinker with the settings in the Property inspector.

BLANK ANSWERS PANEL

My Answers Panel is blank even when I'm connected to the Internet. Does Fireworks not like me?

There are two possible fixes for this scenario. Let's take the easiest approach first. Undock the Answers panel by dragging the panel by its gripper (the dots on the left side of the panel group's title bar). Move the panel to the middle of the workspace. Click the Close button on the upper-left corner of the panel to close the Answers panel. Relaunch the Answers panel (Window, Answers) and you should see content in the panel. If so, redock the panel by dragging it by the gripper back to the other panel groups.

If you don't see content in the Answers panel after trying the first step, you need to restore an initialization file. When Fireworks MX is launched, the Answers panel locates an initialization file (shim_init.xml), which sends content information to the Macromedia Flash file used to display the Answers panel. The following steps force Fireworks to copy out a new ship_init.xml and all related files so that the Answers panel is restored.

Close Fireworks MX and then open the Application Data (Windows) or Application Support (Macintosh) folder:

- **Windows 2000, NT and XP**—C:\Documents and Settings\<username>\Application Data
- **Windows 98 and ME**—C:\Windows\Application Data
- **Macintosh OS X**—Macintosh HD:Users:<username>:Library:Application Support:Macromedia
- **Macintosh OS 9.X**—Macintosh HD:System Folder:Application Support:Macromedia

Move the Fireworks MX folder from the Macromedia folder to the desktop. This folder will now serve as your backup Fireworks MX folder.

In the Application Data (Windows) or Application Support (Macintosh) folder open the Flash Player folder. Open the localhost folder and delete the Fireworks MX folder.

Relaunch Fireworks.

Quit Fireworks and then replace any components such as preferences, commands, styles, and so on from the backup Fireworks MX folder (on the desktop) into the appropriate locations in the new Fireworks MX folder.

The next time you launch Fireworks, the Answers panel should appear with its contents.

STOPPING AND STARTING THE POLYGON LASSO TOOL

After I start using the Polygon Lasso tool, is there a way I can go back a step without having to start all over again?

To go back a step, simply release the mouse button. Hold down the Shift key, press Alt, then release the Alt key to temporarily display an arrow cursor. The selection path will be reset to wherever you click with the arrow cursor. The cursor will then revert back to the Polygon Lasso tool and you can continue your work.

CHAPTER **26**

CREATING GRAPHICS, ROLLOVERS, AND ANIMATIONS

In this chapter

Graphics as Objects   732

Layers   734

Frames   736

Layers and Frames   737

Simple Rollover   738

Swap Image Behavior   739

Navigation Bars with Four-State Buttons   741

Fireworks and Animation   743

Building an Animation   744

This chapter reviews how Fireworks MX 2004 works with graphics, as well as some of the core concepts that you'll need to understand to successfully create graphics for the Web. Then you can take a look at how you can use Fireworks to create navigation rollovers and even some basic animations.

GRAPHICS AS OBJECTS

The two types of graphics used in Fireworks are bitmap graphics and vector graphics (see Figure 26.01). The simplest way to explain the difference between the two is that bitmap graphics are made up of rows and columns of pixels, whereas vector graphics are made up of several vector objects such as rectangles, lines, text, and ovals.

Figure 26.1
Notice the difference in selection between the bitmap graphics on the left and the vector graphics on the right. The bitmap graphics are selected by color, whereas the vector graphics are individually selected.

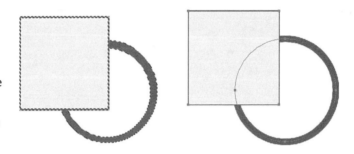

Understanding how Fireworks handles and organizes the elements in your files will help you have a better understanding of how to create graphics for different mediums, as well as increase your productivity.

BITMAP GRAPHICS

If you're familiar with the form of painting called *pointillism*, where tiny primary-color dots are used to generate secondary colors, then working with bitmap graphics is nothing new. If you've never heard of pointillism, fear not. Simply magnify a bitmap graphic such as a photo to see the individual points, or pixels, that create the graphic, as shown in Figure 26.2.

Each pixel can have only one color. When these pixels are arranged in rows and columns, the human eye blends the individual colors together to create the illusion of an image.

The more dots that are used to define an area of an image, the higher the overall quality of the image will be. Accordingly, bitmap images are quantified by the relationship between the number of pixels and the size of the image. This is known as *resolution* and is usually measured in dots per inch (dpi) for print, or pixels per inch (ppi) for the screen.

If you want to edit a bitmap graphic, you have to modify individual pixels. In addition, because a bitmap graphic is rendered with a finite set of pixels, there is no way to enlarge the image without lowering resolution.

Figure 26.2
The photo on the left is at normal (100%) magnification, whereas the photo on the right has been enlarged 800% to show the individual pixels that comprise the mule's muzzle.

Photographs are bitmap images and you will use Fireworks' bitmap tools to modify photographs, as well as use bitmap effects such as blurring and color replacement.

VECTOR GRAPHICS

Vector graphics rely on mathematical instructions that tell the computer how to draw graphics. As an example, a vector might have instructions such as "Draw a circle, starting 100 pixels to the right and 50 pixels down from the top-left corner, with a radius of 200 pixels; draw a red stroke over the circle path that is 2 pixels wide, and fill the circle with a yellow color."

On the other side of the coin, the bitmap version would just describe the pixels that are white (background), red (stroke) and yellow (fill).

Here's where an important concept comes into play. A vector graphic contains instructions for each object it contains. In the circle example, the directions would create a circle object. The same file could have a line object, a square object and a text object. Each object would be completely separate from the others.

Because all graphics are independent of each other and because a specific set of directions is used to construct them, they are always editable. In addition, because vector objects are independent of the canvas behind them, they are also independent of a graphic's resolution. That's the beauty of vector graphics. They're scalable, whereas bitmap graphics are not.

PATHS VERSUS STROKES

The basic shape or line of a vector graphic is called a path. Every vector shape is a path. That path is the representation of a mathematical formula.

Accordingly, each path can have several attributes applied to it. These attributes are what you use to change the path and include stroke and fill color. A path's *stroke* is the coloring that is painted on the path, whereas the path's *fill* is the color, or pattern, that covers the area enclosed by the path (Figure 26.3). Fireworks also enables you to add several more attributes known as effects, such as bevels, glows, drop shadows, and several others.

Figure 26.3
Selecting a polygon helps identify the path, stroke, and fill.

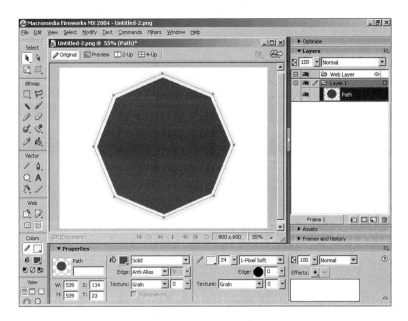

Even if you don't have a stroke, the path is still there. It's a confusing concept for many, but remember that you can have a path without a stroke, but you can't have a stroke without a path.

To sink this home another way, modifying paths and modifying strokes are two different things. When you modify a path, you reshape it. When you modify a stroke, you can change its thickness, color, and visual appearance.

LAYERS

The best way to understand layers is to think of each layer as a sheet of acetate like those used on overhead projectors. Layers are independent images that contain bitmap or vector graphics. The final image will be made up of a stack of all the layers within the image, depending on the order in which the layers are and the transparency levels that are set for each layer. You can work on each layer as if it were an independent image, without interference from any graphical elements that are on other layers.

It is best to place every new element, or addition to an element, on its own layer. You can always merge (combine) layers, and it is much safer and faster to build each element a layer at a time. After you are satisfied with the look, you can then combine the elements that make up that object.

When you place bitmap graphics on top of each other in the same layer, the pixels of the top object replace the pixels of the object beneath it. After all, only one pixel can occupy a space at a time. To keep the bitmap objects separate, you use layers.

Unlike bitmaps, vector objects can be placed on top of one another on a single layer without affecting one another. They create their own sublayers. So, why use layers with vector objects? Simply put, for organization. Using layers, you can organize your content into logical hierarchies.

Any time you create or import an object, it appears in its own layer in Fireworks. A default name is automatically applied to the layer. I use the default name unless I'm working with files where several layers come into play. At that point, it's handy to know how to organize the layers.

LAYERS PANEL BASICS

The Layers panel enables you to control the object layers in your document. The Layers panel main area (Figure 26.4) comprises five main columns:

Figure 26.4
The Layers panel for a simple document with a bitmap image, vector graphic, and text. Note that each object appears in its own layer.

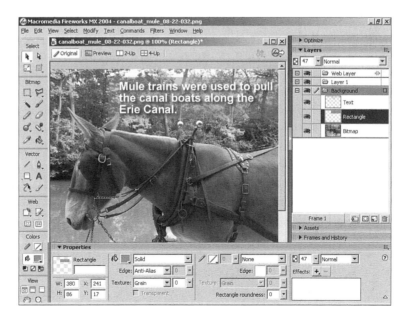

- **Expand/Collapse Layer**—When a collapsed layer contains sublayers, a triangular arrow pointing down (Macintosh) or a + sign (Windows) is shown. Click that arrow or + sign to expand the layer. When the layer is expanded, you see an arrow pointing to the right (Mac) or a – sign (Windows). Click this icon to collapse the layer.

- **Show/Hide Layer**—This column contains the eyeball icon. When you see the eye, the object on the layer is visible. Click the eyeball to hide the object on the layer. The eyeball icon is also hidden. Hidden layers do not affect the contents of the file, and they are not exported with the file.

- **Lock/Unlock Layer**—The padlock icon indicates that a layer is locked and cannot be edited. Click the icon to lock or unlock the layer. You can lock only full layers, not sublayers.

- **Layer Column**—The layer column contains both the layer name and the thumbnail of the layer's contents.

- **Last Column**—The last column doesn't have an official name, so we'll call it the Last Column. It appears beside only full layers, not sublayers. When you select any sublayer, the little blue box (Object in Layer marker) appears in the Last Column for the layer that contains the selected sublayer. If you click the Last Column in any other layer, the selected sublayer is moved to the new layer.

To move layers, or change the stacking order, you can drag the layer or sublayer up or down to a new position in the stack. You can also select a sublayer, then click in the Last Column of the layer where you want it to move. This option does not work on layers; it works only on sublayers.

To rename layers, double-click the layer and the name can be edited. Type the new name and press Return/Enter to seal the deal.

FRAMES

Whereas layers organize objects in space, frames organize objects in time. Why does an image editing program need to worry about time? Because Fireworks is predominantly used to create Web graphics, time comes into play with animated GIFs, Flash animations, and rollovers.

To handle how graphics change over time, Fireworks uses the concept of frames. Fireworks frames work along the same lines as frames in a movie reel, where each frame is the same size and is in the same position, but the contents may change to create the illusion of motion.

FRAMES PANEL BASICS

The Frames panel works much like the Layers panel, except it is divided into three main columns (Figure 26.5):

Figure 26.5
The Frames panel for a simple animation.

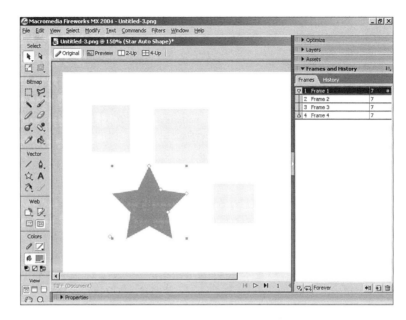

- **Onion Skinning**—Onion Skinning is an animation technique that enables you to view multiple frames at the same time.

- **Frame Name and Number**—The main column displays the frame name, which is set to default to Frame X, where X represents the frame number.

- **Frame Delay**—This column contains the value for the frame delay, which is represented in 100ths of second. The frame is displayed for that duration of time before the animation advances to the next frame. This column also contains the Object in Frame marker, which functions the same as the Object in Layer marker.

To move frames, drag them up or down in the stack.

To duplicate a frame—an excellent way to distribute positioned content across multiple frames—drag the frame to the New/Duplicate Frame button. When the button appears depressed, release the mouse. The frame and all its layers and sublayers are then copied.

To rename a frame, double-click the frame and the name can be edited. Type the new name and press Return/Enter to save the name.

LAYERS AND FRAMES

When you create a new object, it appears on its own sublayer within a layer. As you continue to create your masterpiece, more layers and sublayers are added to the composition.

Let's say you're making an animation and start incorporating frames. Now you have several layers and will be adding several frames. How do layers and frames interact with each other?

SHARED VERSUS UNSHARED LAYERS

The relationship between layers and frames is based on whether or not the layer is shared. Shared layers are the same in every frame. Unshared layers may be different in each frame.

When you add a new frame, Fireworks copies all the unshared layers into the new frame. If you decide to add a new unshared layer in any frame when you're halfway through the project, Fireworks automatically adds that unshared layer to every other frame. Unshared layers is the default setting for layers, by the way.

To share a layer, select the layer. In the Layers panel options menu, select Share This Layer (Figure 26.6). A check appears beside the option and a Shared Layer icon next to the layer name.

Figure 26.6
You decide whether a layer is shared or unshared.

WEB LAYER

A Web layer is always shared. You don't have a say in that. On top of every layer stack in Fireworks is the Web layer. You cannot delete it, rename it, or do anything unsavory with it. The Web layer is where all Web objects, such as slices and hotspots, are stored.

To the right of the Web layer's name is the Shared Layer icon. This icon indicates that the Web layer's contents are available and identical for all frames in your document.

SIMPLE ROLLOVER

The most basic animation is the Simple Rollover. Rollovers are frequently seen in navigation bars and in buttons on Web pages.

The rollover is composed of two images, an Up image and an Over image. When a Web page is first loaded, the Up image is displayed. When the mouse is moved over or rolls over the Up image, it is replaced with the Over image.

Because both images share the same space, they must be the same size. Any variation in size ends up with a "hiccup" during the mouseover.

To create a Simple Rollover button, the first thing you need to do is to create the button's Up and Over states, using frames 1 and 2.

After you've created two images for the button's Up and Over states, use the Slice tool and drag it over the image to create a slice. With the slice still selected, open the Behavior panel (Window, Behaviors) and click the Add Behavior (+) button to open the list of behaviors. Select Simple Rollover from the list and Fireworks creates the rollover.

For ease of use when the rollover graphic is exported to Dreamweaver, you can enter the URL in the Property inspector's Link field as well as the Alt text in the Alt field. You may also want to delete the default slice name and give each slice a more meaningful name.

You can test simple rollovers in Fireworks' preview mode by clicking the Preview button at the top of the document window (Figure 26.7).

Figure 26.7
Use the Preview button in the document window to test the Simple Rollover. The top image is the Up state and the bottom image represents the Over state.

26

SWAP IMAGE BEHAVIOR

Similar to the Simple Rollover is the Swap Image behavior. The Simple Rollover substitutes the contents of a frame slice with the contents of another frame slice. Although the Swap Image behavior can do that as well, it is mostly used to create Disjoint Rollovers.

When rolling over one image causes a different image to change, you have a Disjoint Rollover (Figure 26.8). For example, rolling over Image A causes Image B to change to Image B1.

Figure 26.8
Rolling over the
Home button or the
Search button triggers
a change in the
description image
below the navigation
menu.

An image can have both a Simple Rollover and a Disjoint Rollover. Using the previous example, rolling over Image A would replace Image A with Image A1 and replace Image B with Image B1.

To build a Disjoint Rollover, create all assets in their final positions. You need at least two frames and two slices. Use the Slice tool to add a slicing scheme over the affected areas of the document.

Select the slice covering the trigger image. The trigger image is the image that users will roll over or click to make the disjoint behavior work. Click the Add Behavior (+) button in the Behaviors panel. Select Swap Image from the menu and the Swap Image dialog box appears (Figure 26.9).

Figure 26.9
The Swap Image dia-
log box enables you
to select the target
slice for the Disjoint
Rollover.

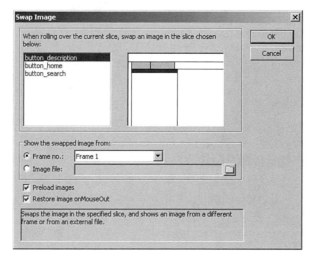

Select the target slice. The target slice is the image that will be affected by the rollover action in the trigger image. You can select the slice in the list or select the slice thumbnail in the slice reconstruction window.

Next, select an image to swap from a different frame or an external file. Because you've already created the image that will be swapped, select another frame.

Preload Images is selected by default to ensure that the swapped image is loaded before the user mouses over the image. I would suggest leaving this option checked to ensure that the swapped image executes quickly, without the new image having to be downloaded at the time of the swap.

Restore Image onMouseOut is also the default if you want the original image to be swapped back in after the user rolls out of the trigger image.

Click OK to apply the behavior and close the Swap Image dialog box.

NAVIGATION BARS WITH FOUR-STATE BUTTONS

Moving up the complexity ladder is a navigation bar with four-state buttons. The Set Nav Bar Image behavior is used to create this type of navigation bar, where the buttons not only have rollovers, but also communicate to the user which page is currently being browsed.

A navigation bar using this behavior has four states. Each state represents the button's appearance in reaction to a mouse event:

- The Up state is the default or untouched appearance of the button.
- The Over state is the way the button appears when the pointer is moved over it.
- The Down state represents the button after it is clicked.
- The Over While Down state is the appearance when the user moves the pointer over a button that is in the Down state.

To add the Set Nav Bar Image behavior, you first need to build a navigation bar. Create a new button symbol for each navigation button by using the Button Symbol Editor. To create a button symbol, select the button (text and background shape) and then use the New Button Symbol command (Modify, Symbol and select Button). Make sure you replace the default Symbol name with a more meaningful name. Click OK to convert the text and image into a button symbol.

Double-click the new button symbol to launch the Button Symbol Editor. Modify the button attributes in the editor for each of the four states (Figure 26.10).

In the Down and the Over While Down states, make sure that the Include in Nav Bar option (located at the top of the editor) is checked. These options should be checked by default.

Repeat this process for the rest of your navigation bar buttons.

To make life easier after you export the navigation bar, take a moment to select each slice and enter a name for the slice, a label for the button, and a URL in the Property inspector.

26

Figure 26.10
Use the Button Symbol Editor to create four states (Up, Over, Down, and Over While Down) to each button in the navigation bar.

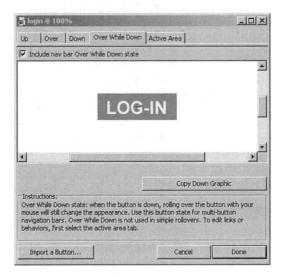

Double-check that everything is going to work by selecting each button and looking in the Behaviors panel. Each slice should have the Set Nav Bar Image behavior with a lock beside it (Figure 26.11).

Figure 26.11
Select each slice and use the Behaviors panel to make sure the Set Nav Bar Image behavior is selected.

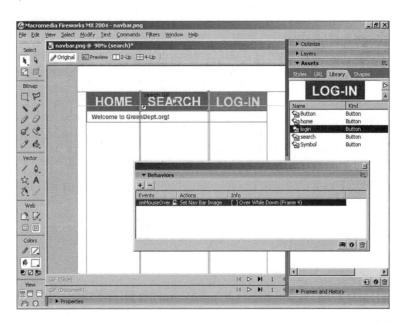

For the ultimate test, you need to export the file to HTML and view it in your browser. Choose File, Export to get started. In the Export dialog box, make sure that HTML and Images is selected in the Save As Type menu.

Click the Options button to launch the HTML Setup dialog box. Click the Document Specific tab. Make sure that the Multiple Nav Bar HTML Pages box is checked. Click OK to close the HTML Setup dialog box so Fireworks will export additional pages for each button in the navigation bar. Click Save to complete the export.

Open the page in your browser to see how it works.

FIREWORKS AND ANIMATION

Creating animations for the Web in Fireworks is a lot more fun to think about than to do. The best animation tool is obviously Flash because the program was designed for the job of creating motion.

That being said, Fireworks can be used to build animations. In fact, there are three different methods you can use to create animations: frame-by-frame, tweened, and animation symbols. Each has its own pros and cons and will be discussed later in this chapter. Before you start tweening away to make the next full-feature animation, we'll take a look at what's involved in building a good animation.

ANIMATION PLANNING

Motion on the Web, or on film, is an illusion. Animation is a series of still images, each with a slight change in appearance from the previous image, that are rapidly presented to the viewer. The human eye processes these images and blends them into a smooth motion. If the images move too slowly, the illusion is gone. This speed is measured as frame rate. Frame rate is measured in frames per second (fps). Most movies and television shows shot on film have a frame rate of 24 fps. Most shows shot on video have a frame rate of 30 fps.

Moving to the Web, we have another concern to throw into the mix. The higher the resolution, the higher the file size, which results in a longer download time. Increasing the frame rate also increases the file size.

Bitmap animations have a sequence of bitmap graphics. Each bitmap graphic is added together to complete the animation in terms of file size. Although file compression helps reduce the file size, bitmap graphics can get large quickly. The most common bitmap animation type is the Animated GIF.

Vector animations have vector graphics on each frame. Vector animations just change object parameters from frame to frame and are accordingly smaller in file size than bitmap animations. The most common vector animation type is Macromedia's Flash SWF format.

Before you build an animation, there is another issue we need to discuss: What is the output format for the final animation?

An Animated GIF typically has a large file size, but is universally compatible with nearly all browsers. This type of animation is restricted by the GIF file format's limited 256-color palette, and it cannot incorporate sound or any other interactivity. The Animated GIF,

26

however, is a piece of cake to implement and you don't need to know Flash to make an animation.

The Flash SWF typically has a small file size and is compatible with most newer browsers that come shipped with the Flash player plug-in. Because Flash is a vector program, certain Fireworks effects such as drop shadows or bevels are lost when converted to Flash. The Flash SWF offers the ability to add sound as well as quite complex interactivity. Mastering Flash, however, takes some expertise.

BUILDING AN ANIMATION

After you have decided the output format for your animation, you can start building your creative masterpiece of motion. Again, Fireworks enables you to build animations using the frame-by-frame method, the tweened method, or the animation symbols method.

FRAME-BY-FRAME ANIMATION

Frame-by-frame animation is the most basic method of the three types of animation you can do in Fireworks. Each element in each frame is repositioned or modified to create the illusion of motion. Remember the stick figures you drew on your school notebooks and how you flipped through the pages to make them move? Those flip books used frame-by-frame animation.

Frame-by-frame animation requires the artist to create each frame by hand. Tweening and animation symbols use the computer to automate the drawing process required between frames.

The simplest way to create an animation is to create an object, add a new frame, place the object on the new frame, and modify it in some way (change color, reposition, and so on). Repeat each step of this process until the animation is built.

The rub with this method is that you cannot see the previous frame as a point of reference if you're moving the object. If you've ever seen hand animators at work, they're constantly flipping between sheets of tracing paper (also known as onion skin) to gather their reference points for the animation.

Fortunately, Fireworks offers two solutions to this dilemma: Onion Skinning and the Distribute to Frames command.

ONION SKINNING

Onion Skinning pays homage to the traditional animation work process, where animators worked on translucent pieces of paper so they could see several layers of drawings simultaneously. In Fireworks, Onion Skinning simulates that process by displaying nearby frames partially grayed out (Figure 26.12).

26

Figure 26.12
Onion Skinning enables you to use surrounding frames to aid in positioning graphics in the animation.

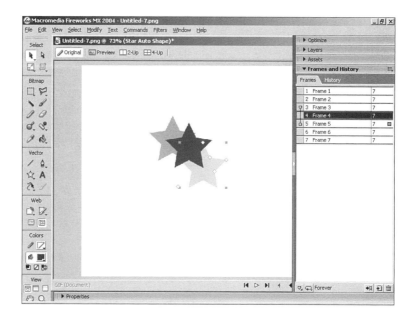

To use Onion Skinning, open the Frames panel. In the lower-left corner is the Onion Skinning button. Click the button to view the Onion Skinning menu (Figure 26.13). The No Onion Skinning option turns off the feature and shows only the active frame. All other options show a user a selected range of frames. Note that all ranges are relative to the active frame. If you select the Multi-Frame Editing option, all visible objects can be edited, including those on inactive frames.

Figure 26.13
The Onion Skinning menu provides several display options.

DISTRIBUTE TO FRAMES

Another option is to use the Distribute to Frames command, which takes a group of selected objects and sends each to its own frame in the order in which it is stacked in the Layers panel.

To use the Distribute to Frames command, create all the objects in one layer. Notice that there are several sublayers, depending on how many objects you create. Use the Layers panel to make sure your objects are in the proper stacking order for the animation. Because objects are distributed from bottom to top, make sure the graphic that starts your animation is the bottom sublayer and the graphic that ends your animation is the top sublayer.

Select all the objects you want to include in the animation with Edit, Select All, or Shift-click if you want to selectively choose graphics. Click the Distribute to Frames button in the Frames panel and Fireworks automatically inserts each graphic in its own frame, in order (Figure 26.14).

Figure 26.14
Use the Distribute to Frames command to automatically place each layered object in its own frame.

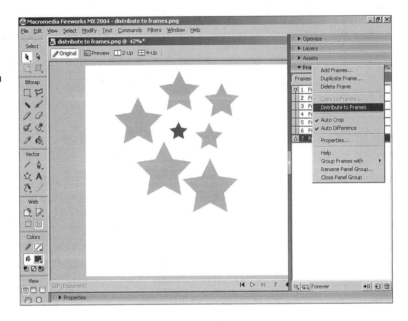

PLAYING YOUR ANIMATION

After you've created your animation, you'll want to see whether you've effectively created the illusion of motion. Built right into the document window is a set of playback controls, similar to those found in a VCR (Figure 26.15).

The animation will be played back a high rate of frames per second and will loop continuously. To change the frame delay, which determines how long the active frame is displayed, double-click in the frame delay of any frame. Remember that frame delay is measured in 100ths of a second. The default frame delay of 7 indicates the frame is delayed seven-tenths of a second. To hold the frame for 3 seconds, enter a value of 300.

To control the looping properties of your animation, click the GIF Animation Looping button at the bottom of the Frames panel (Figure 26.16). Select an option (No Looping, 1–5, 10, 20 and Forever) to set the looping properties.

Figure 26.15
Use the playback controls in the document window to preview your animation.

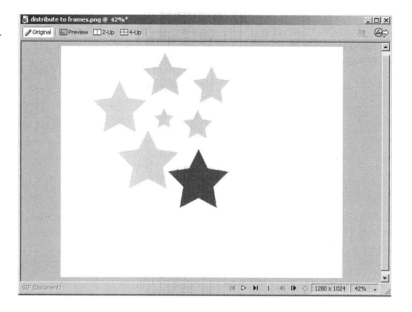

Figure 26.16
The GIF Animation Looping button controls the looping properties for the animation.

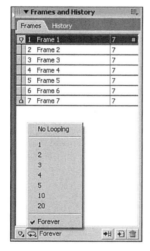

TWEENED ANIMATION

After working with frame-by-frame animations, playing with tweened animations will appear to be a piece of cake. To build a tweened animation, you create a beginning and an end point, then define the number of frames, or steps, in between. Fireworks does the rest.

To create a tweened animation, create an object and convert it to a graphic symbol (Modify, Convert to Symbol, select Graphic Symbol, in the Symbol Properties dialog box) (Figure 26.17). Drag two instances of the symbol onto the canvas. They must be instances of the same symbol.

Figure 26.17
After creating the first object in a tweened animation, convert the object to a graphic symbol.

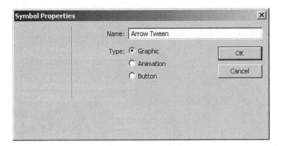

Position and modify each instance as desired. Select both instances and choose Modify, Symbol, Tween Instances (see Figure 26.18). Enter the number of steps in the Tween Instances dialog box. Select the Distribute to Frames option to distribute the symbols across frames. If you want to modify the symbols, leave this option unchecked.

Figure 26.18
Use the Tween Instances command to create the tweened animation.

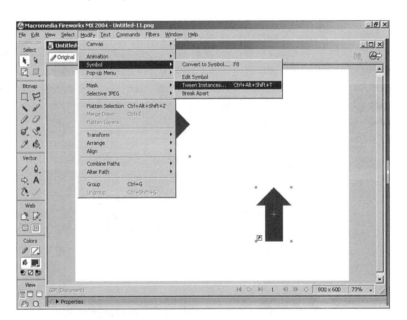

ANIMATION SYMBOLS

Animation symbols are one of the three symbol types in Fireworks (animation, button, and graphic). They are stored in the Fireworks library, and you can use them by simply dragging each symbol onto the canvas. The beauty of using animation symbols is that they hold objects in multi-frame animations together as a single unit. If you move one of the objects, the rest are automatically repositioned.

Although animation symbols are similar to tweened animations, there are a few differences. When you use animation symbols, Fireworks sees the entire animation as single entity. Accordingly, you can make global changes to the entire animation.

Animation symbols are also created from a single selection and parameters that you control (scaling, positioning, and rotation).

Because animation symbols are created from a single selection (tweened animation requires two symbols), you cannot visually set the endpoint. You must numerically designate the endpoint of the animation. But, animation symbols use modifiable motion paths, which allow you to easily change positioning after the animation is created.

CREATING ANIMATION SYMBOLS

The first step in building an animation with animation symbols is to create the symbol. To create the symbol, select one or more objects on the canvas. Choose (Modify, Animation, Animate Selection) to open the Animate dialog box (Figure 26.19).

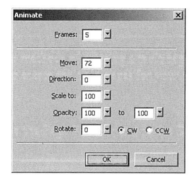

Figure 26.19
The Animate dialog box enables you to set the parameters of an animation symbol.

- **Frames**—Sets the number of frames used in the animation.
- **Move**—Controls the number of pixels the object is moved over the course of the animation. You can visually reposition the object later by modifying the motion path.
- **Direction**—Controls the direction, in degrees, the object is moved.
- **Scale To**—Controls the size of the final object compared to the first object. A relative percentage is used to measure this.
- **Opacity**—Changes the object's opacity. The first number represents the opacity of the first object, whereas the second number represents the opacity of the last object.
- **Rotation**—Controls the number of degrees the object is rotated. The CW and CCW radio button options represent clockwise and counter-clockwise rotation, respectively.

MODIFYING ANIMATION SYMBOLS

You can modify animation symbols in several ways, including modifying the animated object itself, editing the Animate dialog box settings, and modifying the motion path.

To modify the animated object itself, simply double-click an instance and the Symbol Editor window appears (Figure 26.20). You can then add new objects and modify or replace

26

the existing object. Note: All objects in the animation are modified, but the animation itself is not modified.

Figure 26.20
Use the Symbol Editor to modify the animated object.

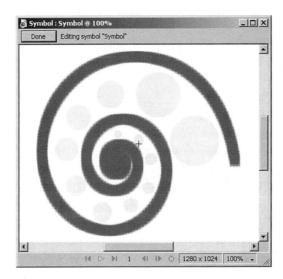

To make changes in the Animate dialog box, simply select the animation and choose (Modify, Animation, Settings) to see the Animate dialog box. Make your changes, press OK, and the symbol is updated.

If you're a numbers person, the Animate dialog box is the way to go to set the motion path. If you're a visual person, use the motion path to modify the object's trajectory in the animation.

After you've created the animation symbol, select an instance and the motion path will appear (Figure 26.21). This path displays the length and direction of the trajectory. To change either setting, drag the first (green) or last (red) point on the path. All intervening frames will be updated.

Note that the motion path is a straight line and not a curve. Because you can modify only the first (red) and last (green) points on the motion path, you can change only the length and direction of the trajectory.

OPTIMIZING YOUR ANIMATION FOR EXPORT AS AN ANIMATED GIF

Now that you've created your animations, you need to get them out there for the adoring public to see. You can use the Export tool or the Export command (File, Export) to start the process of creating an Animated GIF.

The Export Preview dialog box appears. Select Animated GIF from the Format pull-down menu under the Options tab.

Figure 26.21
Modify the animation symbol's trajectory by dragging the points of the motion path.

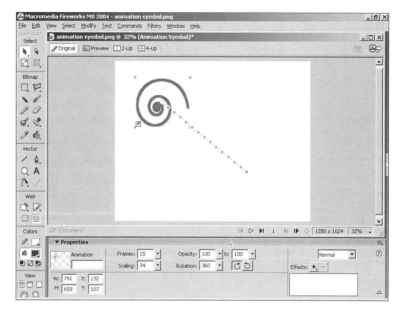

Select the Animation tab to set the compression. A key difference between static exports and animation exports is that animated files require compression across frames.

Fireworks enables you to choose between three levels of frame-to-frame compression (Figure 26.22):

- **None**—This yields the largest file size because there is no compression. The Animated GIF describes complete bitmap images for each frame. None is automatically selected when the Crop Each Frame and Save Differences Between Frames options are not selected.

- **Crop Each Frame**—The Animated GIF describes only the rectangular region where the pixels are changed.

- **Save Differences Between Frames**—The Animated GIF describes only the pixels that change within the rectangular region. Note that Crop Each Frame must be checked for the Save Difference Between Frames to be enabled. Using Saving Differences Between Frames yields the smallest file size.

When you're finished setting the export options, click the Export button, name the file, choose where to save it, and you've created an Animated GIF.

OPTIMIZING YOUR ANIMATION FOR EXPORT TO FLASH

To send your animation to Flash, click the Quick Export button located at the top right of the document window. Select Macromedia Flash and Export SWF (Figure 26.23). Enter a filename and click Save and you're finished.

26

Figure 26.22
Control the frame compression in the Animation tab of the Export Preview dialog box.

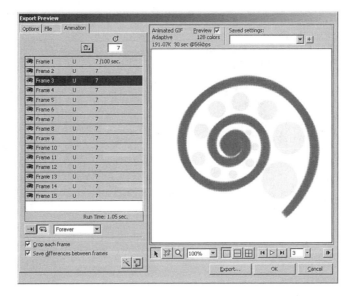

Figure 26.23
Use the Quick Export button to easily send your animation to Flash.

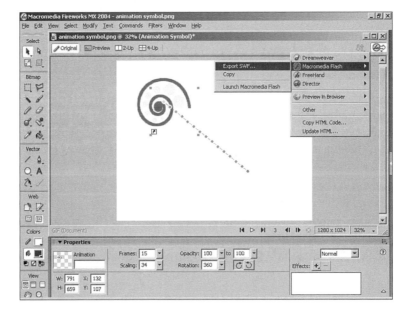

TROUBLESHOOTING

NAVIGATION BAR NOT WORKING WHEN PUBLISHED TO WEB SERVER

I built a cool navigation bar with pop-ups in Fireworks and can't get it to work when I uploaded the HTML page to the Web server. It works on my computer, but not online. What gives?

Locate the file called mm_menu.js that is exported into the same folder as the HTML file you create on export. This is the JavaScript file that runs the navigation rollover effects. You need a copy of that file in every folder on your computer, as well as the Web server, containing pages that have pop-up menus in them of manually updating each page.

MISALIGNED SLICES

No matter how careful I am, my slices keep getting misaligned. What can I do to keep my hand steady other than drinking less caffeine?

Let Fireworks do the work for you. Mark out your slices with guides. Make sure to enable the Snap to Guides command (View, Guides, Snap to Guides). Each time you draw a slice, it snaps to the guides and prevents that migraine-inducing 1-pixel misaligment that often comes from trying to create slices without using this feature.

WHITE BACKGROUND IN BUTTONS

I have made a few buttons on a black background by using the rectangle tool, black fill, no outer line. I converted those buttons to a symbol and adjusted the up, down, and over graphics. Everything is still black, but only the text changes color on the rollover. But when I view the buttons in a browser, they all have white lines! Help!

Check to make sure you are not working on a transparent canvas. To resolve this issue, change the canvas color to the color of the HTML page on which you'll be putting the buttons and you're good to go.

CHAPTER **27**

OPTIMIZING AND EXPORTING GRAPHICS AND WEB PAGES

In this chapter

Optimization Fundamentals   756

File Types   758

Using the Optimize Panel   758

Exporting Fireworks Images   766

In this chapter, we'll explore how to prepare graphics for the Web. As more Internet users have access to broadband connections, reducing the file size of graphics isn't quite as important as it was a few years ago. However, dial-up connections and their slower counterparts are still quite prevalent, and need to be taken into consideration when preparing graphics for the Web.

The process of reducing the file size of an image while preserving its quality is known as *optimization*. There are several concepts involved in the optimization process and a basic understanding of each will help you decide the best method for preparing your graphics for the Web.

OPTIMIZATION FUNDAMENTALS

In a nutshell, graphics optimization is the process of reducing the file size of your graphics so they can be downloaded faster when viewed on the Web. Graphics optimization is an art where you attempt to balance image quality with file size.

Fireworks has a powerful set of optimization tools that can handle the entire optimization process or let you step in and tinker with settings. Before you begin optimizing graphics, it helps to have a basic understanding of what happens when a file is optimized.

COMPRESSION

Compression is the process of reducing the amount of information used to describe, or render, a digital file. Most types of computer files are fairly redundant in that they have the same information listed over and over again. Rather than list a piece of information repeatedly, a compressed file presents a redundant piece of information once and then refers back to it whenever it appears in the original file.

To better understand compression, look at the following sentence: "I left my heart in San Francisco.": Pretend that sentence is a bitmap graphic that Fireworks will compress. The sentence has 7 words, made up of 27 characters and 6 spaces. If each character and space takes up one unit of memory, we get a total file size of 33 units. To get the file size down, we need to look for redundancies. To keep this simple, we'll only look for redundancies in the vowels:

- The letter *a* appears 2 times.
- The letter *e* appears 2 times.
- The lowercase *i* appears 2 times.
- The letter *o* appears once.
- The letter *u* is not present.

After the first *a* appears, each consecutive *a* would be replaced with a number ("1" for example). The number would refer to the first *a* and would naturally begin to reduce the file size.

Now, take that line of thought to a real bitmap graphic such as a JPEG or GIF. To the computer, the image comprises X columns and Y rows of pixels and each pixel has a hexadecimal (six-digit) color value. An uncompressed image would describe the image one pixel at a time and specify the hexadecimal color for each pixel.

LOSSLESS COMPRESSION

Lossless compression can be found in GIF, PNG, and file formats. Lossless compression lists an entire group of the same-colored pixels as single unit. All lossless compression is based on the idea of breaking a file into a smaller form for transmission or storage and then putting it back together on the other end so it can be used again.

The term *lossless* indicates that the file size is reduced without any loss of image quality. If an image has only a few colors, lossless compression can dramatically reduce the file size. However, if the image is made up of hundreds of unique colors, like a color photograph, then lossless compression has a marginal effect on file size.

LOSSY COMPRESSION

Lossy compression takes a completely different approach to reducing file size. This type of compression simply eliminates "unnecessary" bits of information, tailoring the file so that it is smaller. Lossy compression is used for reducing the file size of bitmap pictures, such as photographs and complex drawings. which tend to be fairly bulky. Lossy compression can be found in JPEG file formats.

To see how this works, consider how your computer might compress a scanned photograph. A lossless compression program can't do much with this type of file. Although large parts of the picture may look the same—the lawn is green, for example—most of the individual pixels are different. To make this picture smaller without compromising the resolution, the color value for certain pixels needs to be changed. If the picture had a lot of green grass, Fireworks picks one color of green that can be used for every color variation of a green pixel. Then, Fireworks rewrites the file so that the value for every grass pixel refers back to this information. If the compression scheme works well, you won't notice the change, but the file size will be significantly reduced.

Unfortunately, you can't get the original file back after it has been compressed. For this reason, you can't use this sort of compression for anything that needs to be reproduced exactly.

27

DITHERING

Dithering is most often used in GIFs to fake a color that is not in the file's color palette. Two palette colors from the file are alternated one pixel at a time. The hope is that your eye is tricked into seeing a third color. Dithered images tend to increase file size, the effect doesn't always work that well, and you end up with a grainy appearance to the image.

FILE TYPES

Most file types have fairly distinct advantages and disadvantages. This section focuses only on Web file formats, thus excluding any discussion on TIFF or BMP.

The top three file formats for online graphics are GIF, JPEG, and PNG as a distant third.

→ For more on the GIF, JPEG and PNG file types, **see** Chapter 31, "Integration with the Studio MX Suite," **page 857**.

USING THE OPTIMIZE PANEL

Fireworks provides you with two ways to control the optimization of your graphics: the Export Preview dialog box and the Optimize panel.

Let's take a look at the Optimize panel first. Because the core of image optimization is finding that magical balance between image quality and file size, it's helpful to have a way of comparing images at different optimization settings.

Use the preview buttons (Figure 27.1) to preview your images in one, two, or four panes.

Figure 27.1
The Preview buttons enable side-by-side comparison of various optimization settings.

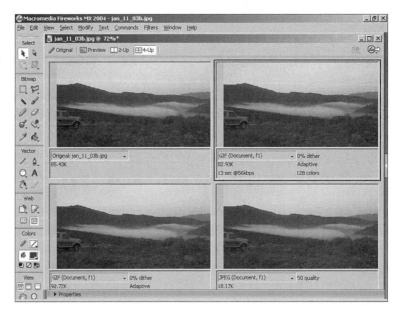

However, when you first view your image in the Preview buttons, you will see the original image in the top left, and the copies of the original in JPEG or GIF format. To change optimization settings, expand the Optimize panel.

Select a Preview pane and a black border appears around it. Enter the desired settings in the Optimize panel (Figure 27.2) and the image preview changes its appearance to reflect the settings.

Figure 27.2
Use the Optimization panel to change optimization settings.

File statistics appear in the bottom of the window (Figure 27.3).

Figure 27.3
File statistics appear in each of the Preview panes to show you how your optimization settings will affect file properties.

The Optimize panel (Figure 27.4) has five sections, no matter which file type is chosen:

- **Title section**—This section comprises three components: the gripper, the panel name, and the Optimize Options menu.
- **Saved Settings section**—This section contains all the saved optimization settings. These settings are presets that are shipped with Fireworks. You can also add or remove your own settings.
- **File Type/Matte section**—This section contains a drop-down list for the file type, as well as an option that lets you select the matte color. The matte color refers to the background color of the file when it is exported.
- **File Type Options section**—The contents of this section change based on the file type selected.
- **Color Palette/Transparency section**—For files with 8-bit or lower color palettes, the entire color palette is displayed here. Also included are tools for adding indexed transparency (GIF and PNG-8 files only) and color palette manipulation.

27

Figure 27.4
The Optimize panel contains five sections.

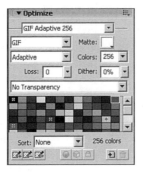

OPTIMIZE TO SIZE COMMAND

The Options menu in the Options Panel contains several options for the optimization process. Many of these options are self-explanatory, or are only in support of specific settings. One option that is worth mentioning is the Optimize to Size command.

This command launches the Optimize to Size dialog box, where you can enter a specific file size for optimized file (Figure 27.5). This command is handy if you are restricted to a specific file size, such as those required for banner advertisements.

Figure 27.5
The Optimize to Size command enables you to optimize an image to a specific file size.

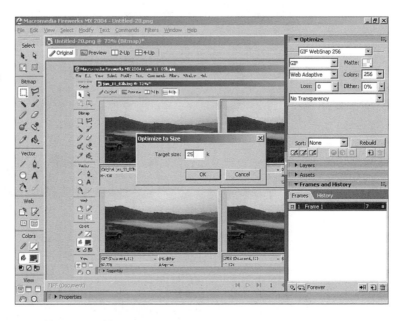

USING SAVED SETTINGS

Fireworks MX 2004 ships with seven predefined optimization settings. These settings represent common configurations and are often good to use "as is" for nearly every Web project. To use one of the settings, simply select one from the Saved Settings drop-down menu at the top of the Optimize panel (Figure 27.6).

Figure 27.6
Fireworks MX 2004 comes with seven Saved Settings for image optimization.

The seven settings are summarized as follows:

- **GIF Web 216**—All colors in the image are forced to the GIF 216-color Web Safe palette. Although image quality is negatively affected, this is a good setting to use if you are concerned about staying within the Web Safe palette.

- **GIF WebSnap 256**—This setting is the same as the GIF Web Snap 128, except there are 256 colors instead of 128.

- **GIF WebSnap 128**—The optimized image contains 128 colors. Colors close to those of the Web Safe palette are changed, whereas colors outside the palette are converted to their closest Web Safe color.

- **GIF Adaptive 256**—The optimized image contains up to 256 colors that are selected to best represent the original colors. It ignores the Web Safe palette.

- **JPEG—Better Quality**—The optimized image is a JPEG with quality setting of 80 and a Smoothing setting of 0.

- **JPEG—Smaller File**—The optimized image is a JPEG with quality setting of 60 and a Smoothing setting of 2.

- **Animated GIF Websnap 128**—The optimized image is an Animated GIF that uses the Websnap 128 palette.

For vector art or text, GIF typically provides a better compression. Use the Preview button to determine the best of the saved GIF settings to use.

For photographs and gradients, JPEG will typically be the best bet. Again, use the Preview button to select the best of the JPEG settings or even some of the GIF settings such as GIF Adaptive 256.

To create your own custom setting, use the Optimize panel to modify an image. Choose Save Settings from the Options menu (Figure 27.7). Enter a name in the Preset Name dialog box and click OK. The new setting is now a part of the settings list.

27

Figure 27.7
Create and save your
own settings, using
the Save Settings
command in the
Options menu.

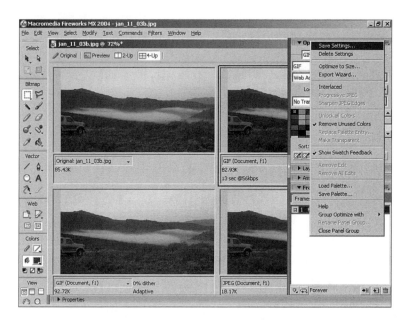

To remove a setting, make sure it is selected in the Saved Settings drop-down menu. Choose Delete Settings from the Optimize panel's Options menu and click OK in the warning dialog box.

USING MANUAL SETTINGS

Although the saved settings are convenient and can be used for most exported Web graphics, there are still some times when you'll need to tweak an image by hand. Fortunately, Fireworks enables you to manually optimize your images in the Optimize panel.

MANUALLY OPTIMIZING JPEGS

Starting with JPEGs, use the Quality setting to control the amount of compression applied to the image. Enter a number between 1 and 100 (or use the Quality slider). The higher the number, the better the quality and lower the compression.

In general, quality settings over 80 are pretty close to the original image. Settings between 60 and 80 are more compressed with generally acceptable quality. Settings below 60 are a gamble as quality begins to degrade quickly (Figure 27.8).

Selective Quality enables you to optimize different regions of the image separately. This control is useful for images with distinct backgrounds and foregrounds. To use selective JPEG compression, identify one region in the image that will use two different compression settings. There can be only one selective JPEG mask.

Use any of the bitmap selection tools (Marquee, Oval Marquee, Lasso, Polygon Lasso, Magic Wand, and so on) to enclose a region. (Figure 27.9).

Figure 27.8
Differences in JPEG quality can be seen between the image on the left, set at 80% quality, and the image on the right, set at 40% quality.

Figure 27.9
Define a selective JPEG mask, using the bitmap selection tools.

While the marquee area is selected, choose Modify, Selective JPEG, Save Selection as JPEG Mask. A translucent pink mask appears over the selected region. In the Optimize panel, double-check that JPEG is the selected file type and use the Quality slider to affect everything outside the mask. In Figure 27.10, the background would be affected.

When you have made your adjustments, look at your handiwork by selecting one of the Preview buttons.

Smoothing blurs the transitions between sharp edges in an image. Smoothing makes it easier for an image to be compressed, but also degrades the quality. Smoothing settings below 3 seem to strike the best balance between image quality and file size.

Sharpen Edges (located in the Options menu) has the opposite effect of Smoothing. Edges are sharpened, often resulting in an improved image quality. File size, however, is increased. You cannot control the degree of sharpness. It is either on or off.

27

Figure 27.10
Use one of the Preview buttons to see how the Quality setting affects the area outside the selected region of the image.

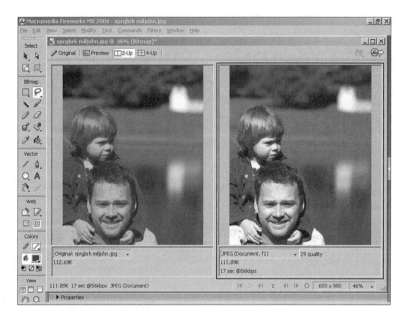

The Progressive setting (located in the Options menu)affects only display, not image quality. There is typically a slight increase in file size, however. When the image is downloaded to the Web browser, a low-resolution version appears first. The details are then gradually filled in. The faster the Internet connection, the more seamless this progression appears.

MANUALLY OPTIMIZING GIFS

The GIF format uses 8-bit or lower indexed color, which means that it uses 256 or fewer colors and tracks each color separately. Accordingly, the trick to getting the best optimization with the GIF format lies with the color palette. To modify that palette, choose the palette type and the number of colors in that palette. Other choices include dithering and whether or not to apply lossy compression.

To choose a palette, use the Indexed Palette drop-down menu in the Optimize panel (or the Export Preview dialog box) (Figure 27.11). Select one of the following choices:

- **Adaptive**—Derived from the actual colors in the document and often produce the highest quality image.

- **Web Adaptive**—Converts colors that are close to the Web Safe palette colors to the appropriate Web Safe color.

- **Web 216**—A palette of the 216 colors common to both Windows and Macintosh computers.

- **Exact**—Contains only the colors used in the original image. If the image contains more than 256 colors, the palette automatically switches to Adaptive.

- **Macintosh**—Contains the 256 colors defined by Macintosh platform standards.

- **Windows**—Contains the 256 colors defined by the Windows platform standards.

- **Grayscale**—Contains a palette of 256 or fewer shades of gray.

- **Black and White**—Converts all pixels to either black or white.

- **Uniform**—Selects colors mathematically, based on RGB pixel values.

- **Custom**—Palettes are loaded from an external palette (ACT file) that you have previously created.

Figure 27.11
Select one of the eight GIF color palettes from the drop-down menu in the Optimize panel.

To choose the number of colors, or color depth, select a number from the Maximum number of colors drop-down menu. Select a color depth that best represents the color integrity of the original image (Figure 27.12)

Although the GIF format uses lossless compression, you can still apply lossy compression by using the Lossy GIF Compression slider. To apply lossy compression to the GIF, drag the slider or enter a number in the field. The higher the number, the higher the compression and the lower the image quality.

Interlacing is similar to the Progressive setting for JPEG. When the image is downloaded to the Web browser, a low-resolution version appears first. The details are then gradually filled in. If there will be a lot of graphics on the Web page, interlacing allows the images to appear onscreen faster, even though they are not the final image. Turn on interlacing by selecting Interlaced from the Options menu.

27

Figure 27.12
Varying the color depth affects file size and image quality.

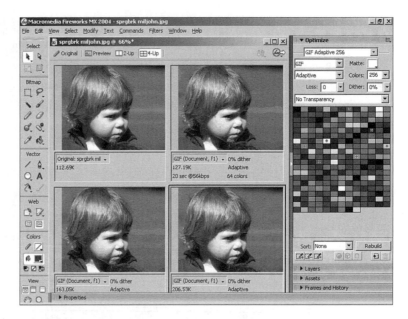

EXPORTING FIREWORKS IMAGES

After you've painstakingly planned, designed, and created your graphics, you need to export the images. There are a number of ways to export Fireworks graphics. You can export a document as a single image in JPEG, GIF, or another graphic file format. You can also export the entire document as an HTML file and associated image files. You can also integrate your Fireworks graphics with Flash and Director.

WEB GRAPHICS

After you have created your Web graphic, you need to export it to a Web-friendly format such as JPEG or GIF. Up to this point, we've explored the strengths and weaknesses of each file format. We've also covered the optimization process. All that's left is to export the image.

Fireworks provides three ways of exporting a Web graphic: the Export command, the Export Area tool, and the Export Wizard.

The Export command exports all the objects on the canvas and excludes objects in the work area. Use the Export command (File, Export) to launch the Export dialog box (Figure 27.13).

Figure 27.13
The Export dialog box provides options for exporting your document.

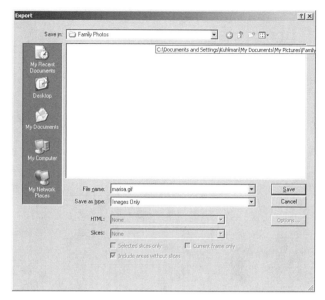

Name the file and be sure that Images Only is selected in the Save As Type drop-down menu. You'll notice that there are several types to choose from, depending on how the exported image is to be used. For the Web, use Images Only. Click the Save button and you're finished.

After you've optimized your image as a GIF or JPEG, that file format will be automatically selected during the export process.

If you want to export only a selected portion of an object or the canvas, use the Export Area tool. Drag the tool to define the area for export (Figure 27.14). Press the Return/Enter key to launch the Export Preview dialog box (Figure 27.15). If you've already optimized your image, these controls will look familiar. The Export Preview dialog box enables you to select the export file type and adjust the optimization settings, as well as preview the effect of the optimization settings.

Using the Export Wizard is the easiest way to configure the optimization of your graphic for export. To access it, select File,Export Wizard. You are prompted to answer a series of questions (Figure 27.16). When you're finished, you are presented with a GIF or JPEG (if you chose the Web or Dreamweaver as your output preference), or TIFF (if you chose an image editing or desktop publishing application).

After you exit the wizard, you find yourself in the Export Preview dialog box, where you can once again select GIF or JPEG if you are exporting for the Web. If you've read this far, you already know what file format you're going to use, so you can skip the Export Wizard altogether.

27

Figure 27.14
Use the Export Area tool to define a specific area for export.

Figure 27.15
The Export Preview dialog box provides the same controls as the Optimize panel and the Preview buttons.

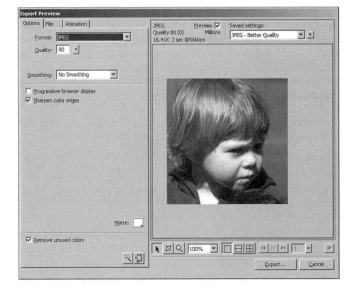

Figure 27.16
The Export Wizard offers a simple, but limited, method of viewing export options.

WEB PAGES

Fireworks generates HTML that can be read by most Web browsers and HTML editors. There are some issues, however, in taking your Fireworks page design and exporting it straight to HTML.

First, HTML is a text-based framework where objects are positioned relative to each other. Fireworks is an object-oriented program where all elements are precisely sized and positioned in pixels relative to the top-left corner of the canvas.

Fireworks elements are constrained to a specific canvas size. HTML is designed to flow to fill a browser window of varying sizes.

In addition, the two major browsers (Internet Explorer and Netscape Navigator) still don't render elements exactly the same. They're getting better about this, but there are still differences that can affect your design.

There are several ways to export Fireworks HTML:

- Export an HTML file, which you can later modify in an HTML editor.
- Copy HTML code to the Fireworks Clipboard, and then paste that code directly into an existing HTML document.
- Export an HTML file, open it in an HTML editor, manually copy sections of code from the file, and paste that code into another HTML document.
- Use the Update HTML command to make changes to an HTML file you've previously created.

To define how HTML is exported in Fireworks, use the HTML Setup dialog box (Figure 27.17). These settings can be document specific or used as your default settings for all HTML that Fireworks exports.

27

Figure 27.17
Adjust the HTML export settings, using the HTML Setup dialog box.

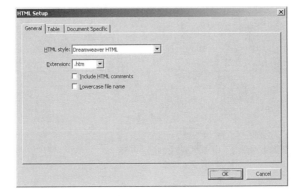

To export an entire page design, your best bet is to use the Slice tool to divide your design in regions (Figure 27.18).

Figure 27.18
Divide your page design into slices for export.

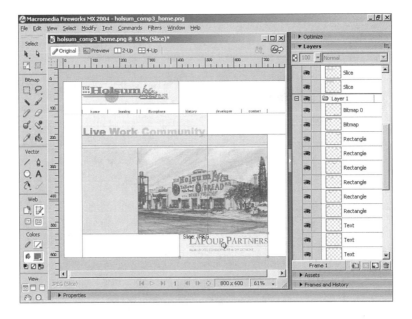

After the page is sliced up, export the page, using the Export command (File, Export). The Export dialog box is launched. Rename the HTML file if necessary and adjust any of the settings to fit your file hierarchy (Figure 27.19).

Click the Save button and all the HTML code necessary to reassemble sliced images, as well as the sliced images themselves, are created. Fireworks HTML contains links to the exported images and sets the Web page background color to the canvas color.

You can then modify the page, using an HTML editor of your choice.

27

Figure 27.19
The Export dialog box.

INTEGRATING WITH DREAMWEAVER

Dreamweaver and Fireworks are two peas in a pod when it comes to integration. Both programs recognize and share many of the same file commands, including changes to links, rollovers, and table slices. Used together, the two programs provide a streamlined workflow for editing, optimizing, and placing Web graphics files in HTML pages.

The first step in creating an integrated work environment is to define a local site in Dreamweaver and to make sure Design Notes are enabled. Design Notes contain information about the graphic files that Fireworks exports. When you launch and edit a Fireworks image from Dreamweaver, Dreamweaver uses this information to locate the source PNG. For example, you created a graphic called candyapple.png. You then exported that graphic as a JPEG image and placed it in your Dreamweaver document. Your source file is candyapple.png.

Setting Fireworks as the external image editor for Dreamweaver lets you effortlessly go between Dreamweaver and Fireworks if you need to edit an image after it is placed in Dreamweaver. Simply select the image and click the Fireworks icon (Figure 27.20) in the Property inspector to launch Fireworks. Edit the image, save it, and the changes are automatically applied to the Dreamweaver file.

27

Figure 27.20
Use the Fireworks
icon in the
Dreamweaver
Property inspector to
launch Fireworks for
image editing.

If planning is not your strong suit, you can build your page in Dreamweaver and add image placeholders if your graphics are not ready. An image placeholder is a graphic you use in your Dreamweaver document until final artwork is ready to be added to the page. You can set the placeholder's size, color, and text label.

After the image placeholder is used in Dreamweaver, you can design the graphic at some later point in Fireworks. After the graphic is created, save it as a PNG and export it as a Web-ready graphic file (GIF or JPEG). When you return to Dreamweaver, the replacement image is updated in the document.

INTEGRATING WITH FLASH

Although Flash has robust drawing capabilities, you may want to create your complex graphics in Fireworks and export them to Flash. There are two ways to accomplish this.

First, you can copy vector objects from Fireworks and paste them into Flash. Select the objects you want to copy and then use the Copy command (Edit, Copy). In Flash, create a new document and then Paste (Edit, Paste). The Fireworks objects are pasted as a group. Ungroup the objects (Modify, Ungroup)—or better yet, use (Modify, Break Apart, which works more consistently—to separate the elements so they can be modified if necessary.

To send an animation to Flash, click the Quick Export button located at the top right of the document window. Select Macromedia Flash and Export to SWF. (Figure 27.21) Enter a file name, click Save, and you're finished.

INTEGRATING WITH DIRECTOR

Because Fireworks enables designers to create and export 32-bit PNG file formats, Fireworks is a popular image and vector artwork design tool for Director developers. Director, which is not covered in this book, is a Macromedia application that enables developers to create interactive content that integrates long video streams, photo-quality images, audio, animation, 3D models, text, and Macromedia Flash content. This content is often used on CDs, DVDs, kiosks, and even the Web.

Exported layers and slices from Fireworks can be used in Director as individual cast members or as composite user interfaces that can be imported as an entire entity onto the stage. Director developers can also use Fireworks to design and script rollovers and navigation interfaces.

27

Figure 27.21
Use the Quick Export button to easily send your animation to Flash.

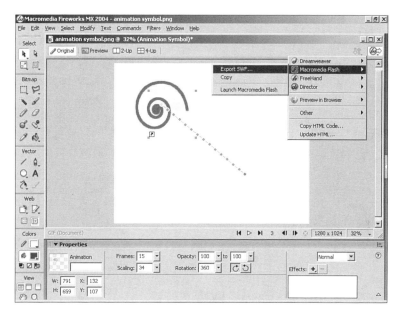

Developers can use Fireworks to create cast libraries from a single Fireworks document by using layers in Fireworks and exporting the Fireworks layers to Director MX. Any Fireworks MX document that contains layers can be exported as Director HTML with the Source pop-up menu in the Export dialog box set to Fireworks Layers. The 32-bit PNG format supports full Alpha transparency, and transparency in a Fireworks document is retained in the Director movie.

If different graphic elements are arranged in separate layers and the developer does not want to generate separate files for each layer, exporting the entire document as a single file, using the PNG32 setting in the Optimize panel, flattens all the layers.

Fireworks can also be used to create a navigational interface. Developers can design the elements in Fireworks, draw slices, add behaviors to the slices, and export the slices to Director MX. Any Fireworks MX document that contains slices can be exported as Director HTML with the Source pop-up menu in the Export dialog box set to Fireworks Slices. This setting enables the images as defined by the slices to be imported into the Director movie, along with the behaviors such as Simple Rollovers, Swap Image, Disjoint Rollovers, and Set Navbar Image behaviors.

When exporting an animated GIF from Fireworks for use in Director, you need to disable Auto Crop and Auto Difference in the Animation tab of the Export Preview. For some reason, Director does not correctly display animated GIFs if those settings are enabled.

27

TROUBLESHOOTING

VECTOR CURVES LOOK BITMAPPED

When I draw vector curves, how come they still look like they're bitmap graphics?

You'll get the best curves in Fireworks if you use a Soft Rounded stroke (Basic, Soft Rounded). The Soft Rounded stroke adds more pixels to smooth the edge of a shape than does the anti-aliasing alone.

EXPORTING ANIMATION SETTINGS TO FLASH

I set frame delay and looping settings on an animation I created in Fireworks. Will they be exported to Flash?

No. Frame delay and looping settings apply only if you are exporting your animation as an Animated GIF. These settings are discarded when you export to Flash SWF.

OPTIMIZATION AND SELECTIVE JPEG COMPRESSION

I keep trying to use the Smoothing optimization setting on a masked object, but it doesn't seem to be doing anything.

Certain optimization settings such as Smoothing can be used only outside a masked area. Anything inside the masked area is off limits. Redraw your mask so the area you want to optimize with Smoothing is outside the mask.

ADOBE GOLIVE AND FIREWORKS

I'm more comfortable using Adobe's GoLive instead of Dreamweaver, but want to use Fireworks to design my Web pages. I'm having problems getting my Fireworks pop-up menus to work in GoLive.

Although GoLive does not recognize pop-up menus created in Fireworks, your menus should still work in a Web browser. When exporting the pop-up menus for use in GoLive, don't use the GoLive style; chooose Generic instead.

FIREWORKS AND PHOTOSHOP FILTERS

On earlier versions of Fireworks and Photoshop, I could use most of Photoshop's filters in Fireworks. That doesn't seem to work anymore. What happened?

Because of the ever-increasing competition between Macromedia and Adobe, Adobe decided to block its filters from being used in Fireworks. Fireworks can still use Photoshop 5.5 and earlier filters. Otherwise, your best bet is to search online for third-party developers to find a filter that matches the Adobe filter you want to use.

CHAPTER 28

AUTOMATING AND EXTENDING FIREWORKS

In this chapter

Automating Tasks   776

Extending Fireworks   780

In this chapter, we'll take a look at how you can use Fireworks to make your life easier. Designing graphics and playing with images is something I enjoy doing. I was fortunate to be able to turn a passion into a career. However, there are days when the passion just isn't there and that 30-page Web site update becomes work. As someone who designs Web sites for a living, I don't want to spend every waking hour staring at a computer screen. This is where the ability to utilize the automation and extension capabilities of Fireworks comes into play. Learn to use these capabilities to be more productive, eliminate tedious tasks, and just make the day go a bit smoother.

The topics covered in this chapter are worthy of a book themselves. A brief overview of the most common applications is presented to give you a primer on automating and extending Fireworks MX 2004.

AUTOMATING TASKS

Designing Web sites often involves repetitive tasks, such as optimizing images or converting images to fit within certain constraints. Think of any major online retailer's Web site and the work that went into resizing, optimizing, and exporting hundreds of product shots.

A wonderful capability of Fireworks is its capability to automate and simplify many of those tedious drawing, editing, and file-conversion tasks.

Fireworks offers three sets of tools that enable you to automate these repetitive tasks:

- **Find and Replace**—Used to search for and replace elements within a file or multiple files. You can specify an asset, such as text, color, URLs, and fonts, and find and replace that asset in a PNG file.

- **Batch Process**—Used to convert entire groups of image files into other formats or to change their color palettes. Batch Process also applies custom optimization settings to groups of files, as well as resize a group of files.

- **Commands**—Used to create shortcuts for commonly used features or to create a script that can perform a complex series of steps. Advanced users can automate complex tasks by writing JavaScript commands and then executing them in Fireworks. These commands are beyond the scope of this book, but we will discuss them briefly later in this chapter in "Extending Fireworks," page 780.

FIND AND REPLACE

Find and Replace comes into play when you need to make global changes to elements of source PNG files. Elements that can be modified using Find and Replace include text, fonts, colors, and URLs.

Note that changes made with Find and Replace are undoable. For example, you search your source PNG files for the word "insomnia" and replace it with the word "sleepless." If you decide to change the word again, you cannot undo that change. However, you can run another Find and Replace. Run a find for the word "sleepless" and replace it with the original word "insomnia."

All Find and Replace commands are handled through the Find panel. Access it by choosing Window, Find, or Edit, Find (Figure 28.1).

Figure 28.1
All Find and Replace operations are handled through the Find panel.

From the Search pop-up menu, choose a source for the search:

- **Search Selection**—Finds and replaces elements in the currently selected objects and text.

- **Search Frame**—Finds and replaces elements in only the current frame.

- **Search Document**—Finds and replaces elements in the active document.

- **Search Files**—Finds and replaces elements across multiple files.

From the Find pop-up menu, select an attribute to search for. The options in the panel change according to your selection.

Next, select a find-and-replace operation:

- **Find**—Locates the next instance of the element.

- **Replace**—Changes a found element with the contents of the Change To option.

- **Replace All**—Finds and replaces every instance of a found element in the search range.

As long as a file is not open, the act of replacing objects in multiple files automatically saves those changes. To give yourself some extra insurance, you can create backups when you use Find and Replace in multiple files.

With the Find panel open, click the Options menu in the top-right corner of the panel. Select Replace Options to launch the Replace Options dialog box (Figure 28.2).

Select from among the following options:

- **Save and Close Files (if checked)**—This option has Fireworks save and close selected files that are not currently open when the Replace operation is completed.

- **Backup Original Files**—This option has three options to choose from: select Choose No Backups to have no file backups made; select Overwrite Existing Backups to create

28

one set of backups and overwrite them if multiple operations are performed; and choose Incremental Backups to create a set of backups for every Find and Replace operation completed.

Click OK to save the settings.

Figure 28.2
The Replace Options dialog box specifies how multiple-file Find and Replace operations are handled.

BATCH PROCESSING

Batch Processing is often performed as a series of simultaneous tasks on a group of files. In contrast to Find and Replace, Batch Processing is used on exported files such as GIFs and JPEGs.

The best way to create a batch process is to use the Batch Wizard (File, Batch Process). The wizard presents three screens, enabling you to accomplish a batch process in a jiffy.

The first screen (Figure 28.3) allows you to add files that will be used to create the batch. Files can be added from more than one directory.

When you have created the batch, click the Next button to continue.

Figure 28.3
The first screen in the Batch Process wizard is where you add files to create the batch.

The second screen (Figure 28.4) is used to add tasks that will tell Fireworks what to do to the files in the batch. The following are some of the most commonly used tasks:

- **Export**—This task specifies how the batch will be re-exported. When selected, all the export presets appear.
- **Scale**—This task scales the graphics to a specific size (like thumbnails), to fit an area, or to a percentage.
- **Find and Replace**—This task opens the Batch Replace dialog box so you can use the Find and Replace operations in PNG files.
- **Rename**—This task allows you to add a prefix or suffix to the files.
- **Commands, Convert to Grayscale**—This command converts the batch images to grayscale and is frequently used in Web design.

When you have added your tasks, click the Next button to continue.

Figure 28.4
The second screen in the Batch Process wizard is where you add tasks that are to be applied to the batch.

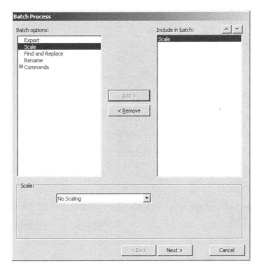

The last screen of the wizard (Figure 28.5) is where you specify the files' output destination, as well as what should happen to the original files. If the results are satisfactory, you can even save the batch process as a Scriptlet. A Scriptlet is a script that you can use again to repeat the exact batch process in the future.

Make your selections and click the Batch button. Fireworks does all the work so you can kick back and take a much deserved break!

28

Figure 28.5
The third screen in the Batch Process wizard is where you choose the output destination and specify the fate of the original files.

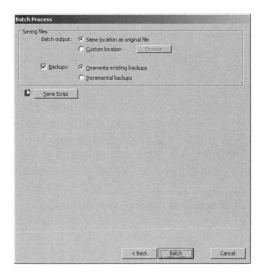

EXTENDING FIREWORKS

The Extension Manager lets you import, install, and delete extensions in Macromedia applications to extend the capabilities of Fireworks. In other words, you can add more features to the program that weren't included when you first installed the application on your computer.

Built into Fireworks is a set of extensibility features. These features are built on an open architecture that enables users and third-party developers to add more goodies to the program.

The most common way to extend Fireworks is through commands. When you save a file, you are using a command. Although this command comes with Fireworks, it was created just like any other custom command script.

Commands are written in a special Fireworks version of JavaScript. If you're a JavaScript ace, the language will come easily to you. If you're not, read on.

CREATING COMMANDS WITH THE HISTORY PANEL

The simplest way to create a custom command is to use the History panel (Window, History). The History panel is a record of all the steps you have recently taken when working in a document. If you want to automate a sequence of those steps, you can use the History panel to create a custom command.

By default, the History panel shows up to 20 steps. You can increase or decrease this number in the General tab of the Preferences dialog (Edit, Preferences).

To create commands with the History panel, execute a series of modifications that are to be used in your command. Using the History panel options menu, highlight the steps you want to use in the command, then select Save As Command (Figure 28.6). The Save Command dialog box appears. Enter a name for your new command. Click OK.

Figure 28.6
Use the Save as Command option to save your History panel options as a custom command.

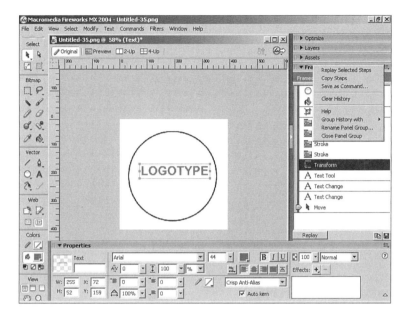

Your very own command now has a home in the Commands menu. Use it again and again. If you find yourself becoming a commands junkie and need to get rid of a few outdated commands, you can rename or delete commands in the Manage Saved Commands dialog box (Commands, Manage Saved Commands) .

USING THE EXTENSION MANAGER

Commands are usually stored in scripts called command scripts. All these scripts are located in the Commands folder on your hard drive. The Commands folder location is specific to settings you used when you installed Fireworks. Fireworks, along with Dreamweaver and Flash, is part of the Macromedia Exchange, a place where developers who create command scripts can distribute and exchange scripts. Macromedia tests each script to make sure it works and contains no harmful code (such as viruses) before posting it on the forum.

Commands from the Exchange are downloaded to your computer and are installed as Extensions. To install an extension, double-click an extension after it has been downloaded and Fireworks takes care of the rest.

To access these Extensions, you need to use the Extension Manager (Help, Manage Extensions) (Figure 28.7). Select File, Go to Macromedia Exchange to connect to the Macromedia Exchange Web site. Peruse the Extensions and download what strikes your fancy.

28

Figure 28.7
The Extension
Manager can be used
install new Extensions
as well as manage
your Extensions col-
lection.

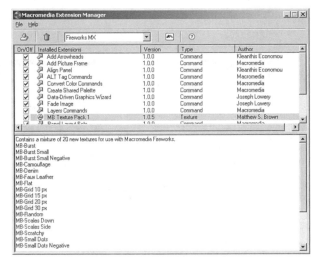

The Extension Manager takes care of the rest.

TROUBLESHOOTING

FIREWORKS AND THE WORLD OF PRINT PUBLISHING

I'd like to print my Fireworks graphics but am having resolution problems.

Fireworks is designed for creating Web graphics. Although you can use it for print graphics, you need to up the resolution. Set the resolution of your image (Properties Inspector, Image Size button) so the number of PPI (pixels per inch) is equal to the number of DPI (dots per inch) your printer uses.

RESETTING STYLES

I created a custom style and accidentally selected Reset Styles from the Styles panel pop-up menu. Are my styles lost forever?

Most definitely. Your painstakingly created styles have been shuttled off to graphics la-la land. Choosing Reset Styles restores the 30 factory defaults and permanently removes any custom styles you may have created. Unfortunately, this action is not undoable.

FREEHAND MX

29   FreeHand MX Environment and Tools   785

30   Using FreeHand in Web Site Planning and Creation   837

31   Integration with the Studio MX suite   857

CHAPTER 29

FreeHand MX Environment and Tools

In this chapter

FreeHand MX Environment   786

Document Window   786

Panels   787

Tools Unique to FreeHand MX   795

Toolbars Unique to FreeHand MX   830

29

In this chapter we will explore FreeHand MX: its work environment and tools. Armed with a basic understanding of the program's collaborative features as well as its robust set of drawing and design tools will enable you to focus on the process of creation instead of the process of production.

The FreeHand MX environment is naturally quite similar to that of the other Studio MX programs.

→ For more on the MX environment, **see** Chapter 3, "Introducing the MX Interface," **page 23**.

However, unlike the other programs, FreeHand enables you to design for both print and Web environments. Accordingly, FreeHand gives you some extra tools and features to use that will enrich your creative options.

FREEHAND MX ENVIRONMENT

Although not as exciting as jumping right into the thick of things, developing an understanding of your working environment is critical to your success in using FreeHand MX. Sure, you can tinker around and explore the program, and that method of learning has its merits if you have the time and patience. Many of us, however, can recall countless times we've smacked our foreheads after spending hours trying to figure out how to do something when the answer was right in front of us in a chapter like this.

Because you'll most likely be using FreeHand in conjunction with other programs in the MX suite, it's helpful to be able to understand differences and similarities between the programs's working environments.

Although you may be tempted to skip ahead to the more exciting goodies, take a few minutes to read this information. Think of this chapter as the driver's manual to your car. You can drive without reading it, but it sure is helpful to know how the jack works before you get a flat tire.

→ For more details on panels, tools, and menus, **see** Chapter 3, **pages 30-42**.

DOCUMENT WINDOW

FreeHand's document window (Figure 29.1) contains the artwork—or graphic file—upon which you are working. The main component of the document window is the canvas, or the "live" area of your art. Anything within the canvas is what will be exported or printed. Anything outside of the canvas, in the gray area known as the work area, is a "dead" area. You can use the work area to store assets or have them bleed off the canvas, if necessary, for print projects.

Figure 29.1
FreeHand's document window.

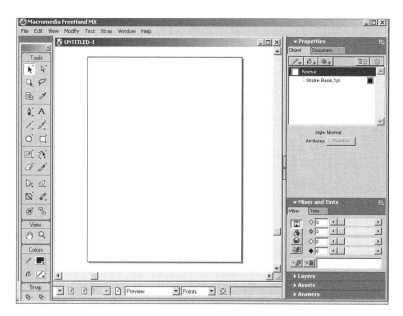

PANELS

Panel groups (Figure 29.2) are docked to the right side of the screen and contain several palettes that let you perform a multitude of tasks, such as changing text and object properties, page attributes, and layer attributes, as well as viewing assets and libraries. There is even a handy panel group that offers assistance and answers to your questions.

Figure 29.2
FreeHand's panels provide an efficient way to modify the document as well as objects.

29

The folks at Macromedia grouped panels into an arrangement that they felt would work best for you. You can move, separate, or combine these customizable panel groups. Panels and panel groups can be opened, closed, docked, expanded, and collapsed. There are five default panel groups, each with a different function. The following is a brief description of what each panel does:

PROPERTIES PANEL GROUP

The Properties Panel group contains the Object Panel and the Document Panel. These two panels are located in the top of the panel for a reason: They are the most frequently used panels to modify objects and the document itself.

- **Object Panel**—The Object panel (Window, Object) allows you to control the stroke, fill, and effects for objects (Figure 29.3). It changes its display depending on the type of object selected. You can use the Object panel to set the size and position of objects, as well as change text attributes.

Figure 29.3
The Object panel enables you to modify objects.

- **Document Panel**—The Document panel (Window, Document) controls the various attributes of your document, including creating and removing pages, page orientation, printer resolution, and bleed (Figure 29.4). You can also use the Document Panel to create Master Pages.

Figure 29.4
The Document panel enables you to modify document attributes.

29

- **Adding Pages**—The Document panel menu enables you add pages by selecting the Add Pages command. To add multiple pages, simply enter a number in the Number of New Pages field.

  If you're working with multiple pages in your document, you need to be able to move from page to page. In FreeHand, you have two ways to navigate through your document.

  The first is to use the Hand tool to drag from one page to another. You can also hold the space bar to temporarily activate the Hand tool.

  The second is to use the Preview Area inside the Document panel (Figure 29.5). Hold the spacebar to temporarily access the Hand tool, drag within the thumbnail pages within the Preview Area to go from page to page, and click on the page you want.

Figure 29.5
The Preview Area not only shows an overall view of pages in the document, but also enables you to rearrange pages.

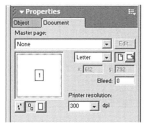

- **Deleting Pages**—If you want to delete a page, select the page you want to delete in the Preview Area of the Document Panel. Choose Remove from the Document Panel menu and your page is deleted. You can also use the Page tool to select the page you want to delete. To delete multiple pages, hold down the Shift key while using the Page tool.

→ For more on the Page tool, **see** "Page Tool," **page 795**, later in this chapter.

- **Page Orientation**—To change your page's orientation, select the portrait or landscape button in the Document Panel. It doesn't get any easier than that!

- **Using Page Bleeds**—Page bleeds are used in printing to extend the color beyond the edge of the page so when the final page is trimmed (as in the cover of this book), there are no white edges or gaps. If you have color that goes right up to the edge of the page, then you need to set a page bleed.

  To set a page bleed in FreeHand, enter the bleed size in the Bleed field of the Document panel (Figure 29.6). Then press Enter or Return and a light gray line appears around your page to indicate the bleed area.

Figure 29.6
Use the Bleed field in the Document panel to control the amount of page bleed in your print documents.

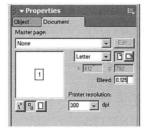

MIXERS AND TINT PANEL GROUP

The Mixers and Tint panel group enables you to select a wide range of colors and tints, as well as create your own custom color swatches that can be saved for different projects.

- **Mixer Panel**—The Mixer panel (Window, Color Mixer) enables you to create and define colors in CMYK, RGB, HLS, and the color picker (either Windows or Macintosh version). Click one of the four icons for the color mode in which you want to work (Figure 29.7). After a color is defined, it can be applied to an object or stored in the Swatches panel.

Figure 29.7
The Mixer panel provides options to create and define colors.

- The CMYK mode defines colors based on the four process colors used in commercial printing: cyan, magenta, yellow, and black. To create CMYK colors, enter values (0%–100%) for the color in the cyan, magenta, yellow, or black fields. You can also drag the sliders to create values for the colors.

- The RGB mode defines colors based on the three colors used in video color systems and computer monitors: red, green, and blue. If you create graphics for the Web or multimedia, you'll be working in the RGB mode. To create RGB colors, enter the values for the color (0–255) in the red, green, or blue field. You can also drag the sliders to create values for the color.

- The HLS mode defines color according to hue, lightness, and saturation. Working in HLS mode gives you more of a visual cue on how to work with complimentary colors. Although you can define colors in HLS mode, its main use is select one color and enable you to view it in HLS mode to find color harmony, or balance, between the selected color and other color selections. For example, if you keep the lightness and saturation values the same, you can select a blue hue and a green hue that appear aesthetically balanced.

Selecting a Color System

With three color modes at your disposal, which one should you use? If you're working for the Web or any medium that uses a video monitor, use the RGB system. This system uses the same colors that are available on monitors and video displays. RGB also has colors that are not available in CMYK.

Because HLS is based on the RGB system, I would suggest you first select your colors in RGB, then switch to HLS if you feel the need to balance your color selections by matching their lightness or saturation.

CMYK is your best bet if your artwork will be sent to a printer who uses the four-color printing process. The values you define in the Color Mixer for cyan, magenta, yellow, and black represent the percentage of ink applied to the paper during printing. The rub is that you're viewing CMYK colors on a monitor that displays RGB colors. Don't trust your eye for color accuracy. Get your hands on a printed process color guide available from Pantone or Trumatch.

- **Tints Panel**—The Tints panel (Window, Tints) controls the tint, or screen, of colors (Figure 29.8). You can apply the tint directly to the object or store it in the Swatches panel.

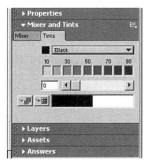

Figure 29.8
Use the Tints panel to control color tint or screen.

29

A tint represents a percentage value of a color. For example, a 25% tint of blue indicates that only one quarter of the saturated value of blue has been applied.

Tints are typically used when working with print graphics that are restricted to one or two colors. Using tints of the same color gives you the illusion of having more colors in your artwork.

LAYERS PANEL GROUP

The Layers panel (Window, Layers) displays all the document layers and lets you add, delete, copy, and arrange layers (Figure 29.9). As your project increases in complexity, use the power of layers to organize the various objects in your document.

Figure 29.9
The Layers panel provides an easy visual reference for document layers.

The following list describes some of ways you can use layers in FreeHand:

- **Nonprinting Layers**—FreeHand also allows you to create nonprinting layers. As the name suggests, these are layers that are visible on your monitor, but do not print. You can use nonprinting layers to hold graphics that are being used for tracing. Nonprinting layers are located below the horizontal line in the Layers panel (Figure 29.10).

  To create a nonprinting layer, drag the layer below the dividing line in the Layers panel (Figure 29.10).

Figure 29.10
The layer "logo-original" was dragged below the dividing line to become a nonprinting layer.

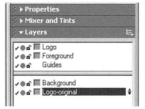

- **Keyline Mode**—FreeHand lets you change the preview for objects on each layer. This feature is typically used for working with complex illustrations such as 3D graphics. In Keyline mode only the outlines of objects are displayed.

To view a layer in Keyline mode, click the gray dot to the left of the layer name. This creates a hollow dot indicating that the layer is now in Keyline mode (see Figure 29.11).

Figure 29.11
The object on the right is displayed in Keyline mode.

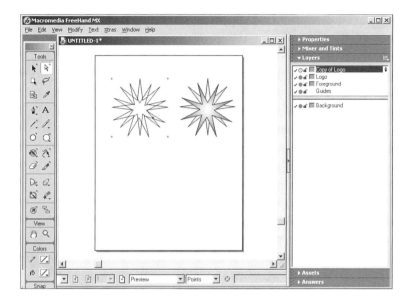

Click the hollow dot to return the layer to Preview mode.

ASSETS PANEL GROUP

The Assets Panel contains objects and settings that you would frequently use for a project: Swatches, Styles, and Library.

- **Swatches Panel**—The Swatches panel (Window, Swatches) lets you store, edit, and rename colors, as well as import and export custom color libraries (Figure 29.12). You can also convert spot colors to process colors and vice versa.

  You can create swatches by using the Eyedropper tool to drag a color from an object to the Swatches panel. You can also create a color in the Color Mixer and drag it to the Swatches panel.

- **Styles Panel**—The Styles panel (Window, Styles) displays the current text style and graphic style in your document (Figure 29.13). You can apply styles to text or graphics by simply dragging the style from the panel to the object. Likewise, you can create a graphic or text style on the document and drag it to the Styles panel to create a new style that you can use on other graphics or text.

Figure 29.12
The Swatches panel enables you to edit and store colors that you will frequently use in a project.

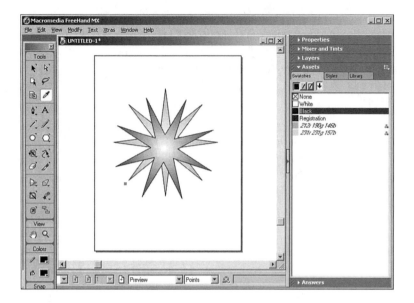

Figure 29.13
FreeHand comes packaged with several creative styles you can apply to objects.

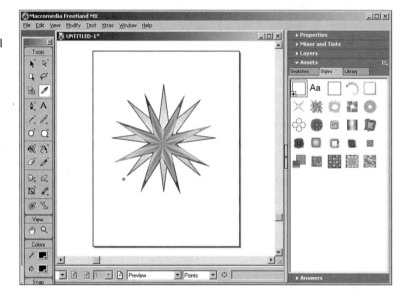

- **Library Panel**—The Library panel (Window, Library) stores master pages, brushes, and symbols that you can reuse throughout the document (Figure 29.14). Using the Library panel enables you to automate your work.

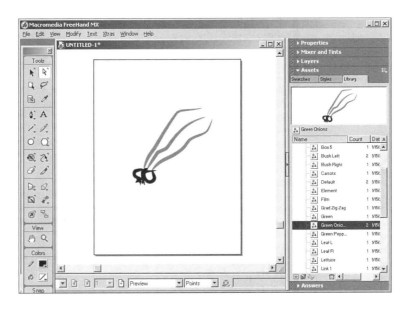

Figure 29.14
The Library panel provides dozens of library elements that you can use to increase your creativity and efficiency.

TOOLS UNIQUE TO FREEHAND MX

Many of the tools used in FreeHand are similar to tools found in other Studio MX programs. For instance, there is little variation in how the selection and drawing tools work between the programs. There are, however, a few "administrative" tools specific to FreeHand, as well as some fun creative tools discussed in the following sections.

PAGE TOOL

The Page tool is used to visually change the size of a page to create custom dimensions. Select the Page tool and click on the page you want to change. A set of handles appears around the page edges (Figure 29.15). Simply drag one of the arrows to change the page size. Note that although the page size changes, the size of your artwork does not.

If you work with a lot of custom page sizes, you can save those dimensions on your list of standard page sizes.

To add a custom page size to your list, follow these steps:

1. Select Edit from the bottom of the preset page size list in the Document panel.
2. The Edit Page Sizes dialog box appears. Click the New button to create a new page size.
3. Enter a name for your new page size.
4. Enter the new page dimensions. The horizontal size goes in the x field; the vertical size goes in the y field.
5. Click the Close button to close the dialog box.
6. Your new custom size now appears with the list of preset page sizes.

Figure 29.15
Use the Page tool to visually change the size of a document page.

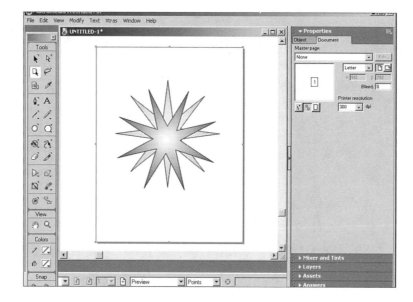

You can also use the Page tool to swap the horizontal and vertical orientation of your pages. Simply select the Page tool and click on the page you want to change. A set of handles appears on the edges of the page. Place your cursor on the outside of a handle so that a curved arrow will appear. Click and drag the handle to rotate the page. Note that the page can only be rotated in 90% increments: from portrait to landscape or from landscape to portrait.

The Page tool also allows you to duplicate pages. Select the Page tool and hold the Alt/Opt key as you drag the tool to duplicate a page (Figure 29.16). Release the mouse button when the new page appears.

The Page tool is also used to move and organize your pages when you are working with multiple pages. Using the Page tool, select a page and drag it to its new location. You can use this feature to change the order of your pages or their location in relation to each other.

OUTPUT AREA TOOL

The Output Area tool is used to define a single area of your document for export. To use this tool, simply select it from the toolbar and click and drag to define the area for export (see Figure 29.17). After you've defined the export area, you can resize or delete it. A nice feature in FreeHand is that the export area is saved as part of the document attributes when you save the document.

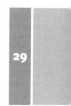

Figure 29.16
The Page tool can also be used to duplicate pages.

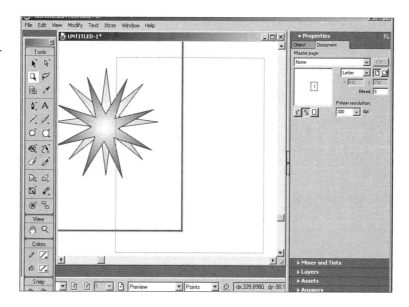

Figure 29.17
The Output Area tool is used to define an area for export.

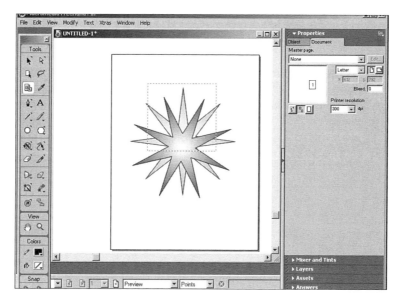

VARIABLE STROKE PEN TOOL

Located in the Pencil tool group, the Variable Stroke Pen tool allows you to draw lines that are both straight and curvy. This tool is designed to replicate a natural brush stroke (Figure 29.18). If you are using a pressure-sensitive tablet, any changes in the pressure you apply changes the thickness of the stroke. The more pressure you apply, the thicker the stroke. The less pressure you apply, the thinner the stroke. If you do not have a pressure-sensitive tablet, you can simulate pressure by using the left (decrease pressure) and right (increase pressure) arrow keys.

Figure 29.18
The Variable Stroke Pen tool replicates a natural brush stroke with the aid of a pressure-sensitive tablet or the left and right arrow keys.

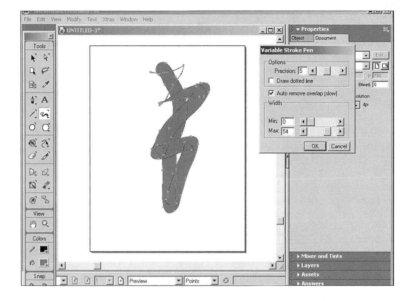

To set properties for your brush strokes, double-click the Variable Stroke Pen tool icon in the toolbar to open the Variable Stroke Pen dialog box. The Precision setting allows you to control how closely the tool follows the path you draw. Setting a low value smoothes out any minor variables as you draw. Setting a high value has your stroke follow any minor variables as you draw.

If you check the box for the Draw Dotted Line option, a dotted line appears if you draw too quickly. The dotted line is replaced by your variable stroke line after you have finished drawing the line. If your computer is having a hard time keeping up with you as you whip through lines, you should consider using this option.

The Auto Remove Overlap option eliminates any parts of the path that overlap (Figure 29.19).

You can also define the minimum and maximum width for your stroke from 1 to 72 points.

CALLIGRAPHIC PEN TOOL

Located in the Pencil tool group, the Calligraphic Pen tool is used to create lines that resemble calligraphic strokes (Figure 29.20). This tool is also pressure sensitive. Using a pressure-sensitive tablet, or the left and right arrow keys, you can alter the thickness of the stroke. Increasing the pressure (or using the right arrow key) increases the stroke's thickness. Decreasing the pressure (or using the left arrow key) decreases the stroke's thickness.

Figure 29.19
The figure on the right was drawn with the Auto Remove Overlap option selected.

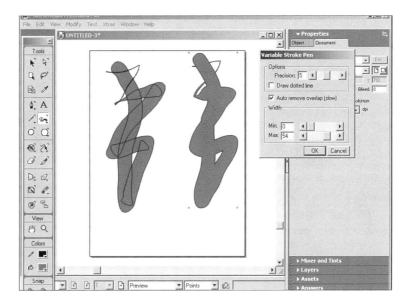

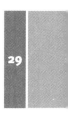

Figure 29.20
Use the Calligraphic Pen tool to create calligraphic strokes.

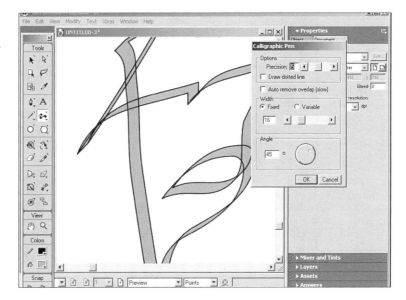

Double-click the Calligraphic Pen tool to open the Calligraphic dialog box. The Precision setting enables you to control how closely the tool will follow the path you draw. Setting a low value smoothes out any minor variables as you draw. Setting a high value has your stroke follow any minor variables as you draw.

If you check the box for the Draw Dotted Line option, a dotted line appears if you draw too quickly. The dotted line is replaced by your variable stroke line after you have finished drawing the line.

29

The Auto remove overlap option eliminates any parts of the path that overlap.

You can also define the minimum and maximum width for your stroke from 1 to 72 points.

Enter a value in the Angle field, or use the wheel, to set the angle for your stroke.

SPIRAL

As someone who has always been a Bezier-impaired individual, I feel that FreeHand's Spiral tool is the best invention since peanut butter and sliced bread. Located in the Line tool group, the Spiral tool gives you several options for creating spirals.

Double-click the Spiral tool to open the Spiral dialog box (Figure 29.21). You can select between a non-expanding spiral and an expanding type. The non-expanding spiral has lines that are evenly spaced. The expanding type increases the distance between lines as the spiral moves out from its center. If you select an expanding spiral, use the slider or enter a number in the Expansion field to change your spiral's properties. The higher the number, the greater the expansion rate.

Figure 29.21
Use the Spiral dialog box to control the attributes for your spiral.

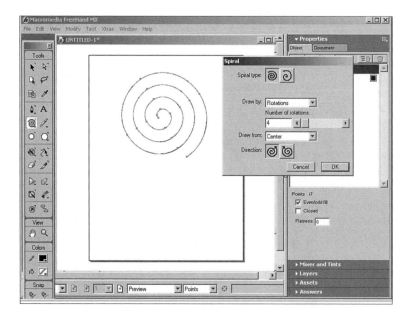

The Draw By List option lets you draw your spiral by specifying the number of rotations or the number of increments (the amount of space between lines in the non-expanding spiral or the starting radius in expanding spirals).

The Draw From List option enables you to draw your spiral starting from the Center, Edge, or Corner.

You can also change the direction of your spiral by selecting the Clockwise or Counterclockwise buttons.

ARC

Another drawing tool that prevents hair pulling is the Arc tool. As the name suggests, the Arc tool enables you to create a variety of arcs.

Located in the Line tool group, double-click the Arc tool to open the Arc dialog box (see Figure 29.22). Here you will find three settings for your arcs:

- Create Open Arc lets you create a simple arc.
- Create Flipped Arc enables you to reflect the arc from one direction to another.
- Create Concave Arc lets you create a...you guessed it...a concave arc.

Figure 29.22
The Arc dialog box lets you select three types of arcs to create.

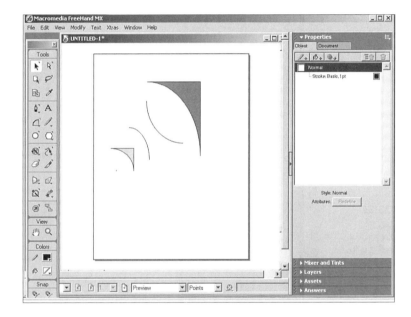

After you start drawing your arc, you can use the Cmd/Ctrl key to close or open the arc. Hold the Shift key to constrain your arc to quarter circles. Use the Opt/Alt key when you're drawing to flip the arc vertically or horizontally.

SCALE

The Scale tool allows you to resize an object. Select an object (or group of objects) and click anywhere on the current document to determine a scale center point, then drag to scale the selected object (Figure 29.23).

Hold the Shift key as you drag to scale an object proportionally. To copy the object as you scale it, hold the Opt/Alt key. The trick here is to release the mouse button first, then the Opt/Alt key, to create the copy.

Figure 29.23
Use the Scale tool to visually resize a selected object.

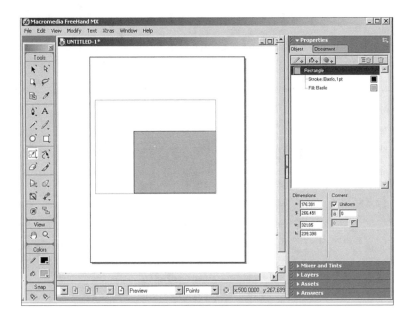

You can also scale an object by using the Transform Panel (Figure 29.24). Double-click the Scale tool to view the Transform Panel. In the Transform Panel, you can

Figure 29.24
Another way to numerically resize a selected object is to use the Transform Panel.

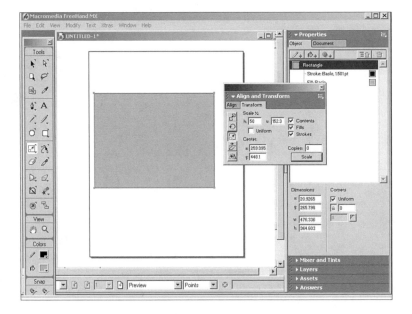

- Enter a percentage value that you want to change your object.
- Uncheck Uniform to adjust X and Y scaling independently.

- Adjust the horizontal scale by changing the X value.

- Adjust the vertical scale by changing the Y value.

- Change the point of transformation from the center of the object by entering coordinates in the x and y fields.

- Check Contents to include any items pasted inside the object.

- Check Fills to scale any fills.

- Check Strokes to scale the size of the stroke as the object is scaled.

- Enter the number of copies created of the scaled object.

ROTATE

The Rotate tool enables you to change the orientation of an object. Select an object (or group of objects) and click anywhere on the current document to determine a rotation center point, then drag to rotate the object (Figure 29.25). Hold the Shift key to constrain the rotation to 45° increments.

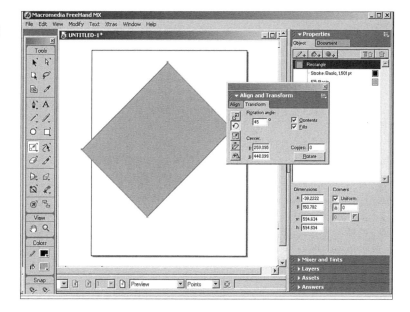

Figure 29.25
Use the Rotation tool to visually rotate an object.

The farther you drag your cursor away from the rotation point, the easier it will be to finesse the rotation.

You can also double-click the Rotate tool to view the Transformation palette (Figure 29.26), where you can

- Set the number of degrees for the rotation.
- Change the point of transformation from the center of the object by entering coordinates in the x and y fields.
- Check Contents to rotate any items pasted inside the object.
- Check Fills to rotate any fills inside the object.

Figure 29.26
Use the Transformation palette to numerically set the degrees of rotation.

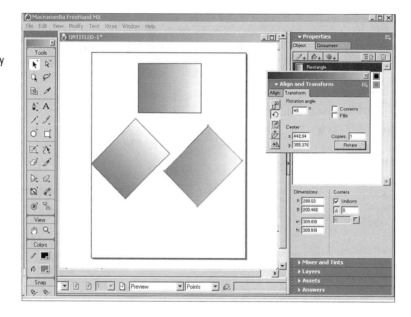

REFLECT

The Reflect tool enables you to create a mirror image of an object. Select an object (or group of objects) and click anywhere on the current document to determine a reflection center point, then drag to reflect the object (Figure 29.27). Hold the Shift key to constrain the rotation to 45° increments. Hold the Opt/Alt key to create a copy.

You can also double-click the Reflect tool to view the Transformation palette, where you can

- Enter the angle amount that you want to reflect around by using the Reflect Axis field.
- Change the point of transformation from the center of the object by entering coordinates in the x and y fields.
- Check Contents to reflect any items pasted inside the object.
- Check Fills to reflect any fills inside the object.
- Enter the number of copies created of the reflected object.

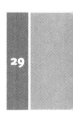

Figure 29.27
The Reflect tool is used to simplify the process of creating a mirror image of an object.

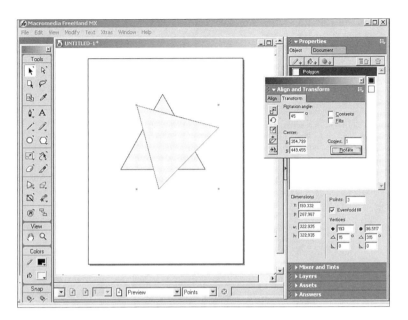

SKEW

The Skew tool enables you to distort an object along an axis. Select an object (or group of objects) and click anywhere on the current document to determine a skew center point, then drag to skew the object (Figure 29.28). Hold the Shift key to constrain the skew to either the horizontal or vertical axis, depending on which way you drag your cursor. Hold the Opt/Alt key to create a copy.

Figure 29.28
Use the Skew tool to distort an object to create the illusion of a third dimension.

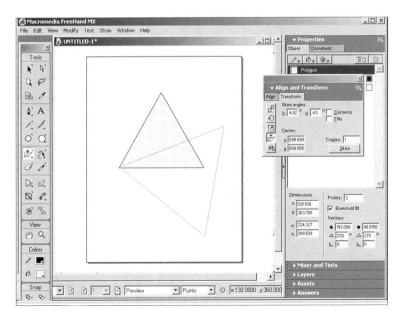

You can also double-click the Skew tool to view the Transformation palette, where you can

- Enter the horizontal and vertical angle amount that you want to skew.
- Change the point of transformation from the center of the object by entering coordinates in the x and y fields.
- Check Contents to skew any items pasted inside the object.
- Check Skew to reflect any fills inside the object.
- Enter the number of copies created of the skewed object.

FREEFORM

The Freeform tool is another gift for us Bezier-impaired individuals. Rather than adjusting points or handles, you can use the Freeform tool to basically knead your object like a piece of dough (Figure 29.29).

Figure 29.29
The object on the right used to look like the object on the left until the Freeform tool was put into play.

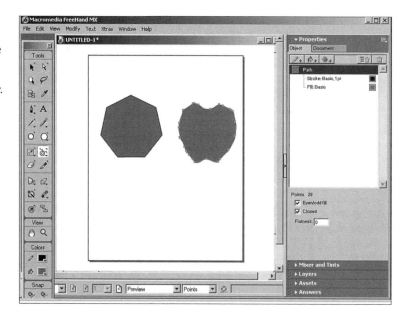

Double-click the Freeform tool to open the Freeform Tool dialog box (Figure 29.30). There are two modes you can use: Push/Pull and Reshape Area.

Select Push/Pull to change the shape of the object, but only the portion that you select. The Freeform Tool dialog box presents you with the following options:

Figure 29.30
Control how the
Freeform tool manip-
ulates an object with
the Freeform Tool dia-
log box.

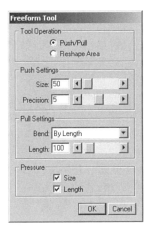

- Set the Size field (use the slider or enter a value between 1–1,000) to control the size of the area you are pushing.

- Set the Precision field (1–10) to control the sensitivity of the tool; the greater the value, the higher the sensitivity.

- Select one of two Pull settings: Bend By Length pulls will pull anywhere along a path; Bend Between Points will pull only between anchor points.

- Set the Length field to control how much the path will be altered.

- If you have a pressure-sensitive tablet, you can check the Size or Length boxes to control how pressure on the tablet affects the tool (Figure 29.31). You can also use the left arrow key to simulate a decrease in pressure and the right arrow key to simulate an increase in pressure.

Figure 29.31
The object on the
right was "cut" while
holding down the left
arrow key to simulate
a decrease in
pressure.

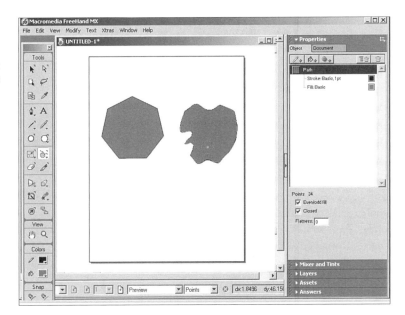

Select Reshape Area to change the shape of the object. This produces a result similar to that of the Push/Pull tool, except that the effect weakens as you drag the pointer. The Freeform Tool dialog box presents you with the following options:

- Set the Size field (use the slider or enter a value between 1–1,000) to control the size of the Reshape Area.

- Set the Strength field (1–50)to control how long the tool will work while you drag it.

- Set the Precision field (1–10) to control the sensitivity of the tool; the greater the value, the higher the sensitivity.

- If you have a pressure-sensitive tablet, you can check the Size or Length boxes to control how pressure on the tablet affects the tool. You can also use the left arrow key to simulate a decrease in pressure and the right arrow key to simulate an increase in pressure.

ROUGHEN

In spite of the name, the Roughen tool does not allow you to intimidate objects on your document. The Roughen tool lets you make smooth paths jagged and irregular (Figure 29.32).

Figure 29.32
The original object on the top and same object on the bottom after it has gone a few rounds with the Roughen tool.

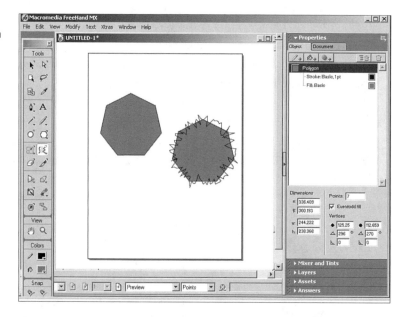

Double-click the Roughen tool to view the Roughen dialog box. Adjust the Amount field to control the number of segments per inch (1–100) that are added when you use the tool. Select a Rough edge to add corner points. Select Smooth edge to add curved points.

The farther you drag the tool, the greater the distortion.

BEND

The Bend tool enables you to warp, in or out, an object's path segments (Figure 29.33). The point where you start to drag becomes the center of the bend and the longer you drag, the more bend you create.

Figure 29.33
Use the Bend tool to distort an object as if you were pulling it like taffy.

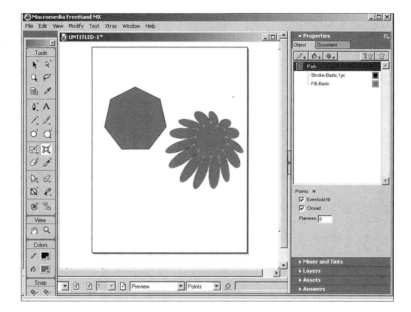

Double-click the Bend tool to open the Bend dialog box. Enter a value or adjust the slider (1–10) to select the number of points per inch that are added.

ERASER

Because FreeHand operates in a vector world, the Eraser tool cannot be used to remove pixels like in Fireworks. The Eraser tool operates by reshaping paths, rather than removing them (Figure 29.34).

Double-click the Eraser tool to view the Eraser Tool dialog box. Use the Min. and Max. fields to set the width of your eraser (1–72 points) if you are using a pressure-sensitive tablet. If you are not using a pressure-sensitive tablet, use the Min. value to change the size of your eraser.

Hold the Opt/Alt key as you drag to erase in a straight line. Hold the Opt/Alt + Shift keys to constrain the eraser in 0°, 45°, and 90° increments.

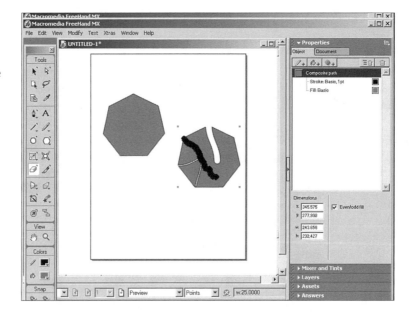

Figure 29.34
Note that the Eraser tool only reshapes paths as seen in the points created by the "erased" section on the left side of the object.

KNIFE TOOL

Use this tool to cut single objects into two or more objects. Select an object (or group of objects) and select the Knife Tool. Click and drag across the object to slice through it. After an object is sliced, deselect it to move portions separately.

Double-click the Knife tool to view the Knife Tool dialog box. Select the Freehand option to create curved or more natural cuts or the Straight option to create only straight-line cuts (Figure 29.35).

Set the Width (0–72 points) to control the space between cuts.

Select Close Cut Paths so that objects cut by the Knife tool are closed when you're finished cutting. Think of it as a self-healing wound. Select Tight Fit if you want the Knife tool to precisely follow your mouse movement.

Use the Opt/Alt key as you drag to temporarily make straight line cuts. Use the Shift key to constrain your cuts to 45° angles.

PERSPECTIVE TOOL

The Perspective tool is used to adjust the Perspective Grid (View, Perspective Grid, Show as seen in Figure 29.36)and to attach objects to the Perspective Grid. If you're not careful, you could be up to the wee hours of the morning just playing with the Perspective tool. It's addicting.

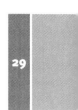

Figure 29.35
Using the knife tool to make (clockwise, starting with the top left object) freehand cuts, straight-line cuts, and freehand cuts with varying widths.

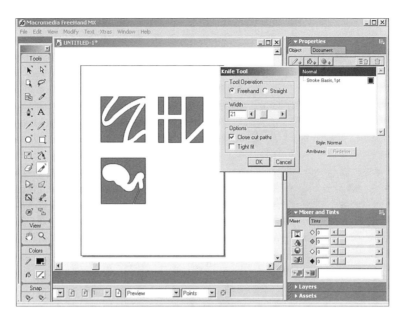

Figure 29.36
Use the Show command in the View menu to see the Perspective Grid.

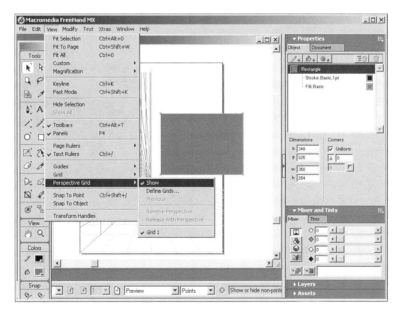

To attach an object to the Perspective Grid, use the Perspective tool to drag the object to a section of the grid. Before letting go of the mouse button, use one of the arrow keys to determine where the object is to be attached:

- Left arrow attaches the object to left grid.
- Right arrow attaches the object to the right grid.

- Down arrow attaches the object to the bottom grid, but lined up with the right vanishing point.

- Up arrow attaches the object to the bottom grid, but lined up with the left vanishing point.

The Perspective tool is also used to move objects along the Perspective grid (Figure 29.37). Hold the Opt/Alt key to copy an object while dragging it on the grid. Hold the Shift key to keep the object's movement within the grid axis.

Figure 29.37
Use the Perspective tool to move objects attached to the Perspective Grid.

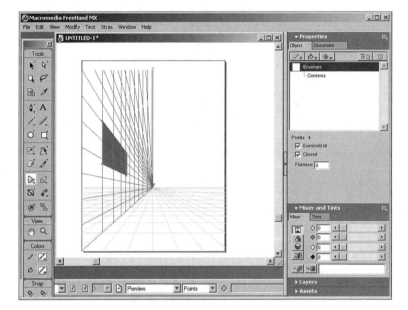

3D ROTATION TOOL

The 3D Rotation tool enables you to apply a three-dimensional rotation to a two-dimensional object. To use the 3D Rotation tool, select the object you want to modify. Choose the 3D Rotation tool, then click and drag the cursor away from the object (Figure 29.38). The farther you drag the line away from the object, the greater the rotation.

Double-click the 3D Rotation tool to view the 3D Rotation dialog box (Figure 29.39). Selecting Easy enables you to change the rotation and distance. The Rotate From Menu option enables you to choose where the rotation point will occur:

Figure 29.38
Use the 3D Rotation
tool make a 2D object
rotate in the third
dimension.

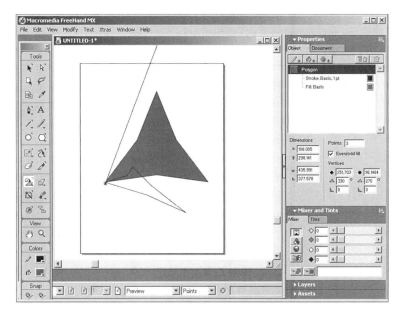

29

Figure 29.39
Change rotation set-
tings in the 3D
Rotation dialog box.

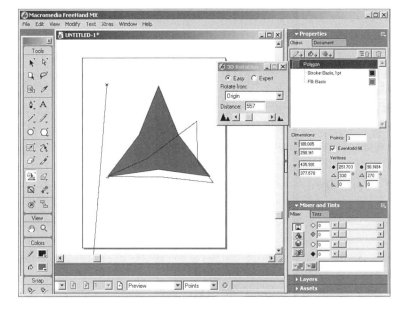

- A mouse click sets the pivot point to the position where you click.
- Center of Selection sets the pivot point to the center of the object.
- Center of Gravity sets the pivot point to the center of an uneven-shaped object.
- Origin sets the pivot point to the bottom-left corner of the object's bounding box.

Selecting the Expert button displays more controls (see Figure 29.40). The Project From Menu option enables you to set the projection point, or vanishing point:

Figure 29.40
Check the Expert button in the dialog box to view more controls for the 3D Rotation tool.

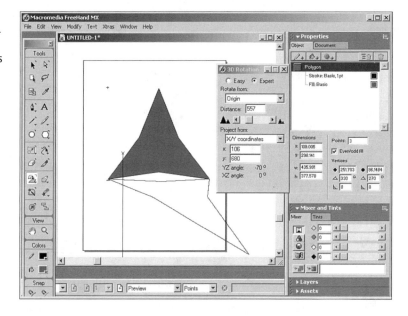

- A mouse click sets the projection point to the position where you click.
- Center of Selection sets the projection point to the center of the object.
- Center of gravity sets the projection point to the center of an uneven-shaped object.
- Origin sets the pivot point to the bottom-left corner of the object's bounding box.
- X/Y coordinates set the projection points from the coordinates you input.

FISHEYE LENS TOOL

The Fisheye Lens tool enables you to create a concave or convex lens effect for your object (Figure 29.41). Select the object you want to modify. If you want to modify text, make sure you have converted the text to paths (Text, Convert to Paths) first. Select the Fisheye Lens tool and drag the cursor to create an oval over the area you want to distort. Use the Opt/Alt key to create a distortion from the center outward. Use the Shift key to constrain the distortion to a circular shape. Release the mouse button to apply the effect.

Double-click the Fisheye Lens tool to open the Fisheye Lens dialog box (Figure 29.42). Enter a value in the Perspective field or use the slider to alter the perspective from Convex (positive numbers) to Concave (negative numbers) .

Figure 29.41
Use the Fisheye Lens tool to distort objects as if they were viewed through a camera's fisheye lens.

Figure 29.42
The Fisheye Lens dialog contains the settings to control the distortion effect.

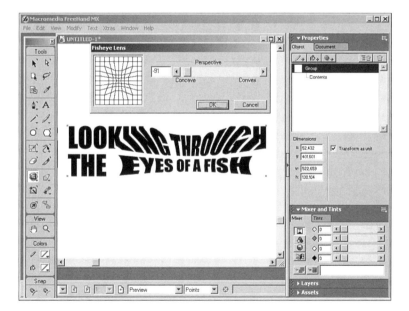

EXTRUDE TOOL

Another extremely addictive tool is the Extrude tool. This sophisticated tool lets you take a 2-D object and project it into a 3-D object. There are several actions you can do with this tool to extrude an object.

To extrude an object, use the Extrude tool to drag in the direction of the extrusion (Figure 29.43). As long as you keep the mouse button depressed, you can increase the depth and angle of the extrusion.

Figure 29.43
Use the Extrude tool to project objects into the realm of 3D.

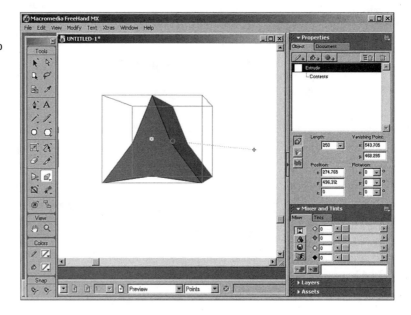

To change the extruded object's orientation, double-click the object with the Extrude tool to enable the orientation controls (Figure 29.44). Drag inside the orientation circle to change the horizontal or vertical orientation; drag outside the orientation circle to change the depth.

Use the Object panel to control the extrusion numerically. Select the Extrude icon to display the numerical equivalents of the modification fields that you can set by eye with the Extrude tool (Figure 29.45).

The Object panel also lets you control the following Surface options by selecting the Surface button:

- Select Flat to apply the surface color with no lighting effects.
- Select Shaded to apply a shaded lighting effect.
- Select Wireframe to display a transparent wireframe of the object.
- Select Mesh to display polygons as the transparent structure of the object.
- Select Hidden Mesh to show the exterior polygons as well as the fill for the object.

Set the number of Steps to increase (higher value) or decrease (lower value) the smoothness of the shading.

Figure 29.44
Using the orientation controls, you can rotate the extruded object along three axes (x, y, and z).

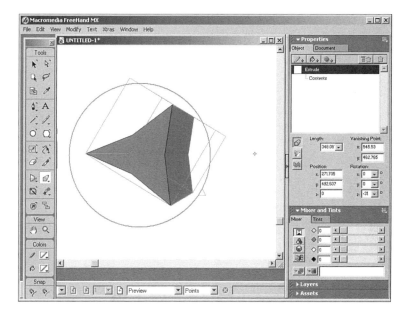

Figure 29.45
You can also rotate an extruded object by entering values in the Object panel.

Use the Ambient control to increase or decrease the amount of light on the extruded object.

Use the Light 1 and Light 2 settings to control the direction and intensity of lighting sources for your object.

With all these controls, you can see how addictive it can be to create extrusions. FreeHand has given us a very powerful tool where apparently the only limits are your imagination.

Smudge Tool

The Smudge tool enables you to add a soft edge to an object. Select the object that you want to modify and then select the Smudge tool. Your cursor changes into the Smudge fingers. Drag the fingers in the direction you want the smudge to go. Release the mouse button to create the smudge.

Hold the Opt/Alt key to create a smudge from the center outward.

Double-click the Smudge tool to open the Smudge dialog box (Figure 29.46). Drag colors from the Swatches panel or the Color Mixer into the Fill and Stroke boxes to change the smudge colors.

Figure 29.46
Use the Smudge tool to smudge the edges of an object to create the appearance of a drop shadow.

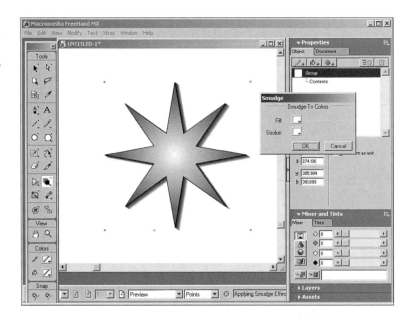

The number of steps in your smudge is determined by the printer resolution in the Document Inspector. To create a smoother smudge effect, increase the printer resolution.

Shadow Tool

Very similar to the Smudge tool, the Shadow tool lets you create sophisticated shadows.

Select the object you want to modify. Double-click the Shadow tool to open the Shadow dialog box (Figure 29.47). From the Type menu:

Figure 29.47
The Shadow tool dialog box enables you to control how the shadow is applied to the object.

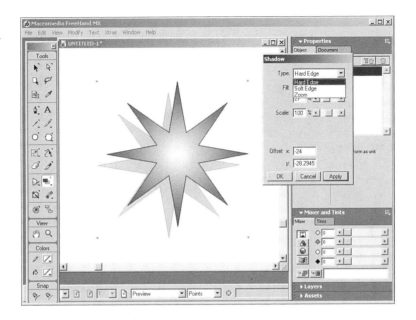

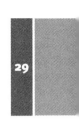

- Select Hard Edge to apply a single object as a shadow.
- Select Soft Edge to apply a blend shadow.
- Select Zoom to apply a blend that is placed to create a 3D effect.

From the Fill menu (Figure 29.48),

Figure 29.48
The Fill menu lets you control the attributes of the shadow's fill color.

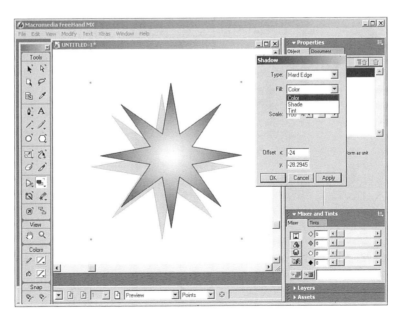

- Select Color to choose a specific color for the shadow.
- Select Shade to create a shadow color that is darker than the original object.
- Select Tint to create a shadow color that is lighter than the original object.
- Use the slider to adjust the lightness or darkness of the shadow.

Set the x and y Offset amounts to determine the shadow's position.

TRACE TOOL

If you've ever had to re-create someone's logo from a business card or a facsimile copy of letterhead, then you're going to love FreeHand's Trace tool. After you've scanned the artwork and imported (File, Import) it into your document, you can use the Trace tool to recognize the shapes in the artwork and convert them into vector paths.

Before you start tracing, you need to double-click the Trace tool to open the Trace tool dialog box so you can get your settings squared away (Figure 29.49). The dialog box lets you set the following properties:

Figure 29.49
The Trace tool dialog box offers several ways to control the accuracy of your tracing.

- **Color Mode**—Select the number of colors or shades of grays (2-256) and between Colors or Gray for the final tracing. If you selected colors, you then have the option of selecting RGB or CMYK color models.
- **Resolution**—Select High resolution to capture the most details, Normal to capture fewer details, and Low to capture the fewest details.

- **Trace layers**—Select All to use all the document layers, Foreground to use only the foreground layers, and Background to use only the background layers.

- **Path conversion**—Select Outline to trace the outside border of the artwork, Centerline to trace the center of the artwork, Centerline/Outline to use both options, and Outer Edge to trace only the outside edge of the artwork.

- **Path overlap**—Select None to trace line art and text, Loose to trace continuous-tone images, or Tight for more precise color tracing.

- **Trace Conformity**—Set a value to determine how closely the traced path will follow the original artwork. Values can range from 0 (less conformity with fewer points) to 10 (greater conformity with more points).

- **Noise Tolerance**—Set a value to eliminate noise, or stray pixels, in a low-quality original (like the facsimile letterhead logo!). Values can range from 0 (more noise retained) to 20 (more noise eliminated).

- **Wand Color Tolerance**—Adjust the slider to control the sensitivity when selecting areas of contiguous colors. Values can range from 0 (narrower range of colors selected) to 255 (wider range of colors selected).

After you've selected your settings, use the Trace tool to drag a selection marquee around the portion of the image to be traced. FreeHand traces it automatically.

Blend Tool

The Blend tool lets you create a transition between two or more paths (Figure 29.50). You can create a blend between two or more identical shapes where only the color changes or two or more different shapes to make one object change its shape and/or color to another object; you can also create a blend to distribute objects by blending one object to a copy of itself.

Select two or more objects that you want to blend. Choose the Blend tool and drag from one object to another. The intermediate steps between the two objects will be displayed. Release the mouse button to complete the blend.

To add another object to the blend, use the Blend tool to drag from the blended objects to the new object, or vice versa.

To change the number of steps in a blend, use the blend controls that appear in the Objects panel (Figure 29.51).

Note that you can also select and move any of the transitional shapes by using the Modify, Ungroup command to ungroup the shapes. Use the Subselect tool to select the transitional shape you want to move.

Figure 29.50
The Blend tool is used to "morph" one object into another.

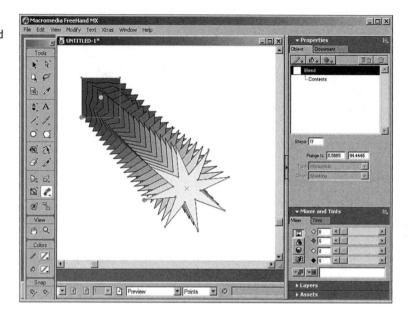

Figure 29.51
The Object panel displays blend controls when the blended objects are selected.

MIRROR TOOL

The Mirror tool lets you create multiple reflected and rotated objects (Figure 29.52). Double-click the Mirror tool to view the Mirror dialog box, where you can choose the axis upon which the reflection takes place:

Figure 29.52
The Mirror tool is used to create a mirror image of a selected object.

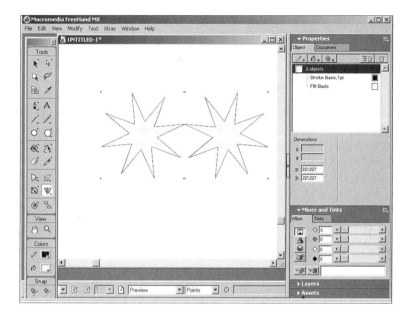

29

- Vertical reflects the object from left to right.
- Horizontal reflects the object from top to bottom.
- Horizontal & Vertical reflects the object along both vertical and horizontal axes.
- Multiple reflects the object around multiple axes. By selecting Multiple, you can use the slider to control the number of axes around which the object will reflect, as well as select Rotate or Reflect.

The preview area shows you how each setting will affect your object.

GRAPHIC HOSE TOOL

Although oddly named in my opinion, the Graphic Hose tool is an interesting tool that lets you paint with stored objects. Stored objects are located in the Graphic Hose panel (Figure 29.53).

Before you start "hosing" the document, you'd better modify some settings so you know what graphics you'll be using. Double-click the Graphic Hose tool to open the Graphic Hose panel (Figure 29.54). Select the Options radio button to display the Options controls.

Control the order in which the objects are placed on the page with the Order menu:

Figure 29.53
The Graphic Hose tool enables you to paint nifty effects using stored objects.

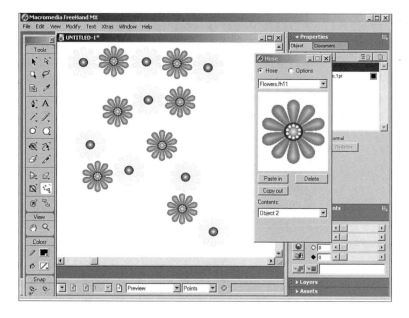

Figure 29.54
Use the Graphic Hose panel to determine how stored objects are displayed on the page when you're painting with the Graphic Hose tool.

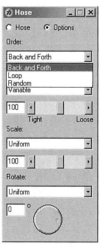

- Loop applies the objects in numerical order.

- Back and Forth applies the objects in forward, then reverse order.

- Random applies the objects in no particular order.

Control the distance between objects with the Spacing menu (Figure 29.55):

Figure 29.55
The Spacing menu enables you to control the amount of space between objects used in the Graphic Hose tool.

- Grid spaces the objects onto a grid as determined by the Grid field.
- Variable spaces the objects in either a Tight or Loose setting.
- Random spaces the objects as the Computer Gods dictate.

Control the size of the objects with the Scale menu (Figure 29.56):

Figure 29.56
Choose between Uniform or Random size of the Graphic Hose objects.

- Uniform sets a certain size for all objects.
- Random once again lets the Computer Gods dictate the size.

Control the rotation of the objects with the Rotate menu and angle wheel (see Figure 29.57):

Figure 29.57
Select one of three rotation controls to apply to the Graphic Hose objects.

- Uniform sets one angle for all objects.

- Incremental applies rotations in specific increments from one object to the next.

- Random rotates the objects with complete disregard for authority. Chaos could ensue so please use this setting with caution.

Although you can have some fun with the FreeHand-supplied Clovers, Flowers, Leaves, and Shapes, the real fun starts when you create your own Graphic Hose objects.

Objects used in the Graphic Hose are stored in sets. For example, one set could include one blue circle, one red square, and yellow star. A set could also include just one object.

Draw the objects you want to put in the set and then double-click the Graphic Hose tool to open the Graphic Hose panel. Click Hose to display the Hose sets. Choose New from the Sets menu to add a new set. A dialog box appears, giving you the opportunity to name your set (Figure 29.58).

Copy the first object and click the Paste In button on the Graphic Hose panel. Continue to Copy and Paste In as necessary to complete your set. You are limited to 10 objects for each set.

CHART TOOL

As the name implies, the Chart tool lets you create charts. To create a chart, select the Chart tool, click a starting point on the document and drag to set the initial size of the chart.

The Chart dialog box automatically appears (Figure 29.59) and lets you start entering data in the cells. You can also Import data from other tab-delimited data sources.

Figure 29.58
You can create custom Graphic Hose objects by copying and pasting objects into the Graphic Hose panel.

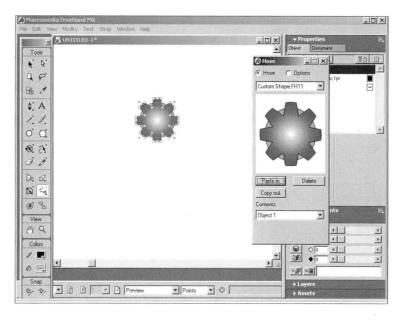

Figure 29.59
Use the Chart dialog box to enter data for your chart.

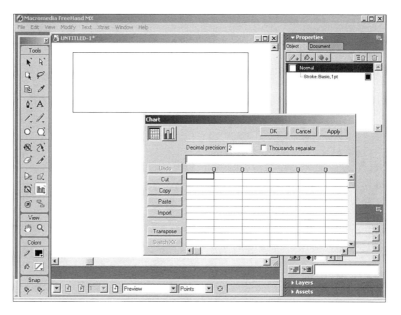

Select the Chart Type button to select one of the following chart types (Figure 29.60):

Figure 29.60
The Chart Type window in the Chart dialog box lets you select from six types of charts.

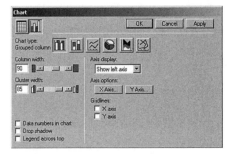

- Grouped Column to compare data using bars. Each bar represents one cell of data.

- Stacked Column to compare the contribution of each value to a total across categories. Each bar represents a row of data.

- Line to show a trend over a period of time. Each line represents a column of data.

- Pie to display data in a circular graph with slices. Each cell of data represents a single slice. Each row of data produces a pie chart.

- Area to display filled areas representing the progress of data over time. This is a cousin to the Stacked Column. Each area represents a column of data in the worksheet. Each column's value is added to the previous column's total.

- Scatter to plot data as paired sets of coordinates to identify trends in data. Each coordinate represents a row of data containing two cells.

In FreeHand, each chart is treated as a series of grouped objects. Ungroup the chart (Modify, Ungroup) to edit individual chart elements such as stroke, fill, scale, and so on. Note that after you ungroup the chart, you can no longer go back and edit the data.

You can apply Pictographs to replace the standard chart bars or lines with an image. Select and copy the FreeHand graphic you'd like to use, then use the Subselect tool to select a column in the chart. Select Xtras, Chart, Pictograph to view the Pictograph dialog box. Click Paste In to place your graphic in the preview window (Figure 29.61).

Check the Repeated check box to fill the columns with repeating copies of your graphic. Uncheck the Repeating check box to fill the column with one scaled object.

ACTION TOOL

The Action tool enables you to apply actions to objects, such as creating links to other pages in the FreeHand document, printing a target page, and loading a target page as a movie (Figure 29.62).

Figure 29.61
Pictographs are used to replace standard chart elements with custom graphics.

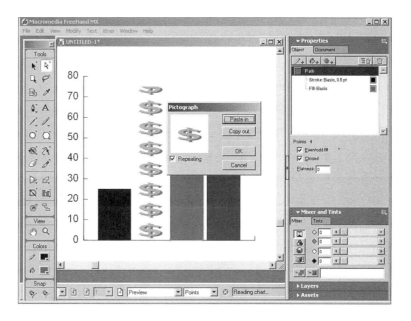

Figure 29.62
You can use the Action tool to create a page link.

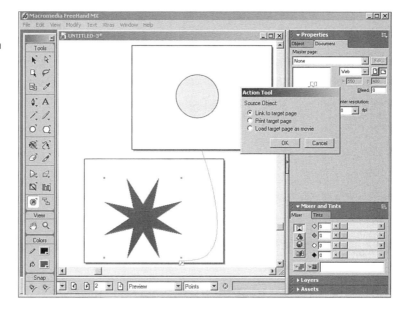

➔ For more on using the Action Tool, **see** Chapter 30, "Using FreeHand in Web Site Planning and Creation," **page 852**.

CONNECTOR TOOL

FreeHand's Connector tool is a fantastic aid for those burdened with creating graphical site maps or organizational charts (Figure 29.63). The Connector tool creates lines that stay

29

connected to objects, no matter where you move them. You can also reshape and move your connector lines after they're drawn.

Figure 29.63
The Connector tool creates dynamic lines that stay glued to objects no matter where you move them.

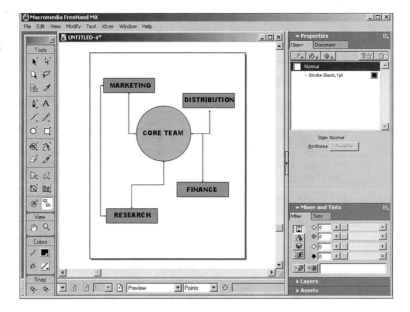

To use the Connector tool, you need to have at least two objects on your document. Select the Connector tool and position the cursor near the side, top, or bottom of the object where you want the connection to begin. Click and drag toward the side, top, or bottom of your second object that you want to connect.

FreeHand automatically places arrowheads on the beginning and end of the connector line. You can modify these lines by using the Stroke Controls in the Objects Panel.

After you have connected your objects, you can rearrange those objects and the connector lines will still stay attached. You can reshape the connector line by placing the cursor over the line. A plus sign and a double-headed arrow appear. Simply drag the cursor to reshape the connector line (see Figure 29.64).

→ For more on using the Connector Tool, **see** Chapter 30, **page 837**.

TOOLBARS UNIQUE TO FREEHAND MX

As a powerful vector-based illustration tool, FreeHand offers the designer some extra, or Xtra, goodies to use during the design process. Xtras are plug-in software extensions developed by Macromedia and third-party companies that expand FreeHand's capabilities.

Xtras included with FreeHand are automatically installed with the software. You can install additional Xtras by dragging the Xtra file into the Xtras folder, which is located in your

FreeHand MX application folder. To remove Xtras, drag the file out of the Xtras folder. Restart FreeHand when you are finished for the install/remove to take effect.

Figure 29.64
Connector lines can be reshaped even though they've been attached to an object.

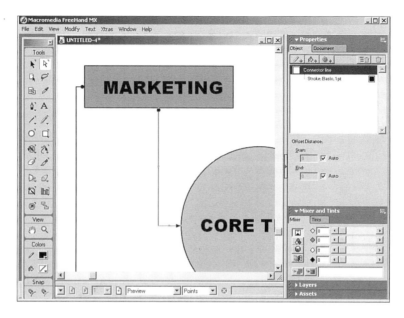

Xtra Operations Toolbar

The Xtra Operations toolbar (Window, Toolbars, Xtra Operations) contains the following tools (Figure 29.65):

Figure 29.65
The Xtra Operations toolbar contains frequently used menu commands in an easy-to-use toolbar format.

- Crop removes portions of selected, closed paths.
- Inset Path creates a new path, following the contour of a closed path at a given distance.
- Expand Stroke converts an open path to a closed path.
- Union combines two or more closed paths into a single path.
- Divide cuts selected paths into sections defined by the areas of overlap.
- Punch removes portions of selected, closed paths.

29

- Intersect creates a path enclosed by the area common to all selected, closed paths.
- Blend creates a transition between two or more paths with respect to shape, stroke, and fill.

→ For more on Blends, **see** "Blend Tool," **page 821**, earlier in this chapter.

- Simplify reduces the number of points in a path.
- Remove Overlap removes overlapping portions of a closed path that crosses over itself.
- Reverse Direction reverses the path's direction.
- Closed paths have one of two directions: clockwise or counterclockwise. When a clockwise path meets a counterclockwise path, these paths yield a transparent, overlapping section in a composite path. When two closed paths of the same direction overlap, these paths yield a filled, overlapping section. If your composite path's overlapping fill does not behave as expected, use the Correct Direction command to alter the path.
- Trap enables you to set color trapping standards.
- Fractalize applies an orderly, geometrical transformation to a path.
- Release to Layers ungroups text, text blocks, groups, blends, or objects attached to a path; creates a new layer for each object; and assigns each ungrouped object to a new layer in consecutive order. This is handy for creating animations in FreeHand.
- Emboss creates a 3D appearance, where the edges of an object are raised or lowered so it appears to be embossed into the background.
- Add Points adds points halfway between every pair of points on a path.

XTRA TOOLS

The Xtra Tools toolbar contains the following tools, which are explained more fully elsewhere in this chapter (Figure 29.66):

Figure 29.66
The Xtra Tools toolbar contains frequently used commands in a convenient toolbar.

- Chart (see page 826)
- Arc (see page 801)
- Spiral (see page 800)
- Roughen (see page 808)
- Bend (see page 809)

29

- 3D Rotation (see page 812)
- Fisheye Lens (see page 814)
- Smudge (see page 818)
- Shadow (see page 818)
- Mirror (see page 822)
- Graphic Hose (see page 823)
- Action Tool (see page 828)

ENVELOPE TOOLBAR

The Envelope toolbar enables you to distort text and other objects within an outer boundary, or envelope. The Envelope toolbar contains 21 preset shapes that you can use (Figure 29.67).

Figure 29.67
The Envelope toolbar contains tools used for distorting objects within an envelope.

To apply an envelope to a graphic, select the object or text you want to modify. Select the envelope preset you want from the Envelope toolbar menu and click the Create Envelope icon to modify the selected object (Figure 29.68).

Figure 29.68
Using an envelope creates an imaginary border where text or objects are forced to match the envelope's shape.

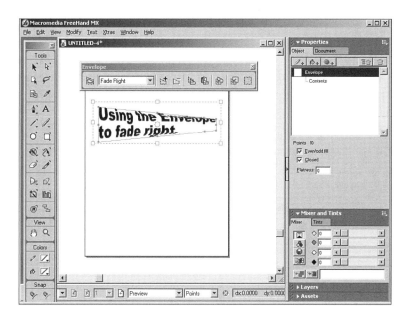

You can use other tools (Scale, Subselect, Freeform, and so on) to modify the preset shape after the effect has been applied.

TROUBLESHOOTING

CHANGING THE SNAP TO THRESHOLD

I'm having trouble changing Snap to Guides in (Edit, Preferences). I can change it up to a threshhold of 3 pixels but nothing beyond that. Is there a setting I am missing?

The Snap Distance cannot exceed the Pick Distance. The Pick Distance refers to how closely you must click to an object for it to be selected. Change both settings to a larger value and your new Snap Distance will be accepted.

REARRANGING TOOLS

I have a particular way I like to work with FreeHand's tools since I commonly use only a few of them. Is there a way I can re-arrange the Toolbox?

Although you can float the Toolbox vertically or horizontally anywhere on your monitor, FreeHand's new tool groupings are designed to make tool selection more convenient. For example, the most common transformation tools--Scale, Skew, Rotate, and Mirror--are all located in one group. If you want to see all four of those tools without clicking and holding the Scale tool icon, rearrange what's visible in the Toolbox by selecting (Window, Toolboxes, Customize). Arrange the tool icons to fit your tastes.

MISSING TOOLBARS

My Toolbox has disappeared. I go to the Windows menu and select Tools, but nothing happens. This is driving me crazy. Help!

This is unfortunately a fairly common experience with FreeHand. When people start customizing their workspace the Toolbox can pull a Jimmy Hoffa and disappear from your screen. This happens when the Toolbox is moved off the screen or the settings file that remembers the location of the toolbar has been corrupted.

To resolve this issue, take a close look at your screen to see if there is a small edge of the Toolbox peeking out. If you see it, try and drag the Toolbox back on the screen. If that doesn't work, you'll have to delete the Toolbox settings profile, but Exit or Quit FreeHand before trying this option:

- **Windows**—C:\Documents and Settings\[username]\Application Data\ Macromedia\FreeHandMX\11\English\Settings\ToolBars\Tools.set
- **Macintosh OS X**—[harddrive] > Users > [username] > Library > Macromedia > FreeHand MX > 11 > English > Settings > Toolbars > Toolbars
- **Macintosh OS 9**—[harddrive] > System Folder > Application Support > Macromedia > FreeHand MX > 11 > English > Settings > Toolbars > Toolbars

If that still doesn't work, delete the Applications preferences. Again, Exit or Quit FreeHand before trying this option:

- **Windows**—C:\Documents and Settings\[username]\Application Data\Macromedia\ FreeHand MX\11\English\Settings\FHprefs.txt

- **Macintosh OS X**—[harddrive] > Users > [username] > Library > Macromedia > FreeHand MX > 11 > English > Settings > Preferences

- **Macintosh OS 9**—[harddrive] > System Folder > Application Support > Macromedia > FreeHand MX > 11 > English > Settings > Preferences

Using FreeHand in Web Site Planning and Creation

In this chapter

Site Architecture   838

Site Design   845

In this chapter we'll take a look at how you can use FreeHand to plan, organize and design Web sites. Although FreeHand is perhaps best known for its ability to work in the print medium, it can be a powerful illustration and presentation tool for the Web.

It's not common for FreeHand to be used to design functioning Web pages. However, the program steps into the spotlight when it comes time to designing and preparing Web site concepts and mock-ups.

Creating Web sites can be an exhilarating process. Typically, site designs begin as a pure mental process. Visions of brilliant graphics and innovative architecture begin to form as a series of images and colors in your brain. Some designers then start doodling with ideas and roughing out concepts on paper. Others may start with a more mechanical approach and build a framework to organize information first before any interface design is considered.

This is all swell until the design goes from concept to reality. In other words, that beautifully-rendered cocktail napkin sketch turns to mush as soon as you try and construct it in Dreamweaver. The fun has now been replaced with tedious experimentation on making your design work…and that's just for the Home page.

Working with larger sites adds an entire new level of complexity to the process. You've gone from the role of a free-spirited designer to a logic-constrained manager of information. Fortunately, FreeHand MX provides the perfect tool to not only design, or conceptualize, a Web site with its powerful design tools, but it also lets you organize the site with the creation of visual site maps and multi-page documents.

Because FreeHand works so well with the other MX Suite products, your designs and pages can be easily imported into Fireworks MX. As soon as you're there, you can slice and dice the design and roll it over to Dreamweaver MX for final construction.

SITE ARCHITECTURE

A Web site's architecture relates to how information is presented to an audience. Creating a good site architecture will save you a lot of "Oops, I forgot that!" curses while building the site.

Although the purpose of this chapter is not to delve into the arcane science of site design, it does cover some basic concepts as you learn how to use FreeHand to maximize your designs.

CREATE A SITE MAP WITH THE CONNECTOR TOOL

First things first. It's helpful to create a preliminary site map to minimize the chances for creating a confusing navigation system. Although this can be accomplished in Dreamweaver, the site map that is created is typically not suitable for presentations to clients or anyone else that will need to see and approve your concept (Figure 30.1). This is where FreeHand comes into play.

Figure 30.1
Dreamweaver's site map is great for the designer, but is not the best way to show a client a site map.

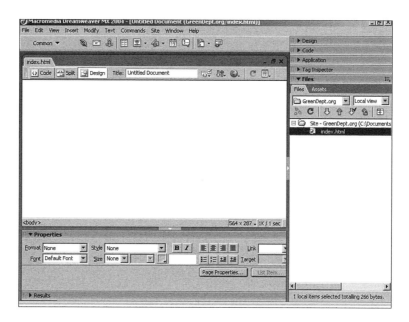

30

For our purposes, we will create a site map for greendept.org, a case study that is being used elsewhere in this book. This site will cater to people who want to find information on anything and everything ecological—environmentally friendly products, services, and events.

Based on the information provided by the client, we know they want to have the following categories showcased on the site:

- Home
- Search
- Log-In
- Events
- About Us
- Contact Us

Create a new document (File, New). Before you start drawing, go ahead and save the file (File, Save) and name it "sitemap."

Start your site map by rendering the top level of the site, which is usually several pages, and includes the home page. Use the Rectangle tool to draw a page icon. Select a fill and stroke. Next, select the Text tool and create a label, "Home," as shown in Figure 30.2.

Figure 30.2
Create a home page icon for the site map by using the Rectangle tool.

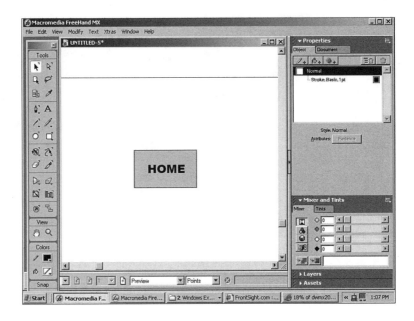

To create page icons for these navigation elements, simply duplicate the Home page icon. Use the Select tool to draw a marquee around the Home page icon to include the rectangle and text block. Copy these objects by using the Copy command (Edit, Copy) and then Paste (Edit, Paste). Use the Select tool to reposition the duplicate icon (Figure 30.3).

Figure 30.3
Duplicate the Home icon by using the Copy command.

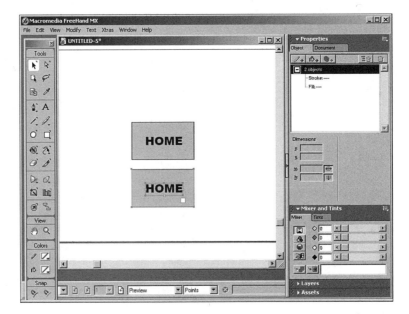

Then use the Type tool to rename the label from "Home" to "Search". Rinse and repeat to create page icons for the remaining main navigation elements, as shown in Figure 30.4.

Figure 30.4
Duplicate the original "Home" page icon and edit the text label until you have your top navigation level represented.

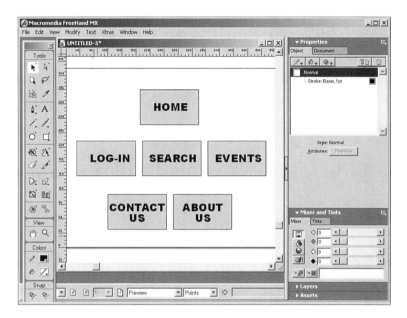

Use the Connector tool to indicate links between the page icons. The Connector tool creates lines that will automatically stay connected to objects. In this case, the objects are the page icons. The beauty of using the Connector tool at this stage of the site design is that you don't have to redraw connections (links) every time there is a change to the structure. This is what makes the Connector tool an ideal site mapping device during the fluid conceptualization process.

To connect the page icons, select the Connector tool from the panel. Position your cursor near the bottom of the "Home" page icon. A small circle appears, indicating that you can begin to draw your connector line. Drag toward the top of the Search page icon. Release the mouse when you see the small circle appear on the cursor once again. The connector line automatically appears, as shown in Figure 30.5. You've just created a visual "link" between your pages.

After you've repeated the process and created links from your Home page icon to all other top-level page icons (Search, Log-In, Events, About Us, Contact Us), you should have a page that looks something like Figure 30.6.

30

Figure 30.5
Use the Connector
tool to create a
dynamic connection
between your page
icons.

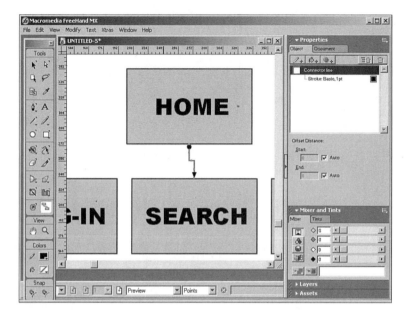

Figure 30.6
The "connected"
site map.

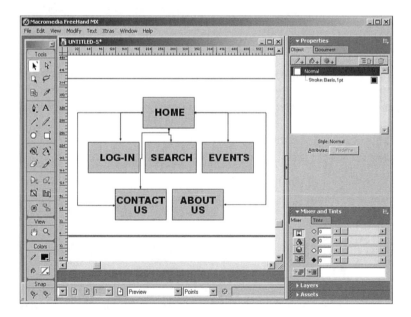

Here's where the magic happens. Go ahead and reposition your page icons and watch the connector lines magically follow your every move. Set up an arrangement that is visually appealing to you (Figure 30.7).

Figure 30.7
When you reposition objects that are connected, the connector lines are automatically redrawn.

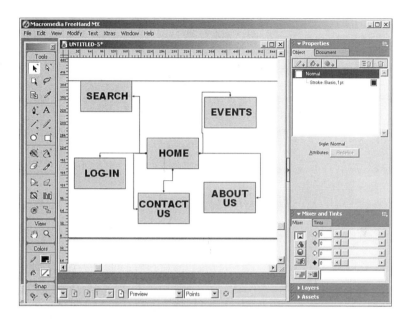

If you don't like the direction your arrows are going between objects, you can reverse the direction. Select the connector line with either of the selection tools or the Connector tool. Use the Reverse Direction command (Modify, Alter Path, Reverse Direction). The arrowhead and the default "ball" are reversed.

Because you are working in the wonderful world of the Web, however, you won't be creating one-way links. Your pages should show that that the links work both ways. This is best accomplished by using an arrowhead at each end of the connector line. Select any existing connector line. In the Objects panel, select Connector Line to view the line's properties. Using either drop-down menu, you can select an arrowhead for either end of the connector line (Figure 30.8).

The second level in a site architecture contains the pages you navigate to by going "down from" the top-level pages.

In this example, a top-level page called Events would have second-level pages that go into more detail about each of the events, as well as provide links to a calendar of future events, as shown in Figure 30.9.

Figure 30.8
Use the Objects panel to change the appearance of your connector lines.

Figure 30.9
Use your second-level pages to show more detail about subtopic content.

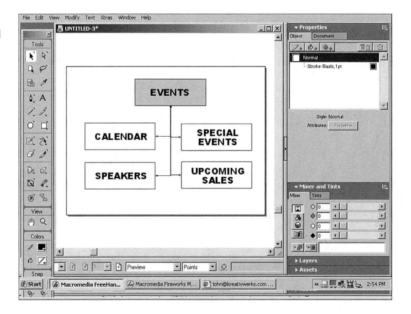

Having a second-level navigation scheme is important so you don't have to go up to the top level just to see the other choices in the same second level you're in.

SITE DESIGN

If you've created a working site outline, as detailed in the previous section, you can now start working on designing your site. This is where FreeHand MX really begins to shine for working with Web graphics. Typically, Fireworks MX is used to create site composites (or "comps"). The final image is then sliced and moved over to Dreamweaver MX, where it is posted online.

If you're working with a large site, you will be rendering several designs for the major pages and a variety of sub-topic pages. The key to keeping your sanity is to use FreeHand MX and Fireworks MX to model your site. In this section, we'll take a look at using FreeHand MX and its feature that allows us to create multi-page documents that are located in one file. This file can then be efficiently imported from FreeHand MX into Fireworks MX where you can prep the image (optimize and slice) for use in Dreamweaver MX.

CREATE A MULTIPAGE DOCUMENT

There are a few methods of creating a multipage document in FreeHand MX. You can use the Page tool to create multiple pages for your document.

→ For more information about the Page tool, **see** "Page Tool," **page 795**, in Chapter 29, "Freehand MX Environment and Tools."

You can also use the Page Preview area in the Document panel (see Figure 30.10).

Figure 30.10
The Page Preview area in the Document Panel.

Continuing with the case study of greendept.org, you need to create a multipage environment for the six top-level pages (Home, Search, Log-In, Events, About Us, Contact Us).

Open a new FreeHand MX document (File, New). Select the Documents tab in the Property inspector. If your Property inspector is not open, select it (Window, Document). From the Page Type menu, select Web (Figure 30.11). The page size is set to a default 550 pixels wide by 400 pixels tall.

Figure 30.11
Set the page size in the Documents tab.

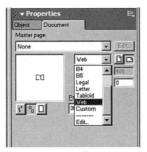

If you need to work with a different screen size, simply select Custom and set your page dimension accordingly.

To add pages to the document, select Add Pages from the Options menu (Figure 30.12).

Figure 30.12
Add pages to the document with the Add Pages command in the Options menu.

This opens the Add Pages dialog, where you can enter the number of pages you want to create, as well as change page dimensions. In this case, you will add five more pages. Click OK.

When the Add Pages dialog disappears, the new pages appear in the Document Preview window as tiny pages. To enlarge or reduce the size of the page thumbnails, click one of the three page magnification buttons (Figure 30.13).

When magnification is set to the middle or highest level, some of the pages in the document may not be visible in the Document panel's pasteboard window.

Note that your pages are now laid out in a linear order. Because you want to replicate the look of the site map created earlier, you need to rearrange the page order.

Select Fit All (Figure 30.14) from the drop-down menu located at the bottom of the document in the Status toolbar.

Figure 30.13
Select one of three page magnification buttons to control how the page thumbnails are displayed in the Document Preview window.

Figure 30.14
Since new pages are added in a vertical stack, select the Fit All option to view all pages in the document.

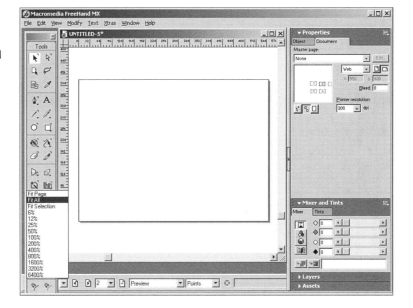

Select the Page tool. Click on a page and drag it to a new position, similar to the site map layout created earlier (Figure 30.15). Repeat for the remaining pages. Notice that the page thumbnails in the Document panel resemble the new arrangement you created. You can also drag these thumbnails in the preview area to rearrange page order. However, if you're working with several pages, some pages will not be viewable in the preview area because it does not allow you to scroll.

Figure 30.15
You can create a new page arrangement by using the Page tool to reposition the pages.

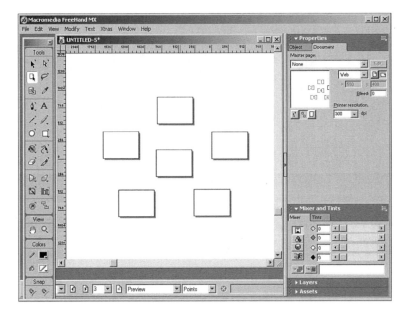

DESIGN THE HOME PAGE

After your house is in order, so to speak, you can start adding the good stuff to your pages. It's time to design.

From the Status toolbar, select the page number you want to work on first. In this case, it will be Page 1, the Home page. Images and text can now be added to create your home page design. The first order of business is to import the client's logo and place it on the home page (Figure 30.16). Select (File, Import) and import the image as a bitmap.

Figure 30.16
Place the imported logo as a bitmap on the canvas.

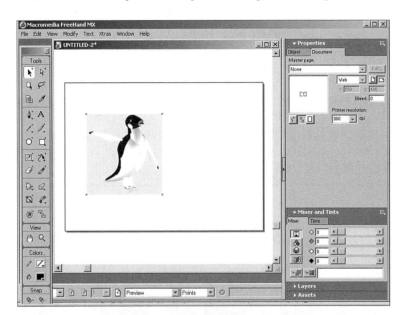

At this point, you'll need to work with some FreeHand MX text effects if you want to spice up the site's typography.

TEXT EFFECTS

FreeHand MX offers several powerful text effects that can add highlights, shadows, and three-dimensional zooms. Because you are designing for the Web, you shouldn't get too crazy with text effects that may not render properly in a low-resolution environment.

One of the more powerful effects in FreeHand is to align text to a path. The path can be closed or open. In this case, you will attach the Web site name (GreenDept.org) to a path around the penguin.

First things first. You need to create a path. Using the Ellipse tool, draw a circle (hold the Shift key while dragging) around the penguin (Figure 30.17).

Figure 30.17
To attach text to a path, you need to create a path first. In this case, use the Ellipse tool to draw a circle around the logo.

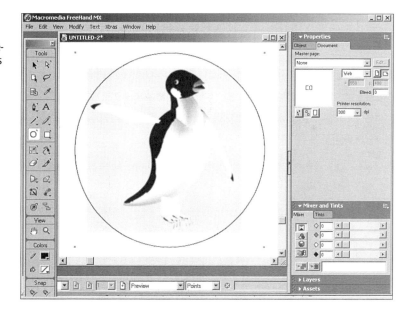

Next, you need to create the text that will be used on the path. Use the Text tool to type **GreenDept.org** (Figure 30.18). Use the Object panel to change the font, size, and fill color.

Select both the circle and the text block by holding the Shift key while using the Select tool. Choose (Text, Attach to Path)(Figure 30.19) and the text will now align to the path. Because you are working with a closed path, insert a paragraph return between the "." and "org" to align the text to both the top and the bottom of the path. Because the "." looked dorky sitting at the top, I deleted it (Figure 30.20).

Figure 30.18
After you've created a
path, add your text.

Figure 30.19
Use the Text, Attach to
Path command to
attach the text to the
path, or circle.

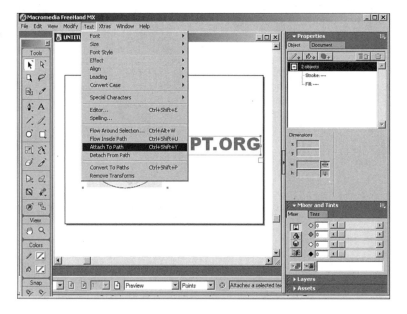

30

Figure 30.20
The text is now attached to the path.

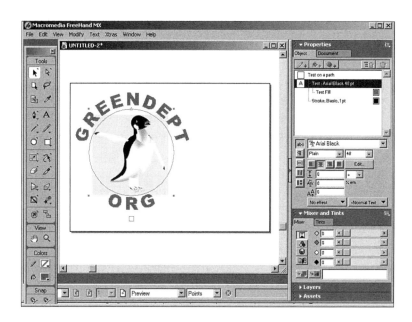

Resize the graphic and text and reposition as your creative eye sees fit (Figure 30.21).

Figure 30.21
The resized and repositioned logo.

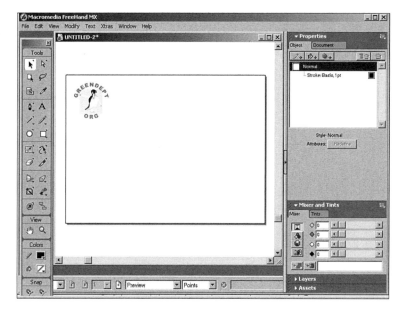

You can change the direction in which the text flows by holding the Opt/Alt key while using the Pointer tool to select just the path. Choose (Modify, Alter Path, Reverse Direction) to have the text flow in the opposite direction.

To reposition text along the path, use the Pointer tool to click the path. A small white triangle appears. Drag the triangle to move the text along the path.

To change the text alignment in regard to the vertical alignment of the text in relation to the path, click on the Text on a path entry in the Object panel. This displays the Text on a path options. The Top and Bottom Text alignment menus control where the text sits in relation to a path. The Top menu controls text before any paragraph return, whereas the Bottom menu controls text after any paragraph return.

Baseline places the baseline of the characters on the path; Ascent places the ascenders (letters in which part of the letter rises above the tops of the other letters, as with the letter *t*) on the path; Descent places the descenders (letters in which part of the letter drops below the baseline, as in the letter *q*). None indicates that no text is on the top or the bottom of the path.

After you've played with text and paths, you can start blocking out the site design. I like to use text headings and rectangles to show clients where the major page elements will be located (Figure 30.22).

Figure 30.22
Block out major page elements in your page concept design to show where key content areas are located.

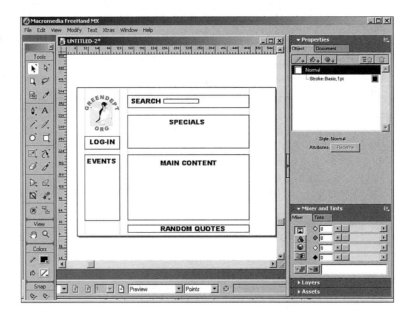

ACTIONS

Another method of presenting a site map is to create a faux working model that will let people navigate between your page designs in FreeHand. You can accomplish this by using FreeHand's Action tool.

To assign an action to an object, double-click the Action tool in the Tools panel to open the Action Tool dialog box. Select one of the following actions:

- Link to Target Page creates a link that moves from one page to another.
- Print Target Page adds a command that prints the target page.
- Load Target Page as a Movie takes objects on one page and adds them to the top of objects on the current page.

In this case, select Link to Target Page because you want to simulate working links between pages. Click OK to close the Action Tool dialog box.

Drag the Action tool from the object you want to act as the button to the target page. Release the mouse button and a curved action line indicates that an action has been applied between the pages (Figure 30.23).

Figure 30.23
Use the Action tool to simulate a working link between the page concepts.

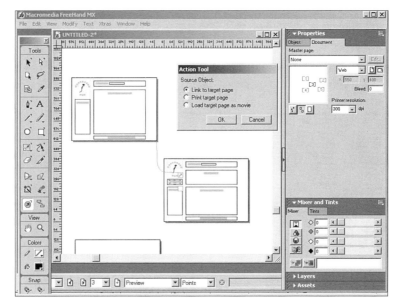

Using the Action tool allows you to apply only three types of Actions. The Navigation panel, however, enables you to apply several other actions. Nearly all these actions relate to incorporating Flash movies in your FreeHand documents.

To assign actions with the Navigation panel (Window, Navigation), select the object that will have the action applied. In the Navigation panel, use the Action menu to select an appropriate action (Figure 30.24).

Figure 30.24
Use the Action menu
to choose an action.

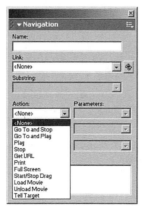

Use the Event menu to select the event that will trigger the action:

- Go To and Stop creates a button that goes to a particular frame or movie. The play action is then stopped.

- Go To and Play creates a button that goes to a particular frame or movie. The movie then continues to play at that point.

- Get URL creates a button that is used to go to the link specified in the Link field.

- Play creates a button that starts a paused movie.

- Stop creates a button stops a movie that is running.

- Print creates a button that specifies a page that can be printed through the Flash Player.

- Full Screen displays the movie in the Flash Player in full-screen mode.

- Start/Stop Drag allows a movie clip to be dragged around a page when an event happens and stop when another event happens.

- Load Movie creates a button that loads the movie from one page onto the movie on the current page.

- Unload Movie creates a button that removes a loaded movie from a page.

- Tell Target creates a button that controls the movies that were loaded onto the current movie.

TROUBLESHOOTING

PROBLEMS WITH PATTERNS

I cannot get my custom patterns and textured fills to display. All I see are circles.

Since custom patterns and textured fills are PostScript, FreeHand will not display them on screen. They will, however, print just fine to a PostScript printer or to Acrobat Distiller. You can also export the pattern or fill to an EPS file. Likewise, your custom pattern or textured fill will not export properly to a TIFF or JPEG format.

Text Not Flowing

I cannot get the text to flow around an object, no matter how many times I try. What am I doing wrong?

FreeHand MX can be a memory hog. If you're like most graphics professionals, you will have several applications running in addition to FreeHand. When you try and flow text around an object (Text, Flow Around Selection) and it doesn't work, you're most likely running low on memory. Quitting FreeHand and reopening the file seems to resolve this issue.

Changing Text Color After Converting to Paths

In FreeHand 10 I could change the color of text after I had converted it to paths, but the only way I can do that in FreeHand MX is by ungrouping the text and filling in each letter one by one.

Once you've converted your text to paths, there are a couple of options to efficiently change the fill or stroke colors. Use the Subselect tool to select the objects you want to modify and then apply new fill or stroke attributes. Or, you could select the object (formerly text) with the Pointer tool. Double-click the Contents item in the Object panel and apply the color modifications.

CHAPTER 31

INTEGRATION WITH THE STUDIO MX SUITE

In this chapter

Moving Designs to the Web   858

Working with Fireworks MX   865

Working with Flash MX   867

MOVING DESIGNS TO THE WEB

This chapter looks at how you can get your FreeHand designs to the Web, as well as coordinate the use of your FreeHand documents with other MX Suite programs such as Dreamweaver, Fireworks, and Flash.

FreeHand MX is a powerful design program for working with traditional print publishing. It is also a powerful tool that lets you incorporate many features for creating Web graphics and Web pages.

FreeHand MX lets you work with colors that work best when viewed online, as well as export graphics that are used in Web designs. In addition, FreeHand allows you to directly convert your graphics into HTML. Although this is a handy feature to have in a design program, it is not a replacement for Fireworks MX or Dreamweaver MX. It's simply another tool to use if you've invested a lot of time designing a newsletter or brochure for print publishing and need to convert it to an HTML Web page without reinventing the wheel. I wouldn't recommend using FreeHand as your primary site-building program.

WEB-SAFE COLORS

The old rule of thumb for Web design was to only work in the 216 colors that could be consistently displayed on both Windows and Macintosh monitors. That rule of thumb was always a limiting factor in Web design and, fortunately, is now mostly a rule of bygone days.

→ For more on the Web-Safe palette, **see** Chapter 3, "Introducing the MX Interface," **page 23**.

To work with Web-Safe colors in FreeHand MX, you have two options:

- Click the Fill or Stroke color box in the Tools panel. The default palette shows Web-Safe colors (Figure 31.1). The first number of the color represents the hexadecimal code and the second number represents the RGB value.

Figure 31.1
The Web-Safe Color Library is the default color palette displayed in the Fill and Stroke color box.

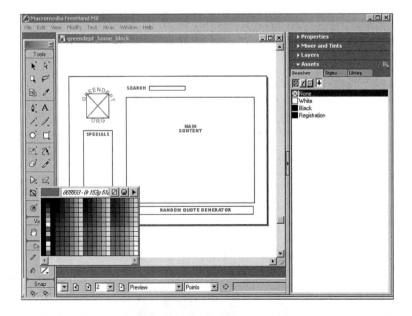

■ Import Web-Safe colors with the Swatches panel (Figure 31.2). Scroll through your color choices and select the colors you want to use in your design. Click OK when you're finished and the colors will appear in the Colors List.

Figure 31.2
The Web-Safe Color Library accessed from the Swatches panel.

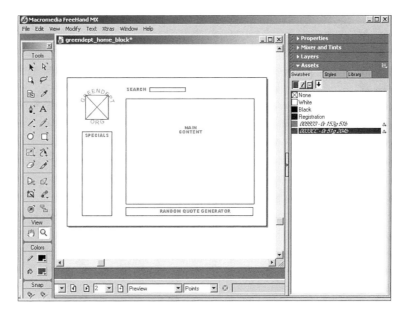

WEB GRAPHICS

FreeHand MX lets you export your designs to three Web file formats: GIF, JPEG, and PNG. But before you look at those formats, it helps to know a bit about a few key color-related terms, indexed color, and color depth.

The GIF file format uses a special type of color palette that limits the maximum number of colors to 256. It also has a unique feature in that each color is tracked, or indexed. For example, instead of indicating that the pixel color in column 3, row 1 is #000000 (black), the GIF format assigns an arbitrary value to each color and assigns that. In this case, #000000 might be color 7 in this file. The pixel in column 3, row 1 would be referred to as 7. As a result of this indexing, the file description is shortened and you end up with a smaller file size.

A plus of this indexing system is the capability to have an indexed transparency. Number 7 could be designated as transparent. As a result of using an indexed transparency, you can effectively turn off the background color.

Color depth refers to the maximum number of colors in an image. A GIF file may contain anywhere from 2, 4, 8, 16, 32, 64, 128, or 256 colors. A JPEG, on the other hand, can have up to 16.8 million colors. As an image's color depth increases, so does image quality and image size.

EXPORTING TO GIF

One of the most popular Web graphic formats is GIF. GIF files are commonly used if you have transparent backgrounds as part of your image. To create a GIF, select the object(s) you want to use to export. Choose File, Export to open the Export Document Dialog box. Select GIF from the Save As Type (Windows) or Format (Macintosh) menu. Click the Setup button to open the Bitmap Export Defaults dialog box (Figure 31.3).

Figure 31.3
Control export options with the Bitmap Export Defaults dialog box.

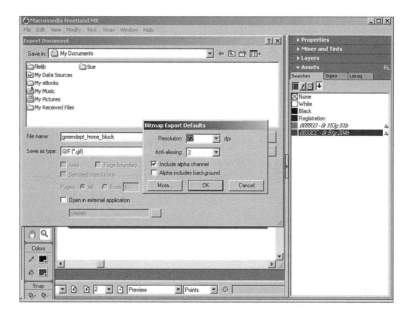

You can set the Resolution. In the online world, this is 72 dpi. You can use the Anti-Aliasing menu to control the amount of softening that will be applied to the image. You can also create an alpha channel that can be used as an image mask as well as include the background area in the alpha channel.

Click the More button to view more options for GIF images (Figure 31.4).

With the GIF Options dialog box open, you have a few options to play with.

Select Interlaced if you want your image to load faster on the Web page. An interlaced image will load in rough form first and then will gradually become clearer. With more broadband and high-speed connections being used every day, interlaced images are not as time-saving as they once were in the days of slooowwww dial-up modems.

Use the Dither menu to select the amount of dithering that will be applied to the colors. One means of extending the usefulness of the limited Web-Safe palette is with dithering. Dithering refers to the interpolation of unavailable colors by mixing pixels of (usually two) available colors in certain patterns and ratios. When the dither pattern is very tight, with available colors in nearly equal quantities, the resulting appearance can be very good, sometimes nearly indistinguishable from a nondithered image. Dithering gets goofy, however, when the pattern is diffuse. Turn off dithering when you're working with photos, text, or detailed artwork. Selecting None from the Dither menu applies no dithering. Selecting High applies the most dithering.

Figure 31.4
The GIF Options dialog box allows you to control settings for your GIF exports.

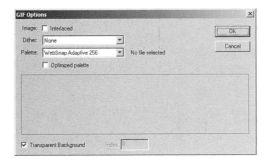

The Palette menu lets you select which colors you want to include in the color palette when you export the image. The fewer colors you use, the smaller the file size of the exported image.

The palette choices are described as follows:

- Exact Palette creates a color palette with only the colors used in your artwork.
- WebSnap Adaptive 256, 128, or 16 create a color palette that is converted to the closest Web-Safe color equivalent.
- Web-Safe 216 includes the standard 216 Web-Safe colors.
- 64 colors, 32 colors, or 16 colors allow you to preset Web-Safe color palettes.
- Macintosh systems use the 256 colors of the Macintosh OS palette.
- Windows systems use the 256 colors of the Windows OS palette.
- 3-3-2 uses the palette of the FreeHand MX GIF Import Export Xtra.
- Grays use a palette of 256 grayscale colors.

Select Optimized Palette to have FreeHand remove any unused colors from the palette. This reduces the file size of the exported image.

Select Transparent if you need your GIF to have a transparent background.

EXPORTING TO JPEG

JPEG is another popular format for Web graphics. Its strength lies in the format's ability to better render details of photographs and color nuances and blends in a compressed file size.

To create a JPEG, select the object(s) you want to use to export. Choose File, Export to open the Export Document dialog box (Figure 31.5). Select JPEG from the Save As Type (Windows) or Format (Macintosh) menu. Click the Setup button to open the Bitmap Export Defaults dialog box.

31

As with GIF, you can set the Resolution as well as the Anti-Aliasing menu to control the amount of softening that will be applied to the image. You can also create an alpha channel that can be used as an image mask as well as include the background area in the alpha channel.

Click the More button to view more options for JPEG images.

Figure 31.5
The JPEG Options dialog box allows you to control settings for your JPEG exports.

Enter a percentage for Image Quality. Low quality settings reduce the quality of the image but decrease the file size. High quality settings give you a better image, but also increase the file size. Select Progressive JPEG to create an effect similar to that of the Interlaced GIF.

EXPORTING TO PNG

One of the relatively newer formats is PNG (Portable Network Graphics). The PNG format was basically designed to replace the GIF format. For the Web, PNG has three main advantages over GIF: alpha channels (variable transparency), gamma correction (cross-platform control of image brightness), and two-dimensional interlacing (a method of progressive display). PNG also compresses slightly better than GIF in most cases. PNG, however, is still not as widely supported as it should be in Netscape Navigator and Internet Explorer. Most professional designers still work with GIF and JPEG for online graphics.

For image editing, PNG is a handy format for the storage of intermediate stages of editing. Unlike JPEG, saving, re-saving, and restoring an image does not degrade its quality.

To create a PNG, select the object(s) you want to use to export. Choose File, Export to open the Export Document dialog box (Figure 31.6). Select PNG from the Save As Type (Windows) or Format (Macintosh) menu. Click the Setup button to open the Bitmap Export Defaults dialog box.

Click the More button in Windows or Setup in the Macintosh dialog box to open the PNG Options dialog box.

Make your selection for the color bit depth. The higher the bit depth, the better the quality.

Select Interlaced PNG to create an effect similar to that of the Interlaced GIF.

Figure 31.6
The PNG Options dialog box enables you to control settings for your PNG exports.

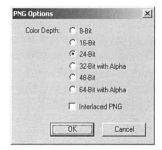

HTML PAGES

Like most popular software programs today, FreeHand MX has a feature that enables you to convert your FreeHand page to an HTML page. This is a handy conversion to have, but is typically not used when creating professional Web sites. Dreamweaver MX and Fireworks MX are specifically geared toward working in the online environment and give you more finesse and control in your work.

Like any other feature, this feature is to be looked upon as a tool for your design toolbox. Some may find it useful; others will find it a solution to a problem that doesn't exist.

To convert your document to HTML, open the HTML Output dialog box (Figure 31.7) by selecting File, Publish as HTML.

Figure 31.7
The HTML Output dialog box enables you create Web pages from your FreeHand documents.

Select a setting from the HTML Setting menu. You can also click the Setup button to create a new setting.

If you want to be alerted to potential HTML output problems, check Show Output Warnings. Check View in Browser or HTML Editor if you want to immediately open the file in Internet Explorer or Netscape Navigator. You can select a browser version or HTML Editor of your liking in the pop-up menu.

When you're ready to go, click the Save as HTML button. The HTML file(s) are created in a folder that is considered the document root in the HTML Setup dialog box. Your images are placed in a separate directory within the root directory.

To create a custom HTML setup, click the Setup button (Figure 31.8).

Figure 31.8
The HTML Setup dialog box allows you to adjust specific elements of the HTML conversion process.

To create a custom HTML setup, click the Setup button. Click the + button to create a new setup. Name your setup and click OK.

Select the folder where you want to save your HTML files by using the Browse button or entering a directory path in the Document root field.

The Layout menu gives you some pretty nifty options that you won't find in other canned "save me to HTML" programs:

■ Positioning with Layers uses Cascading Style Sheets (CSS) to make an accurate rendition of your FreeHand layout.

■ Positioning with Tables uses tables and nested tables to convert your document(s) to HTML. Tables are frequently used in Web design, but nested tables can still get a bit quirky with Netscape.

Use the Encoding menu to select the language for the page. Unless this book is translated into other languages, keep this set to Western (Latin 1). If you are reading this in another language, select the language of your choice.

You can also choose the file format for your exported images: GIF, JPEG, PNG, and SWF (Flash).

Click OK to save the setup.

You can also click the HTML Export Wizard (Windows) or the HMTL Output Assistant (Macintosh) to guide you through the setup process (Figure 31.9).

Figure 31.9
The HTML Export Wizard (Windows) or the HTML Output Assistant (Macintosh) guides you step by step through the process of creating a custom setup for your HTML files.

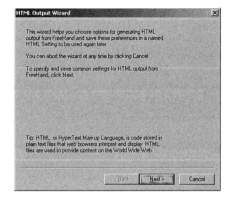

WORKING WITH FIREWORKS MX

FreeHand MX and Fireworks MX can make wonderful music together. FreeHand enables you to import flattened images (multiple layers combined into one layer) from Fireworks that you can place as objects in your document. You can also import Fireworks files that can still be edited in FreeHand.

IMPORTING FIREWORKS MX FILES INTO FREEHAND MX

PNG files created in Fireworks can be imported into FreeHand MX in several ways. Fireworks PNG files can contain separate objects and layers that can then be manipulated in FreeHand. You can also work with flattened Fireworks files, such as GIF, JPEG, TIFF, or exported PNG. These will appear as a single image.

To import a native Fireworks PNG file, select File, Import or File, Open and choose the file you want to bring into FreeHand. The Fireworks PNG Import Settings dialog box appears (Figure 31.10).

Figure 31.10
The Fireworks PNG Import Settings dialog box determines how objects from Fireworks MX are imported into FreeHand MX.

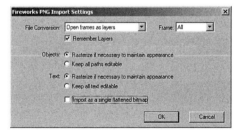

Using the conversion menu, select Open Frames As Pages to open each Fireworks frame as a separate page; or select Open Frames As Layers to convert each Fireworks frame into a FreeHand layer. The Frame menu lets you select a specific frame or all frames for import.

Check Remember Layers to keep the objects on their original layers.

For objects, select one of the following Objects options: Rasterize if Necessary to Maintain Appearance, which may rasterize any imported Fireworks objects; or Keep All Paths Editable, which converts all Fireworks objects into FreeHand objects. Selecting this option may change the object's appearance during the import process.

For text, select one of the following Text options: Rasterize if Necessary to Maintain Appearance, which may rasterize the imported text; Keep All Text Editable, which converts Fireworks text into FreeHand text.

You can also check Import As a Single Flattened Bitmap to turn the Fireworks object(s) into a pixel-based image.

To import a flattened Fireworks file or exported Fireworks file, select File, Import and choose the file you want to bring into FreeHand. A corner symbol appears. Using your mouse, drag or click the corner symbol to place the image in your document.

EDITING FIREWORKS MX IMAGES IN FREEHAND MX

Another nifty feature is the ability to go back and forth between FreeHand and Fireworks with the click of a button. You can use this feature to edit a Fireworks image even after it's been placed in FreeHand.

In FreeHand, select the image you want to edit. Click the Edit with Fireworks button (Figure 31.11) found in the Object panel.

Figure 31.11
The Edit with Fireworks button launches Fireworks.

The Find Source for Editing dialog box appears (Figure 31.12). Click the Yes button to launch Fireworks and open the original fireworks file. If the original object is layered, select Yes. Click the No button to work with the flattened version of the image.

Select one of the three options from the Fireworks Source Files menu: Always Use Source PNG to always open the PNG source file; Never Use Source PNG to preserve the original file and open a flattened file in its place; Ask When Launching to open the dialog box.

Figure 31.12
The Find Source for Editing dialog box allows you to select the original source file.

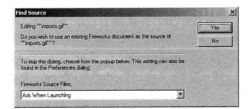

Edit the image to your heart's content. When you're finished, click the Done button (Figure 31.13) in Fireworks to close the file and return to FreeHand. Presto! The changes you made to the original image are automatically carried over to the imported file in FreeHand.

Figure 31.13
The Done button is used to seal the deal when you're done editing the image in Fireworks.

WORKING WITH FLASH MX

Although Flash is powerful, FreeHand packs more power when it comes to sophisticated drawing tools like perspective, enveloping, extrusions, and other special effects. Fortunately, FreeHand plays well with Flash by allowing you to copy and paste or export your graphics into Flash as well as import and export SWF movies.

USING FREEHAND MX OBJECTS IN FLASH MX

The simplest way to incorporate your FreeHand graphics into Flash is to drag and drop the artwork from FreeHand into a Flash frame (Figure 31.14). This requires resizing the program windows so you can fit both applications on the screen.

Select the FreeHand object and use the Pointer tool to drag the object into the Flash window. When you see the rectangle box appear, release the mouse and your object is now imported into Flash.

Figure 31.14
It's a piece of cake to drag and drop FreeHand graphics into Flash.

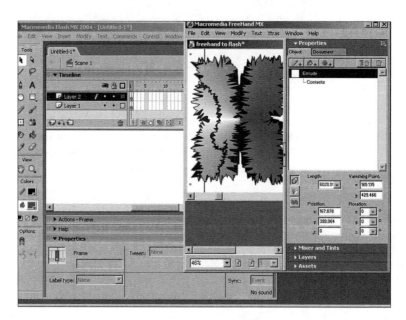

To paste into Flash, select the object and copy (Edit, Copy). Open your Flash file and select paste (Edit, Paste). Your object is now in the Flash file.

When moving from FreeHand to Flash, here are some things to keep in mind:

- Text blocks remain editable in Flash, but text attached to a path is converted to an object.
- Transparency lens fills remain transparent, but other lens fills are changed into masked objects.
- Grouped objects can be ungrouped and edited in Flash.
- Square end caps (the square shape at the end of a line) are changed to round end caps.

USING FLASH MX MOVIES IN FREEHAND MX

Although not used often because designers typically use FreeHand for print publishing, you can import a Flash SWF movie into your FreeHand documents. Similar to the Launch and

Edit relationship to Fireworks, FreeHand also has a Launch and Edit feature to edit the imported Flash movie.

To import an SWF movie into FreeHand, select File, Import and choose the SWF file you want to import. Drag to modify the size of the file or click to place it at its original size.

Use the Object panel to control the settings of the SWF movie. Select the SWF file and choose Show Snapshot in the Object panel to see a thumbnail of one of the movie frames (Figure 31.15).

Figure 31.15
The Show Snapshot check box and Frame slide allow you to control how the SWF movie is displayed in FreeHand.

If the Show Snapshot check box is not selected, the Flash logo is displayed. If the check box is selected, you can use the Frame slider to choose a particular movie frame to be displayed.

EXPORTING FLASH MX MOVIES FROM FREEHAND MX

You can also export an SWF file from FreeHand. Select File, Export to open the Export Document dialog box (Figure 31.16). Choose Macromedia Flash (SWF) from the list and click the Setup button to open the Movie Settings dialog box.

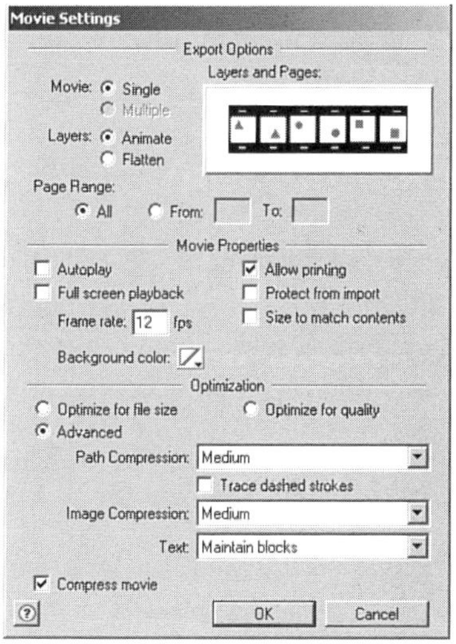

Figure 31.16
FreeHand MX also allows you to export SWF files.

Modify any settings you need to change and click OK. Name the exported file and you are finished.

The Movie Properties section in the Movie Settings dialog box offers a subset of the options available in Flash MX 2004, either in the Document Properties dialog (Modify, Document) or through Publish Settings (File, Publish Settings).

EDITING FLASH MX MOVIES IN FREEHAND MX

Just as with Fireworks, FreeHand lets you edit Flash movies. Because the original Flash movie is not placed in FreeHand, you must use the Launch and Edit command in the Object Inspector (Figure 31.17) to open the original Flash file.

Figure 31.17
The Launch and Edit button in the Object panel enables you to edit the original Flash file.

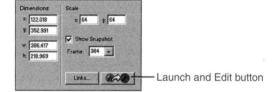

Launch and Edit button

Modify the original Flash file as needed in Flash MX. When you have completed the revisions, click the Done button located near the top of the Flash window. The Flash file closes and the changes are automatically applied to the SWF file you imported into FreeHand. It doesn't get any easier than that!

TROUBLESHOOTING

THE QUICK WAY TO COPY TEXT ATTRIBUTES

I want to have the same formatting on different text blocks but don't want to go through the hassles of creating a style. Is there a shortcut?

If you want to use the same text formatting on different blocks of text in your document, a common approach is to create a style. However, there are times when you just want to do something quick and informal. To use a shortcut, select some of the text you want to copy using the Text tool. Go to (Edit, Copy Attributes). Then select the text y you want to add that formatting to and choose (Edit, Paste Attributes).

CREATING ONE OBJECT FROM MANY

I'm not that handy at drawing complex shapes or modifying existing ones, but I can create the shape I want by combining different shapes like ellipses, rectangles and stars. Is there a way I can turn all of those different objects into one object?

Select all the objects, or parts of objects, you want to combine. Choose (Edit, Join) to create one object from many. If there are any open ends you will also need to close the object either by finishing the shape yourself or by checking Closed in the Object Inspector.

CROPPING IMPORTED PHOTOS

I like to crop my photos after I bring them into FreeHand, but haven't found an easy way of doing this without going back to Fireworks.

After you've imported your photo into FreeHand, select the Rectangle tool and draw a rectangle over the photo as you would like to have it cropped. Select the photo with the Pointer tool and Cut it (Edit, Cut). Select the rectangle and choose (Edit, Paste Contents) to paste the photo inside the rectangle.

PART VI

ColdFusion MX

32 Understanding and Administering ColdFusion   875

33 ColdFusion Markup Language (CFML)   885

CHAPTER 32

UNDERSTANDING AND ADMINISTERING COLDFUSION

In this chapter

Introducing ColdFusion   876

ColdFusion Architecture   877

Using Flash to Access the ColdFusion Server   878

Using the Built-in Web server   880

Configuring Data Sources   880

INTRODUCING COLDFUSION

ColdFusion is easy-to-learn, easy-to-use, yet full-featured server-based infrastructure for data-enabling Web sites.

→ For an introduction to data-enabling Web sites, **see** "Dynamic Content," **page 20,** in Chapter 2, "Studio MX: A Bird's-Eye View").

The developer version of ColdFusion, included with Studio MX, allows you to develop ColdFusion applications and run them on your development machine. Other than that, it can be accessed by only one additional IP address—just enough for testing.

You need a production ColdFusion server to make your applications available on the Web. You can either buy and manage your own production ColdFusion server or pay a monthly fee for a hosting service—the same options you have for an ordinary Web site. You may also be able to find free ColdFusion hosting, which may be appropriate for testing or for non-critical uses that don't put much stress on the server or demand a lot of bandwidth.

→ Dreamweaver is an excellent tool for developing ColdFusion applications. For more on developing ColdFusion applications with Dreamweaver, **see** Chapter 13, "Developing ColdFusion Applications in Dreamweaver," **page 287**.

In addition, the developer version of ColdFusion can be used as a versatile personal automation tool. Three examples:

- For repetitive find-and-replace tasks, ColdFusion offers powerful find and replace functions that use *regular expressions*.

> **NOTE**
>
> *Regular expressions* use special placeholder characters such as * and ? to represent unknown characters. The Windows Explorer supports regular expressions that use * and ? in searching for file names.

- If you regularly gather the same information from the same Web page, or from a number of Web pages, you may find that ColdFusion's *screen scraping* capabilities can automate the whole process.
- You can automate sending email with ColdFusion. You can use a database to store and retrieve names, email addresses, and perhaps other information to personalize the messages.

→ For more on screen-scraping with ColdFusion, see "The cf_scrape Custom Tag," **page 899** in Chapter 33, "ColdFusion Markup Language (CFML)."

After ColdFusion is installed, there are a few of things you need to do before you can start working with it:

- Configure a Web server to work with ColdFusion. There is a built-in Web server that requires no configuration.
- Create or obtain a database file, created by a program such as Microsoft Access, Microsoft SQL Server, or MySQL. (On the CD accompanying this book, there is a Microsoft Access database, greendept.mdb, that you can use for testing.) Typically, you install the database on the ColdFusion server.

- Create a System DSN (Data Source Name), so that Windows applications can access the database. You can create the System DSN with the ColdFusion Administrator.

- If you are not developing (for example, running Dreamweaver) on the same machine that ColdFusion is running on, you may also need an RDS (Remote Development Services) password to log on to the ColdFusion server.

- A final, optional step is to configure debugging options by using the ColdFusion Administrator, so that you get more information when an error occurs.

COLDFUSION ARCHITECTURE

ColdFusion has three basic components: the server, the administrator interface, and ColdFusion Markup Language (CFML). The server is the central element. You use the browser-based administrator interface to manage the server. You use CFML in Web pages destined for the ColdFusion server in much the same way that HTML pages are destined for Web servers.

The ColdFusion server runs side by side with a Web server. As the Web server displays pages, the ColdFusion server watches for ColdFusion pages (pages with the .cfm extension). ColdFusion pages contain a mixture of standard HTML and CFML. The ColdFusion server grabs the ColdFusion pages, turns them into pure HTML, and returns them to the Web server for display. (See Figure 32.1.)

Figure 32.1
The ColdFusion server takes .cfm pages that come to the Web server, performs dynamic data operations (insert, update, retrieve, delete) based on the ColdFusion Markup Language (CFML) in the .cfm file, and returns pure HTML to the Web server, which forwards it to the browser.

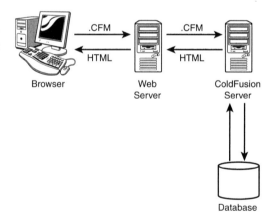

While it has the page in its possession, the ColdFusion server can do four basic types of things:

- **Database operations**, such as retrieving, inserting, updating and deleting data in databases stored on the server. This is the central function of the ColdFusion server. It allows the Web developer to populate Web pages with data from databases created with database management systems such as MySQL, Microsoft Access, or SQL Server (and many others).

- **File operations**, such as reading, writing, and appending to text files, including HTML, XML, and CFML files, that are stored on the server. This means that the developer isn't limited to database information, but can get at anything that's stored in a text file. The ColdFusion server can also upload files to the server from clients.

- **Server-to-server communications**, in which the ColdFusion server exchanges data with other servers, including other ColdFusion servers, servers running Flash Remoting software, and directory servers that use Lightweight Directory Access Protocol (LDAP). It can also communicate with SMTP servers, allowing it to send and receive email. When you use Simple Object Access Protocol (SOAP) to access Web services, the ColdFusion Server also provides a proxy service, which replicates the functions of the Web service. You can create the proxy in 30 seconds using Dreamweaver.

→ For instructions on creating the Web services proxy, **see** "Consuming Web Services," in Chapter 13, **page 316.**

- **Page processing and display operations**, which are numerous and varied, including text formatting, search and replace, and building tables, forms, and charts. ColdFusion can also change information in HTTP headers, which can instruct the Web server to do various things such as prompt the user for a response, or purge the HTML file from its cache after displaying it.

32 USING FLASH TO ACCESS THE COLDFUSION SERVER

Flash can be used to implement the client side of ColdFusion applications. A Flash client typically interacts with a ColdFusion server in one of two ways: using Web services or using Flash Remoting. Figure 32.2 shows the architecture and protocols associated with each approach.

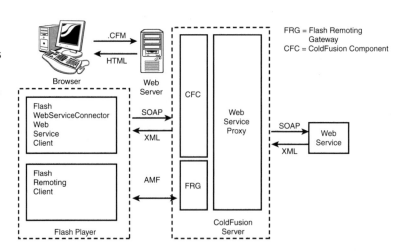

Figure 32.2
The Flash Player (lower left) can access the ColdFusion server either using the WebServiceConnector component, or using Flash Remoting.

→ For more on dynamic data in Flash, **see** Chapter 23, "Using Flash for Dynamic Data," **page 661**.

WEB SERVICES

The Web services architecture allows clients to get dynamic data from servers, making requests using Simple Object Access Protocol (SOAP) and receiving XML replies. By using standard, open protocols, Web services enable any-to-any communication. For example, you can create Web services that run on the ColdFusion server, and they can be accessed by clients using PHP, JSP, ASP.NET, or any other technology that supports Web services standards.

Note, however, that the Flash Player's prohibition on cross-domain data transfers without a cross-domain policy file puts a serious restriction on this potential for universal communication.

In addition, initial experience with the Flash Player and SOAP indicates that it may be best suited to non-demanding and non-critical applications.

→ For a link to results of some early testing on Flash Remoting and SOAP, **see** `SOAPvsRemoting.htm` on the CD accompanying this book.

→ For an introduction to the issue of cross-domain data transfers, **see** "New Security Rules," **page 330**, in Chapter 14, "What's New in Flash MX 2004?". For relevant links, **see** `crossDomainPolicyFiles.htm` on the CD accompanying this book.

Web services are best accessed from the Flash Player through the WebServiceConnector component in Flash MX 2004 Professional. The WebServiceConnector makes it easy to get the basic Web services connection going.

→ For instructions on using the WebServiceConnector, **see** "Web Services," **page 672**, in Chapter 23.

The Web services architecture requires the client to communicate with the server via a proxy, which replicates server behaviors on a local server, such as the ColdFusion server.

Dreamweaver has tools for creating ColdFusion server behaviors for use as Web services. Dreamweaver also makes it easy to create the proxy for the client on the ColdFusion server. Finally, Dreamweaver makes it easy to create simple client interactions with Web services.

→ For more on Dreamweaver's tools for auto-generating the proxy and Web service client code, **see** "Consuming Web Services," **page** 316, in Chapter 13.

FLASH REMOTING

To use Flash Remoting, you have to download the Flash Remoting components from `www.macromedia.com`.

→ For instructions on using Flash Remoting, **see** Chapter 23, "Using Flash for Dynamic Data," **page 661**.

Flash Remoting clients communicate via the Flash Remoting Gateway, a standard feature of the ColdFusion server. The Flash Remoting client invokes a function, created by the ColdFusion developer and often contained in a ColdFusion component (CFC) on the ColdFusion server. The function returns a value to the Flash Remoting client.

Flash Remoting is the most efficient way to communicate with the ColdFusion server. The ColdFusion server and the Flash client store data in the same format, eliminating the need for time-consuming translation required with technologies like XML. In addition, the proprietary Action Message Format (AFM) used for communication between client and server is efficient and compact.

USING THE BUILT-IN WEB SERVER

ColdFusion MX includes a built-in Web server, the JRun Web server, designed to be used for development only. The built-in server can be accessed in the browser via the IP address 127.0.0.1 or using the server name *localhost*.

You don't have to use the built-in Web server. ColdFusion also works with popular Web servers such as Microsoft Internet Information Server (IIS) and the Apache Web Server.

Web servers listen on a particular TCP/IP port number. Port 80 is the default. Thus, if no port number is specified in the URL, port 80 is assumed. So `http://www.greendept.com` and `http://www.greendept.com:80` are equivalent. The default port number for secure HTTP (HTTPS) is 443.

However, ColdFusion's built-in Web server listens on port 8500 by default. Thus, for example, these are two equivalent URLs for accessing the ColdFusion Administrator on the built-in Web server:

```
http://127.0.0.1:8500/CFIDE/administrator/index.cfm
http://localhost:8500/CFIDE/administrator/index.cfm
```

CONFIGURING DATA SOURCES

Here's a simple, typical procedure for configuring a data source:

- Start the ColdFusion MX Administrator (probably accessible at one or both of the URLs provided at the end of the previous section).

> **TIP**
>
> If you haven't already done so, now is a good time to maximize debugging information. In the ColdFusion Administrator, under Debugging and Logging, click Debugging Settings. (See Figure 32.3.) Check all available boxes and click Submit Changes.

- Under Data & Services, click Data Sources. (Refer to Figure 32.3.)
  The Add New Data Source dialog will appear.

- At a minimum, on the Add New Data Source dialog, provide a name for the System DSN and choose a database driver type from the drop-down menu. In Figure 32.4 the DSN happens to be the same as the database file (greendept), but you're making up a new DSN, and it can be anything you want, as long as it has not already been used for another DSN and it conforms to the rules for ColdFusion variable naming. For instance, the name can't contain any spaces. (If you break the rules, you'll get an error message: `Trying to create a datasource with a name that is invalid. Datasource Names must match ColdFusion variable naming conventions.`) Then click the Add button.

Figure 32.3
The ColdFusion
Administrator
browser-based
interface.

Add new DSN here ———

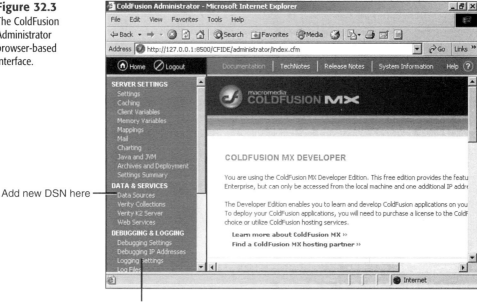

Maximize debugging information here

WARNING

If the DSN contains any spaces, you get an error message when you try to add the name.

32

Figure 32.4
The Add New Data
Source dialog. The
greendept DSN is
about to be added, so
it doesn't yet appear
in the Connected
Data Sources list.

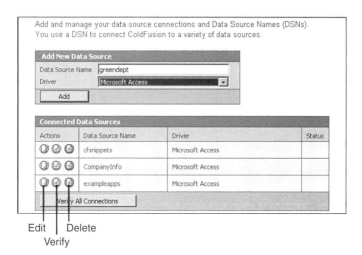

Edit | Delete
Verify

- The Data Source dialog appears for the selected driver. For instance, Figure 32.5 shows the Microsoft Access Data Source dialog.

- In the Database File box, provide the full path to the database file on the ColdFusion server hard disk, which in Figure 32.5 is the local C: drive. You can click the Browse button and navigate to the database file. In Figure 32.5, the path to the database file (only partially visible in the box) is C:\CFusionMX\wwwroot\greendept\assets\greendept.mdb.

Optionally, you can also provide a description of the database in the Description box. Click Submit.

You should see something similar to Figure 32.6, including the Datasource updated successfully message, and the entry in Connected Data Sources, with OK in the Status column.

Figure 32.5
The Microsoft Access Data Source dialog. Fill in the full path and filename for the database file, and optionally a description.

Figure 32.6
This is what you see when you have added a DSN that ColdFusion can access successfully.

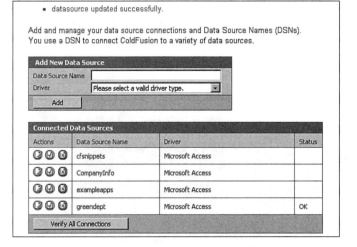

 If you get a message such as Connection verification failed for data source: greendept *or you see "Error" in the Status column, see "Troubleshooting" at the end of this chapter.*

Notice the Actions column on the left in Figure 32.4. You can return to this screen at any time and use the three buttons in this column to edit, verify, or delete the DSN. These actions do not affect the database file itself, only the DSN.

TROUBLESHOOTING

"Connection Verification Failed" Error

If you get a message such as Connection verification failed for data source: greendept, look at what comes after it. A lot of it may not be very helpful, but somewhere in there, there should be a solid clue as to what is wrong. For instance:

Could not find file tells you there is something wrong with the filename or path that you entered in the Database box.

If the file is on your local machine, and the error message says Please check your username, password, URL, and other connectivity info, the database file may be protected by a username and password. Two options are to uncheck Use Default Username and provide the correct username and password in the appropriate boxes (ColdFusion Username and ColdFusion Password), or to un-protect the database by using the database management system.

If all else fails, you might try using the Windows interface for working with DSNs (Start, Settings, Control Panel, Administrative Tools, Data Sources (ODBC), System DSN tab).

CHAPTER 33

COLDFUSION MARKUP LANGUAGE (CFML)

In this chapter

Introducing CFML   886

Variables and Scopes   888

Using ColdFusion for Database Operations   891

Custom Tags   895

Creating and Using ColdFusion Components (CFCs)   903

Creating and Using Web Service CFCs   904

INTRODUCING CFML

CFML is a tag-based programming language, similar to HTML in format. CFML consists of about 100 tags, enclosed in angle brackets like HTML tags.

All CFML tag names start with cf. Not all ColdFusion language elements are tags, however. For instance, there are built-in functions such as iif().

The iif() Function

The iif() function evaluates an expression (condition in the following code). Depending on whether the expression is true or false, iif() dynamically evaluates one of two string expressions (string_expression1 and string_expression2) and returns the result.

It's equivalent to:

```
<cffunction>
    <cfif condition>
        <cfset result = Evaluate(string_expression1)>
    <cfelse>
        <cfset result = Evaluate(string_expression2)>
    </cfif>
    <cfreturn result>
<cffunction>
```

In most cases, when you apply a tag, you use a start tag and an end tag. The end tag has the same name as the start tag but is preceded by a forward slash (/).

For example:

```
<cfoutput>
    Hello
</cfoutput>
```

Table 33.1 lists some commonly used ColdFusion tags. The rest of this chapter illustrates the use of these tags.

TABLE 33.1   SOME COMMONLY USED COLDFUSION TAGS

Tag	Purpose
cfapplication	Defines various client behaviors associated with an application, such as whether the client can log information in a cookie, and whether the client session will time out.
cfargument	Within a function, defines a parameter (data passed to the function).
cfbreak	See cfloop.
cfcatch	See cftry.
cfcomponent	Creates a ColdFusion component (CFC), an object encapsulating procedures (functions, referred to as methods), and data (variables and parameters).

Tag	Purpose
cfdirectory	Returns a list of files in a directory. Can also create, delete, and rename directories.
cfdump	Displays the contents of variables, objects, components, user-defined functions, and other elements. Useful for debugging.
cfelse	See cfif.
cffile	Performs operations such as reading, writing, and appending to files on the ColdFusion server.
cffunction	Defines a ColdFusion function (an object encapsulating a procedure).
cfhttp	Generates an HTTP request and handles the response from the server.
cfif	Executes enclosed code if a condition is true. Can be used with cfelse to define an action to perform if the condition is not true.
cfimport	Imports all ColdFusion pages in a directory into the calling page as a custom tag library.
cfinclude	Adds the contents of the included ColdFusion page to the page containing the cfinclude tag, as if the code on the included page were part of the page containing the cfinclude tag.
cfinvoke or a Web service.	Invokes (runs or executes) either a function (method) in a component.
cflock	Locks (prevents simultaneous access to) a single section of code, two or more different sections of code, or a scope. Locks prevent simultaneous change of the same variable to two different values.
cfloop	Loops through the tag body zero or more times, based on a condition specified by the tag attributes. The cfbreak tag exits a cfloop tag.
cfmail	Sends SMTP mail messages with application variables, query results, or server files. (See also cfpop, for getting mail.)
cfmodule	Invokes a custom tag, providing a workaround for custom tag name conflicts.
cfobject	Loads an object into a variable. Can load a CFC or an object written in other programming languages, including COM (Component Object Model) components, Java objects such as Enterprise JavaBeans, or CORBA (Common Object Request Broker Architecture) objects.
cfoutput	Displays output that can contain the results of processing ColdFusion functions, variables, and expressions.
cfparam	Creates a variable if it doesn't already exist. Optionally, sets the variable to a default value. If the variable already exists, cfparam does not change its value.

33

continues

TABLE 33.1   CONTINUED

Tag	Purpose
cfpop	Retrieves and/or deletes email messages from a POP mail server.
cfquery	Establishes a connection to a database (if a connection does not exist), executes a query operation such as insert, retrieve, update, or delete, and returns results.
cfreturn	Returns a result from a function.
cfset	Sets or resets the value of a ColdFusion variable. If the variable doesn't already exist, cfset creates the variable and sets the value. If the variable does exist, cfset sets the value.
cftry	Used with one or more cfcatch tags to catch and process exceptions (events such as failed database operations that disrupt normal program flow) .

VARIABLES AND SCOPES

A *variable* is a name that represents data, in the same way that a label on a drawer represents the contents of the drawer. The *value* of the data is the contents of the drawer. In ColdFusion, variable values can be set and reset with cfset, or set to an initial default value with cfparam. Variables can be passed as attributes to CFML tags, or as parameters to functions.

Here's a typical cfparam tag:

```
<cfparam name="BirthDate" type="date" default="January 1, 2003">
```

If there is no BirthDate variable in existence yet, ColdFusion creates one and sets its value to January 1, 2003. If the variable BirthDate already exists, its value doesn't change.

To refer to the value stored in a variable, enclose the variable in pound signs, like this: #BirthDate#. For example, to use the cfoutput tag to display this variable, do this:

```
<cfoutput>#BirthDate#</cfoutput>
```

TROUBLESHOOTING WITH DATA TYPE CHECKING

In the cfparam example, the type attribute helps you detect problems in your program by causing ColdFusion to check whether the existing value can be interpreted as a valid date. If not, ColdFusion gives you an Invalid parameter type error. In the following example, the first line creates the variable, whereas the second generates an error:

```
<cfset BirthDate = "hello">
<cfparam name="BirthDate" type="date" default="January 1, 2003">
```

The following lines, on the other hand, don't generate an error:

```
<cfset BirthDate = "1-1-02">
<cfparam name="BirthDate" type="date" default="January 1, 2003">
```

Error checking does not persist after the `cfparam` tag. So, the following generates no error:

```
<cfset BirthDate = "1-1-02">
<cfparam name="BirthDate" type="date" default="January 1, 2003">
<cfset BirthDate = "hello">
```

USING `cftry`/`cfcatch` TO TRAP ERRORS

Normally, you should use the `type` attribute—or any operation that may generate an error—in combination with `cftry`/`cfcatch`, to gracefully recover from the error, or at least give users an error message they will understand.

```
<cftry>
    <cfparam name="BirthDate" type="date" default="January 1, 2003">
    <cfcatch>
        <!--- GRACEFUL RECOVERY OR MEANINGFUL ERROR MESSAGE GOES HERE --->
    </cfcatch>
</cftry>
```

MANAGING VARIABLES IN SCOPES

All variables are stored in *scopes*, categories that define the accessibility and longevity of the variables. If no scope is explicitly specified, as in the examples given so far in this chapter, the variable is created in the default VARIABLES scope. (Although it is not a requirement, scopes are sometimes written in all caps, to make it easier to distinguish them from other CFML elements.)

You specify a scope explicitly by putting it before the variable, separating the two with a period: SESSION.myVar.

Other commonly encountered scopes include APPLICATION, ARGUMENTS, ATTRIBUTES, CALLER, CLIENT, FLASH, FORM, REQUEST, SESSION, and URL.

SCOPES THAT REQUIRE LOCKING

There are four scopes in which data persists past the life of a single request: CLIENT, APPLICATION, SESSION, and SERVER. Because ColdFusion is multi-threaded, at any given moment ColdFusion may be processing multiple requests, even from a single client. For this reason, all four of these scopes present the danger of simultaneously trying to set a single variable to two different values, resulting in unpredictable behavior. To avoid this, use the `cflock` tag to enclose sections of code that change variables in these scopes. For instance:

```
<cflock>
<cfset application.myVar = "true">
</cflock>
```

WARNING

> For locking to work, all code that changes the variable must be enclosed within `cflock` tags. A `cfset` tag not enclosed in `cflock` tags could change a locked variable.

33

NOTE

> Before application variables can be used, the application state management system must be enabled with the `clientmanagement` attribute in the `cfapplication` tag. For example:
>
>   <CFAPPLICATION NAME="greendeptApp"
>   CLIENTMANAGEMENT="Yes">

SCOPING OUT THE SCOPES

Variables in the ATTRIBUTES scope are available only on the page on which they are created and pages included with the `cfinclude` tag. (See also the CALLER scope).

CALLER and ATTRIBUTES are used only with custom tags (files that define procedures and attributes for tags that you create yourself). In a custom tag file, the CALLER scope references the VARIABLES scope of the page that called (used) the custom tag. The ATTRIBUTES scope is for variables that contain values passed by the calling page.

→ The `cf_scrape` custom tag, defined in `scrape.cfm`, uses both the CALLER and ATTRIBUTES scopes. **See** "Custom Tags," **page 895**, in this chapter.

The ARGUMENTS scope contains variables passed to a user-defined function, or to a method (a function contained in a ColdFusion component).

The APPLICATION scope contains variables associated with an entire application. The application name is defined in a `cfapplication` tag, which the programmer usually puts in `application.cfm`.

---

application.cfm
The `application.cfm` file is a special page that is automatically processed before each page in the application is loaded. The `application.cfm` page defines application-level settings, functions, and features, such as default variables, constants, data sources, style settings, and error pages. Anything defined on the `application.cfm` page will always be available on all pages and to all users of the application.

The CLIENT scope contains variables associated with one client. Client variables persist across pages and browser sessions. By default, Client variables are stored in the system registry of the client computer, but you can store them in a cookie or a database.

The FLASH scope contains variables exchanged between a Macromedia Flash MX movie and the ColdFusion MX server.

→ For more on using Flash with ColdFusion, **see** Chapter 23, "Using Flash for Dynamic Data," **page 661**.

The FORM scope contains variables passed from a Form page to its action page when the user submits the form.

The REQUEST scope contains variables associated with one HTTP request. The variables stored in the REQUEST scope are available to all pages processed in response to the request. The REQUEST scope is often used instead of the APPLICATION scope, so that variables don't have to be locked.

The SERVER scope contains variables available to all applications running on the server.

The SESSION scope contains variables associated with one client. Unlike Client variables, however, Session variables do not persist across browser sessions. They disappear when the user closes the browser. They can also be configured to time out after a period of inactivity.

The URL scope contains parameters that were appended to the URL that called the current page. A question mark separates the main body of the URL from the parameters. If there is more than one parameter, they are separated by ampersands (&). For instance:

```
http://www.greendept.com/index.cfm?type="lightbulb"&item="compact fluorescent"
```

➔ For a complete table of scopes, and links to information on scopes and locking, **see** scopes.htm on the CD accompanying this book.

USING COLDFUSION FOR DATABASE OPERATIONS

The main purpose of ColdFusion is to provide a high-level programming interface for data-enabling Web sites. Thus, the kernel of ColdFusion functionality focuses on the four basic database operations: retrieve, update, insert, and delete. One tag, cfquery, handles all four operations. The database functionality is expressed in a Structured Query Language (SQL) statement contained between the start and end tags.

You can greatly enhance your ability to interact with databases in ColdFusion by learning some beyond-the-basics SQL. On the other hand, all the examples provided in this section were auto-generated with Dreamweaver, as described in Chapter 13. You may find it faster and easier to generate basic SQL with Dreamweaver. Even if you do not use Dreamweaver, the material in this section will help you understand the code that Dreamweaver generates, in case you want to modify it.

➔ For more on database operations and SQL, **see** "Database Operations," **page 290**, in Chapter 13, "Developing ColdFusion Applications in Dreamweaver."

RETRIEVING DATA

Retrieving data creates a *recordset*, an object containing zero or more records, which you can access and manipulate with CFML. You retrieve data by enclosing an SQL SELECT statement within a ColdFusion cfquery tag.

NOTE

> SELECT is an SQL *keyword*, a word reserved by SQL for its own use. (Although not a requirement, SQL keywords are often represented in all caps, to make them easier to distinguish from other elements of the SQL statement.)

➔ For a full listing of SQL reserved words, **see** SQLreservedWords.htm on the CD accompanying this book.

The <cfquery> tag specifies the database from which to retrieve data. The SELECT statement specifies the table(s) within the database, and which records in the tables to get.

33

The simplest SELECT statement looks like this:

```
SELECT * FROM Products
```

This statement says, "Retrieve all columns (fields) of all rows (records) from the Products table." The asterisk is a wild-card meaning "all columns." All rows are retrieved, because the statement contains no limiting clause for selecting only a subset of rows. In this case, each row is a different product, and the columns are the attributes of the product, such as the product's unique ID, category, description, name, list price, and so on.

To avoid possible problems with database management systems that automatically create columns, it is best to explicitly name each column you want to retrieve, like this:

```
SELECT ProductID, Category, ProductName,
Description, ProductURLID, ListPrice, Weight,
ProductSize, ProductApplication, AlternativeTo,
Brand, SmallImageName, MediumImageName,
LargeImageName, WhenEntered, Owner
FROM Products
```

You can use a WHERE clause to select only specified rows. For instance, the following statement retrieves only records with the Category code 13001010000 (the category code for books in the greendept.mdb database):

```
SELECT ProductID, Category, ProductName, Description,
  ProductURLID, ListPrice, Weight, ProductSize,
  ProductApplication, AlternativeTo, Brand, SmallImageName,
  MediumImageName, LargeImageName, WhenEntered, Owner
FROM Products
WHERE Category = '13001010000'
```

To use this SQL statement in ColdFusion, enclose it in a cfquery tag. In the following example, the cfquery tag specifies the greendept database, and assigns the name qProducts to the Recordset that is created:

```
<cfquery name="qProducts" datasource="greendept">
SELECT ProductID, Category, ProductName, Description,
  ProductURLID, ListPrice, Weight, ProductSize,
  ProductApplication, AlternativeTo, Brand, SmallImageName,
  MediumImageName, LargeImageName, WhenEntered, Owner
FROM Products
WHERE Category = '13001010000'
</cfquery>
```

→ qProducts.cfm, qProducts2.cfm, qProducts2b.cfm, and qProducts_form.cfm, on the CD accompanying this book, all use some version of the qProducts recordset. These sample .cfm files are discussed in "Retrieving Data," **page 293**, in Chapter 13. qProducts.cfc also uses a recordset named qProducts that is similar to this one but retrieves only four attributes. qProducts.cfc is discussed under "Web Services," **page 672** (Chapter 23) .

UPDATING RECORDS

Updating changes the values stored in fields in an existing record or records. Conceptually, you use two ColdFusion pages to update data: an update form and an update action page. In practice, the two pages can be, and often are, combined on one page.

You create an update form with an HTML `form` tag or a `cfform` tag. On the action page, you can use either a `cfquery` tag (containing an SQL UPDATE statement) or a `cfupdate` tag. The update action page may also contain a "success" message, so that the user knows that the record was successfully updated, or it may redirect the user to a page containing such a message.

The following is a basic UPDATE statement in SQL. As it stands, because no limit is put on which records to update, it sets the Category field to all zeros for all products in the database.

```
UPDATE Products SET Category='00000000000'
```

Multiple fields can be updated with a single UPDATE statement. The assignment statements (for example, `Category='00000000000'`) for the different fields are separated by commas. For example:

```
UPDATE Products SET Category='00000000000', ProductName='Seeking Sanctuary'
```

A WHERE clause limits the update to specified records:

```
UPDATE Products
SET Category='00000000000', ProductName='Seeking Sanctuary'
WHERE ProductID = 1
```

(Note that an SQL statement can be written on multiple lines for readability.)

Form variables provide the values in the assignment statements. Thus, the user's input on the form determines the values used in the update operation. For example:

```
UPDATE Products
SET Category='#FORM.Category#', ProductName='#FORM.ProductName#'
WHERE ProductID = #FORM.ProductID#
```

In addition, you should use a `cfif` tag to check that the form variables actually exist (for example, `cfif IsDefined("FORM.Category")`) and that they are not blank (for example, AND `#FORM.Category# NEQ ""`). (NEQ is "not equal to.") If the form variable doesn't exist or it is empty, one solution is to update the database with a NULL value. Here's an example, with the `cfquery` tag added:

```
<cfquery datasource="greendept">
UPDATE Products SET Category=
<cfif IsDefined("FORM.Category") AND #FORM.Category# NEQ "">
  '#FORM.Category#'
    <cfelse>
    NULL
</cfif>
, ProductName=
<cfif IsDefined("FORM.ProductName") AND #FORM.ProductName# NEQ "">
  '#FORM.ProductName#'
    <cfelse>
    NULL
</cfif>
WHERE ProductID = #FORM.ProductID#
</cfquery>
```

33

Fields present in the database but not in the UPDATE statement remain unchanged.

Attempting to update with a NULL value generates an error if the database has been configured not to accept the NULL value for that field. In that case, you may be able to substitute a more appropriate value for NULL. For instance, the Category field in the greendept database is a required field and does not accept a NULL, but there is a category code for Miscellaneous (00000000010) that might be appropriate:

```
<cfif IsDefined("FORM.Category") AND #FORM.Category# NEQ "">
  '#FORM.Category#'
    <cfelse>
    '00000000010'
</cfif>
```

If the same default value is always appropriate, you can configure it in the database. If a default value has been configured in the database, the database provides that value when you try to update with a NULL.

Relationships between tables can also generate errors when you try to update. For instance, in the greendept database, the Products table has an Owner field, which can contain only a valid user ID from the UserID field in the Users table. Any other value would generate an error if there were no default set in the database (or if a default were set that didn't correspond to a value in the UserID field in the Users table). To handle this situation, a "No User" record has been created in the Users table, with the UserID equal to 1. With the default Owner in Products set to 1, there is a match between Owner and UserID, and no error is generated.

Even where the database accepts a NULL, it may be preferable to insert a dash or some other character indicating an empty field. Dynamic tables may format better with such a character. For instance, the following example uses a dash instead of NULL to indicate "no value":

```
<cfif IsDefined("FORM.ProductName") AND #FORM.ProductName# NEQ "">
  '#FORM.ProductName#'
    <cfelse>
    '-'
</cfif>
```

→ For an illustration of updating, **see** update1.cfm, which was auto-generated with Dreamweaver, on the CD accompanying this book.

INSERTING RECORDS

Inserting adds a new record to the database. As with updating, there is conceptually a form page and an action page for inserting, and the two pages are commonly combined.

Here's a simple INSERT statement, providing three values for three fields:

```
INSERT INTO Products (ProductID, Category, ProductName)
VALUES (1, '00000000000', 'Seeking Sanctuary')
```

Fields present in the database but not in the INSERT statement are filled in according to the rules of the database. Typically, a NULL is inserted if the database permits it and no default value has been defined in the database for that field.

Using form variables, substituting NULL for nonexistent or blank variables, and adding the cfquery tag, the statement looks like this:

```
<cfquery datasource="greendept">
INSERT INTO Products (ProductID, Category, ProductName) VALUES (
<cfif IsDefined("FORM.ProductID") AND #FORM.ProductID# NEQ "">
  #FORM.ProductID#
    <cfelse>
    NULL
</cfif>
,
<cfif IsDefined("FORM.Category") AND #FORM.Category# NEQ "">
  '#FORM.Category#'
    <cfelse>
    NULL
</cfif>
,
<cfif IsDefined("FORM.ProductName") AND #FORM.ProductName# NEQ "">
  '#FORM.ProductName#'
    <cfelse>
    NULL
</cfif>
)
</cfquery>
```

The same problems that arise in attempting to update with NULL can arise when attempting to insert a NULL value with the cfelse clause, and the same solutions also apply.

→ For an illustration of inserting, **see** insert1.cfm, which was auto-generated with Dreamweaver, on the CD accompanying this book.

DELETING RECORDS

Deleting permanently and irrevocably removes records from the database. This simple statement, because it puts no limits on what to delete, totally wipes out an entire table:

```
DELETE FROM Products
```

Relationships can cause delete operations to fail. For example, if you try DELETE FROM Users (delete all records in the Users table) in greendept.mdb, it has no effect, because each UserID in Users is required to maintain a relationship with the Products table. You get an error, The record cannot be deleted or changed because table 'Products' includes related records.

You can apply delete operations to specific records if you use a WHERE clause:

```
<cfquery datasource="greendept">
DELETE FROM Products WHERE ProductID = 1
</cfquery>
```

CUSTOM TAGS

You can extend CFML by creating your own custom tags, which work just like standard CFML tags. Use custom tags to encapsulate application logic so that you can use and re-use it from any ColdFusion page.

33

Thousands of custom tags are also available through the ColdFusion Exchange at www.macromedia.com, many of them freeware or shareware. Browsing there is a good way to familiarize yourself with tags, and also to find out what you don't have to do, because someone else has already done it for you.

→ For more on custom tags, **see** customTags.htm on the CD, which includes a link to the ColdFusion Exchange at www.macromedia.com.

Custom Tags Versus ColdFusion Components

Custom tags and ColdFusion components both encapsulate application logic. However, there are important differences between them. Probably the two most significant have to do with accessibility and persistence.

Custom tags are accessible only locally and only via ColdFusion. CFCs can be accessed in a number of ways, including as Web services or via Flash Remoting, which means they are accessible remotely from a wide variety of environments. If there are capabilities in your program that you want to expose remotely to a variety of platforms, implement them as CFCs. These are likely to be the fundamental services offered by your site. If a database is at the foundation of your site, the most fundamental service usually involves returning data. For instance, if the basic purpose of your site is translation among multiple languages, returning the translated text is the basic service. This is a capability you would most likely expose as a Web service, and therefore one you would implement as a CFC. Capabilities relating to presentation (formatting and viewing), on the other hand, typically apply only to the local mechanism for consuming the service (such as a ColdFusion page that displays the translated text), and therefore might be better implemented with custom tags for encapsulation.

The other big difference is that you can *persist* a CFC and data in it by assigning the CFC to a persistent scope, such as the SESSION or APPLICATION scope.

There is no way to persist a custom tag. Therefore, it can't be used to store data.

There are other, more minor differences too. For instance, a custom tag has a single entry point, so it is best suited for implementing a single procedure. A CFC can contain multiple functions, which provide multiple entry points, so it's well suited for implementing multiple related procedures.

By encapsulating multiple related procedures and persistent data, a CFC takes on the characteristics of an object, whereas the custom tag remains simply a transient procedure.

In addition, Dreamweaver automates creating and deploying CFCs more than custom tags. For example, there is a drag-and-drop procedure for creating a page that calls a function in a CFC. There is nothing like that for custom tags.

One framework for thinking about the implications of the inherent difference between CFCs and custom tags is the model-view-controller (MVC) paradigm for architecting applications. The *view* manages graphical and/or textual output. The *controller* interprets input from the user, and tells the model and/or the view to change appropriately. Finally, the *model* does whatever the application is ultimately designed to do, such as translating for a translation application.

In this framework, CFCs are usually appropriate at the model and controller levels, whereas custom tags are appropriate at the view level, as shown in Figure 33.1.

→ For an example of persistence, **see** the link in persistence.htm on the CD accompanying this book.

→ To learn more about the drag-and-drop procedure for creating a page that calls a function in a CFC, **see** "Invoking a function in a CFC," **page 312**, in Chapter 13.

Figure 33.1
Custom tags are often most appropriate at the view level. CFCs are usually more appropriate at the controller and model levels. (Thanks to: Benoit Hediard. See *benorama.htm* on the CD.)

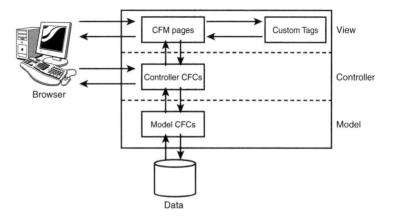

CUSTOM TAG BASICS

Each custom tag is embodied in its own separate file. Although there are several ways of invoking a custom tag, a simple one is to use a tag with the name of the file, with cf_ in front of it. For example, if the custom tag is contained in a file named scrape.cfm, the custom tag is cf_scrape.

> **NOTE**
>
> The other ways of invoking a custom tag use cfmodule and cfimport. They are often favored for managing a large number of custom tags.

> **NOTE**
>
> There are two kinds of custom tags: CFML and CFX. CFX tags are written in C++ or Java. Only CFML tags are covered in this book.

ColdFusion looks for custom tags first in the same directory as the calling page, then in the CFusionMX\CustomTags directory, then in subdirectories of the CFusionMX\CustomTags directory, and finally in directories that you can specify in the ColdFusion MX Administrator.

The calling page can pass data to the custom tag page. Although custom tags do not explicitly return a value, the calling page can easily get a result from a custom tag.

PASSING DATA TO A CUSTOM TAG

To pass data from the calling page to the custom tag page, you have to do two things, one on the calling page and one on the custom tag page:

- On the calling page, invoke the custom tag with one or more name/value pairs.
- On the custom tag page, use the cfparam tag to create a corresponding parameter for each name/value pair. Create the parameter(s) in the ATTRIBUTES scope.

For now, you don't have to worry about the details of the following example, as long as you see the basic outline of the two steps just described.

→ The following example is implemented in screenScrapeTest.cfm (calling page) and screenScrape.cfm (custom tag) on the CD accompanying this book.

→ The details of invoking the screenScrape.cfm custom tag example should be clear after you read the section on "The cf_scrape Custom Tag," **page 879**, in this chapter.

Suppose you have a custom tag for screen scraping—searching a Web page for text contained between a specified start string and a specified end string. If the custom tag is embodied in a file named screenScrape.cfm and requires four parameters, named document, start, end, and matchCase, then on the calling page you will have something like this:

```
<cf_screenScrape
    document = "#myDoc#"
    start = "#startSearch#"
    end = "#endSearch#"
    matchCase = "Yes"
>
```

In the preceding code, document = "#myDoc#" is the first name/value pair, start = "#startSearch#" is the second, and so on. The entire tag, including all name/value pairs, can be on a single line. Using multiple lines, as in the preceding example, may make the code easier to read.

On the custom tag page, screenScrape.cfm, you will have one cfparam statement for each name/value pair, like this:

```
<cfparam name="attributes.document" default="#errordoc#" type="string">
<cfparam name="attributes.start" default="/////" type="string">
<cfparam name="attributes.end" default="////" type="string">
<cfparam name="attributes.matchCase" default="no" type="boolean">
```

Notice that each parameter created is assigned to the ATTRIBUTES scope: name="attributes.document", name="attributes.start", and so on. The calling page automatically puts the name/value pairs in the custom tag's ATTRIBUTES scope. Within the custom tag, you have to specify that scope explicitly when referencing the values.

RETURNING DATA FROM A CUSTOM TAG

Variables created within a custom tag disappear when the tag terminates. Therefore, before the tag terminates (usually just before), you must pass data back to the calling page. The key to accomplishing this is the CALLER scope. The CALLER scope in the custom tag and the VARIABLES scope in the calling page refer to the very same place.

For example, answerMaybe.cfm on the CD is a custom tag consisting of a single line:

```
<cfset "caller.answer" = "maybe">
```

This line sets the answer variable in the calling file to the value "maybe", creating the variable first if it doesn't already exist.

To use answerMaybe.cfm, all you need to do in the calling file (answerMaybeTest.cfm on the CD) is this:

```
<cf_answerMaybe>
<cfoutput>#answer#</cfoutput>
```

This will display the word "maybe."

THE cf_scrape CUSTOM TAG

Matthew Walker's scrape.cfm custom tag illustrates both the mechanics of custom tags and automated text retrieval.

CAUTION

> As Matthew states on his site, the ethics and etiquette of screen-scraping require you to get permission, give credit, and make sure that you're not bogging someone's server down by retrieving too much information too often.

→ For a link to Matthew's site, **see** scrapeLink1.htm on the CD accompanying this book.

There are basically three steps to using scrape.cfm:

- Get some text.
- Pass the text to scrape.cfm, along with instructions on what to search for within the text. If scrape.cfm were looking for people, the instructions would basically say, "Grab the guy between John and Bill"—with the added proviso that there may be more than one John and more than one Bill, and therefore more than one guy to grab.
- Use the result returned by scrape.cfm.

All three of these steps occur in the calling page, not in scrape.cfm.

In scrape.cfm, the action also unfolds in three phases:

- Get the text and the instructions.
- Loop through the text, finding all the desired items and putting them in an array.

→ For more on arrays, see the "Arrays" sidebar below.

- Return the result.

33

Arrays

An array is an ordered, numbered list of data items. The data items are called *elements*. The number that identifies an element's place in the list is called the *index* of that element. If the array is named myArray, the second element in the array is referenced as myArray[2]. That is, you reference elements by using the name of the array, followed by the element's index in square brackets.

A difference between ColdFusion arrays and Flash arrays is that Flash arrays are zero-based. That is, the first element in a Flash array is myArray[0]. In ColdFusion, the first element is myArray[1].

The elements of an array can be any data type, including other arrays. An array of arrays is a two-dimensional array, which you can visualize as a table or spreadsheet in which the rows can be of different lengths. In a two-dimensional array, myArray[1][2] is the second element in the first "row" (that is, in the first array).

ColdFusion can create arrays in one, two, or three dimensions. Here is an example of creating an array with the cfset tag: <cfset myArray=ArrayNew(1)>. This creates a one-dimensional array. Change the number 1 to a 2 or 3 for a two- or three-dimensional array.

In the array returned by scrape.cfm, the elements are *structures*.

Structures

A structure is a collection of key-value pairs, where the keys are text strings and the values can be any ColdFusion data type, including other structures. To create a structure, use the ColdFusion StructNew function. Structures are often named. For example, the following line creates a new, empty structure named myStruct:

```
<cfset myStruct = StructNew()>
```

Then you can add key-value pairs like this:

```
<cfset myStruct.myVar1 = "true">
<cfset myStruct.myVar2 = "false">
```

The two preceding lines add two key-value pairs to the structure. The keys are myVar1 and myVar2. The values are "true" and "false".

You can create an array of structures as follows. The first line creates the array. The second line creates an empty structure as the first element of the array. The third line creates an empty structure as the second element of the array.

```
<cfset myArray=ArrayNew(1)>
<cfset myArray[1] = structNew()>
<cfset myArray[2] = structNew()>
```

Add key-value pairs to these structures like this:

```
<cfset myArray[1].myVar1 = "true">
<cfset myArray[1].myVar2 = "false">
```

All these ways of using structures are employed in scrape.cfm.

In scrape.cfm, each structure in the array has three key-value pairs, in which the keys are start, middle, and end. The values of both start and end are arrays, and the value of middle is a text string. It's usually the middle values that you're interested in getting back from scrape.cfm, but scrape.cfm returns the whole structure. As you'll see in a minute, start and end could be of interest, as well. (I said earlier that the instructions amount to, "Grab the guy between John and Bill." Well, scrape.cfm brings John and Bill back, too, for good measure.)

Now that you know a little bit about what you're getting back from scrape.cfm, it's time to back up and look at the first step in using scrape.cfm: getting the text. Because we're interested in getting information from Web pages, we're going to use the cfhttp tag, which generates an HTTP request and stores the response from the Web server in a variable that can be referenced as #cfhttp.fileContent#. The tag looks like this:

33

```
<cfhttp
    url="http://www.someDomain.com/greendept/index.cfm"
    method="get"
    resolveurl="no"
    timeout="3"
>
```

The url attribute specifies the Web page to which the request is directed. The method attribute indicates the action to be performed, in this case getting information from the Web server. (The other common method is post, which sends data to the server.) The resolveurl attribute determines whether links in the retrieved HTML text remain functional; in this case, they do not. Finally, timeout determines how long, in seconds, the ColdFusion server will wait for a response before deciding that the request has failed.

Now let's look at giving "instructions"—how we specify the "John" and "Bill"—to scrape.cfm. These are specified in two variables: startRegex and endRegex. Much of the power of scrape.cfm lies in the fact that the values of these variables are *regular expressions* rather than just text strings. A regular expression is essentially a formula for finding matching text strings. It's as if, instead of having to say "John," we could say "anyone whose name begins with J," or "anyone whose name has four letters," or "anyone whose name begins with J and has four letters," or a thousand other descriptions. This allows for a much more flexible search.

Regular Expressions

Regular expressions combine literal text strings with special characters to create "formulas" that define a set of text strings with common characteristics. In ColdFusion, regular expressions are used to search for text that matches the formula. There are four built-in ColdFusion functions that use regular expressions: REFind, REFindNoCase, REReplace, and REReplaceNoCase. The "RE" in each of these function names stands for "Regular Expression." The first two functions find text. The second two find and replace.

The special characters used in regular expressions are

+ * ? . [^ $ ( ) { | \

A set of characters enclosed in square brackets [] represents any one of those characters. For example,

- "[blqr]" matches "b", "l", "q," or "r"
- b[ia][lr]k matches "bilk," "balk," "birk," or "bark"
- A dash indicates a range of characters. For example, "[A-Z]" matches any uppercase letter.
- A period (.) matches any character.

An asterisk extends a single-character formula to any number of characters. For instance, "[A-Z]*" matches any number of uppercase letters (including the number zero).

A plus sign (+) extends a single-character formula to any number of characters greater than zero. For instance, "[A-Z]+" matches any non-zero number of uppercase letters.

A pair of parentheses groups a part of a regular expression into a subexpression that you can treat as a single unit. For example, the regular expression "yada" matches just one instance of the string. The regular expression "(yada)+" matches one or more instances.

A backslash "escapes" a special character so that it is interpreted as a literal character. For example, the formula for a literal asterisk is

"*"

33

Use two backslashes together to indicate a literal backslash:

"\\"

There are many more rules for building regular expressions, which you can find in the ColdFusion documentation, Macromedia's livedocs, and many other sources. (However, the rules for regular expressions are not exactly the same in other environments, such as JavaScript and Perl. ColdFusion's rules are quite close to those of Perl, but there are a few exceptions, listed in the ColdFusion documentation.)

Regular expressions are powerful, but they also can be tricky to use. Use the ordinary Find, FindNoCase, Replace, and ReplaceNoCase functions when you just need to search for literal text strings. You'll avoid the complexities of having to escape special characters.

The usage of cf_scrape is illustrated in three ColdFusion files on the CD accompanying this book. You also need to install a small database file, gdQuotes.mdb, to make this example work. These are the three files:

- scrape.cfm is the custom tag file (cf_scrape)
- quotePage.cfm is the page to be scraped. It displays a random quote from the three quotes in the gdQuotes.mdb database.
- quotesScrape.cfm is the calling page. It uses scrape.cfm (cf_scrape) to screen scrape the quote.

Put all the cfm files in CFusionMX/wwwroot/, copy gdQuotes.mdb to your hard disk, and create a system DSN for it named gdquotes. Then you can run quotePage.cfm or quotesScrape.cfm by typing **http://localhost:8500/quotePage.cfm** or **http://localhost:8500/quotesScrape.cfm** in your browser's address bar.

The quotesScrape.cfm file depends on the fact that quotePage.cfm uses CSS tags named quoteText and quoteAuthor to format the quote and the author's name, respectively. Here's how quotesScrape.cfm retrieves the quote text. No special characters are required; the regular expressions are just text strings.

```
<cf_scrape
    document = "#cfhttp.fileContent#"
    startRegex = "span class = quoteText>"
    endRegex = "<"
    return = "quoteText"
    matchCase = "Yes"
>
```

Here's how quotesScrape.cfm retrieves the author's name. No special characters are required in startRegex and endRegex, except the backslashes needed to escape the parentheses.

```
<cf_scrape
    document = "#cfhttp.fileContent#"
    startRegex = "span class = quoteAuthor>\("
    endRegex = "\)<"
    return = "author"
    matchCase = "Yes"
>
```

CREATING AND USING COLDFUSION COMPONENTS (CFCs)

A ColdFusion component consists of one or more functions enclosed in `cfcomponent` tags. Here's an example of a single-function component named demo.cfc (available on the CD) with a function named `demoFunction` that returns the text string "This is the result."

```
<cfcomponent>
    <cffunction name="demoFunction" access="public" returntype="string">
        <cfset result = "This is the result.">
        <cfreturn result>
    </cffunction>
</cfcomponent>
```

Notice that the function explicitly declares a return type of "string". ColdFusion throws an error if you try to return a different data type. In addition, the function explicitly returns a value, using the `cfreturn` tag. It does not use the CALLER scope.

The following code from demo.cfm (also on the CD) invokes the `demoFunction` function in demo.cfc:

```
<cfinvoke component="demo"
    method="demoFunction"
    returnvariable="result">
></cfinvoke>
```

The variable name used within the component to store the return value and variable name used on the calling page to receive the return value happen to be the same here: "result". This was done for the programmer's convenience, as a reminder of their relationship. The names could be different. In contrast to custom tags, components don't have to provide the name of the variable that will receive the data on the calling page.

CFCs use the `cfargument` tag in much the same way that custom tags use `cfparam`: to define data items that will be passed in. To illustrate this, here are the first few lines of code in scrape.cfc on the CD, a component that implements the same functionality as the custom tag scrape.cfm:

```
<cfcomponent>
    <cffunction name="scrape" access="public" returntype="array">
        <cfargument name="document"  type="string" required="true">
        <cfargument name="startRegex" type="string" required="true">
        <cfargument name="endRegex"  type="string" required="true">
        <cfargument name="matchCase"  default="No" type="boolean">
```

From there on in the scrape.cfc component, everything is exactly the same as in scrape.cfm, until it comes time to pass data back to the calling page, in the last line of the function. At that point, scrape.cfc uses `cfreturn`, like this:

```
<cfreturn result>
```

Again, unlike the custom tag, the component is not providing the name of the variable to receive the return value. The calling page defines that variable, and only the calling page

33

needs to know its name. The variable name `result` could be changed in the component to anything else, without requiring any changes in the calling page. Of course, all occurrences of the variable name would have to be changed consistently within the component.

CREATING AND USING WEB SERVICE CFCS

As you saw in the previous section, the differences in format between a custom tag and a single-function component are minor. The difference in potential, however, is significant, because a CFC has the potential to be accessed remotely in three ways: a URL parameter (including a URL parameter generated automatically when a form is submitted), Flash Remoting, or a Web service invocation.

For a function within a CFC to respond as a Web service, it must be formatted with four parameters: `name`, `access` (set to "remote"), `returnType`, and `output` (set to "no" or "false"). For example, this is the start tag for the `getSiteName` function:

```
<cffunction name="getSiteName" access="remote"
    returnType="string" output="false">
```

If the function doesn't return anything, set `returnType` to `"void"`.

The `output` attribute must be set to `"no"` or `"false"` because ColdFusion converts all Web service output to XML.

WARNING

When a CFC is invoked as a Web service, all arguments will be considered required, even if the `required` attribute of the argument is set to `"false"`.

33

There are a number of approaches to passing parameters to CFCs. Here is a CFC with a `getSiteName` function, with one (useless) argument added. (This CFC was largely generated by Dreamweaver, with only the words "The Green Department" added by hand.)

→ The `getSiteName` function was auto-generated in Dreamweaver, as described in "Creating a Web service CFC," **page 314**, in Chapter 13.

```
<cfcomponent displayName="Get Site Name">
    <cffunction name="getSiteName" access="remote" returnType="string"
output="false">
        <!--- getSiteName body --->
        <cfargument name="uselessArgument" required="no">
        <cfreturn "The Green Department">
    </cffunction>
</cfcomponent>
```

When invoking this CFC, you can provide the required argument in three ways. (And it *is* required for Web service access.) The following examples assume that the name of the CFC file is `getSiteName.cfc`, and that it is in the Web service directory under the Web root (wwwroot) .

- With the `cfinvokeargument` tag:

```
<cfinvoke
 webservice="http://www.someDomain.com/webservice/getSiteNameArg.cfc?wsdl"
 method="getSiteName"
 returnvariable="aString">
 <cfinvokeargument name="uselessArgument" value = "useless">
</cfinvoke>
```

- As a named attribute-value pair:

```
<cfinvoke
 webservice="http://www.someDomain.com/webservice/getSiteNameArg.cfc?wsdl"
 method="getSiteName"
 uselessArgument = "useless"
 returnvariable="aString">
</cfinvoke>
```

- As a structure, in the `argumentCollection` attribute:

```
<cfset argumentStruct = StructNew()>
<cfset argumentStruct.uselessArgument = "useless">
<cfinvoke
 webservice="http://www.someDomain.com/webservice/getSiteName.cfc?wsdl"
 method="getSiteName"
 argumentcollection="#argumentStruct#"
 returnvariable="aString">
</cfinvoke>
```

Each of the foregoing methods can be extended to provide any number of arguments.

The last approach can be used to hand over an entire scope to the CFC. For instance, to submit a form to a CFC, you can use

```
argumentcollection="#FORM#"
```

TROUBLESHOOTING

Invoking a function as a Web service, I'm getting an error message like, "Web service operation 'getSiteName' with parameters {} could not be found." I know the CFC with this function is there, and I'm addressing it correctly. Why can't it be found?

The clue to your problem is in the mention of "parameters" in the error message. The function you are invoking requires one or more arguments that you are not providing. (Remember that when you invoke a function as a Web service, even arguments defined as not being required are required.) Basically, ColdFusion is telling you, "I can't find a Web service method (function) with this name *that doesn't take any parameters.*" Provide the parameter(s), and your problem should be solved.

PART VII

APPENDIXES

A ActionScript Reference   909

B Making Flash Accessible   977

ActionScript Reference

In this appendix

The ContextMenu Class   910

Datatype Conversion Rules   911

The MovieClip Class   917

Arithmetic Operators   926

Understanding Bitwise Operators   930

Assignment and Compound Assignment   938

Comparison Operators   939

Using Logical (Boolean) Operators   943

The Conditional Operator   946

The Comma Operator   947

Named Operators   948

The Date Class   951

The Key Object   955

The Math Object   957

The TextField and TextFormat Classes   958

Wrapper Classes: Boolean, Number, String   968

The Camera Class   972

The Microphone Class   974

THE ContextMenu CLASS

The ContextMenu class, available only in Flash Player 7, allows you to replace or add to the context menu, which normally appears when the user right-clicks (Windows) or Ctrl-clicks (Mac) in the Flash Player.

Use the constructor new ContextMenu() to create a ContextMenu object. Then you can use the methods and attributes of the ContextMenu class to control the display of the built-in context menu items (such as Zoom In and Zoom Out), add custom menu items, or create a copy of the custom menu.

To add a custom menu item, you push a ContextMenuItem object onto the customItems array, which is a standard property of every ContextMenu object. Each push() adds a new item to the customItems array, and a new option on the custom menu. Each item has a label, which is displayed to the user, and an event handler, which is called when the user selects the item.

The ContextMenu class generates an onSelect event, called when a user brings up the custom context menu that you have created, but before the menu actually displays. There is one onSelect event for your entire custom menu, and one onSelect event for each custom item on the menu.

Using the menu property of the Button, MovieClip, or TextField class, you can assign a custom menu to the Main Timeline, or to an individual button, movie clip, or text field object. The menu property is new in Flash MX 2004.

ContextMenu has two methods:

- copy, which returns a copy of the specified ContextMenu object.
- hideBuiltInItems, which hides built-in context menu items (with the exception of Settings) while leaving custom menu items visible. This method sets to false the eight Boolean attributes of the builtInItems object: save, zoom, quality, play, loop, rewind, forward_back, and print, removing the menu items of the same names from the ContextMenu.

ContextMenuItem has one method, copy, which makes a copy of the menu item object.

It has four attributes:

- caption—Caption text displayed in the context menu
- enabled—Boolean, enables or disables the menu item
- separatorBefore—A Boolean, false by default, indicating whether a separator bar should appear above the menu item
- visible—A Boolean, true by default, indicating whether the menu item is visible

The following program (contextMenu.fla on the CD accompanying this book) illustrates

- Creating a custom context menu assigned to the Main Timeline, with event handlers for each option on the menu

- Trapping the onSelect event for the entire menu
- Assigning the menu to individual objects on the Stage

Note that existing (built-in) labels (such as Zoom In), even if hidden, cannot be used in your custom menu. In addition, you cannot use the following options: Macromedia, Flash Player, Copy, Save, or Paste. If you try to use any of these, they will simply not show up on your menu. However, you may be able to get around this limitation by putting something after the forbidden phrase, as in Zoom In.... However, this trick does not work with the Macromedia, Flash Player, or Settings options. Any label that even contains these phrases will not show up.

```
// Start basic program
myMenu.hideBuiltInItems();
myMenu.customItems.push( new ContextMenuItem("Zoom In ... ",itemHandler1) );
myMenu.customItems.push( new ContextMenuItem("Calculate   ...",itemHandler2) );
myMenu.customItems.push( new ContextMenuItem("Clear",itemHandler3) );
function itemHandler1() { trace(" pressed Zoom In ... ") };
function itemHandler2() { trace(" pressed Calculate ... ") };
function itemHandler3() { trace(" pressed Clear") };
this.menu = myMenu;
// End basic program
// Start trapping onSelect for entire menu
menuHandler = function (obj:Object, menu:ContextMenu) {
  if(obj instanceof MovieClip) {
    trace("Movie clip: " + obj);
    status = "mc";
  }
  if(obj instanceof TextField) {
    trace("Text field: " + obj);
      status = "txt";
  }
  if(obj instanceof Button) {
    trace("Button: " + obj);
      status = "but";
  }
}
myMenu.onSelect = menuHandler;
// End trapping onSelect for entire menu
// Assign menu to individual objects on the Stage
mybut.menu = myMenu;
but2.menu = myMenu;
status_txt.menu = myMenu;
myClip.menu = myMenu;
```

A

DATATYPE CONVERSION RULES

When the ActionScript interpreter expects one datatype, and you use a different datatype, the interpreter creates a new value of the expected type. For instance, suppose your program contains the following statements:

```
var x;
x = 63 - "my dentist";
trace(x); // ??
```

What will the trace statement display?

If you ask the ActionScript interpreter to subtract a string from a number, it attempts to comply by implicitly converting the string to a number and then subtracting. In this case, the string "my dentist" cannot be successfully converted to a number. It was for cases such as this that the NaN value was created. The ActionScript interpreter converts "my dentist" to NaN, which is officially of the number datatype. Any mathematical operation involving NaN also results in NaN. Therefore, x is equal to NaN.

The same thing happens if you use strong data typing on x and cast "my dentist" to a number:

```
var x:Number;
x = 63 - Number("my dentist");
trace(x); // NaN
```

In this case, the datatype conversion didn't do much good, except that it allowed the program to continue functioning (the alternative to implicit conversion being an error, as in Java). Then again, you gave the ActionScript interpreter an impossible job. On the other hand, if you give it a string such as "3" that *can* be converted to a number, the ActionScript interpreter does something quite helpful:

```
x = 63 - "3";
trace(x); // 60
```

The result of an implicit datatype conversion is always a primitive datatype: string, number, or Boolean. Table A.1 shows the rules for converting to a number.

TABLE A.1   IMPLICIT CONVERSION TO A NUMBER

Supplied Value	Value After Conversion
undefined	FP7: NaN, FP6: 0
null	FP7: NaN, FP6: 0
Boolean false	0
Boolean true	1
A numeric string that can be converted to a base-10 number. (Can contain numerals, a decimal point, a plus sign, a minus sign, and whitespace.)	The equivalent numeric value. (Exception: The + operator concatenates all strings, including numeric strings. See Chapter 13.)
A non-numeric string. (Includes the empty string and any string containing an alphabetic character, including strings starting with "x", "0x", and "FF".)	NaN
"Infinity"	Infinity
"-Infinity"	-Infinity
"NaN"	NaN
Any array	NaN

Supplied Value	Value After Conversion
Any object	NaN
Any movie clip	NaN

Table A.2 shows the rules for converting to a string.

TABLE A.2   IMPLICIT CONVERSION TO A STRING

Supplied Value	Value After Conversion
undefined	FP7: undefined, FP6: "" (the empty string)
null	"null"
Boolean false	"false"
Boolean true	"true"
NaN	"NaN"
0	"0"
Infinity	"Infinity"
-Infinity	"-Infinity"
Any other numeric value	The string equivalent of the numeric value.
Any array	A comma-separated list of element values.
Any object	The return value of the object's toString() method. The default is "[object Object]". The built-in Date object returns a date.
Any movie clip	The absolute path to the movie clip instance; for example, "_level0.myClip".

Table A.3 shows the rules for converting to a Boolean.

TABLE A.3   IMPLICIT CONVERSION TO A BOOLEAN

Supplied Value	Value After Conversion
undefined	false
null	false
NaN	false
0	false
Infinity	true
-Infinity	true
Any other numeric value	true
Empty string	false

continues

TABLE A.3   CONTINUED

Supplied Value	Value After Conversion
Any string that can be converted to a valid nonzero number	`true`
Any string that *cannot* be converted to a valid nonzero number. (Departs from ECMA-262 standard to maintain compatibility with Flash 4.)	`false`
Any array	`true`
Any object	`true`
Any movie clip	`true`

You can explicitly convert any datum to a number, string, or Boolean.

CONVERTING TO A NUMBER

You convert to a number by using the global `Number()` function. For instance, if a user types his or her age into an input text box, it is initially a string. You convert it to a number like this:

```
user1Age = Number(user1Age);
```

If the user types in **"23"**, the interpreter sees the preceding line as follows:

```
user1Age = Number("23");
```

The interpreter sets the user1Age variable to the number 23.

The `Number()` function assumes decimal numbers with optional trailing exponents:

```
Number("2.637e-4"); // 0.0002637
```

You can use hexadecimal numbers if you prefix the string with 0x, as in this instance:

```
greenColor = "0x00FF00"; // hex representation of green color, a string
hexGreen = Number(greenColor); // 65280, the decimal form of 0x00FF00
```

The `parseInt()`and `parsefloat()` functions also convert strings to numbers, but the string must have the following format: The first nonblank character must be the first character of the number you want, and the first character after the number you want must be non-numeric. The following examples use `parseInt()`:

```
1: parseInt("12years") ; // extracts 12
2: parseInt("  12years") ; // extracts 12
3: parseInt("12 years") ; // extracts 12
4: parseInt("12 1 year olds") ; // extracts 12
5: parseInt("twelve 1 year olds") ; // NaN
```

Looking at line 1, the first character after the number is y, which is non-numeric. Line 2 shows that leading blank characters don't matter. Lines 3 and 4 demonstrate that a following blank character counts as non-numeric. In line 5, the first non-blank character is not the first character of a number; therefore, NaN is extracted from this string.

The parseInt() function can also take a second argument that specifies the *radix* (base) of the result. For instance:

```
parseInt("10",16); // extracts 16 - hex 10 (base 16)
parseInt("10",8); // extracts 8 - octal 10 (base 8)
parseInt("10",10); // extracts 10 - decimal 10 (base 10)
```

parseInt() and Hexadecimal Numbers

parseInt() *always* assumes that numbers starting with 0x are hexadecimal:

```
parseInt("0x10"); // 16
```

Trying to override such an implied hexadecimal yields results that aren't usually useful:

```
parseInt("0x10", 10); // 0
parseInt("0x10", 8); // 0
```

Numbers starting with 0 (but not with 0x) are octal by default:

```
parseInt("010"); // 8
```

Unlike with the hexadecimal 0x, you *can* override the implied octal radix and get useful results:

```
parseInt("010", 10); // parsed as decimal, equals 10
```

Don't forget the quotation marks around the string. Sometimes, you can get by with leaving them off, but not always:

```
trace(parseInt(010)); // 0 - not what you want !!!
```

The following examples show how to use parseFloat():

```
trace(parseFloat("12.5years")) ; // extracts 12.5
trace(parseFloat("   12.5years")) ; // extracts 12.5
trace(parseFloat("12.5 years")) ; // extracts 12.5
trace(parseFloat("12.5 1 year olds")) ; // extracts 12.5
trace(parseInt("twelve and a half 1 year olds")) ; // NaN
```

The last example is NaN because the first nonblank character is not numeric.

CONVERTING TO A STRING

You can convert to a string by using either the toString() method or the String() global function. By default, the two accomplish the same thing, though they use different syntax:

```
var x = 6;
x.toString(); // "6"
String(x); // "6"
```

Although methods belong only to objects, implicit datatype conversion allows the toString() method to work with any datatype, according to the rules in Table A.2:

```
var x = 6;
trace(x.toString()); // "6"
y = true;
trace(y.toString()); // "true"
z = null;
trace(z.toString()); // "undefined"
trace(Math.toString()); // "[object Object]" - Math is a built-in object
```

The toString() method has an optional argument that sets the radix (base) of the result, if the supplied datum is a number. For instance, if the number and the radix are the same (such as the number 6 in base 6, the number 7 in base 7), the result is "10":

```
trace(x.toString(x)); // "10" - true if x is any number
```

The following is another example. Note the parentheses required around the number 65280:

```
(65280).toString(16); // "ff00"
```

USING IMPLICIT DATATYPE CONVERSION

You can use a couple of tricks to take advantage of implicit datatype conversion. Their advantage is their very concise syntax. On the downside, when you're reading the code, what they do may not be intuitively obvious.

For instance, the "add and reassign" operator (+=) can accomplish the same thing as the toString() method or the String() global function. It's more obvious with toString() or String() that you are converting to a string, but the "add and reassign" operator is more concise.

Any datum is converted to a string, following the rules of Table A.2, if you add the empty string to it. For example, the second line here accomplishes the same thing as String() or toString():

```
x = 77; // x is a number
x += ""; // x is now a string: "77"
```

"Add and Reassign" and "Subtract and Reassign"

The "add and reassign" operator (+=) adds a second operand to a first operand and assigns the result to the first operand. For example, x += "" is the equivalent of x = x + "".

The "subtract and reassign" operator (-=) subtracts a second operand from a first operand and assigns the result to the first operand. For example, x -= 0 is the equivalent of x = x - 0.

Similarly, subtracting 0 from any datum converts it into a number. For instance:

```
x = new Object(); // x is an object
x -= 0; // x is a number: NaN
```

THE MovieClip CLASS

TABLE A.4 MovieClip **METHODS**

Method	Format	Description
attachMovie	myClip.attachMovie(*idName*, *newName*, *depth* [, *initObject*])	Attaches a movie in the Library to myClip, with the specified depth. The attached movie has all the local properties of the init object. Returns a reference to the attached movie.
createEmptyMovieClip	myClip.createEmptyMovieClip (*instanceName*, *depth*)	Creates an empty movie clip as a child of myClip, with the specified depth.
createTextField	myClip.createTextField (*instanceName*, *depth*, *x*, *y*, *width*, *height*)	Creates an empty text field, with the specified instance name, depth, x and y coordinates, width, and height.
duplicateMovieClip	myClip.duplicateMovieClip (*newName*, *depth* [,*initObject*])	Duplicates myClip, creating a sibling at the specified depth. The new movie has all the local properties of the init object.
getBounds	myClip.getBounds (*targetCoordinateSpace*)	Returns the minimum and maximum x and y coordinates of myClip in relation to a specified coordinate space.
getBytesLoaded	myClip.getBytesLoaded()	Returns the number of bytes loaded for myClip.
getBytesTotal	myClip.getBytesTotal()	Returns the size of myClip in bytes.
getDepth	myClip.getDepth()	Returns the depth number of myClip.

continues

A

TABLE A.4   CONTINUED

Method	Format	Description
getInstanceAtDepth	myClip.getInstanceAtDepth(*depth*)	Returns the name of the child clip of myClip located at the depth number specified by the *depth* parameter. If there is no child movie clip at that depth, returns undefined. FP7 only.
getNextHighestDepth	myClip.getNextHighest Depth()	Returns a number equal to the highest depth number plus one for children of myClip. This is the depth number you need to use to create new child content that will render on top of all existing child content. FP7 only.
getSWFVersion	myClip.getSWFVersion()	Returns an integer specifying the targeted Flash Player version of the SWF loaded into myClip. Returns a -1 error if a JPEG was loaded into myClip. FP7 only.
getTextSnapshot	myClip.getTextSnapshot()	Returns a TextSnapShot object containing the static text from myClip, or an empty string if myClip contains no static text. Works in FP7 only, but myClip can be targeted for FP6 or FP7.
getURL(*URL* [,*window, variables*])	myClip.getURL("http://www. myDomain.com")_	Loads a document into a browser window from the specified URL, sending all the variables from the root of myClip using GET or POST, as specified in the *variables* string.
globalToLocal	myClip.globalToLocal(*point*)	Converts the *point* object from main movie Stage coordinates to the local coordinates of myClip.

A

Method	Format	Description
gotoAndPlay	myClip.gotoAndPlay(*frame*)	Sends the playhead to a specific frame in myClip and then starts playing the movie.
gotoAndStop	myClip.gotoAndStop(*frame*)	Sends the playhead to a specific frame in myClip and then stops the movie.
hitTest	myClip.hitTest(*x, y, shapeFlag*)	Returns true if myClip's bounding box overlaps the point specified by the x and y coordinates. *shapeFlag* is a Boolean value that determines whether the entire shape of myClip is evaluated (true), or just myClip's bounding box (false).
	myClip.hitTest(*target*)	Returns true if myClip's bounding box intersects the bounding box of the target movie clip.
loadMovie	myClip.loadMovie("*url*" [,*variables*])	Loads the movie or JPEG specified in "*url*" into myClip, using GET or POST, as specified in the *variables* string. If targeting FP7, use MovieClipLoader instead of this.
loadVariables	myClip.loadVariables("*url*", *variables*)	Loads variables from a URL or other location into myClip.
localToGlobal	myClip.localToGlobal(*point*)	Converts a point object from the local coordinates of myClip to the global Stage coordinates.
nextFrame	myClip.nextFrame() frame of myClip.	Sends the playhead to the next
play	myClip.play()	Plays myClip.

A

continues

TABLE A.4   CONTINUED

Method	Format	Description
prevFrame	myClip.prevFrame()	Sends the playhead to the previous frame of myClip.
removeMovieClip	myClip.removeMovieClip()	Removes myClip from the Timeline if it was created through the use of attachMovie(), duplicateMovieClip(), or createEmptyMovieClip().
setMask	myClip.setMask (maskMovieClip)	Specifies a movie clip as a mask for myClip.
startDrag	myClip.startDrag([lock, [left, top, right, bottom]])	Makes myClip draggable and begins dragging myClip. If the value of lock is true, the mouse pointer remains centered on myClip's registration point. The left, top, right, and bottom values specify coordinates beyond which myClip cannot be dragged.
stop	myClip.stop()	Pauses myClip.
stopDrag	myClip.stopDrag()	Stops the dragging of any clip that is being dragged (not just myClip). Exact equivalent of global function stopDrag().
swapDepths	myClip.swapDepths(depth)	Puts myClip at the specified depth. If there is a movie clip at that depth, it is moved to myClip's former depth level.
	myClip.swapDepths(target)	Swaps the depth levels of myClip and the target movie clip.
unloadMovie	myClip.unloadMovie()	Removes myClip if it was loaded with loadMovie(). Also works for JPEGs loaded with loadMovie().

Legend: (na) not available (undocumented method)

A

TABLE A.5   MovieClip Attributes

Attribute	Description
_alpha	Transparency/opacity, an integer from 0–100.
_currentframe	Current frame number, an integer, read-only.
_droptarget	A read-only string containing the absolute path in slash syntax notation of the movie clip instance on which a draggable movie clip was dropped.
enabled	A Boolean that determines whether a button movie clip is enabled.
focusEnabled	A Boolean that determines whether a movie clip can receive focus.
_focusrect	A Boolean that determines whether a focused movie clip has a yellow rectangle around it.
_framesloaded	An integer; the number of frames that have been loaded into memory, read-only.
_height	The height of a movie clip instance, in pixels; a floating-point number.
hitArea	The movie clip that defines the hit area for a button movie clip.
_lockroot	"Locks" the reference of _root in an SWF, so it doesn't change when the SWF is loaded into another movie clip.
_quality	A string that determines rendering quality: LOW, MEDIUM, HIGH, BEST.
menu	Works with the new ContextMenu and ContextMenuItem classes to let you create a new context menu for a MovieClip.
_name	The instance name, a string.
_parent	A reference to the movie clip's parent clip.
_rotation	A floating-point number; the number of degrees of rotation from the clip's original orientation.
_soundbuftime	An integer; the number of seconds of sound to prebuffer before starting to play the sound.
tabChildren	A Boolean; determines whether the children of a movie clip are included in automatic tab ordering.
tabEnabled	A Boolean; determines whether a movie clip is included in tab ordering.
tabIndex	Determines the tab order of the clip.
_target	The target path of the clip.
_totalframes	The total number of frames in the clip.
trackAsMenu	A Boolean that determines whether, if the user presses the mouse button over this button movie clip (or button) and releases it over a different one, the second one receives a release event.

continues

A

TABLE A.5 CONTINUED

Attribute	Description
_url	A read-only string; the location of the SWF file from which the clip was downloaded.
useHandCursor	A Boolean that enables and disables the display of the hand cursor for a button movie clip.
_visible	A Boolean value that determines whether a clip instance is hidden or visible.
_width	The width of a movie clip instance, in pixels; a floating-point number.
_x	The x coordinate of a clip instance; a floating-point number.
_xmouse	The x coordinate of the mouse cursor within a clip instance; a floating-point number.
_xscale	A floating-point number specifying a percentage for horizontally scaling a clip instance.
_y	The y coordinate of a clip instance; a floating-point number.
_ymouse	The y coordinate of the cursor within a clip instance; a floating-point number.
_yscale	A floating-point number specifying a percentage for vertically scaling a clip instance.

NOTES ON MOVIE CLIP METHODS AND ATTRIBUTES

Six attributes—_focusrect, enabled, focusEnabled, hitArea, trackAsMenu, and useHandCursor—enable and disable button-like functionality for movie clips and button movie clips. Flash 5 had a _focusrect global variable, which still exists in Flash MX. In addition, buttons and movie clips now have a _focusrect property.

Three movie clip attributes—tabChildren, tabEnabled, and tabIndex—control *tab ordering*, the sequence of text fields, buttons, and/or movie clips that receive keyboard focus as the user presses Tab or Shift+Tab. The typical application is using the Tab key to move from one field to the next while filling out a form.

Enabling and Disabling the Yellow Focus Rectangle

Flash displays a yellow rectangle over a button or button movie clip that has keyboard focus, unless you've done something to suppress this feature. You can enable and disable the yellow focus rectangle on a global basis by using the global _focusrect property. If _focusrect is set to true (the default), the yellow rectangle appears. If _focusrect is set to false, as in the following example, the yellow rectangle does not appear. In that case, buttons and button movie clips display their Over state when they have keyboard focus.

```
_focusrect = false; // focus rectangle is disabled globally
```

You can enable and disable the yellow focus rectangle for an individual movie clip or button instance by using the _focusrect property of the instance. If _focusrect is set to true (the default), the yellow rectangle appears when the instance gets focus. If `_focusrect` is set to `false`, as in the following example, the yellow rectangle does not appear when the instance gets focus. In that case, a button or button movie clip displays its Over state when it has keyboard focus.

```
myButton._focusrect = false; // focus rectangle is disabled for myButton
```

If you do nothing about tab ordering, Flash implements *automatic* tab ordering. That is, it sets up a default order in which items take focus. For example, if you create a form with a number of input text fields in a single column, the default tab ordering, which is simply top-to-bottom, may be perfectly acceptable. Alternatively, you can explicitly set up a *custom* tab order, which disables automatic tab ordering for the entire document, including any SWFs loaded with `loadMovie()` or `loadMovieNum()`. This might be required in a more complex form.

enabled

The `enabled` property enables and disables button-type functionality in a movie clip. The default is `true`. Set `enabled` to `false`, as shown in the following example, and the hand cursor does not appear; button event handlers are no longer called; and `_over`, `_down`, and `_up` frames are disabled:

```
myButtonClip.enabled = false; // no more button functionality
```

Even when `enabled` is `false`, the movie clip continues to be included in tab ordering, and `MovieClip`, `Mouse`, and `Key` event handlers continue to function.

focusEnabled

The `focusEnabled` property allows you to enable and disable focus-related event handlers for movie clips.

Text fields, buttons, button movie clips, and ordinary movie clips can all have `onSetFocus` and `onKillFocus` event handlers that fire in response to `Selection.setFocus()`. For text fields, buttons, and button movie clips, these two focus-related event handlers are *enabled* by default. For ordinary movie clips, these event handlers are *disabled* by default. If you set the `focusEnabled` property of an ordinary movie clip to `true`, its `onSetFocus` and `onKillFocus` event handlers fire in response to `Selection.setFocus()`.

The following example is based on sample movie focusenabled.fla:

```
myClip.onSetFocus = function(oldFocus) {
    trace("focus was "+oldFocus+ ", new focus is myClip");
};
myClip.focusEnabled = true; // allows myClip.onSetFocus above to fire
Selection.setFocus(myClip); // myClip.onSetFocus fires
```

Here are four facts about the `focusEnabled` property:

- By default, it is `undefined`, which is equivalent to `false`.
- It is unnecessary if `tabEnabled` is `true`. (`tabEnabled` enables focus.)

- It has no effect on a text field, button, or button movie clip.
- It enables event handlers associated with a *single* movie clip—myClip in the preceding example. It fires myClip.onSetFocus only when myClip gets focus. If you want myClip.onSetFocus to fire on *every* change of focus (for other objects, as well as myClip), define a listener instead of or in addition to setting focusEnabled to true:

```
Selection.addListener(myClip);
```

If you both define a listener and set focusEnabled to true, myClip.onSetFocus fires twice when myClip gets focus.

You can also use focusEnabled to enable a movie clip to take focus, even though that clip has no onSetFocus event handler. In the following example, focusenabled2.fla on the CD, the movie clip (myMc) takes focus, but another object (myObj) listens for the event.

```
function MyClass () {}
MyClass.prototype.onSetFocus = function(){
 trace("MyClass.prototype.onSetFocus");
}
myObj = new MyClass();
myMc.focusEnabled=true;
Selection.addListener(myObj);
Selection.setFocus(myMc) ;
```

hitArea

The hitArea property enables you to designate any movie clip as a hit area. For button movie clips, as in this example, when the mouse is over the hit area clip, the mouse pointer changes to a hand cursor, and the button movie clip is clickable:

```
myButtonClip.hitArea = myButtonClip.myHitClip;
```

You can reassign hitArea to a different clip at any time. You can change the size or shape of the hitArea clip. And you can make the hitArea clip invisible, without affecting the button movie clip's clickability. If you don't assign a hitArea clip, or you assign one that doesn't actually exist, the button movie clip itself becomes the hit area by default.

Enabling the Hit Area Feature

Just assigning a hit area to an ordinary movie clip has no effect. Even if you add useHandCursor = true (as described in the "useHandCursor" section later in this appendix), you see no effect. You can achieve clickability and get a hand cursor by assigning a button event handler to the movie clip, making it a button movie clip. Then the hit area feature is functional, as well.

---

tabChildren

The tabChildren property allows you to exclude a movie clip's children from tab ordering and later to re-include them. This capability could be useful, for instance, if certain fields in a form needed to be filled in only under certain conditions. When those conditions were met, you would set the tabChildren property to true.

By default, the children of a tab-*enabled* movie clip are tab-*disabled* (not included in tab ordering). So if you have a user interface component made up of multiple movie clips, for instance, and you always want to treat it as a single tab stop, you don't have to do anything special.

If you sometimes want the children tab-enabled and sometimes tab-disabled, you first tab-enable them (for instance, using the `tabEnabled` property). Then, if you later want to disable them again, set `tabChildren` to `false`. When you want to re-enable them, set `tabChildren` to `true`.

If `tabChildren` is `undefined` (the default), the children *are* tab-enabled as soon as you set the `tabEnabled` property to `true` or make the movie clip into a button movie clip.

tabEnabled

The `tabEnabled` property causes the movie clip to be included in either automatic or custom tab ordering, whichever is currently in force in the document. The movie clip can also take focus.

tabIndex

Changing the `tabIndex` property to a positive integer (from its default, which is `undefined`) causes the movie clip to be included in custom tab ordering and enables the movie clip to take focus. The movie clip's place in the tab sequence is determined by the integer: A movie clip with a lower tab index receives focus before a movie clip with a higher tab index.

Setting even one `tabIndex` property in a document disables automatic tab ordering for the entire document.

trackAsMenu

Normally, an `onRelease` event occurs when the user *presses and releases* the mouse button over a single button or button movie clip. With a drop-down menu, you may want the user to press the mouse button over one button, causing the drop-down menu to appear, and then move the mouse to the button representing the desired selection and release it there. The "track as menu" option enables this behavior.

You assign an `onPress` event handler to the button or button movie clip that reveals the drop-down menu. To the other buttons or button movie clips, you assign an `onRelease` event and the "track as menu" tracking behavior.

You can assign the "track as menu" behavior to a button in two ways: through the Property inspector or by using ActionScript and the `trackAsMenu` property. With a button movie clip, you must use ActionScript.

In sample movie options.fla, the "track as menu" tracking behavior is assigned to buttons. ActionScript was used for one option, as shown in the following example, and the Property inspector for the others. Sample movie options2.fla uses button movie clips and ActionScript. Sample movie wapsec.fla demonstrates the default "track as button" behavior.

```
option1.trackAsMenu = true;
```

useHandCursor

Button movie clips display the hand cursor by default. You can suppress this behavior by setting the useHandCursor property to false, as shown in the following example, and re-enable it by setting the useHandCursor property to true:

```
myButtonClip.useHandCursor = false;
```

→ For an example of useHandCursor in action, **see** spacelisten.fla on the CD accompanying this book.

The hand cursor is also suppressed if you set the movie clip's enabled or tabEnabled property to false.

Just setting useHandCursor = true on an ordinary movie clip has no effect. You can achieve clickability and get a hand cursor by assigning a button event handler to the movie clip, making it a button movie clip. Then you can use useHandCursor = false to suppress the hand cursor, if you want.

ARITHMETIC OPERATORS

Arithmetic operators perform mathematical operations on numeric operands to produce numeric results. The ActionScript interpreter automatically converts non-numeric operands to numbers for use with arithmetic operators.

THE SPECIAL VALUE NaN ("NOT A NUMBER")

If an operand used with an arithmetic operator cannot be converted into a number, FP7 will always change it to the special value NaN ("not a number"). FP6, when evaluating undefined or null in a numeric context, returns 0.

It is possible, though rare, to get NaN as a result of manipulating numbers. For instance, if you divide zero by zero, you get NaN:

```
trace(0/0); // NaN
```

More commonly, NaN results from an unsuccessful attempt to convert a string to a number.

Any mathematical operation involving an operand whose value is NaN yields a final result of NaN.

INCREMENTING AND DECREMENTING

The increment operator, which is two plus signs (++), adds 1 to the operand. The decrement operator, which is two minus signs (--), subtracts 1 from the operand, as in these examples:

```
x = 1;
x++; // x is now equal to 2
```

```
y = 2;
y--; // y is now equal to 1
```

Both the increment and the decrement operator can be used as a *prefix* or a *postfix*—that is, before or after the operand. It doesn't matter whether you use the prefix or the postfix form, if all you're doing in the statement is incrementing or decrementing (as shown in the previous example), although postfix is favored by tradition.

If in the same statement, however, you're doing something with the result (storing it in a variable, for instance, or displaying it in the Output window), prefix and postfix act differently. The prefix form changes the operand first and then does something with it. The postfix does something with the operand first and then changes it.

For instance, in the following two statements, the operand x always changes in the same way: It starts with a value of 2 and ends up with a value of 3. With the postfix increment, the variable y ends up with the initial value of x because the assignment is made before x changes. With the prefix increment, y ends up with the final value of x because the assignment is made after x changes. (Visually, when the operator is near y, it affects y. When the operator is away from y, it doesn't affect y.)

```
x = 2;
y = x++; // postfix, result is  x : 3, y : 2
y = ++x; // prefix, result is x : 3, y : 3
```

The same rule applies to the decrement operator. In the following statements, the final and initial values of x are 2 and 1, respectively. The variable y ends up with the initial value of x with the postfix decrement, and the final value of x with the prefix decrement.

```
x = 2;
y = x--; // x : 1, y : 2
y = --x; // x : 1, y : 1
```

Again, for a simple assignment, a decrement operator that faces a variable affects it. In contrast, when x faces y, y just gets the value of x.

Similarly, in the following examples, when the operator faces the `trace` keyword, it affects what is displayed:

```
x = 2;
trace(x++); // displays 2 , x changes, but it doesn't affect the trace

x = 2;
trace(++x); // displays 3 , x changes, and it does affect the trace
```

Increment and decrement operators are commonly used with variables for counting loops in looping sequences.

ADDITION AND SUBTRACTION

Addition and subtraction differ from incrementing and decrementing in two ways:

- They require two operands.
- They do not change the operands. They just produce a result.

Consider this example:

```
a = 6;
b = 2;
c = 1
d = a - b + c; // Now d is 5. No change in a, b, or c, still 6, 2, and 1.
```

Operands can be any expressions that resolve to real numbers. Operands that don't resolve to real numbers are converted to NaN.

If you want the absolute (positive) difference between two numbers, subtract and then apply the Math.abs function to the result:

```
c = Math.abs(a - b); // if b is greater than a, c is still positive
```

WORKING WITH THE POLYMORPHIC + OPERATOR

With numeric operands, the + operator performs simple addition. For instance:

```
2 + 2 // yields 4
```

However, the + operator is *polymorphic*. That is, it performs different operations with different datatypes or classes. Specifically, it concatenates strings and adds numbers. Whenever one of the operands is a string, the result is a string, as in these examples:

```
x = "1" + 6; // "16"
trace(typeof x); // string

x = 6 + "1"; // "61"
trace(typeof x);  // string
```

You can change this behavior by explicitly converting strings to numbers as follows:

```
x = 6 + Number("1"); // 7
trace(typeof x);  // number
```

Other arithmetic operators are not polymorphic and always yield numbers, even if all the operands are strings, as shown here:

```
x = "3" * "7"; // 21, a number; multiplication is not polymorphic
x = "7" - "3"; // 4, a number; subtraction is not polymorphic
x = "6" / "3"; // 2, a number; division is not polymorphic
```

WORKING WITH THE OVERLOADED - OPERATOR

Although the - (minus and unary negation) operator is not polymorphic—it does not perform different operations with different datatypes or classes—it is *overloaded*. That is, it performs different operations within a single datatype or class, depending on the number of operands. In fact, it is considered a different operator, depending on the number of operands.

With a single operand, it is the *unary negation* operator, which reverses the sign of a numeric value. A positive value becomes negative, and a negative value becomes positive, as shown in this example:

```
x = 8;
trace(-x); // displays -8 (negative 8)
```

With two operands, it is the familiar *subtraction* operator, as shown here:

```
2 - 2 // yields 0 (zero)
```

MULTIPLICATION AND DIVISION

Multiplication and division present few problems or peculiarities. They work just as they do in ordinary arithmetic. As usual, ActionScript relies on automatic datatype conversions (rather than errors or exceptions, as in some other languages, such as Java) to deal with illegal operations. For instance, division by zero yields an undefined result in ordinary arithmetic. In Flash, it yields Infinity:

```
x = 0;
y = 8;
z = y / x; // z is Infinity
```

Integer division can produce a fractional result. This point might not even be worth mentioning, except that Macromedia's Lingo (the programming language for Director) always produces an integer result if both operands are integers. The following example illustrates the fact that, in ActionScript, you can get a fractional result by dividing integers:

```
x = 17;
y = 8;
z = x / y; // z is 2. 125
```

MODULO (%) DIVISION

The modulo operator gives you the remainder of a division operation. That is, it performs *modulo division*, in which the result is the remainder, or *modulus*, of the division operation. For instance, 11 % 3 equals 2, because 11 divided by 3 is 3, with a remainder of 2. More examples include the following:

```
4 % 3 // 1
16 % 8 // 0
200 % 100 // 0
18 % 10 // 8
10 % 9.5 // .5
```

Note from the final example that, unlike some other languages (C and C++, for instance), ActionScript can use floats as operands in modulo division.

You also can use modulo division to perform a task at a regular interval, such as the following:

```
onClipEvent (load) {
    var interval = 5;
    var frameCounter = 0;
}
onClipEvent (enterFrame){
    if( ++frameCounter % interval == 0){
        // Do something here. It will happen every five frames.
    }
}
```

A

For instance, sample movie leglift2.fla is a slightly modified version of leglift.fla from Chapter 19. Here, you make the leg move half as fast by using modulo division:

```
onClipEvent(load) {
    var slowdown = 2; // ADDED
    var frameCounter = 0; // ADDED
    var degrees = _rotation;
    function raise() { degrees = 20; }
    function lower() { degrees = 68; }
    function halt() { degrees = _rotation; }
    function lift(degrees) {
        if (_rotation < degrees) rotation++;
        if (_rotation > degrees) rotation--;
    }
}
onClipEvent(enterFrame) {
    if( ++frameCounter % slowdown == 0){ // ADDED
        lift(degrees);
    }
}
```

UNDERSTANDING BITWISE OPERATORS

Bitwise operations provide an efficient and concise alternative to tracking large numbers of binary variables—variables that can have only two values. Using bitwise operators gives you a smaller SWF. In addition, if you often want to set or get multiple values simultaneously, using bitwise operators will probably speed up your program significantly.

Unfortunately, code that incorporates bitwise operators can be hard to read. In addition, to use bitwise operators effectively, you need to understand binary (base 2) arithmetic. Bitwise operators are never an absolute necessity: You can always achieve the same result by using logical (Boolean) operators. Therefore, many programmers avoid bitwise operators. However, bitwise operators are much more concise and efficient for some jobs. You'll almost certainly benefit from having them in your ActionScript toolkit.

Binary arithmetic is based on the *bit*, which is a unit of information that can have just two states. You can think of these states as 0 and 1, on and off, true and false, set and cleared, or whatever other dichotomy you might want to represent.

A

ActionScript binary arithmetic is based on 32-bit binary numbers, as shown in Figure A.1. The power of these numbers comes from the fact that you can look at them in two completely different ways:

- You can get and set them as integers, changing all 32 bits in one operation.
- You can use each number to represent 31 binary variables, which you can get or set in any grouping or combination you want.

Figure A.1
A 32-bit binary number. The number shown here is 1 because the only digit that is "on" is the ones place.

You can switch back and forth between these modes at will, using ordinary arithmetic operators for the first type of operation and the bitwise operators for the second type. It's the second way of looking at binary numbers, in which each digit represents a separate variable, that makes them so powerful in ActionScript.

A Very Short Course in Binary Arithmetic

In base 10, the value of the digits from right to left goes up by powers of 10: 1, 10, 100, 1,000, 10,000, and so on. Each place is 10 times greater than the one to its right. In the binary system, the value of the digits goes up by powers of 2: 1, 2, 4, 8, 16, 32, 64, and so on. Each place is 2 times greater than the one to its right.

This is 1 represented as a 32-bit binary number:

    00000000000000000000000000000001

This is 2:

    00000000000000000000000000000010

This is 4:

    00000000000000000000000000000100

In base 10, each digit can contain a number from 0 to 9. In base 2, each bit can contain either a 0 or a 1. Each place is either on or off. If it's on, you add the value of the place to the number. If it's off, you add nothing.

Consider these examples:

11 in binary is 3: $1 \times 2 + 1 \times 1$.

100 in binary is 4: $1 \times 4 + 0 \times 2 + 0 \times 1$.

1001 in binary is 9: $1 \times 8 + 0 \times 4 + 0 \times 2 + 1 \times 1$.

Figure A.2 shows binary counting from 0 to 8, using four bits. A black oval indicates a 1; a white oval, a 0. At the same time, these bits can be viewed as four on-off switches.

With that background, let's look at the bitwise operators. They fall into two basic categories: I'll refer to the first as "bitwise logical." (They're usually just called "bitwise," to avoid confusion with the Boolean logical operators.) The other category is "bit-shift."

In addition, each bitwise logical and bit-shift operator can be combined with an assignment in the same way that arithmetic operators can.

BITWISE LOGICAL OPERATORS

The four bitwise logical operators are AND (&), NOT (~) OR (|), and XOR (^).

The bitwise NOT operator simply reverses every bit of a 32-bit binary number. So, if all the bits of a number are set to 1, they will all be set to 0, and vice versa.

Figure A.2
Binary counting from
0 to 8. The four digits
can also be viewed as
four on-off switches.

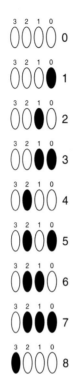

The other three bitwise logical operators compare two 32-bit binary numbers and yield a third 32-bit binary number as a result. They do a bit-by-bit comparison of the two input numbers and use the result of each bitwise comparison to determine the value of the corresponding bit in the third number. You can most easily visualize this comparison by arranging the two input numbers vertically, with the result underneath.

THE BITWISE AND OPERATOR

With the bitwise AND operator, the result bit is a 1 only if both input bits are 1. Figure A.3 illustrates this, using four bits. In the figure, only the least significant bit (LSB), bit 0, is a 1 in both input numbers. Therefore, only the LSB is 1 in the result.

Figure A.3
The result bit of the
bitwise AND operator
is a 1 only if both
input bits are 1.

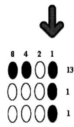

N O T E

> The symbol for the bitwise AND operator is a single character (&), whereas the logical AND operator uses two characters (&&).

You can use the bitwise AND operator to check whether a particular bit or group of bits is on. For instance, consider this code, which embodies the comparison in Figure A.3:

```
x = 13;
y = 1;
result = x & y; // result is 1
```

The result answers the question, "Is the LSB (bit 0) on in x?" If the result is 1, the LSB is on. If the result is 0, the LSB is off. In this case, it's on.

You could also look at the result the other way around, as answering the question, "Are bits 0, 2, or 3 on in y?" Whichever bits are on in the result are on in y. In this case, that is just bit 0.

If you set y = 3, then result = x & y answers the question, "Is either bit 0 or bit 1 on in x?" Table A.6 shows the possible results and their meanings.

TABLE A.6   USING THE BITWISE AND OPERATOR TO DETERMINE THE ON/OFF STATES OF BITS

Result	Bit 1 in x	Bit 0 in x
3	on	on
2	on	off
1	off	on
0	off	off

For example, in a database of houses for sale, bits 0 and 1 could represent a garage and a carport, respectively. With one query, you could find out whether the house in question has just one or the other (and, if so, which one), or if it has both or neither.

Using two bits, you can check four possible combinations. With three bits, you can check eight combinations. Each additional bit doubles the number of combinations you can check. How many combinations can you check with 31 bits? The answer is 2 to the 31st power, or 2,147,483,648! (Check this result in Flash with trace(Math.pow(2,31)).) Not bad for four bytes of information.

THE BITWISE OR OPERATOR

With the bitwise OR operator, the result bit is a 1 if either input bit is 1, as illustrated in Figure A.4.

Figure A.4
The result bit of the bitwise OR operator is a 1 if either input bit is 1.

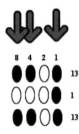

NOTE

> The symbol for the bitwise OR operator is a single character (|), whereas the logical OR operator uses two characters (||).

You can use the bitwise OR operator to turn on a particular bit or group of bits. For instance, consider this code, which embodies Figure A.4:

```
x = 13;
y = 1;
result = x | y; // result is 13
```

Bit 0 will be on in `result`, no matter what x is. As it happens, bit 0 is already on in x, so there is nothing to turn on, and `result` and x are the same.

If the bits in operands x and y represent newspaper articles in online databases, the preceding example would represent the question, "Does either database contain the article represented by bit 0?" If bit 0 is on in `result`, one of the databases has the article. If bit 0 is off in `result`, neither database has the article.

Another way of thinking about the bitwise OR operator is that it combines two sets of information. For instance, in the example of the two databases, `result` combines the information in x and y.

THE BITWISE XOR OPERATOR

With the bitwise XOR operator, the result bit is a 1 only when the input bits differ, as illustrated in Figure A.5. The symbol for the bitwise XOR operator is the caret (^)—Shift+6 on most keyboards.

Figure A.5
The result bit of the bitwise XOR operator is a 1 only when the input bits differ.

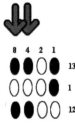

You can use the bitwise XOR operator to reverse a particular bit or group of bits. For instance, consider this code, which embodies Figure A.5:

```
x = 13;
y = 1;
result = x ^ y; // result = 12, because LSB toggled from 1 to 0
```

Bit 0 in result will be reversed from whatever it was in x. In this case, it was on in x, and it is off in result.

If you have on-off buttons in a program, you could track the states of up to 31 buttons in one 32-bit binary number and set the states of multiple buttons simultaneously by using the bitwise XOR operator.

THE BITWISE NOT OPERATOR

The bitwise NOT operator reverses each bit of a 32-bit binary number. If you have on-off buttons in a program, for instance, with their on-off states represented in a 32-bit binary number, you could toggle the state of all your buttons in one operation by using the bitwise NOT operator.

USING MULTIPLE BITWISE LOGICAL OPERATORS

You can use multiple bitwise logical operators in a single statement as follows:

```
x = 13;
y = 1;
z = 2;
result = x & (y | z); // result = 1
```

The final line answers the question, "Is either bit 0 or bit 1 on in x?" Whichever of these two bits is on in result is also on in x.

Using the same values for x, y, and z as in the preceding example, the following line of code answers the question, "Are both bit 0 and bit 1 on in x?"

```
result = (x & (y | z)) == (y | z); // result is false
```

In this case, bit 0 is on in x, but bit 1 is not, so result is false.

To understand the logic of this expression, consider that (y|z) is some group of bits; call it g. Then (x & (y | z)) is the overlap between x and g—the bits that are on in both. This means that result answers the question, "Is the overlap between x and g equal to g?" If so, that is the same as saying that all the on bits in g are also on in x. In this case, y is 1, so bit 0 is on in y; z is 2, so bit 1 is on in z. So g in this example includes both bits 0 and 1. But x is 13, in which bits 3, 2, and 0 are on, but not bit 1. So the overlap between x and g is only bit 0, which is not equal to g.

BIT-SHIFT OPERATORS

The three bit-shift operators move the value in each bit a certain number of steps to the right or left. Bits at the end of the line fall off and are lost.

A

Shifting bits one step to the right is the equivalent of dividing by 2. Shifting bits one step to the left is the equivalent of multiplying by 2.

Shifting bits is analogous to the base-10 phenomenon, in which shifting digits to the right or left divides or multiplies by 10. For instance, if you start with 100 and shift digits one step to the right, you get 10. In other words, you have just divided by 10. The final 0 in 100 falls off and is lost.

Similarly, if you start with binary 100 (which is 4) and shift digits one step to the right, you get binary 10 (which is 2). In this case, you have just divided by 2. The final 0 in the binary 100 falls off and is lost.

Using bit-shift operators to divide or multiply an integer is significantly faster than using the division (/) or multiplication (*) operators. In some tests that I have run, the difference has been about 30%. Of course, using bit-shift operators to divide or multiply works only if your divisor or multiplier is a power of 2. Also, if you bit-shift right (divide) with an odd operand, the result is rounded down because the LSB falls off. Positive results become smaller, and negative results become more negative.

Signed Right Shift

The signed right shift divides by 2, dropping any remainder. It preserves the sign of a negative number.

Preserving the Sign When Shifting Right

Computers set the most significant bit (MSB) to 1 when making a number negative in "twos complement" notation. In positive numbers, the MSB is 0.

As a binary number is shifted to the right, bits fall off on the right, and new bits appear on the left. For negative numbers, the bitwise signed right shift operator sets the new bits to 1. For positive numbers, it sets the new bits to 0. In this way, the signs of numbers are preserved even if you reverse the process and shift left the same number of steps that you shifted right.

The general form of the signed right shift is

```
result = value >> steps
```

NOTE

The symbol for the signed right shift is formed by two greater than signs together: >>.

Consider these examples of the signed right shift:

```
x = 10;
y = 1;
result = x >> y ; // result = 5, which is 10 / 2, no remainder

x = 13;
y = 2;
result = x >> y ; // result = 3, which is 13 / 4, rounded down
```

```
x = -13;
y = 2;
result = x >> y ; // result = -4, which is 13 / 4, rounded down
```

UNSIGNED RIGHT SHIFT

The unsigned right shift shifts digits to the right. However, unlike the signed right shift, the unsigned right shift always adds zeros on the left. Therefore, the result is always positive.

The general form of the unsigned right shift is

```
result = value >>> steps
```

> **NOTE**
> The symbol for the unsigned right shift is formed by three greater than signs together: >>>.

The unsigned right shift sometimes comes in handy when you're "twiddling bits." However, it doesn't have any obvious arithmetic applications. For positive numbers, it yields the same results as the signed right shift. For negative numbers, the 1s in the high bits yield results that are not related to the original number in any obvious way. For instance:

```
x = -13;
y = 1;
result = x >>> y ; // result = 2,147,483, 641
```

SIGNED LEFT SHIFT

The signed left shift multiplies by 2, preserving the sign of a negative number.

The general form of the signed left shift is

```
result = value << steps
```

> **NOTE**
> The symbol for the signed left shift is formed by two less than signs together: <<.

A

Consider these examples of the signed left shift:

```
x = 13;
y = 2;
result = x << y ; // result = 52, which is 13 * 4

x = 10;
y = 1;
result = x << y ; // result = 20, which is 10 * 2

x = -13;
y = 2;
result = x << y ; // result = -52, which is -13 * 4
```

ASSIGNMENT AND COMPOUND ASSIGNMENT

The assignment operator (=) stores the result of an expression in a variable, array element, or object property, as in these examples:

```
x = 2; // stores the number 2 in the variable x
month[11] = "December";// 12th element of the month array is "December"
car.color = 0xFF0000; // color property of car object is 0xFF0000 (red)
```

Ten *compound assignment operators* provide a concise notation for combining the assignment operator with various arithmetic or bitwise operators. For instance, the "add and reassign" operator (+=) combines assignment and addition. Each compound assignment operator performs an operation on two operands and stores the result in the left operand. For instance, x += 2 adds 2 to x and stores the result in x. This is equivalent to x = x + 2.

Table A.7 lists the compound assignment operators with examples and equivalent expressions.

TABLE A.7   COMPOUND ASSIGNMENT OPERATORS

Name	Operator	Example	Equivalent Expression
add and reassign	+=	i += 2	i = i + 2
subtract and reassign	-=	balance -= debit	balance = balance - debit
multiply and reassign	*=	rate *= increase	rate = rate * increase
divide and reassign	/=	price /= discount	price = price / discount
modulo divide and reassign	%=	frameCounter % slowdown	frameCounter = frameCounter % slowdown
bit-shift left and reassign	<<=	answer <<= num	answer = answer << num
bit-shift right and reassign	>>=	result >>= 1	result = result >> 1
bitwise AND and reassign	&=	test &= 4	test = test & 4
bitwise XOR and reassign	^=	finalMask ^= initialMask	finalMask = finalMask ^ initialMask
bitwise OR and reassign	|=	onOff |= on	onOff = onOff	on

The compound assignment operators are not more efficient computationally than their longer equivalents, nor do they result in smaller SWFs. They are strictly a notational convenience.

Note that

```
x *= y + z
```

is equivalent to

```
x = x * (y + z)
```

not

```
x = x * y + z
```

which is the same as

```
x = (x * y) + z
```

COMPARISON OPERATORS

The comparison operators are used to determine whether two operands are equal, or whether one operand is greater than or less than another. The eight comparison operators are as follows:

- Equality (==)
- Inequality (!=)
- Strict equality (===)
- Strict inequality (!==)
- Less than (<)
- Less than or equal to (<=)
- Greater than (>)
- Greater than or equal to (>=)

The first four are also known as *equality* operators, and the last four as *relational* operators. All eight compare two strings or numbers and return `true` or `false`, depending on whether the relationship indicated in the comparison is accurate.

In addition, the relational operators return `undefined` if at least one of the operands is `NaN`. The equality and strict equality operators return `false` in this case, whereas the inequality and strict inequality operators return `true`.

A

UNDERSTANDING EQUALITY OPERATORS

Both the equality (==) and strict equality (===) operators test for "sameness," but the equality operator performs datatype conversions when necessary before comparing. The strict equality operator insists that the operands already be of the same datatype, or else it returns `false`.

For instance, `null == undefined` is true, but `null === undefined` is false. Because `null` and `undefined` are of different datatypes, they are not strictly equal. However, the equality operator converts them both to 0, so they are equal.

The inequality (!=) and strict inequality (!==) operators return the opposite of the equality and strict equality operators. Whenever the former returns `true`, the latter returns `false`, and vice versa.

The equality operator is perhaps the most commonly used operator, and also the source of one of the most common mistakes: using a single equal sign (the assignment operator) when you mean to use two equal signs (the equality operator).

Numbers are compared mathematically. For instance, these expressions all yield `true`:

```
1 + 2 == 3
-20 < -1
80.5 != 80
```

In contrast, these expressions all yield `false`:

```
6 <= 5
5 >= 6
-200 > 0
```

The "code points" of the ISO-8859 (Latin-1) or Unicode character set are used to compare strings. The code point is the number or "character code" associated with each character. For instance, these expressions all yield `true`:

```
"A" < "a" // capital letters come before lowercase
"A" > "1" // numbers come before capital letters
"<" <= ">" // the "less than" sign comes before the "greater than" sign
```

If you want to use the character code of a letter to compare it with a number, use the `charCodeAt()` function. For instance, the character code for a blank space is 32. Therefore, the following expression yields `true`:

```
" ".charCodeAt(0) == 32 // true, the first (0) character is a blank
```

This expression yields `false`:

```
" " == 32
```

AUTOMATIC DATATYPE CONVERSIONS FOR COMPARISONS

The expression `" " == 32` is false because of the way the ActionScript interpreter performs automatic datatype conversion. For primitive datatypes, the interpreter converts operands to ensure that it ultimately compares either two strings or two numbers. Note that the interpreter makes temporary copies of the operands and converts the copies; it does not change the original data that is being compared.

A character string converts to a number only if it literally spells out a number. For example, the following yields `true`:

```
"32" == 32
```

In all other cases, strings are converted to `NaN`. If either operand (or both) is converted to `NaN`, the comparison yields `false` for all the comparison operators except != and !==. As counterintuitive as it seems, even `NaN == NaN` is a false expression, as far as the ActionScript interpreter is concerned! By the same token, NaN != NaN is true. This makes comparison operators an extremely nonintuitive means of determining whether a datum is NaN. The typeof operator doesn't help either; it just yields number. To test whether a value is NaN, use the isNaN() function:

```
x = NaN;
trace(x); // NaN(
trace(x == NaN); // false
trace(typeof x); // number
trace(isNaN(x)); // true
```

The preceding discussion assumes two primitive datatypes. If just one of the operands in a comparison is a composite datatype (object, array, or function), the ActionScript interpreter invokes the valueOf() method of the operand. If valueOf() returns a primitive value, that value is used in the comparison. If not, the comparison yields false.

In Flash 5, the valueOf() method was used in comparing *two* composite types, as well. This is no longer true for equality/inequality comparisons in Flash MX.

In Flash MX, if *both* operands are composite types, equality/inequality comparisons are made *by reference*. This means they are equal only if they reference *the same object*.

Thus, if f1 and f2 refer to function literals, (f1 == f2) is true only if both refer to the same function literal, as is the case in the following example:

```
myfunc = function (){};
f1 = myFunc;
f2 = myFunc;
trace(f1==f2); // true
```

On the other hand, func1 and func2 in the following example are identical in form, but do not refer to the same function literal:

```
function func1(){}
function func2(){}
trace(func1 == func2); // false
```

Using Comparison Operators with Objects and Arrays

By default, >=, <=, >, and < do not yield meaningful results with objects and arrays as operands.

Newly created objects test unequal:

```
trace(o == o2); // false
trace(o != o2); // true
```

However, the results of the following statements, taken together, would lead to the conclusion that the objects are equal:

```
trace(o); // [object Object]
trace(o2); // [object Object]
trace(o <= o2); // true
trace(o >= o2); // true
trace(o > o2); // false
trace(o < o2); // false
```

A

For instance, if o >= o2 is true (o is either greater than or equal to o2) and o > o2 is false (it's not greater than), o must be equal to o2, right? (Wrong. You'll see why in a moment.)

Results for two newly created arrays are similar, except that they display nothing where objects display [object Object].

These results, however, are simply artifacts of the way Flash tests for >= and <=. In both cases, under the covers, Flash actually uses < in the final comparison and then reverses the answer. For example, for o <= o2, Flash asks, "Is o2 < o?" If not, it concludes that o <= o2 must be true! For o >= o2, Flash asks, "Is o < o2?" If not, it concludes that o >= o2 must be true!

These conclusions are valid, assuming numeric operands, or strings that can be reduced to numeric code points. In the case of objects, however, the interpreter converts both objects to NaN. The result of (NaN < NaN) is undefined:

```
trace(typeof (NaN < NaN));  // undefined
```

The ActionScript interpreter converts undefined to false in comparison results. So the interpreter reverses that result and deduces true for the original comparisons, in both cases!

Clearly, by default, >=, <=, >, and < do not produce generally useful results with objects or arrays as operands. However, you can create valueOf() methods for objects or arrays, and these methods can return numeric or string primitives that can usefully be compared using the >=, <=, >, and < operators.

Note that objects and arrays differ from functions in this respect. The valueOf() method does not come into play when comparing two functions. It plays a role only when comparing a function with a primitive datatype.

Movie clips have always been compared by their instance names, and this is still true in Flash MX. Only the equality/inequality comparisons yield meaningful results with movie clips. The >=, <=, >, and < operators yield undefined.

Automatic datatype conversion for comparisons favors numbers over other datatypes: If one operator is a number and the other is a string, Boolean, null, or undefined, the non-numeric operand is converted to a number. This includes non-numeric operands returned by valueOf() functions.

DEPRECATED FLASH 4 COMPARISON OPERATORS

The Flash 4 comparison operators eq, ne, lt, gt, le, and ge are equivalent to ==, !=, <, >, <=, and >=, except that lt, gt, le, and ge are string specific. As of Flash 5, the Flash 4 operators are "deprecated," meaning supported but not recommended, unless you're exporting to Flash 4 format.

You may find situations in which the deprecated objects work better than the newer ones. Rather than use the old ones, you might be wise to create new functions of your own, based on the new operators but compensating for whatever behavior is creating a problem.

Macromedia will drop support for deprecated operators and functions as soon as it is practical to do so. Programs using deprecated syntax live on borrowed time.

USING LOGICAL (BOOLEAN) OPERATORS

Logical operators allow you to make decisions based on evaluating two or more expressions. Typically, you use expressions that naturally and intuitively yield Boolean values.

The three logical operators are AND (&&), OR (||), and NOT (!).

The logical NOT operator returns the Boolean opposite of the single operand that it precedes. Thus, if an expression returns true, with the logical NOT operator, you get false. For instance, say you have a movie clip, myClip, on the Stage, and it is visible:

```
trace(myClip._visible); // true
trace(!myClip._visible); // false
```

Similarly, if an expression returns false and you prefix it with the logical NOT operator, you get true. For instance, say you have a function, checkKillList(), that returns false:

```
trace(checkKillList()); // false
trace(!checkKillList()); // true
```

The AND operator answers the question, "Are both of these expressions true?"

The OR operator answers the question, "Is either of these expressions true?"

The following four pseudocode examples involve two expressions that are either true or false:

Example #1:

```
IF
starting point is San Francisco
AND
destination is Berkeley
THEN
take Bay Area Rapid Transit
```

Example #2:

```
IF
user hits Cancel
OR
an error occurs
THEN
cancel operation
```

Example #3:

```
IF
user provides correct password
AND
user is NOT on "kill" list
THEN
grant user access
```

Example #4:

```
IF
movie clip does NOT exist
```

A

```
OR
movie clip is NOT visible
THEN
tell user "Sorry, that movie clip is unavailable! "
```

NOTE

> The symbol for OR is two vertical lines. On most keyboards, you produce the vertical line by using the Shift key plus the backslash (\) key, at the far right of the QWERTY row.

The preceding four examples might look like this in ActionScript:

Example #1:

```
if ((start == "San Francisco") && (end == "Berkeley") ) {
    wayToGo = "BART";
}
```

Example #2:

```
if ( (input == cancel) || (input == error) ) {
    cancelOperation();
}
```

Example #3:

```
if ( (checkPassword() ) && (!checkKillList() ) {
    grantAccess();
}
```

Example #4:

```
if ( (!myClip) || (!myClip._visible) ) {
    returnError(unavailable)
}
```

You can always duplicate the logic of logical operators by using multiple `if` statements. For instance, the AND operator is the equivalent of two nested `if` statements. Examples #1 and #3 look like this converted into nested `if` statements:

```
if (start == "San Francisco") {
    if (end == "Berkeley") {
        wayToGo = "BART";
    }
}
if (checkPassword()) {
    if (!checkKillList()) {
        grantAccess();
    }
}
```

Mostly, programmers think of the choice between AND and nested `if` statements as just one of taste. Some programmers find nested `if` statements more readable. The AND operator is more concise.

You can replace the OR operator with an `if-else-if` statement. For example, Example #2 looks like this converted into an `if-else-if` statement:

```
if (input == cancel) {
    cancelOperation();
}
else if (input == error) {
    cancelOperation();
}
```

In this case, the `if-else-if` statement has nothing to recommend it. The OR operator is both more concise and more readable.

Actually, `if` statements do not exactly replicate the functionality of the AND or OR operator. The `if` statements return Boolean values, `true` or `false`. The AND and OR operators, on the other hand, actually return one of their operands. The AND operator returns its second operand if both operands resolve to `true`; otherwise, it returns whichever operand resolves to `false`. The OR operator returns its first operand, if it resolves to `true`: otherwise, it returns its second operand. The AND and OR operators are usually used in an `if` statement, and the `if` statement converts the returned operand to a Boolean.

Table A.8 gives some examples of OR statements, their return values as displayed by a `trace()` statement, and to which Boolean the return value resolves.

Note that what is actually returned by the OR statement in each example is identical to one side of the OR statement. For instance, in the statement `["one", "two"] || "hi"`, the array `["one", "two"]` becomes `true` when converted to a Boolean; therefore, the OR statement returns the array, which a `trace()` statement displays as `one, two`.

In practice, the values returned by AND and OR statements are seldom utilized directly. They're just converted into Booleans by `if` statements.

TABLE A.8 OR Statements, Their Returns, and Boolean Equivalents

OR Statement	Trace (Return)	Boolean Equivalent of Return
`"ho" || "hi"`	`hi`	`false`
`"32" || "hi"`	`32`	`true`
`32 || "hi"`	`32`	`true`
`Infinity || "hi"`	`Infinity`	`true`
`["one", "two"] || "hi"`	`one, two`	`true`
`myClip || "hi"`	`_level0.myClip`	`true`
`{eyes : "green", age : 32} || "hi"`	`[object Object]`	`true`

A

THE CONDITIONAL OPERATOR

The conditional operator is a slightly optimized way of implementing if-else logic. It's like an if that *requires* an else, in contrast to the normal if statement, for which the else is optional.

The conditional operator always specifies both a true and a false condition, making it a *ternary* operator, meaning it has three arguments. Because it is the only operator that always has three arguments, it is sometimes also called *the* ternary operator. Its format is

```
condition ? result_if_true : result_if_false;
```

The first part of the conditional expression (condition) is a test that returns true or false. The next two parts are possible return values. If the condition is true, the operator returns part two. If the condition is false, the operator returns part three. In pseudocode, here's a condition that says, "If the journey is greater than 1,000 miles, then fly; if it is not greater than 1,000 miles, then drive."

```
journey is greater than 1000 miles ? fly : drive
```

Here's how that example might look in ActionScript:

```
distance = 2000;
howtoGo = distance > 1000 ? "fly" : "drive";
trace(howToGo); // fly
```

The third line is the equivalent of

```
if (distance > 1000) {
    howtoGo =  "fly"
} else {
    howtoGo = "drive"
}
```

You can use functions in the second and third parts, too, thus using the conditional operator to control program flow. For instance:

```
function fly() {
    trace("fly");
}
function drive() {
    trace("drive");
}
miles = 2000;
miles > 1000 ? fly() : drive(); // displays "fly"
```

You can check multiple conditions with nested conditional operators. For instance, suppose you want to fly if the distance is more than 1,000 miles, walk if it's 3 miles or less, and drive otherwise. In that case, you would add a walk() function to the previous program:

```
function walk() {
    trace("walk");
}
```

Then you can do all this in a single line of code:

```
Ask "Is the distance greater than 1000 miles?"
If yes, fly.
If no, ask, "Is the distance greater than 3 miles?"
If yes, drive.
In no, walk.
```

In the following example, the distance is not greater than 3 miles, so the `walk()` function is executed:

```
miles = 3;
miles > 1000 ? fly() : miles > 3 ? drive() : walk(); // displays "walk"
```

In this case, the conditional operator is faster and produces a smaller SWF than if/else, but not by much.

In the following instance, `if-else` would be slightly lighter and faster, but the conditional operator is more readable:

```
(day == "Monday") ? trace("is fair of face") :
(day == "Tuesday") ? trace("is full of grace") :
(day == "Wednesday") ? trace("is full of woe") :
(day == "Thursday") ?  trace("has far to go") :
(day == "Friday") ? trace("is loving and giving") :
(day == "Saturday") ? trace("works hard for a living"):
(day == "Sunday") ? trace("is bonny and blithe and good and gay.") : null;
```

Notice the use of `null` as the final option. The conditional operator must always return something, so the choice is between using something like `null` or choosing one of the `trace` actions as a default. For instance, to make the final `trace` the default, change the last line to look like this:

```
trace("is bonny and blithe and good and gay.");
```

Using the final `trace` as a default implies that the variable `day` will always have a valid day of the week as a value. Thus, if it isn't "Monday" through "Saturday", it must be "Sunday".

THE COMMA OPERATOR

The comma operator is used primarily to declare two or more variables in a single statement, as in this example:

```
var x=1, y=2, z=3;
```

The preceding is equivalent to

```
var x=1;
var y=2;
var z=3;
```

This operator can come in handy when you want to initialize two or more index variables in a `for` loop, as in this example:

A

```
for (i = 0, j = 0,  k = 0; i < 50;  i++, j -= i, k--) {
    trace(i+" "+j+" "+k);
}
```

The output is as follows:

```
0 0 -10
1 -1 -11
2 -3 -12
3 -6 -13
 . . .
```

The return value of the comma operator, which is the resolved value of the final operand, isn't used in either of the preceding cases. In general, the return value of the comma operator is not useful. For instance, it is useless (though not illegal) to have several comma-separated terms in the middle (test) portion when you're setting up a for loop because only the final term would be evaluated. For instance, the following does exactly the same thing as the previous for loop because j >= k, k < i is ignored and only i < 50 is tested on each loop:

```
for (i = 0, j = 0,  k = -10; j >= k, k < i, i < 50;  i++, j -= i, k--) {
    trace(i+" "+j+" "+k);
}
```

NAMED OPERATORS

A number of operators are referred to by names instead of symbols. They include new, typeof, instanceof, delete, and void.

THE new OPERATOR

You use the new operator with a constructor function to create a datum of the object or array datatype. For instance, in the following examples, the constructor functions are Object(), Array(), and Date():

```
myObj = new Object();
myArray = new Array();
myDate = new Date();
```

THE typeof OPERATOR

The typeof operator returns a string indicating the datatype of an operand. Its format is

```
typeof expression
```

where expression is any legal expression.

THE instanceof OPERATOR

The instanceof operator determines whether an object belongs to a class. Its format is as follows:

```
object instanceof class
```

The `instanceof` operator follows the inheritance chain, to determine whether the object inherits from the class. In the following example, for instance, a is an instance of `Object` because a is an array, which is an object, and all objects inherit from `Object`. On the other hand, a is not an instance of `_global` because `_global` is not a constructor function.

```
a = new Array();
trace(a instanceof Array); // true
trace(a instanceof Object); // true - this is true for all objects
trace(a instanceof _global); // false - _global is not a constructor function
```

In the following example, 6 is not an instance of `Number` because 6 is a primitive datum, not an object. On the other hand, n is an object whose value is 6, and n is an instance of `Number`.

```
trace(6 instanceof Number); // false -  6 is not an object
n = new Number(6);
trace(n instanceof Number); // true
```

THE delete OPERATOR

The `delete` operator attempts to delete a variable, object (including a function), object property, array, or array element. The format is simply

```
delete identifier
```

Here's an example of its use:

```
myVar = "three"; // create a variable
delete myVar; // remove it
```

The `delete` operator returns `true` or `false`, depending on whether the deletion was successful. In the following example, `delete` returns `false` when you try to delete a property a second time:

```
myObj = {a : "one", b: "two"} // create an object
trace(delete myObj.a); // true
trace(delete myObj.a); // false - it's already gone
```

THE void OPERATOR

The ActionScript `void` operator appears to be present just for ECMA compatibility. Its format is

```
void(expression)
```

It causes the interpreter to throw away the results of the expression and return `undefined`.

The Flash ActionScript Dictionary says that the `void` operator "is often used in comparisons using the `==` operator to test for undefined values." I can't find any real-life examples; however, the following does work:

```
a = undefined;
b = 1;
trace(void(b) == a); // true
```

A

Still, using the following approach is easier:

```
a = undefined;
trace(undefined == a); // true
```

The Void datatype is used for strict typing, to indicate that a function doesn't return anything:

```
function myFunc ():Void
{
// function body here
};
```

However, this is Void as a datatype, not void as an operator.

OBJECT PROPERTY ACCESS: THE DOT OPERATOR

The dot (.) operator indicates a property of an object or a nested movie clip. For instance, you set a property to a value as follows:

```
myObject.myProperty = "myValue"; // set a property to a string value
```

Here, you set a variable, clipVar, equal to a movie clip instance name:

```
clipVar = myClipParent.myClipChild; // set a variable to a movie clip name
```

THE ARRAY-ELEMENT/OBJECT PROPERTY OPERATOR

Square brackets can indicate an element of an array or a property of an object. For instance, the following is an array element:

```
months[0] = "January";
```

The following is an object property:

```
computer["display"] = "SVGA";
```

THE PARENTHESES/FUNCTION CALL OPERATOR

In addition to using parentheses for grouping other operators, you can use them as the function call operator, to invoke a function.

The format for *calling*, or invoking, a function is

```
identifier(list)
```

where *identifier* is the name of the function and *list* is an optional comma-separated list of *arguments*, or parameters, passed to the function. The operator here is the parentheses that enclose the arguments.

A

THE Date CLASS

TABLE A.9   METHODS OF THE Date CLASS

Name	Format	Description
Date.getDate	myDate.getDate()	Returns the day of the month from 1 to 31 according to local time.
Date.getDay	myDate.getDay()	Returns the day of the week from 0 (Sunday) to 6 (Saturday) according to local time.
Date.getFullYear	myDate.getFullYear()	Returns the four-digit year according to local time.
Date.getHours	myDate.getHours()	Returns the hour from 0 (midnight) to 23 (11 p.m.) according to local time.
Date.getMilliseconds	myDate.getMilliseconds()	Returns the milliseconds from 0 to 999 according to local time.
Date.getMinutes	myDate.getMinutes()	Returns the minutes from 0 to 59 according to local time.
Date.getMonth	myDate.getMonth()	Returns the month from 0 (January) to 11 (December) according to local time.
Date.getSeconds	myDate.getSeconds()	Returns the seconds from 0 to 59 according to local time.
Date.getTime	myDate.getTime()	Returns the number of milliseconds since midnight January 1, 1970, universal time.
Date.getTimezoneOffset	mydate.getTimezoneOffset()	Returns the difference, in minutes, between the computer's local time and the universal time.
Date.getUTCDate	myDate.getUTCDate()	Returns the day (date) of the month from 1 to 31 according to universal time.
Date.getUTCDay	myDate.getUTCDay()	Returns the day of the week from 0 (Sunday) to 6 (Saturday) according to universal time.

A

continues

TABLE A.9   CONTINUED

Name	Format	Description
Date.getUTCFullYear	myDate. getUTCFullYear()	Returns the four-digit year according to universal time.
Date.getUTCHours	myDate.getUTCHours()	Returns the hour from 0 (midnight) to 23 (11 p.m.) according to universal time.
Date.getUTCMilliseconds	myDate. getUTCMilliseconds()	Returns the milliseconds from 0 to 999 according to universal time.
Date.getUTCMinutes	myDate. getUTCMinutes()	Returns the minutes from 0 to 59 according to universal time.
Date.getUTCMonth	myDate.getUTCMonth()	Returns the month from 0 (January) to 11 (December) according to universal time.
Date.getUTCSeconds	myDate.getSeconds()	Returns the seconds from 0 to 59 according to universal time.
Date.getYear	myDate.getYear()	Returns an integer which, when added to 1900, gives the year according to local time. For instance, a return value of 0 means 1900.
Date.setDate	myDate.setDate(date)	Sets the day of the month to *date*, an integer from 1 to 31, according to local time. Returns the new time in milliseconds.
Date.setFullYear	myDate.setFullYear(*year* [, *month* [, *date*]])	Sets a four-digit *year*, and optionally also the *month* from 0 (January) to 11 (December), and the *date* from 1 to 31, all according to local time. Returns the new time in milliseconds.
Date.setHours	myDate.setHours(*hour* [, *minute* [, *second* [, *millisecond*]]])	Sets the *hour*, from 0 (midnight) to 23 (11 p.m.); and optionally *minute* from 0 to 59; *second* from 0 to 59; and *millisecond* from 0 to 999, all according to local time. Returns the new time in milliseconds.

Name	Format	Description
Date.setMilliseconds	myDate. setMilliseconds (*millisecond*)	Sets the milliseconds according to local time from 0 to 999. Returns the new time in milliseconds.
Date.setMinutes	myDate.setMinutes (*minute* [, *second* [, *millisecond*]])	Sets *minute* from 0 to 59; and optionally *second* from 0 to 59; and *millisecond* from 0 to 999, all according to local time. Returns the new time in milliseconds.
Date.setMonth	myDate.setMonth (*month* [, *date*])	Sets the *month* from 0 (January) to 11 (December) and optionally the *date* from 1 to 31, both according to local time. Returns the new time in milliseconds.
Date.setSeconds	myDate.setSeconds (*second* [, *millisecond*]))	Sets the *second* from 0 to 59, and optionally the *millisecond* from 0 to 999, both according to local time. Returns the new time in milliseconds.
Date.setTime	myDate.setTime (*millisecond*)	Sets the date, expressed in milliseconds since midnight on January 1, 1970. Returns the same number you give it.
Date.setUTCDate	myDate.setUTCDate (*date*)	Sets the date according to universal time, from 1 to 31. Returns the new time in milliseconds.
Date.setUTCFullYear	myDate.setUTCFullYear (*year* [, *month* [, *date*]])	Sets a four-digit *year*, and optionally also the *month* from 0 (January) to 11 (December), and the *date* from 1 to 31, all according to universal time.
Date.setUTCHours	myDate.setUTCHours (*hour* [, *minute* [, *second* [, *millisecond*]]])	Sets the *hour*, from 0 (midnight) to 23 (11 p.m.); and optionally *minute* from 0 to 59; *second* from 0 to 59; and *millisecond* from 0 to 999, all according to universal time. Returns the new time in milliseconds.

A

continues

TABLE A.9 **CONTINUED**

Name	Format	Description
Date.setUTCMilliseconds	myDate. setUTCMilliseconds (*millisecond*)	Sets *millisecond* from 0 to 999 according to universal time. Returns the new time in milliseconds.
Date.setUTCMinutes	myDate.setUTCMinutes (*minute* [, *second* [, *millisecond*]])	Sets *minute* from 0 to 59; and optionally *second* from 0 to 59; and *millisecond* from 0 to 999, all according to universal time. Returns the new time in milliseconds.
Date.setUTCMonth	myDate.setUTCMonth (*month* [, *date*])	Sets the *month* from 0 (January) to 11 (December) and optionally the *date* from 1 to 31, both according to universal time. Returns the new time in milliseconds.
Date.setUTCSeconds	myDate.setUTCSeconds (*second* [, *millisecond*]))	Sets the *second* from 0 to 59, and optionally the *millisecond* from 0 to 999, both according to universal time. Returns the new time in milliseconds.
Date.setYear	myDate.setYear(*year*)	Determines the value that will be retrieved by Date.getYear(). The *year* argument is an integer. If *year* is a one- or two-digit number, Date.getYear() retrieves that number. If *year* is three or more digits, Date.getYear() retrieves that number minus 1900.
Date.toString	myDate.toString()	Returns a string representing the date and time in this format: Sat May 4 12:42:19 GMT-0700 2002.
Date.UTC	Date.UTC(*year, month* [, *date* [, *hour* [, *minute* [, *second* [, *millisecond*]]]]]))	Returns the number of milliseconds between midnight on January 1, 1970, universal time, and the date/time specified in the arguments *year, month, date, hour, minute, second,* and *millisecond*.

THE Key OBJECT

TABLE A.10 KEY OBJECT METHODS AND CONSTANTS

Name	Method/ Attribute/ Event	Format	Description
Key.addListener	M	Key.addListener (myObject)	Registers myObject to receive notification when the onKeyDown and onKeyUp methods are invoked.
Key.getAscii	M	Key.getAscii()	Returns the ASCII value of the last key pressed.
Key.getCode	M	Key.getCode()	Returns the keycode of the last key pressed.
Key.isDown	M	Key.isDown (charCode)	Returns true if the user presses the key whose character code is charCode.
Key.isToggled	M	Key.isToggled (charCode)	Returns true if the key specified in charCode is activated. On the PC, charCode for Caps Lock is 20; for Num Lock, 144; and for Scroll Lock, 145. You can use Key.CAPSLOCK for Caps Lock.
Key.removeListener	M	Key.removeListener (myObject)	If myObject was previously registered with Key.addListener(), myObject is removed from the list of listeners.
Key.BACKSPACE	A	Key.BACKSPACE	Constant associated with the keycode value for the Backspace key (8).
Key.CAPSLOCK	A	Key.CAPSLOCK	Constant associated with the keycode value for the Caps Lock key (20).
Key.CONTROL	A	Key.CONTROL	Constant associated with the keycode value for the Control key (17).
Key.DELETEKEY	A	Key.DELETEKEY	Constant associated with the keycode value for the Delete key (46).

A

continues

TABLE A.10   CONTINUED

Name	Method/ Attribute/ Event	Format	Description
Key.DOWN	A	Key.DOWN	Constant associated with the keycode value for the Down Arrow key (40).
Key.END	A	Key.END	Constant associated with the keycode value for the End key (35).
Key.ENTER	A	Key.ENTER	Constant associated with the keycode value for the Enter key (13).
Key.ESCAPE	A	Key.ESCAPE	Constant associated with the keycode value for the Escape key (27).
Key.HOME	A	Key.HOME	Constant associated with the keycode value for the Home key (36) .
Key.INSERT	A	Key.INSERT	Constant associated with the keycode value for the Insert key (45).
Key.LEFT	A	Key.LEFT	Constant associated with the keycode value for the left arrow key (37).
Key.PGDN	A	Key.PGDN	Constant associated with the keycode value for the Page Down key (34).
Key.PGUP	A	Key.PGUP	Constant associated with the keycode value for the Page Up key (33).
Key.RIGHT	A	Key.RIGHT	Constant associated with the keycode value for the right arrow key (39).
Key.SHIFT	A	Key.SHIFT	Constant associated with the keycode value for the Shift key (16).
Key.SPACE	A	Key.SPACE	Constant associated with the keycode value for the space-bar (32) .

A

Name	Method/ Attribute/ Event	Format	Description
Key.TAB	A	Key.TAB	Constant associated with the keycode value for the Tab key (9).
Key.UP	A	Key.UP	Constant associated with the keycode value for the up arrow key (38).
Key.onKeyDown	E	myObject.onKeyDown = function() { };	Fires when a key is pressed.
Key.onKeyUp	E	myObject.onKeyUp = function() { };	Fires when a key is released.

THE Math OBJECT

TABLE A.11   MATH METHODS AND ATTRIBUTES

Name	Method/ Attribute	Format	Description
abs	M	Math.abs(x)	Computes the absolute value of x.
acos	M	Math.acos(x)	Computes the arccosine of x.
asin	M	Math.asin(x)	Computes the arcsine of x.
atan	M	Math.atan(x)	Computes the arctangent of x.
atan2	M	Math.atan2(y, x)	Computes the arctangent of the ratio y/x, that is, the angle from the positive x-axis to the point (x, y).
ceil	M	Math.ceil(x)	Rounds x up to the nearest integer.
cos	M	Math.cos(x)	Computes the cosine of x.
exp	M	Math.exp(x)	Computes Math.E to the power x.
floor	M	Math.floor(x)	Rounds x down to the nearest integer.
log	M	Math.log(x)	Computes the natural logarithm of x.
max	M	Math.max(x, y)	Returns the larger of integers x and y.
min	M	Math.min(x, y)	Returns the smaller of integers x and y.
pow	M	Math.pow(x, y)	Computes x raised to the power y.
random	M	Math.random()	Returns a pseudo-random number between 0 and 1.

A

continues

TABLE A.11 CONTINUED

Name	Method/Attribute	Format	Description
round	M	Math.round(x)	Rounds x to the nearest integer.
sin	M	Math.sin(x)	Computes the sine of x.
sqrt	M	Math. sqrt(x)	Computes the square root of x.
tan	M	Math.tan(x)	Computes the tangent of x.
E	A	Math.E	Euler's constant and the base of natural logarithms (approximately 2.718), traditionally notated as e.
LN2	A	Math.LN2	The natural logarithm of 2 (approximately 0.693).
LOG2E	A	Math.LOG2E	The base 2 logarithm of Math.E (approximately 1.442).
LN10	A	Math.LN10	The natural logarithm of 10 (approximately 2.302).
LOG10E	A	Math.LOG10E	The base 10 logarithm of Math.E (approximately 0.434).
PI	A	Math.PI	The ratio of the circumference of a circle to its diameter (approximately 3.14159).
SQRT1_2	A	Math.SQRT1_2	The reciprocal of the square root of 2, that is, 1/Math.SQRT2 (approximately 0.707).
SQRT2	M	Math.SQRT2	The square root of 2 (approximately 1.414).

THE TextField AND TextFormat CLASSES

TABLE A.12 TextField ATTRIBUTES, METHODS, AND EVENTS

Name	Method/Attribute/Event/	Format	Description
addListener	M	myTextField.addListener (myObject)	Registers myObject to receive notification of onChanged and onScroller events associated with myTextField.
getDepth	M	myTextField.getDepth()	Returns the depth of myTextField.

Name	Method/ Attribute/ Event/	Format	Description
getFontList	M	TextField.getFontList()	Returns an array of font names. Note: TextField, *not* myTextField.
getNewTextFormat	M	myTextField. getNewTextFormat()	Returns a copy of the TextFormat object applied to new text inserted in myTextField manually or using replaceSel().
removeListener	M	myTextField. removeListener(myObject)	Removes myObject from the array of listeners associated with myTextField, that is, can cels myTextField.addListener(myObject).
removeTextField	M	myTextField. removeTextField()	Removes myTextField, if it was created with MovieClip.createTextField().
setNewTextFormat	M	myTextField. setNewTextFormat (myTextFormat)	Sets myTextFormat as the text format object for new text inserted in myTextField manually or using replaceSel().
replaceSel	M	myTextField.replaceSel (*newText*)	Substitutes the *newText* string for currently selected text.
setTextFormat	M	myTextField. setTextFormat (myTextFormat)	Assigns myTextFormat to text that is already in myTextField.
_alpha	A	myTextField._alpha	The transparency value of myTextField, an integer from 0 to 100.
autoSize	A	myTextField.autoSize	A string specifying the anchor point for myTextField when it is being automatically resized to fit text. See Table A.13.
background	A	myTextField.background	A Boolean that shows (true) or hides (false) background fill.

continues

A

Table A.12   Continued

Name	Method/ Attribute/ Event/	Format	Description
backgroundColor	A	myTextField. backgroundColor	Specifies the color of the background fill. An integer, often in hexadecimal format, for example, 0xFF0000.
border	A	myTextField.border	A Boolean that specifies whether the text field has a border.
borderColor	A	myTextField.borderColor	Specifies the color of the border. An integer, often in hexa decimal format, for example, 0xFF0000.
bottomScroll	A	myTextField.bottomScroll	A read-only integer specifying the bottommost line in myTextField that is visible.
condenseWhite	A	myTextField. condenseWhite	A Boolean that specifies whether "white space" (including spaces, line breaks, and paragraph breaks) are removed from HTML text. Ignored if html attribute is false.
embedFonts	A	myTextField.embedFonts	A Boolean that specifies whether the text field uses embedded font outlines (true) or device fonts (false).
_focusrect	A	myTextField._focusrect	A Boolean that specifies whether a text field has a yellow rectangle around it when it has focus.
_highquality	A	TextField._highquality	References the global _highquality variable. Globally enables smoothing bitmaps and antialiasing. An integer. 0 : none. 1 : antialias, smooth bitmaps if no animation in movie (default). 2 : smooth bitmaps and antialias.

A

Name	Method/ Attribute/ Event/	Format	Description
_height	A	myTextField._height	A read-write integer, the height of myTextField in pixels. Affects bounding box size only, not font size.
hscroll	A	myTextField.hscroll	An integer that specifies, in pixels, the current horizontal scroll position of myTextField.
html	A	myTextField.html	A Boolean that specifies whether myTextField contains HTML text. Must precede myTextField.htmlText.
htmlText	A	myTextField.htmlText	A string containing HTML-formatted text for myTextField.
length	A	myTextField.length	A read-only integer, the number of characters in myTextField.
maxChars	A	myTextField.maxChars	An integer. When myTextField contains this number of characters, Flash disables manual insertion of characters.
maxhscroll	A	myTextField.maxhscroll	A read-only integer value that specifies, in pixels, the maximum possible value of myTextField.hscroll, given the current text.
maxscroll	A	myTextField.maxscroll	A read-only integer value that specifies, in pixels, the maximum possible value of myTextField.scroll, given the current text.
multiline	A	myTextField.multiline	A Boolean that specifies whether myTextField can contain multiple lines.
_name	A	myTextField._name	A string, the instance name, for example, "myTextField".

continues

TABLE A.12 CONTINUED

Name	Method/ Attribute/ Event/	Format	Description
_parent	A	myTextField._parent	A reference to the movie clip or button that is myTextField's parent.
password	A	myTextField.password	A Boolean that specifies whether myTextField is a password field. If it is true, Flash displays asterisks on the screen instead of input characters.
_quality	A	TextField._quality	Global string attribute, specifies the rendering quality of a movie. LOW: Graphics not antialiased; bitmaps not smoothed. MEDIUM: Graphics antialiased using a 2×2 pixel grid; bitmaps not smoothed. Suitable for movies with no text. HIGH: Graphics antialiased using a 4×4 pixel grid; bitmaps smoothed if no animation in movie. (HIGH is the default.) BEST: Graphics antialiased using a 4×4 pixel grid; bitmaps always smoothed.
restrict	A	myTextField.restrict	A string specifying the set of characters that a user can enter into myTextField. A dash indicates a range. A caret (^) means the following characters are excluded, whereas preceding characters are allowed. The following example includes only lowercase letters, but excludes the lowercase letter w: myTextField.restrict = "a-z^w";

Name	Method/ Attribute/ Event/	Format	Description
_rotation	A	myTextField._rotation	A read-write integer value that specifies the current degree of rotation of myTextField.
scroll	A	myTextField.scroll	A read-write integer value that specifies the current vertical scrolling position of myTextField, measured in lines of text.
selectable	A	myTextField.selectable	Boolean, specifies whether myTextField is selectable.
_soundbuftime	A	myTextField._ soundbuftime	References the global _sound buftime variable. Globally sets and gets the amount of time, in seconds, a sound must pre-buffer before it streams. An integer, defaulting to 5.
tabEnabled	A	myTextField.tabEnabled	A Boolean that specifies myTextField is included in automatic tab ordering.
tabIndex	A	myTextField.tabIndex	Specifies the tab order of myTextField.
text	A	myTextField.text	A read-write string, the current text in the text field.
textColor	A	myTextField.textColor	A read-write integer, the color of the current text in the text field. Often in hex format, such as 0xFF0000.
textHeight	A	myTextField.textHeight	A read-only integer value that specifies the height of the actual text (not the bounding box).
textWidth	A	myTextField.textWidth	A read-only integer value that specifies the width of the actual text (not the bounding box).

continues

A

TABLE A.12 **CONTINUED**

Name	Method/ Attribute/ Event/	Format	Description
type	A	myTextField.type	A read-write string, dynamic or input, that specifies whether myTextField is an input text field or dynamic text field.
_url	A	myTextField._url	A read-only string, the URL of the SWF file that created the text field instance.
variable	A	myTextField.variable	A read-write string, the vari able name associated with the text field.
_visible	A	myTextField._visible	A read-write Boolean value that determines whether myTextField is hidden (false) or visible (true).
_width	A	myTextField._width	A read-write integer, the width of myTextField in pixels. This affects only the bounding box of the text field; it does not affect the border thickness or text font size.
wordWrap	A	myTextField.wordWrap	A read-write Boolean that specifies whether the text field word-wraps.
_x	A	myTextField._x	A read-write integer, the x coordinate of myTextField.
_xmouse	A	myTextField._xmouse	A read-only integer, the x coordinate of the cursor rela-tive to myTextField.
_xscale	A	myTextField._xscale	A read-write integer from -100 to 100, specifying the per-centage for horizontally scal-ing myTextField.
_y	A	myTextField._y	A read-write integer, the y coordinate of myTextField.

Name	Method/ Attribute/ Event/	Format	Description
_ymouse	A	myTextField._ymouse	A read-only integer, the y coordinate of the cursor relative to myTextField.
_yscale	A	myTextField._yscale	A read-write integer from -100 to 100, specifying the percentage for vertically scaling myTextField.
onChanged	E	myTextField.onChanged = function (textfieldName) {}	Invoked when the text in the field is changed.
onKillFocus	E	myTextField.onKillFocus = function (newFocus) {}	Invoked when the text field loses focus.
onScroller	E	myTextField.onScroller = function (textfieldName) {}	Invoked when the scroll, maxscroll, hscroll, maxhscroll, or bottomscroll attribute of myTextField changes.
onSetFocus	E	myTextField.onSetFocus = function (oldFocus) {}	Invoked when the text field receives focus.

TABLE A.13   TextField.autoResize **VALUES**

Value	Single Line	Multiline
"none" or false	Do not automatically resize	Do not automatically resize
"left" or true	Expand right	Expand bottom
"center"	Expand right and left	Expand bottom
"right"	Expand left	Expand bottom

A

TABLE A.14   TextFormat ATTRIBUTES AND METHODS

Name	Method/Attribute	Format	Description
getTextExtent	M	myTextFormat.getTextExtent (*text*)	Returns an object with two attributes, width and height, that indicate the dimensions in points of the *text* string when formatted with myTextFormat. (Width may be inaccurate with embedded fonts.)
align	A	myTextFormat.align	A string indicating text alignment: null, "left", "right", or "center".
blockIndent	A	myTextFormat.blockIndent	An integer specifying, in points, an amount to indent all lines in a block of text.
bold	A	myTextFormat.bold	A Boolean indicating whether text is boldface.
bullet	A	myTextFormat.bullet	A Boolean indicating whether to format text in a bulleted list.
color	A	myTextFormat.color	An integer specifying the color of text. Often in hexadecimal format, for example, 0xFF0000.
font	A	myTextFormat.font	A string specifying the font name, for example, New Times Roman.
indent	A	myTextFormat.indent	An integer specifying, in points, the indentation from the left margin to the first character in each paragraph.
italic	A	myTextFormat.italic	A Boolean indicating whether text is italicized.
leading	A	myTextFormat.leading	An integer specifying, in points, the amount of leading (vertical space between lines).
leftMargin	A	myTextFormat.leftMargin	An integer specifying the left margin, in points.
rightMargin	A	myTextFormat.rightMargin	An integer specifying the right margin, in points.

A

Name	Method/Attribute	Format	Description
tabStops	A	myTextFormat.tabStops	An array of positive integers specifying custom tab stops.
target	A	myTextFormat.target	Used with myTextFormat.url. A string specifying the browser window in which to display the hyperlinked page. Values match those of the HTML target attribute, for example, "_blank", "_self", "_top", "_parent".
size	A	myTextFormat.size	An integer specifying, in points, the size of the text.
underline	A	myTextFormat.underline	A Boolean indicating whether text is underlined.
url	A	myTextFormat.url	A string specifying the URL to which the text links.

TABLE A.15 STYLESHEET METHODS AND EVENTS

Name	Method/Event	Format	Description
getStyle	M	myStyleSheet.getStyle("myStyleName")	Returns a copy of the style sheet object associated with the myStyleName style.
getStyleNames	M	myArray = myTextField.myStyleSheet.getStyleNames()	Returns an array that contains the names of all the styles registered in the style sheet object.
load	M	myStyleSheet.load("gdStyles.css")	Begins loading the external gdStyles.css style sheet into the myStyleSheet object. Requires complete path to external style sheet.
parseCSS	M	myStyleSheet.parseCSS(textToParse)	Parses a string of CSS text (textToParse) and creates the specified style.

continues

TABLE A.15 CONTINUED

Name	Method/Event	Format	Description
setStyle	M	myStyleSheet.setStyle ("bodyText", {	fontsize: '12px'}); Adds a new style (bodyText) to the style sheet object, with the specified CSS properties.
onLoad	E	myStyleSheet.onLoad()	Callback handler invoked when a TextField.StyleSheet.load() operation has completed.

WRAPPER CLASSES: Boolean, Number, String

TABLE A.16 METHODS AND ATTRIBUTES OF WRAPPER CLASSES: Boolean, Number, String

Name	Method/Attribute	Format	Description
Boolean.toString	M	myBoolean.toString()	Returns the string representation (true) or (false) of myBoolean.
Boolean.valueOf	M	myBoolean.valueOf()	Returns the primitive value type of myBoolean.
Number.toString	M	myNumber.toString()	Returns the string representation of myNumber.
Number.valueOf	M	myNumber.valueOf()	Returns the primitive value of myNumber.
Number.MAX_VALUE	A	myNumber.MAX_VALUE	A constant, the largest number that ActionScript can represent: 1.79769313486231e+308.
Number.MIN_VALUE	A	myNumber.MIN_VALUE	A constant, the smallest number that ActionScript can represent: 5e-324.

A

Name	Method/ Attribute	Format	Description
`Number.NaN`	A	`myNumber.NaN`	"Not a Number," a constant representing a value that is not a number but is used in a context where a number is expected.
`Number.NEGATIVE_INFINITY`	A	`myNumber.NEGATIVE_INFINITY`	A constant representing a value more negative than `Number.MAX_VALUE`.
`Number.POSITIVE_INFINITY`	A	`myNumber.POSITIVE_INFINITY`	A constant representing a value more positive than `Number.MAX_VALUE`. (Same as the global constant `Infinity`.)
`String.charAt`	M	`myString.charAt(index)`	Returns the character at a specific location in `myString`.
`String.charCodeAt`	M	`myString.charCodeAt(index)`	Returns the Unicode encoding of the character at `myString[index]` as a 16-bit integer between 0 and 65,535.
`String.concat`	M	`myString.concat(value1,...valueN)`	Returns a new string resulting from concatenating (combining) `myString` and the strings specified in arguments (`value1–valueN`).
`String.fromCharCode`	M	`MyString.fromCharCode(charCode1, charCode2, ...charCodeN)`	Returns a new string made up of the characters specified as character codes in the parameters.
`String.indexOf`	M	`myString.indexOf(substring, [startIndex])`	Searches the string, starting at `startIndex`, and returns the index of the first occurrence of `substring`. Returns `-1` if `substring` is not found.

A

continues

TABLE A.16 CONTINUED

Name	Method/Attribute	Format	Description
String.lastIndexOf	M	myString.lastIndexOf (*substring*, [*startIndex*])	Searches the string, starting at *startIndex*, and returns the index of the last occurrence of *substring*. Returns -1 if *substring* is not found.
String.slice	M	myString.slice (*startIndex*, [*endIndex*])	Returns a substring of the original string, starting at the character whose position in myString is *startIndex*, up to but not including the character whose position in myString is *endIndex*. (The index of the first character in the string is 0.)
String.split	M	myString.split ("*delimiter*", [*limit*])	Splits a string into substrings by breaking it wherever the *delimiter* string occurs, and returns the substrings in an array. If you use an empty string ("") as a delimiter, each character in the string is an element in the returned array. If *delimiter* is undefined, the first and only element in the returned array is the entire string. The optional *limit* argument specifies the maximum number of su strings that may be returned.

A

Name	Method/ Attribute	Format	Description
String.substr	M	myString.substr (*startIndex*, [*length*])	Returns a substring that starts at *startIndex* and includes the number of characters specified in the *length* argument, or the rest of the characters in the string (if there is no *length* argument). If *startIndex* is negative, the starting position is determined from the end of the string, with -1 indicating the last character, -2 the second to last, and so on.
String.substring	M	myString.substring (*startIndex*, *endIndex*)	Returns a substring starting at *startIndex* and ending one character before *endIndex*. If *endIndex* is omitted, the returned substring runs to the end of the string. If *startIndex* equals *endIndex*, the method returns the empty string. If *startIndex* is greater than *endIndex*, the Flash interpreter should swap them before running the function; in reality, it sometimes returns the empty string.
String.toLowerCase	M	myString. toLowerCase()	Returns a copy of myString, but with all characters in lowercase. The original value is unchanged.

A

continues

TABLE A.16   CONTINUED

Name	Method/Attribute	Format	Description
String.toUpperCase	M	myString.toUpperCase()	Returns a copy of myString, but with all characters in uppercase. The original value is unchanged.
String.valueOf	M	myString.valueOf()	Returns the primitive value type of the specified String object.
String.length	A	myString.length	The length of the string.

THE Camera CLASS

TABLE A.17   Camera METHODS

Name	Format	Description
get	Camera.get([index])	Returns the video stream from the default camera or the camera specified by index. Returns null if no camera is available. (If more than one camera is installed, the user specifies the default camera in the Flash Player Camera Settings panel.)
setMode	myCamera.setMode(width, height, fps [,favorSize])	Sets attributes of the camera capture mode, including height, width, and frames per second. favorSize is an optional Boolean value. To maximize frame rate at the expense of height and width, set favorSize to false. To favor maintaining height and width over frame rate, set favorSize to true.

A

Name	Format	Description
setMotionLevel	myCamera.setMotionLevel (sensitivity [,timeout])	sensitivity is an integer from 0 to 100 that specifies how much motion is required to invoke Camera.onActivity(true). The default is 50. timeout specifies how many milliseconds must elapse without motion before Camera.onActivity(false) is invoked. The default is 2000 (2 seconds).

TABLE A.18   Camera ATTRIBUTES

Format	Description
myCamera.activityLevel	The amount of motion the camera is detecting, from 0 (none) to 100 (maximum). Prior to a myVideoObject.attachVideo() call, this is -1. Read-only.
myCamera.bandwidth	The maximum amount of bandwidth the current outgoing video feed can use, in bytes. Read-only.
myCamera.currentFps	The rate at which the camera is capturing data, in frames per second. Read-only.
myCamera.fps	The rate at which you would like the camera to capture data, in frames per second. Read-only.
myCamera.height	The current capture height, in pixels. Read-only.
myCamera.index	The index of the camera, as reflected in the array returned by Camera.names. Read-only.
myCamera.motionLevel	The amount of motion required to invoke Camera.onActivity(true). Read-only.
myCamera.motionTimeOut	The number of milliseconds between the time the camera stops detecting motion and the time Camera.onActivity(false) is invoked. Read-only.
myCamera.muted	A read-only Boolean value that specifies whether the user has allowed or denied access to the camera.
myCamera.name	The name of the camera as specified by the camera hardware. Read-only.

continues

A

TABLE A.18 CONTINUED

Format	Description
Camera.names	A class property, an array of strings containing the names of all available video capture devices, including video cards and cameras. Read-only.
myCamera.quality	A number from 1 to 100 that specifies the current level of picture quality. More compression means lower quality: 1 is lowest quality, maximum compression. 100 is highest quality, no compression. Read-only.
myCamera.width	The current capture width, in pixels. Read-only.

TABLE A.19 Camera EVENT HANDLERS

Name	Format	Description
onActivity	myCamera.onActivity = function(activity) {}	Invoked when the camera starts or stops detecting motion. activity is a Boolean value set to true when the camera starts detecting motion, false when it stops.
onStatus	myCamera.onStatus = function(infoObject){}	Invoked when the user allows or denies access to the camera.

THE Microphone CLASS

TABLE A.20 Microphone METHODS

Name	Format	Description
get	Microphone.get([index])	Returns a default or specified audio stream, or null if no microphone is available.
setGain	myMicrophone.setGain(gain)	Specifies the amount by which the microphone should boost the signal, from 0 to 100.

A

Name	Format	Description
setRate	myMicrophone.setRate(*kHz*)	Specifies the rate at which the microphone should capture sound, in kHz.
setSilenceLevel	myMicrophone. setSilenceLevel(*level* [,*timeout*])	Specifies the sound level (from 0 to 100) required to activate the microphone. Optionally also sets *timeout*, specifying milliseconds of inactivity before Flash invokes Microphone.onActivity(fal se). The default value is 2000 (2 seconds). The default value of level is 10.
setUseEchoSuppression	myMicrophone. setUseEchoSuppression (*suppress*)	*suppress* is a Boolean that specifies whether to use the echo suppression feature of the audio codec.

TABLE A.21   Microphone ATTRIBUTES

Format	Description
myMicrophone.activityLevel	The amount of sound the microphone detects, from 0 to 100.
myMicrophone.gain	The amount by which the microphone boosts the signal before transmitting it, from 0 to 100. The default is 50.
myMicrophone.index	The index of the current microphone.
myMicrophone.muted	A Boolean value that specifies whether the user has allowed or denied access to the microphone.
myMicrophone.name	The name of the current sound capture device, as returned by the sound capture hardware.
Microphone.names	A class property, an array of strings containing the names of all available sound capture devices, including sound cards and microphones.
myMicrophone.rate	The sound capture rate, in kHz.

A

TABLE A.22   Microphone **EVENT HANDLERS**

Name	Format	Description
onActivity	myMicrophone.onActivity = function (*activity*){ }	Invoked when the microphone starts or stops detecting sound. *activity* is a Boolean value set to true when the microphone starts detecting sound, and false when it stops.
onStatus	myMicrophone.onStatus = function (*infoObject*){}	Invoked when the user allows or denies access to the microphone. *infoObject* usage similar to that of Camera.onStatus.

MAKING FLASH ACCESSIBLE

In this appendix

Accessibility Guidelines   978

Introduction to Accessibility in Flash MX 2004   978

How to Make Content Accessible   979

ACCESSIBILITY GUIDELINES

Until the release of Macromedia Flash MX, Flash content had been woefully inaccessible to users who required screen readers or were hearing impaired. Now the Flash Player can communicate with screen reader software and other assistive devices to convey visual content.

Flash MX 2004 includes accessibility support in the authoring environment, as well, with keyboard shortcuts for navigating and interface controls, enabling you to use the interface without using the mouse.

Also new in Flash MX 2004 is a new generation of components that offers better accessibility through improved tab focus management and improved support for third-party screen readers and closed-caption programs.

To help designers and developers ensure that Rich Internet Applications are accessible, Macromedia Flash Player 7 and Macromedia Flash MX 2004 include support for updating and generating the accessibility properties via ActionScript. This enables applications to update accessibility information as the content changes.

INTRODUCTION TO ACCESSIBILITY IN FLASH MX 2004

Screen reader software allows people with visual disabilities to use the Internet. Screen readers speak or read text, but cannot convey images or animations. Because much Flash content is inaccessible to screen readers, it's essential to make the most of the new Flash MX accessibility options.

The following five objects are defined as accessible within Flash and are passed from the Flash Player to screen reader software:

- Text
- Input text fields
- Buttons (including button movie clips)
- Movie clips (including components)
- Entire movies

Individual graphics, however, are not exposed to the screen reader. This is especially important to note with text. Any graphical text—text that has been broken apart into shapes—is not accessible, which can mean that entire navigation systems are inaccessible. Keep this fact in mind as you design layouts and ensure that essential menu text is created with text, not shapes.

For each of the five accessible objects, Flash allows you to provide additional text descriptions—much like ALT tags in HTML—which make your content more useful and available to screen readers. The most powerful of these is the Name property, which can be assigned to objects and which is read aloud by screen readers. You can also specify which of the Flash objects are exposed to screen readers.

HOW TO MAKE CONTENT ACCESSIBLE

To specify accessibility options for Flash objects, follow these steps:

1. Select a Flash object on the Stage.

2. In the Property inspector, click the Edit Accessibility Settings button (a blue circle with a white star in it, in the lower right corner), to open the Accessibility panel. If the Edit Accessibility Settings button does not appear, the selection cannot have accessibility applied to it.

   Alternatively, you can press Opt-F2 (Mac) or Alt+F2 (Windows) to open the Accessibility panel.

3. Be sure that Make Object Accessible is checked and then assign a name and description within the Accessibility panel.

You can even assign a keyboard shortcut within the Accessibility panel to trigger buttons or input text fields. To do so, spell out key name abbreviations, such as Alt or Ctrl, and use a plus sign with no spaces to combine key names.

NOTE

Screen reader software is currently available only on the Windows platform. Keep this fact in mind when you're creating shortcuts, and do not use Mac-specific keys such as Cmd.

Be sure to provide names for any accessible objects. Even if an object contains content that is purely visual—such as an animated special effect—it is essential to provide an indication of the content to screen readers. If you do not, users employing assistive devices may be entirely unaware of important content or, in the case of a purely visual effect, may think they are missing vital content. You don't have to provide a name if the object includes a text label: The text label will be read by the screen reader.

When a Flash movie is complete, you must define accessibility for the entire movie for the objects you have made accessible to be exposed to the screen reader. To define accessibility for an entire movie, follow these steps:

1. When a movie is complete and ready to publish, deselect any items on the Stage and then access the Accessibility panel by clicking the Accessibility button in the Property inspector or by choosing Window, Other Panels, Accessibility.

2. Select Make Movie Accessible, which is selected by default. If you want to hide the movie from screen readers, deselect this option.

B

3. Select Make Child Objects Accessible to expose accessible objects within the movie to screen readers.

4. Select Auto Label to use text objects as automatic labels for accessible buttons and input text fields. This option is selected by default.

5. Enter a brief, descriptive title in the Name field.

6. Enter a longer description in the Description field. Imagine that you cannot see the movie, and provide a description that will convey your content without relying upon any visual references.

Although Flash MX 2004 attempts to make content more accessible, designers and developers have to ensure that essential content can be conveyed. Take the initiative and do all that you can to make your content available for as wide an audience as possible.

B

INDEX

Symbols

+= (add and reassign compound assignment operator), 938

& (ampersand), 625, 891

& (AND logical bitwise operator), 932-933

&& (AND logical operator), 943

= (assignment operator), 461, 475, 938-939

* (asterisk), 892

>>= (bit-shift and reassign compound assignment operator), 938

<<= (bit-shift and reassign compound assignment operator), 938

&= (bitwise AND and reassign compound assignment operator), 938

|= (bitwise OR and reassign compound assignment operator), 938

^= (bitwise XOR and reassign compound assignment operator), 938

{} (curly brackets), CSS declarations, 173

— (decrement operator), 926-927

/= (divide and reassign compound assignment operator), 938

. (dot) operator, 467, 542, 547, 950

"" (double quotes)
    HTML/XHTML values, 170
    server-side includes, 634
    strings, 625

// (double slashes), 449

= (equal sign), 170, 625

== (equality operator), 939

(hash mark), 175, 224, 627

++ (increment operator), 926-927

!= (inequality operator), 940

% (modulo) operator, 929-930

%= (modulo divide and reassign compound assignment operator), 938

*= (multiply and reassign compound assignment operator), 938

! (NOT logical operator), 943

+= operator (add and reassign), 916

| (OR logical bitwise operator), 933-934

|| (OR logical operator), 943-944

- (overloaded) operator, 928-929

() [parentheses], 476, 488

. (period), class selectors, 175

+ (plus) operator, 470

+ (polymorphic) operator, 928

? (question mark), 632

; (semicolon), CSS declarations, 173-174

>> (signed right bit-shift operator), 936-937

!== (strict inequality operator), 940

-= (subtract and reassign compound assignment operator), 938

<< (signed left bit-shift operator), 937

/ (slash), 886

[] (square brackets), object property access, 467

=== (strict equality operator), 482, 939

^ (XOR logical bitwise operator), 934-935

>>> (unsigned right bit-shift operator), 937

Numbers

2D objects, converting to 3D, 815

3D objects, 2D objects, converting to, 815

3D animation (Flash), 322

3D Rotation dialog box, 812

3D Rotation tool (FreeHand), 812-814

A

A server timeout has occured. error (Dreamweaver), 317

abs method (Math object), 957

absolute link values, HTML/XHTML, 171

absolute paths, movie clips, 495

absolute URLs, 619

Access (Microsoft), 13

accessibility
context-sensitivity, 246
guidelines
Flash, 978-980
WAI (Web Accessibility Initiative), 245-246
movie clips, 979
testing, 246-247, 262
validation, site management, 245-246
Accessibility button, 979
Accessibility object, 593
Accessibility Panel, opening, 979
accessing
Actions panel (ActionScript), 443-444
array elements, 447
clients, Dreamweaver ColdFusion, 311-316
ColdFusion servers, Flash, 878-880
databases, Flash, 662
Dreamweaver Exchange, 54
extensions, 781
JavaBeans, 65
Movie Explorer (Flash), 344
named properties, arrays, 561
object properties, 447, 467
Preferences, 345
properties, symbol instances (Flash), 387
Recordset, 297
sound (Sound object), 415
symbol instances (Flash), 389
timeline variables, 489
Web services, 879
_accProps variable, 593
acos (arccos) method, 588
acos method (Math object), 957
Action menu commands, Get More Behaviors, 267
Action Message Format (AMF), 662, 880
Action tool, 828, 852-854
Action Tool dialog box, 853-854

actions
Dreamweaver, 221
Flash buttons, 422
frame, 445-446, 503
Link to Target Page, 853
Load Target Page, 853
managing, History panel, 90-91
Navigation panel, 853
objects, 445-446, 503
Print Target Page, 853
triggering, 854
triggering via event handlers, 500-501
button events, 508-511
calling explicitly, 507
deleting/disabling event handlers, 507
dynamic event handlers, 502-505
input events, 504
key events, 511-512
keyboard focus, 507-510
listener registration, 504-505
mouse events, 512
movie clip events, 513-515
scoping, 505-506
selection events, 515
sound events, 515-516
Stage events, 516
static event handlers, 503-505
system events, 504
TextField events, 516-517
this keyword, 505-506
Web sites, assigning, 852-854
Actions command (Window menu), 443
Actions panel (ActionScript), 444-446
Actions toolbox, 444-446
ActionScript (AS1), 540
arithmetic operators, 926-929
assignment operator (=), 938-939
behaviors (Flash interactivity), 418-420

bitwise operators, 930-937
Camera class, 972-974
classes, superclasses, 615
comma operator, 947-948
comparison operators, 939-942
compound assignment operators, 938-939
conditional operator, 946-947
ContextMenu class, 910-911
control blocks
body, 477
conditional statements, 480-483
control constructs, 477
flow control, 480
headers, 477
keywords, 477-479
looping, 476
loops, 483-485
non-looping, 476
databinding, 665
datatype conversion rules, 911-916
Date class, methods, 951-954
event handlers, 500-501
button events, 508-511
calling explicitly, 507
deleting/disabling, 507
dynamic, 502-505
input events, 504
key events, 511-512
keyboard focus, 507-510
listener registration, 504-505
mouse events, 512
movie clip events, 513-515
scoping, 505-506
selection events, 515
sound events, 515-516
Stage events, 516
static, 503-505
system events, 504
TextField events, 516-517
this keyword, 505-506
expressions, 471-474

Flash
Actions panel, 443-446
benefits, 442-443
code hints, 456-457
event handlers, 445-446
functions, 445
interactivity, 442-443
limitations, 442
reachability, 453-456
readability, 448-450
reusability, 451-453
troubleshooting, 458
Flash Remoting connections, 666-668
functions
aliases, 497
arguments, declaring, 490
automatic scoping, 497-500
call operators (), 488
calling, 488, 493
constructor, 493
creating, 486
creating, declarations, 486-487
creating, literals, 487
explicit scoping, 494-497
function.apply() method, 493-494
function.call() method, 493-494
local function variables, 488-489
passing arguments, 489-492
retrieving results via return values, 492-493
timeline variable access, 489
troubleshooting, 487, 536-537
var keyword, 489
identifiers, 462-464
input text fields, borders, 371
JavaScript communication, troubleshooting, 657
Key object, 955-957
keyboard focus, troubleshooting, 537
literals, 470-471

logical (Boolean) operators, 943-945
Math object, 957-958
Microphone class, 974-975
movie clips
bounding boxes, 529
coordinates, 530
creating, 517-520
drag and drop, 533-534
droptarget property, 534
dynamic masks, 534-535
empty, 520
external content, loading/unloading, 520-524
functions, 531-533
hierarchies, 519, 524-525
hitTest() method, troubleshooting, 537-538
init objects, 528-529
loaded, troubleshooting, 537
overlapping, 529-531
positioning, 519
properties, 518
removing, 518-520
stacking, 518, 524-528
timelines, 517
MovieClip class, 917-923
named operators, 948-950
NaN (Not a Number) value, 912
operands, troubleshooting, 535
operators, 471-476
overview, 460
reserved words, 463
scope chains, 498-499
statements, 471-474, 479
StyleSheet class, 967-968
switch statements, troubleshooting, 535
TextField class, 958-965
TextFormat class, 966-967
Timeline, 535-536
undefined return statements, troubleshooting, 536
variables
centralizing code, 462
comments, 460

creating explicitly, 460-461
creating implicitly, 460
data conversion, 469
datatypes, 464-471
declaring, 460-462
Main Timeline organization, 462
naming, 462-464
set statements, 461
value assignments, 461
video playback, 439
ActionScript 2 (AS2)
classes, 540
attribute names, 548
attribute value initialization, 544-546
class features, 543-544
classpaths, entering, 554-556
core, 556-567
core, Date, 569-570
core, Error, 570-572
core, Function, 572
core, Math, 578-589
core, Object, 572-578
core, objects, 557
core, System, 589-592
core, wrapper, 567-569
defining, 541
dynamic, 548-549
dynamic, limitations, 549
feature visibility, 546
get method, 546-548
hierarchies, 550-552
instances, 541-543, 548-554
locating, 554-556
prototype attribute, 542-543
set method, 546-548
static features, 543-544
subclasses, 550
components, building, 612-615
constructor functions, 544-546
movie classes, 592
Accessibility, 593
Button, 593-594

Color, 594-595
ContextMenu, 596
Key, 596
LocalConnection, 596-600
Mouse, 600
PrintJob, 600-602
Selection, 602
Shared Object, 602-603
Stage, 603-605
TextField, 605-611
TextFormat, 605-611
TextSnapshot, 611-612
OOP (object-oriented programming), 330
strict data typing, 331
text files, formatting, troubleshooting, 615
trigonometry, troubleshooting, 615
troubleshooting, 331
ActionScript Editor, 444
ActionScript Editor Preferences (Flash), 349-350
Active Server Pages (ASP), 634
ActiveX, JavaScript/Flash communications, 621
ActiveX controls, 232-234
ActiveX Name property (ActiveX controls), 233
Adaptive Differential Pulse Code Modulation (ADPCM), sound optimization, 416
Adaptive option (Indexed Palette drop-down menu), 764
Add a Page button, 271-272
add and reassign (+=) compound assignment operator, 938
add and reassign operator (+=), 916
Add Behavior (+) button, 739
Add Binding dialog box, 675
Add Columns dialog box, 309
Add New Data Source dialog box, 880-881
Add Noise Live Effect, 691
Add Pages command (Options menu), 846

Add Pages dialog box, 846
Add Points option (Xtra Operations toolbar), 832
Add to Favorites button, 138
Add to Personal button, 153
Add URL dialog box, 139-140
Add Using WSDL dialog box, 316-317
Adding Pages option (Document panel), 789
addition operators, 927
addListener method, 504, 958
addProperty method, 572, 576
addRequestHeader() method, 646-647
Address fields, JavaScript function calls, 621-622
administrator interfaces, ColdFusion, 877
Adobe Acrobat Reader plug-in, 230
Adobe GoLive, Fireworks, 774
ADPCM (Adaptive Differential Pulse Code Modulation), sound optimization, 416
advanced buttons (Flash interactivity), 422-423
Advanced command (Color drop-down menu), 388
Advanced Effect panel, 595
Advanced Effects dialog box, 388
Advanced Encoding dialog box, 437-438
Advanced Settings dialog box, 388
Advanced tab, 104, 107
advanced types, CSS (Cascading Style Sheets), 183
Alias Text button, 327, 370
aliasing
anti-aliasing, 689
Flash, 327
functions, 497
Align command (Modify menu), 213
Align panel, 356, 399

align property, 231, 280, 603-604, 966
Align, Make Same Height (Modify menu), 213
Align, Make Same Width (Modify menu), 213
alignment, 47
bitmap fonts, 369
layers, 213
objects (Flash), 356
pixels, 369
snapping (Flash), 353-354
Stage content, 603
text (Dreamweaver), 97-98
text to paths, 849-852
Alignment command (Text menu), 98
allowDomain event handler, 597-598
allowDomain method, 591
allowInsecureDomain method, 592
allowInsecureDomain() event handler, 597
alpha
movie clips, 594
transforming (movie clips), 595
alpha channels (Flash), 358
Alpha command (Color drop-down menu), 388
_alpha property (MovieClip class), 921
alpha property (TextField class), 959
Alpha transparency, Fireworks, 773
alphanumeric characters, 466
Alt property (Java applets), 235
Alter Path, Reverse Direction command (Modify menu), 843, 851
Alter Path, Simplify command (Modify menu), 42
AMF (Action Message Format), 662, 880
ampersand (&), 625, 891
amplitude, 406, 414
anchor points, 39-41
anchors, named anchors (Flash), 346

AND logical bitwise operator (&), 932-933

AND logical operator (&&), 943

angular blending, shape tweens (Flash), 399

Animate dialog box, 749-750

Animated GIF Websnap 128 option (Optimize panel), 761

animation. *See also* multimedia
   3D (Flash), 322
   bitmap graphics (Flash), 364-365
   controls, 697
   DHTML (Dynamic HTML), Dreamweaver, 19
   Dreamweaver, 19
   Fireworks, 19-20
   Flash, 19-20
   Flash buttons, 423
   frame-to-frame compression, 751
   frames, 392-393
   guidelines, 405
   keyframes, 335, 392-393
   layers
      DHTML, 228
      Flash, 336
   settings (Fireworks), exporting, Flash, 774
   symbols, 748-750
   text, 375
   time-line based, creating, 323

animation (Fireworks)
   bitmap, 743
   creating
      animation symbols, 748-750
      frame-by-frame, 744-746
      tweened, playing, 747-748
   exporting, 750-751
   frame delay, 746
   frame rates, 743
   looping, 746
   output formats, 743
   preparations, 743-744
   rollovers, 738-741
   vector, 743

animation (Flash)
   bitmaps, 391
   cartoon animations, 404
   creating, 391
   frame-by-frame animations, 393
   frames, 391-392
   guidelines, 405
   keyframes, 391-393
   motion guides, troubleshooting, 440
   motion paths, troubleshooting, 440
   nesting symbols, 404
   objects, 391
   previewing, 403
   sequences, 390
   strokes, 394
   symbols, 391
   Timeline Effects, 391, 400-403
   Timeline effects, scrubbing, 403-404
   tweening, 393
      motion tweens, 394-398
      shape tweens, 398-400
   vectors, 390

Animation, Animate Selection command (Modify menu), 749

Animation, Settings command (Modify menu), 750

Answers panel (Fireworks), troubleshooting, 728-729

anti-aliasing
   Fireworks, 689
   Flash, 327
   pixels, 368
   turning off, 370

Apache HTTP Server, 15

Apache Web servers, 880

API
   dynamic masks, creating, 535
   JavaScript API extensions, 691

appendChild(node) command, 642

Apple QuickTime plug-in, 230

Applet Name property (Java applets), 235

applets, Java, 234-235

Application panel, 85-88, 289

APPLICATION scope, 890

Application tab (Dreamweaver), 79

applications. *See* programs

Apply button, 141

apply() method, 572

Arc dialog box, 801

Arc tool (FreeHand), 801

arccos (acos) method, 588

architecture, Web sites, 838-844

arcs, traced bitmaps (Flash), 360

arcsin (asin) method, 588

arctangent (atan) method, 589

area charts, 828

arg parameter, 489

arguments
   declaring, 490
   defined, 312, 451
   functions, 468
   passing to functions, 489-492
   slice() method, 566

arguments object, 490-491

arguments parameter, 622

ARGUMENTS scope, 890

arguments.callee property, 491

arguments.caller property, 492

arguments.length property, 491

arithmetic operators, 472, 926-929

Arrange, Prevent Layer Overlaps command (Modify menu), 214

arranging panel groups (Dreamweaver), 81-83

array class
   creating, 558-559
   elements, 557-562
   empty, 558
   methods, 562-567

array core object, 558-560

array datatype, 465-467

array elements, scope chains, 498

How can we make this index more useful? Email us at indexes@quepublishing.com

array literals, 470-471, 558

Array return values, 574

Array() constructor function, 558-559

array-element/object property operator, 950

arrays, 899
  associative, 494
  comparison operators, 941-942
  data structures, 447
  elements, accessing, 447
  functions, 448
  last-in-first-out (LIFO), stack, 564
  modifying, 566
  named properties, 561
  nested, 564-566
  reusability, code, 451
  reversed, 564
  sparse, 560
  structures, 900

arrow keys (Flash), shape dimensions, 355

Arrow tool. See Selection tool

arrowheads, links (site maps), 843

arrows, drawing, 717

arithmetic, binary arithmetic, 930-931

arithmetic operators, 928-930

.as file extension, 541

AS1. See ActionScript

AS2. See ActionScript 2

ascenders, 852

ASCII, Web page titles, 117

asin (arcsin) method, 588

asin method (Math object), 957

ASP (Active Server Pages), 634

ASP.NET 1.1, 65

ASP.NET pages, creating/testing, 12

assets, Library (Flash), 343

Assets command (Window menu), 123

Assets panel
  assets, 141-142, 157
  categories, 136-141

Dreamweaver, 89-90
Favorites list, 137-139
Library category
  item behaviors, 149-150
  item copies, 150
  item creation, 143-145
  item deletion, 149, 158
  item detachment, 148-149
  item editing, 147-148
  item insertion into sites, 146-147
  similarity to SSIs, 144
  versus templates, 144-145
maintenance of, 141-142
site component tracker (Dreamweaver), 136
Site list, 137, 142
sliced images, piecing back into tables, 157
templates, creating, 123-124

Assets panel group (FreeHand), 793-794

assignment operators, 461, 472, 475, 938-939

associative arrays, 494, 561-562

associativity, operators, 475-476

asterisk (*), 892

atan (arctangent) method, 589, 957

atan2 method (Math object), 957

Attach External Style Sheet dialog box, 181

Attach to Path command (Text menu), 723, 849-850

attachMovie() method, 519-520, 528, 594, 917

attachSound() method, 415, 653

attachVideo method, 656-657

Attribute panel (Dreamweaver), 88

attribute property, 641

attribute values (classes), initializing, 544-546

attributes. See properties

attributes property, 639

ATTRIBUTES scope, 890

audio. See also multimedia; sound

Author option (Extension Manager dialog box), 266

Auto Kern option, 46

Auto Remove Overlap option
  Calligraphic dialog box, 800
  Variable Stroke Pen dialog box, 798

Auto Shapes, adding, 718

Auto Shapes tools, 686-687, 716-718

auto-expanding text blocks, resizing, 43

automated emailing, ColdFusion, 876

automated operations, databases (Dreamweaver ColdFusion)
  CFML (ColdFusion Markup Language) code, 290
  <cfquery> tag, 290
  detail pages, 310-311
  dynamic data, 297-305
  Live Data feature, 298, 306
  master pages, 310-311
  previewing data, 291-293
  records, managing, 308-310
  retrieving data, 293-297
  schema, 290
  Server Behavior panel, 306

automatic datatype conversion, 940-942

automatic depth numbering, 526-527

automatic scoping, 497-500

automatic tab ordering, 923

automation (Fireworks), 776-779

autoSize property (TextField class), 959

Autostretch option (Layout mode), 196

avHardwareDisable property, 589

B

Back and Forth command (Order menu), 824

Background category (Style Definition dialog box), 184

background color layer preference, 208

Background Color property (Flash object), 280

background colors, 58, 118

background image layer preference, 208

background images, 119-120

background property (TextField class), 959

backgroundColor property (TextField class), 960

backgrounds, white, buttons, 753

Backup Original Files option (Replace Options dialog box), 777

Bandwidth Profiler command (View menu), 435

Bandwidth slider, 436

Base property, 234-235

baselines, 852

Basic tab, 126

Batch Process (Fireworks), 778-779

Batch Process command (File menu), 722, 778

batch processing (Fireworks), 684

Batch Wizard, 778-779

Behavior panel (Dreamweaver), 88-89

behaviors
    ActionScript (Flash interactivity), 418-420, 442-443
    Check Browser, 229
    ColdFusion servers, creating with Dreamweaver, 879
    defined, 443
    downloading, 267-268
    Drag Layer, 227-228
    Flash, 323
    JavaScript, 221-223
    Library category, 149-150

Play Sound JavaScript, 236
    rollovers, creating, 224
    Set Nav Bar Image, 741
    Show-Hide, 227
    Swap Image, 225, 739-741
    Swap Image Restore, 225

Behaviors command (Window menu), 222

Behaviors panel
    behaviors, inserting, 222
    data sources, triggering, 678
    events, 227
    navigation bar, editing, 227

Bend dialog box, 809

Bend tool (FreeHand), 809

beveled rectangles, drawing, 717

Bézier curves, 40

Bg Color property (layers), 216

Bg Image property (layers), 215

binary arithmetic, 930-931

binary numbers, shifting bits, 936

binary variables, bitwise operators, 930

Bindings panel, 14, 86, 293

Bindings tab, 675

bit depth, sampling, 408

bit-shift and reassign (>>=) compound assignment operator, 938

bit-shift and reassign (<<=) compound assignment operator, 938

bit-shift bitwise operators, 935-937

bitmap animation, 743

Bitmap Export Defaults dialog box, 860-862

bitmap fonts, 368-370, 376-377

bitmap graphics
    colors, replacing, 687-688
    Fireworks, 732-733
    Flash
        animating, 364-365
        blurry, 365
        breaking apart, 362-363
        compressing, 363-364

fills, 358
    formats, 357
    importing, 357-358
    modifying, 358
    pixels, 352
    saving, 358
    tracing, 358-362, 365
    layers, 735

bitmap layers, creating, 700

bitmap mode (Fireworks), 697

Bitmap Properties dialog box, 363

Bitmap tools
    Blur, 705
    Brush, 703
    Burn, 706
    Dodge, 706
    Eraser, 703
    Gradient, 710-712
    Lasso, 701
    Magic Wand, 701
    Marquee, 700
    Oval Marquee, 701
    Pencil, 703
    Polygon Lasso, 701
    Red-Eye Removal, 710
    Replace Color, 708-710
    Rubber Stamp, 708
    Sharpen, 706
    Smudge, 707

Bitmap, Trace Bitmap command (Modify menu), 360

bitmaps, 36
    animations (Flash), 391
    selecting (Lasso tool), 339

Bitmaps (Clipboard Preferences), 348

bits
    binary arithmetic, 930
    MSB (most significant bit), 936
    on/off states, 933
    reversing, 935
    shifting, 938
    turning on, 934

bitwise AND and reassign (&=) compound assignment operator, 938

bitwise operators, 472, 930
    bit-shift, 935-937
    logical, 931-935

bitwise OR and reassign (|=) compound assignment operator, 938

bitwise XOR and reassign (^=) compound assignment operator, 938

Black and White option (Indexed Palette drop-down menu), 765

Blank Keyframe command (Insert menu), 335

blank keyframes (Flash), 392

_blank special target, 620

Blend option (Xtra Operations toolbar), 832

Blend tool (FreeHand), 821

blending shape tweens (Flash), 399

block elements, 100, 169

block properties option (Style Definition dialog box), 184

blockIndent property (TextFormat class), 966

blocks, character, 374

Blur effect (Timeline), 402

Blur tool, 705

blurring motion blur effects, 688

body, control blocks, 477

Bold button, 46

bold property (TextFormat class), 966

boolean, implicit datatype conversion, 913-914

Boolean (logical) operators, 943-945

Boolean attributes, 591

Boolean datatype, 465-466

Boolean return values, 574

Boolean wrapper class, 568

Boolean.toString method (wrapper classes), 968

Boolean.valueOf method (wrapper classes), 968

border = true property, 607

Border Color property (Property Inspector), 206

border property (TextField class), 960

border styles option (Style Definition dialog box), 185

borderColor property (TextField class), 960

borders
  frames, 206
  input text fields, 370-371
  visual, frames, 204

Borders property (Property Inspector), 206

born objects, 514

bottom parameters, startDrag () method, 533

bottomScroll property (TextField class), 960

Bound To dialog box, 675

bounding boxes, 339, 529

box properties option (Style Definition dialog box), 184

boxes. *See also* dialog boxes
  bounding, 339, 529
  Fill box, 34
  Stroke box, 34

Bradbury Software Web site, 179

Break Apart command (Modify menu), 362, 374, 399

break statement, 482

breaking apart, bitmap graphics (Flash), 362-363

breaking text apart, 374

brightness, video encoding (Flash), 438

Brightness and Contrast button, 277

Brightness command (Color drop-down menu), 387

broadband connections, testing sites online, 251

Browse mode (Contribute 2), 269

Browser Check icon, 244

browser control, 618-621

browser languages
  CSS (Cascading Style Sheets), 188-189
    cascade order, 178
    CSS Styles panel, 179-180
    declarations, 173-175
    design, 172
    displaying, 177

Document window, 179

Document window internal editor, 179

history, 171-172

integration, 177-178

layers, 162

links, 176

managing, 180-182

modifying, 172, 185-187

nesting, 175, 183

new definitions, 182-185

rules, 173-174

selectors, 173-177

versus HTML, 172-173

HTML (Hypertext Markup Language), 162
  attributes, 170
  converting to XHTML, 168
  elements, 169
  SGML (Standard Generalized Markup Language), 163
  values, 170-171
  versus CSS (Cascading Style Sheets), 172-173

HTML 4 (Hypertext Markup Language), 164-166

markup, 163-164

XHTML (Extensible HTML), 162
  attributes, 170
  document conformance, 167
  DTDs (document type definitions), 167
  elements, 169
  history, 164
  syntax rules, 168-169
  troubleshooting, 187
  values, 170-171
  well-formedness, 168

browsers
cross-browser compatibility, 154-155, 244-245
dynamic cross-browser compatibility, code clean up, 154-155
Dynamic Cross-Browser Compatibility Check feature, 66

frames, naming, 620
id attribute, 188
MIME types, 624
OBJECT parameter, troubleshooting, 658
windows, naming, 620
Brush Mode modifier (Brush tool), 340
brush strokes (Variable Stroke Pen), properties, setting, 798
Brush tool, 340-341, 703
built-in labels, custom menu, 911
built-in Web servers (ColdFusion), 880
bullet property (TextFormat class), 966
bulleted lists, creating (Dreamweaver), 98-99
Burn tool, 706
Button class, 593-594
Button component (Flash), 427
Button Symbol Editor, launching, 741
Button, MovieClip, TextField return values, 574
buttons
adding, Flash, 281-282
creating, 594
editing, Flash, 283
events, 508-511
Flash interactivity, 420-423
four-state, navigation bars, 741-743
functions, 55
Insert toolbar (Dreamweaver), 79
instances, keyPress event, 510
Italic, 46
movie clips, 505, 514-515
previewing, Flash, 283
resizing, Flash, 283
rollovers, creating, 421
screen reader software, 978
symbols, 380-381, 741
timelines, 518
white backgrounds, 753

C

call flow control, 480
call() method, 572
CALLER scope, 890, 898
Calligraphic dialog box, 799
Calligraphic Pen tool (FreeHand), 798-800
calling
CFML custom tags, 897
event handlers, explicitly, 507
functions, 488, 493, 531-533, 905, 950
JavaScript functions, 621-622
methods, 493
Camera class, 972-974
Camera Rich Media class, 647
Camera.names property (Camera class), 974
capabilities property, System class, 589-590
capitalization
code, 448-449
identifiers, 464
readable names (readability), 450
caption attribute (copy method), 910
caption element, 192
Cartesian coordinate systems, 383
cartoon animations (Flash), 404
Cascading Style Sheets. *See* **CSS**
cast libraries, creating, 773
casting variables, 469
categories, extensions (Dreamweaver), 267
ceil method (Math object), 957
cells
layout, 193-198
snapping, 195
centralizing code, 453-454, 462
<cfapplication> tag (CFML), 886

<cfargument> tag (CFML), 886, 903
<cfbreak> tag (CFML), 886
<cfcatch> tag (CFML), trapping errors, 889
<cfcomponent> tag (CFML), 886, 903
CFCs (ColdFusion Components), 288, 903
creating, 312, 667
functions, invoking, 312-314
parameters, passing, 904
required arguments, 904-905
versus CFML custom tags, 896
Web services, 904-905
Web services, creating, 314-316
<cfdirectory> tag (CFML), 887
<cfdump> tag (CFML), 887
<cfelse> tag (CFML), 887
<cffile> tag (CFML), 887
<cfform> tag (CFML), 893
<cffunction> tag (CFML), 887
<cfhttp> tag (CFML), 887
<cfif tag >(CFML), 887
<cfimport> tag (CFML), 887
<cfinclude> tag (CFML), 887
<cfinvoke> tag (CFML), 887
<cflock> tag (CFML), 887-889
<cfmail> tag (CFML), 887
CFML (ColdFusion Markup Language), 288, 877
code, creating, 293-294
databases (Dreamweaver ColdFusion), 290
database operations, 891-895
overview, 886-888
server behaviors, creating, 21
tags, 887-888
creating via Insert bar, 313-314
custom, 895-902
slash (/), 886
variables, 888-891

<cfmodule> tag (CFML), 887

<cfobject> tag (CFML), 887

<cfoutput> tag (CFML), 887

<cfparam> tag (CFML),
887-888

<cfpop> tag (CFML), 888

<cfquery> tag, 888, 290
    deleting records, 895
    inserting records, 894-895
    retrieving data, 891-892
    updating records, 892-894

<cfreturn> tag (CFML), 888,
903

<cfset> tag (CFML), 888

<cftry> tag (CFML),
888-889

<cfupdate> tag (CFML), 893

<cf_scrape> custom tag
(CFML), 899-902

CGI (Common Gateway
Interface) scripts, 627-629,
658

Change Property action,
216-217

channels, alpha channels
(Flash), 358

character attributes, 45-47

character blocks, distributing,
374

character codes, 940

Character Options dialog box,
373

character position, 47

character sets, 466

character spacing, 46-47

characters
    delimiter, 563
    special, regular expressions,
    901-902

charCodeAt() function, 940

Chart dialog box, 826

Chart tool (FreeHand),
826-828

charts
    grouping, 828
    types, 827-828

check boxes, Show Tooltips,
457

Check Browser behavior, 229

Check In/Out feature,
252-254

Check Links feature, 92,
258-259

Check Page, Check
Accessibility command (File
menu), 246

Check Page, Check Links
command (File menu), 92

Check Page, Check Target
Browsers command (File
menu), 92, 155

Check Page, Validate Markup
command (File menu), 243

Check Page, Validate
Markup/Validate as XML
command (File menu), 91

Check Spelling command
(Text menu), 153

Check Spelling dialog box,
153

Check Target Browsers
report, 92

CheckBox component (Flash),
427

checking spelling, code clean
up, 153

child nodes, XML (Extensible
Markup Language), 635

childNodes property, 639

children, invisible, 530

Circle Hotspot tool, 719

circles, drawing, 716

class features, 543-544

class keyword, 541

class selectors, 175-176

class tags, 175

class types, CSS (Cascading
Style Sheets), 183

classes, 540
    array, creating, 558-559
    AS2, centralizing code, 462
    attribute values, initializing,
    544-546
    attributes, naming, 548
    Camera, 972-974
    class features, 543-544
    classpaths, entering,
    554-556
    constructor functions, 493
    ContextMenu, 910-911
    core, 556
        array class, 557-567
        Date, 569-570

Error, 570-572
Function, 572
Math, 578-588
Object, 572-578
objects, 557
System, 589-592
wrapper, 567-569
Date, methods, 951-954
defining, 541
dynamic, 548-549
features, visibility, 546
get method, 546-548
hierarchies, 550-552
instance features, 542-543,
548-550
instances, 541-542, 552-554
locating, 554-556
Microphone class, 974-976
movie, 592
    Accessibility, 593
    Button, 593-594
    Color, 594-595
    ContextMenu, 596
    Key, 596
    LocalConnection,
    596-600
    Mouse, 600-605
    TextField, 605-611
    TextFormat, 605-611
    TextSnapshot, 611-612
MovieClip
    methods, 917-923
    properties, 921-926
prototype attribute,
542-543
Rich Media, 647
    NetConnection,
    648-649
    NetStream, 648-651
    Sound, 651-655
    Video, 656-657
set method, 546-548
static features, 543-544
StyleSheet, 967-968
subclasses, 550
superclasses, initialization
code, 615
TextField, 958-965
TextFormat, 966-967
wrapper, 968-972

ClassID property (ActiveX
controls), 233

classpaths, entering, 554-556

Clean Up HTML/XHTML command, options, 150-151

cleaning up code
cross-browser compatibility, 154-155
dynamic cross-browser compatibility, 154-155
estimating download speed, 152-153
HTML, 150-152
manual proofreading, 156
spell checking, 153

cleaning up HTML markup, 152

Clear Keyframes command, 392

clear method, 657

Clear Row Heights option (Layout mode), 196

clearInterval() method, 532

Click Accuracy (Editing Preference), 348

clicks, column headers (DataGrid components), 670-671

client access, Dreamweaver ColdFusion, 311
CFCs (ColdFusion components), 312-314
Web services, consuming, 316

client interfaces, creating, 21

client proxies, ColdFusion servers, 879

CLIENT scope, 890

clip positioning, registration points, 519

Clip property (layers), 216

Clipboard Preferences (Flash), 348

Clipboard Variations command (Edit menu), 722

clips. See movie clips

cloaking version control systems, 255

Clockwise option (Spiral dialog box), 800

clockwise rotation, 582

cloneNode(deep) command, 642

close method, 597-598

Close Panel Group command (Options menu), 83

closing tags, XML (Extensible Markup Language), 637

CMYK (cyan, magenta, yellow, and black) color mode, 791

code
centralizing, 453-454, 462
CFML (ColdFusion Markup Language), creating, 293-294
character codes, 940
cleaning up, 150-156
dynamic tables, Dreamweaver ColdFusion, 300-301
hiding, 454
pseudo-code, 450
reachability, 453-456
readability, 448-450
reusability, 451-453
source code components, 325
SQL, creating, 293

code completion (code hints), 456

code hints, 456-457

Code Inspector (Dreamweaver), 93

Code Inspector command (Window menu), 93

Code panel (Dreamweaver), 84-85

code points, 940

Code property (Java applets), 235

Code view (Dreamweaver), 76-77

codec (coder-decoder), 432

Coder Workspace (Dreamweaver), 75

coder-decoder (codec), 432

coding, hard-coding, 495

coding tools (Dreamweaver), 66-68

col element, 192

ColdFusion, 634
administrator interface, 877
Apache Web servers, 880
arrays, 899
automated emailing, 876
built-in Web servers, 880
data sources, configuring, 880-882
database files, 876
developer version, 876
files, opening, 291
hosting, 876
JRun Web servers, 880
Microsoft IIS (Internet Information Server), 880
overview, 876-877
RDS (Remote Development Services) password, 877
regular expressions, 876
screen scraping, 876
servers, 12, 876
accessing with Flash, 878-880
behaviors, creating, 20-21, 879
client proxies, creating with Dreamweaver, 879
database operations, 877
display operations, 878
file operations, 878
Flash Remoting Gateway, 879
functions, 877-878
page processing, 878
proxy services, 878
server-to-server communications, 878
setting up, 876-877
System DSN (Data Source Name), 877
troubleshooting, Connection Verification Failed error, 883
Web servers, 876

ColdFusion (Dreamweaver)
client access, 311-316
databases
accessing, 289
automated operations, 290-291

automated operations, <cfquery> tag, 290
automated operations, CFML (ColdFusion Markup Language) code, 290
automated operations, detail pages, 310-311
automated operations, dynamic data, 297-305
automated operations, Live Data feature, 298, 306
automated operations, master pages, 310-311
automated operations, previewing data, 291-293
automated operations, record management, 308-310
automated operations, retrieving data, 293-297
automated operations, schema, 290
automated operations, Server Behaviors panel, 306
creating, 289
dynamic, 288-289
ColdFusion 6.1 tags, 65
ColdFusion Administrator, 292, 877, 880-881
ColdFusion Components (CFCs), 288, 903
creating, 312, 667
functions, invoking, 312-314
parameters, passing, 904
required arguments, 904-905
versus CFML custom tags, 896
Web services, 314-316, 904-905
ColdFusion Markup Language. See CFML
colgroup element, 192
collaboration, 252-255
collapsing hierarchical trees, 291

collisions. See overlapping, movie clips
color
background, 58, 118
background color layer preference, 208
borders, frames, 206
dithering, graphics (FreeHand), 860-861
fill color, 34-35
fonts, 45-46, 96
gradients, 36-37
hexadecimal values, 118, 594
links (Dreamweaver), 121-122, 133
modes, 34, 790-791
picking up, Eyedropper tool, 37
replacing, graphics, 687-688
rows, DataGrid component, 669
solid, 35-36
stroke color, 34-35
text, Web pages (Dreamweaver), 120-121
traced bitmaps (Flash), 360
transforming (movie clips), 595
Web-Safe, FreeHand integration, 858-859
Color class, 594-595
color coding, comments, 449
Color command (Fill menu), 820
Color drop-down menu commands
Advanced, 388
Alpha, 388
Brightness, 387
Tint, 387
Color Mixer command (Window menu), 790
Color Mode option (Trace Tool dialog box), 820
Color Palette/Transparency section (Optimize panel), 759
color palettes, Web-safe, 34
Color Picker, 35
color property (TextFormat class), 966

color swatches, colors, changing, 712
Color Threshold (Trace Bitmap dialog box), 360
Colors category (Assets panel), 139
colors mixer, 34-35
columns
DataGrid component, 668-671, 679
Frames panel, 736-737
Layers panel, 735
Combine Nested <font> Tags when Possible option (Clean Up HTML/XHTML command), 151
Combine Paths command (Modify menu), 723
ComboBox component (Flash), 427
comma operator, 947-948
command parameter, 622
commands
Action menu, Get More Behaviors, 267
Clean Up HTML/XHTML, options, 150-151
Clear Keyframes, 392
Color drop-down menu
Advanced, 388
Alpha, 388
Brightness, 387
Tint, 387
Commands menu
Clean up HTML, 151
Manage Extensions, 266
Optimize Image in Fireworks, 276
Compression menu
Lossless (PNG/GIF), 364
MP3, 416
Photo (JPEG), 363
context menu
List, Indent, 98
List, Outdent, 98
Control menu
Disable Keyboard Shortcuts, 596
Enable Simple Buttons, 422

Enter, 404
Play, 404
Return, 404
Test Movie, 399-401, 423, 429
Convert to Blank Keyframes, 393
Convert to Keyframes, 393
Copy Keyframes, 392
creating, 91, 780-781
Debug menu, List Variables, 377
Edit in New Window, 386
Edit menu
    Copy, 840, 868
    Duplicate, 114
    Edit Document, 385-386, 422
    Edit in Place, 385
    Edit Symbols, 386
    File Types/Editors, 179
    Find, 777
    Find and Replace, 328
    Page Properties, 58
    Paste, 840, 868
    Preferences, 55, 74, 275, 345
    Preferences, ActionScript, 449, 457
    Preferences, General, 457
    Preferences, Layers, 208
    Redo, 328
    Undo, 328
    Undo command, 360
Edit Preferences, Validator, 243
exec, 623
File menu
    Batch Process, 778
    Check Page, Check Target Browsers, 92, 155
    Check Page, Validate Markup, 243
    Check Page, Validate Markup/Validate as XML, 91
    Convert, XHTML, 168
    Design Notes, 115-116

Export, 742, 750, 766-767, 770, 860-862, 869
Export Wizard, 767
Export, Export CSS Styles, 182
Import, 327, 433, 865, 869
Import, Import to Library, 357
Import, Import to Stage, 357
Install Extension, 267
New, 111, 123, 202, 394, 694, 839
New, Dynamic Page, 291, 312
New, Flash JavaScript File, 329
Open, 114
Publish as HTML, 863
Publish Settings, 458, 516, 604
Publishing Settings, 410
Save, 77, 839
Save and Compact, 324
Save As, 113
Save As Template, 124
Fill menu
    Color, 820
    Shade, 820
    Tint, 820
Format menu
    GIF, 860
    JPEG, 861
    PNG, 862
fullscreen, 622
Get, 250
Help menu
    Extensions, Extending Dreamweaver, 264
    Manage Extensions, 781
Insert menu
    Blank Keyframe, 335
    Dynamic Table, 298
    Frames, 335
    HTML, Frames, 202
    Image, 197, 275
    Image Objects, Navigation, 226
    Image Objects, Rollover Image, 224

Keyframes, 421
Layout Objects, Layer, 209
Link, 270
Media, ActiveX, 233
Media, Flash, 231
Media, Flash Button, 282
Media, Flash Text, 280
Media, Plugin, 230, 237
Media, Shockwave, 232
Microsoft Office Document, 272
New Symbol, 421
Special Characters, Line Break, 94
Symbol, 381
Template Objects, 124
Template Objects, Editable Regions, 124, 127
Template Objects, Optional Regions, 126
Template Objects, Repeating Region, 128
Template Objects, Repeating Table, 127
Timeline Effects, 400
Timeline, Blank Keyframe, 335
Timeline, Keyframe, 335
Timeline, Layer, 429
Timeline, Motion Guide, 396
JavaScript API extensions, 691
Library Options pop-up menu, Properties, 439
loadMovie(), 632
Modify menu
    Align, 213
    Align, Make Same Height, 213
    Align, Make Same Width, 213
    Alter Path, Reverse Direction, 843, 851
    Alter Path, Simplify, 42
    Animation, Animate Selection, 749
    Animation, Settings, 750

Arrange, Prevent Layer Overlaps, 214
Bitmap, Trace Bitmap, 360
Break Apart, 362, 374, 399
Convert to Symbol, 380, 383
Convert to Symbol, Graphic Symbol, 747
Document, 334
Document, Dimensions, 675
Frameset, 200-201
Group, 30
Library, 145
Library, Update Current Page, 147
Library, Update Pages, 150
Page Properties, 118
Remove Template Markup, 125
Shape, Add Shape Hint, 400
Shape, Optimize, 42, 353, 361
Symbol, Button, 741
Symbol, Duplicate Symbol, 384
Symbol, Tween Instances, 748
Templates, Apply Template to Page, 131
Templates, Make Attribute Editable, 129
Templates, Update Pages, 132
Timeline, Distribute, 374
Ungroup, 821, 828
Onion All, 397
Onion Skinning menu, No Onion Skinning, 745
Options menu
Add Pages, 846
Close Panel Group, 83
Expand Branch, 456
Optimize to Size, 760
Order menu
Back and Forth, 824
Loop, 824

Paste Keyframes, 392
Put, 250
quit, 623
Remove Frames, 392
Rotate menu
Incremental, 826
Random, 826
Uniform, 826
Save as Type menu
GIF, 860
JPEG, 861
PNG, 862
Scale menu
Random, 825
Uniform, 825
Select menu, Deselect, 700
send, 645
sendAndLoad, 645
Shape, 399
Site menu
Get, 110
Manage Sites, 104, 107, 248
Manage Sites, New, 289
Reports, 247, 256
Synchronize, 255
Spacing menu
Grid, 825
Random, 825
Variable, 825
stopAllSounds(), 409
Swap command, Property Inspector, 389
Template menu, Flash with Named Anchors, 346
Text menu
Alignment, 98
Attach to Path, 849-850
Check Spelling, 153
Indent, 98
List, Unordered, 98
Outdent, 98
Paths, 814
Style, 97
Text Type menu
Dynamic Text, 371
Input Text, 370
View menu
Bandwidth Profiler, 435
Grid, Edit Grid, 355
Guides, Lock Guides, 355

Guides, Show Guides, 355
Head Content, 141
JavaScript in Panel, 329
Magnification, 400%, 354
Perspective Grid, 810
Preview Mode, Fast, 361
Preview Mode, Outlines, 361
Rulers, 355
Server Debug, 93
Simulate Download, 435
Snapping, Edit Snap Align, 339
Snapping, Snap to Guides, 355
Snapping, Snap to Objects, 339
Snapping, Snap to Pixels, 354, 369
Table Mode, Layout Mode, 193
Table Mode, Standard Mode, 193
Toolbars, 78
Visual Aids, Frame Borders, 200, 204
Visual Aids, Invisible Elements, 133
Web menu
Track as Button, 425
Track as Menu Item, 425
Window menu
Actions, 443
Assets, 123
Behavior, 222
Code Inspector, 93
Color Mixer, 790
Design Panels, Align, 356
Development Panels, Behaviors, 678
Development Panels, Components, 427
Development Panels, Web Services, 672-673
Document, 788, 845
Find, 777
Frames, 203
Layers, 211-213, 792
Library, 389, 422, 794
Navigation, 853

Object, 788
Other Panels,
 Accessibility, 979
Other Panels, Common
 Libraries, 344
Other Panels, Movie
 Explorer, 344
Panel Sets, Default, 350
Panel Sets, Default
 Layout, 443
Site, 105
Styles, 793
Swatches, 793
Tints, 791
Toolbars, Main, 30
Toolbars, Xtra
 Operations, 831
XML (Extensible Markup
 Language), 642
Commands Folder, 781
Commands menu, 724
Commands menu commands
Manage Extensions, 266
Optimize Image in
 Fireworks, 276
**Commands menu commands
(Clean up HTML), 151**
**Commands, Convert to
Grayscale option (Batch
Wizard), 779**
comments
code, 449
color coding, 449
functions (reusability), 452
Perl, 627
variables, 460-462
**Common Gateway Interface
(CGI) scripts, writing,
627-629, 658**
**Common Libraries (Flash),
creating, 344**
Common tab, 79, 197, 224
communication. *See also* exter-
nal communications (Flash)
ActionScript/JavaScript,
 troubleshooting, 657
ColdFusion servers, Flash
 Remoting Gateway, 879
Flash files,
 LocalConnection class,
 596-600

comparison functions, arrays,
 565
comparison operators, 472,
 939-942
compatibility
cross-browser compatibility,
 154-155, 244-245
dynamic cross-browser
 compatibility, code clean
 up, 154-155
Dynamic Cross-Browser
 Compatibility Check fea-
 ture, 66
Netscape 4 compatibility
 layer preference, 208
**compilers, locating classes
(ActionScript), 554-556**
**Component Inspector, 665,
677-678**
**component instances, Web
services, 674-675**
components
adding, 429
building, 612-615
centralizing code, 462
CFC (ColdFusion
 Components), 667, 896
databinding, 664-666
DataGrid, 668-671
defined, 443
Flash, 426
 adding, 428-430
 layers, inserting, 429
 listeners, 427
 parameters, 427
 skinning, 430-431
 source code, 325
 UI (user interface), 325
 V1, 325
 V2, 325-326
WebServiceConnector, 879
Components panel, 87, 427
composite datatypes,
 464-468
compound assignment operators, 475, 938-939
compression, 756
bitmap graphics (Flash),
 363-364
dithering, 757
Flash video, 433

frame-to-frame, 751
JPEG, troubleshooting, 774
lossless, 757
lossy, 757
Sorensen Spark codec, 433
sound (Flash), 415-416
**Compression menu
commands**
Lossless (PNG/GIF), 364
MP3, 416
Photo (JPEG), 363
**concat() method, 453, 562,
566**
**concatenation, array elements,
563**
concave lens effect, 814
**condenseWhite property, 606,
960**
conditional flow control, 480
conditional operator, 946-947
**conditional statements,
480-483**
configurations
data sources (ColdFusion),
 880-882
global, sound (Flash), 410
Web sites, directory structure (Dreamweaver),
 104-110
**Configure Server dialog box,
248**
Connect button, 110
**Connect Lines (Editing
Preference), 347**
connect method, 597-598, 645
**Connect to Remote Host but-
ton, 157**
**Connection Verification Failed
error, 883**
connections
broadband, testing sites
 online, 251
Flash Remoting, 666-668
**connector lines, page icons,
841-843**
**Connector tool, 829-830,
838-844**
connectors, drawing, 717
**Connects to Remote Host
button, 249-251**

constant value, 466

constructor functions, 493
  Array(), 558
  attribute values, initializing, 544-546
  overloading, 545

constructor property, 572-574

containers, data containers, 557-558

context menu
  commands, 98
  Dreamweaver, opening, 68
  hiding, 623
  managing, 910-911

context-sensitivity, accessibility, 246

ContextMenu class, 596, 910-911

contour gradients, 690, 711

contrast, video encoding (Flash), 438

Contribute, 252

Contribute 2 program
  creating drafts, 272
  creating pages, 270-274
  editing pages, 270
  FlashPaper Printer utility, 269
  markup, 285
  modes, 269
  overview, 268-269
  toolbar, 270

control blocks
  body, 477
  conditional statements, 480-483
  control constructs, 477
  flow control, 480
  headers, 477
  keywords, 477-479
  looping, 476
  loops, 483-485
  non-looping, 476

control constructs, 477

control handles, 40-41

Control menu commands
  Disable Keyboard Shortcuts, 596
  Enable Simple Buttons, 422
  Enter, 404
  Play, 404

Return, 404
Test Movie, 399-401, 423, 429

controlling browsers, 618-621

controlling position, Math class, 586-587

controlling projectors, 622-623

controlling sound, 653-655

controlling speed, Math class, 587-588

controls
  ActiveX, 232-234
  animation, 697

conversion, automatic datatype conversions, 940-942

conversion rules, datatypes, 911-916

Convert to Blank Keyframes command, 393

Convert to Grayscale command (Commands menu), 724

Convert to Keyframes command, 393

Convert to Paths command (Text menu), 723, 814

Convert to Symbol command (Modify menu), 380, 383

Convert to Symbol dialog box, 383-384, 394

Convert to Symbol, Graphic Symbol command (Modify menu), 747

Convert, XHTML command (File menu), 168

converting
  data, variables, 469
  decimal numbers, 595
  documents to Flash, 269
  objects, symbols (Flash), 383-384
  strings, 469, 940
  symbol objects (Flash), 380
  text blocks, 370

convex lens effect, 814

coordinate systems, Caretsian, 383

coordinates, movie clips, 530

Copy command (Edit menu), 840, 868

Copy Keyframes command, 392

copy method, 910

Copy Selected Steps to the Clipboard button, 329

Copy Steps button, 91

Copy to Grid effect (Timeline), 401

core classes, 556
  array class
    creating, 558-559
    elements, 557-562
    empty, 558
    methods, 562-567
  Math
    direction, 585-586
    functions, 578-579
    getting width, 583-584
    position control, 586-587
    random integers, 579
    relative positioning, 580-581
    speed control, 587-588
    trigonometry methods, 581-589
  Object
    addProperty() method, 576
    constructor property, 574
    hasOwnProperty() method, 576
    isPropertyEnumerable() method, 575
    isPrototypeOf() method, 575
    methods, 572-573
    toLocaleString() method, 575
    toString() method, 574-575
    unwatch() method, 576-578
    valueOf() method, 575
    watch() method, 576-578
  objects, 557
  System, 589-592
  wrapper, 567-572

core objects, 557, 560, 569, 951, 969, 972

corner points, 40

Corner Threshold (Trace Bitmap dialog box), 360

corners, traced bitmaps (Flash), 360

cos method (Math object), 957

Counterclockwise option (Spiral dialog box), 800

counterclockwise rotation, 582

Create Component dialog box, 314-315

Create Concave Arc option (Arc dialog box), 801

Create Envelope icon, 833

Create Flipped Arc option (Arc dialog box), 801

Create New Symbol dialog box, 381, 421, 612

Create Open Arc option (Arc dialog box), 801

createElement(nodeName) command, 642

createEmptyMovieClip() method, 517, 520, 917

createTextField method, 606, 917

createTextNode(nodeValue) command, 642

Crop button, 277

Crop Each Frame option (frame-to-frame compression), 751

Crop option (Xtra Operations toolbar), 831

cross-browser compatibility
code clean up, 154-155
site management, 244-245

cross-domain policy files, 330

CSS (Cascading Style Sheets), 14-15, 57, 70-71, 94, 608
applying, 605
cascade order, 178
CSS Styles panel, 179-180
declarations, 173-175
design, 172
displaying, 177
Document window, 179
fonts, 95-97
fonts, troubleshooting, 188
history, 171-172

integrating, 58, 177-178
layers, 162, 209-217
Library items, editing, 148
links, 176
managing, 180-182
modifying, 172, 185-187
nesting, 175, 183
new definitions, 182-185
page properties, 60-61
Property inspector, 59-60
Relevant CSS panel, 58-59
resources, 189
rules, 173-174
selectors, 173-177
site management, 243
StyleSheet object, 609-611
styles, Microsoft integration, 284
tags, text formatting, 42
text formatting, 327
versus HTML, 172-173

CSS Property inspector, 59-60

CSS Style Definition dialog box, 183

CSS Styles panel, 84, 179-180

.css file extension, 177

cue points, creating, 419

curly brackets {}, CSS declarations, 173

_currentframe property (MovieClip class), 921

cursors
hand, displaying, 926
mouse cursors, 600

curve points, 40

Curved Fit (Trace Bitmap dialog box), 360

curved line segments, 41-42

curves
Bézier, 40
drawing, 713
optimizing, 42, 353, 361
segments, 39
smoothing (Flash), 353
vector, troubleshooting, 774

custom functions, calling, 488

custom gradients, creating, 36

custom menu, built-in labels, 911

custom mouse pointers, creating, 512

custom page sizes, creating, 795

Custom palettes option (Indexed Palette drop-down menu), 765

custom tab ordering, 923-925

custom tags, CFML (ColdFusion Markup Language), 895
cf_scrape, 899-902
invoking, 897
passing data, 897-898
returning data, 898-899
versus CFCs (ColdFusion components), 896

D

dashed strokes, 690

data. *See also* dynamic data (Flash)
embedding, LoadVars object, 632-634
previewing, database automated operations (Dreamweaver ColdFusion), 291-293
retrieving, database automated operations (Dreamweaver ColdFusion), 293-297
sending, LoadVars object, 630-632
storing (variables), 448
XML data, parsing, 639

Data components (Flash), 426

data containers, 557-558

data conversion, variables, 469

data movie clip event, 513

data parsing, XML (Extensible Markup Language), 644
attributes, 641
converting text, 638
examining data, 638-640
simple references, 640

data primitives, objects, 447

Data property (ActiveX controls), 234

Data Source dialog box, 881

data sources
  configuring (ColdFusion),
    880-882
  Web services, triggering,
    678-679

data structures, objects, **447**

data type checking (CFML),
  troubleshooting, **888-889**

data typing, strict, **460**

database management system
  (DBMS), **12-13**

database operations, CFML
  (ColdFusion Markup
  Language), **891-895**

databases
  accessing, Flash, 662
  files, ColdFusion, 876
  SourceSafe, remote servers,
    106

databases (Dreamweaver
  ColdFusion)
  accessing, 289
  automated operations
    <cfquery> tag, 290
    CFML (ColdFusion
      Markup Language)
      code, 290
    detail pages, 310-311
    dynamic data, 297-304
    Live Data feature, 298,
      306
    master pages, 310-311
    previewing data,
      291-293
    records, managing,
      308-310
    retrieving data, 293-297
    schema, 290
    Server Behaviors panel,
      306
  creating, 289

Databases panel
  (Dreamweaver), **86**

databinding, **664-666,
  675-678**

DataGrid component, **668-671**

datatype conversion rules,
  911-916

datatype conversions, automatic, **940-942**

datatypes
  arrays, 467
  Boolean, 466
  composite, 464
  function, 468
  movieclip, 468
  null, 467-468, 471
  number, 465-466
  object, 466-467
  primitive, 464
  strings, 466, 470
  undefined, 468-471

Date class, **569-570, 951-954**

Date object, **633**

Date return values, **574**

Date.getDate method (Date
  class), **951**

Date.getDay method (Date
  class), **951**

Date.getFullYear method
  (Date class), **951**

Date.getHours method (Date
  class), **951**

Date.getMilliseconds method
  (Date class), **951**

Date.getMinutes method
  (Date class), **951**

Date.getMonth method (Date
  class), **951**

Date.getSeconds method
  (Date class), **951**

Date.getTime method (Date
  class), **951**

Date.getTimezoneOffset
  method (Date class), **951**

Date.getUTCDate method
  (Date class), **951**

Date.getUTCDay method
  (Date class), **951**

Date.getUTCFullYear method
  (Date class), **952**

Date.getUTCHours method
  (Date class), **952**

Date.getUTCMilliseconds
  method (Date class), **952**

Date.getUTCMinutes method
  (Date class), **952**

Date.getUTCMonth method
  (Date class), **952**

Date.getUTCSeconds method
  (Date class), **952**

Date.getYear method (Date
  class), **952**

Date.setDate method (Date
  class), **952**

Date.setFullYear method
  (Date class), **952**

Date.setHours method (Date
  class), **952**

Date.setMilliseconds method
  (Date class), **953**

Date.setMinutes method
  (Date class), **953**

Date.setMonth method (Date
  class), **953**

Date.setSeconds method
  (Date class), **953**

Date.setTime method (Date
  class), **953**

Date.setUTCDate method
  (Date class), **953**

Date.setUTCFullYear method
  (Date class), **953**

Date.setUTCHours method
  (Date class), **953**

Date.setUTCMilliseconds
  method (Date class), **954**

Date.setUTCMinutes method
  (Date class), **954**

Date.setUTCMonth method
  (Date class), **954**

Date.setUTCSeconds method
  (Date class), **954**

Date.setYear method (Date
  class), **954**

Date.toString method (Date
  class), **954**

Date.UTC method (Date
  class), **954**

dates/times, objects, **569**

DBCS (double-byte character
  set), **466**

DBMS (database management
  system), **12-13**

deblocking property, **656**

Debug menu commands, List
  Variables, **377**

debugging
  ColdFusion Administrator,
    877, 880
  watch() method, 576

decimal numbers, converting,
  595

declarations
    arguments, 490
    CSS (Cascading Style
        Sheets), 173-175
    curly brackets {}, 173
    functions, 486-487, 498
    methods, 498, 553
    semicolon (;), 173-174
    variables, 460-462, 947
decrement operator (—),
    926-927
default features, classes, 542-
    543
default statements, 482
definitions, CSS (Cascading
    Style Sheets), 182-185
degrees, trigonometry meth-
    ods, 584
delays, frames, 737, 746
Delete button, 149
delete operator, 560-561, 949
Delete Record dialog box, 310
Deleting Pages option
    (Document panel), 789
delimiter characters, 563
dependent files, uploading,
    251
deprecated Flash 4 compari-
    son operators, 942
deprecated objects, 942
depth numbering, visual
    stacking order, 526-527
descenders, 852
description property, 593
Deselect command (Select
    menu), 700
design, 13
    CSS (Cascading Style
        Sheets), 14-15
    Dreamweaver Bindings
        panel, 14
    FreeHand, 13-14
    layers, 216-217
    templates, 14
Design Notes
    Dreamweaver, 115-117, 771
    enabling, 275
    versus HTML Comments,
        158

Design Notes command (File
    menu), 115-116
Design Notes dialog box,
    115-116
Design panel (Dreamweaver),
    83
Design Panels, Align com-
    mand (Window menu), 356
Design Time style sheets,
    185-186
Design Time Style Sheets dia-
    log box, 186
Design view (Dreamweaver),
    76-77
Designer Workspace
    (Dreamweaver), 74
designing home pages,
    848-849
designing pages
    (Dreamweaver)
    frames, 218
        benefits, 199
        creating, 200
        deleting, 201
        framesets, 201-203
        modifying, 205-206
        overview, 199-200
        resizing, 201
        selecting, 203-204
        splitting, 200-201
        targeting windows,
            206-207
        visual borders, 204
    layers
        activating, 210
        aligning, 213
        content, adding, 210
        converting to tables, 218
        creating, 209-210
        design, 216-217
        Invisible Elements, 210
        layouts, 209
        nesting, 214
        overlapping, 214-215
        overview, 207-208
        preferences, 208
        properties, 215-216
        renaming, 214
        resizing, 212-213
        selecting, 211-212
        showing/hiding, 217

        stacking order, 214
        visibility, 213
    layout tables, adding con-
        tent, 218
    tables, 192-198
designing programs, 461
designing Web sites, 838
    actions, 852-854
    home pages, 848-849
    multipage files, 845-847
    text effects, 849-852
detail pages, databases,
    Dreamweaver ColdFusion,
    310-311
Development Panels,
    Behaviors command
    (Window menu), 678
Development Panels,
    Components command
    (Window menu), 427
Development Panels, Web
    Services command (Window
    menu), 672-673
device fonts, 373-374, 535
DevNet Resource Kits
    (DRKs), 265
DHTML (Dynamic HTML)
    CSS (Cascading Style
        Sheets), 172
    Dreamweaver, 19
    layer animation, 228
dialog boxes
    3D Rotation, 812
    Action Tool, 853-854
    Add Binding, 675
    Add Columns, 309
    Add New Data Source,
        880-881
    Add Pages, 846
    Add URL, 139-140
    Add Using WSDL,
        316-317
    Advanced Effects, 388
    Advanced Encoding,
        437-438
    Advanced Settings, 388
    Animate, 749-750
    Arc, 801
    Attach External Style Sheet,
        181
    Bend, 809

Bitmap Export Defaults, 860-862
Bitmap Properties, 363
Bound To, 675
Calligraphic, 799
Character Options, 373
Chart, 826
Check Spelling, 153
Configure Server, 248
Convert to Symbol, 383-384, 394
Create Component, 314-315
Create New Symbol, 381, 421, 612
CSS Style Definition, 183
Data Source, 881
Delete Record, 310
Design Notes, 115-116
Design Time Style Sheets, 186
Document Attributes, 334
Document Properties, 870
Drag Layer, 227
Dynamic Checkbox, 303-304
Dynamic Radio Button, 304-305
Dynamic Table, 298
Dynamic Text Configuration, 301-302
Edit Envelope, 413-414
Edit Page, 795
Edit Sites, 254
Editable Tag Attributes, 129
Editing, 434-436
Embedded Video Properties, 439
Encoding, 436-437
Eraser Tool, 809
Export, 742, 766-767, 770
Export Document, 860-862, 869
Export Preview, 699, 750, 767
Export Styles As CSS File, 182
Extension Manager, 266
File Selector, 181
Find Source, 61
Find Source for Editing, 867

Fireworks PNG Import Settings, 865
Fisheye Lens, 814
Frame Tag Accessibility Attributes, 202
Freeform Tool, 806-808
GIF Options, 860-861
HTML Output, 863
HTML Setup, 743, 769, 863
Import, 357, 433
Import to Library, 358
Inconsistent Region Names, 131
Insert Document, 272
Insert Flash Button, 282-283
Insert Flash Text, 280-283
Insert Link, 271
Insert Navigation Bar, 225-226
Insert Repeating Table, 127
Insert Rollover Image, 224
JPEG Options, 862
Knife Tool, 810
Linkage Properties, 415
List/Menu, 306
Magic Wand Settings, 363
Manage Saved Commands, 781
Manage Sites, 104, 107-109, 248
Master Detail Page Set, 311
Microsoft Access Data Source, 881-882
Mirror, 822-823
Movie Settings, 869-870
New CSS Style, 182-184
New Document, 111-112, 123, 180-181
New Editable Region, 124
New from Template, 130
New Optional Region, 126
New Page, 271
New Repeating Region, 128
Open, 114
Optimize Curves, 353, 361
Optimize Images, 62
Optimize to Size, 760
Optional Region, 126

Page Properties, 58-60, 96
background colors, 118
background images, 119-120
link color, 121-122
margins, 120
text color, 120-121
Parameters, 231, 234
Pictograph, 828
PNG Options, 862-863
Preferences, 55, 74
Preset Name, 761
Publish Settings, 334, 346, 416, 604, 870
QuickTime, 434
Record Insertion Form, 308-309
Record Update Form, 309
Recordset, 294-296
Replace Options, 777-778
Reports, 247, 256
Roughen, 808
Save As, 113
Save As Template, 124
Save Command, 781
Scale and Rotate, 332
Select, 237
Select File, 231
Select HTML, 205
Select Image Source, 197
Shadow, 818
Show-Hide Layers, 227
Site Definition, 69, 104-109, 248, 254, 289
Smudge, 818
Snap Align, 339-340
Sound Properties, 410, 415
Spiral, 800
Style Definition, 183-185
Swap Image, 740
Swap Symbol, 389
Symbol Name, 384
Symbol Properties, 747
Synchronize, 255
Tag Editor, 314
Trace Bitmap, 360
Trace Tool, 820-821
Trigger Data Source, 678
Tween Instances, 748
Update Pages, 132, 147-148
Update Template Files, 132

Values, 429
Variable Stroke Pen, 798
Workspace Setup, 74-75
direction, getting/setting, 585-586
directives, #include, 462
Director, integration, 772-773
directories, Web site setup (Dreamweaver), 104-110
Disable Keyboard Shortcuts command (Control menu), 596
disjoint rollovers, 225, 739-741
displayError() function, 489
displays, dimension size (Dreamweaver), 80
Distort FX (Flash), 322
Distort modifier, 341, 375
Distort tool, 698
Distribute button, 356
Distribute to Frames command (Frames panel), 745
Distributed Duplication effect (Timeline), 401
distributing, objects, 356
distributive blending, shape tweens (Flash), 399
dithering
    colors, graphics (FreeHand), 860-861
    compression, 757
divide and reassign (/=) compound assignment operator, 938
Divide option (Xtra Operations toolbar), 831
division, 929
do-while loop statement, 484
docking
    panel groups (Dreamweaver), 83
    panels, 30
DOCTYPE declaration, ensuring compliance (Dreamweaver), 134
docTypeDecl property, 645
Document Attributes dialog box, 334

Document command (Modify menu), 334
Document command (Window menu), 788, 845
Document panel, 788-790
Document Properties dialog box, 870
document reports, running, 246-247
document structure (Flash), 424-425
Document toolbar (Dreamweaver), 78
Document Type Definition (DTD), 165-167, 635
Document window
    CSS editor, 179
    Dreamweaver
        Code view, 76-77
        Design view, 76-77
        menu bar, 77
        status bar, 79-80
        text, 93-98
        title bar, 76
        toolbars, 78-79
    Fireworks, 695-697
    frames, selecting, 204
    framesets, selecting, 204
    FreeHand, 786
    layers, selecting, 211-212
Document, Dimensions command (Modify menu), 675
documents. See files
Dodge tool, 706
domain method, 597-598
dot (.) operator, 467, 542, 547, 950
dot syntax, 447, 495
dots per screen (dpi), 732
double quotes (""), server-side includes, 634
double slashes (//), 449
double-byte character set (DBCS), 466
double-precision floats, 465
Down rollover state, 225
down state, button movie clip events, 515
Down state, navigation bars, 741

Download button, 267
Download indicator, 152
download speeds, 152-153, 156
downloading
    behaviors, 267-268
    Extension Manager, 265-267
    extensions, Dreamweaver, 264-265
    QuickTime 4, 357
dpi (dots per screen), 732
drafts, Contribute 2, 272-274
drag and drop, movie clips, 533-534
Drag Layer behavior, 227-228
Drag Layer dialog box, 227
dragging layers, 227-228
dragOut button event, 509
dragOver button event, 509
Draw By List option (Spiral dialog box), 800
Draw Dotted Line option, 798-799
Draw From List option (Spiral dialog box), 800
Draw Layer button, 209
Draw Layout Cell button, 195
draw() method, 614
drawing
    arrows, 717
    circles, 716
    connectors, 717
    curved line segments, 40
    curves, 713
    ellipses, 716
    freeform lines/shapes, 38
    layout cells, 193-195
    layout tables, 193-194
    lines, 712
    paths, 712-713
    pie charts, 717
    polygons, 716-717
    rectangles, 715-717
    spirals, 717
    squares, 715
    stars, 716
    straight line segments, 39
    strokes, 38

Drawing Settings (Editing Preference), 347

Dreamweaver
A server timeout has occured. error, 317
accessibility testing, 262
actions, 221
adding content, 192-197, 218
animation, 19
Application panel, 289
Assets panel, asset nicknaming, 157
Bindings panel, 293
browser languages
HTML (Hypertext Markup Language), 162-163, 169-173
HTML 4 (Hypertext Markup Language), 164-166
markup, 163-164
XHTML (Extensible HTML), 162, 167-169
browsers, id attribute, 188
client interfaces, creating, 21
code clean up, 150-156
Code Inspector, 93
coding tools, 66-68
ColdFusion
CFML (ColdFusion Markup Language) code, 290
client access, 311-316
databases, 289-305, 308-311
dynamic, 288-289
files, opening, 291
Live Data feature, 298, 306
servers, 879
Server Behaviors panel, 306
Color Picker, 35
Contribute 2 program
creating pages, 270-272
drafts, 274
drafts, creating, 272
Edit Page button, troubleshooting, 284

editing pages, 270
FlashPaper Printer utility, 269
frames, 274
images, 273
importing Word/Excel documents, 272
links, 273
lists, 273
markup, 285
modes, 269
overview, 268-269
tables, 273
text, 273-274
toolbar, 270
copying to Favorites list, 142
CSS (Cascading Style Sheets), 57, 70-71
cascade order, 178
CSS Styles panel, 179-180
declarations, 173-175
design, 172
displaying, 177
Document window, 179
fonts, 188
history, 171-172
integrating, 58, 177-178
layers, 162
links, 176
managing, 180-182
modifying, 172, 185-187
nesting, 175, 183
new definitions, 182-185
page properties, 60-61
Property inspector, 59-60
Relevant CSS panel, 58-59
resources, 189
rules, 173-174
selectors, 173-177
versus HTML, 172-173
deleted content, troubleshooting, 100
Design Notes, enabling, 275
Document window
Code view, 76-77
CSS editor, 179

Design view, 76-77
menu bar, 77
status bar, 79-80
text, 93-98
title bar, 76
toolbars, 78-79
dynamic platforms, 64-65
editing, 142
categories, 137-140
Favorites list, 137-139
extensions, 264-268
external editors, 187
Eyedropper tool, 37
files, optimizing via Fireworks, 61-62
Fireworks integration, 61-63
Flash, 63, 231
font element/valid documents, 100-101
frames, 199-207
frequently changing content, 70
grid layout, troubleshooting, 218
history, 164
HTML tags, managing, 80
Insert bar, 288
integration
Fireworks, 274-278, 771-772
Flash, 278-283
Microsoft, 283-284
interactivity
ActiveX controls, 232-234
Java applets, 234-235
JavaScript, 220-223
layers, 227-229
plug-ins, 229-232
interface, 28-29
item deletion, accidental, 158
Library, 143, 146-150
maintenance of, 141-142
Site list, 137
Library items, accidental deletion of, 158
lists, 98-99
Microsoft applications, copy/paste, 65-66

multimedia
ActiveX controls, 232-234
audio, 235-238
Java applets, 234-235
plug-ins, 229-232
video, 235-238
navigation bars, 223-226
page design, 209-218
panels
Application, 85-88
Assets, 89-90
Attribute, 88
Behavior, 88-89
Bindings, 86
Code, 84-85
Components, 87
CSS Styles, 84
Databases, 86
Design, 83
Files, 88-89
FTP Log, 92
groups, 81-83
History, 90-91
Layers, 84
Link Checker, 92
Reference, 85
Relevant CSS, 88
Results, 91
Search, 91
Server Behaviors, 87
Server Debug, 93
Site Reports, 92-93
Snippets, 84-85
Tag Inspector, 88
Target Browser Check, 92
Validation, 91
placeholders, 275
plug-ins, troubleshooting, 284
Property Inspector, 81
rebuilding, 142
refreshing, 142, 157
rollovers, 223-225
security, FTP (File Transfer Protocol), 69
server behaviors, creating, 20
site component tracker, 136

site management
accessibility, 245-247
cross-browser compatibility, 244-245
CSS (Cascading Style Sheets), 243
document validation, 243-244
overview, 242
site maintenance, links, 258-260
site reports, 256-258
Web standards, 242
XHTML, 243
siteless page editing, 57
source files, troubleshooting, 70
templates, 130-133
text, 18-19
transfers, troubleshooting, 261
troubleshooting, XHTML (Extensible HTML), 167-171, 187
UltraDev CF server objects, troubleshooting, 70
user interface, 54-57
validation errors, 100
validators, troubleshooting, 261
Web pages
adding assets, 141
background colors, setting, 118
background images, setting, 119-120
editable attributes, 129-130
editable regions, 124-127
link colors, 121-122, 133
margins, setting, 120
optional regions, 125-126
repeating regions, 127-128
templates, 122-124
text color, setting, 120-121
titles, 117, 133

Web sites
defining, 104-110
DOCTYPE declaration, ensuring compliance, 134
editing online, remote servers, 157
files, managing, 113-117
refreshing files, 133
testing online, 156-157
Web Standards project, 188
workspaces, layouts, 74-75
Dreamweaver Bindings panel, 14
Dreamweaver Exchange, accessing, 54
Dreamweaver Exchange Extensions forum, 267
Dreamweaver Special Markup option (Clean Up HTML/XHTML command), 151
DRKs (DevNet Resource Kits), 265
Drop Shadow effect (Timeline), 402
droptarget property (movie clips), 534, 921
DTD (Document Type Definition), 635
font elements/valid documents (Dreamweaver), 100
HTML 4, 165-166
XHTML (Extensible HTML), 167
Duplicate command (Edit menu), 114
duplicateMovieClip() global function, 519
duplicateMovieClip() method, 519-520, 528, 917
duration property, 655
DWT files, Templates category (Assets panel), 141
dynamic button events, 508-509
Dynamic Checkbox dialog box, 303-304
dynamic classes, 548-549
dynamic content, 20-21

dynamic cross-browser compatibility, code clean up, 154-155

Dynamic Cross-Browser Compatibility Check feature, 66

dynamic data
automated operations, databases (Dreamweaver ColdFusion), 297-305
loading, LoadVars object, 627-629

dynamic data (Flash)
databinding, 664-666
DataGrid component, 668-671
Flash Remoting, 662-663, 666-668
overview, 662-664
Web services, 662-663, 672
component instances, creating, 674-675
data sources, triggering, 678-679
databindings, 675-678
hierarchy, 673

Dynamic Data button, 298

dynamic Dreamweaver (ColdFusion), 288-289

dynamic event handlers, 5 02-505

Dynamic HTML (DHTML), 19, 172

dynamic masks, 534-535

dynamic movie clip events, 513-515

dynamic pages, creating, 85-88

dynamic platforms (Dreamweaver), 64-65

Dynamic Radio Button dialog box, 304-305

Dynamic Table command (Insert menu), 298

Dynamic Table dialog box, 298

dynamic tables, Dreamweaver ColdFusion, 298-301

dynamic text, 42, 368-371
breaking text apart, 374
device fonts, 373-374

Dreamweaver ColdFusion, 301-302
embedded fonts, 373-374
fields, 378, 607
formatting options, 372
transforming text, 375-376
variables, 372

Dynamic Text command (Text type menu), 371

Dynamic Text Configuration dialog box, 301-302

dynamically creating text fields, 606

E

E property (Math object), 958
Ease slider, 398
easing, tweens (Flash), 397-399
Easy option (3D Rotation dialog box), 812
ECMA-262 (ActionScript), 443
edges, Magic Wand tool, 701
Edit Accessibility Settings button, 979
Edit button, 142, 147, 277, 358
Edit Character Options button, 373
Edit Document command (Edit menu), 385-386, 422
Edit Envelope dialog box, 413-414
Edit in Fireworks button, 63
Edit in New Window command, 386
Edit in Place command (Edit menu), 385
Edit menu commands, 722
Copy, 840, 868
Duplicate, 114
Edit Document, 385-386, 422
Edit in Place, 385
Edit Symbols, 386
Find, 777
Find and Replace, 328
Page Properties, 58
Paste, 840, 868

Preferences, 55, 74, 275, 345
Preferences, ActionScript, 449, 457
Preferences, File Types/Editors, 179
Preferences, General, 457
Preferences, Layers, 208
Preferences, Validator, 243
Redo, 328
Undo, 328, 360

Edit mode (Contribute 2), 269

Edit Multiple Frames button, 339

Edit Page button, 272, 284

Edit Page Size dialog box, 795

Edit property (Flash object), 279

Edit Sites dialog box, 254

Edit Symbols command (Edit menu), 386

Edit with Fireworks button, 866

editable attributes, templates (Dreamweaver), 129-130

editable regions, templates (Dreamweaver)
creating, 124-127
highlighting, 133
Web pages, 131

Editable Tag Attributes dialog box, 129

editing roundtrip (Fireworks), 689

Editing dialog box, 434-436

Editing Options (ActionScript Editor Preferences), 350

Editing Preferences (Flash), 347-348

Editing tab, 726

editors
ActionScript Editor, 444
Button Symbol Editor, launching, 741
external, Dreamweaver, 187
image, Fireworks, setting up, 274-275
Symbol Editor, launching, 749
text editors, XML, 637

effects
  Fireworks, 690-691
  Flash, 322-323, 400-404
  lens, 814
  motion blur effects, 688
  text, Web sites, adding, 849-852
eHelp, RobotHelp, 426
element selectors, 175
elements
  arrays, 899
    adding, 560
    associative arrays, 561-562
    core classes, 557
    elements, accessing, 447
    referencing, 559-560
    removing, 560-561
  block, 100, 169
  Font, 61, 95
  font, valid documents (Dreamweaver), 100-101
  HTML, 169
  inline, 100, 169
  tables, 192
  XHTML, 169
Ellipse tool, 38, 716, 849
ellipses, drawing, 716
emailing, automated (ColdFusion), 876
Embed property (ActiveX controls), 234
embedded fonts, 373-374
embedded sound (Flash), 408-411
embedded style sheets, CSS integration, 177
Embedded Video behaviors, 419
Embedded Video Properties dialog box, 439
embedding
  audio, 236-238
  data, LoadVars object, 632-634
  Java applets, 235
  plug-ins, 230
  video files, 238, 649-650
  video (Flash), 431
    file formats, 432-433
    managing, 438-439

  playback control, 439
  versus linked, 433
  Video Import Wizard, 433-438
embedFonts property (TextField class), 960
Emboss option (Xtra Operations toolbar), 832
empty arrays, 558
Empty Container Tags option (Clean Up HTML/XHTML command), 151
empty movie clips, 520
Enable Simple Buttons command (Control menu), 422
enabled attribute (copy method), 910
enabled property, 593, 921-923
encoding video (Flash), 436-438
Encoding dialog box, 436-437
End Onion Skin marker, 338
endRegex variable, 901
engines, event, 500
Enter command (Control menu), 404
enter frame event handler, 452, 580
enterFrame movie clip event, 513
Envelope handles (sound), 414
Envelope modifier, 341, 375-376
Envelope toolbars (FreeHand), 833-834
environments (FreeHand), 786
equal sign (=), 170, 625
equaliteral polygons, drawing, 717
equality (==) operator, 939
equality operators, 939-940
Erase Fills modifier (Eraser tool), 342
Erase Normal modifier (Eraser tool), 342
Erase Selected Fills modifier (Eraser tool), 342
Erase Shape modifier (Eraser tool), 342

Erase Strokes modifier (Eraser tool), 342
Eraser tool, 342, 703, 809
Eraser Tool dialog box, 809
Error class, 570-572
error trapping, Flash, 570
errors
  A server timeout has occured. (Dreamweaver), 317
  Connection Verification Failed, 883
  Invalid parameter type, 888
  Resolve Library Conflict, 440
  validation (Dreamweaver), 100
Event (synchronization option), 411
event engines, 500
event generators, watch() method, 576
event handlers, 500-501
  ActionScript, 445-446
  allowDomain(), 597
  allowInsecureDomain(), 597
  button events, 508-511
  calling explicitly, 507
  Camera class, 974
  deleting/disabling, 507
  dynamic, 502-505
  enter frame, 452, 580
  focus-related, disabling/enabling, 923
  in-line event handlers, onEnterFrame, 454
  input events, 504
  key events, 511-512
  keyboard focus, 507-510
  listener registration, 504-505
  LocalConnection movie class, 597-598
  mouse events, 512
  movie clip events, 513-515
  scoping, 505-506
  selection events, 515
  sound events, 515-516
  Stage events, 516
  Stage.onResize, 603
  static, 503-505

How can we make this index more useful? Email us at indexes@quepublishing.com

system events, 504
TextField events, 516-517
this keyword, 505-506
var keyword, 489
event sound, 408-411, 652
eventObject parameter, 670-671
events
Behaviors panel, 227
Button class, 593
button events, 425, 508-511
cue points, 419
input, 504
key events, 511-512
Key object, 955-957
Microphone classes, 976
mouse events, 512
movie clip events, 513-515
MovieClipLoader object, 523
onData, 644
onLoad, 625, 643-644
onSoundComplete, 653
onStatus, 597
programming, 507-509
selection events, 515
sound events, 515-516
Stage events, 516
StyleSheet class, 967-968
system, 504
TextField class, 958-965
TextField events, 516-517
trapping, 501
Exact option (Indexed Palette drop-down menu), 764
exactSettings attribute, 591
Excel documents, importing into Web pages, 272
exec command, 623
exp method (Math object), 957
Expand Branch command (options menu), 456
Expand effect (Timeline), 402
Expand Stroke option (Xtra Operations toolbar), 831
Expand/Collapse Layer column (Layers panel), 736
Expanded Tables mode, 195
expanding hierarchical trees, 291

expanding spirals, creating, 800
Expert option (3D Rotation dialog box), 814
explicit data conversion, variables, 469
explicit depth numbering, 526-527
explicit scoping, 494-497
explicitly calling event handlers, 507
Explode effect (Timeline), 402
Export Area tool, 699, 767
Export command (File menu), 742, 750, 766-767, 770
Export dialog box, 247, 742, 766-767, 770
Export Document dialog box, 860-862, 869
Export option (Batch Wizard), 779
Export Preview dialog box, 699, 750, 767
Export Styles As CSS File dialog box, 182
Export Wizard, 767
Export Wizard command (File menu), 767
Export, Export CSS Styles command (File menu), 182
exporting
animations, 750-751
CSS (Cascading Style Sheets), 182
Flash
animation settings, Flash, 774
FLV (Flash Video) files, 324
movies, FreeHand, 869-870
graphics (Fireworks)
Director integration, 772-773
Dreamweaver integration, 771-772
Flash integration, 772
Web graphics, 766-767
Web pages, 769-770
expressions, 471-475
array core classes, 557
regular, 876, 901-902

results, storing, 938
return values (function results), 492
extends keyword, 550
Extensible HTML. See XHTML
Extensible Markup Language. See XML
Extension Manager (Fireworks)
commands, creating, 780-781
Commands Folder, 781
downloading/installing, 265-267
extensions, 781
Extension Manager dialog box, 266
extensions. See also file extensions
accessing, 781
Dreamweaver
behavior downloads, 267-268
categories, 267
downloading, 264-265
help, 267
installing, 267
managing, 265-267
third-party plug-in installations, 268
writing, 264
installing, 781
JavaScript API extensions, 691
extensions option (Style Definition dialog box), 185
Extensions, Extending Dreamweaver command (Help menu), 264
external communications (Flash)
local, 618-623
network-aware, 618
HTTP headers, 646-647
LoadVars object, 625-634
overview, 623-624
Rich Media classes, 647-657
XML, 634-646
overview, 618

external content (movie clips), loading/unloading, 520-524

external editors, Dreamweaver, 187

external files
  CSS (Cascading Style Sheets), 609
  loading, 462

external links, validating, 261

external sites, displaying, 218

external sound (Flash), 408-411

external style sheets
  creating, 180-181
  CSS integration, 177
  links, 181-182

Extrude tool (FreeHand), 815-817

eye icon, 337

eyeball icon, 736

Eyedropper tool, 37

F

fade-ins, movie clips, 594

fade-outs, movie clips, 594

false value, Boolean, 466

Faucet modifier (Eraser tool), 342

Favorites folder, creating, 138-139

Favorites list (Assets panel), 137
  assets, 138, 142
  Favorites folder, creating, 138-139

Favorites tab (Dreamweaver), 79

features, classes
  instance, 542-543, 548-550
  static, 543-544
  visibility, 546

fields
  Address JavaScript function calls, 621-622
  dynamic text fields, troubleshooting, 378
  Frame Rate, 334, 393
  Identifier, 415

input text, borders, 370-371

Instance Name field, 389

Maximum Characters field, 372

text
  creating, 606
  formatting, troubleshooting, 615
  instance names, 377
  properties, 607

text fields, 372

text input, screen reader software, 978

user input, 42

Var, 372

file extensions
  .as, 541
  audio, 236
  bitmap graphics (Flash), 357
  .css, 177
  .fla, 279, 455
  GIF, 119
  imported sound, 412
  JPEG, 119
  .jsfl, 329
  .lbi (Library), 143
  optimization, 758
  output, animation, 743
  PNG, 119
  saving files (Dreamweaver), 113
  .swc, 279
  .swf, 279
  .swt, 279
  video (Flash), 432-433
  video, 236

File menu commands, 721
  Batch Process, 778
  Check Page, Check Accessibility, 246
  Check Page, Check Links, 92
  Check Page, Check Target Browsers, 92, 155
  Check Page, Validate Markup, 243
  Convert, XHTML, 168
  Design Notes, 115-116

Export, 742, 750, 766-767, 770, 860-862, 869

Export Wizard, 767

Export, Export CSS Styles, 182

File menu, 433

Import, 327, 865, 869

Import, Import to Library, 357

Import, Import to Stage, 357

Install Extension, 267

New, 111, 123, 202, 394, 694, 839

New, Dynamic Page, 291, 312

New, Flash JavaScript File, 329

Open, 114

Publish as HTML, 863

Publish Settings, 410, 458, 516, 604

Save, 77, 839

Save and Compact, 324

Save As, 113

Save As Template, 124

File property (Flash object), 279

File Selector dialog box, 181

File Transfer Protocol (FTP)
  Check In/Out feature, 253
  Dreamweaver security, 69
  remote servers, 106-107

File Type Options section (Optimize panel), 759

File Type/Matte section (Optimize panel), 759

file types, Flash, 278-279

filename, sorting site reports by, 258

files
  attributes, setting, 334
  Check In/Out feature, 252-254
  checking in/out (Fireworks), 692
  converting to Flash, 269
  ColdFusion, 291, 876
  cross-domain policy, 330
  dependent, uploading, 251

Dreamweaver files
adding to Web sites, 111-112
automatic refresh cycling, Web sites, 133
deleting, Web sites, 113-114
Design Notes, Web sites, 115-117
duplicating, Web sites, 113-114
opening, Web sites, 114
optimizing via Fireworks, 61-62
renaming, Web sites, 113-114
DWT, Templates category (Assets panel), 141
Excel, importing into Web pages, 272
external, loading, 462
Fireworks, creating, 694
Flash
FLV (Flash Video), exporting, 324, 648-651
importing, 327
improved speed, 322
inserting, Dreamweaver, 231
security, 330
selecting, 323
video, 649-650
*.LCK, 253
MP3, ID3 metadata, 651
multipage, 845-847
policy, 626
predefined framesets, 202-203
saving, 77, 113, 124
size, reducing, 324
sound files, size, 408
source, 61, 70, 205
SWF, 443
validating, 243-244
Web sites
DOCTYPE declaration compliance (Dreamweaver), 134
structure, effect on search engine results, 158-159
Word, importing into Web pages, 272
XML (Extensible Markup Language), 637, 641-645
Files panel, 57, 88-89, 250
Fill box, 34
Fill menu commands
Color, 820
Shade, 820
Tint, 820
Fill Transform tool (Flash), 341
fill-color box, 594
fills, 33
bitmaps, 36, 358
color, 34-35
gradients, 35-37
paths, 734
solid colors, 35-36
filters, troubleshooting (Photoshop), 774. *See also* **effects**
Filters menu, 724
Find and Replace command (Edit menu), 328
Find and Replace feature, 328
Dreamweaver, 67
Fireworks, 776-778
option (Batch Wizard), 779
Find command
Edit menu, 777
Window menu, 777
Find pop-up menu (Find and Replace feature), 777
Find Source dialog box, 61
Find Source for Editing dialog box, 867
Fireworks
animation, 19-20
bitmap, 743
creating, 744-750
exporting, 750-751
frame delay, 746
frame rates, 743
frame-to-frame compression, 751
looping, 746
output formats, 743
preparations, 743-744
rollovers, 738-741
settings, exporting, Flash, 774
vector, 743
Answers panel, troubleshooting, 728-729
anti-aliasing, 689
automating, 776-779
buttons, white backgrounds, 753
deleted styles, troubleshooting, 782
document window, 695-697
documents, creating, 694
Dreamweaver integration, 274-278
effects, 690-691
Extension Manager, 780-781
Eyedropper tool, 37
graphic exports
Director integration, 772-773
Dreamweaver integration, 771-772
Flash integration, 772
Web graphics, 766-767
Web pages, 769-770
graphics, 18
bitmap, 732-733
frames, 736-738
layers, 734-738
modifying in FreeHand, 866-867
resolution, troubleshooting, 782
vector, 732-734
importing files to FreeHand, 865-866
integrating, Dreamweaver, 61-63
interface, 26-29, 684-685
JavaScript API extensions, 691
launching, 866
menus, 696
Commands menu, 724
Edit menu, 722
File menu, 721
Filters menu, 724
Help menu, 725
Modify menu, 723
Select menu, 722

Text menu, 723
View menu, 722
Window menu, 725
navigation bars
    four-state buttons,
        741-743
    troubleshooting, 752
navigation interfaces, creat-
    ing, 773
objects, selecting, 29
optimization
    compression, 756-757,
        774
    file formats, 758
    Optimize panel, 758-765
panels, 696
performance, 684
Photoshop filters, trou-
    bleshooting, 774
Preferences, 725-727
Property inspector, 696,
    721
roundtrip editing, 689
slices, troubleshooting, 753
Start page, 694
text, 18-19, 728
text blocks, resizing, 43
tools, 696
    Auto Shapes, 686-687
    Bitmap, 700-712
    Hide Slice, 721
    Hotspot, 719
    Live Effects panel, 688
    Polygon Lasso, 729
    Polygon Slice, 719
    Red Eye Removal, 687
    Replace Color, 687-688
    Select, 698
    Select, Distort, 698
    Select, Export Area, 699
    Select, Select to Behind,
        698
    Show Slice, 721
    Slice, 719
    Vector, 712-719
    Web, 719
Tools panel, 33
transparence, 773
troubleshooting, Adobe
    GoLive, 774
Unicode support, 691

upgrading, 684
vector curves, troubleshoot-
    ing, 774
vector objects,
    copying/pasting, 772
Web site management, 692
Fireworks PNG Import
    Settings dialog box, 865
firing Key events, 512
firstChild property, 639
Fisheye Lens dialog box, 814
Fisheye Lens tool (FreeHand),
    814
Fixed option (Layout mode),
    196
fixed-width text blocks,
    resizing, 43
.fla file format, 279, 455
Flash
    3D animation, 322
    accessibility guidelines,
        978-980
    ActionScript
        Actions panel, 444-446
        benefits, 442-443
        code hints, 456-457
        event handlers, 445-446
        functions, 445
        interactivity, 442-443
        limitations, 442
        OOP (object-oriented
            programming),
            446-448
        reachability, 453-456
        readability, 448-450
        reusability, 451-453
        troubleshooting, 458
    ActionScript Editor, 444
    aliasing, 327
    alpha channels, 358
    animation, 19-20, 440
        bitmaps, 391
        cartoon animation, 404
        creating, 391
        frame-by-frame, 393
        frames, 391-393
        guidelines, 405
        keyframes, 391-393
        nesting symbols, 404
        objects, 391
        previewing, 403

        sequences, 390
        strokes, 394
        symbols, 391
        Timeline Effects, 391,
            400-403
        tweening, 393-400
        vectors, 390
    arrays, 899
    AS2 (ActionScript 2),
        330-331
    Behaviors, 323
    bitmap graphics
        animating, 364-365
        blurry, 365
        breaking apart, 362-363
        compressing, 363-364
        fills, 358
        formats, 357
        importing, 357-358
        modifying, 358
        pixels, 352
        saving, 358
        tracing, 358-362, 365
    client interfaces, creating,
        21
    ColdFusion servers, access-
        ing, 878
    components, 426
        adding, 428-430
        layers, inserting, 429
        listeners, 427
        parameters, 427
        skinning, 430-431
        source code, 325
        UI (user interface), 325
        V1, 325
        V2, 325-326
    content, publishing in mul-
        tiple languages, 327
    converting documents to,
        269
    database access, 662
    deprecated Flash 4 compar-
        ison operators, 942
    Distort FX, 322
    documents, selecting, 323
    Dreamweaver integration
        adding buttons, 281-282
        editing buttons/text, 283
        Flash file types, 278-279
        Flash object properties,
            279-280

inserting text, 280-281
previewing buttons/text, 283
resizing buttons/text, 283
dynamic data
databinding, 664-666
DataGrid component, 668-671
Flash Remoting, 662-663, 666-668
overview, 662-664
Web services, 662-663, 672-679
effects, 322-323
error trapping, 570
exporting animations as, 751
external communications
local, 618-623
network-aware, 618
network-aware, HTTP headers, 646-647
network-aware, LoadVars object, 625-634
network-aware, overview, 623-624
network-aware, Rich Media classes, 647-657
network-aware, XML, 634-646
overview, 618
Eyedropper tool, 37
files
attributes, setting, 334
importing, 327
improved speed, 322
Find and Replace feature, 328
Flash animation settings, exporting, 774
Flash Remoting, 879-880
FreeHand objects, importing to, 868
graphics, 18
History panel, 328
input events, 504
integrating
Dreamweaver, 63
exporting Fireworks graphics, 772

interactivity
ActionScripting with behaviors, 418-420
buttons, 420-423
menus, 424-425
scripts, 418
interface, 25, 28-29
JSFL (Flash JavaScript), 329-330
keyboard shortcuts, 342-343
layout
Align panel, 356
grids, 354-355
guides, 354-355
shape dimensions, 355
snapping, 353-354
Library, 343-344, 357
masks, creating, 356
media types, 232
movie clips
FreeHand, 868-870
inserting, Dreamweaver, 231
size, 391
testing, 399-400
transforming color, 595
transforming transparency, 595
transparency, 594
Movie Explorer, 344
objects, 29, 256
panels, layouts, 334
Pixel FX, 322
placeholders, 231
plug-in, 231-232
Preferences
ActionScript Editor, 349-350
Clipboard, 348
Editing, 347-348
General, 345-347
Warning, 348-349
Property Inspector, 358
Resolve Library Conflict, 440
rules, showing, 354
security, 330
Selection tool, 352
shapes, 352

sound
amplitude, 406
compressing, 415-417
controlling, 414
embedded, 408-411
event, 408-411
external, 408-411
frequency, 406
global configurations, 410
importing, 412
keyframes, 414-415
layers, 412
looping, 414
modifying, 413-414
overview, 406
pitch, 408
preparations, 407-408
previewing, 412
properties, 412
sampling, 407
Sound object, 415
stream, 408-411
synchronization, 411
troubleshooting, 659
turning off, 417
volume, 413
zooming, 414
spell checker, 326
Subselection tool, 352-353, 365
Swiff Chart, 322
SWiSH Power FX, 322
symbols
button symbols, 380-381
converted objects, 383-384
copying, 439-440
creating, 380-384
duplicating, 384
editing, 385-386
graphic symbols, 380
instances, 380, 386-389
launching timelines, 386
Library, 389-390
movie clips, 381
objects, converting, 380
positioning, 382-383
sorting, 390
storing, 389
synchronization, 409
system events, 504

tabbed interface, 323
task speed, 323-324
templates, 326
text blocks, resizing, 43
text formatting, CSS
  (Cascading Style Sheets),
  327
Text FX, 322
text, pixels, 368-370
third-party extensions/
  add-ins, 322-323
Timeline, 334-339
Timeline Effects, 323
Toolbox, 339-342
Tools panel, 33
tweens, troubleshooting,
  440
vector graphics, 352
versions, 324
video files, 649-650
video integration, 431
  file formats, 432-433
  managing, 438-439
  playback control, 439
  versus linked, 433
  Video Import Wizard,
    433-438
video, compression, 433
Web services, 879

Flash (SWF) category (Assets panel), 140
Flash Elements tab (Dreamweaver), 79
Flash JavaScript (JSFL), 329-330
Flash MX 2004, 324
Flash MX 2004 Professional, 324-326
Flash Player, 322
Flash Remoting, 662-663
  ColdFusion servers, access-
    ing, 879-880
  components, installing, 666
  connections, 666-668
Flash Remoting Gateway (FRG), 662-663, 879
FLASH scope, 890
Flash Video (FLV) files, exporting, 324

Flash with Named Anchors command (Template menu), 346
FlashPaper Printer utility, 269
Flat option (Surface button), 816
floating point numbers (floats), 465
floats, modulo division, 929
floor() method, 579, 957
flow, text, 851
flow control, 480
flowcharts, FreeHand, 14
FLV (Flash Video) files
  exporting, 324
  progressively loading,
    648-651
FLV Exporter, 324
focus
  keyboard focus
    event handlers, 507-510
    Selection object, 515
    TextField events, 516
    troubleshooting, 537
  mouse focus, keyPress
    event, 510
  movie clips, 925
focus shifting, keyPress event, 511
focus-related event handlers, disabling/enabling, 923
focusEnabled property (MovieClip class), 921-924
_focusrectr property, 921-922
focusrect property, 921-922, 960
folders
  Commands Folder, 781
  Favorites, creating, 138-139
  Inetpub, 15
  layers (Flash), 336-338
  Library, 390
  local, Web sites
    (Dreamweaver), 104-106,
    109-110
Folders tab, 727
Font element, 61, 95
font element, valid documents (Dreamweaver), 100-101

font property (TextFormat class), 966
fonts
  antialiasing, 370
  bitmap fonts, 368-369,
    376-377
  colors, 45-46
  CSS (Cascading Style
    Sheets), troubleshooting,
    188
  device, 373-374
  device fonts, 373, 535
  dynamic text, 372
  embedded, 373-374
  point size, 45-46
  serif, text legibility, 376
  styles, 45-46
  text (Dreamweaver), 95-97
for loop statement, 484-485
for-in loop statement, 485
forceSimple property, 593
Form button, 302
FORM scope, 890
Format menu commands
  GIF, 860
  JPEG, 861
  PNG, 862
formatting. See also CSS (Cascading Style Sheets)
  columns, DataGrid compo-
    nents, 670
  Layout mode, 195-196
  options, 372
  text, CSS (Cascading Style
    Sheets), 42, 327
  TextFormat class, 607-608
forms, 302-304
Forms category, 302-303
Forms tab (Dreamweaver), 79
forums, Dreamweaver Exchange Extensions, 267
four-state buttons, navigation bars, 741-743
FP6 movie clips, external content, 521-523
FP7 movie clips, external content, 523-524
fps (frames per second), 334, 743

Fractalize option (Xtra Operations toolbar), 832

Frame command
Edit menu, 722
Insert menu, 335

Frame Delay column (Frames panel), 737

Frame Name and Number column (Frames panel), 737

Frame Rate field, 334, 393

frame rates, animation, 743

Frame Tag Accessibility Attributes dialog box, 202

frame-by-frame animation
creating, 744-745
Flash, 393
playing, 746

frame-to-frame compression, 751

FrameName property (Property Inspector), 205

frames
actions, 445-446, 503
animations, 391-393
benefits, 199
borders, 206
browser frames, naming, 620
button symbols (Flash), 380
copying, 737
creating, framesets, 200
delay, animations, 746
deleting, 201
external sites, 218
Flash, 335, 338, 421
framesets, 201-203
graphics (Fireworks), 736-738
keys, checking, 511
loading, 483
managing, Contribute 2 program, 274
margins, 206
modifying, 205-206
moving, 737
naming, 205, 737
overview, 199-200
printing, 218
resizing, 201
scroll bars, 205
selecting, 203-204

source documents, 205
splitting, 200-201
targeting, 619-620
targeting windows, 206-207
visual borders, 204

Frames button, 202, 414

Frames command (Window menu), 203

Frames panel, 736-737
Distribute to Frames, frame-by-frame animation, 745
frames, selecting, 203
framesets, selecting, 204
Onion Skinning, frame-by-frame animation, 744-745

frames per second (fps), 334, 743

Frameset command (Modify menu), 200-201

frameset HTML 4, 165-166

framesets, 200-206

_framesloaded property (MovieClip class), 921

Free Transform tool, 341, 375

freeform lines, drawing, 38

freeform shapes, drawing, 38

FreeForm tool, 718, 806-808

Freeform Tool dialog box, 806-808

FreeHand, 13
color options, 35
dithering, 860-861
document window, 786
environment, 786
Eyedropper tool, 37
Fireworks files, importing to, 865-866
Flash movies, 868-870
flowcharts, 14
graphics, 18
integration, Web, 858-864
interface, 27-29
interfaced graphics, 860
modifying Fireworks graphics, 866-867
objects, 29, 868
panels, 787
Assets, 793-794
Layers, 792-793

Mixers and Tint, 790-792
Properties, 788-790
text, 18-19
text blocks, resizing, 43-44
toolbars, 830-834
tools
3D Rotation, 812-814
Action, 828
Arc, 801
Bend, 809
Blend, 821
Calligraphic Pen, 798-800
Chart, 826-828
Connector, 829-830
Eraser, 809
Extrude, 815-817
Fisheye Lens, 814
Freeform, 806-808
Graphic Hose, 823-826
Knife, 810
Mirror, 822-823
Output Area, 796
Page, 795-796
Perspective, 810-812
Reflect, 804
Rotate, 803-804
Roughen, 808-809
Scale, 801-803
Shadow, 818-820
Skew, 805-806
Smudge, 818
Spiral, 800
Trace, 820-821
Variable Stroke Pen, 797-798
Web sites
creating, 838-844
designing, 838, 845-854

FreeHand Text (Clipboard Preferences), 348

frequency, 406

FRG (Flash Remoting Gateway), 662-663

fscommand() function, 621

FTP (File Transfer Protocol)
Check In/Out feature, 253
Dreamweaver security, 69
graphics (Fireworks), 692
remote servers, 106-107

FTP Log panel (Dreamweaver), 92
full justification, 47
fullscreen command, 622
function call operators (), 488
Function class, 572
function datatype, 465, 468
function keys, F9, 443
function.apply() method, 493-494
function.call() method, 493-494
functionality, reusability, 451
functions. *See also* methods
  ActionScript, 445
  aliases, 497
  arguments, 468, 489-492
  arguments, declaring, 490
  arrays, 448
  automatic scoping, 497-500
  calling, 488, 493, 531-533, 950
  comparison, arrays, 565
  conditional operator, 946
  constructor, 493
  initializing, 544-546
  constructor functions, Array(), 558
  creating, 486-487
  declarations, scope chains, 498
  defined, 312
  explicit scoping, 494-497
  fscommand(), 621
  function.apply() method, 493-494
  function.call() method, 493-494
  getURL(), 618-619
  global, 468
  iif(), 886
  invoking, CFCs (ColdFusion components), 312-314
  invoking as Web services, 905
  JavaScript, 621-622
  LoadVariables(), 626-627
  local function variables, creating, 488-489
  Math class, 578-579
  objects, 447
  properties, 468
  retrieving results via return values, 492-493
  reusability, code, 451-453
  scoping rules, 453
  stopping, 532
  Timeline, troubleshooting, 536
  timeline variable access, 489
  toString(), 626
  troubleshooting, 487, 536-537
  var keyword, 489

G

gamma
  settings, graphics, 722
  video encoding (Flash), 438
General Preferences (Flash), 345-347
General tab, 112, 726
generators, event generators, 576
Get command, 110, 250
get keyword, 547
get method, 546-548, 630-631, 972-974
Get More Behaviors command (Action menu), 267
getAscii() method, 596
getBeginIndex() method, 602
getBound() method, 529, 917
getBytesLoaded property, 644
getBytesLoaded() method, 626, 655, 917
getBytesTotal property, 644
getBytesTotal() method, 626, 655, 917
getCode() method, 596
getDepth() method, 593, 917, 958
getEndIndex() method, 602
getFontList method (TextField class), 959
getInstanceAtDepth method, 518, 918

getNewTextFormat method (TextField class), 959
getNextHighestDepth method, 518, 918
getRBG() method, 594-595
getStyle method (StyleSheet class), 967
getStyleNames method, 611, 967
getSWFVersion method, 518, 918
getTextExtent method (TextFormat class), 966
getTextSnapShot method, 518, 918
getting files (uploading), site management, 251
getTransform() method, 595
getURL function, 618-619
getURL method (MovieClip class), 918
GIF Adaptive 256 option (Optimize panel), 761
GIF Animation Looping button, 746
GIF command, 860
GIF Options dialog box, 860-861
GIF Web 216 option (Optimize panel), 761
GIF WebSnap 128 option (Optimize panel), 761
GIF WebSnap 256 option (Optimize panel), 761
GIFs
  animated, exporting animations as, 750-751
  background images, 119
  Fireworks, 19
  Flash, 19
  manually optimizing (Optimize panel), 764-765
  Web integration (FreeHand), 859-861
global classpaths, entering, 554-556
global configurations, sound (Flash), 410
global coordinates, movie clips, 530
global functions, 468

global objects (singletons), 592
  Accessibility object, 593
  Button class, 593-594
  Color class, 594-595
  ContextMenu class, 596
  creating dynamically, 606
  Key class, 596
  LocalConnection class, 596-600
  Mouse, 600
  PrintJob, 600-602
  properties, 607
  Selection, 602
  Shared Object, 602-603
  Stage, 603-605
  TextField, 605-611
  TextFormat, 605-611
  TextSnapshot, 611-612
globally modifying text, 44-45
globalToLocal method (MovieClip class), 918
globalToLocal() method, 530, 918
GoLive (Adobe), Fireworks, troubleshooting, 774
gotoAndPlay method (MovieClip class), 919
gotoAndStop method (MovieClip class), 919
gradient pointers, 36
Gradient tool, 710-712
gradients
  attributes, setting, 710
  color, 36-37
  contour, 690, 711
  custom, creating, 36
  editing, 712
  linear, 35
  radial, 35
Gradients (Clipboard Preferences), 348
Graphic Hose tool (FreeHand), 823-826
graphic symbols
  Flash, 380
  objects, converting to, 747

graphics, 19
  adding, layout cells, 197-198
  background, 119-120
  background image layer preference, 208
  bitmap (Flash)
    animating, 364-365
    blurry, 365
    breaking apart, 362-363
    compressing, 363-364
    fills, 358
    formats, 357
    importing, 357-358
    modifying, 358
    pixels, 352
    saving, 358
    tracing, 358-362, 365
  colors, 687-688, 860-861
  Fireworks, 18, 866-867
    bitmap, 732-733
    creating (Dreamweaver integration), 275-276
    exporting, 766-773
    frames, 736-738
    layers, 734-738
    resolution, troubleshooting, 782
    vector, 732-734
  Flash, 18
  FreeHand, 18
  FTP (Fireworks), 692
  gamma settings, 722
  interlaced (FreeHand), 860
  managing, Contribute 2 program, 273
  modifying, Fireworks, 276
  navigation bars, creating, 225
  noise, adding, 691
  off state, 224
  on state, 224
  optimization
    compression, 756-757, 774
    file formats, 758
    Optimize panel, 758-765
  previewing, 685
  red eye, removing, 687
  screen reader software, 978

  sliced, piecing back in to tables (Assets panel), 157
  SVG (Scalable Vector Graphics), 164
  vector graphics
    Fireworks, 732-735
    Flash, 352
  Web integration (FreeHand), 859-862
Grayscale option (Indexed Palette drop-down menu), 765
Grid command (Spacing menu), 825
grid layouts, troubleshooting, 218
Grid, Edit Grid command (View menu), 355
grids
  Flash, 354-355
  Perspective Grid, adjusting, 810
  snapping increments, layers, resizing, 212
grippers, panel groups (Dreamweaver), 83
Group command (Modify menu), 30
grouped column charts, 828
grouping
  declarations, CSS (Cascading Style Sheets), 174-175
  objects, 30
grouping operators, 475-476
groups, panels (Dreamweaver), 81-83
Guide icon, 355
guides (Flash)
  layers, 336-337, 354-355
  locking, 355
  motion, 395-397, 440
  shape dimensions, changing, 355
Guides, Lock Guides command (View menu), 355
Guides, Show Guides command (View menu), 355

H

H property, 235-237

hand cursors
button movie clip events, 514
displaying, 926

Hand tool, 33

handlers. *See* event handlers

handles
Envelope handles (sound), 414
resize, layers, resizing, 212

Hard Edge option (Shadow dialog box), 819

hard-coding, explicit scoping, 495

hasAccessibility property, 589

hasAudio property, 589

hasAudioEncoder property, 589

hasChildNodes property, 639

hash arrays, 561-562

hash mark (#), ID selectors, 175

hasMP3 property, 589

hasOwnProperty() method, 573, 576

hasPrinting property, 589

hasScreenBroadcast property, 589

hasScreenPlayback property, 589

hasStreamingAudio property, 589

hasStreamingVideo property, 589

hasVideoEncoder property, 589

Head Content command (View menu), 141

headerRelease() function, 670

headers, 477
columns, DataGrid component, 669-671
http, customizing, 646-647

height layer preference, 208

_height property (MovieClip class), 921

height property, 279, 603, 656, 961

help
extensions, Dreamweaver, 267
RoboHelp, 426

Help menu, 725

Help menu commands
Extensions, Extending Dreamweaver, 264
Manage Extensions, 781

hexadecimal color values, 118, 594

hexadecimal numbers, parseInt() function, 915

Hidden Mesh option (Surface button), 816

Hide Slice tool, 721

hide() method, 512, 600

hideBuiltInItems method, 910

hiding
code, 454
context menu, 623
layers, 217, 227, 337
panels (Flash), 350

hierarchical trees, collapsing/expanding, 291

hierarchies
classes, 550-552
movie clips, 519, 524-525
parent-child, visual stacking order (movie clips), 525
Web services, 673
XML (Extensible Markup Language), 635-636

High Quality Keyframes option (Encoding dialog box), 437

Highlight Color Options (General Preferences), 346

highlighting templates, editable regions (Dreamweaver), 133

highquality property (TextField class), 960

hints, shape tweens (Flash), 400

History panel, 90-91, 328, 780-781

hit area, button movie clip events, 514

Hit states, 422

hit tests, 530-531

hitArea property (MovieClip class), 921, 924

hitTest() method, 529-530, 537-538, 919

HLS (hue, lightness, and saturation) color mode, 791

home pages, designing, 848-849

HomeSite+, 65

Horizontal & Vertical option (Mirror dialog box), 823

horizontal guidelines (Flash), 354

Horizontal option (Mirror dialog box), 823

horizontal orientation, pages, 796

Horizontal Spacing property (Flash object), 280

horizontal text direction, 46

hosts
ColdFusion, 876
Web Host Industry Review Web site, 104

Hotspot command (Edit menu), 722

Hotspot tool, 719

hotspots, creating, 423, 719

HSB (hue-saturation-brightness), 34

hscroll property (TextField class), 961

HTML (Hypertext Markup Language), 162
attributes, 170
cleaning up, 150-152
comments, versus Design Notes, 158
converting to XHMLT, 168
DOCTYPE declaration, ensuring compliance (Dreamweaver), 134
element selectors, 175
elements, 169
Fireworks graphics, exporting to, 769
importing, Microsoft integration, 284

pages, embedding data, LoadVars object, 632-634

Roundtrip, 163

SGML (Standard Generalized Markup Language), 163

tags, 80, 88

values, 170-171

versus CSS (Cascading Style Sheets), 172-173

versus XML (Extensible Markup Language), 634

Web integration (FreeHand), 863-864

HTML 4, 164-166

HTML Export Wizard, 864

HTML Output Assistant, 864

HTML Output dialog box, 863

html property (TextField class), 961

HTML Setup command (File menu), 722

HTML Setup dialog box, 743, 769, 863

HTML tab, 79, 516, 604-605

HTML, Frames command (Insert menu), 202

htmlText property (TextField class), 961

HTTP headers, customizing, 646-647

hues, Flash, 387, 438

Hypertext Markup Language. See HTML

I

icons
eye, 337
Guide, 355
layers (Flash), 337
page, 840-843
pencil, 337

id attribute, browsers, 188

ID property (ActiveX controls), 234

ID selectors, 175

ID3 metadata, MP3 files, 651

Identifier field, 415

identifiers, 462-464

idle programs, 512

if statement, 480-481, 944-945

if-else statement, 481, 945

ifFrameLoaded conditional statements, 483

Ignore All button, 153

Ignore button, 153

ignoreWhite property, 643

iif() function, 886

IIS (Internet Information Server), 15, 880

Image command (Insert menu), 197, 275

image editing toolbar, 277-278

image editors, setting up (Fireworks), 274-275

Image Objects, Navigation command (Insert menu), 226

Image Objects, Rollover Image command (Insert menu), 224

image placeholders, Dreamweaver integration, 772

image swapping, 223

images. See graphics

Images button, 197

Images category (Assets panel), 139

IMEs (Input Method Editors), 348

implicit data conversion, variables, 469

implicit datatype conversion, 912-916

Import command (File menu), 327, 433, 865, 869

Import dialog box, 357, 433

Import tab, 727

Import to Library dialog box, 358

Import, Import to Library command (File menu), 357

Import, Import to Stage command (File menu), 357

importing
bitmap graphics (Flash), 357-358
files, Flash, 327
Fireworks files to FreeHand, 865-866
Flash movies to FreeHand, 868-869
FreeHand objects to Flash, 868
HTML, Microsoft integration, 284
local folders, Web sites (Dreamweaver), 109-110
remote servers, Web sites (Dreamweaver), 110
sound (Flash), 412
XML (Extensible Markup Language) documents, 643-645, 658-659

in-line event handlers, onEnterFrame, 454

#include directive, 462

Inconsistent Region Names dialog box, 131

increment operator (++), 926-927

Incremental command (Rotate menu), 826

Indent command (Text menu), 98

indent property (TextFormat class), 966

indentation
code, 448-449
text (Dreamweaver), 98

index
array core classes, 558
array elements (referencing), 559
elements, arrays, 899
numbers, elements, 557

Indexed Palette drop-down menu (Optimize panel), 764-765

inequality operator (!=), 940

Inetpub folder, 15

Infinity value, 466

inheritance, styles, 178

init objects, 528-529

initialization code, super-classes, 615

Ink Bottle tool, 37, 341

inline elements, 100, 169

inline styles, CSS (Cascading Style Sheets), 178

input, user input, 596

input events, 504

Input Method Editors (IMEs), 348

input text, 368
  breaking text apart, 374
  device fonts, 373-374
  embedded fonts, 373-374
  fields, 370-371, 978
  formatting options, 372
  transforming text, 375-376
  variables, 372

Input Text command (Text Type menu), 370

Insert bar, 288

Insert button, 141, 146

Insert Document dialog box, 272

Insert Flash Button dialog box, 282-283

Insert Flash Text dialog box, 280-283

Insert Link dialog box, 271

Insert Link method, 270-271

Insert menu commands
  Blank Keyframe, 335
  Dynamic Table, 298
  Frames, 335
  HTML, Frames, 202
  Image, 197, 275
  Image Objects, Navigation, 226
  Image Objects, Rollover Image, 224
  Keyframes, 421
  Layer, Timeline, 429
  Layout Objects, Layer, 209
  Link, 270
  Media, ActiveX, 233
  Media, Flash, 231
  Media, Flash Button, 282
  Media, Flash Text, 280
  Media, Plugin, 230, 237
  Media, Shockwave, 232

Microsoft Office Document, 272
New Symbol, 421
Special Characters, Line Break, 94
Symbol, 381
Template Objects, 124
Template Objects, Editable Regions, 124, 127
Template Objects, Optional Regions, 126
Template Objects, Repeating Region, 128
Template Objects, Repeating Table, 127
Timeline Effects, 400
Timeline, Blank Keyframe, 335
Timeline, Keyframe, 335
Timeline, Motion Guide, 396

Insert Navigation Bar dialog box, 225-226

Insert Record button, 308

Insert Repeating Table dialog box, 127

Insert Rollover Image dialog box, 224

INSERT statements, 894

Insert toolbar, 78-79, 298

insertBefore(nodetoInsert, nodeNum) command, 642

inserting records, CFML (ColdFusion Markup Language), 894-895

Inset Path option (Xtra Operations toolbar), 831

inspectors
  Multiple Layer Inspector, 216
  Property Inspector, 393, 398, 412
    Fireworks, 696, 721
    Flash, 358
    frame properties, 205-206
    graphical previews, 685
    layer properties, 215-216
    Swap command, 389
  rule, 186-187

Install Extension command (File menu), 267

installations
  Extension Manager, 265-267
  extensions, 267, 781
  third-party plug-ins, 268

Installed Extension option (Extension Manager dialog box), 266

Instance Name field, 389

instance names, text fields, 372, 377

instanceof operator, 948-949

instances
  boolean wrapper classes, 568
  classes, 541-542, 552-554
  component, Web services, creating, 674-675
  defined, 540
  features, classes, 542-543, 548-550
  method declarations, 553
  symbols (Flash), 380, 386
    accessing, 389
    Library, 343
    names, 389
    properties, 387-389
    swapping, 389
  wrapper classes, 567

integer division, 929

integers, number datatype, 465

integration
  CSS (Cascading Style Sheets), 58, 177-178
  Dreamweaver
    Fireworks, 274-278
    Flash, 278-283
    Microsoft, 283-284
  Fireworks into Dreamweaver, 61-63
  Flash, 431
    Dreamweaver, 63
    file formats, 432-433
    managing, 438-439
    playback control, 439
    versus linked, 433
    Video Import Wizard, 433-438

Web (FreeHand)
graphics, 859-862
HTML, 863-864
Web-Safe colors,
858-859

interactivity
ActionScript, 442-443
ActiveX controls, 232-234
components, adding, 429
creating, 323
defined, 220
Flash
ActionScripting with
behaviors, 418-420
buttons, 420-423
menus, 424-425
scripts, 418
Java applets, 234-235
JavaScript, 220-223
layers, 227-229
plug-ins, 229-232

interfaces, 24
administrator, ColdFusion,
877
clients, creating, 21
Dreamweaver, 28-29
Fireworks, 26-29, 684-265
Flash, 25, 28-29
FreeHand, 27-29
navigational, creating, 773
tabbed (Flash), 323

interframe compression (temporal compression), 433

interlaced graphics
(FreeHand), 860

interlacing GIFs, manually
optimizing (Optimize panel),
765

internal linking, 258

internal style sheets, CSS
integration, 177

Internet Explorer, Web-safe
color palettes, 34

Internet Information Server
(IIS), 15, 880

Intersect option (Xtra
Operations toolbar), 832

interval identifiers, 532

intervals, calling functions
(movie clips), 531-533

intraframe compression (spatial compression), 433

Invalid parameter type error,
888

invisibility
children, movie clips, 530
Flash buttons, 423

Invisible Elements, layers, 210

invoking. *See* calling

irregular guides (Flash), 354

isActive() method, 593

isDebugger property, 589

isDown() method, 596

isNan() function, 941

isPropertyEnumerable
method, 573-575

isPrototypeOf method,
573-575

isToggled() method, 596

Italic button, 46

italic property (TextFormat
class), 966

iterative control blocks, 476

J

Java applets, 234-235

Java Server Pages (JSP), 65,
634

JavaBeans, accessing, 65

JavaScript
ActionScript communica-
tion, troubleshooting, 657
behaviors, 221-223
creating, 221
functions, calling, 621-622
JSFL (Flash JavaScript),
329-330
overview, 220-221
Scripts category (Assets
panel), 140
snippets, 221

JavaScript API extensions, 691

JavaScript in Panel command
(View menu), 329

join() method, 562-564

JPEG command, 861

JPEG Options dialog box, 862

JPEG-Better Quality option
(Optimize panel), 761

JPEG-Smaller File option
(Optimize panel), 761

JPEGs
background images, 119
compressed bitmaps, 364
compression, troubleshooting, 774
manually optimizing
(Optimize panel), 762-764
Web integration
(FreeHand), 859-862

JRun Web servers, 880

JSFL (Flash JavaScript),
329-330

.jsfl file extension, 329

JSP (Java Server Pages), 634

justification, 45-47, 369

K

kerning, 46-47

key events, 511-512

Key object, 596, 955-957

Key.addListener method (Key
object), 955

Key.BACKSPACE property
(Key object), 955

Key.CAPSLOCK property
(Key object), 955

Key.CONTROL property
(Key object), 955

Key.DELETEKEY property
(Key object), 955

Key.DOWN property (Key
object), 956

Key.END property (Key
object), 956

Key.ENTER property (Key
object), 956

Key.ESCAPE property (Key
object), 956

Key.getAscii() method, 511,
955

Key.getCode() method, 511,
955

Key.HOME property (Key
object), 956

Key.INSERT property (Key
object), 956

Key.isDown() method, 511,
955

Key.isToggled() method, 511, 955

Key.LEFT property (Key object), 956

Key.onKeyDown event (Key object), 957

Key.onKeyUp event (Key object), 957

Key.PGDN property (Key object), 956

Key.PGUP property (Key object), 956

Key.removeListener method (Key object), 955

Key.RIGHT property (Key object), 956

Key.SHIFT property (Key object), 956

Key.SPACE property (Key object), 956

Key.TAB property (Key object), 957

Key.UP property (Key object), 957

keyboard focus
  event handlers, 507-510
  Selection object, 515
  TextField events, 516
  troubleshooting, 537

keyboard shortcuts, 47
  A, 48
  Accessibility panel, 979
  Alt+Ctrl+F2, 343
  Alt+F1, 343
  Alt+F2, 343
  Alt+F3, 343
  Alt+F7, 343
  Cmd-E, 385
  Cmd-F9, 48
  Cmd-F2, 48
  Cmd-F3, 48, 343
  Cmd-F7, 343, 427
  Cmd-F8, 381, 421
  Cmd-I, 343
  Cmd-K, 343, 399
  Cmd-L, 422
  Cmd-N, 394, 398
  Cmd-T, 343
  Cmd-Z, 360
  Ctrl+E, 385
  Ctrl+F2, 48

  Ctrl+F3, 48, 343
  Ctrl+F7, 427
  Ctrl+F8, 381, 421
  Ctrl+F9, 48
  Ctrl+I, 343
  Ctrl+K, 343, 399
  Ctrl+L, 422
  Ctrl+N, 394, 398
  Ctrl+T, 343
  Ctrl+Z, 360
  E, 48
  F, 342
  F1, 48
  F2, 343
  F4, 48
  F5, 335
  F6, 335, 421
  F7, 335
  F9, 343
  F11, 343
  Flash, 342-343
  H, 48
  I, 48
  K, 342
  L, 48
  layers, selecting, 211
  N, 48
  Option-Cmd-T, 343
  Option-F1, 343
  Option-F2, 343
  Option-F3, 343
  Option-F7, 343
  P, 48
  Q, 342
  S, 342
  Shift+F1, 343
  Shift+F2, 343
  Shift+F4, 343
  Shift+F9, 48
  Shift-F1, 343
  Shift-F2, 343
  Shift-F4, 343
  T, 48
  V, 48
  Z, 48

keyboards, user input, 596
keycodes, 596
Keyframe slider, 436
keyframes
  animations, 391-393
  Flash, 335-336

  layers, 392
  selecting, 346
  sound control (Flash), 414-415
  tweened animations, 394

Keyframes command (Insert menu), 421

Keyline Mode option (Layers panel), 792

keyPress button event, 509-511

keys
  checking, 511
  function keys, F9, 433

keywords
  class, 541
  control blocks, 477-479
  extends, 550
  get, 547
  public, 546
  set, 547
  SQL, SELECT, 891
  statements, 479
  static, 543
  this, 493-496, 505-506
  var, 460, 488-489

Knife tool (FreeHand), 810
Knife Tool dialog box, 810

L

L and T property (layers), 215
Label component (Flash), 427
labels, built-in, 911
language property, 589
languages. See also ActionScript; browser languages; SQL (Structured Query Language)
  CFML (ColdFusion Markup Language), 877
  multiple, publishing Flash content in, 327
  OOP (object-oriented programming), ActionScript, 446-448
  Unicode (Fireworks), 691

Lasso tool, 29, 339-340, 362, 701

Last column (Layers panel), 736

last-in-first-out (LIFO) stacks, 564

lastChild property, 639

Launch and Edit settings, 726, 870

Layer Animagic, 229

Layer column (Layers panel), 736

Layer command (Edit menu), 722

layer folders (Flash), 336-338

Layer ID property (layers), 215

layers
    activating, 210
    aligning, 213
    animation, DHTML, 228
    bitmap, creating, 700
    collapsing/expanding, 736
    content, adding, 210
    creating, 209-210
    CSS (Cascading Style Sheets), 162
    design, 216-217
    displaying (frames), 391
    document structure (Flash menus), 424
    Flash, 336-338, 356
    graphics (Fireworks), 734-738
    guides (Flash), 354-355
    hiding/showing, 736
    inserting, components, 429
    interactivity, 227-229
    Invisible Elements, 210
    keyframes, 392
    layouts, 209
    moving, 736
    naming, 736
    nesting, 214
    nonprinting, creating, 792
    overlapping, 214-215
    overview, 207-208
    preferences, 208
    properties, 215-216
    renaming, 214
    resizing, 212-213
    selecting, 211-212
    separating (text blocks), 374
    shared versus unshared, 738
    showing/hiding, 217
    sound (Flash), 412
    stacking order, 214, 736
    unlocking/locking, 736
    visibility, 213
    Web, sharing, 738

Layers command (Window menu), 211-213, 792

Layers panel, 735-736
    Dreamweaver, 84
    FreeHand, 792-793
    layers, selecting, 211
    nesting layers, 214
    opening, 213
    overlapping layers, 214-215
    renaming layers, 214
    stacking order, 214
    visibility, 213

Layout button, 193

Layout mode, 193-198

Layout Objects, Layer command (Insert menu), 209

Layout tab, 79, 193

Layout Table button, 194-195

layout tables
    adding content, troubleshooting, 218
    attributes, setting, 196-197
    drawing, 193-194
    nesting, 193-195, 198
    resizing, 198

layouts
    cells, 193-198
    Flash, 353-356
    grids, troubleshooting, 218
    layers, 209
    panels (Flash), 334
    workspaces (Dreamweaver), 74-75

.lbi file extension (Library), 143

*.LCK files, 253

LDAP (Lightweight Directory Access Protocol), 878

leading property (TextFormat class), 966

least significant bit (LSB), 932

left parameters, startDrag () method, 533

leftMargin property (TextFormat class), 966

legibility, text, 376-377

length method (arrays), 563

length property (TextField class), 961

lens effects, 814

letters, transforming, 376

levels
    visual stacking, 525-528
    Web site architecture, 843-844

lexical program design, 461

lexically scoped, 506

<li>, </li> tags, 98

libraries, cast, creating, 773

Library
    Flash, 343-344, 357
    folders, 390
    imported sound, 412
    items
        accidental deletion of, 158
        behaviors, 149-150
        copying to other sites, 150
        creating, 143-145
        deleting, 149
        detaching, 148-149
        editing, 147-148
        inserting into sites, 146-147
        .lbi file extension, 143
        SSIs (Server-Side Includes), 144
        versus templates, 144-145
    opening, 389
    organizing, 390
    sizing, 389
    sound, attaching, 653
    symbols (Flash), 389-390

Library category (Assets panel), 141

Library command
    Modify menu, 145
    Window menu, 389, 422, 794

Library Options pop-up menu commands, Properties, 439

Library panel, 439, 794

Library, Update Current Page command (Modify menu), 147

Library, Update Pages command (Modify menu), 150

LIFO (last-in-first-out) stacks, 564

Lightweight Directory Access Protocol (LDAP), 878

line breaks, creating (Dreamweaver), 94

line charts, 828

Line tool, 38, 712

linear gradients, 35

lines. *See also* strokes
  connector, page icons (site maps), 841-843
  dashed strokes, 690
  drawing, 712
  freeform, drawing, 38
  segments, 39-42
  text fields, 372

Lingo, 929

Link Checker panel (Dreamweaver), 92

Link Checker report, 259

link color, Web pages (Dreamweaver), 121-122

Link command (Insert menu), 270

Link reports, 258-259

Link to Target Page action, 853

Linkage Properties dialog box, 415

linked video, versus embedded (Flash), 433

links
  audio, 236-237
  colors, troubleshooting (Dreamweaver), 133
  CSS (Cascading Style Sheets), 176
  external style sheets, 181-182
  external, validating, 261
  frames, 206-207
  inserting, 270-271

internal, 258

Live Data feature, 306

managing, Contribute 2 program, 273

null, # (hash mark), 224

page icons, site maps, 841-843

site maintenance, 258-260

video files, 238

List component (Flash), 427

list properties option (Style Definition dialog box), 185

List Variables command (Debug menu), 377

List, Indent command (context menu), 98

List, Outdent command (context menu), 98

List, Unordered command (Text menu), 98

List/Menu dialog box, 306

listener objects, 500

listeners
  Flash components, 427
  registering, 504-505

lists
  Dreamweaver, 98-99
  managing, Contribute 2 program, 273
  ordered. *See* arrays

literals, 471
  functions, 487
  storing, 487
  versus strings, 470

Live Data feature, 298, 306

Live Effects panel, 688

LiveConnect, JavaScript/Flash communications, 621

LN10 property (Math object), 958

LN2 property (Math object), 958

load method, 609, 967

load movie clip event, 513

Load Sound from Library behavior, 420

Load Streaming MP3 File behavior, 420

Load Target Page action, 853

load targets, movie clips versus levels, 527

load() method, 625, 643

loaded movie clips, troubleshooting, 537

loaded property, 643-644

Loader component (Flash), 427

loading
  dynamic data, LoadVars object, 627-629
  external content, movie clips, 520-524
  external files, 462
  frames, 483
  progressively, .flv files, 648-651
  sound, 653

loadMovie() commands, 632

loadMovie() function, 513

loadMovie() global function, 521-522, 525

loadMovie() method, 521, 919

loadMovieNum() global function, 521-522, 525

loadSound() method, 652

loadVariables method (MovieClip class), 919

loadVariables() function, 513, 626-627

LoadVars object
  completing, 625-626
  embedding data, 632-634
  getBytesLoaded() method, 626
  getBytesTotal() method, 626
  loading dynamic data, 627-629
  LoadVariables() function, 626-627
  sending data, 630-632

local coordinates, movie clips, 530

local external communications (Flash), 618-623

local folders, Web sites (Dreamweaver), 104-106, 109-110

local function variables, creating, 488-489

LocalConnection class, 596-600

localFileReadDisable property, 589

localization, strings, 575

localToGlobal() method, 530, 919

lock parameters, startDrag () method, 533

_lockroot property, 518, 921

Lock/Unlock Layer column (Layers panel), 736

locking
layers (Flash), 337
scope, CFML (ColdFusion Markup Language) variables, 889-890

log method (Math object), 957

LOG2E property (Math object), 958

LOG10E property (Math object), 958

logical (Boolean) operators, 943-945

logical bitwise operators, 931-935

logical operators, 472

logical program design, 461

logs, Transfer, 261

Loop command (Order menu), 824

loop flow control, 480

looping
animations, 746
control blocks, 476
sound (Flash), 414

loops, 483-485

Lossless (PNG/GIF) command (Compression menu), 364

lossless compression, 757

lossy compression, 757, 765

LSB (least significant bit), 932

M

Macintosh, Web-safe color palettes, 34

Macintosh option (Indexed Palette drop-down menu), 765

Macro recorder, 65

Macromedia Exchange
Dreamweaver extensions, downloading, 264-265
registering, 266

Macromedia Flash. *See* Flash

Macromedia Flash and Shockwave plug-in, 230

Macromedia Shockwave
Assets panel category, 140
plug-in, 230

Macromedia Web site, 879

Macs, Web-safe color palettes, 34

Magic Wand (Lasso tool), 339, 701

Magic Wand Settings dialog box, 363

magnification window (Fireworks), 697

Magnification, 400% command (View menu), 354

main menu bar, 30

Main Timeline. *See* Timeline

main toolbar, 30

maintaining sites, links, 258-260

Make Widths Consistent option (Layout mode), 196

makeHandler() function, 499

Manage Extensions command
Commands menu, 266
Help menu, 781

Manage Sites command (Site menu), 104, 107, 248

Manage Sites dialog box, 104, 107-109, 248

Manage Sites, New command (Site menu), 289

Managed Saved Commands dialog box, 781

managers, 780-781

managing sites
Dreamweaver
accessibility, 245-247
cross-browser compatibility, 244-245
CSS (Cascading Style Sheets), 243
document validation, 243-244
overview, 242

site maintenance, links, 258-260
site management, 252-254
site reports, 256-258
Web standards, 242
XHTML, 243
uploading pages, 248-252

manual settings (Optimize panel), 762-765

manufacturer property, 589

map view window, 256

Margin Height property (Property Inspector), 206

Margin Width property (Property Inspector), 206

margins
frames, 206
Web pages, setting (Dreamweaver), 120

markers, 338

markup
cleaning up, 150-156
Contribute 2, 285
Dreamweaver, 163
history, 163-164

markup languages. *See* CFML (ColdFusion Markup Language)

Marquee tool, 700

masks
dynamic, 534-535
Flash, creating, 356
layers, 336

Masks command (Modify menu), 723

Master Detail Page Set dialog box, 311

master pages, databases (Dreamweaver ColdFusion), 310-311

Math class
direction, 585-586
functions, 578-579
getting width, 583-584
position control, 586-587
random integers, 579
relative positioning, 580-581
speed control, 587-588
trigonometry methods, 581-589

Math object, 957-958

Math.cos() method, 581-584

Math.sin() method, 581-584

Math.sqrt() method, 580-581

max method (Math object), 957

maxChars property (TextField class), 961

maxhscroll property (TextField class), 961

Maximum Characters field, 372

maxscroll property (TextField class), 961

Media (Rich Media) classes, 647

   behaviors, 419

   components (Flash), 426

   NetConnection, 648-649

   NetStream, 648-651

   Sound, 651-655

   Video, 656-657

Media button, 230, 233, 237

Media, ActiveX command (Insert menu), 233

Media, Flash Button command (Insert menu), 282

Media, Flash command (Insert menu), 231

Media, Flash Text command (Insert menu), 280

Media, Plugin command (Insert menu), 230, 237

Media, Shockwave command (Insert menu), 232

members, defined, 540

memory, deleted movie clips, 520

menu bars

   Dreamweaver, 77

   main, 30

menus

   context, 68, 623

   dynamic data, Dreamweaver ColdFusion, 305

   Fireworks

      Commands menu, 724

      Edit menu, 722

      File menu, 721

      Filters menu, 724

      Help menu, 725

      Modify menu, 723

      Select menu, 722

      Send To menu, 696

      Text menu, 723

      View menu, 722

      Window menu, 725

   Flash interactivity, 424-425

parameter, 623

property, 518, 921

quickstart (Dreamweaver), 54-55

Mesh option (Surface button), 816

metadata

   ID3, MP3 files, 651

   tags, 614

methods, 468

   addRequestHeader(), 646-647

   arrays, 562-567

   attachSound(), 415, 653

   boolean wrapper classes, 568

   calling, 493

   Camera class, 972-973

   Color class, 594-595

   concat(), 453

   ContextMenu class, 910

   Date class, 951-954

   declarations, 498, 553

   get, 546-548

   Key object, 511, 596, 955-957

   LocalConnection class, 597-598

   Math object, 957-958

   Microphone classes, 974-975

   Mouse events, 512

   Mouse movie object, 600

   MovieClip class, 917-923

   MovieClip methods, 919

   MovieClipLoader object, 523

   Object class, 572-578

   objects, 448

   Selection movie object, 602

   set, 546-548

   String wrapper class, 569

   String.split() method, 569

   StyleSheet class, 967-968

   TextField class, 958-965

   TextFormat class, 966-967

   TextFormat movie class, 966

   trigonometry, 581-589

   wrapper classes, 968-972

Microphone class, 974-975

Microphone Rich Media class, 647

Microphone.names property (Microphone class), 975

Microsoft

   applications, copy/paste, 65-66

   Dreamweaver integration, 283-284

Microsoft Access, 13

Microsoft Access Data Source dialog box, 881-882

Microsoft Active Accessibility (MSAA), 593

Microsoft IIS (Internet Information Server), 880

Microsoft Office Document command (Insert menu), 272

Microsoft Visual SourceSafe, 254

MIME (Multipurpose Internet Mail Extension) types, plug-ins, 229, 624, 645

min method (Math object), 957

Minimum Area (Trace Bitmap dialog box), 360

Mirror dialog box, 822-823

Mirror tool (FreeHand), 822-823

Mixer panel, 790-791

Mixers and Tint panel group (FreeHand), 790-792

mixing colors, 34-35

model-view-controller (MVC), 896

modes

   bitmap (Fireworks), 697

   color, 34, 790-791

   Contribute 2, 269

   Expanded Tables, 195

   Layout, 193-198

   Push/Pull (Freeform Tool dialog box), 806-807

Reshape Area (Freeform Tool dialog box), 808
scaling modes, Stage, 604
symbol-editing mode (Flash), 386

modifiers
Distort, 375
Envelope, 375-376
Free Transform tool, 341

Modify menu, 723

Modify menu command
Frameset, 200-201
Timeline, Distribute, 374

Modify menu commands
Align, 213
Align, Make Same Height, 213
Align, Make Same Width, 213
Alter Path, Reverse Direction, 843, 851
Alter Path, Simplify, 42
Animation, Animate Selection, 749
Animation, Settings, 750
Arrange, Prevent Layer Overlaps, 214
Bitmap, Trace Bitmap, 360
Break Apart, 362, 374, 399
Convert to Symbol, 380, 383
Convert to Symbol, Graphic Symbol, 747
Document, 334
Document, Dimensions, 675
Frameset, 200
Group, 30
Library, 145
Library, Update, 150
Library, Update Current Page, 147
Page Properties, 118
Shape, Add Shape Hint, 400
Shape, Optimize, 42, 353, 361
Symbol, Button, 741
Symbol, Duplicate Symbol, 384
Symbol, Tween Instances, 748

Templates, Apply Template to Page, 131
Templates, Make Attribute Editable, 129
Templates, Remove Template Markup, 125
Templates, Update Pages, 132
Ungroup, 821, 828

Modify Onion Markers button, 339

modulo (%) operator, 929-930

modulo divide and reassign (%=) compound assignment operator, 938

modulo division, 929

modulus (remainders), 929

mono, sound, 408

most significant bit (MSB), 936

motion blur effects, 688

Motion Guide Layer icon, 337

motion guides (Flash), 395-397, 440

motion paths (Flash), troubleshooting, 440

motion tweens (Flash), 394-398

mouse
cursors, 600
custom mouse pointers, creating, 512
events, 512

mouse focus, keyPress event, 510

Mouse object, 600

mouseWheelEnabled property, 606

movie classes, 592
Accessibility, 593
Button, 593-594
Color, 594-595
ContextMenu, 596
creating dynamically, 606
Key, 596
LocalConnection, 596-600
Mouse, 600
PrintJob, 600-602
properties, 607
Selection, 602
Shared Object, 602-603

Stage, 603-605
TextField, 605-611
TextFormat, 605-611
TextSnapshot, 611-612
troubleshooting, 615

movie clips, 921
absolute paths, 495
accessibility, 979
bounding boxes, 529
button movie clips, 505
code, organizing, 454
color, transforming, 595
comparing, 942
coordinates, 530
creating, 517-520
custom tab ordering, 925
drag and drop, startDrag() method, 533-534
droptarget property, 534
dynamic masks, 534-535
elements, displaying (Movie Explorer), 455
empty, 520
events, 513-515
external content, loading/unloading, 520-524
Flash, 381
    FreeHand integration, 868-870
    size, 391
    testing, 399-400
focus, 925
frames (Flash), 335
functions, 531-533
hierarchies, 519, 524-525
hit areas, 924
hitTest() method, troubleshooting, 537-538
init objects, 528-529
invisible children, 530
loaded, troubleshooting, 537
managing, Movie Explorer (Flash), 344
multiple hit tests, 531
naming, 463
overlapping, 529-530
perfect hit illusions, 531
positioning, 519
preloaders, 483
properties, 447, 518, 926
reducing hit test misses, 530

removing, 518-520
scope, 462
screen reader software, 978
stacking, 518, 524-528
testing, 429
timelines, 517
transparency, 594-595
visual stacking, levels, 528

Movie Explorer (Flash), 344, 455-456

movie objects
Sound object, sounds (loading/attaching), 653
troubleshooting, 615

movie parameter, 632

Movie Settings dialog box, 869-870

Movieclip behaviors, 420

MovieClip class
methods, 917-923
properties, 921-926

movieclip datatype, 465, 468

MovieClip method, 522, 919

MovieClipLoader object, 523-524

movies. *See* movie clips

Movies category (Assets panel), 140

MP3 (MPEG-1 Audio Layer 3), 412, 416-417, 651

MP3 command (Compression menu), 416

MPEG files, Movie category (Assets panel), 140

MPEG-1 Audio Layer 3 (MP3), 412, 416-417, 651

MSAA (Microsoft Active Accessibility), 593

MSB (most significant bit), 936

multiline = true property, 607

multiline property (TextField class), 961

multimedia
ActiveX controls, 232-234
audio, 235-238
defined, 220
Java applets, 234-235
plug-ins, 229-232
video, 235-238

multipage files, 845-847

multiple conditional statements, 481

multiple layers, 212-213, 216

Multiple Layers inspector, 216

multiple layouts, 194-195

multiple logical bitwise operators, 935

Multiple option (Mirror dialog box), 823

Multiple Passes (Optimize Curves dialog box), 353

multiplication operators, 929

multiply and reassign (*=) compound assignment operator, 938

Multipurpose Internet Mail Extension (MIME) types, plug-ins, 229

MVC (model-view-controller), 896

myCamera.activityLevel property (Camera class), 973

myCamera.bandwidth property (Camera class), 973

myCamera.currentFps property (Camera class), 973

myCamera.fps property (Camera class), 973

myCamera.height property (Camera class), 973

myCamera.index property (Camera class), 973

myCamera.motionLevel property (Camera class), 973

myCamera.motionTimeOut property (Camera class), 973

myCamera.muted property (Camera class), 973

myCamera.name property (Camera class), 973

myCamera.quality property (Camera class), 974

myCamera.width property (Camera class), 974

myMicrophone.activityLevel property (Microphone class), 975

myMicrophone.gain property (Microphone class), 975

myMicrophone.index property (Microphone class), 975

myMicrophone.muted property (Microphone class), 975

myMicrophone.name property (Microphone class), 975

myMicrophone.rate property (Microphone class), 975

N

name property, 206-207, 279, 593, 921, 961

name/value pairs, special characters, 625

Named Anchor on Scenes (General Preferences), 346

named anchors (Flash), 346

Named Object property (layers), 217

named operators, 948-950

named properties, arrays, 561

names
instance, 372, 377
symbol instances (Flash), 389

naming
accessible objects, 979
browsers, 620
frames, 205
style sheets, 181

NaN (not a number) value, 465, 912
arithmetic operators, 926
converting strings, 940

navigation, 19
actions, 852-854
dynamic tables, Dreamweaver ColdFusion, 299-300
site maps
creating, 838-844
page icons, 840-843
Web content, 424
XML (Extensible Markup Language), 636

navigation bars, 223
adding, 225-226
creating, 225
editing, 226

Fireworks, 741-743, 752
images, creating, 225
Navigation command
(Window menu), 853
Navigation panel, actions, 853
navigational interfaces, creating, 773
negative numbers, shifting
bits, 936
negative settings, 46
nested arrays, 564-566
nested conditional operators,
946
nested layout cells, moving,
198
nested layout tables, moving,
198
nesting
CSS (Cascading Style
Sheets), 175, 183
HTML tags, 88
layers, 208, 214
layout tables, 193-195
symbols, animations (Flash),
404
NetConnection Rich Media
class, 647-649
Netscape, Web-safe color
palettes, 34
Netscape 4 compatibility layer
preference, 208
NetServices class, 666
NetStream Rich Media class,
647-651
network-aware external communications (Flash), 618
HTTP headers, 646-647
LoadVars object
completing, 625-626
embedding data,
632-634
getBytesLoaded()
method, 626
getBytesTotal() method,
626
loading dynamic data,
627-629
LoadVariables() function, 626-627
sending data, 630-632
overview, 623-624

Rich Media classes, 647
NetConnection,
648-649
NetStream, 648-651
Sound, 651-655
Video, 656-657
XML
attributes, 637
benefits, 637-638
commands, 642
data parsing, 638-641,
644
documents, 641-645
hierarchy, 635-636
navigation, 636
overview, 634-636
properties, 639, 644-645
readability, 637
sockets, 645-646
tags, 637
New Button command (Edit
menu), 722
New command (File menu),
111, 123, 202, 394, 694, 839
New CSS Style button, 181
New CSS Style dialog box,
182-184
New Document dialog box,
111-112, 123, 180-181, 202,
312, 694
New Editable Region dialog
box, 124
new empty predefined framesets, creating, 202
New Folder icon, 390
New from Template dialog
box, 130
New Library button, 150
New Library Item button, 145
new operator, 467, 948
New Optional Region dialog
box, 126
New Page dialog box, 271
New Repeating Region dialog
box, 128
new statement, 541-542
New Symbol command (Insert
menu), 421
New Template button, 124
New URL button, 139-140

New Value property (layers),
217
New, Dynamic Page command
(File menu), 291, 312
New, Flash JavaScript File
command (File menu), 329
New/Duplicate Frame button,
737
nextFrame method
(MovieClip class), 919
nextSibling property, 639
nicknames
Asset panel, 139
assets (Assets panel), 157
URLs, 140
No Onion Skinning command
(Onion Skinning menu), 745
nodeName property, 639
nodes, XML (Extensible
Markup Language),
635-636, 658-659
nodeType property, 639
nodeValue property, 639
Noise Tolerance option
(Trace Tool dialog box), 821
Non-Dreamweaver HTML
Comments option (Clean Up
HTML/XHTML command),
151
non-expanding spirals,
creating, 800
non-looping control blocks,
476
None option (frame-to-frame
compression), 751
Nonprinting Layers option
(Layers panel), 792
NoResize property (Property
Inspector), 206
Normal view, 361
Not a Number (NaN) value,
465, 912, 940
NOT logical bitwise operator
(), 935
NOT logical operator (!), 943
notes, Design Notes
(Dreamweaver integration),
771
null datatype, 465-468, 471
null links, # (hash mark), 224
number datatype, 465-466

Number return values, 574

number wrapper class, 568

Number() function, 914

Number.MAX VALUE, 465, 968

Number.MIN VALUE, 466, 968

Number.NaN property (wrapper classes), 969

Number.NEGATIVE INFINITY property (wrapper classes), 969

Number.POSITIVE INFINITY property (wrapper classes), 969

Number.toString method (wrapper classes), 968

Number.valueOf method (wrapper classes), 968

numbered lists, creating (Dreamweaver), 99

numbered properties, arrays, 561

numbers
binary numbers, shifting bits, 936
datatype conversion rules, 914-915
decimal numbers, converting, 595
hexadecimal, parseInt() function, 915
implicit datatype conversion, 912-913
negative numbers, shifting bits, 936
pi, 584

numbers datatype, 465

numeric indices, accessing array literals, 470

numeric literals, versus strings, 470

numeric values, HTML/XHTML, 170-171

numericSortFunc() function, 671

NumericStepper component (Flash), 427

O

object actions (static event handlers), 445-446, 503

Object class, 572-578

Object command (Window menu), 788

object datatype, 465-467

object element, inserting ActiveX controls, 233

object literals, 470-471, 655

Object panel, 788

OBJECT parameter, troubleshooting, 658

object properties (Flash), 279-280

object property access operator, 467

Object return values, 574

object-oriented programming (OOP)
ActionScript, 446-448
AS2 (ActionScript 2), 330
functions, 486

objects. *See also* arrays
2D, converting to 3D, 815
animations (Flash), 391
arguments, 490-491
born objects, 514
comparing, 568
comparison operators, 941-942
converting
symbols (Flash), 380, 383-384
to graphic symbols, 747
core classes, 557
data primitives, 447
data structures, 447
date/time, 569
defined, 446
defining, 452
deprecated, 942
distributing, 356
dot syntax, 447
editing panels, 31-32
Flash objects
accessing, 979-980
aligning, 356
functions, 447

global (singletons), 592
Accessibility object, 593
Button class, 593-594
Color class, 594-595
ContextMenu, 596
Key object, 596
LocalConnection object, 596-600
Mouse object, 600
PrintJob class, 600-602
Selection object, 602
Shared Object class, 602-603
Stage, 603-605
TextField, 605-611
TextFormat, 605-611
TextSnapshot, 611-612

grouping, 30

init, 528-529

Key, 955-957

listener, 500

LoadVars
completing, 625-626
embedding data, 632-634
getBytesLoaded() method, 626
getBytesTotal() method, 626
loading dynamic data, 627-629
LoadVariables() function, 626-627
sending data, 630-632

Math, 957-958

methods, 448

MovieClipLoader, 523-524

persistent storage, 602

properties
accessing, 447
function literal storage, 487
scope chains, 498

registering as listeners, 504-505

reusability code, 451-453

scoping, 453, 496-497

selecting, 29-30

Selection, 515

Sound, 415

sound transform objects, 655

transform objects, 595

vector (Fireworks), copying/pasting, 772

off states

bits, 933

images, 224

offset number, 595

<ol>, </ol> tags, 99

on states

bits, 933

images, 224

On/Off option (Extension Manager dialog box), 266

onActivity event, 974-976

onChanged event, 502, 965

onChanged TextField event, 517

onClose event, 503

onConnect event, 503

onData event, 503, 644

onData movie clip event, 513

onDragOut button event, 509

onDragOut event, 502, 593

onDragOver button event, 509

onDragOver event, 502, 593

onEnterFrame event, 503

onEnterFrame in-line event handler, 454

Onion All command, 397

Onion Marker button, 397

Onion Skin button, 338, 397

Onion Skin Outlines button, 339

onion skinning, 338-339

frame-by-frame animation, 744-745

motion tweens (Flash), 398

No Onion Skinning menu command, 745

Onion Skinning column (Frames panel), 737

onKeyDown event, 503

onKeyUp event, 503

onKillFocus button event, 508

onKillFocus event, 502, 593, 965

onKillFocus TextField event, 517

online

editing Web pages, 157

testing Web sites, 156-157

uploading pages, 249-250

onLoad event, 503, 625, 643-644, 968

onLoad movie clip event, 513

onLoad sound event, 515

onMouseDown event, 503

onMouseDown listener, 600

onMouseMove event, 503

onMouseMove listener, 600

onMouseUp event, 503

onMouseUp listener, 600

onPress button event, 508

onPress event, 502, 593

onRelease button event, 509

onRelease event, 502, 593

onReleaseOutside button event, 509

onReleaseOutside event, 502, 593

onResize stage event, 516

onRollOut button event, 509

onRollOut event, 502, 593

onRollOver button event, 509

onRollOver event, 502, 593

onScroller event, 502, 965

onScroller TextField event, 517

onSetFocus button event, 508

onSetFocus event, 502, 593, 965

onSetFocus TextField event, 516

onSoundComplete event, 503, 653

onSoundComplete sound event, 515

onStatus event, 591, 597

Camera class, 974

event handler, 598

Microphone class, 976

onUnload event, 503

onUnload movie clip event, 514

OOP (object-oriented programming)

ActionScript, 446-448

AS2 (ActionScript 2), 330

functions, 486

opacity swatches, transparency, 712

Open command (File menu), 114

Open dialog box, 114

OpenSSH protocol, 69

operands

modulo division, 929

troubleshooting, 535

operators, 471-475

. (dot), 467, 542, 547, 950

add and reassign (+=), 916

arithmetic operators, 472, 926-930

assignment (=), 472, 475

assignment operators (=), 461, 938-939

associativity, 475-476

bitwise operators, 472, 930

bit-shift, 935-937

logical, 931-935

comma operator, 947-948

comparison operators, 472

arrays, 941-942

automatic datatype conversion, 940-942

deprecated Flash 4, 942

equality operators, 939-940

objects, 941-942

compound assignment, 475, 938-939

conditional operator, 946-947

expressions, 475

function calls (), 488

grouping, 475-476

logical operators, 472, 943-945

named operators, 948-950

new operator, 467

object datatype, 466

operands, 475

parentheses (), 476

plus (+), 470

precedence, 475-476

property access, 542
statement, 475
strict equality (===), 482
ternary operator, 946
typeof operator, 464, 469, 941
unary negation operator, 928
optimization (Fireworks)
compression, 756-757, 774
Dreamweaver files, 61-62
file formats, 758
Optimize panel, 759
manual settings, 762-765
Optimize to Size command, 760
Preview buttons, 758
Saved Settings section, 760-762
Optimize Curves dialog box, 353, 361
Optimize Image in Fireworks command (Commands menu), 276
Optimize Images dialog box, 62
Optimize in Fireworks button, 61, 277
Optimize panel, 759-765
Optimize to Size command (Options menu), 760
Optimize to Size dialog box, 760
optimizing
code, 450
curves, 42, 353
traced bitmaps (Flash), 361-362
Optional Region dialog box, 126
optional regions, creating templates (Dreamweaver), 125-126
Options menu commands
Add Pages, 846
Close Panel Group, 83
Expand Branch, 456
Optimize to Size, 760
OR logical bitwise operator (|), 933-934

OR logical operator (||), 943-944
OR statements, boolean equivalents/returns, 945
Order menu commands, 824
ordered lists. See arrays
ordering (tabs), 922-925
orientation
Page Orientation option (Document panel), 790
pages, 796
Rotate tool, 803
text, changing, 45
orphaned Web pages, 258
os property, 590
Other Panels, Accessibility command (Window menu), 979
Other Panels, Common Libraries command (Window menu), 344
Other Panels, Movie Explorer command (Window menu), 344
Outdent command (Text menu), 98
outlines
device fonts, 373
layers (Flash), 337
Output Area tool (FreeHand), 796
output formats, animation, 743
Oval Marquee tool, 701
Oval tool, 38
Over button state, 421
Over graphics, rollovers, 739
Over rollover state, 225
Over state
button movie clip events, 515
navigation bars, 741
Over While Down rollover state, 225
Over While Down state, navigation bars, 741
Overflow property (layers), 216

overlapping
layers, 214-215
movie clips, 529-531
shapes, 33
overloaded (-) operator, 928-929
overloading constructor functions, 545
overriding class hierarchies, 551
overwriting class hierarchies, 551

P

page bleeds, Using Page Bleeds option (Document panel), 790
page design (Dreamweaver)
frames
benefits, 199
creating, 200
deleting, 201
external sites, 218
framesets, 201-203
modifying, 205-206
overview, 199-200
printing, 218
resizing, 201
selecting, 203-204
splitting, 200-201
targeting windows, 206-207
visual borders, 204
layers
activating, 210
aligning, 213
content, adding, 210
converting to tables, 218
creating, 209-210
design, 216-217
Invisible Elements, 210
layouts, 209
nesting, 214
overlapping, 214-215
overview, 207-208
preferences, 208
properties, 215-216
renaming, 214
resizing, 212-213
selecting, 211-212

showing/hiding, 217
stacking order, 214
visibility, 213
layout tables, adding content, 218
tables
elements, 192
Layout mode, 193-198
page icons, site maps, 840-843
Page Orientation option (Document panel), 790
page preview (Fireworks), 697
Page Preview feature, creating multipage files, 845
page properties, CSS, 60-61
Page Properties command
Edit menu, 58
Modify menu, 118
Page Properties dialog box, 58-60, 96
background colors, 118
background images, 119-120
link color, 121-122
margins, 120
text color, 120-121
Page tool (FreeHand), 795-796, 845-847
Paint Behind modifier (Brush tool), 340
Paint Bucket tool, 36-37, 594
Paint Fills modifier (Brush tool), 340
Paint Inside modifier (Brush tool), 341
Paint Selection (Brush tool), 340
palettes
color, Web-safe, 34
Transformation, 803-806
Panel Sets, Default command (Window menu), 350
Panel Sets, Default Layout command (Window menu), 443
panels, 30. *See also* **Property Inspector**
Accessibility, opening, 979
Action (ActionScript), 443-446
Advanced Effect panel, 595

Align, 356, 399
Answers (Fireworks), troubleshooting, 696, 728-729
Application, 289
Assets
assets, nicknaming, 157
categories, 136-137
Favorites list, 137-139
item deletion, 136-137, 157-158
templates, creating, 123-124
Auto Shapes, 686-687
Behaviors
behaviors, inserting, 222
data sources, triggering, 678
events, 227
navigation bar, editing, 227
Bindings, 14, 293
Components, opening, 427
CSS Styles, 179-180
docking/undocking, 30
Dreamweaver
Application, 85-88
Assets, 89-90
Attribute, 88
Behavior, 88-89
Bindings, 86
Code, 84-85
Components, 87
CSS Styles, 84
Databases, 86
Design, 83
Files, 88-89, 250
FTP Log, 92
groups, 81-83
History, 90-91
Layers, 84
Link Checker, 92
organizing, 55-57
Property Inspector, 81
Reference, 85
Relevant CSS, 58-59, 88
Results, 91, 243
Search, 91
Server Behaviors, 87
Server Debug, 93
Site Reports, 92-93
Snippets, 84-85
Tag Inspector, 88

Target Browser Check, 92
Validation, 91
Files, 57
Frames, 736-737
Distribute to Frames, frame-by-frame animation, 745
frames, selecting, 203
framesets, selecting, 204
Onion Skinning, frame-by-frame animation, 744-745
FreeHand, 787
Assets, 793-794
Layers, 792-793
Mixers and Tint, 790-792
Properties, 788-790
hiding (Flash), 350
History, 328, 780-781
Layers, 735-736
layers, selecting, 211
nesting layers, 214
opening, 213
overlapping layers, 214-215
renaming layers, 214
stacking order, 214
visibility, 213
layouts (Flash), 334
Library, 439, 794
Live Effects, 688
maximizing/minimizing, 30
Navigation, actions, 853
Objects, editing, 31-32
opening, 30
Optimize, 759
manual settings, 762-765
Optimize to Size command, 760
Preview buttons, 758
Saved Settings section, 760-762
resizing, 31
Server Behaviors, 306
Strings, 327
Styles, 793
Swatches, 793, 859
Timelines, 228-229

Tools
  Round Rectangle Radius modifier, 38
  View section, 33
  Web-Safe colors, 858
Transform, 802-803
Web Services, 672-673
panning cartoon animations (Flash), 404
paragraph attributes, 45-47
paragraphs (Dreamweaver), 94, 97-98
parameters
  ActiveX controls, 234
  ampersand (&), 891
  components (Flash), 427
  Java applets, 235
  OBJECT parameter, troubleshooting, 658
  Passing, CFCs (ColdFusion Components), 904
  plug-ins, 231
  send() method, 631
  startDrag() method, 533-534
  TextFormat class, 607
  trailing, 607
Parameters button, 234
Parameters dialog box, 231, 234
Parameters property (Flash object), 280
parent property, 921, 962
_parent special target, 620
parent-child hierarchies, movie clips, 524-525
parent-child relationships, movie clips, 519
parentheses ()
  function call operators, 488
  operators, 476
parentheses/function call operator, 950
parentNode property, 639
parseCSS method, CSS (Cascading Style Sheets), 610
parsefloat() function, 914
parseInt() function, 914-915

parsing XML (Extensible Markup Language) data, 638-641, 644
passing
  arguments to functions, 489-492
  data, CFML custom tags, 897-898
password property (TextField class), 962
passwords, RDS (Remote Development Services), 877
Paste command (Edit menu), 840, 868
Paste Keyframes command, 392
Path Conversion option (Trace Tool dialog box), 821
Path Overlap option (Trace Tool dialog box), 821
Path Scrubber tool, 719
paths, 39
  absolute, movie clips, 495
  ascenders, 852
  baselines, 852
  classpaths, entering, 554-556
  creating, 849
  descenders, 852
  drawing, 712-713
  fill, 734
  motion (Flash), troubleshooting, 440
  sinuous, 586
  text
    aligning, 849-852
    converting to, 814
    flowing, 851
  versus strokes (vector graphics), 734
Pen tool, 396, 712-714
  anchor points, 40-41
  control handles, 40-41
  curved line segments, 40-42
  straight line segments, drawing, 39
pencil icon, 337
Pencil tool, 38, 396, 703
performance (Fireworks), 684
period (.), class selectors, 175

Perl
  # (hash mark), 627
  CGI (Common Gateway Interface) scripts, writing, 627-629
  comments, 627
  troubleshooting, 658
persistence, ColdFusion components, 896
persistent storage, 602
Personal Home Pages (PHP), 634
Personal Web Server (PWS), 15
Perspective Grid command (View menu), 810
Perspective tool (FreeHand), 810-812
Photo (JPEG) command (Compression menu), 363
Photoshop, troubleshooting filters, 774
PHP (Personal Home Pages), 65, 634
PI property (Math object), 584, 958
PICT Settings (Clipboard Preferences), 348
Pictograph dialog box, 828
pie charts, 717, 828
pitch, sound, 408
Pixel FX (Flash), 322
pixelAspectRatio property, 590
pixels, 352
  alignment, 369
  anti-aliasing, 368-370
  bitmap graphics, 732-733
  blurring, 705
  compressed bitmaps (Flash), 364
  darkening, 706
  fonts, bitmap, 368-370, 376-377
  justification, 369
  layers, resizing, 212
  lightening, 706
  modifying (bitmaps), 362
  snapping, 353-354, 369
  tables, 196
  text, 368-369
  traced bitmaps (Flash), 360

pixels per inch (ppi), 732
placeholders
    Dreamweaver, 275
    Flash, 231
    Image, Dreamweaver inte-
        gration, exporting
        Fireworks graphics, 772
    text, 370
planning
    CSS (Cascading Style
        Sheets), 14-15
    Dreamweaver Bindings
        panel, 14
    FreeHand, 13-14
    templates, 14
platforms, dynamic
    (Dreamweaver), 64-65
Play command (Control
    menu), 404
play method (MovieClip
    class), 919
Play Sound behavior, 420
Play Sound JavaScript
    behavior, 236
Play/Stop property (Flash
    object), 280
Playback, controlling embed-
    ded video (Flash), 439
playerType property, 590
Plg URL property
    embedded audio files, 237
    plug-ins, 231
plug-ins, 229
    detecting, 229-230
    Dreamweaver, trou-
        bleshooting, 284
    embedding, 230
    Flash, 231-232
    inserting, ActiveX controls,
        234
    parameters, 231
    properties, 230-231
    Shockwave, 232
    third-party, installing, 268
Plugin icon, 230
Plugin Name property
    (plug-ins), 231
Plugin property (embedded
    audio files), 237
plus (+) operator, 470
PNG (Portable Network
    Graphics), 119, 862

PNG command
    Format menu, 862
    Save As Type menu, 862
PNG Fireworks files, import-
    ing to FreeHand, 865
PNG Options dialog box,
    862-863
point size, fonts, 45-46
point-check approach, over-
    lapping movie clips, 530
pointers
    custom mouse pointers,
        creating, 512
    gradient pointer, 36
policy files, 626
Polygon Hotspot tool, 719
Polygon Lasso tool, 701, 729
Polygon modifier (Lasso tool),
    340
Polygon Slice tool, 719
Polygon tool, 716
Polygons, drawing, 716-717
polymorphic (+) operator, 928
pop method (arrays), 562
pop() method, 561, 564
Portable Network Graphics
    (PNG), 119, 862
ports, Web servers, 880
position control, Math class,
    586-587
position property, 655
positioning
    character position, 47
    movie clips, 519
    relative, Math class,
        580-581
    symbols (Flash), 382-383
positioning styles option
    (Style Definition dialog box),
    185
positive settings, 46
POST method, 632
postfixes, operators, 927
pound sign (#)
    null links, 224
    Perl, 627
pow method (Math object),
    957
ppi (pixels per inch), 732
precedence operators,
    475-476

Precision option
    Calligraphic dialog box, 799
    Variable Stroke Pen dialog
        box, 798
predefined framesets,
    201-203
Preferences
    Fireworks, 725-727
    Flash, 345-350
    layers, 208
Preferences command (Edit
    menu), 55, 74, 275, 345, 722
Preferences dialog box, 55, 74
Preferences, ActionScript
    command (Edit menu), 449,
    457
Preferences, File
    Types/Editors command
    (Edit menu), 179
Preferences, General com-
    mand (Edit menu), 457
Preferences, Layers command
    (Edit menu), 208
Preferences, Validator com-
    mand (Edit menu), 243
prefixes, operators, 927
preloaders
    centralizing code, 462
    movie clips, 483
    sound preloaders, 655
Preset Name dialog box, 761
press button event, 508
Pressure modifier (Brush
    tool), 341
prevFrame method
    (MovieClip class), 920
Preview buttons, optimization,
    758
Preview Mode, Fast command
    (View menu), 361
Preview Mode, Outlines com-
    mand (View menu), 361
previewing
    animations (Flash), scrub-
        bing, 403
    data, automated operations,
        291-293
    graphics, 685
    Page Preview feature, creat-
        ing multipage files, 845
    pages (Fireworks), 697
    sound (Flash), 412

previousSibling property, 639

primitive datatypes, 464, 471

Print Target Page action, 853

printing frames, 218

Printing Options (General Preferences), 345

PrintJob class, 600-602

private visibility, class features, 546

processing
 batch (Fireworks), 684
 Batch Process (Fireworks), 778-779

program design, lexical/ logical, 461

programming
 event-based programming, 507-509
 OOP (object-oriented programming), 330, 486

programs
 choosing, 49
 Contribute 2, 270-274
 creating
  editing pages, 270
  FlashPaper Printer utility, 269
  frames, 274
  images, 273
  importing Word/Excel documents, 272
  links, 273
  lists, 273
  modes, 269
  overview, 268-269
  tables, 273
  text, 273-274
  toolbar, 270
 idle programs, 512
 Microsoft, 65-66

progress bars, sound, 655

ProgressBar component (Flash), 427

Progressive option (JPEG compression), 764

progressively loading .flv files, 648-651

Project (Editing Preference), 348

project classpaths, entering, 554-556

Project From Menu option (3D Rotation dialog box), 814

Project Seven, Layer Animagic, 229

projector control, 622-623

projects, Web standards, 188

promoting Web sites, effect of directory structure on search engines, 158-159

properties
 Accessibility object, 593
 ActiveX controls, 233-234
 arguments.callee, 491
 arguments.caller, 492
 arguments.length, 491
 Button class, 593
 Camera class, 973-974
 character, 45-47
 childNodes property (XML), 639
 CSS (Cascading Style Sheets), 610
 defined, 540
 droptarget (movie clips), 534
 editable, templates (Dreamweaver), 129-130
 embedded audio files, 237-238
 embedded video files, 238
 files, setting, 334
 frames, 205-206
 functions, 468
 get/set methods, 546-548
 HTML, 170
 Java applets, 235
 Key object, 955-957
 layers, 215-217
 layout cells, 196-197
 layout tables, 196-197
 Math object, 957-958
 Microphone classes, 975
 movie clips, 518, 528-529, 926
 MovieClip class, 921-926
 movies, 447
 named properties, 206-207, 561
 naming, 548
 numbered properties, arrays, 561

Object class, constructor, 574
 objects
  accessing, 447, 467
  Flash, 279-280
  scope chains, 498
  storing function literals, 487
 pages, CSS, 60-61
 paragraph, 45-47
 plug-ins, 230-231
 PrintJob class, 601
 prototype, 542-543
 sound (Flash), 412
 Stage object, 603-605
 symbol instances (Flash), 387-389
 target, targeting windows, 206-207
 text fields, 607
 TextField class, 958-965
 TextFormat class, 966-967
 TextFormat movie class, 966
 type, 888
 wrapper classes, 968-972
 XHTML, 170
 XML (Extensible Markup Language), 637, 641-645

Properties command (Library Options pop-up menu), 439

Properties panel
 objects, editing, 31-32
 opening, 845

Properties panel group (FreeHand), 788-790

property access operator, 542

Property Inspector, 393, 398, 412
 CSS (Dreamweaver), 59-60
 Dreamweaver, 81
 Fireworks, 696, 721
 Flash, 358
 frame properties, 205-206
 graphical previews, 685
 layer properties, 215-216
 Swap command, 389

Property property (layers), 217

protocols
 AMF (Action Message Format), 662
 FTP (File Transfer Protocol), 69, 106-107, 253
 LDAP (Lightweight Directory Access Protocol), 878
 OpenSSH, 69
 SOAP (Simple Object Access Protocol), 662, 878-879
prototype attribute, 542-543
proxies, ColdFusion servers, creating with Dreamweaver, 879
proxy services, 878
pseudo-code, 450
PSW (Personal Web Server), 15
public keyword, 546
public visibility, class features, 546
Publish as HTML command (File menu), 863
Publish button, 334
Publish Settings command (File menu), 410, 458, 516, 604
Publish Settings dialog box, 334, 346, 416, 604, 870
publishing
 drafts, Contribute 2 program, 274
 Flash content, multiple languages, 327
Punch option (Xtra Operations toolbar), 831
push method (arrays), 562
push technology (XML sockets), 646
push() method, 564
Push/Pull mode (Freeform Tool dialog box), 806-807
Put command, 250
Put File(s) button, 250
putting files (uploading), site management, 250-251
Pythagorean theorem, 581

Q

quality property, 921, 962
Quality property (Flash object), 280
Quality slider, 436
queries, saving, 67
query strings, 630
question mark (?), 632
Quick Compress option (Encoding dialog box), 437
Quick Export button, 751
quickstart menu (Dreamweaver), 54-55
QuickTime
 files, Movies category (Assets panel), 140
 linked video, 433
QuickTime 4, downloading, 357
QuickTime dialog box, 434
quit command, 623
quotation marks ("")
 double quotation marks (), server-side includes, 634
 HTML/XHTML values, 170
 strings, 625

R

radial gradients, 35
radians, 584
RadioButton component (Flash), 427
Random command
 Rotate menu, 826
 Scale menu, 825
 Spacing menu, 825
random integers, Math class, 579
random method (Math object), 957
random() method, 579
rates
 frame rates (Flash), 393, 743
 sampling rates, 407-408
Raw option (sound compression), 417

RDS (Remote Development Services)
 passwords, 877
 remote servers, 106
reachability, ActionScript (Flash), 453-456
readability, ActionScript (Flash), 448-450
readable names, code, 449
reading text, 376-377
real-time audio streams, 653
RealOne Player plug-in, 230
rebuilding Sites list (Assets panel), 142
Recognize Lines (Editing Preference), 347
Recognize Shapes (Editing Preference), 348
Reconstitute Table command (File menu), 722
Record Insertion Form dialog box, 308-309
Record Insertion Form Wizard, 308
Record Update Form dialog box, 309
Record Update Form Wizard, 309
recording macros, 65
records
 CFML (ColdFusion Markup Language), 892-895
 databases, managing (Dreamweaver ColdFusion), 308-310
Recordset dialog box, 294-296
Recordset Navigation bar, 299
Recordset Paging button, 299
Recordsets, 295-297, 891
Rectangle Hotspot tool, 719
Rectangle tool, 38, 399, 715
rectangles, drawing, 715-717
Red Eye Removal tool, 687, 710
Redo command (Edit menu), 328
Redo feature, 328
Redraw Path tool, 714

Redundant Nested Tags option (Clean Up HTML/XHTML command), 151

Reference panel (Dreamweaver), 85

references
explicit scoping, 495
object comparisons, 568
XML (Extensible Markup Language), 640

referencing array elements, 559-560

Reflect tool (FreeHand), 804

Refresh Site List button, 142

Refresh Size button, 62

Refresh Templates button, 272

refreshing
files, Web sites (Dreamweaver), 133
Sites list (Assets panel), 142

regions (Dreamweaver), 125-128, 131

registerClass method, 573

registration
listeners, 504-505
symbols, creating (Flash), 382-383

registration points, clip positioning, 519

Registration settings (Convert to Symbol dialog box), 383

regular expressions, 876, 901-902

relative link values, HTML/XHTML, 171

relative positioning, Math class, 580-581

relative references, explicit scoping, 495

relative URLs, 619

release button event, 509

Release to Layers option (Xtra Operations toolbar), 832

releaseOutside button event, 509

Relevant CSS panel (Dreamweaver), 58-59, 88

Relevant CSS tab, 186-187

remainders (modulus), 929

Remote Development Services (RDS)
passwords, 877
remote servers, 106

remote rollovers, 225

remote servers
siteless file editing, 248
uploading files, 250
Web sites
editing online, 157
importing (Dreamweaver), 110
setting up (Dreamweaver), 106-109
testing online, 157

Remote Site pane, 249

remote sites, setting up, 252

Remove All Spaces option (Layout mode), 196

Remove Frames command, 392

Remove from Favorites button, 138

Remove Nesting option (Layout mode), 196

Remove Overlap option (Xtra Operations toolbar), 832

removeColumnA+() method, 668

removeListener method (TextField class), 959

removeMovieClip method (MovieClip class), 920

removeMovieClip() method, 520

removeNode(nodeNum) command, 642

removeTextField method (TextField class), 959

Rename option (Batch Wizard), 779

Render Text as HTML button, 372

repeating regions, creating templates (Dreamweaver), 127-128

repeating tables, creating (Dreamweaver), 127-128

Replace Color tool, 687-688, 708-710

Replace Options dialog box, 777-778

replaceSel method (TextField class), 959

Report Settings button, 247

reports
Check Links, 92
Check Target Browsers, 92
documents, running, 246-247
Link, 258-259
Link Checker, 259
site, 247, 256-258, 261
Site Report, 92

Reports command (Site menu), 247, 256

Reports dialog box, 256

REQUEST scope, 890

Resample button, 277

reserved target names, 207

reserved words
ActionScript, 463
AS2 (ActionScript 2), 331

Reset Size property (Flash object), 279

Reshape Area mode (Freeform Tool dialog box), 808

resize handles, resizing layers, 212

Resize Selected Objects command (Commands menu), 724

resolution
graphics (Fireworks), troubleshooting, 782
measuring, 732

Resolution option (Trace Tool dialog box), 820

Resolve Library Conflict error, 440

resources
bitmap fonts, 369
CSS (Cascading Style Sheets), 189

restoring panels (Flash), 350

restrict property (TextField class), 962

results (expressions), storing, 938

Results panel, 243

Results panel (Dreamweaver), 91

retrieving data
  automated operations, databases (Dreamweaver ColdFusion), 293-297
  CFML (ColdFusion Markup Language), 891-892

Return command (Control menu), 404

return statement, 492, 536

return values
  comma operator, 948
  function results, retrieving, 492-493
  toString() method, 574

returning data, CFML custom tags, 898-899

reusability, ActionScript (Flash), 451-453

Reverse Direction option (Xtra Operations toolbar), 832

reverse method (arrays), 562

reverse() method, 564

reversed arrays, 564

RGB (red-green-blue) color mode, 34, 791

Rich Media classes, 647
  NetConnection, 648-649
  NetStream, 648-651
  Sound, 651-655
  Video, 656-657

right parameters, startDrag () method, 533

right-angled arrows, drawing, 717

rightMargin property (TextFormat class), 966

RoboHelp, 426

rollOut button event, 509

rollOver button event, 509

Rollover Image icon, 224

rollovers
  creating, 223, 421
  DataGrid component, 671
  Disjoint Rollovers (Fireworks), 739-741

inserting, 224
naming, 224
off state images, 224
on state images, 224
remote, 225
Simple Rollovers (Fireworks), 738-739
states, 225
testing, 739

root depth numbering, 527

Rotate and Skew modifier (Free Transform tool), 341

Rotate and Skew tool, 384

Rotate From Menu option (3D Rotation dialog box), 812

Rotate menu commands, 826

Rotate tool (FreeHand), 803-804

_rotation property (MovieClip class), 921

rotation, 582, 812-814

rotation property (TextField class), 963

Roughen dialog box, 808

Roughen tool (FreeHand), 808-809

round method (Math object), 958

Round Rectangle Radius modifier, 38

round() method, 579

rounded rectangles, drawing, 717

roundtrip editing, 276, 689

Roundtrip HTML, 163

row color, DataGrid component, 669

Rubber Stamp tool, 708

rule inspector, 186-187

rulers, showing (Flash), 354

Rulers command (View menu), 355

rules
  conversion, datatypes, 911-916
  CSS (Cascading Style Sheets), 173-174
  shape dimensions (Flash), changing, 355

Run button, 247

S

sampling
  bit depth, 408
  sound, 407

sans-serif fonts, 370, 373

saturation, video encoding (Flash), 438

Save and Close Files option (Replace Options dialog box), 777

Save and Compact command (File menu), 324

Save As command (File menu), 113

Save As dialog box, 113

Save as HTML button, 863

Save As Template command (File menu), 124

Save As Template dialog box, 124

Save As Type menu commands
  GIF, 860
  JPEG, 861
  PNG, 862

Save command (File menu), 77, 839

Save Command dialog box, 781

Save Differences Between Frames option (frame-to-frame compression), 751

Save Query button, 67

Save Selected Steps as a Command button, 91

Saved Settings section (Optimize panel), 759-762

saving
  bitmap graphics (Flash), 358
  files, 77, 113, 124

Scalable Vector Graphics (SVG), 164

Scale and Rotate dialog box, 332

Scale menu commands, 825

Scale modifier (Free Transform tool), 341

Scale option (Batch Wizard), 779

Scale property (Flash object), 280

Scale slider, 438

Scale tool, 384, 801-803

scaleMode property, 604-605

scaling modes, Stage, 604

scaling projector windows, 622

scatter charts, 828

schema
automated operations, databases (Dreamweaver ColdFusion), 290
XML (Extensible Markup Language), 635

scientific notation, 465

scope chains, 498-499

scopes, 461-462, 889-891

scoping
automatic, 497-500
event handlers, 505-506
explicit scoping, 494-497
lexically scoping, 506
rules, 453
variables, 496

Scr property (embedded audio files), 237

screen reader software, 978-979

screen scraping, 876, 899

screenColor property, 590

screenDPI property, 590

screenResolution property, 590

screenResolutionY property, 590

script data typing, 460

Script icon, 221

Script Navigator, 444

scripts
CGI (Common Gateway Interface), 627-629, 658
Flash interactivity, 418
Perl, troubleshooting, 658

Scripts category (Assets panel), 140

scroll bars, 205, 325

Scroll property
Property Inspector, 205
TextField class, 963

ScrollPane component (Flash), 427

scrubbing Timeline effects, 403

search engines, importance of proper document structure, 158-159

Search panel (Dreamweaver), 91

Search pop-up menu (Find and Replace feature), 777

searches
Find and Replace feature, 67, 328
History panel, 328

Seconds button, 414

Secure FTP (SFTP), 248

security
data text, loading, 626
Flash, 330
Flash Remoting, 663
FTP (Dreamweaver), 69
HTTP headers, customizing, 647
policy files, 626
Web services, 663

segments, 39-42

Select dialog box, 237

Select File dialog box, 231

Select HTML dialog box, 205

Select Image Source dialog box, 197

Select menu, 700, 722

SELECT SQL keyword, 891

Select to Behind tool, 698

Select tools, 698-699

selectable property (TextField class), 963

Selectable Text button, 372

selecting objects, 29-30

selection events, 515

Selection object, 515, 602

Selection Options (General Preferences), 346

Selection tool, 29, 352-354, 395, 399

Selective Quality option (JPEG compression), 762

selectors, CSS (Cascading Style Sheets), 173-177

_self special target, 620

semicolons (;), CSS declarations, 173-174

send command, 645

send method, 597

Send To menu, 696

send() method, 597-598, 631

sendAndLoad command, 645

sendAndLoad() method, 631

sending XML (Extensible Markup Language) documents, 645

separating layers (text blocks), 374

separatorBefore attribute (copy method), 910

sequences, animations (Flash), 390

serif fonts, 373
antialising, 370
text legibility, 376

server behaviors, creating, 20-21

Server Behaviors panel, 87, 306

Server Debug command (View menu), 93

Server Debug panel (Dreamweaver), 93

SERVER scope, 891

Server-Side ActionScript (SSAS), creating server behaviors, 21

Server-Side Includes. See SSIs

servers
Apache HTTP Server, 15
ColdFusion, 876
accessing with Flash, 878-880
behaviors, creating with Dreamweaver, 879
client proxies, creating with Dreamweaver, 879
database operations, 877
display operations, 878

file operations, 878
Flash Remoting Gateway, 879
functions, 877-878
page processing, 878
proxy services, 878
server-to-server communications, 878
IIS (Internet Information Server), 15
Microsoft IIS (Internet Information Server), 880
PWS (Personal Web Server), 15
remote
siteless file editing, 248
uploading files, 250
Web sites, 106-110, 157
SQL Server, 13
Web, 12
Apache, 880
built-in (ColdFusion), 880
ColdFusion, 876
ColdFusion Developer Edition, 12
determining, 15
JRun, 880
MIME types, 624
ports, 880
serverString property, 590-591
services. *See* Web services
SESSION scope, 891
set keyword, 547
set method, 546-548
Set Nav Bar Image behavior, 741
set statement, 461
Set Text of Layer action, 217
setClipboard method, 591
setGain method (Microphone class), 974
setInterval() global function, 531-533
setMask method (MovieClip class), 920
setMask() method, 534
setMode method (Camera class), 972
setMotionLevel method (Camera class), 973

setNewTextFormat method, 608, 959
setPan() method, 654-655
setRate method (Microphone class), 975
setRGB() method, 594-595
setSilenceLevel method (Microphone class), 975
setStyle method
CSS (Cascading Style Sheets), 610
StyleSheet class, 968
setTextFormat method, 608, 959
Settings buttons, 388
setTransform() method, 595, 655
Setup button, 861
setUseEchoSuppression method (Microphone class), 975
setVolume() method, 654
SFTP (secure FTP), 69, 248
SGML (Standard Generalized Markup Language), 163-164
Shade command (Fill menu), 820
Shaded option (Surface button), 816
Shadow dialog box, 818
Shadow tool (FreeHand), 818-820
Shape command, 399
shape tweens (Flash), 398-400, 440
Shape, Add Shape Hint command (Modify menu), 400
Shape, Optimize command (Modify menu), 42, 353, 361
shapes
Auto Shapes, adding, 718
curves (Flash), optimizing, 353
dimensions, changing (Flash), 355
freeform, drawing, 38
overlapping, 33
Selection tool (Flash), 352
smoothing (Flash), 353
straightening (Flash), 353

strokes (Flash), 365
Subselection tool (Flash), 352
shared layers versus unshared layers, 738
Shared Object class, 602-603
sharing Web layers, 738
Sharpen button, 277
Sharpen Edges option (JPEG compression), 763
Sharpen tool, 706
shift method (arrays), 562
shift() method, 567
shifting
bits, 938
focus shifting, keyPress event, 511
Shockwave category (Assets panel), 140
Shockwave plug-in, 232
Shockwave.com Web site, 232
shortcut property, 593
shortcuts. *See* keyboard shortcuts
Show Border Around Text button, 370
Show Log on Completion option (Clean Up HTML/XHTML command), 151
Show Pen Preview (Editing Preference), 347
Show Precise Cursors (Editing Preference), 347
Show Slice tool, 721
Show Solid Points (Editing Preference), 347
Show Tooltips (General Preferences), 346
Show Tooltips check box, 457
Show Totals Message (Optimize Curves dialog box), 362
show() method, 512, 600
Show-Hide behavior, 227
Show-Hide Layers behavior, 217
Show-Hide Layers dialog box, 227
Show/Hide Layer column (Layers panel), 736

showing
 layers, 217, 227
 rulers (Flash), 354
showMenu property, 603
showSettings method, 591
signed left bit-shift operator
 (<<), 937
signed right bit-shift operator
 (>>), 936-937
silent property, 593
simple buttons (Flash interactivity), 421-422
Simple Object Access
 Protocol (SOAP), 662,
 878-879
Simple Rollovers, 738-739
Simplify option (Xtra
 Operations toolbar), 832
simplifying
 code, 450
 curves, 42
Simulate Download (View
 menu), 435
sin method (Math object), 958
single layouts, 194-195
singletons (global objects),
 592
 Accessibility object, 593
 Button class, 593-594
 Color class, 594-595
 ContextMenu class, 596
 Key object, 596
 LocalConnection class,
  596-600
 Mouse object, 600
 PrintJob class, 600-602
 Selection object, 602
 Shared Object class,
  602-603
 Stage object, 603-605
 TextField class, 605-611
 TextFormat class, 605-611
 TextSnapshot, 611-612
sinuous paths, 586
Site button, 142
Site command (Window
 menu), 105
Site Definition dialog box, 69,
 104-109, 248, 254, 289
Site list (Assets panel), 137

site management
 Dreamweaver, 242, 256
 accessibility, 245-247
 collaboration, 252-255
 cross-browser compati-
  bility, 244-245
 CSS (Cascading Style
  Sheets), 243
 document validation,
  243-244
 overview, 242
 site maintenance, links,
  258-260
 site reports, 256-258
 Web standards, 242
 XHTML, 243
 uploading pages, 248-252
Site Map button, 256
Site menu commands
 Get, 110
 Manage Sites, 104, 107, 248
 Manage Sites, New, 289
 Reports, 247, 256
 Synchronize, 255
Site Reports panel
 (Dreamweaver), 92-93
Site Reports tab, 246
siteless page editing
 (Dreamweaver), 57
Sites list (Assets panel), 142
Sites panel. See Files panel
sites. See also Web sites
 file editing, 248
 maps, creating, 838-844
 reports, 247, 256-258, 261
 window, 249-250
Size button, 334
size property (TextFormat
 class), 967
size() method, 614
sizes
 files, reducing, 324
 sound files, 408
Skew tool (FreeHand),
 805-806
skinning
 Flash components, 430-431
 Onion Skinning, 737,
  744-745

slash syntax, explicit scoping,
 495
slashes (/), 449, 886
Slice command (Edit menu),
 722
slice method (arrays), 562
Slice tool, 719
slice() method, 566
sliced images, piecing back in
 to tables (Assets panel), 157
slices
 creating, 719
 troubleshooting
  (Fireworks), 753
 Web pages, exporting, 770
sliders
 Bandwidth slider, 436
 Ease slider, 398
 Keyframe slider, 436
 Quality slider, 436
 Scale slider, 438
 Smoothing slider, 362
SMIL (Synchronized
 Multimedia Integration
 Language), 164
Smooth modifier
 Arrow tool, 339
 Flash, 353
Smoothing (Magic Wand
 Settings dialog box), 363
smoothing curves/shapes
 (Flash), 353
Smoothing option (JPEG
 compression), 763
smoothing property, 656
Smoothing slider, 362
Smudge dialog box, 818
Smudge tool, 707, 818
Snap Align dialog box,
 339-340
Snap to Objects modifier
 (Arrow tool), 339
snapping
 cells, 195
 Flash, 353-354
 grid increments, resizing
  layers, 212
 objects (Flash), 339
 pixels, 369

Snapping, Edit Snap Align command (View menu), 339

Snapping, Snap to Guides command (View menu), 355

Snapping, Snap to Objects command (View menu), 339

Snapping, Snap to Pixels command (View menu), 354, 369

snippets, JavaScript, 221

Snippets panel (Dreamweaver), 84-85

SOAP (Simple Object Access Protocol), 662, 878-879

sockets, XML (Extensible Markup Language), 645-646

Soft Edge option (Shadow dialog box), 819

software, 12
  ActiveX, JavaScript/Flash communications, 621
  DBMS (database management system), 12-13
  LiveConnect, JavaScript/Flash communications, 621
  screen reader software, 978-979
  TopStyle, 179
  Web servers, 12

solid colors, 35-36

Sorensen Spark codec, 432-433

Sorenson Spark Pro Web site, 433

Sorenson Squeeze, 324

sort method (arrays), 562

sort() method, 564-566

sorting
  columns, DataGrid component, 671
  site reports, 258
  symbols (Flash), 390

sortOn method (arrays), 562

sortOn() method, 564-566

sound
  attaching, 653
  Envelope handles, 414
  event, 652
  file size, 408

Flash
  amplitude, 406
  compressing, 415-417
  controlling, 414-415
  embedded, 408-411
  event, 408-411
  external, 408-411
  frequency, 406
  global configurations, 410
  importing, 412
  layers, 412
  looping, 414
  modifying, 413-414
  overview, 406
  pitch, 408
  preparations, 407-408
  previewing, 412
  properties, 412
  sampling, 407
  stream, 408-411
  synchronization, 411
  turning off, 417
  volume, 413
  zooming, 414
Flash buttons, 422
loading, 653
real-time audio streams, 653
streaming, 652
troubleshooting, 659
volume (amplitude), 414

Sound behaviors, 420

_soundbuftime property (MovieClip class), 921

Sound Designer II, 412

sound events, 515-516

Sound movie object, 653

Sound object, 415

Sound Only Quicktime Movies, 412

Sound Properties dialog box, 410, 415

Sound Rich Media class, 647
  controlling sounds, 653-655
  creating, 651
  information, 655
  loading/attaching sounds, 651-653

sound transform objects, creating, 655

soundbuftime property (TextField class), 963

source code components (Flash), 325

source documents, frames, 205

source files, 61, 70

SourceSafe database, remote servers, 106

spacing
  character spacing, 46-47
  code, 448-449

Spacing menu commands, 825

Span Based Selection (General Preferences), 346

sparse array, 560

spatial compression, video, 433

special characters, regular expressions, 901-902

Special Characters, Line Break command (Insert menu), 94

special targets, 620-621

Specific Tag(s) option (Clean Up HTML/XHTML command), 151

speech compression (sound), 417

speed
  downloads, 152-153, 156
  Flash files (SWF), 322

speed control, Math class, 587-588

spell checking
  code clean up, 153
  Flash, 326
  Web pages, dictionary problems, 158

Spiral dialog box, 800

Spiral tool (FreeHand), 800

spirals, drawing, 717

splice method (arrays), 563

splice() method, 566-567

splitting
  frames, 200-201
  strings, 569

SQL (Structured Query Language)
  CFML (ColdFusion Markup Language) database operations, 891-895
  code, creating, 293
  keywords, 891
  tags, 290
SQL Servers, 13
sqrt method (Math object), 958
SQRT2 method (Math object), 958
SQRT1 2 property (Math object), 958
square brackets ([]), object property access, 467
squares, drawing, 715
Squeeze (Sorenson), 324
src parameter, 632
Src property
  plug-ins, 231
  Property Inspector, 205
SSAS (Server-Side ActionScript), creating server behaviors, 21
SSIs (Server-Side Includes)
  double quotes (""), 634
  dynamic data, adding, 633-634
  Library items, 144
stacked column charts, 828
stacking
  layers, 214, 736
  movie clips, visual stacking order, 524-528
stacks, last-in-first-out (LIFO) stacks, 564
Stage
  cartoon animations, panning, 404
  clearing, 392
  content, aligning, 603
  object alignment (Flash), 356
  resizing, 516, 675
  scaling modes, 604
  tracing bitmaps, 360
Stage events, 516
Stage object, 603-605

Stage.onResize event handler, 603
Standard Generalized Markup Language (SGML), 163-164
Standard toolbar (Dreamweaver), 78
standardizing code, 450
stars, drawing, 716
Start (synchronization option), 411
Start Onion Skin marker, 338
Start page (Fireworks), 685, 694
start() method, 410, 653
startDrag method (MovieClip class), 920
startDrag() method, 533-534
startRegex variable, 901
statements, 471-474
  break, 482
  control blocks, 476-479
    body, 477
    conditional statements, 480-483
    control constructs, 477
    flow control, 480
    headers, 477
    keywords, 477-479
    loops, 476, 483-485
    non-looping, 476
  default, 482
  if, 480-481, 944-945
  if-else, 481
  if-else-if, logical operators, 945
  INSERT, 894
  keywords, 479
  new, 541-542
  OR, boolean equivalents/returns, 945
  return, 492
  set, 461
  switch, troubleshooting, 535
  trace(), 945
  UPDATE, 893
  with, 498
states
  button symbols (Flash), 381
  Flash buttons, 421-422
  navigation bars, 741-743

static button events, 508-511
static event handlers, 503-505
static features, classes, 543-544
static frames (Flash), 391
static keyword, 543
static movie clip events, 513-515
static text, 368, 607
statistics, tracking usage, 262
status bar (Dreamweaver), 79-80
status property, 644
Status toolbar, designing home pages, 848
stereo, 408, 417
Stop (synchronization option), 411
Stop All Sounds behavior, 420
stop method (MovieClip class), 920
Stop Sound behavior, 420
stop() method, 653
stopAllSounds() command, 409
stopAllSounds() functions, 654
stopDrag method (MovieClip class), 920
stopDrag() method, 533
storing
  data (variables), 448
  expression results, 938
  function literals, 487
  persistence, 602
  Recordsets, 297
  symbols (Flash), 389
straight line segments, drawing, 39
Straighten modifier
  Arrow tool, 339
  Flash, 353
Straighten or Smooth (Editing Preference), 347
straightening shapes (Flash), 353
Stream (synchronization option), 411

streaming
real-time audio streams, 653
sound, 408-411, 652
video files, Flash, 649-650
strict data typing, 331
strict equality (===) operator, 939
strict equality operator (===), 482
strict HTML 4, 165
strict inequality operator (!==), 940
strict typing, 456, 542
string datatype, 465-466, 470
string literals versus strings, 470
String wrapper class, 569
String() global function, 915
String.charAt method (wrapper classes), 969
String.charCodeAt method (wrapper classes), 969
String.concat method (wrapper classes), 969
String.fromCharCode method (wrapper classes), 969
String.indexOf method (wrapper classes), 969
String.lastIndexOf method (wrapper classes), 970
String.length property (wrapper classes), 972
String.slice method (wrapper classes), 970
String.split method (wrapper classes), 970
String.split() method, 569
String.substr method (wrapper classes), 971
String.substring method (wrapper classes), 971
String.substring() method, 569
String.toLowerCase method (wrapper classes), 971
String.toUpperCase method (wrapper classes), 972
String.valueOf method (wrapper classes), 972

strings
comparing, code points, 940
converting, 469, 940
datatype conversion rules, 915-916
implicit datatype conversion, 913
localization, 575
query strings, 630
quotation marks (), 625
splitting, 569
Strings panel, 327
Stroke box, 34
strokes, 33
animations (Flash), 394
color, 34-35
dashed, 690
drawing, 38
shapes (Flash), 365
versus paths (vector graphics), 734
Structured Query Language. *See* SQL
structures, arrays, 900
Style command (Text menu), 97
Style Definition dialog box, 183-185
style sheets 14-15. *See also* CSS (Cascading Style Sheets)
styles
deleted styles (Fireworks), troubleshooting, 782
fonts, 45-46
inheritance, 178
Styles command (Window menu), 793
Styles panel, 793
StyleSheet class, 967-968
styling text (Dreamweaver), 94-97
subclasses, 550
subscripts, 47
Subselection tool, 29, 41, 352, 355, 375
substrings, 569
subtract and reassign (-=) compound assignment operator, 938

subtraction operators, 927
Sun AU, 412
superclasses, initialization code, 615
superscripts, 47
Surface button, 816
SVG (Scalable Vector Graphics), 164
Swap command (Property Inspector), 389
Swap Image behaviors, 225, 739-741
Swap Image dialog box, 740
Swap Image Restore behaviors, 225
Swap Symbol dialog box, 389
swapDepths method (MovieClip class), 920
swapping
depth numbers (movie clips), 527
images, 223
symbol instances (Flash), 389
Swatches command (Window menu), 793
Swatches panel, 793, 859
.swc file extension, 279
SWF files, 19-20, 322, 443
Swiff Chart (Flash), 322
SWiSH Power FX (Flash), 322
switch statements, troubleshooting, 535
switch/case conditional statements, 481-482
.swt file extension, 279
Symbol command
Edit menu, 722
Insert menu, 381
Symbol Editor, 749
Symbol Name dialog box, 384
Symbol Properties dialog box, 747
Symbol, Button command (Modify menu), 741
Symbol, Duplicate Symbol command (Modify menu), 384
Symbol, Tween Instances command (Modify menu), 748

symbol-editing mode (Flash), 386

symbols
animation, 748-750
buttons, 380-381, 741
graphic symbols (Flash), 380, 747
Library (Flash), 343
modifying, 384

symbols (Flash), 380
animations, 391, 404
button symbols, 380-381
converted objects, 383-384
copying, 439-440
creating, 380-384
duplicating, 384
editing, 385-386
graphic symbols, 380
instances, 380, 386-389
Library, 389-390
movie clips, 381
objects, converting, 380
positioning, 382-383
sorting, 390
storing, 389
timelines, launching, 386

synchronization, 255, 409-411

Synchronize command (Site menu), 255

Synchronize dialog box, 255

Synchronize to Macromedia Flash Document Frame Rate option (Encoding dialog box), 437

Synchronized Multimedia Integration Language (SMIL), 164

Syntax Coloring (color coding), 449

syntax. See code

System 7 Sounds, 412

System class, 589-592

System DSN (Data Source Name)
ColdFusion, 877
database access, 290

system events, 504

T

tab ordering, 922
automatic tab ordering, 923
custom tab ordering, 923-925
movie clip children, 924

tabbed interfaces (Flash), 323

tabChildren property (MovieClip class), 921, 924-925

tabEnabled property, 593
MovieClip class, 921, 925
TextField class, 963

tabIndex property, 593
MovieClip class, 921, 925
TextField class, 963

table element, 192

Table Mode, Layout Mode command (View menu), 193

Table Mode, Standard Mode command (View menu), 193

tables
dynamic, Dreamweaver ColdFusion, 298-301
elements, 192
layers, converting to, 218
layout, 192-198, 218
managing, Contribute 2 program, 273
Microsoft application tables, copy/paste, 65-66
pixels, 196
repeating, creating (Dreamweaver), 127-128

tabStops property (TextFormat class), 967

Tag Editor dialog box, 314

Tag Inspector panel (Dreamweaver), 88

Tag Selector, 80, 211

tags
<cfquery>, 290
CFML (ColdFusion Markup Language), 887-888
creating via Insert bar, 313-314
slash (/), 886
class, 175

ColdFusion 6.1, 65
CSS (Cascading Style Sheets), 183
applying, 178
text formatting, 42
custom, CFML (ColdFusion Markup Language), 895
cf_scrape, 899-902
invoking, 897
passing data, 897-898
returning data, 898-899
versus CFCs (ColdFusion components), 896
HTML, managing, 80, 88
<li>, </li>, 98
metadata, 614
<ol>, </ol>, 99
TextFormat class, 608
<ul>, </ul>, 99
XML (Extensible Markup Language), 637

tan method (Math object), 958

tangent (tan) method, 588

Target Browser Check panel (Dreamweaver), 92

Target Browser Check tab, 244

target browsers, cross-browser compatibility, 155

_target property (MovieClip class), 921

target property
targeting windows, 206-207
TextFormat class, 967

targeting windows, 206-207

targets, 619-621

tbody element, 192

td element, 192

technologies, push (XML sockets), 646

Template menu commands, 346

Template Objects command (Insert menu), 124

Template Objects, Editable Regions command (Insert menu), 124, 127

Template Objects, Optional Regions command (Insert menu), 126

Template Objects, Repeating Region command (Insert menu), 128

Template Objects, Repeating Table command (Insert menu), 127

templates
design/planning, 14
Flash, 326
versus Library items, 144-145

templates (Dreamweaver), 123
creating, 122-124
editable attributes, 129-130
editable regions
creating, 124-127
highlighting, 133
editing, 132-133
files, saving as, 124
optional regions, creating, 125-126
repeating regions, creating, 127-128
Web pages, 130-131

Templates category (Assets panel), 141

Templates tab, 130

Templates, Apply Template to Page command (Modify menu), 131

Templates, Make Attribute Editable command (Modify menu), 129

Templates, Remove Template Markup command (Modify menu), 125

Templates, Update Pages command (Modify menu), 132

temporal compression, video, 433

Test button, 108

Test Movie command (Control menu), 399-401, 423, 429

testing
accessibility
Dreamweaver, 262
site management, 246-247

ASP.NET pages, 12
compressed bitmaps (Flash), 364
embedded fonts, 373
keycodes, 596
movie clips (Flash), 399-400
movies, 429
online, site management, 251-252
rollovers, 739
Web sites, 152, 156-157

text
adding, 43, 197
aligning (Dreamweaver), 97-98
animating, 375
bending, 728
breaking apart, 374
character attributes, 45-47
color, setting in Web pages (Dreamweaver), 120-121
deleted content, troubleshooting (Dreamweaver), 100
Document window (Dreamweaver), 93
dynamic, 42, 368-371
breaking text apart, 374
device fonts, 373-374
Dreamweaver ColdFusion, 301-302
embedded fonts, 373-374
formatting options, 372
transforming text, 375-376
variables, 372
editing (Flash), 283
effects, adding to Web sites, 849-852
Fireworks, 18-19
formatting, CSS (Cascading Style Sheets), 42, 327
FreeHand, 18-19
indenting (Dreamweaver), 98
input, 368-371
breaking text apart, 374
device fonts, 373-374
embedded fonts, 373-374
formatting options, 372

transforming text, 375-376
variables, 372
inserting (Flash), 280-281
legibility, 376-377
line breaks (Dreamweaver), 94
managing, Contribute 2 program, 273-274
modifying globally, 44-45
orientation, changing, 45
paragraph attributes, 45-47
paragraphs (Dreamweaver), 94
paths, 814, 849-852
pixels (Flash), 368-370
placeholder, 370
previewing (Flash), 283
resizing (Flash), 283
screen reader software, 978
serifs, 370
spell checker (Flash), 326
static, 368
styling (Dreamweaver), 94-97
transforming, 375-376

text blocks
auto-expanding, 43
converting, 370
fixed-width, 43
moving, 45
resizing, 43-44

text direction, 46

Text Direction button, 347

text editors, XML, 637

text fields
creating, 606
creating dynamically, 606
dynamic, troubleshooting, 378
input, screen reader software, 978
instance names, 372, 377
lines, 372
Maximum Character field, 372
properties, 607

text files, troubleshooting formatting, 615

text flow, paths, 851

Text FX (Flash), 322

Text menu commands
  Alignment, 98
  Attach to Path, 849-850
  Check Spelling, 153
  Indent, 98
  List, Unordered, 98
  Outdent, 98
  Paths, 814
  Style, 97
text nodes, XML (Extensible Markup Language), 636
text property, 607, 963
Text tab (Dreamweaver), 79
Text tool, 43-44, 399
Text Type menu commands
  Dynamic Text, 371
  Input Text, 370
text-level elements (inline elements), 100, 169
TextArea component (Flash), 427
textColor property (TextField class), 963
TextField class, 605, 958-967
  CSS (Cascading Style Sheets), 608-611
  text fields, 606-607
TextField events, 516-517
TextField.autoResize values, 965
TextFormat class, 605
  CSS (Cascading Style Sheets), 608-611
  formatting, 607-608
  tags, 608
  text fields, 606-607
TextFormat movie class, 966
textHeight property (TextField class), 963
TextInput component (Flash), 427
TextSnapshot class, 611-612
textWidth property (TextField class), 963
tfoot element, 192
th element, 192
thead element, 192
themes, Flash components, 430-431

third-party plug-ins, installing, 268
this keyword, 493
  event handlers, 505-506
  explicit scoping, 495-496
Threshold (Magic Wand Settings dialog box), 363
thumbnails, sizing multipage files, 846
tiling background images (Dreamweaver), 119
Time In (Edit Envelope dialog box), 413
time-line based animations, creating, 323
Timeline, 381, 462
  button symbols (Flash), 380
  buttons, 518
  code, organizing, 454-455
  document structure (Flash), 424-425
  frames (Flash), 335
  function access, troubleshooting, 536
  keyframes (Flash), 335-336
  layers (Flash), 336-338
  Library items, editing, 148
  movie clips, 381, 517
  onion skins (Flash), 338-339
  scope chains, 498
  symbols, launching (Flash), 386
  variable access, troubleshooting, 535-536
  video playback, 439
Timeline Effects (Flash), 323, 391, 400-404
Timeline Effects command (Insert menu), 400
Timeline Options (General Preferences), 346
timeline variables, accessing, 489
Timeline, Blank Keyframe command (Insert menu), 335
Timeline, Distribute command (Modify menu), 374
Timeline, Keyframe command (Insert menu), 335
Timeline, Layer command (Insert menu), 429

Timeline, Motion Guide command (Insert menu), 396
Timelines panel, 228-229
times/dates, objects, 569
Tint command
  Color drop-down menu, 387
  Fill menu, 820
  Window menu, 791
Tints panel, 791-792
title bar (Dreamweaver), 76
Title section (Optimize panel), 759
titles
  lack of, troubleshooting (Dreamweaver), 133
  Web pages, adding (Dreamweaver), 117
To Stage button, 356
Toggle Full Screen Mode behavior, 419
tolerance, Magic Wand tool, 701
toLocaleString method, 573
toLocaleString() method, 575
toolbars
  Contribute 2, 270
  Document (Dreamweaver), 78
  Envelope (FreeHand), 833-834
  image editing, 277-278
  Insert, 78-79, 298
  main, 30
  Standard (Dreamweaver), 78
  Status, home page design, 848
  Xtra Operations (FreeHand), 830-832
  Xtra Tools (FreeHand), 832-833
Toolbars command (View menu), 78
Toolbars, Main command (Window menu), 30
Toolbars, Xtra Operations command (Window menu), 831

Toolbox
Actions, 444-446
Arrow tool (Flash), 339
Brush tool (Flash), 340-341
Eraser tool (Flash), 342
Fill Transform tool (Flash), 341
Free Transform tool, 341, 375
Ink Bottle tool, 37, 341
Lasso tool, 29, 339-340, 362
Paint Bucket, 594

tools, 33
Action, 852-854
Arrow, 375
Arrow (Flash), 339
Brush (Flash), 340-341
choosing, 18-20
coding (Dreamweaver), 66-68
Connector, creating site maps, 838-844
Ellipse, 38, 849
Eraser (Flash), 342
Export Area, 767
Eyedropper, 37
Fill Transform (Flash), 341
fills, 33-37
Free Transform, 341, 375
Hand, 33
Ink Bottle, 37, 341
Lasso, 29, 339-340, 362
Line, 38
Oval, 38
Page, 845-847
Paint Bucket, 36-37
Pen, 39-42, 396
Pencil, 38, 396
Rectangle, 38, 399
Rotate and Skew, 384
Scale, 384
Selection, 29, 352-354, 395-399
strokes, 33-35
Subselection, 29, 41, 352, 355, 375
Text, 43-44, 399
Transform (Fireworks), 341, 684
Zoom, 33

tools (Fireworks), 696-697
Auto Shapes, 686-687
Bitmap
Blur, 705
Brush, 703
Burn, 706
Dodge, 706
Eraser, 703
Gradient, 710-712
Lasso, 701
Magic Wand, 701
Marquee, 700
Oval Marquee, 701
Pencil, 703
Polygon Lasso, 701
Red-Eye Removal, 710
Replace Color, 708-710
Rubber Stamp, 708
Sharpen, 706
Smudge, 707
Hide Slice, 721
Hotspot, 719
Live Effects panel, 688
Polygon Lasso, 729
Polygon Slice, 719
Red Eye Removal, 687
Replace Color, 687-688
Select, 698-699
Show Slice, 721
Slice, 719
Vector
Auto Shapes, 716-718
Ellipse, 716
FreeForm, 718
Line, 712
Path Scrubber, 719
Pen, 712-714
Polygon, 716
Rectangle, 715
Redraw Path, 714
Vector Path, 714
Web, 719

tools (FreeHand)
3D Rotation, 812-814
Action, 828
Arc, 801
Bend, 809
Blend, 821
Calligraphic Pen, 798-800
Chart, 826-828
Connector, 829-830
Eraser, 809
Extrude, 815-817
Fisheye Lens, 814
Freeform, 806-808
Graphic Hose, 823-826
Knife, 810
Mirror, 822-823
Output Area, 796
Page, 795-796
Perspective, 810-812
Reflect, 804
Rotate, 803-804
Roughen, 808-809
Scale, 801-803
Shadow, 818-820
Skew, 805-806
Smudge, 818
Spiral, 800
Trace, 820-821
Variable Stroke Pen, 797-798

Tools panel, 33
Round Rectangle Radius modifier, 38
View section, 33
Web-Safe colors (FreeHand), 858

tooltips (code hints), 456
top parameters, startDrag () method, 533
_top special target, 620
TopStyle software, 179
toString method, 563, 573
toString() function, 626, 642
toString() method, 563-564, 568-569, 574-575, 915
_totalframes property (MovieClip class), 921
tr element, 192
Trace Bitmap dialog box, 360
Trace Conformity option (Trace Tool dialog box), 821
Trace Layers option (Trace Tool dialog box), 821
Trace tool (FreeHand), 820-821
trace() statement, 945
tracing bitmap graphics (Flash), 358-362, 365
Track as Button command (Web menu), 425

Track as Menu Item command (Web menu), 425

trackAsMenu property, 593, 921, 925-926

tracking site components (Dreamweaver), 136

trailing parameters, 607

Transfer log, 261

transfers (Dreamweaver), troubleshooting, 261

Transform effect (Timeline), 403

transform objects, 595

Transform panel, 802-803

Transform tool (Fireworks), 684

Transformation palette, 803-806

transformation percentage number, 595

transformation points, symbols (Flash), 384

transformations, applying (Free Transform tool), 341

transforming
color (movie clips), 595
letters, 376
text, 375-376
transparency (movie clips), 595

Transition effect (Timeline), 403

transitional HTML 4, 165

transparency
alpha channels, bitmaps (Flash), 358
Fireworks, 773
movie clips, 594
opacity swatches, 712
transforming (movie clips), 595

Trap option (Xtra Operations toolbar), 832

trapping
errors (Flash), 570
events, 501

trees, XML (Extensible Markup Language), 635

triangles disabling/enabling yellow focus, 922-923

Trigger Data Source behavior, ActionScript (Flash interactivity), 419

Trigger Data Source dialog box, 678

triggering
actions, 854
actions via event handlers, 500-503
button events, 508-511
calling explicitly, 507
deleting/disabling event handlers, 507
dynamic event handlers, 502-505
input events, 504
key events, 511-512
keyboard focus, 507-510
listener registration, 504-505
mouse events, 512
movie clip events, 513-515
scoping, 505-506
selection events, 515
sound events, 515-516
Stage events, 516
static event handlers, 503-505
system events, 504
TextField events, 516-517
this keyword, 505-506
button events, 425
data sources, Web services, 678-679

trigonometry, 581-589, 615

troubleshooting
ActionScript (Flash), 458
ActionScript/JavaScript communication, 657
Answers panel (Fireworks), 728-729
AS2 (ActionScript 2), 331
bitmaps, 365, 377
CGI scripts, 658
Connection Verification Failed error, 883
CSS fonts, 188
data type checking (CFML), 888-889

DataGrid component columns, 679
deleted content (Dreamweaver), 100
deleted styles (Fireworks), 782
Dreamweaver, 70
dynamic text fields, 378
Edit Page button, Contribute 2, 284
Fireworks, 774, 782
Flash panels, hiding, 350
functions, 487, 536-537
grid layouts, 218
hitTest() method, 537-538
JPEG compression, 774
keyboard focus, 537
layout tables, adding content, 218
link colors (Dreamweaver), 133
links, 259
loaded movie clips, 537
motion guides (Flash), 440
motion paths (Flash), 440
movie classes, 615
movie clips, 530
movie objects, 615
navigation bars, 752
OBJECT parameter, 658
operands, 535
Perl scripts, 658
Photoshop filters, 774
plug-ins (Dreamweaver), 284
programs, choosing, 49
Resolve Library Conflict error, 440
shape tweens (Flash), 440
slices, 753
sound, 659
spell-checker, 158
strokes (Flash), 365
switch statements, 535
text files, formatting, 615
Timeline functions, accessing, 536
Timeline variables, accessing, 535-536
titles, lack of (Dreamweaver), 133

transfers (Dreamweaver), 261

trigonometry, 615

undefined return statements, 536

validation errors (Dreamweaver), 100

validators (Dreamweaver), 261

vector curves, 774

Web services, invoking functions as, 905

XHTML (Extensible HTML), 187

XML, 658-659

true value, Boolean, 466

try/catch/finally conditional statements, 482-483

Tween Instances dialog box, 748

tweening (Flash)
animations (Flash), 393, 747-748
motion tweens, 394-398
shape tweens, 398-400, 440
text, 375
layers (Flash), 336

Twist and Fade command (Commands menu), 724

type attribute, 888

Type category (Style Definition dialog box), 184

Type of Object property (layers), 217

type of operator, 464

Type option (Extension Manager dialog box), 266

type property, 607, 964

typecasting variables, 469

typefaces. *See* fonts

typeof operator, 469, 941, 948

typewriter font, 373

U

UI (user interface) components (Flash), 325

<ul>, </ul> tags, 99

UltraDev CF server objects (Dreamweaver)l troubleshooting, 70

unary negation operator, 928

undefined datatype, 465, 468-471

undefined return statements, troubleshooting, 536

underline property (TextFormat class), 967

Undo command (Edit menu), 328, 360

Undo feature, 278, 328

Undo Levels (General Preferences), 345

undocking panel groups (Dreamweaver), 83

Ungroup command (Modify menu), 821, 828

Unicode (Fireworks), 691

Unicode character set, 466

Uniform command
Rotate menu, 826
Scale menu, 825

Uniform option (Indexed Palette drop-down menu), 765

Uniform Resource Locators. *See* URL

Union option (Xtra Operations toolbar), 831

unlinked style sheets, CSS integration, 177

unload movie clip event, 514

unloading external content (movie clips), 520-524

unloadMovie method (MovieClip class), 920

unloadMovie() global function, 522

unloadMovieNum() global function, 522

Unordered List button, 98

unordered lists, creating (Dreamweaver), 98-99

unshared layers versus shared layers, 738

unshift method (arrays), 563

unshift() method, 567

unsigned right bit-shift operator (>>>), 937

unwatch method, 573

unwatch() method, 576-578

Up button state, 421

Up graphics, rollovers, 739

Up rollover state, 225

Up state
button movie clip events, 515
navigation bars, 741

Update button, 364

Update HTML command (File menu), 722

Update Pages dialog box, 132, 147-148

Update Record button, 309

UPDATE statements, 893

Update Template Files dialog box, 132

updating
files, Web sites (Dreamweaver), 133
records, CFML (ColdFusion Markup Language), 892-894

upgrades, Fireworks, 684

uploading Web pages, 248-252

url attribute, 901

url property
TextField class, 964
TextFormat class, 967

_url property (MovieClip class), 922

URL (Uniform Resource Locator), 619
category (Assets panel), 139-140
scope, 891

usage statistics, tracking, 262

useCodepage attribute, 591

useHandCursor property, 593, 922, 926

user input, 42, 596

user interface
components (Flash), 325
panel organization (Dreamweaver), 55-57
quickstart menu (Dreamweaver), 54-55
streamlined workspace (Dreamweaver), 55-57

user1Age variable, 914

Using Page Bleeds option (Document panel), 790

V

V1 components (Flash), 325
V2 components (Flash), 325-326
Validate button, 244
validating
    accessibility, site management, 245-246
    errors (Dreamweaver), 100
    external links, 261
    files, 243-244
    Web sites, 91
Validation panel (Dreamweaver), 91
validators (Dreamweaver), troubleshooting, 261
valueOf method, 573
valueOf() method, 568-569, 575, 941
values
    array elements (adding), 560
    assigning, variables, 461
    attribute (classes), initializing, 544-546
    Boolean datatype, 466
    HTML, 170-171
    name/value pairs, special characters, 625
    null datatype, 467
    number datatype, 465-466
    return values, 574, 948
    scaleMode property, 604
    text nodes, 636
    TextField.autoResize, 965
    XHTML, 170-171
    XML attributes, 641
Values dialog box, 429
Var field, 372
var keyword, 460, 488-489
Variable command (Spacing menu), 825
variable property, 607, 964
Variable Stroke Pen tool (FreeHand), 797-798
variables, 460
    binary variables, bitwise operators, 930
    centralizing code, 462

CFML (ColdFusion Markup Language), 888-891
    comments, 460
    creating explicitly, 460-461
    creating implicitly, 460
    data, 469, 448
    datatypes
        arrays, 467
        Boolean, 466
        composite, 464
        function, 468
        movieclip, 468
        null, 467-468, 471
        number, 465-466
        object, 466-467
        primitive, 464
        strings, 466, 470
        undefined, 468-471
    declaring, 460-462, 947
    decrement operators, 927
    dynamic text, 372
    function literals, storing, 487
    increment operators, 927
    input text, 372
    local functions, creating, 488-489
    Main Timeline organization, 462
    naming, 462-464
    return values (function results), 492
    scoping, 453, 496
    Timeline, 489, 535-536
    values, assigning, 461
VBScript, Scripts category (Assets panel), 140
vector animation, 390, 743
vector curves, troubleshooting, 774
vector graphics
    Fireworks, 732-735
    Flash, 352
vector objects (Fireworks), copying/pasting, 772
Vector Path tool, 714
Vector tools
    Auto Shapes, 716-718
    Ellipse, 716
    FreeForm, 718

    Line, 712
    Path Scrubber, 719
    Pen, 712-714
    Polygon, 716
    Rectangle, 715
    Redraw Path, 714
    Vector Path, 714
version control systems, 254-255
Version option (Extension Manager dialog box), 266
version property, 590
versions
    Flash, 324
    Web site management (Fireworks), 692
vertical guidelines (Flash), 354
Vertical option (Mirror dialog box), 823
vertical orientation, pages, 796
Vertical Spacing property (Flash object), 280
Vertical Text (Editing Preference), 347
vertical text direction, 46
video (Flash). *See also* **multimedia**
    compression, 433
    embedding files, 649-650
    streaming files, 649-650
Video Import wizard, 327, 433-434, 650
    video edits, 435-436
    video encoding, 436-438
video integration (Flash), 431
    file types, 432-433
    managing, 438-439
    playback control, 439
    versus linked, 433
    Video Import Wizard, 433-438
Video Rich Media class, 647, 656-657
View menu commands
    Bandwidth Profiler, 435
    Grid, Edit Grid, 355
    Guides, Lock Guides, 355
    Guides, Show Guides, 355
    Head Content, 141
    JavaScript in Panel, 329

Magnification, 400%, 354
Perspective Grid, 810
Preview Mode, Fast, 361
Preview Mode, Outlines, 361
Rulers, 355
Server Debug, 93
Simulate Download, 435
Snapping, Edit Snap Align, 339
Snapping, Snap to Guides, 355
Snapping, Snap to Objects, 339
Snapping, Snap to Pixels, 354, 369
Table Mode, Layout Mode, 193
Table Mode, Standard Mode, 193
Toolbars, 78
Visual Aids, Frame Borders, 200, 204
Visual Aids, Invisible Elements, 133
View section (Tools panel), 33
views
Code (Dreamweaver), 76-77
Design (Dreamweaver), 76-77
Normal view, 361
Vis property (layers), 215
visibility layer preference, 208
visibility
class features, 546
layers, 213
visible attribute (copy method), 910
_visible property (MovieClip class), 922
visible property (TextField class), 964
Visual Aids, Frame Borders command (View menu), 200, 204
Visual Aids, Invisible Elements command (View menu), 133
visual borders, frames, 204
Visual SourceSafe (Microsoft), 254

visual stacking
depth numbering, 526-527
levels, 525-528
movie clips, 519, 524-525
parent-child hierarchies, 525
visually impaired, accessibility, 593
void operator, 949-950
volume (sound), 413-414, 654-655

W

W and H property (layers), 215
W property
embedded audio files, 237
Java applets, 235
W3C (World Wide Web Consortium), 57
WAI (Web Accessibility Initiative), 245-246
Web standards, 242
Wand Color Tolerance option (Trace Tool dialog box), 821
Warning Preferences (Flash), 348-349
watch method, 573
watch() method, 576-578
watchpoints, 576-577
Web 216 option (Indexed Palette drop-down menu), 764
Web Accessibility Initiative (WAI) guidelines, 245-246
Web Adaptive option (Indexed Palette drop-down menu), 764
Web behaviors, 420
Web browsers. *See* browsers
Web graphics, exporting, 766-767
Web Host Industry Review Web site, 104
Web integration (FreeHand), 858
graphics, 859-862
HTML, 863-864
Web-Safe colors, 858-859

Web layers, sharing, 738
Web menu commands, 425
Web pages
ASP.NET, creating/testing, 12
assets, adding from Assets panel, 141
background colors, 58, 118
background images, setting (Dreamweaver), 119-120
creating, Contribute 2, 270-272
custom sizes, creating, 795
dynamic, creating, 85-88
editing, Contribute 2, 270
exporting, 769-770
home, designing, 848-849
links, colors (Dreamweaver), 121, 133
margins, setting (Dreamweaver), 120
orientation, 796
orphaned, 258
siteless page editing (Dreamweaver), 57
spell checking, dictionary problems, 158
start (Fireworks), 694
templates (Dreamweaver), 122-123
applying to, 131
creating, 122-124, 130-131
editable attributes, 129-130
editable regions, 124-127, 133
editing with, 131
optional regions, 125-126
repeating regions, 127-128
saving files as, 124
text color, setting (Dreamweaver), 120-121
titles, 117, 133
uploading, 248-252
Web servers
Apache, 880
built-in (ColdFusion), 880
ColdFusion, 876
ColdFusion Developer Edition, 12

determining, 15
JRun, 880
MIME type, 624
ports, 880
Web service CFCs (ColdFusion components), creating, 314-316
Web services, 662-663, 672-673
accessing, 879
CFCs (ColdFusion Components), 904-905
ColdFusion servers, accessing, 879
component instances, creating, 674-675
consuming, Dreamweaver ColdFusion, 316
data sources, triggering, 678-679
databindings, 675-678
functions, invoking as, 905
hierarchy, 673
Web Services panel, 672-673
Web sites
Bradbury Software, 179
components, tracking (Dreamweaver), 136
content navigation, 424
creating, 838
Dreamweaver, 289
site maps, 838-844
defining (Dreamweaver), 104-110
designing, 838
actions, 852-854
home pages, 848-849
multipage files, 845-847
text effects, 849-852
DOCTYPE declaration, ensuring compliance (Dreamweaver), 134
editing online, remote servers, 157
files (Dreamweaver), 111-117, 133
hosting services, 104
importance of proper document structure, 158-159
Library items, inserting, 146-147

Macromedia, 879
managing (Fireworks), 692
markup, cleaning up, 152
remote, setting up, 252
Shockwave.com, 232
Sorenson Spark Pro, 433
testing online, 156-157
usage statistics, tracking, 262
validating, 91
W3C (World Wide Web Consortium), 57
Web Host Industry Review, 104
Web standards, validating files, 242-244
Web Standards project, 188
Web tools
Hide Slice, 721
Hotspot, 719
Polygon Slice, 719
Show Slice, 721
Slice, 719
Web-Safe colors
FreeHand integration, 858-859
palettes, 34
WebDAV (Web-based Distributed Authoring and Versioning), 106, 254
WebObjects, 634
WebServiceConnector component, 879
well-formed XHTML documents, 168
what-you-see-is-what-you-get (WYSIWYG), 76
while loop statement, 484
white backgrounds, buttons, 753
whitespace
line breaks (Dreamweaver), 94
readability code, 449
XML (Extensible Markup Language), 643
Wide Library View button, 389
width layer preference, 208

width property, 603, 656, 922
Flash object, 279
TextField class, 964
wildcards, asterisk (*), 892
Window component (Flash), 427
Window menu commands
Actions, 443
Assets, 123
Behaviors, 222
Code Inspector, 93
Color Mixer, 790
Design Panels, Align, 356
Development Panels, Behaviors, 678
Development Panels, Components, 427
Development Panels, Web Services, 672-673
Document, 788, 845
Find, 777
Frames, 203
Layers, 211-213, 792
Library, 389, 422, 794
Navigation, 853
Object, 788
Other Panels, Accessibility, 979
Other Panels, Common Libraries, 344
Other Panels, Movie Explorer, 344
Panel Sets, Default, 350
Panel Sets, Default Layout, 443
Site, 105
Styles, 793
Swatches, 793
Tints, 791
Toolbars, Main, 30
Toolbars, Xtra Operations, 831
Window Size Selector (Dreamweaver), 80
windowlessDisable property, 590
windows
browsers, 620
Document
Code view (Dreamweaver), 76-77

CSS editor, 179
Design view (Dreamweaver), 76-77
frames, selecting, 204
framesets, selecting, 204
layers, selecting, 211-212
menu bar (Dreamweaver), 77
status bar (Dreamweaver), 79
document (Fireworks), 695-697
document (FreeHand), 786
magnification (Fireworks), 697
map view, 256
projectors, modifying, 622
screen reader software, 979
Tag Selector, 80
targeting, 619-620
reserved target names, 207
target/name attributes, 206-207
Web-safe color palettes, 34
Window Size Selector, 80
text, managing, 93-98
title bar, 76
toolbars, 78-79
Windows Media Player (WMA) plug-in, 230
Windows option (Indexed Palette drop-down menu), 765
Windows/Macintosh Gamma command (View menu), 722
Wireframe option (Surface button), 816
Wireless Markup Language (WML), 164
with statement, 498
wizards
Batch, 778-779
Export, 767
HTML Export, 864
Record Insertion Form Wizard, 308
Video Import, 327, 433-438, 650
WMA (Windows Media Player) plug-in, 230

WML (Wireless Markup Language), 164
Word documents, importing into Web pages, 272
wordWrap = true property, 607
wordWrap property (TextField class), 964
Workspace Setup dialog box, 74-75
workspace layouts (Dreamweaver), 74-75
WOW (World Organization of Webmasters), 243
wrapper classes, 567-569, 968-972
writing extensions (Dreamweaver), 264
WYSIWYG (what-you-see-is-what-you-get), 76

X

x property, 922, 964
XHTML (Extensible HTML), 162
attributes, 170
document conformance, 167
DTD (document type definitions), 167
elements, 169
history, 164
site management, 243
syntax rules, 168-169
troubleshooting, 187
values, 170-171
well-formedness, 168
XML (Extensible Markup Language), 164, 634
attributes, 637
benefits, 637-638
commands, 642
cross-domain policy files, 330
data parsing, 638-641, 644
documents
creating, 637, 641-643
importing, 643-645
sending, 645
hierarchy, 635-636

navigation, 636
overview, 634-636
properties, 639, 644-645
readability, 637
sockets, 645-646
tags, 637
text editors, 637
troubleshooting, 658-659
versus HTML (Hypertext Markup Language), 634
xmlDecl property, 645
xmouse property, 922, 964
XOR logical bitwise operator (^), 934-935
xscale property, 922, 964
Xtra Operation toolbars (FreeHand), 831-832
Xtra Tools toolbars (FreeHand), 832-833

Y-Z

y property, 922, 964
yellow focus triangles, disabling/enabling, 922-923
ymouse property, 922, 965
yscale property, 922, 965

Z-Index property (layers), 215
z-order (stacking order), layers, 214
zero degrees rotation, 582
Zoom (Edit Envelope dialog box), 414
Zoom Edge option (Shadow dialog box), 819
Zoom tool, 33
Zooming sound (Flash), 414